R. Gupta's®

Dictionary of MEDICAL SCIENCES

by

RPH Editorial Board

Ramesh Publishing House, New Delhi

Published by
O.P. Gupta *for* Ramesh Publishing House

Admin. Office
12-H, New Daryaganj Road, Opp. Officers' Mess,
New Delhi-110002 ✆ 23261567, 23275224, 23275124

E-mail: info@rameshpublishinghouse.com
Website: www.rameshpublishinghouse.com

Showroom
• Balaji Market, Nai Sarak, Delhi-6 ✆ 23253720, 23282525
• 4457, Nai Sarak, Delhi-6, ✆ 23918938

Book Code: R-919

ISBN: 978-81-7812-322-6

8th Edition : 1910

HSN Code : 49019100

Price: ₹ 330

Printed at: Deepak Offset, Delhi

Preface

This Dictionary of Medicine covers accurate and latest definitions of terms being used in latest context and also the current usage. It covers all aspect of Medicine and health. The field of medicine has grown so vast in the last few years, that to cover every term is impossible. We have therefore compiled a volume, which is appropriate for all medical workers.

Definitions are comprehensive, include major diseases, disorders, procedures, and drugs and are explained with illustrations. All fields, such as Anatomy, Physiology, Biochemistry, Pharmacy, Surgery, Ophthalmology, Dermatology, E.N.T., Psychiatry, Genetics are covered. This dictionary will prove a valuable reference for practitioners, specialists, consultants and students. Terms are concisely presented and explained in a very lucid manner. Medical students in general will find the dictionary indispensable.

Users of this Dictionary will find it easy to understand the various terms as they are explained in a very lucid manner. It will benefit not only student but also professionals, researchers, and scholars. We owe a great debt to all those scholars and authors in this field whose work we have consulted and who have influenced our understanding of the field. We have not included a bibliography of works consulted for this dictionary because it could not be completed but we express our appreciation. We can only hope that those who consult this book will find it useful. Any suggestions for additional improvement of this book will be greatly valued.

Publisher

Dictionary of Medical Sciences

A Prefix denoting absence of; lacking, e.g. alactasia is absence or deficiency of the enzyme lactase.

A33 A type of monoclonal antibody used in cancer detection or therapy. Monoclonal antibodies are laboratory produced substances that can locate and bind to cancer cells.

AAP (Alanine aminopeptidase) An enzyme that is used as a biomarker to detect damage to the kidneys, and that may be used to help diagnose certain kidney disorders. It is found at high levels in the urine when there are kidney problems.

Abarelix A drug used to reduce the amount of testosterone made in patients with advanced symptomatic prostate cancer for which no other treatment options are available. It belongs to the family of drugs called gonadotropin-releasing hormone (GnRH) antagonists. Also called Plenaxis.

ABCD rating A staging system for prostate cancer that uses ABCD. "A" and "B" refer to cancer that is confined to the prostate. "C" refers to cancer that has grown out of the prostate but has not spread to lymph nodes or other places in the body. "D" refers to cancer that has spread to lymph nodes or to other places in the body. Also called the Jewett staging system or the Whitmore-Jewett staging system.

Abdomen The area of the body between the thorax and pelvis. The abdomen contains the liver, the spleen and most of the digestive organs.

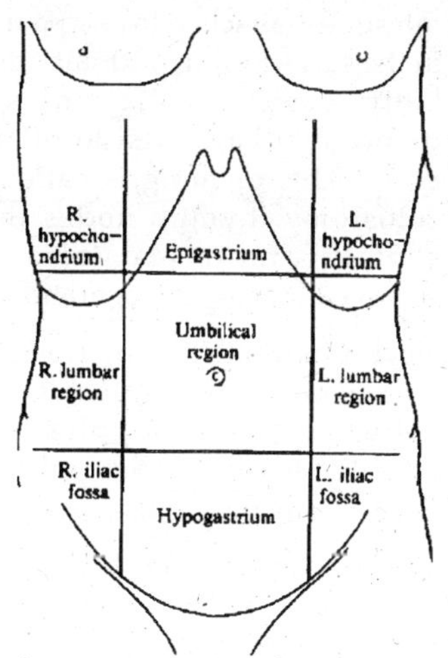

Figure Regions of abdomen

Abdominal Having to do with the abdomen, which is the part of the body between the chest and the hips that contains the pancreas, stomach, intestines, liver, gallbladder and other organs.

Abdominal aorta The continuation into the abdomen of the thoracic aorta, which divides into the two common iliac arteries.

Abdominal ultrasound A diagnostic imaging technique which creates images from the rebound of high-frequency sound waves in the internal organs.

Abdominal X-ray A simple study that will give the physician an idea of how the internal organs look.

Abdominoperineal resection Surgery to remove the anus, the rectum, and part of the sigmoid colon through an incision made in the abdomen. The end of the intestine is attached to an opening in the surface of the abdomen and body waste is collected in a disposable bag outside of the body. This opening is called a colostomy. Lymph nodes that contain cancer may also be removed during this operation.

Abduct A movement away from the medial plane. In the orbit, the abducens nerve supplies the lateral rectus muscle that pulls the eye laterally outward.

Abductor Any muscle that moves any part of the body away from midline of the body.

Ablation In medicine, the removal or destruction of a body part or tissue or its function. Ablation may be performed by surgery, hormones, drugs, radiofrequency, heat or other methods.

Abnormal Not normal. Deviating from the usual structure, position, condition, or behaviour. In referring to a growth, abnormal may mean that it is cancerous or premalig-nant (likely to become cancer).

Abortion An abortion is the removal or expulsion from the uterus of an embryo or fetus, resulting in or caused by its death. This can occur spontaneously as a miscarriage, or be artificially induced through chemical, surgical or other means. Commonly, "abortion" refers to an induced abortion procedure at any point in the pregnancy; medically, it is defined as a miscarriage or induced termination before twenty weeks gestation, which is considered nonviable. There have been various methods of inducing abortion throughout history.

Spontaneous abortion An abortion due to accidental trauma

Induced abortion: An abortion deliberately caused. Induced abortions are further subcategorized into therapeutic abortions and elective abortions:

a. Therapeutic abortion To save the life of the pregnant woman.

To preserve the woman's physical or mental health.

To terminate a pregnancy that would result in a child born with a congenital disorder which would be fatal or associated with significant morbidity.

To selectively reduce the number of fetuses to lessen health risks associated with.

b. Elective abortion An abortion performed for any other reason.

A pregnancy that ends earlier than 37 completed weeks of gestation, and where an infant is born and survives, is termed a premature birth.

In common parlance, the term "abortion" is synonymous with induced abortion of a human fetus. However, in medical texts, the word 'abortion' can also refer to spontaneous abortion (miscarriage).

The distinctions between spontaneous abortion, therapeutic abortion and induced delivery may be blurred. For example, in cases of pre-eclampsia spontaneous abortion may occur, but if it does not, doctors may opt for immediate delivery regardless of the potential viability of the fetus.

Abrasion Loss of tooth structure caused by a hard toothbrush, poor brushing technique, or Bruxism (grinding or clenching the teeth).

Abscess An enclosed collection of pus in tissues, organs, or confined spaces in the body. An abscess is a sign of infection and is usually swollen and inflamed.

Absorbent products Pads and garments, disposable or reusable, worn to absorb leaked urine. Absorbent products include shields, undergarment pads, combination pad-pant systems, diaperlike garments, and bed pads.

Absorption The passage of nutrients in food from the small intestine into the cells in the body.

Abuse When used as a legal term in the business of healthcare, it normally refers to actions that do not involve intentional misrepresentations in billing but which, nevertheless, result in improper conduct. Consequences can result in civil liability and administrative sanctions. An example of abuse is the excessive use of medical supplies.

Abutment Tooth or teeth that support a fixed or removable bridge.

ABX EGF A monoclonal antibody that is being studied in the diagnosis and treatment of some types of cancer. Monoclonal antibodies are made in the laboratory and can locate and bind to cancer cells. Also called panitumumab.

AC/A ratio Accommodative convergence/accommodative (measured in prism diopters/diopters). The convergence response of an individual (amount the eyes turn inward) in relation to the amount of stimulus of accommodation (eye focusing). The normal ratio is 4:1.

Acantholysis The loss of cohesion between epidermal or adnexal keratinacytes.

Acanthosis The increase in the thickness of the stratum malpighii.

Acanthosis nigricans A dermatological disorder present in association with endocrine diseases (i.e., diabetes, obesity, pituitary tumors, or Cushing's disease). It is characterized by brown, velvety hyperkeratotic patches in the body folds.

Acarbose A drug used as a treatment for Type 2 (noninsulin-dependent) diabetes; belongs to a class of drugs called alpha-glucosidase inhibitors.

Acarid A mite or tick.

Accelerated phase chronic myelogenous leukemia A phase of chronic myelogenous leukemia in which the disease is progressing. In this phase, 6% to 30% of the cells in the blood and bone marrow are blast cells (immature blood cells).

Acceptable daily intake (ADI) The amount of chemical that, if ingested daily over a lifetime, appears to be without appreciable effect.

Access The patient's ability to obtain medical care. The ease of access is determined by such components as the availability of medical services and their acceptability to the patient, the location of health care facilities, transportation, hours of operation and cost of care. An individual's ability to obtain appropriate health care services. Barriers to access can be financial (insufficient monetary resources), geographic (distance to providers), organizational (lack of available providers) and sociological (e.g., discrimination, language barriers). Efforts to improve access often focus on providing/improving health coverage.

Accessory cell Cell required for, but not actually mediating, a specific immune response. Often used to describe antigen-presenting cells.

Accessory movement Joint movements which cannot be performed voluntarily or in isolation by the patient.

Acclimatization The biological process whereby an organism adapts to a new environment. One example is the process of developing microorganisms that degrade toxic wastes in the environment.

Accommodation (eye focusing) The eye's ability to adjust its focus by the action of the ciliary muscle, which increases the lens focusing power. When this accommodation skill is working properly, the eye can focus and refocus quickly and effortlessly, which is similar to an automatic focus feature on a camera. The ciliary muscles must contract to adjust for near vision, which causes the eye's crystalline lens, which is flexible, to be squashed. For distant vision, the ciliary muscle must relax and the eye's crystalline lens is stretched out. The ability of the eye to accommodate does decrease with age due to the crystalline lens becoming less flexible causing a condition called presbyopia.

Accommodation schedule Defines all areas that can influence unit operations required for manufacturing, and relationships and flows between them.

Accommodative esotropia (clinical condition) When an individual is focusing on a near object and his or her eyes are turning inward too much. It is caused by either uncorrected hyperopic refractive error and/or a high accommodative convergence/accommodation (AC/A) ratio. The average age of onset is 2 1/2 years. It is most noticeable when the child is tired or sick. This is treated with plus lenses (glasses or contacts) to help straighten the eyes. In some cases, vision therapy and corrective lenses are prescribed.

Accommodative excess (AE) This clinical condition is also called accommodative spasm. It is an over focusing, over stimulation of the focusing action of the crystalline lens causing an inability to relax the focusing system which may result in blurry vision when focusing at distance objects. Other symptoms include holding near work closer than normal, headaches with near work (such as reading or using a computer), eyestrain associated with near work, and possible double vision. Clinical signs include: patient accepts more minus on accommodative rock but blurs with plus lenses, lower NRA than PRA, dynamic retinoscopy findings indication of over accommodation and/or slow relaxation of accommodation, and reduced or erratic distance visual acuity. Treatment includes a low plus lens and/or vision therapy.

Accommodative fatigue This clinical condition is also called Ill-Sustained Accommodation. It is the inability of the eye to adequately sustain sufficient focusing over an extended time period. The most common sign or symptom is blurred vision after prolonged near work such as reading and using a computer. In addition, such patients often have asthenopia (eyestrain), general fatigue, headaches and nausea, excess tearing, and an unusual sensitivity to light. Clinical signs include: normal amplitude of accommodation, decreased PRA, and the patient generally fails the +/−2.00 D flipper test. Plus lenses (glasses or contacts) and vision therapy are effective in treating this condition.

Accommodative infacility A clinical condition in which the individual has difficulty changing eye focus from distance to near. Symptoms include eyestrain associated with near work (such as reading or using a computer), periodic blurring of distance vision especially following sustained near visual work, tendency to hold near work closer than expected, headaches with near work, and possible double vision. Clinical signs include: patient will have difficulty with both the plus and the minus lens (fails +/−2.00 D flipper test), low PRA and NRA, and poor recoveries on Bell Retinoscopy. Vision therapy is an effective treatment option.

Accommodative insufficiency (AI) This clinical condition is also called non-presbyopic accommodative insufficiency. It is an under focusing, a lack of focusing ability at a near distance. Symptoms include eyestrain, blurred vision, occasional or constant when doing near work (such as reading or using a computer), occasional unusual sensitivity to light, excess tearing, headaches, and general fatigue. Clinical signs include: patient will have difficulty with a minus lens, low amplitude of accommodation, low PRA and higher NRA. Vision therapy is an effective treatment option.

Accommodative vergence A convergence response (to turn the eyes inward) which occurs as a direct result of accommodation (eye focusing).

Accrual The amount of money that is set aside to cover expenses. The accrual is the plan's best estimate of what those expenses are, and (for medical expenses) is based on a combination of data from the authorization system, the claims system, lag studies, and the plan's prior history.

ACE inhibitor (Angiotensin-converting enzyme inhibitor) A type of drug that is used to lower blood pressure. ACE inhibitors belong to the family of drugs called antihypertensives.

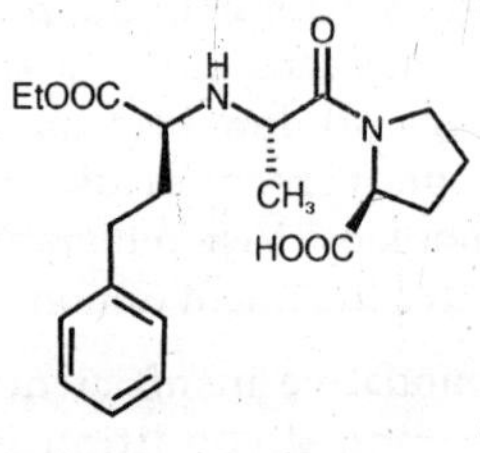

(A type of ACE inhibitor)

Figure Enalapril

Acesulfame K Acesulfame K, or acesulfame potassium is a low-calorie sweetener. It is an organic salt consisting of carbon, nitrogen, oxygen, hydrogen, sulphur and potassium atoms. It is 200 times sweeter than sucrose, has a synergistic sweetening effect with other sweeteners, has a stable shelf-life and is heat stable. It is excreted through the human digestive system unchanged, and is therefore non-caloric.

Acetabulum A large cup-shaped cavity that is the point of articulation between the femur and the os coxae of the pelvis.

Acetaminophen A drug that reduces pain and fever (but not inflammation). It belongs to the family of drugs called analgesics.

Acetohexamide A "first-generation" sulfonylurea pill taken to lower the level of glucose (sugar) in the blood. Only some people with Type 2 diabetes take these pills.

Acetone A chemical formed in the blood when the body uses fat instead of glucose (sugar) for energy. If acetone forms, it usually means that the cells do not have enough insulin, or cannot use the insulin that is in the blood, to use glucose for energy. Acetone passes through the body into the urine. Someone with a lot of acetone in the body can have breath that smells fruity and is called "acetone breath."

Acetylcysteine A drug usually used to reduce the thickness of mucus and ease its removal. It is also used to reverse the toxicity of high doses of acetaminophen. Also called N-acetyl-L-cysteine.

Acetylsalicylic acid An orally administered non-steroidal anti-inflammatory agent. Acetylsalicylic acid binds to and acetylates serine residues in cyclooxygenases, resulting in decreased synthesis of prost-aglandin, platelet aggregation, and inflammation. This agent exhibits analgesic, antipyretic and anticoagulant properties.

Achilles tendinitis Inflammation of the Achilles tendon, particularly the peritendon. It may be predisposed to this type of condition because of biomechanical, muscular, training and footwear factors.

Achilles tendon The tendon of the musclesof the calf of leg, at the back of the ankle and attached to calcaneus, the heel bone.

Achlorhydria A lack of hydrochloric acid in the digestive juices in the stomach. Hydrochloric acid helps digest food.

Acid A compound of an electronegative element or radical with hydrogen; it form salts by replacing all or part of the hydrogen with an electropositive element or radical. Or, a hydrogen-containing substance that when dissolved in water dissociates to produce one or more hydrogen ions (H^+).

Acid fast bacillus Bacteria capable of living in acidic environments, such as inside macrophages. Tuberculosis and MAI/MAC are acid fast bacilli

Acid feed Injection of an acid into a liquid stream to make it less alkaline (pH adjustment).

Acidosis Too much acid in the body. For a person with diabetes, this can lead to diabetic ketoacidosis.

Acini The sac-like part of the milk-producing glands in the breast. These are also called lobules.

Acitretin A substance that is used in the prevention of cancer and in the treatment of psoriasis. It belongs to the family of drugs called retinoids.

Acne A disorder of the skin in which oil glands and hair glands become inflamed.

Acoustic Having to do with sound or hearing.

Acoustic neurofibromatosis A genetic condition in which tumors form on the nerves of the inner ear and cause loss of hearing and balance. Tumors may also occur in the brain and on nerves in the skull and spinal cord, and may cause loss of speech, eye movement, and the ability to swallow. Also called neurofibromatosis type 2.

Acquired condition A condition that can be brought about by an eye disease, trauma or surgery resulting in phthisis, evisceration, enucleation or exenteration of the eye.

Acquired immune deficiency syndrome (AIDS) Severe manifestation of infection with the human immunodeficiency virus (HIV). The Centers for Disease Control and Prevention lists numerous opportunistic infections and neoplasms which, in the presence of HIV infection, constitute an AIDS diagnosis. In addition, a CD4 count below 200/mm^3 in the presence of HIV infection constitutes an AIDS diagnosis.

Acquired immunity The body's ability to fight or prevent a specific infection. This ability can be acquired either actively (by having and recovering from an infection or by being vaccinated against an infection) or passively (by receiving antibodies from an outside source, such as from breast milk or donated blood components).

Acridine carboxamide A substance that is being studied in the treatment of cancer. It belongs to the family of drugs called topoisomerase inhibitors.

Acrodermatitis Inflammation of the skin of the extremities, particularly of the paws or feet, e.g. lethal acrodermatitis - an inherited autosomal recessive disease in bull terriers relating to zinc metabolism.

Acromioclavicular joint The articulation between the acromion process and clavicle.

Acromion process The vertical extension of the scapula, above the glenohumeral joint.

Acrylonitrile A substance used to make plastics, rubber, and textiles. Being exposed to acrylonitrile may increase the risk of developing certain cancers, such as lung, brain, or prostate cancer.

Actinic keratosis A precancerous condition of thick, scaly patches of skin. Also called solar or senile keratosis.

Action point A value set to identify when a parameter has drifted outside the operating range (Acceptance Criteria). A documented response is usually required.

Action study In cancer prevention clinical trials, a study that focuses on finding out whether actions people take can prevent cancer.

Activase A protein that is made by the body and that helps dissolve blood clots. It can also be made in the laboratory and is used in the treatment of heart attack and stroke. It is also being studied in the treatment of cancer. Activase belongs to the family of drugs called systemic thrombolytic agents. Also called tissue plasminogen activator (tPA), recombinant tissue plasminogen activator (r-tPA), and Alteplase.

Activate In biology, to stimulate a cell in a resting state to become active. This causes biochemical and functional changes in the activated cell.

Activated carbon Material used to adsorb organic impurities from water. Derived from wood, lignite, pulp-mill char, blood, etc. The source material is initially charred at high temperature to convert it to carbon. The carbon is then "activated" by oxidation from exposure to high temperature steam. It comes in granular or powdered form.

Active control treatment A control treatment that involves use of a pharmacologically or medically active substance. Active controls are used when there is already an available treatment, so the use of a placebo or no treatment would be unethical.

Active immunity Protection from a specific infection that develops after having and recovering from the infection or being vaccinated against the infection.

Active ingredient Any component that is intended to furnish pharmacological activity or other direct effect in the diagnosis, cure, mitigation, treatment, or prevention of disease, or to affect the structure or any function of the body of man or other animals. The term includes those components that may undergo chemical change in the manufacture of the drug product and are present in the drug product in a modified form intended to furnish the specified activity or effect.

Active site The region of a protein molecule that binds the specific substrate and chemically modifies it into the new product (in an enzyme) or interacts with it (in a receptor).

Active transport Energy-requiring transport of a solution across a membrane in the direction of increasing concentration.

Activities of daily living The tasks of everyday life. Basic ADLs include eating, dressing, getting into or out of a bed or chair, taking a bath or shower, and using the toilet. Instrumental activities of daily living (IADL) are activities related to independent living and include preparing meals, managing money, shopping, doing housework, and using a telephone.

Actos A drug that is used to treat type 2 diabetes and is being studied in the prevention of head and neck cancer. It may be able to stop leukoplakia (a precancerous condition affecting the mouth) from developing into cancer. It belongs to the family of drugs called thiazolidinediones. Also called pioglitazone.

Acuity Clearness of eyesight. Depends on the sharpness of images and the sensitivity of nerve elements in the retina.

Acupressure The application of pressure or localized massage to specific sites on the body to control symptoms such as pain or nausea. It is a type of complementary and alternative medicine.

Acupuncture The technique of inserting thin needles through the skin at specific points on the body to control pain and other symptoms. It is a type of complementary and alternative medicine.

Acustimulation Mild electrical stimulation of acupuncture points to control symptoms such as nausea and vomiting.

Acute Short term, intense symptomatology or pathology, as distinct from chronic. Many diseases have an acute phase (like HIV seroconversion disease) and a chronic phase. This distinction is sometimes used in treatments, as in highdose ganciclovir for acute (or induction) treatment of CMV retinitis, followed by a lower dose for chronic (or maintenance) treatment.

Acute care A pattern of health care in which a patient is treated for an acute (immediate and severe) episode of illness, for the subsequent treatment of injuries related to an accident or other trauma, or during recovery from surgery. Specialized personnel using complex and sophisticated technical equipment and materials usually give acute care in a hospital. Unlike chronic care, acute care is often necessary for only a short time.

Acute HIV infection Also known as primary HIV infection or acute retroviral syndrome (ARS). The period of rapid HIV replication that occurs 2 to 4 weeks after infection by HIV. Acute HIV infection is characterized by a drop in CD4 cell counts and an increase in HIV levels in the blood. Some, but not all, individuals experience flu-like symptoms during this period of infection. These symptoms can include fever, inflamed lymph nodes, sore throat, and rash. These symptoms may last from a few days to 4 weeks and then go away.

Acute leukemia A rapidly progressing cancer that starts in blood-forming tissue such as the bone marrow and causes large numbers of white blood cells to be produced and enter the blood stream.

Acute lymphoblastic leukemia A quickly progressing disease in which too many immature white blood cells (called lymphoblasts) are found in the blood and bone marrow. Also called acute lymphocytic leukemia.

Acute myeloid leukemia A quickly progressing disease in which too many immature white blood cells (not lymphocytes) are found in the blood and bone marrow. Also called acute myelogenous leukemia or acute nonlymphocytic leukemia.

Acute nonlymphocytic leukemia A quickly progressing disease in which too many immature blood-forming cells are found in the blood and bone marrow. Also called acute myeloid leukemia or acute myelogenous leukemia.

Acute pain Pain that comes on quickly, can be severe, but lasts a relatively short time.

Acute promyelocytic leukemia An aggressive (fast-growing) type of acute myeloid leukemia in which there are too many immature blood-forming cells in the blood and bone marrow. It is usually marked by an exchange of parts of chromosomes 15 and 17. Also called promyelocytic leukemia.

Acyclovir A substance used to prevent or treat cytomegalovirus and herpes simplex infections that may occur when the body is immunosuppressed. It belongs to the family of drugs called antivirals.

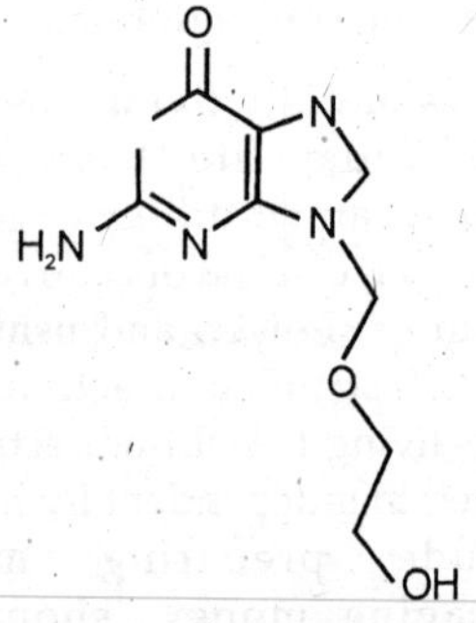

Figure Acyclovir

AD 32 A drug that is used to treat bladder cancer that does not respond to BCG (Bacillus Calmette Guerin). It is an anthracycline and belongs to the family of drugs called antitumor antibiotics. Also called valrubicin.

Ad5CMV p53 gene A replication-defective adenoviral-CMV vector that encodes a wild-type p53 gene. Ad5CMV-p53 induces tumor cells that have been transfected with the vector to produce wild-type p53, a tumor suppressor gene that is deleted or mutated in a significant number of cancers. In transfected tumor cells, the wild-type p-53 gene product exerts an antitumor effect by blocking cell cycle progression at the G1/S regulation point, activating DNA repair proteins in the presence of DNA damage, and initiating apoptosis when DNA damage is irreparable.

Adderall A combination of drugs that is used as a treatment for attention deficit hyperactivity disorder (ADHD) and narcolepsy (a sleep disorder). It belongs to the family of drugs called stimulants. Also called dextroamphetamine-amphetamine.

Addiction Uncontrollable craving, seeking and use of a substance such as a drug or alcohol.

Addison's disease A rare endocrine disease that results from the underproduction of steroid hormones by the adrenal glands. Symptoms include weakness, low blood pressure, anaemia, low blood sugar and electrolyte abnormalities. Addison's disease has several causes, including autoimmune destruction of the adrenal glands by antibodies, as in the Autoimmune Polyglandular Syndrome where it may be linked to type 1A diabetes.

Additive genetic effects When the combined effects of alleles at different loci are equal to the sum of their individual effects.

Additives (food additives) Any natural or synthetic material, other than the basic raw ingredients, used in the production of a food item to enhance the final product. Any substance that may affect the characteristics of any food, including those used in the production, processing, treatment, packaging, transportation or storage of food.

Additus ad antrum The mastoid air spaces connecting the mastoid antrum with the epitympanic recess.

Adduct A movement toward the midline. The adductor magnus muscle in the thigh pulls the leg toward the medial plane.

Adductor tendinitis Commonly occurring in athletes and horse riders, with localised pain over the tendinous origin of adductor longus from the pubis or at its musculotendinous junction.

Adenine (A) A purine base, 6-aminopurine, occurring in RNA (ribonucleic acid) and DNA (deoxyribonucleic acid) and as a component of adenosine triphosphate.

Adeno Gland. e.g. adenitis inflammation of a gland.

Adenocarcinoma Cancer that begins in cells that line certain internal organs and that have glandular (secretory) properties.

Adenoid cystic cancer A rare type of cancer that usually begins in the salivary glands.

Adenoma A benign tumor made up of glandular tissue. For example, an adenoma of the pituitary gland may cause it to produce abnormal amounts of hormones.

Adenopathy Enlargement of glands, especially the lymph nodes.

Adenosine triphosphate (ATP) A substance present in all living cells that provides energy for many metabolic processes and is involved in making RNA. ATP made in the laboratory is being studied in patients with advanced solid tumors to see if it can decrease weight loss and improve muscle strength.

Adenovirus 5 tumor necrosis factor alpha A recombinant agent consisting of a genetically-modified adenovirus 5 vector encoding the protein cytokine tumor necrosis factor (TNF) alpha. TNF exhibits potent anti-tumor cytolytic properties; the adenovirus 5 vector efficiently infects tumor cells, delivering tumor-specific TNF.

Adenovirus One of a number of genetically-engineered adenoviruses designed to insert a gene of interest into a eukaryotic cell where the gene of interest is subsequently expressed. Unlike most other vectors, adenovirus vectors have the ability to infect post-mitotic cells. Thus, these agents are especially useful for gene transfer into neuronal cells.

Adherence Closely following (adhering to) a prescribed treatment regimen. This includes taking the correct dose of a drug at the correct time, exactly as prescribed. Failure to adhere to an anti-HIV treatment regimen can lead to virological failure and drug resistance.

Adhesive dentistry Contemporary term for dental restorations that involve "bonding" of composite resin or porcelain fillings to natural teeth.

Adipose tissue Orbital fatty tissue that cushions the eyeball. It is usually made reference to when its loss, reduction or displacement within the orbit causes facial asymmetry of the eyelids resulting in enophthalmos and/or superior sulcus depression.

Adiposis The breaking down of fatty tissue, or its gravitational displacement following loss of the eye. It can also occur following trauma induced phthisis.

Adjudication Processing claims according to contract.

Adjunct agent In cancer therapy, a drug or substance used in addition to the primary therapy.

Adjunctive therapy Another treatment used together with the primary treatment. Its purpose is to assist the primary treatment.

Adjusted admissions Adjusted admissions are equivalent to the sum of inpatient admissions and an estimate of the volume of outpatient services. This is a measure of all patient care activity undertaken in a hospital, both inpatient and outpatient. This estimate is calculated by multiplying outpatient visits by the ratio of outpatient charges per visit to inpatient charges per admission.

Adjuvant Any substance used in conjunction with another to enhance its activity. Aluminium salts are used as adjuvants in the preparation of DPT vaccines.

Adjuvant chemotherapy Chemotherapy given to kill any remaining cancer cells, usually after all detectable tumor is removed by surgery or radiotherapy.

Adjuvant therapy Treatment that is added to increase the effectiveness of a primary therapy. It usually refers to chemotherapy or radiation added after surgery to increase the chances of curing the disease or keeping it in check locally.

Administration (route of administration) How a drug or therapy is introduced into the body (e.g., intravenously, or orally).

Admissions per 1,000 Number of patients admitted to a hospital or hospitals per 1,000 health plan members. An indicator calculated by taking the total number of inpatient and/or outpatient admissions from a specific group, e.g., employer group HMO population at risk, for a specific period of time (usually one year), dividing it by the average number of covered members in that group during the same period, and multiplying the result by 1,000. This indicator can be calculated for behavioural health or any disease in the aggregate and by modality of treatment, e.g., inpatient, residential, and partial hospitalization, etc.

Adnexa Appendages of the eyeball, which includes the eyelids, muscles and soft tissue.

Adnexal mass A lump in tissue near the uterus, usually in the ovary or fallopian tube. Adnexal masses include ovarian cysts, ectopic (tubal) pregnancies, and benign (noncancerous) or malignant (cancerous) tumors.

Adrenal gland A small gland that produces steroid hormones, adrenaline, and noradrenaline, which help control heart rate, blood pressure, and other important body functions. There are two adrenal glands, one located on top of each kidney.

Adrenaline A drug used to treat anaphylaxis. (It is very similar to the hormone called adrenaline that is produced naturally in our bodies and is responsible for feelings of excitement and stimulation). Also known as Epinephrine in the USA.

Adrenocortical cancer A rare cancer that forms in the outer layer of tissue of the adrenal gland (a small organ on top of each kidney that makes steroid hormones, adrenaline, and noradrenaline to control heart rate, blood pressure, and other body functions). Also called adrenocortical carcinoma and cancer of the adrenal cortex.

Adrenocortical Having to do with or made by the outer layer of the adrenal gland, which produces steroid hormones. There is an adrenal gland on top of each kidney.

Adriamycin An anticancer drug that belongs to the family of drugs called antitumor antibiotics. It is an anthracycline. Also called doxorubicin.

Adsorption Adhesion of the molecules of a gas, liquid or dissolved substance to a surface because of chemical or electrical attraction - typically accomplished with granular activated carbon to remove dissolved organics and chlorine. The attachment of charged particles to the chemically active groups on the surface and in the pores of an ion exchanger.

Adult T-cell leukemia/lymphoma ATLL. An aggressive (fast-growing) type of T-cell non-Hodgkin's lymphoma caused by the human T-cell leukemia virus type 1 (HTLV-1). It is marked by bone and skin lesions, high calcium levels, and enlarged lymph nodes, spleen and liver.

Advance directive A legal document that states the treatment or care a person wishes to receive or not receive if he or she becomes unable to make medical decisions (for example, due to being unconscious or in a coma). Some types of advance directives are living wills and do-not-resuscitate (DNR) orders.

Advanced cancer A stage of cancer in which the disease has spread from the primary site to other parts of the body, directly or by traveling through the network of lymph glands (lymphatics) or in the bloodstream. When the cancer has spread only to the surrounding areas, it is called locally advanced.

Advanced glycation end products (AGEs) A group of compounds that may have a role in diabetes complications such as retinopathy, neuropathy, nephropathy, and vascular disease. At present it is not known if they are the cause or the consequence of the complications observed.

Advanced malignant mesothelioma Malignant mesothelioma that is stage II, III, or IV.

Adventitious agents Acquired, sporadic, accidental contaminants.

Adverse agents Undesired effects or toxicity due to exposure (often but not limited to a drug or medical device).

Adverse drug reaction (ADR) Any drug effect that is unwanted, unpleasant, or potentially harmful. These effects may be mild and may disappear when the drug is stopped or subside as the body adjusts to the drug. Other ADRs, such as skin rashes, anemia, or organ damage, are more serious.

Adverse effect An unwanted side effect of treatment.

Adverse event An unexpected medical problem that happens during treatment with a drug or other therapy. Adverse events do not have to be caused by the drug or therapy, and they may be mild, moderate, or severe.

Adverse experience (AE) A toxic reaction to a treatment under study. Typically, all Grade 4, life-threatening toxicities and deaths are adverse experiences, irrespective of whether or not they are believed to be due to study drug, as are any toxicities that require permanent discontinuation of study drug.

AE-941 A substance made from shark cartilage that is being studied for its ability to prevent the growth of new blood vessels to solid tumors. It belongs to the family of drugs called angiogenesis inhibitors.

AEE788 An orally bioavailable multiple-receptor tyrosine kinase inhibitor. AEE788 inhibits phosphorylation of the tyrosine kinases of epidermal growth factor receptor (EGFR), human epidermal growth factor receptor 2 (HER2), and vascular endothelial growth factor receptor 2 (VEGF2), resulting in receptor inhibition, the inhibition of cellular proliferation, and induction of tumor cell and tumor-associated endothelial cell apoptosis.

AER (Adverse experience report) A document in a pre-specified format used to collect information on all reportable adverse experiences

Aero allergen Allergen that is suspended in the air and breathed into respiratory tract, where it sets up an allergic reaction.

Aerobe An organism that can live and grow only in the presence of oxygen.

1. Facultative aerobe: one which normally thrives in the absence of oxygen, but which may acquire the faculty of living in the presence of oxygen.

2. Obligate aerobe: one that cannot live without air.

Aerobic In biochemistry, reactions that need oxygen to happen or happen when oxygen is present.

Aerobic bacteria Bacteria capable of growing in the presence of Oxygen.

Aerobic exercise Aerobic exercise refers to the kind of fast-paced activity that makes you "huff and puff." It places demands on your cardiovascular apparatus and, over time, produces beneficial changes in your respiratory and circulatory systems.

Aerobic metabolism A chemical process in which oxygen is used to make energy from carbohydrates (sugars). Also known as aerobic respiration, oxidative metabolism, or cell respiration.

Aerobic respiration A chemical process in which oxygen is used to make energy from carbohydrates (sugars). Also known as oxidative metabolism, cell respiration, or aerobic metabolism.

Aerodigestive tract The combined organs and tissues of the respiratory tract and the upper part of the digestive tract (including the lips, mouth, tongue, nose, throat, vocal cords, and part of the esophagus and windpipe).

Aerosol A product that is dispensed by a propellant from a metal can up to a maximum size of 33.8 fluid up to a maximum size of 33.8 fluid ounces (1000 ml) or a glass or plastic bottle up to a size of 4 fluid ounces (118.3 mL), other than a rim-vented container.

Aerosol photometer Light-scattering mass concentration indicating instrument with a threshold sensitivity of at least 10 to the negative third power microgram per liter for 0.3µm diameter DOP (Dioctyl Phthalate) concentrations over a range of 10 to the fifth power times the threshold sensitivity. Photometers may include hand-held remote meter probes that can scan for airborne contaminants in HEPA filters, in penetrations around frames, seals and plenums, and in hoods and work stations.

Aerosolize In medicine, to turn a liquid drug into a fine mist that can be inhaled.

Aerosolized A form of administration in which a drug, such as pentamidine, is turned into a fine spray or mist by a nebulizer, and inhaled.

AFB Acid-fast bacillus.

AFB smear A laboratory technique for visualizing mycobacteria under the microscope. Smear results are usually available within a few days, and they correlate strongly with infectiousness, especially in untreated patients. However, a "positive" result cannot distinguish between TB, MAI or other mycobacterial infections.

Afebrile Without a fever.

Affected relative pair Individuals related by blood, each of whom is affected with the same trait. Examples are affected sibling, cousin, and avuncular pairs.

Affinity A measure of the binding constant of a single antigen combining site with a monovalent antigenic determinant.

Aflatoxin A harmful substance made by certain types of mold (Aspergillus flavus and Aspergillus parasiticus) that is often found on poorly stored grains and nuts. Consumption of foods contaminated with aflatoxin is a risk factor for primary liver cancer.

AFP (Alpha-fetoprotein) A protein normally produced by a developing fetus. AFP levels are usually undetectable in the blood of healthy nonpregnant adults. An elevated level of AFP suggests the presence of either a primary liver cancer or germ cell tumor.

AFP gene hepatocellular carcinoma vaccine A cancer vaccine composed of naked plasmid DNA of the gene for the tumorassociated antigen alphafetoprotein (AFP), a macromolecule that acts as a specific immunologic target for hepatocellular carcinoma. This agent exerts an antitumor effect by inducing cytotoxic T-lymphocytes to attack AFP-expressing tumor cells.

After image The eye's ability to still see an image during eye blinks and even after the viewed object is no longer present. The most common example is seeing light after the flash of a camera.

Agammaglobulinemia Absence or low levels of antibodies in the blood. This condition leaves a person vulnerable to infections.

Agar A complex mixture of polysaccharides obtained from marine red algae, used as an emulsion stabilizer in foods, as a sizing in fabrics, as a gelling agent and as a solid substrate or media for the laboratory culture of microorganisms. Agar melts at 100°C and when cooled below 44°C forms a stiff and transparent gel. Microorganisms are seeded and grown on the surface of the gel.

Agarose A highly purified form of agar.

Agarose gel electrophoresis A method used to separate, identify, and purify molecules of different molecular weight and/or structure. It is specifically applied to the separation of protein or DNA fragments where it is rapid, simple, and accurate and the separated molecules can be visualized directly by staining with dyes. The electrophoretic migration rate of molecules through agarose gel is dependent on the following parameters:

1. Molecular size: molecules pass through the gel at rates that are inversely proportional to the log of their molecular weight.

2. Agarose concentration: a molecule of a given size migrates at different rates through gels containing different concentrations of agarose.

3. Molecular conformation: a molecule of the same molecular weight but of a different conformation will migrate at different rates. Generally, closed circular or globular forms will migrate faster than linear forms.

4. Electric current: at low voltages the rate of migration is proportional to the voltage, but as the voltage is increased the rate of migration of high molecular weight fragments is increased differentially.

Age/sex rates Also called table rates, they are given group products' set of rates where each grouping, by age and sex, has its own rates.

Agenesis Absence, failure of formation or imperfect development of any part.

Agent study In cancer prevention clinical trials, a study that tests whether taking certain medicines, vitamins, minerals, or food supplements can prevent cancer. Also a called chemoprevention study.

Agglomerate Suspended solids clustered together to form larger clumps or masses that are easier to remove by filtration or settling.

Agglutination The aggregation of particulate antigen by antibodies. Agglutination applies to red blood cells as well as to bacteria and inert particles covered with antigen.

Agglutinin A substance that makes particles (such as bacteria or cells) stick together to form a clump or a mass.

Aggressive A quickly growing ca'.cer.

Agg essive lymphoma A type of lymphoma that grows and spreads quickly, and has severe symptoms. It is seen frequently in patients who are HIV-positive (AIDS-related lymphoma). Also called intermediate-grade or high-grade lymphoma.

Agnogenic myeloid metaplasia A progressive, chronic disease in which the bone marrow is replaced by fibrous tissue and blood is made in organs such as the liver and the spleen, instead of in the bone marrow. This disease is marked by an enlarged spleen and progressive anemia. Also called chronic idiopathic myelofibrosis, primary myelofibrosis, myelosclerosis with myeloid metaplasia, and idiopathic myelofibrosis.

Agonist A drug that triggers an action from a cell or another drug.

Agranulocyte A type of white blood cell; monocytes and lymphocytes are agranulocytes.

Agrochemicals Term for artificially produced chemicals (such as feed additives, pharmaceuticals, fertilizers or pesticides) used in agriculture to improve crops or livestack production.

AHF (Antihemophilic factor) In the clotting of blood it is also known as Factor VIII.

AIDS defining condition Any of a list of illnesses that, when occurring in an HIV-infected person, leads to a diagnosis of AIDS, the most serious stage of HIV infection. AIDS is also diagnosed if an HIV-infected person has a CD4 count below 200 cells/mm^3, whether or not that person has an AIDS-defining condition. The Centers for Disease Control and Prevention (CDC) published a list of AIDS-defining conditions in 1993. The 26 conditions include candidiasis, cytomegalovirus disease, Kaposi's sarcoma, mycobacterium avium complex, pneumocystis carinii pneumonia, recurrent pneumonia, progressive multifocal leukoencephalopathy, pulmonary tuberculosis, invasive cervical cancer, and wasting syndrome.

AIDS dementia complex (ADC) Also called HIV-associated dementia. A progressive mental disorder with different nervous system and mental symptoms. Mental symptoms may be memory loss, speech problems, inabilty to concentrate, or poor judgment. There may be behaviour changes, such as not being able to perform daily tasks. There may also be mood changes, such as depression. Motor difficulties may include loss of control of the legs or moving slowly or stiffly. ADC is considered an AIDS-defining condition in people with HIV.

AIDS related cancer Several cancers are more common or more aggressive in people with HIV. These cancers include certain types of immune system cancers (lymphomas), Kaposi's sarcoma, cancers that affect the anus and the cervix, and others. Having HIV appears to play a role in the development and progression of these cancers, although people without HIV can also have them.

AIDS related complex (ARC) A group of complications that commonly occur in the early stage of HIV infection. These may include recurrent fever, unexplained weight loss, swollen lymph nodes, diarrhea, herpes, or fungus infection of the mouth and throat.

AII antagonists A type of drug used to lower blood pressure. They are currently approved for the treatment of essential hypertension. Clinical studies are currently in progress to determine whether they also have a role in the management of heart failure and in the prevention and management of diabetic kidney disease Also called AII Receptor Antagonists. AII is an acronym for Angiotensin II.

Air abrasion Removal of tooth structure by blasting a tooth with air and abrasive, a relatively new technology that may avoid the need for anesthetic.

Air change rate The number of times the total air volume of a defined space is replaced in a given unit of time. This is computed by dividing the total volume of the subject space (in cubic feet) into the total volume of air exhausted from (or supplied to) the space per unit of time.

Air cleaners Filtration systems that may be freestanding or installed in a ceiling or wall to remove contaminants such as bacteria, viruses, and dust from the air. Air cleaners may incorporate HEPA filters.

Air lift bioreactor A reactor in which the source of agitation is air sparged upwards through a draft tube - most widely used for cell culture applications and monoclonal antibody production.

Air velocity meters/monitors Meters to measure and indicate the force and speed of airflow. Meters may use a variety of probes for measuring near HEPA filters and at right angles. Monitors check and record air velocity.

Airflow visualization Using chemical smoke or fog to visualize flow patterns in a cleanroom or clean space.

Airlock A room or space designed to act as a means of segregating areas of different air classification or quality. It may contain a method to remove particulate contamination from clean room garments as personnel pass through, and usually includes HEPA filtered air supply and interlocking doors. Airlocks pressure will "float" between those of the spaces being protected. With all doors closed, the airlock pressure will be somewhere between that of the highest adjoining room and that of the lowest adjoining room as air flows through it from room to room. "Ventilated airlocks" are in neutral ducted air balance (supply CFM = return CFM).

AJCC staging system A system developed by the American Joint Committee on Cancer for describing the extent of cancer in a patient's body. The descriptions include TNM: T describes the size of the tumor and if it has invaded nearby tissue, N describes any lymph nodes that are involved, and M describes metastasis (spread of cancer from one body part to another).

Alanine aminotransferase (ALT) A liver enzyme, measured through a blood test, that indicates the health of the liver. Lower counts are better. Levels may go up because of hepatitis and other infections, or because of drug toxicities

Alanine transferase An enzyme found in the liver and other tissues. A high level of alanine transferase released into the blood may be a sign of liver damage, cancer, or other diseases. Also called serum glutamate pyruvate transaminase or SGPT.

Alanosine An amino acid analog derived from Streptomyces alanosinicus, a purine antagonist, and an adenylosuccinate synthetase inhibitor with antineoplastic properties. L-alanosine deprives MTAP-deficient (salvage pathway) tumor cells of de novo synthesized adenosine and is probably responsible for diminished DNA synthesis. The clinical use of L-alanosine may be narrow due to its toxicity profile.

Alarms Audible or visual signals used to warn of unacceptable conditions at monitored sites. They may be buzzers, horns, speakers, bells, or warning lights. They can be Advisory, Alert, or Action alarms. The first two are for operation and maintenance information, to alert of abnormal situations that do not compromise product SISPQ. The Action alarm is for GMP records, indicating that product SISPQ may have been compromised, but Alert alarms are also usually recorded.

Albinism Pigmentation is deficient or absent. May occur in skin, hair, and eyes. Ocular albinism is a pigmentation deficiency occurring mainly in the eyes. Individuals with albinism including ocular albinism commonly have decreased visual acuity (20/70 - 20/200), strabismus, photophobia, and nystagmus. There is no known treatment. Individuals may benefit from low-vision aids. Treatment options for strabismus and nystagmus does apply to these individuals.

Albumin Commonly, the white of egg is a simple protein widely distributed throughout the tissues and fluid of plants and animals. Soluble in pure water it is also precipitable from a solution by mineral acids, and coagulable by heat in acid or neutral solution.

Albuminoid Resembling albumin, a simple protein present in horny and cartilaginous tissues, insoluble in neutral solvents. Keratin, elastin, and collagen are albuminoids.

Albuminuria More than normal amounts of a protein called albumin in the urine. Albuminuria may be a sign of kidney disease, a problem that can occur in people who have had diabetes for a long time.

Alcohol An organic chemical in which one or more hydroxyl (OH) groups are attached to carbon (C) atoms in place of hydrogen (H) atoms. Common alcohols include ethyl alcohol or ethanol (found in alcoholic beverages), methyl alcohol or methanol (can cause blindness) and propyl alcohol or propanol (used as a solvent and antiseptic). Rubbing alcohol is a mixture of acetone, methyl isobutyl ketone, and ethyl alcohol. In everyday talk, alcohol usually refers to ethanol as, for example, in wine, beer, and liquor. It can cause changes in behaviour and be addictive.

Alcoholic hepatitis Hepatitis with unique pathologic liver injury varying widely in severity and caused by chronic, heavy alcohol ingestion.

Aldesleukin A laboratory-made colony-stimulating factor that stimulates the production of blood cells, especially platelets, during chemotherapy. It is a cytokine that belongs to the family of drugs called hematopoietic (blood-forming) agents. Also called interleukin-2 or IL-2.

Aldose reductase An enzyme that is normally present in the eye and in many other parts of the body. It changes glucose (sugar) into a sugar alcohol called sorbitol. Too much sorbitol trapped in eye and nerve cells seems to damage these cells, and may be part of the cause of diabetic retinopathy and neuropathy. There are medications that interfere with aldose reductase.

Aldose reductase inhibitor A class of drugs that prevent or slow (inhibit) the action of aldose reductase; are being studied as a way to prevent or delay these complications of diabetes.

Alemtuzumab A recombinant DNA-derived humanized monoclonal antibody directed against the cell surface glycoprotein, CD52. Alemtuzumab is an IgG1 kappa with human variable framework and constant regions, and complementarity-determining regions derived from a rat monoclonal antibody. This agent selectively binds to CD52, thereby triggering a host immune response that results in lysis of CD52 + cells. CD52 is a glycoprotein expressed on the surface of essentially all normal and malignant B and T cells, a majority of monocytes, macrophages and natural killer (NK) cells, a subpopulation of granulocytes, and tissues of the male reproductive system.

Alendronate sodium A drug that affects bone metabolism. It is used in treating osteoporosis and Paget's disease, and is being studied in the treatment of hypercalcemia (abnormally high levels of calcium in the blood) and in treating and reducing the risk of bone pain caused by cancer. Alendronate sodium belongs to the family of drugs called bisphosphonates.

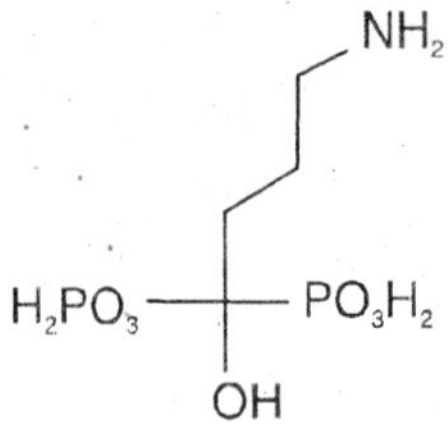

Figure Alendronate

Alert point Used in determining when a parameter is drifting toward extremes of the operating range.

Algin A compound which is extracted from algae and used in puddings, milk shakes and ice cream to make these foods creamier and thicker and to extend shelf life.

Alginate A powdery extract of marine kelp when mixed with water sets into a gelatinous form. It is used to taking impressions of the orbit or globe.

Alignment Proper fusing (uniting) of images to each eye.

Alimta A drug that is used to treat malignant pleural mesothelioma and advanced non-small cell lung cancer and is being studied in the treatment of other types of cancer. It belongs to the family of drugs called enzyme inhibitors. Also called pemetrexed disodium and LY231514.

Aliquot Of, pertaining to, or designating an exact divisor or factor of a quantity, specially of an integer. To divide out a sample to multiple containers for multiple analytical tests.

Alitame A sweetener made from amino acids (L-aspartic acid, D-alanine, and a novel amide (a specific arrangement of chemical bonds between carbon, nitrogen and oxygen)). It offers a taste that is 2000 times sweeter than that of sucrose and can be used in a wide variety of products including beverages, tabletop sweeteners, frozen desserts and baked goods. Only the aspartic acid component of alitame is metabolized by the body. As a result, alitame contains 1.4 kcal/g. Since alitame is such an intense sweetener, however, it is used at very low levels and thus contributes negligible amounts of calories. It is highly stable, can withstand high temperatures in cooking and baking, and has the potential to be used in almost all foods and beverages in which sweeteners are presently used.

Alkaline phosphatase An enzyme normally present in certain cells within the liver, bone, kidney, intestine, and placenta. When cells are destroyed in those tissues, the enzyme leaks into the blood, and levels rise in proportion to the severity of the condition. Measurement of this enzyme is one way to evaluate the health of the liver.

Alkalinity An expression of the total amount of basic anions (hydroxyl groups) present in a solution. In water analysis, it also represents the presence of carbonate, bicarbonate, and occasionally borate, silicate, and phosphate salts that react to produce hydroxyl groups. Bicarbonate and carbonate ions are expected to be in most waters. Hydroxide may occur in water that has been softened by the lime soda process or has been in contact with fresh concrete. Alkalinity furnishes a guide in choosing appropriate treatment of either raw water or plant effluents.

Alkalinization The process by which a substance becomes an alkali. An alkali is the opposite of an acid.

Alkaloid A member of a large group of chemicals that are made by plants and have nitrogen in them. Some alkaloids have been shown to work against cancer.

Alkeran A drug that is used to treat multiple myeloma and ovarian epithelial cancer and is being studied in the treatment of other types of cancer. It belongs to the family of drugs called alkylating agents. Also called melphalan.

Alkylating agent A drug that is used in the treatment of cancer. It interferes with the cell's DNA and inhibits cancer cell growth.

ALL acute lymphoblastic leukemia A quickly progressing disease in which too many immature white blood cells called lymphoblasts are found in the blood and bone marrow. Also called acute lymphocytic leukemia.

All inclusive visit rate Aggregate costs for any one patient visit based upon annual operating costs divided by patient visits per year. This rate incorporates costs for all services at the visit.

All trans retinoic acid A form of vitamin A that is used to treat acute promyelocytic leukemia, usually together with other drugs, and to treat acne. It is also being studied in the treatment and prevention of other types of cancer. Also called tretinoin.

Allantoic fluid The clear white portion of an egg. In influenza vaccine manufacturing, the virus is propagated in the embryonic chick and sloughed into the allantoic fluid that is harvested to produce the vaccine

Allele Alternative form of a genetic locus; a single allele for each locus is inherited from each parent (e.g., at a locus for eye color the allele might result in blue or brown eyes).

Allelic exclusion The ability of heterozygous lymphoid cells to produce only one allelic form of antigen-specific receptor when they have the genetic endowment to produce both. Genes other than those for the specific receptors are usually expressed codominantly.

Allelic Relating to one of a series of two or more alternate forms of a gene that occupy the same position or locus on a specific chromosome.

Allergen (Food allergen) A food allergen is the part of a food (a protein) that stimulates the immune system of food allergic individuals. A single food can contain multiple food allergens. Carbohydrates or fats are not allergens.

Allergenic A predisposition to trigger allergies or cause allergic sensitisation.

Allergenic extract An extract in a solvent of a substance that causes an allergic reaction. They are relative crude drugs by contemporary standards and are manufactured by specialty companies and in some cases, by a practicing allergist. Also, allergenic extracts are generally difficult to filter since they most frequently are extracts of natural substances such as foods, house dust, animal hair, etc.

Allergic march A pattern that evolves as one allergic condition slowly progresses into another as the person grows up.

Allergic rhinitis Medical term for hay fever, a condition due to allergy that mimics a chronic cold. (Hay fever is a misnomer since hay is not a usual cause of this problem and there is no fever. Many substances cause the allergic symptoms in hay fever. Allergic rhinitis is the correct term for this allergic reaction. (Rhinitis means "irritation of the nose" and is a derivative of Rhino, meaning "nose"). Symptoms include nasal congestion, a clear runny nose, sneezing, nose and eye itching, and tearing eyes. Post-nasal dripping of clear mucus frequently causes a cough. Loss of smell is common and loss of taste occurs occasionally. Nose bleeding may occur if the condition is severe. Eye itching, redness, and tearing frequently accompany the nasal symptoms.

Allergic shiners Darkening of skin around eyes that occurs in allergy sufferers.

Allergy A condition in which the body is not able to tolerate eating certain foods, or exposure to certain animals, plants, or other substances.

Allergy (Food allergy) A food allergy is any adverse reaction to an otherwise harmless food or food component (a protein) that involves the body's immune system. To avoid confusion with other types of adverse reactions to foods, it is important to use the terms "food allergy" or "food hypersensitivity" only when the immune system is involved in causing the reaction.

Allergy clinic Specialist clinic to assess and carry out diagnostic allergy tests on GP referral.

Allocation ratio Treatment allocation ratio. For example, 1:1 is equal allocation, 3:1 is 75% in one group, and 25% in the other.

Allocation strata Treatment allocation strata. Allocations are generally balanced within strata.

Allogeneic Taken from different individuals of the same species. Also called allogenic.

Allogeneic bone marrow transplantation A procedure in which a person receives stem cells (cells from which all blood cells develop) from a genetically similar, but not identical, donor.

Allogeneic GM CSF secreting breast cancer vaccine An allogenic vaccine consisting of irradiated breast cancer cells transfected with the granulocyte macrophage-colony-stimulating factor (GM-CSF) gene. Upon vaccination, the genetically modified cells secrete GM-CSF, thereby potentiating a tumor-specific T cell response against breast cancer cell-associated antigens.

Allogeneic lymphocytes A population of lymphocytes therapeutically administered to a recipient individual who is genetically distinct from a donor of the same species.

Allogeneic stem cell transplantation A procedure in which a person receives blood-forming stem cells (cells from which all blood cells develop) from a genetically similar, but not identical, donor. This is often a sister or brother, but could be an unrelated donor.

Allogeneic tumor cell vaccine A vaccine composed of tumor cells isolated from the tumor of one patient, killed and processed, and administered to another patient in order to stimulate cytotoxic immune responses to a similar tumor cell type. The cells found in this type of whole-cell vaccine express many cell-surface tumor-associated antigens. This vaccine is frequently administered with an adjuvant immunostimulant.

Allograft A tissue transplant (graft) between two genetically nonidentical members of a species.

Allopurinol A structural isomer of hypoxanthine. Allopurinol inhibits xanthine oxidase, an enzyme that converts oxypurines to uric acid. By blocking the production of uric acid, this agent decreases serum and urine concentrations of uric acid, thereby providing protection against uric acid-mediated end organ damage in conditions associated with excessive production of uric acid, i.e. the massive cell lysis associated with the treatment of some malignancies.

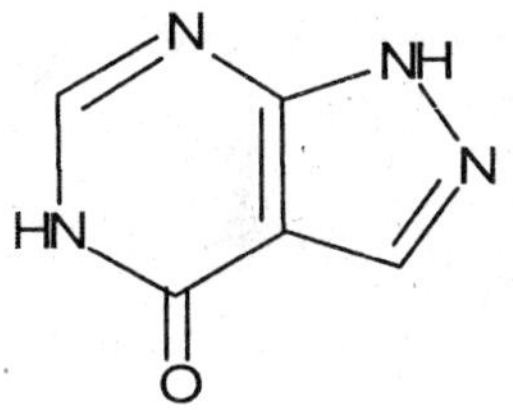

Figure Allopurinol

Allotypes Antigenic determinants that are present in allelic (alternate) forms. When used in association with immunoglobulin, allotypes describe allelic variants of immunoglobulins detected by antibodies raised between members of the same species.

Allovectin-7 A substance that is being studied as a gene therapy agent in the treatment of cancer. It increases the ability of the immune system to recognize cancer cells and kill them.

Ally methyl trisulfide dithiol-thiones A type of sulfide/thiol found in cruciferous vegetables which may provide the health benefits of lowering LDL cholesterol and of maintaining a healthy immune system.

Aloe emodin A substance found in certain plants, including aloe vera. It belongs to a family of compounds called anthraquinones, which have shown anti-inflammatory and anticancer effects.

Alopecia The lack or loss of hair from areas of the body where hair is usually found. Alopecia can be a side effect of some cancer treatments.

Alpha cell A type of cell in the pancreas (in areas called the islets of Langerhans). Alpha cells make and release a hormone called glucagon, which raises the level of glucose (sugar) in the blood.

Alpha fetoprotein plasmid DNA vaccine A vaccine consisting of plasmid DNA encoding alpha fetoprotein. After vaccination, expressed alpha fetoprotein may stimulate a cytotoxic T lymphocyte (CTL) response against tumor cells that express alpha fetoprotein, resulting in tumor cell lysis.

Alpha-carotene A type of carotenoid found in carrots which provides the health benefit of neutralizing free radicals that may cause damage to cells.

Alprostadil The naturally occuring prostaglandin E1 (PGE1) which displays a variety of pharmacologic actions. Alprostadil is a potent vasodilator agent that increases peripheral blood flow, inhibits platelet aggregation, and induces bronchodilation. Used in. the treatment of erectile dysfunction, this agent produces corporal smooth muscle relaxation by binding to PGE receptors, resulting in the activation of adenylate cyclase and the subsequent accumulation of 3′5′-cAMP.

Alteplase A protein that is made by the body and that helps dissolve blood clots. It can also be made in the laboratory and is used in the treatment of heart attack and stroke. It is also being studied in the treatment of cancer. Alteplase belongs to the family of drugs called systemic thrombolytic agents. Also called tissue plasminogen activator (tPA), recombinant tissue plasminogen activator (r-tPA), and Activase.

Alteration A change resulting in something that is different from the original.

Alternate (alternative) pathway The mechanism of complement activation that does not involve activation of the C1, C4, C2 pathway by antigen-antibody complexes, and begins with the activation of C3.

Alternate delivery systems Health services provided in other than an inpatient, acute-care hospital or private practice. A phrase used to describe all forms of health care delivery except traditional fee-for-service, private practice. Examples within general health services include skilled and intermediary nursing facilities, hospice programs, and home health care. Alternate delivery systems are designed to provide needed services in a more cost-effective manner. Most of the services provided by community mental health centers fall into this category.

Alternate site testing Using parts of the body other than the finger tips to obtain blood for blood glucose testing.

Alternative hypothesis In a trial, the alternative hypothesis might be that a treatment of unknown efficacy has more benefit than the standard treatment. The alternative hypothesis is an alternative to the null hypothesis of no difference that specifies some true underlying difference of set of differences between two or more populations or groups with regard to some function, trait, characteristic, or effect. It may be stated in such a way so as to be concerned with a difference(s) in only one direction (one-sided alternative hypothesis) or in either direction (two-sided alternative hypothesis) relative to :he null value.

Alternative medicine Pract ces used instead of standard treatments. They generally are not recognized by the medical community as standard approaches. Alternative medicine includes dietary supplements, megadose vitamins, herbal preparations, special teas, acupuncture, massage therapy, magnet therapy, spiritual healing, and meditation.

Alternative splicing Different ways of combining a gene's exons to make variants of the complete protein

Altretamine An anticancer drug that belongs to the family of drugs called alkylating agents.

Alum A type of immune adjuvant (a substance used to help boost the immune response to a vaccine). Also called aluminum sulfate.

Alum adjuvant An inorganic compound containing aluminum. Used in various immunologic preparations to improve immunogenicity, alum adjuvant consists of aluminium sulfate. In vaccines, this agent binds to the protein conjugate, resulting in improved antigen processing by the immune system.

Aluminum sulfate A type of immune adjuvant (a substance used to help boost the immune response to a vaccine). Also called alum.

ALVAC CEA vaccine A cancer vaccine containing a canary pox virus (ALVAC) combined with the human carcinoembryonic antigen (CEA) gene.

Alveolar bone The jaw bone that anchors the roots of teeth.

Alveoli Tiny air sacs at the end of the

Alveus A layer of myelinated fibers overlying the ventricular surface of the hippocampus. It arises from cells within the hippocampus and converges medially to form the fimbria, the beginning of the fornix.

Alzheimer's disease This disease causes progressive memory loss and dementia in its victims as it kills brain cells (neurons). It is named after Alois Alzheimer who in 1906 first described the Amyloid β Protein (AβP) plaques in the human brain that are caused by this disease. The drug Tacrine appears to slow the progression of Alzheimer's disease, but there is currently no way to stop the disease.

Amalgam A most common filling material, also known as "silver fillings," containing mercury (app 50%), silver, tin, copper and zinc used for fillings.

Amanita phalloides A type of poisonous mushroom that has harmful effects on the kidneys and liver. It is responsible for most fatal cases of mushroom poisoning. Also called death cap.

Ambien A drug used to treat insomnia (inability to sleep), and anxiety. It belongs to a family of drugs known as imidazopyridines (sedative hypnotics). Also called zolpidem.

Ambient The normal environment conditions such as temperature, relative humidity, or room pressure of a particular area under consideration.

Amblyopia (clinical condition) Reduced visual acuity (poorer than 20/20) which is not correctable by glasses or contacts and is not caused by structural or pathological anomalies. This condition is often called "lazy eye" because it is typically the result of disuse. It is usually marked by blurred vision in one eye and favoring one eye over the other. About two percent of the population is affected.

Types of functional (reversible) amblyopia:

Refractive- anisometropia (the two eyes have different refractive powers), or other amblyopiogenic refractive errors (hyperopia, myopia, or astigmatism)

Strabismic- misalignment of the two eyes in which they point in different directions form deprivation (may also be referred to as amblyopia ex anopsia)- caused by conditions that prevent light from entering the eye. These may include congenital ptosis (droopy eyelid), corneal opacity, or cataract.

Treatment options for functional amblyopia are eye patching, prescription lenses, prisms, and vision therapy.

Ambulatory care Health services provided without the patient being admitted. Also called outpatient care. The services of ambulatory care centers, hospital outpatient departments, physicians' offices and home health care services fall under this heading provided that the patient remains at the facility less than 24 hours. No overnight stay in a hospital is required.

AMD3100 A substance that is being studied for its ability to move stem cells out of the bone marrow and into circulating blood where they can be collected for use in stem cell transplantation. Stem cell transplantation is a method of replacing blood-forming stem cells that were destroyed by cancer treatment. AMD3100 belongs to the families of drugs called stem cell mobilizers and CXCR4 inhibitors.

Amelanotic melanoma A type of skin cancer in which the cells do not make melanin. Skin lesions are often irregular and may be pink, red, or have light brown, tan, or gray at the edges.

Ames test A simple bacterial test for carcinogens.

Amethopterin A drug used to treat some types of cancers, including breast, head and neck, lung, blood, and bone, and other disorders. It belongs to the family of drugs called antimetabolites. Also called methotrexate.

Ametropia Any optical error such as hyperopia, myopia, or astigmatism. Also called refractive error.

AMG 706 An orally bioavailable multiple-receptor tyrosine kinase inhibitor with potential antineoplastic activity. AMG 706 selectively targets and inhibits vascular endothelial growth factor (VEGFR), platelet-derived growth factor (PDGFR), kit, and Ret receptors, thereby inhibiting angiogenesis and cellular proliferation.

Amifostine A drug used as a chemoprotective drug to control some of the side effects of chemotherapy and radiation therapy.

Amifostine trihydrate The trihydrate form of a phosphorylated aminosulfhydryl compound. After dephosphorylation of amifostine by alkaline phosphatase to an active free sulfhydryl (thiol) metabolite, the thiol metabolite binds to and detoxifies cytotoxic platinum-containing metabolites of cisplatin and scavenges free radicals induced by cisplatin and ionizing radiation. The elevated activity of this agent in normal tissues results from both the relative abundance of alkaline phosphatase in normal tissues and the greater vascularity of normal tissues compared to tumor tissues.

Amikacin An antibiotic drug used to treat infection. It belongs to the family of drugs called aminoglycoside antibiotics.

Amine A substance that may be derived from ammonia by the replacement of one or more of the hydrogen atoms by hydrocarbon radicals.

Amino acid sequence The arrangement of amino acids in a protein. Proteins can be made from 20 different kinds of amino acids, and the structure and function of each type of protein are determined by the kinds of amino acids used to make it and how they are arranged.

Amino acids Amino acids function as the building blocks of proteins. Chemically, amino acids are organic compounds containing an amino (NH_2) group and a carboxyl (COOH) group. Amino acids are classified as essential, nonessential and conditionally essential. If body synthesis is inadequate to meet metabolic need, an amino acid is classified as essential and must be supplied as part of the diet. Essential amino acids include leucine, isoleucine, valine, tryptophan, phenylalanine, methionine, threonine, lysine, histidine and possibly arginine. Nonessential amino acids can be synthesized by the body in adequate amounts, and include alanine, aspartic acid, asparagine, glutamic acid, glutamine, glycine, proline and serine. Conditionally essential amino acids become essential under certain clinical conditions.

Aminocamptothecin An anticancer drug that belongs to the family of drugs called topoisomerase inhibitors.

Aminoglutethimide An anticancer drug that belongs to the family of drugs called nonsteroidal aromatase inhibitors. Aminoglutethimide is used to decrease the production of sex hormones (estrogen in women or testosterone in men) and suppress the growth of tumors that need sex hormones to grow.

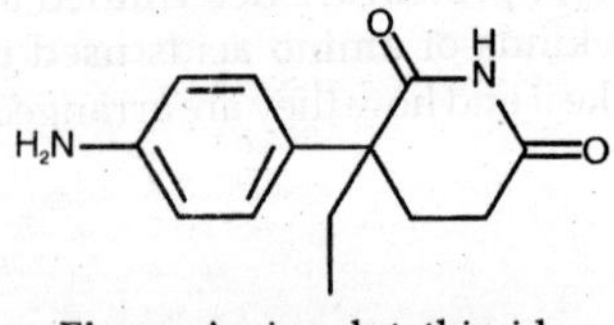

Figure Aminoglutethimide

Aminoglycoside antibiotic A type of antibiotic that works against many types of bacteria and includes streptomycin, gentamicin, and neomycin. Aminoglycosides are used to treat bacterial infections.

Aminolevulinic acid A topically administered metabolic precursor of protoporphyrin IX. After topical administration, aminolevulinic acid (ALA) is converted to protoporphyrin IX (PpIX) which is a photosensitizer. When the proper wavelength of light activates protoporphyrin IX, singlet oxygen is produced, resulting in a local cytotoxic effect.

Aminopterin An anticancer drug that belongs to the family of drugs called antimetabolites.

AML (Acute myelogenous leukemia) A quickly progressing disease in which too many immature blood-forming cells are found in the blood and bone marrow. Also called acute myeloid leukemia or acute nonlymphocytic leukemia.

Amniotic fluid The fluid around the fetus that allows it to move freely and protects against mechanical injury.

Amonafide A substance that is being studied in the treatment of cancer. It belongs to the families of drugs called topoisomerase inhibitors and intercalating agents.

Amonafide dihydrochloride The dihydrochloride salt of amonafide, an imide derivative of naphthalic acid. Amonafide intercalates into DNA and inhibits topoisomerase II, resulting in protein-associated strand breaks and impaired DNA and RNA synthesis.

Amoxicillin An antibiotic drug used to treat infection. It belongs to the family of drugs called penicillins or penicillin derivatives.

Amoxicillin clavulanate potassium A combination of the semisynthetic broad-spectrum antibiotic amoxicillin and the beta-lactamase enzyme inhibitor clavulanate potassium. Clavulanate potassium increases the serum half-life of amoxicillin by inhibiting beta-lactamase-mediated metabolism of amoxicillin. Amoxicillin inhibits bacterial cell wall synthesis by binding to penicillin binding proteins and inhibiting peptidoglycan synthesis, a critical component of bacterial cell walls.

Ampholyte Amphoteric electrolyte. Electrolyte that can either give up or take on a hydrogen ion and can thus behave as either an acid or a base.

Amphoteric Having two opposite characteristics.

Amphotericin B A drug used in the treatment of infections caused by fungi. It belongs to the family of drugs called antifungals.

Ampicillin An antibiotic widely used in clinical treatment and rDNA research. It is a derivative of penicillin, which kills bacteria by interfering with the synthesis of the cell wall.

Amplification The production of additional copies of a chromosomal sequence, found as either intrachromosomal or extra chromosomal DNA.

Amplitude of accommodation (AA) A measurement of the eye's ability to focus clearly on objects at near distances. This eye focusing range for a child is usually about 2-3 inches. For a young adult, it is 4-6 inches. The focus range for a 45-year-old adult is about 20 inches. For an 80-year-old adult, it is 60 inches.

Ampoule or ampule A small glass vial sealed after filling and one of the earliest devices developed for safe storage of sterile injectable unit.

Ampulla A sac-like enlargement of a canal or duct.

Ampulla of vater An enlargement of the ducts from the liver and pancreas at the point where they enter the small intestine.

Amputation Surgery to remove part or all of a limb or appendage.

Amsacrine An aminoacridine derivative with potent antineoplastic properties. Although its mechanism of action is incompletely defined, amsacrine may intercalate into DNA and inhibit topoisomerase II, resulting in DNA double-strand breaks. This agent's cytotoxicity is maximal during the S phase of the cell cycle when topoisomerase levels are greatest.

Amygdalar A complex of nuclei located in the dorsomedial temporal lobe just deep to the uncus. This nuclear complex is in contact with the tail of the caudate nucleus and is a component of the basal ganglia known as the archi striatum. It has olfactory, visceral, endocrine, and behavioural functions and may be involved with emotional changes associated with Alzheimer's disease and in Schizophrenia.

Amygdalin A substance found in the pits of many fruits such as apricots and papayas, and in other foods. It has been tried in some countries as a treatment for cancer, but it has not been shown to work in clinical studies. Also called laetrile.

Amylase A pancreatic enzyme. High levels in the blood may indicate pancreatic damage.

Amyloidosis A group of diseases in which protein is deposited in specific organs (localized amyloidosis) or throughout the body (systemic amyloidosis). Amyloidosis may be either primary (with no known cause) or secondary (caused by another disease, including some types of cancer). Generally, primary amyloidosis affects the nerves, skin, tongue, joints, heart, and liver; secondary amyloidosis often affects the spleen, kidneys, liver, and adrenal glands.

Amyotrophic lateral sclerosis An inherited, fatal degenerative nerve disorder, also known as Lou Gehrig's disease.

Amyotrophy A type of diabetic neuropathy that causes muscle weakness and wasting.

Anabolic steroids Derivatives of the male sex hormone testosterone and are used as performance enhancing, to increase muscle bulk and strength. Can be taken orally or as an injectable.

Anabolism The intracellular process involved in the synthesis of more complex compounds than those involved in catabolism (for example, glucose to glycogen) and requires energy.

Anaerobe A microorganism that thrives best, or only, when deprived of oxygen.

1. Facultative anaerobe: one able to grow in the presence or absence of free oxygen.

2. Obligate or obligatory anaerobe: one that will grow only in the absence of free oxygen.

Anaerobic bacteria Bacteria capable of growing in the absence of Oxygen.

Anaerobic Relating to an anaerobe.

Anaesthesia In modern medical practice, general anaesthesia is a state of total unconsciousness resulting from anesthetic drugs. A variety of drugs are given to the patient that have different effects with the overall aim of ensuring unconsciousness, amnesia and analgesia. The anesthesiologist selects the optimal technique for any given patient and procedure.

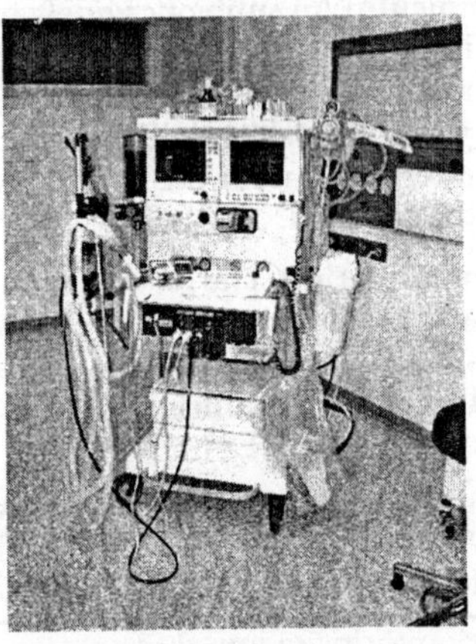

Figure An anaesthetic machine

General anaesthesia is a complex procedure involving:

- Preanaesthetic assessment
- Administration of general anaesthetic drugs
- Cardiorespiratory monitoring
- Analgesia
- Airway management
- Fluid management
- Postoperative pain relief

Muscle relaxation (also known as neuromuscular blockade) with skeletal muscle relaxants is an integral part of modern anaesthesia. The first drug used for this purpose was curare, introduced in the 1940's and now superseded with drugs with fewer side effects, and generally shorter duration.

Muscle relaxation allows surgery within major body cavities, eg. abdomen and thorax without the need for very deep anesthesia, and is also used to facilitate endotracheal intubation.

Acetylcholine, the natural neurotransmitter substance at the neuromuscular junction, causes muscles to contract when released from nerve endings. Muscle relaxants work by preventing acetylcholine from attaching to it's receptor.

Muscle relaxation causes paralysis of the muscles of respiration, ie. the diaphragm and intercostal muscles of the chest, and requires some form of artificial respiration. As the muscles of the larynx are also paralysed, the airway usually needs to be protected by means of an endotracheal tube.

Monitoring of muscle relaxation is most easily provided by means of a peripheral nerve stimulator. This device intermittently sends short electrical pulses through the skin over a peripheral nerve while the contraction of a muscle supplied by that nerve is observed.

The effects of muscle relaxants are commonly reversed at the termination of surgery by anticholinesterase drugs.

Examples of skeletal muscle relaxants in use today are pancuronium, rocuronium, vecuronium, atracurium, mivacurium, and succinylcholine.

Anagrelide A drug that is used to decrease the number of platelets in the blood in order to prevent blood clotting.

Anakinra A recombinant human nonglycosylated interleukin-1 (IL-1) receptor antagonist with potential antineoplastic activity. Anakinra binds to the IL-1 receptor, thereby blocking the binding of the IL-1 to and activation of its receptor. Blockade of IL-1 activity may inhibit the cascade of downstream proangiogenic factors such as vascular endothelial cell growth factor, tumor necrosis factor-alpha, and IL-6, resulting in inhibition of tumor angiogenesis.

Anal cancer Cancer that forms in tissues of the anus. The anus is the opening of the rectum (last part of the large intestine) to the outside of the body.

Anal fissure A small tear in the anus that can cause bleeding, itching, or pain.

Anal Having to do with the anus, which is the posterior opening of the large bowel.

Analgesia Pain relief which may be achieved by use of medication (e.g. aspirin, paracetamol or codeine), modalities (e.g. ultrasound, interferential and laser) or acupuncture.

Analgesic A compound used to reduce or treat pain. Examples of analgesics include aspirin, morphine, and acetaminophen.

Analog (analogue) A chemical compound with a structure similar to that of another but differing from it in respect to a certain component; it may have a similar or opposite action metabolically.

Analysis A process in which anything complex is separated into simple or less complex parts.

Analytical method Small scale process used to characterize and/or separate a mixture, a compound, or an unknown material into its constituent parts or elements.

Anaphylactic shock A life-threatening allergic reaction characterized by a swelling of body tissues (including the throat) and a sudden decline in blood pressure; can be (rarely) triggered by medication.

Anaphylactoid A reaction similar in presentation to anaphylaxis; however, the cause is not IgE-mediated hypersensitivity. Example: Generalized hives due to direct release of histamine from mast cells by morphine.

Anaphylatoxin Substance capable of releasing histamine from mast cells.

Anaphylaxis A rare but potentially fatal condition in which several different parts of the body experience food-allergic reactions simultaneously, causing hives, swelling of the throat and difficulty breathing. It is the most severe allergic reaction to an allergen and requires immediate medical attention when it occurs.

Anaplasia The atypical appearance of nuclei as is found in malignant neoplasia. Anaplastic nuclei are usually large, irregular and hyperchromatic, and may produce bizarre or atypical mitotic figures.

Anaplastic A term used to describe cancer cells that divide rapidly and have little or no resemblance to normal cells.

Anaplastic large cell lymphoma An aggressive (fast-growing) type of non-Hodgkin's lymphoma that is usually of the T-cell type. The cancer cells express a marker called CD30 or Ki-1 on the surface, and may appear in the lymph nodes, skin, bones, soft tissues, lungs, or liver.

Anaplastic thyroid cancer A rare, aggressive type of thyroid cancer in which the malignant (cancer) cells look very different from normal thyroid cells.

Anastomosis A procedure to connect healthy sections of tubular structures in the body after the diseased portion has been surgically removed.

Anastrozole An anticancer drug that is used to decrease estrogen production and suppress the growth of tumors that need estrogen to grow. It belongs to the family of drugs called nonsteroidal aromatase inhibitors.

Ancestim A drug that is being studied for its ability to increase the number of stem cells in the blood. It belongs to the family of drugs called hematopoietic cell growth factors. Also called stem cell factor (SCF) and Stemgen.

Ancillary material Material used in preparing drugs that does not become a component of the drug (e.g. steam, air, N2, DI water).

Ancillary services (ancillary charges) Supplemental services, including laboratory, radiology, physical therapy, and inhalation therapy that are provided in conjunction with medical or hospital care.

Ancillary trial An investigation, stimulated by the trial and intended to generate information of interest to the trial, that is designed and carried out by investigators from one or more of the centers in the trial and that utilizes resources of the trials (e.g., money, study patients, staff time, etc.), but that is not a required part of the design or data collection procedures of the main trial.

Androblastoma A rare type of ovarian tumor in which the tumor cells secrete a male sex hormone. This may cause virilization (the appearance of male physical characteristics in females). Also called arrhenoblastoma and Sertoli-Leydig cell tumor of the ovary.

Androgen A male sex hormone, such as testosterone. Androgens may be used to treat recurrence of breast cancer. Their effect is to block the activity of estrogen, which "feeds" some cancers.

Androgen ablation Treatment to suppress or block the production of male hormones. Androgen suppression is achieved by surgical removal of the testicles, by taking female sex hormones, or by taking other drugs (anti-androgens). Also called androgen suppression.

Androgen suppression Treatment to suppress or block the production of male hormones. Androgen suppression is achieved by surgical removal of the testicles, by taking female sex hormones, or by taking other drugs, antiandrogens. Also called androgen ablation.

Androgen-independent Describes the ability of tumor cells to grow in the absence of androgens (hormones that promote the development and maintenance of male sex characteristics). Many early prostate cancers require androgens for growth, but advanced prostate cancers are often androgen-independent

Anecdotal report An incomplete description of the medical and treatment history of one or more patients. Anecdotal reports may be published in places other than peer-reviewed, scientific journals.

Anemia A condition in which there is a decreased volume of red cells in the blood. There are many causes for anemia, including drug toxicities and chronic infections. The most common way in which anemia is measured is by the titer of hemoglobin (Hgb) in peripheral venous blood.

Anergic Refers to the state of being so immunologically suppressed that one is unable to produce cutaneous delayed type hypersensitivity reaction (DTH). Such patients will usually not test positive for TB on a PPD (mantoux) test.

Anergy Failure of lymphocytes that have been primed by an antigen to respond on second contact with the antigen

Anesthesia The loss of feeling or sensation as a result of drugs or gases. General anesthesia causes loss of consciousness ("puts you to sleep"). Local anesthesia numbs only a specified area.

Anesthesiologist A doctor who specializes in giving drugs or other agents to prevent or relieve pain during surgery or other procedures being done in the hospital.

Anesthetic A substance that causes loss of feeling or awareness. Local anesthetics cause loss of feeling in a part of the body. General anesthetics put the person to sleep.

Anetholtrithione A substance that is being studied in the treatment of cancer.

Aneurysm The dilation of the wall of an artery, vein, or the heart, that forms a sac-like structure.

Angelica root The root of any of a group of herbs called Angelica. It has been used in some cultures to treat certain medical problems, including gastrointestinal problems such as loss of appetite, feelings of fullness, and gas.

Angina (angina pectoris) An intense, steady pain or feeling of pressure in the region of the heart caused by a decreased blood flow to the heart muscle.

Angio (suffix) Vessel e.g. lymphangitis - inflammation of a lymph vessel.

Angioedema Similar to hives in that swelling of the skin occurs, but angioedema affects the deeper, subcutaneous layer of the skin and the swollen areas are not itchy. It usually affects the face, genitalia, hands & feet.

Angiogenesis Blood vessel formation. Tumor angiogenesis is the growth of blood vessels from surrounding tissue to a solid tumor. This is caused by the release of chemicals by the tumor.

Angiogenesis inhibitor A substance that may prevent the formation of blood vessels. In anticancer therapy, an angiogenesis inhibitor prevents the growth of blood vessels from surrounding tissue to a solid tumor.

Angiogram An x-ray of blood vessels; the person receives an injection of dye to outline the vessels on the x-ray.

Angiography A diagnostic procedure in which catheters are passed through the arteries of the heart. Pressures are measured and blood samples are taken from within the heart and its major blood vessels.

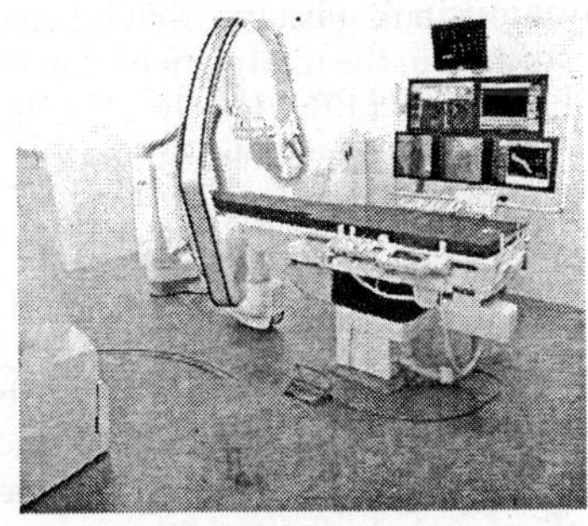

Figure Angiography Machine

Angioimmunoblastic T-cell lymphoma An aggressive (fast-growing) type of T-cell non-Hodgkin's lymphoma marked by enlarged lymph nodes and hypergammaglobulinemia (increased antibodies in the blood). Other symptoms may include a skin rash, fever, weight loss, or night sweats.

Angiopathy Disease of the blood vessels (arteries, veins, and capillaries) that occurs when someone has diabetes for a long time. There are two types of angiopathy: macroangiopathy and microangiopathy. In macroangiopathy, fat and blood clots build up in the large blood vessels, stick to the vessel walls, and block the flow of blood. In microangiopathy, the walls of the smaller blood vessels become so thick and weak that they bleed, leak protein, and slow the flow of blood through the body. Then the cells, for example, the ones in the center of the eye, do not get enough blood and may be damaged.

Angiosarcoma A type of cancer that begins in the cells that line blood vessels or lymph vessels. Cancer that begins in blood vessels is called hemangiosarcoma. Cancer that begins in lymph vessels is called lymphangiosarcoma.

Angiostatin A protein normally made by the body. It can also be made in the laboratory, and is being studied in the treatment of cancer. Angiostatin may prevent the growth of new blood vessels from the surrounding tissue to a solid tumor. It belongs to the family of drugs called angiogenesis inhibitors.

Angiozyme A substance that is being studied in the treatment of kidney cancer. It may prevent the growth of blood vessels from surrounding tissue to the tumor. It belongs to the families of drugs called VEGF receptor and angiogenesis inhibitors. Also called RPI.4610.

Angle of louis The point of junction between the manubrium and the body of the sternum.

Angstrom A unit of length equal to one hundred-millionth of a centimeter (one ten-thousandth of a micron) used especially to specify radiation wavelengths.

Anhydrovinblastine An anticancer drug that belongs to the family of drugs called mitotic inhibitors.

Anidulafungin A cyclic lipopeptide echinocandin derivative with antifungal activity. Anidulafungin inhibits 1,3 beta-D-glucan synthase, an enzyme involved in fungal cell wall synthesis, resulting in cell lysis and death. This agent is active against Candida species and Aspergillus.

Animal model An animal with a disease either the same as or like a disease in humans. Animal models are used to study the development and progression of diseases and to test new treatments before they are given to humans. Animals with transplanted human cancers or other tissues are called xenograft models.

Anion A negatively charged particle or ion.

Anion exchange resin An ion exchange material that removes anions from solution by exchanging them with hydroxyl ions.

Anis, aniso Unequal; dissimilar, e.g. anisokaryosis - inequality in the size of the nuclei of cells.

Aniseikonia A difference in the size or shape of two visual images when the images should be the same size and/or shape.

Anisometropia The condition in which the two eyes have different refractive powers.

Ankle joint A "mortise and tenon" joint between the two bones of the lower leg (tibia and fibula) and the talus of the foot.

Ankle sprain Usually an over stretch of the lateral (outside) ligament of the ankle joint. Can be of varying degrees, from minor over stretch to complete rupture.

Ankylosing spondylitis A disease process of unknown aetiology, characterised by the presence of bilateral sacroiliitis with inflammatory changes in the spinal joints. The onset is most common in males in their late teens to early twenties. As the name suggests, it is a process which results in a gradual stiffening of the axial skeleton, sacroiliac joints and pubic symphysis.

Annamycin A substance that is being studied in the treatment of cancer. It belongs to the family of drugs called anthracycline antibiotics.

Anneal The process by which the complementary base pairs in DNA strands combine.

Annealing A treatment process for steel in which the metal is heated and held at a suitable temperature and then cooled at a suitable rate for the purpose of reducing hardness, improving machinability, facilitating cold working, producing a desired microstructure, or obtaining desired mechanical, physical, or other properties.

Annotation Adding pertinent information such as gene coded for, amino acid sequence, or other commentary to the database entry of raw sequence of DNA bases.

Annulus fibrosis This is the peripheral portion of the intervertebral disc, consisting of collagen fibres arranged in a highly ordered pattern. The posterior fibres of the collagen lamellae are thinner and more tightly packed, hence the posterior aspect of the annulus fibrosis is thinner than the rest of the annulus.

Anomalies Birth defects; abnormalities.

Anomalous retinal correspondence (ARC) A type of retinal projection, occurring frequently in strabismus, in which the foveae (center of the retina that produces the sharpest eyesight) of the two eyes do not facilitate a common visual direction; the fovea of one eye has the same functional direction with an extrafoveal (non-fovea) area of the other eye.

Anophthalmic/anophthalmos Absence of an eye(s). It can be a congenital (born without) or an acquired condition (surgically removed).

Anorectal atresia Absence of a normal opening between the anus and the rectum.

Anorexia An abnormal loss of the appetite for food. Anorexia can be caused by cancer, AIDS, a mental disorder (i.e., anorexia nervosa), or other diseases.

Anorexia nervosa An eating disorder characterized by refusal to maintain a minimally normal weight for height and age. The condition includes weight loss leading to maintenance of body weight 15 percent below normal; an intense fear of weight gain or becoming fat, despite the individual's underweight status; a disturbance in the self-awareness of one's own body weight or shape; and in females, the absence of at least three consecutive menstrual cycles that would otherwise be expected to occur.

Anosmia A loss of the sense of smell.

Ansa lenticularis An efferent fiber bundle arising from the internal division of the globus pallidus. It utlimately joins the thalamic fasciculus which projects to the ventral anterior and lateral thalamic nuclei.

Ansamycin An anticancer drug that belongs to the family of drugs called antineoplastic antibiotics.

Antacids Medicines that neutralize stomach acid.

Antagonism The opposite of synergy. One factor (treatment) reduces or cancels the effect of another treatment.

Antagonist In medicine, a substance that stops the action or effect of another substance. For example, a drug that blocks the stimulating effect of estrogen on a tumor cell is called an estrogen receptor antagonist.

Ante Before in time or space, e.g. ante mortem - before death.

Antenatal Before the time of birth.

Antepartum The time period before childbirth (refers to the mother).

Anterior The front, or forward part of something

Anterior arch (C1) The curved structure located at the forward part of the atlas (ventral side of body).

Anterior chamber Area between the cornea and iris in both the human eye and the ocular prosthesis.

Anterior clinoid process The bony process located on the medial end of the posterior border of the lesser wing of the sphenoid bone.

Anterior cruciate ligament (ACL) Intra-articular ligament of the knee, attaching on the anterior portion of the tibial plateau extending upwards and posteriorly to the medial aspect of the lateral femoral condyle. Very frequently injured during twisting type sports (e.g. Australian Rules football, soccer), or those that involve rapid deceleration (e.g. netball). Extrinsic trauma also has a large part to play in ACL injuries.

Anterior mediastinotomy A procedure in which a tube is inserted into the chest to view the tissues and organs in the area between the lungs and between the breastbone and heart. The tube is inserted through an incision next to the breastbone. This procedure is usually used to get a tissue sample from the lymph nodes on the left side of the chest. Also called the Chamberlain procedure.

Anterior mediastinum The area in the front part of the chest between the lungs. Also called prevascular space.

Anterior rib The portion of the rib locted on the ventral side of the body.

Anterior surface The front of the ocular prosthesis, implant and/or the eye.

Anterior teeth The six upper or six lower front teeth.

Anterior tibial artery Artery originating from the popliteal artery and branching into the posterior and anterior tibial recurrent, and lateral and medial anterior malleolar arteries, and lateral and medial malleolar retes.

Anterior urethra The part of the male urethra that extends from the bulb to the meatus of the glans penis.

Anthocyanidins A type of flavonoid found in various fruits which provides the health benefits of neutralizing free radicals and possibly reducing the risk of cancer.

Anthracenedione An anticancer drug that belongs to the family of drugs called anticancer antibiotics.

Anthracycline A type of antibiotic that comes from the fungus Streptococcus peucetius. Anthracyclines are used as treatments for cancer. Daunorubicin, doxorubicin, and epirubicin are anthracyclines.

Anthraquinone A type of anticancer drug.

Anti Prefix generally meaning "against, opposite or opposing, and contrary." In medicine, anti- often connotes "counteracting or effective against" as in antibacterial, anti-infective, and antiviral. Sometimes medical terms containing anti- take on new meanings as has occurred with antibiotic and antibody. As a prefix, anti- may be shortened to ant- as in antacid. "Anti" is the Greek word for "against."

Anti allergy medication Nose and eye drops, inhalers and capsules that help prevent allergy. Based on chromoglycate, which is derived from a Middle Eastern plant call Khellin.

Anti CD3 x anti HER 2 neu bispecific monoclonal antibody A murine monoclonal antibody with two antigen-recognition sites: one for CD3, an antigen expressed on mature T cells, and one for HER-2-neu, a tumor-associated antigen that promotes tumor growth. This agent attaches to CD3-expressing T cells and HER-2-neu-expressing tumor cells, selectively cross-linking tumor and immunologic cells which results in the recruitment of cytotoxic T cells to the T cell/tumor cell aggregate.

Anti idiotype vaccine A vaccine made of antibodies that see other antibodies as the antigen and bind to it. Anti-idiotype vaccines can stimulate the body to produce antibodies against tumor cells.

Anti inflammatory medication Nose sprays, Inhalers and Creams that contain steroids based on Beclomethasone.

Anti thymocyte globulin A purified gamma immunoglobulin with immunosuppressive properties. Obtained from rabbits that have been immunized with human thymocytes, antithymocyte globulin specifically recognizes and destroys T lymphocytes. Although the exact mechanism of action is not completely understood, it appears to involve T lymphocyte clearance from the circulation and modulation of T lymphocyte activity. Administering antithymocyte globulin with chemotherapy prior to stem cell transplantation may reduce the risk of graft-versus-host disease.

Antiandrogen A drug used to block the production or interfere with the action of male sex hormones.

Antiandrogen therapy Treatment with drugs used to block production or interfere with the action of male sex hormones.

Antiangiogenesis Prevention of the growth of new blood vessels.

Antiangiogenic Having to do with reducing the growth of new blood vessels.

Antiapoptotic Something that prevents apoptosis. Apoptosis is a type of cell death in which a series of molecular steps in a cell leads to its death.

Antibiotic The word means "destructive of life." Antibiotics are chemical substances, produced by living organisms or synthesized (created) in laboratories, for the purpose of killing other organisms that cause disease. Some cancer therapies interfere with the body's ability to fight off infection (they suppress the immune system), so antibiotics may be needed along with the cancer treatment to protect against or kill infectious diseases.

Antibiotic resistance The ability of a bacterium to synthesize a protein that neutralizes an antibiotic.

Antibodies Proteins that the body makes to protect itself from foreign substances. Occasionally, the body also makes proteins against normal parts of the body. These proteins are called autoantibodies.

Exogenous Antibodies: In either Type 1 or Type 2 diabetes, the body sometimes makes antibodies to work against pork or beef insulins because they are not exactly the same as human insulin or because they have impurities. These antibodies can keep the insulin from working well and may rarely cause the person with diabetes to have an allergic or bad reaction to the beef or pork insulins.

Endogenous Antibodies: In Type 1 diabetes, several different autoantibodies against normal tissues are found. These antibodies are associated with the destruction of the beta cells of the pancreas, although their exact role is uncertain. Some of the autoantibodies which are found in diabetes patients include: islet-cell antibodies (ICAs), anti-insulin antibodies (AIAs), and anti-GAD antibodies.

Antibody dependent, cell mediated cytotoxicity (ADCC) A phenomenon in which target cells, coated with antibody, are destroyed by specialized killer cells (NK cells and macrophages), which bear receptors for the Fc portion of the coating antibody (Fc receptors). These receptors allow the killer cells to bind to the antibody-coated target.

Antibody therapy Treatment with an antibody, a substance that can directly kill specific tumor cells or stimulate the immune system to kill tumor cells.

Anticachexia Describes a drug or effect that works against cachexia (loss of body weight and muscle mass).

Anticancer antibiotic A type of anticancer drug that blocks cell growth by interfering with DNA, the genetic material in cells. Also called an antitumor antibiotic or antineoplastic antibiotic.

Anticarcinogenic Having to do with preventing or delaying the development of cancer.

Anticarcinogens Substances which inhibit the formation of cancers or the growth of tumors. More than 600 chemicals are claimed to be anti-cancer agents. These range from natural chemical constituent present in garlic, broccoli, cabbage and green tea to manmade antioxidants, such as butylated hydroxyanisole (BHA) and derivatives of retinoic acid.

Anti-CEA antibody An antibody against carcinoembryonic antigen (CEA), a protein present on certain types of cancer cells.

Anticholinergics Medicines that help calm spasms in the intestine.

Anticipation Each generation of offspring has increased severity of a genetic disorder; e.g., a grandchild may have earlier onset and more severe symptoms than the parent, who had earlier onset than the grandparent.

Anticoagulant A drug that helps prevent blood clots from forming. Also called a blood thinner.

Anticonvulsant A drug that prevents, reduces, or stops convulsions or seizures.

Antidepressant A drug used to treat depression.

Antidiabetic agent A substance that helps a person with diabetes control the level of glucose (sugar) in the blood so that the body works as it should.

Antidiarrheals Medicines that help control diarrhea.

Antiemetic A drug that prevents or relieves nausea and vomiting, which are common side effects from many chemotherapies. Antiemetic drugs are now used before, during or after chemotherapy. Granisetron and ondansetron are examples of antiemetic drugs.

Antiestrogen Any substance (for example, the drug tamoxifen) that blocks the effects of estrogen on tumors. Antiestrogens are used to treat breast cancers that depend on estrogen for growth.

Antifolate A substance that blocks the activity of folic acid. Antifolates are used to treat cancer. Also called folate antagonist.

Antifungal agent A drug used to treat fungal infections.

Antigen Any of various foreign substances such as bacteria, viruses, endotoxins, exotoxins, foreign proteins, pollen, and vaccines, whose entry into an organism induces an immune response (antibody production, lymphokine production, or both) directed specifically against that molecule. Response may be demonstrated as an increased reaction, such as hypersensitivity (usually protein or a complex of protein and polysaccharide, or occasionally a polysaccharide of high molecular weight), a circulating antibody that reacts with the antigen, or some degree of immunity to infectious disease if the antigen was a micro-organism or its products.

Antigen presenting cell (APC) A white blood cell that devours foreign bodies, breaks them down, and carries characteristic antigen peptides to it's surface. The foreign antigen, complexed with MHC I or II is presented to CD4 or CD8 to initiate an immune response specific to that peptide.

Antigen processing Large molecules are broken down (processed) within macrophages into peptides and presented within the groove of MHC molecules.

Antigen receptor The specific antigen-binding receptor on T or B lymphocytes; these receptors are transcribed and translated from rearrangements of V genes.

Antigen-binding site The part of an immunoglobulin molecule that binds antigen specifically.

Antigenemia The presence of detectable amounts of an antigen in the blood.

Antigenic determinant A single antigenic site or epitope on a complex antigenic molecule or particle.

Antigenicity The ability of an antigen to combine with antibodies and T-cell receptors to invoke a reaction from the immune system.

Antiglobulin test A laboratory test to identify antibodies that can bind to the surface of red blood cells or platelets and destroy them. This test is used to diagnose certain blood disorders in which patients make antibodies to their own red blood cells or platelets. It is also used to determine blood type. Also called a Coomb's test.

Antihistamines Medicines that are used to treat allergic reactions. They work by blocking the effect of histamine. Available as liquids, tablets and nasal sprays.

Antihormone therapy Treatment with drugs, surgery, or radiation in order to block the production or action of a hormone. Antihormone therapy may be used in cancer treatment because certain hormones are able to stimulate the growth of some types of tumors.

Anti-inflammatory Having to do with reducing inflammation.

Anti-interferon An antibody to an interferon. Used for the purification of interferons.

Antimetabolites Antimetabolites are substances that interfere with the body's metabolic processes, such as burning calories or division of cells to form new cells. In treating cancer, antimetabolite drugs disrupt DNA production, which in turn prevents cell division and growth of tumors.

Antimicrotubule agent A drug that inhibits cell growth by stopping cell division. Antimicrotubule agents are used as treatments for cancer. Also called antimitotic agents, mitotic inhibitors, and taxanes. Docetaxel and paclitaxel are antimicrotubule agents.

Antimitotic agent A drug that inhibits cell growth by stopping cell division. Antimitotic agents are used as treatments for cancer. Also called antimicrotubule agents, mitotic inhibitors, and taxanes. Docetaxel and paclitaxel are antimitotic agents.

Antineoplastic antibiotic A type of anticancer drug that blocks cell growth by interfering with DNA, the genetic material in cells. Also called an anticancer antibiotic or antitumor antibiotic.

Antineoplaston A substance isolated from normal human blood and urine that is being tested as a type of treatment for some tumors and AIDS.

Antineoplaston A10 A piperidinedione antineoplaston with potential antineoplastic activity. Antineoplaston A10 was originally isolated from human urine but is now synthetically derived. This agent intercalates into DNA, resulting in cell cycle arrest in G1 phase, reduction of mitosis, and decreased protein synthesis. Antineoplaston A10 may also inhibit ras-oncogene expression and activate tumor suppressor gene p53, leading to cell differentiation and apoptosis.

Antineoplaston AS21 A 4:1 mixture of phenylacetate and phenylacetylgluatmine, degradation products of the antineoplaston agent A10. Antineoplaston AS2-1 inhibits the incorporation of L-glutamine into tumor-cell proteins, leading to cell cycle arrest in the G1 phase and inhibition of mitosis. This agent may also inhibit RAS oncogene expression and activate tumor suppressor gene p53, resulting in cell differentiation and apoptosis.

Anti-nuclear antibody test Laboratory test, when positive suggests the presence of some form of autoimmune illness.

Antioxidant Antioxidants protect key cell components by neutralizing the damaging effects of "free radicals," natural byproducts of cell metabolism. Free radicals form when oxygen is metabolized, or burned by the body. They travel through cells, disrupting the structure of other molecules, causing cellular damage. Such cell damage is believed to contribute to aging and various health problems.

Antiparasitic A drug used to treat infections caused by bacteria and parasites. It is also used in the treatment of some cancers.

Antiprotozoal A natural or man-made substance that can kill or stop the growth of single-celled micro-organisms called protozoa.

Antipyretic A compound that reduces fever

Antiretroviral (ARV) A medication that interferes with the ability of a retrovirus (such as HIV) to make more copies of itself.

Antiretroviral therapy (ART) Treatment with drugs that inhibit the ability of retroviruses (such as HIV) to multiply in the body. The antiretroviral therapy recommended for HIV infection is referred to as highly active antiretroviral therapy (HAART), which uses a combination of medications to attack HIV at different points in its life cycle.

Antisense A piece of DNA that produces the mirror image, or antisense messenger RNA, that is exactly opposite in sequence to one that directs the cells to produce a specific protein. Since the antisense RNA binds tightly to its image, it prevents the protein from being made.

Antisense drugs A man-made segment of DNA or RNA that can lock onto a strand of DNA or RNA from a virus or other micro-organism. This marks the organism's genetic instructions for destruction and prevents the organism from making more copies of itself.

Antiseptic Acting against sepsis. An antiseptic agent is one that has been formulated for use on living tissue such as mucous membranes or skin to prevent or inhibit growth or action of organisms. Antiseptics should not be used to decontaminate inanimate objects.

Antiserum The blood serum obtained from an animal after has been immunized with a particular antigen. It contains antibodies specific for that antigen as well as antibodies specific for any other antigens with which the animal has previously been immunized.

Antispasmodics Medicines that help reduce or stop muscle spasms in the intestines.

Antistatic cleaners Liquid cleaners that enhance surface conductivity of cleanroom tabletops, workstations, and other surfaces.

Antitachycardia pacing A method of treating ventricular tachycardia (too-fast heartbeat) by stimulating the heart with a preset rapid series of small electrical pulses.

Antithymocyte globulin A protein used to reduce the risk of or to treat graft-versus-host disease.

Antitoxin An antibody that is capable of neutralizing the specific toxin that stimulated its production in the body. Antitoxins are produced in animals for medical purposes by injection of a toxin or toxoid, with the resulting serum being used to counteract the toxin in other individuals.

Antitrust A legal term encompassing a variety of efforts on the part of government to assure that sellers do not conspire to restrain trade or fix prices for their goods or services in the market.

Antituberculosis Describes a drug or effect that works against tuberculosis (a contagious bacterial infection that usually affects the lungs).

Antitumor antibiotic A type of anticancer drug that blocks cell growth by interfering with DNA, the genetic material in cells. Also called an anticancer antibiotic or antineoplastic antibiotic.

Antiviral A substance, drug, or process which destroys a virus or suppresses its replication. Can apply to anti-HIV activity, or other viruses, such as herpes or CMV.

Antoni type a tissue An arrangement of Schwann cells nuclei forming palisading parallel rows that enclose a homogeneous material that is devoid of nuclei, and has scant or no collagen.

Antrum An entry or opening cavity or chamber.

Antrum of stomach The dilated portion of the pyloric region of the stomach, near the junction with the duodenum.

ANUG An acronym for Acute Necrotizing Ulcerative Gingivitis, commonly known as trench mouth.

Anus The opening at the end of the digestive tract where bowel movements leave the body.

Anxiety Feelings of fear, dread, and uneasiness that may occur as a reaction to stress. A person with anxiety may sweat, feel restless and tense, and have a rapid heart beat. Extreme anxiety that happens often over time may be a sign of an anxiety disorder.

Anxiolytic A drug used in the treatment of anxiety and muscle spasms.

Aorta The main trunk of the arterial system which originates from the left ventricle of the heart and extends to the level of the fourth lumbar vertebra.

Abdominal Aortic Aneurysm

Abdominal Aortic Aneurysm

Abdominal Aortic Aneurysm.

Aortic arch The portion of the aorta which bends over inorder to extend into the thorax.

Aortic bifurcation The point where the abdominal aorta divides into the two common iliac arteries.

Aortic sinus Dilations of the aortic wall superior to each valve.

AP view A front to back view of the body.

APC vaccine A vaccine made of antigens and antigen-presenting cells (APCs). Also called antigen-presenting cell vaccine.

APC8015 Immune system cells that are collected from a patient with prostate cancer and treated in the laboratory with a molecule found on prostate cells. The treated cells are being studied for their ability to stimulate the immune system to kill prostate cancer cells.

Aperture rule A stick-like instrument used in vision therapy to develop convergence and divergence (eye teaming) skills.

Apex of heart The bottom most portion of the heart, formed by the left ventricle.

Aphasia Complete or partial loss of the ability to speak, or understand speech.

Apheresis A procedure in which blood is collected, part of the blood such as platelets or white blood cells is taken out, and the rest of the blood is returned to the donor. Also called pheresis.

Aphthous ulcer A painful shallow sore in the mouth. The sore is usually oval shaped, with a yellow-white center surrounded by a narrow red ring. Aphthous ulcers are 1/8 to 1/4 inch across and have no blisters. They occur on the soft surfaces of the mouth, such as the inner cheeks, inner lips, soft areas of the roof and floor of the mouth, tongue, gums, and throat.

API (Active pharmaceutical ingredient) Also called Drug Substance. Any substance or mixture of substances intended to be used in the manufacture of a drug (medicinal) product and that when used in the production of a drug becomes an active ingredient of the drug product. Such substances are intended to furnish pharmacological activity or other direct effect in the diagnosis, cure, mitigation, treatment, or prevention of disease or to affect the structure and function of the body.

API starting material A material used in the production of an API which is itself or is incorporated as a significant structural fragment into the structure of the API. A starting material may be an article of commerce, a material purchased from one or more suppliers under contract or commercial agreement, or it may be produced in-house. Starting materials are normally of defined chemical properties and structure.

Apicoectomy Surgical removal of the root tip to treat a dead tooth.

Aplasia Defective development or congenital absence of an organ or tissue.

Aplastic anemia A condition in which the bone marrow is unable to produce blood cells.

Apley's test A test of meniscal integrity comprising a compression of the knee (in 90° of flexion, with patient lying prone) and then performing both medial and lateral rotation.

Aplidine A substance that is being studied in the treatment of cancer. It is obtained from a marine organism.

Apocrine gland A type of gland that is found in the skin, breast, eyelid, and ear. Apocrine glands in the breast secrete fat droplets into breast milk and those in the ear help form earwax. Apocrine glands in the skin and eyelid are sweat glands. Most apocrine glands in the skin are in the armpits, the groin, and the area around the nipples of the breast. Apocrine glands in the skin are scent glands, and their secretions usually have an odor. Another type of gland (eccrine gland or simple sweat gland) produces most sweat.

Apoenzyme The protein moiety of an enzyme - determines the specifity of the enzyme reaction.

Apolizumab A humanized monoclonal antibody directed against 1D10, a polymorphic determinant on the HLA-DR beta chain that is expressed on normal and neoplastic B cells. Apolizumab induces complement-mediated cytotoxicity, antibody-dependent cell-mediated cytotoxicity, and apoptosis of 1D10 antigen-positive B cells in vitro.

Apoptosis "cell suicide" Thought to be primarily a way that the body clears out immune cells that respond to the body's own proteins, apoptosis involves a complete physical destruction of a cell, driven by enzymes. Apoptosis also occurs when one receptor on a CD4 cell is triggered without the normal "co-activation" signal. Abnormal apoptosis may be elevated in persons with HIV.

Appendectomy Surgery to remove the appendix (small finger-shaped pouch at the end of the first part of the large intestine).

Appendicitis Irritation, inflammation, and pain in the appendix, caused by infection, scarring, or obstruction (blockage).

Appendix A small pouch attached to the first portion of the large intestine (the cecum); it has no known function.

Apprehension test A test that places the joint in a position that would simulate subluxation or dislocation, with the degree of "positivity" being judged by the level of "apprehension" on the patient's face.

Aqueous Having to do with water.

Aquifer An underground layer of permeable rock, sand, or gravel that contains water for wells or springs.

Arachnoid Matter The middle of the three meninges enclosing the brain and spinal cord. It is a thin, translucent membrane closely adherent to the dura matter. Trabeculae extend from its inner surface across the subarachnoid space to the pia. Also forms the outer membrane of the leptomeninges.

Arachnoid villi (granulations) Microscopic tufts of pia-arachnoid mater that pierce the dura and open into venous sinuses, lacunae or extradural veins. They permit unidirectional flow of cerebrospinal fluid from the subarachnoid space to the venous system.

Arbor vitae The tree-like appearance of the branching white matter core within the folia of the cerebellar vermis as seen in sagittal section.

Arch Describes the alignment of the upper or lower teeth.

Archicerebellum The phylogenetically oldest part of the cerebellum represented by the nodulus and paired flocculi (flocculonodular lobe). Closely related to the vestibular system.

Archistriatum The phylogenetically oldest component of the basal ganglia; the amygdaloid nuclear complex.

Arctigenin A substance found in certain plants, including burdock. It has shown antiviral and anticancer effects. Arctigenin belongs to a group of substances called lignans.

Arctiin A substance found in certain plants, including burdock. It has shown anticancer effects. Arctiin belongs to a group of substances called lignans.

Arcus senilis A white or creamy opacity around the edge of the cornea that is found in the aged.

Areola The dark area of flesh that encircles the nipple of the breast.

Arginine butyrate The butyric acid salt of the amino acid arginine. In EBV-related lymphomas, arginine butyrate induces EBV thymidine kinase transcription and may act synergistically with the antiviral agent ganciclovir to inhibit cell proliferation and decrease cell viability. In addition, the butyrate moiety inhibits histone deacetylase, which results in hyperacetylation of histones H3 and H4. Acetylated histones have a reduced affinity for chromatin; this reduced histone-chromatin affinity may allow chromosomal unfolding, potentially enhancing the expression of genes related to tumor cell growth arrest and apoptosis.

Arm Any of the treatment groups in a clinical trial. Most clinical trials have two arms, but some have three or even more. Each arm receives a different treatment or placebo.

Aromatase inhibitor A drug that prevents the formation of estradiol, a female hormone, by interfering with an aromatase enzyme. Aromatase inhibitors are used as a type of hormone therapy for postmenopausal women who have hormone-dependent breast cancer.

Array A lead consisting of three electronically common elements joined at a yoke. The SQ array is used as part of an AICD system.

Arrayed library Individual primary recombinant clones (hosted in phage, cosmid, YAC, or other vector) that are placed in two-dimensional arrays in microtiter dishes. Each primary clone can be identified by the identity of the plate and the clone location (row and column) on that plate. Arrayed libraries of clones can be used for many applications, including screening for a specific gene or genomic region of interest.

Arrest The stopping of a function. Cardiac arrest is the stopping of the heartbeat and the heart's function.

Arrhenoblastoma A rare type of ovarian tumor in which the tumor cells secrete a male sex hormone. This may cause virilization (the appearance of male physical characteristics in females). Also called androblastoma and Sertoli-Leydig cell tumor of the ovary.

Arrhythmia An abnormal rhythm of the heart beat. Types of arrhythmias include tachycardias (accelerated heartbeats) and bradycardias (slow heartbeats).

Arsenic A poisonous chemical used to kill weeds and pests. Also used in cancer therapy.

Arsenic trioxide A small-molecule arsenic compound with antineoplastic activity. The mechanism of action of arsenic trioxide is not completely understood. This agent causes damage to or degradation of the promyelocytic leukemia protein/retinoic acid receptor-alpha (PML/RARa) fusion protein; induces apoptosis in acute promyelocytic leukemia (APL) cells and in many other tumor cell types; promotes cell differentiation and suppresses cell proliferation in many different tumor cell types; and is pro-angiogenic.

Arterial embolization The blocking of an artery by a clot of foreign material. This can be done as treatment to block the flow of blood to a tumor.

Arteriogram A radiograph of arteries after they have been injected with a contrast material.

Arteriography A procedure to x-ray arteries. The arteries can be seen because of an injection of a dye that outlines the vessels on an x-ray.

Arteriosclerosis A group of diseases in which the walls of the arteries get thick and hard. In one type of arteriosclerosis, fat builds up inside the walls and slows the blood flow. These diseases often occur in people who have had diabetes for a long time.

Artery A large blood vessel that carries blood from the heart to other parts of the body. Arteries are thicker and have walls that are stronger and more elastic than the walls of veins.

Arthr (o) Joint; articulation, e.g. arthrolith - a calculous deposit within a joint.

Arthralgia Joint pain with symptoms such as heat, redness, tenderness to touch, loss of motion, or swelling.

Arthritis A disease that causes inflammation and pain in the joints.

Arthrogram A roentgenographic record of a joint after the introduction of contrast material.

Arthroscopy Using an intra-articular camera to assist, this less invasive procedure allows the Orthopaedic Surgeon to assess, repair or reconstruct various tissues both within and around joints. Now used preferentially to "open" procedures, when permitted.

Articular cartilage Covers the ends of bones and allows the distribution of compressive loads over the cross section of bones, as well as providing a near frictionless and wear resistant surface for joint movement.

Articular fossa A hollow of depressed area within a joint.

Articular surface The surfaces of bone or cartilage which form a joint.

Artificial pancreas A large machine used in hospitals that constantly measures glucose (sugar) in the blood and, in response, releases the right amount of insulin. Scientists are also working to develop a small unit that could be implanted in the body, functioning like a real pancreas.

Artificial sphincter Sometimes complicated cases of incontinence require implantation of a device known as an artificial urinary sphincter. People who might benefit from this treatment include those who are incontinent after surgery for prostate cancer or stress incontinence, trauma victims and people with congenital defects in the urinary system. The artificial sphincter has three components, including a pump, balloon reservoir, and a cuff that encircles the urethra and prevents urine from leaking out. The cuff is connected to the pump, which is surgically implanted in the scrotum (in men) or labia (in women). The pump can be activated (usually by squeezing or pressing a button) to deflate the cuff and permit the bladder to empty. After a brief interval, the cuff refills itself and the urethra is again closed. Because the artificial sphincter is an implant, it is subject to the risks common to implants, such as infection, erosion (breaking down of tissue) and mechanical malfunction. Yet with appropriate pre-surgical evaluation, operative techniques and postoperative follow-up, many problems can be avoided and incontinent patients can experience an improved quality of life with this device.

Arytenoid cartilage Paired cartilage of the larynx which articulates with the lamina of the cricoid cartilage.

Asbestos A natural material that is made of tiny fibers. Asbestos can cause several serious diseases, including cancer.

Ascending aorta The portion of the aorta that originates from the left ventricle and gives rise to the right and left coronary arteries.

Ascending colon The part of the colon that lies between the cecum and the right colic flexure.

Ascites Abnormal build-up of fluid in the abdomen that may cause swelling. In late-stage cancer, tumor cells may be found in the fluid in the abdomen. Ascites also occurs in patients with liver disease.

Ascomycetes A family of fungi marked by long spore-containing cells. Form sexual spores called ascospores, which are contained within a sac (a capsule structure). Ergot, truffles, some molds of the genera Neurospora and Aspergillus, and yeasts belong to this category.

Ascorbic acid Also known as vitamin C, it is essential for the development and maintenance of connective tissue. Vitamin C speeds the production of new cells in wound healing and it is an antioxidant that keeps free radicals from hooking up with other molecules to form damaging compounds that might attack tissue. Vitamin C protects the immune system, helps fight off infections, reduces the severity of allergic reactions and plays a role in the synthesis of hormones and other body chemicals. Green peppers, broccoli, citrus fruits, tomatoes, strawberries, and other fresh fruits and vegetables are good sources of vitamin C.

Asepsis A condition in which living pathogenic (causing or capable of causing disease) organisms are absent.

Aseptic Marked by or relating to asepsis.

Aseptic processing area Area in which sterile product is formulated, filled into containers, and sealed.

Aseptic processing Processing conditions designed to achieve a sterile product.

Aseptic transfer (in Isolators) The key issue in all contained aseptic environments. Aseptic transfer is essential for change parts, components, and even product to enter and exit an isolator system without sterility challenges. There are an increasing number of ways to make an aseptic transfer. The following is a brief list of some of the key techniques:

1. Alpha Beta Systems Double Door Systems: also called RTPs (Rapid Transfer Ports) and HCT (High Containment Transfer). When mated, the two ports act as one door, protecting the internal and external environments.

2. Alpha Beta Dry Heat Sterilized: similar to Alpha Beta port with the additional safeguard of a heat sterilized seal.

3. UV and Pulsed Light: light sterilization/sanitization. Sterilizing the system by making use of a wide spectrum of light within the transfer chamber.

4. One Shot Systems: basically, two halves coming together. Similar to an Alpha Beta port but simpler, cheaper, and capable of only a single connection.

5. Heat Welded Bag Systems: passed in or passed out using a continuous polyethylene liner which is heat sealed and cut to maintain the integrity of the internal and external environments.

6. Steam Sterilized: the liquid component or powder path is

clean steam sterilized after connection and prior to transfer.

7. Autoclave/Depyrogenation/Dryheat: pass through for batch. Use of conventional autoclave to sterilize a canister provided with an Alpha Beta port and filters to allow the passage of steam and safe aspiration on cooling. Depyrogenation/Dryheat uses dry heat to sterilize and at sufficient temperature depyrogenate components, typically glassware, in a batch oven.

8. Depyrogenation Tunnel: standard volume glassware entry. Depyrogenation/Dry heat uses dry heat to sterilize and at sufficient temperature to depyrogenate components, typically glassware, in a tunnel allowing continuous input.

Asparaginase An enzyme isolated from the bacterium Escherichia coli or the bacterium Erwinia carotovora. Asparagine is critical to protein synthesis in leukemic cells, which cannot synthesize this amino acid due to the absence of the enzyme asparagine synthase. Asparaginase hydrolyzes L-asparagine to L-aspartic acid and ammonia, thereby depleting leukemic cells of asparagine and blocking protein synthesis and tumor cell proliferation, especially in the G1 phase of the cell cycle. This agent also induces apoptosis in tumor cells. The E. carotovora-derived form of asparaginase is typically reserved for cases of asparaginase hypersensitivity.

Aspartame Aspartame is a low-calorie sweetener used in a variety of foods and beverages and as a tabletop sweetener. It is about 200 times sweeter than sugar. Aspartame is made by joining two protein components, aspartic acid and phenylalanine.

Aspartate aminotransferase A liver enzyme, measured through a blood test, that indicates the health of the liver. Lower counts are better. Levels may go up because of hepatitis and other infections, or because of drug toxicities

Aspergillosis An infection of the lungs caused by the fungus Aspergillus. The infection may also spread through the blood to other organs. Symptoms include fever, chills, difficulty in breathing, and coughing up blood. If the infection reaches the brain, it may cause dementia.

Aspergillus A family of fungi commonly found in soil. Certain types may cause disease, especially in people who have suppressed immune systems.

Aspirate Fluid withdrawn from a lump (often a cyst) or a nipple.

Aspiration The process of removing fluid or tissue, or both, from a specific area.

Aspirin A drug that reduces pain, fever, inflammation, and blood clotting. Aspirin belongs to the family of drugs called nonsteroidal anti-inflammatory agents. It is also being studied in cancer prevention.

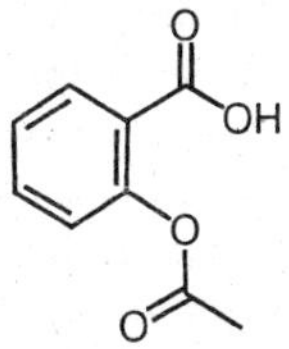

O
OH
O
O

Figure Aspirin

Assay A technique (test) for measuring a biological response or for determining characteristics such as composition, purity, activity, and weight.

Assembly Putting sequenced fragments of DNA into their correct chromosomal positions.

Assimilation The formation of cellular material utilizing small food molecules and energy.

Assisted living Broad range of residential care services, but does not include nursing services. Normally lower in cost than nursing homes.

Assisted reproductive technologies (ART) The new forms of fertility treatment incorporate many methods of sperm retrieval and preparation. Once the sperm have been processed to ensure optimal fertilizing potential, they are used in a variety of procedures that aid the process of conception. These procedures include artificial insemination (AI), in vitro fertilization (IVF), and sperm microinjection techniques.

Assistive device A tool that helps a person with a disability to do a certain task. Examples are a cane, wheelchair, scooter, walker, hearing aid, or special bed.

Assistive technology Any device or technology that helps a disabled person. Examples are special grips for holding utensils, computer screen monitors to help a person with low vision read more easily, computers controlled by talking, telephones that make the sound louder, and lifters to help a person rise out of a chair.

Association Synonyms for association include correlation and relationship. An association between two conditions or states means that if one is present, the other is likely to be so as well. Association does not necessarily imply a causal relationship. In addition, association does not necessarily imply a statistically significant relationship.

AST (Aspertate aminotransferase) Enzyme or protein that leaks from the damaged liver. Measured in blood to assess liver injury.

Asthenia Weakness; lack of energy and strength.

Asthenopia Eyestrain, symptoms include excessive tearing, itching, burning, visual fatigue, and headache. It can be caused from an uncorrected refractive error, accommodation (eye focusing) disorder, binocularity (eye teaming) disorder, or by extended, intense use of the eyes.

Asthma A chronic disease in which the bronchial airways in the lungs become narrowed and swollen, making it difficult to breathe. Symptoms include wheezing, coughing, tightness in the chest, shortness of breath, and rapid breathing. An attack may be brought on by pet hair, dust, smoke, pollen, mold, exercise, cold air, or stress.

Asthmatic 1. Pertaining to asthma as, for example, asthmatic bronchitis.

2. A person with asthma.

Astigmatism Light rays entering the eye do not all meet at the same point (similar to a frayed string), which results in blurred or distorted vision. An abnormally shaped cornea typically causes this condition. Occasionally astigmatism exists in the lens of the eye. This condition is corrected by a cylindrical (toric) eyeglass or contact lens.

Astrocyte Largest and most numerous type of neuroglial cell within the central nervous system. These cells of ectodermal origin are of two types; fibrous and protoplasmic astrocytes

Astrocytoma A tumor that begins in the brain or spinal cord in small, star-shaped cells called astrocytes.

Asymmetrical/asymmetry An imbalance in facial alignment as it relates to the eyes, eyelids or eyebrows.

Asymmetry Lack or absence of balanced proportions between parts of a thing.

Asymptomatic To be without noticeable signs or symptoms of disease. Many cancers can develop and grow without producing symptoms, especially in the early stages. Detection tests, such as mammography, try to discover developing cancers at the asymptomatic stage, when the chances for cure are usually highest.

Asynchrony A condition in which the heart fails to maintain a normal time sequence between atrial and ventricular contractions.

Atamestane A substance that is being studied in the treatment of cancer. Atamestane blocks the production of the hormone estrogen in the body. It belongs to the family of drugs called antiestrogens.

Ataxia Partial or complete loss of coordination of voluntary muscular movements. This can interfere with a person's ability to walk, talk, eat, and perform other tasks of daily living.

Ataxia-telangiectasia A rare, inherited, progressive, degenerative disease of childhood that causes loss of muscle control, a weakened immune system, and an increased risk of cancer.

Ataxic gait Awkward, uncoordinated walking.

Atelectasis Failure of the lung to expand (inflate) completely. This may be caused by a blocked airway, a tumor, general anesthesia, pneumonia or other lung infections, lung disease, or longterm bedrest with shallow breathing. Sometimes called a collapsed lung.

Atherectomy A minimally invasive CAD intervention procedure which involves the excision and removal of blockages by catheters with miniature cutting systems.

Atherosclerosis Narrowing or blockage of arteries caused by a buildup of fat (cholesterol) within the artery wall. The build-up is sometimes referred to as "plaque."

Athrombin K Other name for warfarin.

Athymic nude mouse A type of laboratory mouse that is hairless, lacks a normal thymus gland, and has a defective immune system because of a genetic mutation. Athymic nude mice are often used in cancer research because they do not reject tumor cells, from mice or other species.

Atlas and axis C1 (the atlas) sits atop C2 (the axis) and can rotate about the dens - a vertical post from C2.

ATLL (Adult t-cell leukemia/ lymphoma) An aggressive (fast-growing) type of T-cell non-Hodgkin's lymphoma caused by the human T-cell leukemia virus type 1 (HTLV-1). It is marked by bone and skin lesions, high calcium levels, and enlarged lymph nodes, spleen and liver.

Atomic absorption spectro-photometry A highly sensitive instrumental technique for identifying and measuring metals in water.

Atonic colon Lack of normal muscle strength in the large intestine; caused by overuse of laxatives or by a disease called Hirschsprung's disease.

Atopy A predisposition to develop allergy, which may remain latent until clinical allergy develops. Diagnosed by having at least 1 positive skin prick test response or personal or first degree family history of asthma, eczema or hay fever.

Atovaquone (mepron) Antibiotic sometimes used in treatment of PCP. In trials for prophylaxis of PCP, and for treatment of toxoplasmosis

Atrasentan hydrochloride The orally available hydrochloride salt of pyrrolidine-3-carboxylic acid with potential antineoplastic activity. As a selective antagonist of the endothelin-A (ETA) receptor, atrasentan binds selectively to the ETA receptor, which may result in inhibition of endothelin-induced angiogenesis and tumor cell proliferation.

Atresia Closed; absence of a normal opening or normally patent lumen

Atria The upper chambers of the heart, specifically the right atrium and left atrium. The 2 atria collect blood as it comes into the heart and fill the ventricles (lower chambers) with blood.

Atrial appendage The ear-shaped appendage of either atrium of the heart.

Atrio ventricular synchrony AV synchrony - The normal physiologic sequencing of atrial contraction followed, after a fraction of a second, by a ventricular contraction.

Atrio-ventricular (AV) node A cluster of muscle cells located in the wall between the right and left atrium, just above the ventricles. This part of the heart's electrical pathway helps carry signals from the atria to the ventricles.

Atrium One of two upper chambers of the heart (plural: atria). The atria collect blood as it comes into the heart and fill the lower chambers (ventricles) with blood.

Atrophy A wasting of tissues, organs or the entire body; caused by death and resorption of cells, diminished cellular proliferation, pressure, ischemia, malnutrition, decreased function or hormonal changes.

Attention deficit hyperactivity disorder (ADHD) Commonly called "hyperactivity," Attention Deficit Hyperactivity Disorder is a clinical diagnosis based on specific criteria. These include excessive motor activity, impulsiveness, short attention span, low tolerance to frustration and onset before 7 years of age.

Attention The ability to focus selectively on a selected stimulus, sustaining that focus and shifting it at will. The ability to concentrate.

Attenuated A term used to describe a bacterium or virus that has been changed in the laboratory so that it is not harmful to people. Attenuated viruses are often used as vaccines because they can no longer cause disease, but can still stimulate a strong immune response. Examples include the vaccines against polio (Sabin oral vaccine), measles, mumps, and rubella.

Attenuated virus A weakened virus with reduced ability to infect or produce disease. Some vaccines are based on attenuated viruses.

Attestation The requirement that the attending physician certify, in writing, the accuracy and completion of the clinical information used for DRG assignment.

Attrition Loss of structure due to natural wear.

Atypical hyperplasia A benign (noncancerous) condition in which cells look abnormal under a microscope and are increased in number.

Atypical Not usual; abnormal. Cancer is the result of atypical cell division.

Atypical teratoid/rhabdoid tumor ATT/RHT or AT/RT. An aggressive cancer of the central nervous system, kidney, or liver that occurs in very young children.

Auger electron spectroscopy (AES) An alternative surface analysis that can detect all elements with an atomic number greater than that of helium with the additional ability to analyze sub micron-diameter features. It is not as quantitative as ESCA and cannot determine the chemical state of an element. The primary advantage of Auger is that when combined with etching, a chemical depth profile can be measured rapidly and can image the distribution on the surface of spatial limitation resolution of 100 to 1,000 angstroms (depending on the equipment capability).

Augmerosen A substance that is being studied in the treatment of cancer. It may kill cancer cells by blocking the production of a protein that makes cancer cells live longer and by making them more sensitive to anticancer drugs. It belongs to the family of drugs called antisense oligodeoxyribonucleotides. Also called oblimersen, Genasense, and bcl-2 antisense oligodeoxynucleotide G3139.

Austenite A face-centered cubic crystal with high solubility for carbon (about 2%); an allotropic form of iron resulting from steel being heated above the transformation temperature.

Auto Self, e.g. autolysis self-dissolution; the post-mortem enzymatic degradation of cells.

Auto immune disease A disease in which the body produces an immunogenic response against self-antigens. In some cases, predominantly one organ is affected (e.g. hemolytic anemia and chronic thyroiditis); in others, the disease process is diffused through many tissues (e.g. SLE (Systemic Lupus Erythematosis)).

Autoantibody An antibody directed against the body's own tissue.

Autoclave An apparatus into which moist heat (steam) under pressure is introduced to sterilize or decontaminate materials placed within (e.g. filter assemblies, glassware, etc.). Steam pressure is maintained for pre-specified times and then allowed to exhaust. There are two types of autoclaves: 1. Gravity displacement autoclave: this type of autoclave operates at 121°C. Steam enters at the top of the loaded inner chamber, displacing the air below through a discharge outlet.

2. Vacuum autoclave: this type of autoclave can operate with a reduced sterilization cycle time. The air is pumped out of the loaded chamber before it is filled with steam.

Figure Autoclave

Autoclave-resistant factor A substance found in soybeans that may slow down or stop the spread of cancer. This substance does not break down in an autoclave (a device that uses high-pressure steam to kill microorganisms and clean medical equipment).

Autograft A tissue transplant from one area to another on a single individual.

Autoimmune disease One of the growing number of otherwise unrelated disorders now suspected of being caused by the inflammation and destruction of tissues by the body's own antibodies (autoantibodies). These disorders include Systemic Lupus Erythematosus (SLE), rheumatic fever, and several forms of Thyroid dysfunction including Hashimoto's disease.

Autoimmune polyglandular syndrome A group of autoimmune disorders that involve endocrine glands and which result in failure of the glands to produce their hormones. (Also called autoimmune endocrine failure syndrome, autoimmune polyendocrine syndrome, and immunoendocrinopathy syndrome.)

Type I A disorder that includes hypoparathyroidism, candidiasis and Addison's disease (adrenal gland failure). 15% have autoimmune Type 1 Diabetes. It has recently been shown that there is a mutation in the AIRE (AutoImmune Regulator) gene on chromosome 21.

Type II A disorder in which two or more autoimmune conditions are found. 50% show Type 1 autoimmune diabetes and another associated condition, which may include Addison's disease, the celiac syndrome, vitiligo, pernicious anemia, myasthenia gravis, Graves' disease, and others.

Autoimmunity A condition in which the body's immune system mistakenly fights and rejects the body's own tissues.

Autologous Taken from an individual's own tissues, cells, or DNA.

Autologous bone marrow In transplantation, refers to a person's own bone marrow. Bone marrow is the soft, sponge-like tissue in the center of most large bones that produces white blood cells, red blood cells, and platelets.

Autologous bone marrow transplantation A procedure in which bone marrow is removed from a person, stored, and then given back to the person after intensive treatment.

Autologous dendritic cell adenovirus p53 vaccine An autologous vaccine composed of dendritic cells (DC) that have been transduced with a p53 tumor suppressor gene-modified virus. When the autologous dendritic cell-adenovirus p53 vaccine is administered, the host cytotoxic T lymphocytes (CTL) are directed against p53-positive tumor cells, which may result in tumor cell death and decreased tumor growth.

Autologous EBV transformed B lymphoblastoid tumor fusion cell vaccine A cell-based vaccine composed of autologous tumor cells fused with Epstein-Barr virus transformed B-lymphoblastoid cells. Upon administration, this vaccine may stimulate a cytotoxic T cell response against tumor cells, resulting in tumor cell lysis.

Autologous immunoglobulin idiotype KLH conjugate vaccine A cancer vaccine composed of tumor-specific idiotype determinants derived from an individual's tumor cells which are conjugated to keyhole limpet hemocyanin, an immunostimulant carrier protein. When injected into the individual from whom the tumor cells were isolated, this vaccine may stimulate an antitumoral cytotoxic T-lympho-cytic immune response.

Autologous lymphocyte In transplantation, refers to a

person's own white blood cells. Lymphocytes have a number of roles in the immune system, including the production of antibodies and other substances that fight infection and disease.

Autologous stem cell transplantation A procedure in which bloodforming stem cells (cells from which all blood cells develop) are removed, stored, and later given back to the same person.

Autologous tumor cell A cancer cell from an individual's own tumor.

Autologous tumor cell vaccine A therapeutic agent produced by isolating tumor cells from an individual and processing these tumor cells into a vaccine formulation in vitro; the vaccine is then administered to the individual from whom the tumor cells were isolated. Typically combined with an adjuvant immunostimulant, an autologous cell vaccine may elicit a cytotoxic T-lymphocytic immune response to cell surface-expressed tumor-associated antigens (TAAs), resulting in tumor cell death.

Automated refractor Also called auto refractor This method determines the eye's refractive error and the best corrective lenses to be prescribed by using a computerized device that varies its optical power mechanically and prints out the results.

Automated system Any facility system or piece of equipment that is controlled with limited or no manual intervention.

Automatic implantable cardioverter defibrillator (AICD) A surgically implanted device that monitors the heartbeat and delivers electrical impulses to correct an abnormal rhythm and restore a regular heartbeat. The AICD system usually consists of an implanted pulse generator and one or more leads. The system is adjusted using an external programming device.

Autonomic neuropathy A disease of the nerves affecting mostly the internal organs such as the bladder muscles, the cardiovascular system, the digestive tract, and the genital organs. These nerves are not under a person's conscious control and function automatically. Also called visceral neuropathy.

Autoradiography A technique that uses X-ray film to visualize radioactively labeled molecules or fragments of molecules; used in analyzing length and number of DNA fragments after they are separated by gel electrophoresis.

Autosomal dominant A gene on one of the non-sex chromosomes that is always expressed, even if only one copy is present. The chance of passing the gene to offspring is 50% for each pregnancy.

Autosomal recessive disease An inherited disorder which is equally likely to occur in either sex. Wilson's Disease is an autosomal recessive disease.

Autosome A chromosome not involved in sex determination. The diploid human genome consists of a total of 46 chromosomes: 22 pairs of autosomes, and 1 pair of sex chromosomes (the X and Y chromosomes).

Autotrophs One of two categories in which microorganisms are classified on the basis of their carbon source. Autotrophs use carbon dioxide as a carbon source.

Av groove A groove on the surface of the heart which separates the atria from the ventricles.

Avascular implant A solid orbital implant that will not allow penetration of blood vessels. It is usually encapsulated in fibrous tissue.

Avascular necrosis (AVN) Death of bone (osteonecrosis) caused by a loss of blood supply to the bone tissue. AVN has occured in the hip bones of some people with HIV, but it is not clear if bone death occurs because of HIV infection itself or as a side effect of the medications used to treat HIV. Symptoms include pain in the affected area of the body, limited range of motion, joint stiffness, limping, and muscle spasms. If untreated, AVN can cause progressive bone damage leading to bone collapse.

Avastin A monoclonal antibody used in the treatment of colorectal cancer that has spread. It is also being studied in the treatment of other types of cancer. It may prevent the growth of new blood vessels from surrounding tissue to a solid tumor. Also called bevacizumab.

Average length of stay (ALOS) Refers to the average length of stay per inpatient hospital visit.

Avidity The summation of multiple affinities, for example when a polyvalent antibody binds to a polyvalent antigen.

Avoidable hospital condition Medical diagnosis for which hospitalization could have been avoided if ambulatory care had been provided in a timely and efficient manner.

Avulsion Usually caused when a muscle is forcefully stretched beyond its freely available range of motion, or when it meets a sudden unexpected resistance while contracting forcefully. Can also occur in ligament injuries, where the insertion of the ligament may pull some bone off when it is damaged.

Avuncular relationship The genetic relationship between nieces and nephews and their aunts and uncles.

Axial view The axial imaging plane is a "cross-section" - perpendicular to the long axis of a cylinder.

Axilla The armpit.

Axillary dissection A surgical procedure in which the lymph nodes in the armpit (axillary nodes) are removed and examined, to find out if breast cancer has spread to those nodes.

Axillary lymph node A lymph node in the armpit region that drains lymph channels from the breast.

Axillary lymph node dissection Surgery to remove lymph nodes found in the armpit region. Also called axillary dissection.

Axillary vein The continuation of the basilic vein which ends at the lateral border of the first rib, becoming the subclavian vein.

Axillary Pertaining to the armpit area, including the lymph nodes that are located there.

Axis The alignment of the len's cylindrical part; used for correcting astigmatism. This measurement is given in degrees. The values are typically from 90 degrees to 180 degrees.

Axon The process of a neuron that conducts impulses away from the cell body. Typically a single process, extending for variable distances, enveloped in a myelin sheath and establishing specialized junctional contacts.

Axoplasmic flow This is continually moving cytoplasm within the neurone and provides material synthesized by the cell body to meet the physiological requirements of the cell body, the axon and the target tissues. Disruption to axoplasmic flow results in diminished performance of the neurone.

Azacitidine A pyrimidine nucleoside analogue of cytidine with antineoplastic activity. Azacitidine is incorporated into DNA, where it reversibly inhibits DNA methyltransferase, thereby blocking DNA methylation. Hypomethylation of DNA by azacitidine may activate tumor suppressor genes silenced by hypermethylation, resulting in an antitumor effect. This agent is also incorporated into RNA, thereby disrupting normal RNA function and impairing tRNA cytosine-5-methyltransferase activity.

Azathioprine Drug marketed with trade name Imuran. Used to treat a number of diseases of unknown or autoimmune cause. Also used to treat organ transplant recipients to help prevent graft rejection.

AZD2171 A substance that is being studied in the treatment of some types of cancer. It belongs to the families of drugs called angiogenesis inhibitors and vascular endothelial growth factor receptor (VEGFR) tyrosine kinase inhibitors.

Azithromycin (zithromax) A macrolide antibiotic sometime used as a component in combination therapy for mycobacterium avium complex.

Azoles A family of antifungal drugs (Fluconazole, itraconazole, etc.) that are used to treat fungal infections in persons with HIV, including candida, cryptococcus, histoplasmosis, and others.

Azoxymethane A substance that is used in cancer research to cause colon tumors in laboratory animals. This is done to test new diets, drugs, and procedures for use in cancer prevention and treatment.

AZQ Diaziquone. An anticancer drug that is able to cross the blood-brain barrier and kill cancer cells in the central nervous system.

AZT Also called zidovudine, Retrovir, or azidothymidine. A thymidine (genetic building block) analog that suppresses replication of HIV. It is the only drug approved for the initial treatment of HIV infection. Adverse side effects may include anemia, leukopenia, muscle fatigue, muscle wasting, nausea and headaches.

Azygoesophageal recess An area of lucency on the frontal chest image, representing a portion of the Right lower lobe that crosses the midline anterior to the spine, and ends at the azygous vein and or the esophagus.

Azygous arch The point where the azygous vein arches over the root of the right lung to empty into the superior vena cava.

Azygous lobe A normal variant produced by an indentation in the R. upper lobe of the lung by four layers of pleura (two layers of visceral pleura and two layers of parietal pleura). It is produced by invagination of the azygous vein. This is not a true lobe, since it does not have a separate bronchus.

Azygous vein A vertical paraspinal vein that connects the superior venae cava with abdominal veins.

B

B cell A white blood cell that comes from bone marrow. As part of the immune system, B cells make antibodies and help fight infections. Also called B lymphocyte.

B cell lymphoma A type of cancer that forms in B cells (a type of immune system cell). B-cell lymphomas usually occur in adults and may be either indolent (slow-growing) or aggressive (fast-growing). There are many different types of B-cell lymphomas, and prognosis and treatment depend on the type and stage of cancer.

B lymphocytes B-lymphocytes are blood cells of the immune system derived from the bone marrow and spleen involved in the production of antibodies. B-lymphocytes float through all body fluids, are able to detect the presence of foreign invaders, and produce antibodies on their own and when primed by T-lymphocytes. B-lymphocytes can later differentiate into plasma and memory cells. B-cells mediate the "humoral" immune response.

BID Twice a day dosing instructions.

B3 antigen A protein found on some tumor cells.

B43 PAP immunotoxin A toxic substance linked to an antibody that attaches to tumor cells and kills them.

B7 1 A molecule that helps control immune responses in the body. B7-1 is involved in stimulating T-cells.

BAC (Bacterial Artificial Chromosome) A vector used to clone DNA fragments (100-kb to 300-kb insert size; average, 150-kb) in E. Coli cells. Based on naturally occurring F-factor plasmid found in the bacterium E. coli.

Backbone The bones, muscles, tendons, and other tissues that reach from the base of the skull to the tailbone. The backbone encloses the spinal cord and the fluid surrounding the spinal cord. Also called spine, spinal column, and vertebral column.

Backcross A cross between an animal that is heterozygous for alleles obtained from two parental strains and a second animal from one of those parental strains. Also used to describe the breeding protocol of an outcross followed by a backcross.

Background contamination Contamination introduced accidentally in reagents, dilution water, solvents, rinse water, etc., which can be confused with constituents in samples being analyzed.

Background environment The environment that surrounds a critical area.

Background retinopathy Early stage of diabetic retinopathy; usually does not impair vision. Also called "nonproliferative retinopathy."

Backwash The countercurrent flow of water through equipment, usually to clean or to recover performance, such as in a resin bed (flow-in at the bottom of the exchanger unit and out at the top) to clean and reclassify the bed after exhaustion. This process of reversing flow may also be applied to filters in order to force contaminants out of plugged pores and passages.

Bacteremia The presence of bacteria in the blood

Bacteria A large group of single-cell microorganisms. Some cause infections and disease in animals and humans. The singular of bacteria is bacterium.

Bacterial toxin A toxic substance, made by bacteria, that can be modified to kill specific tumor cells without harming normal cells.

Bactericidal Capable of killing bacteria.

Bactericide An agent that kills vegetative bacteria but not mycobacteria or spores.

Bacteriological specimen Refers to any body fluid, secretion, or tissue sent to the laboratory where smears and cultures for bacteria will be performed. The specimen may consist of blood, sputum, urine, spinal fluid, material obtained at biopsy, etc.

Bacteriophage A virus that exclusively infects bacteria. A protein coat surrounds the genome (DNA or RNA). One of the bacteriophages most extensively studied is the lambda phage, which is also one of the most important viral vectors used in rDNA work. Lambda promoters have been used to express eukaryotic proteins in E.coli.

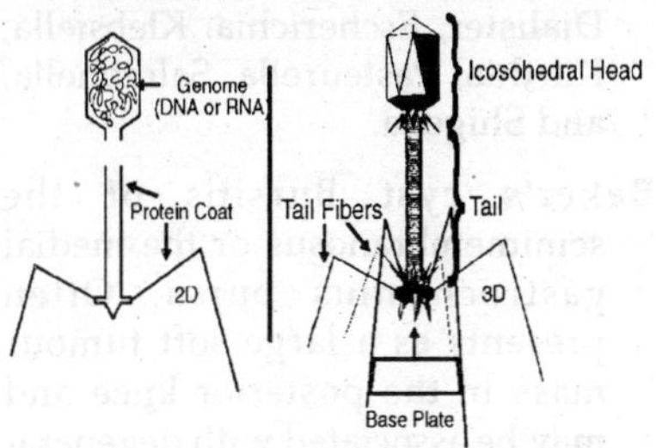

Structural Overview of T Phage

Figure Bacteriophage

Bacteriostatic Capable of inhibiting bacterial growth (but not necessarily capable of killing bacteria).

Bacteriostatic water For Injection, Water that serves the same purposes as Sterile Water for Injection, it meets the same standards, with the exception that it may be packaged in either single-dose or multiple-dose containers of not larger than 30-ml size.

Bacterium Any of a large group of microscopic organisms having round, rod-shaped, spiral, or filamentous unicellular or noncellular bodies that are often aggregated into colonies, are enclosed by a cell wall or membrane (prokaryotes), and lack fully differentiated nuclei. Bacteria range in size from 0.4μm to 2.0μm and may exist as free-living organisms in soil, water, organic matter, or as parasites in the live bodies of plants. Some are disease producing, but most perform necessary functions such as digestion, fermentation, and nitrification. Most of the forms are variously grouped under generic names such as: Alcaligenes, Dialister, Escherichia, Klebsiella, Kurthia, Pasteurella, Salmonella, and Shigella.

Baker's cyst Bursitis of the semimembranosus or the medial gastrocnemius bursa. Often presents as a large soft tumour mass in the posterior knee and may be associated with degeneration of the knee.

BAL (British anti-lewisite) The first drug discovered to be effective in the treatment of Wilson's Disease. It is administered in a long series of painful injections. BAL was originally developed as an antidote for Lewisite. Lewisite a chemical warfare agent similar to mustard gas.

Ballooning degeneration A cytoplasmic swelling of epidermal cells with loss of intercellular bridges as seen in viral vesicles.

Bankart lesion An anterior pouch that is formed when the humeral head dislocates anteriorly, and remains following reduction, leaving a deficit in the anterior restraining mechanisms.

Barbiturate A drug used to treat insomnia, seizures, and convulsions, and to relieve anxiety and tension before surgery. It belongs to the family of drugs called central nervous system (CNS) depressants.

Barium A liquid used to coat the inside of organs so they will show up on an x-ray.

Barium enema A procedure done to evaluate the large intestine for abnormalities. A fluid called barium that shows up well on x-rays is given into the rectum as an enema. An x-ray of the abdomen shows strictures (narrowed areas), obstructions (blockages), and other problems.

Barium solution A liquid containing barium sulfate that is used in x-rays to highlight parts of the digestive system.

Barium swallow A series of x-rays of the esophagus. The x-ray pictures are taken after the person drinks a solution that contains barium. The barium coats and outlines the esophagus on the x-ray. Also called an esophagram and upper GI series.

Barrett's esophagus A condition in which normal cells that line the esophagus, called squamous cells, turn into abnormal cells, called specialized columnar cells. Damage to the lining of the esophagus causes the cells to change; often occurs with long-term acid reflux.

Barrier isolator A containment device that utilizes barrier technology for the enclosure of a controlled workspace. There are two main types of isolator:

1. Type 1 Isolator: An isolator designed to protect the product from process-generated and external factors that would compromise its quality.

2. Type 2 Isolator: An isolator designed to protect the product from process-generated and external factors that would compromise its quality and to protect the operator from hazards associated with the product.

Barrier technology The technology of using separating environments, whether protecting the world from a product or the product from the world. Containment, barrier isolation and isolation all refer to the same technology, which is enclosing an environment. There are, however, some redefining terms that are gaining favour:

1. Containment - protect the world from the product (as in the case of highly potent compounds or a toxic). 2. Isolation - protect the product from the world (as in the case of a sterile product).

Basal cell A small, round cell found in the lower part (or base) of the epidermis, the outer layer of the skin.

Basal cell carcinoma A type of skin cancer that arises from the basal cells, small round cells found in the lower part (or base) of the epidermis, the outer layer of the skin.

Basal cell nevus syndrome A genetic condition that causes unusual facial features and disorders of the skin, bones, nervous system, eyes, and endocrine glands. People with this syndrome have a higher risk of basal cell carcinoma. Also called Gorlin syndrome and nevoid basal cell carcinoma syndrome.

Basal ganglia Subcortical masses of grey matter (nuclei) located within the medullary center of each cerebral hemisphere. Usually includes the caudate nucleus, putamen, globus pallidus, amygdala and claustrum. The ter m is now used to refer to the corpus striatum, subthalamic nucleus and substantia nigra.

Basal metabolism Basal metabolism is the energy (calories) a body burns when completely at rest. Basal metabolism rate (BMR) is the level of energy needed to keep involuntary body processes going. These processes include heartbeat, breathing, generating body heat, perspiring to keep cool, and transmitting messages to the brain. For a sedentary person, BMR accounts for about 60-70 percent of daily energy expenditure; the remaining 30-40 percent is from physical activity and from body heat produced after a meal. Physical activity is responsible for as much as 50-60 percent of the total energy expenditure in people who include frequent aerobic activity into their lifestyles

Basal rate Refers to a continuous supply of low levels of insulin, as in insulin pump therapy.

Basal/bolus insulin administration (poor man's pump) Using several daily injections of fast-acting insulin (e.g., NovoLog, Humalog, or Regular), at mealtimes – the bolus doses – together with one or more daily injections of long acting insulin (e.g., Lantus, UltraLente, or NPH) – the basal doses – to achieve blood sugar control in a manner similar to that used by people who use insulin pumps.

Base An electropositive element or radical that unites with an acid to form a salt. Or, a substance that when dissolved in water, dissociates to produce one or more hydroxyl ions (OH^-).

Base down (BD) prism A wedge-shaped lens which is thicker on one edge than the other. The thicker edge (base) is turned down. Prisms bend light (opposite direction from its thicker end) so the base-down prism turns the light upward thus causing the eye to also move up. This prism is used to measure an eye misalignment and/or treat a binocular dysfunction (eye teaming problem). Prisms are sometimes added to glasses to help improve eyesight due to a misalignment or visual field loss.

Base in (BI) prism A wedge-shaped lens which is thicker on one edge than the other. The thicker edge (base) is turned inward, closest to the nose. Prisms bend light (opposite direction from its thicker end) so the base-in prism turns the light outward (toward the ear) thus causing the eye to also move outward. This prism is used to measure an eye misalignment and/or treat a binocular dysfunction (eye teaming problem). Prisms are sometimes added to glasses to help improve eyesight due to a misalignment or visual field loss.

Base pair (BP) Two nitrogenous bases (adenine and thymine or guanine and cytosine) held together by weak bonds. Two strands of DNA are held together in the shape of a double helix by the bonds between base pairs.

Base sequence The order of nucleotide bases in a DNA molecule; determines structure of proteins encoded by that DNA.

Base sequence analysis A method, sometimes automated, for determining the base sequence.

Base up (BU) prism A wedge-shaped lens which is thicker on one edge than the other. The thicker edge (base) is turned up. Prisms bend light (opposite direction from its thicker end (base)) so the base-up prism turns the light downward thus causing the eye to also move down. This prism is used to measure an eye misalignment and/or treat a binocular dysfunction (eye teaming problem). Prisms are sometimes added to glasses to help improve eyesight due to a misalignment or visual field loss.

Baseline In some analytical procedures a sample is dissolved in water or combined with other reagents for analysis. A "blank" or standard consisting of the same reagents may be analyzed without sample present. This provides a comparative reference point, or baseline, so that the test results can be attributed solely to the sample itself.

Baseline characteristic A variable that is measured, observed, or assessed on a patient at or shortly before treatment assignment and the initiation of treatment.

Baseline data 1. The set of data collected on a specific patient or set of patients prior to randomization.

Baseline examination An examination that is carried out as part of the baseline visit and that is designed to assess a patient's eligibility for enrollment into the trial and to produce required baseline data.

Basic science years A term that usually refers to the initial two years of a medical school's program. However, in some schools, this may entail more or less than two years. With the introduction of new learning methodologies such as Problem-Based Learning (PBL) and early exposure to patients, basic science learning has become more integrated with clinical instruction and the division between basic science years and clinical years has eroded.

Basidiomycetes Reproduce by basidiospores, which are extended from the stalks of specialized cells called the basidia. The class comprises Photobasidiomycetes (smuts and rusts) and the Hymenomycetes (mushrooms and puffballs).

Basilar artery The artery that originates from the junction of the two (L & R) vertebral arteries (VA) and runs along the dorsal clivus (base of the skull), anterior to the brainstem, before dividing in a terminal bifurcation into the two posterior cerebral arteries (PCA).

Basis of design A design document that describes what the purpose of a given system is and how the system will accomplish its required task. This document is created and approved before the issuance of bid specifications and is often used to develop them. Until the system is developed this is a conceptual document.

Basis pedunculi Ventral most part of the midbrain cerebral peduncle consisting of corticospinal, corticobulbar, and corticopontine fiber tracts. Also known as the crus cerebri.

Basophil A polymorphonuclear leukocyte., whose basophils granules contain heparin, histamine and other vasoactive amines. Within tissues, these cells are known as mast cells.

Batch A specific quantity of material produced in a process or series of processes so that is expected to be homogeneous within specified limits. In the case of continuous production a batch may correspond to a defined fraction of the production, characterized by its intended homogeneity. The batch size may be defined either by fixed quantity or the amount produced in a fixed time interval.

Batch fermentation The process in which a fixed volume of sterile medium in a vessel is inoculated with a desired organism. The broth is fermented for a defined period to completion, without further additions of media. After discharging the batch, the fermenter is cleaned and rebatched with medium for another cycle. Two other types of fermentation cycles are fed batch and continuous.

Batchwise Control The use of validated in-process sampling and testing methods such that results prove the process has done what it purports to do for the specific batch concerned, assuming control parameters have been appropriately maintained.

Batch number A unique combination of numbers and/or letters which specifically identify a batch or lot and from which the production and distribution history can be determined.

Batimastat An anticancer drug that belongs to the family of drugs called angiogenesis inhibitors. Batimastat is a matrix metalloproteinase inhibitor.

BB 10901 An immunoconjugate of a humanized murine monoclonal antibody (huN-901) and DMI, a semi-synthetic derivative of the plant-derived ansa macrolide maytansine. The antibody moiety of BB-10901 selectively attaches to CD56 antigen, a neural cell adhesion molecule (NCAM)) expressed on the surface of cells of small cell lung cancer (SCLC) and other neuroendocrine (NE) tumors. Thus, the DMI conjugate is targeted specifically to CD56-expressing tumor cells, where it inhibits tubulin polymerization and assembly, resulting in inhibition of mitosis and cell cycle arrest in the S phase.

BBBD (Blood-brain barrier disruption) The use of drugs to create openings between cells in the blood-brain barrier. The blood-brain barrier is a protective network of blood vessels and tissue that protects the brain from harmful substances, but can also prevent anticancer drugs from reaching the brain. Once the barrier is opened, anticancer drugs may be infused into an artery that goes to the brain, in order to treat brain tumors.

BCG An attenuated strain of Mycobacterium bovis with non-specific immunoadjuvant and immunotherapeutic properties. Although the mechanism of its anti-tumor activity is unclear, immunization with BCG (Bacillus Calmette-Guerin) likely activates a Th1 cytokine response that includes induction of interferon. Vaccination with BCG may be immunoprotective against infection with Mycobacterium tuberculosis.

BCG solution A form of biological therapy for superficial bladder cancer. A catheter is used to place the BCG solution into the bladder. The solution contains live, weakened bacteria (bacillus Calmette-Guérin) that activate the immune system. The BCG solution used for bladder cancer is not the same thing as BCG vaccine, a vaccine for tuberculosis.

Bcl-2 antisense oligodeoxy-nucleotide G3139 A substance that is being studied in the treatment of cancer. It may kill cancer cells by blocking the production of a protein that makes cancer cells live longer and by making them more sensitive to anticancer drugs. It belongs to the family of drugs called antisense oligodeoxyribonucleotides. Also called oblimersen, augmerosen, and Genasense.

BCX-1777 A substance that is being studied in the treatment of some types of leukemia and lymphoma. It belongs to the family of drugs called purine nucleoside phosphorylase (PNP) enzyme inhibitors. Also called forodesine.

BDNA (Branched DNA assay) A DNA test for detecting and measuring HIV in the blood plasma of people with HIV. The bDNA test is faster and probably more accurate than plasma culture, the test currently used‹it is less sensitive than PCR, another new test. bDNA testing may eventually be useful to monitor the effectiveness of anti-HIV drugs and to gauge HIV disease progression. It is not yet approved, nor is it widely available.

Beckwith Wiedemann syndrome A rare, overgrowth disorder in which babies are large at birth and may develop low blood sugar. Other common symptoms are a large tongue, large internal organs, and defects of the abdominal wall near the navel. Beckwith-Wiedemann syndrome increases the risk of developing certain cancers, especially Wilms' tumor.

Beclomethasone A drug being studied in the treatment of graft-versus-host disease. It belongs to a family of drugs called corticos-teroids.

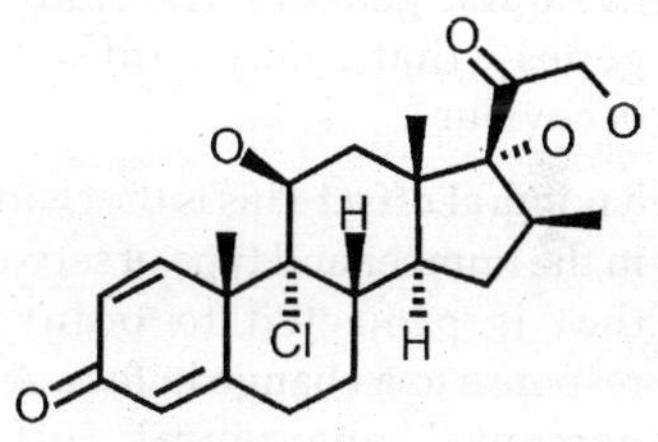

Figure Beclomethasone

Beconase Other name for beclome-thasone dipropionate.

Bed Column of carbon, sand, chromatography, or ion exchange resins through which a liquid passes during operation.

Bed days Number of inpatient hospital days per 1,000 health plan members for a specified period, usually annual.

Bed depth The height of the exchange or capture material in a column after proper backwashing for effective operation.

Bed expansion The effect produced during backwashing; resin particles separate and rise in the column. Regulating backwash flow may control bed expansion caused by the increase in space between resin particles.

Bedside teaching A part of clinical rounds where both student and instructor attends the patient's bedside to discuss the case and/ or demonstrate a clinical procedure. This is the student's opportunity to see how the attending physician relates to the patient and to get hands-on instruction in interviewing a patient, physical examination, and counseling skills.

Behavioural genetics The study of genes that may influence behaviour.

Behavioural offset This is the change in the number and type of services that is projected to occur in response to a change in fees. A 50 percent behavioural offset suggests that 50 percent of the savings from fee reductions will be offset by increased volume and intensity of services.

Behavioural optometrist (Functional optometrist or developmental optometrist) An optometrist who specializes in all aspects of vision as it is related to an individual's development and to the role of vision in relation to reading, computer monitor use, and sports. The optometrist may use prescription lenses and/or vision therapy to improve an individual's visual function and performance. Behavioural optome-try had its origins in orthoptics, which is a non-surgical treatment for strabismus, and in case analysis systems which were developed to resolve eyestrain symptoms that include excessive tearing, itching, burning, visual fatigue, and headache in nonstrabismic individuals. Behavioural optometry's emphasize of visual care is in prevention, remediation, rehabilitation, and enhancement.

Behavioural techniques Different methods to help "retrain" the bladder and get rid of the urgency to urinate.

Bellini duct carcinoma A rare type of kidney cancer that grows and spreads quickly. It begins in the duct of Bellini in the kidney.

Bence Jones protein A small protein made by plasma cells (white blood cells that produce antibodies). It is found in the urine of most people with multiple myeloma (cancer that begins in plasma cells).

Bendamustine A substance that is being studied in the treatment of cancer. It belongs to the family of drugs called alkylating agents. Also called SDX-105.

Benign Not cancerous. Benign tumors may grow larger but do not spread to other parts of the body.

Benign breast disease A common condition marked by benign (noncancerous) changes in breast tissue. These changes may include irregular lumps or cysts, breast discomfort, sensitive nipples, and itching. These symptoms may change through-out the menstrual cycle and usually stop after menopause. Also called fibrocystic breast disease, fibrocystic breast changes, and mammary dysplasia.

Benign growth A swelling or growth that is not cancerous and does not spread from one part of the body to another.

Benign proliferative breast disease A group of noncancerous conditions that may increase the risk of developing breast cancer. Examples include ductal hyperplasia, lobular hyperplasia, and papillomas.

Benign prostatic hypertrophy (BPH) A benign (noncancerous) condition in which an overgrowth of prostate tissue pushes against the urethra and the bladder, blocking the flow of urine. Also called benign prostatic hyperplasia.

Benign tumor A noncancerous growth that does not invade nearby tissue or spread to other parts of the body.

Benzaldehyde A colorless oily liquid used as a flavoring agent and to make dyes, perfumes, and pharmaceuticals. Benzaldehyde is chemically related to benzene.

Figure Benzaldehyde

Benzene A chemical that is used widely by the chemical industry, and is also found in tobacco smoke, vehicle emissions, and gasoline fumes. Exposure to benzene may increase the risk of developing leukemia.

Benzoporphyrin derivative monoacid ring A A synthetic light activated agent with photodynamic activity. Upon systemic administration, verteporfin accumulates in neovessels in the eye and, once stimulated by nonthermal red light in the presence of oxygen, produces highly reactive short-lived singlet oxygen and other reactive oxygen radicals, resulting in local damage to neovascular endothelium and blood vessel occlusion.

Benzoylphenylurea A low molecular weight agent with antineoplastic activity. Benzoylphenylurea binds to the colchicine binding site on tubulin, thereby blocking tubulin polymerization and disrupting mitotic function. This agent also inhibits DNA polymerase, and has been shown to arrest leukemia cells in the G1-S transition phase of the cell cycle.

Benzydamine A substance that is being studied as a mouth rinse treatment for oral mucositis (painful mouth sores) caused by cancer therapy. It belongs to the family of nonsteroidal anti-inflammatory drugs (NSAIDS).

Benzydamine hydrochloride An indazole non-steroidal anti-inflammatory drug (NSAID) with analgesic, antipyretic, and anti-edema properties. Unlike other NSAIDs, benzydamine hydrochloride does not inhibit cyclooxygenases (COX) but stabilizes membranes, resulting in local anesthesia; inhibits the production of pro-inflammatory cytokines; inhibits the generation of reactive oxygen species by neutrophils; inhibits leukocyte aggregation and adhesion; and exhibits antimicrobial properties.

Bereavement A state of sadness, grief, and mourning after the loss of a loved one.

Beriplast P A substance used in surgical wound healing to cause a blood clot to form. It consists of blood-clotting factors found naturally in human blood.

Best evidence medical education (BEME) Methods and approaches used by teachers of medical education based on the best available evidence as opposed to opinion-based education. BEME should take into account these factors: how reliable the evidence is as well as its utility, extent, strength, validity and relevance. It calls for critical appraisal of available literature and existing databases and identifying any existing gaps.

Best evidence-based assessment (BEBA) An evaluation performed by properly selected measurement methods under methodological rigor with which the instruments are constructed and administered; assessment must be congruent with evaluation questions and designed to demonstrate acquired competencies. Proper choice of measurement methods and construction of measurement instruments is a crucial step in the evaluation process because it determines the quality of data that will be collected securing robust and valid results. The methodological rigor is necessary for reliability and validity of the evaluation.

The best evidence-based assessment approach reflects a present focus on the quality of evaluation process and has been initiated by recent developments of so-called quantified tests, standardized patient examinations and computer case simulations and the use of relevant research data and information to validate the preferred assessment procedures.

Best practice In medicine, treatment that experts agree is appropriate, accepted, and widely used. Health care providers are obligated to provide patients with the best practice. Also called standard therapy or standard of care.

Beta 2 microglobulin A small protein normally found on the surface of many cells, including lymphocytes, and in small amounts in the blood and urine. An increased amount in the blood or urine may be a sign of certain diseases, including some types of cancer, such as multiple myeloma or lymphoma.

Beta agonist Drugs used to relax the bronchial airways, but it also increases heart rate and blood pressure. Bronchodilator medications are beta-agonists

Beta alethine A substance that is being studied in the treatment of cancer. It belongs to a family of chemicals called disulfides.

Beta carotene A form of carotene, precursor to vitamin A; a red-orange pigment found in plants and plant-eating animals, and also found in dark green and dark yellow fruits and vegetables. Beta carotene may have beneficial effects on the immune system.

Beta cell A type of cell in the pancreas in areas called the Islets of Langerhans. Beta cells make and release insulin, a hormone that controls the level of glucose (sugar) in the blood.

Beta glucan A polysaccharide isolated from the cell walls of bacteria, plants, and fungi with immunostimulant and antineoplastic activities. In a solubilized form, beta-glucan binds to a lectin site within complement receptor C3 (CR3) on leukocytes, priming the receptor to trigger cytotoxic degranulation of leukocytes when leukocyte CR3 binds to complement 3 (iC3b)-coated tumors. Thus, the attachment of beta-glucan to CR3 of circulating leukocytes simulates leukocytes to kill iC3b-coated tumor cells in the same way as they kill iC3b-coated yeast.

Beta hemolytic streptococcus group B A type of bacteria often found in the vagina. It can cause systemic infections in people with suppressed immune systems.

Beta-endorphin A substance produced in the brain, especially in the pituitary gland, that blocks the sensation of pain. It is produced in response to pain, exercise, and other forms of stress. It belongs to a group of chemicals called polypeptide hormones.

Beta-human chorionic gonadotropin ß-hCG. A hormone normally found in the blood and urine during pregnancy. It may also be produced by some tumor cells. An increased level of ß-hCG may be a sign of cancer of the testis, uterus, ovary, liver, stomach, pancreas, or lung. ß-hCG may also be produced in response to certain conditions that are not cancer. ß-hCG is being studied in the treatment of Kaposi's sarcoma.

Bevacizumab A monoclonal antibody used in the treatment of colorectal cancer that has spread. It is also being studied in the treatment of other types of cancer. It may prevent the growth of new blood vessels from surrounding tissue to a solid tumor. Also called Avastin.

Bexarotene A synthetic retinoic acid agent with potential antineoplastic, chemopreventive, teratogenic and embryotoxic properties. Bexarotene selectively binds to and activates retinoid X receptors (RXRs), thereby inducing changes in gene expression that lead to cell differentiation, decreased cell proliferation, apoptosis of some cancer cell types, and tumor regression.

Bexxar regimen A combination of monoclonal antibodies used to treat certain types of non-Hodgkin's lymphoma. The monoclonal antibody tositumomab is given with iodine I 131 tositumomab (a form of tositumomab that has been chemically changed by adding radioactive iodine). Monoclonal antibodies are laboratory-produced substances that can locate and bind to cancer cells.

BG00001 A recombinant replication-defective adenovirus which encodes the gene for the cytokine human interferon-beta (IFN-beta). Once inserted into and replicating in host tumor cells, recombinant adenovirus-hIFN-beta expresses human IFN-beta, which may stimulate an antiproliferative natural killer (NK) cell response against tumor cells and induce caspase-mediated tumor cell apoptosis.

Bi lateral integration/ gross motor coordination Visual guidance of body movements and the coordination between both sides of the body.

Bi ocularity Using both eyes, but not together as a team.

Biafine cream A topical preparation to reduce the risk of, and treat skin reactions to, radiation therapy.

Biarthrodial muscles Muscles that span over two joints and have a function over those joints e.g. biceps brachii - shoulder flexion and elbow flexion.

Bias Bias occurs when problems in study design lead to effects that are not related to the variables being studied. An example is selection bias, which occurs when study subjects are chosen in a way that can misleadingly increase or decrease the strength of an association. Choosing experimental and control group subjects from different populations would result in a selection bias.

Bicalutamide A synthetic, nonsteroidal antiandrogen. Bicalutamide competitively binds to cytosolic androgen receptors in target tissues, thereby inhibiting the receptor binding of androgens. This agent does not bind to most mutated forms of androgen receptors.

Bicuspid or pre-molar Transitional teeth behind the cuspids.

BID Common abbreviation for "twice a day"

Bidi A cigarette made by rolling tobacco by hand in a dried leaf from the tendu tree (a member of the ebony family). Most bidis are made in India and they come in different flavours.

Bifocal glasses Used to correct vision at two distances, composed of two ophthalmic lenses such as a plus lens for near vision and a minus lens for distance vision.

Bifurcation The point where a structure divides into two branches (e.g. the abdominal aorta bifurcates into the common iliac aa. and the trachea bifurcates into the L and R mainstem bronchi).

Bilateral Affecting both sides of the body; for example, bilateral breast cancer is cancer occurring in both breasts at the same time (synchronous) or at different times (metachronous).

Bilateral nephrectomy Surgery to remove both kidneys.

Bilateral prophylactic mastectomy Surgery to remove both breasts in order to reduce the risk of developing breast cancer. Also called preventive mastectomy.

Bilateral salpingo-oophorectomy Surgery to remove both ovaries and both fallopian tubes.

Bile Fluid produced by liver cells and carried by bile ductules into the bile duct and stored in gall bladder between meals. Contains substances needed to aid in the digestion of food. Provides a method for the body to eliminate toxic substances that are broken down by the liver.

Bile ducts Tubes that take bile from the liver to the gallbladder and small intestine to aid in digestion.

Bile ductule Microscopic bile duct that collects bile from liver cells and delivers it to the large bile duct outside the liver.

Biliary atresia Bile ducts do not have normal openings, preventing bile from leaving the liver. This causes jaundice (a yellow skin colour) and liver damage known as cirrhosis. Biliary atresia is a birth defect.

Biliary Having to do with the liver, bile ducts, and/or gallbladder.

Bilirubin A yellowish substance excreted by the liver. Its measurement can be used as an indication of the health of the liver. Large quantities of bilirubin may cause the skin to take on a yellow tint (jaundice), and very high levels may cause brain damage.

Binary explosive An explosive material composed of separate components, each of which is safe for storage and transportation and would not in itself be considered as an explosive.

Binary outcome measure An outcome measure that can assume only one of two values, such as in a trial with death as the outcome measure.

Binding agent A substance that makes a loose mixture stick together. For example, binding agents can be used to make solid pills from loose powders.

Binocular fusion dysfunction A clinical condition in which the eyes are not working as a team. Vision therapy is an effective treatment option.

Binocular vision The simultaneous use of the two eyes.

Binocularity The ability to use both eyes as a team and to be able to fuse (unite) two visual images into one, **three-dimensional** image.

Bio compatible implant A porous implant that can be infiltrated with living tissue.

Bioactivity A protein's ability to function correctly after it has been delivered to the active site of the body (in vivo).

Bioassay The determination of the biological activity of a substance (e.g. a drug) by observing its effect on an organism (or organ) compared to a standard preparation.

Bioaugmentation A strategy involved in bioremediation that increases the activity of an organism to break down or metabolize a pollutant. This involves reseeding a waste site with bacteria as they die.

Bioavailability The rate and extent to which a substance is absorbed and circulated in the body.

Bioavailable The ability of a drug or other substance to be absorbed and used by the body. Orally bioavailable means that a drug or other substance that is taken by mouth can be absorbed and used by the body.

Bioburden The level and type of microorganisms which may be present in raw materials, API (Active Pharmaceutical Ingredient) starting materials, intermediates, or APIs which have defined limits and should not affect the quality of the API. Bioburden should not be considered contamination unless the levels have been exceeded or defined objectionable organisms have been detected.

Biochanin A An isoflavone found in soy products. Soy isoflavones are being studied to see if they help prevent cancer.

Biochemical reactions In living cells, chemical reactions that help sustain life and allow cells to grow.

Biochemistry The study of chemical processes in living things. Despite the dramatic differences in the appearance of living things, the basic chemistry of all organisms is strikingly similar. Even tiny, one-celled creatures carry out essentially the same reactions that each cell of a complex organism, such as man, carries out.

Biocide An agent that can kill all pathogenic and non-pathogenic living organisms, including spores. More general than bacteriocide, biocide includes insecticides and any compound toxic to any living thing.

Biodegradable Describes any material that can be broken down by biological action (e.g., dissimilation, digestion, denitrification). The breakdown of material (chemicals) by microorganisms (bacteria, fungus, etc.).

Bioequivalency A scientific basis on which generic and brand name drugs are compared with one another. Drugs are bioequivalent if they enter circulation at the same rate when given in similar doses under similar conditions.

Biofeedback A method of learning to voluntarily control certain body functions such as heartbeat, blood pressure, and muscle tension with the help of a special machine. This method can help control pain.

Biogenerator A contained system, such as a fermentor, into which biological agents are introduced along with other materials so as to effect their multiplication or their production of other substances by reaction with the other materials. Biogenerators are generally fitted with devices for regulation, control, connection, material addition, and material withdrawal.

Biohazard An infectious agent (s), or part thereof, presenting a real or potential risk to human, other animals, or plants, directly through infection or indirectly through disruption of the environment.

Bioinformatics The science of managing and analyzing biological data using advanced computing techniques. Especially important in analyzing genomic research data.

Biologic A therapeutic agent derived from living things.

Biologic response modifiers A class of compounds that are produced in the body. Among the roles they play, biologic response modifiers boost the body's immune system to fight against cancer.

Biological Pertaining to biology or to life and living things. In medicine, refers to a substance made from a living organism or its products. Biologicals may be used to prevent, diagnose, treat or relieve of symptoms of a disease. For example, antibodies, interleukins, and vaccines are biologicals. Biological also refers to parents and children who are related by blood.

Biological activity The effect (change in metabolic activity upon living cells) caused by specific compounds or agents. For example, the drug aspirin causes the blood to thin, that is to clot less easily.

Biological agent A substance that is made from a living organism or its products and is used in the prevention, diagnosis, or treatment of cancer and other diseases. Biological agents include antibodies, interleukins, and vaccines. Also called biologic agent or biological drug.

Biological barrier An impediment (naturally occurring or introduced) to the infectivity and/or survival of a microbiological agent or eukaryotic cell once it has been released into the environment.

Biological controls An integrated pest management method which includes the use of living organisms to reduce the extent of pest problems. This includes the use of beneficial or predatory insects such as ladybugs and parasitic wasps to control crop-destroying bugs.

Biological drug A substance that is made from a living organism or its products and is used in the prevention, diagnosis, or treatment of cancer and other diseases. Biological drugs include antibodies, interleukins, and vaccines. Also called biologic agent or biological agent.

Biological Impurities Impurities resulting from living matter (bacteria, virus, algae, protozoa, microfungi) and their by-products, including pyrogens (endotoxins).

Biological indicators Resistant microorganisms placed into or on various materials to confirm that a sterilization process is effective. They may for instance be placed within a filter in order to determine if a proposed autoclave cycle is effective. After autoclave, they are removed and culture tests are performed to see if the microorganisms were killed.

Biological reactivity tests, in vivo This classification is based on responses to a series of in vivo tests for which extracts, materials and routes of administration are specified. Six Plastic Classes are defined:

1. Class I - Uses a specified dosage of an extract of sample in Sodium Chloride Injection applied either intravenously or intracutaneously into a mouse or a rabbit.

2. Class II - Same as Class I but in addition uses an extract of sample in 1 in 20 Solution of Alcohol in Sodium Chloride Injection applied either intravenously or intracutaneously into a mouse or a rabbit.

3. Class III - Same as Class II but in addition uses an extract of sample in Polyethylene Glycol 400, and an extract of sample in Vegetable Oil, both applied either intraperitoneally or intra-cutaneously into a mouse.

4. Class IV - Same as Class II but in addition uses an extract of sample in Vegetable Oil applied intraperitoneally or intra-cutaneously into a mouse or a rabbit. Also uses implant strips of sample into a rabbit.

5. Class V - Same as Class II but in addition uses an extract of sample in Polyethylene Glycol 400, and an extract of sample in Vegetable Oil applied intraperitoneally or intracutaneously into a mouse or a rabbit.

6. Class VI - Same as Class V but in addition uses implant strips of sample into a rabbit.

These tests are designed to determine the biological response of animals to elastomerics, plastics and other polymeric material with direct or indirect patient contact, or by the injection of specific extracts prepared from the material under test. Three tests are described:

1. Systemic Injection Test - Designed to determine the systemic biological responses of animals to plastics and other polymers by the single-dose injection of specific extracts prepared from a sample.

2. Intracutaneous Test - Designed to determine the local biological responses of animals to plastics and other polymers by the single-dose injection of specific extracts prepared from a sample.

3. Implantation Test - Designed to evaluate the reaction of living tissue to the plastic and other polymers by the implantation of the sample (specimen under test) itself into animal tissue. With the exception of the Implantation Test, the procedures are based on the use of extracts that, depending on the heat resistance of the material, are prepared at one of the three standard temperatures: 50°, 70°, and 121°. Therefore, the class designation of a plastic must be accompanied by an indication of the temperature of extraction e.g., IV - 121°, which represents a class IV plastic extracted at 121°).

Biological response modifiers (BRMS) Substances, either natural or synthesized, that boost, direct, or restore normal immune defenses. BRMs include interferons, interleukins, thymic hormones, and monoclonal antibodies.

Biological response modifier therapy (BRM therapy) Treatment to stimulate or restore the ability of the immune system to fight cancer, infections, and other diseases. Also used to lessen certain side effects that may be caused by cancer treatment. Also called immunotherapy, biotherapy, or biological therapy.

Biological therapy Treatment to stimulate or restore the ability of the immune system to fight cancer, infections, and other diseases. Also used to lessen certain side effects that may be caused by some cancer treatments. Also called immunotherapy, biotherapy, or biological response modifier (BRM) therapy.

Biomarker A substance sometimes found in the blood, other body fluids, or tissues. A high level of biomarker may mean that a certain type of cancer is in the body. Examples of biomarkers include CA 125 (ovarian cancer), CA 15-3 (breast cancer), CEA (ovarian, lung, breast, pancreas, and gastrointestinal tract cancers), and PSA (prostate cancer). Also called tumor marker.

Biomass The entire assemblage of living organisms (both plant and animal), of a particular region, considered collectively.

Biometabolism Physical and chemical processes that occur within a cell or an organism, for example, the conversion of nutrients into energy.

Biometrics A method of verifying an individual's identity based on measurement of his/her physical feature (s) or repeatable action (s) where those features and/or actions are both measurable and unique to that individual. The main types of biometrics are: face recognition, finger scanning, hand geometry, finger geometry, iris recognition, palm, retina, signature, and voice recognition.

Bionics An interscience discipline for constructing artificial systems, which resemble or have the characteristics of living systems.

Bioperine Other name for piperine extract standardized.

Biopesticide A biopesticide is any material of natural origin used in pest control derived from living organisms, such as bacteria, plant cells or animal cells.

Biopharmaceuticals Ethical pharmaceutical drugs derived through bioprocessing.

Bioprocess engineering Process that uses complete living cells or their components (e.g., enzymes, chloroplast) to effect desired physical or chemical changes.

Bioprocessing The creation of a product utilizing a living organism.

Biopsy The removal of cells or tissues for examination by a pathologist. The pathologist may study the tissue under a microscope or perform other tests on the cells or tissue. When only a sample of tissue is removed, the procedure is called an incisional biopsy. When an entire lump or suspicious area is removed, the procedure is called an excisional biopsy. When a sample of tissue or fluid is removed with a needle, the procedure is called a needle biopsy, core biopsy, or fine-needle aspiration.

Biopure water Water that is sterile, pyrogen free and has a total solids content of less than 1 ppm.

Bioreactor A closed system used for bioprocessing (flask, roller bottle, tank, vessel, or other container), which supports the growth of cells, mammalian or bacterial, in a culture medium. A bacterial reaction usually is said to take place in a fermenter, and cell culture in a bioreactor.

Bioremediation The use of biological organisms such as plants or microbes to aid in removing hazardous substances from an area.

Biosphere All the living matter on or in the earth, the oceans and seas, and the atmosphere.

Biosynthesis The production, by biological synthesis or degradation, of compounds by a living organism (e.g. amino acid synthesis, nucleotide synthesis).

Biosynthetic human insulin A man-made insulin that is very much like human insulin.

Biotechnology An industry that creates, develops, and markets a variety of techniques that use living organisms, or substances from those organisms, to make or modify a product by microbial and biochemical processes. A common misconception is that biotechnology refers only to recombinant DNA or gene splicing work. Recombinant DNA is only one of the many techniques used to derive products for organisms, plants, and parts of both for the biotechnology industry. A list of areas covered by the term biotechnology would more properly include: plant tissue culture, cell fusion techniques (especially for the production of monoclonal antibodies), enzyme systems, plant breeding, meristem culture, fermentation, and others.

Bioterrorism or biological warfare The unlawful use, wartime use, or threatened use, of microorganisms or toxins to produce death or disease in humans. Often viewed as the preferred choice of warfare of less powerful groups of people in attempt to wage war or protect themselves from more powerful groups or nations. However, biological agents could be used by individuals or by powerful nations as well.

Biotherapy Treatment to stimulate or restore the ability of the immune system to fight cancer, infections, and other diseases. Also used to lessen certain side effects that may be caused by cancer treatment. Also called biological therapy, immunotherapy, or biological response modifier (BRM) therapy.

Biowaste Inactivation The inactivation or "killing" of biological organisms using heat or chemicals. This step is done at the end of the processing to ensure that there are no living organisms remaining in the effluent that is sent to the sanitary sewer system.

Heat is usually applied at 130°C (266°F) for mammalian cells. Chemicals used include caustic or acid.

Biphasic insulin A type of insulin that is a mixture of intermediate- and fast-acting insulin.

BI-RADS A method used by radiologists to interpret and report in a standardized manner the results of mammography, ultrasound, and MRI used in breast cancer screening and diagnosis.

Birefringence The property of appearing bright white in a dark field when examined with polarized light. Collagen, hair and silica are some of the more common birefringent materials.

Birt hogg dube syndrome An inherited condition in which benign tumors develop in hair follicles on the head, chest, back, and arms. People who have this disorder may be at increased risk of developing colon or kidney cancer.

Birth defect Any harmful trait, physical or biochemical, present at birth, whether a result of a genetic mutation or some other non genetic factor.

Bismuth Bi213 monoclonal antibody M195 A radioimmunoconjugate consisting of murine monoclonal antibody (M195) and bismuth 213 (Bi213). Monoclonal antibody M195 binds to CD33, a surface antigen expressed by myelogenous leukemia cells. Bi213 is an isotope that emits short-ranged high-energy alpha particles. This radioimmunoconjugate selectively delivers alpha particle-mediated cytotoxicity to leukemic cells, thereby limiting the exposure of normal tissues to ionizing radiation.

Bispecific antibody An antibody developed in the laboratory to recognize more than one protein on the surface of different cells. Examples include bispecific antibodies 2B1, 520C9xH22, mDX-H210, and MDX447.

Bispecific monoclonal antibody A monoclonal antibody that binds two different types of antigen. Bispecific monoclonal antibodies do not occur naturally; they must be made in the laboratory.

Bisphosphonate A type of drug used to treat osteoporosis and the bone pain caused by some types of cancer. Also called diphosphonate.

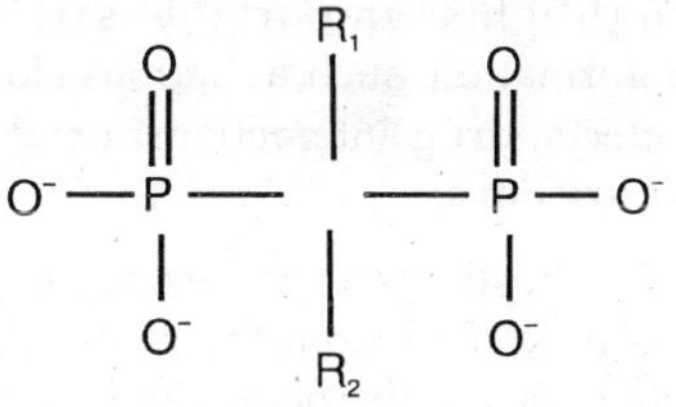

Figure Basic structure of bisphosphonate

Bite Relationship of the upper and lower teeth on closure (occlusion).

Bizelesin An anticancer drug that belongs to the family of drugs called alkylating agents. It is also an antitumor antibiotic.

BL22 immunotoxin A recombinant immunotoxin consisting of the Fv portion of the anti-CD22 antibody RFB4 fused to a fragment of Pseudomonas exotoxin-A with potential antineoplastic activity. BL22 immunotoxin binds to CD22, an antigen expressed in B-cell malignancies, thereby delivering its toxin directly to tumor cells. The toxin moiety induces caspase-mediated apoptosis of tumor cells via a mechanism involving mitochondrial damage; it also blocks translational elongation via binding to elongation factor-2 in eukaryotic cells.

BLA (Biologics license application) The required application for marketing a biologic product. Most biopharmaceuticals are biologics.

Black box warning Information found at the beginning of a drug's prescribing information, manufacturer labeling, and promotional material. This information highlights important safety information, such as serious side effects, drug interactions, or use restrictions.

Black cohosh A triterpene-containing herb isolated from the roots and rhizomes of the plant Cimicifuga racemosa (also known as Actaea racemosa). While the mechanism of action of black cohosh is not completely understood, it appears to act as a selective estrogen receptor modulator. In vitro, this preparation has been shown to induce cell cycle arrest and caspase-dependent apoptosis of estrogen-sensitive breast cancer cells.

Black hairy tongue Elongated papillae on the tongue, promoting the growth of microorganisms.

Black snakeroot Cimicifuga racemosa. A substance obtained from the root of the plant has been used in some cultures to treat a number of medical problems. It is being studied in the treatment of hot flashes and other symptoms of menopause. The plant is also called black cohosh, rattlesnake root, bugwort, and bugbane.

Bladder cancer Cancer that forms in tissues of the bladder (the organ that stores urine). Most bladder cancers are transitional cell carcinomas (cancer that forms in cells in the innermost tissue layer of the bladder). Other types include squamous cell carcinoma (cancer that begins in flat cells lining the inside of the bladder) and adenocarcinoma (cancer that begins in cells that make and release mucus and other fluids).

Bladder The musculomembraneous sac used for urine collection from the kidneys (via the ureters) and discharge through the urethra.

Bladder training A behavioural technique that teaches the patient to resist or inhibit the urge to urinate, and to urinate according to a schedule rather than urinating at the urge.

Blank A preliminary analysis omitting only the sample to provide an unbiased reference point or baseline for comparison. It is important to minimize extraneous contamination that could be confused with constituents in the sample itself.

Blast A computer program that identifies homologous (similar) genes in different organisms, such as human, fruit fly, or nematode.

Blast crisis A phase of chronic myelogenous leukemia in which tiredness, fever, and an enlarged spleen occur during the blastic phase, when more than 30% of the cells in the blood or bone marrow are blast cells (immature blood cells).

Blastic phase chronic myelogenous leukemia A phase of chronic myelogenous leukemia in which more than 30% of the cells in the blood or bone marrow are blast cells (immature blood cells). When tiredness, fever, and an enlarged spleen occur during the blastic phase, it is called blast crisis.

Bleaching Chemical or laser treatment of natural teeth for whitening effect.

Bleomycin A mixture of glycopeptide antineoplastic antibiotics isolated from the fungus Streptomyces verticillus. Bleomycin forms complexes with iron that reduce molecular oxygen to superoxide and hydroxyl radicals which cause single- and double-stranded breaks in DNA; these reactive oxygen species also induce lipid peroxidation, carbohydrate oxidation, and alterations in prostaglandin synthesis and degradation.

Blepharal Reference to the eyelids.

Blepharitis Inflammation of the eyelid margin.

Blepharochalasis Excessive relaxation of the eyelid caused by loss of muscle tone.

Blepharophimosis An abnormally small eyelid aperture.

Blepharoplasty A corrective surgical procedure of the eyelid.

Blepharoptosis A drooping of the upper eyelid.

Blessed thistle Cnicus benedictus. A plant whose leaves, stems,. and flowers have been used in some cultures to treat certain medical problems. Blessed thistle may have anti-inflammatory and anticancer effects. Also called St. Benedict's thistle, cardin, holy thistle, and spotted thistle.

Blind (Single or double) experiment In a single blind experiment, the subjects do not know whether they are receiving an experimental treatment or a placebo. In a double blind experiment, neither the researchers nor the participants are aware of which subjects receive the treatment - until after the study is completed.

Blinded study A type of study in which the patients (single-blinded) or the patients and their doctors (double-blinded) do not know which drug or treatment is being given. The opposite of a blinded study is an open label study.

Blip A temporary increase in viral load in someone who previously had undetectable virus and who later returns to having undetectable virus. The viral load during a blip is usually low (50 to 500 copies/mL).

Block 1. A group, quantity, section, or segment that is considered as a unit for some purpose, procedure, process, or action.

2. (Clinical trials) Treatment block. Analyses are conducted for each block, and then combined over blocks.

Block injection Anesthesia of a nerve trunk that covers a large area of the jaw; a mandibular block injection produce numbness of the lower jaw, teeth, half the tongue.

Block size 1. The number of individual elements making up a block.

2. Treatment block size.

Blocking The process of establishing defined groups, as in a treatment allocation schedule designed to ensure a specific allocation ratio.

Blocking antibody A functional term for an antibody molecule capable of blocking the interaction of antigen with other antibodies or with cells.

Blood The familiar red fluid in the body that contains white and red blood cells, platelets, proteins, and other elements. The blood is transported throughout the body by the circulatory system. Blood functions in two directions: arterial and venous. Arterial blood is the means by which oxygen and nutrients are transported to tissues while venous blood is the means by which carbon dioxide and metabolic by-products are transported to the lungs and kidneys, respectively, for removal from the body.

Blood brain barrier A selective barrier between brain blood vessels and brain tissues whose effect is to restrict what may pass from the blood into the brain. Certain compounds readily cross the blood brain barrier. Others are completely blocked.

Blood cell count A test to check the number of red blood cells, white blood cells, and platelets in a sample of blood. Also called complete blood count (CBC).

Blood cells Minute structures produced in the bone marrow; they consist of red blood cells, white blood cells, and platelets.

Blood chemistry study A procedure in which a sample of blood is examined to measure the amounts of certain substances made in the body. An abnormal amount of a substance can be a sign of disease in the organ or tissue that produces it.

Blood corpuscle A cell that circulates in the blood.

Blood count The number of red blood cells, white blood cells, and platelets in a sample of blood.

Blood doping In its usual form, this involves withdrawal of blood from an athlete, followed by re-infusion after a suitable period of time, usually 4 - 8 weeks, during which time the level of red blood cells had returned to its pre-withdrawal state. The addition of the extra blood would increase the amount of cells available to carry oxygen. This practice has been used to improve endurance. This is a banned practice at elite levels of sport and may be potentially dangerous.

Blood glucose The main sugar that the body makes from the three elements of food-proteins, fats, and carbohydrates-but mostly from carbohydrates. Glucose is the major source of energy for living cells and is carried to each cell through the bloodstream. However, the cells cannot use glucose without the help of insulin.

Blood glucose meter/Blood glucose monitoring A way of testing how much glucose (sugar) is in the blood. A drop of blood, usually taken from the fingertip, is placed on the end of a specially coated strip, called a testing strip. The strip has a chemical on it that makes it change color according to how much glucose is in the blood. A person can tell if the level of glucose is low, high, or normal in one of two ways. The first is by comparing the color on the end of the strip to a color chart that is printed on the side of the test strip container. The second is by inserting the strip into a small machine, called a meter, which "reads" the strip and shows the level of blood glucose in a digital window display. Some meters have a memory that can store results from multiple tests. Blood testing is more accurate than urine testing in monitoring blood glucose levels because it shows what the current level of glucose is, rather than what the level was an hour or so previously.

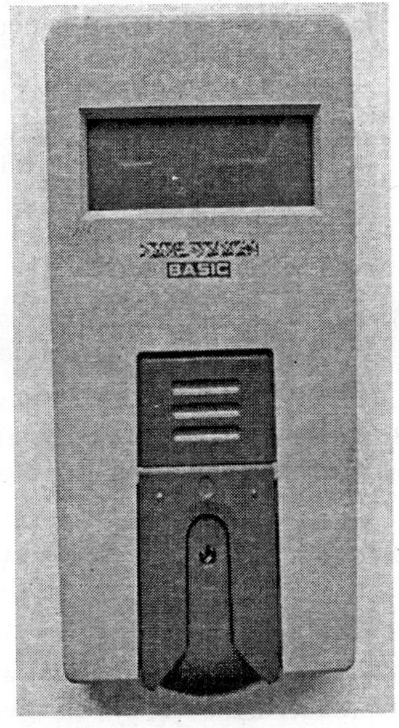

Figure Blood glucose meter

Blood plasma Blood from which all blood corpuscles, with the exception of platelet cells, have been removed (e.g. by centrifugation) resulting in a clear, straw-colored fluid, which clots as easily as whole blood.

Blood platelets Small, disc-shaped, metabolically active cells circulating in the blood. They are essential in the blood clotting process since they aggregate to form a plug on the injured surface of the blood vessel.

Blood pressure The blood pressure is the pressure of the blood within the arteries. It is produced primarily by the contraction of the heart muscle. It's measurement is recorded by two numbers. The first (systolic pressure) is measured after the heart contracts and is highest. The second (diastolic pressure) is measured before the heart contracts and lowest. A blood pressure cuff is used to measure the pressure. Elevation of blood pressure is called "hypertension".

Blood serum The liquid expressed from clotted blood or clotted blood plasma.

Blood thinner A drug that helps prevent blood clots from forming. Also called an anticoagulant.

Blood transfusion The administration of blood or blood products into a blood vessel.

Blood urea nitrogen (BUN) A waste product of the kidneys. Increased levels of BUN in the blood may indicate early kidney damage.

Blood vessels Tubes that act like a system of roads or canals to carry blood to and from all parts of the body. The three main types of blood vessels are arteries, veins, and capillaries. The heart pumps blood through these vessels so that the blood can carry with it oxygen and nutrients that the cells need or take away waste that the cells do not need.

Blood-borne pathogens Infectious microorganisms that are carried in the blood of infected humans or animals and that can be transmitted through contact with infected blood, body fluids, tissues, or organs. Blood-borne pathogens are implicated in diseases such as malaria, syphilis, brucellosis, tuberculosis, hepatitis B, and AIDS (Acquired Immuno-deficiency Syndrome). Workplace transmission of a blood-borne pathogen can occur via accidental inoculation with a contaminated "sharp" exposure through open cuts, skin abrasions, and mucous membranes of eyes and mouth indirect transmission (e.g., touching mouth, eyes, nose or open cuts with contaminated hands).

Blood-sampling devices A small instrument for pricking the skin with a fine needle to obtain a sample of blood to test for glucose (sugar).

Blowdown The bleeding-off of fixed quantities of accumulated feed water to reduce concentrated impurities. If these impurities are permitted to accumulate, they may pass through the distillation process and contaminate the distillate or foul the distillation system.

Blurred vision Lack of visual clarity or acuity.

BMD (Bone mineral density) A measure of the amount of calcium contained in a certain volume of bone. Calcium gives bones their strength and helps keep them from breaking. Bone density measurements may be used to diagnose osteoporosis, to see how well osteoporosis treatments are working, and to figure out how likely the bones are to break. Also called bone density and bone mass.

BME (Basic medium eagles) One of the most common tissue culture media composed of isotonic salts, carbohydrates and vitamins. When combined with animal serum. BME is a good medium for cell proliferation.

BMS 214662 A nonsedating benzodiazepine derivative with antineoplastic activity. BMS-214662 inhibits the enzyme farnesyl protein transferase, resulting in apoptosis of tumor cells. Farnesyl protein transferase modifies several proteins posttranslationally (farnesylation), including Ras, an oncoprotein implicated in the pathogenesis of many human tumors. BMS-214662 may also reverse the malignant phenotype of H-Ras-transformed cells. This agent has been shown to be active against tumor cells with and without Ras mutations.

Board certified (Boarded, diplomate) Describes a physician who has passed a written and oral examination given by a medical specialty board and who has been certified as a specialist in that area.

Body fluids Term used for a number of fluids manufactured within the body. Usually used when referring to semen, blood, urine, and saliva.

Body habitus changes Abnormal changes in the body's physical characteristics.

Body mass index (BMI) Method used for determining overweight and obesity in adults. BMI is a calculation that divides a person's weight in kilograms by height in meters squared (BMI = (kg/m^2). BMI can also be calculated in pounds and inches: BMI= (lbs/in^2) X 703. The general guideline currently recommended by the Center for Disease Control and Prevention is that individuals with a BMI of 25 to 29.9 are considered overweight and those individuals with a BMI greater than 30 are considered obese.

Body of pancreas The mid portion of the pancreas. The pancreas has both endocrine ("internal") and exocrine ("external") glands, including the islets of Langerhans - cell clusters that produce insulin and the pancreatic acini that secrete pancreatic digestive juices for the small intestine.

Body of sternum The portion of the sternum between the angle of Louis and the xiphoid process.

Bolus A single dose of drug usually injected into a blood vessel over a short period of time. Also called bolus infusion.

Bolus infusion A single dose of drug usually injected into a blood vessel over a short period of time. Also called bolus.

Bonding Adhesive dental restoration technique; a tooth-colored composite resin to repair and/or change the colour or shape of a tooth.

Bone (skeletal) survey X-rays of the entire skeleton.

Bone cancer Primary bone cancer is cancer that forms in cells of the bone. Some types of primary bone cancer are osteosarcoma, Ewing's sarcoma, malignant fibrous histiocytoma, and chondrosarcoma. Secondary bone cancer is cancer that spreads to the bone from another part of the body (such as the prostate, breast, or lung).

Bone density A measure of the amount of calcium contained in a certain volume of bone. Calcium gives bones their strength and helps keep them from breaking. Bone density measurements may be used to diagnose osteoporosis, to see how well osteoporosis treatments are working, and to figure out how likely the bones are to break. Also called bone mineral density (BMD) and bone mass.

Bone marrow The soft, sponge-like tissue in the center of most bones. It produces white blood cells, red blood cells, and platelets.

Bone marrow ablation The destruction of bone marrow using radiation or drugs.

Bone marrow biopsy and aspiration The procedure by which a needle is inserted into a bone to withdraw a sample of bone marrow.

Bone marrow cancer Cancer that forms in the blood-forming cells of the bone marrow (soft sponge-like tissue in the center of most bones). Bone marrow cancer includes leukemias, multiple myeloma, and others.

Bone marrow metastases Cancer that has spread from the original (primary) tumor to the bone marrow.

Bone marrow suppression Damage to the bone marrow stem cells that produce new blood cells. Suppression of the bone marrow may be caused by drugs, toxic chemicals, or radiation.

Bone marrow transplant A complex treatment that may be used when breast cancer is advanced or has recurred. The bone marrow transplant, which was first proved successful in treating leukemia, makes it possible to use exceedingly high doses of chemotherapy that would otherwise be impossible. Autologous bone marrow transplant means that the patient's own bone marrow is used. When this is not possible, it becomes necessary to find a donor whose biologic characteristics (such as blood type) match or very closely match the patient's. A portion of the patient's or donor's bone marrow is withdrawn, cleansed, treated and stored. The patient is then given high doses of chemotherapy that kill the cancer cells but also destroy the remaining bone marrow, thus robbing the body of its natural ability to fight infection. The cleansed and stored marrow is given by transfusion (transplanted) to rescue the patient's immune defenses. Although this method has been widely reported by the media, and it has given good results in many people, it is not yet scientifically proven to be effective in breast cancer. It is a risky procedure that involves a lengthy and expensive hospital stay that may not be covered by the patient's health insurance. The best place to have a bone marrow transplant is in a clinical trial at a comprehensive cancer center or other facility that has the technical skill and experience to perform it safely.

Bone mass A measure of the amount of calcium contained in a certain volume of bone. Calcium gives bones their strength and helps keep them from breaking. Bone density measurements may be used to diagnose osteoporosis, to see how well osteoporosis treatments are working, and to figure out how likely the bones are to break. Also called bone density and bone mineral density (BMD).

Bone metastases Cancer that has spread from the original (primary) tumor to the bone.

Bone mineral density (BMD) A measure of the amount of calcium contained in a certain volume of bone. Calcium gives bones their strength and helps keep them from breaking. Bone density measurements may be used to diagnose osteoporosis, to see how well osteoporosis treatments are working, and to figure out how likely the bones are to break. Also called bone density and bone mass.

Bone resorption Decrease in bone supporting the roots of teeth; a common result of periodontal (gum disease).

Bone scan An imaging method that gives important information about the growth and health of bones, including the location of cancer that may have spread to the bones. It can be done as an outpatient procedure and is painless, except for the needle stick when a low-dose radioactive dye is injected into a vein.

Bone-seeking radioisotope A radioactive substance that is given through a vein, and collects in bone cells and in tumor cells that have spread to the bone. It kills cancer cells by giving off low-level radiation.

Booster An additional dose or doses of a vaccine taken after the initial dose to enhance the immune response to the vaccine. Also used as a term to describe a medicine given to enhance another medicine, such as using ritonavir (RTV) as a "booster" for other PIs.

Borderline diabetes A term no longer used.

Boron neutron capture therapy A type of radiation therapy. The person is given an intravenous infusion containing the element boron, which concentrates in the tumor cells. The person then receives radiation therapy with atomic particles called neutrons from a small research nuclear reactor. The radiation is absorbed by the boron, killing the tumor cells without harming normal cells.

Boronophenylalanine-fructose complex BPA-F. A substance used in a type of radiation therapy called boron neutron capture therapy. BPA-F is injected into a vein, and becomes concentrated in tumor cells. The patient then receives radiation treatment with atomic particles called neutrons. The neutrons react with the boron in BPA-F, producing radioactive particles that kill the tumor cells without harming normal cells.

Bortezomib A drug that is used to treat multiple myeloma and is being studied in the treatment of other types of cancer. It belongs to the families of drugs called proteosome inhibitors and dipeptidyl boronic acids. Also called Velcade and PS-341.

Botryoid Shaped like a bunch of grapes.

Botulinum toxin type A (oculinum, botox) An injection of this poison has been used as an alternative to conventional surgery in selected strabismic patients. It causes a temporary paralysis of an extraocular muscle that leads to a change in eye position. This change has been reported to result in long-lasting and permanent alteration in eye alignment. Although one injection is often sufficient to produce positive results, one-third to one-half of patients may require additional injections. This technique has been most successful when used in adults with small-angle misalignments. It is not commonly used in children. This treatment is also used in patients who have blepharospam (an uncontrollable eye lid spasm).

Bovine spongiform encephalopathy (BSE) Bovine spongiform encephalopathy, or BSE, is also known as "mad cow disease." It is a rare, chronic degenerative disease affecting the brain and central nervous system of cattle. Cattle with BSE lose their coordination, develop abnormal posture and experience changes in behaviour. Clinical symptoms take 4-5 years to develop, followed by death in a period of several weeks to months unless the affected animal is destroyed sooner.

Bowel function The way the intestines work in terms of how often there are bowel movements, the ability to control when to have a bowel movement, and whether the stools are hard and dry as in constipation or watery as in diarrhea.

Bowel The long tube-shaped organ in the abdomen that completes the process of digestion. There is both a small and a large bowel. Also called the intestine.

Bowen's disease A skin disease marked by scaly or thickened patches on the skin and often caused by prolonged exposure to arsenic. The patches often occur on sun-exposed areas of the skin and in older, white men. These patches may become malignant (cancerous). Also called precancerous dermatosis or precancerous dermatitis.

Bowman's capsule Bowman's capsule is a blind sac at the beginning of the tubular component of a nephron in the mammalian kidney. A glomerulus is enclosed in the sac. Fluids from blood in the glomerulus are collected in the Bowman's capsule (i.e., glomerular filtrate) and further processed along the nephron to form urine. Bowman's capsule is named after Sir William Bowman (1816-1892), a British surgeon and anatomist.

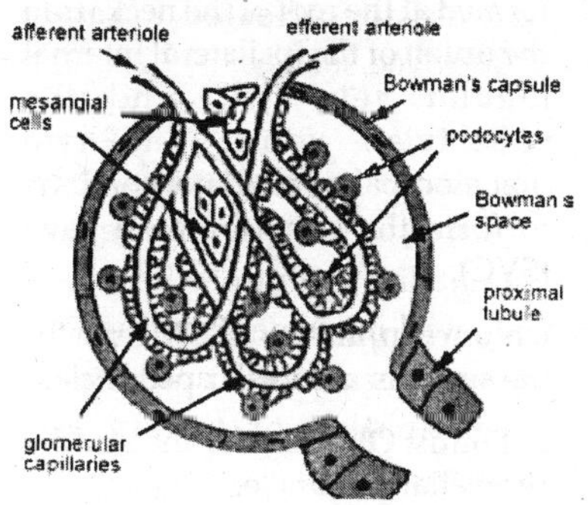

Figure Bowman's capsule

Together with the glomerulus it is known as a renal corpuscle, or a Malpighian corpuscle, named after Marcello Malpighi (1628-1694), an Italian physician and biologist. This name is not used widely anymore, probably to avoid confusion with a Malpighian corpuscle in the spleen. The barrier between the blood and the lumen of the nephron here is formed of three layers: the squamous endothelium of the capillaries; the basement membrane; and the endothelial podocytes forming the nephron. The barriers are 'leaky' in the sense that relatively large molecules can pass through unfiltered.

The process of filtration of the blood in the Bowman's capsule is ultra-filtration or glomerular filtration, the normal rate of glomerular filtration is 125 ml/min, equivalent to 10x the blood volume daily. Any proteins under ~30,000 daltons in size can pass freely through the membrane, although there is some extra hindrance for negatively charged molecules due to the negative charge of the basement membrane and the podocytes. Any small molecules such as water, glucose, salt (NaCl), amino acids and urea pass freely into the nephron but cells, platelets and large proteins do not. The filtrate leaving the Bowman's capsule is very similar to plasma fluid in composition and passes on into the distal convoluted tubule.

Bowman birk inhibitor concentrate An extract of soybeans enriched in Bowman-Birk inhibitor (BBI), a soybean-derived, 71-amino acid, polypeptide and serine protease inhibitor with potential chemopreventive activity. Bowman-Birk inhibitor contains distinct inhibitory sites for trypsin and chymotrypsin. Although the exact mechanism by which BBI suppresses carcinogenesis is unknown, its antiproliferative activity appears to be linked to the chymotrypsin inhibitory region.

BPC (Bulk Pharmaceutical Chemical) A pharmaceutical product derived by chemical synthesis, in bulk form, for later dispensing, formulation or compounding, and filling in a pharmaceutical finishing facility.

Breakthrough Passage of a substance through a bed, filter, or process designed to eliminate it. For ion exchange processes, the first signs are leakage of ions (in mixed beds, usually Silica) and the resultant increase in conductivity. For organic removal beds, usually small, volatile compounds (Trihalomethanes (THMs) are common in activated carbon).

BPU (Benzoylphenylurea) A substance that is being studied in the treatment of cancer. It belongs to the family of drugs called antitubulin agents.

Braces Devices used by orthodontists to gradually reposition teeth to a more favorable alignment.

Brachial plexopathy A condition marked by numbness, tingling, pain, weakness, or limited movement in the arm or hand. It is caused by an impairment of the brachial plexus, a network of nerves that affect the arm and hand.

Brachial plexus A network of nerves that sends signals from the spine to the arm and hand.

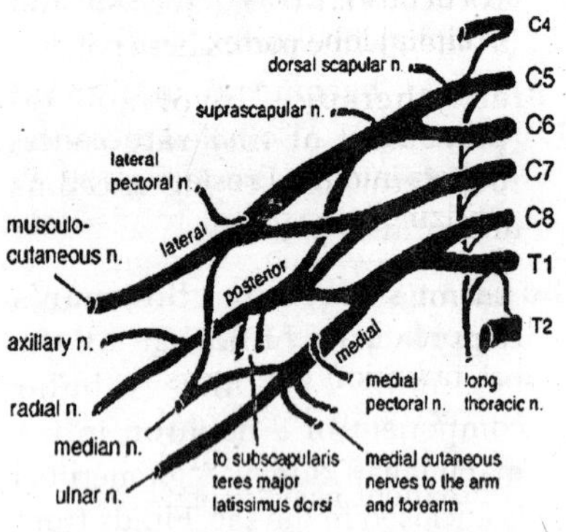

Figure Brachial plexus

Brachiocephalic trunk (innominate) The first branch of the arch of the aorta which further divides into the right common carotid and right subclavian arteries. ("innominate" - literally "nameless").

Brachiocephalic vein Two veins formed at the root of the neck from the union of the ipsilateral internal jugular vein (IJV) and the subclavian veins. The two brachiocepalic veins later combine to form the superior vena cava (SVC).

Brachium conjunctivum Old term for the superior cerebellar peduncle.

B. Pontis: Old term for the middle cerebellar peduncle.

B. of the Inferior Colliculus: Nerve fiber bundle of the auditory pathway running from the inferior colliculus to the medial geniculate body.

B. of the Superior Coilliculus: Nerve fiber bundle extending from the optic tract and lateral geniculate body to the superior colliculus. Consists mainly of corticotectal fibers arising from occipital lobe cortex.

Brachytherapy Involves . the placement of tiny radioactive pellets into the Prostate gland. By utilizing ultrasound to place the seed pellets, damage to surrounding tissues is minimized. Approximately 13,500-16,000 rads of radiation energy is delivered directly to the Prostate. This procedure is performed on an outpatient basis. It is a one time procedure with very effective results. The 10-year follow-up outcome data parallels that of Radical Prostatectomy.

Brady pacing A method of treating a slow or irregular heartbeat by periodically stimulating the heart with small electrical pulses.

Bradycardia A slow heartbeat, typically less than 60 beats per minute. It may be caused by the sinoatrial node not working properly, or by a condition called heart block.

Brain metastasis Cancer that has spread from the original (primary) tumor to the brain.

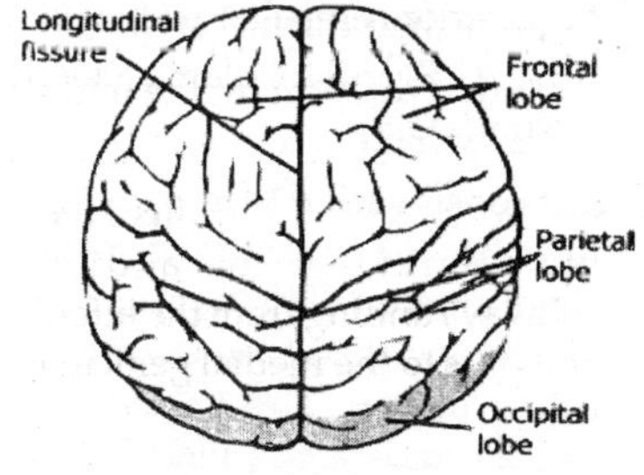

Figure The Brain

Brain scan An imaging method used to find abnormalities in the brain, including brain cancer and cancer that has spread to the brain from other places in the body. This procedure can be done in an outpatient clinic. It is painless, except for the needle stick when a radioactive dye is injected into a vein.

Brain stem The portion of the brain that connects from the cerebral hemispheres to the cervical spinal cord.

Brain stem glioma A tumor located in the part of the brain that connects to the spinal cord (the brain stem). It may grow rapidly or slowly, depending on the grade of the tumor.

Brain stem tumor A tumor in the part of the brain that connects to the spinal cord (the brain stem).

Brain tumor The growth of abnormal cells in the tissues of the brain. Brain tumors can be benign (non-cancerous) or malignant (cancerous).

Branched chain DNA assay A test that measures a person's viral load (level of HIV RNA in the blood) to identify HIV infection and monitor disease progression and treatment effectiveness. Results are reported as number of HIV RNA copies per mL of blood. bDNA assay is an alternative to measuring viral load by reverse transcriptase-polymerase chain reaction (RT-PCR).

Brazing A metal joining process wherein coalescence is produced by use of a nonferrous filler metal having a melting point above 427°C (800°F), but lower than that of the base metals being joined. The filler metal is distributed between the closely fitted surfaces of the joint by capillary action.

BRCA1 A gene located on the short arm of chromosome 17. When this gene is damaged (mutated), it places a woman at greater risk of developing breast and / or ovarian cancer, compared with women who do not have the mutation. In a woman with a BRCA1 mutation, the risk of developing breast cancer by age 50% is 58%, compared with 2% in the general population. A person who has this mutated gene has a 50% chance of passing on the gene to each of her children. Scientists are working on a blood test that can be used to detect BRCA1 mutations in the general population, but this test is still several years away.

BRCA2 A gene on chromosome 13 that normally helps to suppress cell growth. A person who inherits an altered version of the BRCA2 gene has a higher risk of getting breast, ovarian, or prostate cancer.

Break point The point at which a person can no longer fuse (unite) two images into one. A blur point will occur before the this point.

Breakthrough pain Intense increases in pain that occur with rapid onset even when pain-control medication is being used. Breakthrough pain can occur spontaneously or in relation to a specific activity.

Breast A "modified sebaceous gland" in the superficial tissues of the anterior chest wall. Consists of a variable mixture of milk-producing glandular tissue, fat, and supporting connective tissue (Cooper's ligaments). Several major medical groups recommend routine mammograms for early detection of breast cancer. There is continued discussion about the benefits of screening mammograms.

Breast cancer Cancer that starts in the breast. How rapidly it grows, whether it will spread (metastasize) or not, and what the outcome will be varies, depending on many factors, including the type of cancer, where it begins, how soon it was detected, whether it is estrogen-receptor positive or negative, and whether it responds to the type of treatment chosen. Some of the factors that contribute to the course of breast cancer are still unknown, but one area that is under study is the effect of diet. The main types of breast cancer are ductal carcinoma in situ, infiltrating ductal carcinoma, invasive lobular carcinoma, lobular carcinoma in situ, medullary carcinoma, and Paget's disease of the nipple.

Breast cancer in situ Abnormal cells that are confined to the ducts or lobules in the breast. There are two forms, called ductal carcinoma in situ (DCIS) and lobular carcinoma in situ (LCIS).

Breast conservation therapy Surgery to remove a breast cancer and a small amount of tissue around the cancer, without removing any other part of the breast. This procedure is also called lumpectomy, segmental excision, limited breast surgery, or tylectomy. The method may require an axillary dissection and or radiation therapy in addition to the breast conservation surgery.

Breast density Describes the relative amount of different tissues present in the breast. A dense breast has less fat than glandular and connective tissue. Mammogram films of breasts with higher density are harder to read and interpret than those of less dense breasts.

Breast duct endoscopy A method used to examine the lining of the breast ducts to look for abnormal tissue. A very thin, flexible, lighted tube attached to a camera is inserted through the nipple, and threaded into the breast ducts deep in the breast. Tissue and fluid samples may be removed during the procedure.

Breast imaging reporting and data system BI-RADS. A method used by radiologists to interpret and report in a standardized manner the results of mammography, ultrasound, and MRI used in breast cancer screening and diagnosis.

Breast implant A manufactured sac that is filled with silicone gel (a synthetic material containing silicon) or saline (sterile saltwater). The sac is surgically inserted to increase breast size or restore the appearance of a breast after mastectomy. Because of concern about possible (but as yet unproven) side effects of silicone, silicone implants are presently available only to women who agree to participate in a clinical trial in which side effects are carefully monitored.

Breast reconstruction Surgery that rebuilds the breast contour after mastectomy. A breast implant or the woman's own tissue provides the contour. If desired, the nipple and areola may also be re-created. Reconstruction can be done at the time of mastectomy or any time later.

Breast self exam (BSE) A technique of checking one's own breasts for lumps or suspicious changes. The method is recommended for all women over age 20, to be done once a month, usually at a time other than the days before, during, or immediately after her menstrual period.

Breast specialist A term describing health professionals who have a dedicated interest in breast health. While they may acquire specialized knowledge in this area, medical schools and licensing boards do not teach or certify a specialty in breast care.

Breast-conserving surgery An operation to remove the breast cancer but not the breast itself. Types of breast-conserving surgery include lumpectomy (removal of the lump), quadrantectomy (removal of one quarter, or quadrant, of the breast), and segmental mastectomy (removal of the cancer as well as some of the breast tissue around the tumor and the lining over the chest muscles below the tumor). Also called breast-sparing surgery.

Breast-sparing surgery An operation to remove the breast cancer but not the breast itself. Types of breast-sparing surgery include lumpectomy (removal of the lump), quadrantectomy (removal of one quarter, or quadrant, of the breast), and segmental mastectomy (removal of the cancer as well as some of the breast tissue around the tumor and the lining over the chest muscles below the tumor). Also called breast-conserving surgery.

Breath control shields Typically made of acrylic or plastic materials, shields protect product, equipment, or the work from particulate contamination expelled by people.

Breathing The process of respiration, during which air is inhaled into the lungs through the mouth or nose due to muscle contraction, and then exhaled due to muscle relaxation.

Bregma Craniometric term denoting the point on surface of skull where the sagittal and coronal sutures meet.

Brewster stereoscope An instrument used in orthoptics/vision therapy to improve eye teaming skills and near focusing skills. It consists of two parallel viewing tubes with a +5.00 D lens. The distance from the target can be adjusted as well as the pupillary distance. The Bernell-O-Scope and Keystone Ophthalmic Telebinocular are designed essentially the same.

Bridge Stationary dental prosthesis (appliance) fixed to teeth adjacent to a space; replaces one or more missing teeth, cemented or bonded to supporting teeth or implants adjacent to the space.

Brief pain inventory A questionnaire used to measure pain.

Brivudine A substance that is being studied in the treatment of infections caused by herpesvirus, including herpes-zoster (shingles). It belongs to the family of drugs called antivirals.

Broad spectrum Over a wide range. A broad-spectrum disinfectant is effective against a wide range of microorganisms including bacterial spores, mycobacteria, nonlipid and lipid viruses, fungi, and vegetative bacteria.

Bromelain An enzyme found in pineapples that breaks down other proteins, such as collagen and muscle fiber, and has anti-inflammatory properties. It is used as a meat tenderizer in the food industry.

Bronchi The hollow branches of the pulmonary tree which connect the trachea to the alveoli.

Bronchial adenoma Cancer that forms in tissues of the bronchi (large air passages in the lungs including those that lead to the lungs from the windpipe).

Bronchial Having to do with the bronchi, which are the larger air passages of the lungs, including those that lead from the trachea (windpipe) to the lungs and those within the lungs.

Bronchiole The small airways that carry air into and out of the lungs. In people with asthma they become inflamed, narrowed, contracted, and sticky with mucus.

Bronchitis An inflammation of the bronchial tubes, generally accompanied by coughing, pain, or shortness of breath.

Bronchodilator A medicine based on adrenaline that is used to treat asthma, such as Salbutamol, used in relievers.

Bronchogenic carcinoma A cancer originating in the lungs or airways.

Bronchoscope A thin, lighted tube used to examine the inside of the trachea and bronchi, the air passages that lead to the lungs.

Bronchoscopy A procedure in which a thin, lighted tube is inserted through the nose or mouth. This allows examination of the inside of the trachea and bronchi (air passages that lead to the lung), as well as the lung. Bronchoscopy may be used to detect cancer or to perform some treatment procedures.

Bronchospasm The sudden, involuntary contraction of the smooth muscle of the bronchi, as occurs in asthma.

Bronchus A large air passage that leads from the trachea (windpipe) to the lung.

Bronchus intermedius On the right, the segment of bronchus between the origin of the upper lobe bronchus (of the lung) and the bifurcation into the middle and lower lobe bronchi.

Brostallicin A substance that is being studied in the treatment of cancer. It belongs to the family of drugs called DNA intercalators.

Broth The liquid culture medium in which fermentation or cell culture takes place.

Broxuridine A drug that makes cancer cells more sensitive to radiation and is also used as a diagnostic agent to determine how fast cancer cells grow.

Bruxism Grinding of the teeth, which may be a predisposing factor to temporomandibular joint (TMJ) dysfunction.

Bruxomania Persistent "nervous" grinding of the teeth while the patient is awake.

Bryostatin 1 A macrocyclic lactone isolated from the bryozoan Bugula neritina with antineoplastic activity. Bryostatin-1 binds to and inhibits the cell-signaling enzyme protein kinase C, resulting in the inhibition of tumor cell proliferation, the promotion of tumor cell differentiation, and the induction of tumor cell apoptosis. This agent may act synergistically with other chemotherapeutic agents.

BSE (Bovine spongiform encephalopathy) See Bovine spongiform encephalopathy.

BSH Sodium borocaptate. A substance used in a type of radiation therapy called boron neutron capture therapy. BSH is injected into a vein and becomes concentrated in tumor cells. The patient then receives radiation treatment with atomic particles called neutrons. The neutrons react with the boron in BSH and make radioactive particles that kill the tumor cells without harming normal cells.

BT (Bacillus Thuringiensis) One of the most common microorganisms used in biologically based pesticides is the Bacillus thuringiensis or Bt bacterium. Several of the proteins produced by the Bt, principally in the coating the bacteria forms around itself, are lethal to individual species of insects. By using Bt in pesticide formulations, target insects can be controlled using an environmentally benign, biologically-based agent. Bt-based insecticides have been widely used by home gardeners for many years as well as on farms.

BTU (British Thermal Unit) The unit used to measure the amount of heat in a substance. One BTU is the heat required to produce a temperature rise of 1°F. in one lb. of water.

Bubble point test A filter leakage test in which the filter is wetted and air pressure is applied and slowly increased until water is expelled from the largest pores and bubbles appear from a submerged tube in a downstream collection vessel. Vigorous bubbling, as opposed to a diffusional airflow or occasional bubbles, is indicative of reaching the bubble point. This visual test can be fairly accurate for low area filters, such as discs. When used to evaluate high area filters, it is subject to limitations in observation, test time, collection conditions, and pressurization rates. The bubble point test is not recommended for integrity testing of filter cartridges.

Buccal mucosa Tissue in the mouth that is used for split or full thickness grafts in reconstruction of the fornices.

Bucket handle tear A description given to a type of tear of the meniscus of the knee joint, usually medial. The tear is one that extends along the length of the meniscus, within the body of the meniscus. This tear allows for the internal portion of the torn meniscus to slip into the joint. A common cause of a "locked" knee.

Budding The final step in the HIV life cycle, when an individual virus pushes out ("buds") from the host cell, stealing part of the cell's outer envelope and freeing itself to attach to and infect another host cell.

Budesonide A drug used in the treatment of asthma and rhinitis. It is also being studied in the treatment of cancer. Budesonide belongs to the family of drugs called steroids.

(16,17- (butylidenebis (oxy))-11,21-dihydroxy-, (11-â,16-á)-pregna-1,4-diene-3,20-dione)

Figure Budesonide

Buffer A substance capable of neutralizing both acids and bases in solution, thereby maintaining the original acidity or causticity of the solution.

Buffer prep Area Section of most biotech facilities devoted to the preparation of controlled bio-burden buffer solutions for use in the chromatographic separation area of those facilities.

Bugbane /Bugwort Cimicifuga racemosa. A substance obtained from the root of the plant has been used in some cultures to treat a number of medical problems. It is being studied in the treatment of hot flashes and other symptoms of menopause. The plant is also called black cohosh, black snakeroot, rattlesnake root, and bugwort.

Bulbar conjunctiva The tissue covering the scleral of the eyeball.

Bulimia nervosa An eating disorder characterized by rapid consumption of a large amount of food in a short period of time, with a sense of lack of control during the episode and self-evaluation unduly influenced by body weight and shape. There are two forms of the condition, purging and non-purging. The first type regularly engages in purging through self-induced vomiting or the excessive use of laxatives or diuretics. Alternatively, the non-purging type controls weight through strict dieting, fasting or excessive exercise.

Bulk handling The transferring of flammable or combustible liquids from tanks or drums into smaller containers for distribution.

Bulk oxygen system An assembly of equipment, such as storage containers, pressure regulators, safety devices, vaporizers, manifolds, and interconnecting piping that has a storage capacity of more than 12,000 cubic feet (340 m^3) of oxygen at normal temperature and pressure, connected in service or ready for service, or more than 25,000 cubic feet (708 m^3) of oxygen, including unconnected reserve on hand at the site.

Bulla A cavity of at least 5 mm in diameter forming within or below the epidermis.

Bunion A bump or bulge on the first joint of the big toe caused by the swelling of a sac of fluid under the skin. Shoes that fit well can keep bunions from forming. Bunions can lead to other problems such as serious infections.

Bupropion hydrochloride The hydrochloride salt of an aminoketone antidepressant. The molecular mechanism of the antidepressant effect of bupropion is unknown. This agent does not inhibit monoamine oxidase and, compared to classical tricyclic antidepressants, is a weak blocker of the neuronal uptake of serotonin and norepinephrine. Buproprion also weakly inhibits the neuronal re-uptake of dopamine.

Burdock Arctium lappa. A plant whose seeds and root have been used in some cultures to treat certain medical problems. It may have antioxidant effects. Also called lappa and happy major.

Burkitt's leukemia A rare, fast-growing cancer of the blood. Also called B-cell acute lymphocytic leukemia or B-cell acute lymphoblastic leukemia.

Burkitt's lymphoma An aggressive (fast-growing) type of B-cell non-Hodgkin's lymphoma that occurs most often in children and young adults. The disease may affect the jaw, central nervous system, bowel, kidneys, ovaries, or other organs. There are three main types of Burkitt's lymphoma (sporadic, endemic, and immunodeficiency related). Sporadic Burkitt's lymphoma occurs throughout the world, and endemic Burkitt's lymphoma occurs in Africa. Immunodeficiency-related Burkitt's lymphoma is most often seen in AIDS patients.

Burr hole A small opening in the skull made with a surgical drill.

Bursa A tissue space lined by joint tissue; bursas are found in between tendon and bone, skin and bone and muscles.

Bursa of fabricius An outpouching of the cloaca in birds; site of development of B cells in birds.

Bursitis Inflammation (swelling, pain, and warmth) of a bursa. A bursa is a flat, fluid-filled sac found between a bone and a tendon or muscle. It forms a cushion to help the tendon or muscle slide smoothly over the bone. Bursitis may be caused by long-term overuse, trauma, rheumatoid arthritis, gout, or infection. It usually affects the shoulder, knee, elbow, hip, or foot.

Buserelin A synthetic analog of gonadotropin-releasing hormone (GnRH). Buserelin binds to and activates pituitary gonadotropin releasing hormone (GnRH) receptors. Prolonged administration of buserelin results in sustained inhibition of gonadotropin production, suppression of testicular and ovarian steroidogenesis, and reduced levels of circulating gonadotropin and gonadal steroids. Buserelin is more potent that GnRH.

Buspirone hydrochloride The hydrochloride salt of an anxiolytic agent chemically and pharmacologically unrelated to benzodiazepines, barbiturates, or other sedative/hypnotic drugs.

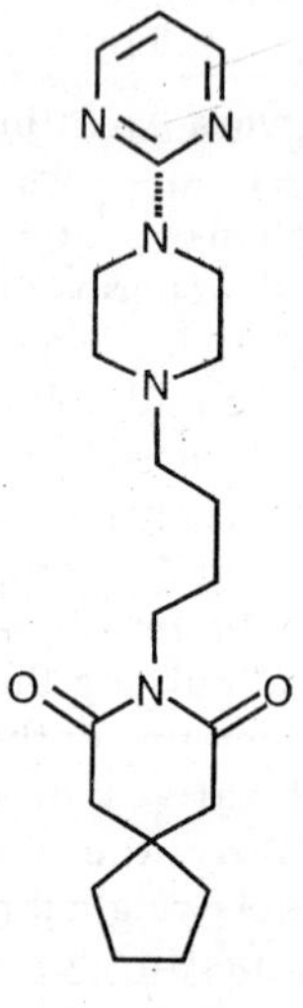

Figure Buspirone

Although its exact mechanism of action is unknown, buspirone may exert its anti-anxiety effects via serotonin (5-HT1A) and dopamine receptors (D2) and may indirectly affect other neurotransmitter systems. Unlike typical benzodiazepine anxiolytics, this agent does not exert anticonvulsant or muscle relaxant effects and lacks prominent sedative effects.

Busulfan An anticancer drug that belongs to the family of drugs called alkylating agents.

Buthionine sulfoximine A synthetic amino acid. Buthionine sulfoximine irreversibly inhibits gamma-glutamylcysteine synthetase, thereby depleting cells of glutathione, a metabolite that plays a critical role in protecting cells against oxidative stress, and resulting in free radical-induced apoptosis. Elevated glutathione levels are associated with tumor cell resistance to alkylating agents and platinum compounds. By depleting cells of glutathione, this agent may enhance the in vitro and in vivo cytotoxicities of various chemotherapeutic agents in drug-resistant tumors. Buthionine sulfoximine may also exhibit antiangiogenesis activity.

Butylated hydroxyanisole (BHA) A phenolic chemical compound used to preserve foods by preventing rancidity. It may also be used as a defoaming agent for yeast. BHA is found in foods high in fats and oils; also in meats, cereals, baked goods, beer, and snack foods.

BVD (Bovine viral diarrhea) Viral contaminant found in bovine sera. Able to be filtered out using 0.1 μm nylon filters.

Bovine Of, relating to, or from a cow: such as Bovine Blood: blood from a cow.

Bypass A surgical procedure in which the doctor creates a new pathway for the flow of body fluids.

Byte An abbreviation for binary term. A storage unit capable of holding eight bits or the space required for a single letter or number, a single character.

C cell A type of cell in the thyroid. C cells make calcitonin, a hormone that helps control the calcium level in the blood.

C peptide A substance that the pancreas releases into the bloodstream in equal amounts to insulin. A test of C-peptide levels will show how much insulin the body is making.

CA 19-9 assay A test that measures the level of CA 19-9 in the blood. CA 19-9 is a tumor marker released into the bloodstream from both cancer cells and normal cells. Higher than normal amounts of CA 19-9 in the blood can be a sign of gallbladder or pancreatic cancer or other conditions.

CA-125 A substance sometimes found in an increased amount in the blood, other body fluids, or tissues and that may suggest the presence of some types of cancer.

CA-125 test A blood test that measures the level of CA-125, a substance found in blood, other body fluids and some tissues. Increased levels of CA-125 may be a sign of cancer.

Cachexia Loss of weight, muscle wasting, fatigue, weakness, and decrease of appetite in someone who is not actively trying to lose weight. Usually associated with serious disease.

CAD (Coronary artery disease) A disease in which there is a narrowing or blockage of the coronary arteries (blood vessels that carry blood and oxygen to the heart). CAD is usually caused by atherosclerosis (a build up of fatty material and plaque inside the coronary arteries). The disease may cause chest pain, shortness of breath during exercise, and heart attacks. The risk of CAD is increased by having a family history of CAD before age 50, older age, smoking tobacco, high blood pressure, high cholesterol, diabetes, lack of exercise, and obesity. Also called coronary heart disease.

Cadmium A metallic element that occurs naturally in tiny amounts in air, water, soil, and food. It is a byproduct of zinc refining, and is used to make batteries, pigments, plastics, alloys, and electroplate. It is also found in cigarette smoke. Exposure to high levels of cadmium may cause certain cancers and other health problems.

Caffeic acid A type of phenol found in various fruits, vegetables and citrus fruits which have antioxidant like activities that may reduce the risk of degenerative diseases, heart disease and eye disease.

Caffeine Caffeine is a naturally-occurring substance found in the leaves, seeds or fruits of over 63 plant species worldwide and is part of a group of compounds known as methylxanthines. The most commonly known sources of caffeine are coffee and cocoa beans, cola nuts and tea leaves. Caffeine is a pharmacologically active substance and, depending on the dose, can be a mild central nervous system stimulant. Caffeine does not accumulate in the body over the course of time and is normally excreted within several hours of consumption.

Calamus scriptorius The tapered caudal part of the fourth ventricle in the region of the vagal and hypoglossal trigones. Likened to the nib of a pen in shape.

Calcaneal spur Also called calcaneal enthesiopathy, where there is repetitive microtrauma at the attachment of the Achilles tendon resulting in the formation of a spur, extending from the calcaneum into the tendon.

Calcaneus The "heel bone" of the foot, located at the back of the tarsus.

Calcar avis Projection or eminence located along the medial wall of the occipital horn of the lateral ventricle caused by the deep calcarine fissure.

Calcification Deposits of calcium in the tissues. Calcification in the breast can be seen on a mammogram, but cannot be detected by touch. There are two types of breast calcification, macrocalcification and microcalcification. Macrocalcifications are large deposits and are usually not related to cancer. Microcalcifications are specks of calcium that may be found in an area of rapidly dividing cells. Many microcalcifications clustered together may be a sign of cancer.

Calcitonin A hormone formed by the C cells of the thyroid gland. It helps maintain a healthy level of calcium in the blood. When the calcium level is too high, calcitonin lowers it.

Calcitriol The active form of vitamin D. Calcitriol is formed in the kidneys or made in the laboratory. It is used as a drug to increase calcium levels in the body in order to treat skeletal and tissue-related calcium deficiencies caused by kidney or thyroid disorders.

Calcium A mineral that builds bones and strengthens bones, helps in muscle contraction and heartbeat, assists with nerve functions and blood clotting. Teens 18 years and younger should strive to consume about 1,300 milligrams per day. Individuals 50 years and older need about 1,200 milligrams per day. Everyone else should strive for about 1,000 milligrams per day. Milk and other diary foods such as yogurt and most cheeses are the best sources of calcium. In addition, dark green leafy vegetables, fish with edible bones, and calcium fortified foods supply significant amounts.

Calcium carbonate A mineral taken primarily as a supplement to prevent osteoporosis. It is also being studied for cancer prevention.

Calcium carbonate equivalent The value obtained when salts are calculated in terms of equivalent quantities of calcium carbonate. This is a convenient method of reducing all salts to a common basis for comparison.

Calcium channel blocker A drug used to lower blood pressure.

Calcium citrate The citrate salt of calcium. An element necessary for normal nerve, muscle, and cardiac function, calcium as the citrate salt helps to maintain calcium balance and prevent bone loss when taken orally. This agent may also be chemopreventive for colon and other cancers.

Calcium gluconate The gluconate salt of calcium. An element or mineral necessary for normal nerve, muscle, and cardiac function, calcium as the gluconate salt helps to maintain calcium balance and prevent bone loss when taken orally. This agent may also be chemopreventive for colon and other cancers.

Calculus Hard residue, commonly known as "tarter," that forms on teeth due to inadequate plaque control, often stained yellow or brown.

Calendula ointment A substance made from the flower of the marigold plant Calendula officinalis. Calendula-based skin products have been used to treat minor cuts, burns, and skin irritation. Another product, Calendula ointment, is being studied in France in the prevention of dermatitis in patients having radiation therapy for breast cancer.

Calibration The demonstration that a particular instrument or device produces results within specified limits by comparison with those produced by a reference or traceable standard over an appropriate range of measurements.

Callus A small area of skin, usually on the foot, that has become thick and hard from rubbing or pressure. Calluses may lead to other problems such as serious infection. Shoes that fit well can keep calluses from forming.

Caloric intake Refers to the number of calories (energy content) consumed.

Calorie A measurement of the energy content of food. The body needs calories as "fuel" to perform all of its functions, such as breathing, circulating the blood, and physical activity. When a person is sick, their body may need extra calories to fight fever or other problems.

Calorimetry Analytical method that measures heat loss or gain resulting from physical or chemical changes in a sample. Differential scanning calorimetry compares the results of heating a sample to those for heating a reference material. For example, a method to measure the temperature at which the sample crystallizes, changes phases, or decomposes.

CAM (Complementary and alternative medicine) Forms of treatment that are used in addition to (complementary) or instead of (alternative) standard treatments. These practices generally are not considered standard medical approaches. Standard treatments go through a long and careful research process to prove they are safe and effective, but less is known about most types of CAM. CAM may include dietary supplements, megadose vitamins, herbal preparations, special teas, acupuncture, massage therapy, magnet therapy, spiritual healing, and meditation.

Campath-1H A monoclonal antibody used to treat leukemia. Monoclonal antibodies are laboratory-produced substances that can locate and bind to cancer cells. Also called alemtuzumab.

Camphor A substance that comes from the wood and bark of the camphor tree or is made in the laboratory. It has a very unique smell and taste and is used in commercial products (for example, mothballs). Camphor is used in topical anti-infective and anti-pruritic (anti-itching) agents.

Camptothecin An anticancer drug that belongs to the family of drugs called topoisomerase inhibitors.

Camptothecin analog An anticancer drug related in structure to camptothecin, a topoisomerase inhibitor. One such drug is aminocamptothecin.

Cancell A liquid that has been promoted as a treatment for a wide range of diseases, including cancer. The ingredients thought to be in Cancell have been tested, and none of them has been shown to be effective in treating any form of cancer. Also called Entelev, Sheridan's Formula, Jim's Juice, Crocinic Acid, JS-114, JS-101, 126-F, and Cantron.

Cancer A term for diseases in which abnormal cells divide without control. Cancer cells can invade nearby tissues and can spread through the bloodstream and lymphatic system to other parts of the body. There are several main types of cancer. Carcinoma is cancer that begins in the skin or in tissues that line or cover internal organs. Sarcoma is cancer that begins in bone, cartilage, fat, muscle, blood vessels, or other connective or supportive tissue. Leukemia is cancer that starts in blood-forming tissue such as the bone marrow, and causes large numbers of abnormal blood cells to be produced and enter the bloodstream. Lymphoma and multiple myeloma are cancers that begin in the cells of the immune system.

Cancer care team The group of health professionals who cooperate in the diagnosis, planning, treatment, after-care, and counselling of people with cancer. The team may include any or all of the following and others: primary care physician and / or gynecologist, nurse, pathologist, oncology specialists (medical oncologist, radiation oncologist, hematologist), surgeon, oncology nurse specialist, oncology social worker. Whether the team is linked formally or informally, there is usually one person who takes the job of "referee".

Cancer cell A cell that divides and reproduces abnormally and can spread throughout the body.

Cancer cluster The occurrence of a larger-than-expected number of cases of cancer within a group of people in a geographic area over a period of time.

Cancer in situ The stage where the cancer is still confined to the tissue in which it started.

Cancer of the adrenal cortex A rare cancer that forms in the outer layer of tissue of the adrenal gland (a small organ on top of each kidney that makes steroid hormones, adrenaline, and noradrenaline to control heart rate, blood pressure, and other body functions). Also called adrenocortical cancer and adrenocortical carcinoma.

Cancer of unknown primary origin A case in which cancer cells are found in the body, but the place where the cells first started growing (the origin or primary site) cannot be determined.

Cancer related checkup A routine health examination for cancer in persons without obvious signs or symptoms of cancer. The goal of the cancer-related check-up is to find the disease, if it exists, at an early stage, when chances for cure are greatest. Clinical breast examination, Pap smears and skin examinations are examples of methods used in cancer-related check-ups.

Cancer vaccine A vaccine designed to prevent or treat cancer.

Cancidas Other name for caspofungin acetate.

Candida albicans A yeast-like fungi, commonly found in the normal flora of the mouth, skin, intestinal tract, and vagina. Generally, candida is harmless, but can become clinically infectious in immune compromised people.

Candida kruseii Another candida species, similar to Candida albicans, but often less susceptible to the common drugs used to treat C Albicans.

Candida Yeast that causes irritation and infection, especially of the mucous membranes of the body such as the mouth, vagina, and anus.

Candidate gene A gene located in a chromosome region suspected of being involved in a disease.

Candidemia Candida albicans in the blood

Candidiasis A condition in which Candida albicans, a type of yeast, grows out of control in moist skin areas of the body. It is usually a result of a weakened immune system, but can be a side effect of chemotherapy or treatment with antibiotics. Thrush usually affects the mouth (oral thrush); however, rarely, it spreads throughout the entire body. Also called candidosis or thrush.

Canker sore Mouth sore appearing whitish, often with a red halo, of ten to fourteen day duration.

Canthi (Plural) The juncture where the upper and lower eyelids meet.

Canthus Reference to either the medial (inner) and the lateral (outer) extent of the eyelids.

Cantilever bridge Fixed bridge that attaches to adjacent teeth only on one end.

Cantron A liquid that has been promoted as a treatment for a wide range of diseases, including cancer. The ingredients thought to be in Cantron have been tested, and none of them has been shown to be effective in treating any form of cancer. Also called Entelev, Sheridan's Formula, Jim's Juice, Crocinic Acid, JS–114, JS–101, 126–F, and Cancell.

Canvaxin Other name for polyvalent melanoma vaccine.

CAP 1 (Carcinoembryonic antigen peptide-1) A protein that can stimulate an immune response.

Cap Common term for dental crown.

Capecitabine A fluoropyrimidine carbamate belonging to the class of antineoplastic agents called antimetabolites. As a prodrug, capecitabine is selectively activated by tumor cells to its cytotoxic moiety, 5-fluorouracil (5-FU); subsequently, 5-FU is metabolized to two active metabolites, 5-fluoro-2-deoxyuridine monophosphate (FdUMP) and 5-fluorouridine triphosphate (FUTP) by both tumor cells and normal cells. FdUMP inhibits DNA synthesis and cell division by reducing normal thymidine production, while FUTP inhibits RNA and protein synthesis by competing with uridine triphosphate for incorporation into the RNA strand.

Capillary array Gel-filled silica capillaries used to separate fragments for DNA sequencing. The small diameter of the capillaries permit the application of higher electric fields, providing high speed, high throughput separations that are significantly faster than traditional slab gels.

Capillary leak syndrome A condition in which fluid and proteins leak out of tiny blood vessels and flow into surrounding tissues, resulting in dangerously low blood pressure. Capillary leak syndrome may lead to multiple organ failure and shock.

Capillary The smallest type of blood vessel. A capillary connects an arteriole (small artery) to a venule (small vein) to form a network of blood vessels in almost all parts of the body. The wall of a capillary is thin and leaky, and capillaries are involved in the exchange of fluids and gases between tissues and the blood.

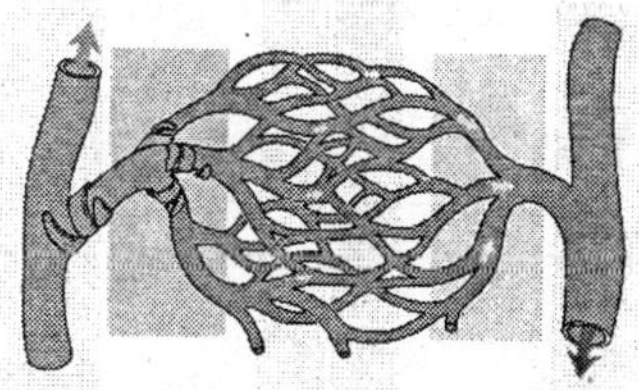

Figure A network of capillaries

Capital expenditure review A review of proposed capital expenditures of hospitals or providers to determine the need for, and appropriateness of, the proposed expenditures. The review is usually done by a designated regulatory agency and has a sanction attached that prevents or discourages unneeded expenditures.

Capsaicin A component of certain plants, including cayenne and red pepper, used topically for peripheral nerve pain. Also being studied for controlling mucositis pain after chemotherapy and radiation therapy.

Capsid The external protein shell or coat of a virus particle.

Capsule formation Scar tissue that may form around a breast (or other type of) implant as the body tries to "wall off" or encapsulate the foreign object. Sometimes called a contracture.

Captopril A sulfhydryl-containing analog of proline with antihypertensive activity and potential antineoplastic activity.

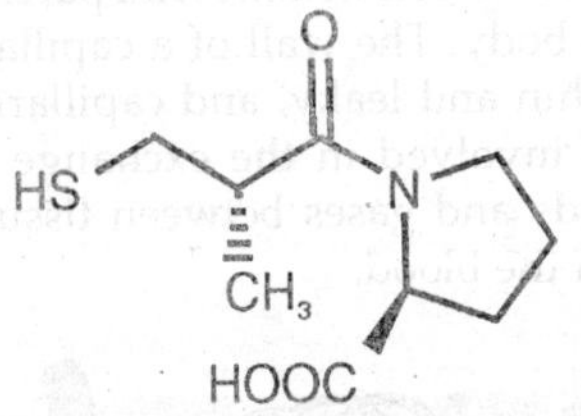

Captopril (1-[(2S)-3-mercapto-2-methylpropionyl]-l-proline)

Figure Captopril

Captopril competitively inhibits angiotensin converting enzyme (ACE), thereby decreasing levels of angiotensin II, increasing plasma renin activity, and decreasing aldosterone secretion. This agent may also inhibit tumor angiogenesis by inhibiting endothelial cell matrix metalloproteinases (MMPs) and endothelial cell migration. Captopril may also exhibit antineoplastic activity independent of effects on tumor angiogenesis.

Carbendazim An anticancer drug that belongs to the family of drugs called antifungal agents.

Carbogen An inhalant consisting of hyperoxic gas (95%-98% oxygen and 2%-5% carbon dioxide) with radiosensitizing properties. Inhaled carbogen reduces diffusion-limited tumor hypoxia, increasing tumor radiosensitivity due to the increased availability of molecular oxygen for cytotoxic radiation-induced oxygen free radical production.

Carbohydrate Carbohydrates are organic compounds that consist of carbon, hydrogen and oxygen. They vary from simple sugars containing from three to seven carbon atoms to very complex polymers. Only the hexoses (sugars with six carbon atoms) and pentoses (sugars with five carbon atoms) and their polymers play important roles in nutrition. Carbohydrates in food provide 4 calories per gram.

Plants manufacture and store carbohydrates as their chief source of energy. The glucose synthesized in the leaves of plants is used as the basis for more complex forms of carbohydrates. Classification of carbohydrates relates to their structural core of simple sugars, saccharides. Principal monosaccharides that occur in food are glucose and fructose. Three common disaccharides are sucrose, maltose and lactose. Polysaccharides of interest in nutrition include starch, dextrin, glycogen and cellulose.

Carbon 11 acetate The acetate salt of the radioisotope carbon-11. Although the mechanism is unclear, carbon-11 acetate preferentially accumulates in tumor tissue, serving as a tracer for imaging tumors with positron emission tomography (PET).

Carbon filter A vessel loaded with activated carbon and used to remove organics, chlorine, tastes, and odors from liquids, operating on the principle of adsorption.

Carbon thickness A measurement of surface organic material. Carbon thickness values typically range from 5 to 20 angstroms (Å). Significantly contaminated surfaces can show surface carbon thickness of 20 angstroms (Å) or more.

Carbonate hardness That hardness in water caused by bicarbonates and carbonates of calcium and magnesium. If alkalinity exceeds total hardness, all hardness is carbonate hardness; if hardness exceeds alkalinity, the carbonate hardness equals the alkalinity.

Carboplatin A second-generation platinum compound with a broad spectrum of antineoplastic properties. Carboplatin contains a platinum atom complexed with two ammonia groups and a cyclobutane-dicarboxyl residue. This agent is activated intracellularly to form reactive platinum complexes that bind to nucleophilic groups such as GC-rich sites in DNA, thereby inducing intrastrand and interstrand DNA cross-links, as well as DNA-protein cross-links. These carboplatin-induced DNA and protein effects result in apoptosis and cell growth inhibition. This agent possesses tumoricidal activity similar to that of its parent compound, cisplatin, but is more stable and less toxic.

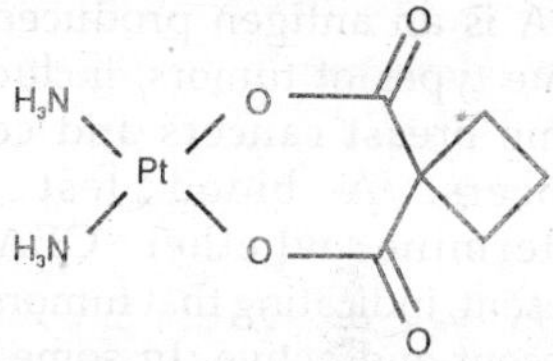

Carboplatin (Diammine (cyclobutane-1, 1-dicarboxylato (2-)-O,O′)platinum)

Figure Carboplatin

Carboxyamidotriazole An orally-active agent with potential antineoplastic activity. Carboxyamidotriazole binds to and inhibits non-voltage-operated Ca^{2+} channels, blocking both Ca^{2+} influx into cells and Ca^{2+} release from intracellular stores and resulting in the disruption of calcium channel mediated signal transduction and inhibition of vascular endothelial growth factor (VEGF) signaling, endothelial proliferation, and angiogenesis.

This agent may also inhibit tumor cell growth, invasion and metastasis.

Carboxypeptidase G2 A zinc-dependent enzyme isolated from a strain of the bacterium Pseudomonas. Because carboxy-peptidase-G2 rapidly hydrolyzes methotrexate into inactive metabolites, it may be useful as a rescue agent for methotrexate induced nephrotoxicity. In antibody directed enzyme prodrug therapy (ADEPT), this agent is conjugated with an antibody that binds to a specific tumor cell type, allowing for carboxypeptidase-G2-catalyzed activation of a co-administered prodrug at the site of the tumor.

Carcinoembryonic antigen (CEA) CEA is an antigen produced by some types of tumors, including some breast cancers and colon cancers. A blood test can determine whether CEA is present, indicating that tumors are present and active. In some, but not all, cases of breast cancer that has spread (metastasized), the CEA test helps determine whether the treatment method is working. The CEA test is not useful for routine cancer-related check-ups.

Carcinogen A substance that causes the development of cancerous growths in living tissue. A chemical is considered to be a carcinogen if it has been evaluated by the International Agency for Cancer Research (IARC) and found to be a carcinogen or potential carcinogen, or if it is listed in the Annual Report on Carcinogens published by the National Toxicology Program, or if it is regulated by OSHA as a carcinogen.

Carcinogenesis The process by which normal cells are transformed into cancer cells.

Carcinogenic Cancer-causing. Many agents that are carcinogenic are mutagens.

Carcinoid A slow-growing type of tumor usually found in the gastrointestinal system (most often in the appendix), and sometimes in the lungs or other sites. Carcinoid tumors may spread to the liver or other sites in the body, and they may secrete substances such as serotonin or prostaglandins, causing carcinoid syndrome.

Carcinoid syndrome A combination of symptoms caused by the release of serotonin and other substances from carcinoid tumors of the gastrointestinal tract. Symptoms may include flushing of the face, flat angiomas (small collections of dilated blood vessels) of the skin, diarrhea, bronchial spasms, rapid pulse, and sudden drops in blood pressure.

Carcinoma A malignant tumor that begins in the lining (epithelial) cells of organs. Carcinomas can occur in almost any part of the body. At least 80% of all cancers are carcinomas, and almost all breast cancers are carcinomas.

Carcinoma in situ An early stage of cancer, in which the tumor is still only in the structures of the organ where it first developed, and the disease has not invaded other parts of the organ or spread (metastasized). Most in situ carcinomas are highly curable.

Carcinomatosis A condition in which cancer is spread widely throughout the body, or, in some cases, to a relatively large region of the body. Also called carcinosis.

Carcinosarcoma A malignant tumor that is a mixture of carcinoma (cancer of epithelial tissue, which is skin and tissue that lines or covers the internal organs) and sarcoma (cancer of connective tissue, such as bone, cartilage, and fat).

Carcinosis A condition in which cancer is spread widely throughout the body, or, in some cases, to a relatively large region of the body. Also called carcinomatosis.

Carcinostatic Pertaining to slowing or stopping the growth of cancer.

Cardiac arrest The heart stops completely, so that no blood is being pumped out to the body.

Cardiac arrhythmia An abnormal heartbeat. Types of arrhythmias include tachycardias (accelerated heartbeats) and bradycardias (slow heartbeats).

Cardiac catheterization (Angiography) A diagnostic procedure in which catheters are passed through the arteries of the heart. Pressures are measured and blood samples are taken from within the heart and its major blood vessels.

Cardiac Having to do with the heart.

Cardiac rhythm management (CRM) The field of cardiovascular disease which relates to the detection and treatment of abnormally fast tachycardia (Tachy) and abnormally slow bradycardia (Brady) heart rhythms.

Cardiac sarcoma A rare cancer that develops in tissues of the heart. Also called heart cancer.

Cardin Cnicus benedictus. A plant whose leaves, stems, and flowers have been used in some cultures to treat certain medical problems. Cardin may have anti inflammatory and anticancer effects. Also called blessed thistle, St. Benedict's thistle, holy thistle, and spotted thistle.

Cardiologist A doctor who sees and takes care of people with heart disease; a heart specialist.

Cardiomegaly An enlargement of the heart.

Cardiomyopathy A condition that weakens the heart muscle or causes a change in heart muscle structure. Cardiomyopathy is associated with inadequate heart pumping or other heart function abnormalities. Cardiomyopathy may occur in HIV-infected people with advanced disease. Irregular heartbeat, abnormal heart and breath sounds, decreased heart function, or heart enlargement may indicate cardiomyopathy.

Cardiophrenic angle The angle formed by the heart ("cardio") and the diaphragm ("phrenic") - usually refers to pleural space or a region on the frontal chest film.

Cardiopulmonary Having to do with the heart and lungs.

Cardiotoxicity Toxicity that affects the heart.

Cardiovascular Relating to the heart and blood vessels (arteries, veins, and capillaries); the circulatory system.

Cardioversion The stopping of a fast heart rate by an electrical impulse that is delivered at the same time as the heartbeat. It uses low to moderate energy to restore the heart's normal rhythm.

Caries Tooth decay or "cavities".

Carina (Trachea) A ridge at the tracheal bifurcation, formed by the last tracheal cartilage that runs anteroposteriorly between the orifices of the two main bronchi. (from "carina" - the "v" shape of the bottom of a boat).

Carmustine An antineoplastic nitrosourea. Carmustine alkylates and cross-links DNA during all phases of the cell cycle, resulting in disruption of DNA function, cell cycle arrest, and apoptosis. This agent also carbamoylates proteins, including DNA repair enzymes, resulting in an enhanced cytotoxic effect. Carmustine is highly lipophilic and crosses the blood-brain barrier readily.

Carnitine A substance made in the muscles and liver, and also found in certain foods such as meat, poultry, fish, and some dairy products. The body needs carnitine to make energy from fat.

Carotenoid A substance found in yellow and orange fruits and vegetables and in dark green, leafy vegetables. Carotenoids may reduce the risk of developing cancer.

Carotid artery A major artery that carries blood from the heart to the head. There is a carotid artery on each side of the neck, and each one splits into two branches. The interior branch carries blood to the brain and eyes, and the exterior branch carries blood to the face, tongue, and outside parts of the head.

Carotid bifurcation The point of division of the common carotid arteries into the internal and external carotid arteries.

Carpal tunnel A "tunnel" formed at the wrist, by the flexor retinaculum and the carpal bones.

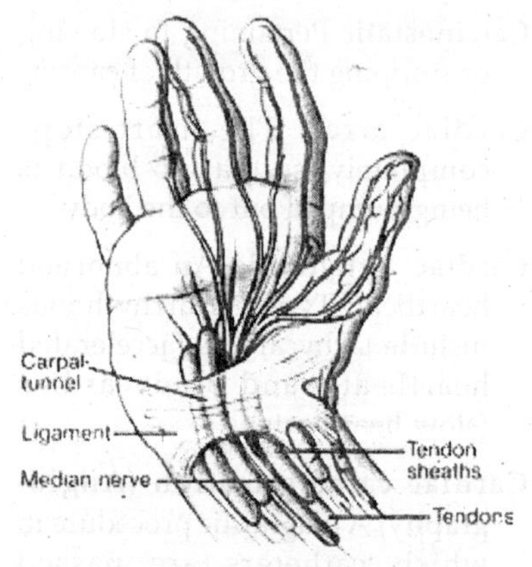

Figure Carpal tunnel

Carpal tunnel syndrome Where there is compression of the median nerve in the carpal tunnel, resulting in sensory and motor disturbances of the hand.

Carrageenan A compound extracted from Irish moss (a type of seaweed) that is used in puddings, milk shakes and ice cream to stabilize and keep color and flavor even.

Cartilage A tough, flexible tissue that lines joints and gives structure to the nose, ears, larynx, and other parts of the body.

Carzelesin An anticancer drug that belongs to the family of drugs called alkylating agents.

Case control study A study that involves the identification of persons with the disease or condition of interest (cases) and a suitable group of persons without the disease or condition of interest (controls). Cases and controls are compared with respect to some existing or past attribute or exposure believed to be causally related to the disease or condition. Also referred to as a retrospective study because the research approach proceeds from effect to cause. The term applies even if cases and controls are accumulated in a prospective manner.

Case report A detailed report of the diagnosis, treatment, and follow-up of an individual patient. Case reports also contain some demographic information about the patient (for example, age, gender, ethnic origin).

Case series A group or series of case reports involving patients who were given similar treatment. Reports of case series usually contain detailed information about the individual patients. This includes demographic information (for example, age, gender, ethnic origin) and information on diagnosis, treatment, response to treatment, and follow-up after treatment.

Case severity A measure of intensity or gravity of a given condition or diagnosis for a patient. May have direct correlation with the amount of service provided and the associated costs or payments allowed.

Caseation necrosis Identical to coagulation necrosis and ischemic necrosis. The affected tissue has lost its structural outline and appears as pale eosinophilic, amorphous and finely granular. Until the necrosis is far advanced some shrunken or fragmented nuclei are present.

Casein A milk protein; casein is precipitated out of milk in acid conditions; it is the principal protein of cheese.

Caseous Having a consistency like that of cottage cheese.

Caspid The protein covering of some viruses - made up of capsomeres; may stimulate the body's immune response.

Caspofungin acetate The acetate salt of an antimycotic echinocandin lipopeptide, semisynthetically derived from a fermentation product of the fungus Glarea lozoyensis. Caspofungin inhibits 1,3-beta-glucan synthase, resulting in decreased synthesis of beta (1,3)-D-glucan (an essential component of the fungal cell wall), weakening of the fungal cell wall, and fungal cell wall rupture. This agent is active against Aspergillus and Candida species.

Cast or model Reproduction of structures made by pouring plaster or stone into a mold.

Castleman's disease A rare disorder in which noncancerous growths develop in lymph node tissue.

Castration Removal or destruction of the testicles or ovaries using radiation, surgery, or drugs. Medical castration refers to the use of drugs to suppress the function of the ovaries or testicles.

CAT scan Computerized axial tomography scan. A series of detailed pictures of areas inside the body, taken from different angles; the pictures are created by a computer linked to an x-ray machine. Also called computed tomography (CT scan) or computerized tomography.

Catabolism The intracellular phase of metabolism involved in the energy-yielding degradation of nutrient molecules (for example, glucose to CO_2 and H_2O). Waste products are called catabolites.

Catalase An enzyme that catalyzes the decomposition of hydrogen peroxide and molecular oxygen and water.

Catalyst A compound that increases the rate of a chemical reaction without being consumed or changed. In the biosciences, the term enzyme is used. Enzymes catalyze biological reactions.

Cataract A condition of the crystalline lens, in which the normally clear lens becomes clouded or yellowed, causing blurred or foggy vision. Cataracts may be caused by aging, eye injuries, disease, heredity, or birth defects. Surgery is a treatment option. The affected lens is removed and is replaced with a substitute (implant) lens or with a special type of contact lens. Generally the success rate of cataract surgery is over 90%, if the eye is otherwise healthy.

Catarrh Inflammation of a mucous membrane with free discharge.

Catechins A type of flavonoid found in tea which provides the health benefits of neutralizing free radicals and possibly reducing the risk of cancer.

Catechol A chemical originally isolated from a type of mimosa tree. Catechol is used as an astringent, an antiseptic, and in photography, electroplating, and making other chemicals. It can also be man-made.

Catheter A hollow flexible tube used to infuse or drain fluids into or from the body. Example: A catheter is used to transfer insulin from an insulin pump to a needle that is placed in the skin of the person using an insulin pump.

Catheterization A test in which a catheter is inserted through the veins or arteries and into the heart to measure pressure, take blood samples and test for abnormalities in the heart.

Cation A positively charged particle or ion.

Cation exchange resin An Ion

exchange resin, which removes positively charged ions (cations) by exchanging them for hydrogen ions.

Catoptric image A reflective light image cast upon the cornea of the human eye and the ocular prosthesis. A balanced reflective image on the corneas would signify symmetrical alignment.

Cauda equina The lumbar and sacral nerve roots within the lumbar cistern as they descend to emerge from their respective intervertebral and sacral foramina.

Caudate nucleus One of the nuclei belonging to the basal ganglia located lateral to the thalamus. The nucleus consists of an enlarged head that bulges into the lateral wall of the frontal horn of the lateral ventricle, a body adjioning the dorsolateral thalamus and an attenuated tail that extends into the temporal horn of the lateral ventricle within its roof.

Causal agent A factor associated with the definitive onset of an illness. An example of a causal agent is the bacteria causing a specific infection. The relationship is more direct than in the case of a risk factor, and in general the specific ill health will only occur if the causal agent is present. Causal agent is often confused with risk factor.

Causation There is causation only when one factor necessarily alters the possibility of a second. Statistical methods alone cannot establish a causal relationship between factors. Examples of criteria to test causation include:

1. strength of the association,

2. biologic credibility of the association,

3. consistency of the findings with other investigations,

4. temporal relationship of the association,

5. presence of a dose-response relationship. Randomization allows assessment of causation.

Cauterization The destruction of tissue with a hot instrument, an electrical current, or a caustic substance.

Cauterize To destroy tissue with a hot instrument, an electrical current, or a caustic substance. This process may be used to kill certain types of small tumors or to seal off blood vessels to stop bleeding.

Cavitating Eroding, or creating holes. Often used to describe the characteristic destruction of lung tissue accompanying active tuberculosis.

Cavitation A condition of liquid flow where, after partial vaporization of the liquid, the subsequent collapse of vapor bubbles can produce surface damage.

Cavitron Dental tool that uses high frequency ultrasonic waves to clean teeth.

Cavum septum pellucidum Space enclosed within the laminae of the septum pelludicum, the membranous partition that seperates the frontal horns of the ventricle.

CBC (Complete blood count) A test to check the number of red blood cells, white blood cells, and platelets in a sample of blood. Also called blood cell count.

CBR96-doxorubicin immuno-conjugate A substance that is being studied in the treatment of cancer. It combines a monoclonal antibody with the anticancer drug doxorubicin. Monoclonal antibodies are substances that are made in the laboratory and that can locate and bind to cancer cells. cBR96-doxorubicin immuno-conjugate belongs to the family of drugs called antibody drug conjugates. Also called SGN-15.

CC49-streptavidin A substance that is being studied in the treatment of cancer. It is made by combining the monoclonal antibody CC49 with a chemical called streptavidin. It can find tumor cells that have the protein TAG-72 on their surface, including colon, prostate, breast, and ovary cancer cells. After CC49-streptavidin binds to cancer cells, a radioactive compound called yttrium Y 90 DOTA-biotin will find those cells and kill them.

CD34 antigen A protein found on the surface of some bone marrow and blood cells.

CD4 (T4) A protein embedded in the cell surface of helper T-lymphocytes; also found to a lesser degree on the surface of monocyte/macrophage, langerhans cells, astrocytes, keratinocytes, and glial cells. One of the ways HIV invades cells is by first attaching to the CD4 molecule (CD4 receptor).

CD4 cell "helper" T-cell responsible for coordinating much of the immune response. CD4 cells are one of the main targets damaged by HIV.

CD4 cell count A measurement of the number of CD4 cells in a sample of blood. The CD4 count is one of the most useful indicators of the health of the immune system and the progression of HIV/AIDS. A CD4 cell count is used by health care providers to determine when to begin, interrupt, or halt anti-HIV therapy; when to give preventive treatment for opportunistic infections; and to measure response to treatment. A normal CD4 cell count is between 500 and 1,400 cells/mm^3 of blood, but an individual's CD4 count can vary. In HIV-infected individuals, a CD4 count at or below 200 cells/mm^3 is considered an AIDS-defining condition.

CD4 percentage The percent of lymphocytes (white blood cells) that are CD4 cells. This measurement is less likely to vary in between blood tests than CD4 count, but CD4 count remains a more reliable measure of immune function than CD4 percentage for most people.

CD4 receptor A specific molecule present on the surface of a CD4 cell. HIV recognizes and binds to a CD4 receptor and a co-receptor to gain entry into a host cell.

CD40 ligand A recombinant therapeutic agent which is chemically identical to or similar to CD40-ligand. CD40-ligand, also known as CD40L/TRAP and CD154, is a type II membrane protein which binds to CD40, a cell surface receptor that belongs to the tumor necrosis factor receptor family; CD40 is expressed on B lymphocytes, monocytes, dendritic cells (DC), hematopoietic progenitors, endothelial cells and epithelial cells. Recombinant CD40-ligand may be used to activate DC ex vivo via CD40 binding; CD40-ligand-activated DC may provide or augment a protective antitumor immunity when administered in dendritic cell cancer vaccines.

CD8 cell Also called a cytotoxic T lymphocyte (CTL), killer T cell, or suppressor T cell. A type of white blood cell that is able to identify and kill cells infected with bacteria, viruses, or other foreign invaders.

CD8 count The number of killer/ suppresser T-lymphocytes in a cubic millimeter of blood.

CEA (Carcinoembryonic antigen) A substance that is sometimes found in an increased amount in the blood of people who have certain cancers, other diseases, or who smoke. It is used as a tumor marker for colorectal cancer.

CEA assay A laboratory test to measure carcinoembryonic antigen (CEA), a substance that is sometimes found in an increased amount in the blood of people who have certain cancers.

Cecum A pouch that forms the first part of the large intestine. It connects the small intestine to the colon, which is part of the large intestine.

Cefepime A drug used to treat infection. It belongs to the family of drugs called cephalosporin antibiotics.

Cefixime A broad-spectrum, third-generation cephalosporin antibiotic derived semisyn-thetically from the marine fungus Cephalosporium acremonium with antibacterial activity. As does penicillin, the beta-lactam antibiotic cefixime inhibits bacterial cell wall synthesis by disrupting peptidoglycan synthe-sis, resulting in a reduction in bacterial cell wall stability and bacterial cell lysis. Stable in the presence of a variety of beta-lactamases, this agent is more active against gram-negative bacteria and less active against gram-positive bacteria compared to second-generation cephalosporins.

Ceflatonin Other name for homoharringtonine.

Ceftriaxone A drug used to treat infection. It belongs to the family of drugs called cephalosporin antibiotics.

Cele (Suffix) Tumor; herniation, e.g. meningocoele - hernial protrusion of meninges.

Celecoxib A drug that reduces pain. Celecoxib belongs to the family of drugs called nonsteroidal anti-inflammatory agents. It is being studied in the prevention of cancer.

Celiac artery The artery which originates from the abdominal aorta and divides into the left gastric, splenic, and common hepatic arteries.

Celiac disease A digestive disease that is caused by an immune response to a protein called gluten, which is found in wheat, rye, barley, and oats. Celiac disease damages the lining of the small intestine and interferes with the absorption of nutrients from food. A person with celiac disease may become malnourished no matter how much food is consumed.

Celiac syndrome (also spelled coeliac syndrome) An autoimmune disorder of the upper intestinal mucosa that is triggered by cereal proteins, especially wheat gluten, and which leads to a malabsorption of all nutrients, primarily of fat. It can be detected by the presence of anti-transglutaminase antibodies. If these are positive it would be justifiable to take a mucosal biopsy and if this is positive, then dietary treatment is all that is required.

About 5% of people with autoimmune diabetes have positive anti-transglutaminase antibodies. Celiac syndrome may also be part of the Autoimmune Polyglandular Syndrome.

Cell bank Master Cell Bank: The bank of cells, which contain the original unused mutated cells from which, the Manufacturing Working Cell Bank is taken. This is usually kept under lock with very limited access.

Manufacturing Working Cell Bank: The bank of cells derived from the Master Cell Bank, which are used to seed the fermentation manufacturing process.

Cell culture The in vitro propagation of cells removed from organisms in a laboratory environment that has strict sterility, temperature, and nutrient requirement; also used to refer to any particular individual sample. Usually, cell culture takes place in a bioreactor.

Cell differentiation The process whereby descendants of a common parental cell achieve and maintain specialization of structure and function. Muscle cells become muscle cells and bone cells develop. In humans all the different types of cells differentiate from the simple sperm and egg.

Cell fusion The fusing together of two or more cells to become a single cell. This technique has had important consequences in immunology, developmental biology, and genetics. For example, monoclonal antibodies are produced by fusing a spleen cell (producing an antibody specific for the antigen of interest) with a mouse myeloma cell to produce a hybridoma which has an indefinitely long life because of the myeloma component and which secretes a specific antibody. When a human cell is fused with a mouse cell, the human chromosomes are progressively lost from the resultant hybrid and by correlating the presence of proteins in the hybrid with the presence of particular human chromosomes, genes can be assigned to individual chromosomes.

Cell lines When cells from the first culture (taken from the organism) are used to make subsequent cultures, a cell line is established.

"Immortal" cell lines can replicate indefinitely.

Cell mediated An event accomplished with the assistance of certain cells

Cell mediated cytotoxicity (CMC) Killing (lysis) of a target cell by an effector lymphocyte.

Cell mediated immunity (CMI) A branch of the immune system responsible for the reaction to foreign material by specific defense cells (T-lymphocytes, killer cells, macrophage and other white blood cells) rather than antibodies.

Cell motility The ability of a cell to move.

Cell proliferation An increase in the number of cells as a result of cell growth and cell division.

Cell respiration A chemical process in which oxygen is used to make energy from carbohydrates (sugars). Also called oxidative metabolism, aerobic metabolism, or aerobic respiration.

Cell The basic unit of which all living things are made. Cells carry out basic life processes. Organs are clusters of cells that have developed specialized tasks. In scientific language, cytecell, and therefore cytology is the study of cells, cytotoxic means "toxic to cells," an erythrocyte is a red blood cell, and so on. Cells replace themselves by splitting and forming new cells (mitosis), and it is this process that is disrupted in cancer. chemoprevention. Prevention or reversal of disease using drugs, chemicals, vitamins or minerals. While this idea is not ready for widespread use, it is a very promising area of study. The Breast Cancer Prevention Trial is one such study, in which the drug tamoxifen is being tried to see if it will prevent breast cancer.

Cell to cell signaling The transfer of information from one cell to another.

Cell-cycle regulation Any process that controls the series of events by which a cell goes through the cell cycle. During the cell cycle, a cell makes a copy of its DNA and other contents, and divides in two. When cell cycle regulation doesn't happen correctly, cells may divide in an uncontrolled way, and diseases such as cancer can occur.

Cellular adhesion The close adherence (bonding) to adjoining cell surfaces.

Cellular adoptive immunotherapy A treatment used to help the immune system fight cancer. A cancer patient's T cells (a type of white blood cell) are collected and grown in the laboratory to increase the number of T cells that are able to kill the person's cancer cells. These cancer-specific T cells are given back to the patient to help the immune system fight the cancer.

Cellular metabolism The sum of all chemical changes that take place in a cell through which energy and basic components are provided for essential processes, including the synthesis of new molecules and the breakdown and removal of others.

Cellulitis A diffuse inflammatory process within solid tissues characterized by edema, redness, pain and interference with function. Cellulitis often occurs in the loose tissues beneath the skin, but may also occur in mucous membranes and in muscle bundles surounding organs.

Celsius Of or pertaining to a temperature scale that registers the freezing point of water as 0°C and the boiling point as 100°C under normal atmospheric pressure. Also called "centigrade". The designation Celsius has been official since 1948, but centigrade remains in common use.

Cementum Hard tissue that covers the roots of teeth.

Censoring A term used in survival or time-to-event analyses to denote an individual who has not experienced the event of interest as of a specific point in follow-up, e.g. time of interim analysis, end of study, or time at lost to follow-up. The process by which patient outcome data cannot be obtained beyond a specific point in time.

Centesis Puncture, e.g. thoracentesis - puncture of the pleural cavity.

Centi Prefix meaning one one-hundredth, as in a centimeter, which is a hundredth of a meter.

Centimeter A measure of length in the metric system. A centimeter is one hundredth of a meter. There are 2½ centimeters in an inch.

Centimorgan (CM) A unit of measure of recombination frequency. One centimorgan is equal to a 1% chance that a marker at one genetic locus will be separated from a marker at a second locus due to crossing over in a single generation. In human beings, one centimorgan is equivalent, on average, to one million base pairs.

Cento A prefix meaning a hundred times, as in centogram, a hundred grams.

Central canal (of spinal cord) Narrow ependymal lined channel that extends from the fourth ventricle through the length of the spinal cord within the midline of the transverse gray commissure (lamina X of Rexed). It is usually not patent beyon d the 20th year of life.

Central nervous system (CNS) The part of the nervous system made up of the brain, spinal cord, and spinal nerves. These serve as the main "processing center" for the whole nervous system, and together control all the workings of the body. HIV can infect and damage parts of the central nervous system.

Central nervous system metastasis (CNS metastasis) Cancer that has spread from the original (primary) tumor to the central nervous system (CNS).

Central nervous system primitive neuroectodermal tumor (CNS PNET) A type of cancer that arises from a particular type of cell within the brain or spinal cord.

Central nervous system prophylaxis CNS prophylaxis. Chemotherapy or radiation therapy given to the central nervous system (CNS) as a preventive treatment. It is given to kill cancer cells that may be in the brain and spinal cord, even though no cancer has been detected there. Also called CNS sanctuary therapy.

Central nervous system sanctuary therapy (CNS sanctuary therapy) Chemotherapy or radiation therapy given to the central nervous system (CNS) as a preventive treatment. It is given to kill cancer cells that may be in the brain and spinal cord, even though no cancer has been detected there. Also called CNS prophylaxis.

Central nervous system tumor (CNS tumor) A tumor of the central nervous system, including brain stem glioma, craniopharyngioma, medulloblastoma, and meningioma.

Central venous access catheter A tube surgically placed into a blood vessel for the purpose of giving intravenous fluid and drugs. It also can be used to obtain blood samples. This device avoids the need for separate needle insertions for each infusion or blood test. Examples of these devices include Hickman catheters, which require clamps to make sure the valve is closed, and Groshong catheters, which have a valve that opens as fluid is withdrawn or infused and remains closed when not in use.

Centrifugation Mechanical means of separation based on differences in sedimentation rates due to differences in density between the suspended particles in the liquid.

Centrifuge A centrifuge operates on the principle of centrifugal force, the inertial reaction by which a body tends to move away from a center about which it revolves. This technique is commonly used to separate solids from liquids or liquids of different densities. Centrifugal equipment is divided into two major types, sedimenters and filters:

Centromere A specialized chromosome region to which mitotic or meiotic spindle fibers attach during cell division.

Centrum semi (ovale) The semioval area of white matter within either cerebral hemisphere as seen when the brain is cut horizontally just above the level of the corpus callosum or the oval area seen when the two hemispheres are taken together.

CEP-2563 dihydrochloride A growth factor antagonist that may stop tumor cells from growing.

Cephalexin An antibiotic drug that belongs to the family of drugs called cephalosporins.

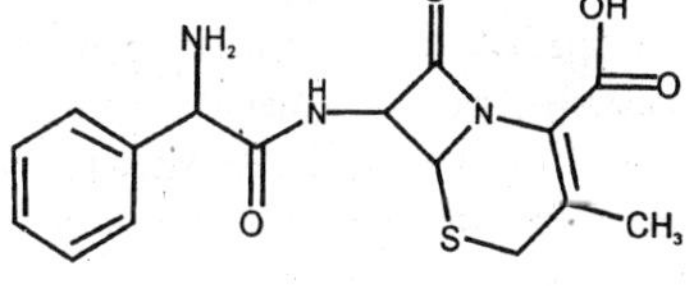

Figure Cephalexin

Cephalic vein Originates from the dorsal venous arch in the hand and joins the axillary vein.

Cephalosporin A drug used to treat bacterial infections. It belongs to the family of drugs called antibiotics.

Ceramide A type of fat produced in the body. It may cause some types of cells to die and is being studied in cancer treatment.

Cerebellar hemangioblastoma A benign, slow-growing tumor in the cerebellum (part of the brain at the back of the head), made up of abnormal blood vessel growth. People with von Hippel-Landau disease have an increased risk of developing hemangioblastomas.

Cerebellar tonsil A paramedian portion of the cerebellum that is continuous with the uvula of vermis that forms part of the caudal lobe of the cerebellar hemisphere.

Cerebellopontine Having to do with two structures of the brain, the cerebellum (located at the lower back of the brain) and the pons (located at the base of the brain in front of the cerebellum) and the area between them.

Cerebellum Sub-division of the rhombencephalon located in the posterior cranial fossa. It straddles the pons and medulla to which it is connected along with the midbrain by 3 peduncles. It functions in the motor sphere; coordination of muscle activity in movement, maintenance of equilibrium, and muscle tone.

Cerebral aqueduct (of sylvius) The narrow cerebrospinal fluid filled channel of the midbrain that joins the third and fourth ventricles of the brain.

Cerebral hemisphere Pair of rounded structures on either side of the midline of the brain that are partially separated by the longitudinal (interhemispheric) cerebral fissure.

Cerebral peduncle The ventral part of the midbrain consisting of the tegmentum and basis pedunculi (or crus cerebri).

Cerebral Relating to the brain.

Cerebrospinal fluid A watery, clear, colourless liquid produced largely by the choroid plexuses and contained within the cerebral ventricles, central canal of the spinal cord and the subarachnoid spaces surrounding the central nervous system.

Cerebrospinal fluid diversion A process used to drain fluid that has built up around the brain and spinal cord. A shunt (a long, thin tube) is placed in a ventricle of the brain and threaded under the skin to another part of the body, usually the abdomen. The shunt carries excess fluid away from the brain so it may be absorbed elsewhere in the body.

Cerebrovascular disease Damage to the blood vessels in the brain, resulting in a stroke. The blood vessels become blocked because of fat deposits or they become thick and hard, blocking the flow of blood to the brain. Sometimes, the blood vessels may burst, resulting in a hemorrhagic stroke. People with diabetes are at higher risk of cerebrovascular disease.

Cerebrum The largest part of the brain. It is divided into two hemispheres, or halves, called the cerebral hemispheres. Areas within the cerebrum control muscle functions and also control speech, thought, emotions, reading, writing, and learning.

Ceruloplasmin A simple protein found in the blood which binds itself to copper so that copper may be moved about the body by the circulatory system. Over 90% of Wilson's Disease patients have abnormally low levels of blood ceruloplasmin.

Cervene Other name for TGFa-PE38 immunotoxin .

Cervical Relating to the neck, or to the neck of any organ or structure. Cervical lymph nodes are located in the neck. Cervical cancer refers to cancer of the uterine cervix, which is the lower, narrow end (the "neck") of the uterus.

Cervical cancer Cancer that forms in tissues of the cervix (organ connecting the uterus and vagina). It is usually a slow-growing cancer that may not have symptoms, but can be found with regular Pap smears (procedure in which cells are scraped from the cervix and looked at under a microscope).

Cervical carcinoma A cancer of the cervix (the neck of the uterus).

Cervical dysplasia The abnormal growth of cervical cells, usually with no symptoms. It can be detected by a Pap smear and treatment can prevent it from progressing to cervical cancer.

Cervical intraepithelial neoplasia (CIN) A general term for the growth of abnormal cells on the surface of the cervix. Numbers from 1 to 3 may be used to describe how much of the cervix contains abnormal cells.

Cervical nodes Lymph nodes in the neck.

Cervical spine Seven vertebrae - C1 - C7. Articulate with the occiput superiorly and the T1 vertebra inferiorly. Commonly known as the neck.

Cervix The lower end portion of the uterus connecting the isthmus and the ostium uteri with the vaginal canal.

Cetuximab A monoclonal antibody specific for the epidermal growth factor receptor (EGFR), a tyrosine kinase that triggers cell division. Cetuximab binds to and inhibits EGFRs, which are overexpressed on the cell surfaces of many types of tumors. This agent blocks the tumor growth, invasion, and metastasis associated with the overexpression of cell-surface EGFRs.

Cevimeline A substance that increases production of saliva and tears. It is being studied as a treatment for dry mouth caused by radiation therapy to the head and neck. It belongs to the family of drugs called cholinergic enhancers.

CFU (Colony forming unit) A measure of the number of bacteria present in the environment or on the surfaces of an aseptic processing room, measured as part of qualification and ongoing monitoring. Also applied to the testing of purified water samples.

Chamberlain procedure A procedure in which a tube is inserted into the chest to view the tissues and organs in the area between the lungs and between the breastbone and heart. The tube is inserted through an incision next to the breastbone. This procedure is usually used to get a tissue sample from the lymph nodes on the left side of the chest. Also called anterior mediastinotomy.

Chance Random variation, i.e., the happening of events without an apparent cause.

Chancre A hard, syphilitic primary ulcer, the first sign of syphilis, appearing approx. 2 to 3 weeks after infection. The ulcer begins as a painless lesion or papule that ulcerates. Occurs generally singly, but sometimes may be multiple.

Chancroid A sexually transmitted disease (STD) caused by a bacterium called Hemophilus ducreyi. Often causes swollen lymph nodes and painful sores on the penis, vagina, or anus. The lesions appear after an incubation period of 3 to 5 days and may facilitate HIV transmission.

Channeling Cleavage, cracking, and furrowing of a resin bed due to resin age, a change in one of the feed solutions, or faulty operational procedures. The solution being treated follows the path of least resistance, runs through these furrows, and fails to contact active resin material in other parts of the bed.

Chaplain A member of the clergy in charge of a chapel or who works with the military or with an institution, such as a hospital.

Characteristics Traits or attributes: those qualities that define a describe a thing or person

Characterization Precisely deciphering and describing all the characteristics of a drug substance that affect its efficacy and its purity. Or the chemical, physical, and sometimes biological properties that are attributes of a specific drug substance.

Charcot foot A foot complication associated with diabetic neuropathy that results in almost painless destruction of joints and soft tissue. Also called "Charcot's joint" and "neuropathic arthropathy."

Chart Log of dental or medical records.

Chart stimulated recall oral examination (CSR) A measurement tool for assessing clinical decision making and the application of medical knowledge using actual patients and a standardized oral examination. A trained and experienced physician/examiner questions the examinee about the provided care, probing for the reasons behind the work-up diagnoses, interpretation of clinical findings and treatment plans. The examiners rate the examinee using an established protocol and scoring procedure. In an efficiently designed CSR, each patient case (test item) takes 5 to 10 minutes. A typical CSR exam involves one or two physicians as examiners per separate 30 to 60-minute sessions. The examinee's performance is measured by combining scores from all the cases tested for a pass/fail decision overall, or by scoring for each session. Exam score reliabilities have been reported between 0.65 and 0.88. In assessing recall ability or medical knowledge, multiple-choice questions (MCQ) are more effective than CSR exams.

Checklist evaluation A method that is useful for assessing any competency or competency component that can be broken down into specific behaviours or actions. To obtain consistent scores and satisfactory reliability of observed performance using checklists, trained evaluators are required. To ensure the validity of content and scoring rules, checklist development requires consensus by several experts on the essential behaviours, actions and criteria for evaluating performance. The usefulness of checklists is well documented for evaluation of patient care skills (history and physical examination) and interpersonal and communication skills. Checklists have also been used for self-assessment of practice-based learning skills, and in addition are very useful in providing feedback on performance.

Checksum A record of the number of bits transmitted and included with the transmission so that the receiving program can check to see whether the same number of bits arrived. If the counts match, it is assumed that the complete transmission was received.

Cheiroscope An instrument used in orthoptics/vision therapy to train binocular skills and accommodation skills. The Keystone Correct-Eye Scope is an example of a Cheiroscope.

Chelate A particular type of chemical reaction with a metal (such as copper). Many drugs used to treat Wilson's Disease "chelate" copper into a form which patients' bodies can eliminate.

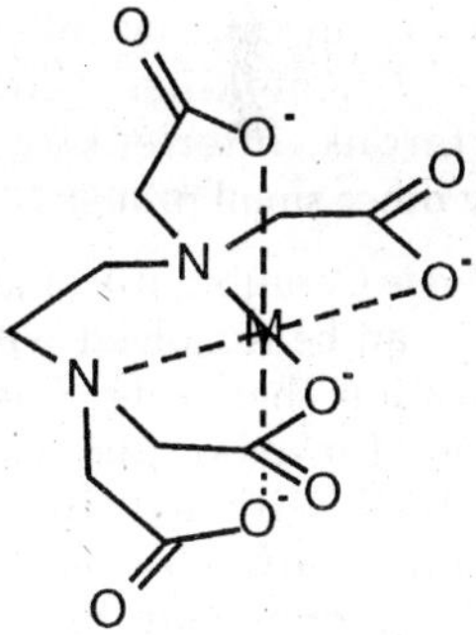

Figure Chelate

Chelating agents Organic compounds that can withdraw ions from solution, forming insoluble complexes.

Chemoautotrophs Facultative autotrophs that obtain their energy from the oxidation of inorganic compounds.

Chemoembolization A procedure in which the blood supply to the tumor is blocked surgically or mechanically and anticancer drugs are administered directly into the tumor. This permits a higher concentration of drug to be in contact with the tumor for a longer period of time.

Chemoimmunotherapy Chemotherapy combined with immunotherapy. Chemotherapy uses different drugs to kill or slow the growth of cancer cells; immunotherapy uses treatments to stimulate or restore the ability of the immune system to fight cancer.

Chemokines Proteins that serve as chemical messengers to control the activities of the immune system. Chemokines are involved in a wide variety of processes, including the control of infectious diseases, cancers, and inflammation. Chemokines include interferons, interleukins, and many other small proteins.

Chemolysis Certain types of kidney stones can be dissolved with the application chemicals. Uric acid stones, for example, can be dissolved with a solution of sodium bicarbonate in saline. Cystine stones may be treated successfully with a combination of acetylcysteine and sodium bicarbonate in saline. Struvite and carbon apatite stones can be treated with an acidic solution of hemiacidrin. The procedure involves infusing the chemical solution into the affected area by means of a ureteral catheter in a series of treatments over time until the stone is dissolved. The patient's urine must be cultured regularly throughout the course of treatment to guard against urinary infection and prevent the buildup of excessive chemical levels, particularly magnesium, which can cause other health problems.

Chemoprevention studies In cancer prevention clinical trials, studies test whether taking certain medicines, vitamins, minerals, or food supplements can prevent cancer. Also called agent studies.

Chemoprophylaxis Prevention of disease by chemical means.

Chemoprotective A quality of some drugs used in cancer treatment. Chemoprotective agents protect healthy tissue from the toxic effects of anticancer drugs.

Chemoradiation Treatment that combines chemotherapy with radiation therapy. Also called chemoradiotherapy.

Chemoradiotherapy Treatment that combines chemotherapy with radiation therapy. Also called chemoradiation.

Chemosensitivity assay A laboratory test that measures the number of tumor cells that are killed by a cancer drug. The test is done after the tumor cells are removed from the body. A chemosensitivity assay may help in choosing the best drug or drugs for the cancer being treated.

Chemosensitivity The susceptibility of tumor cells to the cell-killing effects of anticancer drugs.

Chemosensitizer A drug that makes tumor cells more sensitive to the effects of chemotherapy.

Chemosis A severe swelling of the bulbar conjunctiva.

Chemostat A growth chamber that keeps a bacterial culture at a specific volume and rate of growth by limiting nutrient medium and removing spent culture.

Chemotaxis Movement of a cell or organism to the stimulus of a gradient of chemical concentration.

Chemotherapeutic agent A drug used to treat cancer.

Chemotherapy Treatment using anticancer drugs, which kill or prevent the growth and division of cells. The drugs enter the bloodstream and travel through the body killing mostly cancer cells, but also some healthy cells.

Chest wall The muscles, bones, and joints that make up the area of the body between the neck and the abdomen.

Chest x-ray An x-ray of the structures inside the chest. An x-ray is a type of high-energy radiation that can go through the body and onto film, making pictures of areas inside the chest, which can be used to diagnose disease.

Chiasma An anatomy term for an X-shaped crossing (for example, of nerves or tendons).

Child-life worker A professional who is responsible for making a child's hospital and treatment experience less scary.

Chimera An organism that contains cells or tissues with a different genotype. These can be mutated cells of the host organism or cells from a different organism or species.

Chimeraplasty An experimental targeted repair process in which a desirable sequence of DNA is combined with RNA to form a chimeraplast. These molecules bind selectively to the target DNA. Once bound, the chimeraplast activates a naturally occurring gene-correcting mechanism. Does not use viral or other conventional gene-delivery vectors.

Chimeric An organism, especially a plant, containing tissues from at least two genetically distinct parents. Type of antibody, partially human and partially mouse.

Chinese herbal treatment A form of traditional Chinese medicine that is helpful for some people with eczema.

Chinese rhubarb Rheum palmatum or Rheum officinale. The root of this plant has been used in some cultures to treat certain medical problems. It may have anti-inflammatory and anticancer effects. Also called rhubarb, dahuang, Indian rhubarb, and Turkish rhubarb.

Chitin A type of polysaccharide (sugar molecule) that is made by some plants and animals. The hard outer shell of shrimp, lobsters, and many insects is made of chitin.

Chlamydia A sexually transmitted disease (STD) caused by a bacterium called Chlamydia trachomatis. The bacteria infect the genital tract and if left untreated can cause damage to the female and male reproductive systems, resulting in infertility.

Chlorambucil An orally-active antineoplastic aromatic nitrogen mustard. Chlorambucil alkylates and cross-links DNA during all phases of the cell cycle, resulting in disruption of DNA function, cell cycle arrest, and apoptosis.

Chloramine A chlorine compound formed by reaction with organic amines or ammonia.

Chlorinated vinyls Thermoplastic chlorinated vinyls include PVC, CPVC, and VDC. PVC and CPVC are very similar materials, the primary difference being the addition of more chlorine to the PVC molecule to synthesize CPVC. This results in a higher glass transition temperature that equates to a higher use temperature for CPVC. The polymerization with chlorine also makes these materials inherently flame resistant. In addition to being resistant to higher temperatures, CPVC is more resistant to process chemicals.

Chlorination Adding chlorine or chlorine compounds to water for disinfection.

Chlorine An element used to kill microorganisms in water. At room temperature and atmospheric pressure a greenish yellow gas.

Chlorine demand Amount of chlorine used up by reacting with oxidizable substances in water before chlorine residual can be measured.

Chlorine residual Portion of free or combined chlorine that remains active after specified contact period.

Chloroma A malignant, green-colored tumor of myeloid cells (a type of immature white blood cell). This tumor is usually associated with myelogenous leukemia. Also called granulocytic sarcoma.

Chloroplast chromosome Circular DNA found in the photosynthesizing organelle (chloroplast) of plants instead of the cell nucleus where most genetic material is located.

Chloroplasts Relatively large, chlorophyll containing, green organelles responsible for photosynthesis in photosynthetic eukaryotes, such as algae and plant cells. Every chloroplast contains an outer membrane and a large number of inner membranes called thylakoids.

Chloroquinoxaline sulfonamide (CQS) A substance that is being studied in the treatment of cancer. It belongs to the family of drugs called halogenated sulfanilamides.

Chlorpropamide A pill taken to lower the level of glucose (sugar) in the blood. Only some people with noninsulin-dependent diabetes take these pills.

CHO (Chinese hamster ovary) cells In cell culture, the cells of a female hamster's reproductive organs, which historically have proven to be excellent expression systems in analytical studies and for producing pharmaceutical proteins.

Chol Bile, e.g. cholelith - gallstone; bile stone.

Cholangiocarcinoma A rare type of cancer that develops in cells that line the bile ducts in the liver. Cancer that forms where the right and left ducts meet is called Klatskin tumor.

Cholangiography X-rays of the bile ducts.

Cholangiosarcoma A tumor of the connective tissues of the bile ducts.

Cholecalciferol A nutrient that helps the body use calcium and phosphorus and make strong bones and teeth. It is found in fatty fish, eggs, and dairy products. The skin can also make cholecalciferol when exposed to sunshine. Not getting enough cholecalciferol can cause a bone disease called rickets. Cholecalciferol is being studied in the prevention and treatment of some types of cancer. Also called vitamin D.

Cholecystectomy An operation to remove the gallbladder.

Cholelith Solid material that forms in the gallbladder or common bile duct. Choleliths are made of cholesterol or other substances found in the gallbladder. They may occur as one large stone or as many small ones, and vary from the size of a golf ball to a grain of sand. Also called gallstone.

Cholestasis Any condition in which the release of bile from the liver is blocked. The blockage can occur in the liver (intrahepatic cholestasis) or in the bile ducts (extrahepatic cholestasis).

Cholesterol A fat-like substance found in blood, muscle, liver, brain, and other tissues in people and animals. The body makes and needs some cholesterol. Too much cholesterol, however, may cause fat to build up in the walls of the larger arteries and cause a disease called atherosclerosis. Butter and egg yolks are examples of foods that have a lot of cholesterol.

Cholesterol is composed of several components:

HDL-Cholesterol (high-density lipoprotein cholesterol): This component of cholesterol seems to have protective effects, and higher levels are considered to be good to have.

LDL-Cholesterol (low-density lipoprotein cholesterol) .

VLDL-Cholesterol (very low-density lipoprotein cholesterol) .

Cholesterol is a lipid.

Chondrocyte Cartilage cell. Chondrocytes make the structural components of cartilage.

Chondroitin sulfate The major glycosaminoglycan (a type of sugar molecule) in cartilage.

Chondromalacia patellae Common name given to softening of the articular cartilage on the undersurface of the patella. Commonly seen in adolescents and commonly associated with functional and biomechanical deficiencies of the patello-femoral joint.

Chondrosarcoma A malignant tumor of cartilage that usually occurs near the ends of the long bones.

ChoPat strap An infrapatellar strap, commonly used in the treatment of patellar tendinitis or chondromalacia patellae.

Chordoma A type of bone cancer that usually starts in the lower spinal cord.

Chorioadenoma destruens A type of cancer that grows into the muscular wall of the uterus. It is formed after conception (fertilization of an egg by a sperm). It may spread to other parts of the body, such as the vagina, vulva, and lung. Also called invasive hydatidiform mole.

Chorioallantoic membrane The membrane in hen's eggs that helps chicken embryos get enough oxygen and calcium for development. The calcium comes from the egg shell.

Choriocarcinoma A rare cancer in women of childbearing age in which cancer cells grow in the tissues that are formed in the uterus after conception. Also called gestational trophoblastic disease, gestational trophoblastic neoplasia, gestational trophoblastic tumor, or molar pregnancy.

Choroid plexus A vascularized epithelium projecting into the ventricles of the brain that produces the cerebrospinal fluid.

Choroid plexus tumor A rare type of cancer that occurs in the ventricles of the brain. It usually occurs in children younger than 2 years.

Choroid The vascular membrane between the sclera and the retina of the eye, that extends from the ora serrata to the optic nerve.

CHPP (Continuous hyperthermic peritoneal perfusion) A procedure that bathes the abdominal cavity in fluid that contains anticancer drugs. This fluid is warmer than body temperature. This procedure appears to kill cancer cells without harming normal cells.

Chromatids Copies of a chromosome produced by replication.

Chromatin The complex of DNA and protein in the nucleus of the interphase cell, originally recognized by its reaction with stains specific for DNA.

Chromatography Procedure by which solutes (e.g., proteins and other chemical products) are selectively separated by a dynamic differential migration process in a system consisting of two or more phases, one of which moves continuously in a given direction and in which the individual substances exhibit different mobilities by reason of differences in adsorption, partition, solubility, vapor pressure, molecular size, or ionic charge density. The individual substances thus obtained can be identified or determined by analytical methods. There are several types of chromatography in use with different operating principles:

1. Adsorption - separates products by their different affinities for the surface of a solid medium, either an inorganic carrier such as silica gel, alumina, or hydroxyapatite, or an organic polymer.

2. Ion Exchange - uses ion exchange resin to which ionized functional groups have been

attached. At an appropriate pH, target proteins acquire a net surface charge that allows them to selectively bind to an ion exchange resin. Other impurities are eluted through the column.

3. Gel Filtration - employs a neutral cross-linked carrier with a defined pore size for molecular fractionation. Molecules larger than the largest pores cannot enter the matrix and pass directly through the column; smaller molecules enter the carrier and are retarded. Gel filtration thus separates on the basis of molecular size, eluting larger molecules first, followed by progressively smaller species.

4. Affinity - relies on the propensity of each biomolecule to have an affinity for another highly specific biomolecule, such as an antibody-antigen relationship. Once bound together, the drug molecules can be detached by altering various chemical attributes in the column.

5. Hydrophobic - separates by molecule polarity and reverse interaction with water.

6. High Pressure Liquid Chromatography (HPLC).

Chromium enrichment layer thickness In stainless steel, the same as its maximum depth of enrichment, unless a surface iron layer is present in which case the chromium enrichment layer is calculated as the maximum depth of enrichment minus the thickness of the surface iron oxide layer.

Chromomere One of the serially aligned beads or granules of a eukaryotic chromosome, resulting from local coiling of a continuous DNA thread.

Chromosomal deletion The loss of part of a chromosome's DNA.

Chromosomal inversion Chromosome segments that have been turned 180 degrees. The gene sequence for the segment is reversed with respect to the rest of the chromosome.

Chromosome painting Attachment of certain fluorescent dyes to targeted parts of the chromosome. Used as a diagnositic for particular diseases, e.g. types of leukemia.

Chromosome region p A designation for the short arm of a chromosome.

Chromosome The self-replicating genetic structure of cells containing the cellular DNA that bears in its nucleotide sequence the linear array of genes. In prokaryotes, chromosomal DNA is circular, and the entire genome is carried on one chromosome. Eukaryotic genomes consist of a number of chromosomes whose DNA is associated with different kinds of proteins.

Chronic A disease or condition that persists or progresses over a long period of time.

Chronic care Long term care of individuals with long standing, persistent diseases or conditions. It includes care specific to the problem as well as other measures to encourage self-care, to promote health, and to prevent loss of function.

Chronic eosinophilic leukemia A disease in which too many eosinophils (a type of white blood cell) are found in the bone marrow, blood, and other tissues. Chronic eosinophilic leukemia may stay the same for many years, or it may progress quickly to acute leukemia.

Chronic granulocytic leukemia A slowly progressing disease in which too many white blood cells (not lymphocytes) are made in the bone marrow. Also called chronic myelogenous leukemia or chronic myeloid leukemia.

Chronic hepatitis Prolonged inflammation and death of liver cells persisting for six months or more caused by hepatitis viruses, autoimmune factors, and on occasion, unknown conditions.

Chronic idiopathic demyelinating polyneuropathy (CIPD) Chronic, spontaneous loss or destruction of myelin, a white fatty material that protects and insulates nerve cells. People with CIPD show progressive, usually symmetrical weakness in the arms and legs. CIPD can be one of the symptoms of lactic acidosis or progressive multifocal leukoencephalopathy.

Chronic idiopathic myelofibrosis A progressive, chronic disease in which the bone marrow is replaced by fibrous tissue and blood is made in organs such as the liver and the spleen, instead of in the bone marrow. This disease is marked by an enlarged spleen and progressive anemia. Also called agnogenic myeloid metaplasia, primary myelofibrosis, myelosclerosis with myeloid metaplasia, and idiopathic myelofibrosis.

Chronic leukemia A slowly progressing cancer that starts in blood-forming tissues such as the bone marrow, and causes large numbers of white blood cells to be produced and enter the blood stream.

Chronic lymphoblastic leukemia A slowly progressing disease in which too many immature white blood cells (called lymphoblasts) are found in the body.

Chronic lymphocytic leukemia (CLL) A common type of indolent (slowly progressing) cancer in which too many lymphocytes (white blood cells) are found in the peripheral blood and bone marrow. Most patients with CLL are older than 50 years and have no symptoms at the time of their diagnosis.

Chronic myeloid leukemia (CML) A slowly progressing disease in which too many white blood cells (not lymphocytes) are made in the bone marrow. Also called chronic myelogenous leukemia or chronic granulocytic leukemia.

Chronic myelomonocytic leukemia (CMML) A slowly progressing type of myelodysplastic/myeloproliferative disease in which too many myelomonocytes (a type of white blood cell) are in the bone marrow, crowding out other normal blood cells, such as other white blood cells, red blood cells, and platelets.

Chronic neutrophilic leukemia A disease in which too many neutrophils (a type of white blood cell) are found in the blood. The extra neutrophils may cause the spleen and liver to become enlarged. Chronic neutrophilic leukemia may stay the same for many years or it may progress quickly to acute leukemia.

Chronic pain Pain that can range from mild to severe, and persists or progresses over a long period of time.

Chronic phase Refers to the early stages of chronic myelogenous leukemia or chronic lymphocytic leukemia. The number of mature and immature abnormal white blood cells in the bone marrow and blood is higher than normal, but lower than in the accelerated or blast phase.

Chronic phase chronic myelogenous leukemia A phase of chronic myelogenous leukemia in which 5% or fewer of the cells in the blood and bone marrow are blast cells (immature blood cells). This phase may last from several months to several years, and there may be no symptoms of leukemia.

Cidofovir A drug used in the treatment of infections caused by viruses.

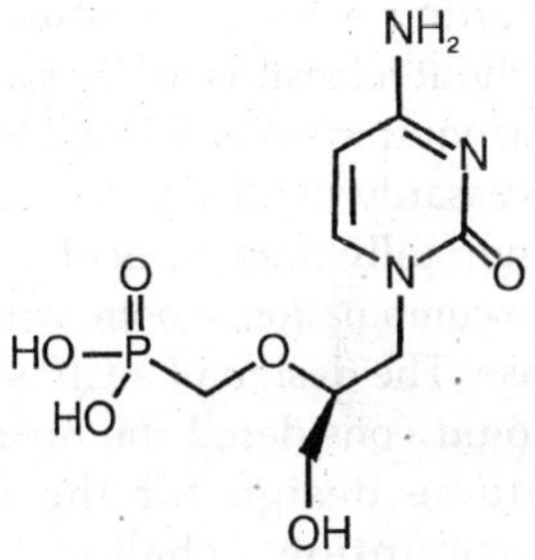

Figure Cidofovir

Cilengitide A cyclic Arg-Gly-Asp peptide with potential antineoplastic activity. Cilengitide binds to and inhibits the activities of the alpha (v) beta (3) and alpha (v) beta (5) integrins, thereby inhibiting endothelial cell-cell interactions, endothelial cell-matrix interactions, and angiogenesis.

Cilia The eyelashes.

Ciliary body A structure directly behind the iris of the eye and contains the ciliary muscle.

Ciliary muscle A band of muscle and fibers that are attached to the lens that controls the shape of the lens and allows the lens to accommodate (change focus).

Cimetidine A drug usually used to treat stomach ulcers and heartburn. It is also commonly used in a regimen to prevent allergic reactions.

Cingulum An association bundle of the cerebrum located within the cingulate gyrus which almost encircles the corpus callosum having connections along its course with adjacent frontal, parietal and temporal lobe cortex.

CIP (Clean in place) Internally cleaning a piece of equipment without relocation or disassembly. The equipment is cleaned but not necessarily sterilized. The cleaning is normally done by acid, caustic, or a combination of both, with WFI rinse. The design of a CIP system should considered the operating volume design for the water consumption, chemical and biowaste effluent, and energy required to clean a given circuit or piece of equipment.

Ciprofloxacin A synthetic broad spectrum fluoroquinolone antibiotic. Ciprofloxacin binds to and inhibits bacterial DNA gyrase, an enzyme essential for DNA replication. This agent is more active against Gram-negative bacteria than Gram-positive bacteria.

Figure Ciprofloxacin

Circle of willis The polygonal (hexagon/ pentagon) anastomosis that is made up of the internal carotid, anterior and posterior cerebral arteries, the anterior communicating artery, and the posterior communicating arteries - all in the region of the suprasellar cistern.

Circulation The flow of blood through the heart and blood vessels of the body.

Circulatory system The system that contains the heart and the blood vessels and moves blood throughout the body. This system helps tissues get enough oxygen and nutrients, and it helps them get rid of waste products. The lymph system, which connects with the blood system, is often considered part of the circulatory system.

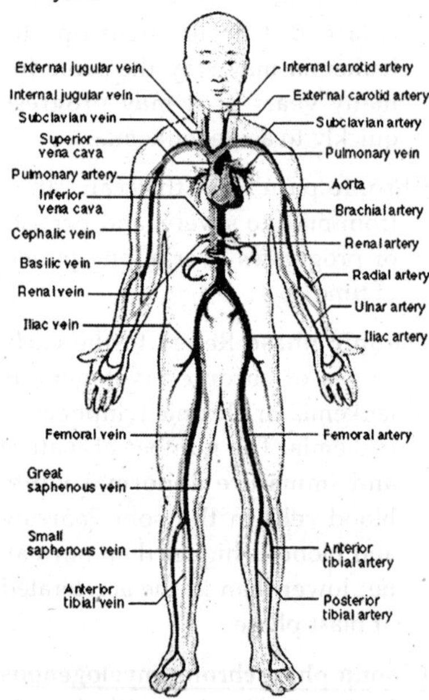

Figure Circulartory system

Circumduction Movement of a limb or extremity so that the distal end describes a circle while the proximal end remains fixed.

Circumflex artery Any of several paired curving arteries.

Cirrhosis A chronic problem makes it hard for the liver to remove toxins (poisonous substances) from the body. Alcohol, medications, and other substances may build up in the bloodstream and cause problems. Cirrhosis is a result of scarring and damage from other diseases, like biliary atresia and alcoholism.

Cisplatin An inorganic platinum agent (cis-diamminedichloroplatinum) with antineoplastic activity. Cisplatin forms highly reactive, charged, platinum complexes which bind to nucleophilic groups such as GC-rich sites in DNA, inducing intrastrand and interstrand DNA cross-links, as well as DNA-protein cross-links. These cross-links result in apoptosis and cell growth inhibition.

Cisterna chyli The dilated protion of the thoracic duct (a lymphatic channel) in the lumbar region that recieves fluid from the intestinal, lumbar, and descending intercostal lymph vessels.

Citric acid/potassium-sodium citrate A drug used in the treatment of metabolic acidosis (a disorder in which the blood is too acidic).

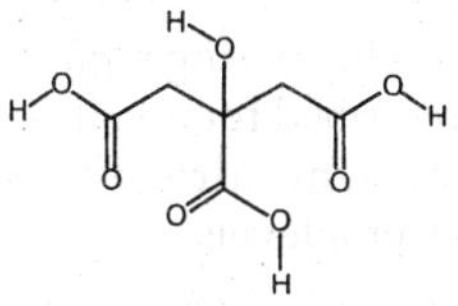

Figure Citric acid

Civatte or colloid body Eosinophilic, round homogeneous structures seen in the epidermis or upper dermis. They form through degeneration of epidermal cells and are most commonly seen in lichenoid tissue reactions.

C-kit receptor A protein on the surface of some cells that binds to stem cell factor (a substance that causes certain types of cells to grow). Altered forms of this receptor may be associated with some types of cancer.

Clade A group of organisms that are genetically similar and descended from a single parent organism. With HIV, the term "clade" refers to a group of specific HIV-1 strains within an HIV subtype. For example, HIV-1 subtype M contains clades A through H, J, and K. Clades B and C account for the majority of HIV infections around the world.

Cladribine A purine nucleoside antimetabolite analogue. Cladribine triphosphate, a phosphorylated metabolite of cladribine, incorporates into DNA, resulting in single strand breaks in DNA, depletion of nicotinamide adenine dinucleotide (NAD) and adenosine triphosphate (ATP), and apoptosis. Because this agent is resistant to adenosine deaminase, an enzyme that inactivates some antineoplastic agents, it is selectively toxic to lymphocytes and monocytes which exhibit little deoxynucleotide deaminase activity.

Clarithromycin A semisynthetic 14-membered ring macrolide antibiotic. Clarithromycin binds to the 50S ribosomal subunit and inhibits RNA-dependent protein synthesis in susceptible organisms. Clarithromycin has been shown to eradicate gastric MALT (mucosa-associated lymphoid tissue) lymphomas, presumably due to the eradication of tumorigenic Helicobacter pylori infection. This agent also acts as a biological response modulator, possibly inhibiting angiogenesis and tumor growth through alterations in growth factor expression.

Clarke's test Compression of the patella with resisted knee extension. Commonly used as a test of chondromalacia patellae but has not been shown to be reliable.

Clasp Device that retains a removable partial denture to stationary teeth.

Class 1,000 Classification of an area where particle count should not exceed 1,000 particles (35,300 particles per cubic meter) 0.5μm or larger, per cubic foot of air. Supplied by HEPA filtered air. Class 1,000 is not a pharmaceutical GMP expectation.

Class 10,000 Classification of an area where particle count should not exceed 10,000 particles (353,000 particles per cubic meter) 0.5μm or larger, per cubic foot of air. Minimum of 20 air changes per hour, HEPA filtered air.

Class 100 Classification of an aseptic processing area where particle count should not exceed 100 particles (3,530 particles per cubic meter) 0.5μm or larger, per cubic foot of air, and no more than 0.1 CFU (Colony Forming Units) per cubic foot. Target uniform air velocity is 90 fpm plus or minus 20%, HEPA filtered air.

Class 30% ashrae area This area would have 30% efficient filtration.

Class 65% ashrae area This area would have 65% efficient filtration.

Class 95% ashrae area These areas would have 95% efficient supply air filtration, unlike classified areas, which would have HEPA filtration.

Class I, II and III MHC molecules Proteins encoded by genes in the major histocompatibility complex. Class I molecules are designated HLA-A, B, or C. Class II molecules are designated DP, DQ or DR.

Class sparing regimen An anti-HIV drug regimen that purposefully does not include one or more classes of anti-HIV drugs. A class-sparing regimen may be prescribed to "save" certain classes of drugs for later use or to avoid side effects specific to a class. For example, a PI-sparing regimen would not include any PIs. Because some PIs may cause an increase in cholesterol in the blood, a PI-sparing regimen might be prescribed for an HIV-infected person who already has high cholesterol levels.

Classical pathway The mechanism of complement activation initiated by antigen-antibody aggregates and proceeding by way of C1, C4 and C2.

Classical pharmaceuticals Small-molecule, nonbiotech drugs produced by chemical synthesis.

Classified space A space in which the number of airborne particles is limited. This is accomplished by the strict use of HVAC systems. Areas are classified as Class 10, Class 100, Class 1,000, Class 10,000, and Class 100,000. In pharmaceutical production, only classes 100, 10,000, and 100,000 are used.

Claus model A computer program that uses statistics to predict a person's risk for developing breast cancer based on family history.

Claustrum A thin vertical sheet of gray matter that underlies the cortex of the insula. It is located between the extreme capsule laterally and the external capsule medially. Considered a component of the basal ganglia but with no functional relationship.

Clava The protuberance on the dorsal surface of the medulla overlying the gracile nucleus. Also known as the Gracile tubercle.

Clavicle The "collar bone". A curved bone which articulates medially with the sternum and laterally with the scapula, forming the anterior portion of the shoulder girdle.

Clean air device Stand-alone equipment for treating and distributing clean air to achieve defined environmental conditions.

Clean air projector Fan and filter unit used to locally clean room air and deliver it to a desired location. Often called a fan/filter unit.

Clean area An area where particulate and microbial levels are specified (e.g., Filling Room - Class 10,000 "In Operation").

Clean space A room or volume controlled to meet a certain airborne particulate limit (Class or Grade). In pharmaceutical facilities, clean spaces are usually classified and controlled only for aseptic processing facilities, but may also be defined for certain biotech processes. Final non-sterile bulk facilities, oral product, most topical product manufacturing facilities, and warehouses are normally not classified as clean spaces.

Clean steam Steam free from boiler additives that may be purified, filtered, or separated. When condensed, clean steam meets the specification for WFI. Usually utilized to sterilize process equipment.

Clean zone A dedicated space in which the concentration of airborne particles is controlled, and which is constructed and used in a manner to minimize the introduction, generation, and retention of particles inside the zone and in which other relevant parameters, e.g. temperature, humidity, and pressure, are controlled as necessary.

Cleaning Removal of plaque and calculus (tarter) from teeth, generally above the gum line.

Cleanroom A specially constructed space environmentally controlled with respect to airborne particles (size and count), temperature, humidity, air pressure, airflow patterns, air motion, and lighting. ISO 14644-1 defines it as "a room in which the concentration of airborne particles is controlled, and which is constructed and used in a manner to minimize the introduction, generation, and retention of particles inside the room, and in which other relevant parameters, e.g. temperature, humidity, and pressure, are controlled as necessary."

Cleanroom classification The maximum number of particles greater than or equal to 0.5µm in diameter that may be present in a cubic foot of room air.

Clear cell A type of cell that looks clear inside when viewed under a microscope.

Clear Cell Adenocarcinoma A rare type of tumor, usually of the female genital tract, in which the inside of the cells look clear when viewed under a microscope. Also called clear cell carcinoma and mesonephroma.

Clear cell sarcoma of the kidney A rare type of kidney cancer. Clear cell sarcoma can spread from the kidney to other organs, most commonly the bone, but also including the lungs, brain, and soft tissues of the body.

Cleavage The splitting up of a complex molecule into two or more simpler molecules. The series of cell divisions occurring in the ovum immediately following its fertilization.

Cleaved Having to do with the appearance of cells when viewed under a microscope. The nucleus of cleaved cells appears divided or segmented.

Clergy Ordained individuals who perform spiritual and/or religious functions.

Clerkships A rotation around the clinical settings of the medical school. Some clerkships are obligatory (e.g., internal medicine, pediatrics, surgery), while others are elective or selective.

Clindamycin An antibiotic sometimes used in the treatment of PCP and toxoplasmosis. Clindamycin usage has been associated with severe diarrhea caused by the bacteria c. dificile.

Clinic coordinator The study nurse or other staff person who is primary administrator and contact person for a research effort.

Clinical anophthalmos Birth defect: Complete absence of an optic vesicle (eye).

Clinical competence The mastery of relevant knowledge and the acquisition of a range of relevant skills at a satisfactory level including interpersonal, clinical and technical components at a certain point of education, such as at graduation. In the case of clinical training, which is primarily based on an apprenticeship model, teachers define what the student is expected to do and then test their ability to do it. However, in actuality, most clinical actions are concerned with problems for which there are no clear answers and no single solution. In such situations, an experienced doctor searches his or her mind and sifts through a wide range of options and in some cases the solution will be something he or she has never arrived at before. Therefore, competence itself is only of value as a prerequisite for performance in a real clinical setting and does not always correlate highly with performance in practice.

Clinical data repository That component of a computer-based patient record (CPR) which accepts, files, and stores clinical data over time from a variety of supplemental treatment and intervention systems for such purposes as practice guidelines, outcomes management, and clinical research. May also be called a data warehouse.

Clinical decision support The capability of a data system to provide key data to physicians and other clinicians in response to "flags" or triggers which are functions of embedded, provider-created rules. A system that would alert case managers that a client's eligibility for a certain service is about to be exhausted would be one example of this type of capacity. Also a key functional requirement to support clinical or critical pathways.

Clinical endpoint A measurement used in clinical trials to evaluate the effect of the treatment being tested. Examples of clinical endpoints for HIV disease include death, serious drug toxicity, or development of an AIDS-defining illness. Because these endpoints may be difficult to measure without long-term follow-up, surrogate (substitute) short-term endpoints, such as a change in viral load or CD4 count, may also be used as clinical endpoints.

Clinical event committee A group of physicians used to review endpoints in trials, and to evaluate their certainty.

Clinical failure The occurrence or recurrence of HIV-related infections or a decline in physical health despite taking an HIV treatment regimen for a minimum of three months. Clinical failure may occur as a result of virologic or immunologic failure.

Clinical or critical pathways A "map" of preferred treatment/ intervention activities. Outlines the types of information needed to make decisions, the timelines for applying that information, and what action needs to be taken by whom. Provides a way to monitor care "in real time." These pathways are developed by clinicians for specific diseases or events. Proactive providers are working now to develop these pathways for the majority of their interventions and developing the software capacity to distribute and store this information.

Clinical oral examination (COE) Unstructured clinical and oral examination which is the traditional form of clinical examination and continues to be popular in many parts of the world. With face-to-face contact, examiners explore both the breadth and depth of a student's understanding in real-life clinical situations. Aspects of competence which can be tested include the ability to respond to new information, a variety of interpersonal skills, and those aspects of competence that cannot be easily measured by more objective methods, such as an OSCE. Case variability can be reduced by recruiting a small group of patients with the same condition and similar symptoms or by the use of simulated patients. The use of videotapes of students undertaking a long-case examination with subsequent scoring of the performance by the examiner, who then discusses the results with the examinee, enhances the value of this form of examination. Proper briefing and training of examiners and a very structured approach to scoring contribute to the quality of this exam.

Clinical Pertaining to or founded on actual observation and treatment of patients, as distinguished from theoretical or basic science.

Clinical practice guidelines Recommendations by panels of expert health care practitioners designed to assist clinicians and patients in making decisions about appropriate health care for specific diseases and conditions.

Clinical resistance The failure of a cancer to shrink after treatment.

Clinical science review committee An internal committee at the division of AIDS in charge of prioritizing research, approving trial designs, coordinating intra- and extramural efforts, and clearing specific protocols for implementation.

Clinical series A case series in which the patients receive treatment in a clinic or other medical facility.

Clinical study A type of research study that tests how well new medical approaches work in people. These studies test new methods of screening, prevention, diagnosis, or treatment of a disease. Also called a clinical trial.

Clinical trial A research study that uses human volunteers to answer specific health questions. Carefully conducted clinical trials are regarded as the fastest and safest way to find effective treatments for diseases and conditions, as well as other ways to improve health. Interventional trials use controlled conditions to determine whether experimental treatments or new ways of using known treatments are safe and effective. Observational trials gather information about health issues from groups of people in their natural settings.

Clivus A triangular bone, that slopes upward from the foramen magnum to the dorsum sellae, in the posterior cranial fossa. (clivus = "wedge" or "slide").

Clodronate A drug used in the treatment of hypercalcemia (abnormally high levels of calcium in the blood) and cancer that has spread to the bone (bone metastases). It may decrease pain, the risk of fractures, and the development of new bone metastases.

Clofarabine A substance that is being studied in the treatment of cancer. It belongs to the family of drugs called nucleoside analogs.

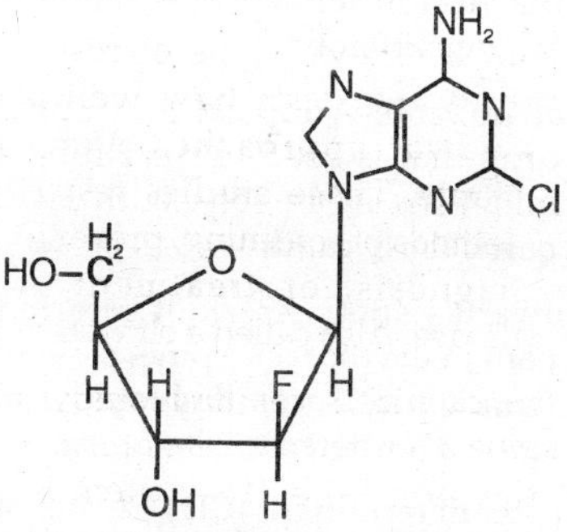

Figure Clofarabine

Clofazimine An anti-leprosy drug that is used as a component in combination therapy of Mycobacterium avium complex.

Clonal deletion The loss of lymphocytes of a particular specificity due to contact with either "self" or artificially introduced antigen.

Clonal selection theory The prevalent concept that specificity and diversity of an immune response are the result of selection by antigen of specifically reactive clones from a large repertoire of preformed lymphocytes, each with individual specificities.

Clone A group of individuals produced from one individual through asexual processes that do not involve the interchange or combination of genetic material. As a result, members of a clone have identical genetic compositions. Protozoa and bacteria, for example, frequently reproduce asexually by a process called binary fission. In binary fission, a single-celled organism undergoes cell division and the result is two cells with identical genetic composition. Next, these two identical cells undergo division and the result is four cells with identical genetic composition. These identical offspring are all members of a clone.

Cloning Using specialized DNA technology to produce multiple, exact copies of a single gene or other segment of DNA to obtain enough material for further study. This process is used by researchers in the Human Genome Project, and is referred to as cloning DNA. The resulting cloned (copied) collections of DNA molecules are called clone libraries. A second type of cloning exploits the natural process of cell division to make many copies of an entire cell. The genetic makeup of these cloned cells, called a cell line, is identical to the original cell. A third type of cloning produces complete, genetically identical animals such as the famous Scottish sheep, Dolly.

Cloning vector DNA molecule originating from a virus, a plasmid, or the cell of a higher organism into which another DNA fragment of appropriate size can be integrated without loss of the vector's capacity for self-replication; vectors introduce foreign DNA into host cells, where the DNA can be reproduced in large quantities. Examples are plasmids, cosmids, and yeast artificial chromosomes; vectors are often recombinant molecules containing DNA sequences from several sources.

Clopidogrel bisulfate A thienopyridine with antiplatelet activity. Clopidogrel bisulfate irreversibly alters the platelet receptor for adenosine diphosphate (ADP), thereby blocking the binding of ADP to its receptor, inhibiting ADP-mediated activation of the glycoprotein complex GPIIb/IIIa, and inhibiting fibrinogen binding to platelets and platelet adhesion and aggregation.

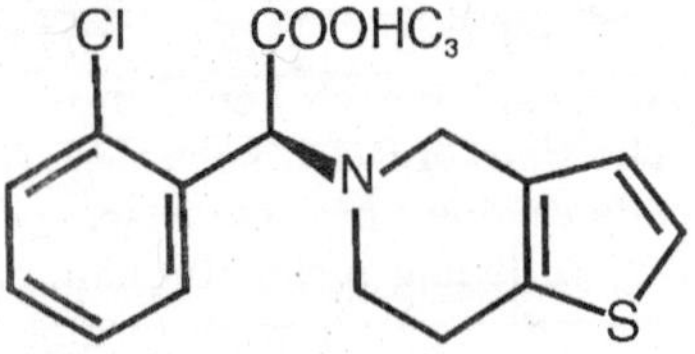

Clopidogrel ((+)- (S)-methyl 2-(2-chlorophenyl)-2- (6,7-dihydrothieno[3,2-c]pyridin-5 (4H)-yl)acetate)

Figure Clopidogrel bisulfate

Closed system System sterilized-in-place or sterilized while closed prior to use, is pressure or vacuum tight to some predefined leak rate, can be utilized for its intended purpose without breach to the integrity of the system, can be adapted for fluid transfers in or out while maintaining asepsis, and is connectable to other closed systems while maintaining integrity of all closed systems. (From PDA TR-28 for sterile product manufacture).

Clostridium difficile (Also known as C. diff or C. difficile.) Bacteria normally found in the large intestine, which can cause a serious intestinal infection and diarrhea in some people who are taking antibiotics.

Clotrimazole A topical antifungal drug that is used to treat fungal infections in persons with HIV, particularly candida.

Cloward's spots Areas of referred pain in the thoracic spine, close to the scapulae, secondary to cervical spine disorders.

Cluster determinant (CD) Cluster of antigens with which antibodies react that characterize a cell surface marker.

CMAX The maximum (peak) amount of drug measurable in the blood after a dose is administered.

CMC (Chemistry, manufacturing, and controls) The section on a BLA (Biologics License Application) or IND (Investigational New Drug) describing the composition, manufacture, and specifications of a drug product and its ingredients.

CMIN The lowest (trough) amount of drug measurable in the blood after a dose is administered.

CMV (Cytomegalovirus) A virus that may be carried in an inactive state for life by healthy individuals. It is a cause of severe pneumonia in people with a suppressed immune system, such as those undergoing bone marrow transplantation or those with leukemia or lymphoma.

CMV pp65 peptide A peptide derived from cytomegalovirus (CMV) internal matrix protein pp65. CMV pp65 peptide antigen is used in recombinant vaccinia virus as an HLA-A-restricted epitope to produce vaccines and specific CD8+ and CD4+ cell responses against CMV infection, a serious complication of allogeneic bone marrow transplantation (BMT). In BMT, CMV infection may be prevented by passive immunization with donor-derived CMV-pp65-specific T-cell clones if provided early post-BMT.

CNGRC peptide TNF alpha conjugate A cytokine-peptide conjugate composed of the cytokine tumor necrosis factor alpha (TNF-alpha) chemically linked to the peptide CNGRC. The peptide moiety CNGRC, a ligand for the membrane-bound metalloprotease CD13, binds to endothelial cells of the angiogenic vasculature that express CD13 (also known as aminopeptidase N); subsequently, the TNF-alpha moiety induces apoptosis in endothelial cells expressing CD13, thereby inhibiting tumor-associated angiogenesis.

Cnicin A substance found in certain plants, including blessed thistle. It has been used in some cultures to treat certain medical problems. It may have anti-inflammatory and anticancer effects. Cnicin belongs to a group of substances called sesquiterpene lactones.

Co infection Infection with more than one virus, bacterium, or other micro-organism at a given time. For example, an HIV-infected individual may be co-infected with hepatitis C virus (HCV) or tuberculosis (TB).

Co morbid condition Any disease or condition that occurs at the same time as another disease or condition. The second disease may worsen or be worsened by the initial disease. For example, tubuculosis (TB) may occur as a co-morbid conditon in an individual infected with HIV, and the HIV infection may worsen the TB.

Co receptor A protein on the surface of a cell that serves as a second binding site for a virus or other molecule. Although the CD4 protein is HIV's primary receptor, the virus must also bind either the CCR5 or CXCR4 co-receptor to get into a host cell.

Coactivated T cell A T cell that has been coated with monoclonal antibodies to enhance its ability to kill tumor cells.

Coagulation Adding insoluble compounds to water to neutralize the electrical charge on colloids, causing them to coalesce to form larger particles that can be removed by settling.

Coaguligand A VTA (Vascular Targeting Agent) that utilizes a human coagulation protein to induce tumor blood vessel clotting.

Cobalamin A vitamin that is needed o make red blood ce'ls and DNA (the genetic material in cells) and to keep nerve cells healthy. It is found in eggs, meat, poultry, shellfish, milk, and milk products. Cobalamin, along with folate, may be given to help reduce side effects in cancer patients being treated with drugs called antimetabolites. Also called vitamin B12.

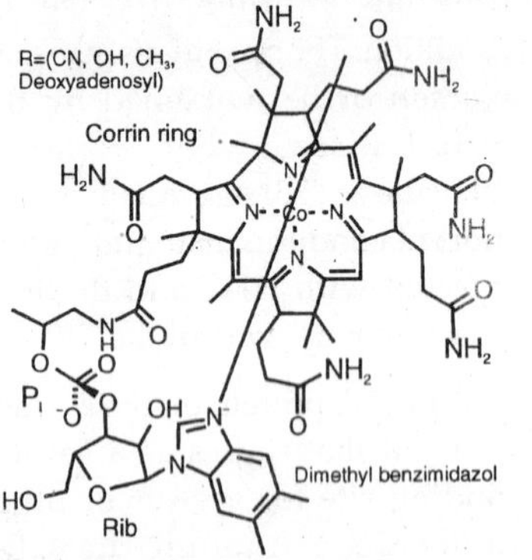

Chemical structure of cyanocobalamin

Figure Cobalamin

Cobalt 60 A radioactive form of the metal cobalt, which is used as a source of radiation to treat cancer.

Coccidioidomycosis Also called desert fever, San Joaquin Valley fever, or valley fever. An infectious disease caused by the inhalation of spores of Coccidioides immitis. The disease is especially common in hot, dry regions. It is an AIDS-defining condition in people with HIV.

Coccus A bacterium of round, spheroidal, or ovoid form, including micrococcus, staphylococcus, streptococcus, and pneumococcus.

Coccydynia Pain around the coccyx. Often caused by local trauma, but may also be a referred pain syndrome from the lumbar spine.

Coccyx The "tail bone" - a caudal extremity of the vertebral column formed by the fussion of four rudimentary vertebrae.

Cochlea A spiral bone tube of the inner ear, which lies against the lateral end of the internal acoustic meatus. The cochlea ("snail") contains the auditory sensory structure.

Cockayne syndrome A genetic condition characterized by short stature, premature aging, sensitivity to light, and possibly deafness and mental retardation.

Co-culture A mixture of two or more different kinds of cells that are grown together.

COD (Chemical oxygen demand) The amount of oxygen needed to completely oxidize all oxidizable organic and inorganic substances in water.

Coding sequence The region of a gene (DNA) that encodes the amino acid sequence of a protein.

Codominance Situation in which two different alleles for a genetic trait are both expressed.

Codon A sequence of 3 bases that specifies a particular amino acid; a building block of the cell's genetic material, DNA and RNA.

Coeliac disease An inflammatory disease of the intestine, possibly caused by a delayed allergic reaction to gluten, a protein found in wheat, rye, barley and oats.

Coenzyme A non-polypeptide molecule required for the action of certain enzymes; often contains a vitamin as a component.

Coenzyme Q10 A naturally occurring benzoquinone important in electron transport in mitochondrial membranes. Coenzyme-Q functions as an endogenous antioxidant; deficiencies of this enzyme have been observed in patients with many different types of cancer and limited studies have suggested that coenzyme-Q may induce tumor regression in patients with breast cancer. This agent may have immuno-stimulatory effects.

Cofactor A substance, microorganism or environmental factor that activates or enhances the action of another entity such as a disease-causing agent. Cofactors may influence the progression of a disease or the likelihood of becoming ill. Possible cofactors that have been suggested in AIDS are the herpes viruses, parasites, mycoplasma (a form of life intermediate between bacteria and viruses) and non-HIV retrovirii.

Cognitive impairment Loss of the ability to process, learn, and remember information. The progression of HIV disease may lead to cognitive impairment.

Cognitive Pertaining to thought, awareness, or the ability to rationally apprehend the world and abstract meaning.

Cohort A group of individuals who are alike in some way. For example, the people in a cohort of HIV-infected individuals are all infected with HIV.

Cohort study A research study that compares a particular outcome (such as lung cancer) in groups of individuals who are alike in many ways but differ by a certain characteristic (for example, female nurses who smoke compared with those who do not smoke).

Coisogenic or congenic Nearly identical strains of an organism; they vary at only a single locus.

COL-3 A substance that is being studied in the treatment of cancer. COL-3 may block tumor growth by preventing the growth of new blood vessels into tumors. It belongs to the families of drugs called matrix metalloproteinase inhibitors and angiogenesis inhibitors.

Cold nodule When radioactive material is used to examine the thyroid with a scanner, nodules that collect less radioactive material than the surrounding thyroid tissue are considered "cold." A nodule that is cold does not make thyroid hormone. Cold nodules may be benign or cancerous. Cold nodules are sometimes called hypofunctioning nodules.

Colectomy An operation to remove all or part of the colon. When only part of the colon is removed, it is called a partial colectomy. In an open colectomy, one long incision is made in the wall of the abdomen and doctors can see the colon directly. In a laparoscopic-assisted colectomy, several small incisions are made and a thin, lighted tube attached to a video camera is inserted through one opening to guide the surgery. Surgical instruments are inserted through the other openings to perform the surgery.

Colic A condition in an otherwise healthy baby characterized by excessive crying.

Coliform bacteria A group of bacteria found in mammalian intestines and soil, used as a measure of fecal pollution in water. They are easy to identify and count in the laboratory because of their ability to ferment lactose.

Colitis Inflammation of the colon (large intestine). This may lead to intestinal bleeding, ulcers, or perforations (holes) in the colon.

Collagen An albuminoid present in connective tissue, bone (ossein), and cartilage (chondrin), notable for its high content of the imino acids proline and hydroproxilone. On boiling with water it is converted into gelatin.

Collagen disease A term previously used to describe chronic diseases of the connective tissue (e.g., rheumatoid arthritis, systemic lupus erythematosus, and systemic sclerosis), but now is thought to be more appropriate for diseases associated with defects in collagen, which is a component of the connective tissue.

Collagen hydrolysate A functional component of gelatin which may help improve some symptoms associated with osteoarthritis.

Collateral eminence An elevation along the floor of the posterior part of the temporal horn of the lateral ventricle, lateral to the hippocampus caused by the deep collateral sulcus.

Collateral targeting The therapeutic strategy of targeting structures and cell types other than cancer cells common to all solid tumors as a means to attack a solid tumor.

Collateral trigone That part of the lateral ventricle where the occipital horn, temporal horn, and posterior part of the body become confluent.

Collecting duct The last part of a long, twisting tube that collects urine from the nephrons (cellular structures in the kidney that filter blood and form urine) and moves it into the renal pelvis and ureters. Also called renal collecting tubule.

Colle's fracture A common fracture to the distal radius, usually brought about by a fall onto the outstretched hand.

Colliculus C. Superior : Bilateral rounded eminences projecting from the surface of the rostral midbrain tectum associated with the visual system.

C. Inferior: Bilateral rounded eminences extending from the surface of the caudal midbrain tectum associated with the auditory system.

C. Facial: Small elevation on the floor of the fourth ventricle medial to the sulcus limitans, produced by the underlying abducent nerve nucleus and the internal genu of the facial nerve.

Colliquative necrosis Necrosis associated with the formation of pus.

Colloid A translucent, yellowish material of the consistency of glue, less fluid than mucoid or mucinoid, found in the cells and tissues in a state of colloid degeneration or colloid carcinoma.

A substance, such as gelatin or cytoplasm that because of the size of its molecules, is slowly diffusible rather than soluble in water and is incapable of passing through an animal membrane.

Coloanal anastomosis A surgical procedure in which the colon is attached to the anus after the rectum has been removed. Also called coloanal pull-through.

Coloanal pull-through A surgical procedure in which the colon is attached to the anus after the rectum has been removed. Also called coloanal anastomosis.

Colon The longest part of the large intestine, which is a tube-like organ connected to the small intestine at one end and the anus at the other. The colon removes water and some nutrients and electrolytes from partially digested food. The remaining material, solid waste called stool, moves through the colon to the rectum and leaves the body through the anus.

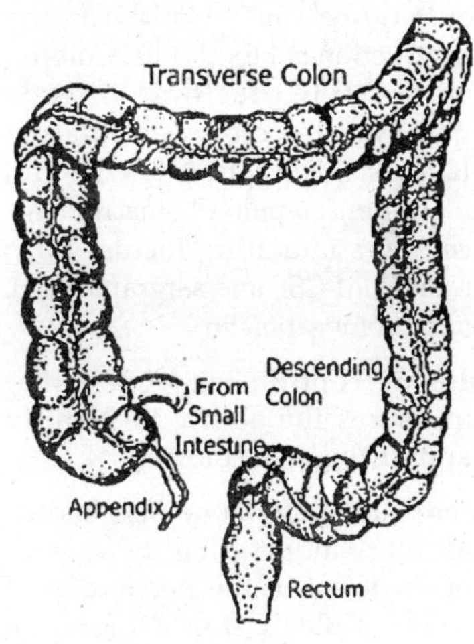

Figure Colon

Colon cancer Cancer that develops in the tissues of the colon.

Colon polyp An abnormal growth of tissue in the lining of the bowel. Polyps are a risk factor for colon cancer.

Colonization Residence of bacteria in, or on, part of the body and causing neither disease nor a response by the individual's immune system.

Colonoscope A thin, lighted tube used to examine the inside of the colon.

Colonoscopy An examination of the inside of the colon using a thin, lighted tube, called a colonoscope, inserted into the rectum. Samples of tissues may be collected for examination under a microscope.

Colony A growth of microorganisms on a solid medium. The growth is visible without magnification.

Colony-stimulating factor A substance that stimulates the production of blood cells. Colony-stimulating factors include granulocyte colony-stimulating factors (also called G-CSF and filgrastim), granulocyte-macrophage colony-stimulating factors (also called GM-CSF and sargramostim), and promegapoietin.

Color perception test A test that measures the ability to identify and distinguish colors.

Color vision deficiency Also known as colorblindness. It is the absence of or defect in the perception of colors. Color vision is based on perception of red, green, and blue. If there is a defect in the perception of one of these colors, a color will be perceived as if it were composed only of the other two colors. Based on the color or colors for which there is defective perception, a person may suffer from red, green, or blue blindness. Color blindness in which all colors are perceived as gray is termed monochromasia. For people with the common, inherited, types of color deficiency there is no cure.

Colorectal Having to do with the colon or the rectum.

Colorectal cancer Cancer that develops in the colon (large intestine) and/or the rectum (the last several inches of the large intestine before the anus).

Colostomy A procedure done when there is an abnormality in the large intestine or rectum that allows stool to leave the body by a different route. Through an operation, an opening is made in the abdomen and the colon (large intestine) is connected to it. Stool passes through the opening to a collection bag on the abdomen. A colostomy may be temporary or permanent, depending on the health of the colon.

Colposcope A lighted magnifying instrument used to examine the vagina and cervix.

Colposcopy Examination of the vagina and cervix with an instrument called a colposcope.

Coma A sleep-like state; not conscious. May be due to a high or low level of glucose (sugar) in the blood.

Comatose In a coma; not conscious.

Combination therapy Two or more drugs used together to achieve optimal results in controlling HIV infection. Combination therapy has proven more effective in decreasing viral load than monotherapy (single-drug therapy), which is no longer recommended for the treatment of HIV. An example of combination therapy is the use of two NRTIs plus a PI or an NNRTI.

Combinatorial joining The joining of segments of DNA to generate essentially new genetic information, as occurs with Ig genes during the development of B cells.

Combinatorial joining allows multiple opportunities for 2 sets of genes to combine in different ways.

Combretastatin A4 phosphate A water-soluble prodrug derived from the African bush willow (Combretum caffrum) with tumor vascular-targeting activity. In vivo, combretastatin A4 phosphate is dephosphorylated to its active metabolite, combretastatin A4, which binds to tubulin and inhibits microtubule depolymerization, resulting in morphological changes in proliferating endothelial cells. As a result, the permeability of tumor vasculature is increased, leading to reduced tumor blood flow and ischemic necrosis of tumor tissue. In vitro, combretastatin A4 phosphate has been shown to be directly cytotoxic to proliferating endothelial cells and tumor cells.

Combustible dust Any finely divided solid material that is 420μ or 0.017 inches or less in diameter, or any material capable of passing through an US No. 40 standard sieve that when dispersed in air in the proper proportions, could be ignited by a flame, spark or other source of ignition.

Combustible liquid A liquid having a closed cup flash point at or above 100°F (37.8°C). Combustible liquids do not include compressed gases or cryogenic fluids. Combustible liquids are subdivided as follows:

1. Class II - Liquids having a closed cup flash point at or above 100°F (37.8°C) and below 140°F (60°C).

2. Class III-A - liquids having a closed cup flash point at or above 140°F (60°C) and below 200°F (93.3°C).

Class III-B - liquids having a closed cup flash point at or above 200°F (93.3°C).

Comedo carcinoma A type of ductal carcinoma in situ (very early-stage breast cancer).

Comfort care Care given to improve the quality of life of patients who have a serious or life-threatening disease. The goal of comfort care is to prevent or treat as early as possible the symptoms of the disease, side effects caused by treatment of the disease, and psychological, social, and spiritual problems related to the disease or its treatment. Also called palliative care, supportive care, and symptom management.

Comitant strabismus A condition in which the magnitude of deviation remains essentially the same in all positions of gaze and with either eye fixating.

Commensal An organism that lives in close association with another of a different species without either harming or benefiting it. For example, some microorganisms living in the gut obtain both food and a suitable habitat but neither harm nor benefit man.

Commissioning The documented process, verifying that equipment and systems are installed according to specifications, placing the equipment and systems into active service and verifying its proper operation. Commissioning is done for good business, but can include many Qualification activities.

Commissure Compact bundles of nerve fibers that cross the midline and interconnect corresponding regions in opposite cerebral hemispheres. The principal commissures are the corpus callosum, anterior and posterior c ommissures.

Common bile duct Carries bile from the liver and gallbladder into the duodenum (the upper part of the small intestine).

Common carotid artery The major artery for the head and neck, that divides into the internal and external carotid arteries. On the right, it begins at the bifurcation of the brachiocephalic trunk, and on the left - it is a direct branch from the aorta.

Common rule Under HIPAA, it outlines the necessity of obtaining informed consent from patients.

Communicating veins Veins found in the thigh, lower leg, and foot that connect superficial and deep veins.

Communication skills Proficiency in the interchange of information. These are essential skills for clinical practitioners because of the large and varied number of people they must communicate with every day. The idea that doctors automatically learn communication through experience or that doctors are inherently either good or bad communicators is being largely abandoned. It is now widely believed that such skills can be taught to both students and doctors by a variety of professionals including doctors and specialists in communication skills as an important part of undergraduate as well as postgraduate and continuing medical education.

Communication The process by which information and feelings are shared by people through an exchange of verbal and non-verbal messages. In the context of medical education, its primary function is to establish understanding between patient and doctor. In an atmosphere of effective communication, patients improve faster, cope better with post-operative pain, require less psychotropic drugs, and experience numerous other health benefits.

Community A group of individuals living together in some form of social organization with cohesion in planning and operation and/or manifesting some unifying trait or common interest. In health care organization, it refers to the most local level of the health system. The form of services provided to a locality will vary according to each country's political, economic, social, cultural and epidemiological patterns.

Community advisory board A lay panel. consisting of patients and affected others, who provide guidance and feedback to clinical trials sites with respect to accrual, retention, compliance, access, and ethical issues surrounding clinical trials.

Community based education (CBE), community-based learning (CBL), or community-based teaching (CBT) A form of instruction where trainees learn professional competencies in a community setting focusing on population groups and also individuals and their everyday problems. The amount of time students spend in the community and organizational settings may vary. Instruction may take place at a general practice, family planning clinic, community health center or a rural hospital. During their training in the community, students learn about social and economic aspects of illness, about health services in the community and methods of health promotion, about working in teams, and about frequency and types of problems encountered outside a hospital setting.

Community based organization (CBO) A service organization that provides social services to local clients. CBOs include nonprofit organizations and free clinics targeted at helping people with HIV.

Community diagnosis Appraisal of the health status of a community in general or limited to specific health conditions, determinants or subgroups.

Community health center (CHC) An ambulatory health care program (defined under section 330 of the Public Health Service Act) usually serving a catchment area which has scarce or nonexistent health services or a population with special health needs; sometimes known as the neighborhood health center. Community Health Centers attempt to coordinate national, state and local resources into a single organization capable of delivering both health and related social services to a defined population. While such a center may not directly provide all types of health care, it usually takes responsibility to arrange all medical services needed by its patient population.

Community health information network (CHIN) An integrated collection of computer and telecommunication capabilities that permit multiple providers, payers, employers, and related healthcare entities within a geographic area to share and communicate client, clinical, and payment information. Also known as community health management information system.

Community medicine The speciality that deals with the health and disease of a population or of a specified community. The goal is to identify health problems and needs, to identify means by which these needs may be met, and to evaluate the extent to which health services do so. Community medicine is concerned with specified populations rather than individuals.

Comorbid condition A medical condition that, along with the principal diagnosis, exists at admission and is expected to increase hospital length of stay by at least one day for most patients.

Comparative genomics The study of human genetics by comparisons with model organisms such as mice, the fruit fly, and the bacterium E. coli.

Compartment syndrome Exercise, or effort, induced pain syndrome, whereby the pain is due to the inability of the muscles within the compartment to expand. Often confirmed by using catheter pressure testing.

Compassionate use General term used to describe any program that provides an experimental therapy outside of clinical trials to patients who do not have any approved treatment options (for example, HIV-infected individuals who have extensive drug resistance to approved anti-HIV drugs). To enroll in compassionate use programs, an individual has to meet strict medical critera.

Competence Possession of a satisfactory level of relevant knowledge and acquisition of a range of relevant skills that include interpersonal and technical components at a certain point in the educational process. Such knowledge and skills are necessary to perform the tasks that reflect the scope of professional practices. Competence may differ from "performance", which denotes actions taken in a real life situation. Competence is therefore not the same as "knowing" on the contrary, it may well be about recognizing one's own limits. The more experienced the professional being tested, the more difficult it is to create a tool to assess their actual understandings and the complex skills of the tasks they undertake. A holistic integration of understandings, abilities and professional judgments i.e. a "generic" model, is one where competence is not necessarily directly observable, but rather can be inferred from performance.

Competitive bidding Can be viewed by some as a pricing method that elicits information on costs through a bidding process to establish payment rates that reflect the costs of an efficient health plan or health care provider. Competitive bidding is also the process of offering reduced rates to health plans to obtain exclusive contracts from payers.

Complement A group of proteins in normal blood serum and plasma that, in combination with antibodies, causes the destruction of antigens (particularly bacteria and foreign blood corpuscles).

Complement cascade A precise sequence of events, usually triggered by an antigen-antibody complex, in which each component of the complement system is activated in turn, inactivating and occasionally destroying pathogens.

Complement components An enzymatic system of serum proteins triggered by the classical and alternative pathways, and resulting in target cell lysis, phagocytosis, opsonization and chemotaxis.

Complement receptor A structure found on erythrocytes, lymphocytes, neutrophils, monocytes and macrophages that binds C3 fragments.

Complementary and alternative medicine Forms of treatment that are used in addition to (complementary) or instead of (alternative) standard treatments. These practices generally are not considered standard medical approaches. Standard treatments go through a long and careful research process to prove they are safe and effective, but less is known about most types of CAM. CAM may include dietary supplements, megadose vitamins, herbal preparations, special teas, acupuncture, massage therapy, magnet therapy, spiritual healing, and meditation.

Complementary DNA (C DNA) DNA that is synthesized in the laboratory from a messenger RNA template.

Complementary medicine Practices often used to enhance or complement standard treatments. They generally are not recognized by the medical community as standard or conventional medical approaches. Complementary medicine may include dietary supplements, megadose vitamins, herbal preparations, special teas, acupuncture, massage therapy, magnet therapy, spiritual healing, and meditation.

Complementary sequence Nucleic acid base sequence that can form a double-stranded structure with another DNA fragment by following base-pairing rules (A pairs with T and C with G). The complementary sequence to GTAC for example, is CATG.

Complete hysterectomy Surgery to remove the entire uterus, including the cervix. Sometimes, not all of the cervix is removed. Also called total hysterectomy.

Complete metastasectomy Surgery to remove all metastases (tumors formed from cells that have spread from the primary tumor).

Complete remission The disappearance of all signs of cancer in response to treatment. This does not always mean the cancer has been cured. Also called a complete response.

Complex trait Trait that has a genetic component that does not follow strict Mendelian inheritance. May involve the interaction of two or more genes or gene-environment interactions.

Compliance date This is specified date by which health plans and providers are to be in compliance with rules. Under HIPAA, this is the date by which a covered entity must comply with a standard, an implementation specification, or a modification. This is usually 24 months after the effective data of the associated final rule for most entities, but 36 months after the effective data for small health plans. For future changes in the standards, the compliance date would be at least 180 days after the effective data, but can be longer for small health plans and for complex changes.

Complication A medical condition that arises during a course of treatment and is expected to increase the length of stay by at least one day for most patients.

Composite rate Group rate billed to all subscribers of a given group.

Composite resin Material composed of plastic with small glass or ceramic particles; usually cured with filtered light or chemical catalyst.

Compound In science, a substance that is made up of more than one ingredient.

Compound nevus A type of mole formed by groups of nevus cells found in the epidermis and dermis (the two main layers of tissue that make up the skin).

Compounding The bringing together of excipient and solvent components into a homogeneous mix of active ingredients.

Compression bandage A bandage designed to provide pressure to a particular area.

Computed tomographic colonography (CTC) A procedure in which a detailed picture of the colon is created by an x-ray machine linked to a computer. Also called computed tomography (CT) scan or computerized axial tomography (CAT) scan of the colon.

Computer based patient record (CPR) A term for the process of replacing the traditional paper-based chart through automated electronic means; generally includes the collection of patient-specific information from various supplemental treatment systems, i.e., a day program and a personal care provider; its display in graphical format; and its storage for individual and aggregate purposes. Also called "digital medical record" or "electronic medical record".

Computer vision syndrome (CVS) The complex of eye and vision problems related to near work that are experienced during or related to computer use. Its symptoms include eyestrain, dry or burning eyes, blurred vision, headaches, double vision, distorted color vision, and neck and backaches. The condition is caused by various internal and external factors. Treatment options may include prescription glasses and/or vision therapy.

Concentration polarization The phenomenon in ultrafiltration (UF) in which solutes form a dense, polarized layer next to the membrane surface eventually blocking further flow. UF systems counteract this by continuously flushing the solute away from the membrane surface.

Conception In biology, the beginning of pregnancy, marked by fertilization of an egg by a sperm.

Concomitant drugs At the same time.

Concurrent process validation Establishing documented evidence that a process does what it purports to do based on information generated during actual implementation of the process.

Concurrent review Review of a procedure or hospital admission done by a health care professional (usually a nurse) other than the one providing the care, during the same time frame that the care is provided. Usually conducted during a hospital confinement to determine the appropriateness of hospital confinement and the medical necessity for continued stay.

Concurrent therapy A treatment that is given at the same time as another.

Condensate Distillate just after it has been cooled from steam into the liquid state.

Condenser The heat exchanger used in distillation to cool steam in order to convert it from the vapor to the liquid state.

Conditioned stimulus A situation in which one signal, or stimulus, is given just before another signal. After this happens several times, the first signal alone can cause the response that would usually need the second signal.

Conductivity The reciprocal of resistivity (C=1/R). A measure of the ability to conduct an electric current. Since ionized impurities increase the conductivity of water, it is also an accurate measure of ionic purity. Conductivity is normally expressed in micromhos/cm (μmho/cm) or microsiemens/cm (μS/cm). To measure it, current is passed between two electrodes a fixed distance apart.

Condyloma A raised growth on the surface of the genitals caused by human papillomavirus (HPV) infection. The HPV in condyloma is very contagious and can be spread by skin-to-skin contact, usually during oral, anal, or genital sex with an infected partner. A female with condyloma is at an increased risk for developing cervical cancer. Also called genital wart and condylomata acuminata.

Condylomata acuminata A raised growth on the surface of the genitals caused by human papillomavirus (HPV) infection. The HPV in condylomata acuminata is very contagious and can be spread by skin-to-skin contact, usually during oral, anal, or genital sex with an infected partner. A female with condylomata acuminata is at an increased risk for developing cervical cancer. Also called condyloma and genital wart.

Cone A receptor cell which is sensitive to light and is located in the retina of the eye. It is responsible for color vision.

Cone biopsy Surgery to remove a cone-shaped piece of tissue from the cervix and cervical canal. Cone biopsy may be used to diagnose or treat a cervical condition. Also called conization.

Confidence interval Population descriptor of interest.

Confidentiality In genetics, the expectation that genetic material and the information gained from testing that material will not be available without the donor's consent.

Configuration The three-dimensional shape or form of a macromolecule.

Confluence (of the sinuses) (Confluens sinuum, torcular herophili) An area where the dural venous sinuses (superior sagittal, straight sinus, right and left transverse sinuses) converge near the internal occipital protuberance.

Conformation The characteristic three-dimensional shape (tertiary structure) of a macromolecule.

Conformer, plastic/silicone A concave oval shape piece placed into the socket following surgical removal of the eye. It aids in retention of the upper and lower cul-de-sac, and to prevent inversion of the eyelashes. It also has two small holes to allow drainage of secretion and to apply post-operative antibiotics.

Conformer, pressure stem The application of external force by means of an attached 'mushroom' shaped stem. Used when the anophthalmic cavity is unable to retain a prosthesis. Also, used to expand the orbital tissue and palpebral fissure.

Confounding variable or confounding factor A "hidden" variable that may cause an association which the researcher attributes to other variables.

Congenital Existing at birth, referring to certain mental or physical traits or peculiarities, malformations, diseases, which may be either hereditary or due to some influence occuring during gestation even up to the moment of birth.

Congenital anomaly An abnormal condition that affected the complete development of the eyeball (s).

Congenital cystic adenomatoid malformation (CCAM) A congenital cystic adenomatoid malformation (CCAM) is an abnormality of one or more lobes in which the lobe appears as a fluid-filled sac – called a cyst – that does not function as normal lung tissue. These cysts occur with equal frequency on either side of the lung, but rarely occur on both sides.

Congenital defects Problems or conditions that are present at birth.

Congenital diaphragmatic hernia (CDH) A congenital diaphragmatic hernia is a hole in the muscle between the chest and abdomen that requires only a one-inch incision in the mother. Most babies with this defect can be treated after birth but a few with the most severe form of this defect may be treated while in the womb.

Congestive heart failure Heart failure caused by loss of pumping power by the heart, resulting in fluids collecting in the body. Congestive heart failure often develops gradually over several years, although it also can happen suddenly. It can be treated by drugs and in some cases, by surgery.

Conization Surgery to remove a cone-shaped piece of tissue from the cervix and cervical canal. Conization may be used to diagnose or treat a cervical condition. Also called cone biopsy.

Conjoint tendon The common tendinous insertion of transversus abdominis and internal oblique at the pectineal line.

Conjugated estrogens Purified orally bioavailable female sex hormones isolated from pregnant mare urine or synthetically derived from plant materials and primarily conjugated as sulfate esters. Estrogen binds to and activates specific nuclear receptors, which, in turn, bind to estrogen response elements (EREs) in target genes, resulting in histone acetylation, alteration of chromatin conformation, and initiation of transcription.

Conjugated lenoleic acid (CLA) A type of fatty acid found in cheeses and some meat products which may provide the health benefits of improving body composition and decreasing the risk of certain cancers.

Conjugated protein A protein containing a metal or an organic prosthetic group or both. Hemoglobin is a conjugated protein.

Conjunctiva The mucous membrane tissue which lines the under part of the eyelid (palpebral) and the eyeball (bulbar).

Conjunctival flap A portion of superior bulbar conjunctiva is drawn over the cornea and sutured to the inferior bulbar conjunctiva.

Conjunctivitis An inflammation of the conjunctiva, the transparent layer covering the inner eyelid and the white portion (sclera) of the eyeball. Conjunctivitis can be caused by a virus, bacteria, or fungus (infectious conjunctivitis, or "pink eye", may be contagious); by allergies to pollen, fabrics, animals, or cosmetics (allergic conjunctivitis); or by air pollution or noxious fumes such as swimming pool chorine (chemical conjunctivitis). Symptoms include red or watery eyes, blurred vision, inflamed inner eyelids, scratchiness in the eyes, or (with infectious conjunctivitis) a puss like or watery discharge and matted eyelids. Conjunctivitis is usually treated with antibiotic eye drops and/or ointment.

Connective tissue Tissue that surrounds other more highly ordered tissues and organs; blood, cartilage and bone.

Consecutive case series A clinical study that includes all eligible patients identified by the researchers during the study registration period. The patients are treated in the order in which they are identified. This type of study usually does not have a control group.

Conserved sequence A base sequence in a DNA molecule (or an amino acid sequence in a protein) that has remained essentially unchanged throughout evolution.

Consolidation therapy A type of high-dose chemotherapy often given as the second phase (after induction therapy) of a cancer treatment regimen for leukemia. Also called intensification therapy.

Constant region (C region) The invariant carboxyl-terminal portion of an antibody molecule, as distinct from the variable region which is at the amino-terminal of the chain.

Constipation A condition in which stool becomes hard, dry, and difficult to pass, and bowel movements don't happen very often. Other symptoms may include painful bowel movements, and feeling bloated, uncomfortable, and sluggish.

Constitutive ablation Gene expression that results in cell death.

Constructed response questions A method of written examination in which examinees are required to construct their responses as opposed to selecting them from a set of options.

Contact dermatitis A type of eczema that occurs when the skin reacts to a substance that comes into direct contact with it. The reaction usually takes 24 hours to develop.

Contagious Easily passable between people through normal day-to-day contact. For example, chicken pox is both an infectious (causing infection) and a contagious disease. In contrast, HIV is an example of an infectious disease that is not a contagious disease (it cannot be passed from person to person through casual contact).

Containment The action of confining within a defined space a microbiological agent or other entity that is being cultured, stored, manipulated, transported, or destroyed in order to prevent or limit its contact with people and/or the environment. Methods to achieve containment include physical and biological barriers and inactivation using physical or chemical means.

1. Primary Containment. Addresses the protection of personnel and the immediate laboratory environ-ment from exposure to infectious agents. It involves the use of closed containers or safety biological cabinets along with secure operating procedures.

2. Secondary Containment. A system of containment that prevents the escape of infectious agents into the environment external to the laboratory. It involves the use of rooms with specially designed air handling, the existence of airlocks and/or sterilizers for the exit of materials and secure operating procedures. In many cases it may add to the effectiveness of primary containment.

1. Appendix G - Physical Containment specifies physical containment for standard laboratory experiments and defines Biosafety Level 1 (BL1) through Biosafety Level 4 (BL4).

2. Appendix I - Biological Containment specifies levels of biological containment (host vector systems) for prokaryotes and defines Host Vector 1 Systems (HV1) and Host Vector 2 Systems (HV2).

3. Appendix K - Physical Containment for Large Scale Uses of Organisms Containing Recombinant DNA Molecules specifies physical containment guidelines for large scale (over 10 liters) research or production involving viable organisms containing recombinant DNA molecules, and defines GLSP (Good Large Scale Practice) through Biosafety Level 3-LS (Large Scale).

4. Appendix P - Physical and Biological Containment for Recombinant DNA Research Involving Plants specifies physical and biological containment conditions and practices suitable to the greenhouse conduct of experiments involving recombinant DNA-containing plants, plant-associated microorganisms, and small animals, and defines Biosafety Level 1-Plants (BL1-P) through Biosafety Level 4-Plants (BL4-P).

5. Appendix Q - Physical and Biological Containment for Recombinant DNA Research Involving Animals specifies containment and confinement practices for research involving whole animals, both those in which the animal's genome has been altered by stable introduction of recombinant DNA, and experiments involving viable recombinant DNA-modified microorganisms tested on whole animals, and defines Biosafety Level 1-Animals (BL1-N) through Biosafety Level 4-Animals (BL4-N).

Contaminant Any unwanted or undesired component in a process fluid or controlled environment.

Contamination The undesired introduction of impurities of a chemical or microbiological nature, or of foreign matter, into or onto a raw material, intermediate, or API (Active Pharma ceutical Ingredient) during production, sampling, packaging or repackaging, storage or transport.

Contig Group of cloned (copied) pieces of DNA representing overlapping regions of a particular chromosome.

Contig map A map depicting the relative order of a linked library of small overlapping clones representing a complete chromosomal segment.

Contiguous Touching or very close together.

Contiguous lymphoma Lymphoma in which the lymph nodes containing cancer are next to each other.

Continent reservoir A pouch formed from a piece of small intestine to hold urine after the bladder has been removed.

Contingency management In medicine, a treatment plan that gives immediate rewards for desired changes in behaviour. It is based on the principle that if a good behaviour is rewarded, it is more likely to be repeated. This is often used in the treatment of drug and alcohol abuse, and is being studied as a smoking cessation method.

Continuing medical education (CME) A continuous process of acquiring new knowledge and skills throughout one's professional life. As under graduate and postgraduate education is insufficient to ensure lifelong physicians' competencies, it is essential to maintain the competencies of physicians, to remedy gaps in skills, and to enable professionals to respond to the challenges of rapidly growing knowledges and technologies, changing health needs and the social, political and economic factors of the practice of medicine. Continuing medical education depends highly upon learner motivation and self-directed learning skills.

Continuous fermentation A process in which sterile medium is added without interruption to the fermentation system with a balancing withdrawal (or "harvesting") of broth for product extraction. The length of fermentation can be measured in weeks or months. Commercial applications of continuous fermentation are limited in number, with ethanol production by yeast the most important example.

Continuous infusion The administration of a fluid into a blood vessel, usually over a prolonged period of time.

Continuous passive motion (CPM) A form of passive mobilisation, assisting in the recovery of cartliage. Used commonly following knee reconstructions.

Continuous quality improvement (CQI) An approach to health care quality management borrowed from the manufacturing sector. It builds on traditional quality assurance methods by putting in place a management structure that continuously gathers and assesses data that are then used to improve performance and design more efficient systems of care. Also known as quality improvement (QA) and total quality management (TQM).

Contract A legal agreement between a payer and a subscribing group or individual which specifies rates, performance covenants, the relationship among the parties, schedule of benefits and other pertinent conditions. The contract usually is limited to a 12-month period and is subject to renewal thereafter. Contracts are not required by statute or regulation, and less formal agreements may be made.

Contract provider Any hospital, physician, skilled nursing facility, extended care facility, individual, organization, or agency licensed that has a contractual arrangement with an insurer for the provision of services under an insurance contract.

Contraction The rhythmic squeezing of the heart muscle that causes blood to be pumped out of the heart chambers and into the body. This contraction produces a heartbeat.

Contraindication A symptom or medical condition that makes a particular treatment or procedure inadvisable because a person is likely to have a bad reaction. For example, having a bleeding disorder is a contraindication for taking aspirin because treatment with aspirin may cause excess bleeding.

Contralateral Having to do with the opposite side of the body.

Contrast material A dye or other substance that helps show abnormal areas inside the body. It is given by injection into a vein, by enema, or by mouth. Contrast material may be used with x-rays, CT scans, MRI, or other imaging tests.

Control animal An animal in a study that does not receive the treatment being tested. Comparing the health of control animals with the health of treated animals allows researchers to evaluate the effects of a treatment more accurately.

Control area A building or portion of a building within which the exempted amounts of hazardous materials may be stored, dispensed, handled, or used.

Control group The group of subjects in a study to whom a comparison is made in order to determine whether an observation or treatment has an effect. In an experimental study it is the group that does not receive a treatment. Subjects are as similar as possible to those in the test or treatment group.

Control parameters Those operating variables that can be assigned values and are used as control levels.

Control serum Serum used as a standard for clinical chemistry lab tests. Most often produced from outdated whole blood plasma. Most often turbid and difficult to filter.

Controlled 1. Constrained, monitored, or watched.

2. A system of observation and data collection that provides a basis for comparison, as with a comparison group.

Controlled area An area constructed and operated in such a manner that some attempt is made to control the introduction of potential contamination, and the consequences of accidental release of living organisms. The level of control exercised should reflect the nature of the organism employed in the process. At a minimum, the area should be maintained at a pressure negative to the immediate external environment and allow for the efficient removal of small quantities of airborne contaminants.

Controlled clinical trial A clinical trial involving one or more test treatments, at least one control treatment, and concurrent enrollment, treatment, and follow-up of all patients in the trial.

Controlled disease Taking care of oneself so that a disease has less of an effect on the body. People with diabetes can "control" the disease by staying on their diets, by exercising, by taking medicine if it is needed, and by monitoring their blood glucose. This care will help keep the glucose (sugar) level in the blood from becoming either too high or too low.

Controlled experiment In this type of research, study subjects (whether animal or human) are selected according to relevant characteristics, and then randomly assigned to either an experimental group, or a control group. Random assignment ensures that factors known as variables, which may affect the outcome of the study, are distributed equally among the groups and therefore could not lead to differences in the effect of the treatment under study. The experimental group is then given a treatment (sometimes called an intervention), and the results are compared to the control group, which does not receive treatment. A placebo, or false treatment, may be administered to the control group. With all other variables controlled, differences between the experimental and control groups may be attributed to the treatment under study.

Controlled study An experiment or clinical trial that includes a comparison (control) group.

Controlled trial A control is a standard against which experimental treatments may be compared and evaluated for safety and effectiveness. In clinical trials, one group of patients may be given an experimental drug, while another group (the control group) is given either a standard treatment for the disease or a placebo.

Contusion A bruise, often associated with blunt trauma.

Conus medullaris The cone-shaped terminal part of the spinal cord. Located at lower border of the first lumbar vertebra.

Conventional therapy A system of diabetes management practiced by most people with diabetes; the system consists of one or two insulin injections each day, daily self-monitoring of blood glucose, and a standard program of nutrition and exercise. The main objective in this form of treatment is to avoid very high and very low blood glucose (sugar). Also called: "standard therapy."

Conventional treatment A currently accepted and widely used treatment for a certain type of disease, based on the results of past research. Also called conventional therapy.

Convergence excess (CE) A clinical condition in which the eyes have a tendency to turn excessively inward when viewing an object at a near distance. Symptoms may include visual fatigue while reading or using a computer, occasional blurred or double vision, and inability to comprehend or concentrate while reading. Clinical signs include: greater esophoria at near than distance, high AC/A ratio, and a high lag of accommodation. Can be improved with vision therapy and/or glasses.

Convergence insufficiency (CI) (clinical condition) The inability of the eyes to turn inward and/or sustain an inward turn. Symptoms include eye strain with reading and using a computer, headaches, loss of comprehension, difficulty concentrating, blurred or double vision, and eye fatigue. Clinical signs include: near point of convergence of greater than 4 inches (10 cm), greater exophoria at near than at distance, and low AC/A ratio. Vision therapy is an effective treatment option.

Convergence The ability to use both eyes as a team and to be able to turn the eyes inward to maintain single vision up close.

Conversion factor (CF) The dollar amount used to multiply the Relative Value Schedule (RVS) of a procedure to arrive at the maximum allowable for that procedure.

Conversion factor update Annual percentage change to a conversion factor, either set annually by the government or by the formula reflecting actual expenditure growth from two years falling below or above the original target rate.

Convexity A condition in which the surface of a welded joint is extended relative to the surface of the tube or pipe. Convexity is measured as a maximum distance from the outside or inside diameter surface of a welded joint along a line perpendicular to a line joining the weld toes.

Coombs' test A test named for its originator, R.R.A. Coombs, used to detect non-agglutinating antibodies on red blood cells by addition of an anti-immunoglobulin antibody.

Cooperative clinical trial Term frequently used to denote a multicenter trial.

Coordinating center A center in the structure of a study that is responsible for receiving, editing, processing, analyzing, and storing data generated in a study and that, in addition, has responsibility for coordination of activities required for execution of the study.

CoQ10 A substance found in most tissues in the body, and in many foods. It can also be made in the laboratory. It is used by the body to produce energy for cells, and as an antioxidant. It is being studied in the treatment of cancer and in the relief of side effects caused by some cancer treatments. Also called coenzyme Q10, Q10, vitamin Q10, and ubiquinone.

Coracoid process A projection of bone that originates from the upper part of the neck of the scapula and overhangs the shoulder joint.

Cordectomy An operation on the vocal cords or on the spinal cord.

Cordycepin An anticancer drug that belongs to a family of drugs called antitumor antibiotics.

Core biopsy The removal of a tissue sample with a needle for examination under a microscope.

Core The inner protective coat of protein that surrounds the genetic material of most viruses. In HIV, the core is mostly made up of the p24 protein, which surrounds two copies of HIV's genetic material.

Corn steep liquor An ingredient in the culture medium for producing penicillin. A natural nitrogenous material that is a by-product of the corn milling industry.

Cornea The transparent, blood-free tissue covering the central front of the eye (over the pupil, iris, and aqueous humor) that initially refracts or bends light rays as light enters the eye. Contact lenses are fitted over the cornea.

Coronal suture This calvarial (vault) synostosis is the coronal plane between the frontal and parietal bones.

Coronal view Longitudinal section passing through the body at right angles to the median plane, in a "frontal" or "facing" orientation. This is the plane of the coronal suture of the skull - and vice versa.

Coronary angiogram A procedure in which catheters are passed into the heart and coronary arteries. Radiopaque dye (x-ray dye) is injected so that x-ray pictures of the heart and arteries may be taken.

Coronary arteries The blood vessels that carry blood from the aorta to the heart muscle. The three major coronary arteries are: the right coronary artery (RCA), the left anterior descending (LAD) and the circumflex (CX).

Coronary artery bypass graft (CABG) An operation performed to circumvent blocked coronary arteries and deliver blood to areas of the heart receiving insufficient blood flow.

Coronary artery disease (CAD) A disease in which there is a narrowing or blockage of the coronary arteries (blood vessels that carry blood and oxygen to the heart). Coronary artery disease is usually caused by atherosclerosis (a build up of fatty material and plaque inside the coronary arteries). The disease may cause chest pain, shortness of breath during exercise, and heart attacks. The risk of coronary artery disease is increased by having a family history of coronary artery disease before age 50, older age, smoking tobacco, high blood pressure, high cholesterol, diabetes, lack of exercise, and obesity. Also called coronary heart disease.

Coronary ligament Lies on the anterior aspect of the knee and attaches the anterior horn of the medial meniscus to the tibial plateau.

Coronary sinus The end portion of the cardiac vein which empties into the right atrium.

Corpora quadrigemina Term applied to the four protuberances on the dorsal surface of the midbrain; the two superior and two inferior colliculi.

Corps grains, corps ronds Acantholytic, dyskeratotic, basophilic cells. Corps ronds have round nuclei with a perinuclear halo. Grains have an elongeated "grain shaped" nucleus. These cells are seen in Darier's, Grover's and warty dyskeratoma.

Corpus collosum Literally "hard body". A large bundle of white matter, found in the longitudinal fissure, forming a "commissure" by interconnecting the two cerebral hemispheres.

Corpus The body of the uterus.

Correlation An association, or when one phenomenon is found to be accompanied by another. A correlation does not prove cause and effect. Correlation may also be defined statistically.

Corrosive A chemical that causes visible destruction or irreversible alterations in living tissue by chemical action at the site of contact. A chemical is considered corrosive if, when tested on the intact skin of albino rabbits by the method described in Appendix A of CFR 49 Part 173, it destroys or changes irreversibly the structure of the tissue at the site of contact following an exposure period of four hours. This term shall not refer to action on inanimate surfaces.

Corrosive liquid A liquid which when in contact with living tissue, will cause destruction or irreversible alteration of such tissue by chemical action. Examples include acidic, alkaline, or caustic materials.

Corrugated Having a ripple-like distortion.

Cortex cerebral The superficial layer of gray matter that covers the cerebral hemispheres. It varies in thickness from 1.5 (striate cortex) to 4.5 (motor cortex) mm in thickness and consists of from 3 to 6 horizontal layers of cells.

Cortex The outer layer of a body or organ structure. From the Latin word for "bark". (Like the "cortex" of the kidney or brain).

Corticosteroids Any of a number of steroid substances obtained from the cortex of the adrenal gland or manufactured synthetically. Corticosteroids are immunosuppressive and people with HIV should be cautious about taking them for longer than a few weeks. Steroids appear to be an effective adjunct to standard PCP treatments in people with moderate to severe PCP.

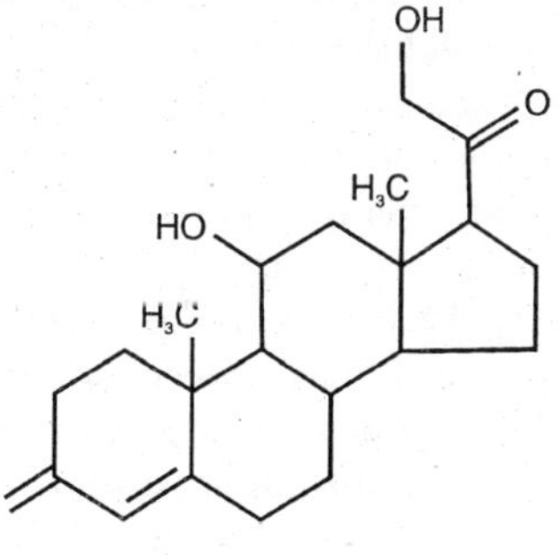

OH
O
H_3C
HO
H_3C

Figure Corticosteroid

Corticotropin A form of the hormone adrenocorticotropic hormone

(ACTH). It belongs to the family of drugs called corticosteroids.

Cortisol One of several hormones made in the adrenal glands. The primary responsibility of cortisol is to activate the immune system; it also is involved with the metabolism of glucose, and can cause elevation of the blood sugar level.

Cortisol is in the class of hormones called corticosteroids (or steroids). It, and synthetic versions such as prednisone, are available as prescription medications for treating severe illnesses including asthma and arthritis; they are sometimes also used for severe cases of minor illnesses like poison ivy rashes.

Cortisone A natural steroid hormone produced in the adrenal gland. It can also be made in the laboratory. Cortisone reduces swelling and can suppress immune responses.

Corynebacterium granulosum A bacterium that may stimulate the immune system to fight cancer.

Corynebacterium granulosum P40 An insoluble fraction isolated from the bacterium Corynebacterium granulosum with potential cancer immunotherapeutic activity. As a non-specific immunostimulant, Corynebacterium granulosum P40 activates the reticulo-endothelial system; induces the production of certain cytokines; enhances macrophage activity; and potentiates a delayed-type hypersensitivity response when co-administered with an antigen.

Cosmesis Mirror image symmetry of the eye and lids. A return to a normal appearance.

Cosmetic (Aesthetic) dentistry Treatments performed to enhance appearance; not a recognized specialty.

Cosmid Artificially constructed cloning vector containing the cos gene of phage lambda. Cosmids can be packaged in lambda phage particles for infection into E. coli; this permits cloning of larger DNA fragments (up to 45kb) than can be introduced into bacterial hosts in plasmid vectors.

Cost containment Control of inefficiencies in the consumption, allocation, or production of health care services that contribute to higher than necessary costs. Inefficiencies are thought to exist in consumption when health services are inappropriately utilized; inefficiencies in allocation exist when health services could be delivered in less costly settings without loss of quality; and, inefficiencies in production exist when the costs of producing health services could be reduced by using a different combination of resources. Cost containment is a word used freely in healthcare to describe most cost reduction activities by providers.

Cost of illness analysis (COI) An assessment of the economic impact of an illness or condition, including treatment costs.

Cost outlier A case that is more costly to treat compared with other patients in a particular diagnosis related group. Outliers also refer to any unusual occurrence of cost, cases that skew average costs or unusual procedures.

Costochondral junction Junction between rib and costal cartilage. Commonly disrupted in contact sports.

Costophrenic angle Point of junction between the costal and diaphragmatic pleurae.

Costophrenic sulcus (recess) The space, or potential space, between the ribs ("costo-") of the lateral chest wall and the diaphragm ("phrenic").

Co-trimoxazole A drug used in the treatment of infections caused by bacteria and protozoa. It is a combination of two anti-infection drugs, sulfamethoxazole and trimethoprim.

Coumestan An estrogen-like substance (phytoestrogen) made by some plants. Coumestans may have anticancer effects.

Coumestrol A type of coumestan. Coumestans are estrogen-like substances (phytoestrogens) made by some plants. Coumestans may have anticancer effects.

Counterregulatory An attempt by the body to correct a perceived abnormality. The correction may be in the form of an endocrine, neuronal, or other mechanism. In diabetes, this is a term that is usually used to describe the body's normal response through other hormones, epinephrine and glucocorticoids (which are called "counterregulatory hormones") to correct blood sugars that are too low.

Cover test A test of eyeball alignment in which each eye is covered with an occluder (eye cover) and then uncovered to observe eye movements.

COX inhibitor A type of drug that is used to treat inflammation and pain, and is being studied in the prevention and treatment of cancer. COX inhibitors belong to the family of drugs called nonsteroidal anti-inflammatory drugs (NSAIDs). Also called cyclooxygenase inhibitor.

COX-2 inhibitor Cyclooxygenase-2 inhibitor. A nonsteroidal anti-inflammatory drug used to relieve pain and inflammation. COX-2 inhibitors are being studied in the prevention of colon polyps, and as anticancer drugs.

Coxsackie B4 virus An agent that has been shown to damage the beta cells of the pancreas in lab tests. This virus may be one cause of insulin-dependent diabetes.

CP (Cyclic polarization) An electrochemical test (ASTM G61) for metals that measures the point at which pitting corrosion begins. CP uses an electrolytic cell to directly measure the corrosion rate. By using the test piece as the working electrode, initiation of localized corrosion is shown by the potential at which the current density increases rapidly. This point is called the "pitting potential". The lower the current density at this point, the more resistance to pitting corrosion. The current density is measured in micro-amps per square centimeter.

CP 724,714 An orally bioavailable quinazoline with potential antineoplastic activity. CP-724,714 selectively binds to the intracellular domain of HER2, reversibly inhibiting its tyrosine kinase activity and resulting in suppression of tumor cell growth. HER2, a member of the epidermal growth factor receptor (EGFR) family, is overexpressed in many adenocarcinomas, particularly breast cancers.

CPR (Cardiopulmonary resuscitation) Artificial procedures employed by a rescuer after cessation of breathing or heart stoppage.

CPT 11 An anticancer drug that belongs to a family of drugs called topoisomerase inhibitors. It is a camptothecin analogue. Also called irinotecan.

CQS (Chloroquinoxaline sulfonamide) A substance that is being studied in the treatment of cancer.

Cranial autonomic ganglia Groups of nerve cell bodies located outside the brain and associated with cranial nerves III, VII, IX and ,X. They represent the location of postganglionic prasymapthetic neurons.

Cranial nerve ganglia Groups of nerve cell bodies located outside the brain and associated with certain of the cranial nerves. They represent the location of cell bodies of sensory neurons.

Cranial nerve lesion An injury from any of a number of causes to a cranial nerve, its nuclei of origin or termination and/or its supranuclear projections that results in some pathological alteration in its function.

Cranial nerve nuclei Groups or columns of nerve cells within the brainstem representing the sites of origin and termination of the various cranial nerves.

Craniopharyngioma A benign brain tumor that may be considered malignant because it can damage the hypothalamus, the area of the brain that controls body temperature, hunger, and thirst.

Craniotomy An operation in which an opening is made in the skull.

Cranium The part of the skull (8 bones) which encloses and protects the brain. It excludes the 14 bones of the face.

Crazing Stress fractures in the plastic that can be caused by improper curing or a chemical reaction from a non-compatible substance (alcohol).

Creatinine A protein found in muscles and blood and excreted by the kidneys into the urine. The level of creatinine in the blood or urine provides a measure of kidney function. Increased levels of creatinine indicate abnormal or impaired kidney function.

Creatinine kinase (Creatinine phospho kinase) An enzyme

found in the muscles. High levels in the blood indicate breakdown of muscle tissue. In AIDS, may be diagnostic of myopathy.

Crepitus A grinding noise or sensation within a joint. Commonly felt in knees, particularly on change of position after a long period of time.

Crib death The sudden and unexpected death of a healthy child who is younger than one year old, usually during sleep. The cause of crib death is not known. Also called sudden infant death syndrome (SIDS).

Cribriform Pierced with small holes as in a sieve. Refers to the appearance of a tumor when viewed under a microscope. The tumor appears to have open spaces or small holes inside.

Cribriform plate (of the ethmoid bone) Perforated plate of the ethmoid bone through which the fila olfactoria (cranial nerve I) enter the cranial cavity.

Cricoid cartilage The cartilage that forms the lower and back portion of the larynx, just above the trachea.

Crisnatol mesylate An anticancer drug that interferes with the DNA in cancer cells.

Crista galli A midline cocks come-like projection of the ethmoid bone into the anterior cranial fossa to which the falx cerebri attaches anteriorly.

Critical A material, process step, or process condition, test requirement, or any other relevant parameter is considered critical when non-compliance with predetermined criteria directly influences the quality attributes of the API (active pharmaceutical ingredient) in a detrimental manner.

Critical area An area where (sterile) product or contact surface is exposed, normally Class 100 (e.g., Point of Fill).

Critical device A device that directly ensures that a GMP Critical Parameter is maintained within predetermined limits (e.g., terminal HEPA filter, point of use filter). A malfunction of such a device would place product quality directly at risk.

Critical instrument An instrument that measures a GMP Critical Parameter, used to monitor and document that parameter.

Critical parameter A GMP or product quality parameter (e.g., differential pressure, unidirectional airflow pattern) that must be maintained within predefined limits to ensure product SISPQ (Strength, Identity, Safety, Purity, or Quality).

Critical point The combination of pressure and temperature at which the gas and liquid phases of a substance become indistinguishable.

Critical process step For sterile products, this normally is an activity where product or product contact parts are exposed to the surrounding environment.

Critical step (s) The point or points in the process which, if not carried out properly or if contaminated, will not allow drug substances to be made such that they will meet their intended characterizations and impurity profiles.

Critical surface The part of the working surface to be protected from particulate contamination. It is within the Critical Zone.

Critical system A structural, mechanical, or electrical system that can impact the processing parameters and attributes of the finished product or regulatory study. Critical systems may include utilities, process equipment, and systems.

Crocinic acid A liquid that has been promoted as a treatment for a wide range of diseases, including cancer. The ingredients thought to be in Crocinic Acid have been tested, and none of them has been shown to be effective in treating any form of cancer. Also called Entelev, Sheridan's Formula, Jim's Juice, Cancell, JS-114, JS-101, 126-F, and Cantron.

Crohn's disease A chronic illness that causes irritation in the digestive tract. It occurs most commonly in the ileum (lower small intestine) or in the colon (large intestine). It is a form of inflammatory bowel disease.

Crop residues Plant materials remaining from the former crop that are left on the soil surface after planting form crop residues. Crop residues reduce soil erosion, air and surface water pollution, conserve soil moisture, and improve the soil by adding organic matter.

Cross bite Reverse biting relationship of upper and lower teeth; aka "under bite," as in Class III malocclusuion (prognathic jaw).

Cross contamination The measurable and detrimental contamination of a material or product with another material or product.

Cross reactivity The interaction of an antigen with an antibody formed against a different antigen with which the first antigen shares identical or closely related properties

Cross resistance Cross resistance occurs when a micro-organism has changed (mutated) in such a way that it loses its susceptibility to multiple drugs simultaneously. For example, HIV resistance to one NNRTI drug usually produces resistance to the entire NNRTI drug class.

Cross sensitivity Occurrence of a drug reaction that may occur again with the use of a different, but related, drug. Cross sensitivity can occur within a drug class, such as when a person reacts to all NNRTIs similarly after treatment with just one. Cross sensitivity can also occur among chemically similar drug classes. For example, a person who has a negative side effect to a sulfa-based antibiotic is at risk for the same negative side effect if he or she takes any other sulfa-based drug.

Crossed treatments Two or more study treatments that are used in sequence (e.g., as in a crossover design) or in combination (e.g., as in a factorial treatment structure).

Crossing over The breaking during meiosis of one maternal and one paternal chromosome, the exchange of corresponding sections of DNA, and the rejoining of the chromosomes. This process can result in an exchange of alleles between chromosomes.

Crossover design Crossover treatment design. Patients are given treatments in sequence, and crossover is determined by time, not clinical outcomes.

Cross-reactivity The ability of an antibody, specific for one antigen, to react with a second antigen; a measure of relatedness between two different antigenic substances.

Crown 1. The portion of a tooth above the gum line;

2. Dental restoration covering all or most of the natural tooth.

Cruciate ligaments The "cross-shaped" ligaments situated in the knee joint between the femoral condyles and the proximal tibia (tibial spines) that form a cross-shaped structure.

Cruciferous vegetable A member of the family of vegetables that includes kale, collard greens, broccoli, cauliflower, cabbage, brussels sprouts, and turnips. These vegetables contain substances that may protect against cancer.

Crus cerebrii Another name for basis pedunculi of the cerebral peduncle.

Crus of diaphragm The fibromuscular bands originating from the upper three or four lumbar vertebrae and inserting into the central tendon of the diaphragm.

Crustacean Any of the various aquatic arthropods, including lobsters, crabs, shrimps and barnacles. Characteristically have segmented bodies, chitinous exoskeletons and paired, jointed limbs.

Cryogenic liquid A fluid that has a normal boiling point below -150°F (-101.1°C).

Cryopreservation The process of cooling and storing cells, tissues, or organs at very low or freezing temperatures to save them for future use.

Cryosurgery A procedure performed with an instrument that freezes and destroys abnormal tissues.

Cryotherapy The use of liquid nitrogen to freeze and destroy a lesion or growth to prevent further spread of the growth. In people with HIV, it is used to treat lesions caused by Kaposi's sarcoma and condyloma acuminatum (genital warts).

Cryptococcal meningitis A life-threatening infection of the membranes surrounding the brain and the spinal cord caused by the fungus Cryptococcus neoformans. Symptoms include headache, dizziness, stiff neck, and, if untreated, coma and death. Immunocompromised individuals are more susceptible to this infection. It is con ·idered an AIDS-defining condition in people with HIV.

Cryptococcosis An infection caused by the fungus Cryptococcus neoformans. This fungus typically enters the body through the lungs and usually spreads to the brain, causing cryptococcal meningitis. In some cases, it can also affect the skin, skeletal system, and urinary tract. It is considered an AIDS-defining condition in people with HIV.

Cryptococcus neoformans A fungus, pathogenic in the immune suppressed, which is acquired via the respiratory tract. Cryptococcosis most frequently causes meningitis, with symptoms of headache and stiff neck.

Cryptography The mathematical science of deliberately scrambling and unscrambling information. Information is protected by being transformed (encrypted) into an unreadable format, called cipher text. Only those who posses a secret key can decypher (or decrypt) that message into plain text.

Cryptorchidism A condition in which one or both testicles fail to move from the abdomen, where they develop before birth, into the scrotum. Cryptorchidism may increase the risk for development of testicular cancer. Also called undescended testicles.

Cryptosporidiosis A diarrheal disease caused by the protozoa Cryptosporidium. Symptoms include abdominal cramps and severe chronic diarrhea. It is considered an AIDS-defining condition in people with HIV.

Cryptosporidium parvum A waterborne enterocyte protozoan, c. parvum is often deposited in water supply by wild or domestic animals. c parvum has caused at least one large epidemic of diarrheal disease through contamination of a municipal water supply.

Cryptosporidium The protozoan that causes cryptosporidiosis. It is found in the intestines of animals and may be transmitted to humans by direct contact with an infected animal, by eating contaminated food, or by drinking contaminated water.

Cryptosporldiosis An opportunistic infection caused by a protozoan parasite (Cryptosporidium parvum). Cryptosporidiosis causes diarrhea and abdomen pain.

Crystalline lens Transparent disc located behind the iris which changes shape to focus on objects at different distances from the eye.

CSF (Cerebrospinal fluid) This is the fluid that surrounds and protects the brain and spinal cord. It is made primarily by the choroid plexus and is absorbed by the arachnoid villi and granulations of the dural sinuses and veins.

Cuboid A cube-shaped bone in the foot.

Cul de sac The shallow pocket where palpebral and bulbar conjunctiva meet in the lower eyelid, and the deeper recess in the upper eyelid.

Cultural controls An integrated pest management method which includes annual crop rotation to discourage pests and weed production.

Culture medium Any nutrient system for the artificial cultivation of bacteria or other cells; usually a complex mixture of organic and inorganic materials. current good manufacturing practices (cGMP's)

Culture The process of growing bacteria or other microorganisms in the laboratory so that organisms can be identified.

Cultured cell A human, plant, or animal cell that has been adapted to grow in the laboratory.

Cultured cell line Cells of a single type (human, animal, or plant) that have been adapted to grow continuously in the laboratory and are used in research.

Cumulative dose In medicine, the total amount of a drug or radiation given to a patient over time; for example, the total dose of radiation given in a series of radiation treatments.

Cuneate tubercle A swelling on the dorsal surface of the medulla oblongata that marks the location of the underlying cuneate nucleus.

Cuneiforms A wedged-shaped bone in the foot.

Cuneus A region of the occipital lobe of the brain located on the medial surface of the cerebral hemisphere between the parieto-occipital and calcarine sulci.

Curcumin A phytopoylphenol pigment isolated from the plant Curcuma longa, commonly known as tumeric, with a variety of pharmacologic properties. Curcumin blocks the formation of reactive-oxygen species, possesses anti-inflammatory properties as a result of inhibition of cyclo-oxygenases (COX) and other enzymes involved in inflammation; and disrupts cell signal transduction by various mechanisms including inhibition of protein kinase C. These effects may play a role in the agent's observed antineoplastic properties, which include inhibition of tumor cell proliferation and suppression of chemically induced carcinogenesis and tumor growth in animal models of cancer.

Cure To heal or restore health; a treatment to restore health.

Curettage Removal of tissue with a curette (a spoon-shaped instrument with a sharp edge).

Curette A spoon-shaped instrument with a sharp edge.

Curriculum An educational plan that spells out which goals and objectives should be achieved, which topics should be covered and which methods are to be used for learning, teaching and evaluation.

Cusp Mound on posterior teeth.

Cuspid or canine The four "eye teeth".

Cut An enzymatic break that occurs in both strands of a DNA molecule opposite one another by restriction enzymes.

Cut point 1. The point or value in an ordered sequence of values that is used to separate those values into two subparts.

2. Subgrouping cut-point.

Cutaneous Having to do with the skin.

Cutaneous breast cancer Cancer that has spread from the breast to the skin.

Cutaneous T-cell lymphoma A disease in which certain cells of the lymph system (called T lymphocytes) become cancerous (malignant) and affect the skin.

CXCR4 Chemokine receptor 4 (CXCR4, also known as fusin) is a protein on the surface of some immune system cells. It is one of two co-receptors that HIV can use along with the CD4 receptor to bind to and enter host cells (the other co-receptor is CCR5).

Cyanogenic glucoside A plant compound that contains sugar and produces cyanide.

Cyanosis Blue-colored skin caused by too little oxygen in the blood.

Cyclamate A sweetener which is 30 times sweeter than sucrose, calorie free and heat stable and works synergistically with other sweeteners. It is approved for tabletop use in Canada and more than 50 countries in Europe, Asia, South America and Africa. Since 1970, however, the use of cyclamate has been banned in the United States on the basis of a study that suggested that cyclamates may be related to the development of bladder tumors in rats. Although 75 subsequent studies have failed to show that cyclamate is carcinogenic.

Cyclooxygenase inhibitor A type of drug that is used to treat inflammation and pain, and is being studied in the prevention and treatment of cancer. COX inhibitors belong to the family of drugs called nonsteroidal anti-inflammatory drugs (NSAIDs). Also called COX inhibitor.

Cyclooxygenase-2 inhibitor COX-2 inhibitor. A nonsteroidal anti-inflammatory drug used to relieve pain and inflammation. COX-2 inhibitors are being studied in the prevention of colon polyps, and as anticancer drugs.

Cyclophosphamide A synthetic alkylating agent chemically related to the nitrogen mustards with antineoplastic and immuno-suppressive activities. In the liver, cyclophosphamide is converted to the active metabolites aldophos-phamide and phosphoramide mustard, which bind to DNA, thereby inhibiting DNA replication and initiating cell death.

Cycloplegic refraction One method available to eye doctors to determine the eye's refractive error and the best corrective lenses to be prescribed if needed. The eye is dilated with the muscles of accommodation (eye focusing muscles) being temporarily paralyzed with specialized eye drops or spray (Atropine, Homatropine, Cyclogyl, or Mydriacyl). This is a good method for non-responsive or non-communicative patients such as young children. The technique of retinoscopy is used with this method.

Cyclosporine A natural cyclic polypeptide immunosuppressant isolated from the fungus Beauveria nivea. The exact mechanism of action of cyclosporine is not known but may involve binding to the cellular protein cytophilin, resulting in inhibition of the enzyme calcineurin. This agent appears to specifically and reversibly inhibit immunocompetent lymphocytes in the G0-or G1-phase of the cell cycle. T-lymphocytes are preferentially inhibited with T-helper cells as the primary target. Cyclosporine also inhibits lymphokine production and release.

Cylinder lens An ophthalmic lens that has at least one non-spherical surface. Used to correct astigmatism. The values are typically from -0.75 to -1.25. The cylinder measurement is given with a "-" sign.

Cyproheptadine A drug that is used to treat asthma, allergies, and colds, and to relieve itching caused by certain skin disorders. It has also been used to stimulate appetite and weight gain, and is being studied in the treatment of weight loss caused by cancer and its treatment. Cyproheptadine belongs to the family of drugs called antihistamines.

Cyproterone A synthetic steroidal anti-androgen with antineoplastic activity. Cyproterone, in its acetate form, binds the androgen receptor (AR), thereby preventing androgen-induced receptor activation and inhibiting the growth of testosterone-sensitive tumor cells. This agent also exerts progesterogenic activity, resulting in a reduction in testicular androgen secretion and total androgen blockade.

Cyst A lump filled with either fluid or soft material, occurring in any organ or tissue; may occur for a number of reasons but is usually harmless unless its presence disrupts organ or tissue function.

Cystectomy Surgical removal of the bladder.

Cystic duct The connection between the neck of the gallbladder and the common bile duct.

Cystic fibrosis A common hereditary disease in which exocrine (secretory) glands produce abnormally thick mucus. This mucus can cause problems in digestion, breathing, and body cooling.

Cystitis An inflammation of the bladder.

Cystocele A herniation of bladder into vagina

Cystogram A radiograph of the bladder opacified (filled with radiopaque contrast).

Cystosarcoma phyllodes (CSP) A type of tumor found in breast tissue. It is often large and bulky and grows quickly. It is usually benign (not cancer), but may be malignant (cancer). Also called phyllodes tumor.

Cystoscope A thin, lighted instrument used to look inside the bladder and remove tissue samples or small tumors.

Cystoscopy Examination of the bladder and urethra using a thin, lighted instrument (called a cystoscope) inserted into the urethra. Tissue samples can be removed and examined under a microscope to determine whether disease is present.

Cyt (o) Cell, e.g. cytomegaly - marked enlargement of cells.

Cytarabine An antimetabolite analogue of cytidine with a modified sugar moiety (arabinose instead of ribose). Cytosine arabinoside is converted to the triphosphate form within the cell and then competes with cytidine for incorporation into DNA. Because the arabinose sugar sterically hinders the rotation of the molecule within DNA, DNA replication ceases, specifically during the S phase of the cell cycle. This agent also inhibits DNA polymerase, resulting in a decrease in DNA replication and repair.

Cytochlor A radio-sensitizing pyrimidine nucleoside with potential antineoplastic activity. Cytochlor is metabolized first to a phosphate derivative, CldCMP, by the enzyme deoxycytidine kinase and then to the active uracyl derivative, CldUMP, by the enzyme dCMP deaminase; deoxycytidine kinase and dCMP deaminase have been found in abnormally high concentrations in most cancers. CldUMP, the active metabolite, incorporates into DNA and, upon exposure to radiation, induces the formation of uracil radicals and double-strand DNA breaks.

Cytochrome P450 (CYP450) A system of enzymes, located primarily in the liver, that participate in the break-down of drugs. Many drugs inhibit or enhance the activity of these enzymes. Any change in CYP450 enzyme activity may cause an increase or decrease in blood levels of drugs broken down through this system.

Cytogenetics The study of chromosomes and chromosomal abnormalities.

Cytokine A chemical messenger protein released by certain white blood cells, including macrophages, monocytes or lymphocytes, the cytokines include the interferons, the interleukins, Tumor necrosis factor, and many others. Cytokines produced by lymphatic cells are also called "Lymphokines"

Cytological band An area of the chromosome that stains differently from areas around it.

Cytological map A type of chromosome map whereby genes are located on the basis of cytological findings obtained with the aid of chromosome mutations.

Cytology The study or examination of cells: their origin, structure, function and pathology to determine whether they are cancerous or benign.

Cytolysis The dissolution of cells particularly by destruction of their cell membrane.

Cytolytic Having a destructive effect on cells, causing them to erupt or burst open.

Cytomegalovirus (CMV) A herpesvirus that can cause infections, including pneumonia (infection of the lungs), gastroenteritis (infection of the gastrointestinal tract), encephalitis (inflammation of the brain), or retinitis (infection of the eye), in immunosuppressed people. Although CMV can infect most organs of the body, HIV-infected people are most susceptible to CMV retinitis.

Cytomegalovirus retinitis An infectious eye disease caused by cytomegalovirus (CMV). People with CMV retinitis can lose their vision, and CMV retinitis is the most common cause of blindness among people infected with HIV.

Cytometry The counting of cells, especially blood cells, using a cytometer (a standardized, ruled glass slide or small glass chamber of known volume).

Cytopathic Damaging to cells.

Cytopenia A condition in which the production of one or more kind of blood cells is greatly reduced or stops completely. Some medications used to treat HIV or cancer may cause cytopenia.

Cytoplasm The fluid inside a cell but outside the cell's nucleus. Most chemical reactions in a cell take place in the cytoplasm.

Cytoplasmic trait A genetic characteristic in which the genes are found outside the nucleus, in chloroplasts or mitochondria. Results in offspring inheriting genetic material from only one parent.

Cytosine (C) A nitrogenous base, one member of the base pair GC (guanine and cytosine) in DNA.

Cytoskeleton Protein filaments that extend through the cytoplasm of cells and enable them to move and change shape.

Cytostatic agents Therapeutics that inhibit cell division and growth.

This term can refer to machinery, such as those that would freeze cells.

Cytotoxic An agent or process which is toxic to cells that results in suppression of function or cell death.

Cytotoxic T cell A type of white blood cell that can directly destroy specific cells. T cells can be separated from other blood cells, grown in the laboratory, and then given to a patient to destroy tumor cells. Certain cytokines can also be given to a patient to help form cytotoxic T cells in the patient's body.

Cytotoxic chemotherapy Anticancer drugs that kill cells, especially cancer cells.

D

D & C (Dilation and curettage) A minor operation in which the cervix is expanded enough (dilation) to permit the cervical canal and uterine lining to be scraped with a spoon-shaped instrument called a curette (curettage). Also called dilatation and curettage.

D gene A small segment of immunoglobulin heavy-chain and T-cell receptor DNA, coding for the third hypervariable region of most receptors.

D value The time under a stated set of exposure conditions (temperature in an autoclave) required to reduce a microbial population by a factor of 90% (e.g. from 10,000 to 1,000).

D1/3 MAGE 3 his fusion protein A recombinant, chimeric protein derived from a melanoma antigenic epitope (MAGE-3) and recognized by specific cytotoxic T lymphocytes. MAGE-3, a human peptide epitope present in the cytosol of melanoma cells, may be expressed as the fusion protein D1/3-Mage-3; this fusion protein may boost antitumoral immune responses when used in a vaccine formulation.

D5W (5 D/W) One of the most prevalent of LVPs. Five percent dextrose in water. Presence of dextrose presents significant filtration problems. Usually requires activated charcoal pretreatment.

Da huang Rheum palmatum or Rheum officinale. The root of this plant has been used in some cultures to treat certain medical problems. It may have anti-inflammatory and anticancer effects. Also called rhubarb, Chinese rhubarb, Indian rhubarb, and Turkish rhubarb.

DACA Acridine carboxamide. A substance that is being studied in the treatment of cancer. It belongs to the family of drugs called topoisomerase inhibitors.

Dacarbazine A triazene derivative with antineoplastic activity. Dacarbazine alkylates and cross-links DNA during all phases of the cell cycle, resulting in disruption of DNA function, cell cycle arrest, and apoptosis.

Dacliximab A monoclonal antibody that is being studied in the treatment of adult T-cell leukemia and in the treatment of cytopenia (low blood cell count). Also called daclizumab.

Daclizumab A recombinant monoclonal antibody interleukin-2 receptor antagonist. Daclizumab binds specifically to the alpha subunit of the human interleukin-2 (IL-2) receptor expressed on the surface of activated lymphocytes in vivo, thereby inhibiting IL-2 binding and IL-2-mediated lymphocyte activation, a critical cellular immune response pathway.

Dactinomycin A chromopeptide antineoplastic antibiotic isolated from the bacterium Streptomyces parvulus. Dactinomycin intercalates between adjacent guanine-cytosine base pairs, blocking the transcription of DNA by RNA polymerase; it also causes single-strand DNA breaks, possibly via a free-radical intermediate or an interaction with topoisomerase II.

DAIDS The division of AIDS at the National Institute of Allergy and Infectious Diseases, DAIDS coordinates all of NIAID's AIDS research, and supervises extramural networks, including ACTG, DATRI, AVEU and spirat.

Daidzein An isoflavone found in soy products. Soy isoflavones are being studied in the prevention of cancer.

Dalteparin A low molecular weight, synthetic heparin. As an anticoagulant/antithrombotic agent, dalteparin binds to antithrombin and enhances the inhibition of Factor Xa. Compared to unfractionated heparins, the use of dalteparin is associated with lower incidences of osteoporosis and heparin-induced thrombocytopenia.

Dalton The unit of molecular weight, equal to the weight of a hydrogen atom.

Danazol A synthetic hormone that belongs to the family of drugs called androgens and is used to treat endometriosis. It is being evaluated in the treatment of endometrial cancer.

Dander Animal dander is the tiny particles of skin that are shed by animals such as cats and dogs. These are a major cause of allergies such as asthma and eczema. All furry animals shed dander including hamsters, gerbils, guinea pigs, rats, mice, rabbits and horses.

Dapsone An antibiotic active against Pneumocystis carinii, leprosy, and other pathogens, and to a lesser degree against toxoplasma gondii and MAC. Often used as a second line PCP prophylaxis in those unable to tolerate trimethoprim-sulphamethoxazole.

Darbepoetin alfa A recombinant analog of the endogenous cytokine erythropoietin, an erythropoiesis-stimulating protein. Due to the addition of two carbohydrate chains, darbepoetin alfa exhibits a three-fold greater half-life than does erythropoietin. Similar to erythropoietin, darbopoietin alfa binds to and activates epoetin receptors, thereby inducing the differentiation and maturation of erythrocyte progenitors, stimulating endothelial cell proliferation, and stimulating B-cell proliferation and immunoglobulin production.

Dark field microscope A microscope (device used to magnify small objects) in which objects are lit at a very low angle from the side so that the background appears dark and the objects show up against this dark background.

Dasatinib An orally bioavailable synthetic small molecule-inhibitor of SRC-family protein-tyrosine kinases. Dasatinib binds to and inhibits the growth-promoting activities of these kinases. Apparently because of its less stringent binding affinity for the BCR-ABL kinase, dasatinib has been shown to overcome the resistance to imatinib of chronic myeloid leukemia (CML) cells harboring BCR-ABL kinase domain point mutations. SRC-family protein-tyrosine kinases interact with variety of cell-surface receptors and participate in intracellular signal transduction pathways; tumorigenic forms can occur through altered regulation or expression of the endogenous protein and by way of virally-encoded kinase genes.

Data Factual information, such as measurements, observations, or statistics, which is used as a basis for reasoning, discussion, or calculation.

Data aggregation Combining of sets of protected health information by a business associate to permit data analysis.

Data collection visit Any visit by a patient to a study clinic that is used for data collection in the trial.

Data condition A description of the circumstances in which certain data is required.

Daunorubicin hydrochloride The hydrochloride salt of an anthracycline antineoplastic antibiotic with therapeutic effects similar to those of doxorubicin. Daunorubicin exhibits cytotoxic activity through topoisomerase-mediated interaction with DNA, thereby inhibiting DNA replication and repair and RNA and protein synthesis.

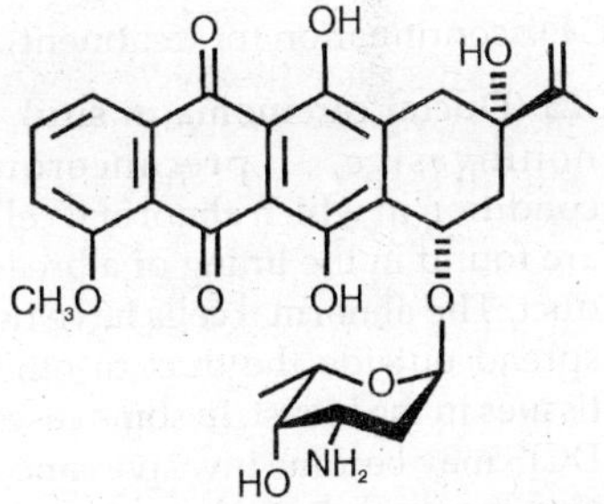

(8-acetyl-10- ((3-amino-2,3,6-trideoxy-alpha-L-lyxo-hexopyranosyl)oxy)-7,8,9,10-tetrahydro-6,8,11-trihydroxy-1-methoxy-, (8S,10S)-5,12-naphthacenedione)

Figure Daunorubicin

Dawn phenomenon A sudden rise in blood glucose levels in the early morning hours. This condition sometimes occurs in people with insulin-dependent diabetes and (rarely) in people with noninsulin-dependent diabetes. Unlike the Somogyi effect, it is not a result of an insulin reaction. People who have high levels of blood glucose in the mornings before eating may need to monitor their blood glucose during the night. If blood glucose levels are rising, adjustments in evening snacks or insulin dosages may be recommended.

Day outlier A patient with an atypically long length of stay compared with other patients in a particular diagnosis related group.

DBPC (Double blind placebo controlled) Test in which neither the physician nor the patient knows whether a placebo (dummy) is being administered or a drug or specific food is being administered.

DC Discontinuation (of treatment).

DCIS (Ductal carcinoma in situ) A noninvasive, precancerous condition in which abnormal cells are found in the lining of a breast duct. The abnormal cells have not spread outside the duct to other tissues in the breast. In some cases, DCIS may become invasive cancer and spread to other tissues, although it is not known at this time how to predict which lesions will become invasive. Also called intraductal carcinoma.

DDC (Direct digital control) A collection of control units (analog and discrete) connected into a data highway, usually with a host or alarming/recording computer attached.

DDS (Denys-drash syndrome) A rare disorder that causes kidney failure before age 3, abnormal develop-ment of the sexual organs, and, in most cases, Wilms' tumor (a type of kidney cancer). Children with Denys-Drash syndrome are also at high risk of some other types of cancer.

De minimis release The release of viable microbiological agents or eukaryotic cells that does not result in the establishment of disease in healthy people, plants, or animals; or in uncontrolled proliferation of any microbiological agents or eukaryotic cells.

De novo In cancer, the first occurrence of cancer in the body.

De quervain's disease Inflammation of the tendons and sheath of abductor pollicis longus and extensor pollicis brevis, in the first dorsal compartment of the wrist, with subsequent thickening and stenosis.

Dead leg An area of entrapment in a vessel or piping run that could lead to contamination of the product. In a piping system, a non-flowing pocket, tee, or extension from a primary piping run that exceeds a defined number of pipe diameters from the ID of the primary pipe. Denoted by the term L/D or L/A, where L is equal to the leg extension perpendicular to the normal flow pattern or direction, A is the annular gap width, and D is equal to the ID (or inside dimension) of the extension or leg. In some existing standards, the dimension L is measured from the centerline of the primary pipe. For bioprocessing systems, an L/D of 2:1 is achievable with today's component technology for most valving and piping configurations.

Death cap Amanita phalloides. A type of poisonous mushroom that has harmful effects on the kidneys and liver. It is responsible for most fatal cases of mushroom poisoning.

Debridement The removal of infected, hurt, or dead tissue.

Debulk To drastically reduce in size, decrease the amount of mass.

DECA Preferences meaning ten times, as in decagram, or ten grams.

Decapitation secretion Apocrine secretion where part of the apocrine cell "pinches off" and is released into the lumen of the gland.

Decaspray Other name for dexamethasone.

Decay Destruction of tooth structure caused by toxins produced by bacteria.

Decedents Deceased individuals. Afforded privacy rights under the HIPAA Privacy Rule, even though not considered "human subjects" protected under the Common Rule. As is the current practice, all research protocols involving the review of medical records of deceased subjects or of living and deceased subjects require review and approval by the HRC/IRB and can be conducted without informed consent and authorization only if the protocol satisfies the criteria for a waiver. If the research includes access to the records of decedents, the investigator will be asked to document that the decedents will only be used for research and that the information is necessary for the research. The covered entity may require the investigator to provide proof of death.

DECI Prefix meaning one tenth, as in decigram, or a tenth of a gram.

Deciduous teeth Commonly called "baby teeth," the first set of (usually) twenty teeth.

Decitabine A cytidine antimetabolite analogue with potential antineoplastic activity. Decitabine incorporates into DNA and inhibits DNA methyltransferase, resulting in hypomethylation of DNA and intra-S-phase arrest of DNA replication.

Decongestants Medicines that help to relieve the blocked nose associated with allergies such as hay fever and perennial allergic rhinitis. Available as tablets and nasal sprays based on Ephedrine. They relieve congestion by causing vascular constriction

Decontamination A process that reduces contaminating substances to a defined acceptance level.

Decortication Removal of part or all of the external surface of an organ.

Decussation A location in the brain where nerve fibers cross the midline (i.e. decussation of the superior cerebellar peduncle).

Deductible carry over credit Charge incurred during the last three months of a year that may be applied to the deductible and which may be carried over into the next year.

Deep Extending well inward from an outer surface.

Deep lymph nodes Small masses of lymphatic tissue that connect lymph vessels in the deep fascia.

Deep transverse frictions Cross fibre, deep massage. Often a technique utilised on scar tissue and chronic tendon disorders.

Deep vein thrombosis (DVT) Blockage of the deep veins, particularly common in the calf. Often mistaken for calf strain, the DVT is characterised by sharp pain in the calf, swelling, worsening with foot dependency and relief with elevation, tenderness and possibly some ecchymosis.

Defensive medicine Doctors in recent years have admitted to and have been accused of prescribing additional tests or procedures to justify their care, strengthen support for their decisions or simply to corroborate their diagnosis. This defensiveness is a result of lawsuits, malpractice claims and the onslaught of external UR entities questioning care decisions. Defensive medicine is said to be one of the primary causes of the increasing cost of health care. Many physicians fight for reform to reduce the need for defensive medicine. However, patient groups and patient advocates, not in favour of reform, explain that the right to sue for malpractice is a valid method of holding physicians accountable for mistakes made.

Deferasirox A synthetic, orally available, achiral, tridentate triazole derived from salicylic acid with iron chelator properties. Deferasirox chelates iron at a 2:1 (ligand:iron) ratio. Because of its oral availablity, and long plasma half-life, this agent may be superior to desferrioxamine (desferal, DFO), which is orally inactive and has a short plasma half-life.

Deferoxamine An iron-chelating agent that removes iron from tumors by inhibiting DNA synthesis and causing cancer cell death. It is used in conjunction with other anticancer agents in pediatric neuroblastoma therapy.

Defibrillation The stopping of a fast heart rate by delivering a high-energy electrical shock to restore the heart's normal rhythm. Electrical current is used to restore the heart's natural pacemaker function which resumes a normal heartbeat. The shock is administered through electrodes placed on the chest wall (external defibrillation) or in the heart (internal defibrillation).

Defibrillator An internal or external device that can deliver an electric shock to stop extremely rapid and irregular heartbeats and return the heart to normal rhythm.

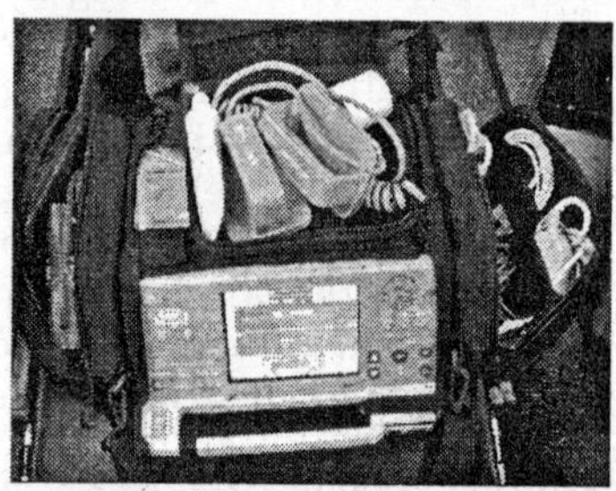

Figure An external defibrillator

Defibrotide A substance that is being studied in the prevention of veno-occlusive disease, a rare complication of high-dose chemotherapy and stem cell transplantation in which small veins in the liver become blocked.

Deficiency In medicine, a shortage of a substance (such as a vitamin or mineral) needed by the body.

Deficit Lack, or shortfall.

Deflagration An exothermic reaction, such as the extremely rapid oxidation of a combustible dust or flammable vapor in air, in which the reaction progresses through the unburned material at a rate less than the velocity of sound. A deflagration can have an explosive effect.

Degarelix A long-acting, synthetic peptide with gonadotrophin-releasing hormone (GnRH) antagonistic properties. Degarelix targets and blocks GnRH receptors located on the surfaces of gonadotroph cells in the anterior pituitary, thereby reducing secretion of luteinizing hormone (LH) by pituitary gonadotroph cells and so decreasing testosterone production by interstitial (Leydig) cells in the testes.

Degeneration Deterioration; change from a higher to lower form, especially as in change to less functional or healthy tissue.

Degenerative disease A disease in which the function or structure of the affected tissues or organs changes for the worse over time. Osteoarthritis, osteoporosis, and Alzheimer's disease are examples.

Degrading Deterioration of a surface finish so that pieces of the finish (or substrate) material large enough to be visible to the unaided eye, dislodge without any direct physical contact and fall from the surface of the material.

Dehiscence A splitting or gaping of the conjunctiva at a suture line or exposure of an implant.

Dehydration A condition caused by the loss of too much water from the body. Severe diarrhea or vomiting can cause dehydration.

Dehydroepiandrosterone A synthetic form of dehydroepiandrosterone with potential chemopreventive activity. Produced endogenously, dehydroepiandrosterone (DHEA) is an intermediate in the conversion of cholesterol to androgens and estrogens. Although the mechanisms of action of exogenously administered DHEA have not been fully illuminated, they may result in both direct and indirect physiologic effects. Direct effects include GABA-a receptor complex and NMDA receptor modulation, and enhanced pancreatic beta cell insulin secretion and antiglucocorticoid activities.

Deionization Removing dissolved ions from solution by passing the solution through a bed of ion exchange resin, consisting of polymer beads that exchange hydrogen ions for cations and hydroxyl ions for anions in solution. The ionic impurities remain bound to the resins and the hydrogen and hydroxyl ions combine with each other to form water.

Delamination The splitting apart or separation of layers, usually in the painted iris, when pigments used are incompatible to the acrylic.

Delayed type hypersensitivity (DTH) A cell-mediated immune response that produces a cellular infiltrate and edema (swelling), redness and induration (hardness) between 48 and 72 hours after exposure to an antigen. DTH response is the basis for PPD testing of tuberculosis exposure.

Deletion A loss of part of the DNA from a chromosome; can lead to a disease or abnormality.

Deletion map A description of a specific chromosome that uses defined mutations – specific deleted areas in the genome– as 'biochemical signposts,' or markers for specific areas.

Delta cell A type of cell in the pancreas in areas called the islets of Langerhans. Delta cells make somatostatin, a hormone that is believed to control how the beta cells make and release insulin and how the alpha cells make and release glucagon.

Demand A need or desire for a product or service. Price, availability and quality of the product all affect demand. Demand for health services is often difficult to assess and surveys of willingness to pay may be necessary to estimate its scope or extent.

Demarcate To separate, or to indicate the interface between two areas.

Dementia Chronic intellectual impairment (loss of mental capacity) with organic origins, that affects a person's ability to function in a social or occupational setting.

Demineralization Sometimes used interchangeably with deionization, it refers to the removal of minerals and mineral salts using ion exchange. Water softening is a common form of demineralization.

Denaturation The loss of the native structure of a macromolecule resulting, from heat treatment, extreme pH changes, chemical treatment, etc. It is accompanied by loss of biological activity. For example, proteins may be denatured by heat, pH extremes, or addition of agents such as urea or guanidinium hydrochloride.

Dendrite The highly branched tree-like process of a neuron that serves as a receptive field and conducts impulses toward the cell body.

Dendritic cells A type of antigen-presenting cell that picks up foreign substances from the bloodstream and "presents" them to other parts of the immune system, activating an immune response against the foreign invader.

Dendritic cell MART 1 peptide vaccine A cancer vaccine consisting of dendritic cells harvested from a patient with cancer and pulsed or transduced with a peptide fragment of MART-1 (melanoma antigen recognized by T-cells), an antigen expressed by melanoma cells. When the altered dendritic cells are returned to the patient, they stimulate the host immune system to mount a cytotoxic T-lymphocyte immune response against tumor cells expressing MART-1.

Denileukin diftitox A cytotoxic recombinant protein consisting of interleukin-2 (IL-2) protein sequences fused to diphtheria toxin. The IL-2 protein sequence moiety of denileukin difitox directs the cytocidal action of diphtheria toxin to cells that express IL-2 receptors. After the toxin moiety is internalized into target IL-2 receptor-expressing cells, its catalytic domain catalyzes the transfer of the ADP-ribose moiety of NAD to a posttranslationally modified histidine residue of elongation factor 2 (EF-2), called diphthamine. This covalent modification inactivates EF-2 and disrupts polypeptide chain elongation, resulting in cell death.

Dennie line Crease seen under eyelid in allergy sufferer.

Dent A typical stainless steel interior surface anomaly that refers to a large, smooth-bottomed depression whose diameter or width is greater than its depth and which will not produce an indication.

Dental caries Popularly known as cavities, dental caries occur when bacteria in the mouth feed on fermentable carbohydrates and produce acids that dissolve tooth enamel. Various conditions affect this process, such as heredity and the composition and flow of saliva. Any fermentable carbohydrate (starches and sugars) can serve as food for cavity-causing bacteria. The amount of carbohydrate is not as important as how often these foods are eaten and how long they stay in the mouth. Widespread use of fluoride in water supplies and oral health products is credited with the dramatic decline in dental caries among children and adults alike over the past 20 years.

Dental implant A metal, root-shaped device that is placed surgically in the jawbone. It acts as an anchor for attaching false teeth (crowns or bridges).

Dentate gyrus A slender gyrus with a scalloped appearance that runs along the hyppocampal sulcus; a component of the hippocampal formation. Like the hippocampus it consists of 3 cellular layers whose proce sses do not extend beyond the hippocampal formation.

Dentate nucleus The largest and most lateral of the cerebellar nuclei. It is located deep within the white matter of cerebellum and is shaped like a crumpled purse with its hilus directed medially.It is associated functionally with the neoce rebellum.

Denticulate ligament Condensation of spinal pia mater that laterally anchors the spinal cord along its length to the dura-arachnoid sleeve.

Dentin Inner layer of tooth structure, immediately under the surface enamel.

Dentist A health professional who specializes in caring for the teeth, gums, and other tissues in the mouth.

Dentition The arrangement of natural or artificial teeth in the mouth.

Denture Removable (partial or complete) set of artificial teeth.

Denturism The production of dentures dispensed directly by laboratory technicians.

Deoxycytidine A drug that protects healthy tissues from the toxic effects of anticancer drugs

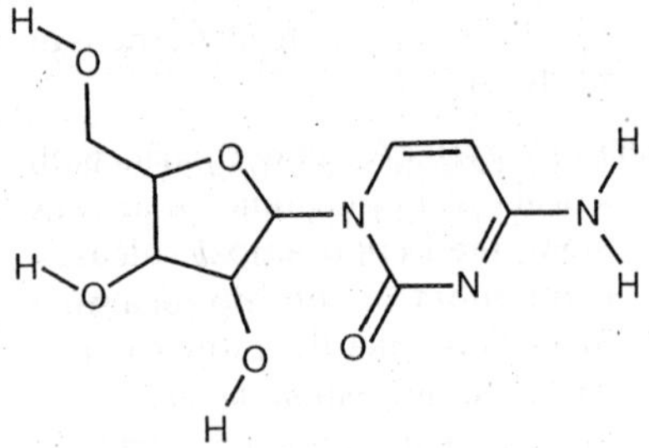

Figure Deoxycytidine

Deoxyribonucleic acid (DNA) Chemical structure that contains the genetic instructions for reproduction and protein synthesis for all cells and for many viruses.

Deoxyribose A type of sugar that is one component of DNA (deoxyribonucleic acid).

DepoFoam encapsulated cytarabine The anticancer drug cytarabine formulated inside small particles of a synthetic lipid material called DepoFoam. This dosage form slowly releases the drug and provides a sustained action.

Depression A mental condition marked by ongoing feelings of sadness, despair, loss of energy, and difficulty dealing with normal daily life. Other symptoms of depression include feelings of worthlessness and hopelessness, loss of pleasure in activities, changes in eating or sleeping habits, and thoughts of death or suicide. Depression can affect anyone, and can be successfully treated. Depression affects 15-25% of cancer patients.

Depsipeptide A substance that is made naturally by some bacteria, fungi, and other organisms, and can also be made in the laboratory. Depsipeptides are being studied in the treatment of cancer.

Depth perception test A test to measure the ability of the vision system to discern the relative distances of various objects. (Also called a "Stereopsis Test").

Depth perception The ability to judge relative distances of objects.

Depyrogenation The removal or destruction of endotoxins.

Derivative In chemistry, a compound produced from or related to another.

Derma, dermat (o) Skin, e.g. dermatitis - inflammation of the skin.

Dermal Relating to the skin.

Dermatitis Another name for eczema which includes Atopic Dermatitis and Contact Dermatitis.

Dermatochalasis Excessive eyelid skin caused by loss of its elasticity.

Dermatofibrosarcoma protuberans A type of tumor that begins as a hard nodule and grows slowly. These tumors are usually found in the dermis (the inner layer of the two main layers of tissue that make up the skin) of the limbs or trunk of the body. They can grow into surrounding tissue but do not spread to other parts of the body. These tumors are related to giant cell fibroblastoma.

Dermatographism A red, raised wheal that develops if the skin is firmly stroked. Commonly seen in people with Urticaria.

Dermatologist A doctor who has special training to diagnose and treat skin problems.

Dermatome Area of skin supplied by one spinal segment.

Dermatophagoides pteronyssius A type of house dust mite. Most common cause of asthma in the UK & NZ.

Dermatophyte A fungus belonging to any one of the genera (Microsporum, Trichophyton, and Epidermophyton) that can feed on keratin and cause ringworm (tinea)

Dermatoses Any disease of the skin, particularly one without inflammation

Dermis The lower or inner layer of the two main layers of tissue that make up the skin.

Dermis fat Autogenous tissue used to implant within the anophthalmic cavity for reduction of enophthalmos.

DES (Diethyl stilbestrol)A synthetic form of the hormone estrogen that was prescribed to pregnant women between about 1940 and 1971 because it was thought to prevent miscarriages. DES may increase the risk of uterine, ovarian, or breast cancer in women who took it. DES also has been linked to an increased risk of clear cell carcinoma of the vagina or cervix in daughters exposed to DES before birth.

Desalination The removal of dissolved salts from brine to produce potable water.

Descending aorta The protion of the aorta from the arch to its division in the abdomen into the common iliac arteries.

Descending colon The part of the colon between the left colic flexure ("splenic flexure") and the sigmoid colon (at the pelvic brim).

Desensitization A method to reduce or stop a response such as an allergic reaction to something. For instance, if a person with diabetes has a bad reaction to taking a full dose of beef insulin, the doctor gives the person a very small amount of the insulin at first. Over a period of time, larger doses are given until the person is taking the full dose. This is one way to help the body get used to the full dose and to avoid having the allergic reaction.

Desiccant Chemical salt used to dehumidify air, to control moisture in materials contacting that air.

Desiccators Closed containers, usually made of glass or plastic, with an airtight seal used for drying materials.

Design condition The specified range or accuracy of a controlled variable used by the designer to determine performance requirements of an engineered system.

Design specification A specification that defines the design of a system or system component.

Deslorelin A synthetic nonapeptide analogue of the natural gonadotrophin releasing hormone (GnRH) with potential antineoplastic activity. Deslorelin binds to and activates pituitary gonadotropin releasing hormone (GnRH) receptors. Continuous, prolonged administration of goserelin in males results in pituitary GnRH receptor desensitization and inhibition of pituitary secretion of follicle stimulating hormone (FSH) and luteinizing hormone (LH), leading to a significant decline in testosterone production; in females, prolonged administration results in a decrease in estradiol production.

Desmoid tumor A tumor of the tissue that surrounds muscles, usually in the abdomen. A desmoid tumor rarely metastasizes (spreads to other parts of the body). Also called aggressive fibromatosis, especially when the tumor is outside the abdomen.

Desmoplastic Causing or forming adhesions or fibrous connective tissue within a tumor.

Desmoplastic melanoma A rare form of malignant melanoma marked by nonpigmented lesions on sun-exposed areas of the body, most commonly on the head and neck.

Desmoplastic small round cell tumor A rare, aggressive cancer that usually affects young males and usually is located in the abdomen.

Desquamating Shedding or losing skin, particularly as in grade 3 and 4 rashes

Detection Finding disease. Early detection means that the disease is found at an early stage, before it has grown large or spread to other sites. Mammography is the principal way to detect breast cancer early. A mammogram can show a developing breast tumor before it can be felt by the woman herself or even by a highly skilled health professional. Women participate in early detection by performing monthly breast self-examination, getting medical attention immediately for any suspicious lumps or discomfort in the breast, and having mammograms on the schedule.

Determinant Part of the antigen molecule which binds to an antibody-combining site or to a receptor on T cell.

Detonation An exothermic reaction characterized by the presence of a shock wave in a material that establishes and maintains the reaction. The reaction zone progresses through the material at a rate greater than the velocity of sound. The principal heating mechanism is one of shock compression. Detonations have an explosive effect.

Detox B adjuvant A cancer vaccine adjuvant that consists of an oil droplet emulsion of monophosphoryl lipid A and mycobacterial cell wall skeleton. Detox-B adjuvant is a non-specific immunostimulant that may enhance the host immune response to certain cancer vaccines. Detox-B differs from Detox adjuvant in that Detox-B contains lecithin.

Deuteromycetes Molds that cannot reproduce by sexual means. Some pathogenic fungi such as Trichophyton, which causes athlete's foot, belong to this family.

Developmental disorder When a delay in an individual's normal development has occurred.

Developmental vision analysis More comprehensive than a routine eye exam, examination will evaluate all of the patient's visual abilities such as visual acuity, eye focusing skills, eye teaming skills, eye tracking skills, visual motor skills, and visual perceptual skills.

Dexamethasone A synthetic steroid (similar to steroid hormones produced naturally in the adrenal gland). Dexamethasone is used to treat leukemia and lymphoma and may be used to treat some of the problems caused by other cancers and their treatment.

Dexmethylphenidate A substance that is being studied in the treatment of fatigue and nervous system side effects caused by chemotherapy. It belongs to the family of drugs called central nervous system stimulants.

Dexrazoxane hydrochloride The hydrochloride salt of a bisdioxopiperazine with cardioprotective and antineoplastic activities. After hydrolysis to an active form that is similar to ethylenediaminetetraacetic acid (EDTA), dexrazoxane chelates iron, thereby preventing the metal-catalyzed formation of reactive oxygen radicals produced by anthracycline antibiotics such as doxorubicin. This agent also inhibits the catalytic activity of topoisomerase II, resulting in cell growth inhibition.

Dextroamphetamine-amphetamine A combination of two synthetic agents with central nervous system stimulant activity. Both agents are non-catecholamine, sympathomimetic agents that elevate blood pressure and cause bronchodilation. These agents are commonly abused psychostimulant drugs that induce psychologic dependence manifested by elevated mood, increased wakefulness, concentration, physical performance and a feeling of well-being. Tolerance to various effects develops unequally, so that tachycardia and enhanced alertness diminish while psychotoxic effects (hallucinations and delusions) may occur.

Dextromethorphan acetic acid An anticancer drug that belongs to the family of drugs called angiogenesis inhibitors.

Dextrose A simple sugar found in the blood. It is the body's main source of energy. Also called glucose.

DFMO (Difluoromethylornithine) A substance that is being studied in the treatment of cancer.

DHA paclitaxel A prodrug comprised of the naturally occurring omega-3 fatty acid docosahexaenoic acid (DHA) covalently conjugated to the anti-microtubule agent paclitaxel. Because tumor cells take up DHA, DHA-paclitaxel is delivered directly to tumor tissue, where the paclitaxel moiety binds to tubulin and inhibits the disassembly of microtubules, thereby resulting in the inhibition of cell division. Paclitaxel also induces apoptosis by binding to and blocking the function of the apoptosis inhibitor protein Bcl-2 (B-cell Leukemia 2). DHA-paclitaxel exhibits improved pharmacokinetic and toxicity profiles when compared to conventional paclitaxel and has demonstrated antineoplastic activity in animal models of cancer.

DHL vaccine A tri-valent vaccine. Also, the most common veterinary vaccine that has a combination of viral and bacterial vaccines. Used for distemper, hepatitis (canine), and leptospira.

Di hydrofolate reductase (DHR) The bacterial (or protozoal) enzyme targeted by trimethoprim-sulphamethoxazole: DHR is necessary for pneumocystis or Toxoplasmosis to survive.

Dia Through; between; ss, e.g. diarrhea - fecal matter flowing through the bowel.

Diabetes control and complications trial (DCCT) A 10-year study (1983-1993) funded by the National Institute of Diabetes and Digestive and Kidney Diseases to assess the effects of intensive therapy on the long-term complications of diabetes. The study proved that intensive management of insulin-dependent diabetes prevents or slows the development of eye, kidney, and nerve damage caused by diabetes.

Diabetes insipidus A disease of the pituitary gland or kidney, not diabetes mellitus. Diabetes insipidus is often called "water diabetes" to set it apart from "sugar diabetes." The cause and treatment are not the same as for diabetes mellitus. "Water diabetes" has diabetes in its name because most people who have it show most of the same signs as someone with diabetes mellitus-they have to urinate often, get very thirsty and hungry, and feel weak. However, they do not have glucose (sugar) in their urine.

Diabetes mellitus A disease that occurs when the body is not able to use sugar as it should. The body needs sugar for growth and energy for daily activities. It gets sugar when it changes food into glucose (a form of sugar). A hormone called insulin is needed for the glucose to be taken up and used by the body. Diabetes occurs when the body cannot make use of the glucose in the blood for energy because either the pancreas is not able to make enough insulin or the insulin that is available is not effective. The beta cells in areas of the pancreas called the islets of Langerhans usually make insulin.

There are two main types of diabetes mellitus: insulin-dependent (Type 1) and noninsulin-dependent (Type 2). In insulin-dependent diabetes (IDDM), the pancreas makes little or no insulin because the insulin-producing beta cells have been destroyed. This type usually appears suddenly and most commonly in younger people under age 30. Treatment consists of daily insulin injections or use of an insulin pump, a planned diet and regular exercise, and daily self-monitoring of blood glucose.

In noninsulin-dependent diabetes (NIDDM), the pancreas makes some insulin, sometimes too much. The insulin, however, is not effective. NIDDM is controlled by diet and exercise and daily monitoring of glucose levels. Sometimes oral drugs that lower blood glucose levels or insulin injections are needed. This type of diabetes usually develops gradually, most often in people over 40 years of age. NIDDM accounts for 90 to 95 percent of diabetes.

The signs of diabetes include having to urinate often, losing weight, getting very thirsty, and being hungry all the time. Other signs are blurred vision, itching, and slow healing of sores. People with untreated or undiagnosed diabetes are thirsty and have to urinate often because glucose builds to a high level in the bloodstream and the kidneys are working hard to flush out the extra amount. People with untreated diabetes often get hungry and tired because the body is not able to use food the way it should.

In insulin-dependent diabetes, if the level of insulin is too low for a long period of time, the body begins to break down its stores of fat for energy. This causes the body to release acids (ketones) into the blood. The result is called ketoacidosis, a severe condition that may put a person into a coma if not treated right away.

The causes of diabetes are not known. Scientists think that insulin- dependent diabetes may be more than one disease and may have many causes. They are looking at hereditary (whether or not the person has parents or other family members with the disease) and at factors both inside and outside the body, including viruses.

Noninsulin-dependent diabetes appears to be closely associated with obesity and with the body resisting the action of insulin.

Diabetic amyotrophy A disease of the nerves leading to the muscles. This condition affects only one side of the bod-y and occurs most often in older men with mild diabetes.

Diabetic coma A severe emergency in which a person is not conscious because the blood glucose (sugar) is too low or too high. If the glucose level is too low, the person has hypoglycemia; if the level is too high, the person has hyperglycemia and may develop ketoacidosis.

Diabetic dermopathy A characteristic skin disorder found in up to 50% of male adults and 30% of female adults with diabetes. The lesions may be round or oval and usually are red or reddish brown, and usually measure 1-3 inches. They usually occur on the thigh or shin, but may appear also on the scalp, forearm and trunk. There is not an effective treatment and the lesions tend to disappear spontaneously after several years.

Diabetic ketoacidosis (DKA) Severe, out-of-control diabetes (high blood sugar) that needs emergency treatment. DKA is caused by a profound lack of circulating insulin. This may happen because of illness, taking too little insulin, or getting too little exercise. The body starts using stored fat for energy, and ketone bodies (acids) build up in the blood.

Ketoacidosis starts slowly and builds up. The signs include nausea and vomiting, which can lead to loss of water from the body, stomach pain, and deep and rapid breathing. Other signs are a flushed face, dry skin and mouth, a fruity breath odor, a rapid and weak pulse, and low blood pressure. If the person is not given fluids and insulin right away, ketoacidosis can lead to coma and even death.

Diabetic myelopathy Spinal cord damage found in some people with diabetes.

Diabetic osteopathy Loss of foot bone as viewed by x-ray; usually temporary. Also called "disappearing bone disease."

Diabetic retinopathy A disease of the small blood vessels of the retina of the eye. When retinopathy first starts, the tiny blood vessels in the retina become swollen, and they leak a little fluid into the center of the retina. The person's sight may be blurred. This condition is called background retinopathy. About 80 percent of people with background retinopathy never have serious vision problems, and the disease never goes beyond this first stage.

However, if retinopathy progresses, the harm to sight can be more serious. Many new, tiny blood vessels grow out and across the eye. This is called neovascularization. The vessels may break and bleed into the clear gel that fills the center of the eye, blocking vision. Scar tissue may also form near the retina, pulling it away from the back of the eye. This stage is called proliferative retinopathy, and it can lead to impaired vision and even blindness.

Diabetogenic Causing diabetes; some drugs cause blood glucose (sugar) to rise, resulting in diabetes.

Diabetologist A doctor who sees and treats people with diabetes mellitus.

Diagnosis related groups (DRGs) An inpatient or hospital classification system used to pay a hospital or other provider for their services and to categorize illness by diagnosis and treatment. Groupings of diagnostic categories drawn from the International Classification of Diseases and modified by the presence of a surgical procedure, patient age, presence or absence of significant comorbidities or complications, and other relevant criteria. System involving classification of medical cases and payment to hospitals on the basis of diagnosis.

Diagnosis The process of determining health status and the factors responsible for producing it; it may be applied to an individual, family, group or community. The diagnosis should take into account etiology, pathology, and severity of the clinical state.

Diagnostic mammogram X-ray of the breasts used to check for breast cancer after a lump or other sign or symptom of breast cancer has been found.

Diagnostic procedure A method used to identify a disease.

Diagnostic trial A research study that evaluates methods of detecting disease.

Diagonal band (of broca) An association bundle of fibers located immediately rostral to the optic tract and forming the posterior border of the of the anterior perforated substance. It interconnects the paraterminal gyrus and subcallosal area (septal area) and septal nuclei with the hippocampus and lateral olfactory area.

Diallyl sulfide A type of sulfide/thoil found in onions, garlic, olives, leeks and scallions which may provide the health benefits of lowering LDL cholesterol and of maintaining a healthy immune system.

Dialysis A method for removing waste such as urea from the blood when the kidneys can no longer do the job. The two types of dialysis are: hemodialysis and peritoneal dialysis. In hemodialysis, the patient's blood is passed through a tube into a machine that filters out waste products. The cleansed blood is then returned to the body.

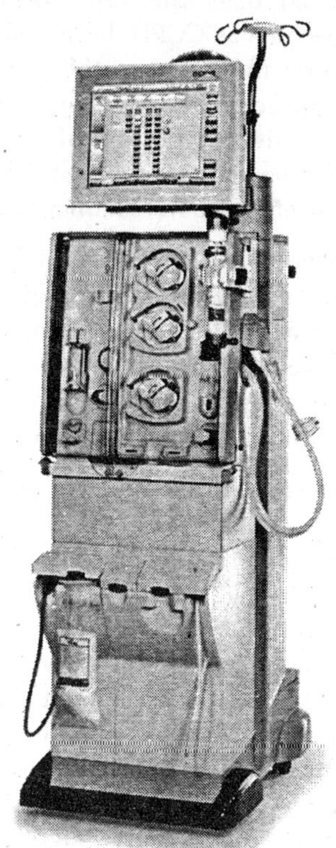

Figure Dialysis machine

In peritoneal dialysis, a special solution is run through a tube into the peritoneum, a thin tissue that lines the cavity of the abdomen. The body's waste products are removed through the tube. There are three types of peritoneal dialysis. Continuous ambulatory peritoneal dialysis (CAPD), the most common type, needs no machine and can be done at home. Continuous cyclic peritoneal dialysis (CCPD) uses a machine and is usually performed at night when the person is sleeping. Intermittent peritoneal dialysis (IPD) uses the same type of machine as CCPD, but is usually done in the hospital because treatment takes longer. Hemodialysis and peritoneal dialysis may be used to treat people with diabetes who have kidney failure.

Diameter The length of a straight line that extends from one edge of a tumor or other object, through its center and to the opposite edge. It is usually used to measure the size of round or spherical shapes.

Diaphanography Also called transillumination, this is a method of examining the breast. It is used primarily in younger women (40 years of age or less), for whom mammography is not appropriate. The technique uses bright light to illuminate inner structures, in much the same way that children observe the blood and bones in their hands with a flashlight. It has limitations and by itself is not an adequate method of examination for suspicious lumps or thickenings in the breast.

Diaphragm The muscle and membrane separating the abdominal and thoracic cavities of the body. Major inspiratory muscle.

Diaphragma sellae Horizontal partition of dura mater which roofs over the sella turcica (hypophysial fossa) enclosing the pituitary stalk and separating the pituitary gland from the ypothalamus.

Diaphysis The shaft of a long bone between the two "metaphyses"; tube of compact bone surrounding the marrow cavity.

Diarrhea Uncontrolled, loose, watery, and frequent bowel movements caused by diet, infection, medication, or irritation or inflammation of the intestine. Severe or long-lasting diarrhea can lead to weight loss and malnutrition. The most common infectious organisms causing HIV-related diarrhea include cytomegalovirus (CMV); the parasites Cryptosporidium, Microsporidia, and Giardia; and the bacteria Mycobacterium avium and Mycobacterium intracellulare. Bacteria and parasites that cause diarrheal symptoms in otherwise healthy people may cause more severe, prolonged, or recurrent diarrhea in people with HIV or AIDS.

Diastema Space between teeth.

Diathermy The use of heat to destroy abnormal cells. Also called cauterization or electrodiathermy.

Diatom Any minute, unicellular or colonial algae of the class Bacillariophyceae having siliceous cells walls consisting of two overlapping symmetrical parts.

Diatomaceous earth, diatomite, kiselguhr (DE) Fine silicaceous powder used as a filter aid.

Diaziquone AZQ An anticancer drug that is able to cross the blood-brain barrier and kill cancer cells in the central nervous system.

Didanosine (DDI) A nucleoside analogue reverse transcriptase inhibitor, didanosine is in the same family of antiviral drugs as AZT. It's primary toxicities are pancreatitis and neuropathy.

Diencephalon Subdivision of the forebrain (prosencephalon) located between the telencephalon (end brain) and the mesencephalon (mid brain). It consists of the thalamus, hypothalamus, sub-thalamus and epithalamus and has important sensory, motor, endocrine , and visceral functions.

DIEP flap A type of breast reconstruction in which blood vessels called deep inferior epigastric perforators (DIEP), and the skin and fat connected to them are removed from the lower abdomen and used for reconstruction. Muscle is left in place.

Diet The things a person eats and drinks.

Dietary supplement Vitamins, minerals, or other substances taken by mouth, and intended as an addition to the diet.

Dietitian An expert in nutrition who helps people with special health needs plan the kinds and amounts of foods to eat. A registered dietitian (R.D.) has special qualifications. The health care team for diabetes should include a dietitian, preferably an R.D.

Differentiated A type of cell, which specializes in one specific task or has one specific purpose.

Differentiation In cancer, refers to how mature (developed) the cancer cells are in a tumor. Differentiated tumor cells resemble normal cells and tend to grow and spread at a slower rate than undifferentiated or poorly differentiated tumor cells, which lack the structure and function of normal cells and grow uncontrollably.

Differentiation antigen A cell surface antigenic determinant found only on cells of a certain lineage and at a particular developmental stage; used as an immunologic marker.

Diffuse large B-cell lymphoma A type of B-cell non-Hodgkin's lymphoma (cancer of the immune system) that is usually aggressive (fast-growing). It is the most common type of non-Hodgkin's lymphoma, and is marked by rapidly growing tumors in the lymph nodes, spleen, liver, bone marrow, or other organs. Other symptoms include fever, night sweats, and weight loss. There are several subtypes of diffuse large B-cell lymphoma.

Diffusion The random thermal motion of particles, which causes them to flow from a region of higher concentration to one of lower concentration until they are uniformly distributed.

Digestion How the body breaks down food and uses it for energy, cell repair, and growth. Starts in the mouth, continues in the stomach and small intestine, and is completed in the large intestine. The liver and pancreas add enzymes and juices that aid in this process.

Digestive system The organs that are responsible for getting food into and out of the body and for making use of it. These organs include the salivary glands, the mouth, esophagus, stomach, small intestine, liver, gallbladder, pancreas, colon, rectum, and anus.

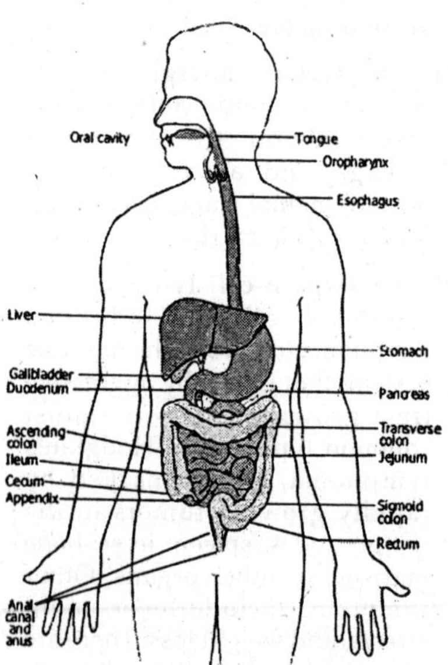

Figure Digestive system

Digital A series of on and off pulses arranged to convey information.

Digital mammography A technique that uses a computer, rather than x-ray film, to record x-ray images of the breast.

Digital rectal examination (DRE) An examination in which a doctor inserts a lubricated, gloved finger into the rectum to feel for abnormalities.

Digital representation Biometric parameters such as a fingerprint or retinal pattern are turned into data that a computer understands: the digital representation of the biometric. The pattern in the biometric divides it into a grid of boxes, and a zero or a one, depending on whether the box is filled in, marks each box.

Digital signature An electronic signature based upon cryptographic methods of originator authentication, computed by using a set of rules and a set of parameters such that the identity of the signer and the integrity of the data can be verified.

Dihematoporphyrin ether Used in photodynamic therapy, a drug that is absorbed by tumor cells; when exposed to light, it becomes active and kills the cancer cells.

Dilatation (Dilation) Gradual opening of the narrowed coronary artery by cracking and compressing the narrowing or obstructing plaque.

Dilate To widen or enlarge an opening or hollow structure beyond its usual size, such as the pupil of the eye or a blood vessel.

Dilated pupil examination A necessary part of an examination for diabetic eye disease. Special drops are used to enlarge the pupils, enabling the doctor to view the back of the eye for damage.

Dilator A device used to stretch or enlarge an opening.

Dilution factor The ratio of solvent to solute by volume.

Dilution Lowering the concentration of a solution by adding more solvent.

Dimesna A synthetic derivative of dithio-ethane sulfonate with uroprotective properties. In the kidney, dimesna undergoes reduction to the free thiol compound, mesna, which reacts chemically with the urotoxic ifosfamide metabolites acrolein and 4-hydroxy-ifosfamide, resulting in their detoxification. This agent also inhibits cyclophosphamide-induced hemorrhagic cystitis.

Dimethyl sulfoxide A colourless liquid that readily dissolves many chemicals and penetrates animal and plant tissues. It is used in human medicine, veterinary medicine, and pharmaceuticals.

Dimethylxanthenone acetic acid A fused tricyclic analogue of flavone acetic acid with potential antineoplastic activity. Dimethylxanthenone acetic acid induces the cytokines tumor necrosis alpha (TNF-alpha), serotonin and nitric oxide, resulting in hemorrhagic necrosis and a decrease in angiogenesis. This agent also stimulates the anti-tumor activity of tumor-associated macrophages.

Dimpling A pucker or indentation of the skin; on the breast, it may be a sign of cancer.

Diopter (D) A measurement of the refractive (light bending) power of a lens or a prism (pd). The strength of prescription glasses and contacts are measured in these units. For example a lens that is 0.50 diopter (D) is very weak, where as a lens that is 10.0 diopter (D) is very strong.

Diphosphonate A drug used to treat osteoporosis and the bone pain caused by some types of cancer. Also called bisphosphonate.

Diphtheritic membrane A thin coating on the surface of an epithelial lined organ (e.g. intestine) that is composed of necrotic cellular debris, inflammatory cells and fibrin.

Diploic space The medullary space between the dense cortical bone of inner and outer tables of the flat calvarial bones of the skull, composed of cancellous bone and bone marrow.

Diploid A full set of genetic material consisting of paired chromosomes, one from each parental set. Most animal cells except the gametes have a diploid set of chromosomes. The diploid human genome has 46 chromosomes.

Diplophase A phase in the life cycle of an organism where the organism has two copies of each gene. The organism is said to be diploid.

Diplopia A single object is perceived as two rather than one; double vision.

Diptera A large group of insects, including mosquitoes, gnats and houseflies that possess a single pair of wings.

Dipyridamole A drug that prevents blood cell clumping and enhances the effectiveness of fluorouracil and other chemotherapeutic agents.

Direct occlusion Covering the non-amblyopic eye.

Direct patient contact Patient contacts that are initiated by the study clinic for the purpose of patient recruitment or data collection and that are directed at specified patients without any reliance on interviewing persons, agencies, institutions, or generalized advertising campaigns to make contacts.

Directed evolution A laboratory process used on isolated molecules or microbes to cause mutations and identify subsequent adaptations to novel environments.

Directed mutagenesis Alteration of DNA at a specific site and its reinsertion into an organism to study any effects of the change.

Directed sequencing Successively sequencing DNA from adjacent stretches of chromosome.

Directionality/laterality Directionality relates to the awareness of the relationship of one object in space to another / laterality relates to the internal awareness of the two sides of the body. Directionality/ Laterality can also be called spatial relations.

Directionality/laterality disorder A condition in which an individual has poor development of left/ right awareness. Symptoms of this disorder include confusion of right and left direction and letters and/ or numbers reversals. Vision therapy is a helpful treatment option.

Disallowance When a payer declines to pay for all or part of a claim submitted for payment.

Disaster Any event (i.e. fire, earthquake, power failure etc.), which could have a detrimental effect upon an automated system or its associated information.

Disc and disc space The space between the vertebrae, formed from a fibrous ring (the annulus) and a central "cushion" (nucleus pulposis).

Disc herniation Often used interchangeably with disc prolapse, disc bulge, slipped disc etc. Disruption to the normal integrity of the intervertebral disc, causing the nucleus pulposus to breach the annular fibres internally. There are varying degrees, from minor bulging, to bursting through the outer annular fibres into the spinal canal.

Discectomy Surgical removal of prolapsed nucleus pulposus.

Discipline based approach Teaching of the individual classical medical disciplines such as anatomy, biochemistry, pathology, surgery or community medicine as separate educational building blocks. It is expected that this approach lays the foundation for contact with patients which tends to occur later, after completion of the basic science course. In this approach, it is left to the student to put together the knowledge gained in each discipline to form an overall picture of medicine.

Discolouration (Welding) Any change in surface colour from that of the base metal. Usually associated with oxidation occurring on the weld and heat affected zone (HAZ) on the outside diameter and inside diameter of the weld joint as a result of heating the metal during the welding. Colours may range from pale bluish-gray to deep blue, and from pale straw colour to a black crusty coating.

Discordant couple A pair of long-term sexual partners in which one person is infected with a sexually transmitted infection (such as HIV) and the other is not.

Discrete variable A variable is capable of assuming only certain values over a defined range.

Disease A general term used to refer to any departure from health in which a patient suffers. It can be defined as disorder of bodily function or destructive processes in organs, organs' systems or in an organism with recognizable signs and symptoms, and in many cases a known cause. The words disease, illness and sickness are used often interchangeably but are not synonymous. Rather, whereas disease relates to a physiological or psychological dysfunction, an illness is the subjective state of a patient who feels unwell and sickness encompasses a state of social dysfunction, such as the role that the individual assumes when ill.

Disease management A type of product or service now being offered by many large pharmaceutical companies to get them into broader healthcare services. Bundles use of prescription drugs with physician and allied professionals, linked to large databases created by the pharmaceutical companies, to treat people with specific diseases. The claim is that this type of service provides higher quality of care at more reasonable price than alternative, presumably more fragmented, care. The development of such products by hugely capitalized companies should be the entire indicator necessary to convince a provider of how the healthcare market is changing. Competition is coming from every direction—other providers of all types, payers, employers who are developing their own in-house service systems, the drug companies.

Disease progression Cancer that continues to grow or spread.

Disease-associated genes Alleles carrying particular DNA sequences associated with the presence of disease.

Disease-free survival Length of time after treatment during which no cancer is found. Can be reported for an individual patient or for a study population.

Disease-specific survival The percentage of subjects in a study who have survived a particular disease for a defined period of time. Usually reported as time since diagnosis or treatment. In calculating this percentage, only deaths from the disease being studied are counted. Subjects who died from some other cause are not included in the calculation.

Disinfection Process by which viable microbiological agents or eukaryotic cells are reduced to a level unlikely to produce disease in healthy people, plants, or animals. These processes may use chemical agents, heat, ultraviolet light, etc. to destroy most (but not necessarily all) of the harmful or objectionable microorganisms, pathogens, and potential pathogens. Disinfection does not necessarily result in sterilization. 1. "High level disinfection" inactivates fungi, viruses, and bacteria. High-level chemical disinfectants may be ineffective against bacterial spores if they are present in large numbers. Extended exposure times may be required.

2. "Intermediate level disinfection" destroys fungi, some viruses (lipid and most non-lipid medium-size and small viruses), mycobacteria, and bacteria.

3. "Low level disinfection" kills vegetative forms of bacteria, some fungi, and some medium-size and lipid-containing viruses. Low-level disinfectants do not reliably kill bacterial spores, mycobacteria, or small or non-lipid viruses.

Disorder In medicine, a disturbance of normal functioning of the mind or body. Disorders may be caused by genetic factors, disease, or trauma.

Dispensing The pouring or transferring of any material from a container, tank or similar vessel, whereby vapours, dusts, fumes, mists or gases may be liberated to the atmosphere.

Dissection Surgery to divide, separate, or remove tissues.

Disseminate Scatter or distribute over a large area or range.

Dissimilation The breakdown of food material to yield energy and building blocks for cellular synthesis.

Dissolved solids The amount of nonvolatile matter dissolved in a water sample, usually expressed in parts per million (PPM) by weight.

Distal In medicine, refers to a part of the body that is farther away from the center of the body than another part. For example, the fingers are distal to the shoulder. The opposite is proximal.

Distal pancreatectomy Removal of the body and tail of the pancreas.

Distance acuity The eye's ability to distinguish an object's shape and details at a far distance such as 20 feet (6 meters).

Distant cancer Refers to cancer that has spread from the original (primary) tumor to distant organs or distant lymph nodes. Also known as distant metastasis.

Distant metastasis Refers to cancer that has spread from the original (primary) tumor to distant organs or distant lymph nodes. Also known as distant cancer.

Distention Swelling or bloating, usually referring to the abdomen.

Distillation The process of separating water from impurities by heating until it changes into vapour and then cooling the vapour to condense it into purified water.

Distraction In medicine, a pain relief method that takes the patient's attention away from the pain.

Distribution, normal (gaussian) distribution A symmetrical distribution which has a shape defined by its mean and standard deviation. Mean=median=mode. Often called the bell-shaped curve.

Disulfiram A drug that slows the metabolism of retinoids, allowing them to act over a longer period of time.

Figure Disulfiram

Diuretic A drug that increases the amount of water in the urine, removing excess water from the body; used in treating high blood pressure and fluid retention

Divergence EXCESS (DE) (clinical condition) The eye's tendency to drift out relative to the direction of a distant object being viewed. Symptoms include: double vision at distance, headaches, eyestrain, nausea, dizziness, and blurred vision. Clinical signs include: exophoria greater at distance than near, high AC/A ratio, and reduced positive fusional vergence at distance. Can be improved with vision therapy.

Divergence insufficiency (DI) (clinical condition) The eye's tendency to turn more inward than necessary when viewing a distant object. Symptoms include: double vision, headaches, eyestrain, nausea, dizziness, and blurred vision. Clinical signs: esophoria greater at distance than near, low AC/A ratio, and reduced negative fusional vergence at distance. Treated with corrective lenses and vision therapy.

Divergence The ability to use both eyes as a team and be able to turn the eyes out toward a far object.

Diverticulosis A condition marked by small sacs or pouches (diverticula) in the walls of an organ such as the stomach or colon. These sacs can become inflamed and cause a condition called diverticulitis, which may be a risk factor for certain types of cancer.

Diverticulum A small pouch in the wall of the large intestine, which usually do not cause a problem unless it becomes irritated or infected.

Division of aids treatment research initiative An extramural program funded by NIAID to due technically challenging cutting edge AIDS clinical research.

DMD (Doctor of medical dentistry) Equivalent to DDS.

DNA (Deoxyribonucleic acid) The molecule of which the genetic material is composed. It consists of two chains joined together as a double helix. Each chain is composed of a polymer of nucleotides (consisting of a nitrogenous base, a deoxyribosesugar ring, and a phosphate group) joined together by phosphodiester bonds between the 5'-phosphate of one nucleotide and the 3'-hydroxyl of the next. The two chains run in opposite directions and are held together by hydrogen bonds between the bases in equivalent positions in the two chains. There are various forms of double helical DNA. They are: 1. B-DNA (first described by Crick and Watson) is a right-handed helix with 10.6 base pairs per turn and is probably the main form of cellular DNA.

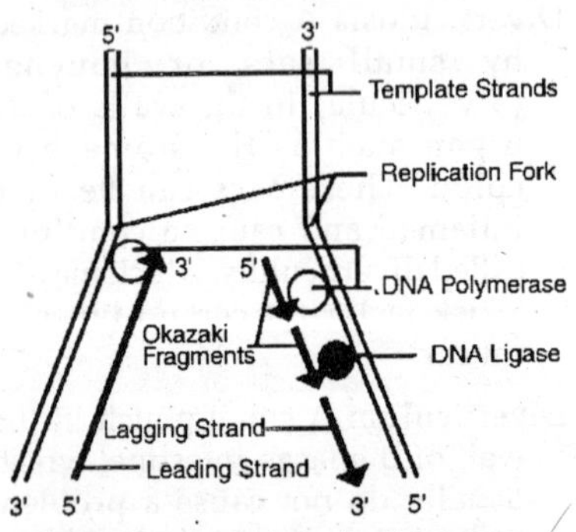

DNA replication. In the first step, a very light, non-fattening portion of the double helix is unwound by a helicase. Next, a molecule of DNA polymerase binds to one strand of the DNA.

Figure DNA

2. A-DNA is also a right-handed helix but is somewhat skewed and contains about 11 base pairs per turn. It is the form taken By DNA-RNA hybrid double helixes.

3. Z-DNA is a left-handed helix with 11 base pairs per turn. It is favored by regions rich in guanine cutosine base pairs and probably occurs infrequently in cellular DNA.

DNA array Spots of DNA arranged on a slide support such as glass or silicon "DNA chip" (or microarray), used for screening, sequencing, genetic mapping, and so on.

DNA bank A service that stores DNA extracted from blood samples or other human tissue.

DNA repair genes Genes encoding proteins that correct errors in DNA sequencing.

DNA replication The use of existing DNA as a template for the synthesis of new DNA strands. In humans and other eukaryotes, replication occurs in the cell nucleus.

DNA sequence The relative order of base pairs, whether in a DNA fragment, gene, chromosome, or an entire genome.

DNA vector A DNA vehicle for transferring generic information from one cell to another.

DNAse (Deoxyribonuclease) An enzyme that degrades DNA.

DNR order (Do not resuscitate order) A type of advance directive in which a person states that healthcare providers should not perform cardiopulmonary resuscitation (restarting the heart) if his or her heart or breathing stops.

Docetaxel A semi-synthetic, second-generation taxane derived from a compound found in the European yew tree, Taxus baccata. Docetaxel displays potent and broad antineoplastic properties; it binds to and stabilizes tubulin, thereby inhibiting microtubule disassembly which results in cell- cycle arrest at the G2/M phase and cell death. This agent also inhibits pro-angiogenic factors such as vascular endothelial growth factor (VEGF) and displays immunomodulatory and pro-inflammatory properties by inducing various mediators of the inflammatory response. Docetaxel has been studied for use as a radiation-sensitizing agent.

Dock Rumex acetosella. A plant that has been used in some cultures to treat certain medical problems. It may have anticancer effects. Also called sheep sorrel and sorrel.

Documentation Written or pictorial information describing, defining, specifying, and/or reporting of certifying activities, requirements, procedures or results.

Dolasetron mesylate An indole derivative with antiemetic activity. As a selective serotonin receptor antagonist, dolasetron mesylate competitively blocks the action of serotonin at 5HT3 receptors, resulting in suppression of chemotherapy- and radiotherapy-induced nausea and vomiting.

Domain A compact segment of an immunoglobulin molecule, made up of about 110 amino acids around an S-S bond, and encoded by a unique segment of DNA, surrounded by nontranslated sequences.

Dominant allele A gene that is expressed, regardless of whether its counterpart allele on the other chromosome is dominant or recessive. Autosomal dominant disorders are produced by a single mutated dominant allele, even though its corresponding allele is normal.

Dominant An allele that is almost always expressed, even if only one copy is present.

Dominant eye The eye that "leads" it partner during eye movements. Humans also have dominant hand, foot, eye, and side of the brain (not necessarily all on the same side).

Donepezil hydrochloride The hydrochloride salt of a piperidine derivative with neurocognitive-enhancing activity. Donepezil reversibly inhibits acetylcholinesterase, thereby blocking the hydrolysis of the neurotransmitter acetylcholine and, consequently, increasing its activity. This agent may improve neurocognitive function in Alzheimer's disease, reduce sedation associated with opioid treatment of cancer pain, and improve neurocognitive function in patients who have received radiation therapy for primary brain tumors or brain metastases.

DOP (Dioctyl phthalate) A mono-dispersed test aerosol of sub-micron particles, generated to challenge (evaluate integrity) of HEPA filters for HVAC.

Dormant At rest; clinically silent.

Dorsal Being or located near, on, or toward the back or posterior part of the human body.

Dorsalis pedis artery The continuation of the anterior tibial artery, that branches into the lateral and medial tarsal, arcuate, and deep plantar arteries.

Dorsocervical fat pad A type of lipodystrophy (problem in the way the body produces, uses, and distributes fat) in which fatty tissue builds up on the upper back and neck. It most often occurs in HIV-infected people as a result of PI or NRTI drug treatment. This fat buildup, also known as "buffalo hump," may also be associated with other metabolic side effects, such as high insulin levels.

Dorsum sellae The posterior bone margin of the pituitary **fossa, that** is the superior limit of the sphenoid bone. The dorsum sellae forms the boundary between the middle and posterior cranial fossae in the midline.

Dosage A specific quantity of a biologically active compound.

Dosage form The form in which drug is delivered to the patient. This could be parenteral, topical, tablet, oral (liquid or dissolved powder), suppository, inhalation, transdermal, etc.

Dosage group A group of subjects in a clinical trial receiving the same dosage (amount) of a drug being tested.

Dose dense chemotherapy A chemotherapy treatment plan in which drugs are given with less time between treatments than in a standard chemotherapy treatment plan.

Dose dependent Refers to the effects of treatment with a drug. If the effects change when the dose of the drug is changed, the effects are said to be dose-dependent.

Dose limiting Describes side effects of a drug or other treatment that are serious enough to prevent an increase in dose or level of that treatment.

Dose ranging The establishment of the optimal dosage of a new drug by repeated trials of varying dosages

Dose rate The strength of a treatment given over a period of time.

Dose response relationship The relationship between the dose of a drug and its corresponding effect on the body. If a drug exhibits a dose-response effect, it means that as the dose increases, so does the effect.

Dose The amount of medicine taken, or radiation given, at one time.

Dosimetrist A person who determines the proper radiation dose for treatment.

Dosimetry Measurement of radiation exposure from x-rays, gamma rays, or other types of radiation used in the treatment or detection of diseases, including cancer.

Double blind test Used in Clinical Trials, this is a method to ensure that any one party cannot improperly influence the test. The product (either in a single strength dosage or in multiple dosages) and the placebo are packaged and given a code name known to only the initiating party. These are then sent to another party who gives the coded packages yet another code name or number, and makes a matrix of the previous name/number to the new name/number. This is then sent to the physician who administers these to the patient. At the end of the test, the physician provides records of which patient received which code name/number product. This is then cross-referenced to the intermediate matrix to determine the original code name/number. The results of the treatment are then correlated to determine the efficacy of the drug.

The structure of DNA as proposed by Watson and Crick. It consists of two right-handed helical polynucleotide chains coiled around the same axis. The two chains are anti-parallel with their 3rd to 5th internucleotide phosphodiester bonds running in opposite directions. Under most conditions, the coiling of the chains is such that if the ends are held still, as in circular DNA or in a large chromosome, the chains cannot be separated except by cleavage of one of the strands.

Double contrast barium enema A procedure in which x-rays of the colon and rectum are taken after a liquid containing barium is put into the rectum. Barium is a silver-white metallic compound that outlines the colon and rectum on an x-ray and helps show abnormalities. Air is put into the rectum and colon to further enhance the x-ray.

Double crush syndrome Defined as a serial impingement of a nerve tract. An initial injury to a nerve (e.g. nerve injury in the neck) may lead to a secondary lesion (e.g. median nerve in the carpal tunnel).

Double helix The twisted-ladder shape that two linear strands of DNA assume when complementary nucleotides on opposing strands bond together.

Double-blind placebo-controlled study Considered the "gold standard" of clinical research studies, the double-blind placebo-controlled study provides dependable findings that are free of bias introduced by either the subject or the researcher. In this type of study, neither the subject nor the researcher conducting the study know whether the test substance or a placebo has been administered. For the results to be valid and to ensure that the subject cannot violate the "blindness," the placebo and the test substance must be virtually identical (i.e., look, smell and taste similar). The "blindness" of the study is crucial.

It eliminates the possibility that a participant's personal beliefs will undermine the study's validity. It also prevents the researcher's expectations from influencing the test results.

Doubling time The time it takes for a cell to divide and double itself. The doubling time of breast cancer cells depends on many things, such as the type of tumor, the resistance of the individual's body, and the location in which it tries to grow. A single cell needs 30 doublings to reach noticeable size (1 cm) – a billion cells. Cancers vary in doubling time from 8 to 600 days, averaging 100 to 120 days. Thus, a cancer may be present for many years before it can be felt.

Douche A procedure in which water or a medicated solution is used to clean the vagina and cervix.

Down syndrome A disorder caused by the presence of an extra chromosome 21 and characterized by mental retardation and distinguishing physical features.

Doxercalciferol A synthetic analog of vitamin D with potential antineoplastic activity. In the liver, doxercalciferol is converted to its biologically active vitamin D metabolites, which control the intestinal absorption of dietary calcium, the tubular reabsorption of calcium by the kidney and, in conjunction with parathyroid hormone (PTH), the mobilization of calcium from the skeleton. Through interaction with specific receptor proteins in target tissues, these vitamin D metabolites act directly on osteoblasts to stimulate skeletal growth, and on the parathyroid glands to suppress PTH synthesis and secretion. This agent has also been shown to inhibit the growth of retinoblastomas, and may exhibit some antiproliferative activity against prostate cancer cells.

Doxorubicin HCl liposome A liposome-encapsulated form of the hydrochloride salt of the anthracycline antineoplastic antibiotic doxorubicin. Liposomal delivery of doxorubicin HCl improves drug penetration into tumors and decreases drug clearance, thereby increasing the duration of therapeutic drug effects. Doxorubicin intercalates into DNA and interacts with topoisomerase II, consequently inhibiting DNA replication and repair and RNA and protein synthesis. This agent also produces toxic free-radical intermediates and interacts with cell membrane lipids causing lipid peroxidation.

Doxorubicin hydrochloride The hydrochloride salt of doxorubicin, an anthracycline antineoplastic antibiotic isolated from the fungus Streptococcus peucetius var. caesius. Doxorubicin intercalates into DNA and interacts with topoisomerase II, thereby inhibiting DNA replication and repair and RNA and protein synthesis. This agent also produces toxic free-radical intermediates and interacts with cell membrane lipids causing lipid peroxidation.

Doxorubicin magnetic targeted carrier complex Anthracycline antineoplastic antibiotic doxorubicin bound to microscopic beads of activated carbon and iron (magnetic targeted carriers). With placement of a magnet on the body surface overlying a tumor site, this carrier complex delivers doxorubicin directly to the tumor, thereby prolonging the duration of the therapeutic effects while decreasing its systemic toxicity. Doxorubicin intercalates into DNA and interacts with topoisomerase II, thereby inhibiting DNA replication and repair and RNA and protein synthesis. This agent also produces toxic free-radical intermediates and interacts with cell membrane lipids causing lipid peroxidation.

Doxycycline An antibiotic drug used to treat infection.

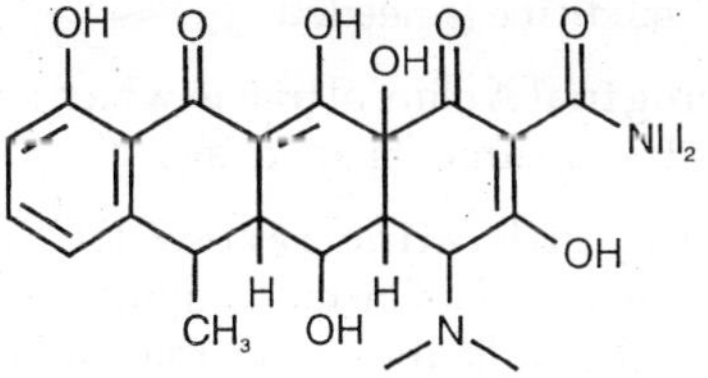

OH O OH O O OH NH2 OH H H CH3 OH N

Figure Doxycycline

DPPE Belongs to a group of antihormone drugs.

DPT A combined vaccine against diphtheria, whooping cough, and tetanus.

DR antigens MHC class II molecules found on B cells and antigen-presenting cells of humans.

Draft sequence The sequence generated by the HGP as of June 2000 that, while incomplete, offers a virtual road map to an estimated 95% of all human genes. Draft sequence data are mostly in the form of 10,000 base pair-sized fragments whose approximate chromosomal locations are known.

Drain In medicine, to remove fluid as it collects; or, a tube or wick-like device used to remove fluid from a body cavity, wound, or infected area.

DRE (Digital rectal examination) An examination in which a doctor inserts a lubricated, gloved finger into the rectum to feel for abnormalities.

Dronabinol A synthetic pill form of delta-9-tetrahydrocannabinol (THC), an active ingredient in marijuana that is used to treat nausea and vomiting associated with cancer chemotherapy.

Drop-out A patient enrolled in a clinical trial who is either unwilling or unable to return to the study clinic for regular follow-up visits.

Drug antagonism An interaction between two or more drugs in which one drug blocks or reverses the effect of another drug.

Drug Any substance, other than food, that is used to prevent, diagnose, treat or relieve symptoms of a disease or abnormal condition. Also refers to a substance that alters mood or body function, or that can be habit-forming or addictive, especially a narcotic.

Drug drug interaction A change in the way a drug works when it is taken along with another drug. The effect may be an increase or a decrease in the action of either drug, or it may be a side effect that does not normally occur with either drug alone.

Drug formulary Varying lists of prescription drugs approved by a given health plan for distribution to a covered person through specific pharmacies. Health plans often restrict or limit the type and number of medicines allowed for reimbursement by limiting the drug formulary list. Formularies are either "closed," including only certain drugs or "open," including all drugs. Both types of formularies typically impose a cost scale requiring consumers to pay more for certain brands or types of drugs.

Drug hepatitis Hepatitis caused by a drug. Causative drugs include isoniazid (INH), Alpha Methyl-dopa, and Dilatin.

Drug interaction An effect that can occur when one drug is taken with another drug or when the drug is taken with particular foods. Possible effects include changes in absorption from the digestive tract, changes in the rate of the drug's breakdown in the liver, new or increased side effects, or changes in the drug's activity.

Drug product A finished dosage form, for example, tablet, capsule, solution, etc., that contains one or more APIs (Active Pharmaceutical Ingredients) generally, but not necessarily, in association with inactive ingredients. The term also includes a finished dosage form, which does not contain an API but is intended to be used as a placebo.

Drug rash with eosinophilia and systemic symptoms (DRESS) A rare but life-threatening allergic drug reaction that sometimes occurs in people taking certain NNRTIs. Symptoms include severe rash along with fever, blood abnormalities, and organ inflammation.

Drug resistance The failure of cancer cells, viruses, or bacteria to respond to a drug used to kill or weaken them. The cells, viruses, or bacteria may be resistant to the drug at the beginning of treatment, or may become resistant after being exposed to the drug.

Drug tolerance A condition that occurs when the body gets used to a medicine so that either more medicine is needed or different medicine is needed.

Drug trial A clinical trial in which the test treatments are drugs.

Drug utilization review (DUR) Review of an insured population's drug utilization with the goal of determining how to reduce the cost of utilization. Reviews often result in recommendations to practitioners, including generic substitutions, use of formularies, use of copayments for prescriptions and education. In some cases, practitioners are now penalized or rewarded depending on their drug prescription related costs and utilization. Some speculate that these incentives can adversely effect doctor decisions.

Dry air Air from which all water vapour and contaminants have been removed. Its composition by volume is:

1. Nitrogen 78.08%
2. Oxygen 20.95%
3. Argon 0.93%
4. Carbon Dioxide 0.03
5. Other gases 0.00003

Dry eye syndrome A deficiency in tear film components (tears, mucus).

Dry Heat sterilization Sterilization utilizing a heating oven or continuous tunnel (gas or electric heated), as opposed to steam sterilization in an autoclave, usually used for glassware and metal parts. In depyrogenation temperatures of 250°C result in sterilization and the inactivation of endotoxin present on the surface of the equipment.

Dry orgasm Sexual climax without the release of semen from the penis.

DTGM fusion protein An anticancer drug formed by the combination of diphtheria toxin and a colony-stimulating factor (GM-CSF). The colony-stimulating factor is attracted to cancer cells, and the diphtheria toxin kills the cells.

DU 145 A cell line made from human prostate cancer cells that is used in the laboratory to study the way prostate cancer cells grow.

Dual energy x-ray absorptiometry scan (DEXA) A painless test that uses low energy x-rays to measure the mineral content of bones. DEXA scans are commonly used to test for osteopenia or osteoporosis, and are also used to evaluate lipodystropy.

Dual-chamber pacemaker A pacemaker that monitors and paces a chamber of the upper heart and a chamber of the lower heart at the same time. A dual-chamber pacemaker usually has two leads one located in the right atrium and the other located in the right ventricle.

Dual-chamber pacing To pace and/or sense heart rhythm in both the atrium and the ventricle.

Duct A pathway. In the breast, a passage through which milk passes from the lobule (which makes the milk) to the nipple.

Duct ectasia Widening of the ducts of the breast, often related to a breast inflammation called periductal mastitis. Duct ectasia is a benign (not cancerous) condition. Symptoms of this condition are a nipple discharge, swelling, dimpling (retraction) of the nipple, or a lump that can be felt.

Ductal carcinoma The most common type of breast cancer. It begins in the cells that line the milk ducts in the breast.

Ductal lavage A method used to collect cells from milk ducts in the breast. A hair-size catheter (tube) is inserted into the nipple, and a small amount of salt water is released into the duct. The water picks up breast cells, and is removed. The cells are checked under a microscope. Ductal lavage may be used in addition to clinical breast examination and mammography to detect breast cancer.

Ductal papillomas Small, finger-like, non-cancerous growths in the breast ducts that cause a bloody nipple discharge. These are most often found in women 45 to 50 years of age. When many papillomas exist, breast cancer risk is slightly increased.

Duction test A test of the eye's ability to turn inward or outward while maintaining single, binocular vision with the gradual introduction of progressively stronger base-in or base out prisms.

Dukes' classification A staging system used to describe the extent of colourectal cancer. Stages range from A (early stage) to D (advanced stage).

Dumping syndrome A condition that occurs when food or liquid moves too fast into the small intestine. Symptoms include cramps, nausea, diarrhea, sweating, weakness, and dizziness. Dumping syndrome sometimes occurs in people who have had part or all of their stomach removed.

Duodenal bulb The portion of the duodenum that forms the superior flexure with the pylorus.

Duodenal ulcer An open sore in the duodenum (first part of the small intestine).

Duodenitis Inflammation of the duodenum (the first part of the small intestine that connects to the stomach).

Duodenum The first part of the small intestine, nearest to the stomach.

Dupuytren's contracture A fibrous proliferation in the palmar fascia of the hand, that gradually produces a flexion deformity of the metacarpophalangeal and proximal interphalangeal joints.

Dura mater The outermost tough fibrous covering of the brain and spinal cord. Also referred to as the Pachymeninx.

Durability The ability to withstand the rigors of the environment without degrading or requiring repair.

Dural septae Folds of dura mater that reflect off the surface of the skull and incompletely divide the cranial cavity into compartments.

Dust Dusting deterioration of the finish at the surface so it is easily loosened from the surface by light physical contact (such as wiping one's hand across the surface), mechanically induced air movements or naturally occurring air movements.

Dust mites Microscopic creatures that live off human dead skin and are a common source of allergy.

Dynamic conditions Environmental conditions of a manufacturing room occupied by the normal number of workers appropriately garbed and with production equipment in operation. However, dynamic conditions for some dusty operations, such as aseptic powder filling, may be measured in the absence of product.

Dynamometer Mechanical instrumentation that allows for measurement of concentric and eccentric muscle action, muscle endurance and muscle balance ratios. Usually associated with isokinetic testing, providing variable, accomodating resistance.

Dys Difficult; bad; abnormal, e.g. dysplasia - abnormal formation, e.g. dyspnea - shortness of breath; difficulty breathing.

Dyscrasia Disease. Usually refers to diseases of the blood.

Dyseidetic Poor sight recognition of words. Dyseidetic is a subtype of dyslexia. Children with this form of dyslexia have trouble analyzing and remembering written symbols. They continue to confuse the orientation. For example, they will write numbers and letters backwards long after other children have mastered these skills. They often confuse letter sequences in reading, and in spelling often get all the letters but in the wrong sequence (spelling "dose" for "does", "on " for "no", etc.). Their visual memory for words is poor, and after learning a new word they may fail to recognize that same new word later in the sentence. They have trouble learning to read and spell phonetically irregular words. For example, they may read " laugh" as "log" and spell it as "laff", both of which are phonetically consistent. Their spelling will have many mistakes, but will be phonetically consistent and one can usually tell what the word was they were trying to spell. When they are attempting to read an unknown word they will usually attempt to sound it out and do so very slowly.

Dysesthesia A condition in which a sense, especially touch, is distorted. Dysesthesia can cause an ordinary stimulus to be unpleasant or painful. It can also cause insensitivity to a stimulus.

Dysfunction Impaired action of the orbits extraocular and/or eyelid muscles causing a lack of synchronized eye/prosthesis movement and/or asymmetrical eyelid opening.

Dysfunctional globe An impairment of function, possible loss of vision, disfigured globe

Dysgenesis Defective embryonic development.

Dysgeusia A bad taste in the mouth. Also called parageusia.

Dyskeratosis Faulty and premature keratinization of individual keratinocytes. Dyskeratotic cells are usually intensely eosinophilic and may contain a small, dense, basophilic nuclear remnant. Dyskeratotic cells may also be densely basophilic as seen in Darier's disease.

Dyslexia A specific language-based disorder. The individual has difficulty with letter or word recognition, spelling, reading, writing, and sometimes naming pictures of objects. Dyslexia varies in degree from mild to very sever. It is caused by an inability of the brain's language centers to decode print or phonetically make the connection between the word's written symbols and their appropriate sounds. Dyslexia is not caused by a vision disorder. Children often are of normal or above normal intelligence. Dyslexia cannot be cured and will never be outgrown. Appropriate teaching methods can be taught to help those with dyslexia overcome their weakness. The Dyslexia Determination test which is used by many optometrists who specialize in vision related vision problems investigates if the patient has one of the three forms of dyslexia: Dyseidetic - poor sight recognition of words, Dysphonesia inability to "sound out" words, and Dysphoneidesia - a combination of characteristics from both types. Vision therapy is NOT considered a direct treatment for dyslexia.

Dyslipidemia Abnormal levels of fat in the blood, usually referring to abnormally high levels. Dyslipidemia may occur as a result of HIV infection or as a side effect of some anti-HIV drugs.

Dysmenorrhea Difficult and painful menstruation.

Dyspepsia Digestive upset.

Dysphagia Difficulty in swallowing. It is common for the swallowing reflex to be impaired in persons with Wilson's Disease, things oftentimes "go down the wrong tube."

Dysphoneidesia Inability to "sound out" words and poor sight recognition of words. Dysphoneidesia is a subtype of dyslexia. Its characteristics are a combination of the other two forms of dyslexia: Dysphonesia and Dyseidetic.

Dysphonesia Inability to "sound out" words. Dysphonesia is a subtype of dyslexia. Children with this form of dyslexia have difficulty sequentially analyzing and remembering what and where the sounds are in words. The resulting phonemic processing problems make it difficult to sound out new words, learn phonics, and make them dependent on their sight vocabulary. When they come to an unknown word they will often substitute a word using context clues. For example, "pony" for "horse", even though the substituted word doesn't look or sound anything like the original word. When spelling unknown words it is often difficult to determine what the original word is. For example, they may write "fmlue" for "familiar" or "**lap**" for "lamp". They cannot learn **phonics** because they cannot process where the sounds are. Their short term sequential auditory memory can be poor and result in repeating "8167" as "8671", or remember to go to their room but forgetting to get the item requested.

Dysplasia Cells that look abnormal under a microscope but are not cancer.

Dysplasia An abnormality in size, appearance, and organization of adult cells, but this condition is not cancer. A biopsy is needed for diagnosis.

Dysplastic nevus An atypical mole; a mole whose appearance is different from that of a common mole. A dysplastic nevus is generally larger than an ordinary mole and has irregular and indistinct borders. Its colour frequently is not uniform and ranges from pink to dark brown; it is usually flat, but parts may be raised above the skin surface.

Dyspnea Difficult or painful breathing; shortness of breath.

Dysregulation Refers to interruption or interference of normal process (es).

Dystonia Involuntary movements and prolonged muscle contraction. The type of dystonia caused by Wilson's Disease causes patients to hold part of their body in an unnatural position.

Dystopia Displacement.

Dysuria Difficult or painful urination.

E coli (Escherichia coli) A fast growing, Gram-negative bacteria commonly found in the body with a comparatively simple structure. The genetic make up of E. coli is the best known of any organism, having been widely studied during the development of genetic engineering. It has been used extensively as the host cell for novel proteins made by rDNA technology.

E health A term that refers to all forms of electronic health services provided over the Internet. It includes all educational, information and commercial services and products offered by professionals, non-professionals, businesses and consumers. Based on the unique capabilities of Internet, E-Health is enabling the delivery of clinical services that previously have been domain of telemedicine and telehealth. E-health differs from telemedicine and telehealth in that it is not "professional-centric" and is motivated by the financial gain, whereas telemedicine and telehealth are not. As it is Internet-based, E-health is making the provision of health care more efficient.

E numbers Method of labeling all food additives in the European Union. For example, E102 is the food colourant Tartrazine.

E7389 A synthetic analogue of halichondrin B, a substance derived from a marine sponge (Lissodendoryx sp.) with antineo-plastic activity. E7389 binds to the vinca domain of tubulin and inhibits the polymerization of tubulin and the assembly of microtubules, resulting in inhibition of mitotic spindle assembly, induction of cell cycle arrest at G2/M phase, and, potentially, tumor regression.

Early and periodic screening, diagnosis, and treatment (EPSDT) EPSDT program covers screening and diagnostic services to determine physical or mental defects in recipients under age 21, as well as health care and other measures to correct or ameliorate any defects and chronic conditions discovered.

Early menopause A condition in which the ovaries stop working before age 40. Symptoms include hot flashes, mood swings, night sweats, vaginal dryness, and infertility. Some cancer treatments, such as chemotherapy, radiation therapy, and surgery can cause early menopause. Early menopause caused by cancer treatment may be temporary or permanent and may be treated with hormone replacement therapy. Also called premature ovarian failure or primary ovarian insufficiency.

Early stage breast cancer Breast cancer that has not spread beyond the breast or the axillary lymph nodes. This includes ductal carcinoma in situ and stage I, stage IIA, stage IIB, and stage IIIA breast cancers.

Early stopping 1. A condition or provision incorporated into the design of a clinical trial that enables investigators to terminate patient recruitment or treatment if data accumulated during the trial strongly indicate an adverse or beneficial treatment effect.

2. A term used to characterize an action involving termination of a study treatment in a trial because of adverse or beneficial treatment effects.

Eating disorders Eating disorders may be classified as anorexia, bulimia, compulsive overeating, binge eating, or any combination of these. Each is based on specific diagnostic criteria.

EBV (Epstein barr virus) A common virus that remains dormant in most people. It has been associated with certain cancers, including Burkitt's lymphoma, immunoblastic lymphoma, and nasopharyngeal carcinoma.

EBV specific cytotoxic T lymphocytes A preparation of lymphocytes harvested from a patient with an Epstein-Barr virus (EBV)-positive tumor. Ex vivo, the lymphocytes are activated against EBV-specific antigens and then returned to the patient, where they mount a specific immune response against EBV-positive tumor cells.

Eccentric Controlled, active lengthening contraction of a muscle.

Eccentric fixation The deviating eye does not use the central foveal (center of the retina that produces the sharpest eyesight) area for fixation. Commonly, individuals with amblyopia and some individuals with strabismus will have this visual adaptation. In esotropia, the eccentrically located retinal point used for fixation is usually in the nasal retina. In exotropia, the eccentrically located retinal point used for fixation is usually in the temporal retina. Vision therapy is a treatment option for those with amblyopia and/or strabismus. It is not a treatment option for an individual with a fovea that has been destroyed.

Ecchymosis A purplish patch caused by extravasation of blood into the tissues differing from petechiae only in size.

Eccrine gland A type of simple sweat gland that is found in almost all regions of the skin. These glands produce sweat that reaches the surface of the skin by way of coiled ducts (tubes). The body is cooled as sweat evapourates from the skin.

Echocardiography A procedure that uses ultrasonic waves directed over the chest wall to obtain a graphic record of the heart's position, motion of the walls, or internal parts such as the valves.

Ecologist An individual who studies the interrelationships between organisms and their environment.

Ecology The study of the interrelationships between organisms and their environment.

Ectasis (suffix) To stretch; dilate, e.g. bronchiectasis - dilatation of bronchi. The noun form is ectasia.

Ectocervical Having to do with the part of the cervix that protrudes into the vagina and is lined with epithelial cells.

Ectomy (suffix) Excision, e.g. cholecystectomy - excision of the gallbladder.

Ectropion The turning outward of the eyelashes and eyelid. Ectropion (of the upper eyelid) is accompanied with retrotarsal atrophy.

Ectropion (of the lower eyelid) is caused by orbicularis muscle weakness, and/or prolapse of adipose tissue.

Eculizumab A monoclonal antibody that is being studied in the prevention of red blood cell destruction in patients with paroxysmal nocturnal hemoglobinuria (a red blood cell disorder).

Eczema A group of skin conditions characterised by dry, red, flaky, itchy skin. The most common form of eczema is allergic or Atopic Eczema (also called Infantile Eczema or Atopic Dermatitis).

ED50 Short for "Effective dose 50"; the dosage of a drug or poison that kills, or stops replication in 50% of the organisms it is tested against. Often applies to dose of drug against microorganisms.

Edatrexate An anticancer drug that belongs to a family of drugs called antimetabolites.

Edema A swelling or puffiness of some part of the body such as the ankles. Water or other body fluids collect in the cells and cause the swelling.

Edge failure A control parameter value that, if exceeded, may result in adverse effect on state of control and/or fitness for use of the product.

Edotecarin A synthetic indolocarbazole with antineoplastic activity. Edotecarin inhibits the enzyme topoisomerase I through stabilization of the DNA-enzyme complex and enhanced single-strand DNA cleavage, resulting in inhibition of DNA replication and decreased tumor cell proliferation.

Edrecolomab A type of monoclonal antibody used in cancer detection or therapy. Monoclonal antibodies are laboratory-produced substances that can locate and bind to cancer cells.

Educational or instructional objectives Statements that describe what learners should be able to master. A major aim is the acquisition of facts, concepts and principles. Developing instructional objectives involves learning the fundamentals and vocabulary of each discipline and developing a logical progression of concepts in each discipline. Resources and materials are more effectively deployed when instructional objectives are explicit. It is important to assure that objectives are measurable and that they delineate a specific level of competence. One can and should distinguish between knowledge, skill and attitude objectives.

Efaproxiral A synthetic small molecule with radiosensitizing activity. Efaproxiral increases oxygen levels in hypoxic tumor tissues by binding non-covalently to the hemoglobin tetramer and decreasing hemoglobin-oxygen binding affinity. Increasing tumor oxygenation reduces tumor radioresistance.

Effectiveness A measure of the extent to which a specific intervention, procedure, regimen, or service, when deployed in the field in routine circumstances, does what it is intended to do for a specified population. In the health field, it is a measure of output from those health services that contribute towards reducing the dimension of a problem or improving an unsatisfactory situation.

Effector cell A cell that performs a specific function in response to a stimulus; usually used to describe cells in the immune system.

Efficiency An ability to perform well or achieve a result without wasted energy, resources, effort, time or money. Efficiency can be measured in physical terms (technical efficiency) or terms of cost (economic efficiency). Greater efficiency is achieved where the same amount and standard of services are produced for a lower cost, if a more useful activity is substituted for a less useful one at the same cost or if needless activities are eliminated.

Effluent The output or discharge from a process, such as a waste-water treatment process.

Effusion A collection of fluid in a body cavity, usually between two adjoining tissues. For example, a pleural effusion is the collection of fluid between two layers of the pleura (the lung's covering).

Eflornithine A difluoromethylated ornithine compound with antineoplastic activity. Eflornithine irreversibly inhibits ornithine decarboxylase, an enzyme required for polyamine biosynthesis, thereby inhibiting the formation and proliferation of tumor cells. Polyamines are involved in nucleosome oligomerization and DNA conformation, creating a chromatin environment that stimulates neoplastic transformation of cells. This agent has been shown to induce apoptosis in leiomyoma cells.

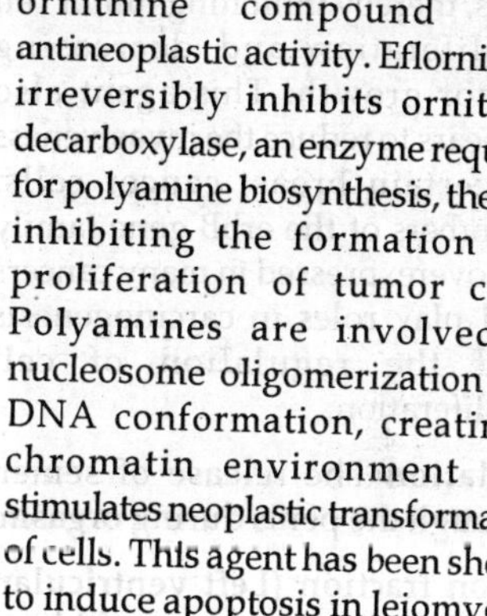

Eflornithine (2-difluoromethyl 2,5-diamino pentanoic acid)

Figure Eflornithine

EGFR (Epidermal growth factor receptor) The protein found on the surface of some cells and to which epidermal growth factor binds, causing the cells to divide. It is found at abnormally high levels on the surface of many types of cancer cells, so these cells may divide excessively in the presence of epidermal growth factor. Also known as ErbB1 or HER1.

EGFR antisense DNA A synthetic sequence of DNA constructed in the antisense orientation to a sequence of DNA in epidermal growth factor receptor (EGFR), a member of the erbB gene family. EGFR antisense DNA suppresses the expression of EGFR by tumor cells, thereby inhibiting tumor cell proliferation and decreasing tumor growth. This agent also appears to reduce the invasiveness of certain breast cancer cells. Members of the erbB gene family are overexpressed in many cancers and play roles in carcinogenesis and the regulation of cell proliferation.

Ejaculation The release of semen through the penis during orgasm.

Ejection fraction (Left ventricular: LVEF) The percentage of blood filling the left ventricle during each heartbeat that flows out of the ventricle into the body's circulatory system. This reading is a direct measure of the "pumping" capability of the heart. Damaged/ diseased hearts may have an ejection fraction below 50%.

EKB-569 A substance that is being studied in the treatment of cancer. It belongs to the family of drugs called epidermmal growth factor receptor inhibitors.

Elastin An albuminoid, or scleroprotein present especially in yellow elastic fibrous tissue.

Elastomer Long chain co-polymers or terpolymers (two or three different monomers in one chain) that contain adequate crosslinks among individual chains. Fluorinated elastomers are more stable than hydrocarbon or silicon elastomers because C-F bonds are approximately 30% stronger than C-H bonds. There are five major compliant elastomers used in the pharmaceutical and biopharmaceutical industries: EPDM (ethylene-propylene-diene rubber), fluororelastomers (FKM), platinum-cured silicon (pt-Si), and finally Kalrez parts using compounds KLR-6221 and KLR-6230, which are perfluoroelastomers.

Elastomeric material A material that can be stretched or compressed repeatedly and, upon immediate release of stress, will return to its approximate original size.

Elbow joint The large joint for the upper extremity, between the distal humerus and the proximal radius and ulna.

Electrical stimulation Provides a situation whereby there is an electrical generation of action potentials, giving rise to therapeutically significant physiological responses e.g. increased muscle strength, stmulated lymph and blood flow, analgesia, kinaesthetic awareness and autonomic nervous system responses.

Electroacupuncture A procedure in which pulses of weak electrical current are sent through acupuncture needles into acupuncture points in the skin. This procedure is being studied in the prevention of nausea and vomiting in patients undergoing chemotherapy.

Electrocardiogram (ECG/EKG) A method of recording the electrical impulses given off by the heart as it beats. This may be done while resting or exercising.

Electrocautery The use of electrical currents to stop bleeding during surgery.

Electrode Transmits or receives electrical impulses from one point to another.

Electrodesiccation The drying of tissue by a high-frequency electric current applied with a needle-shaped electrode.

Electrodialysis (ED) A membrane separation method used for the separation of charged molecules from a solution by application of a direct current. The membranes contain ion-exchange groups and have a fixed electrical charge. This method is very effective in the concentration of electrolytes and proteins.

Electrogram (EGM) A picture of the electrical activity of the heart as sensed from within the heart. This is different from an ECG, which is a picture of your heart's electrical activity sensed from the surface of your skin.

Electrohydraulic lithotripsy (EHL) This technique uses a special probe to break up small stones with shock waves generated by electricity. Through a flexible ureteroscope, the physician positions the tip of the probe 1 mm from the stone. Then, by means of a foot switch, the physician projects electrically generated hydraulic shock waves through an irrigating fluid at the stone until it is broken into small fragments. These can be passed by the patient or removed through the previously described extraction methods. EHL has some limitations. It requires general anesthesia, and is generally not used in close proximity to the kidney itself, as the shock waves can cause tissue damage. Fragments produced by the hydraulic shock also tend to scatter widely, making retrieval or extraction more difficult.

Electrolarynx A battery-operated device that makes a humming sound. It is used to help a person talk after removal of the larynx (voice box).

Electrolyte A substance that breaks up into ions (electrically charged particles) when it is dissolved in body fluids or water. Some examples of electrolytes are sodium, potassium, chloride, and calcium. Electrolytes are primarily responsible for the movement of nutrients into cells and the movement of wastes out of cells.

Electromagnetic field Low-energy radiation that comes from the interaction of electric and magnetic fields. Sources include power lines, electric appliances, radio waves, microwaves, and others. Also called electromagnetic radiation.

Electromagnetic interference (EMI) Produced by an electromagnetic field – if strong enough, it may interfere with the operation of an AICD system. This happens only on very rare occasions.

Electromagnetic radiation Low-energy radiation that comes from the interaction of electric and magnetic fields. Sources include power lines, electric appliances, radio waves, microwaves, and others. Also called electromagnetic field.

Electromyography Quantified information regarding overall muscle performance and function.

Electron beam A stream of electrons (small negatively charged particles found in atoms) that can be used for radiation therapy.

Electron microscope A microscope (device used to magnify small objects) that uses electrons (instead of light) to produce an enlarged image. An electron microscope shows tiny details better than any other type of microscope.

Electron microscopy (EM) A technique for visualizing material that uses beams of electrons instead of light rays and that permits greater magnification than is possible with an optical microscope. Electron microscopes have been used to examine the structure of viruses and bacteria, to identify and classify pollen grains, etc.

Electronic medical record (EMR) A computer-based record containing health care information. This technology, when fully developed, meets provider needs for real-time data access and evaluation in medical care. Together with clinical workstations and clinical data repository technologies, the EMR provides the mechanism for longitudinal data storage and access. A motivation for healthcare entities to implement this technology derives from the need for medical outcome studies, more efficient care, speedier communication among providers and management of health plans. This record may contain some, but not necessarily all, of the information that is in an individual's paper-based medical record.

Electrophoresis A method of separating large molecules (such as DNA fragments or proteins) from a mixture of similar molecules. An electric current is passed through a medium containing the mixture, and each kind of molecule travels through the medium at a different rate, depending on its electrical charge and size. Agarose and acrylamide gels are the media commonly used for electrophoresis of proteins and nucleic acids.

Electrophysiology (EP) test or study An observation and measurement of the electrical impulses running through the heart as it beats. This test can help a doctor to recognize abnormal heart rhythms, to determine the origin of arrhythmias and to determine how well medicines are working. A doctor may also use the test to observe the implantable defibrillator to see how well it functions during an abnormal heart rhythm.

Electropolishing Also known as "chemical machining" and "reverse plating", electropolishing is an electrochemical process far superior to any available mechanical process for the removal of minute surface imperfections in stainless steel. It levels and brightens the material surface by anodic dissolution in an electrolyte flowing solution with an imposed electrical current. When the proper combination of electrolyte current and temperature is attained, the high points of surface irregularities, or high current density areas, are selectively removed at a greater rate than the remainder of the surface, resulting in improved surface smoothness. During electropolishing, the polarized surface film is subjected to the combined effects of gassing (oxygen) that occurs with electromechanical metal removal, saturation of the surface with dissolved metal, and the agitation and temperature of the electrolyte.

Electroporation A process using high-voltage current to make cell membranes permeable to allow the introduction of new DNA; commonly used in recombinant DNA technology.

Electroporation therapy (EPT) Treatment that generates electrical pulses through an electrode placed in a tumor to enhance the ability of anticancer drugs to enter tumor cells.

Electrostatic fluidized bed A container holding powder coating material which is aerated from below so as to form an air-supported expanded cloud of such material which is electrically charged with a charge opposite to the charge of the object to be coated. Such object is transported through the container immediately above the charged and aerated materials in order to be coated.

Electrotherapy Modalities used in the treatment of musculoskeletal disorders e.g. ultrasound, short wave diathermy, interferential therapy, biofeedback, transcutaneous electrical nerve stimulation and laser.

Eligibility criteria In clinical trials, requirements that must be met for an individual to be included in a study. These requirements help make sure that patients in a trial are similar to each other in terms of specific factors such as age, type and stage of cancer, general health, and previous treatment. When all participants meet the same eligibility criteria, it gives researchers greater confidence that results of the study are caused by the intervention being tested and not by other factors.

ELISA (Enzyme linked immunosorbent assay) A laboratory test to determine the presence of antibodies to HIV in the blood.

Ellagic acid A natural-cancer fighting agent found in strawberries.

Ellence Other name for epirubicin hydrochloride.

Ellinghausen's medium A complex medium for growing Leptospira. Contains numerous salts, nutrients, and BSA (bovine serum albumin).

Eloxatin A drug that is used to treat colourectal cancer and is being studied in the treatment of other types of cancer. It belongs to the family of drugs called platinum compounds. Also called oxaliplatin.

Figure Eloxatin

Elute To separate one solute from another by washing. Elution may include the removal by means of a suitable solvent of one material (absorbed material) from another (adsorbent) that is insoluble in that solvent.

Embolism The sudden blocking of an artery by a clot of material (embolus). The process of the formation of an embolus.

Embolus A clot, usually part or all of a thrombus, carried by a larger vessel and forced into a smaller vessel, thus obstructing blood flow.

Embriology The study of the early stages in the development of an organism. In these stages a single highly specialized cell, the egg, is transformed into a complex, many-celled organism resembling its parents.

Embryo Early stage in the development of a plant or an animal. In vertebrate animals (have a backbone or spinal column), this stage lasts from shortly after fertilization until all major body parts appear. In particular, in humans, this stage lasts from about 2 weeks after fertilization until the end of the seventh or eighth week of pregnancy.

Embryoma A mass of rapidly growing cells that begins in embryonic (fetal) tissue. Embryomas may be benign or malignant, and include neuroblastomas and Wilms' tumors. Also called embryonal tumor.

Embryonal rhabdomyosarcoma A soft-tissue tumor that affects children. It begins in muscle cells, and usually occurs in the head, neck, arms, legs, or genitourinary tract.

Embryonal tumor A mass of rapidly growing cells that begins in embryonic (fetal) tissue. Embryonal tumors may be benign or malignant, and include neuroblastomas and Wilms' tumors. Also called embryoma.

Embryonic Having to do with an embryo, which is an early stage in the development of a plant or animal.

Embryonic stage A state of being an embryo, underdeveloped, rudimentary.

Embryonic stem (ES) cells An embryonic cell that can replicate indefinitely, transform into other types of cells, and serve as a continuous source of new cells.

Emcyt Other name for estramustine phosphate sodium.

Emergency Sudden unexpected onset of illness or injury which requires the immediate care and attention of a qualified physician, and which, if not treated immediately, would jeopardize or impair the health of the Member, as determined by the payer's Medical Staff. Significant in that Emergency may be the only acceptable reason for admission without pre-certification.

Emergency center, emergi-center Non-hospital affiliated health facility that provides short-term care for minor medical emergencies or procedures needing immediate treatment; also called urgi-center, urgent center or free standing emergency medical service center.

Emergency medical identification Cards, bracelets, or necklaces with a written message used by people with diabetes or other medical problems to alert others in case of a medical emergency such as coma.

Emesis (Suffix) Vomit, e.g. hematemesis vomiting blood.

Emia (Suffix) Blood, e.g. lipidemia - excess lipid in the blood.

Emissary veins Veins which pierce the skull and connect the dural venous sinuses with the extracranial veins.

Emitefur An anticancer drug that belongs to the family of drugs called antimetabolites.

Emmetropia Normal vision, no correction needed.

Emodin A substance found in certain plants, including rhubarb. It belongs to a family of compounds called anthraquinones, which have shown anti-inflammatory and anticancer effects.

Emollients Special moisturisers - available as bath oils, creams and ointments - that are used to help prevent eczema and hydrate the skin. Usually contain Liquid Paraffin, Cetomacrogol and Emulsifying Wax.

Emphysema Pulmonary emphysema is a disorder affecting the alveoli (tiny air sacs) of the lungs. The transfer of oxygen and carbon dioxide in the lungs takes place in the walls of the alveoli. In emphysema, the alveoli become abnormally inflated, damaging their walls and making it harder to breathe. People who smoke or have chronic bronchitis have an increased risk of emphysema.

Empirical fit A trial and error method of fitting preformed shapes in order to make a custom made prosthesis.

Enalapril An antihypertensive agent that can also be used to slow or prevent the progression of heart disease in people with childhood cancer treated with drugs that may be harmful to the heart.

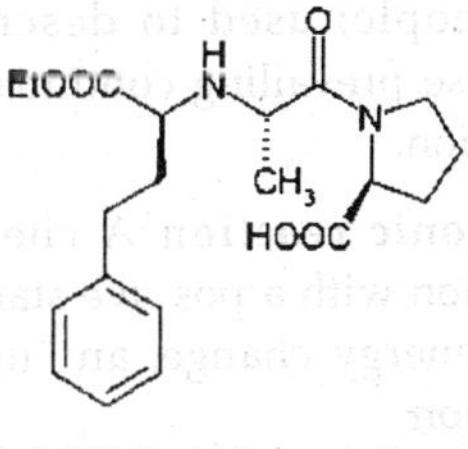

((S)-1-[N-[1- (ethoxycarbonyl)-3 phenylpropyl] -l-alanyl]-l-proline)

Figure Enalapril

Enamel Hard tissue covering the portion of tooth above the gum line.

Encapsulated Confined to a specific, localized area and surrounded by a thin layer of tissue.

Encephalitis A general term denoting inflammation of the brain.

Encephalopathy A disorder of the brain that can be caused by disease, injury, drugs, or chemicals.

Enchancing antibodies Antibodies which enhance the survival of a graft or of a tumour.

Enchondroma A benign (noncancerous) growth of cartilage in bones or in other areas where cartilage is not normally found.

Encopresis Constipation and intestinal obstruction (blockage) lead to an involuntary leakage of loose stool.

End stage renal disease (ESRD) The final phase of kidney disease; treated by dialysis or kidney transplantation.

Endemic A disease present in a community or among a group of people; used to describe a disease prevailing continually in a region.

Endergonic reaction A chemical reaction with a positive standard free energy change, an "uphill" reaction.

Endfeel Physiotherapist appreciation of the "feel" at the end of the range of motion, either of joint or other tissue. This is a sensation felt during passive movement, by the Therapist.

Endo Within, e.g. endocardium - the inner lining of the heart, e.g. endometrium - the mucous membrane lining of the uterus.

Endocardial lead A long, thin insulated wire that runs from a pulse generator through a vein into the heart. The lead transmits signals from the heart to the pulse generator and transmits therapy from the pulse generator to the heart.

Endocardial The inside surface of the heart. Endocardial leads are inserted into the heart through the veins.

Endocervical canal The portion of the uterine cavity that lies within the cervix - the passage that connects the vaginal canal with the main uterine cavity (lumen).

Endocervical curettage A procedure in which the mucous membrane of the cervical canal is scraped using a spoon-shaped instrument called a curette.

Endocrine cancer Cancer that occurs in endocrine tissue, the tissue in the body that secretes hormones.

Endocrine disruption Not considered as an adverse endpoint per se but as a step or mechanism that could lead to toxic outcomes, such as cancer or adverse reproductive effects.

Endocrine glands The glands that secrete their products (hormones) into the blood that then carries them to their specific target organs. Endocrine glands are the pituitary, thyroids, adrenals, pancreas, ovaries (in females), and testes (in males). Endocrine glands are found in some invertebrates as well as in vertebrates.

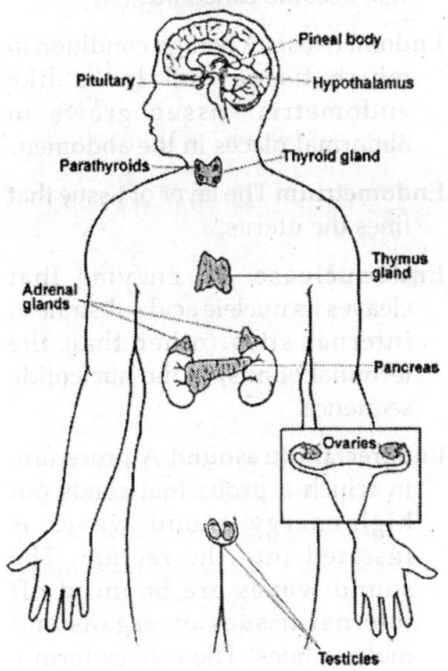

Figure Endocrine system

Endocrine hormones The products secreted by the endocrine glands. These help control long-term processes, such as growth, lactation, sex cycles, and metabolic adjustment. The endocrine system and the nervous system are interdependent and are often referred to collectively as the neuroendocrine system. For example, the juvenile hormone, found in insects and annelids, affects sexual maturation. There is currently great interest in the possible use of such hormones in the control of destructive insects.

Endocrine pancreas cell A pancreatic cell that produces hormones (e.g., insulin and glucagon) that are secreted into the bloodstream. These hormones help control the level of glucose (sugar) in the blood. Also called an islet cell and an islet of Langerhans cell.

Endocrine pancreas The part of the pancreas that produces hormones that govern sugar metabolism.

Endocrine therapy Treatment that adds, blocks, or removes hormones. For certain conditions (such as diabetes or menopause), hormones are given to adjust low hormone levels. To slow or stop the growth of certain cancers (such as prostate and breast cancer), synthetic hormones or other drugs may be given to block the body's natural hormones. Sometimes surgery is needed to remove the gland that makes a certain hormone. Also called hormone therapy, hormonal therapy, or hormone treatment.

Endocrinologist A doctor who treats people who have problems with their endocrine glands. Diabetes is an endocrine disorder.

Endocytosis The process in which cells take in fluids or other large molecules.

Endodontist Specialist who treats injuries, diseases and infections of the tooth pulp (nerve chamber).

Endogenous antibodies In Type 1 diabetes, several different autoantibodies against normal tissues are found. These antibodies are associated with the destruction of the beta cells of the pancreas, although their exact role is uncertain. Some of the autoantibodies which are found in diabetes patients include islet-cell antibodies (ICA's), anti-insulin antibodies (AIA's) and anti-GAD antibodies.

Endogenous Produced or made inside the body; for instance, insulin made by a person's own pancreas is endogenous insulin.

Endometrial biopsy A procedure in which a sample of tissue is taken from the endometrium (inner lining of the uterus) for examination under a microscope. A thin tube is inserted through the cervix into the uterus, and gentle scraping and suction are used to remove the sample.

Endometrial cancer Cancer that forms in the tissue lining the uterus. Most endometrial cancers are adenocarcinomas (cancers that begin in cells that make and release mucus and other fluids).

Endometrial carcinoma A cancer of the lining of the uterus.

Endometrial disorder Abnormal cell growth in the endometrium (the lining of the uterus).

Endometrial Having to do with the endometrium (the layer of tissue that lines the uterus).

Endometrial hyperplasia An abnormal overgrowth of the endometrium (the layer of cells that lines the uterus). There are four types of endometrial hyperplasia: simple endometrial hyperplasia, complex endometrial hyperplasia, simple endometrial hyperplasia with atypia, and complex endometrial hyperplasia with atypia. These differ in terms of how abnormal the cells are and how likely it is that the condition will become cancerous.

Endometriosis A benign condition in which tissue that looks like endometrial tissue grows in abnormal places in the abdomen.

Endometrium The layer of tissue that lines the uterus.

Endonuclease An enzyme that cleaves its nucleic acid substrate at internal sites (other than the terminal bonds) in the nucleotide sequence.

Endorectal ultrasound A procedure in which a probe that sends out high-energy sound waves is inserted into the rectum. The sound waves are bounced off internal tissues or organs and make echoes. The echoes form a picture of body tissue called a sonogram. ERUS is used to look for abnormalities in the rectum and nearby structures, including the prostate. Also called transrectal ultrasound.

Endorphins Endogenous opiates having morphine-like effects consisting of small polypeptides such as enkephalin and leuenkephalin and longer polypeptides such as alpha-, ß-, and gamma-endorphins. They bind to opiate receptors in the brain. Endorphins induce analgesia when injected intraventricularly but not when administered peripherally, presumably because of their inability to cross the blood/brain barrier. The amino acid sequence of the endorphins is short enough to allow the gene sequences coding for them to be synthesized.

Endoscope A small, flexible tube with a light and a camera lens at the end, used to examine the inside of the digestive tract. It can also be used to take tissue samples for testing from inside the digestive tract.

Endoscopic A type of surgery that eliminates the need for a large incision by using telescopes to see and insert miniature instruments.

Endoscopic retrograde cholangiopancreatography (ERCP) A procedure to x-ray the pancreatic duct, hepatic duct, common bile duct, duodenal papilla, and gallbladder. In this procedure, a thin, lighted tube (endoscope) is passed through the mouth and down into the first part of the small intestine (duodenum). A smaller tube (catheter) is then inserted through the endoscope into the bile and pancreatic ducts. A dye is injected through the catheter into the ducts, and an x-ray is taken.

Endoscopic ultrasound (EUS) A procedure in which an endoscope (a thin, lighted tube) is inserted into the body. A probe at the end of the endoscope is used to bounce high-energy sound waves (ultrasound) off internal organs to make a picture (sonogram). Also called endosonography.

Endoscopy A procedure looking at the inside of body cavities, such as the esophagus (food pipe) or stomach.

Endosonography A procedure in which an endoscope (a thin, lighted tube) is inserted into the body. A probe at the end of the endoscope is used to bounce high-energy sound waves (ultrasound) off internal organs to make a picture (sonogram). Also called endoscopic ultrasound (EUS).

Endospore A highly heat and chemical resistant dormant inclusion (spore) occurring within the substance of certain genera of bacteria, mainly Bacillus and Clostridium.

Endostatin A drug that is being studied for its ability to prevent the growth of new blood vessels into a solid tumor. Endostatin belongs to the family of drugs called angiogenesis inhibitors.

Endotak An implantable lead system used to sense heart rhythms and deliver energy to the heart.

Endothelial cell The main type of cell found in the inside lining of blood vessels, lymph vessels, and the heart.

Endothelin receptor antagonist A drug that blocks the hormone endothelin and may prevent prostate cancer from spreading to the bones. It may also prevent the growth and spread of other types of cancer, including colourectal cancer.

Endothelin-1 protein receptor antagonist A substance that blocks the binding of the endothelin-1 protein to its receptor. Endothelin-1 is a small molecule that causes changes in blood vessels and helps regulate blood pressure. It can also stimulate the growth of some types of cells.

Endothelium The cells or membrane lining organs.

Endotoxin A poisonous complex molecule (lipopolysaccharide) that forms an integral part of the bacterial (gram-negative bacteria) cell wall and is only released when the integrity of the wall is disturbed. Certain organisms may release endotoxins (e.g. E. coli) during biosynthesis of a recombinant DNA product, thus necessitating purification steps to ensure their removal. In water treatment, it most often refers to pyrogens.

Endotracheal tube (ET) An airway catheter (tube) that is inserted into the trachea to assist breathing and ventilation of the lung. ET tubes are used with mechanical ventilation for critical patients.

Endpoint A primary or secondary outcome variable used to judge the effectiveness of a treatment. This term is confusing because it often incorrectly implies that patients in a study are no longer followed after they experience an endpoint. This is obviously true where the event is death, but need not be so for nonfatal events. In fact, the design of the trial may require continued treatment and follow-up of patients over the entire course of the trial, regardless of the number of nonfatal "endpoints" observed.

Enema A liquid placed into the rectum to either clear stool out of the large intestine, or to examine the large intestine with an x-ray (barium enema).

Energy balance In biology, the state at which the number of calories eaten equals the number of calories used. Energy balance is affected by physical activity, body size, amount of body fat and muscle, and genetics.

Eniluracil An anticancer drug that increases the effectiveness of fluorouracil. Also called ethynyluracil.

Enophthalmos The overall 'sinking in' appearance following loss of the eyeball, or partial loss of ocular volume.

Enoxaparin A drug used to prevent blood clots. It belongs to the family of drugs called anticoagulants.

Enriched foods Enriched foods are those that nutrients have been added to replace the nutrients which were lost during food processing. For example, B vitamins are lost in processing wheat to white flour and these are then added back to the flour.

ENT A doctor who specializes in treating diseases of the ear, nose, and throat. Also called an otolaryngologist.

Entelev A liquid that has been promoted as a treatment for a wide range of diseases, including cancer. The ingredients thought to be in Entelev have been tested, and none of them has been shown to be effective in treating any form of cancer.

Enter (o) Intestine, e.g. enteritis - inflammation of the intestine.

Enteral nutrition A form of nutrition that is delivered into the digestive system as a liquid. Drinking nutrition beverages or formulas and tubefeeding are forms of enteral nutrition. People who are unable to meet their needs with food and beverages alone, and who do not have vomiting or uncontrollable diarrhea may be given tubefeedings. Tubefeeding can be used to add to what a person is able to eat or can be the only source of nutrition. A small feeding tube may be placed through the nose into the stomach or the small intestine, or it may be surgically placed into the stomach or the intestinal tract through an opening made on the outside of the abdomen, depending on how long it will be used.

Enteric Relating to, or of the intestines or gastrointestinal tract.

Enterocele Herniation of small bowel into vagina.

Enterostomal therapist A health professional trained in the care of persons with stomas, such as colostomies or urostomies.

Enthalpy A thermodynamic property that indicates the total energy in a sample of dry air and water vapour, measured in Btu/lb dry air. Dry air at zero degrees Fahrenheit and atmospheric pressure is designa-ted as zero enthalpy.

Entrapment neuropathy Pathological situation where a nerve is trapped in an abnormally produced anatomical or physiological site.

Entropion The inward turning of the eyelashes and eyelid. This is usually accompanied by contraction of the palpebral conjunctiva (under part of the eyelid).

Enucleation In medicine, the removal of an organ or tumor in such a way that it comes out clean and whole, like a nut from its shell.

Enveloped virus A virus that has an outer wrapping or envelope. This envelope comes from the infected cell, or host, in a process called "budding off". During the budding process, newly formed virus particles become "enveloped" or wrapped in an outer coat that is made from a small piece of the cell's plasma membrane. The envelope may play a role in helping a virus survive and infect other cells.

Environmental protection agency (EPA) The EPA's mission is to protect human health and safeguard the natural environment—air, water and land—upon which life depends. Through regulation, EPA tries to ensure the human population and the environment are protected from environmental risks and exposures.

Environmental tobacco smoke (ETS) Smoke that comes from the burning of a tobacco product and smoke that is exhaled by smokers (second-hand smoke). Inhaling ETS is called involuntary or passive smoking.

Enzastaurin A substance that is being studied in the treatment of cancer. It belongs to the families of drugs called protein kinase C inhibitors and angiogenesis inhibitors.

Enzastaurin hydrochloride The hydrochloride salt of enzastaurin, a synthetic macrocyclic bisindolemaleimide with potential antineoplastic activity. Binding to the ATP-binding site, enzastaurin selectively inhibits protein kinase C beta, an enzyme involved in the induction of vascular endothelial growth factor (VEGF)-stimulated neo-angiogenesis. This agent may decrease tumor blood supply and so tumor burden.

Enzyme Any of numerous proteins or conjugated proteins produced by living organisms and functioning as complex biochemical catalysts. They not only promote reactions but also function as regulators making sure the organism does not produce too much or too little of any chemical substance. Although all enzymes are proteins, many contain additional non-protein compo-nents essential for catalytic activity. Such enzymes are termed haloenzymes. The protein part of this enzyme is termed an apoenzyme and the non-amino acid part is termed a coenzyme.

Eosinophil chemotactic factor of anaphylaxis (ECF A) A substrate released from mast cells during anaphylaxis which attracts eosinophils.

Eosinophilia A condition in which the number of eosinophils (a type of white blood cell) in the blood is greatly increased. Eosinophilia is often a response to infection or allergens (substances that cause an allergic response).

Eosinophils White blood cells containing chemical filled granules that when released kill parasites. Also, eosinophils found in the blood or mucous secretions indicates the presence of allergy.

EP 2101 A proprietary cancer DNA vaccine that contains multiple natural and modified epitopes derived from the four tumor associated antigens, CEA, HER2/neu, p53, and MAGE 2/3. EP-2101 also includes CAP1-6D, a heteroclitic CEA analog, and PADRE, a proprietary universal T-cell epitope that serves to enhance the immunogenicity of the epitopes. This agent has been shown to elicit cytotoxic T-lymphocyte responses against tumor cells expressing these multiple epitopes.

Ependyma Single uninterrupted layer of ciliated squamous to columnar epithelial-like cells that line the cerebral ventricles and central canal of the spinal cord.

Ependymal tumor A brain tumor that usually begins in the central canal of the spinal cord. Ependymal tumors may also develop in the cells lining the ventricles of the brain, which produce and store the special fluid (cerebrospinal fluid) that protects the brain and spinal cord. Also called an ependymoma.

Ependymoma A type of brain tumor that may arise in the ventricles of the brain or in the spinal cord. Also called an ependymal tumor.

Epi Upon; over, e.g. epibulbar - situated upon the eyeball.

Epicardial The outside surface of the heart. Epicardial leads are placed on the heart during open-chest surgery.

Epicardium The inner layer of the serous pericardium which is in contact with the heart.

Epidemic A disease attacking many people in a community simultaneously; distinguished from endemic, since the disease is not continuously present but has been introduced from outside.

Epidemiology The study of distribution and determinants of diseases or other health outcomes in human populations. It seeks to expose potential associations between aspects of health (such as cancer, heart disease, etc.) and diet, lifestyle, habits or other factors within populations. Epidemiological studies may suggest relationships between two factors, but do not provide the basis for conclusions about cause and effect. Possible associations inferred from epidemiological research can turn out to be coincidental.

Epidermis The upper or outer layer of the two main layers of tissue that make up the skin.

Epidermoid carcinoma Cancer that begins in squamous cells, which are thin, flat cells that look like fish scales. Squamous cells are found in the tissue that forms the surface of the skin, the lining of the hollow organs of the body, and the lining of the respiratory and digestive tracts. Also called squamous cell carcinoma.

Epidermolytic hyperkeratosis Also called granular degeneration. It is characterized by:

perinuclear clear spaces in the upper stratum malpighii,

indistinct cellular boundaries,

a markedly thickened granular layer with increased numbers of keratohyalin granules, and

hyperkeratosis.

Epidermotropism The presence of mononuclear cells in the epidermis, without the presence of spongiosis. Occurs in mycosis fungoides. Not to be confused with exocytosis.

Epidural block An injection of an anesthetic drug into the space between the wall of the spinal canal and the covering of the spinal cord.

Epidural Having to do with the space between the wall of the spinal canal and the covering of the spinal cord. An epidural injection is given into this space.

Epidural space Narrow space situated between the dura mater and the bony skull or vertebral column.

Epigastric Having to do with the upper middle area of the abdomen.

Epiglottis The cartilagenous structure which overhangs the larynx - it acts like a flap valve to prevent food entering the airway when swallowing.

Epilepsy A group of disorders marked by problems in the normal functioning of the brain. These problems can produce seizures, unusual body movements, a loss of consciousness or changes in consciousness, as well as mental problems or problems with the senses.

Epinephrine A substance produced by the medulla (inside) of the adrenal gland. The name epinephrine was coined in 1898 by the American pharmacologist and physiologic chemist (biochemist) John Jacob Abel who isolated it from the adrenal gland which is located above (epi-) the kidney ("nephros" in Greek). (Abel also crystallized insulin). Technically speaking, epinephrine is a sympathomimetic catecholamine. It causes quickening of the heart beat, strengthens the force of the heart's contraction, opens up the airways (bronchioles) in the lungs and has numerous other effects. The secretion of epinephrine by the adrenal is part of the fight-or-flight reaction. Adrenaline is a synonym of epinephrine and is the official name in the British Pharmacopoeia.

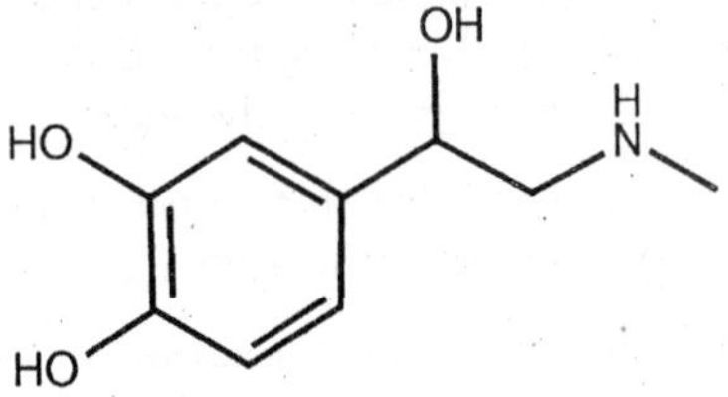

OH
HO
H
N
HO

Epinephrine (4- (1-hydroxy-2 (methylamino) ethyl)benzene-1,2-diol)

Figure Epinephrine

Epiphora An overflow of tears.

Epipodophyllotoxin A drug used to treat a variety of childhood cancers. Epipodophyllotoxins belong to a larger class of drugs called topoisomerase II inhibitors.

Epirubicin hydrochloride The hydrochloride salt of the 4'-epi-isomer of the anthracycline antineoplastic antibiotic doxorubicin. Epirubicin intercalates into DNA and interacts with topoisomerase II, thereby inhibiting DNA replication and repair and RNA and protein synthesis. This agent also produces toxic free-radical intermediates and interacts with cell membrane lipids causing lipid peroxidation.

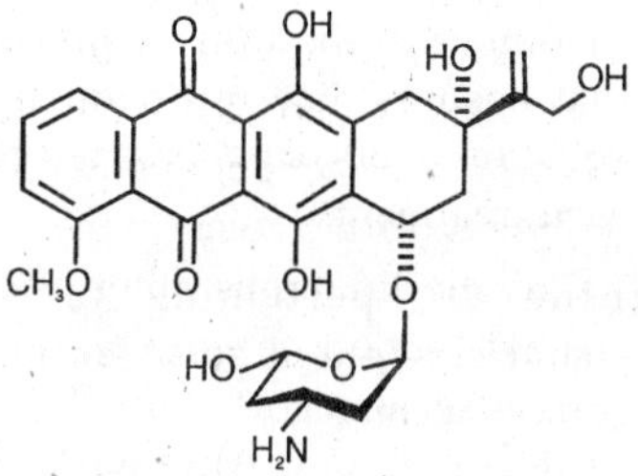

Epirubicin (10- ((3-amino-2,3,6-trideoxy-beta-L-arabino-hexopyranosyl)oxy)-7,8,9,10-tetrahydro-6,8,11-trihydroxy-8-(hydroxyacetyl)-1-methoxy- (8S-cis)-5,12-naphthacenedione)

Figure Epirubicin hydrochloride

Epistasis One gene interfers with or prevents the expression of another gene located at a different locus.

Epithalamus The postero-dorsal part of the diencephalon located above the thalamus at the point where the cerebral aqueduct joins the third ventricle. Consists of the habenular nuclei, pineal body, subcimmissural organ, posterior and habenular commissures.

Epithelial Refers to the cells that line the internal and external surfaces of the body.

Epithelial carcinoma Cancer that begins in the cells that line an organ.

Epithelial ovarian cancer Cancer that occurs in the cells lining the ovaries.

Epithelioid cells Cells derived from macrophages, seen in granulomas and characterized by a large, usually oval, pale, vesicular nucleus with a clearly visible nuclear membrane. The cytoplasm is abundant,. ill-defined and slightly eosinophilic.

Multinucleated epithelioid or giant cells arise from mature macrophages that fuse rather than divide. Langhans giant cells have nuclei in a semicircle at the cell periphery. Foreign body giant cells have nuclei distributed randomly.

Epithelium The layer (s) of cells between an organism or its tissues or organs and their environment (skin cells, inner linings of lungs or digestive organs, outer linings of kidneys, etc.).

Epitope A unique shape or marker carried on an antigen's surface which triggers a corresponding antibody response.

Epitympanic recess The upper portion of the tympanic membrane, above the level of the tympanic membrane.

EPO (Erythropoietin) A glycoprotein hormone that stimulates the production of red blood cells. It is a commercialized product of recombinant DNA technology.

Epoetin alfa A recombinant therapeutic agent which is chemically identical to or similar to the endogenous cytokine human erythropoietin (EPO). Produced primarily by cells of the peritubular capillary endothelium of the kidney in response to hypoxia, circulating EPO binds to EPO receptors on the surface of committed erythroid progenitors in the bone marrow resulting in their replication and maturation into functional erythrocytes.

Epoetin beta A substance that is made in the laboratory and that stimulates the bone marrow to make red blood cells. It belongs to the family of drugs called antianemics. It is also called recombinant human erythropoietin.

Epothilone A drug obtained from bacteria that interferes with cell division. Some epothilones are being studied as treatments for cancer.

Epothilone B A substance that is being studied as a treatment for cancer. It belongs to the family of drugs called epothilones. Also called EPO906.

Epothilone D A natural polyketide compound isolated from the myxobacterium Sorangium cellulosum. Also known as desoxyepothilone B, epothilone D binds to tubulin and inhibits the disassembly of microtubules, resulting in the inhibition of mitosis, cellular proliferation, and cell motility.

Epratuzumab A recombinant, humanized monoclonal antibody directed against CD22, a cell surface glycoprotein present on mature B-cells and on many types of malignant B-cells. After binding to CD22, epratuzumab's predominant antitumor activity appears to be mediated through antibody-dependent cellular cytotoxicity (ADCC).

Equal treatment allocation A scheme in which the assignment probability in the randomization process for any one treatment is the same as for every other treatment in the trial. A process that ensures that approximately equal numbers of patients receive each treatment.

Equine Of, pertaining to, or characteristic of a horse, such as equine hormones.

Equipment suitability The established capacity of process equipment and ancillary systems to operate consistently within established limits and tolerances.

Equity A state of being fair or equal; equity in health implies the ideal that everyone should have a fair opportunity to attain his or her full health potential. More pragmatically, it implies that no one should be disadvantaged by being prevented from achieving this potential. The term inequity refers to differences in health, which are not only unnecessary and avoidable but, in addition, are considered unfair and unjust.

Equivalence zone In a precipitin reaction, the region in which the concentration of antigen and antibody leads to maximal precipitation.

ER (Estrogen receptor) Protein found on some cancer cells to which estrogen will attach.

ER- (Estrogen receptor negative) Describes cells that do not have a protein to which the hormone estrogen will bind. Cancer cells that are ER- do not need estrogen to grow, and usually do not stop growing when treated with hormones that block estrogen from binding.

ER+ (Estrogen receptor positive) Describes cells that have a protein to which the hormone estrogen will bind. Cancer cells that are ER+ need estrogen to grow, and may stop growing when treated with hormones that block estrogen from binding.

Erectile dysfunction An inability to have an erection of the penis adequate for sexual intercourse. Also called impotence.

Erection In medicine, the swelling of the penis with blood, causing it to become firm.

Erector spinae Muscles of the spine that lie posteriorly. These are commonly known as the "anti-gravity" muscles.

Erector spinea muscle Intermediate muscles of the back that produce extention in the vertebral column. It originates from the sacrum, iliac crest, and spines of the lumbar and eleventh and twelfth thoracic vertebrae, splitting into the iliocostals, longissimus, and spinalis muscles.

Ergonomics The account of how the workplace relates to the human and its function.

Erlotinib hydrochloride The hydrochloride salt of a quinazoline derivative with antineoplastic properties. Competing with adenosine triphosphate, erlotinib reversibly binds to the intracellular catalytic domain of epidermal growth factor receptor (EGFR) tyrosine kinase, thereby reversibly inhibiting EGFR phosphorylation and blocking the signal transduction events and tumorigenic effects associated with EGFR activation.

Eroded Having a shallow or superficial ulceration.

Erosion An area where the epidermis is lost without dermal loss.

ERT (Estrogen replacement therapy) Hormones (estrogen, progesterone, or both) given to postmenopausal women or to women who have had their ovaries surgically removed. Hormones are given to replace the estrogen no longer produced by the ovaries.

Eruption Process of teeth protruding through the gums.

Erythema Redness of the skin.

Erythrocyte sedimentation rate (ESR) The distance red blood cells travel in one hour in a sample of blood as they settle to the bottom of a test tube. The sedimentation rate is increased in inflammation, infection, cancer, rheumatic diseases, and diseases of the blood and bone marrow. Also called sedimentation rate.

Erythrocyte The red blood cell consisting largely of hemoglobin and carrying nearly all the oxygen contained in the blood. Erythrocytes are biconcave discs that are manufactured in the bone marrow.

Erythrodysplasia A condition in which immature red blood cells (erythroid cells) in the bone marrow are abnormal in size, shape, organization, and/or number. Erythrodysplasia may be caused by vitamin deficiency or chemotherapy, or it may be a sign of refractory anemia, which is a myelodysplastic syndrome. Also called erythroid dysplasia.

Erythroleukoplakia An abnormal patch of red and white tissue that forms on mucous membranes in the mouth and may become cancerous. Tobacco (smoking or chewing) and alcohol may increase the risk of erythroleukoplakia.

Erythromycin An antibiotic that binds to the 50S subunit of prokaryotic ribosomes and inhibits translocation of mRNA along the ribosome.

Erythroplakia An abnormal patch of red tissue that forms on mucous membranes in the mouth and may become cancerous. Tobacco (smoking and chewing) and alcohol may increase the risk of erythroplakia.

Esophageal Having to do with the esophagus, the muscular tube through which food passes from the throat to the stomach.

Esophageal atresia During pregnancy, the baby's esophagus does not develop properly, and ends before reaching the stomach. Food cannot pass from the mouth into the stomach.

Esophageal cancer Cancer that forms in tissues lining the esophagus (the muscular tube through which food passes from the throat to the stomach). Two types of esophageal cancer are squamous cell carcinoma (cancer that begins in flat cells lining the esophagus) and adenocarcinoma (cancer that begins in cells that make and release mucus and other fluids).

Esophageal manometry A test that measures the muscle tone in the esophagus.

Esophageal pH monitoring A test used to monitor the amount of acid in the esophagus, which helps evaluate gastroesophageal reflux disease (GERD).

Esophageal reflux The backward flow of stomach acid contents into the esophagus (the tube that connects the mouth to the stomach). Also called gastroesophageal reflux or gastric reflux.

Esophageal speech Speech produced by trapping air in the esophagus and forcing it out again. It is used after removal of a person's larynx (voice box).

Esophageal stricture A narrowing in the esophagus, often caused by irritation from long-term presence of acid in the esophagus with chronic gastroesophageal reflux disease (GERD).

Esophageal varices Dilated vessels in the lower end of the esophagus that result from portal hypertension. Often results in gastrointestinal bleeding, a life threatening complication of cirrhosis.

Esophagectomy An operation to remove a portion of the esophagus.

Esophagitis Inflammation of the esophagus (the tube that carries food from the mouth to the stomach).

Esophagogastroduodenoscopy (EGD) A test using an endoscope to look at the inside of the esophagus, stomach, and upper part of the small intestine. Tissue samples can also be taken to test for diseases.

Esophagoscopy Examination of the esophagus using a thin, lighted tube.

Esophagram A series of x-rays of the esophagus. The x-ray pictures are taken after the person drinks a solution that contains barium. The barium coats and outlines the esophagus on the x-ray. Also called a barium swallow and upper GI series.

Esophagus The musculomembraneous tube connecting the pharynx to the stomach.

Esophoria (Eso) (clinical condition) A tendency of the eyes to want to turn more inward than necessary when an individual is viewing an object at near or at distance, which may cause the individual to experience eyestrain and other symptoms. Symptoms of basic esophoria include: eyestrain, headaches, blurred or double vision, apparent movement of print, and difficulty concentrating on and comprehending reading material. Clinical signs of basic esophoria include: AC/A ratio is normal, equal esophoria at distance and near, and normal near point of convergence. Sometimes esophoria is caused by a refractive error such as hyperopia (farsightedness), and glasses or contacts can correct the problem alone. However, sometimes vision therapy is needed to to help re-train the eyes to function more appropriately.

Esotropia (ET) (Clinical condition) A condition in which an eye is turned either constantly or intermittently inward toward the nose. Esotropia is a type of strabismus. It is caused by a reduction in visual acuity, reduced visual function, high refractive error, traumatic brain injury, oculomotor nerve lesion, or eye muscle injury. Treatment options may include one or more of the following: glasses or contacts, bifocal lenses, prisms, vision therapy, surgery, or Botulinum Toxin Type A (Oculinum, Botox) injections. In some cases, esotropia is caused by a refractive error such as hyperopia (farsightedness), and glasses or contacts alone may allow the eyes to straighten. Vision therapy is most appropriate when there are small degrees of misalignment. Surgery, to reposition or shorten the eye muscles, may be required for high degrees of misalignment. If surgery is required, a combination of surgery and vision therapy often yields the best results.

Essays or open-ended questions An assessment method, distinguished from short-answer questions by the scope, the length of required answers, and the relative lack of specific cues for recall. Essay questions typically deal with larger issues and are based on information that is spread out over a number of learning sources. Students' answers should reflect both how much is known about a topic and how well organized knowledge of the subject is. As essay questions and answers are comparatively complex, more abilities are displayed than with other question types. They may be used to assess knowledge of basic and clinical science and its application to clinical problems. They provide information about the respondent perceptions, reasoning abilities, attitudes, feelings, and experiences. Because such questions typically require extensive knowledge as well as analytical and writing skills, they perhaps are best suited for deciding who the top students in a course are. The essential weakness of essay questions is that they can be ambiguous, difficult to grade reliably and require scorers with relevant knowledge and training.

Essential amino Acids Amino acids that cannot be synthesized by human and other vertebrates and must be obtained from the diet.

Essential community providers Providers such as community health centers that have traditionally served low-income populations.

Essential fatty acids The group of polyunsaturated fatty acids of plants required in the human diet.

Essential thrombocythemia An increased number of thrombocytes (platelets) in the blood, without a known cause. Also called essential thrombocytosis.

Essiac A herbal tea mixture that contains burdock root, Indian rhubarb root, sheep sorrel, and slippery elm bark. It has been claimed to remove toxins from the body, make the immune system stronger, relieve pain, control diabetes, treat AIDS, reduce tumor size, increase cancer survival, and improve quality of life. No clinical trial using Essiac in humans has been reported in a peer-reviewed, scientific journal.

EST (Expressed sequence tag) ethical pharmaceutical A controlled substance for the diagnosis or treatment of disease.

Estimated sample size The number of patients required for a study, as derived from a sample size calculation or in some other way.

Estradiol A steroid sex hormone vital to the maintenance of fertility and secondary sexual characteristics in females. Typically esterified, estradiol derivatives are formulated for oral or parenteral administration. As the primary, most potent estrogen hormone produced by the ovaries, estradiol binds to and activates specific nuclear receptors. Estradiol exhibits mild anabolic and metabolic properties, and increases blood coagulability.

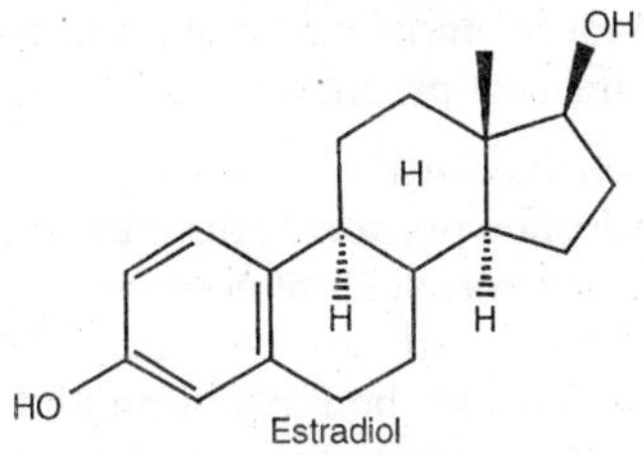

OH
H
H H
HO
Estradiol

Figure Estradiol

Estramustine A combination of the hormone estradiol (an estrogen) and nitrogen mustard (an anticancer drug). Used in the palliative therapy of prostate cancer.

Estramustine phosphate sodium The orally available disodium salt, monohydrate, of estramustine phosphate, a synthetic molecule that combines estradiol and nornitrogen mustard through a carbamate link. Estramustine and its major metabolite estramustine bind to microtubule-associated proteins (MAPs) and tubulin, thereby inhibiting microtubule dynamics and leading to anaphase arrest in a dose-dependent fashion. This agent also exhibits anti-androgenic effects.

Estrogen A female sex hormone produced primarily in the ovaries, possibly in the adrenal cortex, and produced in men in the testis (in much smaller amounts than in women). In women, levels of estrogen fluctuate on nature's carefully orchestrated schedule, regulating the development of secondary sex characteristics, including breasts; regulating the monthly cycle of menstruation; and preparing the body for fertilization and reproduction. In breast cancer, estrogen may feed the growth of cancer cells.

Estrogen receptor A protein found inside the cells of the female reproductive tissue, some other types of tissue, and some cancer cells. The hormone estrogen will bind to the receptors inside the cells and may cause the cells to grow.

Estrogen receptor assay A test to see if a breast tumor's cells are nourished by estrogen (estrogen receptor positive) or not (estrogen-receptor negative).

Estrogen receptor test A lab test to find out if cancer cells have estrogen receptors (proteins to which estrogen will bind). If the cells have estrogen receptors, they may need estrogen to grow, and this may affect how the cancer is treated.

Etanercept A recombinant soluble dimeric fusion protein consisting of the extracellular ligand-binding region of recombinant human tumor necrosis factor (rhTNF) receptor attached to the constant (Fc) region of human immunoglobulin G (FcIgG). The receptor moiety of etanercept binds to circulating TNF (2 molecules of TNF per receptor) and inhibits its attachment to endogenous TNF cell surface receptors, thereby rendering TNF inactive and inhibiting TNF-mediated mechanisms of inflammation.

Etanidazole A drug that increases the effectiveness of radiation therapy.

Ethambutol (myambutol) An antibiotic used as a component in combination therapy to treat tuberculosis or mycobacterium avium complex.

Ethanol A colourless organic liquid also known as ethyl alcohol or grain alcohol. Ethanol's primary physiologic effects involve the central nervous system. Depending on the dose delivered, ethanol behaves as an anxiolytic, a depressant, or a general anesthetic. Ethanol-induced immunosuppression involves dysregulation of CD4+ T cells.

Ethics The branch of philosophy that deals with distinctions between right and wrong and with the moral consequences of human actions. Examples of ethical issues that arise in medical practice and research include informed consent, confidentiality, respect for human rights, and scientific integrity.

Ethinyl estradiol A semisynthetic estrogen. Ethinyl estradiol binds to the estrogen receptor complex and enters the nucleus, activating DNA transcription of genes involved in estrogenic cellular responses. This agent also inhibits 5-alpha reductase in epididymal tissue, which lowers testosterone levels and may delay progression of prostatic cancer. In addition to its antineoplastic effects, ethinyl estradiol protects against osteoporosis. In animal models, short-term therapy with this agent has been shown to provide long-term protection against breast cancer, mimicking the antitumor effects of pregnancy.

Ethiodized oil A synthetic iodine addition product of the ethyl ester of the fatty acids of poppyseed oil. Ethiodized oil contains 37% organically bound iodine and is used as a diagnostic radiopaque medium or, labeled with I-131, as an antineoplastic agent. Selectively retained in tumor vessels for long periods, ethiodized oil is used for imaging organs such as liver, lung, stomach, and thyroid. Labelled with I-131 or other beta emitters (Y-90 or P-32), ethiodol can deliver a high internal radiation dose to certain tumors with minimal effect on healthy tissues.

Ethmoid sinus The paranasal sinus located within the ethmoid bone, between the orbits, below the brain, and above the nasal cavity.

Ethylene oxide (ETO) A toxic compound used in gaseous form as a sterilizing agent, usually as a 10% mixture with carbon dioxide or 12% mixture with freon (referred as 12-88). Sterilization using ETO leaves residual chemicals such as ethylene chlorohydrin and ethylene glycol.

Etidronate A drug that belongs to the family of drugs called bisphosphonates. Bisphosphonates are used as treatment for hypercalcemia (abnormally high levels of calcium in the blood) and for cancer that has spread to the bone (bone metastases).

Etiologic agent A disease-causing organism or toxin.

Etiology Study of the cause of disease. In cancer, there are probably many etiologies, although research is showing that genetics are a major factor in many cancers.

Etoposide A semisynthetic derivative of podophyllotoxin, a substance extracted from the mandrake root Podophyllum peltatum. Possessing potent antineoplastic properties, etoposide binds to and inhibits topoisomerase II and its function in ligating cleaved DNA molecules, resulting in the accumulation of single- or double-strand DNA breaks, the inhibition of DNA replication and transcription, and apoptotic cell death. Etoposide acts primarily in the G2 and S phases of the cell cycle.

EU A prefix denoting: 1. Good, well or easy.

2. Normal e.g. euthyroid - having a thyroid gland that functions normally.

Eugenics The study of improving a species by artificial selection; usually refers to the selective breeding of humans.

Euglycemia A normal level of glucose (sugar) in the blood.

Eukaryote An organism that carries its genetic material physically constrained within a nuclear membrane, separate from the cytoplasm. All animal and plant cells except bacteria, viruses, and bluegreen algae are eukaryotic. Eukaryotes are five to ten times larger than prokaryotes in diameter.

Eustachian tube A hollow cartilagenous tube connecting the tympanic cavity (middle ear) and the nasopharynx. An open tube can equilibrate the pressure in the middle ear. Yawning opens the tube to allow the ears to "pop!" when changing altitude.

Eutectic Of, pertaining to, or formed at the lowest possible temperature of solidification for any mixture of specified constituents. A common term used to describe metal alloys.

Evaluable disease Disease that cannot be measured directly by the size of the tumor but can be evaluated by other methods specific to a particular clinical trial.

Evaluable patients Patients whose response to a treatment can be measured because enough information has been collected.

Evaluation A process that attempts to systematically and objectively determine the relevance, effectiveness, and impact of activities in light of their objectives. Evaluation can be related to structure, process, or outcome. One can distinguish these various types:

Formative individual evaluation provides feedback to an individual (usually a learner) in order to improve that individual's performance. This type of evaluation identifies areas for improvement and provides specific suggestions for improvement serving as an educational tool.

Summative individual evaluation measures whether specific objectives were accomplished by an individual in order to place a value on the performance of that individual. It may certify competency or lack of competency in performance in a particular area.

Formative program evaluation provides information in order to improve a program's performance. It usually takes the form of surveys of learners to obtain feedback about and suggestions for improving a curriculum. Quantitative information such as ratings of various aspects of the curriculum can help identify areas that need revision. Qualitative information, such as responses to open-ended questions about program strengths and weaknesses, as well as suggestions for change, provide feedback in areas that may not have been anticipated and provide ideas for improvement. Information can also be obtained from faculty or other observers, such as nurses and patients.

Summative program evaluation measures the success of a curriculum in achieving learner objectives for all targeted learners, its success in achieving its process objectives, and/or its success in engaging, motivating, and pleasing its learners and faculty. In addition to quantitative data, summative program evaluation may include qualitative information about unintended barriers or unanticipated effects encountered in program implementation.

Formative evaluations generally require the least amount of rigor, whereas summative individual and summative program evaluation for external use (e.g., certification of competence) requires the greatest amount of rigor. When a high degree of methodological rigor is required, the measurement instrument must be appropriate in terms of content, reliability, validity, and practicality.

Evapourator Apparatus used in distillation to heat a liquid and create a phase change from the liquid to the vapour state. A steam boiler is an evapourator.

Event 1. An occurrence, incident, or experience, especially one of some significance.

2. Binary outcome measure.

3. Clinical event.

4. The actual occurrence of a condition, trait, or characteristic that is defined by a binary outcome measure.

Event driven data Data whose collection is triggered by clinically manifest occurrence, as opposed to on a particular schedule.

Event rate The number of events experienced by a specified number of patients in a specified unit of time.

Everolimus A derivative of the natural macrocyclic lactone sirolimus with immuno-suppressant and anti-angiogenic properties. In cells, everolimus binds to the immunophilin FK Binding Protein-12 (FKBP-12) to generate an immunosuppressive complex that binds to and inhibits the activation of the mammalian Target of Rapamycin (mTOR), a key regulatory kinase. Inhibition of mTOR activation results in the inhibition of T lymphocyte activation and proliferation associated with antigen and cytokine (IL-2, IL-4, and IL-15) stimulation and the inhibition of antibody production.

Evidence-based medicine Evidence-based health care is the conscientious use of current best evidence in making decisions about the care of individual patients or the delivery of health services. Term used in quality improvement and peer review programs in hospitals and health plans.

Evisceration Complete removal of the contents of the eye, this could include the cornea.

Ewing's family of tumors (EFTs) A group of cancers that includes Ewing's tumor of bone (ETB or Ewing's sarcoma of bone), extraosseus Ewing's (EOE) tumors, primitive neuroectodermal tumors (PNET or peripheral neuroepithelioma), and Askin's tumors (PNET of the chest wall). These tumors all come from the same type of stem cell.

Ewing's sarcoma A type of bone cancer that usually forms in the middle (shaft) of large bones. Also called Ewing's sarcoma/primitive neuroectodermal tumor (PNET).

Ex (o) Out of; away from; outside of, e.g. exophytic - projecting out from a surface.

Exatecan mesylate A semisynthetic, water-soluble derivative of camptothecin with antineoplastic activity. Exatecan mesylate inhibits topoisomerase I activity by stabilizing the cleavable complex between topoisomerase I and DNA and inhibiting religation of DNA breaks, thereby inhibiting DNA replication and triggering apoptotic cell death. This agent does not require enzymatic activation and exhibits greater potency than camptothecin and other camptothecin analogues.

Exchange lists A grouping of foods by type to help people on special diets stay on the diet. Each group lists food in serving sizes. A person can exchange, trade, or substitute a food serving in one group for another food serving in the same group. The lists put foods in six groups:

starch/bread

meat

vegetables

fruit

milk

fats

Within a food group, each serving has about the same amount of carbohydrate, protein, fat, and calories.

Excipient A more or less inert substance added in a prescription drug compound as a diluent or vehicle or to give form or consistency when the remedy is given in a pill form; simple syrup, aromatic powder, honey, and various elixirs are examples of excipients.

Excision Surgical removal.

Excisional biopsy A surgical procedure in which an entire lump or suspicious area is removed for diagnosis. The tissue is then examined under a microscope.

Excisional skin surgery A surgical procedure used to remove moles, cysts, skin cancer, and other skin growths using local anesthesia. To treat skin cancer, the doctor uses a scalpel to remove the entire tumor and some of the healthy tissue around it.

Excoriation The destruction and removal of the surface of the skin or the covering of an organ by scraping.

Excrete Remove waste from the body.

Exemestane A synthetic androgen analogue. Exemestane binds irreversibly to and inhibits the enzyme aromatase, thereby blocking the conversion of cholesterol to pregnenolone and the peripheral aromatization of androgenic precursors into estrogens.

Exenteration The removal of the orbital contents which could include the eyelids.

Exergonic reaction Referring to a chemical reaction that takes place with release of negative standard energy to its surroundings, a "downhill" reaction.

Exfiltration Leakage of air out of a room through cracks in doors and pass-throughs through material transfer openings, etc. due to a difference in room pressures.

Exfoliate Process of shedding deciduous (baby) teeth.

Exhaustion Occurs when absorbents, such as activated carbon or ion exchange resins, have depleted their capacity by using up all active sites. Ion exchange resins may be regenerated to reverse the process.

Exisulind An inactive metabolite of the nonsteroidal, anti-inflammatory agent sulindac. After oral administration, sulindac undergoes extensive biotransformation including irreversible oxidation to sulindac sulfone. Approximately, one half of an administered dose of sulindac is eliminated through the urine, mostly as the conjugated sulfone metabolite.

Exocrine cancer A type of pancreatic cancer in which malignant (cancer) cells are found in the non-insulin producing tissues of the pancreas.

Exocrine pancreas cell A pancreatic cell that produces enzymes that are secreted into the small intestine. These enzymes help digest food as it passes through the gastrointestinal tract.

Exocytosis The presence of mononuclear cells in the epidermis with spongiosis (or microvesiculation). Occurs in inflammatory conditions. Not to be confused with epidermotropism.

Exodontia Practice of dental extractions.

Exogenous DNA DNA originating outside an organism that has been introducted into the organism.

Exogenous Produced or made outside the body; for instance, insulin that is commercially produced (made from pork or beef pancreas or by biosynthetic processes) is exogenous insulin when given to people.

Exon The region of DNA coding for a protein or a segment of a protein.

Exonuclease An enzyme that cleaves nucleotides sequentially from free ends of a linear nucleic acid substrate.

Exophoria (Exo) (clinical condition) A tendency of the eyes to want to turn more outward than necessary when an individual is viewing an object at near or at distance, which may cause the individual to experience eyestrain and other symptoms. Symptoms of basic exophoria include: eyestrain, headaches, blurred or double vision, apparent movement of print, and difficulty concentrating on and comprehending reading material. Clinical signs of basic exophoria include: normal AC/A ratio, equal exophoria at distance and near, and decreased near point of convergence. Vision therapy is an effective treatment option.

Exophthalmos Abnormal protrusion of the eyeball.

Exotic organism A biological agent where either the corresponding disease does not exist in a given country or geographical area, or where the disease is the subject of prophylactic measures or an eradication program undertaken in the given country or geographical area.

Exotoxins Proteins produced by bacteria that are able to diffuse into a medium through the bacterial cell membrane and cell wall. They are generally more potent and specific in their actions than endotoxins.

Exotropia (XT) (clinical condition) A condition in which an eye is either constantly or intermittently turned outward toward the ear. Exotropia is a type of strabismus. It may also be called divergent strabismus, wandering eye, or wall eye (s). It is caused by a reduction in visual acuity, reduced visual function, high refractive error, traumatic brain injury, oculomotor nerve lesion, or eye muscle injury. Treatment options may include one or more of the following: glasses or contacts, bi-focal lenses, prisms, vision therapy, surgery, or Botulinum Toxin Type A (Oculinum, Botox) injections.

Vision therapy is most appropriate when there are small degrees of misalignment. If surgery is required, a combination of surgery and vision therapy often yields the best results.

Expanded access A general term for methods of distributing experimental drugs to patients who are unable to participate in ongoing clinical efficacy trials and have no other treatment options. Specific types of expanded-access mechanism-s include parallel track, Treatment IND, and compassionate use.

Expanded access trial A way to provide an investigational therapy to a patient who is not eligible to receive that therapy in a clinical trial, but who has a serious or life-threatening illness for which other treatments are not available. Expanded access allows a patient to receive promising but not yet fully studied or approved cancer therapies when no other treatment option exists. Also called compassionate use trial.

Expectorant A medication that helps bring up mucus and other material from the lungs, bronchi, and trachea. An example of as expectorant is guaifenesin which promotes drainage of mucus from the lungs by thinning the mucus and also lubricates the irritated respiratory tract. Sometimes the term "expectorant" is incorrectly extended to any cough medicine. From the Latin expectorare, to expel from the chest, from ex-, out of pectus, chest.

Experimental drug A substance that has been tested in a laboratory and has gotten approval to be tested in people. A drug may be approved for use in one disease or condition but be considered experimental in other diseases or conditions. Also called an investigational drug.

Experimental group The group of subjects in an experimental study which receives a treatment.

Expiration date The date placed on the container/labels of an API (Active Pharmaceutical Ingredient) designating the time during which the API is expected to remain within established shelf life specifications if stored under defined conditions, and after which it should not be used.

Explanation of benefits (EOB) A statement sent to covered individuals explaining services provided, amount to be billed, and payments made. A summary of benefits provided subscribers by the carrier.

Explanatory trial Trials that are designed to explain how a treatment works, in which patients are typically analyzed by treatment received and not as assigned.

Explorer Sharp instrument used to detect decay on the surface of teeth.

Explosion resistance A type of construction used to house solvents in sufficiently large quantities, to qualify the space electrically as an explosion potential area. Typically the internal walls, ceiling, and floor are constructed of material strong enough to withstand a specified intensity of explosion, and at least one wall has explosion relief devices that direct the explosion outwardly. In a single story arrangement, or if the explosion resistant area is on the top floor, the roof may also have devices that can be used to relieve the explosion.

Explosive A chemical that causes a sudden, almost instantaneous release of pressure, gas and heat when subjected to sudden shock, pressure, or high temperatures, or a material or chemical, other than a blasting agent, that is commonly used or intended for the purpose of producing an explosive effect.

Exposed or open process The drug substance is exposed to the room environment during processing.

Express To translate the genetic information stored in the DNA into protein.

Expression system A host organism combined with a genetic vector (such as virus or circular DNA molecule called a plasmid) that is loaded with a gene of interest. The expression system provides the genetic context in which a gene will function in the cell - that is, the gene will be expressed as a protein.

Extended care facility (ECF) A nursing or convalescent home offering skilled nursing care and rehabilitation services on a 24-hour basis.

Extension An unbending movement around a joint in a limb that increases the angle between the bones of the limb at the joint.

Extensive-stage small cell lung cancer Cancer has spread outside of the lung in which it began or to other parts of the body.

External acoustic (auditory) canal The opening in the external surface of the temporal bone, behind the condyle of the mandible and in front of the mastoid air cells that conducts air and sound toward the tympanic membrane.

External auditory meatus The opening for the passage from the external ear toward the tympanic membrane. Also called the External Auditory Canal.

External beam radiation therapy A 25-28 treatment protocol that utilizes External Beam Radiation. Approximately 6800-7400 rads of radiation energy is delivered to the Prostate. There can be some radiation effect on surrounding tissues.

External capsule The thin association fiber layer of white matter immediately overlying the lateral convex surface of the putamen.

External iliac vein The continuation of the femoral vein, beginning at the level of the inguinal ligament, and joining the internal iliac vein at the sacroiliac articulation to form the common iliac vein.

External oblique muscle Muscles that run from the lower eight ribs at the costal cartilages to the crest of ilium and linea alba, that are responsible for flexing and rotating the torso and vertebral column.

External-beam radiation Radiation therapy that uses a machine to aim high-energy rays at the cancer. Also called external radiation.

Extra-articular That which lies external to the joint.

Extracellular Outside the cells.

Extracerebral Outside the brain or skull.

Extracorporeal Outside the body.

Extracorporeal photopheresis A procedure in which blood is removed from the body and treated with ultraviolet light and drugs that become active when exposed to light. The blood is then returned to the body. It is being studied in the treatment of some blood and bone marrow diseases and graft-vs-host disease (GVHD). Also called photopheresis.

Extracorporeal shock wave lithotripsy (ESWL) Extracorporeal shock wave lithotripsy uses highly focused impulses projected from outside the body to pulverize kidney stones.

Extracranial germ cell tumor A rare cancer that forms in germ cells in the testicle or ovary, or in germ cells that have traveled to areas of the body other than the brain (such as the chest, abdomen, or tailbone). Germ cells are reproductive cells that develop into sperm in males and eggs in females.

Extract In medicine, a preparation of a substance obtained from plants, animals, or bacteria and used as a drug or in drugs.

Extractables Undesirable foreign substances that are leached or dissolved by water or process streams from the materials of construction used in filters, storage vessels, distribution piping, and other wetted surfaces.

Extragonadal germ cell tumor A rare cancer that develops in germ cells that are found in areas of the body other than the ovary or testicle (such as the brain, chest, abdomen, or tailbone). Germ cells are reproductive cells that develop into sperm in males and eggs in females.

Extrahepatic Located or occurring outside the liver.

Extrahepatic bile duct The part of the common hepatic bile duct (tube that collects bile from the liver) that is outside the liver. This duct joins a duct from the gallbladder to form the common bile duct, which carries bile into the small intestine when food is being digested.

Extramural Research that is conducted outside of NIH, supported by either contract or grant support.

Extraneural That which lies external to neural tissue.

Extraocular muscles The muscles attached to the outside of the eyeball which control eye movement. Each eye has six muscles (lateral rectus, medial rectus, superior oblique, inferior oblique, superior rectus, and inferior rectus) that are coordinated by the brain.

Extrapleural pneumonectomy Surgery to remove a diseased lung, part of the pericardium (membrane covering the heart), part of the diaphragm (muscle between the lungs and the abdomen), and part of the parietal pleura (membrane lining the chest). This type of surgery is used most often to treat malignant mesothelioma.

Extrapulmonary Outside the lungs.

Extravasation The leaking of intravenous fluids or medications into tissue surrounding the infusion site. Extravasation may cause tissue damage.

Extreme capsule Thin layer of association fibers between the claustrum and cortex of the insula.

Extrusion An expulsion of an orbital implant.

Eye The organ of sight or vision. In man, and the vertebrates generally, it is properly the movable ball or globe in the orbit, but the term often includes the adjacent parts.

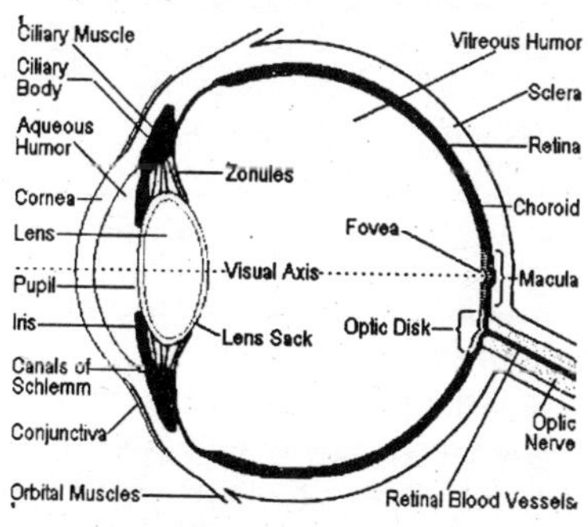

Figure Cross section view of Eye

The essential parts of the eye are enclosed in a tough outer coat, the sclerotic, to which the muscles moving it are attached, and which in front changes into the transparent cornea. A little way back of cornea, the crystalline lens is suspended, dividing the eye into two unequal cavities, a smaller one in front filled with a watery fluid, the aqueous humor, and larger one behind filled with a clear jelly, the vitreous humor. The sclerotic is lined with a highly pigmented membrane, the choroid, and this is turn is lined in the back half of the eyeball with the nearly transparent retina, in which the fibres of the optic nerve ramify. The choroid in front is continuous with the iris, which has a contractile opening in the center, the pupil, admitting light to the lens which brings the rays to a focus and forms an image upon the retina, where the light, falling upon delicate structures called rods and cones, causes them to stimulate the fibres of the optic nerve to transmit visual impressions to the brain.

Eye cancer Cancer that forms in tissues of and around the eye. Some of the cancers that may affect the eye include melanoma (a rare cancer that begins in cells that make the pigment melanin in the eye), carcinoma (cancer that begins in tissues that cover structures in the eye), lymphoma (cancer that begins in immune system cells), and retinoblastoma (cancer that begins in the retina and usually occurs in children younger than 5 years).

Eye fitter An ancillary eye care provider who does not fabricate, but does fit stock prostheses.

Eye hand coordination The ability of our eyes to guide our hands, also called visual motor integration.

Eye tracking The ability of the eyes to smoothly and effortlessly follow a moving target.

Eyeteeth The four upper and lower canine (cuspid) teeth.

Fab Fragment of antibody containing the antigen-binding site, generated by cleavage of the antibody with the enzyme papain, which cuts at the hinge region N-terminally to the inter-H-chain disulphide bond and generates two Fab fragments from one antibody molecule.

Fabella A sesamoid bone that is within the lateral head of gastrocnemius, which often articulates with the femoral condyle.

Faber test Flexion - Abduction - External Rotation test of the hip.

Face velocity The velocity obtained by dividing the air quantity by the component face area (NEBB).

Facial artery A branch of external carotid that branches into the ascending palatine, tonsillar, submental, inferior labial, superior labial, septal, lateral nasal, angular, and glandular arteries.

Facility flexibility A qualitative measure of the number of different products that can be produced in a facility or area of a facility.

Facility of accommodation A measure of the ease and speed of the eye (s) to change focus.

Facility user The end user of a facility, often called the Owner, represented by operating, maintenance, and quality control personnel.

Facing Tooth coloured overlay on the visible portion of a crown; may be acrylic, composite or porcelain.

Factor VIII (Hemophilia factor) Also known as antihemophilic factor or AHF (Brinkhous) in the clotting of blood, Factor VIII is a labile protein of the blood-clotting system that assists in the conversion of Factor IX into plasma factor X (Stuart factor). Deficiency of factor VIII is associated with classic hemophilia A, a hereditary, sex-linked, hemorrhagic tendency that occurs almost exclusively in men; clotting time is prolonged, less thromboplastin is formed, and the conversion of prothrombin is diminished.

Factorial treatment structure A treatment structure in which one study treatment is used in combination with at least one other study treatment in a trial, or where multiples of a defined dose of a specified treatment are used in the same trial.

Faculty development Because faculty members may be experts in their subject but may not have received special training in educating others, faculty development programs exist to enable these teachers to acquire the necessary professional knowledge, skills, attitudes and tools. It is an essential component for obtaining high reliability and validity of applied assessment on a day-to-day basis. It also enhances ongoing formative evaluation so that students are given feedback to help them improve continuously. Faculty development activities can be organized as series of special workshops, readings, or individualized feedback sessions. Since teaching is considered a very important aspect of a physician's work, such educational programs are often viewed as a form of Continuing Medical Education.

Faculty ratings questionnaires Questionnaires completed by faculty members that are used in the assessment of student deficiencies and achievements as well as professional behaviour and competence. They provide indirect, inexpensive measures of clinical skills attainment and real-life students' performance. However, Faculty-Ratings Questionnaires are subject to rating biases.

Failure to thrive A condition that occurs when a baby does not gain weight and grow normally; caused by many factors, including disease or poor nutrition.

Falciform ligament (of liver) An extension of the coronary ligament of the liver that attaches the liver to the diaphragm and separates the right and left lobes of the liver.

Fallopian tube A slender tube through which eggs pass from an ovary to the uterus. In the female reproductive tract, there is one ovary and one fallopian tube on each side of the uterus.

False negative test result A test result that indicates that a person does not have a specific disease or condition when the person actually does have the disease or condition.

False positive error The probability of rejecting the null hypothesis of no treatment difference when there is no treatment difference, that is, falsely claiming a treatment difference. Also called type I error.

False positive test result A test result that indicates that a person has a specific disease or condition when the person actually does not have the disease or condition.

False vocal cord A fold of mucous membrane in the larynx that separates the vestibule from the laryngeal ventricle, all above the true vocal cords (glottis).

Falx cerebri Sickle-shaped fold of dura mater that extends vertically in the midline between the two cerebral hemispheres.

F. Cerebelli: Sickle-shaped fold of dura mater that extends vertically between the cerebellar hemispheres along the posterior midline of the posterior cranial fossa.

Famciclovir (Famvir) A drug chemically related to acyclovir, used in the treatment of herpetic diseases

Familial adenomatous polyposis (FAP) An inherited condition in which numerous polyps (growths that protrude from mucous membranes) form on the inside walls of the colon and rectum. It increases the risk for colourectal cancer. Also called familial polyposis.

Familial atypical multiple mole melanoma syndrome (FAMMM) syndrome An inherited condition marked by the following:

1. one or more first- or second-degree relatives (parent, sibling, child, grandparent, grandchild, aunt, or uncle) with malignant melanoma;

2. many moles, some of which are atypical (asymmetrical, raised, and/or different shades of tan, brown, black, or red) and often of different sizes; and

3. moles that have specific features when examined under a microscope. FAMMM syndrome increases the risk of melanoma and may increase the risk of pancreatic cancer.

Familial cancer Cancer that occurs in families more often than would be expected by chance. These cancers often occur at an early age, and may indicate the presence of a gene mutation that increases the risk of cancer. They may also be a sign of shared environmental or lifestyle factors.

Familial dysplastic nevi A condition that runs in certain families in which at least two members have dysplastic nevi (atypical moles) and have a tendency to develop melanoma.

Familial polyposis An inherited condition in which numerous polyps (growths that protrude from mucous membranes) form on the inside walls of the colon and rectum. It increases the risk of colourectal cancer. Also called familial adenomatous polyposis or FAP.

Family history A record of a person's current and past illnesses, and those of his or her parents, brothers, sisters, children, and other family members. A family history shows the pattern of certain diseases in a family, and helps to determine risk factors for those and other diseases.

Fanconi's anemia A rare and often fatal inherited disease in which the bone marrow fails to produce red blood cells, white blood cells, platelets, or a combination of these cells. The disease may transform into myelodysplastic syndrome or leukemia. Also called Fanconi's syndrome.

Fansidar A combination of two antibiotics, Pyrimethamine and sulfadoxine, Fansidar was once used in the treatment of PCP. It proved highly toxic, however, with a high rate of allergic reactions and rash, including Stevens-Johnson syndrome. Rarely used anymore.

Farmer's lung An occupational lung disease caused by an allergy to fungal spores that grow in inadequately dried stored hay, straw or grain. Also known as Allergic Alveolitis.

Fascia A sheet or thin band of fibrous tissue that covers muscles and various organs of the body.

Fasciculus Bundles of nerve fibers (tract) within the central nervous system which have a common origin, course, and termination, and function.

Fasciotomy Division of fascia. Often associated with compartment syndromes of the lower leg.

Faslodex A drug that blocks estrogen activity in the body and is used in the treatment of estrogen-dependent tumors such as breast cancer. It belongs to the family of drugs called antiestrogens. Also called fulvestrant and ICI 182780.

Fastigial nuclei Paired cerebellar nuclei located on either side of the midline deep within the white matter of the cerebellar vermis. Associated with the vestibulo-cerebellum.

Fastigium The mid-dorsal apex of the fourth ventricle that extends into the medullary substance of the cerebellum.

Fasting plasma glucose (FPG) A method for finding out how much sugar (glucose) is in the blood. The test can show if a person has diabetes. A blood sample is taken in a lab or doctor's office. The test is usually done in the morning, after not eating for eight hours. The normal, nondiabetic range for fasting plasma glucose is less than 100 mg/dl (6.1 mmol/L). If the level is 126 mg/dl (7 mmol/L) or higher, it usually means the person has diabetes. Previous name for this test was fasting blood sugar (FBS).

Fat necrosis The death of fat cells, usually following injury. Fat necrosis is a benign condition, but it can cause a lump, pulling of the skin, or skin changes that can be confused with breast cancer.

Fat pad A "filler" in caverns. The most common is the infrapatellar fat pad.

Fat replacers Fat replacers are developed to duplicate the taste and texture of fat, but contain fewer calories per gram than fat. Fat replacers generally fall into three categories: carbohydrate, protein or fat-based. The ingredients that are used to replace fat depend on how the food product will be eaten or prepared. For example, not all fat replacer ingredients are heat stable. Thus, the fat replacer that worked well in a salad dressing may not work well in a muffin mix.

Fatigue A condition marked by extreme tiredness and inability to function due lack of energy. Fatigue may be acute or chronic.

Fats (Dietary fats) Fats are referred to in the plural because there is no one type of fat. Fats are composed of the same three elements as carbohydrates – carbon, hydrogen and oxygen, However, fats have relatively more carbon and hydrogen and less oxygen, thus supplying a higher fuel value of nine calories per gram (versus four calories per gram from carbohydrates and protein).

One molecule of fat can be broken down into three molecules of fatty acids and one molecule of glycerol. Thus, fats are known chemically as triglycerides.

Fats are a vital nutrient in a healthy diet. Fats supply essential fatty acids, such as linoleic acid, which is especially important to childhood growth. Fat helps maintain healthy skin, regulate cholesterol metabolism and is a precursor of prostaglandins, hormone-like substances that regulate some body processes. Dietary fat is needed to carry fat-soluble vitamins A, D, E and K and to aid in their absorption from the intestine.

Fatty acid Fatty acids are generally classified as saturated, monounsaturated or polyunsaturated. These terms refer to the number of hydrogen atoms attached to the carbon atoms of the fat molecule. In general, fats that contain a majority of saturated fatty acids are solid at room temperature, although some solid vegetable shortenings are up to 75 percent unsaturated. Fats containing mostly unsaturated fatty acids are usually liquid at room temperature and are called oils.

Fatty-replaced breast tissue A term used in mammography that refers to the replacement of breast tissue with fatty tissue. This commonly occurs as a woman ages.

Favourable selection Selection of subscribers or covered lives based on data that shows a tendency for utilization of health services in that population group to be lower than expected or estimated.

Fazarabine An anticancer drug that belongs to the family of drugs called antimetabolites.

FC Fragment of antibody without antigen-binding sites, generated by cleavage with papain; the Fc fragment contains the C-terminal domains of the heavy immunoglobulin chains.

Fc receptor (FcR) A receptor on a cell surface with specific binding affinity for the Fc portion of an antibody molecule. Fc receptors are found on many types of cells.

Febrile With a fever.

Febrile neutropenia A condition marked by fever and decrease in the number of neutrophils in the blood. A neutrophil is a type of white blood cell that helps fight infection. Having too few neutrophils increases the risk of infection.

Fecal fat test Assesses how well the body can break down and absorb fat. A fat free diet is eaten for two to three days, and then stool samples are collected and examined for the amount of fat they contain.

Fecal incontinence Inability to hold stool in the rectum.

Fecal occult blood test (FOBT) A test to check for blood in the stool. Small samples of stool are placed on special cards and sent to a doctor or laboratory for testing. Blood in the stool may be a sign of colourectal cancer.

Fed-batch fermentation The most common operating mode for rDNA fermentation. After an initial partial charge of media to the fermenter and seed transfer, sterile media is added at measured rates during the balance of the fermentation cycle. Cell mass and broth are withdrawn only at the end of the cycle.

Feedback loop A central concept in industrial controls in which the value of a process variable is compared with the desired value (setpoint), and any discrepancy (error) is converted into a modified output signal.

Feedwater The water entering a treatment process.

Feingold diet A diet that purports to treat many illnesses by the elimination of artificial food colouring, preservatives and salicylates from the diet. It has been recommended for the treatment of hyperactivity syndrome, but is of unproven value.

Femoral artery A continuation of the external iliac that branches into the superficial epigastric, superficial circumflex iliac, external pudendal, deep femoral, and descending geniculate arteries.

Femoral condyles (Medial and lateral) Two articulating surfaces located on the distal end of the femur and articulate with the proximal head of the tibia.

Femoral head The round ball-shaped proximal end of the Femur that articulates with the socket formed by the ischium, pubis, and acetabulum (joined together by the triradiate cartilage).

Femoral vein The continuation of the popliteal vein that becomes the external iliac at the inguinal ligament.

Femur The proximal bone of the lower extremity. It is the largest bone in the body. AKA "thigh bone".

Fenestrated Having many small holes (to allow excess impression gel to flow through).

Fentanyl A narcotic opioid drug that is used in the treatment of pain.

Fermentation The process of growing microorganisms within an enclosed tank (fermenter) under controlled conditions of aeration, agitation, temperature, and pH. The different types organisms used as a basis for fermentation are:

1. Bacteria (E. coli)
2. Yeasts
3. Molds
4. Chinese Hamster Ovary (CHO) cells
5. Kidney cells
6. Vaccines to viruses.

Fermenter A tank or vessel used for carrying out fermentation. There are various choices of fermenters, depending on whether cells are suspended in the medium or attached to some type of support:

1. In suspension reactors
2. Attached growth reactors
3. Stirred-tank reactors
4. Airlift fermenters
5. Packed bed reactors
6. Two-chamber reactors
7. Hollow-fiber reactors

Ferritin Iron-containing serum protein measured by laboratory to help establish a diagnosis of hemochromatosis.

Fertile Able to produce children.

Fertility The ability to produce children.

Fertility drug Any of a number of medications designed to increase a couple's chances of pregnancy, primarily by improving a woman's ability to ovulate. Women usually begin with pills and proceed, if unsuccessful, to more expensive needle injections. None of the drugs guarantees pregnancy.

Fertilization Penetration of the woman's egg by a sperm cell. It is the first interaction that can lead to a child, though pregnancy does not necessarily result.

Fertilizer Any organic or inorganic material, either natural or synthetic, used to supply elements (such as nitrogen, phosphate and potash) essential for plant growth. If used in excess or attached to eroding soil, fertilizers can become a source of water pollution.

Ferulic acid A type of phenol found in various fruits and vegetables and citrus fruits which has antioxidant like activities that may reduce the risk of degenerative diseases, heart disease and eye disease.

Ferumoxtran-10 A substance that is being studied as a way of improving magnetic resonance imaging (MRI) in diagnosing cancer and finding lymph nodes to which cancer has spread. Ferumoxtran-10 is made of nanoparticles (ultrasmall pieces) of iron oxide coated with dextran (a type of sugar). It is injected into the blood of the patient and the particles collect in lymph nodes, liver, spleen, or brain tissue where they can be seen using MRI. Ferumoxtran-10 later breaks down and passes from the body in urine.

Ferumoxytol A nanoparticle form of iron made in the laboratory that is being studied for use in iron replacement therapy, and as a contrast agent for magnetic resonance imaging. Contrast agents are substances that are injected into the body and taken up by certain tissues, making the tissues easier to see in imaging scans.

Fetal calf serum The liquid portion remaining after natural coagulation of blood drawn from the heart of an unborn calf. Because of the absence of gamma globulin, fetal calf serum is a good tissue culture serum.

Fetal hemoglobin A kind of hemoglobin usually present during fetal (intrauterine) life, which has a different chemical structure from normal adult hemoglobin. After birth, the fetal hemoglobin in the red blood cells is gradually replaced by the adult type of hemoglobin, this process is usually complete during the first 6 months of life.

Fetendo Surgery on a fetus using telescopes and eliminating the need for a large uterine incision in the mother.

Fetus The developing offspring from 7 to 8 weeks after conception until birth.

FEV (Forced expiratory volume) The speed with which air is exhaled during the first second in a pulmonary function test.

Fever Also known as pyrexia, a human body temperature above the normal 98.6°F (37°C).

Fiber Dietary fiber generally refers to parts of fruits, vegetables, grains, nuts and legumes that can't be digested by humans. Meats and dairy products do not contain fiber. Studies indicate that high-fiber diets can reduce the risks of heart disease and certain types of cancer. There are two basic types of fiber - insoluble and soluble. Soluble fiber in cereals, oatmeal, beans and other foods has been found to lower blood cholesterol. Insoluble fiber in cauliflower, cabbage and other vegetables and fruits helps move foods through the stomach and intestine, thereby decreasing the risk of cancers of the colon and rectum.

Fibrin A plasma protein that, in its aggregated state, is the major component of a blood clot. It is produced from fibrinogen, a soluble precursor, by the action of the proteolytic enzyme, thrombin.

Fibrin sealant A plasma-derived fibrin sealant consisting of two separate components that are combined on application. One component is a concentrated solution of clottable fibrinogen; the other component is a thrombin solution containing CaCl2. When combined, the two preparations rapidly form a clot, reproducing the final stages of the coagulation cascade.

Fibrinogen In the clotting of blood it is known as Factor I. The plasma protein that becomes converted to a clot at the end of the coagulation process. Present in plasma; absent in serum.

Fibroadenoma An adenoma in the breast, composed of fibrous tissue. On clinical examination or breast self-examination, it feels like a firm lump. These usually occur in young women and are benign.

Fibroblast A connective tissue cell that makes and secretes collagen proteins.

Fibrocystic breast disease A common condition marked by benign (noncancerous) changes in breast tissue. These changes may include irregular lumps or cysts, breast discomfort, sensitive nipples, and itching. These symptoms may change throughout the menstrual cycle and usually stop after menopause. Also called benign breast disease, fibrocystic breast changes, and mammary dysplasia.

Fibroid A benign smooth-muscle tumor, usually in the uterus or gastrointestinal tract. Also called leiomyoma.

Fibromatosis A condition in which multiple fibromas develop. Fibromas are tumors (usually benign) that affect connective tissue.

Fibrosarcoma A type of soft tissue sarcoma that begins in fibrous tissue, which holds bones, muscles, and other organs in place.

Fibrosis Formation of fibrous (tough or scar) tissue. This can occur anywhere in the body.

Fibrositis A benign, intermittently recurring and protracted disease process, with a lack of underlying pathology. The condition is often associated with muscular pain and stiffness.

Fibrous Containing or resembling fibers.

Fibrovascular Ingrowth infiltration of blood vessels and fibrous tissue. A means of stabilizing/anchoring a porous type implant.

Fibula The thin bone of the lower leg. The large bone is the Tibia.

Fifth cranial nerve The main sensory nerve of the head and face, and the motor nerve of the muscles used in chewing. Also called the trigeminal nerve.

Fig: ground The ability to recognize distinct shapes from their background, such as objects in a picture, or letters on a chalkboard.

Filgrastim A recombinant therapeutic agent which is chemically identical to or similar to the endogenous cytokine human granulocyte colony-stimulating factor (G-CSF). Produced endogenously by monocytes, fibroblasts, and endothelial cells, G-CSF binds to and activates specific cell surface receptors, stimulating neutrophil progenitor proliferation and differentiation and selected neutrophil functions.

Fill and finish (Parenteral drugs) Preparation of parenteral drugs, either LVPs or SVPs, demands the highest level of contamination control, because the human body's normal defenses against infection are bypassed when parenteral medications are introduced either intramuscularly (I.M.) or intravenously (I.V.) directly into the body. The processing of raw materials into finished dosage forms must comply at all times with cGMPs and must be able to support process validation. Mechanical design should include HVAC Classifications considered essential to attain global regulatory acceptance. Terminal sterilization may be accomplished using autoclaves that apply overpressure to balance the pressures that are developed across the inside and outside of the containers. Because of product sensitivities, biologics, and blood products are not appropriate applications for terminal sterilization.

Filler An inactive substance used to make a product bigger or easier to handle. For example, fillers are often used to make pills or capsules because the amount of active drug is too small to be handled conveniently.

Filling Restoration of lost tooth structure with metal, porcelain or resin materials.

Filovirus The thread-like virus family which includes such viruses as Ebola and Marburg; very deadly.

Filters Filtering centrifuges accommodate a range of liquid-solid separations. The two batch types, basket and peeler centrifuges, can separate almost any liquid-solid slurry. For continuous operation, there are pusher and conical centrifuges. (a) Pusher - with a horizontal axis, the pusher centrifuge operates at a constant fixed speed. It has a perforated bowl, generally with a bar-type screen. One end of the bowl is open while the opposite end is closed with a reciprocating diaphragm, or disc, which rotates with the bowl. (b) Conical - the standard conical centrifuge consists of a cone with a small closed end and a large open end to which is attached a coarsely woven drainage screen, topped with a filter screen or perforated plate. A compartmentalized casing surrounds the bowl. There are two variations of the basic conical centrifuge: the tilting conical centrifuge and the conveyor conical type.

Filtration Removal of suspended matter from a fluid by passing it through a porous matrix that prevents particles from getting through, usually by entrapment on or in the filter matrix.

Filum terminale Thread-like filament of pia mater within the lumbar cistern extending from the end of the spinal cord to the coccyx.

Fimbria Efferent fiber bundle arising from the hippocampus and continuing as the fornix.

Final bulk product The final drug product after chemical or biological processing and purification, ready for concentration, drying, and filling into containers prior to dispensing and final filling.

Finasteride A drug used to reduce the amount of male hormone (testosterone) produced by the body.

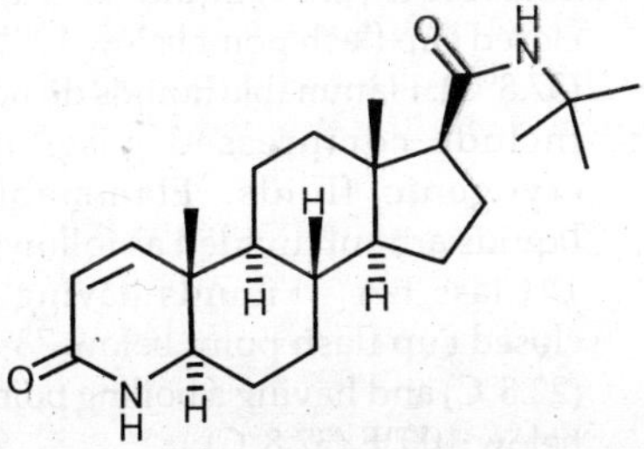

Figure Finasteride

Fine motor skills The ability to coordinate hand and finger movements.

Fine-needle aspirate A procedure in which a needle is inserted, under local anesthesia, to obtain a sample for the evaluation of suspicious tissue.

Fingerprinting In genetics, the identification of multiple specific alleles on a person's DNA to produce a unique identifier for that person.

Finished DNA sequence High-quality, low error, gap-free DNA sequence of the human genome. Achieving this ultimate 2003 HGP goal requires additional sequencing to close gaps, reduce ambiguities, and allow for only a single error every 10,000 bases, the agreed-upon standard for HGP finished sequence.

Finished product A medicinal product that has undergone all stages of production, including packaging in its final container.

Finkelstein's test Test for de Quervain's syndrome, whereby the patient clenches the fingers over the thumb and performs an ulnar deviation. To be positive, pain in the correct region must be elicited.

First line treatment The preferred therapy for a particular condition (e.g., trimethoprim-sulfamethoxazole (TMP-SMX) is the first-line treatment for PCP).

First phase insulin release Release of insulin into the bloodstream from the beta cell within a few minutes after the blood glucose level rises. It is thought that this almost immediate release is due to release of insulin that was previously manufactured, and was being stored in the beta cell.

First-line therapy The first type of therapy given for a condition or disease.

FISH (Fluorescent in situ hybridization) A physical mapping approach that uses fluorescein tags to detect hybridization of probes with metaphase chromosomes and with the less condensed somatic interface chromatin.

Fissile material A radioisotope that could undergo a nuclear fission reaction and is usually found at reactor sites or as part of a nuclear weapon.

Fissure Certain deep clefts (sulci) which separate various parts of the central nervous system (i.e. lateral fissure of Sylvius, primary fissure etc.)

Fistula An abnormal, tube-like passage from a hollow organ to the surface, or from one organ to another, e.g. esophageal fistula - a communication between the esophagus and some portion of the respiratory tract.

Five year survival To survive cancer for five years after treatment of the disease. This is a "milestone" for most cancer patients, indicating that treatment was successful.

Fixation disparity (FD) Over-convergence or under-convergence, or vertical misalignment of the eyes under binocular (both eyes) viewing conditions small enough in magnitude so that fusion is present.

Fixation The ability to direct and maintain steady visual attention on a target. Fixations are a form of pursuits.

Fixed costs Costs that do not change with fluctuations in census or in utilization of services.

Fixed dose combination A capsule or tablet containing two or more drugs. This type of drug formulation allows a patient to take multiple medications at one time to decrease pill burden.

Flaggelae Thin, helical filaments attached to the surface of bacterial and eukaryotic (e.g. sperm, protozoa) cells. They are motile structures containing microtubules (composed of proteins called tubulin) that enable cells possessing them to move.

Flagyl A drug that is used to treat infection and is being studied in the treatment of cancer. It belongs to the families of drugs called antibacterials, antiprotozoals, and anthelmintics. Also called metronidazole.

Flammable liquid A liquid having a closed cup flash point below 100°F (37.8°C). Flammable liquids do not include compressed gases or cryogenic fluids. Flammable liquids are subdivided as follows:
1. Class I-A - Liquids having a closed cup flash point below 73°F (22.8°C) and having a boiling point below 100°F (37.8°C).

2. Class I-B - liquids having a closed cup flash point below 73°F (22.8°C) and having a boiling point at or above 100°F (37.8°C).

3. Class I-C - liquids having a closed cup flash point at or above 73°F (22.8°C) and below 100°F (37.8°C).

Flammable solid A solid substance, other than one which is defined as a blasting agent or explosive, that is liable to cause fire through friction or as a result of retained heat from manufacture, which has an ignition temperature below 212°F (100°C), or which burns so vigorously or persistently when ignited that it creates a serious hazard. Flammable solids include finely divided solid materials which when dispersed in air as a cloud could be ignited and cause an explosion.

Flap surgery Lifting of gum tissue to expose and clean underlying tooth and bone structures.

Flavones A type of flavonoid found in various fruits and vegetables which provides the health benefits of neutralizing free radicals and possibly reducing the risk of cancer.

Flavonoid A member of a group of substances found in many plants and plant-based foods. Flavonoids have shown antioxidant effects.

Flavopiridol A synthetic N-methylpiperidinyl chlorophenyl flavone compound. As an inhibitor of cyclin-dependent kinase, flavopiridol induces cell cycle arrest by preventing phosphorylation of cyclin-dependent kinases (CDK) and by down-regulating cyclin D1 and D3 expression, resulting in G1 cell cycle arrest and apoptosis. This agent is also a competitive inhibitor of adenosine triphosphate activity.

Flaws Metallic flaws are unintentional irregularities that occur at one place or at relatively infrequent or widely varying intervals on the surface. Flaws include such defects such as cracks, blowholes, inclusions, pits, checks, ridges, scratches, and other surface abnormalities.

Flaxseed Seed isolated from one of several species of the plant genus Linum. Flaxseed-derived foods, lignans, and essential fatty acids such as alpha-linolenic acid, possess anti-inflammatory, lipid-lowering, antioxidant, and antineoplastic properties.

Flecainide A drug that is used to treat abnormal heart rhythms. It may also relieve neuropathic pain, the burning, stabbing, or stinging pain that may arise from damage to nerves caused by some types of cancer or cancer treatment.

Flexion A bending movement around a joint in a limb that decreases the angle between the bones of the limb at the joint.

Floc Mass having a fluffy or wooly appearance.

Flocculation A technique for liquid/ solids separation. Cationic or anionic polyelectrolytes (e.g. polyacrylamides) are added to highly colloidal water causing coagulation and subsequent settling. The phenomena could be charge neutralization or a bridging effect between separate particles.

Flocculent Having downy or flaky shreds.

Flocculus Small hemispherical component of the ventral cerebellum located at the cerebello-medullary-pontine angle. It is connected by a stalk to the nodulus in the vermal midline to form the flocculonodular lobule (vestibulocerebellum or archicerebellum).

Floor of orbit The inferior portion of the bony cavity that contains the eyeball, made up of the maxilla, zygomatic, and palatine bones.

Floor of sella The inferior portion of the sella turcica (pituitary fossa).

Flouroquinolones A family of antibiotics, including Ciprofloxacin, ofloxacin, and Sparfloxacin. Sometimes used as components of combination therapy for mycobacterium avium complex.

Flow cytometry A method of measuring the number of cells in a sample, the percentage of live cells in a sample, and certain characteristics of cells, such as size, shape, and the presence of tumor markers on the cell surface. The cells are stained with a light-sensitive dye, placed in a fluid, and passed in a stream before a laser or other type of light. The measurements are based on how the light-sensitive dye reacts to the light.

Flow decay Measuring the decline in flow rate through a filter to establish a Silt Index for the water being filtered. The Silt Index is a measure of suspended solids and their ability to clog the filter.

Flow karyotyping Use of flow cytometry to analyze and separate chromosomes according to their DNA content.

Flow restrictor A flow-limiting orifice used to control flow rate or pressure drop in a liquid stream.

Floxuridine A fluorinated pyrimidine monophosphate analogue of 5-fluoro-2'-deoxyuridine-5'-phosphate (FUDR-MP) with antineoplastic activity. As an antimetabolite, floxuridine inhibits thymidylate synthetase, resulting in disruption of DNA synthesis and cytotoxicity. This agent is also metabolized to fluorouracil and other metabolites that can be incorporated into RNA and inhibit the utilization of preformed uracil in RNA synthesis.

Fluconazole A synthetic triazole with antifungal activity. Fluconazole preferentially inhibits fungal cytochrome P-450 sterol C-14 alpha-demethylation, resulting in the accumulation of fungal 14 alpha-methyl sterols, the loss of normal fungal sterols, and fungistatic activity. Mammalian cell demethylation is much less sensitive to fluconazole inhibition.

Flucytosine (5 FC) Antifungal drug used as an adjunct to amphotericin for the treatment of cryptococcal meningitis.

Fludarabine A fluorinated nucleotide antimetabolite analog of the antiviral agent vidarabine (ara-A) with antineoplastic activity. Administered parente-rally as a phosphate salt, fludarabine phosphate is rapidly dephosphorylated to 2-fluoro-ara-A and then phosphorylated intracellularly by deoxycytidine kinase to the active triphosphate, 2-fluoro-ara-ATP. This metabolite may inhibit DNA polymerase alpha, ribonucleotide reductase and DNA primase, thereby interrupting DNA synthesis and inhibiting tumor cell growth.

Fludeoxyglucose F 18 A positron-emitting radiopharmaceutical containing radioactive 2-deoxy-2-(18F) fluoro-D-glucose. With similar cell uptake as glucose (high in tumor cells), fludeoxyglucose F 18 is not dephosphorylated and further metabolized.

Fludrocortisone A synthetic corticosteroid. It is used to replace steroid hormones normally produced by the adrenal gland.

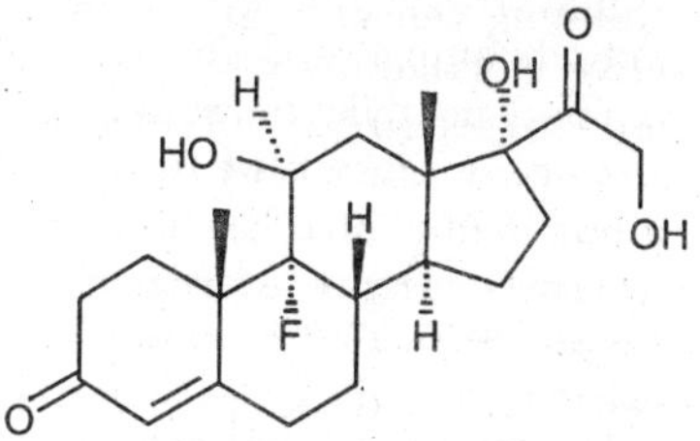

Figure Fludrocortisone

Fluidized bed A container holding powder coating material which is aerated from below so as to form an air-supported expanded cloud of such material through which the preheated object to be coated is immersed and transported.

Fluorescein An orange-red compound, $C_{20}H_{12}O_5$, which exhibits intense fluorescence in alkaline solution.

Fluorescein angiography A method of taking a picture of the flow of blood in the vessels of the eye by tracing the progress of an injected dye.

Fluorescent antibody An antibody coupled with a fluorescent dye, used with a fluorescence microscope to detect antigen on cells, tissues, or microorganisms.

Fluoride Fluoride is a natural component of minerals in rocks and soils. Widespread use of fluoride in water supplies and oral health products is credited with the dramatic decline in dental caries among children and adults alike. All water contains fluoride, but it is sometimes necessary to add it to some public supplies to attain the optimal amount for dental health. Fluoride makes tooth enamel stronger and more resistant to decay. It also prevents the growth of harmful bacteria and interferes with converting fermentable carbohydrates to acids in the mouth.

Fluorinated plastics Fluorinated plastics are thermoplastic paraffinic polymers where the hydrogen has been replaced by fluorine, and in some cases, chlorine. These materials are some of the more popular in the CPI because of good chemical resistance to a wide variety of aggressive chemicals, and relatively high heat resistance of 400°F to 500°F. They include FEP, PTFE, PFA, PCTFE, ETFE, PVDF, and PVF.

Fluoropyrimidine One of a group of substances used to treat cancer. Fluoropyrimidines belong to the family of drugs called antimetabolites. Examples are capecitabine, floxuridine, and fluorouracil (5-FU).

Fluoroscope An x-ray machine that makes it possible to see internal organs in motion.

Fluoroscopy It is an imaging technique commonly used by physicians to obtain real-time images of the internal structures of a patient through the use of a fluoroscope. In its simplest form, a fluoroscope consists of an x-ray source and fluorescent screen between which a patient is placed. However, modern fluoroscopes couple the screen to an x-ray image intensifier and CCD video camera allowing the images to be played and recorded on a monitor. The use of x rays, a form of ionizing radiation, requires that the potential risks from a procedure be carefully balanced with the benefits of the procedure to the patient. While physicians always try to use low dose rates during fluorscopy procedures, the length of a typical procedure often results in a relatively high absorbed dose to the patient. Recent advances include the digitization of the images captured and flat-panel detector systems which reduce the radiation dose to the patient still further.

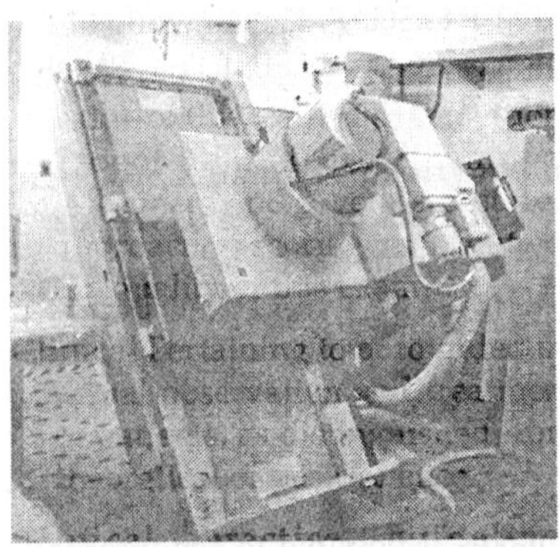

Figure Fluoroscopy machine

Fluorouracil An antimetabolite fluoropyrimidine analog of the nucleoside pyrimidine with antineoplastic activity. Fluorouracil and its metabolites possess a number of different mechanisms of action. In vivo, fluoruracil is converted to the active metabolite 5-fluoro-xyuridine monophosphate (F-UMP); replacing uracil, F-UMP incorporates into RNA and inhibits RNA processing, thereby inhibiting cell growth. Another active metabolite, 5-5-fluoro-2'-deoxyuridine-5'-O-monophosphate (F-dUMP), inhibits thymidylate synthase, resulting in the depletion of thymidine triphosphate (TTP), a necessary constituent of DNA. Other fluorouracil metabolites incorporate into both RNA and DNA; incorporation into RNA results in major effects on both RNA processing and functions.

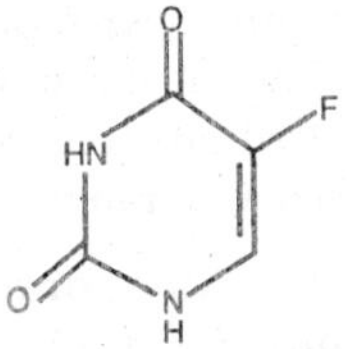

O, F, HN, O, N, H

Figure Fluorouracil (5-fluoro-2,4 (1H,3H)-pyrimidinedione)

Fluorouracil-uracil A formulated therapeutic oral agent consisting of a combination of 5-fluorouracil (5-FU) and uracil (1:4). Because of its higher concentration in the combination, uracil saturates the uracil-reducing enzymatic activity of dihydropyrimidine dehydrogenase, thereby inhibiting firstpass dihydropyrimidine dehydrogenase-mediated hepatic metabolism of the uracil analogue 5-FU and permitting oral administration of 5-FU. 5-FU inhibits the enzyme thymidylate synthase, resulting in decreased thymidine synthesis and so reduced DNA synthesis and tumor cell cytotoxicity.

Fluoxetine A drug used to treat depression. It belongs to the family of drugs called antidepressants.

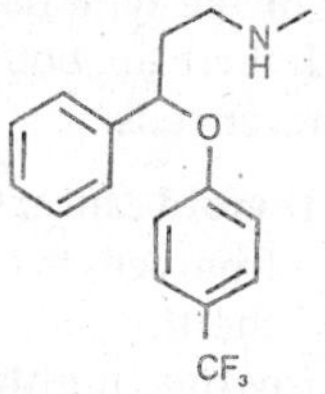

Figure Fluoxetine

Flutamide A toluidine derivative and nonsteroidal antiandrogen that is structurally related to bicalutamide and nilutamide. Flutamide and its more potent active metabolite 2-hydroxyflutamide competitively block dihydrotestosterone binding at androgen receptors, forming inactive complexes which cannot translocate into the cell nucleus. Formation of inactive receptors inhibits androgen-dependent DNA and protein synthesis, resulting in tumor cell growth arrest or transient tumor regression.

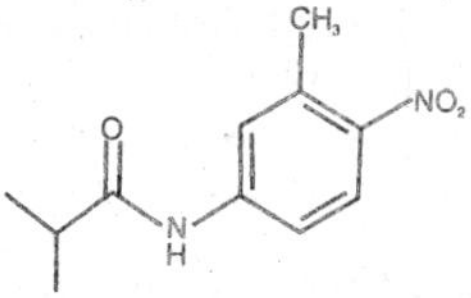

(2-methyl-N-[4-nitro-3-(trifluoromethyl) phenyl]-propanamide)

Figure Flutamide

Flux removers Chlorinated solvents with alcohols that may be sprayed from aerosol cans to remove welding flux.

Foam cell A lipid-laden macrophage.

Focal In terms of cancer, limited to a specific area.

Folate A salt or ester of folic acid, a crystalline vitamin of the B complex. Drugs such as trimethoprim sulfa and trimetrexate work by "starving" bacteria of folate, without starving the human body.

Folate antagonist A substance that blocks the activity of folic acid. Folate antagonists are used to treat cancer. Also called antifolate.

Folfox An abbreviation for a type of combination chemotherapy that is used to treat colourectal cancer. It includes fluorouracil, leucovorin, and oxaliplatin.

Folic acid Folic acid, folate, folacin, all form a group of compounds functionally involved in amino

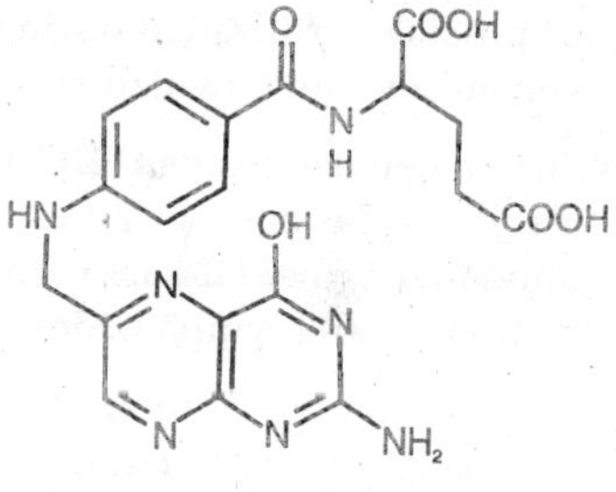

(N-[4 (2-Amino-4-hydroxy-pteridin-6-ylmethylamino)-benzoyl]-L (+)-glutamic acid.)

Figure Folic acid

acid metabolism and nucleic acid synthesis. Good dietary sources of folate include leafy, dark green vegetables, legumes, citrus fruits and juices, peanuts, whole grains and fortified breakfast cereals.

Recent studies show, if all women of childbearing age consumed sufficient folic acid (either through diet or supplements), 50 to 70 percent of birth defects of the brain and spinal cord could be prevented. Folic acid is critical from conception through the first four to six weeks of pregnancy when the neural tube is formed. This means adequate diet or supplement use should begin before pregnancy occurs.

Recent research findings also show low blood folate levels can be associated with elevated plasma homocysteine and increased risk of coronary heart disease.

Folium One of the narrow transverse folds of the cerebellar surface.

Follicle A small sac in the ovary that contains an egg, which is released for possible fertilization during a woman's monthly ovulation.

Follicular dendritic cells (FDCs) A specific type of dendritic cell found in lymphoid tissues such as the thymus and lymph nodes.

Follicular large cell lymphoma A rare type of non-Hodgkin's lymphoma (cancer of the lymphatic system) with large cells that look cleaved (split) or non-cleaved under the microscope. It is an indolent (slow-growing) type of lymphoma.

Follicular lymphoma A type of B-cell non-Hodgkin's lymphoma (cancer of the immune system) that is usually indolent (slow-growing). The tumor cells grow as groups to form nodules. There are several subtypes of follicular lymphoma.

Follicular mixed cell lymphoma An indolent (slow-growing) type of B-cell non-Hodgkin's lymphoma (cancer of the lymphatic system) in which there are both small and large cancer cells.

Follicular thyroid cancer Cancer that develops from cells in the follicular areas of the thyroid. One of the slow-growing, highly treatable types of thyroid cancer.

Folliculitis An infection or inflammation of the follicle, at the root of a hair. Folliculitis may be aseptic, as in eosinophilic folliculitis.

Follow up data Data collected on a patient, or a set of patients, after enrollment into a trial.

Follow up Monitoring a person's health over time after treatment. This includes keeping track of the health of people who participate in a clinical study or clinical trial for a period of time, both during the study and after the study ends.

Follow up visit Any patient clinic visit that takes place after the randomization visit for study-related purposes.

Food additive Chemical added to food to enhance flavour, colour and prevent spoiling, but which might cause adverse reaction. Example is Monosodium Glutamate (MSG).

Food aversion Fear that a food will cause an adverse reaction.

Food challenge Test carried out in hospital to identify suspected food allergens by giving traces of food concealed in capsules or broth.

Open Food Challenge is when the food is not concealed.

Food idiosyncrasy Non-allergic reaction to food or food component that occurs through unknown mechanisms.

Food intolerance A general term for any adverse reaction to a food or food component that does not involve the body's immune system.

Food intolerance or food sensitivity A sensitivity or bad reaction to certain foods that does not involve the immune system so is not an allergy. Examples are Lactose and Caffeine Intolerance.

Food irradiation The exposure of food to sufficient radiant energy (gamma rays, x-rays and electron beams) to destroy microorganisms and insects. Irradiation is used in food production and processing to promote food safety.

Food preservatives All preservatives prevent spoilage either by slowing the growth of organisms that live on food or by protecting the food from oxygen. Antimicrobials are preservatives that protect food by slowing the growth of bacteria, molds and yeasts. Antioxidants are preservatives that protect by preventing food molecules from combining with oxygen (air).

Food safety Food safety is a relative and not absolute matter. Relative food safety can be defined as the practical, certainty that injury or damage will not result from food or ingredient used in reasonable and customary manner and quantity.

Food toxicity Reaction to a poison contained in a food.

Foodborne disease Disease, usually gastrointestinal, caused by organisms or their toxins carried in ingested food. Also commonly known as "food poisoning."

Foot care Taking special steps to avoid foot problems such as sores, cuts, bunions, and calluses. Good care includes daily examination of the feet, toes, and toenails and choosing shoes and socks or stockings that fit well. People with diabetes have to take special care of their feet because nerve damage and reduced blood flow sometimes mean they will have less feeling in their feet than normal. They may not notice cuts and other problems as soon as they should.

Foramen A communication between two cavities such as the brain ventricles or an opening in bone for passage of vessels and/or nerves.

Foramen magnum The large opening that connects the vertebral canal to the cranial cavity, located in the anterior and inferior portion of the occipital bone, and allows passage of CSF and connection of the medulla oblongata to the cervical spinal cord.

Foramen ovale The passage for the mandibular (3rd) branch of the trigeminal (Vth) nerve through the medial and posterior part of the greater wing of the sphenoid bone.

Foramen rotundum The opening that allows the passage of the maxillary (2nd) branch of the trigeminal (Vth) nerve through the medial part of the greater wing of the sphenoid bone.

Foramen spinosum The opening near the posterior angle of the greater wing of the sphenoid bone, posterior to the spinous process, that allows passage of the middle meningeal artery.

Foramen transversium The opening in the transverse process which allows the vertebral vessels to pass through the cervical vertebra.

Forceps major Fibers of the splenium of the corpus callosum which extend laterally and posteriorly into the occipital lobe interconnecting comparable cortical regions.

F. Minor: Fibers of the genu of the corpus callosum that extend laterally and anteriorly interconnecting comparable regions of the frontal lobe.

Forensic dentistry Practice of gathering legal evidence for body identification or judicial issues.

Forensics The use of DNA for identification. Some examples of DNA use are to establish paternity in child support cases; establish the presence of a suspect at a crime scene, and identify accident victims.

Form constancy The ability to recognize two objects that have the same shape but different size or position. This ability is needed to tell the difference between "b" and "d", "p" and "q", "m" and "w".

Formaldehyde A chemical used in manufacturing and chemical industries, and as a preservative by anatomists, embalmers, and pathologists. Being exposed to formaldehyde may increase the risk of developing leukemia and brain cancer.

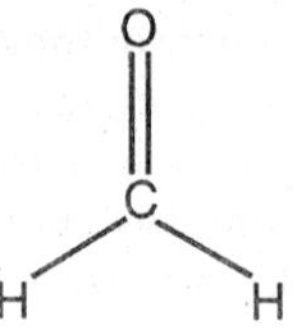

Figure Formaldehyde

Formatting and protocol standards Data exchange standards which are needed between CPR systems, as well as CPT and other provider systems, to ensure uniformity in methods for data collection, data storage and data presentation. Proactive providers are current in their knowledge of these standards and work to ensure their information systems conform to the standards.

Formulation The physical form in which a drug is administered. Examples include tablets, capsules, liquids, and injectables. A single drug may be available in multiple formulations.

Fornix Efferent fiber tract that arises from the hippocampus, arches forward over the thalamus, then courses downward to terminate mainly in the mammillary body of the hypothalamus.

Forodesine hydrochloride The hydrochloride salt of the synthetic high-affinity transition-state analogue forodesine. Forodesine binds preferentially to and inhibits purine nucleotide phosphorylase (PNP), resulting in the accumulation of deoxyguanosine triphosphate and the subsequent inhibition of the enzyme ribonucleoside diphosphate reductase and DNA synthesis. This agent selectively causes apoptosis in stimulated or malignant T-lymphocytes. A transition state analogue is a substrate designed to mimic the properties or the geometry of the transition state of reaction.

Fortified foods Fortified foods have nutrients added to them that were not present originally. For example, milk is fortified with vitamin D, which helps your body absorb calcium and phosphorus found naturally in milk.

Forward flow test An objective and quantitative method of determining filter integrity. A test in which the filter is wetted and a predetermined constant air pressure is applied. A measurement of pure diffusional airflow through the wetted membrane is made. If the diffusional airflow across the membrane is below the maximum allowable value given, then the filter is acceptable.

Foscarnet (Foscavir) An antiviral drug for the treatment of cytomegalovirus (CMV) retinitis and other diseases caused by CMV. It is also used to treat acyclovir-resistant herpes virus infections. Adverse side effects may include kidney toxicity, muscle twitching, nausea and skin ulcers.

Fossa A depression (i.e. posterior cranial fossa).

Fotemustine A chloroethylating nitrosourea with antineoplastic activity. Fotemustine alkylates guanine by forming chloroethyl adducts at the 6 position of guanine, resulting in N1-guanine and N3-cytosine cross linkages, inhibition of DNA synthesis, cell cycle arrest, and finally apoptosis. This agent is lipophilic and crosses the blood-brain barrier.

Fouling Occurs when gelatinous coatings, colloidal masses, or dense bacterial growth form a compacted crust on membrane or filter surfaces which blocks further flow.

Fourth ventricle The cavity in the rhombencephalon located between the medulla oblongata, the pons, and the isthmus ventrally and anterior and the cerebellum dorsally and posterior.

Fovea capitus The depression where the ligamentum teres attaches to the head of the femur, containing the vascular supply for the intracapsular portion of the femur (head and proximal neck).

Fovea Center of the retina that can produce the sharpest eyesight and contains the most cones.

Fowlpox CEA TRICOM vaccine A cancer vaccine comprised of a recombinant fowlpox viral vector encoding the carcinoembryonic antigen (CEA) and TRICOM. TRICOM is comprised of three co-stimulatory molecule transgenes (B7-1, ICAM-1 and LFA-3). This agent may enhance CEA presentation to antigen presenting cells (APC) and activate cytotoxic T-cells against CEA-expressing tumors.

Fowlpox NY ESO 1 vaccine A cancer vaccine consisting of a recombinant fowlpox virus vector encoding an immunogenic peptide derived from the cancer-testis antigen NY-ESO-1, an antigen found in normal testis and various tumors, including bladder, breast, hepatocellular, melanoma, and prostate cancers. Vaccination with NY-ESO-1 peptide vaccine may stimulate the host immune system to mount a humoral and cytotoxic T lymphocyte (CTL) response against tumor cells expressing NY-ESO-1 antigen, resulting in tumor cell lysis.

Fowlpox virus vaccine vector A recombinant fowlpox virus-based vaccine vector designed to express various tumor-associated peptide antigens. Strong CD8 cytotoxic T cell responses may be induced after prolonged immunization with fowlpox virus vaccines and have been associated with tumor regression. Fowlpox virus is an attractive vector because its genome is easy to manipulate and it does not multiply in human tissues.

Fowlpox-tyrosinase vaccine A recombinant fowlpox virus vaccine with potential antineoplastic activity. Binding to the melanoma antigen tyrosinase, the fowlpox-tyrosinase vaccine generates cellular immune responses against melanoma cells expressing the tyrosinase antigen; this effect is enhanced by the co-administration of interleukin 2 (IL-2). Fowlpox virus is an attractive vector because its genome is easy to manipulate and it is replication incompetent in mammalian cells.

Fractional urine Urine that a person collects for a certain period of time during 24 hours; usually from breakfast to lunch, from lunch to supper, from supper to bedtime, and from bedtime to rising. Also called "block urine."

Fractionation Dividing the total dose of radiation therapy into several smaller, equal doses delivered over a period of several days.

Fraternal twin Siblings born at the same time as the result of fertilization of two ova by two sperm. They share the same genetic relationship to each other as any other siblings.

Free radical A highly reactive chemical that often contains oxygen and is produced when molecules are split to give products that have unpaired electrons (a process called oxidation). Free radicals can damage important cellular molecules such as DNA or lipids or other parts of the cell.

Freeway space Distance between the upper and lower teeth with the lower jaw in rest position.

Freeze dried A method used to dry substances, such as food, to make them last longer. The substance is frozen and then dried in a vacuum.

Freiberg's disease Considered as an osteochondritis dissecans, due to an osteochondral fracture, with avascular necrosis of the bone, usually involving the head of the second metatarsal.

Frenectomy Removal or reshaping of thin muscle tissue that attaches the upper or lower lips to the gum, or the tongue to the floor of the mouth.

Freund's complete adjuvant A water-in-oil emulsion that contains an immunogen, an emulsifying agent, and killed mycobacteria which enhance the immune response to the immunogen; termed "incomplete" Freund's adjuvant if mycobacteria are not included.

Friable Breaks apart or crumbles easily.

Frontal bone The bone that closes the frontal part of the cranial cavity.

Frontal horn The extension of the lateral ventricle into the frontal lobe of the brain.

Frontal lobe The portion of the anterior cerebral hemisphere from the frontal pole to the sulcus centralis (central sulcus).

Frontal sinus A paired paranasal sinus within the frontal bone that is connected to the middle meatus of the nasal cavity by the nasofrontal duct. Both functionally, and embryologically, the frontal sinus represents the most anterior ethmoid air cell.

Frozen section Microscopic examination of a specimen of tissue that has been quick-frozen. This method gives a quick diagnosis, sometimes while the surgeon is waiting to complete a procedure. The diagnosis is confirmed in a few days by a more detailed study called a permanent section.

Frozen shoulder Alternate name for "capsulitis" of the shoulder, which undergoes four distinct stages of pathology: Pain; Pain and stiffness; Stiffness; Resolution. These four stages usually run a protracted course, varying in length from 9 - 18 months.

Fructo oliogosaccharides (FSO) A type of prebiotic/probiotic found in Jerusalem artichokes, shallots and onion powder which may improve gastrointestinal health.

Fructosamine A term referring to the linking of blood sugar onto protein molecules in the bloodstream. The fructosamine value depends upon the average blood sugar level during the past three weeks. The fructosamine test could be viewed as complementary to the glycohemoglobin, as the two tests are different reflections of diabetes control: glycohemoglobin looks back approximately eight to twelve weeks, and the fructosamine test looks back about three weeks.

Fructose Fructose is a monosaccharide found naturally in fruits, as an added sugar in a crystalline form and as a component of high-fructose corn syrup (HFCS).

Fruit and vegetable extracts Extracts from fruits and vegetables that contain fiber, vitamins, minerals, and other natural substances with antioxidant, lipid-lowering, and antiproliferative properties. Used in chemoprevention therapy, these extracts may prevent the development or recurrence of cancer.

Fulguration Destroying tissue using an electric current.

Full denture Removable dental prosthesis (appliance) replacing all upper or lower teeth.

Full gene sequence The complete order of bases in a gene. This order determines which protein a gene will produce.

Full mouth reconstruction Extensive restorations of natural teeth with crowns and or fixed bridges to manage bite problems.

Fulminating Serious acute, active infection

Fulvestrant A synthetic estrogen receptor antagonist. Unlike tamoxifen (which has partial agonist effects) and the aromatase inhibitors (which reduce the estrogen available to tumor cells), fulvestrant binds competitively to estrogen receptors in breast cancer cells, resulting in estrogen receptor deformation and decreased estrogen binding. In vitro studies indicate that fulvestrant reversibly inhibits the growth of tamoxifen-resistant, estrogen-sensitive, human breast cancer cell lines.

Fume hoods Units that collect fumes from chemicals, solvents, acids, and other hazardous materials. Hoods may include HEPA filters if powders are present, or carbon filters to filter fumes from the work surface and return cleaned air to the room. Most fume hoods are 100% exhausted to outdoors. A glass, Plexiglas or acrylic front panel may be included for worker safety.

Functional component Those components in food that provide special health benefits. The abilities of these functional components may reduce cancer risk, aid digestion, decrease risk of tooth decay or improve various other body functions or reduce disease risk.

Functional disease A condition in which a patient complains of symptoms for which no physical cause can be found. Such a condition is frequently an indication of a psychological disorder. Compare Organic disorder.

Functional foods Foods that may provide health benefits beyond basic nutrition. Examples include tomatoes with lycopene, thought to help prevent the incidence of prostate and cervical cancers; fiber in wheat bran and sulfur compounds in garlic also believed to prevent cancer.

Functional gene tests Biochemical assays for a specific protein, which indicates that a specific gene is not merely present but active.

Functional genomics The study of genes, their resulting proteins, and the role played by the proteins the body's biochemical processes.

Functional health status Refers to a patient's ability to perform typical daily physical and social/role functions, plus other measures of self-perceived health status such as well-being, vitality and mental health.

Functional magnetic resonance imaging A noninvasive tool used to observe functioning in the brain or other organs by detecting changes in chemical composition, blood flow, or both.

Functionality Suitability for the intended purpose.

Fundoscopic exam Visual inspection of the interior of the eye. Often used to diagnose CMV retinitis.

Fundus of stomach The portion of the stomach that lies above and to the left of the entrance of the esophagus.

Fundus of the eye The back or deep part of the eye, including the retina.

Fundus The larger part of a hollow organ that is farthest away from the organ's opening. The bladder, gallbladder, stomach, uterus, eye, and cavity of the middle ear all have a fundus.

Funduscopy A test to look at the back area of the eye to see if there is any damage to the vessels that bring blood to the retina. The doctor uses a device called an ophthalmoscope to check the eye.

Fungating lesion A type of skin lesion that is marked by ulcerations (breaks on the skin or surface of an organ) and necrosis (death of living tissue) and that usually has a bad smell. This kind of lesion may occur in many types of cancer, including breast cancer, melanoma, and squamous cell carcinoma, and especially in advanced disease.

Fungemia The presence of fungus in the blood.

Fungi Plural of fungus. Low forms of plant life unable to form protein and carbohydrates (heterotrophs) that are widespread in nature. Fungal cells are larger than bacterial cells, and their typical internal structures, such as nucleus and vacuoles, can be seen easily with a light microscope. On the basis of their mode of sexual reproduction, fungi are grouped in four classes: Phycomycetes, Ascomycetes, Deuteromycetes (Fungi Imperfectii), and Basidiomycetes. Two major groups of fungi are the yeasts and molds.

Fungicide A chemical that is mixed with wax and applied to fruits or vegetables to prevent mold and rot from developing.

Fungus A group of primitive organisms including mushrooms, yeasts, rusts, and molds, some of which can infect humans and cause disease. For example, mouth thrush is caused by the fungus Candida.

Funiculus Refers to three broad columns of white matter within the spinal cord that contain several different ascending and descending tracts or fasciculi.

F. (Dorsal): Column of white matter located between the dorsal roots and dorsal median septum of the spinal cord.

F. (Lateral): Spinal cord white matter located between the emerging dorsal and ventral roots.

F. (Ventral): Column of spinal cord white matter located between the emerging ventral roots and ventral median fissure.

Fusiform Descriptive term applied to structures that taper at both ends (i.e. muscle spindle).

Fusion inhibitors A class of anti-HIV drugs that inhibits the fusing of HIV's outer envelope with the host cell membrane, preventing infection of the cell.

Fusion protein A protein created by joining two genes together. Fusion proteins may occur naturally or can be created in the laboratory for research.

Fusion test Determines the eyes ability to unite the images from each eye into a single image.

Fusion The union of images from each eye into a single image. There are three degrees of fusion. 1st degree fusion is the superimposition of two dissimilar targets. 2nd degree fusion is flat fusion with a two-dimensional target. 3rd degree fusion is depth perception (stereopsis) with a three-dimensional target.

Fusion welding Welding in which the base material is fused together without the addition of filler material to the weld.

Fusional vergence A convergence response which serves to maintain (fusion) the union of images from each eye into a single image. The eyes will turn with a slow smooth tonic movement or a fast jumping movement called phasic.

FVC (Forced vital capacity) The amount of air that can be forced from the lungs over 14 to 20 seconds.

G CSF (Granulocyte colony-stimulating factor) A colony-stimulating factor that stimulates the production of neutrophils (a type of white blood cell). It is a cytokine that belongs to the family of drugs called hematopoietic (blood-forming) agents. Also called filgrastim.

Gabapentin A substance that is being studied as a treatment for relieving hot flashes in women with breast cancer. It belongs to the family of drugs called anticonvulsants.

GAD (Glutamic acid decarboxylase) A normal enzyme found in all cells that initiates the metabolism of a substance called glutamic acid. Glutamic acid is a component of all proteins and is also part of the cycle for the disposal of a waste product called ammonia. The presence of antibodies to GAD (called anti-GAD antibodies) in the blood is an early indication of the start of the autoimmune process in Type 1A Diabetes.

Gadolinium texaphyrin A substance that is being studied in the treatment of cancer. It may make tumor cells more sensitive to radiation therapy, improve tumor images using magnetic resonance imaging (MRI), and kill cancer cells. It belongs to the family of drugs called metalloporphyrin complexes. Also called motexafin gadolinium.

Gadopentetate dimeglumine A gadolinium complex of diethylene-triamine pentaacetic acid with ionic paramagnetic properties. Gado-pentetate dimeglumine may provide contrast enhancement during magnetic resonance imaging (MRI) of intracranial lesions with abnormal vascularity or of abnormalities in the blood-brain barrier (BBB).

Gail model A computer program that uses personal and family history to estimate a woman's chance of developing breast cancer.

Gait The pattern of locomotion. Alterations to this pattern may be altered weight distribution, lack of mobility in hips, knees, ankles or presence of a Trendelenburg sign.

Galactocele Clogged milk duct; a cyst filled with milk. It may occur in the breast during breastfeeding.

Galactose A monosaccharide occurring in both levo (L) and dextro (D) forms as a constituent of plant and animal oligosaccharides (lactose and raffinose) and polysaccharides (agar and pectin). Galactose is the sugar derived from digesting lactose ('milk sugar").

Galiximab A monoclonal antibody that is being studied in the treatment of follicular non-Hodgkin's lymphoma. Monoclonal antibodies are made in the laboratory and can locate and bind to cancer cells. Galiximab binds to the protein CD80, which is found on certain normal and cancerous white blood cells.

Gall bladder The reservoir for bile located between the right and quadrate lobe on the posteroinferior surface of the liver.

Gallbladder cancer Cancer that forms in tissues of the gallbladder. The gallbladder is a pear-shaped organ below the liver that collects and stores bile (a fluid made by the liver to digest fat). Gallbladder cancer begins in the innermost layer of tissue and spreads through the outer layers as it grows.

Gallbladder disease There are several different forms of gallbladder disease:

1. Gallstones without symptoms. About 20% of women and 8% of men will develop gallstones. In most of these cases, gallstones do not produce symptoms and thus usually do not require treatment.

2. Biliary colic. This condition occurs when a gallstone intermittently blocks the duct that drains the gallbladder (cystic duct). Biliary colic usually causes severe, steady pain that lasts from 15 to 60 minutes to up to 6 hours.

3. Inflammation of the gallbladder (acute cholecystitis). This condition occurs when a gallstone becomes stuck in the cystic duct, causing severe abdominal pain that lasts longer then 6 hours. It is the most common complication of gallstone disease.

4. Chronic cholecystitis. This condition develops when there is long term (chronic) inflammation of the gallbladder. The wall of the gallbladder may be thickened and rigid.

5. Common bile duct stones (choledocholithiasis). This condition occurs when a gallstone passes through the cystic duct into the common bile duct. About 8 to 15% of people who have gallstones also have common bile duct stones. Most people who have common bile duct stones do not have symptoms. However, people who do have symptoms may develop life-threatening complications, such as infection and inflammation of the bile duct or pancreas.

Gallium nitrate A drug that lowers blood calcium. Used as treatment for hypercalcemia (too much calcium in the blood) and for cancer that has spread to the bone (bone metastases).

Gallium scan A procedure to detect areas of the body where cells are dividing rapidly. It is used to locate cancer cells or areas of inflammation. A very small amount of radioactive gallium is injected into a vein and travels through the bloodstream. The gallium is taken up by rapidly dividing cells in the bones, tissues, and organs and is detected by a scanner.

Gallstone Solid material that forms in the gallbladder or common bile duct. Gallstones are made of cholesterol or other substances found in the gallbladder. They may occur as one large stone or as many small ones, and vary from the size of a golf ball to a grain of sand. Also called cholelith.

Gamete Mature male or female reproductive cell (sperm or ovum) with a haploid set of chromosomes (23 for humans).

Gamma globulin A blood protein that plays a major role in the process of immunity. Sometimes the term "gamma globulin" refers to a whole group of blood proteins that are known as antibodies or immunoglobulins (Ig). Most often, however, it applies to a particular immunoglobulin, designated as IgG, believed to be the most abundant type of antibody in the body.

Gamma irradiation A type of radiation therapy that uses gamma radiation. Gamma radiation is a type of high-energy radiation that is different from x-rays.

Gamma knife Radiation therapy in which high-energy rays are aimed at a tumor from many angles in a single treatment session.

Gamma ray A type of high-energy radiation that is different from an x-ray.

Gamma scanning A procedure to find areas in the body where cells, such as tumor cells, are dividing rapidly. A small amount of radioactive material is injected into a vein or swallowed, and travels through the bloodstream. A machine called a scanner measures the radioactivity and produces pictures (scans) of internal parts of the body. The pictures can show abnormal changes in the area of the body containing the radioactive material. Examples of gamma scans include PET scans, gallium scans, and bone scans. Also called radionuclide scanning.

Ganciclovir (Cytovene) An antiviral drug to treat cytomegalovirus (CMV) retinitis and to prevent CMV disease in transplant patients at risk for CMV. It has also been used to treat CMV colitis, CMV esophagitis, AIDS-related meningoencephalitis and AIDS-related polyradiculopathy; generally administered intraveno-usly. An oral form of the drug is under study for the treatment and prevention of CMV disease in people with HIV infection.

Ganglion A collection of nerve cell bodies located outside the central nervous system serving a common function, either sensory or autonomic.

Ganglioside A complex molecule that contains both lipids (fats) and carbohydrates (sugars) and is found in the plasma (outer) membrane of many kinds of cells. Several different types of gangliosides have been identified.

Gangrene The death of body tissue. It is most often caused by a loss of blood flow, especially in the legs and feet.

Garden heliotrope Valeriana officinalis. A plant whose roots are used as a sedative and to treat certain medical conditions. It is being studied as a way to improve sleep in cancer patients undergoing treatment. Also called valerian, garden valerian, Indian valerian, Pacific valerian, Mexican valerian, and Valerianae radix.

Garden valerian Valeriana officinalis. A plant whose roots are used as a sedative and to treat certain medical conditions. It is being studied as a way to improve sleep in cancer patients undergoing treatment. Also called valerian, Indian valerian, Pacific valerian, Mexican valerian, garden heliotrope, and Valerianae radix.

Gas Air that collects in the stomach and intestines as a natural result of digesting food. Passed out of the body via the rectum or the mouth.

Gas metal arc welding (GMAW) An arc welding process that produces coalescence of metals by heating them with an arc between a continuous filler metal (consumable) electrode and the work. Shielding is obtained entirely from an externally supplied gas or gas mixture. Some variations of this process are called MIG (metal inert gas) Or CO_2 welding, nonpreferred terms.

Gas room A separately ventilated, fully enclosed room in which only toxic and highly toxic compressed gases and associated equipment and supplies are stored or used.

Gas tungsten arc welding (GTAW) An arc welding process that produces coalescence of metals by heating them with an arc between a tungsten (nonconsumable) electrode and the work. Shielding is obtained from a gas or gas mixture. Pressure may or may not be used and filler material may or may not be used. (This process is sometimes called TIG (Tungsten Inert Gas) welding, a nonpreferred term).

Gastrectomy An operation to remove all or part of the stomach.

Gastric Having to do with the stomach.

Gastric atrophy A condition in which the stomach muscles shrink and become weak. The digestive (peptic) glands may also shrink, resulting in a lack of digestive juices.

Gastric cancer Cancer that forms in tissues lining the stomach. Also called stomach cancer.

Gastric reflux The backward flow of stomach acid contents into the esophagus (the tube that connects the mouth to the stomach). Also called esophageal eflux or gastroesophageal reflux.

Gastrinoma A tumor that causes overproduction of gastric acid. It usually occurs in the islet cells of the pancreas but may also occur in the esophagus, stomach, spleen, or lymph nodes.

Gastritis Inflammation of the lining of the stomach.

Gastro esophageal reflux (GER) The backward flow of gastric juices from the stomach into the esophagus.

Gastrocnemius Calf muscle made up of medial and lateral heads.

Gastroduodenal artery The artery which originates from the common hepatic artery and branches into the supraduodenal and posterior superior pancreaticoduodenal arteries.

Gastroenteritis Irritation or infection of the stomach and intestines. May be caused by bacteria or parasites, irritating food, stress, or emotional upset.

Gastroenterologist A physician whose specialty is digestive diseases.

Gastroenterology The diagnosis and treatment of diseases of the digestive system

Gastroesophageal junction The point where the stratified squamous epithilium of the esophagus meets the simple columnar epithilium of the cardia of the stomach. The GE junction may be above the diaphragm when there is a hiatal hernia. In turn, hiatal hernia may be associated with GERD (Gastroesophageal Reflux Disease).

Gastroesophageal reflux disease (GERD) Movement of food, fluids, and digestive juices from the stomach back up into the esophagus; causes irritation of the esophagus with acid, resulting in discomfort. GERD occurs when the muscle between the stomach and the esophagus, known as the lower esophageal sphincter, opens when it should stay closed, or is weak.

Gastrointestinal GI. Refers to the stomach and intestines.

Gastrointestinal carcinoid tumor An indolent (slow-growing) cancer that forms in cells that make hormones in the lining of the gastrointestinal tract (the stomach and intestines). It usually occurs in the appendix (a small fingerlike pouch of the large intestine), small intestine, or rectum. Having gastrointestinal carcinoid tumor increases the risk of forming other cancers of the digestive system.

Gastrointestinal stromal tumor (GIST) A type of tumor that usually begins in cells in the wall of the gastrointestinal tract. It can be benign or malignant.

Gastrointestinal tract (Also called the digestive tract.) The parts of the body that break down food into small particles, allowing nutrients from food to be used for energy and growth: the mouth, esophagus, stomach, pancreas, liver, gallbladder, small intestine, and large intestine.

Gastrointestinal tract The stomach and intestines.

Gastronomy The study and appreciation of good food and good eating, and a culture's culinary customs, style and lore. Any interest or study of culinary pursuits as relates essentially to the kitchen and cookery, and to the higher levels of education, training and achievement of the chef apprentice or professional chef.

Gastroparesis A form of nerve damage that affects the stomach. Food is not digested properly and does not move through the stomach in a normal way, resulting in vomiting, nausea, or bloating and interfering with diabetes management.

Gastroscopy An examination of the inside of the stomach using a thin, lighted tube (called a gastroscope) passed through the mouth and esophagus.

Gastrostomy A surgically created opening in the stomach and the abdominal muscles. A tube is passed through these openings, into the stomach, to allow for feeding of a person who cannot eat normally.

Gatekeeper A primary care physician, utilization review, case management, local agency or managed care entity responsible for determining when and what services a patient can access and receive reimbursement for. An arrangement in which a primary care provider serves as the patient's agent, arranges for and coordinates appropriate medical care and other necessary and appropriate referrals. A PCP is involved in overseeing and coordinating all aspects of a patient's medical care. In order for a patient to receive a specialty care referral or hospital admission, the PCP must preauthorize the visit, unless there is an emergency. The term gatekeeper is also used in health care business to describe anyone (EAP, employer based case manager, UR entity, etc.) that makes the decision of where a patient will receive services.

Gatekeeping The process by which a primary care physician directly provides primary care and coordinates all diagnostic testing and specialty referrals required for a patient's medical care. Referrals and procedures usually are preauthorized by gatekeepers except in cases of emergency care.

GC rich area Many DNA sequences carry long stretches of repeated G and C which often indicate a gene-rich region.

Gefitinib An anilinoquinazoline with antineoplastic activity. Gefitinib inhibits the catalytic activity of numerous tyrosine kinases including the epidermal growth factor receptor (EGFR), which may result in inhibition of tyrosine kinase-dependent tumor growth. Specifically, this agent competes with the binding of ATP to the tyrosine kinase domain of EGFR, thereby inhibiting receptor autophosphorylation and resulting in inhibition of signal transduction. Gefitinib may also induce cell cycle arrest and inhibit angiogenesis.

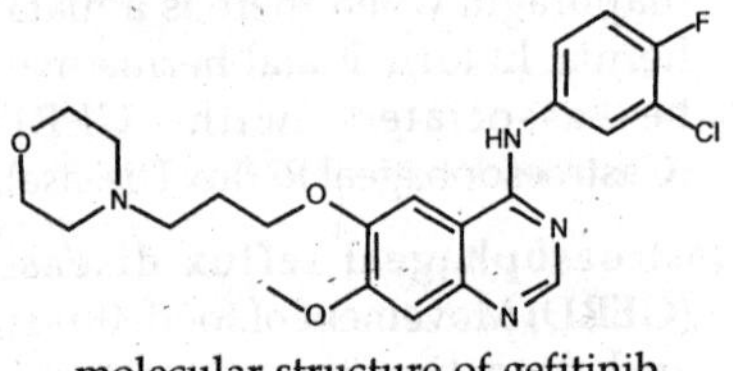

molecular structure of gefitinib

(N- (3-chloro-4-fluorophenyl)-7-methoxy-6- (3- morpholinopropoxy) quinazolin-4-amine)

Figure Gefitinib

Gel A colloid, where the dispersed phase is liquid and the dispersion medium is solid.

Gel electrophoresis A DNA separation technique that is very important in DNA sequencing. Standard sequencing procedures involve cloning DNA fragments into special sequencing cloning vectors that carry tiny pieces of DNA. The next step is to determine the base sequence of the tiny fragments by a special procedure that generates a series of even tinier DNA fragments that differ in size by only one base. These nested fragments are separated by gel electrophoresis, in which the DNA pieces are added to a gelatinous solution, allowing the fragments to work their way down through the gel. Smaller pieces move faster and will reach the bottom first. Movement through the gel is hastened by applying an electrical field to the gel.

Gel polarization The phenomenon of formation of a layer of insoluble/semi-soluble material at a liquid/filter interface. It is a common occurrence with excessive linear velocity flow through filters of colloidal suspensions and macromolecular solutions.

Gelatin A derived protein formed from the collagen of the tissues by boiling in water, sometimes called an albuminoid, though it lacks the characteristic albuminoid properties. Glue, size, and isinglass are forms of gelatin.

Gelatin sponge (absorbable) A sterile hemostatic agent composed of purified porcine-derived gelatin. In regional chemotherapy, absorbable gelatin sponge may be used to embolize arteries in the region of a tumor in order to block or retard blood flow; this blockage results in a locally increased concentration of chemotherapeutic agents delivered to the tumor when chemotherapeutic agents are infused into the embolized arterial circulation upstream of the blockage.

Geldanamycin analogue A class of agents containing analogues of the benzoquinone antineoplastic antibiotic geldanamycin. A geldanamycin analogue binds to HSP90, a chaperone protein that aids in the assembly, maturation, and folding of proteins. Subsequently, the function of Hsp90 is inhibited, leading to the degradation and depletion of client proteins such as kinases and transcription factors involved with cell cycle regulation and signal transduction.

Gemcitabine hydrochloride The hydrochloride salt of an analogue of the antimetabolite nucleoside deoxycytidine with antineoplastic activity. Gemcitabine is converted intracellularly to the active metabolites difluorodeoxycytidine di- and triphosphate (dFdCDP, dFdCTP). dFdCDP inhibits ribonucleotide reductase, thereby decreasing the deoxynucleotide pool available for DNA synthesis; dFdCTP is incorporated into DNA, resulting in DNA strand termination and apoptosis.

Gemtuzumab ozogamicin A recombinant, humanized anti-

CD33 monoclonal antibody attached to the cytotoxic antitumor antibiotic calicheamicin. In this conjugate, the antibody binds to and is internalized by tumor cells expressing CD33 antigen (a sialic acid-dependent glycoprotein commonly found on the surface of leukemic blasts), thereby delivering the attached calicheamicin to CD33-expressing tumor cells. Calicheamicin binds to the minor groove of DNA, causing double strand DNA breaks and resulting in inhibition of DNA synthesis.

Genasense A substance that is being studied in the treatment of cancer. It may kill cancer cells by blocking the production of a protein that makes cancer cells live longer and by making them more sensitive to anticancer drugs. It belongs to the family of drugs called antisense oligodeoxyribonucleotides. Also called oblimersen, augmerosen, and bcl-2 antisense oligodeoxynucleotide G3139.

Gene A natural unit of hereditary material that is the physical basis for the transmission of the characteristics of living organisms from one generation to another. The basic genetic material is fundamentally the same in all living organisms. It consists of deoxyribonucleic acid (DNA) in most organisms and ribonucleic acid (RNA) in certain viruses, and is usually associated in a linear arrangement that, in part, constitutes the chromosome. The average length of a gene is 1µm and thus, about one million genes could be contained in a one-meter stretch of DNA. The segment of DNA that is involved in producing a polypeptide chain, it includes regions preceding (leader) and following (trailer) the coding region as well as intervening sequences (introns) between individual coding segments (exons).

Gene amplification Repeated copying of a piece of DNA; a characteristic of tumor cells.

Gene chip technology Development of cDNA microarrays from a large number of genes. Used to monitor and measure changes in gene expression for each gene represented on the chip.

Gene deletion The total loss or absence of a gene.

Gene expression The process by which a gene's coded information is converted into the structures present and operating in the cell. Expressed genes include those that are transcribed into mRNA and then translated into protein and those that are transcribed into RNA but not translated into protein (e.g., transfer and ribosomal RNAs).

Gene family Group of closely related genes that make similar products.

Gene mapping Determination of the relative positions of genes on a DNA molecule (chromosome or plasmid) and of the distance, in linkage units or physical units, between them.

Gene markers Landmarks for a target gene, either detectable traits that are inherited along with the gene, or distinctive segments of DNA.

Gene pool All the variations of genes in a species.

Gene prediction Predictions of possible genes made by a computer program based on how well a stretch of DNA sequence matches known gene sequences

Gene product The biochemical material, either RNA or protein, resulting from expression of a gene. The amount of gene product is used to measure how active a gene is; abnormal amounts can be correlated with disease causing alleles.

Gene sequencing The determination of the sequence of bases in a DNA strand. The two most widely used methods are the chain-termination method, developed by Sanger in the mid-seventies, and the chemical method developed by Maxam & Gilbert around the same time.

Gene splicing The enzymatic attachment of one gene or part of a gene to another.

Gene therapy Treatment that alters a gene. In studies of gene therapy for cancer, researchers are trying to improve the body's natural ability to fight the disease or to make the cancer cells more sensitive to other kinds of therapy.

Gene transfer Incorporation of new DNA into and organism's cells, usually by a vector such as a modified virus. Used in gene therapy.

Gene-modified Cells that have been altered to contain different genetic material than they originally contained.

General anesthesia Controlled state of unconsciousness, accompanied by a partial or complete loss of pain sensation, protective reflexes, and the ability to respond purposefully to physical stimulation or verbal command.

General binocular vision disorder Inability to efficiently utilize and/or sustain binocular vision. Symptoms include eyestrain, headaches, decreased comprehension, inability to concentrate while reading, excessive tearing, and blurred vision. A patient will have difficulty with both base-in and base-out prisms. Vision therapy is an effective treatment option.

Generalizability The extent to which the results of a study are able to be applied to the general population of people that is comparable to the population studied.

Generic drug A drug produced and marketed under its chemical or "generic" name (e.g. acetaminophen) as opposed to "Tylenol", a brand name for the former produced by Johnson & Johnson. A generic drug can be sold only after a proprietary drug goes off patent (i.e. when the patent runs out after 17 years). There are numerous generic drug manufacturers. While generic drugs are cheaper for consumers, they still must meet the standards.

Genesis (Suffix) Origin, e.g. spermatogenesis - formation of sperm.

Genetic The study of how particular traits are passed from parents to children. Identifiable genetic information receives the same level of protection as other health care information.

Genetic analysis The study of a sample of DNA to look for mutations (changes) that may increase risk of disease or affect the way a person responds to treatment.

Genetic code The sequence of nucleotides, coded in triplets (codons) along the mRNA, that determines the sequence of amino acids in protein synthesis. A gene's DNA sequence can be used to predict the mRNA sequence, and the genetic code can in turn be used to predict the amino acid sequence.

Genetic counseling A communication process between health care provider and client that emphasizes providing accurate and up-to-date information about a genetic disorder in a sensitive and supportive, non-directive manner.

Genetic discrimination Prejudice against those who have or are likely to develop an inherited disorder.

Genetic diseases Diseases that occur because a mutation in the genetic material.

Genetic engineering Artificially changing an organism's genetic material (DNA or RNA) in order to change particular characteristics of that organism. This laboratory technique can produce proteins for use as drugs and vaccines. For example, a virus such as canarypox virus (which does not cause disease in humans) can be genetically engineered so that it produces specific HIV proteins. The modified canarypox virus can then be tested as an experimental HIV vaccine.

Genetic illness Sickness, physical disability, or other disorder resulting from the inheritance of one or more deleterious alleles.

Genetic marker Alteration in DNA that may indicate an increased risk of developing a specific disease or disorder.

Genetic mosaic An organism in which different cells contain different genetic sequence. This can be the result of a mutation during development or fusion of embryos at an early developmental stage.

Genetic mutation A change in hereditary characteristic due to a permanent change in a gene.

Genetic polymorphism Difference in DNA sequence among individuals, groups, or populations (e.g., genes for blue eyes versus brown eyes).

Genetic predisposition Susceptibility to a genetic disease. May or may not result in actual development of the disease.

Genetic screening Testing a group of people to identify individuals at high risk of having or passing on a specific genetic disorder.

Genetic susceptibility An inherited increase in the risk of developing a disease.

Genetic testing Analyzing an individual's genetic material to determine predisposition to a particular health condition or to confirm a diagnosis of genetic disease.

Genistein A soy-derived isoflavone and phytoestrogen with antineoplastic activity. Genistein binds to and inhibits protein-tyrosine kinase, thereby disrupting signal transduction and inducing cell differentiation. This agent also inhibits topoisomerase-II, leading to DNA fragmentation and apoptosis, and induces G2/M cell cycle arrest. Genistein exhibits antioxidant, antiangiogenic, and immunosuppressive activities.

Genital ulcer disease Sores on the genitals, usually caused by a sexually transmitted disease (STD) such as herpes, syphilis, or chancroid. The presence of genital ulcers may increase the risk of becoming infected with HIV through sexual intercourse.

Genital warts Also known as condyloma acuminatum and venereal warts. Growths or bumps that appear in and around the vagina, anus, or cervix in females or on the penis, scrotum, groin, or thigh in males. They can be raised or flat, single or multiple, small or large. Some cluster together to form a cauliflower-like shape. They are caused by the human papillomavirus (HPV) and are usually flesh-coloured and painless.

Genitourinary tract Also called genitourinary system, urogenital system, or urogenital tract. The organs involved in the production and excretion of urine and in reproduction.

Genome All the genetic material in the chromosomes of a particular organism; its size is generally given as its total number of base pairs.

Genome project Research and technology development effort aimed at mapping and sequencing some or all of the genome human beings and other organisms.

Genomic library A collection of clones made from a set of randomly generated overlapping DNA fragments representing the entire genome of an organism.

Genomic sequence The order of the subunits, called bases, that makes up a particular fragment of DNA in a genome. DNA is a long molecule made up of four different kinds of bases, which are abbreviated A, C, T, and G. A DNA fragment that is 10 bases long might have a base sequence of, for example, ATCGTTCCTG. The particular sequence of bases encodes important information in an individual's genetic blueprint, and is unique for each individual (except identical twins).

Genomics The study of the complete genetic material, including genes and their functions, of an organism.

Genotype The genetic composition of an organism (including expressed and nonexpressed genes), which may not be readily apparent.

Genotypic assay (GART) Also known as Genotypic Antiretroviral Resistance Test (GART). A test that determines if HIV is resistant to particular anti-HIV drugs. The test analyzes a sample of the virus from an individual's blood to identify any genetic mutations that are associated with resistance to specific drugs.

Genu Refers to a number of different angled or bent structures within the nervous system resembling the knee.

G. of the Corpus Callosum: Anterior part of corpus callosum continuous with the rostrum below and the body posteriorly.

G. of the Facial Nerve (Internal): Loop of facial nerve fibers over the rostral pole of the abducent nucleus within the floor of the 4th ventricle. The elevation left by these structures on the floor of the ventricle is referred to as the faci al colliculus.

G. of the Facial Nerve (External) Abrupt bend of the facial nerve within the facial canal of the petrous temporal bone.

G. of the Internal Capsule: The point of junction between the anterior and posterior limbs of the internal capsule.

Genu varum Seen at the knee. Commonly known as "bowed legs".

Geographic tongue Benign changes in the usual colour and texture of tongue; does not require treatment.

Gerdy's tubercle Lateral tubercle at upper end of tibia, being the site of partial insertion of iliotibial band. Common site of pathology due to friction of iliotibial band on bone.

Geriatric cases The older patient with an atonal condition of the external orbital tissue and muscles.

Germ cell Sperm and egg cells and their precursors. Germ cells are haploid and have only one set of chromosomes (23 in all), while all other cells have two copies (46 in all).

Germ cell tumor A type of tumor that begins in the cells that give rise to sperm or eggs. Germ cell tumors can occur almost anywhere in the body and can be either benign or malignant.

Germ line gene therapy An experimental process of inserting genes into germ cells or fertilized eggs to cause a genetic change that can be passed on to offspring. May be used to alleviate effects associated with a genetic disease.

Germ line Refers to genes in germ cells as opposed to somatic cells, that is, genes in their unrearranged state rather than those rearranged for production of a protein.

Germ-free Free of bacteria, disease-causing viruses, and other organisms that can cause infection.

Germicidal lamps Light sources that emit ultraviolet radiation at a wavelength of 254 nanometers. These lights are commonly found in biological safety cabinets and used to inactivate bacteria, viruses and fungi which are either airborne or on exposed surfaces.

Germicide An agent that destroys microorganisms, especially pathogenic microorganisms ("germs"). Sterilants, disinfectants, and antiseptics are germicides.

Germinoma The most common type of germ cell tumor in the brain.

Germline mutation A gene change in the body's reproductive cells (egg or sperm) that becomes incorporated into the DNA of every cell in the body of offspring; germline mutations are passed on from parents to offspring. Also called hereditary mutation.

Germplasm The total genetic variability, represented by germ cells or seeds, available to a particular population of organisms.

Gerota's capsule A fibrous envelope of tissue that surrounds the kidney. Also called renal fascia and Gerota's fascia.

Gerson therapy A diet plan that has been claimed to be a treatment for cancer, migraine, tuberculosis, and other diseases. It is a vegetarian diet that includes eating organic fruits and vegetables and 13 glasses of fresh juice each day. It also includes supplements with iodine, vitamin B-12, potassium, thyroid hormone, liver extract, and pancreatic enzymes. No clinical trial to test Gerson therapy has been reported.

Gestation The length of pregnancy.

Gestational diabetes mellitus (GDM) A type of diabetes mellitus that can occur when a woman is pregnant. In the second half of the pregnancy, the woman may have glucose (sugar) in the blood at a higher than normal level. However, when the pregnancy ends, the blood glucose levels return to normal in about 95 percent of all cases.

Gestational trophoblastic disease A rare cancer in women of childbearing age in which cancer cells grow in the tissues that are formed in the uterus after conception. Also called gestational trophoblastic tumor, gestational trophoblastic neoplasia, molar pregnancy, or choriocarcinoma.

Gestational trophoblastic neoplasia A rare cancer in women of childbearing age in which cancer cells grow in the tissues that are formed in the uterus after conception. Also called gestational trophoblastic disease, gestational trophoblastic tumor, molar pregnancy, or choriocarcinoma.

GGTP (Gamma glutamyl transpeptidase) Enzyme or protein synthesized by the liver in large amounts when there is obstruction of the bile ducts to the normal flow of bile. Measured in blood by laboratory to assess function of liver.

Giant cell fibroblastoma A rare type of soft tissue tumor marked by painless nodules in the dermis (the inner layer of the two main layers of tissue that make up the skin) and subcutaneous (beneath the skin) tissue. These tumors may come back after surgery, but they do not spread to other parts of the body. They occur mostly in boys and are related to dermatofibrosarcoma protuberans.

Giant Cell Large multinucleated cells. Epidermal multinucleated giant cells are characteristic of herpes virus infections. Histiocytic giant cells whose nuclei form a horseshoe arrangement are called Langhans type giant cells. Touton type giant cells have a ring of nuclei surrounding foamy cytoplasm with cytoplasm usually also visible around the nuclei. Foreign-body giant cells have a haphazard nuclear arrangement.

Giardia lamblia A parasite found in spoiled food or unclean water that can cause diarrhea.

Giardiasis A common protozoal infection of the small intestine spread via contaminated food and water and direct person-to-person contact.

GIGA Prefix meaning a billion times.

Gimatecan A substance that is being studied in the treatment of cancer. It belongs to the family of drugs called topoisomerase inhibitors. Also called ST1481.

Ginger A rhizome herb isolated from the plant Zingiber officinale with potential antineoplastic activity. Ginger contains a number of different phenolic compounds, some of which have displayed antineoplastic, anti-inflammatory, and antioxidant activities. This agent also exhibits antiemetic properties.

Gingiva Gum tissue.

Gingivectomy Surgical removal of gum tissue.

Gingivitis An inflammation of the gums that if left untreated may lead to periodontal disease, a serious gum disorder. Signs of gingivitis are inflamed and bleeding gums.

Ginseng An herb with a root that has been used in some cultures to treat certain medical problems. It may have anticancer effects.

Gland An organ that makes one or more substances, such as hormones, digestive juices, sweat, tears, saliva, or milk. Endocrine glands release the substances directly into the bloodstream. Exocrine glands release the substances into a duct or opening to the inside or outside of the body.

Glaucoma An eye disease associated with increased pressure within the eye. Glaucoma can damage the optic nerve and cause impaired vision and blindness.

Gleason score A system of grading prostate cancer cells based on how they look under a microscope. Gleason scores range from 2 to 10 and indicate how likely it is that a tumor will spread. A low Gleason score means the cancer cells are similar to normal prostate cells and are less likely to spread; a high Gleason score means the cancer cells are very different from normal and are more likely to spread.

Gleevec A drug that is being studied for its ability to inhibit the growth of certain cancers. It interferes with a portion of the protein produced by the bcr/abl oncogene. Also called imatinib mesylate and STI571.

Glenoid fossa The a shallow "cup" on the lateral edge of the scapula that is the point of articulation between with the head of the humerus.

Gliadel wafer A biodegradable wafer that is used to deliver the anticancer drug carmustine directly into a brain tumor site after the tumor has been removed by surgery. Also called polifeprosan 20 carmustine implant.

Glial cell A type of cell that surrounds nerve cells and holds them in place. Glial cells also insulate nerve cells from each other.

Glial tumor A general term for tumors of the central nervous system, including astrocytomas, ependymal tumors, glioblastoma multiforme, and primitive neuroectodermal tumors.

Glioblastoma A general term that refers to malignant astrocytoma, a type of brain tumor.

Glioblastoma multiforme A type of brain tumor that forms from glial (supportive) tissue of the brain. It grows very quickly and has cells that look very different from normal cells. Also called grade IV astrocytoma.

Glioma A cancer of the brain that begins in glial cells (cells that surround and support nerve cells).

Gliosarcoma A type of glioma (cancer of the brain that comes from glial, or supportive, cells).

Global-rating of live or recorded performance forms Ratings by faculty supervisors to assess trainees' medical knowledge, interpersonal and communication skills and patient care clinical skills which are completed retrospectively and are based on general impressions collected over a period of time. They are derived from multiple sources of information such as direct observations or interactions, input from other faculty, residents or patients; review of work products or written materials. They differ from other rating forms in that a rater judges general categories of ability and skills rather than specific skills, tasks or behaviours. The rating forms contain scales used by the evaluator to judge knowledge, skills, and behaviours listed on the form. Scoring these forms entails combining numeric ratings with comments to obtain a useful judgment about performance based upon more than one rater. Reproducibility appears easier to achieve for ratings of knowledge and more difficult to achieve for patient care and interpersonal and communication skills. To improve reproducibility, the rater should be well trained; otherwise the scores can be highly subjective and competencies may be rated similarly regardless of performance.

Globe The eyeball.

Globose nucleus Several small cell groups embedded in the white matter of the cerebellum medial to the emboliform and lateral to the fastigial nucleus.

Globus pallidus Component of the lenticular nucleus situated between the putamen and the internal capsule. The principal efferent nucleus of the corpus striatum. Also known as the paleostriatum.

Glomerular filtration rate Measure of the kidneys' ability to filter and remove waste products.

Glomeruli Network of tiny blood vessels in the kidneys where the blood is filtered and waste products are removed.

Glossectomy Surgical removal of all or part of the tongue.

Glossoepiglottic fold The folds of mucous memrane located between the tongue and epiglottis.

Glottis A synonym for the vocal cords.

Glucagon A hormone that raises the level of glucose (sugar) in the blood. The alpha cells of the pancreas, in areas called the islets of Langerhans, make glucagon when the body needs to put more sugar into the blood.

An injectable form of glucagon is available as a prescription item, for use to treat severe insulin reactions. The glucagon is injected and raises blood glucose levels within a half-hour. It is frequently recommended that people with Type 1 diabetes, and other people taking insulin injections, have a family member learn how to administer glucagon.

Glucagonoma A rare pancreatic tumor that produces a hormone called glucagon. Glucagonomas can produce symptoms similar to diabetes.

Glucocorticoid A compound that belongs to the family of compounds called corticosteroids (steroids). Glucocorticoids affect metabolism and have anti-inflammatory and immunosuppressive effects. They may be naturally produced (hormones) or synthetic (drugs).

Gluconeogenesis The process of making glucose (sugar) from its own breakdown products or from the breakdown products of lipids (fats) or proteins. Gluconeogenesis occurs mainly in cells of the liver or kidney.

Glucose A type of sugar; the chief source of energy for living organisms.

Glucose tolerance test A test to see if a person has diabetes. The test is given in a lab or doctor's office in the morning before the person has eaten. A first sample of blood is taken from the person. Then the person drinks a liquid that has glucose (sugar) in it. After one hour, a second blood sample is drawn, and, after another hour, a third sample is taken. The object is to see how well the body deals with the glucose in the blood over time.

Glue ear Low-grade eardrum inflammation associated with fluid in middle ear cavity.

Glufosfamide An anticancer drug that belongs to the family of drugs called alkylating agents.

Glutamate Glutamate is an amino acid. It is necessary for metabolism and brain function, and is manufactured by the body. Glutamate is found in virtually every protein food we eat. In food, there is "bound" glutamate and "free" glutamate. Glutamate serves to enhance flavors in foods when it is in its free form and not bound to other amino acids in protein. Some foods have greater quantities of glutamate than others. Foods that are rich in glutamate include tomatoes, mushrooms, parmesan cheese, milk and mackerel.

Glutamine A nonessential amino acid. Glutamine can donate the ammonia on its side chain to the formation of urea (for eventual excretion by the kidneys) and to purines (necessary for the synthesis of nucleic acids). Glutamine may become a conditionally essential nutrient during certain catabolic states.

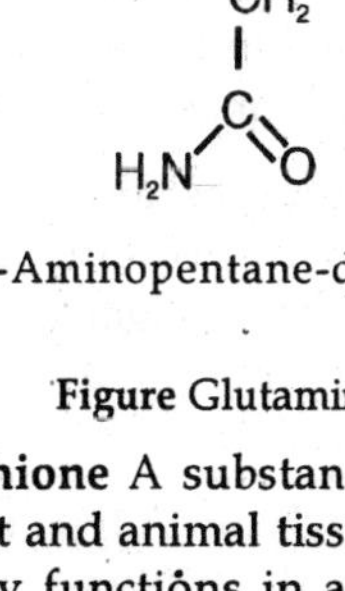

((S)-2-Aminopentane-dioic acid 5-amide)

Figure Glutamine

Glutathione A substance found in plant and animal tissues that has many functiôns in a cell. These include activating certain enzymes and destroying toxic compounds and chemicals that contain oxygen.

Glutathione S-transferase A family of enzymes involved in metabolism and in making toxic compounds less harmful to the body.

Gluten A protein in grains such as wheat, oats, rye, and barley.

Gluteus maximus Muscle originating form the lateral surface of the ilium, dorsal surface of the sacrum and coccyx, and the sacrotuberus ligament, and inserting into the iliotibial tract of the facia lata, and the gluteal tuberosity of femur. It is responsible for the extension. abduction, and lateral rotation of the thigh.

Gluteus medius Muscle originating between the anterior and posterior gluteal lines at the lateral surface of the ilium, and inserting at the greater trochanter of the femur. It is responsible for abduction of the thigh.

Gluteus minimus Muscle originating between the anterior and posterior gluteal lines at the lateral surface of the ilium, and inserting at the greater trochanter of the femur. It is responsible for the abduction and medial rotation of the thigh.

Glycemia A medical term that indicates the level of glucose in the blood.

Glycemic index A ranking of foods based on their immediate effect on blood sugar levels. The Glycemic Index measures how much your blood sugar increases over a period of two or three hours after a meal. Carbohydrate foods that break down quickly during digestion have the highest glycemic index.

Glycemic response The effect of different foods on blood glucose (sugar) levels over a period of time. Researchers have discovered that some kinds of foods may raise blood glucose levels more quickly than other foods containing the same amount of carbohydrates.

Glycerin A syrupy type of alcohol derived from sugar which is used in food flavourings to maintain desired food consistency.

Glycerol A colourless, odourless, syrupy liquid—chemically, an alcohol—that is obtained from fats and oils and used to retain moisture and add sweetness to foods.

Glycinamide ribonucleotide formyltransferase inhibitor A drug that blocks DNA synthesis and may prevent tumor growth. It is being studied as a treatment for cancer.

Glycine max A plant of Asian origin that produces beans used in many food products. Soy products contain isoflavones (estrogen-like substances) that are being studied for the prevention of cancer, hot flashes that occur with menopause, and osteoporosis (loss of bone density). Soy products in the diet may lower cholesterol levels and reduce the risk of heart disease. Also called soy, soya, and soybean.

Glycogen A substance made up of sugars. It is stored in the liver and muscles and releases glucose (sugar) into the blood when needed by cells. Glycogen is the chief source of stored fuel in the body.

Glycogenesis (or glucogenesis) The process by which glycogen is formed from glucose.

Glycolysis A process in which glucose (sugar) is partially broken down by cells in enzyme reactions that do not need oxygen. Glycolysis is one method that cells use to produce energy. When glycolysis is linked with other enzyme reactions that use oxygen, more complete breakdown of glucose is possible and more energy is produced.

Glycopeptide A short chain of amino acids (the building blocks of proteins) that has sugar molecules attached to it. Some glycopeptides have been studied for their ability to stimulate the immune system.

Glycoprotein 100 A tumor-specific antigen used in the development of cancer vaccines.

Glycoprotein A substance composed of both a protein and a carbohydrate (a sugar molecule) joined together by a chemical linkage.

Glycosaminoglycan A type of long, unbranched polysaccharide molecule. Glycosaminoglycans are major structural components of cartilage and are also found in the cornea of the eye.

Glycosuria, glucosuria Having glucose (sugar) in the urine.

Glycosylated hemoglobin test (Glycohemoglobin) A blood test that measures a person's average blood glucose (sugar) level for the 2- to 3-month period before the test.

GM CSF (Granulocyte-macrophage colony-stimulating factor) A substance that helps make more white blood cells, especially granulocytes, macrophages, and cells that become platelets. It is a cytokine that belongs to the family of drugs called hematopoietic (blood-forming) agents. Also called sargramostim.

GM.CD40L cell vaccine A cell-based vaccine composed of irradiated tumor cells transduced with granulocyte-macrophage colony-stimulating factor (GM-CSF) and CD10 ligand (CD10L) genes. Upon administration, this vaccine may stimulate an anti-tumoral dendritic cell-mediated host immune response.

GM2 KLH vaccine A cancer vaccine consisting of GM2 ganglioside, a melanoma-specific antigen, conjugated with the immuno-stimulant keyhole limpet hemocyanin. Vaccination with GM2-KLH vaccine may stimulate the host immune system to mount a cytotoxic T lymphocyte (CTL) response against GM2 ganglioside-expressing melanoma cells, resulting in tumor growth inhibition.

GMP facility A production facility or clinical trial materials pilot plant for the manufacture of pharmaceutical products. It includes the manufacturing space, the storage warehouse for raw and finished product, and support lab areas.

Goal A general aim, object or end-effect which one strives to achieve.

Goiter An enlarged thyroid. It may be caused by too little iodine in the diet or by other conditions. Most goiters are not cancer.

Golgi bodies Very small particles composed of membrane aggregates and responsible for the secretion of certain enzymes and macromolecules. Golgi bodies are the deposition and packaging site for many excreted products.

Gonad The part of the reproductive system that produces and releases eggs (ovary) or sperm (testicle/testis).

Gonadotropin-releasing hormone agonist A hormone made in the laboratory that has the same effect as the gonadotropin-releasing hormone (GnRH) produced naturally by the body.

Goniometer Apparatus for measuring range of motion at a joint. Error rate quite high as there are often problems locating the exact axis of movement, particularly for complex movements.

Gonorrhea A sexually transmitted disease (STD) caused by the bacterium Neisseria gonorrhoeae. Many people with gonorrhea have no symptoms. If symptoms do occur, they may be burning on urination, frequent urination, yellow or green discharge from the genitals, redness or swelling of the genitals, and a burning or itching sensation of the genitals. Active gonorrhea infection may increase the risk of becoming infected with HIV through sexual intercourse.

Gonzalez regimen An alternative therapy that is being studied as a treatment for pancreatic cancer. It includes a special diet, nutritional supplements, pancreatic enzymes, and coffee enemas.

Gorlin syndrome A genetic condition that causes unusual facial features and disorders of the skin, bones, nervous system, eyes, and endocrine glands. People with this syndrome have a higher risk of basal cell carcinoma. Also called nevoid basal cell carcinoma syndrome and basal cell nevus syndrome.

Goserelin A synthetic decapeptide analog of luteinizing hormone-releasing hormone (LHRH) with antineoplastic activity. Goserelin binds to and activates pituitary gonadotropin releasing hormone (GnRH) receptors. Prolonged administration of goserelin inhibits the secretion of pituitary gonadotropin, thereby decreasing levels of testosterone (in males) and estradiol (in females). Administration of this agent in a depot formulation may result in the regression of sex hormone-sensitive tumors and a reduction in sex organ size and function.

Gossypol An anticancer drug extracted from the cotton plant.

Gout Metabolic disease associated with hyperuricaemia, with symptoms occurring as a result of uric acid crystals being deposited into the tissues.

Gp100 antigen A melanoma-associated antigen. When administered in a vaccine formulation, GP100 antigen may stimulate a cytotoxic T cell HLA-A2.1-restricted immune response against tumors that express this antigen, which may result in a reduction in tumor size.

GP120 Another protein on the outer shell, or envelope, of HIV. GP120 is the portion of HIV that binds to a helper T-cell's surface protein, CD4. The "120" refers to its molecular weight.

GP120 glycoprotein 120 One of the proteins embedded in the outer envelope of HIV. GP120 projects from the surface of HIV and binds to the CD4 receptor on CD4 cells, initiating the process by which HIV enters and infects a host cell.

Gp160 glycoprotein 160 A precursor of HIV envelope proteins GP41 and GP120. GP160 is cut by HIV protease to form GP120 and GP41.

Gp41 Glycoprotein 41. One of the proteins embedded in the outer envelope of HIV. GP41 plays a key role in HIV's infection of CD4 cells by fusing HIV's envelope with the host cell membrane, allowing the virus to enter the cell.

Gracilis Muscle that originates at the inferior ramus of the pubis, and inserts into the medial surface of the tibial shaft. It is responsible for adduction of the thigh and flexion of the knee.

Grade 1 follicular lymphoma An indolent (slow-growing) type of non-Hodgkin's lymphoma marked by enlarged lymph nodes and small cells that have cleaved (u-shaped) nuclei.

Grade 3 follicular lymphoma A type of non-Hodgkin's lymphoma marked by large cells and enlarged lymph nodes. Grade 3 follicular lymphoma is less common, and more aggressive than grades 1 or 2 follicular lymphoma.

Grade IV astrocytoma A type of brain tumor that forms from glial (supportive) tissue of the brain. It grows very quickly and has cells that look very different from normal cells. Also called glioblastoma multiforme.

Grade The grade of a tumor depends on how abnormal the cancer cells look under a microscope and how quickly the tumor is likely to grow and spread. Grading systems are different for each tmype of cancer.

Grades of movement Stardardised means of documenting techniques of mobilisation, relating it to the true feel of joint movement.

Grading A system for classifying cancer cells in terms of how abnormal they appear when examined under a microscope. The objective of a grading system is to provide information about the probable growth rate of the tumor and its tendency to spread. The systems used to grade tumors vary with each type of cancer. Grading plays a role in treatment decisions.

Graduate training or internship The phase of acquiring widening clinical experience through the practice of basic clinical skills and judgment. This is normally used to designate the period of hospital clerkship. The periods of undergraduate education and graduate training together comprise the doctor's basic medical education.

Graft Healthy skin, bone, or other tissue taken from one part of the body and used to replace diseased or injured tissue removed from another part of the body.

Graft versus host reaction (GVH) The pathologic consequences of a response initiated by transplanted immunocompetent T lymphocytes into an allogeneic, immunologically incompetent host. The host is unable to reject the grafted T cells and becomes their target.

Graft versus-tumor An immune response to a person's tumor cells by immune cells present in a donor's transplanted tissue, such as bone marrow or peripheral blood.

Granisetron A drug that prevents or reduces nausea and vomiting. It belongs to the family of drugs called antiemetics.

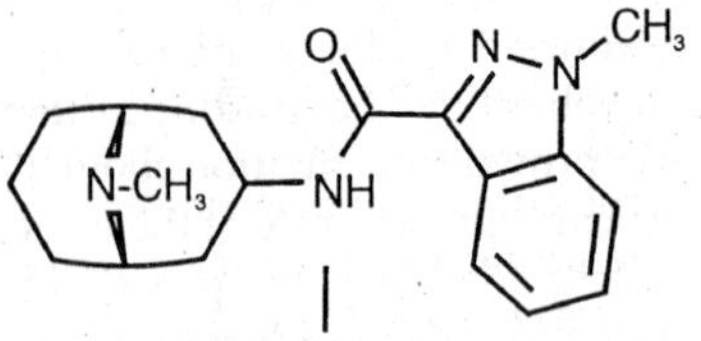

Figure Granisetron

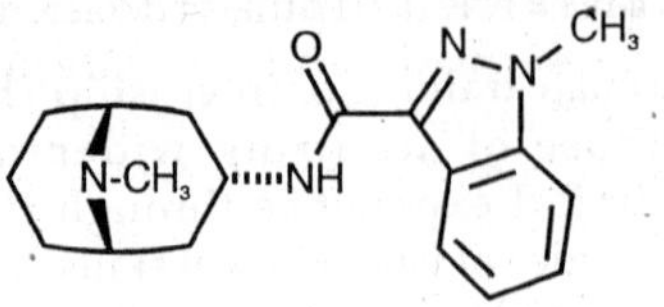

(1-methyl-N- (9-methyl-9-azabicyclo [3.3.1]non-3-yl)indazole-3-carboxamide)

Figure Granisetron

Granisetron hydrochloride The hydrochloride salt of an indazole derivative with antiemetic properties. As a selective serotonin receptor antagonist, granisetron competitively blocks the action of serotonin at 5-hydroxytryptamine3 (5-HT3) receptors, resulting in the suppression of chemotherapy- and radiotherapy-induced nausea and vomiting.

Granulation tissue Newly formed dermis arising in healing wounds and characterized by numerous fibroblasts and new capillaries and an infiltrate consisting of lymphoid cells, macrophages, and plasma cells.

Granulocytes A white blood cell type of the immune system filled with granules of toxic chemicals that enable them to digest microorganisms. Basophils., neutrophils, eosinophils, and PMNs are examples of granulocytes.

Granulocytic sarcoma A malignant, green-coloured tumor of myeloid cells (a type of immature white blood cell). This tumor is usually associated with myelogenous leukemia. Also called chloroma.

Granulocytopenia A lack or low level of granulocytes in the blood. Often used interchangeably with "neutropenia"

Granuloma A chronic proliferative lesion consisting of mononuclear cells and epithelioid cells or multinucleated giant cells or both. These cells lie in groups and are often surrounded by lymphoid cells. "Naked" granulomas have few to none of these surrounding lymphoid cells.

Granulomatous Composed of granulomas.

Granulosa cell tumor A type of slow-growing, malignant tumor that usually affects the ovary.

Graphic stress telethermometry (GST) A method of measuring surface heat from a distance. Some have used this method, plus computer analysis of heat patterns in the breast, to measure breast cancer risk. This is not a reliable method and is not in standard practice.

Graves' disease A form of thyroid disease, with overactivity of the thyroid function, enlargement of the size of the gland, and bulging eyes (exophthalmos) being common features. Named after a 19th century Irish physician.

Graves' is autoimmune in nature. It is found somewhat more commonly than expected in people with type 1 diabetes.

Gray elm Ulmus fulva or Ulmus rubra. The inner bark of this plant has been used in some cultures to treat certain medical problems. It may have antioxidant effects. Also called slippery elm, Indian elm, red elm, and sweet elm.

Greater curvature (stomach) The lateral and inferior border of the stomach.

Greater trochanter (femur) Process on the lateral surface of the proximal femur, the point of attachment for the gluteus medius and minimus.

Greater tuberosity (humerus) Prominence on the lateral surface of the proximal humerus. Point of attachment for the infraspinatus, supraspinatus, and teres minor muscles.

Greater wing of sphenoid Winged-shaped process of the sphenoid bone that helps form the floor and lateral walls of the middle cranial fossa and the lateral wall of the orbit.

Green tea extract A defined, decaffeinated green tea polyphenol mixture isolated from Camellia sinensis, a plant native to Asia, with antiviral and antioxidant activities and potential chemopreventive activity. Green tea extract contains antioxidant compounds, including flavonoids, vitamins and polyphenols such as epigallocatechin-3-gallate (EGCG), which may have antineoplastic properties. Consumption of green tea extract may confer chemopreventive protection against various cancers including those of the prostate, stomach, and esophagus.

Grenz zone A narrow area of uninvolved dermis between the epidermis and a dermal inflammatory or neoplastic infiltrate. "Grenz" is German for "border".

Grey matter The grey nervous tissue of the brain and spinal cord consisting of the cell bodies and dendrites of nerve cells rather than the myelinated axons.

Groin injuries Description of injury to any one of the following muscles: sartorius; long head of rectus femoris; any or all of the adductor muscles; the abdominals or the iliopsoas.

Groin The area where the thigh meets the abdomen.

Grommet A flanged metal or plastic tube that is inserted in the eardrum in cases of glue ear. It allows air to enter the middle ear, bypassing the patient's non-functioning Eustachian tube.

Group practice A group of persons licensed to practice medicine, who, as their principal professional activity, and as a group responsibility, engage or undertake to engage in the coordinated practice of their profession primarily in one or more group practice facilities, and who in their connection share common overhead expenses if and to the extent such expenses are paid by members of the group, medical and other records, and substantial portions of the equipment and the professional, technical, and administrative staffs. Group practices use the acronyms PA, IPA, MSO and others. Group practices are far more common now than a decade ago because physicians seek to lower costs, increase contracting power and share payer contracts.

Group practice without walls (GPWW) Similar to an independent practice association, this type of physician group represents a legal and formal entity where certain services are provided to each physician by the entity, and the physician continues to practice in his/her own facility. It can include marketing, billing and collection, staffing, management, and the like. Also called clinic without walls.

Growth factor A substance made by the body that functions to regulate cell division and cell survival. Some growth factors are also produced in the laboratory and used in biological therapy.

Grumose Lumpy or clotted.

GTI 2040 A 20-mer antisense oligonucleotide complementary to a coding region in the mRNA of the R2 small subunit component of human ribonucleotide reductase. GTI-2040 decreases mRNA and protein levels of R2 in vitro and may inhibit tumor cell proliferation in human tumors in vivo.

GTR (Guided tissue regeneration) A new technique for replacing bone tissue.

Guaiac test A test that checks for hidden blood in the stool.

Guanine (G) A nitrogenous base, one member of the base pair GC (guanine and cytosine) in DNA.

Guar gum A substance made from the seeds of the guar plant which acts as a stabilizer in food systems. Is found as a food additive in cheese, including processed cheese, ice cream and dressings.

Gum recession Exposure of dental roots due to shrinkage of the gums as a result of abrasion, periodontal disease or surgery.

Gyandromorph Organisms that have both male and female cells and therefore express both male and female characteristics.

Gynecologic cancer Cancer of the female reproductive tract, including the cervix, endometrium, fallopian tubes, ovaries, uterus, and vagina.

Gynecologic Having to do with the female reproductive tract (including the cervix, endometrium, fallopian tubes, ovaries, uterus, and vagina).

Gynecologic oncologist A doctor who specializes in treating cancers of the female reproductive organs.

Gynecologist A doctor who specializes in treating diseases of the female reproductive organs.

Gyrus The convolutions on the surface of the cerebral hemispheres separated by sulci or fissures.

H 2 complex The major histocompatibility complex situated on chromosome 17 of the mouse; contains subregions K, I and D.

H pylori (Helicobacter pylori) A type of bacteria that causes inflammation and ulcers in the stomach or small intestine. People with H. pylori infections may be more likely to develop cancer in the stomach, including MALT (mucosa-associated lymphoid tissue) lymphoma.

H_2 blockers Medications used to treat gastroesophageal reflux disease (GERD) that decrease the amount of acid made by the stomach. The stomach lining has sites that react to a chemical normally found in the body called histamine. When histamine attaches to these sites, the stomach produces acid that aids in digestion of food. H_2 blockers prevent the stomach from reacting to histamine, thereby decreasing stomach acid.

Ha20 A monoclonal antibody that is being studied in the treatment of refractory B-cell non-Hodgkin's lymphoma. Monoclonal antibodies are made in the laboratory and can locate and bind to cancer cells. hA20 binds to the protein CD20, which is found on B cells (a type of immune system cell), and some types of lymphoma cells. Also called IMMU-106 and HCD20.

HAART (Highly active antiretroviral therapy) Treatment for human immunodeficiency virus (HIV) infection that uses a combination of several antiretroviral drugs. The drugs inhibit the ability of the virus to multiply in the body, and they slow down the development of AIDS.

Habenular nuclei Nuclei (medial and lateral) underlying the habenular trigone and part of the epithalamus. They receive afferents from the preoptic, anterior thalamic, and septal areas via the stria medullares and sen d fibers to the brain stem interpeduncular, raphe nuclei and reticular formation.

H. Trigone: Small eminences on the dorsomedial aspect of the posterior thalamus lateral to the stalk of the pineal body formed by the habenular nuclei.

H. Commissure: Small commissural band of transverse fibers located above the stalk of the pineal body connecting the two habenular areas accross the midline.

Habit training A behavioural technique that calls for scheduled toileting at regular intervals on a planned basis. Unlike bladder training, there is no systematic effort to motivate the patient to delay voiding and resist urge.

HACCP (Hazard analysis and critical control points) The underlying approach under HACCP for preventing foodborne illness and promote quality is to identify the danger spots and try to avoid them. Instead of putting the burden on government to discover that a food safety problem exists, HACCP shifts responsibility onto the industry to ensure that the food it produces is safe. Food producers will have to prevent bacterial contamination from occurring in the first place. HACCP works by the following principles:

Identify the likely health hazards to consumers in a given product.

Identify the critical points in the processing where the hazards may occur.

Establish safety measures to prevent the hazard from occurring.

Monitor to make sure the safety measures are working.

Establish an appropriate remedy if monitoring shows a problem.

Establish detailed record keeping to document monitoring and remedies taken.

Verify that the whole system is working.

Haemarthrosis Bleeding within a joint. If swelling of a joint occurs quickly (i.e. within 3 - 4 hours) it is probably an haemarthrosis and, in the knee, in 75% of all cases indicates an ACL injury.

Haematoma Bleeding into tissues, usually as a result of blunt trauma.

Haemoptysis The coughing up of blood.

Hair follicle A shaft or opening on the surface of the skin through which hair grows.

Hairpin A double helical region formed by base pairing between adjacent (inverted) complementary sequences in a single strand of RNA or DNA.

Hairy cell leukemia A rare type of leukemia in which abnormal B-lymphocytes (a type of white blood cell) are present in the bone marrow, spleen, and peripheral blood. When viewed under a microscope, these cells appear to be covered with tiny hair-like projections.

Hairy leukoplakia A whitish, slightly raised lesion that appears on the side of the tongue. Thought to be related to Epstein-Barr virus infection, it was not observed before the HIV epidemic.

Half life The amount of time required for half of a given substance to be eliminated from the body.

Halitosis Bad breath of oral or gastrointestinal origin.

Hallux rigidus Loss of range of the movement of the metatarsophalangeal (MTP) joint of the first (great) toe, particularly extension.

Hallux valgus Deformity of the metatarsophalangeal (MTP) joint of the first toe, whereby the toe deviates into the lateral position.

Haloenzyme An enzyme that contains a non-protein component.

Halofuginone hydrobromide A substance that is being studied for its ability to slow the growth of connective tissue and prevent the growth of new blood vessels to a solid tumor. It belongs to the family of drugs called quinazolinone alkaloids.

Halogen One of the chlorine group (bromine, chlorine, fluorine, iodine) of elements, all univalent; they form monobasic acids with hydrogen, and their hydroxides (fluorine forms none) are monobasic acids. The radioactive element, astatine, also belongs to the halogen group.

Halophile An organism that displays accelerated growth or is dependent on high salt concentrations.

Halsted radical mastectomy Surgery for breast cancer in which the breast, chest muscles, and all of the lymph nodes under the arm are removed. For many years, this was the breast cancer operation used most often, but it is used rarely now. Doctors consider radical mastectomy only when the tumor has spread to the chest muscles. Also called radical mastectomy.

Hamartoma A benign (noncancerous) growth made up of an abnormal mixture of cells and tissues normally found in the area of the body where the growth occurs.

Hammer toe Deformity of the toe whereby there is PIP flexion and DIP extension. The MTP is usually extended or neutral.

Hamstrings Muscles located in the posterior compartment of the thigh. Made up of the semitendinosus, semimembranosus and biceps femoris muscles. Some anatomists will also include the "hamstring" head of adductor magnus.

Hand The portion of the upper limb distal to the radiocarpal joint,

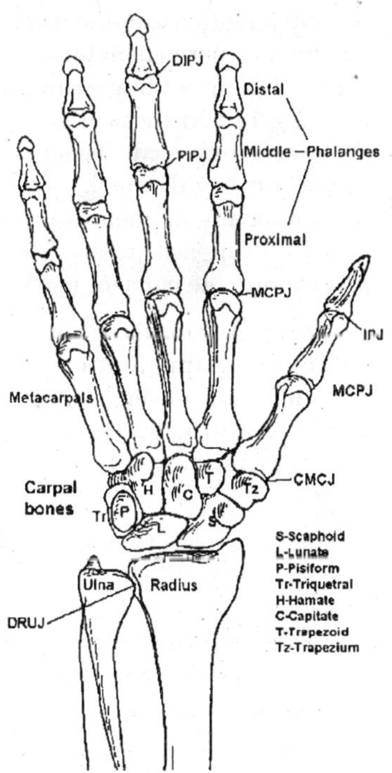

Figure Bones of Hand

comprised of the wrist, palm, and fingers.

Hand-foot syndrome A condition marked by pain, swelling, numbness, tingling, or redness of the hands or feet. It sometimes occurs as a side effect of certain anticancer drugs. Also known as palmar-plantar erythodysthesia.

Handshake Requires the recipient of an electronic data record to acknowledge to the sender that the record has been received.

Handwritten signature The scripted name or legal mark of an individual handwritten by that individual and executed or adopted with the present intention to authenticate a writing in a permanent form. The act of signing with a writing or marking instrument such as a pen or stylus is preserved. The scripted name or legal mark, while conventionally applied to paper, may also be applied to other devices that capture the name or mark.

Haphazard A process occurring without any apparent order or pattern. Distinct from random, in that there is no mathematical basis for characterizing a haphazard process.

Haploid A single set of chromosomes (half the full set of genetic material) present in the egg and sperm cells of animals and in the egg and pollen cells of plants. Human beings have 23 chromosomes in their reproductive cells.

Haplotype A particular combination of closely linked genes on a chromosome inherited from one patient.

Happy major Arctium lappa. A plant whose seeds and root have been used in some cultures to treat certain medical problems. It may have antioxidant effects. Also called burdock and lappa.

Hapten A compound, usually of low molecular weight, that is not itself immunogenic but that, after conjugation to a carrier protein or cells, becomes immunogenic and induces antibody, which can bind the hapten alone in the absence of carrier.

Hard endpoint Any outcome measure that is not subject to serious errors of interpretation or measurement. Usually death, infection or some other explicit clinical event.

Hard palate The anterior (bone) portion of the horizontal partition separating the nasal cavity (above) from the oral cavity (below). The posterior half of the partition is the "soft palate".

Hardness Concentration of calcium and magnesium salts in water. Hardness originally referred to the soap-consuming power of water; as such it is sometimes also taken to include iron and manganese. "Permanent hardness" also known as "noncarbonated hardness " is the excess of hardness over alkalinity. "Temporary hardness" also known as "carbonated hardness" is equal or less than the alkalinity. Permanent hardness can cause boiler or pipe scale and failure of reverse osmosis membranes.

Harvesting The separation of cells from growth media. It can be accomplished by filtration, precipitation, or centrifugation.

Haustra The indentations of mucosa in the wall of the colon - between the teniae coli - that create segments or sacculations of the colon.

Hay fever An allergy caused by breathing in pollen and by pollen getting into the eyes. Affects the delicate lining of the nose and eyes. Also known as seasonal allergic rhinitis.

Hazardous chemical reaction A reaction which generates pressure or byproducts which could cause injury, illness or harm to humans, domestic animals, livestock or wildlife.

Hazardous substance A substance which by reason of being explosive, flammable, toxic, poisonous, corrosive, oxidizing, irritant or otherwise harmful, is likely to cause injury.

Haze The abnormal appearance of a localized diminishing in brightness or luster of a surface when compared to the adjacent surfaces.

HCA (Heterocyclic amine) A chemical that is formed when meat, poultry, or fish is cooked at high temperatures, such as frying, broiling, and barbecuing. HCAs are carcinogens (substances that may cause cancer).

HCD20 A monoclonal antibody that is being studied in the treatment of refractory B-cell non-Hodgkin's lymphoma. Monoclonal antibodies are made in the laboratory and can locate and bind to cancer cells. HCD20 binds to the protein CD20, which is found on B cells (a type of immune system cell), and some types of lymphoma cells. Also called IMMU-106 and hA20.

HCF diet A high-carbohydrate, high-fiber diet.

HCRF (Human corticotropin-releasing factor) A substance that is being studied in the treatment of brain cancer. It is made naturally by the hypothalamus (a part of the brain) and can also be made in the laboratory. HCRF may help reduce symptoms caused by edema (swelling) of the brain. It belongs to the family of drugs called neurohormones.

HDR (High-dose radiation) An amount of radiation that is greater than that given in typical radiation therapy. HDR is precisely directed at the tumor to avoid damaging healthy tissue, and may kill more cancer cells in fewer treatments.

Head and neck cancer Cancer that arises in the head or neck region (in the nasal cavity, sinuses, lip, mouth, salivary glands, throat, or larynx (voice box)).

Head of rib The posterior end of a rib, that articulates with the body of the vertebrae.

Health In accordance with the Constitution of the World Health

Organization (1948), health is "a state of complete physical, mental and social well-being and not merely the absence of disease or infirmity". Health is defined here as a positive concept, emphasizing social and personal resources as well as physical capabilities.

Health care Services provided to individuals or communities by a health care system or by professionals to promote, maintain, monitor, or restore health. Health care contains a broad spectrum of services and activities delivered by a team of health personnel. This contrasts with medical care, which concentrates on diagnostic and therapeutic actions performed by or under the supervision of an individual physician.

Health care provider Providers of medical or health care or researchers who provide health care are health care providers. Normally health care providers are clinics, hospitals, doctors, dentists, psychologists and similar professionals.

Health economics A discipline which concentrates on application of the principles and rules of economics in the sphere of health. In broad terms, it includes analysis and evaluation of health policy and the health system from an economic perspective. In particular, it includes health system planning, market mechanisms, demand for and supply of health care, micro-economic evaluation of individual diagnostic and therapeutic procedures, determinants of health and its valuation, and evaluation of the performance of health care systems in terms of equity and allocative efficiency.

Health hazard Classification of a chemical for which there is statistically significant evidence based on at least one study conducted in accordance with established scientific principles that acute or chronic health effects may occur in exposed persons. The term "health hazard" includes chemicals that are carcinogens, toxic or highly toxic agents, reproductive toxins, irritants, corrosives, sensitizers, hepato-toxins, nephrotoxins, neurotoxins, agents that act on the hematopoietic system, and agents that damage the lungs, skin, eyes or mucous membranes.

Health information Information in any form (oral, written or otherwise) that relates to the past, present or future physical or mental health of an individual. That information could be created or received by a health care provider, a health plan, a public health authority, an employer, a life insurer, a school, a university or a health care clearinghouse.

Health insurance Financial protection against the health care costs of the insured person. May be obtained in a group or individual policy.

Health maintenance services Any health care service or program that helps maintain an individual's good health. This includes all preventive medical practices such as immunizations and periodic examinations, as well as health education and special self-help programs.

Health management Systematic use of the full range of human, technical and financial resources of the health system through planning, organizing, leading and controlling the effort of members to achieve stated goals and to render optimum services at minimum cost. Health managers achieve desired goals by directing and influencing subordinates, and organizing others to perform essential tasks to ensure that the organization is moving towards its goal of improving health.

Health plan A term that has different meanings depending upon the context. "Health plan" can be used to mean an HMO; a "health benefits plan" is provided by an employer to its employees, or services offered by an insurer or third party administrator to employers and/or employees.

Health policy A set of decisions or commitments to pursue courses of action aimed at achieving defined goals of improving health. Policies usually state or imply the values that underpin the policy position. They may also specify the source of funding that can be applied to planning and implementation of policy and to relevant institutions to be involved in this process.

Health promotion The process of enabling individuals to increase control over and improve their health. It involves the population as a whole in the context of their everyday lives, rather than focusing on people at risk for specific diseases, and is directed toward action on the determinants or causes of health.

Health risks appraisal A method of describing an individual's probability of becoming ill or dying from selected causes. Starting from the average risk of death for that individual's age and sex, various lifestyle and physical factors are considered and it is determined whether the individual is at greater or lesser than average risk from the commonest causes of death for their age and sex. Health risk appraisal also indicates the reduction in risk which could be achieved by the individual's altering any of the causal factors (such as cessation of cigarette smoking).

Health services Services performed by health care professionals or by others under their direction for the purpose of promoting, maintaining, or restoring health. In addition to personal health care, health services include health protection, health promotion, and disease prevention.

Health status The state of health of a specified individual, group, or population. It may be measured by obtaining proxies such as people's subjective assessments of their health; by one or more indicators of mortality and morbidity in the population, such as longevity or maternal and infant mortality; or by using the incidence or prevalence of major diseases (communicable, chronic, or nutritional). Conceptually, health status is the proper outcome measure for the effectiveness of a specific population's medical care system, although attempts to relate effects of available medical care to variations in health status have proved difficult.

Health system A complex of interrelated elements that contribute to health in homes, educational institutions, workplaces, public places, and communities. A health system is usually organized at multiple levels, starting at the most local level, also known as community or primary health care level, and proceeding through the intermediate (district, regional or provincial) to the central level, providing progressively more complex and more specialized care and support.

Healthy behaviour The combination of knowledge, practices and attitudes that together contribute to motivate actions we take regarding our own health. Healthy behaviour may promote and preserve good health. On the other hand, behaviours harmful to health such as tobacco smoking, alcohol drinking, drug abuse and lack of physical exercise may be determinants of disease.

Heart The muscle that pumps blood received from veins into arteries throughout the body. It is positioned in the chest behind the sternum (breastbone; in front of the trachea, esophagus, and aorta; and above the diaphragm muscle that separates the chest and abdominal cavities. The normal heart is about the size of a closed fist, and weighs about 10.5 ounces. It is cone-shaped, with the point of the cone pointing down to the left. Two-thirds of the heart lies in the left side of the chest with the balance in the right chest.

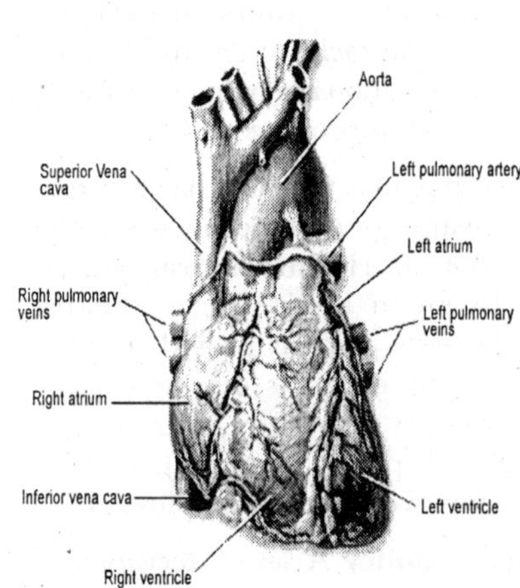

Figure Heart (Anterior View)

Heart attack A myocardial infarction (MI). This occurs when an artery that feeds the heart becomes blocked. As a result, blood does not get to some parts of the heart and some of the heart tissue dies. Symptoms may include nausea, shortness of breath and pain in the chest, arm or neck.

Heart block A condition in which the natural pacemaker signals sent out by the S-A node are delayed or fail to reach the ventricles.

Heartburn A burning feeling in the chest or area just above the stomach, caused by acid moving up the esophagus from the stomach.

Heart cancer A rare cancer that develops in tissues of the heart. Also called cardiac sarcoma.

Heart disease Any disorder that affects the heart. Sometimes the term "heart disease" is used narrowly and incorrectly as a synonym for coronary artery disease. Heart disease is synonymous with cardiac disease but not with cardiovascular disease which is any disease of the heart or blood vessels. Among the many types of heart disease Angina; Arrhythmia; Congenital heart disease; Coronary artery disease (CAD); Dilated cardiomyopathy; Heart attack (myocardial infarction); Heart failure; Hypertrophic cardiomyopathy; Mitral regurgitation; Mitral valve prolapse; and Pulmonary stenosis.

Heart rhythm Another term for heartbeat. You may hear your doctor refer to your rhythm as being normal or irregular, meaning there is an abnormality. A normal heart rate typically ranges from 60 to 100 beats per minute at rest.

Heat A form of energy associated with the motion of atoms or molecules in solids and capable of being transmitted through solid and fluid media by conduction, through fluid media by convection, and through empty space by radiation. Two important characteristics of heat are: 1. Heat cannot be destroyed, only transferred from on body to another, or converted to another form of energy.

2. Heat always flows from the warmer to the colder substance.

Heat affected zone (HAZ) That portion of the base metal that has not been melted but whose microstructure or mechanical properties have been altered by the heat of welding, brazing, soldering, forming, or cutting.

Heat labile Able to be destroyed or altered by high temperature. Heat labile pharmaceuticals are sterilized by filtration.

Heat number An alphanumeric identification of a stated tonnage of metal obtained from a continuous melting in a foundry furnace.

Heat of vapourization The amount of heat needed to change a unit volume from a liquid to a vapour at a given pressure without a temperature change.

Heavy chain (H chain) The larger of the two types of chains that comprise a normal immunoglobulin or antibody molecule.

Heavy metals High molecular weight metal ions, such as lead. Known for their interference with many processes, and "poisoning" of catalysts, membranes, and resins.

Heberden's nodes Bony swellings around the margins of joints, associated with degenerative changes of arthritis.

Hedyotis diffusa An herb used in traditional Chinese medicine to treat certain medical problems. It has been used to boost the immune system and may have anticancer effects.

Heel lock Technique of strapping, to ensure sub-talar joint stability.

Heimlich maneuver Techinque employed by rescuer for obstruction of victim's airway.

HeLa cells An established line of human cervical carcinoma cells used to study the biochemistry and genetics of human cell growth.

Helical computed tomography A detailed picture of areas inside the body. The pictures are created by a computer linked to an x-ray machine that scans the body in a spiral path. Also called spiral CT scan.

Helicobacter A genus of Gram-negative bacteria. The species H. pylori (formerly classified as Campylobacter pylori) is found in the stomach. It is associated with duodenal ulcer.

Helix A spiral, staircase-like structure with a repeating pattern described by two simultaneous operations (rotation and translation). It is one of the natural conformations exhibited by biological polymers.

HELLP Syndrome A term that stands for Hemolysis, Elevated Liver enzyme levels, and a Low Platelet count. This is a rare but serious complication that can develop in the third trimester of pregnancy. Symptoms may include liver, blood pressure, and bleeding problems that can harm both the mother and the baby. Pregnant women taking NRTIs for HIV infection are at an increased risk for developing HELLP syndrome.

Helper T cell A type of white blood cell that helps stimulate immune system reactions. Helper T cells help activate cytotoxic T cells and macrophages by secreting cytokines. They also stimulate B cells to make antibodies.

Helper-suppresser ratio The ratio of helper (CD4+) T-cells to suppresser (CD8+) T-cells.

Hema, hemato, haemo (british) Blood, e.g. hematocrit - the volume percentage of erythrocytes in whole blood.

Hemagglutinin-neuraminidase A protein found in the outer coat of paramyxoviruses. This protein helps virus particles bind to cells, making infection easier.

Hemangio Blood vessel, e.g. hemangiosarcoma - malignant tumor of a blood vessel.

Hemangiopericytoma A type of cancer involving blood vessels and soft tissue.

Hemangiosarcoma A type of cancer that begins in the cells that line blood vessels.

Hematide Other name for synthetic peptide-based erythropoiesis stimulating agent .

Hematin An iron protoporphyrin differing from heme in that the central iron atom is in the ferric (Fe^{+++}) rather than the ferrous (Fe^{++}) state; the prosthetic group of methemoglobin.

Hematocrit A laboratory measurement that determines the percentage of red blood cells in a sample of blood. In women, red blood cells are normally 37 to 47 percent of the blood. In men, red blood cells are normally 40 to 54 percent of the blood.

Hematogenous Originating in the blood or spread through the bloodstream.

Hematologic malignancy A cancer of the blood or bone marrow, such as leukemia or lymphoma. Also called hematologic cancer.

Hematologic Pertaining to, or involving the blood, or it's constituent cells.

Hematologist A physician who specializes in diagnosis and treatment of conditions that arise in the blood and blood-forming tissues, including bone marrow.

Hematology The science that studies the blood.

Hematoma A collection of blood outside a blood vessel caused by a leak or injury; for example, the bruise that may appear after blood is drawn for lab work. Hematomas that occur in the breast after injury may feel like a lump. As with other breast lumps, it's important to have this checked to be sure that it is indeed a hematoma and not a more serious problem.

Hematopoiesis The forming of new blood cells.

Hematopoietic growth factor A group of proteins that causes blood cells to grow and mature.

Hematopoietic Pertaining to the formation of blood cells.

Hematopoietic tissue Tissue in which new blood cells are formed.

Hematoporphyrin derivative A drug used in photodynamic therapy that is absorbed by tumor cells. When exposed to light, it becomes active and kills the cancer cells.

Hematotoxic Toxic or destructive to the blood or bone marrow.

Hematuria Blood in the urine.

Hemidiaphragm One side (one "half") of the diaphragm that separates the chest (thorax) from the abdominal cavity.

Hemilaryngectomy An operation to remove one side of the larynx (voicebox).

Hemiparesis Paralysis of only one side of the body.

Hemizygous Having only one copy of a particular gene. For example, in humans, males are hemizygous for genes found on the Y chromosome.

Hemoccult (Guaiac) test A test that checks for hidden blood in the stool.

Hemochromatosis A condition in which the body absorbs more iron from food than it needs. The extra iron is stored in and may damage the liver, heart, and pancreas. It may cause organ failure, cancer, heart problems, and liver disease. Hemochromatosis may also cause bronze skin, diabetes, pain in the joints and abdomen, tiredness, and impotence.

Hemodialysis A mechanical method of cleaning the blood for people who have kidney disease.

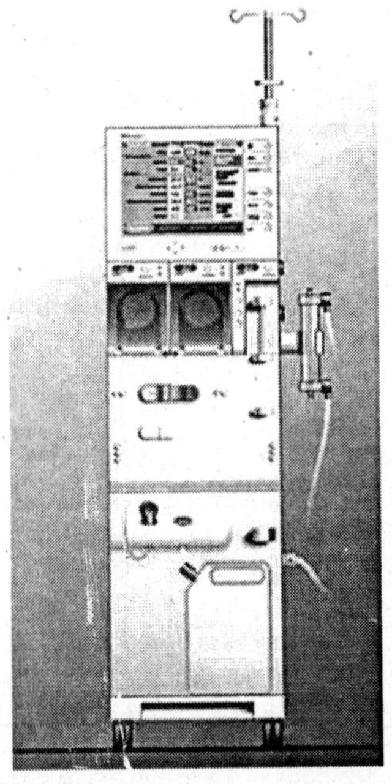

Figure A hemodialysis machine

Hemoglobin The chemical substance (an iron containing protein) of the red blood cell which carries oxygen to the tissues, and gives the cell its red colour.

Hemoglobin A1C (HbA1C) The substance of red blood cells that carries oxygen to the cells and sometimes joins with glucose (sugar). Because the glucose stays attached for the life of the cell (about 4 months), a test to measure hemoglobin A1C shows what the person's average blood glucose level was for that period of time.

Hemoglobin C trait (AC) The inheritance of one gene for the usual hemoglobin (A), and one gene for hemoglobin (C). A person who has hemoglobin C Trait (AC) is a carrier of the hemoglobin C gene, and is not affected by the gene.

Hemoglobin electrophoresis A laboratory technique to determine the type of hemoglobin the individual has. When you pass an electric charge through a solution of hemoglobin, distinct hemoglobins move different distances, depending on their composition. This technique differentiates between usual hemoglobin (A), sickle hemoglobin (S) and many other different kinds of hemoglobin (such as C, D, E, etc.).

Hemolysis Rupture of red blood cell membranes, causing a release of hemoglobin.

Hemolytic anemia Anemia due to the destruction (rather than underproduction) of red blood cells.

Hemophilia A hereditary blood defect that occurs almost exclusively in males and is characterized by delayed clotting of the blood. This leads to difficulty in controlling bleeding, even after minor injuries.

Hemorrhage In medicine, loss of blood from damaged blood vessels. A hemorrhage may be internal or external, and usually involves a lot of bleeding in a short time.

Hemorrhagic fever A condition characterized by non-stop internal or external bleeding resulting from a viral infection which has caused blood vessel damage.

Hemorrhoid An enlarged or swollen blood vessel, usually located near the anus or the rectum.

Hemothorax A collection of blood in the pleural cavity.

HEPA filters (High efficiency particulate air filters) Filters capable of removing 0.3-micron diameter with an efficiency of at least 99.97%.

Heparin A sulphur containing polysaccharide that stops blood from clotting by preventing the conversion of prothrombin to thrombin and by neutralizing thrombin. It is contained in the mast cells and is extractable from various tissues, notably the lung.

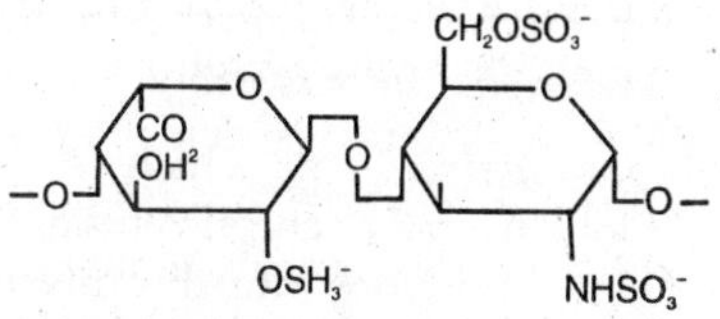

(6- [5- acetylamino- 4,6- dihydroxy-2-(sulfooxymethyl)tetrahydropyran- 3-yl]oxy- 3- [5- (6- carboxy- 4,5-dihydroxy- 3- sulfooxy-tetrahydropyran- 2- yl)oxy- 6-hydroxymethyl)- 3-sulfoamino- 4-sulfooxy- tetrahydropyran- 2- yl]oxy- 4-hydroxy- 5- sulfooxy-tetrahydropyran-2- carboxylicacid)

Figure Heparin

Hepatectomy Surgery to remove all or part of the liver.

Hepatic Relating to the liver.

Hepatic arterial infusion A procedure to deliver chemotherapy directly to the liver. Catheters are put into an artery in the groin that leads directly to the liver, and drugs are given through the catheters.

Hepatic artery The artery which originates from the celiac trunk and branches into the right gastric, gastroduodenal, and hepatic proper arteries.

Hepatic flexure A bend in the right/ superior large intestine, where the ascending colon becomes the transverse colon.

Hepatic necrosis Death of liver cells.

Hepatic portal vein A blood vessel that carries blood to the liver from the stomach, small and large intestines, spleen, pancreas, and gallbladder. Also called portal vein.

Hepatic steatosis Accumulation of too much fat inside liver cells. Also known as "fatty liver."

Hepatic veins Veins which receive blood from the central veins of the liver and flow into the inferior vena cava on the posterior side of the liver.

Hepatic veno-occlusive disease A condition in which some of the veins in the liver are blocked. It is sometimes a complication of high-dose chemotherapy given before a bone marrow transplant and is marked by increases in weight, liver size, and blood levels of bilirubin.

Hepatitis Disease of the liver causing inflammation. Symptoms include an enlarged liver, fever, nausea, vomiting, abdominal pain, and dark urine.

Hepatitis A A form of infectious hepatitis caused by the hepatitis A virus. The virus may be spread by fecal-oral contact, fecal-infected food or water, and may also be spread by a blood-borne infection (which is rare).

Hepatitis A antibody (Anti HA) Main laboratory test used to detect hepatitis A. Detects antibody produced by patient's immune system in response to hepatitis A virus.

Hepatitis A vaccine An inactivated virus vaccine that provides active immunization against hepatitis A virus (HAV). Immunization with hepatitis A vaccine induces the formation of anti-HAV antibodies which provide protection against hepatitis A infection.

Hepatitis B A viral liver disease that can be acute or chronic and even life-threatening, particularly in people with poor immune resistance. Like HIV, the hepatitis B virus can be transmitted by sexual contact, contaminated needles or contaminated blood or blood products. Unlike HIV, it is also transmissible through close casual contact.

Hepatitis B core antibody (Anti HBc) Laboratory test that detects antibody produced by patient's immune system in response to internal components of the hepatitis B virus.

Hepatitis B surface antigen (HBsAg) Main laboratory test used to establish a diagnosis of hepatitis B. Detects component of hepatitis B virus circulating in patient's serum.

Hepatitis B virus (HBV) The virus that causes hepatitis B, an inflammation of the liver that can lead to liver damage and liver cancer. HBV is spread through contact with the blood of an infected person, through sexual intercourse, or from mother to child during childbirth. A vaccine is available to prevent infection with this virus, and hepatitis B can be treated with several drugs.

Hepatitis B virus DNA (HBV DNA) Laboratory test that detects internal component of hepatitis B virus.Reflects degree of activity or rate of multiplication of the virus.

Hepatitis Be antigen (HBeAg) Laboratory test that helps to determine degree of activity, or rate of multiplication, of hepatitis B virus.

Hepatitis C A form of infectious hepatitis caused by the hepatitis C virus. Transmission of the hepatitis C virus occurs primarily from contact with infected blood, but can also occur from sexual contact or from an infected mother to her baby.

Hepatitis C antibody (Anti HC) Laboratory test that detects antibodies produced by patient's immune system in response to presence of the hepatitis C virus. Laboratory test methods include enzyme immunoassay (EIA) and radioimmunoblot assay (RIBA).

Hepatitis C RNA (HC RNA) Laboratory test that measures the levels of components of the hepatitis C virus in the patient's serum.

Hepatitis C virus (HCV) The virus that causes hepatitis C, an inflammation of the liver that can lead to liver damage and liver cancer. HCV is primarily spread through contact with the blood of an infected person. There is no vaccine for HCV, and the only current treatment for hepatitis C is a combination of the drugs peginterferon and ribavirin.

Hepatitis D A form of infectious hepatitis caused by the hepatitis (Delta) virus. This form of hepatitis can only occur in the presence of hepatitis B. Transmission of hepatitis D occurs the same way as hepatitis B.

Hepatitis D antibody (Anti HD) Laboratory test that detects antibodies in serum produced by patient's immune system in response to the presence of hepatitis D virus.

Hepatitis E A form of infectious hepatitis caused by the hepatitis E virus. This form of hepatitis is similar to hepatitis A. Transmission occurs through fecal-oral contamination. Hepatitis E is most common in poorly developed countries and is rarely seen in the US.

Hepatitis G The newest form of infectious hepatitis. Transmission is believed to occur through blood and is seen in IV drug users, individuals with clotting disorders, such as hemophilia, and individuals who require hemodialysis for renal failure.

Hepatobiliary Having to do with the liver, bile ducts, and/or gallbladder.

Hepatoblastoma A type of liver tumor that occurs in infants and children.

Hepatocellular carcinoma (Hepatoma) Most common malignant tumor of the liver. Arises from the main cells of the liver.

Hepatocyte A liver cell.

Hepatomegaly An enlargement of the liver.

Hepatosplenomegaly Enlargement of the liver and spleen.

Hepatotoxicity A general term for liver damage. Often caused by medications, including those used to treat HIV infection. Symptoms of hepatotoxicity include nausea, vomiting, abdominal pain, loss of appetite, diarrhea, unusual tiredness or weakness, jaundice (yellowing of the skin and eyes), and unusual swelling or weight gain. Laboratory testing may show increased levels of liver enzymes in the blood.

Hepatotoxin A toxin that is destructive to parenchymal (specific tissue) cells of the liver.

HER1 (Epidermal growth factor receptor) The protein found on the surface of some cells and to which epidermal growth factor binds, causing the cells to divide. It is found at abnormally high levels on the surface of many types of cancer cells, so these cells may divide excessively in the presence of epidermal growth factor. Also known as EGFR or ErbB1.

HER2/neu (Human epidermal growth factor receptor 2) The HER2/neu protein is involved in the growth of some cancer cells. Also called c-erbB-2.

HER2/neu gene The gene that makes the human epidermal growth factor receptor 2. The protein produced is HER2/neu, which is involved in the growth of some cancer cells. Also called c-erbB-2.

Herba scutellaria barbatae A Chinese herb isolated from the plant Scutellaria barbata D. Don (Lamiaceae) with potential antineoplastic activity. Containing the antioxidant flavone scutellarin, herba scutellariae barbatae has been shown to induce apoptosis of ovarian and breast tumor cells in vitro.

Herbicides Herbicides are a class of crop protection and specialty chemicals used to control weeds on farms and in forests, as well as in non-agricultural applications such as golf courses, public tracts of land and residential lawns.

Herceptin A type of monoclonal antibody used to detect or treat some types of cancer. Monoclonal antibodies are laboratory-produced substances that can locate and bind to cancer cells. Herceptin blocks the effects of the growth factor protein HER2, which transmits growth signals to breast cancer cells. Also called trastuzumab.

Hereditary Transmitted from parent to child by information contained in the genes.

Hereditary cancer Cancer that occurs due to the inheritance of an altered gene within a family.

Hereditary cancer syndrome One or several types of conditions associated with cancers that occur within multiple family members, because of an inherited, mutated gene.

Hereditary leiomyomatosis and renal cell cancer syndrome (HLRCC) A rare inherited disorder that increases the risk of developing benign (noncancerous) tumors of the skin and the uterus (leiomyomas) and malignant (cancerous) tumors of the uterus (leiomyosarcoma) and the kidney.

Hereditary material Material responsible for the transmission of qualities from ancestor to descendant through genes.

Hereditary mutation A gene change in the body's reproductive cells (egg or sperm) that becomes incorporated into the DNA of every cell in the body of offspring; hereditary mutations are passed on from parents to offspring. Also called germline mutation.

Hereditary nonpolyposis colon cancer (HNPCC) An inherited disorder in which affected individuals have a higher-than-normal chance of developing colourectal cancer and certain other types of cancer, often before the age of 50. Also called Lynch syndrome.

Hernia A section of intestine or other internal organ that pushes through an opening in an abdominal muscle.

Herniorrhaphy An operation done to repair a hernia.

Herpes simplex The most common virus that causes sores often seen around the mouth, commonly called cold sores.

Herpes simplex virus 1 (HSV 1) A virus that can cause painful "cold sores" or blisters on the lips ("fever blisters") or in the mouth or around the eyes. The symptomatic disease stage occurs at unpredictable intervals of weeks, months or years. The latent (inactive) virus can reactivate due to emotional stress, physical trauma, other infections, or suppression of the immune system. HSV-1 responds well to treatment with acyclovir.

Herpes simplex virus 2 (HSV 2) A virus closely related to HSV-1 that causes similar lesions. However, HSV-2 is usually transmitted sexually, and its lesions generally are in the anogenital area.

Herpes varicella zoster virus (HVZ/VZV) The varicella virus causes chicken pox in children and may reappear in adulthood as herpes zoster. Herpes zoster, also called shingles, consists of very painful blisters on the skin that follow nerve pathways.

Hetero Dissimilar, e.g. heterocellular - composed of more than one type of cell.

Heterogenic Derived from a different source or species. Also called heterogenous.

Heterophile antigen A cross-reacting antigen that appears in widely ranging species such as humans and bacteria.

Heterophoria Tendency of the eyes to deviate from their normal position for visual alignment. This condition may be observed when one eye is covered.

Hete otrophs One of two categories ir which microorganisms are c.assified on the basis of their carbon source. Heterotrophs use organic compounds such as carbohydrates, lipids, and hydrocarbons as a carbon and energy source.

Heterozygosity The presence of different alleles at one or more loci on homologous chromosomes.

Hexyl 5-aminolevulinate A substance that is used to find and kill tumor cells. It enters tumor cells and becomes activated when exposed to a special type of light. A chemical reaction causes the cells to produce fluorescent light and die.

HHV8 (Human herpesvirus 8) A type of herpesvirus that may cause Kaposi's sarcoma (a rare cancer that can cause skin lesions) and a type of lymphoma (cancer that begins in the lymph system), especially in patients who have a weak immune system. Also called Kaposi's sarcoma-associated herpesvirus (KSHV).

High blood pressure When the blood flows through the vessels at a greater than normal force. High blood pressure strains the heart; harms the arteries; and increases the risk of heart attack, stroke, and kidney problems. Also called hypertension.

High dose chemotherapy An intensive drug treatment to kill cancer cells, but that also destroys the bone marrow and can cause other severe side effects. High-dose chemotherapy is usually followed by bone marrow or stem cell transplantation to rebuild the bone marrow.

High dose rate remote radiation therapy A type of internal radiation treatment in which the radioactive source is removed between treatments. Also called high-dose-rate remote brachytherapy or remote brachytherapy.

High energy photon therapy A type of radiation therapy that uses high-energy photons (units of light energy). High-energy photons penetrate deeply into tissues to reach tumors while giving less radiation to superficial tissues such as the skin.

High fructose corn syrup (HFCS) HFCS are formulations generally containing 42 percent, 55 percent or 90 percent fructose (the remaining carbohydrate being primarily glucose) depending on the product application. HCFS are used in products such as soft drinks or cake mixes.

High grade When referring to cancerous and precancerous growths, a term used to describe cells that look abnormal under a microscope. These cells are more likely to grow and spread quickly than cells in low-grade cancerous and precancerous growths.

High grade lymphoma A type of lymphoma that grows and spreads quickly, and has severe symptoms. It is seen frequently in patients who are HIV-positive (AIDS-related lymphoma). Also called aggressive or intermediate-grade lymphoma.

High grade squamous intraepithelial lesion (HSIL) A precancerous condition in which the cells of the uterine cervix are moderately or severely abnormal.

High purity process systems The equipment that includes the stainless steel vessels, tube, pipe, fittings, and valves used to manufacture and transport drug products.

High risk Having a higher risk of developing cancer, compared with the general population. Some of the factors that can place a person at higher risk are heredity (a family history of breast cancer increases risk of breast cancer), lifestyle choices (smoking increases risk of lung cancer), and the environment (exposure to sunlight increases risk of skin cancer).

High risk cancer Cancer that is likely to recur (come back), or spread.

Highly conserved sequence DNA sequence that is very similar across several different types of organisms.

High-throughput sequencing A fast method of determining the order of bases in DNA.

Hilar Refers to the area where nerves and blood vessels attach to an organ.

Hilar vessels The vascular pedicle for the lung, including the lymphatics, pulmonary arteries and veins.

Hill-sachs lesion Following anterior dislocation of the shoulder, the head of the humerus can sustain a compression fracture. This consequent depression of the humeral head is known as a Hill-Sachs lesion.

Hinge region A flexible, open segment of an antibody molecule that allows bending of the molecule. The hinge region is located between Fab and Fc and is susceptible to enzymatic cleavage.

Hip joint One of the largest joints in the body (it depends on how you measure). Each ball-and-socket hip supports about 3/8 of the total body weight.

Hip pointer Contusion of the iliac crest. Usually due to a severe knock against the iliac crest.

Hippocampal formation Consists of the dentate gyrus, hippocampus, subicular cortex (part of the parahippocampal gurus) and associated nerve fibers.

Hippocampus A long cortical eminence (cornu ammonis) invaginated into the medial wall and floor of the temporal horn of the lateral ventricle. This is phylogenetically old 3 layer archicortex of which the pyramidal cell laye r is the most characteristic. Regional variations in morphology, development, and connectivity subdivide the hippocampus into sectors designated CA1 to CA4.

Hippocratic oath An affirmation usually taken by physicians about to enter the practice of medicine. It is attributed to Greek physician, Hippocrates of Cos, who is called the "Father of Medicine" (circa 460- 377 B.C). Its content reflects the ethical code of the physicians' attitudes and behaviour and obligations towards patients, colleagues and society. The complete text can be found here.

Hirschsprung's disease Caused by malformation of a baby's large intestine during pregnancy. Some of the nerve cells that are normally present are missing, causing problems moving stool through the intestine. This can cause obstruction (blockage) of the intestine.

Histaminase An enzyme widely distributed in the body, which is responsible for the inactivation of histamine.

Histamine A natural chemical that is released by Mast Cells in the body initiating an allergic reaction which leads to inflammation in affected parts of the body.

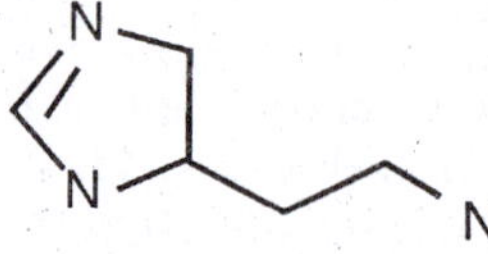

The structure of histamine

Figure Histamine

Histidine An amino acid from which histamine is derived.

Histiocyte A large, phagocytic cell of the reticuloendothelial system; a macrophage.

Histiocytic lymphoma An outdated term referring to non-Hodgkin's lymphomas made up of large abnormal lymphoid cells. Histiocytic lymphomas include mature B-cell and T-cell non-Hodgkin's lymphomas. Many tumors that were once called histiocytic lymphomas are now considered to be a type of large cell lymphoma.

Histiocytoma A common neoplasm of young dogs composed of round histiocytic cells, thought to be Langerhan's cells. Most tumors spontaneously regress.

Histocompatibility Literally, the ability of tissues to get along; in immunology, it means identity in all transplantation antigens. These antigens, in turn, are collectively referred to as histocompatibility antigens.

Histologic examination The examination of tissue specimens under a microscope.

Histology The study of tissues and cells under a microscope.

Histone A type of protein found in chromosomes. Histones bind to DNA, help give chromosomes their shape, and help control the activity of genes.

Histone deacetylase (HDAC) An enzyme that changes the way histone binds to DNA. HDAC inhibitors are being studied as a treatment for cancer.

Histoplasmosis A lung disease caused by the fungus Histoplasma capsulatum. Symptoms are similar to those of influenza. People with severely damaged immune systems, such as those with AIDS, are vulnerable to a very serious form of the disease called progressive disseminated histoplasmosis. This form of histoplasmosis typically lasts a long time and involves other organs besides the lungs. Histoplasmosis is considered an AIDS-defining condition in people with HIV.

Historic cohort study A research study in which the medical records of groups of individuals who are alike in many ways but differ by a certain characteristic (for example, female nurses who smoke and those who do not smoke) are compared for a particular outcome (such as lung cancer). Also called a retrospective cohort study.

Historical control group A group of patients (may be loosely or explicitly defined) considered to have the same disease or condition as the study group, but who were diagnosed and treated in a period of time prior to that of the study group and who received the conventional form of therapy for that time. Historical control groups are generally only useful for evaluations of treatments involving rare diseases with highly predictable outcomes and where it is considered impractical or unethical to carry out a controlled clinical trial.

Historical control subject An individual treated in the past and used in a comparison group when researchers analyze the results of a clinical study that had no control group. The use of a control, or comparison, group helps researchers determine the effects of a new treatment more accurately.

Human immunodeficiency virus (HIV) The virus that causes Acquired Immunodeficiency Syndrome (AIDS). HIV is in the retrovirus family, and two types have been identified: HIV-1 and HIV-2. HIV-1 is responsible for most HIV infections throughout the world, while HIV-2 is found primarily in West Africa.

HIV 1 The HIV type responsible for the majority of HIV infections worldwide.

HIV 2 A virus closely related to HIV-1 that also causes immune suppression and AIDS. Although the two viruses are very similar, immunodeficiency seems to develop more slowly and to be milder in people infected with HIV-2. The majority of HIV-2 cases have been found in West Africa. Not all drugs used to treat HIV-1 infection are effective against HIV-2.

HIV antibody A substance produced by certain white blood cells in reaction to contact with HIV, the human immunodeficiency virus.

HIV positive Infected with the human immunodeficiency virus (HIV), the cause of acquired immunodeficiency syndrome (AIDS).

HIV prevention trials network (HPTN) A worldwide clinical trials network established by the National Institutes of Health (NIH) to develop and evaluate the safety and efficacy of non-vaccine HIV prevention methods designed to prevent the transmission of HIV.

HIV vaccine trials network (HVTN) An international group of scientists and educators that was formed in 1999 by the Division of AIDS of the National Institute of Allergy and Infectious Diseases (NIAID). The main goal of HVTN is to find a safe and effective preventive HIV vaccine. HVTN staff and volunteers around the world are also involved in helping community members understand the general science of HIV/AIDS vaccines, as well as research methods and clinical trials processes.

Hives (urticaria) A skin reaction that results in slightly elevated patches that are redder or paler than the surrounding skin and often are accompanied by itching.

HLA (human lymphocyte antigen) One of a group of proteins found on the surface of white blood cells and other cells that play an important part in the body's immune response to foreign substances. These antigens vary from person to person, and an HLA test is done before organ transplantation to find out if tissues match between a donor and a recipient. Also called human leukocyte antigen.

HLA A1, A2, B35 restricted survivin peptides/Montanide ISA 51 vaccine A peptide vaccine comprised of synthetic HLA-A1, -A2 and -B35 restricted survivin epitopes combined with the adjuvant Montanide ISA-51 with potential antineoplastic activity. Upon administration, HLA-A1, -A2 and -B35 restricted survivin peptides/Montanide ISA-51 may stimulate a cytotoxic T cell response against tumor cells that overexpress survivin, resulting in tumor cell lysis. Montanide ISA-51 (also known as incomplete Freund's adjuvant or IFA), a stabilized water-in-oil emulsion adjuvant containing mineral oil with mannide oleate added as a surfactant, non-specifically stimulates cell-mediated immune responses to antigens.

HMG-CoA reductase inhibitor Hydroxymethylglutaryl-coenzyme A reductase inhibitor. A substance that blocks an enzyme needed by the body to make cholesterol and lowers the amount of cholesterol in the blood. HMG-CoA reductase inhibitor drugs are called statins.

Hodgkin's disease A cancer of the immune system that is marked by the presence of a type of cell called the Reed Sternberg cell. Symptoms include the painless enlarged lymph nodes, spleen, or other immune tissue. Other symptoms include fever, weight loss, fatigue, or night sweats. Also called Hodgkin's lymphoma.

Hollow fiber Refers to reverse osmosis and ultrafiltration membranes formed into small diameter (about 0.05" I.D.) tubes. The inner surface is a very thin (RO or UF) membrane skin supported by a thicker porous outer layer that gives the tube its strength. Hollow fibers are used in bundles of 1,000 or more in a single cartridge shell. Water is forced through the center (upstream surface) of each tube and purified permeate is collected from the outer wall (downstream surface).

Holy thistle Cnicus benedictus. A plant whose leaves, stems, and flowers have been used in some cultures to treat certain medical problems. Holy thistle may have anti-inflammatory and anticancer effects. Also called blessed thistle, St. Benedict's thistle, cardin, and spotted thistle.

Home blood glucose monitoring A way a person can test how much glucose (sugar) is in the blood. Also called self-monitoring of blood glucose.

Home health care Full range of medical and other health related services such as physical therapy, nursing, counseling, and social services that are delivered in the home of a patient, by a provider.

Homeo, homo Similar; same, e.g. homeotypical - resembling the normal or usual type.

Homeobox A short stretch of nucleotides whose base sequence is virtually identical in all the genes that contain it. Homeoboxes have been found in many organisms from fruit flies to human beings. In the fruit fly, a homeobox appears to determine when particular groups of genes are expressed during development.

Homeopathic medicine An alternative approach to medicine based on the belief that natural substances, prepared in a special way and used most often in very small amounts, restore health. According to these beliefs, in order for a remedy to be effective, it must cause in a healthy person the same symptoms being treated in the patient. Also called homeopathy.

Homeopathy A system of medicine based on the theory that 'like cures like'. The patient is treated with extremely small quantities of drugs that are themselves capable of producing symptoms of the particular disease.

Homeostatis When the body is working as it should because all of its systems are in balance.

Homoharringtonine A cytotoxic plant alkaloid isolated from the evergreen tree Cephalotaxus with potential antineoplastic activity. Homoharringtonine binds to the 80S ribosome in eukaryotic cells and inhibits protein synthesis by interfering with chain elongation. This agent also induces differentiation and apoptosis in some cancer cell types.

Homolog A member of a chromosome pair in diploid organisms or a gene that has the same origin and functions in two or more species.

Homologous chromosome Chromosome containing the same linear gene sequences as another, each derived from one parent.

Homologous recombination Swapping of DNA fragmments between paired chromosomes.

Homology Similarity in DNA or protein sequences between individuals of the same species or among different species.

Homozygote An organism that has two identical alleles of a gene.

Honeymoon period The period of time shortly after the diagnosis of Type 1 diabetes during which there is some restoration of insulin production and the blood sugar levels improve to normal, or near-normal levels. Unfortunately, like other honeymoons, this diabetes honeymoon doesn't last forever; it may last for weeks, months, or occasionally, years.

Horizontal integration, horizontal consolidation Merging of two or more firms at the same level of production in some formal, legal relationship. In hospital networks, this may refer to the grouping of several hospitals, the grouping of outpatient clinics with the hospital or a geographic network of various health care services. Integrated systems seek to integrate both vertically with some organizations and horizontally with others. When local health plans (or local hospitals) merge. This practice was popular in the late 1990s and was used to expand regional business presence.

Horizontal transmission A term used to describe transmission of a disease from one individual to another, except from parent to offspring. For example, HIV can be spread horizontally through sexual contact or exposure to infected blood. In contrast, spread of disease from parent to offspring is called vertical transmission.

Hormonal therapy Treatment that adds, blocks, or removes hormones. For certain conditions (such as diabetes or menopause), hormones are given to adjust low hormone levels. To slow or stop the growth of certain cancers (such as prostate and breast cancer), synthetic hormones or other drugs may be given to block the body's natural hormones. Sometimes surgery is needed to remove the gland that makes a certain hormone. Also called hormone therapy, hormone treatment, or endocrine therapy.

Hormone A chemical substance that is released into the body by the endocrine glands, such as the thyroid or ovaries. The substance travels through the bloodstream and sets in motion various body functions. For example, prolactin, which is produced in the pituitary gland, begins and sustains the production of milk in the breast after childbirth.

Hormone receptor A protein on the surface of a cell that binds to a specific hormone. The hormone causes many changes to take place in the cell.

Hormone receptor assay A test to see whether a breast tumor is affected by hormones or if it can be treated with hormones.

Hormone receptor test A test to measure the amount of certain proteins, called hormone receptors, in cancer tissue. Hormones can attach to these proteins. A high level of hormone receptors may mean that hormones help the cancer grow.

Hormone replacement therapy (HRT) Hormones (estrogen, progesterone, or both) given to women after menopause to replace the hormones no longer produced by the ovaries. Also called meno-pausal hormone therapy.

Hormone therapy Treatment that adds, blocks, or removes hormones. For certain conditions (such as diabetes or menopause), hormones are given to adjust low hormone levels. To slow or stop the growth of certain cancers (such as prostate and breast cancer), synthetic hormones or other drugs may be given to block the body's natural hormones. Sometimes surgery is needed to remove the gland that makes a certain hormone. Also called hormonal therapy, hormone treatment, or endocrine therapy.

Horner's syndrome A condition in which one side of the face is flushed, does not produce sweat, and has a constricted pupil and drooping eyelid. It can be caused by an injury to, or paralysis of, nerves in the neck, or by a tumor.

Hospice A concept of supportive care to meet the special needs of patients and family during the terminal stages of illness. The care may be delivered in the home or hospital by a specially trained team of professionals.

Hospital Any institution duly licensed, certified, and operated as a Hospital. In no event shall the term "Hospital" include a convalescent facility, nursing home, or any institution or part thereof which is used principally as a convalescence facility, rest facility, nursing facility, or facility for the aged.

Hospital alliances Groups of hospitals joined together to share services and develop group-purchasing programs to reduce costs. May also refer to a spectrum of contracts, agreements or handshake arrangements for hospitals to work together in developing programs, serving covered lives or contracting with payers or health plans.

Host A cell or organism that supports the growth of a parasite or virus.

Host cell A cell that is infected by a virus or another type of microorganism.

Hot can (active can) Electrical current flows from the lead in the heart to the surface of the pulse generator.

Hot flash A sudden, temporary onset of body warmth, flushing, and sweating (often associated with menopause).

Hot nodule When radioactive material is used to examine the thyroid with a scanner, nodules that collect more radioactive material than the surrounding thyroid tissue are considered "hot." Hot nodules are rarely malignant. Hot nodules are sometimes called hyperfunctioning nodules.

Hotspot In genetics, an area of DNA that is likely to mutate (change).

House dust mite A tiny 0.5mm long spider-like insect that inhabits carpets, bedding and soft furnishings. It eats human skin flakes and thrives in humid environments. Their droppings cause allergies such as Asthma, Eczema and Rhinitis.

Housemaid's knee Inflammation of the superficial infrapatellar bursa.

HPLC (High pressure liquid chromatography) Sometimes called high-performance liquid chromatography, is a separation technique based on a solid stationary phase and a liquid mobile phase. Separations (into distinct bands) are achieved by partition, adsorption, or ion-exchange processes, depending upon the type of stationary phase used. Each band is then profiled as the solvent flows through a UV detector, or by fluorescence, or refractive index detectors.

HPPH 2-(1-hexyloxyethyl)-2-devinyl pyropheophorbide-a. A drug that is used in photodynamic therapy that is absorbed by tumor cells; when exposed to light, it becomes active and kills the cancer cells.

HPV (Human papillomavirus) A member of a family of viruses that can cause abnormal tissue growth (for example, genital warts) and other changes to cells. Infection with certain types of HPV may increase the risk of developing some types of cancer.

HSA (Human serum albumin) The main protein constituent of human serum. It has no prosthetic group and is soluble in water and dilute salt solution. It is sometimes used in the treatment of shock, hypoproteinemia, and erythroblastosis fetalis.

HTLV 1 (Human t-cell leukemia virus type 1) A retrovirus that infects T-cells (a type of white blood cell) and can cause leukemia and lymphoma. HTLV-1 is spread by sharing syringes or needles used to inject drugs, through sexual contact, and from mother to child at birth or through breast-feeding.

HTS computerized binocular home vision therapy system A computer program which is prescribed by an eye doctor. The computer program is for improving eye tracking, eye teaming, and/or eye focusing.

Huang lian A Chinese herb that has been used as a treatment for a variety of medical problems. It is being studied as an anticancer drug.

HuHMFG1 A monoclonal antibody that binds to the protein MUC1, which is found on breast, ovarian, pancreatic, gastric, and colon cancer cells. Monoclonal antibodies are laboratory-produced substances that can locate and bind to cancer cells. HuHMFG1 is being studied in the treatment of some types of cancer.

Human artificial chromosome (HAC) A vector used to hold large DNA fragments.

Human gene therapy Insertion of normal DNA directly into cells to correct a genetic defect.

Human genome initiative Collective name for several projects begun in 1986 by DOE to create an ordered set of DNA segments from known chromosomal locations, develop new computational methods for analyzing genetic map and DNA sequence data, and develop new techniques and instruments for detecting and analyzing DNA. This DOE initiative is now known as the Human Genome Program. The joint national effort, led by DOE and NIH, is known as the Human Genome Project.

Human genome project This project is, in simplest terms, a sequencing of the human genome. Information from the Human Genome Project is making it possible, for example, to identify the exact gene (or genes) that influences a person's susceptibility to a disease, to develop new and better drugs, and to identify thousands of different polymorphisms. The full scope of the Human Genome Project's potential to improve human health is only beginning to be appreciated.

Human growth hormone (HGH) A protein produced in the pituitary gland that stimulates the liver to produce somatomedins, substances that stimulate growth of bone and muscle.

Human insulin Man-made insulins that are similar to insulin produced by your own body. Human insulin has been available since October 1982.

Human prostate-specific membrane antigen plasmid DNA vaccine A vaccine consisting of a plasmid DNA encoding the human prostate-specific membrane antigen (PSMA). Upon administration, expressed PSMA may stimulate a cytotoxic T cell response against tumor cells that express this antigen, resulting in tumor cell lysis.

Human subject Under HIPAA rules, this term refers to a living subject participating in research about whom directly or indirectly identifiable health information or data are obtained or created.

Humatin Brand name of Paromomycin.

Humerus The large single bone of the proximal arm (upper extremity).

Humidifier A machine that puts moisture in the air.

Humoral immune response The immune response that is mediated by B-cells and involves production of antibodies. Humoral immunity (also known as TH-1 immune response) is associated with the production of the cytokines interleukin-4 and interleukin-10.

Humoral immunity Any immune reaction that can be transferred with immune serum is termed humoral immunity (as opposed to cell-mediated immunity). In general, this term refers to resistance that results from the presence of specific antibody.

Hürthle cell neoplasm An uncommon type of thyroid tumor that can be benign or malignant.

Hyalin Homogenous eosinophilic material that is PAS-positive and diastase-resistant and has glycoprotein as a major component.

Hyaluronidase Substance that assists in the resolution of a haematoma. Usually prepared in a cream form.

Hybrid systems Combination of electronic and paper records, common in today's analytical labs, in which raw data is recorded electronically to reconstruct the analysis, but the final results are printed and signed on paper.

Hybrid The offspring of genetically different parents.

Hybridization of crops The mating of two plants from different species or genetically very different members of the same species to yield hybrids possessing some of the characteristics of each parent. Those (hybrid) offspring tend to be more healthy, productive and uniform than their parents—a phenomenon known as "hybrid vigour."

Hybridization The process of joining two complementary strands of DNA or one each of DNA and RNA to form a double-stranded molecule.

Hybridoma A hybrid cell resulting from the fusion of a specific antibody producing spleen cell with a myeloma cell. The hybrid cell has the growth characteristics of the myeloma component and the antibody secreting characteristics of the spleen cell and will multiply to become a source of large quantities of pure, monoclonal antibody.

Hycamtin A drug used to treat some types of cancer. It belongs to the family of drugs called topoisomerase inhibitors. Also called topotecan.

Hydatid disease From the Greek, for "watery" cyst - usually an echinococcus cyst.

Hydatidiform mole A condition in women of childbearing age in which grape-like cysts grow in the uterus after conception (fertilization of an egg by a sperm). Hydatidiform moles may change into a type of cancer called choriocarcinoma or gestational trophoblastic tumor. Also called molar pregnancy.

Hydration Combining with water.

Hydrazine sulfate A substance that has been studied as a treatment for cancer and as a treatment for cachexia (body wasting) associated with advanced cancer.

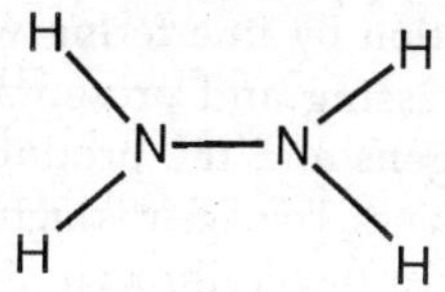

The structure formula of Hydrazine

Figure Hydrazine

Hydro, hygro Water; fluid, e.g. hydronephrosis - distension of the renal pelvis and calices with urine.

Hydrocele A painless swelling of the scrotum, caused by a collection of fluid around the testicle; commonly occurs in middle-aged men.

Hydrocephalus A condition in which there is either overproduction, obstructed circulation or impaired absorption of CSF resulting in abnormal progressive accumulation of fluid within the cerebral ventricles and/o r subarachnoid spaces, dilation of the venricles, compression of brain substance, raised intracranial pressure and consequent neurological and functional disturbances.

Hydrochloric acid Acid made by the stomach that breaks down proteins in the foods we eat.

Hydrocortisone A drug used to relieve the symptoms of certain hormone shortages and to suppress an immune response.

Hydrogen breath test A test that measures the amount of hydrogen in the breath, and helps diagnose lactose intolerance. If the body is unable to digest lactose properly, it will make excess amounts of hydrogen.

Hydrogen peroxide (H_2O_2) A colourless, heavy, strongly oxidizing, unstable liquid used principally in aqueous solutions as an antiseptic, bleaching agent, oxidizing agent, and laboratory reagent. In the vapour phase, as an airborne sterilant.

Hydrogenation Hydrogenation is the process of adding hydrogen molecules directly to an unsaturated fatty acid from sources such as vegetable oils to convert it to a semi-solid form such as margarine or shortening. Hydrogenation contributes important textural properties to food. The degree of hydrogenation influences the firmness and spreadability of margarines, flakiness of pie crust and the creaminess of puddings. Hydrogenated oils are sometimes used in place of other fats with higher proportions of saturated fatty acids such as butter or lard.

Hydrolysis A chemical reaction between water and organic compounds, particularly esters, ketones, and alcohols. This reaction can lead to breakdown of some proteins.

Hydromorphone A drug used to relieve pain.

Hydronephrosis Abnormal enlargement of a kidney, which may be caused by blockage of the ureter (such as by a kidney stone) or chronic kidney disease that prevents urine from draining into the bladder.

Hydrophilic Having a strong affinity for water. Its opposite, hydrophobic.

Hydrophobic Non-wetting; water repelling.

Hydropic degeneration of basal cells Also called liquefaction degeneration, it is a type of degeneration causing vacuolization of the basal cells. This process may lead to pigment incontinence. It is seen in lupus erythematosus, dermatomyositis, LS&A, ashy dermatosis and in early lichen planus.

Hydrops Excessive accumulation of watery fluid in any of the tissues or cavities of the body.

Hydrotest A pressure test of piping, pressure vessels, or pressure-containing parts, usually performed by pressurizing the internal volume with water at a pressure determined by the applicable code or to test the integrity of a process system.

Hydrotherapy Rehabilitation exercises performed in a appropriately designed pool.

Hydroureter Distension of the ureter with fluid due to obstruction. Hydroureter is often accompanied by hydronephrosis if the obstruction is in the bladder trigone or more distal.

Hydroxychloroquine A 4-aminoquinoline with antimalarial and immunosuppressive pro-perties. Although its precise mechanism of action is unknown, hydroxychloroquine may suppress immune function by interfering with the processing and presentation of antigens and the production of cytokines. This agent is highly active against the erythrocytic forms of P. vivax and malariae and most strains of P. falciparum but not the gametocytes of P. falciparum.

Hydroxymethylglutaryl-coenzyme A reductase inhibitor HMG-CoA reductase inhibitor. A substance that blocks an enzyme needed by the body to make cholesterol and lowers the amount of cholesterol in the blood. HMG-CoA reductase inhibitor drugs are called statins.

Hydroxyurea A monohydroxyl-substituted urea (hydroxycarbamate) antimetabolite. Hydroxyurea selectively inhibits ribonucleoside diphosphate reductase, an enzyme required to convert ribonucleoside diphosphates into deoxyribonucleoside diphosphates, thereby preventing cells from leaving the G1/S phase of the cell cycle. This agent also exhibits radiosensitizing activity by maintaining cells in the radiation-sensitive G1 phase and interfering with DNA repair.

Hygiene The science of health, and the practice of cleanliness that promotes good health and well-being.

Hygienic Of, or pertaining to, equipment and piping systems that by design, materials of construction, and operation provide for the maintenance of cleanliness (pyrogen free but not sterile) so that products produced by these systems will not adversely affect human or animal health.

Hygienic clamp joint A tube outside diameter union consisting of two neutered ferrules having flat faces with a concentric groove and mating gasket that is secured with a clamp, providing a nonprotruding, recessless product contact surface. Tri-clamp is a Tri-Clover proprietary name; consequently, it should not be used to describe the above-mentioned fitting unless that particular brand is used.

Hygienist Dental auxiliary who cleans teeth and provides patient education; administers local anesthetic, nitrous oxide and performs periodontal scaling.

Hygroscopicity The affinity for absorbing water.

Hyoid bone The horse shoe shaped bone that lies above the thyroid cartilage at the base of the tongue.

Hyper Ammasia - excessive pigmentation.

Hyperalimentation A form of nutrition that is delivered into a vein. Hyperalimentation does not use the digestive system. It may be given to people who are unable to absorb nutrients through the intestinal tract because of vomiting that won't stop, severe diarrhea, or intestinal disease. It may also be given to those undergoing high-dose chemotherapy or radiation and bone marrow transplantation. It is possible to give all of the protein, calories, vitamins and minerals a person needs using parenteral nutrition. Also known as parenteral or total parenteral nutrition (TPN).

Hyperbaric oxygen Oxygen that is administered at a higher pressure compared to standard (i.e. sea-level) atmospheric pressure. Administration of oxygen under hyperbaric conditions enhances the delivery of oxygen to hypoxic tumor cells, thereby increasing their sensitivity to radiation and chemotherapy. In addition, hyperbaric oxygen may improve the healing of radiation-induced injuries by improving oxygen delivery to damaged tissue.

Hyperbilirubinemia Too much bilirubin in the bloodstream, due to liver problems. Causes a yellow colour of the skin known as jaundice.

Hypercalcemia Abnormally high blood calcium.

Hyperemia Presence of an increased amount of blood in a part or an organ.

Hyperextension Active or passive force which takes the joint into extension, but beyond its normal physiological range.

Hyperfractionation A way of giving radiation therapy in smaller-than-usual doses two or three times a day instead of once a day.

Hypergammaglobulinemia Abnormally high levels of antibodies in the blood. Common in persons with HIV.

Hyperglycemia Too high a level of glucose (sugar) in the blood; a sign that diabetes is out of control. Many things can cause hyperglycemia. It occurs when the body does not have enough insulin or cannot use the insulin it does have to turn glucose into energy. Signs of hyperglycemia are a great thirst, a dry mouth, and a need to urinate often.

Hypericum perforatum An herbal preparation isolated from the plant St. John's Wort with photodynamic, antineoplastic, and antidepressant properties. Hypericin, one of the active compounds found in hypericum perforatum, is a photosensitizer that, when exposed to a particular wavelength and intensity of light, may induce tumor cell apoptosis. Another compound, hyperforin, induces caspase-dependent apoptosis in certain tumor cell lines. Hypericum perforatum preparations may also stimulate the activity of cytochrome P450 enzymes and P-glycoprotein drug transporters, resulting in increased metabolism and decreased efficacy of various chemotherapeutic agents and other drugs.

Hyperinsulinism Too high a level of insulin in the blood. This term most often refers to a condition in which the body produces too much insulin. Researchers believe that this condition may play a role in the development of noninsulin-dependent diabetes and in hypertension.

Hyperkeratosis A condition marked by thickening of the outer layer of the skin, which is made of keratin (a tough, protective protein). It can result from normal use (corns, calluses), chronic inflammation (eczema), or genetic disorders (X-linked ichthyosis, ichthyosis vulgaris).

Hyperlipidemia Elevated concentration of lipids (cholesterol, triglycerides, or both) in the blood. Hyperlipidemia increases the risk of serious heart diseases. In HIV-infected inidividuals, hyperlipidemia may occur as a side effect of PI treatment.

Hypermobility A condition characterized in which the pelvic floor muscles can no longer provide the necessary support to the urethra and bladder neck. As a result, the bladder neck drops when any downward pressure is applied and causing involuntary leakage. This condition is the most common cause of stress urinary incontinence.

Hypernephroma The most common type of kidney cancer. It begins in the lining of the renal tubules in the kidney. The renal tubules filter the blood and produce urine. Also called renal cell cancer.

Hyperopia Farsightedness, an individual will have difficulty seeing clearly up close. Light entering the eye focuses behind the retina when the eye is at rest and is corrected with a plus lens. Vision therapy is not prescribed for hyperopia. Children, up to about the age of 8 years, are often farsighted.

Hyperphoria A condition in which one eye has a tendency to point higher than the other eye, causing eyestrain. Sometimes improved by prisms in glasses.

Hyperplasia An abnormal increase in the number of cells in a specific area, such as the lining of the breast ducts. This overgrowth may be due to hormonal stimulation, injury or continuous irritation. By itself, hyperplasia is not cancerous, but when the proliferating cells are atypical (unlike normal cells), the risk of cancer developing is greater.

Hypersensitivity Exaggerated reactions of the immune system. Gell and Coombs described 4 types: Type I, allergy; Type II, cytotoxic reactions (organ transplantation rejection); Type III, immune complex (serum sickness); and Type IV, delayed-type hypersensitivity (contact dermatitis).

Hypertension Hypertension is the persistently elevated arterial blood pressure. It is the most common public health problem in developed countries. Emphasis on lifestyle modifications has given diet a prominent role for both the primary prevention and management of hypertension.

Hyperthermia therapy A type of treatment in which body tissue is exposed to high temperatures to damage and kill cancer cells or to make cancer cells more sensitive to the effects of radiation and certain anticancer drugs.

Hyperthermic perfusion A procedure in which a warmed solution containing anticancer drugs is used to bathe, or is passed through the blood vessels of, the tissue or organ containing the tumor.

Hyperthyroidism Too much thyroid hormone. Symptoms include weight loss, chest pain, cramps, diarrhea, and nervousness. Also called overactive thyroid.

Hypertrophy An increase in the size of a cell, tissue or organ usually as a physiologic response to a stimulus.

Hypertropia Strabismus, one eye turned in an upward direction.

Hyperuricemia A buildup of uric acid (a byproduct of metabolism) in the blood; a side effect of some anticancer drugs.

Hypervariable regions Portions of the light and heavy immuno globulin chains that are highly variable in amino acid sequence from one immunoglobulin molecule to another, and that, together, constitute the antigen-binding site of an antibody molecule. Also, portions of the T-cell receptor which constitute the antigen-binding site.

Hyperventilation Breathing at an abnormally rapid rate at rest, this causes a reduction in carbon dioxide concentration in arterial blood, leading to dizziness, tingling (paraesthesia) in the lips, limbs and tightness across the chest. If continued hyperventilation can cause loss of consciousness. This sequence of events occurs in the Hyperventilation Syndrome (HVS), which has been estimated to contribute to 10% of outpatient referrals to hospital.

Hypnosis A trance-like state in which a person becomes more aware and focused and is more open to suggestion.

Hypo-allergenic A substance which is unlikely to provoke an allergy. Used to describe milk formula, foods medication or creams.

Hypochlorite A weak, unstable salt of hypochlorous acid used in aqueous solutions as a bleach, oxidizer, deodorant, and disinfectant.

Hypogammaglobulinemia A deficiency of gamma globulins (antibodies) in the blood. This condition may occur in late stages of HIV disease when the immune system has been severely damaged.

Hypoglossal trigone An elevation located on the floor of the fourth ventricle on either side of the caudal midline overlying the motor nucleus of the hypoglossal nerve.

Hypoglycemia Too low a level of glucose (sugar) in the blood. This occurs when a person with diabetes has injected too much insulin, eaten too little food, or has exercised without extra food. A person with hypoglycemia may feel nervous, shaky, weak, or sweaty, and have a headache, blurred vision, and hunger. Taking small amounts of sugar, sweet juice, or food with sugar will usually help the person feel better within 10-15 minutes.

Hypoglycemia unawareness A situation in which the usual epinephrine-induced symptoms of a fall in blood sugar are, for a variety of reasons, either not felt or not recognized.

This situation may be dangerous, as the patient may go from functioning normally to unconscious within a short time. It is generally thought that if such a patient is allowed to maintain somewhat elevated blood sugar levels for several weeks, that the hypoglycemic unawareness may resolve.

Hypogonadism Inadequate activity of the ovaries or testes. This can result in abnormally low levels of gonadal hormones (androgens and estrogens) and problems with sperm or egg production. Hypogonadism may occur in men and women with HIV disease.

Hypomobility A decrease in the normal range of joint movement. Often characterised by the loss of accessory movements.

Hypopharyngeal cancer Cancer that forms in tissues of the hypopharynx (the bottom part of the throat). The most common type is squamous cell carcinoma (cancer that begins in flat cells lining the hypopharynx).

Hypopharynx The portion of the pharynx, under the epiglottis, that opens into the larynx and esophagus.

Hypophoria A condition in which one eye has a tendency to point lower than the other eye. This condition may be observed when one eye is covered.

Hypophysis (cerebri) Endocrine gland (pituitary) which occupies the hypophysial fossa of the sphenoid bone. It is attached to the base of the brain (hypothalamus) by the infundibular stalk and consists of the adenohypophysial and neurohypophysial lobes, both of which are under neural control.

Hypoplasia Underdevelopment of a tissue or organ usually due to a decrease in the number of cells.

Hypotension Low blood pressure or a sudden drop in blood pressure. A person rising quickly from a sitting or reclining position may have a sudden fall in blood pressure, causing dizziness or fainting.

Hypothalamus A small subdivision of the diencephalon located below the thalamus on either side of the third ventricle. It is the only part of the diencephalon visible externally at the base of the brain. It is bounded by the optic chiasma anter iorly, the optic tracts laterally and the mammillary bodies caudally. It is concerned with the regulation of visceral, autonomic and endocrine function. and its destruction is incompatible with life.

Hypothesis, alternative The investigator's initial supposition that the study will demonstrate that "something is going on," i.e., results observed are more than the outcome of chance. Common examples include that there is a difference in outcome measures between groups, correlation between factors of interest, or association between exposure and disease, i.e., observations are the result of real differences or correlations.

Hypothesis, null The investigator's initial supposition that the study will demonstrate that "nothing is going on," i.e., results observed are the outcome of chance. Common examples include that there is no difference in outcome measures between groups, no correlation between factors of interest, or no association between exposure and disease, i.e., observations are the result of random variation. Generally, the goal is to "falsify" the null hypothesis.

Hypothyroidism Too little thyroid hormone. Symptoms include weight gain, constipation, dry skin, and sensitivity to the cold. Also called underactive thyroid.

Hypotonia Abnormally decreased tonicity, tension or strength; ocular hypotony refers to low intraocular pressure.

Hypotropia Strabismus, one eye turned in a downward direction.

Hypoxia A condition in which there is a decrease in the oxygen supply to a tissue. In cancer treatment, the level of hypoxia in a tumor may help predict the response of the tumor to the treatment.

Hysterectomy Surgery to remove the uterus and sometimes, the cervix. When the uterus and part or all of the cervix are removed, it is called a total hysterectomy. When only the uterus is removed, it is called a partial hysterectomy.

Hysterical amblyopia A non specific visual loss with an unknown cause. Upon examination the doctor is unable to find corroborating objective evidence of this abnormality. The most common symptom is an isolated visual acuity impairment, followed by combined visual acuity impairment and visual field constriction, and whereas an isolated visual field constriction occurred most infrequently. This vision loss may be due to anxiety or emotional repression.

Hysterosalpingogram (HSG) A radiographic procedure that uses contrast (radiopaque) material injected into the uterus and fallopian tubes. May be used to diagnose fertility problems and anomalies of the female genital tract.

IA "immune response-associated" Proteins, found on B cells and antigen-presenting cells of mice; an old term now replaced with MHC (major histocompatibility complex) class II moslecules.

Ibandronate A synthetic nitrogen-containing bisphosphonate. Ibandronate inhibits farnesyl pyrophosphate synthase, resulting in a reduction in geranylgeranyl GTPase signaling proteins and apoptosis of osteoclasts. This agent increases bone mineral density, decreases bone remodeling, inhibits osteoclast-mediated bone resorption, and reduces metastasesrelated and corticos-teroid-related bone pain.

IBC (Intermediate bulk container) A container for storing, transporting, and handling dry materials. Normally bigger than ½ cubic meter but smaller than 3 cubic meters, dust free, able to receive and discharge a variety of materials, and capable of automation.

IBMFS (Inherited bone marrow failure syndrome) A rare disorder in which a person's bone marrow is unable to make enough blood cells and there is a family history of the same disorder. There are several different inherited bone marrow failure syndromes. Patients with an IBMFS are at high risk of forming acute leukemia or certain solid tumors.

Ice therapy Cooling of deeper tissues, with vasoconstriction and reduction of localised bleeding.

Ichthyosis Any of a group of disorders, usually hereditary, in which there is noninflammatory scaling of the skin.

Idarubicin A semisynthetic anthracycline antineoplastic antibiotic derived from daunorubicin. Idarubicin intercalates into DNA and interacts with topoisomerase II, thereby inhibiting DNA replication and repair and RNA and protein synthesis. Due to its high lipophilicity, idarubicin penetrates cell membranes better than other anthracycline antibiotics. Idarubicin hydrochloride is the therapeutic form of this drug.

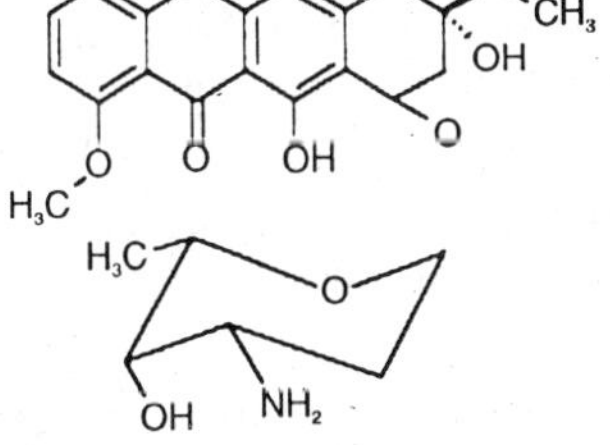

Figure Idarubicin

IDEC-Y2B8 An anticancer drug that is a combination of a monoclonal antibody and a radioisotope (yttrium-90). Monoclonal antibodies are laboratory-produced substances that can locate and bind to cancer cells. Also called yttrium Y90 ibritumomab tiuxetan.

Identical twin Twins produced by the division of a single zygote; both have identical genotypes.

Idiopathic Denoting a disease or condition the cause of which is not known or that arise spontaneously.

Idiopathic myelofibrosis A progressive, chronic disease in which the bone marrow is replaced by fibrous tissue and blood is made in organs such as the liver and the spleen, instead of in the bone marrow. This disease is marked by an enlarged spleen and progressive anemia. Also called chronic idiopathic myelofibrosis, agnogenic myeloid metaplasia, primary myelofibrosis, and myelosclerosis with myeloid metaplasia.

Idiopathic pain Pain without well defined physiological correlates.

Idiopathic thrombocytopenia purpura (ITP) A rare autoimmune disorder characterized by a shortage of platelets in the blood, which results in bruising and spontaneous bleeding.

Idiosyncrasy An unusual or unexpected sensitivity exhibited by an individual to a particular drug or food.

Idiotype The combined antigenic determinants (idiotopes) found on antibodies of an individual that are directed at a particular antigen; such antigenic determinants are found only in the variable region.

IDLH (Immediately dangerous to life and health) A concentration of airborne contaminants, normally expressed in parts per million (ppm) or milligrams per cubic meter, which represents the maximum level from which one could escape within 30 minutes without any escape-impairing symptoms or irreversible health effects. This level is established by the national institute of occupational safety and health (NIOSH).

Idoxifene A drug that blocks the effects of estrogen.

Idoxuridine A drug that reduces the risk of cancer cell growth by interfering with the cells' DNA.

IFOBT (Immunoassay fecal occult blood test) A test to check for blood in the stool. A brush is used to collect water drops from around the surface of a stool while it is still in the toilet bowl. The samples are then sent to a laboratory, where they are checked for a human blood protein. Blood in the stool may be a sign of colourectal cancer. Also called immunologic fecal occult blood test and immuno-chemical fecal occult blood test.

Ifosfamide An anticancer drug that belongs to the family of drugs called alkylating agents.

IgE E-class immunoglobulin (antibody). The type of immunoglobin that triggers release of Histamine from Mast Cells and sets off an acute allergic reaction.

IgG An antibody that reaches peak levels after IgM and sustains the body's defense.

IL 1 (Interleukin-1) A type of biological response modifier that stimulates immune system cells that fight disease, and is involved in inflammatory responses. There are two forms of IL-1, IL-1 alpha and IL-1 beta. Both forms of IL-1 are produced by the body, and can also be made in the laboratory.

IL 1 alpha (Interleukin-1-alpha) A type of biological response modifier (a substance that can improve the body's response to infection and disease). IL-1-alpha stimulates the growth and action of immune system cells that fight disease. IL-1-alpha is normally produced by the body, but it can also be made in the laboratory.

IL 11 (Interleukin-11) A type of biological response modifier (a substance that can improve the body's natural response to disease) that stimulates immune response and may reduce toxicity to the gastrointestinal system resulting from cancer therapy. These substances are normally produced by the body. They are also made in the laboratory for use in treating cancer and other diseases. Also called oprelvekin.

IL 12 (Interleukin-12) A type of biological response modifier (a substance that can improve the body's natural response to disease) that enhances the ability of the immune system to kill tumor cells and may interfere with blood flow to the tumor. These substances are normally produced by the body. They are also made in the laboratory for use in treating cancer and other diseases.

IL 6 (Interleukin-6) A type of biological response modifier (a substance that can improve the body's natural response to infection and disease). These substances are normally produced by the body, but they can also be made in the laboratory.

Ileal vessels Branches of the Superior Mesenteric Artery (SMA) that form the vascular supply to the "ileum" or distal portion of the small intestine.

Ileocecal valve The valve-like structure formed by the flaps of the ileocecal opening. May prevent reflux of colonic contents into the small intestine.

Ileocolic artery The artery which originates from the superior mesenteric and branches into the anterior and posterior cecal, appendicular, colic, and ileal rami arteries.

Ileostomy An opening into the ileum, part of the small intestine, from the outside of the body. An ileostomy provides a new path for waste material to leave the body after part of the intestine has been removed.

Ileum The lowest of the three portions of the small intestines.

Iliac crest The arching ridge of bone on the upper border of the ilium.

Iliac lymph nodes Lymph nodes situated along the iliac vessels.

Iliacus muscle Muscle that originates at the iliac fossa and base of the sacrum, and inserts into the lesser trochanter of the femur. It contributes to the flexion of the thigh and trunk against the lower limb.

Iliolumbar artery Artery which originates from the internal iliac and branches into the iliac and lumbar branches and lateral sacral arteries.

Iliopsoas Deep hip flexor, with attachments to the lumbar spine. Often tight in the presence of lower back pain.

Iliopsoas muscle A compound muscle made up of the iliacus and psoas muscles, a flexor of the hip, inserts onto the lesser trochanter of the proximal femur. The psoas arises along the lateral border of the lumbar spine.

Iliotibial band Laterally situated structure in the thigh. Has action over the hip (muscular attachments of tensor fascia lata and gluteus medius) and over the knee (can act as a flexor at >30° of knee flexion and as an extensor at <30° of flexion). Tends to be a victim of overuse, rather than trauma.

Iliotibial band friction syndrome Pain over the lateral compartment of the knee where the iliotibial band passes over the femoral condyle. Usually brought on by running. Palpation often tender and with compression of the iliotibial band during flexion and extension, pain should be reproduced.

Ilium The superior portion of the hip or pelvic bone.

Ill sustained accommodation This clinical condition is also called Accommodative Fatigue. It is the inability of the eye to adequately sustain sufficient focusing over an extended time period. The most common sign or symptom is blurred vision after prolonged near work such as reading and using a computer. In addition, such patients often have asthenopia (eyestrain). Clinical signs include: normal amplitude of accommodation, decreased PRA, and the patient generally fails the +/-2.00 D flipper test. Plus lenses (glasses or contacts) and vision therapy are effective in treating this condition.

Iloprost A prostacyclin analogue with potential chemopreventive activity. Iloprost binds to the prostacyclin receptor in various target cells, thereby causing vasodilation, inhibition of platelet aggregation, and decreased tumor cell adhesion to endothelium among other effects. Prostacyclin is a naturally occurring eicosanoid with anti-inflammatory, antineoplastic, and anti-metastatic properties.

(E)- (3aS,4R,5R,6aS)-hexahydro-5-hydroxy-4- [(E)- (3S,4RS)-3-hydroxy-4-methyl-1-octen-6-ynyl]- Ä2 (1H),Å-pentalenevaleric acid.

Figure Iloprost

Imaging Any method used to produce an image of internal body structures. Some imaging methods used to detect cancer or metastasis of cancer are x-rays (a breast x-ray is called a mammogram), magnetic resonance imaging (MRI), bone scans, scintigraphy, computerized axial tomography (CAT scans), and ultraso-nography.

Imaging procedure A method of producing pictures of areas inside the body.

Imatinib mesylate The mesylate salt of an antineoplastic agent that inhibits the Bcr-Abl fusion protein tyrosine kinase, an abnormal enzyme produced by chronic myeloid leukemia cells that harbor the Philadelphia chromosome. Imatinib also inhibits the receptor tyrosine kinases for platelet-derived growth factor (PDGF) and stem cell factor (SCF)/c-kit; the SCF/c-kit receptor tyrosine kinase is activated in gastrointestinal stromal tumor (GIST). This agent inhibits proliferation and induces apoptosis in cells that overexpress these oncoproteins.

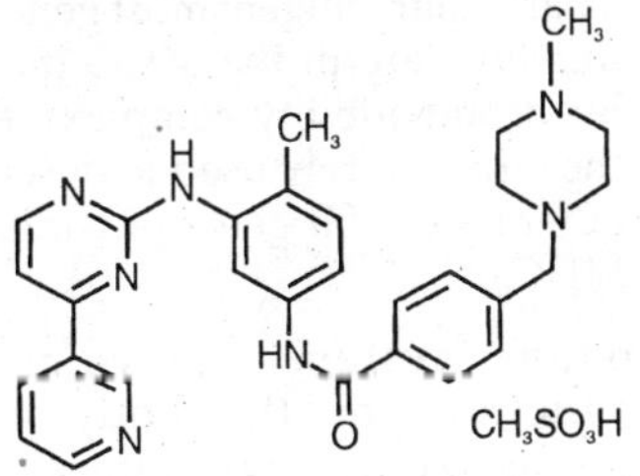

(4-[(4-methyl-1-piperazinyl)methyl]-N-[4-methyl-3-[[4- (3-pyridinyl)-2-pyrimidinyl]amino]-phenyl]benzamide methanesulfonate)

Figure Imatinib mesylate

Imipenem An antibiotic drug used to treat severe or very resistant infection. It belongs to the family of drugs called carbapenems.

Imiquimod A substance that improves the body's natural response to infection and disease. It is used to treat early basal cell skin cancer and other conditions. It is being studied as a topical agent (something used on the surface of the body) for the prevention of some types of cancer. It belongs to the family of drugs called biological response modifiers.

Immediate hypersensitivity: allergy An IgE-mediated response of the immune system. Gell and Coombs Type 1.

Immediate-type hypersensitivity Hypersensitivity tissue reaction occurring within minutes after the interaction of antigen and antibody.

Immobilization Prevention of movement, presumably to allow for natural healing to take place. Side effects include disuse atrophy, deconditioning of muscles and stiffness.

Immune Protected against a particular infection by the presence of specific antibodies against the organisms concerned.

Immune adherence The adherence of particulate antigen coated with C3b to tissue having cells with C3b receptors.

Immune adjuvant A drug that stimulates the immune system to respond to disease.

Immune complex A cluster of interlocking antibodies and antigens.

Immune deficiency A breakdown or inability of certain parts of the immune system to function, thus making a person more susceptible to certain diseases to which the person would not ordinarily be subject. In disease associated with HIV, cell mediated immunity related to the function of T-helper lymphocytes deteriorates, increasing the likelihood of disease from a number of pathogens, many of which are ubiquitous (opportunistic infection).

Immune globulin A preparation of plasma proteins derived from the pooled plasma of adult donors. Largely comprised of IgG antibodies, therapeutic immune globulin provides passive immunization by increasing the recipient's serum levels of circulating antibodies. IgG antibodies have multiple functions, including binding to and neutralizing bacterial toxins; opsonization of pathogens; activation of complement; and suppression of pathogenic cytokines and phagocytes through binding to CD5, interleukin-1a (IL-1a), interleukin 6 (IL-6), tumor necrosis factor-alpha (TNF-alpha), and T-cell receptors. Therapeutic immune globulin may diminish pathogenic mechanisms in some autoimmune diseases by binding to and inhibiting the activity of autoantibodies.

Immune modulators Substances that control the expression of the immune response.

Immune reconstitution syndrome (IRS) Also known as immune restoration disease (IRD) or immune reconstitution inflammatory syndrome (IRIS). An inflammatory reaction that can occur when an immuno-compromised person's immune system improves, such as when a person with HIV disease begins anti-HIV treatment and experi-ences a rise in CD4 cell count. Fever, along with swelling, redness, or discharge at the site of an injury or infection, may signal that an infection previously unnoticed by a weak immune system is now a target of a stronger immune system. Although IRS indicates that a person's immune system has grown healthier, it can be a serious, sometimes fatal condition and must be treated aggressively.

Immune response The response of the immune system to antigens. There are two types of immune response produced by two populations of lymphocytes. B-lymphocytes are responsible for humoral immunity, producing free antibodies that circulate in the blood stream; and T-lymphocytes are responsible for cell-mediated immunity.

Immune response (IR) gene A gene controlling an immune response to a particular antigen; most genes of this type are in the MHC (major histocompatibility complex), and the term is rarely used to describe other types of Ir genes outside the MHC.

Immune system The complex functions of the body that recognize foreign agents or substances, neutralize them, and recall the response later when confronted with the same challenge.

Immune system tolerance The failure of the immune system to respond to an antigen that previously caused an immune response.

Immune thrombocytopenic purpura (ITP) An HIV-related loss of platelets in the blood. Its exact cause is unclear.

Immunity A natural or acquired resistance to a specific disease. Immunity may be partial or complete, long lasting or temporary.

Immunization The production of immunity by artificial means. Passive immunity, which is temporary, may be conferred by the injection of an antiserum, but the production of active immunity calls for the use of treated antigens, to stimulate the body to produce its own antibodies: this is the procedure of vaccination (also called inoculation). The material used for immunization (the vaccine) may consist of live bacteria or viruses so treated that they are harmless while remaining antigenic or completely dead organisms or their products (e.g. toxins) chemically or physically altered to produce the same effect.

Immuno electrophoresis The separation of different antigen-antibody systems by diffusion in an agar gel; a separate precipitation band in the gel detects each system.

Immunoassay A test that uses the binding of antibodies to antigens to identify and measure certain substances. Immunoassays may be used to diagnose disease. Also, test results can provide information about a disease that may help in planning treatment (for example, when estrogen receptors are measured in breast cancer).

Immunocompetence The ability to produce a normal immune response.

Immunocompromised Having a weakened immune system caused by certain diseases or treatments.

Immunocytochemistry A method of detecting cancer in tissues. Monoclonal antibodies are used to stain the tissues and cells before examination under a microscope.

Immunodeficiency The decreased ability of the body to fight infection and disease.

Immunodeficiency syndrome The inability of the body to produce an immune response.

Immunogen A substance capable of inducing an immune response (as well as reacting with the products of an immune response).

Immunogenicity The ability of an antigen or vaccine to stimulate an immune response.

Immunoglobulin A protein that acts as an antibody to help the body fight off disease. There are 5 classes: IgG, IgA, IgD, IgM and IgE. Recombinant and pooled immunoglobulins from blood donations have been used successfully to help HIV-infected children and some adults resist bacterial infections.

Immunoglobulin A (IgA) The body's first line of defense against infectious diseases and is present in seromucous secretions such as saliva, tears, nasal fluids, sweat and secretions of the lung and genito-urinary and gastro-intestinal tracts.

Immunologic failure An HIV-infected individual is said to be experiencing immunologic failure if the individual's CD4 count decreases below his or her baseline count or does not increase above the baseline count within the first year of anti-HIV treatment. People with virologic failure who do not switch to an effective drug regimen usually progress to immunologic failure within about 3 years. Immunologic failure may be followed by clinical failure.

Immunological adjuvant A substance used to help boost the immune response to a vaccine so that less vaccine is needed.

Immunology Study of how the body resists disease or invasion by foreign substances. Knowledge gained in this field is important to understanding how and why cancers develop. Many cancer treatments are based on the principles of immunology.

Immunomodulation Change in the body's immune system, caused by agents that activate or suppress its function.

Immunomodulator Any substance that influences the immune system. Generally the term "immunomodulator" is used.

Immunophenotyping A process used to identify cells, based on the types of antigens or markers on the surface of the cell. This process is used to diagnose specific types of leukemia and lymphoma by comparing the cancer cells to normal cells of the immune system.

Immunoproteins All the proteins concerned with the immune system (antibodies, interferon, and cytokines).

Immunoscintigraphy An imaging procedure in which antibodies labeled with radioactive substances are given to the person. A picture is taken of sites in the body where the antibody localizes.

Immunostimulant A substance that increases the ability of the immune system to fight infection and disease.

Immunosuppression A naturally occurring or induced state in which the ability of the body's immune system to respond is decreased. Certain cancer therapies, including cytotoxic (cancer-cell killing) drugs, radiation, and bone marrow transplant cause immuno-suppression.

Immunosuppressive drugs Drugs that block the body's ability to fight infection or foreign substances that enter the body. A person receiving a kidney or pancreas transplant is given these drugs to stop the body from rejecting the new organ or tissue. Cyclosporin is a commonly used immunosuppressive drug.

Immunotherapeutic Aiming at reconstituting an impaired immune system.

Immunotherapy Treatment to stimulate or restore the ability of the immune system to fight cancer, infections, and other diseases. Also used to lessen certain side effects that may be caused by cancer treatment. Also called biological therapy, biotherapy, or biological response modifier (BRM) therapy.

Immunotoxin An antibody linked to a toxic substance. Some immunotoxins can bind to cancer cells and kill them.

Impaction Partial or completely unexposed tooth that is wedged against another tooth, bone, or soft tissue, precluding the eruption process.

Impaired glucose tolerance (IGT) Blood glucose (sugar) levels higher than normal but not high enough to be called diabetes. People with IGT may or may not develop diabetes. Other names (no longer used) for IGT are "borderline," "subclinical," "chemical," or "latent" diabetes.

Imperforate anus Caused by improper development of the baby's rectum and anus during pregnancy. The opening at the end of the rectum or anus is absent, so stool cannot leave the body normally.

Impetigo A skin infection due to the Staphylococcus Bacterium, it forms scabs and has a 'honey-crust' appearance.

Implant Any inert foreign or autogenous material embedded within the living tissue in the orbit.

Implant radiation A procedure in which radioactive material sealed in needles, seeds, wires, or catheters is placed directly into or near a tumor. Also called brachytherapy, internal radiation, or interstitial radiation.

Implantable cardioverter defibrillator (ICD) A device implanted in the abdomen or pectoral region which is used to treat potentially fatal fast heart rhythms by delivering electrical energy to the heart to restore the heart's normal rhythms.

Implantable insulin pump A small pump placed inside of the body that delivers insulin in response to commands from a hand-held device called a programmer.

Implanted Placed inside the body. The AICD system is an implanted system.

Impotence The loss of a man's ability to have an erect penis and to emit semen. Some men may become impotent after having diabetes for a long time because the nerves or blood vessels have become damaged. Sometimes the problem has nothing to do with diabetes and may be treated with counseling.

Impression Mold made of the teeth and soft tissues.

Impression moulding technique An adapted version from the dental profession for obtaining an accurate copy of the anophthalmic socket, and/or affected eye with a suitable impression tray.

Impression tray An acrylic scleral shell with multiple fenestration's and an attached tube for injection of an alginate impression gel. The excess gel will flow through the holes. Once set the gel and tray can be removed as a unit.

Imprinting A phenomenon in which the disease phenotype depends on which parent passed on the disease gene. For instance, both Prader-Willi and Angelman syndromes are inherited when the same part of chromosome 15 is missing. When the father's complement of 15 is missing, the child has Prader-Willi, but when the mother's complement of 15 is missing, the child has Angelman syndrome.

Impurity Any component present in the intermediate or API (Active

Pharmaceutical Ingredient) that is not the desired entity. It may be either process or product related.

Impurity profile A description of the identified and unidentified impurities present in a typical batch of API (Active Pharmaceutical Ingredient) produced by a specific controlled production process. It includes the identity or some qualitative analytical designation (e.g. retention time), the range of each impurity observed, and type of each identified impurity. For each API there should be an impurity profile describing the identified and unidentified impurities present in a typical batch. The impurity profile is normally dependent upon the process or origin of the API.

In line An integral part of the flow path. In a fluid stream, something is said to be in-line if the entire fluid stream flows directly through or past it.

In process control Checks performed during production in order to monitor and if necessary to adjust the process and/or to ensure that the intermediate or API (Active Pharmaceutical Ingredient) conforms to its specification. (Also called process control).

In situ cancer Early cancer that has not spread to neighbouring tissue.

In situ hybridization Use of a DNA or RNA probe to detect the presence of the complementary DNA sequence in cloned bacterial or cultured eukaryotic cells.

In utero Latin for "in the uterus," or womb.

In vitro fertilization The most common type of assisted reproductive technology, in which eggs are removed from the ovary, fertilized in a laboratory and transferred days later into the uterine cavity.

In vivo Latin for "in life" : Studies conducted within a living organism, e.g., animal or human studies.

Inactivated vaccine Dead microorganisms used as antigens to produce immunity.

Inactivation Any process that destroys the ability of a specific microbiological agent or eukaryotic cell to self-replicate.

Inactive control treatment A control treatment that is not considered to have any pharmacological or physiological effect. A placebo treatment or sham procedure.

Inactive ingredient Any component other than an active ingredient.

Incidence In epidemiology, the number of cases of disease, infection, or some other event having their onset during a prescribed period of time in relation to the unit of population in which they occur. Incidence measures morbidity or other events as they happen over a period of time. Examples include the number of accidents occurring in a manufacturing plant during a year in relation to the number of employees in the plant, or the number of cases of mumps occurring in a school during a month in relation to the number of pupils enrolled in the school. It usually refers only to the number of new cases, particularly of chronic diseases. Hospitals also track certain risk management or quality problems with a system called incidence reporting.

Incidence rate A measure of morbidity based on the number of new episodes of illness arising in a population over an estimated period. It can be expressed in terms of sick persons or episodes per 1000 individuals at risk. Compare prevalence rate.

Incidental release The discharge of a microbilogical agent or eukaryotic cell from a containment system that is expected when the system is appropriately designed and properly operated and maintained. Incidental releases are de minimis in nature.

Incision The cut or wound produced by cutting into the body in order to perform surgery; the cut becomes a scar after surgery.

Incision and drainage Surgical incision of an abscess to drain suppuration (pus).

Incisional biopsy A surgical procedure in which a portion of a lump or suspicious area is removed for diagnosis. The tissue is then examined under a microscope.

Incisors Four upper and four lower front teeth, excluding the cuspids (canine teeth).

Inclusion body Condensed particles of protein formed inside E. coli and other bacteria formed when the cells are forced to make large amounts of a product protein. The cells must be broken to harvest inclusion bodies.

Inclusion/exclusion criteria A specific set of selection rules that determine whether a person is eligible to enroll in a particular clinical trial. For example, some trials may not accept people with chronic liver disease or with certain drug allergies. Others may exclude men or women, or only include people with a certain CD4 count or viral load.

Incomitant strabismus A condition also known as Noncomitant Strabismus. It occurs when the magnitude of deviation is not the same in the different positions of gaze or with either eye fixating. There is an abnormal restriction to movement or an over-action of one or more of the extraocular muscles. Generally, the magnitude must change by at least 5 PD to be incomitant (nonconcomitant).

Incomplete Freund's adjuvant A water-in-oil emulsion that stimulates the T-cell immune response to antigens and may be used in various types of cancer vaccines.

Incontinence Inability to control the flow of urine from the bladder (urinary incontinence) or the escape of stool from the rectum (fecal incontinence).

Incubated Grown in the laboratory under controlled conditions. (For instance, white blood cells can be grown in special conditions so that they attack specific cancer cells when returned to the body.)

Incubation period (latent period) The interval between exposure to an infection and the appearance of the first symptoms.

Incus The middle ossicle of the ear, that helps to conduct vibrations from the tympanic membrane to the oval window of the inner ear.

Together, the incus and malleus look like an ice cream cone.

I ıdependent assortment During meiosis each of the two copies of a gene is distributed to the germ cells independently of the distribution of other genes.

Indian cress Nasturtium officinale. Parts of the flowering plant have been used in some cultures to treat certain medical problems. It may have anticancer effects. Also called watercress.

Indian elm Ulmus fulva or Ulmus rubra. The inner bark of this plant has been used in some cultures to treat certain medical problems. It may have antioxidant effects. Also called slippery elm, gray elm, red elm, and sweet elm.

Indian filing An extension of single rows of cells between and around collagen bundles.

Indian rhubarb Rheum palmatum or Rheum officinale. The root of this plant has been used in some cultures to treat certain medical problems. It may have anti-inflammatory and anticancer effects. Also called rhubarb, da-huang, Chinese rhubarb, and Turkish rhubarb.

Indian valerian Valeriana officinalis. A plant whose roots are used as a sedative and to treat certain medical conditions. It is being studied as a way to improve sleep in cancer patients undergoing treatment. Also called valerian, garden valerian, Pacific valerian, Mexican valerian, garden heliotrope, and Valerianae radix.

Indication Sign or symptom. Also, in terms of drug approval, the exact cause or purpose for which a drug is approved to be prescribed. Also called "label indication"

Indicator A variable that helps to measure changes directly or indirectly and permits one to assess the extent to which objectives and targets of a program are being attained. In medicine, indicators help to measure changes in the health situation of a population.

Indigestion Feeling of nausea, bloating, gas, and/or heartburn caused by poor digestion.

Indinavir A drug that interferes with the ability of a virus to make copies of itself.

Indirect impact system An engineering system considered having no direct impact on product quality.

Indole 3 carbinol A naturally occurring, orally available cleavage product of the glucosinolate glucobrassicanin, a natural compound present in a wide variety of plant food substances including members of the family Cruciferae with antioxidant and potential chemopreventive properties. Indole-3-carbinol scavenges free radicals and induces various hepatic cytochrome P450 mono-oxygenases. Specifically, this agent induces the hepatic monooxygenase cytochrome P4501A1 (CYP1A1), resulting in increased 2-hydroxylation of estrogens and increased production of the chemoprotective estrogen 2-hydroxyestrone.

Indolent A type of cancer that grows slowly.

Indolent lymphoma A type of lymphoma that tends to grow and spread slowly, and has few symptoms. Also called low-grade lymphoma.

Indomethacin A synthetic nonsteroidal indole derivative with anti-inflammatory activity and chemopreventive properties. As a nonsteroidal anti-inflammatory drug (NSAID), indomethacin inhibits the enzyme cyclooxygenase, thereby preventing cyclooxygenase-mediated DNA adduct formation by heterocyclic aromatic amines. This agent also may inhibit the expression of multidrug-resistant protein type 1, resulting in increased efficacies of some antineoplastic agents in treating multi-drug resistant tumors. In addition, indomethacin activates phosphatases that inhibit the migration and proliferation of cancer cells and downregulates survivin, which may result in tumor cell apoptosis.

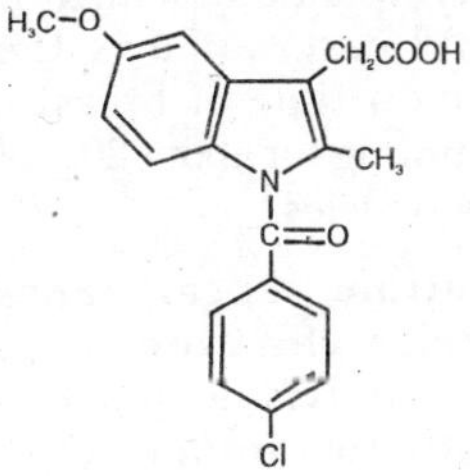

H_3C–O CH_2COOH CH_3 N   C=O   Cl

Indomethacin (1- (4-chlorobenzoyl)-5-methoxy-2-methyl-1-H-indole-3-acetic acid)

Figure Indomethacin

Induced sputum A test where saline mist is breathed to induce a cough. Resultant sputum is then cultured or stained to look for micro-organisms, often pneumocystis carinii.

Induction The initiation of a particular therapy.

Induction therapy Treatment designed to be used as a first step toward shrinking the cancer and in evaluating response to drugs and other agents. Induction therapy is followed by additional therapy to eliminate whatever cancer remains.

Indurated Abnormally hard.

Indusium griseum A thin vestigial layer of gray matter located on the upper surface of the corpus callosum (supracallosal gyrus) continuous posteriorly with the fasciolar and dentate gyri. Imbedded within the indusium griseum are two longitudinal strands of white matter, the medial and lateral longitudinal striae which are rudimentary in man.

Inert Does not dissolve in water or react chemically with other substances.

Infarct A localized area of ischemic necrosis produced by the occlusion of the blood vessels - either arterial supply or venous drainage.

Infection Invasion and multiplication of germs in the body. Infections can occur in any part of the body and can spread throughout the body. The germs may be bacteria, viruses, yeast, or fungi. They can cause a fever and other problems, depending on where the infection occurs. When the body's natural defense system is strong, it can often fight the germs and prevent infection. Some cancer treatments can weaken the natural defense system.

Infectious agent A biological organism that can establish a process of infection.

Infectious Capable of being transmitted by infection, with or without actual contact.

Inferior (temporal) horn The portion of the lateral ventricle which stretches from the pars centralis, behind the thalamus, into the temporal lobe.

Inferior gluteal artery The artery which originates from the internal iliac and branches into the sciatic artery.

Inferior mesenteric artery Artery which originates from the abdominal aorta and branches into the left colic, sigmoid, and superior rectal arteries.

Inferior mesenteric vein The vein that parallels the inferior mesenteric artery and drains into the splenic vein.

Inferior orbital fissure Located in the inferolateral wall of the orbit, it allows for the passage of the infraorbital and zygomatic nerves and infraorbital vessels. It is surrounded by the greater wing of the sphenoid and the orbital process of the maxilla.

Inferior pubic ramus Portion of the pubic bone which projects postero-inferolaterally to join the ramus of the ischium.

Inferior vena cava The vein that begins at the junction of the two common iliac veins, at the level of the fifth lumbar vertebra, and empties into the right atrium. It drains blood from the lower extremities, and the pelvic and abdominal viscera.

Infertile Unable to produce children.

Infertility A failure to conceive during a year of unprotected intercourse. For couples who are older or have had problems with their reproductive organs, doctors sometimes consider them infertile after six months.

Infiltrates Something seeping or filling in a space or cavity.

Infiltrating cancer Cancer that has spread beyond the layer of tissue in which it developed and is growing into surrounding, healthy tissues. Also called invasive cancer.

Infiltrating ductal carcinoma A cancer that starts in the milk passages (ducts) of the breast and then breaks through the duct wall, where it invades the fatty tissue of the breast. When it reaches this point, it has the potential to spread (metastasize) elsewhere in the breast, as well as to other parts of the body through the bloodstream and lymphatic system. Infiltrating ductal carcinoma is the most common type of breast cancer, accounting for about 80% of breast malignancies.

Infiltration Local anesthetic procedure effective for upper teeth and soft tissue; placement of anesthetic under the gum, allowing it to seep into bone.

Inflammation The body's response to injury, which may be acute or chronic. Acute inflammation is the immediate defensive reaction of the tissue to any injury. It involves pain, heat, redness, swelling, and loss of function of the affected part. In certain circumstances healing does not occur and chronic inflammation.

Inflammatory Having to do with inflammation (redness, swelling, pain, and a feeling of heat that helps protect tissues affected by injury or disease).

Inflammatory bowel disease (IBD) Diseases that cause irritation and ulcers in the intestinal tract. Crohn's disease and ulcerative colitis are the most common inflammatory bowel diseases.

Inflammatory breast cancer A type of breast cancer in which the breast looks red and swollen and feels warm. The skin of the breast may also show the pitted appearance called peau d'orange (like the skin of an orange). The redness and warmth occur because the cancer cells block the lymph vessels in the skin.

Infliximab A monoclonal antibody that blocks the action of a cytokine called tumor necrosis factor alfa. It is being studied in the treatment and prevention of weight loss and loss of appetite in patients with advanced cancer. It belongs to the family of drugs called monoclonal antibodies.

Informatics The study of the application of computer and statistical techniques to the management of information. In genome projects, informatics includes the development of methods to search databases quickly, to analyze DNA sequence information, and to predict protein sequence and structure from DNA sequence data.

Information management A method used to organize information to avoid information overload and to keep information in a format that is efficient to retrieve whenever needed. Filing systems, cognitive maps, manuals, and electronic databases are examples of devices that can prove useful in information management. A network of consultants is an additional way to ensure that necessary information will be readily available.

Informed consent A process in which a person learns key facts about a clinical trial, including potential risks and benefits, before deciding whether or not to participate in a study. Informed consent continues throughout the trial.

Infra Beneath, e.g. infraorbital - beneath the eye.

Infraclavicular nodes Lymph nodes located beneath the clavicle (collar bone); a part of the network of axillary (armpit) nodes.

Infrapatellar bursa Fluid filled sac located between the patellar ligament and the skin.

Infrapatellar fat pad Lies deep to the patellar ligament and fills the space between the condyles of the tibia and the femur.

Infrared coagulation A technique in which abnormal tissue is exposed to a burst of infrared light (a type of radiation). This causes blood in veins in the tissue to coagulate (harden) and the abnormal tissue to shrink. It is being studied in the prevention of anal cancer in some patients with HIV.

Infraspinatus muscle Muscle responsible for the lateral rotation of the humerus. It originates from below the scapula spine (infraspinous fossa) and inserts onto the greater tubercle of the humerus.

Infratentorial Below the tentorium cerebelli and within the posterior cranial fossa.

Infundibulum Funnel-shaped evagination of the floor of the third ventricle from which the pituitary stalk arises.

Infusion A method of putting fluids, including drugs, into the bloodstream. Also called intravenous infusion.

Infusion pump A device that delivers measured amounts of fluids or medications into the bloodstream over a period of time.

Ingenol 3 angelate A selective small-molecule activator of protein kinase C (PKC) isolated from the plant Euphorbia peplus with potential antineoplastic activity. Ingenol 3-angelate (I3A) activates various protein kinase C (PKC) isoforms, thereby inducing apoptosis in some tumor cells, including myeloid leukemia cells, melanoma cells, and basal cell carcinoma cells. The PKC family consists of signaling isoenzymes that regulate many cell processes including proliferation, differentiation, and apoptosis.

Ingestion Taking food, water, or medicine into the body by mouth.

Inguinal hernia Part of the small intestine that pushes through an opening in the abdominal muscle, causing a bulge underneath the skin in the groin area.

Inguinal lymph nodes Lymph nodes situated along the inguinal vessels.

Inguinal orchiectomy An operation in which the testicle is removed through an incision in the groin.

Inhalant allergen An allergy provoking protein suspended in the air that we breathe.

Inhalation In medicine, refers to the act of taking a substance into the body by breathing.

Inhaler A device for giving medicines in the form of a spray that is inhaled (breathed in) through the nose or mouth. Inhalers are used to treat medical problems such as bronchitis, angina, emphysema, and asthma. They are also used to help relieve symptoms that occur when a person is trying to quit smoking.

Inherit To receive certain defined characteristics from a parent by transmission of the genes in the egg and sperm.

Inherited Transmitted through genes that have been passed from parents to their offspring (children).

Inion A craniometric landmark located at the apex of the external occipital protuberance.

Injection A preparation intended for parenteral administration and/or constituting or diluting a parenteral article prior to administration. The introduction of parenterals may be into the subcutaneous cellular tissue (subcutaneous or hypodermic), or the muscular tissue (Intramuscular).

Injection drug user (IDU, IVDU, AVDA) Also known as intravenous drug user (IVDU), or intravenous drug abuser (IVDA). None of these terms are very precise: often IVDU will be used to describe someone who injects IM or Sub-Q, and the distinction between "user" and "abuser" is a controversial and emotionally charged one. Nevertheless, a working definition for an IDU is anyone who regularly injects any substances, whether pharmaceutically or illicitly made, not under medical prescription and supervision.

Injection site rotation Changing the places on the body where a person injects insulin. Changing the injection site keeps lumps or small dents from forming in the skin. These lumps or dents are called lipodystrophies. However, people should try to use the same body area for injections that are given at the same time each day-for example, always using the stomach for the morning injection or an arm for the evening injection. Using the same body area for these routine injections lessens the possibility of changes in the timing and action of insulin.

Injection sites Places on the body where people can inject insulin most easily. These are:

The outer area of the upper arm.

Just above and below the waist, except the area right around the navel (a 2-inch circle).

The upper area of the buttock, just behind the hip bone.

The front of the thigh, midway to the outer side, 4 inches below the top of the thigh to 4 inches above the knee.

These areas can vary with the size of the person.

Inlay indirect Filling made by a dental laboratory that is cemented or bonded into place, direct - placement of dental composite resin restoration at chairside.

Inner table of skull The inner layer of compact bone of the flat bones of the skull. The periosteal layer of the dura is attached to the inner table.

Innocuous Safe, not contaminated.

Inoculum 1. Fermentation: an aliquot of a pure culture of microorganism added to the primary seed tank to initiate fermentation.

Inoperable Describes a condition that cannot be treated by surgery.

Inositol A type of sugar that has a different chemical structure than glucose (the chief source of energy for living organisms). It is a basic part of cell membranes, and is important in nerve, brain, and muscle function. Inositol is found in many foods that come from plants, and is being studied in the prevention of cancer.

Inositol hexaphosphate (IP6) A substance found in many foods that come from plants, including corn, wheat, rice, and soybeans, and in large amounts in cereals and legumes. It is being studied in the prevention of cancer. Also called phytic acid.

Inpatient care Care given a registered bed patient in a hospital, nursing home or other medical or post acute institution.

INS316 A substance that is being studied in the diagnosis of lung diseases, including lung cancer. It helps bring up a sample of mucus from deep in the lungs and improves the quality of the sample for testing. It belongs to the family of drugs called nucleoside triphosphates.

Insecticide Insecticides are a class of crop protection and specialty chemicals used to control insects on farms and forests, as well as non-agricultural applications such as residential lawncare, golf courses and public tracts of land.

Insemination The placement of semen into a woman's uterus, cervix, or vagina.

Insertion A chromosome abnormality in which a piece of DNA is incorporated into a gene and thereby disrupts the gene's normal function.

Insoluble fiber A type of dietary fiber found in wheat bran, cauliflower, cabbage and other vegetables and fruits which helps move foods through the digestive system and thereby may decrease the risks of cancers of the colon and rectum. Insoluble fiber may also help reduce the risk of breast cancer.

Insomnia Difficulty in going to sleep or getting enough sleep.

Insterstitial A space or gap in a tissue: in the context of "interstitial infiltrates", means between the air passage in a lung

Instillation In medicine, a method used to put a liquid into the body slowly or drop by drop.

Insula Cerebral cortical area within the depths of the lateral fissure (of Sylvius) beneath the frontal, temporal, and parietal opercula. It overlies the putamen and claustrum. Also known as the Island of Reil and sometimes consider ed the 5th "lobe".

Insulin A hormone made by the islet cells of the pancreas. Insulin controls the amount of sugar in the blood by moving it into the cells, where it can be used by the body for energy.

Insulin allergy When a person's body has an allergic or bad reaction to taking insulin made from pork or beef or from bacteria, or because the insulin is not exactly the same as human insulin or because it has impurities.

The allergy can be of two forms. Sometimes an area of skin becomes red and itchy around the place where the insulin is injected. This is called a local allergy.

In another form, a person's whole body can have a bad reaction This is called a systemic allergy. The person can have hives or red patches all over the body or may feel changes in the heart rate and in the rate of breathing. A doctor may treat this allergy by prescribing purified insulins or by desensitization.

Insulin analog A synthetic modification of insulin where specific amino acids have been substituted for the natural ones at one or more places on the insulin molecule.

Insulin antagonist Something that opposes or fights the action of insulin. Insulin lowers the level of glucose (sugar) in the blood, whereas glucagon raises it; therefore, glucagon is an antagonist of insulin.

Insulin binding When insulin attaches itself to something else. This can occur in two ways. First, when a cell needs energy, insulin can bind with the outer part of the cell. The cell then can bring glucose (sugar) inside and use it for energy. With the help of insulin, the cell can do its work very well and very quickly. But sometimes the body acts against itself. In this second case, the insulin binds with the proteins that are supposed to protect the body from outside substances (antibodies). If the insulin is an injected form of insulin and not made by the body, the body sees the insulin as an outside or "foreign" substance. When the injected insulin binds with the antibodies, it does not work as well as when it binds directly to the cell.

Insulin induced atrophy Small dents that form on the skin when a person keeps injecting a needle in the same spot. They are harmless.

Insulin pen An insulin injection device the size of a pen that includes a needle and holds a vial of insulin. It can be used instead of syringes for giving insulin injections.

Insulin pump A device that delivers a continuous supply of short-acting insulin into the body. The insulin flows from the pump through a plastic tube (called a catheter) that is connected to a needle inserted into the skin and taped in place.

Insulin is delivered at different rates, which can be either manually set or preprogrammed: a low, steady rate (called the basal rate) for continuous day-long coverage, and extra boosts of insulin (called bolus doses) to cover meals or when extra insulin is needed. Both the basal and bolus rates are adjustable by the user, in response to blood sugar tests done with standard methods; no available pump can measure the sugar level and calculate what changes to make in the insulin doses.

The pump runs on batteries and can be worn clipped to a belt or carried in a pocket. It is usually used by people with insulin-dependent diabetes, although it is occasionally recommended for people with other forms of diabetes.

Insulin reaction Too low a level of glucose (sugar) in the blood; also called hypoglycemia. This occurs when a person with diabetes has injected too much insulin, eaten too little food, or exercised without extra food. The person may feel hungry, nauseated, weak, nervous, shaky, confused, and sweaty. Taking small amounts of sugar, sweet juice, or food with sugar will usually help the person feel better within 10-15 minutes.

Insulin receptors Areas on the outer part of a cell that allow the cell to join or bind with insulin that is in the blood. When the cell and insulin bind together, the cell can take glucose (sugar) from the blood and use it for energy.

Insulin resistance A state in which a given level of serum insulin produces a less than expected biological effect. Patients may vary from normoglycemic to severely diabetic despite large doses of insulin. Many people with Type 2 diabetes produce enough insulin, but their bodies do not respond to the action of insulin. This may happen because the person is overweight and does not respond well to insulin. Also, as people age, their body cells lose some of the ability to respond to insulin. Insulin resistance is also linked to high blood pressure and high levels of fat in the blood

Another kind of insulin resistance may rarely happen in people who take insulin injections. They may have to take very high doses of insulin every day (e.g., 200 units or more (in adults)) to bring their blood glucose down to the normal range. This has also been called "insulin insensitivity."

Insulin sensitizer Any of several diabetes medications that reduce insulin resistance. Examples include metformin (Glucophage) and the thiazolidinediones (or "glitazones") rosiglitazone (Avandia) and pioglitazone (Actos).

Insulin-induced hypertrophy Small lumps that form under the skin when a person keeps injecting a needle in the same spot.

Insulinoma A tumor of the beta cells in areas of the pancreas called the islets of Langerhans. Although not usually cancerous, such tumors may cause the body to make extra insulin and may lead to a blood glucose (sugar) level that is too low.

Integrase An HIV protein that plays an important role in the virus's life cycle. Integrase inserts HIV's genetic information into the infected cell's own DNA.

Integrase inhibitors A class of anti-HIV drugs that prevents the HIV integrase protein from inserting HIV's genetic information into an infected cell's own DNA.

Integrated Associated with moveable ocular implants: Attachment of the recti (eye muscles) to the implant.

Integrated teaching A method of teaching that interrelates or unifies subjects frequently taught in separate academic courses or departments. In integrated teaching, subjects are presented together as a meaningful whole. Integration may be vertical or horizontal. Horizontal integration functions between parallel disciplines such as anatomy, histology, biochemistry or medicine, surgery and pharmacology. Vertical integra-tion functions between disciplines traditionally taught in different phases of curriculum; it can occur throughout the curriculum with medical and basic sciences beginning together in the early years.

Integration The process by which HIV integrase inserts HIV's genetic material into an infected cell's own DNA. This crucial step in HIV's life cycle is targeted by the class of anti-HIV drugs called integrase inhibitors.

Intellectual property rights Patents, copyrights, and trademarks.

Intensification Adding additional anti-HIV drugs to an existing treatment regimen, usually because that regimen failed to adequately control HIV replication.

Intensification therapy A type of high-dose chemotherapy often given as the second phase (after induction therapy) of a cancer treatment regimen for leukemia. Also called consolidation therapy.

Intensity modulated radiation therapy (IMRT) A type of 3-dimensional radiation therapy that uses computer-generated images to show the size and shape of the tumor. Thin beams of radiation of different intensities are aimed at the tumor from many angles. This type of radiation therapy reduces the damage to healthy tissue near the tumor.

Intensive care management Intensive community services for individuals with severe and persistent mental illness that are designed to improve planning for their service needs. Services include outreach, evaluation, and support.

Intensive management A form of treatment for insulin-dependent diabetes in which the main objective is to keep blood glucose (sugar) levels as close to the normal range as possible. The treatment consists of three or more insulin injections a day or use of an insulin pump; four or more blood glucose tests a day; adjustment of insulin, food intake, and activity levels based on blood glucose test results; dietary counseling; and management by a diabetes team.

Intention to treat analysis A method of data analysis in which the primary tabulations, summaries and comparisons of patient outcome data are by assigned treatment, regardless of compliance to therapy or the protocol.

Inter Between, e.g. intercellular - between two cells.

Interaction A situation in which the magnitude of the test-control treatment difference for the outcome of interest depends upon the value assumed by a third factor, such as age or prior disease state of the study patients.

Interaction effect Treatment interaction effect.

Intercalator In biochemistry, a type of molecule that binds to DNA and inserts itself into the DNA structure. Some intercalators are used as treatments for cancer.

Intercondylar eminences A projection on the proximal end of the tibia, set in between two tubercles.

Intercostal muscles Muscles lying between ribs and are often injured by rotary stress of the thorax.

Intercurrent Occurring at the same time, or accompanying.

Interface A means of communication between two computer systems, two software applications or two modules. Real time interface is a key element in healthcare information systems due to the need to access patient care information and financial information instantaneously and comprehensively. Such real time communication is the key to managing health care in a cost effective manner because it provides the necessary decision-making information for clinicians, providers and payers.

Interferon (IFN) A cytokine (protein that regulates immune system activity) that the body produces to fight viruses. Laboratory-made versions of IFN are used in the treatment of some virus infections and cancers. There are three main types of interferon: alpha, beta, and gamma. IFN alpha is used to treat hepatitis C virus (HCV) infection and many cancers, including Kaposi's sarcoma.

Interferon alpha A class of naturally-isolated or recombinant therapeutic peptides used as antiviral and anti-tumor agents. Alpha interferons are cytokines produced by nucleated cells (predominantly natural killer (NK) leukocytes) upon exposure to live or inactivated virus, double-stranded RNA or bacterial products. These agents bind to specific cell-surface receptors, resulting in the transcription and translation of genes containing an interferon-specific response element. The proteins so produced mediate many complex effects, including antiviral effects (viral protein synthesis); antiproliferative effects (cellular growth inhibition and alteration of cellular differentiation); anticancer effects (interference with oncogene expression); and immune-modulating effects (natural killer cell activation, alteration of cell surface antigen expression, and augmentation of lymphocyte and macrophage cytotoxicity).

Interferon gamma A recombinant therapeutic agent which is chemically identical to or similar to the endogenous lymphokine interferon gamma (IFN-gamma) with antineoplastic, immunoregulatory, and antiviral activities. Therapeutic IFN-gamma binds to and activates the cell-surface IFN-gamma receptor, stimulating antibody-dependent cytotoxicity and enhances natural killer cell attachment to tumor cells. This agent also activates caspases, thereby inducing apoptosis in malignant cells.

Interhemispheric fissure The cleft between the two cerebral hemispheres, containing CSF and the falx cerebri.

Interim analysis Any data analysis done before the trial is finished, for whatever reason, but usually concerned with assessments of treatment effects.

Interim result 1. Any test-control treatment difference observed during the trial.

2. A test-control treatment difference observed during the trial that results in a treatment protocol change.

Interleukin A biological response modifier (substance that can improve the body's natural response to infection and disease) that helps the immune system fight infection and cancer. These substances are normally produced by the body. They are also made in the laboratory for use in treating cancer and other diseases.

Interleukin 1 beta A recombinant therapeutic agent which is chemically identical to or similar to the endogenous protein cytokine interleukin 1 (IL-1)-beta. Produced by monocytes and activated macrophages, endogenous mature IL-1 is generated through proteolytic cleavage by proteases such as IL-

1-beta converting enzyme (ICE). This agent promotes angiogenesis, fibroblast proliferation, and neutrophil chemotaxis; it also regulates the functions of lymphocytes and epithelial cells and is involved in the 'acute phase response' to infection.

Intermediate gray (zone) Zone of spinal cord gray matter that lies between the anterior and posterior horns corresponding to lamina VII of Rexed. This zone includes the nucleus dorsalis (of Clarke), intermediomedial, intermediolateral, and sacral autonomic nuclei.

Intermediate-grade lymphoma A type of lymphoma that grows and spreads quickly, and has severe symptoms. It is seen frequently in patients who are HIV-positive (AIDS-related lymphoma). Also called aggressive or high-grade lymphoma.

Intermediolateral nucleus Cell column which occupies lateral part of lamina VII (of Rexed) in thoracic and upper lumbar segments (T1-L2) of the spinal cord only. It marks the location of neuronal cell bodies that give rise to preganglionic sym pathetic fibers.

Intermittent claudication Pain in the muscles of the leg that occurs off and on, usually while walking or exercising, and results in lameness (claudication). The pain results from a narrowing of the blood vessels feeding the muscle. Drugs are available to treat this condition.

Internal auditory meatus The channel that allows for the passaage of the facial, intermediate, and vestibuloco-chlear nerves, and the labrynthine artery to pass.

Internal capsule Concentration of protection fibers within the depths of each cerebral hemisphere between the thalamus, caudate and lenticular nuclei. It consists of an anterior limb, genu, and posterior (lenticulothalamic) limb. The corticipit al and corticofugal fibers contained within this confined region are on their way to and from widespread areas of the cerebral cortex.

Internal iliac artery Artery which is a continuation of the common iliac and branches into the iliolumbar, obturator, superior gluteal, inferior gluteal, umbilical, inferior vesicle, uterine, middle rectal, and internal pudendal arteries.

Internal iliac vein The vein originating from the parietal branches at the level of the greater sciatic notch, and extends to the brim of the pelvis where it joins the external iliac to form the common iliac vein.

Internal image A spatial configuration of the combining site of an anti-idiotype antibody which resembles the epitope to which the idiotype is directed.

Internal mammary nodes Lymph nodes beneath the breast bone on each side. The lymph glands of the breast drain into the internal mammary nodes.

Internal medicine Generally, that branch of medicine that is concerned with diseases that do not require surgery, specifically, the study and treatment of internal organs and body systems; it encompasses many subspecialties; internists, the doctors who practice internal medicine, often serve as family physicians to supervise general medical care.

Internal oblique muscle Muscles which originates at the inguinal ligamen, iliac crest, and lumbar aponeurosis, and inserts into the lower three or four costal cartilages, the linea alba, and the conjoined tendon to the pubis. It is responsible for flexion and rotation of the vertebral column and compression of the abdominal viscera.

Internal radiation A procedure in which radioactive material sealed in needles, seeds, wires, or catheters is placed directly into or near a tumor. Also called brachytherapy, implant radiation, or interstitial radiation therapy.

Internal thoracic artery Artery which orginates from the subclavian, and branches into the mediastinal, thymic, bronchial, tracheal, sternal, perforating, medial mammary, lateral musculophrenic, and superior epigastric arteries.

Internal thoracic veins The two veins created from the junction of the venae comitantes of the internal thoracic arteries, and empties into the brachiocephalic vein.

Internship A first postgraduate training year in which graduates practice medicine under supervision. In some countries this is a requirement for licensure. In many countries and for many specialties such as internal medicine, pediatrics and surgery, this is the first year of residency. However, as there are some specialties that are too narrow to provide a broad medical practice experience, those residents may have to attend a transitional year in one of the above specialties or a rotating internship.

Interocclusal Space between upper and lower teeth.

Interpeduncular fossa Depression along the midline of the ventral surface of the midbrain between the two cerebral peduncles.

Interphase The period in the cell cycle when DNA is replicated in the nucleus; followed by mitosis.

Interproximal Surfaces of adjoining teeth.

Interstim continence control therapy A therapy used in treating urge incontinence. A device, about the size of a pacemaker, that is implanted into the sacral nerves of the lower spine, where it delivers electrical impulses that help regulate bladder function.

Interstitial laser A laser probe is placed within prostatic tissue. Laser energy is then used to destroy prostatic tissue which makes urination easier.

Interstitial nephritis A kidney disorder caused by inflammation of the small spaces between parts of the kidney. The condition is a potential side effect of certain anti-HIV drugs.

Interstitial radiation therapy A procedure in which radioactive material sealed in needles, seeds, wires, or catheters is placed directly into or near a tumor. Also called brachytherapy, internal radiation, or implant radiation.

Interthalamic adhesion (massa intermedia) Midline nuclear mass found in about 80% of human brains which represents the fusion of the medial surfaces of the thalami across the third ventricle.

Intertrochanteric line The line that extends obliquely downward from the superior tubercle and then around the medial side of the femur, between the greater and lesser trochanter.

Intervention group The group receiving the study agent that is being tested in a clinical trial or clinical study.

Intervention strategy A generic term used in public health to describe a program or policy designed to have an impact on an illness or disease. Hence a mandatory seat belt law is an intervention designed to reduce automobile-related fatalities.

Intervention study A comparison of the outcome between 2 or more groups of patients that are deliberately subjected to different regimes (usually of treatment but sometimes of a preventative measure, such as vaccination). Wherever possible those entering the trial should be allocated to the respective groups by means of random numbers, and one such group (controls) should have no active treatment (randomised controlled trial). Ideally neither the patient nor the person assessing the outcome should be aware of which therapy is allocated to which patient (blind trial), nor should the doctor responsible for the treatment (double-blind trial), and the groups should exchange treatment after a pre-arranged period (cross-over trial).

Interventricular septum The musculomembreanous division that separates the left ventricle from the right ventricle of the heart.

Intervertebral disc The disc forms a cartilaginous joint between the vertebral bodies, providing extremely efficient shock absorption. Made up of the annulus fibrosis, nucleus pulposus and the cartilage end plates. Research implies the disc is the most commonly damaged structure, being the most common cause of lumbar spine disorders.

Intestinal Having to do with the intestines.

Intestinal flora The normal bacteria, yeast, and fungi found in the intestines that aid in digestion.

Intestinal mucosa The lining of the intestines, through which nutrients and water are absorbed into the body.

Intestinal villi Tiny hair-like projections that line the inside of the small intestine. They contain blood vessels and help absorb nutrients.

Intestine Digestive organs found in the abdomen, also known as either the large or small bowel. The small intestine removes nutrients from food to be used for energy, while the large intestine absorbs water from the digested food and processes it into stool.

Intolerance Allergy to a food or other substance.

Intoplicine An anticancer drug that belongs to the family of drugs called topoisomerase inhibitors.

Intra-articular Being within the joint.

Intracarotid infusion The introduction of fluids and drugs directly into the carotid artery, the main artery in the neck that carries blood from the heart to the brain.

Intracavitary Within a cavity or space, such as the abdomen, pelvis, or chest.

Intracavitary radiation A procedure in which a radioactive source (implant) is placed in a body cavity such as the chest cavity or the vagina.

Intracellular Inside a cell.

Intracolonic Within the colon.

Intracranial tumor A tumor that occurs in the brain.

Intradermal Within the dermis, which is the layer of skin below the epidermis (outermost layer).

Intraductal carcinoma A noninvasive, precancerous condition in which abnormal cells are found in the lining of a breast duct. The abnormal cells have not spread outside the duct to other tissues in the breast. In some cases, intraductal carcinoma may become invasive cancer and spread to other tissues, although it is not known at this time how to predict which lesions will become invasive. Also called ductal carcinoma in situ.

Intraductal papilloma A benign (noncancerous), wart-like growth in a milk duct of the breast. It is usually found close to the nipple and may cause a clear, sticky, or bloody discharge from the nipple. It may also cause pain and a lump in the breast that can be felt or seen. It usually affects women aged 35-55 years. Having an intraductal papilloma does not increase the risk of developing breast cancer.

Intraepithelial Within the layer of cells that form the surface or lining of an organ.

Intrahepatic Within the liver.

Intrahepatic bile duct A bile duct that passes through and drains bile from the liver.

Intrahepatic infusion The delivery of anticancer drugs directly to the blood vessels of the liver.

Intralesional Within a cancerous area, for example, within a tumor in the skin.

Intraluminal intubation and dilation A procedure in which a plastic or metal tube is inserted through the mouth into the esophagus (the tube that carries food to the stomach) to keep it open. This procedure may be used during radiation therapy for esophageal cancer.

Intramural Research that is done at the National Institutes of Health, by one or more institute, often within the NIH clinical research facility.

Intramuscular (IM) Relating to the area within a muscle. Intramuscular also refers to an injection made directly into a muscle.

Intraneural Being within neural tissue.

Intraocular Within the eyeball.

Intraocular melanoma A rare cancer of melanocytes (cells that produce the pigment melanin) found in the eye. Also called ocular melanoma.

Intraoperative radiation therapy (IORT) Radiation treatment aimed directly at a tumor during surgery.

Intraoral camera A smal video camera used to view and magnify oral conditions; images may be printed.

Intrapartum The time period spanning labor and delivery.

Intraperitoneal (IP) Within the peritoneal cavity (the area that contains the abdominal organs).

Intraperitoneal chemotherapy Treatment in which anticancer drugs are put directly into the abdominal cavity through a thin tube.

Intraperitoneal infusion A method of delivering fluids and drugs directly into the abdominal cavity through a thin tube. Also called peritoneal infusion.

Intraperitoneal radiation therapy Treatment in which a radioactive liquid is put directly into the abdomen through a thin tube.

Intrapleural Within the pleural cavity.

Intrathecal Describes the fluid-filled space between the thin layers of tissue that cover the brain and spinal cord. Drugs can be injected into the fluid or a sample of the fluid can be removed for testing.

Intrathecal chemotherapy Treatment in which anticancer drugs are injected into the fluid-filled space between the thin layers of tissue that cover the brain and spinal cord.

Intratumoral Within a tumor.

Intrauterine insemination The most common type of artificial insemination, in which a doctor places a man's sperm into the uterine cavity.

Intravaginal Having to do with the inside of the vagina (the birth canal).

Intravenous (IV) A method of supplying fluids and medications, using a needle inserted in a vein.

Intravenous immunoglobulin (IVIG) A solution of antibodies taken from healthy donors and injected into the veins of people with low or abnormal antibody production to help protect them from infections.

Intravenous pyelogram (IVP) A series of x-rays of the kidneys, ureters, and bladder. The x-rays are taken after a dye is injected into a blood vessel. The dye is concentrated in the urine, which outlines the kidneys, ureters, and bladder on the x-rays.

Intraventricular infusion The delivery of a drug into a fluid-filled cavity within the heart or brain.

Intravesical Within the bladder.

Intravltreal Injected in to the vitreous humor of the eye.

Intrinsic sphincter deficiency (ISD) Weakening of the urethra sphincter muscles. As a result of this weakening the sphincter does not function normally regardless of the position of the bladder neck or urethra. This condition is a common cause of stress urinary intinence.

Intron A segment of DNA that does not code for protein; the intervening sequence of nucleotides between coding sequences or exons.

Intussusception A disorder in which the intestine folds into itself in a telescope fashion, causing obstruction (blockage).

Invasive cancer Cancer that has spread beyond the layer of tissue in which it developed and is growing into surrounding, healthy tissues. Also called infiltrating cancer.

Invasive cervical cancer Cancer that has spread from the surface of the cervix to tissue deeper in the cervix or to other parts of the body.

Invasive hydatidiform mole A type of cancer that grows into the muscular wall of the uterus. It is formed after conception (fertilization of an egg by a sperm). It may spread to other parts of the body, such as the vagina, vulva, and lung. Also called chorioadenoma destruens.

Invasive lobular carcinoma A cancer that arises in the milk-producing glands (lobules) of the breast and then breaks through the lobule walls. From this site, it may then spread elsewhere in the breast. About 15% of mvas1ve breast cancers 1S invasive lobular carcinoma. It is often difficult to detect by physical examination or even by mammography. Up to 25% of women with this type of cancer will at some point develop an additional cancer in the opposite breast.

Invasive procedure A medical procedure that invades (enters) the body, usually by cutting or puncturing the skin or by inserting instruments into the body.

Inverse occlusion Covering the amblyopic eye.

Inverted papilloma A type of tumor in which surface epithelial cells grow downward into the underlying supportive tissue. It may occur in the nose and/or sinuses or in the urinary tract (bladder, renal pelvis, ureter, urethra). When it occurs in the nose or sinuses, it may cause symptoms similar to those caused by sinusitis, such as nasal congestion. When it occurs in the urinary tract, it may cause blood in the urine.

Inviable Not able to survive.

Iodine An element that is necessary for the body to make thyroid hormone. It is found in shellfish and iodized salt.

Iodine I 124 iododeoxyuridine A radiopharmaceutical comprised of the thymidine analog, 5-iodo-2-deoxyuridine (idoxuridine), labeled with the positron emitter iodine I 124. After incorporation into tumor cell DNA, positron emission tomography (PET) is used to image iodine I 124 localized to tumor cells for determining and monitoring tumor burden.

Iodine I 125 A radioactive isotope of iodine, a nonmetallic element of the halogen group. With a half-life of 60 days, iodine 125 occurs naturally and can be produced artificially. This agent has both therapeutic and diagnostic uses, particularly in thyroid disease.

Iodine I 131 A radioactive isotope of iodine with an atomic mass of 131, a half life of eight days, and potential antineoplastic activity. Selectively accumulating in the thyroid gland, iodine I 131 emits beta and gamma particles, thereby killing thyroid cells and decreasing thyroid hormone production.

Iodine I 131 lipiodol A cytotoxic radioconjugate consisting of lipiodol, an iodinated ethyl ester derived from poppy seed oil, labeled with iodine 131 (I-131). I-131 Lipiodol accumulates in hepatocellular carcinoma and hepatoblastoma tumor cells, resulting in targeted cytotoxicity to tumor cells while sparing surrounding normal cells and tissues.

Iodine I 131 metaiodobenzylguanidine An I 131 radioiodinated synthetic analogue of the neurotransmitter norepinephrine. Meta-iodobenzylguanidine localizes to adrenergic tissue and, in radioiodinated forms, may be used to image or eradicate tumor cells that take up and metabolize norepinephrine.

Iododoxorubicin A substance that is being studied as a treatment for cancer, and for primary systemic amyloidosis (a disease in which proteins are deposited in specific organs). It belongs to the family of drugs called anthracycline analogs.

Ionizing radiation A type of radiation made (or given off) by x-ray procedures, radioactive substances, rays that enter the Earth's atmosphere from outer space, and other sources. At high doses ionizing radiation increases chemical activity inside cells and can lead to health risks, including cancer.

Ionomycin An antibiotic drug used to treat infection.

IPI 504 A small-molecule inhibitor of heat shock protein 90 (HSP90) with antiproliferative and antineoplastic activity. IPI-504 binds to and inhibits the cytosolic chaperone functions of HSP90, which maintains the stability and functional shape of many oncogenic signaling proteins and may be overexpressed or overactive in tumor cells. IPI-504-mediated inhibition of HSP90 promotes the proteasomal degradation of oncogenic signaling proteins in susceptible tumor cell populations, which may result in the induction of apoptosis.

Ipsilateral Affecting or pertaining to the same side.

Irinotecan An anticancer drug that belongs to a family of drugs called topoisomerase inhibitors. It is a camptothecin analog. Also called CPT 11.

Irinotecan hydrochloride The hydrochloride salt of a semisynthetic derivative of camptothecin, a cytotoxic, quinoline based alkaloid extracted from the Asian tree Camptotheca acuminata. Irinotecan, a prodrug, is converted to a biologically active metabolite 7-ethyl-10-hydroxy-camptothecin (SN-38) by a carboxylesteraseconverting enzyme. One thousand-fold more potent than its parent compound irinotecan, SN-38 inhibits topoisomerase I activity by stabilizing the cleavable complex between topoisomerase I and DNA, resulting in DNA breaks that inhibit DNA replication and trigger apoptotic cell death. Because ongoing DNA synthesis is necessary for irinotecan to exert its cytotoxic effects, it is classified as an S-phase-specific agent.

Iris The coloured part of the eye located between the lens and cornea; it regulates the entrance of light.

Irofulven A semisynthetic sesquiterpene derivative of illudin S, a natural toxin isolated from the fungus Omphalotus illudens. Irofulven alkylates DNA and protein macromolecules, forms adducts, and arrests cells in the S-phase of the cell cycle. This agent requires NADPH-dependent metabolism by alkenal/one oxidoreductase for activity. Irofulven is more active in vitro against tumor cells of epithelial origin and is more resistant to deactivation by p53 loss and MDR1 than other alkylating agents.

Iron An important mineral the body needs to make hemoglobin, a substance in the blood that carries oxygen from the lungs to tissues throughout the body. Iron is also an important part of many other proteins and enzymes needed by the body for normal growth and development. It is found in red meat, fish, poultry, lentils, beans, and foods with iron added, such as cereal.

Iron lung An iron lung is a large machine that enables a person to breathe when normal muscle control has been lost or the work of breathing exceeds the person's ability. Properly, it is called a negative pressure ventilator.

Figure An iron lung. The patient lies within the chamber, which when sealed provides an effective oscillating atmospheric pressure

Persons using the iron lung are placed into the central chamber, a cylindrical steel drum. A door allowing the head and neck to remain free is then closed, forming a sealed, air-tight compartment enclosing the rest of the person's body. Pumps that control airflow periodically decrease and increase the air pressure within the chamber. When the pressure falls below that within the lungs, air from outside is sucked in via the person's nose and airways to fill the lungs; when the pressure rises above that within the lungs, the reverse occurs, and air is expelled. In this manner, the iron lung mimics the physiologic action of breathing: by periodically altering intrathoracic pressure, it causes air to flow in and out of the lungs. The iron lung is a form of non-invasive therapy

Irradiation The use of high-energy radiation from x-rays, gamma rays, neutrons, and other sources to kill cancer cells and shrink tumors. Radiation may come from a machine outside the body (external-beam radiation therapy) or from materials called radioisotopes. Radioisotopes produce radiation and can be placed in or near the tumor or in the area near cancer cells. This type of radiation treatment is called internal radiation therapy, implant radiation, interstitial radiation, or brachytherapy. Systemic radiation therapy uses a radioactive substance, such as a radiolabeled monoclonal antibody, that circulates through-out the body. Irradiation is also called radiation therapy, radio-therapy, and x-ray therapy.

Irreversible toxicity Side effects that are caused by toxic substances or something harmful to the body and do not go away.

Irritability Represented by the amount of activity necessary to worsen the condition, the extent of the exacerbation and the duration of the response. Based on a movement rather than a static posture, as this would give an idea of the amount of activity necessary to worsen the conditon. This has implications for the amount of assessment and treatment provided to the patient.

Irritable bladder Involuntary contractions of muscles in the bladder, which can cause lack of control of urination.

Irritable bowel syndrome (IBS) A common condition, in which recurrent abdominal pain with constipation and/or diarrhoea, continues for years, without any general deterioration in health. There is no detectable structural disease. The cause is unknown, but the condition is often associated with stress or anxiety.

Ischemia A local deficiency of blood due in part to functional constriction or actual mechanical obstruction of a blood vessel.

Ischial spine Process of bone projecting from the posterior border of the ischium, at the level of the lower border of the acetabulum, backward and medially.

Ischial tuberosity Elongated projection on the inferoposterior margin of the body of the ischial bone, that serves as the point of attachment for a number of muscles.

Ischiorectal fossa The space between the pelvic diaphragm and the skin below it. The fat in this region is almost a liquid at body temperature, allowing for changes in the size and shape of the rectum.

Ischium The inferior dorsal portion of the hip bone.

Iseganan hydrochloride A substance that is being studied as a treatment for oral mucositis (painful mouth sores) caused by cancer therapy. It belongs to the family of drugs called synthetic protegrin analogs.

Islet cell A pancreatic cell that produces hormones (e.g., insulin and glucagon) that are secreted into the bloodstream. These hormones help control the level of glucose (sugar) in the blood. Also called an endocrine pancreas cell and an islet of Langerhans cell.

Islet cell antibodies (ICA's) Specialized proteins, called antibodies, that are found in the blood of many people with Type 1 diabetes at the time of diagnosis. Most people with Type 1 diabetes have antibodies to a variety of islet cell proteins that are apparently released as a consequence of damage to the beta cells of the pancreas. The presence of these antibodies therefore is a useful indicator that the autoimmune process has begun.

The antibodies that are presently routinely assayed include:

IAA antiinsulin

GAD65 anti glutamic acid decarboxylase.

ICA512 a specific islet cell antibody

EMA antiendomyseal antibodies (a test for celiac synmdrome, another autoimmune disorder occurring in 5% of new-onset Type 1 diabetes)

Anti 21-hydroxylase (a test for Addison's disease, also an autoimmune condition found in 2% of new onset Type 1 diabetes)

Islet cell cancer Cancer arising from cells in the islets of Langerhans, which are found in the pancreas. Also called endocrine cancer.

Islet cell transplantation Moving the beta (islet) cells from a donor pancreas and putting them into a person whose pancreas has stopped producing insulin. The beta cells make the insulin that the body needs to use glucose (sugar) for energy. Although transplanting islet cells may one day help people with diabetes, the procedure is still in the research stage. Transplantation of the pancreas itself is surgically feasible, and is sometimes advised for some patients.

Isoenzyme An enzyme performing the same function as another enzyme but having a different set of amino acids. The two enzymes may function at different speeds.

Isoflavone An estrogen-like substance made by some plants, including the soy plant. Soy isoflavones are being studied in the prevention of cancer, hot flashes that occur with menopause, and osteoporosis (loss of bone density).

Isograft A tissue transplanted between two genetically identical individuals.

Isohemagglutinins Antibodies to major red blood cell antigens present normally as a result of inapparent immunization by cross-reactive antigens in bacteria, food, etc.

Isointense Having the same intensity as another object. Used to describe the results of imaging tests, such as x-rays, MRIs, or CT scans.

Isokinetic Applies to muscle contraction in which a constant joint angular velocity is maintained by accommodating resistance.

Isolated hepatic perfusion A procedure in which a catheter is placed into the artery that provides blood to the liver; another catheter is placed into the vein that takes blood away from the liver. This temporarily separates the liver's blood supply from blood circulating throughout the rest of the body and allows high doses of anticancer drugs to be directed to the liver only.

Isolated limb perfusion A technique that may be used to deliver anticancer drugs directly to an arm or leg. The flow of blood to and from the limb is temporarily stopped with a tourniquet, and anticancer drugs are put directly into the blood of the limb. This allows the person to receive a high dose of drugs in the area where the cancer occurred. Also called limb perfusion.

Isolated lung perfusion A surgical procedure during which the circulation of blood to the lungs is separated from the circulation of blood through the rest of the body, and a drug is delivered directly into the lung circulation. This allows a higher concentration of chemotherapy to reach tumors in the lungs.

Isomer One of two or more compounds that have the same chemical formula but different arrangements of the atoms within the molecules and that may have different physical/chemical properties.

Isometric Muscle contraction without movement at the joint.

Isoniazid An antibiotic that is one of the most common components in treatment for tuberculosis, either alone or in combination.

Isosporiasis A Protozoal infection, isosporiasis is usually restricted to the lower gastrointestinal tract. Symptomatically similar to cryptosporidiosis, isosporiasis usually responds well to treatment.

Isosulfan blue A synthetic visual lymphatic imaging agent. Injected into the periphery of the tumor site, isosulfan blue localizes to the lymphatic system and aids in the surgical identification of tumor sentinel nodes which stain blue.

Isotonic Refers to a solution whose salinity is the same as human blood.

Isotretinoin A drug that belongs to the family of drugs called retinoids. It is used in the treatment of acne and psoriasis and is being studied in cancer prevention. Also called 13-cis retinoic acid.

Isotype switch The shift of a B cell or its progeny from the secretion of antibody of one isotype or class of antibody with the same V regions but a different heavy- chain constant region and, hence, a different isotype (class switch).

Isotypes Classes of antibody that differ in the constant region of their heavy chain (Fc portion); distinguishable also on the basis of reaction with antisera raised in another species. These differences also result in different biological activities of the antibodies.

Isthmus A narrow part inside the body that connects two larger structures.

Itis (suffix) Inflammation, e.g. appendicitis inflammation of the appendix.

Itraconazole A synthetic triazole agent with antimycotic properties. Formulated for both topical and systemic use, itraconazole preferentially inhibits fugal cytochrome P450 enzymes, resulting in a decrease in fungal ergosterol synthesis. Because of its low toxicity profile, this agent can be used for long-term maintenance treatment of chronic fungal infections.

IU (International unit) A unit of measurement based on the International System of Units. This system defines units to measure length, time, mass, electric current, temperature, light intensity, and the amount of a substance. It can be used to express measurements of fat-soluble vitamins and some hormones, enzymes, and drugs.

Ixabepilone A semisynthetic analogue of epothilone B with antineoplastic activity. Ixabepilone (BMS-247550) binds to tubulin and promotes tubulin polymerization and microtubule stabilization, thereby arresting cells in the G2-M phase of the cell cycle and inducing tumor cell apoptosis. This agent demonstrates antineoplastic activity against taxane-resistant cell lines.

J chain (Joining chain) A polypeptide involved in the polymerization of immunoglobulin molecules IgM and IgA.

J gene A gene segment coding for the J or joining segment in immunoglobulin DNA; V genes translocate to J segments in L chains, and to D and J segments in H chains. Also, codes for a portion of the T-cell receptor.

J pouch coloanal anastomosis A surgical procedure in which the colon is attached to the anus after the rectum has been removed. A 2-4 inch section of the colon is formed into a J-shaped pouch in order to replace the function of the rectum and store stool until it can be eliminated. This procedure is similar to the side-to-end coloanal anastomosis but a larger pouch is formed.

Jacket Crown for a front tooth, usually made of porcelain.

Infant undergoing home phototherapy for jaundice using a bili blanket

Figure Jaundice

Jaundice A yellowing of the skin and whites of the eyes usually caused by diseases of the liver or bile ducts.

Jc papovavirus Suggested as a possible cause of progressive multifocal leukoencephalopathy.

Jejunum (Jejunal loops) The portion of the small intestine located between the duodenum and the ileum (distal to the duodenum/ proximal to the ileum).

Jet injector A device that uses high pressure to propel insulin through the skin and into the body. When used properly, injections are painless. However, the devices are more complicated to use than a syringe and often require cleaning.

Jewett staging system A staging system for prostate cancer that uses ABCD. "A" and "B" refer to cancer that is confined to the prostate. "C" refers to cancer that has grown out of the prostate but has not spread to lymph nodes or other places in the body. "D" refers to cancer that has spread to lymph nodes or to other places in the body. Also called the ABCD rating or the Whitmore-Jewett staging system.

Jim's juice A liquid that has been promoted as a treatment for a wide range of diseases, including cancer. The ingredients thought to be in Jim's Juice have been tested, and none of them has been shown to be effective in treating any form of cancer. Also called Entelev, Sheridan's Formula, Cancell, Crocinic Acid, JS–114, JS–101, 126–F, and Cantron.

JMML (Juvenile myelomonocytic leukemia) A rare form of childhood leukemia in which cancer cells often spread into tissues such as the skin, lung, and intestines.

Joint capsule An membranous envelope consisting of a fibrous and synovial membrane that encloses the cavity of a synovial joint and attaches to the bone adjacent to the articular surfaces of the bones involved. A small amount of lubricating "synovial fluid" is contained within the capsule.

Joint locking An extremely painful condition, usually caused by entrapment of a loose body within the joint, between the joint surfaces.

Joint space The area between the acticular cartilage surfaces making up a synovial joint. The synovial fluid lubricates the opposing articular cartilage. Normal cartilage is very smooth - like Teflon.

Jordan frame A specialised stretcher developed for transport of suspected spinal injured patients.

JS–101 A liquid that has been promoted as a treatment for a wide range of diseases, including cancer. The ingredients thought to be in JS–101 have been tested, and none of them has been shown to be effective in treating any form of cancer. Also called Entelev, Sheridan's Formula, Jim's Juice, Crocinic Acid, Cancell, JS–114, 126–F, and Cantron.

Jumper's knee Associated with a small area of degeneration at the tendon attachment at the lower pole of the patella, characterized by pain and extreme local tenderness. Often associated with activities that require jumping off one leg e.g. high jumpers. Often associated with aptellar tendinitis.

Junctional nevus A mole found in the junction (border) between the epidermis and dermis layers of the skin. These moles may be pigmented and slightly raised, and have a higher risk of developing into malignant melanoma.

Junk DNA Stretches of DNA that do not code for genes; most of the genome consists of so-called junk DNA which may have regulatory and other functions. Also called non-coding DNA.

Juven An orally bioavailable nutritional supplement. Juven contains the amino acids glutamine and arginine in addition to beta-hydroxy-beta-methylbutyrate (HMB). This agent may promote muscle protein synthesis and increase muscle mass.

Juvenile onset diabetes Former term for insulin-dependent or type 1 diabetes.

K cell An effector lymphocyte with Fc receptors which allow it to bind to and kill antibody-coated target cells.

Kahler's disease A type of cancer that begins in plasma cells (white blood cells that produce antibodies). Also called multiple myeloma, myelomatosis, or plasma cell myeloma.

Kaplan-meier curve A way of graphing patient progress (how many are still alive or free of infection) against time: A lifetable curve showing the percent of people free of a specific event at times following randomization. The Kaplan-Meier method is especially well suited to situations with censored data , such as those encountered in clinical trials, where patients are enrolled over a period of time and followed to a common calendar time point.

Kaposi's sarcoma (KS) A tumor of the wall of blood vessels, or the lymphatic system. Usually appears as pink to purple, painless spots on the skin but may also occur internally in addition to or independent of lesions.

Kaposi's sarcoma-associated herpesvirus (KSHV) A type of herpesvirus that may cause Kaposi's sarcoma (a rare cancer that can cause skin lesions) and a type of lymphoma (cancer that begins in the lymph system), especially in patients who have a weak immune system. Also called human herpesvirus 8 (HHV8).

Karenitecin A synthetic silicon-containing agent related to camptothecin with antineoplastic properties. Karenitecin stabilizes the cleavable complex between topoisomerase I and DNA, resulting in DNA breaks and consequently triggering apoptosis. Because it is lipophilic, karenitecin exhibits enhanced tissue penetration and bio-availability compared to water-soluble camptothecins.

Karnofsky performance status (KPS) A standard way of measuring the ability of cancer patients to perform ordinary tasks. The karnofsky performance scores range from 0 to 100. A higher score means the patient is better able to carry out daily activities. KPS may be used to determine a patient's prognosis, to measure changes in a patient's ability to function, or to decide if a patient could be included in a clinical trial.

Karnofsky score A score between 0 and 100 assigned by a health professional after watching a patient perform common tasks. A score of 100 means that the patient has normal physical abilities with no signs of disease. Decreasing numbers mean that the patient has less ability to perform activities of daily living.

Karyorrhexis The fragmentation of nuclei, producing nuclear dust.

Karyotype A photomicrograph of an individual's chromosomes arranged in a standard format showing the number, size, and shape of each chromosome type; used in low-resolution physical mapping to correlate gross chromosomal abnormalities with the characteristics of specific diseases.

Kayser fleischer rings discoloration of the outer membrane of the iris caused by copper deposits. Although the ring is not present in all patients, it is never present in a person without Wilson's Disease.

Kegel exercises Exercises is to strengthen the muscles of the pelvic floor, which leads to more control and prevents leakage.

Keloid A thick, irregular scar caused by excessive tissue growth at the site of an incision or wound.

Kelp Laminaria digitata. A type of seaweed. The stem-like parts of this plant have been used in some cultures to treat certain medical problems. It may have immunostimulatory and anticanc-er effects.

Keratan sulphate A glycosaminoglycan (a type of polysaccharide) found in cartilage and in the cornea of the eye.

Keratinocyte growth factor (KGF) A substance that stimulates the growth of epithelial cells that line the surface of the mouth and intestinal tract. There are several forms of KGF. Recombinant human KGF (rHuKGF) is being studied in the prevention of graft-versus-host disease (GVHD) that may occur after tissue transplantation, and in the treatment of mucositis caused by chemotherapy and radiation therapy. rHuKGF is also called palifermin.

Keratins Insoluble protective or structural proteins consisting of parallel polypeptide chains in a-helical or b-conformation.

Keratoacanthoma A benign (noncancerous), rapidly growing skin tumor that usually occurs on sun-exposed areas of the skin and that can go away without treatment.

Keratoconus A conical cornea.

Keratohyalin The deeply basophilic, irregularly shaped granules in the stratum granulosum. These form the interfibrillary matrix which cements keratin fibrils, and the marginal band of the horny cells.

Keratosis pilaris Dry sandpaper-rough skin texture found commonly in allergy sufferers.

Ketoconazole A synthetic derivative of phenylpiperazine with broad antifungal properties and potential antineoplastic activity. Ketoconazole inhibits sterol 14-a-dimethylase, a microsomal cytochrome P450-dependent enzyme, thereby disrupting synthesis of ergosterol, an important component of the fungal cell wall.

Figure The structure of Ketoconazole

Ketones (Ketone bodies) Chemicals that the body makes when there is not enough insulin in the blood and it must break down fat for its energy. Ketone bodies can poison and even kill body cells. When the body does not have the help of insulin, the ketones build up in the blood and then "spill" over into the urine so that the body can get rid of them. The body can also rid itself of one type of ketone, called acetone, through the lungs. This gives the breath a fruity odor. Ketones that build up in the body for a long time lead to serious illness and coma.

Ketonuria Having ketone bodies in the urine; a warning sign of diabetic ketoacidosis (DKA).

Ketorolac A drug that belongs to a family of drugs called nonsteroidal anti-inflammatory agents. It is being studied in cancer prevention.

Ketose A simple monosaccharide having its carbonyl groups at other than a terminal position. Kilobase (kb) Unit of length for DNA fragments equal to 1000 nucleotides (kilo base pairs of DNA).

Ketosis A condition of having ketone bodies build up in body tissues and fluids. The signs of ketosis are nausea, vomiting, and stomach pain. Ketosis can lead to ketoacidosis.

Ketotic hypoglycemia A poorly-understood disorder of childhood, marked by hypoglycemia and ketosis. There is carbohydrate deprivation, with consequent dependence on fat stores for energy. Ketotic hypoglycemia can often be effectively treated by simple dietary changes involving frequent feedings of carbohydrate and protein.

Keyhole limpet hemocyanin A natural protein isolated from the marine mollusc keyhole limpet. Keyhole limpet hemocyanin is an immunogenic carrier protein that, in vivo, increases antigenic immune responses to haptens and other weak antigens such as idiotype proteins.

Kidney A pair of "bean shaped" organs in the upper posterior

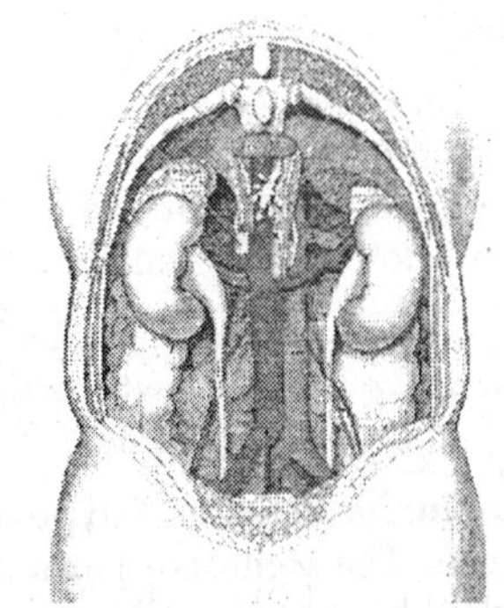

Human kidneys viewed from behind with spine removed

Figure Kidney

abdomen, behind the peritoneal cavity (retroperitoneal) that filter waste products from the blood. Water, sugar and other valuable materials are reabsorbed and conserved, while the "waste water" is drained by the ureters into the bladder.

Kidney cancer Cancer that forms in tissues of the kidneys. Kidney cancer includes renal cell carcinoma (cancer that forms in the lining of very small tubes in the kidney that filter the blood and remove waste products) and renal pelvis carcinoma (cancer that forms in the center of the kidney where urine collects). It also includes Wilms' tumor, which is a type of kidney cancer that usually develops in children under the age of 5.

Kidney disease Any one of several chronic conditions that are caused by damage to the cells of the kidney. People who have had diabetes for a long time may have kidney damage. Also called nephropathy.

Kidney failure A condition in which the kidneys stop working and are not able to remove waste and extra water from the blood or keep body chemicals in balance. Acute kidney failure happens suddenly (for example, after an injury) and may be treated and cured Chronic kidney failure develops over years (related to high blood pressure or diabetes, for example) and cannot be cured. Chronic kidney failure may lead to total and permanent kidney failure, called end-stage renal disease (ESRD), and requires dialysis (process of cleaning the blood by passing it through a membrane or filter) or a kidney transplant.

Kidney stone A hard mass composed of substances from the urine that form in the kidneys.

Kidney threshold The point at which the blood is holding too much of a substance such as glucose (sugar) and the kidneys "spill" the excess sugar into the urine.

Killer T cell A T cell with a particular immune specificity and an endogenously produced receptor for antigen, capable of specifically killing its target cell after attachment to the target cell by this receptor. Also called cytotoxic T cell.

Kilo Prefix meaning a thousand time, as in kilogram, a thousand grams.

Kilobase (kb) Unit of length for DNA fragments equal to 1000 nucleotides.

Kilogram A measure of weight. A kilogram is equal to 2.2 pounds.

Kinaret A substance that is used to treat rheumatoid arthritis, and is being studied in the treatment of cancer. Kinaret blocks the action of interleukin 1 (IL-1). It belongs to the family of drugs called interleukin receptor antagonists. Also called anakinra.

Kinase An enzyme that mediates the addition of phosphorus to chemical groups. The AZT nucleoside must be phosphorylated to become a genetically active nucleotide.

Kinesthesia The sensation of bodily position, presence, or movement resulting chiefly from stimulation of sensory nerve ending in muscles, tendons, and joints.

Klatskin tumor Cancer that develops in cells that line the bile ducts in the liver, where the right and left ducts meet. It is a type of cholangiocarcinoma.

Klebsiella A bacteria that frequently causes lung, urinary tract, intestinal, and wound infections.

Klinefelter's syndrome A genetic disorder in males caused by having an extra X chromosome. Males with this disorder may have larger than normal breasts, a lack of facial and body hair, a rounded body type, and small testicles. They may learn to speak much later than other children and may have difficulty learning to read and write. Klinefelter's syndrome increases the risk of developing testicular cancer.

Knee The major joint of the leg, between the distal femur (condyles) and the proximal tibia (plateau).

Knee cap (Patella) The roughly triangular sesamoid bone located in front of the knee, within the tendon of the quadriceps femoris muscle, a major extensor of the lower leg.

Knee reconstruction Surgical restoration of "normal" biomechanics of the knee, using tendon grafts to replace damaged tissues. Commonly seen with ACL injuries, when there is a concurrent rotary instability caused by damage to other structures, knee reconstructions are often the only way to restore acceptable mechanics. If the knee is unstable, reconstructive procedures are undertaken to restore function stability.

Knockout Deactivation of specific genes; used in laboratory organisms to study gene function.

Knowledge The acquisition or awareness of facts, data, information, ideas or principles to which one has access through formal or individual study, research, observation, experience or intuition.

Kretek A cigarette made of a mixture of tobacco and clove.

Krukenberg tumor A tumor in the ovary caused by the spread of stomach cancer.

Kussmaul breathing The rapid, deep, and labored breathing of people who have ketoacidosis or who are in a diabetic coma. Kussmaul breathing is named for Adolph Kussmaul, the 19th century German doctor who first noted it. Also called "air hunger."

Kyphosis Exaggerated curvature of the spine, in the flexion/extension axis. In the thoracic spine, in adolescents, the most common cause of kyphosis is Sheuermann's disease. In the elderly, the most common cause of kyphosis is disc dengeneration. Localised kyphosis may be caused by collapse of one or more thoracic vertebrae which, in the elderly, may be associated with osteoporosis.

L leucovorin The active l-isomer of the racemic mixture of the 5-formyl derivative of tetrahydrofolic acid. Metabolically active, l-leucovorin, also known levoleucovorin, does not require bioactivation by dihydrofolate reductase, an enzyme inhibited by folic acid antagonists. This agent may enhance the effects of fluoropyrimidines by stabilizing their binding to the enzyme thymidylate synthase.

L threo dihydrosphingosine A saturated derivative of sphingosine. As an inhibitor of protein kinase C (PKC), L-threo-dihydrosphingosine competitively binds to the regulatory phorbol-binding domain of PKC, a kinase involved in tumorigenesis. This agent has been shown to act synergistically with other chemotherapeutic agents and may potentiate chemotherapy drug-induced apoptosis in vitro and in vivo.

Labile Unstable or unsteady; not fixed; characterized by adaptability to alteration or modification, i.e., relatively easily changed, as in cleavage of a molecule or molecular rearran-gement in a compound or complex chemical material.

Labile diabetes A term used to indicate when a person's blood glucose (sugar) level often swings quickly from high to low and from low to high. Also called brittle diabetes.

Laboratory study Research done in a laboratory. These studies may use test tubes or animals to find out if a drug, procedure, or treatment is likely to be useful. Laboratory studies take place before any testing is done in humans.

Laboratory test A medical procedure that involves testing a sample of blood, urine, or other substance from the body.

Lachman's test Drawing forward of the tibia, relative to the femur, in 10 - 20° of knee flexion. A test for ACL disruption.

Lacrimal apparatus The tear-forming and tear-conducting system which

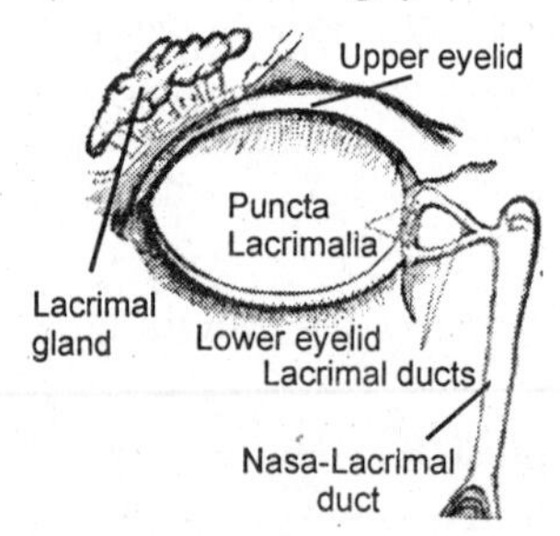

includes the lacrimal glands, eyelid margins, conjunctival sac, and the tear drainage system.

Lacrimal duct The tear ducts remove the tears as they flow toward the inner canthus. Excessive tearing or blockage of the ducts will cause the tears to flow down the cheek.

Lacrimal glands The tear producing glands that are located in a bone depression (fossae) in the upper outer angle of the orbit. Tears serve several functions, including lubrication, moisturizing, and antisepsis for the eyeball. Tears have both a mucus layer, as well as a more liquid layer.

Lactase An enzyme in the small intestine needed to digest lactose, a sugar found in milk and milk products.

Lactase deficiency Lack of an enzyme made by the small intestine called lactase, which prevents the body from digesting lactose (a sugar found in milk and milk products) properly.

Lactate dehydrogenase (LDH) One of a group of enzymes found in the blood and other body tissues and involved in energy production in cells. An increased amount of LDH in the blood may be a sign of tissue damage and some types of cancer or other diseases. Also called lactic acid dehydrogenase.

Lactation Production of milk in the breast.

Lactic acidosis A condition caused by a buildup of lactate, a cellular waste product, in the blood. Symptoms, if any, may include stomach and breathing problems and general weakness. Severe, untreated lactic acidosis can be life threatening. Increased lactate levels, often combined with hepatic steatosis, may occur in HIV-infected individuals taking NRTIs.

Lactobacillus A type of prebiotic/ probiotic found in yogurt and some other dairy products which may improve gastrointestinal health.

Lactoferrin A protein that is found in milk, tears, mucus, bile, and some white blood cells and is being studied in the treatment and prevention of cancer. It is involved in fighting against infection and inflammation and it acts as an antioxidant.

Lactose A sugar naturally occurring in milk, also known as "milk sugar," that is the least sweet of all natural sugars and used in baby formulas and candies.

Lactose intolerance Lactose intolerance is an inherited inability to properly digest dairy products, due to a deficiency in the amount of the enzyme, â-galactosidase in the small intestine. This enzyme is necessary for the hydrolysis of lactose (a disaccharide) into its constituent monosaccharides, glucose and galactose. Symptoms of lactose intolerance, including abdominal cramps, flatulence and frothy diarrhea, can increase with age.

Lacuna A slitlike intraepidermal vesicle or bulla as is seen in Darier's disease.

Laetrile A substance found in the pits of many fruits such as apricots and papayas, and in other foods. It has been tried in some countries as a treatment for cancer, but it has not been shown to work in clinical studies. Also called amygdalin.

Lag of accommodation A measure of the eye's ability to focus accurately on a given target. The dioptric difference between the eye's focusing response and the stimulus to focus.

Lagophthalmos Voluntary or involuntary (incomplete) closure of the eyelid.

LAL (limulus amoebocyte lysate) A material obtained by rupturing the cellular components of the blood of a horseshoe crab (Limulus Poliphemus). This material coagulates in the presence of LPS (lypopolysaccharides) and is a test used to quantitate bacterial endotoxins (pyrogens).

Lamina Any thin bone. The lamina of the spine (arcus vertebrae) is a thin bone plate extending posteriorly from the pedicles and fusing to provide the dorsal portion of the neural arch (surrounding the spinal cord), forming the base for the spinous process.

Lamina propria A type of connective tissue found under the thin layer of tissues covering a mucous membrane.

Laminar flow Non-turbulent fluid flow is usually considered laminar if the Reynolds number is less than 2000 in a pipe. Depending upon many possible varying conditions, the flow may be laminar at a Reynolds number as low as 1,200 or as high as 40,000; however, such conditions are not experienced in normal practice. In the pharmaceutical industry, this term incorrectly refers to the air discharge of a clean air bench or wall.

Laminate Thin plastic or porcelain veneer produced in a dental laboratory and then bonded to a tooth.

Laminectomy Surgical procedure, which includes removal of a portion of the lamina, to provide more room in the vertebral canal. Usually for disc herniation or spinal canal stenosis.

Lamivudine A synthetic nucleoside analogue with activity against hepatitis B virus (HBV) and HIV. Intracellularly, lamivudine is phosphorylated to its active metabolites, lamiduvine triphosphate (L-TP) and lami-duvine monophosphate (L-MP). In HIV, L-TP inhibits HIV-1 reverse transcriptase (RT) via DNA chain termination after incorporation of the nucleoside analogue into viral DNA. In HBV, incorporation of L-MP into viral DNA by HBV polymerase results in DNA chain termination. L-TP is a weak inhibitor of mammalian DNA polymerases alpha and beta, and mitochondrial DNA polymerase.

Lamotrigine A drug that is used to help control some types of seizures. It is being studied in the prevention of peripheral neuropathy caused by some chemotherapy drugs. It belongs to the family of drugs called anticonvulsants.

Lancet A fine, sharp-pointed blade or needle for pricking the skin.

Langelier index A measure of the degree of saturation of calcium carbonate in water that is based on pH, alkalinity and hardness. If the Langelier Index is negative, the water is corrosive (pH value below 7 or acidic). If the Langelier Index is positive, calcium carbonate can precipitate out of solution to form scale (pH value above 7 or basic). The Langelier Index will vary for cold water and for warm water.

Langerhans cell A type of dendritic cell found in the skin.

Laparoscope A tube with a camera lens attached that looks inside organs to check for abnormalities. Often used in surgery to look inside the body and avoid making large incisions.

Laparoscopic lymph node dissection If a perineal prostatectomy is contemplated then prior to the operation the pelvic lymph nodes are sampled via three small incisions made in the abdomen, much like the procedure used to remove gallbladders.

Laparoscopic prostatectomy Surgery to remove all or part of the prostate with the aid of a laparoscope (a thin, lighted tube).

Laparoscopic-assisted colectomy Surgery done with the aid of a laparoscope (a thin, lighted tube) to remove all or part of the colon through several small incisions made in the wall of the abdomen. A laparoscope attached to a video camera is inserted through one opening to guide the surgery. Surgical instruments are inserted through the other openings to perform the surgery. When only part of the colon is removed, it is called a partial colectomy.

Laparoscopy A procedure that uses a tube with a light and a camera lens at the end (laparoscope) to examine organs, check for abnormalities, or perform minimally invasive surgeries. Laparoscopy is a surgery which avoids making large incisions. Tissue samples may also be taken for examination and testing.

Laparotomy A surgical incision made in the wall of the abdomen.

Lapatinib A synthetic, orally-active quinazoline with potential antineoplastic properties. Lapatinib reversibly blocks phosphorylation of the epidermal growth factor receptor (EGFR), ErbB2, and the Erk-1 and-2 and AKT kinases; it also inhibits cyclin D protein levels in human tumor cell lines and xenografts. EGFR and ErbB2 have been implicated in the growth of various tumor types.

Lappa Arctium lappa. A plant whose seeds and root have been used in some cultures to treat certain medical problems. It may have antioxidant effects. Also called burdock and happy major.

Large cell carcinoma Lung cancer in which the cells are large and look abnormal when viewed under a microscope.

Large granular lymphocyte A type of white blood cell that contains granules with enzymes that can kill tumor cells or microbial cells. Also called a natural killer cell.

Large intestine The long, tube-like organ that is connected to the small intestine at one end and the anus at the other. The large intestine has four parts: cecum, colon, rectum, and anal canal. Partly digested food moves through the cecum into the colon, where water and some nutrients and electrolytes are removed. The remaining material, solid waste called stool, moves through the colon, is stored in the rectum, and leaves the body through the anal canal and anus.

Large urban area An urban statistical region with population of one million or more.

Laryngeal Having to do with the larynx.

Laryngeal cancer Cancer that forms in tissues of the larynx (area of the throat that contains the vocal cords and is used for breathing, swallowing, and talking). Most laryngeal cancers are squamous cell carcinomas (cancer that begins in flat cells lining the larynx).

Laryngectomy An operation to remove all or part of the larynx (voice box).

Laryngitis Inflammation of the larynx.

Laryngoscopy Examination of the larynx (voice box) with a mirror (indirect laryngoscopy) or with a laryngoscope (direct laryngoscopy).

Larynx Head/Tomogram/hn033.html The cartilage support structures that connect the superior trachea, the pharynx inferior to the tongue, and the hyoid bone. It supports the sphincter at the entrance to the trachea (the glottis or true vocal cords) and is therefore also the organ responsible for voice.

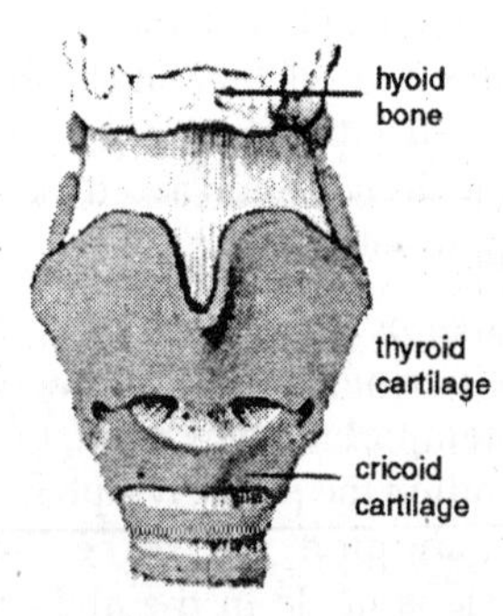

Figure Larynx

Laser A device that concentrates light into an intense, narrow beam used to cut or destroy tissue. It is used in microsurgery, photodynamic therapy, and for a variety of diagnostic purposes.

Laser surgery A surgical procedure that uses the cutting power of a laser beam to make bloodless cuts in tissue or to remove a surface lesion such as a tumor.

Laser therapy Use of low powered lasers, for treatment of pain, swelling, inflammation and promotion of healing.

Late effects Side effects of cancer treatment that appear months or years after treatment has ended. Late effects include physical and mental problems and second cancers.

Latency The time period when an infectious organism is in the body but is not producing any noticeable symptoms. In HIV disease, latency usually occurs in the early years of infection. Also refers to the period when HIV has integrated its genome into a cell's DNA but has not yet begun to replicate.

Latent Describes a condition that is present but not active or causing symptoms.

Latent allergy When allergy testing is positive but no clinical allergy has yet developed to that allergen.

Latent autoimmune diabetes in adults (LADA) Autoimmune diabetes (Type 1A diabetes) occurring in individuals who are older than the usual age of onset of type 1 diabetes (that is, over 30 years of age at diagnosis). Sometimes, patients with LADA are mistakenly thought to have Type 2 diabetes, based on their age at the time of diagnosis. However, positive antibody tests would help make the diagnosis of LADA.

Latent diabetes Former term for impaired glucose tolerance.

Latent heat The amount of heat needed to change a unit of substance, such as water, from a solid to a liquid without change in temperature or pressure.

Latent hyperopia Hyperopia (farsightedness) is compensated by accommodation and the tonicity (tension) of the ciliary muscle; identified by cycloplegic refraction. In mild cases of hyperopia (farsightedness), the eyes are able to compensate without corrective lenses; otherwise a plus lens (glasses or contacts) is prescribed. Vision therapy is not prescribed.

Latent infection Viral infection in which the virus responsible is able to avoid the hosts immune system and defenses.

Lateral To, or on, the side.

Lateral (view) Lateral is the opposite of medial/median.

Lateral epicondylitis Also described as "tennis elbow", but often with no history of sporting endeavour. Condition affecting the lateral compartment of the elbow. Pathology affecting the junctional tissue associated with the origin of the common extensor tendon at the lateral humeral epicondyle, specifically the tendinous origin of the extensor carpi radialis brevis.

Lateral mass (C1) The lateral portions of the atlas bone (C1) that connect the arches (anterior/posterior), the articulating surfaces (superior/inferior), and the transverse processes for the first vertebral segment.

Lateral pterygoid plate A pair of projections (medial/lateral) from the greater wing of the sphenoid bone that forms the medial wall of the infratemporal fossa. The medial and lateral pterygoid muscles attach the mandible to the pterygoids.

Lateral release Surgical procedure whereby there is division of the lateral patellar retinaculum, from the patellar tendon to within the muscle fibres of vastus lateralis. Usually as a treatment of patellofemoral dysfunction, following failed conservative measures.

Lateral semicircular canal Part of the vestibular system of the inner ear that provides sensation for balance and "inertial guidance". The lateral semicircular canal contains the ductus semicircularis lateralis.

Lateral ventricle The CSF filled cavities located in each cerebral hemisphere.

Latex Rubber derivative commonly found in hospitals in surgical gloves, catheters and intravenous drip-sets. May cause severe allergic reactions during operations.

Lattisimus dorsi flap procedure A method of breast reconstruction that uses the long flat muscle of the back, by rotating it to the chest area.

Lattisimus dorsi Muscle that originates from the spines of the thoracic and lumbar vertebrae, thoracolumbar fascia, iliac crest, lower ribs, and inferior angle of the scapula, and inserts into the humerus (along the crest of the intertubercular sulcus). It is responsible for the adduction, extension, and medial rotation of the humerus.

Laughing gas Nitrous oxide; odourless inhalation agent that produces relative analgesic (sedation); reduces anxiety and creates a state of relaxation.

Laxative A substance that promotes bowel movements.

L-carnitine A form of carnitine, which is a substance made in the muscles and liver. It can be given as a supplement to prevent and treat carnitine deficiency in patients who are receiving chemotherapy for cancer or undergoing dialysis for kidney disease. Also called levocarnitine.

(Chemical structure of carnitine)

Figure L-carnitine

LD50 Short for "lethal dose 50"; the dosage of a drug or poison that is toxic to 50% of the organisms it is tested against. Often applies to does of drug against microorganisms.

Lead An insulated wire that carries the heart signal to the pulse generator and energy from the pulse generator to the heart. The leads are attached to the surface of the heart or passed into your heart through the veins.

Learning disability (LD) A disorder that affects people's ability to either interpret what they see and hear or to link information from different parts of the brain. Learning disabilities can be divided into five broad categories: speech and language disorders, reading disorder, arithmetic disorder, writing disorder, and attention disorders. The term learning disability does not include children who have learning problems that are primarily the result of visual, hearing, or motor disorders.

Lecithin A by-product of the refining for soybean oil and is also found in eggs, red meats, spinach and nuts. Historically, lecithin has been used commercially in food processing as an emulsifier, instantizing agent and lubricating agent. Lecithin is a source of choline when digested; and is a critical component of the lipoproteins which transport fat and cholesterol molecules in the blood stream. Lecithin (choline) promotes synthesis of high-density lipoproteins (i.e., HDLP also known as "good" cholesterol) by the liver, when it is consumed by humans.

Lectin A complex molecule that has both protein and sugars. Lectins are able to bind to the outside of a cell and cause biochemical changes in it. Lectins are made by both animals and plants.

LED therapy (Light-emitting diode therapy) Treatment with drugs that become active and may kill cancer cells when exposed to light. LED therapy is a type of photodynamic therapy, which uses a special type of light to activate the drug.

LEEP (Loop electrosurgical excision procedure) A technique that uses electric current passed through a thin wire loop to remove abnormal tissue. Also called loop excision.

Leflunomide An anticancer drug that works by inhibiting a cancer cell growth factor. Also called SU101.

Left atrium Chamber on the left side of the heart that recieves blood from the pulmonary veins, directing it to the left ventricle through the mitral valve.

Left colic artery Artery which originates from the inferior mesenteric, and supplies the descending colon.

Left common carotid artery The artery that originates directly from the aortic arch and splits into the left internal and external carotid arteries.

Left gastroepiploic artery Originating from the splenic artery it branches into the gastric and omental arteries.

Left mainstem bronchi Derived from the trachea, the left main bronchos that conducts air into the left lung.

Left marginal artery Artery which originates from the circumflex artery, and follows the left border of the heart, supplying the left ventricle.

Left pulmonary artery Artery originating from the main pulmonary trunk and branching into the arteries of the superior and inferior lobes of the left lung.

Left ventricle The major systemic pumping chamber of the heart that directs blood out through the aorta and into the systemic arteries.

Leg length A measure from the anterior superior iliac spine, to the tip of the medial malleolus, although this may be inaccurate in the presence of pelvic rotation or asymmetry. Leg length discrepancies may not be significant if they are less than 6 mm, as many asymptomatic patients have a leg length difference of up to 12 mm.

Legend drug Drug that the law says can only be obtained by prescription.

Legionella pneumophilae An ubiquitous bacteria causing pneumonia, or "legionnaire's disease". Recognized fairly recently, L. pneumophilae may be the cause of many pneumonias of indeterminate etiology. Most exposure is from tap water, often aerosolized by a shower head or air-conditioner

Leio Smooth. e.g. leiomyoma - a benign tumor of smooth muscle cells.

Leiomyoma A benign smooth muscle tumor, usually in the uterus or gastrointestinal tract. Also called fibroid.

Leiomyosarcoma A malignant (cancerous) tumor of smooth muscle cells that can arise almost anywhere in the body, but is most common in the uterus, abdomen, or pelvis.

Lenalidomide A thalidomide analog with potential antineoplastic activity. Lenalidomide inhibits TNF-alpha production, stimulates T cells, reduces serum levels of the cytokines vascular endothelial growth factor (VEGF) and basic fibroblast growth factor (bFGF), and inhibits angiogenesis. This agent also promotes G1 cell cycle arrest and apoptosis of malignant cells.

Length of stay (LOS) The duration of an episode of care for a covered person. The number of days an individual stays in a hospital or inpatient facility. May also be reviewed as Average Length of Stay (ALOS).

Lenox hill brace A commonly used brace, developed in New York for the use in ACL deficient knees, with particular emphasis on its derotation properties.

Lens The transparent biconvex structure of the eye that is located between the posterior chamber and vitreous body. The lens is living tissue, but is almost "crystalline" in composition and is "crystal clear". It is one of the driest tissues in the body, and therefore has low signal intensity on MR.

Lensometer Also called Verometer, is a device used to measure the refractive power of eyeglasses and contact lenses.

Lente insulin A type of insulin that is intermediate-acting.

Lentinan A beta-glucan (a type of polysaccharide) from the mushroom Lentinus edodes (shiitake mushroom). It has been studied in Japan as a treatment for cancer.

Lentivirus A subgroup of the retrovirus family that includes HIV. Lentiviruses are characterized by a long time period between infection and the onset of symptoms.

Leokocytosis An abnormal high number of white blood cells in the circulating blood.

LEP-ETU A form of the anticancer drug paclitaxel that may have fewer side effects and work better than paclitaxel. It is being studied in the treatment of cancer. It belongs to the family of drugs called mitotic inhibitors. Also called PNU-93914 and paclitaxel liposome.

Lepirudin A drug that inhibits blood clotting. It is being studied in cancer treatment.

Leptomeningeal cancer A tumor that involves the tissues that cover the brain and spinal cord.

Leptomeningeal Having to do with the two innermost layers of tissues that cover the brain and spinal cord.

Leptomeningeal metastases Cancer that has spread from the original (primary) tumor to the tissues that cover the brain and spinal cord.

Leptospira A genus of the family Treponemataceae, thin coiled organisms, flagellated at the extremities, one or both of which are bent back like a hook. Both pathogenic and innocent forms have been isolated.

Leridistim A substance that is being studied for its ability to stimulate the production of blood cells during chemotherapy. It belongs to the family of drugs called colony-stimulating factors. Also known as SC-70935.

Lerisetron A drug that prevents or reduces nausea and vomiting.

Lesion A change in tissue caused by disease; a point or localized patch of a skin disease. Other words that mean approximately the same thing as lesion are "sore" or "spot."

Lesser curvature (stomach) The medial/superior border of the stomach, site of attachment for the gastric mesentery.

Lesser trochanter (femur) A process on the medial surface of the posterior border of the neck of the femur.

Lesser wing of sphenoid The triangular plate of bone that extends from the anterior portion of the sphenoid bone and helps form the roof of the orbit and floor of the anterior cranial fossa.

Lestaurtinib An orally bioavailable indolocarbazole derivative with antineoplastic properties. Lestaurtinib inhibits autophosphorylation of FMS-like tyrosine kinase 3 (FLT3), resulting in inhibition of FLT3 activity and induction of apoptosis in tumor cells that overexpress FLT3.

Letrozole A nonsteroidal inhibitor of estrogen synthesis that resembles paclitaxel in chemical structure. As a third-generation aromatase inhibitor, letrozole selectively and reversibly inhibits aromatase, a cytochrome P-450 enzyme complex found in many tissues including those of the premenopausal ovary, liver, and breast; aromatase catalyzes the aromatization of androstenedione and testosterone into estrone and estradiol, the final step in estrogen biosynthesis. In estrogen-dependent breast cancers, anastrozole may inhibit tumor growth.

Leuc, leuk White. e.g. leukocyte - a white blood cell. e.g. leukopenia - reduction in the number of leukocytes in the blood.

Leucovorin A drug used to protect normal cells from high doses of the anticancer drug methotrexate. It is also used to increase the antitumor effects of fluorouracil and tegafur-uracil, an oral treatment alternative to intravenous fluorouracil.

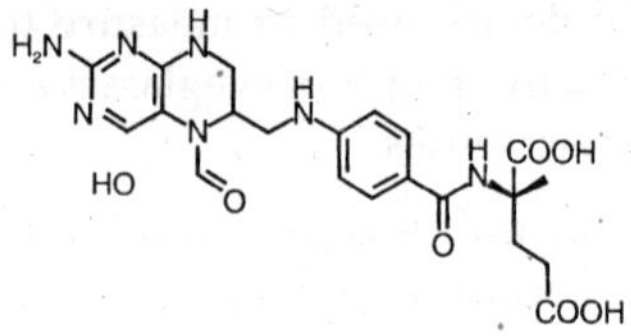

Folinic acid (5-formyl-tetrahydropteroylglutamate)

Figure Leucovorin

Leucovorin calcium An active metabolite of folic acid (also called folinic acid and citrovorum factor), which does not require metabolism by dihydrofolate reductase, the molecular target of folate antagonist-type che-motherapeutic drugs. Leucovorin calcium counteracts the toxic effects of these medications, 'rescuing' the patient while permitting the antitumor activity of the folate antagonist. This agent also potentiates the effects of fluorouracil and its derivatives by stabilizing the binding of the drug's metabolite to its target enzyme, thus prolonging drug activity.

Leukapheresis Removal of the blood to collect specific blood cells; the remaining blood is returned to the body.

Leukemia Cancer of the organs that form the blood, such as lymph nodes and bone marrow. People with leukemia often have a noticeable increase in leukocytes (white blood cells). Leukemia can develop as a consequence of some types of breast cancer therapy.

Leukocyte A white blood cell. Refers to a blood cell that does not contain hemoglobin. White blood cells include lymphocytes, neutrophils, eosinophils, macrophages, and mast cells. These cells are made by bone marrow and help the body fight infection and other diseases.

Leukocytoclasis The disintegration of leukocytes (primarily pmn's) resulting in nuclear dust as seen in leukocytoclastic vasculitis.

Leukoencephalitis Inflammation of the white matter of the brain.

Leukopenia A condition in which the number of leukocytes (white blood cells) in the blood is reduced.

Leukoplakia An abnormal patch of white tissue that forms on mucous membranes in the mouth and other areas of the body. It may become cancerous. Tobacco (smoking and chewing) and alcohol may increase the risk of leukoplakia in the mouth.

Leukotriene antagonists New anti-inflammatory oral medication for Asthma.

Leuprolide acetate The acetate salt of a synthetic nonapeptide analogue of gonadotropin-releasing hormone. Leuprolide binds to and activates gonadotropin-releasing hormone (GnRH) receptors. Continuous, prolonged administration of leuprolide in males results in pituitary GnRH receptor desensitization and inhibition of pituitary secretion of follicle stimulating hormone (FSH) and luteinizing hormone (LH), leading to a significant decline in testosterone production; in females, prolonged administration results in a decrease in estradiol production. This agent reduces testosterone production to castration levels and may inhibit androgen receptor-positive tumor progression.

Leuvectin An agent that delivers the gene for interleukin-2 (IL-2) into cells to increase production of IL-2 by the cells.

Levamisole An antiparasitic drug that is also being studied in cancer therapy with fluorouracil.

Levator muscle It controls the elevation of the upper eyelid.

Levator palpebrae muscle Muscle responsible for raising the upper eyelid. It originates at the upper border of the optic foramen/ orbital rim and inserts into the tarsal palate (cartilage) of the upper eyelid.

Level of product protection The level of protection required for an area based on an assessment by the manufacturer of contamination risk.

Levels of evidence A ranking system used to describe the strength of the results measured in a clinical trial or research study. The design of the study (such as a case report for an individual patient or a randomized double-blinded controlled clinical trial) and the endpoints measured (such as survival or quality of life) affect the strength of the evidence.

Levocarnitine A form of carnitine, which is a substance made in the muscles and liver. It can be given as a supplement to prevent and treat carnitine deficiency in patients who are receiving chemotherapy for cancer or undergoing dialysis for kidney disease. Also called L-carnitine.

Levofloxacin A substance used to treat bacterial infections. It belongs to the family of drugs called quinolone antibiotics.

LGD1069 An anticancer drug used to decrease the growth of some types of cancer cells. It belongs to the family of drugs called retinoids. Also called bexarotene.

Lhermitte's sign A sensation similar to an electrical shock radiating from the back of the head down the spine as the neck is bent forward.

LH-RH (Luteinizing hormone-releasing hormone) A hormone that stimulates the production of sex hormones in men and women.

Liarozole An anticancer drug that promotes differentiation by increasing the levels of retinoic acid within the tumor.

Library An unordered collection of clones (i.e., cloned DNA from a particular organism) whose relationship to each other can be established by physical mapping.

Lichenification The thickening of the epidermis layer of the skin, caused by excessive scratching and rubbing.

Lidocaine A substance that is used to relieve pain by blocking signals at the nerve endings in skin. It can also be given intravenously to stop heart arrhythmias. It belongs to the families of drugs called local anesthetics and antiarrhythmics.

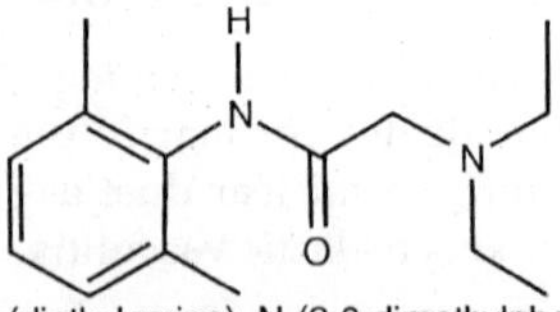

2-(diethylamino)–N-(2,6-dimethylphenyl) acetamide monohydrochloride

Figure Lidocaine

Life-long learning Continuous training over the course of a professional career. Because medical science changes so rapidly, it is vital that its practitioners are committed to and engage in life-long learning.

Lifestyle A general manner of living based on the interplay between living conditions in the broad sense and individual patterns of behavior as determined by socio-cultural factors and personal characteristics. The range of behavior patterns open to individuals may be limited or extended by social environmental factors. For this reason, lifestyles are usually considered in the context of both collective and individual experiences and general conditions of life. A change of lifestyle may include such activities as stopping cigarette smoking, changing the pattern of nutrition or engaging in regular physical exercise.

Lifetable analysis A method of analysis that relies on a count of the number of events observed and the time points at which those events occurred, relative to some zero point. The event may be death or some other event. In clinical trials, the time to an event for a patient is usually measured from the time of randomization. Treatment effects are assessed by comparing event rates in the different treatment groups.

Li-fraumeni syndrome A rare, inherited predisposition to multiple cancers, caused by an alteration in the p53 tumor suppressor gene.

Ligand A molecule or ion that is bound to protein.

Ligase An enzyme used to catalyze the joining of single-stranded DNA segments.

Ligation The process of tying off blood vessels so that blood cannot flow to a part of the body or to a tumor.

Light chain (L chain) The light chain of immunoglobulin is a structural feature that occurs in two forms: kappa and lambda.

Light microscope A microscope (device to magnify small objects) in which objects are lit directly by white light.

Lignans A type of phytoestrogen found in flax, rye and various vegetables which may provide the health benefits of lowering LDL cholesterol, total cholesterol and triglycerides thereby protecting against heart disease and some cancers.

Limb perfusion A technique that may be used to deliver anticancer drugs directly to an arm or leg. The flow of blood to and from the limb is temporarily stopped with a tourniquet, and anticancer drugs are put directly into the blood of the limb. This allows the person to receive a high dose of drugs in the area where the cancer occurred. Also called isolated limb perfusion.

Limbus The boundary between the cornea and scleral.

Limited breast surgery Also called lumpectomy, segmental excision, and tylectomy. It removes the breast cancer and a small amount of tissue around the cancer, but preserves most of the breast. It is almost always combined with axillary lymph node removal and is followed by radiation therapy.

Limited joint mobility A form of arthritis involving the hand; it causes the fingers to curve inward and the skin on the palm to tighten and thicken. This condition mainly affects people with IDDM.

Limited-stage small cell lung cancer Cancer is found in one lung, the tissues between the lungs, and nearby lymph nodes only.

Linac A machine that uses electricity to form a stream of fast-moving subatomic particles. This creates high-energy radiation that may be used to treat cancer. Also called linear accelerator and MeV linear accelerator (mega-voltage linear accelerator).

Linear accelerator A machine that uses electricity to form a stream of fast-moving subatomic particles. This creates high-energy radiation that may be used to treat cancer. Also called linac and MeV linear accelerator (mega-voltage linear accelerator).

Linkage The proximity of two or more markers (e.g., genes, RFLP markers) on a chromosome; the closer together the markers are, the lower the probability that they will be separated during DNA repair or replication processes (binary fission in prokaryotes, mitosis or meiosis in eukaryotes), and hence the greater the probability that they will be inherited together.

Linkage disequilibrium Where alleles occur together more often than can be accounted for by chance. Indicates that the two alleles are physically close on the DNA strand.

Linkage map A map of the relative positions of genetic loci on a chromosome, determined on the basis of how often the loci are inherited together. Distance is measured in centimorgans (cM).

Linseed The seed of the flax plant. It is a rich source of omega-3 fatty acid, fiber, and a compound called lignin. It is being studied in the prevention of prostate cancer. Also called flaxseed.

Liothyronine sodium A thyroid hormone. Also called triiodothyronine or T-3.

Lip (o) Fat; lipid. e.g. lipoma - a benign tumor of fat cells.

Lipid A term for fat. The body stores fat as energy for future use just like a car that has a reserve fuel tank. When the body needs energy, it can break down the lipids into fatty acids and burn them like glucose (sugar).

The two most commonly measured kinds of lipids are triglycerides and cholesterol.

Lipid profile A group of blood tests that are often ordered together to evaluate an individual's risk for heart disease or stroke. These tests include measurement of total cholesterol, HDL-cholesterol ("good" cholesterol), LDL-cholesterol ("bad" cholesterol), and triglycerides.

Lipids Hydrophobic biological compounds (fats and fatlike materials) that are insoluble in water, but soluble in nonpolar solvents such as benzene, chloroform, and ether. The major components in most lipids are fatty acids.

Lipoatrophy Loss of body fat from particular areas of the body, especially the arms, legs, face, and buttocks. Lipoatrophy is a potential side effect of some NRTIs.

Lipodystrophy Lumps (lipohypertrophy) or depressions (lipoatrophy) below the surface of the skin that form when a person keeps injecting insulin into the same spot. Both forms of lipodystrophies are harmless. People can decrease this problem by changing (rotating) the places where they inject their insulin. Using purified insulins may also help.

Lipohypertrophy Also known as hyperadiposity. Abnormal buildup of fat, particularly in the breasts, on the back of the neck and upper shoulders ("buffalo hump"), deep within the abdomen ("protease paunch"), or in fatty growths known as lipomas. Lipohypertrophy may occur with the use of some PIs and NRTIs.

Lipophilic Able to dissolve, be dissolved in, or absorb lipids (fats).

Lipoprotein A conjugated protein containing a lipid, prosthetic group.

Liposarcoma A rare cancer of the fat cells.

Liposomal A drug preparation that contains the active drug in very tiny fat particles. This fat-encapsulated drug is absorbed better, and its distribution to the tumor site is improved.

Liposomal SN-38 A form of the anticancer drug irinotecan that may have fewer side effects and work better than irinotecan alone. It is being studied in the treatment of cancer. It belongs to the family of drugs called irinotecan (CPT-11) derivatives.

Liposome An artificial phospholipid vesicle. Liposomes can be useful for the enclosure of macromolecules such as nucleic acids or, after loading with an appropriate drug. They may be used therapeutically to achieve slow release of the drug into circulation.

Liquid-based pap test A type of Pap test. A Pap test is a procedure in which cells are scraped from the cervix for examination under a microscope. It is used to detect cancer or changes that may lead to cancer. A Pap test can also show noncancerous conditions, such as infection or inflammation. In a liquid-based Pap test, the cells are rinsed into a small container of liquid. The cells are then placed onto slides by a special machine and examined under a microscope to see if the cells are abnormal.

Lisofylline A drug that may protect healthy cells from chemotherapy and radiation without inhibiting the effects of these therapies on tumor cells.

Lispro insulin Lispro insulin is an insulin analog in which the position of two amino acids are switched. The resulting lispro insulin does not form hexamers (clumps of six molecules linked together) and is thus faster acting than regular insulin. It can be injected immediately before a meal, compared with regular which should be injected 30 minutes or more before a meal.

Listeria Listeria monocytogenes is a Gram-positive bacterium, found in at least 37 mammalian species, as well as 17 species of birds and possibly some fish and shellfish. The bacteria can be isolated from soil, and is resistant to heat, freezing and drying.

Listeria has been associated with foods such as raw milk, soft-ripened cheeses, ice cream, raw vegetables, raw and cooked poultry, raw meat and raw and smoked fish. Unlike other pathogenic bacteria, such as salmonella, listeria can survive and grow at temperatures as low as 5°C (41°F).

Acute infection with listeria may result in flu-like symptoms including persistent fever, followed by septicemia, meningitis, encephalitis, and intrauterine or cervical infections in pregnant women. Possible gastrointestinal symptoms include nausea, vomiting and diarrhea, alone or couple with other symptoms (mentioned above).

Lith Stone, e.g. lithotomy - removal of a stone.

Lithotripsy A procedure done to break up stones in the urinary tract using ultrasonic shock waves, so that the fragments can be easily passed from the body.

Liver The liver is the largest solid organ in the body, just under the right upper quadrant of the abdoment, just under the diaphragm. It's primary role is in support of digestion, where it processes nutrients absorbed by the intestinal mucosa. The venous drainage from the intestines enters the liver through the portal veins. The liver also has a separate arterial supply, and the hepatic veins empty directly into the inferior vena cava. The liver also secretes bile, and "filters" the gastrointestinal blood. The liver has 'reticuloendothelial cells' that can trap microsopic particles from the blood. The liver may be imaged by US, CT, MR and functional Nuclear Medicine studies.

Liver biopsy Procedure used to take a sample of the liver to study under a microscope to determine the degree of liver damage or the type of liver injury. Can be performed by passing a needle between the ribs on the right side or at the time of surgical procedure where the abdomen is opened.

Liver cancer A disease in which malignant (cancer) cells are found in the tissues of the liver.

Liver failure A term used to refer to the clinical picture produced by end-stage cirrhosis manifested by esophageal variceal hemorrhage, ascites, and/or hepatic encephalopathy.

Liver function tests Blood tests that measure the levels of liver enzymes (proteins made and used by the liver) to determine if the liver is working properly. The liver enzymes that are routinely measured as part of liver function tests are aspartate aminotransferase (AST), alanine aminotransferase (ALT), gammaglutamyltransferase (GGT), serum glutamic oxaloacetic transaminase (SGOT), and serum glutamic pyruvic transaminase (SGPT). Increased levels of these enzymes indicate that the liver has been damaged.

Liver metastases Cancer that has spread from the original (primary) tumor to the liver.

Liver scan An image of the liver created on a computer screen or on film. A radioactive substance is injected into a blood vessel and travels through the bloodstream. It collects in the liver, especially in abnormal areas, and can be detected by the scanner.

Living will A type of legal advance directive in which a person describes specific treatment guidelines that are to be followed by health care providers if he or she becomes terminally ill and cannot communicate. A living will usually has instructions about whether to use aggressive medical treatment to keep a person alive (such as CPR, artificial nutrition, use of a respirator).

LMB 2 immunotoxin A fusion protein consisting of the Fv portion of a monoclonal antibody attached to a 38-kDa fragment of the Pseudomonas exotoxin A (with amino acids 365-380 deleted). LMB-2 immunotoxin targets the interleukin 2 receptor (also known as IL-2R or CD25) which is expressed on activated normal T and B cells and macrophages and on the cells of various hematologic malignancies. The antibody attaches to the IL-2R on the cell membrane, facilitating the entry of the exotoxin. The exotoxin moiety induces caspase-mediated apoptosis of tumor cells via a mechanism involving mitocho-ndrial damage; it also catalyzes the transfer of ADP ribose from nicotinamide adenine din-ucleotide (NAD) to elongation factor-2 in eukaryotic cells, thereby inactivating elongation factor 2 and inhibiting protein synthesis.

LMB 9 immunotoxin A recombinant disulfide stabilized anti-Lewis Y IgG immunotoxin containing a 38 KD toxic element derived from the Pseudomonas aeruginosa exotoxin A and a monoclonal antibody fragment, designed to attack adenocarcinomas expressing Lewis Y. LMB-9 immunotoxin attaches to tumor cells, facilitating he entry of the exotoxin. The exotoxin moiety induces caspase-mediated apoptosis of tumor cells via a mechanism involving mitochondrial damage; it also catalyzes the transfer of ADP ribose from nicotinamide adenine dinucleotide (NAD) to elongation factor-2 in eukaryotic cells, thereby inactivating elongation factor 2 and inhibiting protein synthesis

Lobaplatin An anticancer drug that belongs to the family of drugs called platinum compounds.

Lobe A portion of an organ, such as the liver, lung, breast, thyroid, or brain.

Lobectomy The removal of a lobe.

Lobradimil A substance that is being studied for its ability to help other drugs reach the brain. It belongs to the family of drugs called bradykinin agonists. Also called RMP-7.

Lobular carcinoma (of the breast infiltrating or invasive) A type of breast cancer that starts within the lobules. It may be multicentric (occurring in multiple lobules). Compared with other types of breast cancer, this type has a higher chance of occurring in the opposite breast, as well. It can often be difficult to diagnose, even with careful physical examination or mammography.

Lobular carcinoma in situ A very early type of breast cancer that develops within the milk-producing glands (lobules) of the breast and does not penetrate through the wall of the lobules. Researchers think that lobular carcinoma in situ does not eventually become an invasive lobular cancer; rather, having this type of cancer places a woman at increased risk of developing an invasive breast cancer later in life. For this reason, it's important for women with lobular carcinoma in situ to have a physical examination three or four times a year and an annual mammogram.

Lobule A small lobe or a subdivision of a lobe.

Local anesthesia Drugs that cause a temporary loss of feeling in one part of the body. The patient remains awake but has no feeling in the part of the body treated with the anesthetic.

Local cancer An invasive malignant cancer confined entirely to the organ where the cancer began.

Local excision Removal of a lesion or tumor that is confined to one area.

Local therapy Treatment that affects cells in the tumor and the area close to it.

Localization The process of determining or marking the location or site of a lesion or disease. May also refer to the process of keeping a lesion or disease in a specific location or site.

Localize Determination of the original position (locus) of a gene or other marker on a chromosome.

Localized breast cancer A cancer that arose in the breast and is confined to the breast.

Localized gallbladder cancer Cancer found only in the tissues that make up the wall of the gallbladder. Localized gallbladder cancer can be removed completely in an operation.

Localized malignant mesothelioma Cancer is found in the lining of the chest wall and may also be found in the lining of the lung, the lining of the diaphragm (the thin muscle below the lungs and heart that separates the chest from the abdomen), or the lining of the sac that covers the heart on the same side of the chest. Also called stage I malignant mesothelioma.

Locally advanced cancer Cancer that has spread only to nearby tissues or lymph nodes.

Loci Plural of locus; a place; usually, a specific site.

Locus The position on a chromosome of a gene or other chromosome marker; also, the DNA at that position. The use of locus is sometimes restricted to mean expressed DNA regions.

Lometrexol A substance that is being studied as a treatment for cancer. It belongs to the family of drugs called antifolates.

Lomustine A nitrosourea with antineoplastic activity. Lomustine alkylates and crosslinks DNA, thereby inhibiting DNA and RNA synthesis. This agent also carbamoylates DNA and proteins, resulting in inhibition of DNA and RNA synthesis and disruption of RNA processing. Lomustine is lipophilic and crosses the blood-brain barrier.

Lonafarnib A synthetic tricyclic derivative of carboxamide with antineoplastic properties. Lonarfanib binds to and inhibits farnesyl transferase, an enzyme involved in the post-translational modification and activation of Ras proteins. Ras proteins participate in numerous signalling pathways (proliferation, cytoskeletal organization), and play an important role in oncogenesis. Mutated ras proteins have been found in a wide range of human cancers.

Long face syndrome Facial Appearance of the chronic nasal allergy sufferer.

Long term nonprogressors People who have been infected with HIV for a number of years (usually at least 7), but have had stable CD4 cell counts of 600 or more, no HIV-related diseases, and no need for anti-HIV therapy.

Long terminal repeat (LTR) Genetic material at the beginning of the HIV genome that helps control replication.

Long-range restriction mapping Restriction enzymes are proteins that cut DNA at precise locations. Restriction maps depict the chromosomal positions of restriction-enzyme cutting sites. These are used as biochemical "signposts," or markers of specific areas along the chromosomes. The map will detail the positions where the DNA molecule is cut by particular restriction enzymes.

Longus capitus muscle Muscle responsible for flexing the head. It originates at the transverse processes of the third to the sixth cervical vertebrae, and inserts into the basal portion of the occipital bone.

Longus colli muscle The long muscles of the neck, responsible for flexion and support of the cervical vertebrae.

Loop of Henle A u-shaped turn in the medullary portion of a renal tubule, with a descending limb from the proximal convoluted tubule and an ascending limb to the distal convoluted tubule.

Loose body A title given to an object, located within a joint, that has become detached. A common cause of locking of a joint.

Loperamide hydrochloride An antidiarrheal drug.

Lordosis Curve of the spine, whereby there is hollowing. Normal lordosis is seen in the lumbar spine, although variances do exist.

Losoxantrone An anticancer drug that belongs to the family of drugs called antipyrazoles.

Lost to follow up A patient who can no longer be followed for the outcome of interest, e.g., a patient who is unwilling or unable to return to the clinic for follow-up examinations in the case of a clinical trial using an outcome measured at the clinic, or a patient who cannot be located for subsequent follow-up in the case of a trial involving mortality or some other outcome that can be measured outside the clinic setting.

Lovastatin A lactone metabolite isolated from the fungus Aspergillus terreus with cholesterol-lowering activity and potential antineoplastic activity. Lovastatin is hydrolyszed to the active beta-hydroxyacid form, which competitively inhibits 3-hydroxyl-3-methylgutarylcoenzyme A (HMG-CoA) reductase, an enzyme involved in the cholesterol biosynthesis. In addition, this agent may inhibit tumor cell proliferation and reduce tumor cell invasiveness, thereby decreasing tumor metastatic potential; induce tumor cell apoptosis, possibly by inhibiting protein geranylgeranylation and; arrest cells in the G1 phase of the cell cycle, an effect that sensitizes tumor cells to the cytotoxic effects of ionizing radiation.

Low grade When referring to cancerous and precancerous growths, a term used to describe cells that look nearly normal under a microscope. These cells are less likely to grow and spread quickly than cells in high-grade cancerous or precancerous growths.

Low grade lymphoma A type of lymphoma that tends to grow and spread slowly, and has few symptoms. Also called indolent lymphoma.

Low grade squamous intraepithelial lesion (LSIL) A condition in which the cells of the uterine cervix are slightly abnormal. LSIL is not cancer.

Low-calorie sweetener Low-calorie sweeteners are non-nutritive sweeteners, also referred to as intense sweeteners. Low-calorie sweeteners can replace nutritive sweeteners in most foods at a caloric savings of approximately 16 calories per teaspoon. Thus, caloric reduction may be achieved when low-calorie sweetened foods and beverages are substituted for their full-calorie counterparts.

Lower esophageal sphincter A muscle at the top portion of the stomach relaxes to allow food to pass from the esophagus to the stomach when we eat, and closes to keep food from moving back into the esophagus from the stomach.

Lower flammability level (LFL) The minimum concentration of vapour in air at which propagation of flame will occur in the presence of an ignition source. LFL is sometimes referred to as LEL or Lower Explosive Limit.

Lower GI series A study that looks at the rectum, the large intestine, and the lower part of the small intestine. A fluid called barium that shows up well on x-rays is given into the rectum as an enema. X-rays of the abdomen shows strictures (narrowed areas), obstructions (blockages), and other problems.

Lower limit of normal The bottom of the normal range for a particular laboratory: helps assure between-lab comparability.

LP needle Lumbar puncture needle.

LPS (Lipopolysaccharide) Molecule found in the outer cell walls of some bacteria that trigger the immune response resulting in fever. Also referred to as pyrogens or as endotoxins, though, strictly speaking, they are not endotoxins but predominant components of endotoxins produced by gram-negative bacteria. Common cause of pyrogenic reactions in parenteral products.

Lubricant An oily or slippery substance.

Lumbar artery A segmental artery which originates from the abdominal aorta and branches into dorsal and spinal branches.

Lumbar puncture A procedure in which a needle is put into the lower part of the spinal column to collect cerebrospinal fluid or to give anticancer drugs intrathecally. Also called a spinal tap.

Lumbar spine Portion of the vertebral column located between the thorax and the pelvis.

Lumen The cavity or channel within a tube or tubular organ such as a blood vessel or the intestine.

Lump Any kind of mass that can be felt in the breast or elsewhere in the body.

Lumpectomy Surgery to remove the tumor and a small amount of surrounding normal tissue.

Lungs The lungs are a pair of breathing organs located with the chest which remove carbon dioxide from and bring oxygen to the blood. There is a right and left lung.

Lung cancer Cancer that forms in tissues of the lung, usually in the cells lining air passages. The two main types are small cell lung cancer and non-small cell lung cancer. These types are diagnosed based on how the cells look under a microscope.

Lung metastases Cancer that has spread from the original (primary) tumor to the lung.

Lung to head ratio (LHR) Congenital diaphragmatic hernia (CDH) usually is diagnosed before birth using ultrasound, in which sound waves form a picture of the fetus that can determine the severity of the defect. The two factors used to grade the severity of the CDH are the position of the liver and the lung-to-head ratio. Liver position refers to whether or not any portion of liver has herniated, or moved up into the chest of the fetus. Fetuses with a liver in the chest have a more severe condition and a low survival rate. The lung-to-head ratio is a numeric estimate of the size of the lungs based on measuring the amount of visible lung. High lung-to-head ratios are associated with a good outcome.

Lupus A chronic, inflammatory, connective tissue disease that can affect the joints and many organs, including the skin, heart, lungs, kidneys, and nervous system. It can cause many different symptoms; however, not everyone with lupus has all of the symptoms. Also called systemic lupus erythematosus (SLE).

Lurtotecan An anticancer drug that belongs to the family of drugs called topoisomerase inhibitors.

Luschka, joints of Known as neurocentral joints, uncovertebral joints or lateral interbody joints, these joints are located near the posterolateral margin of the cervical discs.

Lutein A type of carotenoid found in most green vegetables which positively contributes to maintenance of eye vision.

Luteinizing hormone-releasing hormone (LH-RH) A hormone that stimulates the production of sex hormones in men and women.

Luteinizing hormone-releasing hormone agonist A drug that inhibits the secretion of sex hormones. In men, LH-RH agonist causes testosterone levels to fall. In women, LH-RH agonist causes the levels of estrogen and other sex hormones to fall.

Lutetium texaphyrin A substance that is being studied in the treatment of cancer using photodynamic therapy. It belongs to the family of drugs called metallotexaphyrins. Also called motexafin lutetium.

Lycopene A linear, unsaturated hydrocarbon carotenoid, the major red pigment in fruits such as tomatoes, pink grapefruit, apricots, red oranges, watermelon, rosehips, and guava. As a class, carotenoids are pigment compounds found in photosynthetic organisms (plants, algae, and some types of fungus), and are chemically characterized by a large polyene chain containing 35-40 carbon atoms; some carotenoid polyene chains are terminated by two 6-carbon rings. In animals, carotenoids such as lycopene may possess antioxidant properties which may retard ageing and many degenerative diseases. As an essential nutrient, lycopene is required in the animal diet.

Lymph Clear fluid that passes within the lymphatic system and contains cells known as lymphocytes. These cells fight infections. They have a lesser role in fighting cancer.

Lymph gland A rounded mass of lymphatic tissue that is surrounded by a capsule of connective tissue. Lymph glands filter lymph (lymphatic fluid), and they store lymphocytes (white blood cells). They are located along lymphatic vessels. Also called a lymph node.

Lymph nodes Small bean-sized organs of the immune system, distributed widely throughout the body. Lymph fluid is filtered through the lymph nodes in which all types of lymphocytes take up temporary residence. Antigens which enter the body find their way into lymph or blood and are filtered out by lymph nodes or the spleen respectively, for attack by the immune system.

Lymph node dissection A surgical procedure in which the lymph nodes are removed and examined to see whether they contain cancer. For a regional lymph node dissection, some of the lymph nodes in the tumor area are removed; for a radical lymph node dissection, most or all of the lymph nodes in the tumor area are removed. Also called lymphadenectomy.

Lymph node drainage The flow of lymph from an area of tissue into a particular lymph node.

Lymph node mapping The use of dyes and radioactive substances to identify lymph nodes that may contain tumor cells. Also called lymphatic mapping.

Lymph vessel A thin tube that carries lymph (lymphatic fluid) and white blood cells through the lymphatic system. Also called lymphatic vessel.

Lymphadenectomy A surgical procedure in which the lymph nodes are removed and examined to see whether they contain cancer. For a regional lymphadenectomy, some of the lymph nodes in the tumor area are removed; for a radical lymphadenectomy, most or all of the lymph nodes in the tumor area are removed. Also called lymph node dissection.

Lymphadenopathy Swollen, firm and possibly tender lymph nodes. The cause may range from an infection such as HIV, the flu, mononucleosis, or lymphoma (cancer of the lymph nodes).

Lymphadenopathy syndrome (LAS) Swollen, firm, and possibly tender lymph nodes. The causes range from infection such as HIV, the flu, or mononucleosis to lymphoma (cancer of the lymphoid tissue).

Lymphangiectasia Dilation of the lymphatic vessels; may be congenital or acquired.

Lymphangiogram An x-ray of the lymphatic system. A dye is injected into a lymphatic vessel and travels throughout the lymphatic system. The dye outlines the lymphatic vessels and organs on the x-ray.

Lymphangiography An x-ray study of the lymphatic system. A dye is injected into a lymphatic vessel and travels throughout the lymphatic system. The dye outlines the lymphatic vessels and organs on the x-ray.

Lymphangiosarcoma A type of cancer that begins in the cells that line lymph vessels.

Lymphatic basin A group of lymph nodes that receives and filters lymph that flows from a certain area of the body. Special dyes may be used to stain and identify the lymphatic basin in the tissues around a tumor, so that lymph nodes that may contain cancer can be removed and checked by a pathologist.

Lymphatic fluid The clear fluid that travels through the lymphatic system and carries cells that help fight infections and other diseases. Also called lymph.

Lymphatic mapping The use of dyes and radioactive substances to identify lymph nodes that may contain tumor cells. Also called lymph node mapping.

Lymphatic system The tissues and organs (including bone marrow, spleen, thymus, and lymph nodes) that produce and store lymphocytes (cells that fight infection) and the channels that carry the lymph fluid. The entire lymphatic system is an important part of the body's immune system. lymphedema – Swelling in the arm caused by excess fluid that collects after lymph nodes and vessels are removed by surgery or treated by radiation. This condition is usually painful and can be persistent.

Lymphatic vessels A bodywide network of channels, similar to the blood vessels, which transport lymph to the immune organs and into the bloodstream.

Lymphedema A condition in which excess fluid collects in tissue and causes swelling. It may occur in the arm or leg after lymph vessels or lymph nodes in the underarm or groin are removed or treated with radiation.

Lymphoblast A lymphocyte that has gotten larger after being stimulated by an antigen. Lymphoblasts look like immature lymphocytes, and were once thought to be precursor cells.

Lymphocyte A type of white blood cell. Lymphocytes have a number of roles in the immune system, including the production of antibodies and other substances that fight infection and diseases.

Lymphocyte proliferation assay A laboratory test that measures the ability of lymphocytes (infection-fighting white blood cells) to recognize an antigen and make more copies of themselves (proliferate) in response to the antigen encounter.

Lymphocytic Referring to lymphocytes, a type of white blood cell.

Lymphocytic leukemia A type of cancer in which the bone marrow makes too many lymphocytes (white blood cells).

Lymphoepithelioma A type of cancer that begins in the tissues covering the nasopharynx (the upper part of the throat behind the nose).

Lymphogranuloma venereum (LGV) A sexually transmitted disease (STD) caused by a species of the chlamydia bacterium. It is characterized by genital lesions and swelling of lymph nodes in the groin.

Lymphography An x-ray study of lymph nodes and lymphatic vessels made visible by the injection of a special dye.

Lymphoid Referring to lymphocytes, a type of white blood cell. Also refers to tissue in which lymphocytes develop.

Lymphoid interstitial pneumonitis (LIP) A lung disorder that causes hardening of the parts of the lung that aid in oxygen absorption. The cause of LIP is unknown, and there is no clear treatment. LIP is an AIDS-defining condition in HIV-infected children.

Lymphoid tissue Tissue made up white blood cells and lymphatic vessels.

Lymphokine A substance produced by lymphocytes, that has an effect on other cells involved in the immune system. An example is Interleukin 2 (IL-2).

Lymphokine-activated killer (LAK) cells Killer cell lymphocytes activated in the presence of interleukin-2 (IL-2). Lymphokine-activated killer cells (LAKs) are cytotoxic effector cells with an exceptionally wide target cell spectrum including normal and malignant cells of different origins. LAK cells exhibit a profound heterogeneity with regard to phenotype surface marker expression; it remains to be determined if they represent a unique cell lineage.

Lymphokines Cytokines (chemical messengers that affect the immune response) secreted by white blood cells.

Lymphoma Cancer that begins in cells of the immune system. There are two basic categories of lymphomas. One kind is Hodgkin's lymphoma, which is marked by the presence of a type of cell called the Reed-Sternberg cell. The other category is non-Hodgkin's lymphomas, which includes a large, diverse group of cancers of immune system cells. Non-Hodgkin's lymphomas can be further divided into cancers that have an indolent (slow-growing) course and those that have an aggressive (fast-growing) course. These subtypes behave and respond to treatment differently. Both Hodgkin's and non-Hodgkin's lymphomas can occur in children and adults, and prognosis and treatment depend on the stage and the type of cancer.

Lymphomatoid granulomatosis Destructive growth of lymph cells, usually involving the lungs, skin, kidneys, and central nervous system. Grades I and II are not considered cancerous, but grade III is considered a lymphoma.

Lymphopenia A lower than normal number of white blood cells.

Lymphoplasmacytic lymphoma An indolent (slow-growing) type of non-Hodgkin's lymphoma marked by abnormal levels of IgM antibodies in the blood and an enlarged liver, spleen, or lymph nodes. Also called Waldenström's macroglobulinemia.

Lymphoproliferative disorder A disease in which cells of the lymphatic system grow excessively. Lymphoproliferative disorders are often treated like cancer.

Lymphosarcoma An obsolete term for a malignant tumor of lymphatic tissue.

Lymphoscintigraphy A method used to identify the sentinel lymph node (the first draining lymph node near a tumor). A radioactive substance that can be taken up by lymph nodes is injected at the site of the tumor, and a doctor follows the movement of this substance on a computer screen. Once the lymph nodes that have taken up the substance are identified, they can be removed and examined to see if they contain tumor cells.

Lynch syndrome An inherited disorder in which affected individuals have a higher-than-normal chance of developing colon cancer and certain other types of cancer, usually before the age of 60. Also called hereditary nonpolyposis colon cancer.

Lyophilization Also known as freeze drying, it is a means of stabilizing wet substances by freezing them, then evaporating the resulting ice, to leave a substantially dry, porous residue which has the same size and shape of the original frozen mass.

Lyophilizer A freeze dryer.

Lysate A product of lysis, which is the disintegration or dissolution of the cell walls.

Lyse To rupture or destroy a cell.

Lysine As essential, basic amino acid obtained from many proteins by hydrolysis.

Lysis In biology, lysis refers to the breakdown of a cell caused by damage to its plasma (outer) membrane. Lysis can be caused by chemical or physical means (for example, strong detergents or high-energy sound waves) or by an infection.

Lysosome A sac-like compartment inside a cell that has enzymes that can break down cellular components that need to be destroyed.

Lytic Having to do with lysis. In biology, lysis refers to the disintegration of a cell by disruption of its plasma membrane. Lysis can be caused by chemical or physical means (e.g., high-energy sound waves) or by a virus infection.

Lytic lesion Destruction of an area of bone due to a disease process, such as cancer.

M protein An antibody or part of an antibody found in unusually large amounts in the blood or urine of people with multiple myeloma and other types of plasma cell tumors. Also called monoclonal protein.

M200 A monoclonal antibody that is being studied in the treatment of some types of cancer. Monoclonal antibodies are made in the laboratory and can locate and bind to cancer cells. M200 binds to a protein that is found on cells that line some tumor blood vessels. It belongs to the family of drugs called angiogenesis inhibitors. Also called volociximab.

Macro Large, e.g. macrophage - a large, mononuclear, phagocytic blood cell.

Macroglobulinemia A condition in which the blood contains high levels of large proteins and is too thick to flow through small blood vessels. One type is Waldenstrom's macroglo-bulinemia, which is a type of cancer.

Macrolides A family of antibiotics with wide spectrum activity, including Clarithromycin, Azithromycin, and erythromycin. Some macrolides are sometimes used as parts of combination therapy for mycobacterium avium.

Macromolecules Molecules whose molecular weights are greater than about 5,000 Daltons.

Macroparticle Particle with an equivalent diameter greater than 5 μm. ISO/FDIS 14644-1.

Macrophage A large scavenger cell that ingests degenerated cells, blood tissue and foreign particles, and secretes messenger proteins (monokines) involved in inflammatory reactions, lymphocyte activation and acute systemic immune responses. Macrophages exist in large numbers throughout the body and are key to the development of immunity to a variety of organisms. Along with their precursor blood cell, the monocyte, macrophages are a major reservoir of HIV infection.

Macrophage-activating factor (MAF) Actually several lymphokines, including interferon, released by activated T cells, which together induce activation of macrophages, making them more efficient in phagocytosis and cytotoxicity.

Macrophthalmos An abnormally large eyeball, usually related to infantile glaucoma.

Macrorestriction map Map depicting the order of and distance between sites at which restriction enzymes cleave chromosomes.

Macroreticular resin An ion exchange resin with a reticular porous matrix that makes it effective for removing colloids and bacteria from process streams, as well as dissolved anions. It is especially useful for preventing colloidal and organic fouling of mixed-bed resins and premature clogging of final filters.

Macrosomia Abnormally large; in diabetes, refers to abnormally large babies that may be born to women with diabetes.

Macrovascular disease A disease of the large blood vessels that sometimes occurs when a person has had diabetes for a long time. Fat and blood clots build up in the large blood vessels and stick to the vessel walls Three kinds of macrovascular disease are coronary disease, cerebrovascular disease, and peripheral vascular disease.

Macula The most sensitive part of the retina that is about the size of a pinhead and is where our most detailed vision occurs.

Macular degeneration A deterioration of the central portion of the retina known as the macula.

Macular edema A swelling (edema) in the macula, an area near the center of the retina of the eye that is responsible for fine or reading vision. Macular edema is a common complication associated with diabetic retinopathy.

Mafosfamide A synthetic oxazaphos-phorine derivative with antineoplastic properties. Mafosfamide alkylates DNA, forming DNA cross-links and inhibiting DNA synthesis. Although closely related to cyclophosphamide, mafosfamide, unlike cyclophosphamide, does not require hepatic activation to generate its active metabolite 4-hydroxycyclophosphamide; accordingly, mafosfamide is potentially useful in the intrathecal treatment of neoplastic meningitis.

Magnesium In medicine, a mineral used by the body to help maintain muscles, nerves, and bones. It is also used in energy metabolism and protein synthesis.

Magnetic field therapy Employs an alternating magnetic field to generate an electric current inside the tissues, resulting in changes to blood flow.

Magnetic resonance imaging (MRI) A procedure in which radio waves and a powerful magnet linked to a computer are used to create detailed pictures of areas inside

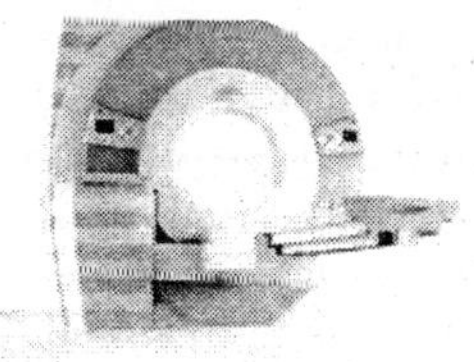

Figure MRI Machine

the body. These pictures can show the difference between normal and diseased tissue. MRI makes better images of organs and soft tissue than other scanning techniques, such as CT or x-ray. MRI is especially useful for imaging the brain, spine, the soft tissue of joints, and the inside of bones. Also called nuclear magnetic resonance imaging.

Magnetic resonance perfusion imaging A special type of magnetic resonance imaging (MRI) that uses an injected dye in order to see blood flow through tissues. Also called perfusion magnetic resonance imaging.

Magnetic resonance spectroscopic imaging (MRSI) A noninvasive imaging method that provides information about cellular activity (metabolic information). It is used along with magnetic resonance imaging (MRI) which provides information about the shape and size of the tumor (spacial information). Also called 1H-nuclear magnetic resonance spectroscopic imaging and proton magnetic resonance spectroscopic imaging.

Magnetic-targeted carrier A tiny bead made from particles of iron and carbon that can be attached to an anticancer drug. A magnet applied from outside the body then can direct the drug to the tumor site. This can keep a larger dose of the drug at the tumor site for a longer period of time, and help protect healthy tissue from the side effects of chemotherapy.

Main pulmonary artery Artery originating from the conus arteriosus of the right ventricle, and dividing into the right and left pulmonary arteries under the arch of the aorta. Carries deoxygenated blood to the lungs.

Maintainability Ease with which maintenance can be performed.

Maintenance therapy Treatment that is given to help a primary (original) treatment keep working. Maintenance therapy is often given to help keep cancer in remission.

Major determinants The part of an antigen molecule that is responsible for the specific interaction with an antibody. Penicilloyl is the major determinant of penicillin because it is responsible for 95% of the anaphylaxis that occurs in penicillin allergic individuals

Major histocompatibility complex (MHC) A cluster of genes on chromosome 6 in humans, encoding cell surface molecules that are polymorphic and that code for antigens which lead to rapid graft rejection between members of a single species which differ at these loci. Several classes of protein such as MHC class I and II proteins are encoded in this region. These in humans, are known as 'Human leukocyte antigens' (HLA).

Malabsorption syndrome A condition that occurs when the intestines have problems absorbing nutrients. Malabsorption syndrome is associated with

HIV infection and can cause loss of appetite, muscle pain, and weight loss.

Malacia (suffix) Softening, e.g. osteomalacia - softening of the bone.

Malaise A general feeling of discomfort or not feeling well.

Male breast cancer Cancer that forms in tissues of the breast in men. Most male breast cancer begins in cells lining the ducts. It is very rare and usually affects older men.

Malignancy A cancerous tumor that can invade and destroy nearby tissue and spread to other parts of the body.

Malignant Cancerous. Malignant tumors can invade and destroy nearby tissue and spread to other parts of the body.

Malignant ascites A condition in which fluid containing cancer cells collects in the abdomen.

Malignant fibrous cytoma A soft tissue sarcoma that usually occurs in the limbs, most commonly the legs, and may also occur in the abdomen. Also called malignant fibrous histiocytoma.

Malignant fibrous histiocytoma A soft tissue sarcoma that usually occurs in the limbs, most commonly the legs, and may also occur in the abdomen. Also called malignant fibrous cytoma.

Malignant meningioma A rare, quickly growing tumor that occurs in the membranes that cover and protect the brain and spinal cord (meninges).

Malignant mesothelioma A rare type of cancer in which malignant cells are found in the sac lining the chest or abdomen. Exposure to airborne asbestos particles increases one's risk of developing malignant mesothelioma.

Malignant mixed Müllerian tumor (MMMT) A rare type of tumor that is a mixture of carcinoma and sarcoma cells. MMMT usually occurs in the uterus.

Malignant peripheral nerve sheath tumor (MPNST) A type of soft tissue sarcoma that develops in cells that form a protective sheath (covering) around peripheral nerves, which are nerves that are outside of the central nervous system (brain and spinal cord).

Malingering A voluntary or intentional reduction in visual acuity or other examination data.

Malleolus Rounded bone process located at either side of the ankle joint. The medial malleolus is part of the distal tibia, the lateral malleolus is the distal fibula.

Mallet finger A common condition due to the rupture of the long extensor tendon of the finger, at its insertion into the base of the distal phalanx of the finger.

Malleus The largest auditory ossicle (small bone), which attaches to the tympanic membrane (ear drum) and connects to the incus. Through mechanical linkages, the sound vibrations are amplified and transmitted to the oval window of the cochlea.

Malnutrition A disorder caused by a lack of proper nutrition or an inability to absorb nutrients from food.

Malocclusion "bad bite" Or misalignment of the upper and lower teeth.

Malondialdehyde A byproduct of lipid (fat) metabolism in the body. It is also found in many foods and can be present in high amounts in rancid food.

Malposition Faulty or abnormal position of a part of the body.

Mammaplasty, mammoplasty Plastic surgery to reconstruct the breast or to change the shape, size, or position of the breast. Reduction mammaplasty reduces the size of the breast. Augmentation mammaplasty enlarges a woman's breast, usually with implants.

Mammary Having to do with the breast.

Mammary dysplasia A common condition marked by benign (noncancerous) changes in breast tissue. These changes may include irregular lumps or cysts, breast discomfort, sensitive nipples, and itching. These symptoms may change throughout the menstrual cycle and usually stop after menopause. Also called benign breast disease, fibrocystic breast disease, and fibrocystic breast changes.

Mammary gland Glandular organ located on the chest. The mammary gland is made up of connective tissue, fat, and breast tissue that contains the glands that can make milk. Also called breast.

Mammillary bodies Two small protuberances located on the ventral surface of the cerebrum. They are created by the underlying medial, intermediate and lateral mammillary nuclei and mark the most posterior border of the ventral hypothalamus. The medial mamillary nucleus receives the postcommissural fornix and gives rise to the mammilothalamic and mammillotegmental tracts.

Mammogram, mammography An x-ray of the breast; the principal method of detection of breast cancer in women over 40. Mammography is performed on a

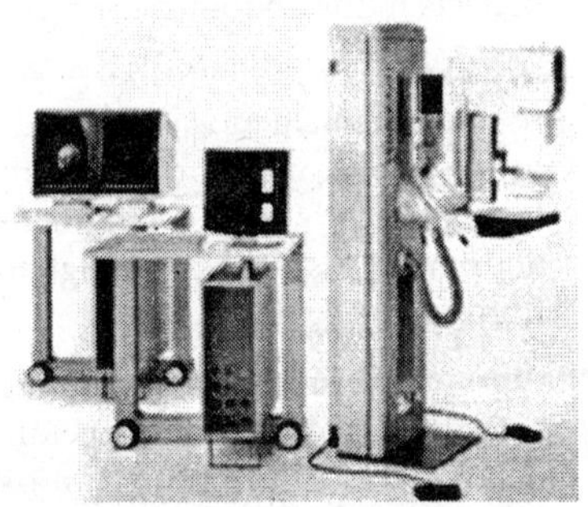

Figure Digital Mammogram machine

special type of x-ray machine that is used only for this purpose. It has two plates. The lower plate is metal and has a drawer for the film cassette. The bare breast is placed on this plate. The upper plate, which is clear plastic, is lowered onto the breast. Thus compressed, it is possible to obtain a clear image of the interior structures of the breast (mammogram). The compression is maintained for only a few seconds – long enough for the technician to go to the control panel and snap the image. The procedure is then repeated with the other breast. A mammogram can show a developing breast tumor before it is large enough to be felt by a woman or even by a highly skilled health professional.

Mammotome A device that uses a computer-guided probe to perform breast biopsies. A Mammotome biopsy can be done on an outpatient basis with a local anesthetic, removes only a small amount of healthy tissue, and doesn't require sutures (stitches) because the incision is very small.

Management trial A trial that is designed primarily to provide information on the value of a treatment in normal usage, typically analyzed by intention to treat.

Mancozeb A pesticide currently in use that contains manganese. When exposed to excessive quantities of Mancozeb, symptoms that indicate bodily poisoning include irritation of the eyes and respiratory tract. Chronic skin disease has been noted in certain cases of occupational exposure.

Mandible The lower jaw bone.

Mandibular condyles Posterior superior process of the mandibular ramus that articulates with the mandibular fossa of the temporal bone. (You can feel this while chewing, by putting your finger in your external ear canal.

Maneb A pesticide currently in use that contains manganese. Maneb is considered carcinogenic to humans and can cause reproductive and developmental anomalies. Excessive exposure may also lead to issues of neurotoxicity causing a severe decrease in mental and physical capabilities.

Manganese A naturally occurring metal that can be found throughout the world in soil, water, and many types of food such as grains and cereals. Manganese is also found in pesticides and is used as a fuel additive in some gasolines. Another common use of manganese is in a steel alloy compound that produces stronger steel resistant to wear. Although necessary in the human diet in trace amounts, excessive quantities may lead to manganese poisoning.

Manganese pneumonitis Inflammation of the lungs affecting the lower airways, caused by the inhalation of manganese particles. Manganese pneumonitis, a form of manganese poisoning, may be fatal or it may be chronic and recurring.

Manganese sulfate A naturally forming chemical nutrient found in fertilizers, necessary for proper photosynthesis in palms, trees, shrubs, and other plants. Excessive quantities of the chemical will damage plant health and distorting and hindering growth. Excessive human contact with the chemical in fertilizers has been linked to health problems including a decrease of motor skills and psychological problems.

Manganism A disease caused by excess exposure to manganese typically by inhalation of dust particles or fumes. Symptoms of Manganism are very similar to Parkinson's disease symptoms and include neurotoxicity resulting in diminished motor and speech skills, partial physical paralysis, inflammation of the respiratory system and decreased mental capacity.

Manifestation The signs or symptoms by which a disease state is known.

Mantle cell lymphoma An aggressive (fast-growing) type of B-cell non-Hodgkin's lymphoma that usually occurs in middle-aged or older adults. It is marked by small- to medium-size cancer cells that may be in the lymph nodes, spleen, bone marrow, blood, and gastrointestinal system.

Mantle field The area of the neck, chest, and lymph nodes in the armpit that are exposed to radiation.

Manual of operations A document or collection of documents that describes the procedures used in a center or set of centers in a clinical trial (e.g., manual of operations for study clinics, coordinating center manual of operations.)

Manual therapy The art of passive movement techniques.

Manubrium The cranial part of the sternum that articulates with the first two pairs of ribs and the clavicles.

Mapping population The group of related organisms used in constructing a genetic map.

Margin The edge or border of the tissue removed in cancer surgery. The margin is described as negative or clean when the pathologist finds no cancer cells at the edge of the tissue, suggesting that all of the cancer has been removed. The margin is described as positive or involved when the pathologist finds cancer cells at the edge of the tissue, suggesting that all of the cancer has not been removed.

Marijuana A type of plant. Extracts of marijuana are being studied for their ability to control severe nausea and vomiting caused by chemotherapy and/or opioid drugs such as morphine.

Marimastat An anticancer drug that belongs to the family of drugs called angiogenesis inhibitors. Marimastat is a matrix metalloproteinase inhibitor.

Marker An identifiable physical location on a chromosome (e.g., restriction enzyme cutting site, gene) whose inheritance can be monitored. Markers can be expressed regions of DNA (genes) or some segment of DNA with no known coding function but whose pattern of inheritance can be determined.

Market area The targeted geographic area or areas of greatest market potential. The market area does not have to be the same as the post acute facility's catchment area.

MART 1 antigen A tumor-associated melanocytic differentiation antigen. Vaccination with MART-1 antigen may stimulate a host cytotoxic T-cell response against tumor cells expressing the melanocytic differentiation antigen, resulting in tumor cell lysis.

Maryland bridge A bridge that is bonded to the back of the adjacent teeth; requires minimum tooth reduction.

Mass spectrometry An instrument used to identify chemicals in a substance by their mass and charge.

Massage A mechanical form of therapy, whereby the soft tissues are made more pliable with different techniques, promoting increased blood flow and subsequent healing.

Masseter muscle One of the muscles of mastication (chewing). Muscle raises the mandible and closes the jaw.

Mast cell tumor A growth or lump of mast cells (a type of white blood cell). Mast cell tumors can involve the skin, subcutaneous tissue, and muscle tissue. Also called mastocytoma.

Mast cells The cells that release histamine during an allergic reaction after being triggered by an allergen binding to IgE on its surface.

Mastectomy Surgery to remove all or part of the breast. Extended radical mastectomy removes the breast, skin, pectoral muscles (both major and minor), and all axillary and internal mammary lymph nodes on the same side. Halsted radical mastectomy removes the breast, skin, both pectoral muscles, and all axillary lymph nodes on the same side. Modified radical mastectomy removes the breast, skin, nipple, areola, and most of the axillary lymph nodes on the same side, leaving the chest muscles intact. Partial mastectomy removes less than the whole breast, taking only part of the breast in which the cancer occurs and a margin of healthy breast tissue surrounding the tumor. Prophylactic mastectomy is removal of the interior of one or both breasts, before any evidence of cancer can be found, for the purpose of preventing cancer. This procedure is sometimes recommended for women at very high risk of breast cancer, but its efficacy is not proven. Quadrantectomy is a partial mastectomy in which the quarter of the breast that contains tumor is removed. Segmental mastectomy is a partial mastectomy. Simple mastectomy is a term once used to describe what is now called total mastectomy. Total mastectomy removes only the breast.

Mastectomy radical Removal of the entire breast along with underlying muscle and lymph nodes of the armpit.

Mastectomy segmental (lumpectomy) Removal of the lump and a small amount of surrounding breast tissue.

Mastectomy simple (modified mastectomy) Removal of the entire breast.

Mastication Process of chewing food.

Mastitis Inflammation or infection of the breast.

Mastocytoma A growth or lump of mast cells (a type of white blood cell). Mast cell tumors can involve the skin, subcutaneous tissue, and muscle tissue. Also called mast cell tumor.

Mastoid air cells The air spaces within the mastoid process of the temporal bone. The communicate with the pharynx via the eustachian tube.

Mastoid process Process projecting inferoanteriorly from the petrous portion of the temporal bone, anterior to the ear.

Mastopexy Surgery to lift a breast that sags.

Matching placebo A pill (capsule or tablet) that is designed to resemble in shape, texture, size, taste, etc., a therapeutically active drug and that is used as the control treatment.

Matrix metalloproteinase A member of a group of enzymes that can break down proteins, such as collagen, that are normally found in the spaces between cells in tissues (i.e., extracellular matrix proteins). Because these enzymes need zinc or calcium atoms to work properly, they are called metalloproteinases. Matrix metalloproteinases are involved in wound healing, angiogenesis, and tumor cell metastasis.

Mature T cell lymphoma One of a group of aggressive (fast-growing) non-Hodgkin's lymphomas that begin in mature T lymphocytes (T cells that have matured in the thymus gland and gone to other lymphatic sites in the body, including lymph nodes, bone marrow, and spleen.) Also called peripheral T-cell lymphoma.

Maturity onset diabetes of the young (MODY) A form of diabetes characterised by early age of onset (usually less than 25 years of age), autosomal dominant inheritance (that is, it is inherited by 50% of a parent's children) with diabetes in at least 2 generations of the patient's family. MODY diabetes that can often be controlled with meal planning or diabetes pills, at least in the early stages of diabetes. It differs from type 2 diabetes in that patients have a defect in insulin secretion or glucose metabolism, and are not resistant to insulin. MODY accounts for about 2% of diabetes worldwide and 6 genes have so far been found that cause MODY, although not all MODY patients have one of these genes. Because MODY runs in families, it is useful for studying diabetes genes and has given researchers useful information about how insulin is produced and regulated by the pancreas.

Matuzumab A monoclonal antibody that is being studied in the treatment of some types of cancer. Monoclonal antibodies are made in the laboratory and can locate and bind to cancer cells. Matuzumab binds to the epithelial growth factor receptor (EGFR) on tumor cells and blocks growth signals.

Mauriac syndrome A condition that occurs as the result of chronic poor control of diabetes. It leads to an enlarged liver due to excessive glycogen deposition, short stature and delayed puberty. There is usually a history of repeated hospitalizations for ketoacidosis and hemoglobin A1c tests can be as high as twice the upper level of normal. Kidney function is usually not affected although it may be an additional complication of poor control. Eating disorders are sometimes an accompaniment.

Maxilla The upper jaw bone that contributes to the formation of the orbit, nasal cavity, and the palate.

Maxillary antrum The large paranasal sinus under the cheekbones, also called the maxillary sinus.

Maxillary artery Originates from the external carotid artery and gives these branches: pterygoid rami, deep auricular, anterior tympanic, inferior alveolar, middle meningeal, masseteric, deep temporal, buccal, posterior superior alveolar, infraorbital, descending palatine, sphenopalatine, and artery of the pterygoid canal ("Vidian artery").

Maxillary sinus One of the paransal sinuses, located on either side of the body of the maxillary bone.

Maxillofacial prosthesis A term describing an external/orbital prosthesis (Lids and Eye).

McMurray test A test for assessing the knee for the presence of a medial meniscal lesion. Performed with the knee in external rotation and abduction, with the knee in 90° of flexion, the knee is extended from 90°.

MDI (Multiple daily injections (of insulin)) One of several terms that are used to describe insulin programs that are designed to obtain tight control of blood sugar by giving several shots every day.

MDX 060 monoclonal antibody A monoclonal antibody with potential antineoplastic activity. MDX-060 is a fully humanized antibody that targets CD30, a member of the tumor necrosis factor receptor superfamily found on activated lymphocytes. CD30 is over-expressed in various lymphoproliferative disorders, Hodgkin's disease and other lymphomas, and other cancers.

Meal plan A guide for controlling the amount of calories, carbohydrates, proteins, and fats a person eats. People with diabetes can use such plans as the Exchange Lists or the Point System to help them plan their meals so that they can keep their diabetes under control.

Mean A statistics term. The average value in a set of measurements. The mean is the sum of a set of numbers divided by how many numbers are in the set.

Mean corpuscular volume (MCV) The average volume of erythrocytes, conventionally expressed in cubic micrometers per red blood cell.

Mean survival time The average time that patients in a clinical study remained alive. The time is measured beginning either at diagnosis or the start of treatment.

Measurable disease A tumor that can be accurately measured in size. This information can be used to judge response to treatment.

Meatus A short passage on the posterior surface of the petrous temporal bone that transmits the facial and vestibulocochlear nerves and the labyrinthine artery.

Mechlorethamine A synthetic agent related to sulphur mustard with antineoplastic and immunosuppressive properties. Nitrogen mustard (a member of a family of chemotherapy agents including cyclophosphamide and chlorambucil) is an irritant and carcinogenic agent metabolized to a highly reactive ethylene immonium derivative; the ethylene immonium derivative alkylates DNA and inhibits DNA replication. This agent also exhibits lympholytic properties.

Meckel's diverticulum A problem that occurs as a baby is developing during pregnancy, in which a small pouch (or sac) forms in the ileum.

Media (plural of medium) Substances used to provide sterile nutrients to the fermentation or cell growth process supporting the growth of the live microorganisms. Media may be liquid (broth) or solid, and generally include sucrose or glucose as a carbon source, various minerals, a nitrogen source, and selected growth factors.

Media prep The act of preparing nutrient media for cell culture or fermentation.

Medial articular facet (tibial plateau) The articulating surface of the proximal tibia, forming a joint with the medial and lateral condyles of the distal femur.

Medial geniculate boby (nucleus) Nuclear mass that is part of the ventrocaudal thalamus (metathalamus). It is the auditory relay nucleus which receives afferents from the inferior colliculus via the brachium of the inferior colliculus and giv es rise to the auditory radiation.

Medial Lying or extending toward the median axis of the body.

Medial meniscus A semicircular disk of fibrocartilage between the medial condyle and medial tibial plateau, attached to the medial margin of the superior articulating surface of the tibia.

Medial pterygoid plate On of a pair of projections from the greater wing of the sphenoid bone that help form the lateral wall of the nasal cavity.

Medial supraclavicular lymph node A lymph node located above the collar bone and between the center of the body and a line drawn through the nipple to the shoulder.

Median The value such that for a series of ranked quantities, one half are above the median, and one half are below. For example, the median for a set of CD4 counts is that value which half the counts are less than, and half more.

Median eminence (of the tuber cinereum) Midline part of the tuber cinereum that forms the floor of the thid ventricle

Median nerve A large nerve, comprising segments from the cervical spine, that is involved in neural function of the upper limb. Commonly entrapped in the carpal tunnel of the wrist, to create a carpal tunnel syndrome.

Median survival time The time from either diagnosis or treatment at which half of the patients with a given disease are found to be, or expected to be, still alive. In a clinical trial, median survival time is one way to measure how effective a treatment is.

Mediastinal pleura The thin membrane that lines the chest cavity in the area between the lungs.

Mediastinoscopy A procedure in which a tube is inserted into the chest to view the organs in the area between the lungs and nearby lymph nodes. The tube is inserted through an incision above the breastbone. This procedure is usually performed to get a tissue sample from the lymph nodes on the right side of the chest.

Mediastinum The area between the lungs. The organs in this area include the heart and its large blood vessels, the trachea, the esophagus, the bronchi, and lymph nodes.

Medical Informatics Medical informatics is a scientific field that deals with the storage, retrieval and optimal use of information and data. Rapid development is due to advances in computing, communication technology and an increasing awareness that the knowledge base of medicine is essentially unmanageable by traditional paper-based methods.

Medical allied manpower This category includes some sixty occupations or specialties that can be divided into two large categories based on time required for occupational training. The first category includes those occupations that require at least a baccalaureate degree, for example, clinical laboratory scientists and technologists, dietitians and nutritionists, health educators, medical record librarians, and occupational speech and rehabilitation therapists. The second group includes those occupations that require less than a baccalaureate degree, such as aides for each of the above categories as well as physician assistants and radiological technicians.

Medical castration Refers to the use of drugs to suppress the function of the ovaries or testicles.

Medical code sets Codes that characterize a medical condition or treatment. These code sets are usually maintained by professional societies and public health organizations. Compare to administrative code sets.

Medical devices Any health care product that does not achieve its principal intended purposes by chemical action in or on the body or by being metabolized. The term "devices" also includes components, parts, or accessories of medical devices, diagnostic aids such as reagents, antibiotic sensitivity disks, and test kits for in vitro diagnosis of diseases and other conditions. There are three classes of medical devices: 1. Class I, General Controls (registration of manufacturers, recordkeeping and labeling requirements, compliance with GMPs).

2. Class II, Special Controls (including performance standards, posmarket survei-llance, and patient regis-tries).

3. Class III, Premarket Approval (implanted and life supporting or life sustaining devices).

Medical education The process of teaching, learning and training of students with an ongoing integration of knowledge, experience, skills, qualities, responsibility and values which qualify an individual to practice medicine. It is divided into undergraduate, postgraduate and continuing medical education, but increasingly there is a focus on the "lifelong" nature of medical education.

Undergraduate education or basic medical education refers to the period beginning when a student enters medical school and ends with the final examination for basic medical qualification. This period of education comprises a pre-clinical and a clinical period. It can result in granting a license to practice, which may be provisional and subject to conditions as to supervision; or permitting the start of postgraduate education.

Postgraduate education, graduate medical education or specialty training is used to designate the more or less continuous period of post-basic training which, when it occurs, normally directly follows undergraduate training and is designed to lead to competence in a chosen branch of medical practice.

Medical management information system (MMIS) A data system that allows payers and purchasers to track health care expenditure and utilization patterns. May also be referred to as Health Information System (HIS), Health Information Management (HIM) or Infor-mation System (IS).

Medical oncologist A doctor who specializes in diagnosing and treating cancer using chemotherapy, hormonal therapy, and biological therapy. A medical oncologist often is the main health care provider for someone who has cancer. A medical oncologist also gives supportive care and may coordinate treatment given by other specialists.

Medical review, medical review criteria Screening of healthcare utilization and the criteria used for this screening. Medical reviews are usually conducted by insurance companies, third-party payers, review organizations and case managers. This is the underlying basis for reviewing the quality and appropriateness of care provided to selected cases. Insurance companies rely heavily on medical review and their own criteria as cost control. Through medical review, payers are able to limit or reduce the utilization of health care services. Medical review may sometimes put patients at odds with their insurance companies or hospitals and doctors in conflict with payers.

Medical services organization (MSO) An organized group of physicians, usually from one hospital, into an entity able to contract with others for the provision of services.

Medical Educator A professional who focuses on the educational process necessary to transform students into physicians. Some medical educators are physicians, but an increasing number have backgrounds in education, behavioral or other health sciences.

Medically necessary, medical necessity, medical necessary services Services or supplies which meet the following tests: They are appropriate and necessary for the symptoms, diagnosis, or treatment of the medical condition; They are provided for the diagnosis or direct care and treatment of the medical condition; They meet the standards of good medical practice within the medical community in the service area; They are not primarily for the convenience of the plan member or a plan provider; and They are the most appropriate level or supply of service which can safely be provided.

Medical school A higher education or university level institution offering a prescribed course of medicine. The following are examples of the names that such institutions may bear and which vary from one country to another or even within countries.

Medication 1. A drug or medicine.

2. The administration of a drug or medicine.

Medication event monitoring system (MEMS) A method of measuring drug adherence that uses a computer chip embedded in a pill bottle lid to record the date and time each dose is taken. Current obstacles to its use include its large size, the possibility of malfunction when refrigerated, and inaccurate reporting when pillboxes are used in place of the original bottle.

Medicinal product Any substance or combination of substances presented for treating or preventing disease in human beings or animals. Any substance or combination of substances that may be administered to human beings or animals with a view to making a medical diagnosis or to restoring, correcting or modifying physiological functions in human beings or in animals is likewise considered a medicinal product.

Medilla oblongata The tapering posterior most division (myelencephalon) of the hindbrain or rhombencephalon. It is interposed between the pons and the spinal cord.

Medlars Medical Literature Analysis Retrieval System: The computer on which "Medline" and "AIDS Line" reside at the National Library of Medicine.

Medline Medical Literature Analysis Retrieval System on Line. A computer searchable database of published medical literature.

MedlinePlus A database of health information developed by the National Library of Medicine (NLM). MedlinePlus has information on several hundred diseases and conditions as well as other health information.

Medroxyprogesterone A synthetic derivative of progesterone administered as an acetate salt (medroxyprogesterone acetate) with antiestrogenic activity. As a do all progestins, medroxyprogesterone binds to and activates nuclear receptors which subsequently bind to and activate target genes for transcription. As an antiestrogen, this agent may inhibit the growth-stimulating effects of estrogen on estrogen-sensitive tumor cells.

Medulla (oblongata) The cone of nerve tissue anterior to the cerebellum and connecting the pons with the cervical spinal cord. It contains nerves responsible for respiration, circulation and special senses.

Medullary breast carcinoma A rare type of breast cancer that often can be treated successfully. It is marked by lymphocytes (a type of white blood cell) in and around the tumor that can be seen when viewed under a microscope.

Medullary carcinoma A special type of infiltrating breast cancer in which the tumor appears well-defined, with obvious boundaries between tumor tissue and normal tissue. About 5% of breast cancers are medullary carcinomas. The outlook (prognosis) for this kind of cancer is considered to be better than averave.

Medullary cavity Within a long bone, the portion of the diaphysis containing marrow.

Medullary thyroid cancer Cancer that develops in C cells of the thyroid. The C cells make a hormone (calcitonin) that helps maintain a healthy level of calcium in the blood.

Medulloblastoma A malignant brain tumor that begins in the lower part of the brain and that can spread to the spine or to other parts of the body. Medulloblastomas are a type of primitive neuroectodermal tumor (PNET).

Mega Great, e.g. megakaryocyte - the giant cell of the bone marrow that has a greatly lobulated nucleus and gives rise to blood platelets.

Mega voltage linear accelerator (MeV linear accelerator) A machine that uses electricity to form a stream of fast-moving subatomic particles. This creates high-energy radiation that may be used to treat cancer. Also called linear accelerator and linac.

Megabase (Mb) Unit of length for DNA fragments equal to 1 million nucleotides and roughly equal to 1 cM.

Megace A drug used to block estrogen and suppress the effects of estrogen and androgens. It is used to treat breast and endometrial cancer, and is being studied in the treatment of other types of cancer. It is also used to improve appetite in patients with cancer. Megace belongs to the group of hormones called progestins. Also called megestrol.

Megaly (suffix) Great, large, e.g. splenomegaly - enlargement of the spleen.

Meibomian glands Pores in the eyelids that secrete an oily substance to prevent your normal tear flow from running down your cheek.

Meiosis The process of two consecutive cell divisions in the diploid progenitors of sex cells. Meiosis results in four rather than two daughter cells, each with a haploid set of chromosomes.

Melan A A tumor-associated melanocytic differentiation antigen. Vaccination with MART-1 antigen may stimulate a host cytotoxic T-cell response against tumor cells expressing the melanocytic differentiation antigen, resulting in tumor cell lysis.

Melanin The substance that gives color to skin and eyes.

Melanocyte A cell in the skin and eyes that produces and contains the pigment called melanin.

Melanoma A form of skin cancer that begins in melanocytes (the cells that make the pigment melanin). Melanoma usually begins in a mole.

Melanoma helper peptide vaccine A multivalent vaccine consisting of peptides derived from melanoma-associated antigens and an adjuvant peptide derived from tetanus toxoid. Vaccination with this agent may stimulate a host cytotoxic T-cell response against tumor cells expressing melanoma-associated antigens, resulting in tumor cell lysis.

Melanoma vaccine A cancer vaccine prepared from human melanoma cancer cells. It can be used alone or with other therapy in treating melanoma.

Melanophage A macrophage that has ingested melanin.

Melatonin A recombinant therapeutic analog of melatonin, a natural serotonin-derived indole with antioxidant properties. Melatonin hormone synthesis occurs in the pineal gland and depends on beta-adrenergic receptor function. Melatonin is involved in numerous biological functions: circadian rhythm, sleep, stress response, aging, and immunity.

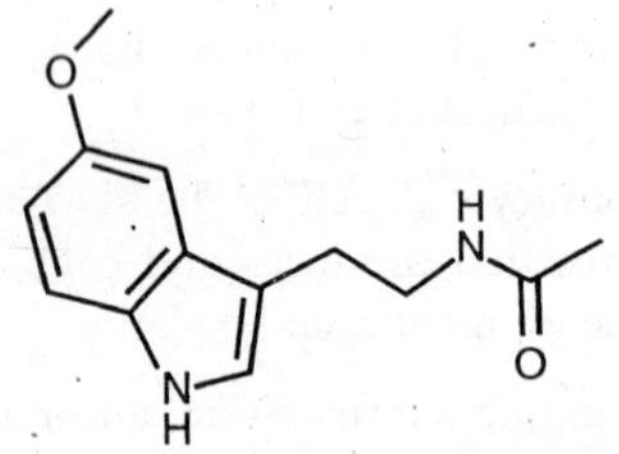

Figure Melatonin

Melphalan A drug that is used to treat multiple myeloma and ovarian epithelial cancer and is being studied in the treatment of other types of cancer. It belongs to the family of drugs called alkylating agents. Also called Alkeran.

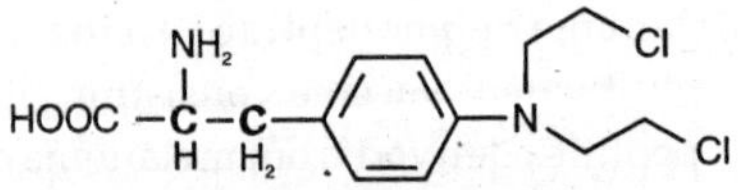

Figure Melphalan

Membrane A barrier, usually thin, that only permits the passage of particles of a certain size or special nature. Filtration membranes are thin polymer films that are permeable to water and other fluids: 1. Microporous membrane filters have measurable pore structures that physically remove particles or microorganisms larger than pore size.

2. Ultrafiltration membranes (sometimes called molecular sieves) also remove molecules larger than a specified molecular weight.

3. Reverse osmosis membranes are permeable to water molecules and very little else, rejecting even dissolved ions and endotoxins in water.

Membraneous urethra The portion of the urethra located between the pars prostatica ("prostatic urethra") and pars spongiosa ("penile urethra") in the male.

Memory In the immune system, memory denotes an active state of immunity to a specific antigen, such that a second encounter with that antigen leads to a larger and more rapid response.

Memory T cells A specific type of infection-fighting T cell that can recognize foreign invaders that were encountered during a prior infection or vaccination. At a second encounter with the invader, memory T cells can reproduce to mount a faster and stronger immune response than the first time the immune system responded to the invader.

Men1 syndrome Multiple endocrine neoplasia type 1 syndrome. A rare, inherited disorder that affects the endocrine glands and can cause tumors in the parathyroid and pituitary glands and the pancreas. These tumors (usually benign) cause the glands to secrete high levels of hormones, which can lead to other medical problems, such as kidney stones, fertility problems, and severe ulcers. In some cases, tumors inside the pancreas can become cancerous. Also called multiple endocrine adenomatosis and Wermer's syndrome.

Menarche The first menstrual period. Early menarche (before age 12) is a risk factor for breast cancer, possibly because the earlier a woman's periods begin, the longer the exposure to estrogen.

Mendelian inheritance One method in which genetic traits are passed from parents to offspring. Named for Gregor Mendel, who first studied and recognized the existence of genes and this method of inheritance.

Mengingioma A hard, firm, or rubbery, slowly growing extraaxial neoplasm, hypervascular, and arising from the arachnoid. They are usually attached to the dura. Meningiomas may cause erosion and thinning of the skull, as well as hyperostosis (bone thickening).

Meningeal Refers to the meninges, the tissue covering the brain and spinal cord.

Meningeal metastases Cancer that has spread from the original (primary) tumor to the tissue covering the brain, spinal cord, or both.

Meninges Membranes surrounding the brain or spinal cord. Part of the so-called "blood-brain barrier"

Meningioma A type of tumor that occurs in the meninges, the membranes that cover and protect the brain and spinal cord. Meningiomas usually grow slowly.

Meningitis Inflammation of the membranes surrounding the brain or spinal cord. Meningitis can be caused by a bacterium, fungus, or virus such as HIV.

Meningo Membrane; meninges, e.g. meningoencephalitis - inflammation of the brain and its meninges.

Meniscectomy Removal of a torn section (or complete) of meniscus. Usually performed arthroscopically.

Meniscus The mensci are fibrocartilaginous structures that function as "washers" - to deepen the joint surfaces, shock absorbers, assist in joint lubrication and provide joint stabilisation. Often damaged, particularly in the knee, when there is a rotational force.

Menkes disease another genetic disorder of copper metabolism in which copper accumulates in excessive amounts in the liver, and is deficient in most other tissues of the body. Also known as Kinky Hair Disease.

Menopausal hormone therapy Hormones (estrogen, progesterone, or both) given to women after menopause to replace the hormones no longer produced by the ovaries. Also called hormone replacement therapy or HRT.

Menopause The time in a woman's life when monthly cycles of menstruation cease forever and the level of hormones produced by the ovaries decreases. Menopause usually occurs in the late 40s or early 50s, but it can also be induced by surgical removal of the ovaries (oophorectomy) or the ovaries and uterus (total hysterectomy), or by some chemotherapies that destroy ovarian function. Among such chemotherapies are some that are used for breast cancer.

Menorrhagia Abnormally heavy menstrual bleeding.

Menstruation Periodic discharge of blood and tissue from the uterus. From puberty until menopause, menstruation occurs about every 28 days when a woman is not pregnant.

Mental health A person's overall psychological and emotional condition. Good mental health is a state of well-being in which a person is able to cope with everyday events, think clearly, be responsible, meet challenges, and have good relationships with others.

Mental health counselor A specialist who can talk with patients and their families about emotional and personal matters, and can help them make decisions.

Mercaptopurine A drug used to treat acute lymphatic leukemia. It belongs to the family of drugs called antimetabolites. Also called Purinethol.

Mercury A silver-white, poisonous metal that is a liquid at ordinary temperatures. It is commonly used in thermometers and amalgams, and has been used as an ingredient in some homeopathic medicines and in very small amounts as a preservative in viral vaccines.

Meristem The growing point or area of rapidly dividing cells at the tip of a stem, root, or branch.

Merkel cell cancer A rare type of cancer that forms on or just beneath the skin. Merkel cell cancer is divided into three types called trabecular, intermediate, and small cell.

Mesencephalon The middle of the three primary brain vesicles in the embryonic brain. The adult derivative of which is the midbrain which is located between the diencephalon and the pons.

Mesenchymal Refers to cells that develop into connective tissue, blood vessels, and lymphatic tissue.

Mesenteric membrane The peritoneal membrane that attaches the intestines to the abdominal wall near the back.

Mesh Medical subject heading. Term used by National Library of Medicine, and employed in their medline system

Mesna A drug that helps protect the kidneys and bladder from the toxic effects of anticancer drugs such as ifosfamide and cyclophosphamide.

Mesonephroma A rare type of tumor, usually of the female genital tract, in which the inside of the cells looks clear when viewed under a microscope. Also called clear cell carcinoma and clear cell adenocarcinoma.

Mesophile An organism that grows best in the temperature range of 20°C to 50°C (68°F to 122°F).

Mesothelioma A benign (noncancerous) or malignant (cancerous) tumor affecting the lining of the chest or abdomen. Exposure to asbestos particles in the air increases the risk of developing malignant mesothe-lioma.

Mesothelium The layer of flat cells lining the body cavity of the embryo; in the adult, it forms the simple squamous epithelium that covers the true serous membranes of the body. Mesothelium is derived from mesoderm.

Messenger RNA (mRNA) A molecule that carries genetic instructions for building a particular protein from the cell's DNA to the place in a cell where proteins are assembled. There, the messenger RNA serves as a blueprint for the construction of a specific protein.

Meta-analysis A quantitative method for combining the results of many studies into one set of conclusions. Generally done from a literature review, a meta-analysis is more a review than an analysis, properly speaking.

Metabolic Refers to the process of building the body's molecular structures from nutrients (anabolism) and of breaking them down for energy production and excretion (catabolism).

Metabolic acidosis A condition in which the blood is too acidic. It may be caused by severe illness or sepsis (bacteria in the bloodstream).

Metabolic syndrome A combination of health conditions that place a person at high risk for heart disease. These conditions are type 2 diabetes, hypertension (high blood pressure), hyperlipidemia (high levels of fat in the blood), and obesity. According to theory, all of these conditions are associated with high blood insulin levels, and it is claimed that the underlying problem in patients with the Metabolic Syndrome is faulty insulin release from the beta cells of the pancreas.

Metabolic therapy Treatment to correct changes in metabolism that can be caused by disease.

Metabolism The entire set of enzyme-catalyzed transformations of organic nutrient molecules (to sustain life) in living cells. Conversion of food and water into nutrients that can be used by the body's cells, and the use of those nutrients by those cells (to sustain life, grow, etc.).

Metabolite Any of the various organic compounds produced by metabolism.

Metachromasia The phenomenon of reacting with a different colour from that of the dye used in staining. For example amyloid shows reddish metachromasia when stained with crystal violet.

Metadata Electronic records that include processing parameters and audit trail logs. Metadata allows reviewers to replay the original result, or reconstruct a final report from raw data. In chromatography, metadata include integration parameters and calibration tables. An example of metadata can be in long division "1,000 ÷ 5" would be the raw data, the work you had to show on your paper in fourth grade math class would be the metadata, and "200" would be your result.

Metaphase A stage in mitosis or meiosis during which the chromosomes are aligned along the equatorial plane of the cell.

Metaphysis Portion of a long bone, usually funnel-shaped between the shaft (diaphysis) and the epiphyseal (growth) plate. This is a region of growth and remodelling during development.

Metaplasia The change of one type of tissue to another, such as metaplastic ossification seen in certain cutaneous tumors.

Metaplastic carcinoma A general term used to describe cancer that begins in cells that have changed into another cell type (for example, a squamous cell of the esophagus changing to resemble a cell of the stomach). In some cases, metaplastic changes alone may mean there is an increased chance of cancer developing at the site.

Metastasectomy Surgery to remove one or more metastases (tumors formed from cells that have spread from the primary tumor). When all metastases are removed, it is called a complete metastasectomy.

Metastasis In cancer, it is the appearance of neoplasms in parts of the body remote from the seat of the primary tumor. It also applies to the transportation of bacteria from one part of the body to another through the blood streams (hematogenous metastasis) or through lymph channels (lymphogenous metastasis).

Metastasize To spread from one part of the body to another. When cancer cells metastasize and form secondary tumors, the cells in the metastatic tumor are like those in the original (primary) tumor.

Metastatic A tumor that has transfered from one organ (or part) to another not directly connected to it.

Metastatic cancer Cancer that has spread from the place in which it started to other parts of the body.

Metastatic lesion The transfer of any pathologic process from one body part to another. Metastasis is usually distinguished from "local extension". Metastasis can be carried by blood-flow ("hematogenous metastasis"), by lymphatic fluid, through the CSF dissemination, by the bronchi (lepidic spread), along the urinary tract, etc.

Metasynchronous Occurring at nearly the same time.

Metatarsal-phalangeal joint The point of junction between the metatarsals and phalanges of the foot.

Metatarsals The five long tubular bones of the foot between the tarsus and the phalanges.

Metathalamus A ventrocaudal subdivision of the thalamus which consists of the medial and lateral geniculate bodies.

Metencephalon The rostral subdivision of the hindbrain or rhombencephalon in the embryonic brain. It is situated between the midbrain (mesencephalon) and the medulla oblongata (myelence-phalon). The adult derivative is the pons and cerebellum.

Meteorism Swelling of the abdomen caused by gas in the intestines or peritoneal cavity. Also called tympanites.

Metformin A drug used as a treatment for Type 2 diabetes; belongs to a class of drugs called biguanides.

Methionine An essential amino acid; furnishes (to organism) both labile methyl groups and sulfur necessary for normal metabolism.

Methionine C 11 A synthetic amino acid radiolabeled with carbon-11. Acting as a methyl donor, methionine C 11 is incorporated into macromolecules, where it serves as a positron emission tomography (PET) imaging agent for detecting tumors with high rates of protein synthesis.

Methods validation Establishing, through documented evidence, a high degree of assurance that an analytical method will consistently yield results that accurately reflect the quality characteristics of the product tested.

Methotrexate A drug used to treat some types of cancers, including breast, head and neck, lung, blood, and bone, and other disorders. It belongs to the family of drugs called antimetabolites. Also called amethopterin.

Methoxsalen A naturally occurring substance isolated from the seeds of the plant Ammi majus with photoactivating properties. As a member of the family of compounds known as psoralens or furocoumarins, methoxsalen's exact mechanism of action is unknown; upon photoactivation, methoxsalen has been observed to bind covalently to and crosslink DNA.

Methoxypolyethylene glycol epoetin beta A substance that is being studied in the treatment of anemia in patients who are receiving chemotherapy. It is a form of erythropoietin (a substance produced in the kidneys that stimulates the production of red blood cells) that has been changed in the laboratory.

Methyl 5 aminolevulinate A drug used in photodynamic therapy; it is absorbed by tumor cells and, when exposed to light, becomes active and kills the cancer cells.

Methyl cellulose A number of gummy substances, produced through reaction between cellulose and methyls. It is found in fruit butters and jellies and serves to keep these products from separating.

Methylene blue A synthetic basic dye. Methylene blue stains to negatively charged cell components like nucleic acids; when administered in the lymphatic bed of a tumor during oncologic surgery, methylene blue may stain lymph nodes draining from the tumor, thereby aiding in the visual localization of tumor sentinel lymph nodes. When administered intravenously in low doses, this agent may convert methemoglobin to hemoglobin.

Methylene dimethane sulfonate A member of the homologous series of dimethane sulphonic acid esters with alkylating properties. Methylene dimethane sulfonate alkylates DNA, resulting in interstrand DNA crosslinking, inhibition of DNA replication, disruption of the cell cycle, and cell death.

Methylnaltrexone A methyl derivative of noroxymorphone with selective, opioid-receptor antagonistic activity. Methylnaltrexone displaces opioids from peripheral opioid receptors in the gastrointestinal tract, the bladder, and the skin, resulting in decreases in opioid-related constipation, urinary retention, and pruritis, respectively. Methylnaltrexone does not cross the blood-brain barrier and does not affect the centrally-mediated analgesic effect of opioids.

Methylphenidate hydrochloride The hydrochloride salt of a synthetic central nervous system stimulant. Methylphenidate appears to activate the brain stem arousal system and cortex to produce its stimulant effect and, in some clinical settings, may improve cognitive function.

Methylprednisolone A synthetic corticosteroid with anti-inflammatory and immunomodulating properties. Methylprednisolone binds to and activates specific nuclear receptors, resulting in altered gene expression and inhibition of proinflammatory cytokine production. This agent also decreases the number of circulating lymphocytes, induces cell differentiation, and stimulates apoptosis in sensitive tumor cell populations.

Metoclopramide A drug that prevents or reduces nausea and vomiting.

Metronidazole A drug that is used to treat infection and is being studied in the treatment of cancer. It belongs to the families of drugs called antibacterials, antiprotozoals, and anthelmintics. Also called Flagyl.

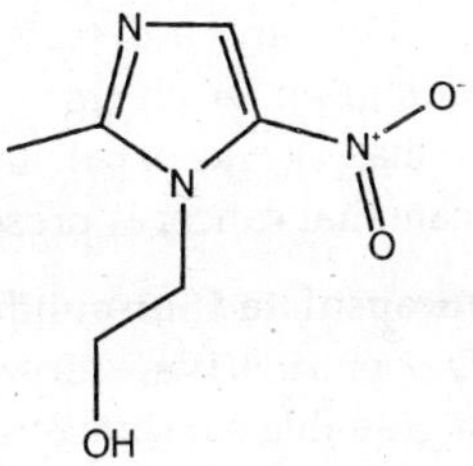

((2-methyl-5-nitro-1H-imidazol-1-yl)ethanol)

Figure Metronidazole

Metronomic therapy Continuous or frequent treatment with low doses of anticancer drugs, often given with other methods of therapy.

Mexican valerian Valeriana officinalis. A plant whose roots are used as a sedative and to treat certain medical conditions. It is being studied as a way to improve sleep in cancer patients undergoing treatment. Also called valerian, garden valerian, Indian valerian, Pacific valerian, garden heliotrope, and Valerianae radix.

Mg/dl The unit of measurement of how much of a substance (such as sugar) is in a specific amount of fluid (such as blood or urine).

MGUS (Monoclonal gammopathy of undetermined significance) A benign condition in which there is a high level of a protein called M protein in the blood. Patients with MGUS are at an increased risk of developing cancer.

MHC class I molecule A molecule encoded to genes of the MHC which participates in antigen presentation to cytotoxic T (CD8+) cells.

MHC class II molecule A molecule encoded by genes of the MHC which participates in antigen presentation to helper T (CD4+) cells.

MHC restriction The ability of T lymphocytes to respond only when they 'see' the appropriate antigen in association with "self" MHC class I or class II proteins on the antigen presenting cells.

Mho Unit of measurement for conductance; the reciprocal of ohm (resistance).

Micro Prefix mean small, or one one-millionth, as in microgram, a millionth of a gram.

Microabscess Small collection of inflammatory cells.

Munro microabscesses are composed of degenerated pmn's in the horny layer and are seen in psoriasis and seb derm.

Spongiform pustules of Kagoj are multilocular pustules in the upper stratum malpighii within a sponge-like network made up of flattened keratinocytes. They are seen in psoriasis, Reiter's disease, geographic, tongue and rarely in candidiasis.

Pautrier microabscesses are a collection of 3 or more atypical mononuclear cells within the epidermis in mycosis fungoides.

Microalbumin Small amounts of protein in the urine that cannot be detected by the usual "dipstick" test done for routine urinanalysis testing for other reasons. Specialized dipsticks, or urine collections over a period of 12-24 hours, are used to measure the amount of microalbumin. If there is persistent microalbumin over several repeated tests at different times, the risk of diabetic nephropathy and macrovascular disease are both higher.

Microaneurysm A small swelling that forms on the side of tiny blood vessels. These small swellings may break and bleed into nearby tissue. People with diabetes sometimes get microaneurysms in the retina of the eye.

Microarray Sets of miniaturized chemical reaction areas that may also be used to test DNA fragments, antibodies, or proteins.

Microbes Living organisms that can be seen only through a microscope, including bacteria, protozoa, viruses, and fungi.

Microbial genetics The study of genes and gene function in bacteria, archaea, and other microorganisms. Often used in research in the fields of bioremediation, alternative energy, and disease prevention.

Microbicide A natural or man-made substance that kills microbes. Researchers are studying the use of microbicides to prevent the transmission of sexually transmitted diseases (STDs), including HIV infection.

Microbiology The study of microscopic life such as bacteria and viruses.

Microcalcification A tiny deposit of calcium in the breast that cannot be felt but can be detected on a mammogram. A cluster of these very small specks of calcium may indicate that cancer is present.

Microencapsulated Surrounded by a thin, protective layer of biodegradable substance referred to as microsphere.

Microglia Small supporting cells of the central nervous system-(neuroglia) derived from the mesoderm (blood histiocytes) and having a phagocytic function.

Microgram One millionth of a gram.

Microhmo A measure of conductance equal to one millionth of a mho.

Microinch A unit of length equal to one millionth of an inch (0.000001 inches).

Microinjection A technique for introducing a solution of DNA into a cell using a fine microcapillary pipet.

Micrometastases Small numbers of cancer cells that have spread from the primary tumor to other parts of the body and are too few to be picked up in a screening or diagnostic test.

Micromolar A concentration of 1/1,000,000 (one millionth) molecular weight per liter (mol/L).

Micron or micrometer A unit of length equal to one millionth of a meter (μm) or thousandth of a millimeter (25μm are approximately 0.001 inch.). Bacteria range in size from 0.5μm to 20μm.

Micronuclei Chromosome fragments that are not incorporated into the nucleus at cell division.

Micronutrient A trace element; an organic compound like a vitamin that is essential but only in small amounts for physical health, growth and metabolism.

Microorganism An organism that can be seen only through a microscope. Microorganisms include bacteria, protozoa, algae, and fungi. Although viruses are not considered living organisms, they are sometimes classified as microorganisms.

Microphthalmic/microphthalmos A congenital anomaly (abnormal development). Partially developed eyeball(s).

Microsatellite A short sequence of DNA, usually 1 to 4 basepairs (a unit of DNA), that is repeated together in a row along the DNA molecule. There is variation from person to person in the number of repeats. There are hundreds of places in human DNA that contain microsatellites.

Microsatellite instability (MSI) A change that occurs in the DNA of certain cells (such as tumor cells) in which the number of repeats of microsatellites (short, repeated sequences of DNA) is different than the number of repeats that was in the DNA when it was inherited. The cause of MSI may be a defect in the ability to repair mistakes made when DNA is copied in the cell.

Microscopic Too small to be seen without a microscope.

Microsporidiosis Disease resulting from infection with a protozoal pathogen from the Microsporidia order; similar in symptoms (diarrhea, cramps) and often misdiagnosed as cryptosporidiosis.

Microstaging A technique used to help determine the stage (extent) of melanoma and certain squamous cell cancers. A sample of skin that contains tumor tissue is examined under a microscope to find out how thick the tumor is and/or how deeply the tumor has grown into the skin or connective tissues.

Microstrabimus Also called microtropia, monofixation syndrome, and small angle strabismus. A small angle deviation (inward or outward, commonly inward) that is less than five degrees with some amount of stereopsis (depth perception) and anomalous retinal correspondence (ARC). Possible mild amblyopia, eccentric fixation, and/or anisometropia may also be present. It frequently results from the treatment of a larger-angle deviation (esotropia or exotropia) by optical correction, vision therapy, pharmacological agents, and/or extraocular muscle surgery. Treatment for microstrabimus consists mostly of correcting significant refractive errors and any coexisting amblyopia. The use of vision therapy and prisms to establish bifoveal fusion has been successful in selected cases.

Microvascular disease Disease of the smallest blood vessels that sometimes occurs when a person has had diabetes for a long time. The walls of the vessels become abnormally thick but weak, and therefore they bleed, leak protein, and slow the flow of blood through the body. Then some cells, for example, the ones in the center of the eye, may not get enough blood and may be damaged.

Microwave (targis) A catheter is placed within the bladder and positioned within the prostate, then the antenna emits microwaves. This procedure increases the passageway allowing for easier urination.

Microwave thermotherapy A type of treatment in which body tissue is exposed to high temperatures to damage and kill cancer cells or to make cancer cells more sensitive to the effects of radiation and certain anticancer drugs. Also called microwave therapy.

Midbrain (Mesencephalon) The portion of the brain developed from the middle of the three primary vesicles in the embryo. In cross-section, the midbrain resembles "Mickey Mouse": the ears are the cerebral peduncles.

Middle colic artery Artery which originates from the superior mesenteric artery, and supplies the transverse colon.

Middle ear bone complex The small bones [malleus ("hammer"), incus ("anvil") and stapes ("stirrup")] that conduct sound from the tympanic membrane ("ear drum") to the oval window of the inner ear.

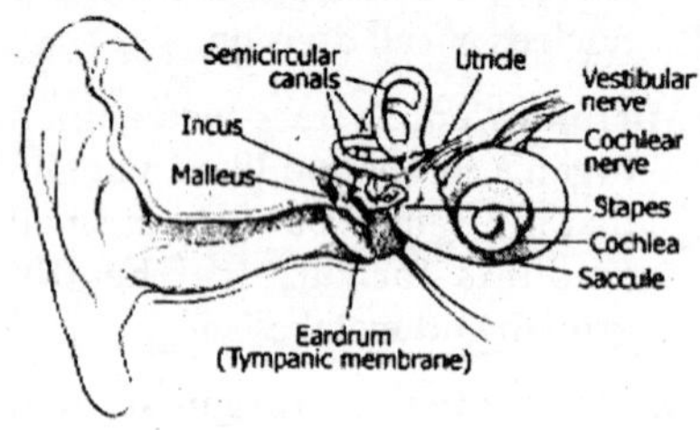

Figure Ear parts

Middle sacral artery The continuation of the abdominal aorta, that branches into the lowest lumbar artery.

Mifepristone An anticancer drug that blocks the action of progesterone, a hormone that affects the growth of some cancers.

(11â-[p- (Dimethylamino)phenyl]-17â-hydroxy -17- (1-propynyl)estra-4,9-dien-3-one)

Figure Mifepristone

Migration inhibition factor (MIF) A lymphokine that inhibits the motility of macrophages in culture.

Mildew Microscopic fungi, the spores of which can cause asthma in some people. Cladosporium and Alternaria spores are most allergenic.

Milk teeth Deciduous (baby) teeth.

Milk thistle A plant that has been used in some cultures to treat certain medical problems, including stomach, liver, and gallbladder disorders. The active extract of milk thistle seeds is called silymarin. It is being studied in the prevention of liver damage caused by some cancer treatments. Also called Silybum marianum.

Milli Prefix meaning one one-thousandth, as in milligram, a thousandth of a gram.

Milliequivalent To simplify the calculation of ion exchange resin capacity, total dissolved ion concentrations are usually converted into equivalent concentrations of calcium carbonate, the most common source of dissolved ions in water. Resin capacity is normally given in ppm as $CaCO_3$, or in grains per gallon as $CaCO_3$ (7,000 grains = 1 pound). However, it may also be given as milliequivalents per litre (meq/L). Since calcium carbonate has a molecular weight of 100 and an equivalent weight of 50 (because calcium has a valence of two) ppm as $CaCO_3$ can be converted to meq/L by dividing by 50. Thus, 1 ppm of $CaCO_3$ = 0.02 meg/L.

Milligram A measure of weight. A milligram is approximately 450,000 times smaller than a pound and 28,000 times smaller than an ounce.

Millilitre A measure of volume for a liquid. A millilitre is approximately 950 times smaller than a quart and 30 times smaller than a fluid ounce. A millilitre of liquid and a cubic centimetre (cc) of liquid are the same.

Millimetre A measure of length in the metric system. A millimetre is one thousandth of a metre. There are 25 millimetres in an inch.

Mindfulness relaxation A type of meditation based on the concept of being "mindful," or having increased awareness, of the present. It uses breathing methods, guided imagery, and other practices to relax the body and mind and help reduce stress.

Mineral A nutrient required to maintain health.

Minienvironment The actual localized control space limited by a defined enclosure that separates or isolates the inside from the outside environment, such that the transfer of potential contamination from one side to the other is minimized or completely eliminated, depending on the design. Minienvironments are not always isolators.

Minimally invasive surgery (MIS) Procedural techniques which limit the size of the abdominal incisions by using small incisions to gain access to the surgical site.

Minimum inhibitory concentation The smallest amount of a substance, when diluted, which kill pathogens or stop them from reproducing. Usually means concentration required to achieve ED90.

Minimum essential requirements This specifies the knowledge, skills and attitudes related to the sciences basic to medicine, clinical practice, professional behavior and ethical values. The graduate of undergraduate medical education should possess these to ensure that he or she is prepared to begin further graduate medical education (specialty training) or to start practicing medicine under supervision.

Minor histocompatibility antigens These antigens, encoded outside the MHC, are numerous, but do not generate rapid graft rejection or primary responses of T cells in vitro. They do not serve as restricting elements in cell interactions.

Minus (-) lens Concave lens, stimulates focusing and diverges light. The lens is thinner in the center than the edges. It is used in glasses or contact lenses for people who are nearsighted (myopia).

Miraluma test A type of breast imaging test that is used to detect cancer cells in the breasts of some women who have had abnormal mammograms, or who have dense breast tissue. The Miraluma test is not used for screening, or in place of a mammogram. In this test, a woman receives an injection of a small amount of a radioactive substance called technetium 99, which is taken up by cancer cells, and a gamma camera is used to take pictures of the breasts. Also called scintimammography and sestamibi breast imaging.

Miscellaneous expenses Hospital charges, other than room and board, such as those for x-rays, drugs, laboratory fees, and other ancillary services.

Misoprostol A radioprotective agent that belongs to the family of drugs called prostaglandins.

Mistletoe An extract of the whole plant Viscum album (mistletoe) with potential biological response modifier (BRM) activity. Mistletoe extract may both stimulate the antitumoral functions of the immune system and have a direct toxic effect on tumor cells.

Mistletoe lectin A substance that comes from the mistletoe plant and that is being studied as a treatment for cancer. A lectin is a complex molecule that has both protein and sugars. Lectins are able to bind to the outside of a cell and cause biochemical changes in it. Lectins are made by both animals and plants.

Mitigate To make milder or less painful.

Mitochondria Organelles within the cytoplasm of the cells, mitochrondia have their own independent DNA, and serve as a source of energy for the cell.

Mitochondrial antibody Laboratory test used to help establish a diagnosis of primary biliary cirrhosis.

Mitochondrial DNA The genetic material found in mitochondria, the organelles that generate energy for the cell. Not inherited in the same fashion as nucleic DNA.

Mitochondrial toxicity A condition in which mitochondria are damaged. This condition is a potential side effect of NRTIs and can cause problems in the heart, nerves, muscles, pancreas, kidneys, and liver.

Mitogen A substance that stimulates the proliferation of many different clones of lymphocytes.

Mitolactol An anticancer drug that belongs to the family of drugs called alkylating agents.

Mitomycin An anti-tumor antibiotic with alkylating properties. Bioreductively activated mitomycin generates oxygen radicals and alkylates DNA, forming interstrand cross-links and inhibiting DNA synthesis.

Mitosis The process of division of somatic cells in which each daughter cell receives the same amount of DNA as the parent cell.

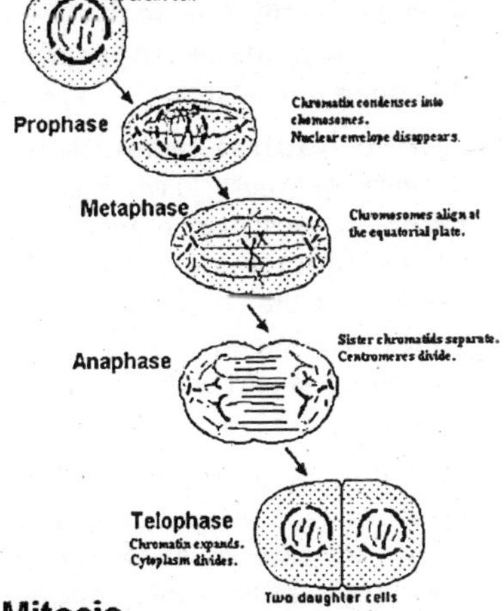

Parent cell
Prophase — Chromatin condenses into chromosomes. Nuclear envelope disappears.
Metaphase — Chromosomes align at the equatorial plate.
Anaphase — Sister chromatids separate. Centromeres divide.
Telophase — Chromatin expands. Cytoplasm divides.
Two daughter cells

Mitosis

Mitotane A synthetic derivative of the insecticide dichlorodiphenyl trichloroethane (DDT) with anti-adrenocorticoid properties. Following its metabolism in the adrenal cortex to a reactive acyl chloride intermediate, mitotane covalently binds to adrenal proteins, specifically inhibiting adrenal cortical hormone production.

Mitotic activity Having to do with the presence of dividing (proliferating) cells. Cancerous tissue generally has more mitotic activity than normal tissues.

Mitotic index In a population of cells, the ratio of the number of cells undergoing mitosis (cell division) to the number of cells not undergoing mitosis.

Mitotic inhibitor A drug that inhibits cell growth by stopping cell division. Mitotic inhibitors are used as treatments for cancer. Also called antimitotic or antimicrotubule agents and taxanes. Docetaxel and paclitaxel are mitotic inhibitors.

Mitoxantrone A drug used to treat advanced prostate cancer that does not respond to hormones, adult acute nonlymphocytic leukemia, and advanced or chronic multiple sclerosis. It is also being studied in the treatment of other cancers. It belongs to the family of drugs called antitumor antibiotics. Also called Novantrone.

Mivobulin isethionate An anticancer drug that belongs to the family of drugs called mitotic inhibitors.

Mixed dose Combining two kinds of insulin in one injection. A mixed dose commonly combines regular insulin, which is fast acting, with a longer acting insulin such as NPH. A mixed dose insulin schedule may be prescribed to provide both short-term and long-term coverage.

Mixed glioma A brain tumor that occurs in more than one type of brain cell, including astrocytes, ependymal cells, and oligodendrocytes.

Mixed Incontinence Having both stress and urge incontinence.

Mixed lymphocyte reaction (MLR) When lymphocytes from two individuals are cultured together, a proliferative response is generally observed, as the result of reactions of T cells of one individual to MHC antigens on the other individual's cells.

Mixed-bed ion exchange Mixing both anion and cation resins in the same deionizer results in higher efficiency, but lower capacity, than separate-bed deionizers.

Mmol/L (millimols per litre) The unit of measurement of how much of a substance (such as sugar) is in a specific amount of fluid (such as blood or urine). Most of the world uses mmol/L.

MMR A combined vaccine against measles, mumps and German measles (rubella).

Mobilization Passive movement technique that is performed that is always in the control of the patient. Usually performed as oscillatory movements in either the physiological or accessory range of a joint.

Modafinil A synthetic central nervous system stimulant with wakefulness-promoting activity. Modafinil appears to inhibit dopamine reuptake, resulting in an increase in extracellular dopamine. This agent exhibits pronounced wakefulness-promoting activity (without sympathomimetic activity) and may improve cognitive function in certain clinical settings.

Modality A method of treatment. For example, surgery and chemotherapy are treatment modalities.

Model organisms A laboratory animal or other organism useful for research.

Modeling The use of statistical analysis, computer analysis, or model organisms to predict outcomes of research.

Modified radical mastectomy Surgery for breast cancer in which the breast, most or all of the lymph nodes under the arm, and the lining over the chest muscles are removed. Sometimes the surgeon also removes part of the chest wall muscles.

Modified essay question (MEQ) A measurement instrument which allows for assessment of clinical reasoning skills, understanding and knowledge of clinical and basic science and application of basic science to clinical problems. MEQ's constitute a series of questions which must be answered in the sequence asked, with no review and no possibility of correcting previous answers. Questions must be answered within the allocated time which may vary from 40 to 90 minutes. In general, a brief patient clinical scenario (presentation) is followed by a few questions exploring diagnostic hypotheses and mechanisms underlying the clinical presentation. Subsequent questions may focus on applied basic science, interpretation of diagnostic information, management issues, disease complications, ethical issues or prognosis, for example. The initial scenario is either repeated or reformulated as the reporting process progresses, and as further information is provided, the assessed area narrows. Thus the medical problem is progressively defined with questions being directed to increasingly specific areas. A well-written MEQ assesses the approach of students to a problem, their reasoning skills and understanding of concepts, rather than recall of factual knowledge.

Modulate To adjust, or change.

Mohs micrographic surgery A surgical procedure used to treat skin cancer. Individual layers of cancerous tissue are removed and examined under a microscope one at a time until all cancerous tissue has been removed. Also called Mohs surgery.

Moiety A part or portion of a molecule, generally complex, having a characteristic chemical or pharmacological property.

Moist air A binary mixture of dry air and water vapour. Each component behaves as if the other is not present and each occupies the complete volume of the mixture.

Molar pregnancy A condition in women of childbearing age in which grape-like cysts grow in the uterus after conception (fertilization of an egg by a sperm). Molar pregnancies may change into a type of cancer called choriocarcinoma or gestational trophoblastic tumor. Also called hydatidiform mole.

Molars Three back teeth in each dental quadrant used for grinding food.

Mold A form or die plate made from any preformed or custom moulded model that will later be reproduced.

Mole A benign growth on the skin (usually tan, brown, or flesh-coloured) that contains a cluster of melanocytes and surrounding supportive tissue.

Molecular biology The study of the structure, function, and makeup of biologically important molecules.

Molecular farming The development of transgenic animals to produce human proteins for medical use.

Molecular genetics Deals with the study of the nature and biochemistry of genetic material. Includes the technologies of genetic engineering.

Molecular mass The sum of the atomic masses of all atoms in a molecule, based on a scale in which the atomic masses of hydrogen, carbon, nitrogen, and oxygen are 1, 12, 14, and 16, respectively. For example, the molecular mass of water, which has two atoms of hydrogen and one atom of oxygen, is 18 (i.e., 2 + 16).

Molecular medicine The treatment of injury or disease at the molecular level. Examples include the use of DNA-based diagnostic tests or medicine derived from DNA sequence information.

Molecular risk assessment A procedure in which biomarkers (for example, biological molecules or changes in tumor cell DNA) are used to estimate a person's risk for developing cancer. Specific biomarkers may be linked to particular types of cancer.

Molecular weight The weight of a molecule that may be calculated as the sum of the atomic weights of its constituent atoms. Atomic weight is the weight of an element in relation to some element taken as the standard, usually oxygen (16) or carbon (12).

Molecularly targeted therapy In cancer treatment, substances that kill cancer cells by targeting key molecules involved in cancer cell growth.

Molecule The smallest particle of a substance that has all of the physical and chemical properties of that substance. Molecules are made up of one or more atoms. If they contain more than one atom, the atoms can be the same (an oxygen molecule has two oxygen atoms) or different (a water molecule has two hydrogen atoms and one oxygen atom). Biological molecules, such as proteins and DNA, can be made up of many thousands of atoms.

Molluscum contagiosum A disease of the skin and mucous membranes caused by a virus. The condition causes pearly white or flesh-colored bumps on the face, neck, underarms, hands, and genital region. In people with HIV, molluscum contagiosum can get worse with time and often becomes resistant to treatment.

Moniliasis (thrush) Opportunistic fungal infection after administration of antibiotic; not uncommon in the mouth.

Mono & di glycerides Emulsifying agents found in shortening, margarine, cacao products and bakery products. Usually derived from soybean fat, these food additives keep food products from separating.

Monoclonal Literally, coming from a single clone. A clone is the progeny of a single cell. In immunology, monoclonal generally describes a preparation of antibody that is monogenous, or cells of a single specificity.

Monoclonal antibodies Antibodies manufactured in the laboratory and designed to seek out specific foreign agents (antigens) on cancer cells as targets. Monoclonal antibodies are being studied for their potential to "deliver" chemotherapy and radiotherapy directly to a cancer, thus killing the cancer cell and not harming healthy tissue. Other studies are being done to see if monoclonal antibodies can be produced to detect or locate small groups of cancer cells.

Monoclonal antibody CAL A humanized monoclonal antibody directed against parathyroid hormone-related protein (PTH-rP). As a poly-hormone with diverse biological roles, PTH-rP is expressed by normal tissues, acting in local tissue environments in a variety of ways; it is commonly overexpressed by breast, prostate, and other cancers, acting systemically by promoting bone resorption, inhibiting calcium excretion from the kidney, inducing hypercalcemia, and possibly playing a role in the formation of bony metastases. By blocking the effects of PTH-rP on calcium metabolism, monoclonal antibody CAL may inhibit cancer-related hypercalcemia.

Monoclonal gammopathy of undetermined significance (MGUS) A benign condition in which there is a high level of a protein called M protein in the blood. Patients with MGUS are at an increased risk of developing cancer.

Monoclonal protein An antibody or part of an antibody found in unusually large amounts in the blood or urine of people with multiple myeloma and other types of plasma cell tumors. Also called M protein.

Monocular vision Only one eye having useful vision.

Monocyte Large circulating white cell, 2-10% of total white cells, phagocytic, indented nucleus. Migrates to tissues, where it is known as a macrophage.

Monogenic disorder A disorder caused by mutation of a single gene.

Monokines Soluble substances secreted by monocytes, which have a variety of effects on other cells.

Monomer The basic subunit from which, by repetition of a single reaction, polymers are made. For example, amino acids (monomers) condense to yield polypeptides or proteins (polymers).

Mononeuropathy A form of diabetic neuropathy affecting a single nerve. The eye is a common site for this form of nerve damage.

Monosaccharides The building blocks of carbohydrates, hence known as "simple sugar". They are classified by the number of carbon atoms in the molecule, pentoses have five and hexoses six.

Monosomy Possessing only one copy of a particular chromosome instead of the normal two copies.

Monotherapy A single drug, prescribed by itself.

Montanide ISA 51 A water-in-oil emulsion that stimulates the T-cell immune response to antigens and may be used in various types of cancer vaccines.

Morbid map A diagram showing the chromosomal location of genes associated with disease.

Morbid obesity This is a state of adiposity or overweight, in which body weight is 100 percent above the ideal and a body mass index of 45 or greater.

Morbidity A disease or the incidence of disease within a population. Morbidity also refers to adverse effects caused by a treatment.

Morbidity rate The sickness rate; the number of people who are sick or have a disease compared with the number who are well.

Morbilliform Describing a skin rash resembling that of measles.

Morinda citrifolia A tropical shrub. An extract from the fruit is being studied as a treatment for cancer, and extracts from the fruit, leaves, or roots have been used in some cultures to treat other diseases. Also called noni.

Morphine A narcotic drug used in the treatment of pain.

Morphologic diagnosis The interpretation of the abnormalities in terms of severity, time, lesion and anatomic site. For example: severe, chronic, glomerulonephritis.

Morphology The science of the form and structure of organisms (plants, animals, and other forms of life).

Mortality Death. Used to describe the relation of deaths to the population in which they occur. The mortality rate (death rate) expresses the number of deaths in a unit of population within a prescribed time and may be expressed as crude death rates (e.g., total deaths in relation to total population during a year) or as death rates specific for diseases and, sometimes, for age, sex, or other attributes (e.g., number of deaths from cancer in white males in relation to the white male population during a given year).

Mortality rate The death rate; the number of people who die of a certain disease compared with the total number of people. Mortality is most often stated as deaths per 1,000, per 10,000, or per 100,000 persons.

Morton's neuroma Painful swelling of one of the digital branches of the plantar nerves. Occurs usually at the bifurcation of the nerve as it lies between the two adjacent metatarsal heads. The most common site is between the third and fourth metatarsal heads.

Motexafin gadolinium A substance that is being studied in the treatment of cancer. It may make tumor cells more sensitive to radiation therapy, improve tumor images using magnetic resonance imaging (MRI), and kill cancer cells. It belongs to the family of drugs called metalloporphyrin complexes. Also called gadolinium texaphyrin.

Motexafin lutetium A substance that is being studied in the treatment of cancer using photodynamic therapy. It belongs to the family of drugs called metallotexaphyrins. Also called lutetium texaphyrin.

Mother liquor The residual liquid that remains after the crystallization or isolation processes. A mother liquor may contain unrecovered products (i.e., unreacted starting materials, intermediates, levels of the API and/or impurities). It may be used for further processing.

Mother to child transmission (MTCT) The passage of HIV from an HIV-infected mother to her infant. The infant may become infected while in the womb, during labor and delivery, or through breastfeeding.

Motility The movement of food through the digestive tract, aided by contractions of muscles in the stomach and intestines known as peristalsis.

Motor In medicine, having to do with the movement of body parts.

Mould Is a specific term applied to the action of taking an impression (mould) of the cavity or dysfunctional globe.

Movement diagram Diagrammatic and graphical depiction of the palpation of a joint. Effective as a teaching tool to describe grades of movement.

Moxifloxacin hydrochloride The hydrochloride salt of a fluoroquinolone antibacterial antibiotic. Moxifloxacin binds to and inhibits the bacterial enzymes DNA gyrase (topoisomerase II) and topoisomerase IV, resulting in inhibition of DNA replication and repair and cell death in sensitive bacterial species.

MSG (Monosodium glutamate) MSG is the sodium salt of glutamic acid. Glutamic acid, or glutamate, is one of the most common amino acids found in nature.

In the early part of the century, MSG was extracted from seaweed and other plant sources. Today, MSG is produced in many countries around the world through a fermentation process of molasses from sugar cane or sugar beets, as well as starch and corn sugar.

Mucin/peptide A protein/sugar compound made by some cancer cells.

Mucinous Containing or resembling mucin, the main compound in mucus.

Mucinous carcinoma A type of cancer that begins in cells that line certain internal organs and produce mucin (the main component of mucus).

Mucocutaneous Relating to mucous membranes and the skin (for example, the mouth, lips, eyes, vagina, or anal area).

Mucogingival junction (MGJ) Meeting of thick, protective gingival tissue around the teeth and the friable mucous lining of the cheeks and lips.

Mucosa The moist, inner lining of some organs and body cavities (such as the nose, mouth, lungs, and stomach). Glands in the mucosa make mucus (a thick, slippery fluid). Also called mucous membrane.

Mucosa-associated lymphoid tissue lymphoma (MALT lymphoma) A type of cancer that arises in cells in mucosal tissue that are involved in antibody production.

Mucosal Pertaining specifically to the mucous membranes

Mucosal fold A fold of mucous membrane protruding into the lumen (cavity).

Mucositis A complication of some cancer therapies in which the lining of the digestive system becomes inflamed. Often seen as sores in the mouth.

Mucous A viscid secretion derived from the mucous membrane.

Müllerian tumor A rare cancer of the uterus, ovary, or fallopian tubes.

Multi epitope melanoma peptide vaccine A peptide cancer vaccine consisting of a combination of peptides derived form several melanoma epitopes. Vaccination with multi-epitope melanoma peptide vaccine stimulates the host immune system to mount a cytotoxic T lymphocyte (CTL) response against tumor cells expressing the corresponding antigens, resulting in tumor cell lysis. This vaccine may stimulate a broader CTL response compared to single-antigen vaccines.

Multicellular Referring to organisms composed of more than one cell - often billions of them, arranged in various organs, tissues, and systems.

Multicenter clinical trial A clinical trial involving two or more clinical centers and a common study protocol.

Multicenter study A clinical trial that is carried out at more than one medical institution.

Multicentric breast cancer Breast cancer in which there is more than one tumor, all of which have formed separately from one another. The tumors are likely to be in different quadrants (sections) of the breast. Multicentric breast cancers are rare.

Multidisciplinary In medicine, a term used to describe a treatment planning approach or team that includes a number of doctors and other health care professionals who are experts in different specialties (disciplines). In cancer treatment, the primary disciplines are medical oncology (treatment with drugs), surgical oncology (treatment with surgery), and radiation oncology (treatment with radiation).

Multidrug resistance Adaptation of tumor cells to anticancer drugs in ways that make the drugs less effective.

Multidrug resistance inhibition Treatment used to make cancer cells less resistant to anticancer drugs.

Multifidus Deep lumbar spine muscle. Its primary function is to stabilise the lumbar spine.

Multimodality treatment Therapy that combines more than one method of treatment.

Multiple comparisons A term used to refer to the fact that two or more treatment comparisons, each involving the same outcome measure, are made or are to be made at a designated time point in the course of the trial. The comparison may involve all members of the treatment groups or subsets (e.g., as in analyses involving subgroups of patients defined by the presence or absence of some baseline characteristic). Also applies to comparisons among several subgroups and/or use of several endpoints.

Multiple drug resistant tuberculosis (MDR TB) A tuberculosis (TB) infection that does not respond to two or more standard anti-TB drugs. MDR-TB usually occurs when inadequate or improper treatment allows the bacteria that cause TB to continue multiplying and become drug resistant.

Multiple endocrine adenomatosis A rare, inherited disorder that affects the endocrine glands and can cause tumors in the parathyroid and pituitary glands and the pancreas. These tumors (usually benign) cause the glands to secrete high levels of hormones, which can lead to other medical problems, such as kidney stones, fertility problems, and severe ulcers. In some cases, tumors inside the pancreas can become cancerous. Also called multiple endocrine neoplasia type 1 syndrome and Wermer's syndrome.

Multiple endocrine neoplasia syndrome An inherited tendency to develop thyroid cancer and other cancers of the endocrine system. The altered gene can be detected with a blood test.

Multiple endocrine neoplasia type 1 syndrome (MEN1 syndrome) A rare, inherited disorder that affects the endocrine glands and can cause tumors in the parathyroid and pituitary glands and the pancreas. These tumors (usually benign) cause the glands to secrete high levels of hormones, which can lead to other medical problems, such as kidney stones, fertility problems, and severe ulcers. In some cases, tumors inside the pancreas can become cancerous. Also called multiple endocrine adenomatosis and Wermer's syndrome.

Multiple myeloma A type of cancer that begins in plasma cells (white blood cells that produce antibodies). Also called Kahler's disease, myelomatosis, or plasma cell myeloma.

Multiple outcomes A term used to refer to the fact that a trial involves several different outcome measures, each of which is used or is to be used to make treatment comparisons.

Multiple sclerosis A disorder of the central nervous system marked by weakness, numbness, a loss of muscle coordination, and problems with vision, speech, and bladder control. Multiple sclerosis is thought to be an autoimmune disease in which the body's immune system destroys myelin. Myelin is a substance that contains both protein and fat (lipid), serving as a nerve insulator and helping in the transmission of nerve signals.

Multiplexing A laboratory approach that performs multiple sets of reactions in parallel (simultaneously); greatly increasing speed and throughput.

Multiplicity A large number or variety.

Multi-specialty group A group of doctors who represent various medical specialties and who work together in a group practice.

Multivitamins A dietary supplement containing all or most of the vitamins that may not be readily available in the diet. Vitamins may be classified according to their solubility either in lipids (vitamins A, D, E, K, F) or in water (vitamins C, B-complex). Present in minute amounts in various foods, vitamins are essential to maintaining normal metabolism and biochemical functions.

Munchausen's syndrome A mental disorder in which the patient persistently tries to obtain medical treatment, for an illness that is non-existent: it is an extreme form of malingering. In Munchausen's Syndrome by proxy, the patient inflicts harm on others (often children) in order to attract medical attention.

Mung bean A type of bean grown in warm climates, usually for its seed and for bean sprouts. Mung bean may have anticancer effects.

Murine Relating to a member of the rodent family Muridae, including rats and mice; such as murine monoclonal antibodies derived from mice.

Muromonab-CD3 A type of monoclonal antibody used in cancer detection or therapy. Monoclonal antibodies are laboratory-produced substances that can locate and bind to cancer cells.

Musculoskeletal Having to do with muscles, bones, and cartilage.

Mustargen A drug used to treat some types of cancer and some precancerous skin conditions. It belongs to the family of drugs called alkylating agents. Also called mechlorethamine.

Mutagen An agent that causes a permanent genetic change in a cell. Does not include changes occurring during normal genetic recombination.

Mutagenesis The induction of mutation in the genetic material of an organism; researchers may use physical or chemical means to cause mutations that improve the production of capabilities of organisms.

Mutagenicity The capacity of a chemical or physical agent to cause permanent genetic alterations.

Mutant The altered cell resulting from mutation of the original wild type or any subsequent alteration.

Mutate To change the genetic material of a cell. The changes (mutations) can be harmful, beneficial, or have no effect.

Mutation A change or adaptation that can be passed down to future generations. Mutations can occur only when a virus is actively replicating, and not when anti-HIV drugs have suppressed the viral load to undetectable. If HIV replication is not well controlled, an individual's original HIV strain can adapt to infect different cell types or resist different anti-HIV drugs.

My, myo Muscle, e.g. leiomyosarcoma - a malignant tumor of smooth muscle cells.

Myalgia Muscle pain or tenderness that spreads throughout the body and is usually accompanied by a general feeling of discomfort or weakness.

Mycelium The mat or complex group of protoplasmic units, or the entangled mass of tubelike or filamentous structures, i.e., hyphae, that represents the "body" of plant forms classified as Eumycetes (including Phycomycetes, Ascomycetes, Deuteromycetes (Fungi Imperfectii), and Basidiomycetes).

Mycobacterium A genus of the family Mycobacteriaceae containing slender, aerobic, usually acid fast, Gram positive, rod-shaped organisms of various forms, club shaped, swollen, but seldom branched or with filaments; it includes many species which were formerly and are still called bacilli, such as the pathogens of tuberculosis and leprosy.

Mycobacterium avium complex (MAC) A common opportunistic infection caused by two very similar mycobacterial organisms, Mycobacterium avium and M. intracellulare. In PWAs, it can spread through the bloodstream to infect lymph nodes, bone marrow, liver, spleen, spinal fluid, lungs and intestinal tract. Symptoms of MAC include prolonged wasting, fever, fatigue and enlarged spleen. MAC infection is one of the disease making up the AIDS definition.

Mycobacterium kansasii Another member of the mycobacteria family, sometime mistaken for MAC.

Mycophenolate mofetil The morpholinoethyl ester of mycophenolic acid (MPA) with potent immunosuppressive properties. Mycophenolate stops T-cell and B-cell proliferation through selective inhibition of the de novo pathway of purine biosynthesis. In vivo, the active metabolite, MPA, reversibly inhibits inosine 5'-monophosphate dehydrogenase, an enzyme involved in the de novo synthesis of guanine nucleotides. MPA displays high lymphocyte specificity and cytotoxicity due to the higher dependence of activated lymphocytes on both salvage and de novo synthesis of guanine nucleotides relative to other cell types.

Mycoplasma A class of microorganism, simpler than a bacteria, but more complex than a virus. Some mycoplasma may play a role in HIV pathogenesis, although the evidence is unclear.

Mycosis Any disease caused by a fungus including Aspergillosis.

Mycosis fungoides A type of non-Hodgkin's lymphoma that first appears on the skin and can spread to the lymph nodes or other organs such as the spleen, liver, or lungs.

Mycosis fungoides plaque In mycosis fungoides, an area of skin that is thickened, raised, red, scaly, and itchy.

Mycostatin A drug that treats infections caused by fungi.

Mycotoxins Toxins produced by fungi. More than 350 different mycotoxins are known to man. Almost all mycotoxins possess the capacity to harmfully alter the immune systems of animals. Consumption by humans and animals of certain mycotoxins (e.g., via eating infected corn, nuts, peanuts cottonseed products, etc.) can result in liver toxicity, gastrointestinal lesions, cancer and muscle necrosis.

Myelencephalon The caudal subdivision of the hindbrain or rhombencephalon which develops into the medulla oblongata in the adult.

Myelin The lipid substance forming a sheath around the axons of certain nerve fibers.

Myelitis Inflammation of the spinal cord, or of the bone marrow.

Myeloablation A severe form of myelosuppression. Myelosuppression is a condition in which bone marrow activity is decreased, resulting in fewer red blood cells, white blood cells, and platelets. It is a side effect of some cancer treatments.

Myelodysplasia Abnormal bone marrow cells that may lead to myelogenous leukemia.

Myelodysplastic syndrome Disease in which the bone marrow does not function normally. Also called preleukemia or smoldering leukemia.

Myelofibrosis A disorder in which the bone marrow is replaced by fibrous tissue.

Myelogenous Having to do with, produced by, or resembling the bone marrow. Sometimes used as a synonym for myeloid; for example, acute myeloid leukemia and acute myelogenous leukemia are the same disease.

Myelogram A roentgenogram of the spinal cord taken after contrast material has been injected (through an LP needle) into the subarachnoid space of the spinal canal.

Myeloid Having to do with or resembling the bone marrow. May also refer to certain types of hematopoietic (blood-forming) cells found in the bone marrow. Sometimes used as a synonym for myelogenous; for example, acute myeloid leukemia and acute myelogenous leukemia are the same disease.

Myeloma A malignant tumor of the bone marrow associated with the production of abnormal proteins.

Myelomatosis A type of cancer that begins in plasma cells (white blood cells that produce antibodies). Also called multiple myeloma, Kahler's disease, or plasma cell myeloma.

Myelomeningocele Spina bifida, also called myelomeningocele, is a condition in which there is an opening in the spinal column or backbone of the fetus.

Myelopathy A degenerative process involving the spinal cord.

Myeloproliferative disorder A disease in which too many blood cells are made in the bone marrow.

Myelosclerosis with myeloid metaplasia A progressive, chronic disease in which the bone marrow is replaced by fibrous tissue and blood is made in organs such as the liver and the spleen, instead of in the bone marrow. This disease is marked by an enlarged spleen and progressive anemia. Also called chronic idiopathic myelofibrosis, agnogenic myeloid metaplasia, primary myelofibrosis, and idiopathic myelofibrosis.

Myelosuppression A condition in which bone marrow activity is decreased, resulting in fewer red blood cells, white blood cells, and platelets. Myelosuppression is a side effect of some cancer treatments. When myelosuppression is severe, it is called myeloablation.

Myelotoxic Toxic to the bone marrow.

Mylohyoid muscle Muscle which originates at the mylohyoid line of the mandible, and inserts into the body of the hyoid bone and median raphe. It elevates the hyoid bone and supports the floor of the mouth.

Myo inositol A substance in the cell that is thought to play a role in helping the nerves to work. Low levels of myo-inositol may be involved in diabetic neuropathy.

Myocardial infarction (MI) Also called a heart attack. This occurs when an artery that feeds the heart becomes blocked. As a result, blood does not get to some parts of the heart and some of the heart tissue dies. Symptoms may include nausea, shortness of breath and pain in the chest, arm or neck.

Myocardial ischemia Oxygen deprivation of the heart muscle caused by a blockage in the blood vessels serving a particular region of the heart.

Myofascial trigger point Areas of focal muscle tenderness and spasm, usually precipitated by a central cause of symptoms e.g. lumbar or cervical spines.

Myometrium The muscular outer layer of the uterus.

Myopathy A disease of muscle tissue. Myopathy may be caused by certain anti-HIV drugs or as a consequence of HIV infection itself.

Myopia Nearsightedness, an individual will have difficulty seeing clearly at distance. Light entering the eye focuses in front of the retina when the eye is at rest and is corrected with a minus lens. A condition known as high myopia occurs when myopia is greater than 6 diopters. Typically, vision therapy is not prescribed for myopia.

Myositis ossificans Ossification of a haematoma, secondary to a blunt trauma. Should the haematoma be unresolved, calcification and subsequent ossification, can occur after approximately 3 weeks. Surgical intervention may then be necessary

Myotome Segmental innervation of muscle. Testing of specific nerve root function can be performed by testing myotomes at different levels.

Myx Mucus, e.g. myxedema - mucinous edema (swelling).

N acetylcysteine An antioxidant drug that may keep cancer cells from developing or reduce the risk of growth of existing cancer.

N butyl N (4 hydroxybutyl) nitrosamine A substance that is used in cancer research to cause bladder tumors in laboratory animals. This is done to test new diets, drugs, and procedures for use in cancer prevention and treatment.

Nadir The lowest level to which viral load (the amount of HIV in the blood) falls after a person starts anti-HIV treatment. Also refers to the lowest CD4 count a person reaches during HIV infection.

Naive t cell A newly formed T cell that has not yet been exposed to antigen.

Naloxone A substance that is being studied as a treatment for constipation caused by narcotic medications. It belongs to the family of drugs called narcotic antagonists.

HO
O
OH
N
O

Figure Naloxone

Nano Prefix meaning one one-billionth, as in nanogram, a billionth of a gram.

Nanogram A measure of weight. One nanogram weighs a billion times less than one gram, and almost a trillion-times less than a pound.

Nanometre One-millionth of a millimetre.

Nanophthalmos Abnormally small eye with proportionately small surrounding eye struc-ture. (Congenital Anomaly)

Nanotechnology The field of research that deals with the engineering and creation of things from materials that are less than 100 nanometres (one-billionth of a meter) in size, especially single atoms or molecules. Nanotechnology is being studied in the detection, diagnosis, and treatment of cancer.

Narcotic An agent that causes insensibility or stupor; usually refers to opioids given to relieve pain.

Nasal By or having to do with the nose.

Nasal concha (turbinate bone) Any of the three thin scroll-like bones that form the sides of the nasal cavity. The superior and middle nasal conchae are part of the ethmoid bone; the inferior nasal conchae are a separate pair of bones.

Nasal salute Rubbing of itchy nose due to nasal allergies.

Nasal septum The vertical (sagittal) midline partition separating the left and right nasal cavities.

Nasal turbinates Curved plates of cartilage and bone, located on the lateral walls of the nasal cavities. Covered by mucous membrane and vascular tissue, they serve to warm and humidfy the air for respiration.

Nasopharyngeal cancer Cancer that forms in tissues of the nasopharynx (upper part of the throat behind the nose). Most nasopharyngeal cancers are squamous cell carcinomas (cancer that begins in flat cells lining the nasopharynx).

Nasopharynx The upper part of the throat behind the nose. An opening on each side of the nasopharynx leads into the ear.

Nasoscope A thin lighted tube used to examine the nose. Also called a rhinoscope.

Nasoscopy A procedure in which a thin, lighted tube is inserted into the nose to look for abnormal areas. Also called rhinoscopy.

Natal Relating to birth.

Natural history of disease 1. The course of a disease when left untreated.

2. The course of a disease when treated with standard modes of therapy.

Natural history study A prospective follow-up study designed to yield information on the natural course of a disease or condition. Such studies generally focus on the control-treated group in a clinical trial (especially one in which the control treatment is a placebo or standard medical care).

Natural killer (NK) cell A type of lymphocyte (white blood cell) that lyses infected or cancerous cells. NK response does not require antigen presentation to lymphocytes.

Nausea A feeling of sickness or discomfort in the stomach that may come with an urge to vomit. Nausea is a side effect of some types of cancer therapy.

Navicular A "boat shaped" bone of the hand and foot. Also called the "scaphoid".

FX Scaphoid (Carpal Navicular)

FX Tarsal Navicular.

Near acuity The eye's ability to distinguish an object's shape and details at a near distance such as 16 inches (40 cm).

Near point of convergence (NPC) The closest point at which the two eyes can maintain a single united image.

Near point of convergence test Measures the patient's ability to point the eyes at an approaching object and to keep them fixed on the object as it reaches the patient's nose. Normal range is 0 to 4 inches away from the nose.

Nebulizer A device used to reduce liquid medication to extremely fine cloudlike particles; useful in delivering medication to deeper parts of the respiratory tract (e.g., into the lungs).

Neck dissection Surgery to remove lymph nodes and other tissues in the neck.

Necr Death, e.g. necrosis - the morphologic changes indicative of cell death, indicated by characteristic nuclear and cytoplasmic changes.

Necrobiosis Altered collagen that loses its normal eosinophilic coloration and fibrillar appearance, becoming slightly bluish and "smudged".

Necrobiosis lipoidica diabeticorum A skin condition usually on the lower part of the legs. The lesions can be small or extend over a large area. They are usually raised, yellow, and waxy in appearance and often have a purple border. Young women are most often affected. This condition occurs in people with diabetes, or it may be a sign of diabetes. It also occurs in people who do not have diabetes.

Necropsy Examination of a body after death.

Necrosis The pathological death of one or more cells, or of a portion of tissue or organ, resulting from irreversible damage to the nucleus.

Necrotizing enterocolitis A situation that may affect underweight or premature infants, and occurs when part of the intestine is damaged or destroyed by a bacterial infection.

Needle aspiration Removal of fluid from a cyst, or cells from a tumor. In this procedure, a needle and syringe (like those used to give injections) is used to pierce the skin, reach the cyst or tumor, and with suction, draw up (aspirate) specimens for biopsy analysis. If the needle is thin, the procedure is called fine needle aspiration or "FNA." If a needle with a large bore (or core) is used, the procedure is called a core biopsy.

Needle biopsy The removal of tissue or fluid with a needle for examination under a microscope. Also called fine-needle aspiration.

Needle localization A procedure used to do a breast needle biopsy when the lump is difficult to locate or in areas that look suspicious on the x-ray but do not have a distinct lump. After an injection of local anesthesia to numb the area, a thin needle is inserted into the breast. X-rays are taken and used to guide the wire to the area to be biopsied. A tiny hook on the end of the wire holds it in place. Then a hypodermic needle (like the type used to give injections) is injected, using the path of the wire as a guide, and the biopsy is completed.

Negative axillary lymph node A lymph node in the armpit that is free of cancer.

Negative control Inactive control treatment.

Negative relative accommodation (NRA) A measure of the maximum ability to relax accommodation while maintaining clear, single binocular vision.

Negative test result A test result that fails to show the specific disease or condition for which the test was being done.

Nelarabine An arabinonucleoside antimetabolite with antineoplastic activity. Nelarabine is deme-thoxylated by adenosine deaminase to become biologically active 9-beta-D-arabinosy-lguanine (ara-G); ara-G incorporates into DNA, thereby inhibiting DNA synthesis and inducing an S phase-dependent apoptosis of tumor cells.

Nelfinavir mesylate A drug that interferes with the ability of a virus to make copies of itself.

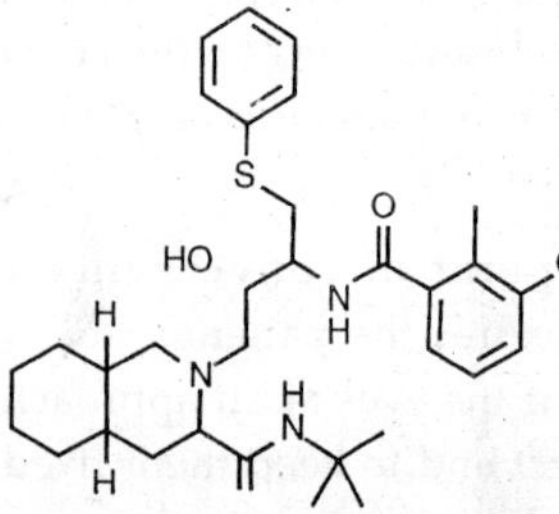

{3S[2 (2S,3S),3α,4aβ,8aβ]-N- (1,1-Dimethylethyl) decahydro-2-2-hydroxy-3-[(3-hydroxy-2- methylbenzoyl)amino]-4-(phenylthio)butyl-3-isoquinolinecarboxamide monomethanesulphonate; (3S,4aS,8aS)-N-tert-Butyldecahydro-2-[(2R,3R)-3- (3-hydroxy-o-toluamido)-2-hydroxy-4-(phenylthio)butyl]isoquinoline-3-carboxamide monomethanesulphonate}

Figure Nelfinavir

Neoadjuvant therapy Treatment given before the primary treatment. Examples of neoadjuvant therapy include chemotherapy, radiation therapy, and hormone therapy.

Neocerebellum The most recently evolved part of the cerebellum and comprising its largest expanse. It includes mainly the lateral or hemispherical part of the cerebellum situated between the primary and posterolateral fissures (posterior lobe).

Neonatal intensive care unit (Neo ICU) A hospital unit with special equipment for the care of premature and seriously ill newborn infants.

Neonatal The time period from birth through the first 4 weeks after birth.

Neopallium The most recently evolved part of the cerebral cortex. It consists of six layers and forms most of the cerebral cortex in man. Also known as neocortex or isocortex.

Neoplasia Abnormal and uncontrolled cell growth.

Neoplasm An abnormal mass of tissue that results when cells divide more than they should or do not die when they should. Tumors may be benign (not cancerous), or malignant (cancerous). Also called tumor.

Neoplastic meningitis A condition in which cancer cells spread into the meninges (membranes that surround the brain and spinal cord).

Neostriatum Phylogenetically, the most recently evolved component of the corpus striatum. It is equivalent to the caudate nucleus and the putamen. Sometimes abbreviated to Striatum.

Neovascularization The term used when new, tiny blood vessels grow in a new place, for example, out from the retina.

Nephelometry The semiquantitative estimation of the concentration of particles in a suspension (e.g. bacterial cells in an antigenic preparation), by means of comparing it with the standard suspensions in a nephelometer.

Nephr Kidney, e.g. nephrectomy - surgical removal of the kidney.

Nephrectomy Surgery to remove a kidney or part of a kidney. In a partial nephrectomy, part of one kidney or a tumor is removed, but not an entire kidney. In a simple nephrectomy, one kidney is removed. In a radical nephrectomy, an entire kidney, nearby adrenal gland and lymph nodes, and other surrounding tissue are removed. In a bilateral nephrectomy, both kidneys are removed.

Nephritis Inflammation of the kidney that can occur as a side effect of some anti-HIV drugs.

Nephrologist A doctor who specializes in diagnosing and treating kidney disease.

Nephropathy Any disease of the kidneys.

Kidney damage caused by diabetes, called diabetic nephropathy, can occur in several ways. The typical form of diabetic nephropathy, called diabetic glomerulosclerosis, has large amounts of urine protein, hypertension, and is slowly progressive. It usually doesn't occur until after many years of diabetes, and can be delayed by tight control of the blood sugar. Usually the best lab test for early detection of diabetic nephropathy is measurement of microalbumin in the urine.

Nephrostomy Surgery to make an opening from the outside of the body to the renal pelvis (part of the kidney that collects urine). This may be done to drain urine from a blocked kidney or blocked ureter into a bag outside the body. It may also be done to look at the kidney using an endoscope (thin, lighted tube attached to a camera), to place anticancer drugs directly into the kidney, or to remove kidney stones.

Nephrotomogram A series of x-rays of the kidneys. The x-rays are taken from different angles and show the kidneys clearly, without the shadows of the organs around them.

Nephrotoxic Poisonous or damaging to the kidney.

Nephrotoxin A cytotoxin that is specific for cells of the kidney.

Nephroureterectomy Surgery to remove a kidney and its ureter. Also called ureteronephrectomy.

Nerve A bundle of fibers that receives and sends messages between the body and the brain. The messages are sent by chemical and electrical changes in the cells that make up the nerves.

Nerve block A procedure in which medicine is injected directly into or around a nerve or into the spine to block pain.

Nerve cell A type of cell that receives and sends messages from the body to the brain and back to the body. The messages are sent by a weak electrical current. Also called a neuron.

Nerve conduction velocity (NCV) studies and electromyography (EMG) Tests used to diagnose neuropathy and check for nerve damage. These tests are usually both run at the same time, using the same equipment.

Nerve grafting Replacing a damaged nerve with a section of a healthy nerve that has been removed from another part of the body. This procedure is being studied in the prevention of erectile dysfunction in men having surgery for prostate cancer.

Nerve root The portion of a nerve adjacent to the CNS centers of the brain and spinal cord that they innervate.

Nerve-sparing radical prostatectomy Surgery to remove the prostate in which an attempt is made to save the nerves that help cause penile erections.

Nerve-sparing surgery A type of surgery that attempts to save the nerves near the tissues being removed.

Nesidioblastosis A group of rare conditions occurring in infancy in which excessively large amounts of insulin are secreted by the beta cells in relation to the prevailing blood sugar level. Sometimes the condition occurs later in life, and sometimes it is due to an autosomal recessive genetic defect. Also called Persistent Hyperinsulinemic Hypoglycemia of Infancy (PHHI).

Neulasta A drug used to increase numbers of white blood cells in patients who are receiving chemotherapy. It belongs to the family of drugs called colony stimulating factors. Also called pegfilgrastim and filgrastim-SD-01.

Neural Having to do with nerves or the nervous system, including the brain and the spinal cord.

Neural foramen The passage for a nerve. For the spine, the spinal nerves and vessels, pass through the intervertebral neural foramen, formed by the inferior notch of the pedicle above, and a superior notch of the pedicle below.

Neuralgia Sharp, shooting pain along a nerve pathway.

Neurobehavioural Having to do with the way the brain affects emotion, behavior, and learning. Some cancers or their treatment may cause neurobehavioural problems.

Neuroblastoma Cancer that arises in immature nerve cells and affects mostly infants and children.

Neurocognitive Having to do with the ability to think and reason. This includes the ability to concentrate, remember things, process information, learn, speak, and understand.

Neuroectodermal tumor A tumor of the central or peripheral nervous system.

Neuroendocrine Having to do with the interactions between the nervous system and the endocrine system. Neuroendocrine describes certain cells that release hormones into the blood in response to stimulation of the nervous system.

Neuroendocrine tumor A tumor derived from cells that release a hormone in response to a signal from the nervous system. Some examples of neuroendocrine tumors are carcinoid tumors, islet cell tumors, medullary thyroid carcinoma, and pheochromocytoma. These tumors secrete hormones in excess, causing a variety of symptoms.

Neuroepithelial Having to do with tissue made up of sensory cells, such as tissue found in the ear, nose, and tongue.

Neurofibroma A benign tumor that develops from the cells and tissues that cover nerves.

Neurofibromatosis type 1 NF1 A rare genetic condition that causes brown spots and tumors on the skin, freckling in skin areas not exposed to the sun, tumors on the nerves, and developmental changes in the nervous system, muscles, bone, and skin.

Neurofibromatosis type 2 NF2 A genetic condition in which tumors form on the nerves of the inner ear and cause loss of hearing and balance. Tumors may also occur in the brain and on nerves in the skull and spinal cord, and may cause loss of speech, eye movement, and the ability to swallow. Also called acoustic neurofibromatosis.

Neuroglia The non-neuronal supporting cells of the central nervous system which includes the macroglia (astrocytes and oligodendrocytes) and the microglia.

Neuroglycopenic Shortage of glucose in the nerve cells of the brain. Since the brain cells depends upon glucose as their main fuel, low blood sugars can quickly result in malfunction of the brain (with change in mental function, and possible loss of consciousness or seizures). In patients with Hypoglycemia Unawareness, where the patient may not recognize low sugar levels because other symptoms such as sweating, tremor, and rapid heart rate, are absent, the first symptoms are neuroglycopenic – namely, loss of mental functioning.

Neurohypophysis Division of the hypophysis cerebri (pituitary) consisting of the median eminence, infundibular stem and the infundibular process (neural lobe).

Neurologic Pertaining to the brain or nervous system.

Neurological exam A series of questions and tests to check brain, spinal cord, and nerve function. The exam checks a person's mental status, coordination, ability to walk, and how well the muscles, sensory systems, and deep tendon reflexes work.

Neurologist A doctor who specializes in the diagnosis and treatment of disorders of the nervous system.

Neuroma A tumor that arises in nerve cells.

Neuron A type of cell that receives and sends messages from the body to the brain and back to the body. The messages are sent by a weak electrical current. Also called a nerve cell.

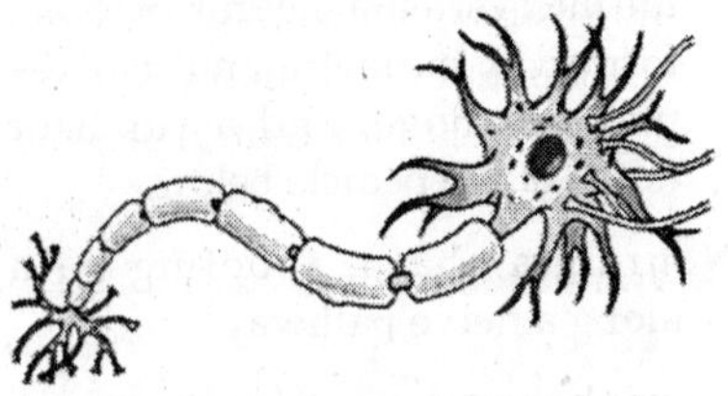

Figure Neuron

Neuro-oncologist A doctor who specializes in diagnosing and treating brain tumors and other tumors of the nervous system.

Neuropathologist A pathologist who specializes in diseases of the nervous system. A pathologist identifies disease by studying cells and tissues under a microscope.

Neuropathy A problem in peripheral nerve function (any part of the nervous system except the brain and spinal cord) that causes pain, numbness, tingling, swelling, and muscle weakness in various parts of the body. Neuropathies may be caused by physical injury, infection, toxic substances, disease (e.g., cancer, diabetes, kidney failure, or malnutrition), or drugs such as anticancer drugs. Also called peripheral neuropathy.

Neuropeptide A member of a class of protein-like molecules made in the brain. Neuropeptides consist of short chains of amino acids, with some functioning as neurotransmitters and some functioning as hormones.

Neuropil The feltwork of unmyelinated neuronal processes (axonal and dendritic) within the gray matter of the central nervous system.

Neuroradiologist A doctor trained in radiology who specializes in creating and interpreting pictures of the nervous system. The pictures are produced using forms of radiation, such as x-rays, sound waves, or other types of energy.

Neurosurgeon A doctor who specializes in surgery on the brain, spine, and other parts of the nervous system.

Neurotoxicity The tendency of some treatments to cause damage to the nervous system.

Neurotoxin A substance that is poisonous to nerve tissue.

Neurotropism An ability to invade and live in neural tissue. This term is usually used to describe the ability of viruses to infect nerve tissue.

Neutralizing antibody An antibody that neutralizes (renders harmless) the infectivity of microorganisms, particularly viruses.

Neutropenia A lower than normal number of neutrophils (a type of white blood cell) in the blood. Moderate to severe neutropenia can increase the chance of developing bacterial infections. Neutropenia may occur as a result of HIV infection or as a side effect of some anti-HIV drugs.

Neutrophils One of the white blood cells called granulocytes, filled with granules of toxic chemicals that can digest microorganisms. Neutrophils are comprised of two kinds of cells, polymorphonuclear cells ("polys" or PMNs), and bands, which are immature polys. Neutrophils are one of the key components of the immune response, especially to bacterial infection, and the neutrophil count is often elevated in acute infection.

Nevaripine An antiretroviral drug of the non-nucleoside reverse transcription inhibitor family. These drugs target the same enzyme as AZT and the other nucleoside drugs, but are chemically different.

Nevoid basal cell carcinoma syndrome A genetic condition that causes unusual facial features and disorders of the skin, bones, nervous system, eyes, and endocrine glands. People with this syndrome have a higher risk of basal cell carcinoma. Also called Gorlin syndrome and basal cell nevus syndrome.

Nevus A benign growth on the skin, such as a mole. A mole is a cluster of melanocytes and surrounding supportive tissue that usually appears as a tan, brown, or flesh-colored spot on the skin. The plural of nevus is nevi.

Newcastle disease virus (NDV) A bird virus that is being studied in the treatment of cancer. It may be used to kill cancer cells directly, or it may be given as a cancer vaccine to stimulate the body's immune system. Newcastle disease virus belongs to the families of drugs called biological response modifiers and vaccine therapy.

NG-monomethyl-L-arginine An amino acid derivative used to counteract high blood pressure caused by interleukin-2.

NHL (Non-hodgkin's lymphoma) Any of a large group of cancers of the immune system. NHLs can occur at any age, and are often marked by enlarged lymph nodes, fever, and weight loss. There are many different types of NHL, and they can be divided into aggressive (fast-growing) and indolent (slow-growing) types, and are classified as either B-cell or T-cell NHL. B-cell NHLs include Burkitt's lymphoma, diffuse large B-cell lymphoma, follicular lymphoma, immunoblastic large cell lymphoma, precursor B-lymphoblastic lymphoma, and mantle cell lymphoma. T-cell NHLs include mycosis fungoides, anaplastic large cell lymphoma, and precursor T-lymphoblastic lymphoma. Lymphomas related to lymphoproliferative disorders following bone marrow or stem cell transplantation are usually B-cell NHLs. Prognosis and treatment depend on the stage and type of disease.

NHSA (Normal human serum albumin) A blood plasma fraction usually prepared by Cohn cold ethanol precipitation. Dispensed as a 5% to 25% protein solution.

Niacinamide The active form of vitamin B3 and a component of the coenzyme nicotinamide adenine dinucleotide (NAD). Niacinamide acts as a chemo- and radio-sensitizing agent by enhancing tumor blood flow, thereby reducing tumor hypoxia. This agent also inhibits poly (ADP-ribose) polymerases, enzymes involved in the rejoining of DNA strand breaks induced by radiation or chemotherapy.

Nicotiana tabacum Tobacco. A plant with leaves that have high levels of the addictive chemical nicotine. The leaves may be smoked (in cigarettes, cigars, and pipes), applied to the gums (as dipping and chewing tobacco), or inhaled (as snuff). Tobacco leaves also contain many cancer-causing chemicals, and tobacco use and exposure to secondhand tobacco smoke have been linked to many types of cancer and other diseases.

Nicotinamide A vitamin being studied to increase the effect of radiation therapy on tumor cells. Also called niacinamide.

Nicotine An addictive, poisonous chemical found in tobacco. It can also be made in the laboratory. When it enters the body, nicotine causes an increased heart rate and use of oxygen by the heart, and a sense of well-being and relaxation. It is also used as an insecticide.

Nicotine gum A chewing gum that contains a small dose of nicotine, which enters the blood by being absorbed through the lining of the mouth. This helps stop nicotine cravings and relieves symptoms that occur when a person is trying to quit smoking. A prescription is not needed for nicotine gum.

Nicotine inhaler A device used to inhale (breathe in) small doses of nicotine through the mouth. The nicotine is absorbed through the lining of the mouth and goes into the blood. This helps stop nicotine cravings, and relieves symptoms that occur when a person is trying to quit smoking. A prescription is needed for nicotine inhalers.

Nicotine lozenge A hard candy-like tablet that contains a small dose of nicotine. The nicotine is absorbed through the lining of the mouth and goes into the blood. This helps stop nicotine cravings, and relieves symptoms that occur when a person is trying to quit smoking. A prescription is not needed for nicotine lozenges.

Nicotine nasal spray A nose spray that contains a small dose of nicotine, which enters the blood by being absorbed through the lining of the nose. This helps stop nicotine cravings and relieves symptoms that occur when a person is trying to quit smoking. A prescription is needed for nicotine nasal spray.

Nicotine patch A patch that sticks on the skin and contains a small dose of nicotine, which enters the blood by being absorbed through the skin. This helps stop nicotine cravings and relieves symptoms that occur when a person is trying to quit smoking. A prescription is not needed for nicotine patches.

Nicotine replacement therapy A type of treatment that uses special products to give small, steady doses of nicotine to help stop cravings and relieve symptoms that occur when a person is trying to quit smoking. These products include nicotine gum, nicotine inhaler, nicotine nasal spray, nicotine lozenges, and nicotine patch. They do not contain any of the other chemicals found in tobacco products.

Night guard Acrylic appliance used to prevent wear and temporomandibular damage caused by grinding or gnashing of the teeth during sleep.

Nilutamide A synthetic, nonsteroidal agent with antiandrogenic properties. Nilutamide preferentially binds to androgen receptors and blocks androgen receptor activation by testosterone and other androgens; this agent may inhibit androgen-dependent growth of normal and neoplastic prostate cells.

Nimodipine Belongs to a family of drugs called calcium channel blockers. It is being investigated for use with anticancer drugs to prevent or overcome drug resistance and improve response to chemotherapy.

Nimustine A nitrosourea with antineoplastic activity. Nimustine alkylates and crosslinks DNA, thereby causing DNA fragmentation, inhibition of protein synthesis, and cell death.

Nipple The tip of the breast; the pigmented projection in the middle of the areola. The nipple contains the opening of milk ducts from the breast.

Nipple discharge Any fluid coming from the nipple. It may be clear, milky, bloody, tan, gray, or green.

Nissen fundoplication An operation that helps treat gastroesophageal reflux disease (GERD). The fundus (top of the stomach) is pulled around the esophagus and sewn. This helps prevent food from moving back from the stomach into the esophagus by creating a muscular band at the top of the stomach, which becomes tighter as the stomach fills up.

Nitric acid A toxic, corrosive, colorless liquid used to make fertilizers, dyes, explosives, and other chemicals.

Nitrocamptothecin A semisynthetic agent related to camptothecin with potent antitumor and antiviral properties. Rubitecan binds to and inhibits the enzyme topoisomerase I and induces protein-linked DNA single-strand breaks, thereby blocking DNA and RNA synthesis in dividing cells; this agent also prevents repair of reversible single-strand DNA breaks.

Nitrogenous base A nitrogen-containing molecule having the chemical properties of a base. DNA contains the nitrogenous bases adenine (A), guanine (G), cytosine (C), and thymine (T).

Nitrosourea An anticancer drug that can cross the blood-brain barrier. Carmustine and lomustine are nitrosoureas.

Nitrous oxide A gas used to reduce patient anxiety.

NK cell Naturally occurring, large, granular, lymphocyte-like killer cells that kill various tumour cells; they may play a role in resistance to tumours. Also, they participate in ADCC. They do not exhibit antigenic specificity, and their number does not increase by immunization.

Nocturnal hypoglycemia Hypoglycemia occurring while the patient is asleep (between the evening injection and getting up in the morning). Nocturnal hypoglycemia typically has symptoms such as restlessness, nightmares, profuse sweating, and frequently is noted by the bed-partner or parent rather than by the sleeping patient, or sometimes is unrecognized.

NOD mouse A strain of mice in which the female has an especially high incidence of a diabetes similar to Type 1 in humans. Much used as a research model for prevention and new onset treatment.

Nodal status A count of the number of lymph nodes in the armpit (axillary nodes) to which cancer has spread (node-positive) or has not spread (node-negative). The number and site of positive axillary nodes help forecast the risk of cancer recurrence.

Node Lymph glands.

Node-negative Cancer that has not spread to the lymph nodes.

Node-positive Cancer that has spread to the lymph nodes.

Nodular parenchyma A small mass of tissue within a gland or organ that carries out the specialized functions of the gland or organ.

Nodule A small, solid lump that can be located by touch.

Nolatrexed dihydrochloride A water-soluble lipophilic quinazoline folate analog with antineoplastic activity. Nolatrexed occupies the folate binding site of thymidylate synthase, resulting in inhibition of thymidylate synthase activity and thymine nucleotide synthesis with subsequent inhibition of DNA replication, DNA damage, S-phase cell cycle arrest, and caspase-dependent apoptosis. This agent also exhibits radiosensitizing activity.

Nolvadex Trade name for tamoxifen, an antiestrogen drug commonly used in breast cancer therapy.

Nominal (rating of filter) An arbitrary micrometer value indicated by filter manufacturers. Based upon removal of some percentage of particles of a given size or larger, but rarely well defined and consequently not reproducible.

Nominal outside diameter A numerical identification of outside diameter to which tolerances apply.

Nominal pore size Based on retention efficiency, a filter should retain 99.9% of particles larger than its nominal rated pore size.

Nominal wall thickness A numerical identification of wall thickness to which tolerances apply.

Nomogram A mathematical device or model that shows relationships between things. For example, a nomogram of height and weight measurements can be used to find the surface area of a person, without doing the math, to determine the right dose of chemotherapy. Nomograms of patient and disease characteristics can help predict the outcome of some kinds of cancer.

Non nucleoside reverse transc-riptase inhibitor (NNRTI) A class of drugs including nevaripine and delaviridine that targets the same reverse transcriptase enzyme of HIV as the nucleoside drugs like AZT, ddI, etc. NNRTIs have been characterized by strong antiviral activity, followed by extremely rapid acquisition of resistance by exposed virus.

Non steroidal anti inflammatory drugs (NSAIDs) A class of drugs that can reduce inflammation, swelling, stiffness, and joint pain. They are used to treat arthritis and mild to moderate pain. Some common NSAIDs are aspirin and ibuprofen.

Non surgical 'cure' Ability to restore a normal appearance by means of an eye prosthesis without requiring an oculoplastic procedure.

Nonblinded Describes a clinical trial or other experiment in which the researchers know what treatments are being given to each study subject or experimental group. If human subjects are involved, they know what treatments they are receiving.

Noncancerous Benign; not malignant; no cancer is present.

Noncarbonate hardness Hardness in water caused by chlorides, sulfates, and nitrates of calcium and magnesium.

Noncompliant 1. The absence of a compliant state in relation to a designated procedure.

2. Term used to describe a patient who is unable or unwilling to follow the assigned treatment regimen.

Nonconsecutive case series A clinical study that includes some, but not all, of the eligible patients identified by the researchers during the study registration period. This type of study does not usually have a control group.

Noncontiguous lymphoma Lymphoma in which the lymph nodes containing cancer are not next to each other, but are on the same side of the diaphragm (the thin muscle below the lungs that helps breathing and separates the chest from the abdomen).

Non-GMP technology Facility design requirement resulting from decisions to address issues outside the realm of GMPs or manufacturer preferences. Often these do affect GMP related design features.

Nonhematologic cancer Cancer that does not begin in the blood or bone marrow.

Noni Morinda citrifolia. A tropical shrub. An extract from the fruit is being studied as a treatment for cancer, and extracts from the fruit, leaves, or roots have been used in some cultures to treat other diseases.

Noninvasive blood glucose monitoring A way to measure blood glucose without having to prick the finger to obtain a blood sample. Several noninvasive devices are currently being developed.

Nonketotic coma (Hyperglycemic hyperosmolar nonketotic syndrome, Hyperglycemic hyperosmolar nonketotic coma) A complication of diabetes caused by a lack of insulin and dehydration. It is diagnosed when the patient has:

very high levels of glucose (sugar) in the blood;

absence of ketoacidosis;

severe dehydration;

a sleepy, confused, or comatose state.

Nonketotic coma is more likely to be associated with Type 2 diabetes, and is sometimes the initial presenting situation for Type 2 diabetes. Nonketotic coma is uncommon in Type 1 Diabetes.

Nonlytic In biology, refers to viruses that do not kill infected cells by disrupting their plasma membranes.

Nonmalignant Not cancerous.

Nonmalignant hematologic disorder A disorder of the blood. Some nonmalignant hematologic disorders may lead to leukemia.

Nonmelanoma skin cancer Skin cancer that arises in basal cells or squamous cells but not in melanocytes (pigment-producing cells of the skin).

Nonmelanomatous Having to do with skin cancer that develops in basal cells or squamous cells but not in melanocytes (pigment-producing cells of the skin).

Nonmetastatic Cancer that has not spread from the primary (original) site to other sites in the body.

Nonopioid A drug that is not an opioid. Examples include acetaminophen and nonsteroidal anti-inflammatory drugs (NSAIDS), such as aspirin and ibuprofen.

Nonprescription A medicine that can be bought without a prescription (doctor's order). Examples include analgesics (pain relievers) such as aspirin and acetaminophen. Also called over-the-counter (OTC).

Nonrandomized clinical trial A clinical trial in which the participants are not assigned by chance to different treatment groups. Participants may choose which group they want to be in, or they may be assigned to the groups by the researchers.

Nonrequired follow up visit Any visit by the patient to the clinic after the randomization visit that is not required for data collection purposes. The visit may be initiated by the patient or by study personnel, and includes interim follow-up visits, monitoring for toxicities, and post-trial follow-up visits. Event driven data such as adverse experiences and overtly clinical events may be collected, otherwise data generated at such visits are not generally used to satisfy data collection needs for required follow-up visits, unless they take place within the time windows for those visits and all necessary procedures are carried out during the visits.

Nonseminoma A group of testicular cancers that begin in the germ cells (cells that give rise to sperm). Nonseminomas are identified by the type of cell in which they begin and include embryonal carcinoma, teratoma, choriocarcinoma, and yolk sac carcinoma.

Non-small cell lung cancer A group of lung cancers that includes squamous cell carcinoma, adenocarcinoma, and large cell carcinoma.

Nonspecific immune cell A cell (such as a phagocyte or a macrophage) that responds to many antigens, not just one antigen.

Nonsteroidal anti-inflammatory drug A drug that decreases fever, swelling, pain, and redness.

Nonsteroidal aromatase inhibitor A drug that decreases the production of sex hormones (estrogen or testosterone) and slows the growth of tumors that need sex hormones to grow.

Nontoxic Not harmful or destructive

Nonunidirectional airflow Air distribution where the first air entering the controlled space mixes with the internal air by means of induction. The airflow that does not meet the definition of unidirectional airflow, previously referred to as "turbulent" or "non-laminar" airflow.

Norgestrel A synthetic progestin commonly used alone or in combination with an estrogen for contraception. Norgestrel suppr-esses the secretion of luteinizing and follicle-stim-ulating hormones (LH and FSH), thickens cervical mucus, and slows the transit of ova through the fallopian tubes. This agent also exhibits antiproliferative activity in endometrial tissue and may exhibit chemopreventive and antineoplastic activities in endometrial carcinoma.

Normal hormonal changes Changes in breast and other tissues that are caused by fluctations in levels of female hormones during the menstrual cycle.

Normal retinal correspondence (NRC) The foveas of the two eyes are corresponding neural points in the visual cortex and binocular vision can occur.

Normal saline A very common LVP that has a physiologic (0.9gm%) concentration of sodium chloride

Northern blot A gel-based laboratory procedure that locates mRNA sequences on a gel that are complementary to a piece of DNA used as a probe.

Nosocomial infections Infections that are acquired while a patient is in a hospital are referred to as nosocomial infections; a term derived from 'nosos' the Greek word for 'disease'. Often nosocomial infections become apparent while the patient is still in the hospital but in some cases symptoms may not show up until after the affected patient is discharged. About one patient in ten acquires an infection as a direct result of being hospitalized. Infection control can be very cost-effective. Approximately one third of nosocomial infections are preventable.

Not exposed or closed Drug substance is protected from exposure to the environment during processing.

Novantrone A drug used to treat advanced prostate cancer that does not respond to hormones, adult acute nonlymphocytic leukemia, and advanced or chronic multiple sclerosis. It is also being studied in the treatment of other cancers. It belongs to the family of drugs called antitumor antibiotics. Also called mitoxantrone.

Novobiocin An antibiotic drug used to treat infection.

Novocain Older brand name for a local anesthetic, currently replaced by safer, more effective agents.

NPH insulin A type of insulin that is intermediate-acting.

Nplanid A term used by CMS for a proposed standard identifier for health plans. CMS had previously used the terms PayerID and PlanID for the health plan identifier.

NPO A Latin abbreviation for "nothing by mouth."

Nuclear dust Fragmented nuclei scattered in the dermis, predominantly around blood vesses.

Nuclear grade An evaluation of the size and shape of the nucleus in tumor cells and the percentage of tumor cells that are in the process of dividing or growing. Cancers with low nuclear grade grow and spread less quickly than cancers with high nuclear grade.

Nuclear magnetic resonance (NMR) A method of taking images of the interior structures of the body.

Nuclear magnetic resonance imaging (NMRI) A procedure in which radio waves and a powerful magnet linked to a computer are used to create detailed pictures of areas inside the body. These pictures can show the difference between normal and diseased tissue. NMRI makes better images of organs and soft tissue than other scanning techniques, such as CT or

X-ray. NMRI is especially useful for imaging the brain, spine, the soft tissue of joints, and the inside of bones. Also called magnetic resonance imaging (MRI).

Nuclear medicine Radioactive materials with specific biological properties can be used to produce images, diagnose illness, and in some cases can be used to treat diseases.

Nuclear medicine scan A method for viewing internal organs such as the brain, liver, or bone, in which small amounts of a radioactive substance (isotope) are injected into the bloodstream. The isotope is concentrated in organs that absorb it, where it can be traced and used to produce an image of the organ. Except for the injection, this method of imaging is painless.

Nuclear transfer A laboratory procedure in which a cell's nucleus is removed and placed into an oocyte with its own nucleus removed so the genetic information from the donor nucleus controls the resulting cell. Such cells can be induced to form embryos. This process was used to create the cloned sheep "Dolly".

Nuclease An enzyme that breaks down nucleic acids. Exonucleases cleave the nucleotides only at the ends of polynucleotide chains (e.g. phosphodiesterase). Endonucleases attack certain linkates wherever they occur in the polynucleotide chain

Nucleic acid Chemical structure that stores genetic information. There are two types of nucleic acid, DNA and RNA. Human genetic information is stored as DNA, while HIV's genetic information can be stored as both DNA and RNA.

Nucleic acid hybridization Matching of either DNA or RNA (depending on the organism) from an unknown organism with DNA or RNA from a known organism. This method is used in tropical disease research for identifying species and strains of organisms.

Nucleic acid test A laboratory test that can detect very small amounts of specific genetic material in blood, plasma, or other tissue. This test can detect several types of viruses and is used to screen blood from blood donors.

Nucleoid The compact body that contains the genome in a bacterium.

Nucleolar organizing region A part of the chromosome containing rRNA genes.

Nucleolus A discrete region of the nucleus created by the transcription of rRNA genes. The nucleolus disappears during mitosis, or cell division.

Nucleoside A precursor to a building block of DNA or RNA. Nucleosides must be chemically changed into nucleotides before they can be used to make DNA or RNA.

Nucleoside analogue reverse transcriptase inhibitor A class of anti-HIV drug. Nucleoside analogues are faulty versions of the building blocks necessary for HIV reproduction. When HIV's reverse transcriptase enzyme uses a nucleoside analogue instead of a normal nucleoside, reproduction of the virus's genetic material is halted. Also called nucleoside analogues or "nukes."

Nucleotide A subunit of DNA or RNA consisting of a nitrogenous base (adenine, guanine, thymine, or cytosine in DNA; adenine, guanine, uracil, or cytosine in RNA), a phosphate molecule, and a sugar molecule (deoxyribose in DNA and ribose in RNA). Thousands of nucleotides are linked to form a DNA or RNA molecule.

Nucleus The cellular organelle present in eukaryotes cells and separated from the cytoplasm by a nuclear membrane. It contains the genetic material and is essential for the continued life of the cell.

Nukes Slang term for nucleoside/nucleotide reverse transcriptase inhibitors (NRTIs).

Null cells An early population of lymphocytes bearing neither T-cell nor B-cell differentiation antigens.

Null hypothesis 1. (Statistics) A hypothesis that postulates no underlying difference in the populations or groups being compared with regard to the factor, trait, characteristic, or condition of interest.

2. Null treatment hypothesis.

Nulliparous A woman who has never given birth to a child.

Nurse A health professional trained to care for people who are ill or disabled.

Nurse practitioner (NP) A registered nurse qualified and specially trained to provide primary care, including primary health care in homes and in ambulatory care facilities, long-term care facilities, and other health care institutions. Normally, NPs are licensed and possess masters degrees. Nurse practitioners generally function under the supervision of a physician but not necessarily in his/her or her presence.

Nursing home A place that gives care to people who have physical or mental disabilities and need help with activities of daily living (such as taking a bath, getting dressed, and going to the bathroom) but do not need to be in the hospital.

Nutraceutical A food or dietary supplement that is believed to provide health benefits.

Nutrient A chemical compound (such as protein, fat, carbohydrate, vitamins, or minerals) that make up foods. These compounds are used by the body to function and grow.

Nutrition The taking in and use of food and other nourishing material by the body. Nutrition is a 3-part process. First, food or drink is consumed. Second, the body breaks down the food or drink into nutrients. Third, the nutrients travel through the bloodstream to different parts of the body where they are used as "fuel" and for many other purposes. To give the body proper nutrition, a person has to eat and drink enough of the foods that contain key nutrients.

Nutritionist A health professional with special training in nutrition who can help with dietary choices. Also called a dietitian.

Nystagmus Rhythmic oscillations or tremors of the eyes which occur independent of the normal eye movements. Generally nystagmus is not curable, but it is manageable. Treatments include prescription glasses or contact lenses, prisms, and vision therapy.

Nystatin A drug that treats infections caused by fungi.

O6 benzylguanine A guanine analogue with antineoplastic activity. O (6)-benzylguanine binds the DNA repair enzyme O (6)-alkylguanine DNA alkyltransferase (AGT), transferr-ing the benzyl moiety to the active-site cysteine and resulting in inhibition of AGT-mediated DNA repair. Co-administration of this agent potentiates the effects of other chemotherapeutic agents that damage DNA.

Oat cell cancer An aggressive (fast-growing) cancer that usually forms in tissues of the lung and spreads to other parts of the body. The cancer cells look small and oval-shaped when looked at under a microscope. Also called small cell lung cancer.

Obese Having an abnormally high, unhealthy amount of body fat.

Obesity When people have 20 percent (or more) extra body fat for their age, height, sex, and bone structure. Fat works against the action of insulin. Extra body fat is thought to be a risk factor for diabetes.

Obex The apex of the caudal midline boundary of the fourth ventricle.

Object database management system (ODBMS) A database management system specifically designed to manage and store complex objects and their complex relationships; that is, such items are stored as objects rather than as tables or fields. They support modeling and creation of data as objects, allowing for greater flexibility in tracking parent method sets and subcomponents.

Objective In medical education, it is what the learner will be able to know or do after taking part in educational activities. Objectives should result from assessment of the needs ofthepatientorpopulation.

Objective improvement An improvement that can be measured by the health care provider (for example, when a tumor shrinks or there are fewer cancer cells in the blood).

Objective response A measurable response.

Objective structured clinical examination (OSCE) A method introduced in 1972 as a more standardized way of assessing clinical competencies. It provides a standardized means to assess physical examination and history-taking skills, communication skills with patients and family members, breadth and depth of knowledge, ability to summarize and document findings, and ability to make a differential diagnosis or plan treatment. The examiners carefully plan the tested areas and objectives of the test are identified and recorded. The clinical competency to be tested is broken down into its various components such as taking a history, auscultation of the heart, interpretation of an ECG, or making a conclusion on a basis of findings. Candidates rotate through a series of "stations", usually 12-20, and in a specified time perform a standardized task.

The format of individual OSCE varies significantly. Clinical models and standardized patients or simulated patients can be used to allow large numbers of students to be tested on the same clinical problem without causing fatigue or stress to real patients. Direct or indirect observations as well as checklists and rating scales measure the performance against predetermined standards resulting in a more objective examination than with traditional methods. This provides a more valid and more reliable examination permitting the move away from testing factual knowledge to testing a wide range of skills. The variables of the examiner and the patient are, to a large extent, removed. OSCE is particularly suited to situations where a pass/fail decision has to be taken and where a decision has to be made as to whether a student has reached a prescribed standard. It is cost-effective when many candidates are examined at once, as it is difficult to create and administer and requires resources and expertise. With succeeding examinations, less time is required and both time and effort can be reduced if a bank of objective test items and checklists is maintained.

Use of OSCE for formative assessment has great potential and value as the learners can gain insights into the elements making up clinical competencies as well as feedback on personal strengths and weaknesses. However, in the OSCE, the student's knowledge and skills are tested in compartmentalized fashion and he/she is not tested on the ability to look at a patient as a whole being. Still, OSCE may be combined with other forms of assessment, such as the clerking of cases in the wards. The previously used term for this assessment method was Multiple Station Exercises/Exam (MSE).

Oblimersen A phosphorothioate antisense oligonucleotide. Targeted to the initiation codon region of the bcl-2 mRNA, oblimersen inhibits bcl-2 mRNA translation, resulting in decreased expression of the bcl-2 protein, an apoptotic inhibitor expressed in some types of cancer and linked to tumor drug resistance. This agent may enhance the efficacy of standard cytotoxic chemotherapy.

Oblique orbital line The radiographic shadow of the greater wing of the sphenoid bone, projected through the orbit.

Oblique view A view or perspective that is rotated off axis from the three cardinal imaging planes: Sagittal - Coronal -- Axial.

OBOB mouse (Obese obese mouse) A variety of mouse that tends to be fat, and diabetic. A model for research on NIDDM.

O'brien fleming monitoring boundary A set of criteria used to determine how data can be looked at during interim reviews, and how much potential error may be caused through looking. Used in constructing the stopping rules for a trial

Observation Closely monitoring a patient's condition but withholding treatment until symptoms appear or change. Also called watchful waiting.

Observational study A type of study in which individuals are observed or certain outcomes are measured. No attempt is made to affect the outcome (for example, no treatment is given).

Observed treatment difference The actual treatment difference observed either at the end of the trial or at some designated time point during the trial.

Obstetrician A doctor who sees and gives care to pregnant women and delivers babies.

Obstruction A blockage in the digestive tract that prevents the forward movement of foods and liquids as they are digested.

Obtundation A dulled or reduced level of alertness or consciousness.

Obturator externus muscle Muscle which originates at the pubis, ischium, and the superficial surface of the obturator membrane, and inserts into the trochanteric fossa of the femur. It contributes to the lateral (external) rotation of the thigh.

Obturator foramen The opening between the os pubis and the ischium.

Obturator internus muscle Muscle which originates at the pelvic surface of the hip bone, the margin of the obturator foramen, the ramus of ischium, the inferior ramus of pubis, and the internal surface of the obturator membrane, and inserts into the greater trochanter of the femur. It contributes to lateral rotation of the thigh.

Occipital artery Originates from the external carotid and branches into the auricular, meningeal, mastoid, descending occipital, and sternocleidomastoid rami arteries.

Occipital bone The bone situated at the inferior and posterior portion of the cranium, articulates with the two parietal bones (at the lambdoid suture) and the temporal bones as well as the sphenoid bone and the atlas (C1).

Occipital lobe That part of the cerebral hemisphere delimited from the parietal lobe on the medial surface by the parieto-occipital fissure and on the lateral surface by an arbitrary line extending from the parieto-ccipital sulcus to the preoccipital notch. The primary visual cortex resides on the medial surface of this small lobe.

Occlusion To block out light. An eye can be completely or partially blocked. This procedure is used to promote the use of one eye or both eyes. This therapy procedure may be used for people with amblyopia, strabismus, or closed head trauma. It may also be used in a vision therapy program for someone with amblyopia, eye focusing (accommodation) disorder, or poor eye tracking (oculomotor) skill. An eye patch, black contact, or another device may be used to block out light from an eye.

Occult blood Blood in the stool that is not visible to the naked eye.

Occult stage non-small cell lung cancer Cancer cells are found in sputum (mucus coughed up from the lungs), but no tumor can be found in the lung by imaging or bronchoscopy, or the primary tumor is too small to be assessed.

Occupancy The purpose for which a building or part thereof is used or intended to be used.

Occupancy rate A measure of inpatient health facility use, determined by dividing available bed days by patient days. It measures the average percentage of a hospital's beds occupied and may be institution-wide or specific for one department or service.

Occupational health OSHA, county health departments and regulatory bodies oversee occupational health hazards in workplaces, including hospitals. Occupational health programs include the employer activities undertaken to protect and promote the health and safety of employees in the workplace, including minimizing exposure to hazardous substances, evaluating work practices and environments to reduce injury, and reducing or eliminating other health threats. Many health providers offer occupational health consultations as well as occupational health screenings, treatments and case-management. Employers and health providers often enter agreements whereby health providers will provide these services as well as managed the related workers compensation case management and rehabilitation programs. Employers seek to remain in compliance with regulations and reduce costs associated with employee injury and benefit utilization. Often, EAPs and drug prevention or drug testing programs are also combined under this category.

Occupational therapist A health professional trained to help people who are ill or disabled learn to manage their daily activities.

OCN (Oncology certified nurse) A registered nurse who has met the requirements and successfully completed a certification examination in oncology.

Octreotide The synthetic acetate salt of a long-acting cyclic octapeptide with pharmacologic properties mimicking those of the natural hormone somatostatin. Similar to somatostatin, octreotide suppresses the luteinizing hormone response to gonadotropin-releasing hormone, decreases splanchnic blood flow, and inhibits the release of serotonin, gastrin, vasoactive intestinal peptide (VIP), secretin, motilin, pancreatic polypeptide, and thyroid stimulating hormone.

Octreotide scan A type of radionuclide scan used to find carcinoid and other types of tumors. Radioactive octreotide, a drug similar to somatostatin, is injected into a vein and travels through the bloodstream. The radioactive octreotide attaches to tumor cells that have receptors for somatostatin. A radiation-measuring device detects the radioactive octreotide, and makes pictures showing where the tumor cells are in the body. This procedure is also called somatostatin receptor scintigraphy (SRS).

Ocular Pertaining to the eye.

Ocular melanoma A rare cancer of melanocytes (cells that produce the pigment melanin) found in the eye. Also called intraocular melanoma.

Ocular motility Pertaining to binocular alignment and eye muscle movement.

Ocular motor (OM) General eye movement ability, which include pursuits (to visually track and/or follow moving objects) and saccades (to direct and coordinate eye movement as the eye quickly and voluntarily shift from one target to another).

Ocular motor dysfunction Poor eye movement skills. Vision therapy is an effective treatment option.

Ocularist A paramedical technician who fabricates and fits custom made artificial eyes. The highest degree would be Board Certified Ocularist by NEBO.

Oculomotor skills The ability to quickly and accurately move our eyes. These are sensory motor skills that allow us to move our eyes so we can fixate on objects (fixation), move our eyes smoothly from point to point as in reading (saccades), and to track a moving object (pursuits).

Oculus dexter (OD) Right eye.

Oculus sinister (OS) Left eye.

Odontoid process (DENS) (C1) The "tooth-like" projection from the superior surface of the axis, which ascends to articulate with the atlas, allowing the head to rotate on the cervical spine.

Ofloxacin A fluoroquinolone antibacterial antibiotic. Ofloxacin binds to and inhibits bacterial topoisomerase II (DNA gyrase) and topoisomerase IV, enzymes involved in DNA replication and repair, resulting in cell death in sensitive bacterial species.

OGF (Opioid growth factor) A substance made by the body and in the laboratory. It is being studied in the treatment of cancer. It belongs to the families of drugs called angiogenesis inhibitors and biological response modifiers.

OGX 011 A mixed-backbone antisense oligodeoxynucleotide with chemosensitizing properties. OGX-011 inhibits testosterone-repressed prostate message-2 (TRPM-2). Administration of OGX-011 abrogates the anti-apoptotic effect of TRPM-2, thereby sensitizing cells to chemotherapy and resulting in tumor cell death. TRPM-2 is an anti-apoptotic clusterin that is overexpressed by prostate cancer cells and is associated with chemoresistance.

Oid (suffix) Like, resembling, e.g. leukemoid - like leukemia.

Olecranon process The bony projection of the distal ulna at the elbow, which helps form the trochlear notch. On extension of the arm, the olecranon "hides" in the olecranon fossa of the distal humerus.

Olfactory trigone The point at which the olfactory tracts as they pass toward the anterior perforated substance divide into medial, lateral and intermediate stria.

Oligo Few; scanty, e.g. oligochromemia - deficiency of hemoglobin in the blood.

Oligoastrocytoma A rare type of brain tumor made up of two kinds of cells, oligodendrocytes and astrocytes, which are brain cells that nourish and support nerve cells. Also called mixed glioma.

Oligodendroglia Neuroglial cells of ectodermal origin (from bipotential O-2A progenitor cells) introduced by Del Rio Hortega and forming part of the non-neuronal interstitium the central nervous system. Interfascicular oligos are common to white matter whereas perineuronal forms are found in gray matter. These cells make myelin and can be identified by their content of carbonic anhydrase, surface galactocerebroside, myelin, and MBP.

Oligodendroglial tumor A rare, slow-growing tumor that begins in the oligodendrocytes (brain cells that nourish and support nerve cells). Also called an oligodendroglioma.

Oligogenic A phenotypic trait produced by two or more genes working together.

Oligohydramnios Too little amniotic fluid.

Oligonucleotide A molecule usually composed of 25 or fewer nucleotides; used as a DNA synthesis primer.

Olive A smooth ovale eminence located on the ventrolateral surface of the rostral medulla oblongata. It marks the location of the underlying inferior olivary nucleus.

Ologous (suffix) Relating to, e.g. homologous - of similar structure.

Oltipraz A drug used in cancer prevention.

Oma (suffix) Tumor, e.g. osteoma - tumor of bone.

Omega 3 fatty acid A type of fat obtained in the diet and involved in immunity.

Omentectomy Surgery to remove part or all of the omentum.

Omentum A fold of the peritoneum (the thin tissue that lines the abdomen) that surrounds the stomach and other organs in the abdomen.

Omeprazole A benzimidazole with selective and irreversible proton pump inhibition activity. Omeprazole forms a stable disulfide bond with the sulfhydryl group of the hydrogen-potassium (H^+ - K^+) ATPase found on the secretory surface of parietal cells, thereby inhibiting the final transport of hydrogen ions (via exchange with potassium ions) into the gastric lumen and suppressing gastric acid secretion. This agent exhibits no anticholinergic properties and does not antagonize histamine H_2 receptors.

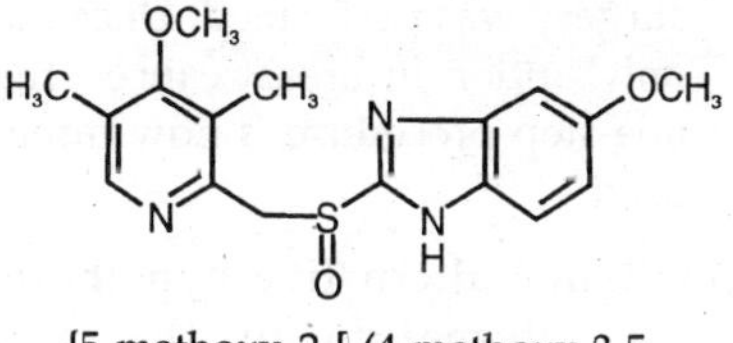

{5-methoxy-2-[(4-methoxy-3,5-dimethyl-pyridin-2-yl)methylsulfinyl]-3H-benzoimidazole}

Figure Omeprazole

Ommaya reservoir A device surgically placed under the scalp and used to deliver anticancer drugs to the fluid surrounding the brain and spinal cord.

Oncogene A gene that normally directs cell growth. If altered, an oncogene can promote or allow the uncontrolled growth of cancer. Alterations can be inherited or caused by an environmental exposure to carcinogens.

Oncologist A doctor who is specially trained in the diagnosis and treatment of cancer. Medical oncologists specialize in the use of drugs and chemotherapy to treat cancer. Radiation oncologists specialize in the use of x-rays (radiation) to kill tumors. Medical and radiation oncologists often cooperate in giving complicated treatments.

Oncology The study and treatment of cancer. Doctors who specialize in oncology are called oncologists.

Oncology clinical nurse specialist A registered nurse with a master's degree who specializes in the education and treatment of cancer patients.

Oncology nurse specialist A nurse who has taken highly specialized training in the field of cancer, after completing the RN (registered nurse) degree. Oncology nurse specialists may mix and administer treatments, monitor patients, prescribe and provide aftercare, and teach and counsel patients and their families. Many oncology nurse specialists are also certified nurse practitioners.

Oncology pharmacy specialist A person who works with an oncologist to prepare anticancer drugs.

Oncology social worker A person with a master's degree in social work who has specialized in the field of cancer. The oncology social worker provides counselling and assistance to people with cancer and their families, especially in dealing with the crises that can result from cancer but are not medical, such as financial problems, housing when treatments must be taken at a facility far away from home, and child care.

Oncolysate An extract made from cancer cells that are infected with a lytic strain of virus. The extract contains both cancer cell proteins and virus proteins. Oncolysates are being studied as cancer vaccines.

Oncolysis The breakdown, or lysis, of a tumor. This can occur by mechanical means, chemicals, or infectious agents such as viruses. Oncolytic viruses do not lyse most normal cells.

Oncolytic adenovirus encoding GM CSF A recombinant oncolytic adenovirus encoding the immunohematopoietic cytokine granulocyte-macrophage colony stimulating factor (GM-CSF) with potential antineoplastic activity. Upon administration, the oncolytic adenovirus selectively infects and replicates in tumor cells, which may result in tumor cells lysis. Synergistically, GM-CSF (sargramostim) expressed by the oncolytic adenovirus may promote a cytotoxic T cell response against tumor cells harboring the oncolytic adenovirus, resulting in an immune-mediated tumor cell death.

Oncolytic Refers to viruses that kill cancer cells more often than they kill normal cells.

Ondansetron A carbazole derivative with antiemetic activity. As a selective serotonin receptor antagonist, ondansetron competitively blocks the action of serotonin at 5HT3 receptors, resulting in suppression of chemotherapy- and radiotherapy-induced nausea and vomiting.

One sided alternative hypothesis One-tailed alternative hypothesis.

One sided test (statistics) One-tailed test.

One step procedure Surgery in which a breast treatment (such as mastectomy, if the diagnosis is indeed breast cancer) is performed in a single operation. The patient is given general anesthesia and does not know until awakened if the diagnosis was cancer or surgery was performed. Once the only option in breast cancer, the one-step procedure is now rarely used.

One tailed alternative hypothesis An alternative to the null hypothesis that specifies a range of permissible values of all which lie to one side of the null value (e.g., all favoring one treatment).

Onlay Laboratory produced restoration covering one or more cusps of a tooth.

Onset of action The length of time it takes for a medicine to start to work.

Oophorectomy Surgery to remove one or both ovaries.

Opacified Made to be opaque to X-ray irradiation, due to the introduction of contrast material - as in a barium study (Upper GI, Barium Enema), arteriogram, myelogram, etc.

Opathy (suffix) Disease, e.g. nephropathy - any disease of the kidney.

Open Exposed to the environment, not closed.

Open access A term describing a member's ability to self-refer for specialty care. Open access arrangements allow a member to see a participating provider without a referral from another doctor. Health plan members' abilities, rights or invitation to self refer for specialty care. Also called Open Panel.

Open biopsy A procedure in which a surgical incision (cut) is made through the skin to expose and remove tissues. The biopsy tissue is examined under a microscope by a pathologist. An open biopsy may be done in the doctor's office or in the hospital, and may use local anesthesia or general anesthesia. A lumpectomy to remove a breast tumor is a type of open biopsy.

Open colectomy An operation to remove all or part of the colon through a long incision made in the wall of the abdomen. When only part of the colon is removed, it is called a partial colectomy.

Open label trial 1. A clinical trial in which a study physician or study patient decides on the treatment to be administered. Nonrandom clinical trial.

2. A non blinded clinical trial.

3. A clinical trial with an open sequential design.

Open nephrolithotomy is the most invasive procedure for removing kidney stones. Because it is so traumatic, most kidneys can withstand no more than two such operations. Deep anesthesia is required, after which the surgeon makes a large (10-20 centimeter) incision in the patient's back or abdomen, depending upon where the stone is located. Either the ureter or the kidney isopened and the stone extracted. Most patients require prolonged hospitalization afterward, and recovery may take up to two months.

Open reading frame (ORF) The sequence of DNA or RNA located between the start-code sequence (initiation codon) and the stop-code sequence (termination codon).

Open system A system that fails to meet one or more of the requirements that set the criteria for a closed system.

Operable Describes a condition that can be treated by surgery.

Operating parameter Any information entered into an automated system that is used for automated equipment operation. Or, a parameter indicative of the operating condition of a system.

Operating range The validated acceptance criteria within which a control parameter must remain, wherein acceptable product is being manufactured.

Operating system (OS) The most important program run on a computer because it manages all the other programs. Operating systems perform basic tasks, such as recognizing input from the keyboard, sending output to the display screen, keeping track of files and directories on the disk, and controlling peripheral devices such as disk drives and printers. For large systems, the OS has even greater responsibilities and powers. It regulates traffic, making sure that different programs and users running at the same time do not interfere with each other. The operating system also is responsible for security, ensuring that unauthorized users do not access a system. Microsoft Windows NT, LINUX, and UNIX are operating systems.

Operating variables All factors of operation, including control parameters that may potentially affect process state of control and/ or fitness for use of the product.

Operation Room condition when normal process operations are undertaken.

Operational cleanroom ISO 14644-1 defines "operational" occupancy state as "condition where the installation is functioning in the specified manner, with the specified number of personnel present and working in the manner agreed upon".

Operculum Adjoining parts of the frontal, parietal and temporal lobes which overhang and conceal the insula from view.

Operon A set of genes transcribed under the control of an operator gene.

Ophthalmic artery Originates from the internal carotid and branches into the lacrimal, supraorbital, central artery of the retina, ciliary, posterior and anterior ethmoid, palpebral, supratrochlear, and dorsal nasal arteries.

Ophthalmics Pertaining to products for the eyes. GMP requirements for the preparation of ophthalmics are essentially identical to those for parenterals.

Ophthalmologist A physician (doctor of medicine (M.D.) or doctor of osteopathy (D.O.) who specializes in the comprehensive care of the eyes and visual system in the prevention of eye disease and injury. The ophthalmologist has completed four or more years of college premedical education, four or more years of medical school, one year of internship, and three or more years of specialized medical and surgical training and experience in eye care. The ophthalmologist is a physician who is qualified by lengthy medical education, training and experience to diagnose, treat and manage all eye and visual system problems, and is licensed by a state regulatory board to practice medicine and surgery. The ophthalmologist is the medically trained specialist who can deliver total eye care: primary, secondary and tertiary care services (i.e., vision services, contact lenses, eye examinations, medical eye care and surgical eye care), and diagnose general diseases of the body. An ophthalmologist is not trained to provide vision therapy.

Ophthalmopathy Eye disease. There are several disorders that can affect vision in people with diabetes; the most severe is diabetic retinopathy.

Ophthalmoscope A device used to illuminate the inside of the eye and enlarge the image for examining the retina, optic nerve entrance, arteries, and veins.

Ophthalmoscopy Visual examination of the eye.

Opiate A drug used to treat pain. It contains opium or a substance made from opium (such as morphine).

Opioid A drug used to treat moderate to severe pain. Opioids are similar to opiates such as morphine and codeine, but they do not contain and are not made from opium.

Opportunistic infections (OIs) Illnesses caused by various organisms that occur in people with weakened immune systems, including people with HIV/AIDS. OIs common in people with AIDS include Pneumocystis carinii pneumonia; cryptosporidiosis; histoplasmosis; toxoplasmosis; other parasitic, viral, and fungal infections; and some types of cancers.

Opsonin A substance, usually antibody or complement component, which coats a particle such as a bacterium and enhances phagocytosis by phagocytic cells.

Opsonization Literally means "preparation for eating". The coating of a bacterium with antibody and/or complement that leads to enhanced phagocytosis of the bacterium by phagocytic cells.

Optic chiasm A Landmark for the rostral-most border of the hypothalamus on the ventral surface of the brain. It is the point of convergence of the optic nerves and where optic nerve fibers from the nasal halves of each retina cross the midline on their way to the contralateral thalamus and visual cortex.

Optic nerve The second cranial nerve, responsible for the special sensation of sight. This is not really a "nerve", but is actually a post-synaptic white-matter tract that connects the retinal ganglion cells to the occipital (visual) cortex, via the chiasm, lateral geniculate body, and the optic radiations.

Optician Is a professional in the field of designing, finishing, fitting and dispensing of eyeglasses and contact lenses, based on an eye doctor's prescription. The optician may also dispense colored and specialty lenses for particular needs as well as low-vision aids and artificial eyes.

Optometric vision therapy (VT) Optometric vision therapy is a treatment plan used to correct or improve specific dysfunctions of the vision system. It includes, but is not limited to, the treatment of strabismus (turned eye), other dysfunctions of binocularity (eye teaming), amblyopia (lazy eye), accommodation (eye focusing), ocular motor function (general eye movement ability), and visual-perception-motor abilities.

Optometric vision therapy is based upon a medically necessary plan of treatment which is designed to improve specific vision dysfunctions determined by standardized diagnostic criteria. Treatment plans encompass lenses, prisms, occlusion (eye patching), and other appropriate materials, modalities, and equipment. (Vision therapy can also be called visual or vision training, orthoptics, eye training, or eye exercises.) However Optometric Vision Therapy is NOT the same as the Bates Method, vision therapy using Bates, integrated vision therapy, or natural eye exercises. These holistic programs use some form of eye exercises associated with relaxation techniques, which claim to improve nearsightedness, farsightedness, astigmatism, decreasing vision with age, and other disorders. There is virtually no statistical studies/results indicating the success of these methods.

Optometrist A health care professional who is state licensed to provide primary eye care service. These services include comprehensive eye health and vision examinations; diagnosis and treatment of eye disease and vision disorders; the detection of general health problems; the prescribing of glasses, contact lenses, low vision rehabilitation, vision therapy, and medications; the performing of certain surgical procedures; and the counseling of patients regarding their surgical alternatives and vision needs as related to their occupations, avocations and lifestyle. The optometrist has completed pre-professional undergraduate education in a college or university and four years of professional education at a college of optometry, leading to the doctor of optometry (O.D.) degree. Some optometrists complete a residency.

OQ (Operational qualification) Documented verification that aspects of a facility system that can affect product quality perform as intended throughout anticipated operating ranges.

Oral By or having to do with the mouth.

Oral allergy syndrome A localised oral allergic reaction to fruit, vegetables and nuts in Hay Fever sufferers.

Oral and maxillofacial surgeon A dental specialist who manages the diagnosis & surgical treatment of diseases, injuries, and deformities of the mouth and supporting structures; Requires four additional years of training after dental school.

Oral and maxillofacial surgery Surgical procedures on the mouth including extractions, removal of cysts or tumors, and repair of fractured jaws.

Oral cancer Cancer that forms in tissues of the lip or mouth. This includes the front two thirds of the tongue, the upper and lower gums, the lining inside the cheeks and lips, the bottom of the mouth under the tongue, the bony top of the mouth, and the small area behind the wisdom teeth.

Oral cavity Cavity of the mouth including the inside of the cheek, palate, oral mucosa, teeth, tongue, and glands that open into the cavity itself.

Oral hairy leukoplakia (OHL) A white-colored, hairy, or ribbed patch that appears on the side of the tongue and inside the cheeks. It develops mainly in people with weakened immune systems, including people with HIV. It is caused by Epstein-Barr virus (EBV), a member of the herpesvirus family.

Oral hygiene Process of maintaining cleanliness of the teeth and related structures.

Oral hypoglycemic agents Pills or capsules that people take to lower the level of glucose in the blood. The pills work for some people with Type 2 diabetes if their pancreas still makes some insulin. They can help the body in several ways such as causing the cells in the pancreas to release more insulin. Types of these pills for sale are:

sulfonylureas (many varieties)

biguanides: metformin (Glucophage)

alpha-glucosidase inhibitors: acarbose (Precose); miglitol (Glyset)

thiazolidinediones (or "glitazones"): rosiglitazone (Avandia); pioglitazone (Actos)

meglitinides: repaglinide (Prandin); nateglinide (Starlix)

Oral pathologist Dentist specializing in the study of oral diseases.

Oral product A pharmaceutical product meant to be introduced through the mouth in the form of a tablet, capsule, or suspension.

Oral solid dosage drug Formulated in a solid or powder form for patient to ingest orally.

Oral surgeon A dentist with special training in surgery of the mouth and jaw.

Orbicularis muscle The muscle that circles the eyelid. Its function is to close the eyelids.

Orbital welding Automatic or machine welding of tubes or pipe in-place with the electrode rotating (or orbiting) around the work. Orbital welding can be done with the addition of filler material or as a fusion process without the addition of filler.

Orchidectomy Surgery to remove one or both testicles. Also called orchiectomy.

Orchitis Inflammation of a testicle.

Oregovomab A murine monoclonal antibody that attaches to the tumor-associated antigen CA125. Vaccination with monoclonal antibody B43.13 may stimulate a host cytotoxic immune response against tumor cells that express CA125.

Organ A part of the body that performs a specific function. For example, the heart is an organ.

Organ-based teaching In this approach, medical competence is gained by focusing on one organ system at a time. It is an approach that integrates different disciplines (subjects) such as biochemistry, physiology and anatomy, and has ultimately led to the more common problem-based approach, which is currently more commonly used.

Organelles Membrane-surrounded structures found in eukaryotic cells; they contain enzymes and other components required for specialized cell function.

Organic Organic matter is a broad category that includes both natural and man-made molecules containing carbon and hydrogen. All living matter in water is made up of organic molecules. The most common are by-products of vegetative decay such as tannins, lignins, and humic acid.

Organic amblyopia Gradual or sudden loss of central vision (partial loss) affecting visual acuity with no treatment options.

Types of organic (irreversible) amblyopia:

nutritional amblyopia- vision loss caused by low levels of vitamin B12 due to poor nutrition and poor absorption associated with drinking alcohol.

tobacco-alcohol amblyopia- clinical evidence exists that a nutritional deficiency is the underlying cause of this vision loss; however, many still believe that the toxic effects of alcohol and/or tobacco are contributing factors.

toxic amblyopia- caused by exposure to toxins such as ethambutol, methyl alcohol (moonshine), ethylene glycol (antifreeze), cyanide, lead, and carbon monoxide.

Organic chemical Any Chemical based on carbon. Frequently including oxygen, hydrogen, and nitrogen.

Organic peroxide An organic compound that contains the bivalent -0-0- structure and which may be considered to be a structural derivative of hydrogen peroxide where on or both of the hydrogen atoms have been replaced by an organic radical. Organic peroxides can present an explosion hazard (detonation or deflagration) or they can be shock sensitive. They can also decompose into various unstable compounds over an extended period.

Organism A single, autonomous living thing. Bacteria and yeasts are organisms; mammalian and insect cells used in culture are not.

Organized care system Often used to discuss a more evolved form of IDSs and CCNs, this relatively new term describes the result of mergers and alliances between and among physicians, health systems, and managed care organizations. These systems often have the same performance imperatives as IDSs and CCNs: improve health status, integrate delivery, demonstrate value, improve efficiency of care delivery and prevention, and meet patient and community needs.

Origin Location where the process of replication in a nucleic acid begins.

Oropharyngeal cancer Cancer that forms in tissues of the oropharynx (the part of the throat at the back of the mouth, including the soft palate, the base of the tongue, and the tonsils). Most oropharyngeal cancers are squamous cell carcinomas (cancer that begins in flat cells lining the oropharynx).

Oropharynx The part of the throat at the back of the mouth. It includes the soft palate, the base of the tongue, and the tonsils.

Orphan drug The status granted to one company for a drug that is believed to substantially increase the life expectancy of the treated patient for a particular disease. This excludes other companies from receiving a license to produce a similar drug for a finite period (usually 7 years), thereby allowing the company producing the drug to recuperate their R&D expenses.

Orrhea (suffix) Flow; discharge, e.g. leukorrhea - white discharge.

Orthodontics Dental speciality that treats misalignment of teeth.

Orthophoria (Ortho) The absence of either esophoria or exophoria. The eyes do not have a tendency to want to turn more inward than necessary or want to turn more outward than necessary when pointed on an object.

Orthoptics The science of correcting defects in binocular vision. The technique of eye exercises to correct strabismus (esotropia or exotropia), convergence insufficiency (exophoria), or convergence excess (esophoria), amblyopia, and ocular motility disorders. Orthoptics was pioneered by French ophthalmologist Javal in the mid to late 1800's. Today ophthalmologists use specialty-trained healthcare professionals called orthoptists to evaluate patients and treat them with orthoptics. Orthoptics is a limited form of optometric vision therapy.

Oscopy (suffix) View, e.g. endoscopy - to view the inside, specifically: the intestine.

Osis (suffix) A process, especially a morbid one, e.g. diverticulosis - involvement with diverticula.

Osmolality The concentration of particles dissolved in a fluid. The osmolality of serum can help diagnose several medical conditions such as dehydration, diabetes, and shock.

Osmosis The diffusion of a solvent through a semipermeable membrane from a solution of higher concentration to one of lower concentration until there are equal concentrations of fluid on both sides of the membrane.

Osmotic Having to do with osmosis (the passage of a liquid through a membrane from a less concentrated solution to a more concentrated solution). This makes the concentrations in both solutions more equal.

Osmotic pressure Pressure generated by the osmotic flow of water through a membrane into a (aqueous) phase containing a solute in a higher concentration.

Osseous Boney.

Osteitis deformans A chronic condition in which both the breakdown and regrowth of bone are increased. Osteitis deformans occurs most frequently in the pelvic and leg bones, skull, and lower spine. It is most common in older individuals, and may lead to bone pain, deformities, and fractures. Also called Paget's disease of bone.

Osteo Bone, e.g. osteomyelitis - inflammation of bone.

Osteogenic sarcoma A cancer of the bone that usually affects the large bones of the arm or leg. It occurs most commonly in young people and affects more males than females. Also called osteosarcoma.

Osteoid Resembling bone.

Osteolytic Causing the breakdown of bone.

Osteonecrosis Also referred to as avascular necrosis. A medical condition in which bone tissue dies. Osteonecrosis affects some people with HIV, but it is unclear if it develops as a complication of HIV infection or as a side effect of anti-HIV drugs.

Osteopenia A medical condition in which bones lose their minerals and become less dense, making them weaker and easier to break.

Osteoporosis Break-down or disintegration of bone, resulting in diminished and porous bone mass. Osteoporosis can result from cancer (including breast cancer) that has spread to the bones), some cancer therapies, and estrogen deficiency (estrogen is an important participant in maintaining bone). Osteoporosis can cause pain, deformity (especially of the spine), pathologic fractures (fractures caused by weakened bone), or traumatic fractures (for example, wrist or hip fracture from a fall).

Osteosarcoma A cancer of the bone that usually affects the large bones of the arm or leg. It occurs most commonly in young people and affects more males than females. Also called osteogenic sarcoma.

Ostia (Ostium pl.) The opening of a tubular organ or between two cavities.

Ostomy An operation that is done when there is damage to a section of intestine. It creates an opening in the wall of the abdomen, and brings a portion of intestine through the opening so stool can leave the body.

OTC (Over the counter) A medicine that can be bought without a prescription (doctor's order). Examples include analgesics (pain relievers) such as aspirin and acetaminophen. Also called nonprescription.

Otitis Inflammation of the ear.

Otolaryngologist A doctor who specializes in treating diseases of the ear, nose, and throat. Also called an ENT (ear, nose, and throat) doctor.

Otomy (suffix) Cut, e.g. cholecystotomy - incision into the gallbladder.

Otorhinolaryngology The study of ear, nose, and throat diseases (i.e. ENT disorders).

Ounce A measure of weight (one-sixteenth pound) and volume (one-eighth cup).

Out of specification An examination, measurement, or test result that does not comply with preestablished criteria.

Outcome All possible demonstrable results that stem from casual factors or activities. In medical education, outcome refers to a new skill, knowledge or stimulus to improve the quality of patient care. Setting outcomes can be very useful for developing a framework of various results expected from various educational activities. Outcomes may be related to the educational process (process outcomes), to the product of undergraduate medical education (learning outcomes), or to the professional role of the physician (performance outcomes).

Outcome-based education This approach emphasizes educational outcomes rather than the educational process and focuses on the product of medical education such as what kind of doctors will be produced, and with what professional knowledge, skills, abilities, values and attitudes. Educational outcomes must be clearly specified as they determine the curriculum content, the teaching methods, the courses offered, the assessment process and the educational environment. The scope and definition of competence and the levels of its attainment is defined in terms of student development within the natural progression in medical school. Consequently, the assessmen-t system will ensure that the expected variation of levels of attainment is defined and assessed.

An example of such a framework is the 12-outcomes paradigm of Dundee- a model presented in the form of three-circles which describes the following:

What the doctor is able to do: clinical skills; practical procedures; patient investigations; patient management; health promotion; disease prevention and communication.

How the doctor approaches his practice: appropriate understanding of basic, social and clinical sciences and underlying principles; with appropriate attitudes and ethical unders-tanding and legal responsibilities and with the appropriate decision-making skills and clinical reasoning and judgment.

The doctor as a professional: understanding of the doctor's role within the health system and the understanding of personal development.

In addition, some medical schools have already incorporated advanced levels of progression in the early phases of their curriculum such as problem-based learning programs, early clinical exposure, and self-directed learning programs.

Outcomes measurement System used to systematically track clinical treatment and responses to that treatment. The methods for measuring outcomes are quite varied among providers. Much disagreement exists regarding the best practice or tools to utilize to measure outcomes. In fact, much disagreement exists in the medical field about the definition of outcome itself. A tool to assess the impact of health services in terms of improved quality and/or longevity of life and functioning.

Outcomes research Research on measures of changes in patient outcomes, that is, patient health status and satisfaction, resulting from specific medical and health interventions. Attributing changes in outcomes to medical care requires distinguishing the effects of care from the effects of the many other factors that influence patients' health and satisfaction. With the elimination of the physician's fiduciary responsibility to the patient, outcomes data is gaining increasing importance for patient advocacy and consumer protection. Outcomes research will also be used in the future by payers to identify potential partners on the basis of good outcomes.

Outer table of skull The outer layer of compact bone, part of the flat bones of the skull.

Outlier A patient whose length of stay or treatment cost differs substantially from the stays or costs of most other patients in a diagnosis related group. Under DRG reimbursement, outliers are given exceptional treatment subject to peer review and organization review.

Outlier thresholds The day and cost cutoff points that separate inlier patients from outlier patients.

Outpatient A patient who visits a health care facility for diagnosis or treatment without spending the night. Sometimes called a day patient.

Outpatient care Care given a person who is not bedridden. Also called ambulatory care. Many surgeries and treatments are now provided on an outpatient basis, while previously they had been considered reason for inpatient hospitalization. Some say this is the fastest growing segment of healthcare.

Output In the health field, this indicates the immediate result of professional or institutional health care activities, usually expressed as units of service such as patient hospital days, outpatient visits or laboratory tests performed.

Ovarian Having to do with the ovaries, the female reproductive glands in which the ova (eggs) are formed. The ovaries are located in the pelvis, one on each side of the uterus.

Ovarian ablation Surgery, radiation therapy, or a drug treatment to stop the functioning of the ovaries. Also called ovarian suppression.

Ovarian cancer Cancer that forms in tissues of the ovary. Most ovarian cancers are either ovarian epithelial carcinomas (cancer that begins in cells that line the ovary) or malignant germ cell tumors (cancer that begins in egg cells).

Ovarian cancer peptide vaccine A cancer vaccine comprised of synthetic peptides corresponding to naturally-occurring peptides derived from ovarian cancer cell antigens. Ovarian cancer peptide vaccine may elicit a cytotoxic T-cell response against tumor cells expressing the related ovarian cancer cell antigens.

Ovarian epithelial cancer Cancer that occurs in the cells lining the ovaries.

Ovarian germ cell tumor An abnormal mass of tissue that forms in germ (egg) cells in the ovary (female reproductive gland in which the eggs are formed). These tumors usually occur in teenage girls or young women, usually affect just one ovary, and can be benign (not cancer) or malignant (cancer). The most common ovarian germ cell tumor is called dysgerminoma.

Ovarian suppression Surgery, radiation therapy, or a drug treatment to stop the functioning of the ovaries. Also called ovarian ablation.

Ovary Reproductive organ in the female pelvic region. Normally a woman has two ovaries. They contain the eggs (ova) that, joined with sperm, result in pregnancy. Ovaries are also the primary site of production of estrogen.

Overactive bladder A condition characterized by involuntary bladder muscle contractions during the bladder filling phase which the patient cannot suppress.

Overactive thyroid Too much thyroid hormone. Symptoms include weight loss, chest pain, cramps, diarrhea, and nervousness. Also called hyperthyroidsm.

Overall Survival The percentage of subjects in a study who have survived for a defined period of time. Usually reported as time since diagnosis or treatment. Also called the survival rate.

Overbite Vertical overlap of the front teeth.

Overdenture Denture that fits over residual roots or dental implants.

Overexpress An excess of a particular protein on the surface of a cell.

Overflow UI Leakage of small amounts of urine from a bladder that is always full.

Overgrowth syndrome A group of genetic disorders in which there is an abnormal increase in the size of the body or a body part that is often noted at birth. Examples of overgrowth syndromes include neurofibromatosis, Sotos syndrome, Beckwith-Wiedemann syndrome, Simpson-Golabi-Behmel syndrome, Weaver syndrome, Proteus syndrome, Sturge-Weber syndrome, and fragile X syndrome. Many of these syndromes increase the risk of cancer.

Overjet Horozontal overlap of the front teeth.

Overt diabetes Diabetes in the person who shows clear signs of the disease such as a great thirst and the need to urinate often.

Over-the-wire (OTW) catheters Balloon catheters which are delivered over a separate guidewire to position the balloon across the lesion.

Overweight Being too heavy for one's height. Excess body weight can come from fat, muscle, bone, and/or water retention. Being overweight does not always mean being obese.

Ovulation The release of an egg from an ovary during the menstrual cycle.

Oxaliplatin An organoplatinum complex in which the platinum atom is complexed with 1,2-diaminocyclohexane (DACH) and with an oxalate ligand as a 'leaving group.' A 'leaving group' is an atom or a group of atoms that is

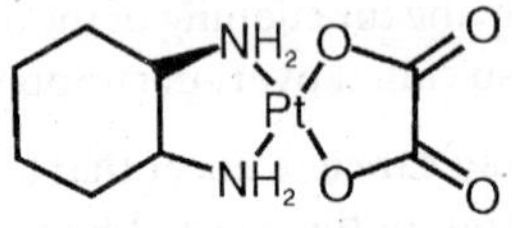

NH_2 O O Pt NH_2 O O

{cis-[(1R,2R)-1,2-cyclohexanediamine-N,N'] [oxalato (2-) -O,O'] platinum}

Figure Oxaliplatin

displaced as a stable species taking with it the bonding electrons. After displacement of the labile oxalate ligand leaving group, active oxaliplatin derivatives, such as monoaquo and diaquo DACH platinum, alkylate macromolecules, forming both inter- and intra-strand platinum-DNA crosslinks, which result in inhibition of DNA replication and transcription and cell-cycle nonspecific cytotoxicity. The DACH side chain appears to inhibit alkylating-agent resistance.

Oxandrolone A synthetic, anabolic steroid hormone analog of testosterone. Similar to testosterone, oxandrolone binds to and activates specific nuclear receptors. This agent may be used for testosterone replacement therapy in hypogonadal men, in HIV-wasting syndrome, and in other conditions in order to increase nitrogen retention and fat-free muscle mass.

Oxidation Process in which molecules are split to give products that have unpaired electrons.

Oxidative metabolism A chemical process in which oxygen is used to make energy from carbohydrates (sugars). Also known as aerobic respiration, cell respiration, or aerobic metabolism.

Oxidative stress Physiological effects of increased levels of free radicals and oxidating molecules, associated with disease and aging; effects include cell membrane damage and cell death.

Oxide layer In welding, an area usually located in the heat-affected zone (HAZ) of the weldment where an oxidation reaction has taken place.

Oxide thickness The depth at which the oxide signal has fallen to half the maximum peak height. Typical values for well electropolished 316L stainless steel range from 20 to 50 angstroms (Å).

Oxidizer A material other than a blasting agent or explosive, that readily yields oxygen or other oxidizing gas, or that readily reacts to promote or initiate combustion of combustible materials. Oxidizers are subdivided as follows: 1. Class 4 - An oxidizer that can undergo an explosive reaction due to contamination or exposure to thermal or physical shock. In addition, the oxidizer will enhance the burning rate and may cause spontaneous ignition of combustible materials.

2. Class 3 - An oxidizer that will cause a severe increase in the burning rate of combustible materials with which it comes in contact or that will undergo vigorous, self-sustained decomposition due to contamination or exposure to heat.

3. Class 2 - An oxidizer that will cause a moderate increase in the burning rate or that may cause spontaneous ignition of combustible materials with which it comes in contact.

4. Class 1 - An oxidizer whose primary hazard is that it slightly increases the burning rate but does not cause spontaneous ignition when it comes in contact with combustible materials.

Oxygenated Carrying oxygen within. Blood that is carrying oxygen from the lungs to all the body tissue is oxygenated.

Ozone Formed by an electric discharge or by the slow combustion of phosphorus, ozone is a modified and condensed form of oxygen, in which three atoms of oxygen are combined to form the molecule, O_3. Because it is a powerful oxidizing agent it is used in deionized water systems to kill bacteria and to reduce by oxidation the amount of Total Organic Carbon (TOC) in the water. Air containing a perceptible amount of ozone has an odor suggesting chlorine or sulfurous acid gas.

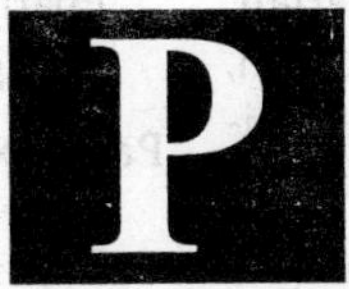

P 32 A radioactive form of phosphorus used in the treatment of cancer.

P value A statistics term. A measure of probability that a difference between groups during an experiment happened by chance. For example, a p-value of .01 (p = .01) means there is a 1 in 100 chance the result occurred by chance. The lower the p-value, the more likely it is that the difference between groups was caused by treatment.

P1 derived artificial chromosome (PAC) One type of vector used to clone DNA fragments (100- to 300-kb insert size; average, 150 kb) in Escherichia coli cells. Based on bacteriophage (a virus) P1 genome.

P24 antigen A core protein making up the nucleocapsid of the HIV Virus, p24 was thought at one time to be a surrogate marker for disease progression. Now it is recognized that some long term asymptomatics have relatively high elevations of p24, while others die never having been positive (anything less than 10 picograms/mole is effectively negative)

P53 gene A tumor suppressor gene that normally inhibits the growth of tumors. This gene is altered in many types of cancer.

P53 peptide vaccine A peptide-based cancer vaccine composed of amino acids 264 to 272 of the wild-type protein encoded by the P53 gene. p53 peptide vaccine may elicit an HLA-A2.1-restricted cytotoxic T lymphocyte immune response against tumor cells that overexpress p53 protein.

Pacemaker lead An electrically insulated conductor that carries signals between the pulse generator (pacemaker) and the heart. Some leads enter the heart through a vein, and other leads attach to the outer surface of the heart.

Pacemaker system A two-part electrical system that includes a pulse generator (pacemaker) and one or two leads. It helps pace the heart when the natural rate is too slow to pump enough blood to the body.

Pacific valerian Valeriana officinalis. A plant whose roots are used as a sedative and to treat certain medical conditions. It is being studied as a way to improve sleep in cancer patients undergoing treatment. Also called valerian, garden valerian, Indian valerian, Mexican valerian, garden heliotrope, and Valerianae radix.

Pack year A way to measure the amount a person has smoked over a long period of time. It is calculated by multiplying the number of packs of cigarettes smoked per day by the number of years the person has smoked. For example, 1 pack year is equal to smoking 1 pack per day for 1 year, or 2 packs per day for half a year, and so on.

Package insert Also known as prescribing information or product label. A document prepared by the manufacturer of a drug to describe approved uses, dosages, contraindications, and potential side effects of the drug. This information is inserted inside each manufactured drug bottle and attached to any promotional or labeling materials.

Packaged equipment An assembly of individual pieces or stages of equipment, complete with interconnecting piping and connections for external piping. The assembly may be mounted on a skid or other structure prior to delivery.

Packaging All operations, including filling and labeling, which a bulk product has to undergo in order to become a finished product.

Packaging material Any material intended to protect an intermediate or API (Active Pharmaceutical Ingredient) during storage and transport.

Paclitaxel A compound extracted from the Pacific yew tree Taxus brevifolia with antineoplastic activity. Paclitaxel binds to tubulin and inhibits the disassembly of microtubules, thereby resulting in the inhibition of cell division. This agent also induces apoptosis by binding to and blocking the function of the apoptosis inhibitor protein Bcl-2 (B-cell Leukemia 2).

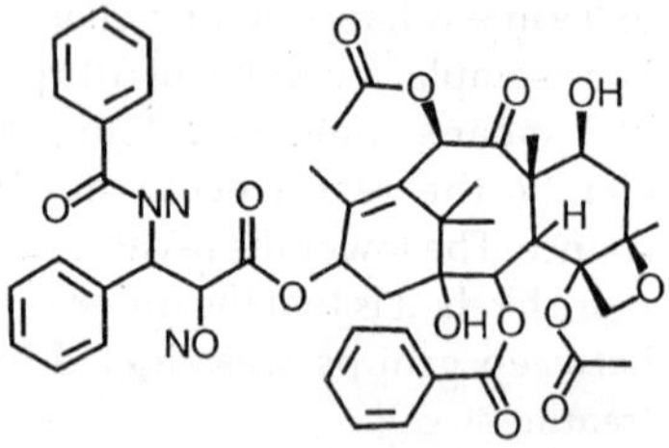

{β- (benzoylamino)-α-hydroxy-,6,12b-bis (acetyloxy)-12- (benzoyloxy)-2a,3,4,4a,5,6,9,10,11,12,12a,12b-dodecahydro-4,11-dihydroxy-4a,8,13,13-tetramethyl-5-oxo-7,11-methano-1H-cyclodeca (3,4) benz (1',2-b)oxet-9-yl ester, (2aR- (2a-α,4-β,4a-β,6-β,
9-α (α-R,β-S),11-α,12-α,12a-α,2b-α))-benzenepropanoic acid}

Figure Paclitaxel

Paclitaxel liposome A form of the anticancer drug paclitaxel that may have fewer side effects and work better than paclitaxel. It is being studied in the treatment of cancer. It belongs to the family of drugs called mitotic inhibitors.

Paclitaxel poliglumex The agent paclitaxel linked to a

biodegradable, water-soluble polyglutamate polymer with antineoplastic properties. The polyglutamate residue increases the water solubility of paclitaxel and allows delivery of higher doses than those achievable with paclitaxel alone. Paclitaxel promotes microtubule assembly and prevents microtubule depolymerization, thus interfering with normal mitosis.

Paclitaxel-loaded polymeric micelle A biodegradable poly (ethylene glycol)-poly .(D,L-lactide) copolymer miceller nanoparticle-entrapped formulation of paclitaxel with antineoplastic properties. Paclitaxel promotes microtubule assembly and prevents depolymerization, thus interfering with normal mitosis. The copolymer residue increases the water-solubility of paclitaxel and allows delivery of higher doses than those achievable with paclitaxel alone.

Paget's disease of bone A chronic condition in which both the breakdown and regrowth of bone are increased. Paget's disease of bone occurs most frequently in the pelvic and leg bones, skull, and lower spine. It is most common in older individuals, and may lead to bone pain, deformities, and fractures. Also called osteitis deformans.

Paget's disease of the nipple A form of breast cancer that begins in the milk passages (ducts) and involves the skin of the nipple and areola. A sign of Paget's disease is a crusting, scaly, red, inflamed tissue (dermatitis) lesion on the nipple. With true Paget's disease, cancer is usually also present within the breast. This is a rare type of breast cancer that occurs in only 1% of cases. If no lump can be felt, it generally has a good outcome (prognosis).

Pain threshold The point at which a person becomes aware of pain.

Pala A substance that is being studied for its ability to increase the effectiveness of the anticancer drug fluorouracil.

Palate The roof of the mouth. The front portion is bony (hard palate), and the back portion is muscular (soft palate).

Palatine uvula The soft flap of tissue that hangs down at the back of the mouth (at the edge of the soft palate). Also called uvula.

Paleocerebellum Phyolgenetically old part of the cerebellum represented by the anterior lobe in man. It is concerned with regulation of muscle tone.

Paleopallium (or paleocortex) Remnants of phylogenetically old 3 layered cortex found in the rhinencephalon or olfactory areas in man

Paleostriatum Oldest component of the corpus striatum, the globus pallidus.

Palladium Pd 103 A radioisotope of the metal palladium used in brachytherapy implants or 'seed'.

With a half-life of 17 days, palladium 103 administered with brachytherapy allows continuous, tumor-site specific low-energy irradiation to the tumor cell population while sparing normal adjacent tissues from radiotoxicity.

Palliative A treatment which provides symptomatic relief, but not a cure.

Palliative care Care given to improve the quality of life of patients who have a serious or life-threatening disease. The goal of palliative care is to prevent or treat as early as possible the symptoms of the disease, side effects caused by treatment of the disease, and psychological, social, and spiritual problems related to the disease or its treatment. Also called comfort care, supportive care, and symptom management.

Pallidal Pertaining to the globus pallidus or paleostriatum.

Pallium Cerebral cortex.

Palmar-plantar erythodysthesia A condition marked by pain, swelling, numbness, tingling, or redness of the hands or feet. It sometimes occurs as a side effect of certain anticancer drugs. Also known as hand-foot syndrome.

Palpable disease A term used to describe cancer that can be felt by touch, usually present in lymph nodes, skin, or other organs of the body such as the liver or colon.

Palpation Examination by pressing on the surface of the body to feel the organs or tissues underneath.

Palpebral conjunctiva The posterior (under part) of the eyelid tissue.

Palpebral fissure The eyelid opening, the aperture.

Pamidronate A synthetic bisphosphonate agent. Although its mechanism of action is not completely understood, pamidronate appears to adsorb to calcium phosphate crystals in bone, blocking their dissolution by inhibiting osteoclast-mediated bone resorption. This agent does not inhibit bone mineralization and formation.

Panacea A cure-all.

Pancoast tumor A type of lung cancer that begins in the upper part of a lung and spreads to nearby tissues such as the ribs and vertebrae. Most Pancoast tumors are non-small cell cancers. Also called pulmonary sulcus tumor.

Pancreas A glandular organ located in the abdomen. It makes pancreatic juices, which contain enzymes that aid in digestion, and it produces several hormones, including insulin. The pancreas is surrounded by the stomach, intestines, and other organs.

Pancreas transplant A surgical procedure that involves replacing the pancreas of a person who has diabetes with a healthy pancreas that can make insulin. The healthy pancreas comes from a donor who has just died or from a living relative. A person can donate half a pancreas and still live normally.

At present, pancreas transplants are usually performed in persons with Type 1 diabetes who have severe complications. This is because after the transplant the patient must take immunosuppressive drugs that are highly toxic and may cause damage to the body.

Pancreatectomy Surgery to remove all or part of the pancreas. In a total pancreatectomy, part of the stomach, part of the small intestine, the common bile duct, gallbladder, spleen, and nearby lymph nodes also are removed.

Pancreatic Having to do with the pancreas.

Pancreatic cancer A disease in which malignant (cancer) cells are found in the tissues of the pancreas. Also called exocrine cancer.

Pancreatic duct The main excretory duct of the pancreas that flows into the common bile duct. Pancreatic secretions are basic and neutralize the acid from the gastric contents.

Pancreatic enzyme A protein secreted by the pancreas that aids in the digestion of food.

Pancreatic juice Fluid made by the pancreas. Pancreatic juices contain proteins called enzymes that aid in digestion.

Pancreaticoduodenal branches The branches of the SMA (superior mesenteric artery) that supply the pancreas and duodenum.

Pancreatitis Inflammation of the pancreas that can cause severe pain. Laboratory tests that indicate pancreatitis include increased blood levels of triglycerides and the pancreatic enzyme amylase.

Pancytopenia A lower than normal number of all types of blood cells, including red and white blood cells and platelets.

Pandemic An outbreak of an infectious disease, such as HIV, that affects people or animals over an extensive geographical area. Also known as a global epidemic.

Pandemic disease An epidemic over an especially wide geographic area.

Panitumumab A human monoclonal antibody produced in transgenic mice that attaches to the transmembrane epidermal growth factor (EGF) receptor. Monoclonal antibody ABX-EGF may inhibit autocrine EGF stimulation of tumor cells that express the EGF receptor, thereby inhibiting tumor cell proliferation.

Panniculitits A rare, multifactorial inflammatory condition involving subcutaneous fat.

Panniculus A layer of membrane.

PAP (Prostatic acid phosphatase) An enzyme produced by the prostate. It may be found in increased amounts in men who have prostate cancer.

Pap smear A method for the early detection of cancer and other abnormalities of the female genital tract. A Pap smear is done by placing a speculum in the vagina, locating the cervix, and then scraping a thin layer of cells from the cervix. The cells are placed on a slide, sent to a laboratory, and analyzed for abnormalities. HIV-infected women often have abnormal results of Pap smear tests, usually as a result of human papillomavirus (HPV) infection.

Papaverine An opiate alkaloid isolated from the plant Papaver somniferum and produced synthetically. As a direct-acting smooth muscle relaxant, papaverine is not closely related to the other opium alkaloids in structure or pharmacological actions; its mechanism of action may involve the non-selective inhibition of phosphodiesterases and direct inhibition of calcium channels. This agent also exhibits antiviral activity against respiratory syncytial virus, cytomegalovirus, and HIV.

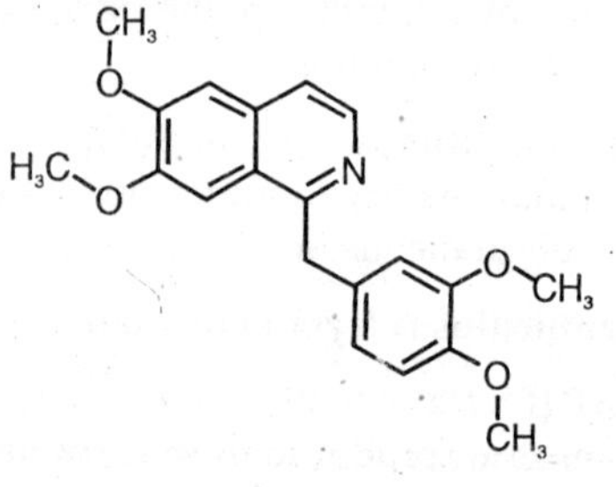

{1-[(3,4-dimethoxyphenyl)methyl]-6,7-dimethoxy-isoquinoline}

Figure Papaverine

Papillary Having small nipple-shaped projections.

Papillary serous carcinoma An aggressive cancer that usually affects the uterus/endometrium, peritoneum, or ovary.

Papillary thyroid cancer Cancer that forms in cells in the thyroid and grows in small finger-like shapes. It grows slowly, is more common in women than in men, and often occurs before age 40. It is the most common type of thyroid cancer.

Papillary tumor A tumor shaped like a small mushroom, with its stem attached to the epithelial layer (inner lining) of an organ.

Papilledema Swelling around the optic disk, the area where the optic nerve (the nerve that carries messages from the eye to the brain) enters the eyeball. Papilledema occurs when increased brain pressure caused by tumors or other problems results in swelling of the optic nerve.

Papilloma A tumor that grows on the skin, such as a wart or polyp. Human papillomavirus (HPV) is the virus that causes papillomas, including genital warts.

Papillomatosis Upward proliferation of epidermis and subepidermal papillae causing the surface epidermis to show irregular undulation.

Papillomavirus A family of papova viruses associated with sexually transmitted diseases, including condylomata. Certain papillomavirus variants have also been associated with cervical cancer, particularly in HIV infected women.

Papules A small circumscribed, solid, elevated lesion of the skin.

PAR (Proven acceptable range) A range for a critical parameter that has been determined to be achievable and appropriate for the process or processes with which it is associated. It is established by knowledge gained through relevant documentation and actual testing. A process should perform consistently and as intended when all critical parameters are held within the established PARs.

Para Beside, e.g. para-aortic - beside the aorta, e.g. parauterine - beside the uterus.

Paraaortic lymph nodes The abdominal lymphnodes that are adjacent to the aorta.

Paracentesis A procedure in which a thin needle or tube is put into the abdomen to remove fluid from the peritoneal cavity (the space within the abdomen that contains the intestines, the stomach, and the liver).

Paraganglioma A rare, usually benign tumor that develops from cells of the paraganglia. Paraganglia are a collection of cells that came from embryonic nervous tissue, and are found near the adrenal glands and some blood vessels and nerves. Paragangliomas that develop in the adrenal gland are called pheochromocytomas. Those that develop outside of the adrenal glands near blood vessels or nerves are called glomus tumors or chemodectomas.

Parageusia A bad taste in the mouth. Also called dysgeusia.

Parahippocampal gyrus A convolution located on the medial surface of the temporal lobe bounded by the collateral and hippocampal sulci and continuous posteriorly with the lingual gyrus. It is separated from the occipitotemporal (fusiform) gyrus laterally by the collateral and rhinal sulci.

Parailiac lymph nodes The lymphnodes that are adjacent to the iliac arteries.

Parakeratosis Retention of nuclei in the stratum corneum. This is a normal finding on mucous membranes.

Parallel track A system of distributing experimental drugs to patients who are unable to participate in ongoing clinical efficacy trials and have no other treatment options.

Paralysis Loss of ability to move all or part of the body.

Paramyxovirus A type of virus that has hemagglutinin-neuraminidase proteins in the outer coat and RNA as the genetic material. Measles (rubeola) virus, mumps virus, and Newcastle disease virus are paramyxoviruses.

Paranasal sinus and nasal cavity cancer Cancer that forms in tissues of the paranasal sinus (hollow spaces behind the lower part of the forehead, nose, and cheeks, or below the eyes) or nasal cavity (the inside of the nose from the nostrils to the part of the throat between the nose and windpipe). The most common type of this cancer is squamous cell carcinoma (cancer that begins in flat cells lining the paranasal sinus and nasal cavity).

Paranasal sinuses The air-filled spaces, lined with mucous membrane, within some of the bones of the skull. They open into the nasal cavity, via the meatuses, and are named according to the bone in which they are situated. They comprise the frontal sinuses and the maxillary sinuses (one pair each), the ethmoid sinuses (consisting of many spaces inside the ethmoid bone), and the two sphenoid sinuses.

Paraneoplastic syndrome A group of symptoms that may develop when substances released by some cancer cells disrupt the normal function of surrounding cells and tissue.

Parasite A plant or organism that lives on or in the host, deriving nourishment from it. Some cause inflammation, but others cause infection and destroy tissue. Human parasites include fungi, yeast, bacteria, protozoa, worms and viruses.

Parasitic Having to do with or being a parasite (an animal or plant that gets nutrients by living on or in an organism of another species).

Parasthesia A partial loss of sensation; may be temporary or permanent.

Parasympathetic Craniosacral division of the autonomic nervous system that functions to conserve energy, build up reserves and restore the resting state of the body.

Paraterminal gyrus Vertical cortical convolution located just rostral to the lamina terminalis and anterior commissure. It is sometimes also referred to as the subcallosal gyrus. The paraterminal gyrus along with the subcallosal area comprise the septal area.

Parathormone A substance made by the parathyroid gland that helps the body store and use calcium. Also called parathyroid hormone, parathyrin, or PTH.

Parathyroid cancer A rare cancer that forms in tissues of one or more of the parathyroid glands (four pea-sized glands in the neck that make parathyroid hormone, which helps the body store and use calcium).

Parathyroid gland One of four pea-sized glands found on the thyroid. The parathyroid hormone produced by these glands increases the calcium level in the blood.

Paratope An antibody combining site that is complementary to an epitope.

Paratracheal stripe The soft-tissue line produced by air inside the trachea and air in the lung outlining the wall of the trachea. Seen on the frontal (PA or AP) chest film, it is thin (usually 2-3 mm, always < 5mm).

Parenchyma The essential or functional elements of an organ.

Parenteral Any route into the body other than through the digestive system. For example, through the veins (intravenous), into the muscles (intramuscular), or through the skin (subcutaneous).

Parenteral drug A parenteral drug is defined as one intended for injection through the skin or other external boundary tissue, rather than through the alimentary canal, so that active substances they contain are administered, using gravity or force, directly into a blood vessel, organ, tissue, or lesion. They are infused when administered intravenously (IV), or injected when administered intramuscularly (IM), or subcutaneously into the human body. A large volume parenteral (LVP) is a unit dose container of greater than 100ml that is terminally sterilized by heat. Small volume parenteral (SVP) is a "catch-all" for all non-LVP parenterals products except biologicals.

Parenteral nutrition A form of nutrition that is delivered into a vein. Parenteral nutrition does not use the digestive system. It may be given to people who are unable to absorb nutrients through the intestinal tract because of vomiting that won't stop, severe diarrhea, or intestinal disease. It may also be given to those undergoing high-dose chemotherapy or radiation and bone marrow transplantation. It is possible to give all of the protein, calories, vitamins and minerals a person needs using parenteral nutrition. Also known as hyperalimentation or total parenteral nutrition (TPN).

Paresis A paralysis that when occurring in ocular muscles causes double vision when looking in some directions.

Paresthesia Abnormal sensations such as burning, tingling, or a "pins-and-needles" feeling that occur without external stimulation. Paresthesia can occur as a symptom of peripheral neuropathy or as a side effect of certain anti-HIV drugs.

Paricalcitol A synthetic noncalcemic, nonphosphatemic vitamin D analogue. Paricalcitol binds to the vitamin D receptor and has been shown to reduce parathyroid hormone (PTH) levels. This agent also increases the expression of PTEN ('Phosphatase and Tensin homolog deleted on chromosome Ten'), a tumor-suppressor gene, in leukemic cells and cyclin-dependent kinase inhibitors, resulting in tumor cell apoptosis and tumor cell differentiation into normal phenotypes.

Parietal lobe Bounded by the central fissure, lateral fissure, parieto-occipital sulcus and an imaginary line extending from the superior margin of the parieto-occipital sulcus to the pre-occipital notch. This lobe includes the primary somesthetic area association cortex concerned with understanding and interpreting multisensory (auditory, visual, somatic) input.

Parietal pericardium The outer layer of the pericardium, which is a thin sac of tissue that surrounds the heart.

Parkinson's disease A progressive systemic disorder that primarily attacks the brain cells that produce neurotransmitters necessary for the normal functioning of the central nervous system. Parkinson's disease is characterized by tremulous or slow movement, facial paralysis, and difficulty with walking and general coordination.

Parkinson's syndrome Any of a class of degenerative diseases that have symptoms similar to those associated with Parkinson's disease, and often having a specific cause as from exposure to toxic drugs or chemicals in an occupational setting.

Paromomycin (humatin) An antibiotic used for treating intestinal infections.

Parotidectomy Surgery to remove all or part of the parotid gland (a large salivary gland located in front of and just below the ear). In a radical parotidectomy, the entire gland is removed.

Paroxetine hydrochloride A drug used to treat depression and anxiety disorders. It belongs to the family of drugs called selective serotonin reuptake inhibitors (SSRI). Also called Paxil.

Paroxysmal nocturnal hemoglobinuria (PNH) A rare disorder in which red blood cells are easily destroyed by certain immune system proteins. Symptoms include blood clots, and red or brownish urine in the morning. Aplastic anemia (decreased production of blood cells) may lead to PNH, and people with PNH are at increased risk of acute myelogenous leukemia.

Partial cystectomy The removal of the cancer as well as some of the bladder tissue around the tumor. Also called segmental cystectomy.

Partial denture Removable dental prosthesis (appliance) replacing one or more natural teeth.

Partial hysterectomy Surgery to remove the uterus only. When the uterus and part or all of the cervix are removed, it is called a total hysterectomy.

Partial laryngectomy An operation to remove part of the larynx (voice box).

Partial mastectomy The removal of cancer as well as some of the breast tissue around the tumor and the lining over the chest muscles below the tumor. Usually some of the lymph nodes under the arm are also taken out. Also called segmental mastectomy.

Partial nephrectomy Surgery to remove part of one kidney or a kidney tumor, but not an entire kidney.

Partial oophorectomy Surgery to remove part of one ovary or part of both ovaries.

Partial remission A decrease in the size of a tumor, or in the extent of cancer in the body, in response to treatment. Also called partial response.

Partially blinded clinical trial 1. A clinical trial in which some, but not all, of the study treatments are administered in a single- or double-blinded fashion.

2. A clinical trial in which some, but not all, of the staff in a clinic are blinded to treatment assignment.

Participating physician A primary care physician in practice in the payer's managed care service area who has entered into a contract.

Particle Solid or liquid object which for purposes of classification of air cleanliness, falls within a cumulative distribution that is based upon a threshold (lower limit) size in the range from 0,1 µm to 5 µm.

Particle concentration Number of individual particles per unit volume of air.

Particle size The apparent maximum linear dimension of a particle in the plane of observation as seen with a microscope or the equivalent diameter of a particle detected by automatic instrumentation. The equivalent diameter is the diameter of a reference sphere having known properties and producing the same response in the sensing instrument as the particle being measured.

Particulate Usually a solid particle large enough to be removed by filtration. Nonfilterable solids are usually referred to as colloids.

Passivation A final chemical treatment/cleaning process that removes exogenous iron or iron compounds from the surface of stainless steel piping and equipment by the use of a mild oxidant, such as a nitric acid solution, or by "in-situ electropolishing. The purpose of passivation is to restore and/or enhance the spontaneous formation of the chemically inert surface or protective passive film.

Passive antibody therapy Treatment with injections of antibodies made in another animal or in the laboratory.

Passive immunity The body's ability to prevent or fight a specific infection after receiving antibodies from another person. The most common example of passive immunity is when an infant receives the mother's antibodies by consuming her breast milk.

Passive immunization Immunization by the admin-istration of preformed antibody into a nonimmune individual.

Passive immunotherapy The transfer of antibodies from one person to another to help the recipient fight infection. An example of passive immunotherapy is the use of plasma donated by healthy HIV-infected people who have high CD4 counts and high levels of anti-HIV antibodies. The plasma is administered to people with AIDS who have lost CD4 cells and can no longer make their own antibodies. Passive immunotherapy has been used with limited success in treating advanced HIV disease in adults, but it is still sometimes used in HIV-infected children.

Passive layer A passive oxidized film that forms naturally on a stainless steel surface when exposed to air or similar oxidizing environment thus protecting the underlying base metal from corrosion. Welding disturbs the passive layer by reducing the chromium and increasing the iron, thus altering the chromium/iron ratio (measure of corrosion resistance). Upon completion and approval of the weld, the weld surface and adjacent boundary area must be brought back to a passive state. Additionally, normal operating conditions in typical Water For Injection, reverse osmosis, deionized water, clean steam, Clean In Place, and process piping often lead to formation of the most prevalent form of self catalyzing corrosion called "rouge" (French for red), which is a colloidal form of rust containing iron oxide, chromium and nickel in various forms. This problem is further accentuated by high temperature. The rouge layer acts as a passive layer until it becomes so thick that it "sloughs off" into the process or water stream.

Passivity The state in which a stainless steel exhibits a very low corrosion rate. Also known as passivity, is the loss (or minimizing) of chemical reactivity exhibited by certain metals and alloys under special environmental conditions.

Pasteurization The heating of milk, wines, fruit juices, etc., for about thirty minutes at 68°C (154.4°F) whereby the living bacteria are destroyed, but the flavour or bouquet is preserved; the spores are unaffected, but are kept from developing by immediately cooling the liquid to 10°C (50°F) or lower.

Patch test Skin tests that can show which substances are causing allergic contact dermatitis or eczema. The test patch is usually applied to the skin on the person's back for 48 hours.

Patella The roughly triangular sesamoid bone located in front of the knee, within the tendon of the quadriceps femoris muscle, a major extensor of the lower leg.

Patent Open, exposed or unobstructed, e g patent ductus arteriosus - an abnormal persistence after birth of an open lumen in the ductus arteriosus, between the pulmonary artery and the aorta.

aterson Kelly syndrome A disorder marked by anemia caused by iron deficiency, and a web-like growth of membranes in the throat that makes swallowing difficult. Having Paterson-Kelly syndrome may increase the risk of developing esophageal cancer. Also called Plummer-Vinson syndrome and sideropenic dysphagia.

ıthogen Any microbiological or eukaryotic cell containing sufficient genetic information, which upon expression of such information is capable of producing disease in healthy people, plants, or animals.

thogenesis The natural evolution of a disease process in the body without intervention (i.e., without treatment); Description of the development of a particular disease, especially the events, reactions and mechanisms involved at the cellular level.

thogenic Causing or capable of causing disease.

thogenic organisms Organisms capable of causing disease, either directly (by infecting) or indirectly (by producing a toxin that causes illness).

hological fracture A break in a bone usually caused by cancer or some disease condition.

hological staging A method used o determine the stage of cancer. Tissue samples are removed during surgery or a biopsy. The stage is determined based on how the cells in the samples look under a microscope.

Pathologist A physician who specializes in the identification of abnormalities and disease by examining body tissue under a microscope and organs. The pathologist determines whether a lump is benign or cancerous.

Pathology The study of disease by the examination of tissues and body fluids under the microscope. A doctor who specializes in pathology is called a pathologist.

Pathology report The description of cells and tissues made by a pathologist based on microscopic evidence, and sometimes used to make a diagnosis of a disease.

Patient close out stage The stage of a trial in which patients leave a trial. The end of treatment and follow-up.

Patient controlled analgesia (PCA) A method in which the patient controls the amount of pain medicine that is used. When pain relief is needed, the person can receive a preset dose of pain medicine by pressing a button on a computerized pump that is connected to a small tube in the body.

Patient follow up A process involving periodic contact with patients enrolled in a clinical trial for the purpose of administering the assigned treatment (s), observing the effects of treatment (s), modifying the course of treatment (s), or for collecting required data.

Patient identification number A unique sequence of numbers, or numbers and letters, that are used to identify a patient.

Patient management problem (PMP) A written method that attempts to assess clinical problem-solving abilities. To improve its validity, recent improvements include an attempt to focus testing on the key features within a clinical case, which represents the diagnostic or problem-solving challenge. The main advantage of this innovation is that many more 'clinical cases' can be administered to candidates in a given period of time than with conventional PMP.

Computer-Based Patient Management Problem (e-PMP) is a related method that has been used for some years, which more recently has been enriched with the ability to link computers to various audiovisual inputs such as videodiscs and optical holograms produced by lasers extending realism of the simulations and conceivably providing enhanced educational opportunities. The cost of developing, establishing and maintaining the required facility may constitute a significant constraining factor for broader use.

Patient origin study A study, generally undertaken by an individual health program or health planning agency, t determine the geographi distribution of the residences o the patients served by one or mor health programs. Such studie help define catchment and medica trade areas and are useful i locating and planning th development of new services.

Patient recruitment goal The numbe of patients scheduled to b enrolled into the trial. Usually se before the trial starts, or shortl thereafter, via a sample siz calculation or via practica considerations.

Patient recruitment The process c identifying suitable patients fc enrollment into a clinical trial.

Patient surveys Questionnaire use to assess patient satisfaction wit different aspects of their healt care. The questions addres general aspects of the physician care such as the amount of tin spent with the patient, overa quality of care, physicia competency (skills and kn wledge), courtesy, and interest empathy. Specific patient ca competencies can be assesse including interpersonal ar communication skills, profess onal behavior, listening skil provision of information abo examination findings etc. Ea rating may generate a single sco overall or separate scores f different clinical care activities settings. Most patient satisfacti surveys are completed at the tir of service and require less than minutes. Improvements to this tool may include utilizing more effective survey design and using computers to collect and summarize survey data.

CD, immotile cilia syndrome (ICS) and kartagener's syndrome (KS) Refer to the same condition, with the exception that in KS the heart is located on the right side of the body.

eak action The time period when the effect of something is as strong as it can be such as when insulin in having the most effect on lowering the glucose (sugar) in the blood.

eak flow meter Device to measure lung expiration and used to monitor asthma severity.

eau d'orange A dimpled condition of the skin of the breast, resembling the skin of an orange, sometimes found in inflammatory breast cancer.

ectoral The area near the breast or upper chest.

ectoral muscles Muscles attached to the front of the chest wall and upper arms. The larger group is called pectoralis major, and a smaller group is called pectoralis minor. Because these muscles are in close proximity to the breast, they may become involved in breast cancer or surgery to treat it.

ectoralis major Muscle which contributes to the adduction, flexion, and medial rotation of the arm. It originates at the clavicle, sternum, six upper ribs, and the aponeurosis of obliquus externus abdominus, and inserts into the crest of intertubercular groove of the humerus. The major muscle of the upper chest wall.

Pectoralis minor Muscle which originates at the third, fourth and fifth ribs, and inserts into the coracoid process of the scapula. It contributes to drawing the shoulder forward and downward.

Pediatric Relating to the medical specialty concerned with the development, care and treatment of children from birth through adolescence.

Pediatric endocrinologist A doctor who sees and treats children with problems of the endocrine glands; diabetes is an endocrine disorder.

Pediatric gastroenterologist A physician who treats infants and children with diseases of the digestive system.

Pediatric hematologist A doctor who specializes in treating blood disorders in children.

Pediatric nurse specialist A registered nurse with an advanced degree in nursing who specializes in the care of children.

Pediatric surgeon A surgeon who specializes in the treatment of children. A surgeon removes or repairs a part of the body by operating on the patient.

Pedicle The short tubular bone process of the vertebral arch that forms the connection between the lamina and vertebral body (centrum).

Pedigree A record of one's ancestors, offspring, siblings, and their offspring that may be used to determine the pattern of certain genes or disease inheritance within a family.

Pedodontics or pediatric dentistry Dental specialty focusing on treatment of children.

Peduncle Generic term usually denoting a stalk-like bundle of connecting nerve fibers.

P. Cerebral: The robust bundles of fibers located bilaterally in the ventral midbrain.

P. Cerebellar: Large bundles of fibers that connect the cerebellum with the midbrain (superior cerebellar peduncle or brachium conjunctivum), pons (middle cerebellar peduncle or brachium pontis) and medulla oblongata (inferior cerebellar peduncle or restiform body).

Pedunculated Elevated, as on a stem (peduncle).

Peer review The mechanism used by the medical staff to evaluate the quality of total health care provided by the Managed Care Organization. The evaluation covers how well all health personnel perform services and how appropriate the services are to meet the patients' needs. Evaluation of health care services by medical personnel with similar training. Generally, the evaluation by practicing physicians or other professionals of the effectiveness and efficiency of services ordered or performed by other members o the profession (peers). Frequently peer review refers to the activitie of the Professional Review Organizations, and also to review of research by other researchers This is the most common metho utilized in managed care fo monitoring the utilization by physicians. In other words, othe physicians will review th decisions made by a physician Much controversy has surfaced in this area in recent years. Som physicians are reluctant to b reviewed by physicians over th phone or by having their writte records read. Some consumer suspect that peer review is not tru peer review since both th providers and the reviewers ofte have personal financial incentive to reduce or increase medical care Nonetheless, peer review i utilized in all managed car settings.

PEG intron A drug used to trea hepatitis C infections. It is als being studied in the treatment an prevention of cancer. It is a cytokine that is modified in th laboratory. It belongs to the family of drugs called biological respons modifiers.

Pegaspargase A complex o polyethylene glycol conjugate with L-asparaginase. Aspara ginase hydrolyzes L-asparagine t L-aspartic acid and ammonia thereby depleting these cells o asparagine and blocking protei synthesis and tumor cel proliferation, especially in the G phase of the cell cycle. The agent also induces apoptosis in tumor cells. Pegylation decreases the enzyme's antigenicity. Asparagine is critical to protein synthesis in leukemic cells, which cannot synthesize this amino acid due to the absence of the enzyme asparagine synthase.

Pegasys A drug used to treat hepatitis C infections. It is also being studied in the treatment and prevention of cancer. It is a cytokine that is modified in the laboratory. It belongs to the family of drugs called biological response modifiers. Also called PEG-interferon alfa-2a.

Pegfilgrastim A long-acting pegylated form of a recombinant therapeutic agent which is chemically identical to or similar to an endogenous human granulocyte colony-stimulating factor (G-CSF). Produced endogenously by monocytes, fibroblasts, and endothelial cells, G-CSF binds to and activates specific cell surface receptors, stimulating neutrophil progenitor proliferation and differentiation and selected neutrophil functions. Conjugation of the cytokine with a branched polyethylene glycol molecule (pegylation) significantly increases its therapeutic half-life.

PEG-MGDF A form of megakaryocyte growth and development factor (MGDF) that is made in the laboratory. MGDF comes from the protein thrombopoietin, which is normally made in the body to help make platelets. PEG-MGDF is being studied as a way to increase the number of platelets in patients receiving chemotherapy. Also called polyethylene glycosylated recombinant human megakaryocyte growth and development factor (PEG-rhMGDF).

PEG-rhMGDF Polyethylene glycosylated recombinant human megakaryocyte growth and development factor. A form of megakaryocyte growth and development factor (MGDF) that is made in the laboratory. MGDF comes from the protein thrombopoietin, which is normally made in the body to help make platelets. PEG-rhMGDF is being studied as a way to increase the number of platelets in patients receiving chemotherapy. Also called PEG-MGDF.

Pegylated doxorubicin HCL liposome A liposome-encapsulated form of the hydrochloride salt of the anthracycline antineoplastic antibiotic doxorubicin. Liposomal delivery of doxorubicin HCL improves drug penetration into tumors and decreases drug clearance, thereby increasing the duration of therapeutic drug effects. Doxorubicin intercalates into DNA and interacts with topoisomerase II, consequently inhibiting DNA replication and repair and RNA and protein synthesis. This agent also produces toxic free-radical intermediates and interacts with cell membrane lipids causing lipid peroxidation.

Pegylated interferon alfa A covalent conjugate of recombinant interferon alpha and polyethylene glycol (PEG), used as an antiviral and antineoplastic agent. The biological activity of this agent is derived from its interferon alpha protein moiety. Interferons alfa bind to specific cell-surface receptors, leading to the transcription and translation of genes whose protein products mediate antiviral, antiproliferative, anticancer, and immune-modulating effects. The PEG moiety lowers the clearance of interferon alpha, thereby extending the duration of its therapeutic effects, but may also reduce interferon-mediated stimulation of an immune response.

PEITC (Phenethyl isothiocyanate) A substance that is being studied in the prevention of cancer. It is a naturally occurring compound found in some cruciferous vegetables.

Peldesine A substance that is being studied for the treatment of cancer.

Pelvic Having to do with the pelvis (the lower part of the abdomen located between the hip bones).

Pelvic diaphragm The floor of the pelvis formed by the coccygei and levatores ani muscles and their fascia. The pelvic diaphgram is fenestrated (holes) for the anus and vagina.

Pelvic exam A physical examination of the vagina, cervix, uterus, fallopian tubes, ovaries, and rectum.

Pelvic exenteration Surgery to remove the lower colon, rectum, and bladder, and create stomata (openings) through which urine and stool are passed out of the body. In women, the cervix, vagina, ovaries, and nearby lymph nodes are also removed.

Pelvic inflammatory disease (PID) An infection of the upper female genital tract affecting the uterus, fallopian tubes, and ovaries. It is usually caused by the bacteria responsible for two common sexually transmitted diseases (STDs), gonorrhea and chlamydia. If left untreated, PID can cause severe pain, tubal pregnancy, and infertility. Severe cases may even spread to the liver and kidneys, causing dangerous internal bleeding and death.

Pelvic lymphadenectomy Surgery to remove lymph nodes in the pelvis for examination under a microscope to see if they contain cancer.

Pelvic muscle exercises Pelvic muscle exercises are intended to improve your pelvic muscle tone and prevent leakage for sufferers of Stress Urinary Incontinence. Also called Kegel exercises.

Pelvic wall The muscles and ligaments that line the part of the body between the hips.

Pelvis A group of bones that join the lower extremity to the spine: sacrum, ilium, ischium, pubis.

Pemetrexed disodium A drug that is used to treat malignant pleural mesothelioma and advanced non-small cell lung cancer and is being studied in the treatment of other types of cancer. It belongs to the family of drugs called enzyme inhibitors.

Penalization To prevent sight out of the good eye and force the weaker, amblyopic eye, to function. A filter, eye patch, or eye drops such as atropin or miotics are used on the good eye.

Penclomedine A substance that is being studied in the treatment of cancer. It belongs to the family of drugs called alkylating agents.

Penetrance The probability of a gene or genetic trait being expressed. "Complete" penetrance means the gene or genes for a trait are expressed in all the population who have the genes. "Incomplete" penetrance means the genetic trait is expressed in only part of the population. The percent penetrance also may change with the age range of the population.

Penia (suffix) Poverty, e.g. thrombocytopenia - decrease in blood platelets.

Penicillamine Perhaps the most commonly use drug for the treatment of Wilson's Disease. It is a variant of penicillin and is also used in the treatment of rheumatoid arthritis. It's brand names are Cuprimine and Depen.

SH

NH_2

CH_3 — C — CH — COOH

CH_3 NH_2

{3-mercapto-D-valine}

Figure Penicillamine

Penicillin An antibiotic containing a β-lactam ring that inhibits an enzyme responsible for making peptide cross-links in the bacterial cell wall. It is obtained from cultures of the molds Penicillium Notatum or Penicillium Chrysogenum.

Penicillium The genus of mold causing a zone of inhibition in an agar plate of bacteria. It is the organism, which produces natural penicillin.

Penile cancer A rare cancer that forms in the penis (the external male reproductive organ). Most penile cancers are squamous cell carcinomas (cancer that begins in flat cells lining the penis).

Penile implant A firm rod or inflatable device that is placed in the penis during a surgical procedure. The implant makes it possible to have and keep an erection. Penile implants are used to treat erectile dysfunction or impotence.

Penis An external male reproductive organ. It contains a tube called the urethra, which carries semen and urine to the outside of the body.

Pentamidine An antibiotic effective in an IV formulation against PCP. An aerosolized form is used to prevent PCP.

Pentetic acid calcium A synthetic chelating agent related to EDTA. Pentetic acid calcium chelates with the metallic radioisotopic moieties of unbound, extracellular radioimmunotherapeutic agents, resulting in higher specific tumor cell binding of radioimmunotherpeutic agents, and so improved tumor cell radiocytotoxicity, while sparing normal cells and tissues from the radiocytotoxic effects of these agents.

Pentosan polysulfate A drug used to relieve pain or discomfort associated with chronic inflammation of the bladder. It is also being evaluated for its protective effects on the gastrointestinal tract in people undergoing radiation therapy.

Pentostatin A purine nucleotide analogue antibiotic isolated from the bacterium Streptomyces antibioticus. Also known as 2'-deoxycoformycin, pentostatin binds to and inhibits adenine deaminase (ADA), an enzyme essential to purine metabolism; ADA activity is greatest in cells of the lymphoid system with T-cells having higher activity than B-cells and T-cell malignancies higher ADA activity than B-cell malignancies. Pentostatin inhibition of ADA appears to result in elevated intracellular levels of dATP which may block DNA synthesis through the inhibition of ribonucleotide reductase. This agent may also inhibit RNA synthesis and may selectively deplete CD26+ lymphocytes.

Pentoxifylline A drug used to prevent blood clotting and as a treatment that may help decrease weight loss in people with cancer.

People living with aids (PLWA) Infants, children, adolescents, and adults infected with HIV/AIDS.

Peptic Related to the stomach and the upper part of the small intestine (duodenum).

Peptic ulcer A sore in the lining of the esophagus, stomach, or duodenum (beginning of the small intestine); often caused by a bacteria called Helicobacter pylori.

Peptide A secondary protein derivative defined as "a definitely characterized combination of two or more amino acids, the carboxyl (COOH) group of one being united with the amino (NH_2) group of the other, with the elimination of a molecule of water". They form a peptide bond.

Peptide 946 A protein that causes white blood cells to recognize and destroy melanoma cells.

Peptide hormones A diverse class of hormones that are synthesized and excreted at various sites within the body. Examples include: insulin, relaxin, glucagons, growth hormone, vasopressin, ACTH (Adrenocorticotropic Hormone), endorphins, and encephalins.

Perceptual skills Includes the identification, discrimination, spatial awareness, and visual-sensory integration. These are visual cognitive skills used to processes visual information to the brain to be organized and interpreted.

Percutaneous Through the skin.

Percutaneous ethanol injection An injection of ethanol (alcohol) through the skin directly into the tumor to kill cancer cells.

Percutaneous nephro-lithotomy (PCN) Percutaneous means "though the skin." In PCN, the surgeon or urologist makes a 1-centimeter incision under local anesthesia in the patient's back, through which an instrument called a nephroscope is passed directly into the kidney and, if necessary, the ureter. Smaller stones may be manually extracted. Large ones may need to be broken up with ultrasonic, electro-hydraulic or laser- tipped probes before they can be extracted. A tube may be inserted into the kidney for drainage.

Percutaneous transhepatic biliary drainage A procedure to drain bile to relieve pressure in the bile ducts caused by a blockage. An x-ray of the liver and bile ducts locates the blockage of bile flow. Images made by ultrasound guide placement of a stent (tube), which remains in the liver. Bile drains through the stent into the small intestine or into a collection bag outside the body. This procedure may relieve jaundice before surgery. Also called percutaneous transhepatic cholangiodrainage (PTCD).

Percutaneous transhepatic cholangiography (PTC) A procedure to x-ray the hepatic and common bile ducts. A contrasting agent is injected into the liver or bile duct; and the ducts are then x-rayed to find the point of obstruction.

Percutaneous transluminal coronary angioplasty (PTCA) Percutaneous (through the skin) transluminal (through the blood vessel) coronary (of the heart) angioplasty (plastic repair of the blood vessels) is a minimally invasive procedure which uses balloon dilation catheters to enlarge and treat blocked coronary arteries.

Perennial allergic rhinitis An allergic condition that has similar symptoms to hay fever but occurs all the year round and is confused with a 'permanent' cold.

Perforation A hole in the wall of an organ.

Performance Denotes what an individual actually does in a real life situation. In medicine, it denotes what a student or doctor actually does in an encounter with a patient when applying learned knowledge and skills, mediated by clinical judgment and the use of interpersonal communication skills. From this standpoint, competence implies professional maturity and ease in making difficult decisions. And, although these elements are inherent in good practice, it is not easy to demonstrate them. Assessment of clinical performance is of the greatest importance but is often difficult to measure.

Performance gap The occurrence, trend, or incident that shows that a clinician's performance falls short of expected performance levels, particularly when the clinician ignores accumulated scientific evidence supporting other clinical interventions or when the clinician does not reach benchmarked targets.

Performance measurement Measures and results that describe the health care being provided and the outcomes. Performance may be stated in terms of health outcome, quality of care, timeliness, correctness, percentage of goals attained or percentage of mistakes made. Performance measures may also indicate whether a health plan or provider has appropriately provided certain services expected to lead to desirable outcomes. Closely related to Continuous quality of improvement (CQI) and utilization review (UR).

Performance standards Standards set by the MCO or payer that the provider will need to meet in order to maintain it's credentialing, renew its contract or avoid penalty. These will vary from payer to payer, and contract to contract. Standards an individual provider is expected to meet, especially with respect to quality of care. The standards may define volume of care delivered per time period. Thus, performance standards for obstetrician/gynecologist may specify some or all of the following office hours and office visits per week or month, on-call days, deliveries per year, gynecological operations per year, etc.

Performance status A measure of how well a patient is able to perform ordinary tasks and carry out daily activities.

Performance-based assessment An evaluation that demands trainees be engaged in specified clinical activities. This permits evaluation of an ability to perform clinical tasks and not merely the recitation of medical knowledge. Typical measurement tools for this form of testing are checklists, observation logs, and anecdotal reports.

Perfusion A feature available on balloon catheters where holes in the catheter shaft on either side of the balloon allow uninterrupted blood flow to the heart muscle during inflation.

Perfusion magnetic resonance imaging A special type of magnetic resonance imaging (MRI) that uses an injected dye in order to see blood flow through tissues. Also called magnetic resonance perfusion imaging.

Peri Around, e.g. peribronchial - around the bronchus.

Periamygdaloid area Small region of the anterior parahippocampal gyrus (near the uncus) dorsal and rostral to the amygdaloid nuclear complex.

Perianal Around the anus.

Periapical (PA) Region at the end of the roots of teeth.

Pericardial effusion An abnormal collection of fluid inside the sac that covers the heart.

Pericardium The fibroserous sac enclosing the heart and the roots of the great vessels of the heart. It is composed of a fibrous external layer and a serous inner layer.

Perifosine An orally active alkyl-phosphocholine compound with potential antineoplastic activity. Targeting cellular membranes, perifosine modulates membrane permeability, membrane lipid composition, phospholipid metabolism, and mitogenic signal transduction, resulting in cell differentiation and inhibition of cell growth. This agent also inhibits the anti-apoptotic mitogen-activated protein kinase (MAPK) pathway and modulates the balance between the MAPK and pro-apoptotic stress-activated protein kinase (SAPK/JNK) pathways, thereby inducing apoptosis. Perifosine has a lower gastrointestinal toxicity profile than the related agent miltefosine.

Perikaryon The cytoplasmic component of a nerve cell body excluding the nucleus and processes. The term is often used synonymously with neuron and soma.

Perillyl alcohol A substance that is being studied in the prevention of cancer. It belongs to the family of plant drugs called monoterpenes.

Perimenopausal The time of a woman's life when menstrual periods become irregular. Refers to the time near menopause.

Perimetry The measurement of a visual field function (the total area that can be seen while looking straight ahead) using targets of different sizes and brightness (light levels). The visual field is measured in degrees. In a normal eye the peripheral field of vision is about 180 degrees. An instrument called a perimeter is used for mapping all areas of a person's eyesight, including peripheral (side) vision. Visual field testing can help detect certain patterns of visual loss, indicating specific types of eye diseases or vision conditions. It is the single best test for diagnosing glaucoma.

Perinatal Relating to the period around the time of birth.

Perinatal transmission The passage of HIV from an HIV-infected mother to her infant. The infant may become infected while in the womb, during labor and delivery, or through breastfeeding.

Perineal colostomy An opening made surgically to allow the colon to exit the body through the perineum (the area of the body between the anus and the vulva in females, and between the anus and the scrotum in males). A colostomy provides a new path for waste material to leave the body after part of the colon has been removed.

Perineal prostatectomy Surgery to remove the prostate through an incision made between the scrotum and the anus.

Perineum The area of the body between the anus and the vulva in females, and between the anus and the scrotum in males.

Perineural Around a nerve or group of nerves.

Periodontal chart Record measuring the depth of gum pockets around the teeth.

Periodontal disease Damage to the gums. People who have diabetes are more likely to have gum disease than people who do not have diabetes.

Periodontal surgery Recontouring or esthetic management of diseased gum and supporting tissue.

Periodontist Dental specialist treating the gums and supporting soft and hard tissues retaining natural teeth and the surgical placement of dental implants.

Perioperative Around the time of surgery. This usually lasts from the time the patient goes into the hospital or doctor's office for surgery until the time the patient goes home.

Peripheral blood Blood circulating throughout the body.

Peripheral blood lymphocyte therapy A treatment for Epstein-Barr virus infection or overgrowth of white blood cells (lymphocytes) after an organ or bone marrow transplant. Specific lymphocytes from a sibling donor are infused into the patient to try and reverse these conditions.

Peripheral blood mononuclear cell (PBMC) A general term for white blood cells containing one nucleus, particularly lymphocytes and macrophages.

Peripheral blood smear A procedure in which a sample of blood is viewed under a microscope to count different circulating blood cells (red blood cells, white blood cells, platelets, etc.)

Peripheral nervous system The cranial nerves (12 pair), spinal nerves (31 pair), nerve plexuses, and the spinal and autonomic ganglia associated with them.

Peripheral neuropathy Condition characterized by sensory loss, pain, muscle weakness, and wasting of muscle in the hands, legs, or feet. It may start with burning or tingling sensations or numbness in the toes and fingers. In severe cases, paralysis may occur. Peripheral neuropathy may result from HIV infection itself or may be a side effect of certain anti-

HIV drugs, particularly NRTIs.

eripheral primitive neuroectodermal tumor (PPNET) A type of cancer that forms in bone or soft tissue. Also called Ewing's sarcoma.

eripheral stem cell An immature cell found circulating in the bloodstream. New blood cells develop from peripheral stem cells.

eripheral stem cell support A method of replacing blood-forming cells destroyed by cancer treatment. Immature blood cells (stem cells) in the circulating blood that are similar to those in the bone marrow are given to the patient after treatment. This helps the bone marrow recover and continue producing healthy blood cells. Transplantation may be autologous (an individual's own blood cells saved earlier), allogeneic (blood cells donated by someone else), or syngeneic (blood cells donated by an identical twin). Also called peripheral stem cell transplantation.

'eripheral stem cell transplantation A method of replacing blood-forming cells destroyed by cancer treatment. Immature blood cells (stem cells) in the circulating blood that are similar to those in the bone marrow are given to the patient after treatment. This helps the bone marrow recover and continue producing healthy blood cells. Transplantation may be autologous (an individual's own blood cells saved earlier), allogeneic (blood cells donated by someone else), or syngeneic (blood cells donated by an identical twin). Also called peripheral stem cell support.

Peripheral T cell lymphoma One of a group of aggressive (fast-growing) non-Hodgkin's lymphomas that begin in mature T lymphocytes (T cells that have matured in the thymus gland and gone to other lymphatic sites in the body, including lymph nodes, bone marrow, and spleen.) Also called mature T-cell lymphoma.

Peripheral vascular disease (PVD) Disease in the large blood vessels of the arms, legs, and feet. People who have had diabetes for a long time may get this because major blood vessels in their arms, legs, and feet are blocked and these limbs do not receive enough blood. The signs of PVD are aching pains in the arms, legs, and feet (especially when walking) and foot sores that heal slowly. Although people with diabetes cannot always avoid PVD, doctors say they have a better chance of avoiding it if they take good care of their feet, do not smoke, and keep both their blood pressure and diabetes under good control.

Peripheral vision The ability to see or be aware of what is surrounding us, our side vision.

Peristalsis The rippling motion of muscles in the intestine or other tubular organs characterized by the alternate contraction and relaxation of the muscles that propel the contents onward.

Peristaltic pump A type of positive displacement pump that operates by pulsations of flow caused by passing rollers over flexible tubing. Operating pressure limited by tubing tolerance.

Peritoneal Having to do with the parietal peritoneum (the tissue that lines the abdominal wall and pelvic cavity) and visceral peritoneum (the tissue that covers most of the organs in the abdomen, including the intestines).

Peritoneal cancer Cancer of the tissue that lines the abdominal wall and covers organs in the abdomen.

Peritoneal cavity The thin space between the parietal and the visceral peritoneum, normally containing a small amount of serous fluid.

Peritoneal dialysis A way to clean the blood of people who have kidney disease.

Peritoneal infusion A method of delivering fluids and drugs directly into the abdominal cavity through a thin tube. Also called intraperitoneal infusion.

Peritoneal perfusion A method of delivering fluids and drugs directly to tumors in the peritoneal cavity.

Peritoneum The tissue that lines the abdominal wall and covers most of the organs in the abdomen.

Peritonitis Inflammation of the peritoneum (tissue that lines the abdominal wall and covers most of the organs in the abdomen). Peritonitis can result from infection, injury, or certain diseases. Symptoms may include swelling of the abdomen, severe pain, and weight loss.

Periurethral bulking injections A surgical procedure in which injected implants are used to "bulk up" the area around the neck of the bladder allowing it to resist increases in abdominal pressure which can push down on the bladder and cause leakage.

Permanent section Preparation of tissue for microscopic examination. The tissue is soaked for up to 12 hours in formaldehyde, processed in various chemicals overnight, then sliced very thin and stained. It provides clear definition of the specimen so that the presence or absence of cancer can be determined.

Permanent teeth (usually) Thirty-two adult teeth in a complete dentition.

Permeability The ability of a body to pass a fluid under pressure.

Permeate In reverse osmosis, the water that diffuses through the membrane, thereby becoming purified water.

Permissible exposure limit (PEL) The maximum permitted eight-hour time-weighted average concen-tration of an airborne contaminant.

Permissions or privileges Security codes that define or restrict which users can read, write, and execute the associated files, directories, or programs. Some departments need to look only at data, some need to input data or run programs, and others may not need to look at the data at all.

Pernicious anemia A type of anemia (low red blood cell count) caused by the body's inability to absorb vitamin B12.

Peroneal artery (fibular artery) Originates from the posterior tibial artery and branches into the superficial epigastric, superficial circumflex iliac, external pudendal, deep femoral, and descending geniculate arteries.

Peroxisome Very small membrane-bound particles responsible for photorespiration in plants. Similar to lysosome in structure, but not in function.

Perpendicular plate of ethmoid The thin bony plate that projects off the inferior surface of the cribriform plate of the ethmoid bone that helps form the nasal septum.

Persistent generalized lymphadenopathy (PGL) Chronic and persistent swollen lymph nodes in at least two areas of the body for at least three months. PGL occurs in people with persistent bacterial, viral, or fungal infections, and in individuals with weakened immune systems, including people with HIV.

Personal development plan (PDP) A list of educational needs, development goals and actions and processes, compiled by learners and used in systematic management and periodic reviews of learning. It is an integral part of reflective practice and self-directed learning for professionals. It can be equally valuable in teacher-directed medical training for maintaining learner-centered approaches and shared objectives. PDP can be used to manage learning needs systematically, to set development and performance improvement goals, organize learning activities and review outcomes. Some educational organizations accept completed plans for accredited professional development and health managers link them with appraisals.

Perturbation A disruption or disturbance.

Pertuzumab A humanized recombinant monoclonal antibody directed against the extracellular dimerization domain of the HER-2 tyrosine kinase receptor. Binding of the antibody to the dimerization domain of the HER-2 tyrosine kinase receptor protein directly inhibits the ability of the HER-2 tyrosine kinase receptor protein (the most common pairing partner) to dimerize with other HER tyrosine kinase receptor proteins; inhibiting receptor protein dimerization prevents the activation of HER signaling pathways, resulting in tumor cell apoptosis.

Pes hippocampi The enlarged anterior foot-like part of the hippocampus located in the floor of the inferior horn of the lateral ventricle.

Pesticide A chemical that is used to kill insects and other pests.

PET scan (Positron emission tomography scan) A procedure in which a small amount of radioactive glucose (sugar) is injected into a vein, and a scanner is used to make detailed, computerized pictures of areas inside the body where the glucose is used. Because cancer cells often use more glucose than normal cells, the pictures can be used to find cancer cells in the body.

Petechia A pinpoint, non-raised, purpiish-red spot caused by intradermal or subcutaneous hemorrhage. Plural is petechiae. These are tell-tale symptoms of Ebola and Lassa Fevers.

Petechiae Tiny areas of bleeding under the skin, usually caused by a low platelet count.

Petrolatum White petrolatum is a purified mixture of semi-solid hydrocarbons obtained from petroleum. It is a common base or carrier for ointments. It can be sterile filtered at elevated temperatures.

Petrous pyramid A pyramid of dense bone within the temporal bone, located at the base of the cranium, and housing the hearing and vestibular sensory structures.

Petrous ridge The lateral division between the middle and posterior cranial fossae, oriented at about 45 degrees between sagittal and coronal in the axial plane.

Peutz jeghers syndrome (PJS) A genetic disorder in which polyps form in the intestine and dark spots appear on the mouth and fingers. Having PJS increases the risk of developing gastrointestinal and many other types of cancer.

Peyer's patches Ovoid, elevated patches of closely packed lymphoid follicles in the mucosa and submucosa of the small intestine. Also called aggregated lymphoid follicles.

PH The pH value of an aqueous solution is a number describing its acidity or alkalinity. A pH is the negative logarithm (base 10) of the concentration of hydrogen ions (equivalent per liter). The pH value of a neutral solution is 7. An acidic solution has a pH less than 7, while a basic solution has a pH greater than 7, up to 14.

Phage (suffix) Eat; devour, e.g. macrophage - a cell which devours (phagocytoses).

Phago Eat; devour, e.g. phagocyte - any cell that ingests foreign material, other cells or microorganisms.

Phagocystosis The consumption and destruction of foreign materials by white blood cells like macrophages

Phagocyte A cell that engulfs foreign particles from its surroundings by a process called phagocytosis. The cell releases hydrolytic enzymes from intracellular bodies called lysosomes that partially digest the foreign particle, after which it is further degraded in the phagocyte cytoplasm.

Phalanges The small tubular bones of the fingers and toes.

Phantom limb pain The sensation of pain or other unpleasant feelings in the place of a missing (phantom) limb.

Pharmaceutical A medicinal drug, or relating to or engaged in pharmacy or the manufacture and sale of pharmaceuticals. A pharmaceutical product is generally one that is made up using available chemical compounds.

Pharmaceutical area A general manufacturing area classification designated by the need for a change of clothing (e.g., Packing Hall).

Pharmacist A professional who fills prescriptions, and in the case of a compounding pharmacist, makes them. Pharmacists are familiar with medication ingredients, interactions, cautions, and hints.

Pharmacogenomics The study of the interaction of an individual's genetic makeup and response to a drug.

Pharmacokinetics The interaction of a drug with the body over a period of time. General pharmacokinetic processes are absorption, distribution, metabolism, and excretion. These processes are usually measured through blood and urine samples.

Pharmacology The branch of medical science that studies the chemistry, effects, and uses of drugs. Pharmacology includes the study of a drug's therapeutic value, toxicology, and interaction with the body (pharmacokinetics).

Pharmacopoeia A book describing chemicals, drugs, and other substances and how they are used as medicines. It is prepared by a recognized authority.

Pharyngeal cancer Cancer that forms in tissues of the pharynx (the hollow tube inside the neck that starts behind the nose and ends at the top of the windpipe and esophagus). Pharyngeal cancer includes cancer of the nasopharynx (the upper part of the throat behind the nose), the oropharynx (the middle part of the pharynx), and the hypopharynx (the bottom part of the pharynx). Most pharyngeal cancers are squamous cell carcinomas (cancer that begins in flat cells lining the pharynx). Also called throat cancer.

Pharyngeal recess A lateral extension in the wall of the nasopharynx that is situated cranial and dorsal to the pharyngeal orifice of the auditory (Eustachian) tube.

Pharynx The hollow tube inside the neck that starts behind the nose and ends at the top of the trachea (windpipe) and esophagus (the tube that goes to the stomach). The pharynx is about 5 inches long, depending on body size. Also called the throat.

Phase I detoxification A process in which the liver uses one of two major enzyme pathways to change a toxic substance, such as an anticancer drug, into a less toxic substance that is easier for the body to excrete.

Phase I trial The first step in testing a new treatment in humans. These studies test the best way to give a new treatment (for example, by mouth, intravenous infusion, or injection) and the best dose. The dose is usually increased a little at a time in order to find the highest dose that does not cause harmful side effects. Because little is known about the possible risks and benefits of the treatments being tested, phase I trials usually include only a small number of patients who have not been helped by other treatments.

Phase II detoxification A process in which the liver uses one of two major enzyme pathways to change a toxic substance, such as an anticancer drug, into a less toxic substance that is easier for the body to excrete. In phase II detoxification, liver cells add a substance (such as cysteine, glycine, or a sulfur molecule) to a toxic chemical or drug, to make it less harmful.

Phase II trial The second stage in testing a new drug in humans. Performed as part of an approved Investigational New Drug Application under Food and Drug Administration guidelines. Generally carried out on patients with the disease or condition of interest. The main purpose is to evaluate activity, and possibly provide preliminary information on treatment efficacy and to supplement information on safety obtained from phase I trials. Usually, but not always, designed to include a control treatment and random allocation of patients to treatment.

Phase III trial The third and usually final stage in testing a new drug in humans. Performed as part of an approved Investigational New Drug Application under Food and Drug Administration guidelines. Concerned primarily with assessment of dosage effects and efficacy and safety. Usually designed to include a control treatment and random allocation to treatment. Once this phase is completed the drug manufacturers may request permission to market the drug by submission of a New Drug Application to the Food and Drug Administration, assuming the results of the phase I, II and III trials are consistent with such a request.

Phase IV trials Clinical studies that occur after a drug has been approved to determine long-term safety and effectiveness. They are sometimes referred to as "post-marketing studies." This trial phase recruits the largest population of patients to gain additional information about the drug's risks, benefits, and optimal use.

Phasic Fast, jump movement.

Phenobarbital A drug that is used to treat seizures and as a sedative. It is being studied in the treatment of diarrhea and for its ability to increase the antitumor effect of other therapies. It belongs to the family of drugs called barbiturates.

Phenocopy A trait not caused by inheritance of a gene but appears to be identical to a genetic trait.

Phenol An organic acid often used as a disinfectant. Proper strength for a bacteriocidal preparation is 5%. Sometimes dispersed as an aerosol "fog" in manufacturing rooms.

Phenotype The physical characteristics of an organism or the presence of a disease that may or may not be genetic.

Phenotypic assay A laboratory test that determines by direct experiment whether a particular strain of HIV is resistant to anti-HIV drugs. This is different from a genotypic assay, which uses an indirect method to find out if a particular strain of HIV has specific genetic mutations that are associated with drug resistance.

Phenoxodiol A synthetic flavonoid derivative. Phenoxodiol activates the mitochondrial caspase system, inhibits X-linked inhibitor of apoptosis (XIAP), and disrupts FLICE inhibitory protein (FLIP) expression, resulting in tumor cell apoptosis. This agent also inhibits DNA topoisomerase II by stabilizing the cleavable complex, thereby preventing DNA replication and resulting in tumor cell death.

Phentolamine mesylate The mesylate salt of a synthetic imidazoline with alpha-adrenergic antagonist activity. As a competitive alpha-adrenergic antagonist, phentolamine binds to alpha-1 and alpha-2 receptors, resulting in a decrease in peripheral vascular resistance and vasodilatation. This agent also may block 5-hydroxytryptamine (5-HT) receptors and stimulate release of histamine from mast cells.

Phenylacetate A substance that is being studied in the treatment of cancer.

Phenylbutyrate An orally active derivative of the short-chain fatty acid butyrate with potential antineoplastic activity. 4-Phenylbutyrate inhibits histone deacetylase, resulting in cell cycle gene expression modulation, reduced cell proliferation, increased cell differentiation, and apoptosis. This agent also initiates fragmentation of genomic DNA, resulting in decreased DNA synthesis and the inhibition of tumor cell migration and invasion.

Phenylketonuria (PKU) An inherited disorder that causes a build-up of phenylalanine (an amino acid) in the blood. This can cause mental retardation, behavioral and movement problems, seizures, and delayed development. Using a blood test, PKU can easily be found in newborns, and treatment is a diet low in phenylalanine.

Pheochromocytoma A tumor of the adrenal gland that causes it to produce too much adrenaline. Pheochromocytomas are usually benign (noncancerous), but can cause dangerously high blood pressure and other symptoms, including pounding headaches, heart palpitations, flushing of the face, nausea, and vomiting.

Pheresis A procedure in which blood is collected, part of the blood such as platelets or white blood cells is taken out, and the rest of the blood is returned to the donor. Also called apheresis.

Philadelphia chromosome An abnormality of chromosome 22 in which part of chromosome 9 is transferred to it. Bone marrow cells that contain the Philadelphia chromosome are often found in chronic myelogenous leukemia.

Philosophical Having to do with the deeper questions of life and with a person's basic beliefs, ideas, and attitudes.

Phleb Vein, e.g. phlebitis - inflammation of the vein.

Phlebitis A painful inflammation of the veins.

Phlebotomy The puncture of a vein with a needle for the purpose of drawing blood. Also called venipuncture.

Phlegm (Obsolete word, no longer used) Thick, gluey, stringy mucus secreted in the respiratory passages as a result of inflammation, irritation or infection of the airways, and discharged through the mouth. (Often synonymous with mucus)

Phospholipid A lipid (fat) that contains phosphorus. Phospholipids are a major part of cell membranes.

Phospholipid complex A chemical or drug that is attached to a lipid (fat) that contains phosphorus.

Phosphorus A nonmetallic element that is found in the blood, muscles, nerves, bones, and teeth and is a component of adenosine triphosphate (ATP; the primary energy source for the body's cells).

Phosphorus P32 A radioactive isotope of phosphorus with beta particle-emitting radiocytotoxic activity. Emitted by phosphorus-32, beta particles directly damage cellular DNA and, by ionizing intracellular water to produce several types of cytotoxic free radicals and superoxides, indirectly damage intracellular biological macromolecules, resulting in tumor cell death.

Phosphorylation The process of adding phosphorus to a

compound. Often done within the body by enzymes named "kinases". The nucleoside drugs, like AZT, ddI, ddC, etc. all need to be phosphorylated in the body before they become active.

Photo oxidation The mechanism by which ultraviolet light reduces Total Organic Carbon (TOC) to Carbon Dioxide. If halogenated organics are present, both CO_2 and mineral acids can be formed.

Photoactivity The effect produced when certain substances are exposed to light. In cancer treatment, some drugs become active when exposed to light and are then able to kill tumor cells.

Photoautotrophs Facultative autotrophs that obtain their energy from light.

Photocoagulation Using a special strong beam of light (laser) to seal off bleeding blood vessels such as in the eye. The laser can also burn away blood vessels that should not have grown in the eye. This is the main treatment for diabetic retinopathy.

Photodynamic therapy Treatment with drugs that become active when exposed to light. These drugs kill cancer cells.

Photofrin A drug used to treat some types of cancer. When absorbed by cancer cells and exposed to light, porfimer sodium becomes active and kills the cancer cells. It belongs to the family of drugs called photodynamic therapy agents. Also called porfimer sodium.

Photoluminescent The property of emitting light as the result of absorption of visible or invisible light, which continues for a length of time after excitation.

Photopheresis A procedure in which blood is removed from the body and treated with ultraviolet light and drugs that become active when exposed to light. The blood is then returned to the body. It is being studied in the treatment of some blood and bone marrow diseases and graft-vs-host disease (GVHD). Also called extracorporeal photopheresis.

Photophobia A condition in which the eyes are more sensitive than normal to light.

Photosensitivity Increased sensitivity of skin to sunlight or ultraviolet light. Photosensitivity commonly causes reddening and blistering of the skin and in time increases a person's risk of skin cancer. Photosensitivity may occur as a side effect of some drugs or as a result of HIV infection.

Photosensitizer A drug used in photodynamic therapy. When absorbed by cancer cells and exposed to light, the drug becomes active and kills the cancer cells. Also called photosensitizing agent.

Photosensitizing agent A drug used in photodynamic therapy. When absorbed by cancer cells and exposed to light, the drug becomes active and kills the cancer cells. Also called photosensitizer.

Phthisis/phthisical Phthisis and Phthisical refers to an eye that has shrunk down due to loss of its fluid. This is an acquired condition that is caused by a disease, trauma or possibly surgery. (Acquired condition would indicate that you had a normal size eye prior to this event.) Also, if the globe is Microphthalmic, it would indicate that it is a congenital problem. It never developed to full size.

Phycomycetes Algalike fungi that do not posses chlorophyll and cannot photosynthesize. Aquatic and terrestrial molds belong to this category.

Phyllodes tumor A type of tumor found in breast tissue. It is often large and bulky and grows quickly. It is usually benign (not cancer), but may be malignant (cancer). Also called cystosarcoma phyllodes.

Physical barrier Any equipment, facilities, or devices, (e.g., fermentors, factories, filters, thermal oxidizers) that are designed to achieve containment.

Physical examination An exam of the body to check for general signs of disease.

Physical hazard A classification of a chemical for which there is scientifically valid evidence that it is a combustible liquid, compressed gas, cryogenic, explosive, flammable gas, flammable liquid, flammable solid, organic peroxide, oxidizer, pyrophoric, unstable, (reactive), or water-reactive material.

Physical manipulation A process other than a chemical reaction that may change the purity of the physical properties of the material, including but not limited to, crystallization, recrystallization, gel filtration, chromatography, milling, drying, or blending.

Physical map A map of the locations of identifiable landmarks on DNA (e.g., restriction enzyme cutting sites, genes), regardless of inheritance. Distance is measured in base pairs. For the human genome, the lowest-resolution physical map is the banding patterns on the 24 different chromosomes; the highest resolution map would be the complete nucleotide sequence of the chromosomes.

Physical therapist A health professional who teaches exercises and physical activities that help condition muscles and restore strength and movement.

Physical therapy The use of exercises and physical activities to help condition muscles and restore strength and movement. For example, physical therapy can be used to restore arm and shoulder movement and build back strength after breast cancer surgery.

Physician A professional, qualified by education and authorized by law to practice medicine. The essence of being a professional is an ability to find solutions to difficult problems for which there are no easily discovered answers and to effectively handle medical situations where no two patients are identical even if they have the same condition. This differentiates the professional, who must deal with complex problems that tend not to have unambiguous, clear-cut solutions, from the technician.

Physician attestation The requirement that the attending physician certify, in writing, the accuracy and completion of the clinical information used for assignment.

Physician organization This term describes physician linkages and alliances that allow physicians to manage risk and capitation. Information systems, physician relationships, and financial integration allow these organizations to be more integrated than the traditional solo practice or IPA relationship between healthcare providers and/or managed care organizations that are working to develop a "seamless" continuum of healthcare services. Sometimes physician organizations are simply group practices or professional organizations without intention of acting as a contracting entity.

Physiologic Having to do with the functions of the body. When used in the phrase "physiologic age," it refers to an age assigned by general health, as opposed to calendar age.

Physiological diplopia A normal diplopia (double vision) that occurs when an individual is not pointing his/her eyes on a certain object.

Physis (growth plate) The portion of long bones concerned with growth in length.

Phytic acid A substance found in many foods that come from plants, including corn, wheat, rice, and soybeans, and in large amounts in cereals and legumes. It is being studied in the prevention of cancer. Also called inositol hexaphosphate (IP6).

Phytochemical A substance found in plants. Some phytochemicals may reduce the risk of cancer.

Phytoestrogen An estrogen-like substance found in some plants and plant products. Phytoestrogens may have anticancer effects.

Phytophotodermatitis An eruption of large blisters occurring after exposure to light in people who have been in contact with certain plants, such as wild parsnip, to which they are sensitive.

Phytosterol A plant-based compound that can compete with dietary cholesterol to be absorbed by the intestines, resulting in lower blood cholesterol levels. Phytosterols may have some effect in cancer prevention. Also called plant sterol.

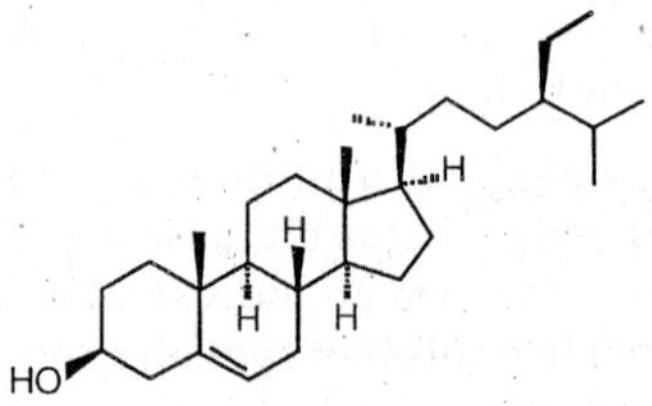

β-sitosterol
Figure Phytosterol

PI 88 A sulfated oligosaccharide. PI-88 inhibits heparanase activity and heparan sulfate binding to fibroblast growth factor (FGF) and vascular endothelial growth factor (VEGF), resulting in decreased tumor proliferation, inhibition of angiogenesis, and inhibition of metastasis.

Pia mater The innermost of the three meninges investing the brain and spinal cord. It is a delicate vascular connective tissue membrane that is closely adherent to the neural surface. Together with the arachnoid comprises the leptomeninges.

Pickle An acid or other chemical solution used as a bath to remove scale and oxides from the surface of metals before plating or finishing.

Pico Prefix meaning a one one-trillionth, as in picogram, a trillionth of a gram.

Picoplatin A new generation organic platinum analog with an extended spectrum of antineoplastic activity. Designed to overcome platinum drug resistance, picoplatin alkylates DNA, forming both inter- and intra-strand cross-linkages, resulting in inhibition of DNA replication and transcription, and the induction of apoptosis.

Pigment A class of substances that provide color, including in the human body. The areola and nipple of the breast are pigmented with melanin. Normally a brownish tint, melanin in these areas of the breast can range from pale pink to deep brown.

Pigment incontinence The deposition of melanin in the dermis, which when not in association with a pigmented lesion implies prior basal layer damage.

Pill burden The number and schedule of pills taken each day in a particular anti-HIV drug regimen. A high pill burden may lead to decreased treatment adherence because of the difficulty of taking a large number of pills properly.

Pilocarpine A drug used to increase salivation in people who have dry mouth caused by opioids or radiation therapy. Pilocarpine belongs to the family of drugs called alkaloids.

Pilocytic Made up of cells that look like fibers when viewed under a microscope.

Pilot study A preliminary study designed to indicate whether a larger study is practical.

PIN (Prostatic intraepithelial neoplasia) Noncancerous growth of cells lining the internal and external surfaces of the prostate gland. Having high-grade PIN may increase the risk of developing prostate cancer.

Pineal body A tiny organ in the cerebrum that produces melatonin. Also called pineal gland or pineal organ.

Pineal gland A small cone-shaped component of the epithalamus attached in the midline by a stalk to the dorsocaudal 3rd ventricle. Also known as the epiphysis cerebri. This endocrine organ secretes serotonin and melatonin in sync with light cycles. Prior to puberty the pineal exerts an inhibitory influence of the reproductive system. After the age of 16 the gland becomes infiltrated with calcareous material which renders it a useful landmark for determining the presence of space-occupying intracranial masses in radiographs.

Pineal region tumorA type of brain tumor that occurs in or around the pineal gland, a tiny organ near the center of the brain.

Pineocytoma A slow growing type of brain tumor that occurs in or around the pineal gland, a tiny organ near the center of the brain.

Pink puffer Term describing the COPD or emphysematic patient whose symptoms are breathlessness, hyperinflation, mild hypoxemia and a low PCO_2.

Pinkeye A condition in which the conjunctiva (membranes lining the eyelids and covering the white part of the eye) become inflamed or infected. Also called conjunctivitis.

Pinna The projecting part of the ear; also known as the auricle.

Pinocytosis Ingestion of liquid or very small particles by vesicle formation in a cell.

PioglitazoneA drug that is used to treat type 2 diabetes and is being studied in the prevention of head and neck cancer. It may be able to stop leukoplakia (a precancerous condition affecting the mouth) from developing into cancer. It belongs to the family of drugs called thiazolidinediones. Also called Actos.

Pioglitazone hydrochloride The hydrochloride salt of an orally-active thiazolidinedione with antidiabetic properties and potential antineoplastic activity. Pioglitazone activates peroxisome proliferator-activated receptor gamma (PPAR-gamma), a ligand-activated transcription factor, thereby inducing cell differentiation and inhibiting cell growth and angiogenesis. This agent also modulates the transcription of insulin-responsive genes, inhibits macrophage and monocyte activation, and stimulates adipocyte differentiation.

Pipe A pressure-tight cylinder used to convey a fluid or to transmit a fluid pressure ordinarily designated "pipe" in applicable material specifications. Materials designated "tube" or "tubing" in

the specifications are treated as pipe when intended for pressure service. Types of pipe, according to the method of manufacture, are:
1. Electric resistance-welded pipe (ERW)

2. Furnace butt welded pipe, continuous welded

3. Electric-fusion welded pipe

4. Double submerged-arc welded pipe

5. Seamless pipe

6. Spiral welded pipe.

Pipe size Pipe size is determined by diameter and schedule. For bioprocessing equipment, pipe does not include tube.

Piperacillin-tazobactam A drug combination that is used to treat infection in people with cancer. Piperacillin is a synthetic penicillin; tazobactam enhances the effectiveness of piperacillin.

Piperine extract (standardized) A standardized extract containing the active alkaloid piperine, derived from the fruit of the plant Piper nigrum (black pepper) and/ or the plant Piper longum L. (long pepper), with thermogenic properties. Co-ingestion of piperidine enhances the bioavailability of various nutrients, including beta-carotene, curcumin, selenium, pyridoxine and coenzyme Q10. In addition, this agent may exert anti-inflammatory and anti-tumor activities and may enhance the production of serotonin.

Pirfenidone An orally active synthetic antifibrotic agent structurally similar to pyridine 2,4-dicarboxylate. Pirfenidone inhibits fibroblast, epidermal, platelet-derived, and transforming beta-1 growth factors, thereby slowing tumor cell proliferation. This agent also inhibits DNA synthesis and the production of mRNA for collagen types I and III, resulting in a reduction in radiation-induced fibrosis.

Piriform sinus Fossa in the wall of the laryngeal pharynx that is lateral to the arytenoid cartilage and medial to the thyroid cartilage.

PiritreximA substance that is being studied in the treatment of cancer. It belongs to the family of drugs called folate antagonists.

Pit A small surface void resulting from a localized loss of base metal by corrosion or etching, or by the removal of surface inclusions during electropolishing or passivation. A pit may or may not be detectable during liquid penetrant inspection.

Pitch To cause to be set at a particular angle or slope. Degree of slope or elevation.

Pituitary An endocrine organ located at the base of the skull in the sella turcica ("turkish saddle"), and connected to the hypothalamus by a thin stalk.

Pituitary Adenoma

Pituitary Adenoma.

Pituitary gland An endocrine gland in the small, bony cavity at the base of the brain. Often called "the master gland," the pituitary serves the body in many ways-in growth, in food use, and in reproduction.

Pituitary tumor A tumor that forms in the pituitary gland. The pituitary is a pea-sized organ in the center of the brain above the back of the nose. It makes hormones that affect other glands and many body functions, especially growth. Most pituitary tumors are benign (not cancer).

Pityrosporum A genus of yeast, producing superficial infection of the skin.

Pixantrone A synthetic noncardiotoxic aza-anthracenedione analogue. Pixantrone intercalates into DNA and induces topoisomerase II-mediated DNA strand crosslinks, resulting in inhibition of DNA replication and tumor cell cytotoxicity.

PKC (Protein kinase C) An enzyme found throughout the body's tissues and organs. Several forms of PKC are involved in many cellular functions. PKC is being studied in the treatment of cancer.

PKC412 A synthetic indolocarbazole protein kinase C (PKC) inhibitor. As a nonspecific inhibitor of protein kinase C enzymes, midostaurin inhibits oncogenic PKC signal transduction pathways involved in the regulation of the cell cycle in tumor cells, thereby initiating tumor cell apoptosis.

Placebo controlled Refers to a clinical study in which the control patients receive a placebo.

Placebo controlled study A study that identifies the true effect of a treatment by comparing results in patients taking the actual treatment to those in patients taking an inactive look-alike, or placebo, treatment.

Placebo effect The effect produced by a placebo due to the expectations of the patient. The effect in placebo-controlled clinical trials is generally measured by comparison of the effect observed in patients receiving the placebo treatment with the effect observed in patients receiving the active treatment.

Placebo Sometimes called a "sugar pill." A pill or other treatment that looks like the treatment being tested in a clinical trial but does not actually contain the active ingredient. Placebos are used in some clinical trials to control for what is called the "placebo effect": an effect that is caused by the power of suggestion alone. The effects of the placebo are then compared to the effects of the active ingredient to determine if the ingredient is truly effective.

Placebo-controlled clinical trial A clinical trial in which patients assigned to the control treatment receive a placebo.

Placenta A combination of fetal and maternal cells that serves as the organ of exchange for nutrients and other chemicals between mother and fetus during pregnancy.

Placental blood transplantation The transfer of blood from a placenta to an individual whose own blood production system is suppressed. Placental blood contains high levels of stem cells needed to produce new blood cells. It is being studied in the treatment of cancer and severe blood disorders such as aplastic anemia. Also called umbilical cord blood transplant.

Placentomegaly Abnormal thickening of the placenta.

Plankton Those microorganisms that are passively floating or drifting in a body of water.

Plano lens A lens that has no prescription. No variance between the curvature of the front and back lens surfaces. It is a flat lens.

Plaque A clear zone in a bacterial culture grown on an agar plate caused by localized destruction of bacterial cells by a bacteriophage. Applying the fluid to a culture and counting the number of plaques formed can estimate the concentration of infective virus in a fluid.

Plasia (suffix) To form, e.g. hyperplasia - an increase in the number of cells in a tissue or organ, usually as a physiologic response to a stimulus.

Plasma The liquid portion of blood in which the cellular elements are suspended. As a fresh liquid obtained by centrifugation, plasma is a clear, amber-coloured solution containing eight to nine percent solids; of these, 85 percent are proteins while the other components are the lipids, which include the neutral fats, fatty acids, lecithin, and cholesterol. Also present are sodium, chloride and bicarbonate, potassium, calcium and magnesium. A most essential function of plasma is the maintenance of blood pressure and the exchange with tissue of nutrients for waste. Contains fibrinogen.

Plasma cell A cell derived from a B-lymphocyte and solely responsible for the production of antibodies. Each plasma cell forms only one type of antibody and is characterized by an eccentric nucleus, a prominent Golgi zone, bulky basophilic cytoplasm (due to an extensive endoplasmic reticulum) and large numbers of mitochondria.

Plasma cell myeloma A type of cancer that begins in plasma cells (white blood cells that produce antibodies). Also called multiple myeloma, Kahler's disease, or myelomatosis.

Plasma cell tumor A tumor that begins in plasma cells (white blood cells that produce antibodies). Multiple myeloma, monoclonal gammopathy of undetermined significance (MGUS), and plasmacytoma are types of plasma cell tumors.

Plasma membrane The physical barrier that surrounds the

cytoplasm of all cells. It is composed of lipid, protein, and carbohydrate and is semi-permeable.

Plasma proteins The proteins found in plasma, usually divided into albumin, globulin and fibrinogen fractions.

Plasmacytic Having to do with plasma cells (a type of white blood cells).

Plasmacytoma A type of cancer that begins in plasma cells (white blood cells that produce antibodies). A plasmacytoma may turn into multiple myeloma.

Plasmapheresis The process of separating certain cells from the plasma in the blood by a machine; only the cells are returned to the person. Plasmapheresis can be used to remove excess antibodies from the blood.

Plasmid Autonomously replicating extra-chromosomal circular DNA molecules, distinct from the normal bacterial genome and nonessential for cell survival under nonselective conditions. Some plasmids are capable of integrating into the host genome. A number of artificially constructed plasmids are used as cloning vectors.

Plastics High molecular weight polymers or copolymers. The wide range in physical properties of polymeric materials allows for utilization as elastomers, fibers, adhesives, rigid castings, composites, and laminates. ASTM D883 defines a plastic as a material that contains as an essential ingredient, one or more organic polymeric substances of large molecular weight, is solid in its finished state, and, at some stage in its manufacture into finished articles, can be shaped by flow. Plastics, or more appropriately polymers, are composed primarily of carbon, hydrogen, oxygen, silicon, chlorine, fluorine, and nitrogen, in various combinations and permutations. Plastics are grouped into two categories: 1. Thermoplastics: can be melted, cooled and remelted without destroying the physical or mechanical characteristics of the polymer. This property permits components to be molded or extruded. Thermoplastic polymers include: Chlorinated Vinyls, Fluorinated plastics, Ketone, Nitrile, Nylon, Polyamide-imide, Polyolefin, Polycarbonate, and Acrylonitrile butadiene styrene (ABS).

2. Thermosets: begin as a liquid or powder that through chemical reaction with a second reactant or through catalyzed polymerization result in anew product with characteristics different from either starting material. Thermoset resins include: Epoxy, Phenolic, Polyurethane, Silicone, Urea and Melamine, Polyester, Vinyl ester, Furan, Bisphenol A fumarate.

Plastic surgeon A surgeon who specializes in reducing scarring or disfigurement that may occur as a result of accidents, birth defects, or treatment for diseases.

Plastic surgery An operation that restores or improves the appearance of body structures.

Platelet count The number of platelets in a blood sample.

Platelets A type of cell in the blood responsible for clotting. When blood vessels are damaged, platelets help to form a plug that prevents the loss of blood.

Platinol AQ Other name for cisplatin.

Platinum A metal that is an important component of some anticancer drugs, such as cisplatin and carboplatin.

Pleiotropy One gene that causes many different physical traits such as multiple disease symptoms.

Plena The plural of plenum.

Plenaxis A drug used to reduce the amount of testosterone made in patients with advanced symptomatic prostate cancer for which no other treatment options are available. It belongs to the family of drugs called gonadotropin-releasing hormone (GnRH) antagonists. Also called abarelix.

Plenum An enclosure in which air or other gas is at a pressure greater than that outside the enclosure.

Pleomorphic Occurring in various distinct forms. In terms of cells, having variation in the size and shape of cells or their nuclei.

Pleomorphism The variation in the appearance of the nuclei of the same cell type. If pronounced and associated with large, irregular, hyperchromatic nuclei it is termed anaplasia and is often an indication of malignancy.

Pleoptics A method of eye exercises created to stimulate and train an amblyopic eye. The goal is to have eyesight which is produced by the fovea.

Plethysmography or body box An airtight chamber with clear doors where you sit to have your lung volumes measured. Breathing is accomplished through a mouthpiece.

Pleura (Ploor a) A thin layer of tissue covering the lungs and lining the interior wall of the chest cavity. It protects and cushions the lungs. This tissue secretes a small amount of fluid that acts as a lubricant, allowing the lungs to move smoothly in the chest cavity while breathing.

Pleural cavity The space enclosed by the pleura, which is a thin layer of tissue that covers the lungs and lines the interior wall of the chest cavity.

Pleural effusion An abnormal collection of fluid between the thin layers of tissue (pleura) lining the lung and the wall of the chest cavity.

Pleural space The fluid-filled "space" between the two pleural walls (visceral and parietal pleura).

Pleurisy Inflammation of the pleura with or without diffusion of an exudate into the pleural cavity

Pleurodesis A medical procedure that uses chemicals or drugs to cause inflammation and adhesion between the layers of the pleura (the tissue that covers the lungs and lines the interior wall of the chest cavity). This prevents the buildup of fluid in the pleural cavity. It is used as a treatment for severe pleural effusion.

Pleuropneumonia A specific infectious disease in cattle characterized by inflammation of the lung and pleura, generally called contagious pleuropneumonia. It is due to a virus.

Pleuropulmonary blastoma A rare and very aggressive (fast-growing) cancer that forms in tissues of the lung and pleura (a thin layer of tissue covering the lungs and the inside wall of the chest cavity). Pleuropulmonary blastoma is most common in children.

Plexiform neurofibroma A nerve that has become thick and misshapen due to the abnormal growth of cells and tissues that cover the nerve.

Plexopathy A disorder affecting a network of nerves, blood vessels, or lymph vessels.

PLL (Prolymphocytic leukemia) A type of chronic lymphocytic leukemia (CLL) in which too many immature white blood cells (prolymphocytes) are found in the blood and bone marrow. PLL usually progresses more rapidly than classic CLL.

Ploidy A measure of the amount of DNA contained in a cell. Ploidy is a characteristic (marker) that helps determine how cancerous a tumor's cells are, compared with healthy cells. Most cancer cells are aneuploid (an'-u-ploid), which means there is an abnormal amount of DNA in them.

Plummer Vinson syndrome A disorder marked by anemia caused by iron deficiency, and a web-like growth of membranes in the throat that makes swallowing difficult. Having Plummer-Vinson syndrome may increase the risk of developing esophageal cancer. Also called Paterson-Kelly syndrome and sideropenic dysphagia.

Pluripotency The potential of a cell to develop into more than one type of mature cell, depending on environment.

Pluripotent Able to mature or develop in any of several ways.

Pluripotent stem cell A cell that is able to develop into several different types of cells or tissues in the body.

Plus (+) lens Convex lens (thicker in the middle) relaxes focusing and converges light. It is typically used in glasses or contact lenses for people who are farsighted (hyperopic). Although it may also be prescribed for other visual conditions as well.

PM 81 A monoclonal antibody that is being studied in the detection and treatment of cancer. Monoclonal antibodies are produced in the laboratory and can locate and bind to cancer cells.

PN401 A substance that is being studied for its ability to protect against the gastrointestinal side effects caused by fluorouracil. Also called triacctyluridine. It belongs to the family of drugs called cytoprotective agents.

Pnea (suffix) Breath, e.g. dyspnea - labored or difficult breathing.

Pneumatic larynx A device that is used to help a person talk after a laryngectomy. It uses air to produce a humming sound, which is converted to speech by movement of the lips, tongue, or glottis.

Pneumocystis carinii pneumonia An opportunistic pneumonitis often seen in HIV-infected patients. PCP generally produces a dry, hacking cough. Although previously thought to be a protozoa, and responsive to anti-protozoal treatment, recent genetic analysis suggest that p carinii is closer to the funguses.

Pneumocystis jiroveci A type of fungus that can cause severe pneumonia in humans, particularly in people with weakened immune systems and especially common in people with AIDS. P. jiroveci is related to P. carinii, the species for which PCP (pneumocystis carinii pneumonia) is named.

Pneumocystis jiroveci pneumonia (PCP) A lung infection caused by Pneumocystis jiroveci, a fungus related to Pneumocystis carinii (the species for which PCP was originally named). PCP occurs in people with weakened immune systems, including people with HIV. It is considered an AIDS-defining condition in HIV-infected individuals. The first signs of infection are difficulty breathing, high fever, and dry cough.

Pneumonectomy An operation to remove an entire lung.

Pneumonia An inflammatory infection that occurs in the lung.

Pneumothorax (PTX) Presence of air in the pleural cavity, caused by by rupture of the plural membrane or by trauma through the chest wall; often referred to as a collapsed lung. Compare to Spontaneous Pneumothorax

Pngvl4a sig/E7 (detox)/HSP70 DNA vaccine An antigen-specific DNA cancer vaccine consisting of the coding sequences of a signal peptide (pNGVL4a-Sig), a detox form of the human papillomavirus type 16 (HPV-16) antigen E7, and the heat shock protein 70 (HSP70). Upon administration, this vaccine may generate potent cytotoxic CD8 (+) T-cell responses against E7-expressing tumor cells, resulting in tumor cell death.

PNU 166148 A substance that is being studied in the treatment of cancer. It belongs to the family of drugs called topoisomerase inhibitors.

PNU-93914 A form of the anticancer drug paclitaxel that may have fewer side effects and work better than paclitaxel. It is being studied in the treatment of cancer. It belongs to the family of drugs called mitotic inhibitors. Also called LEP-ETU and paclitaxel liposome.

PO Abbreviation for "by mouth" (as opposed to Intravenous, intramuscular, etc.).

Podiatrist A doctor who treats and takes care of people's feet.

Podiatry The care and treatment of human feet in health and disease.

Point of service plan (POS) A health services delivery organization that offers the option to its members to choose to receive a service from participating or a nonparticipating provider. Generally the level of coverage is reduced for services associated with the use of non-participating providers. Managed care plan that specifies that those patients who go outside of the plan for services may pay more out of pocket expenses. A health insurance benefits program in which subscribers can select between different delivery systems when in need of health care services and at the time of accessing the services, rather than making the selection between delivery systems at time of open enrollment at place of employment. Typically, the costs associated with receiving care from the "in network" or approved providers are less than when care is rendered by non-contracting providers. This is a method of influencing patients to use certain providers without restricting their freedom of choice too severely.

Point system A rarely-used system of meal planning for diabetes in which foods are rated based upon calorie content, regardless of blood glucose effect or nutritional content. One "calorie point" equals 75 calories. The system may have a role to help with weight loss, but is not typically presently recommended for type 1 diabetes.

Poison Any substance which when taken into the body in a single dose of 1.0 gm. or less, is injurious to health or dangerous to life.

Polaroid lens A lens used in sunglasses and sometimes 3D glasses which consists of two glass or plastic surfaces with a plastic lamination between the two surfaces, and designed to reduce reflected glare. In optometric vision therapy, these lens are used with 3D pictures such as vectograms and stereograms, which are also polarized.

Polifeprosan 20 with carmustine implant A synthetic, biodegradable wafer containing the agent carmustine with antineoplastic activity. Used to deliver drug directly into a brain tumor site and typically implanted post-surgically, the wafer is made of a biodegradable poly-anhydride copolymer and contains the nitrosourea carmustine. As an antineoplastic nitrosourea, carmustine alkylates and cross-links DNA during all phases of the cell cycle, resulting in disruption of DNA function, cell cycle arrest, and apoptosis. Carmustine also carbamoylates proteins, including DNA repair enzymes, resulting in an enhanced cytotoxic ffect. Carmustine is highly lipophilic and crosses the blood-brain barrier readily.

Polished water High purity water after it has undergone a second treatment step. Ultrapure water usually undergoes two or more treatment steps. More economical pretreatment processes (e.g., reverse osmosis) are used to remove all but a very small fraction of the impurities. Highly efficient polishing processes (e.g., mixed-bed deionization) are used to remove the impurities that remain.

Pollen The male 'seed' of plants (grasses, flowers, trees) that consists of microscopic dust-like particles. Can cause hay fever, conjunctivitis and asthma.

Poly ICLC A synthetic complex of carboxymethylcellulose, polyinosinic-polycytidylic acid, and poly-L-lysine double-stranded RNA. Poly ICLC may stimulate the release of cytotoxic cytokines and, by inducing interferon-gamma production, may increase the tumoricidal activities of various immuno-hematopoietic cells.

Polyalphaolefin (PAO) A synthetic oil used in lieu of DOP for HEPA filter testing.

Polyclonal activator A substance that induces activation of many individual clones of either T or B cells.

Polycystic ovary syndrome (PCOS) A syndrome associated with bilateral polycystic ovaries and insulin resistance. Symptoms frequently include decreased menstrual flow, irregular menses, anovulation, and infertility.

Polycythemia Too many red blood cells. The condition exists when the hemoglobin, red blood cell (RBC) count, and total RBC volume are all above normal. .

Polycythemia vera A disease in which there are too many red blood cells in the bone marrow and blood, causing the blood to thicken. The number of white blood cells and platelets may also increase. The extra blood cells may collect in the spleen and cause it to become enlarged. They may also cause bleeding problems and make clots form in blood vessels.

Polydipsia Excessive thirst; may be a symptom of uncontrolled diabetes.

Polyethylene glycosylated recombinant human mega-karyocyte growth and development factor A form of megakaryocyte growth and development factor (MGDF) that is made in the laboratory. MGDF comes from the protein thrombopoietin, which is normally made in the body to help make platelets. Polyethylene glycosylated recombinant human megakaryocyte growth and development factor is being studied as a way to increase the number of platelets in patients receiving chemotherapy. Also called PEG-MGDF.

Polygam S/D Other name for immune globulin.

Polygenic disorder Genetic disorder resulting from the combined action of alleles of more than one gene (e.g., heart disease, diabetes, and some cancers). Although such disorders are inherited, they depend on the simultaneous presence of several alleles; thus the hereditary patterns are usually more complex than those of single gene disorders.

Polyglutamate camptothecin A therapeutic formulation consisting of camptothecin, an alkaloid isolated from the Chinese tree Camptotheca acuminata, conjugated with polyglutamate. During the S phase of the cell cycle, camptothecin selectively stabilizes topoisomerase I-DNA covalent complexes, thereby inhibiting religation of topoisomerase I-mediated single-strand DNA breaks and producing potentially lethal double-strand DNA breaks when encountered by the DNA replication machinery. Conjugation with polyglutamate renders this agent more water soluble and less toxic than the parent molecule.

Polyglutamate paclitaxel A protein that can be linked to a chemotherapy drug to deliver the drug directly to the tumor with fewer side effects. It is being studied as a treatment for cancer. Also called CT-2103.

Polyhydramnios An excess amount of amniotic fluid.

Polymer A macromolecule (long chain) consisting of five or more repeating units called monomers. Examples include polyethylene, polystyrene, and PTFE (polytetrafluoroethylene).

Polymerase An enzyme that catalyzes production of nucleic acid molecules.

Polymerase chain reaction (PCR) A method for amplifying a DNA base sequence using a heat-stable polymerase and two 20-base primers, one complementary to the (+) strand at one end of the sequence to be amplified and one complementary to the (-) strand at the other end. Because the newly synthesized DNA strands can subsequently serve as additional templates for the same primer sequences, successive rounds of primer annealing, strand elongation, and dissociation produce rapid and highly specific amplification of the desired sequence. PCR also can be used to detect the existence of the defined sequence in a DNA sample.

Polymerase, DNA or RNA Enzyme that catalyzes the synthesis of nucleic acids on preexisting nucleic acid templates, assembling RNA from ribonucleotides or DNA from deoxyribonucleotides.

Polymerization The curing (with heat) of the raw acrylic (monomer and polymer) and forming a polymeric compound.

Polymethylmethacrylate (PMMA) Acrylic (plastic) with Trade Names of Lucite and Plexiglas.

Polymorphism Difference in DNA sequence among individuals. Genetic variations occurring in more than 1% of a population would be considered useful polymorphisms for genetic linkage analysis.

Polymorphonuclear leukocyte White cell, granular cytoplasm. Neutral staining (neutrophil) - most frequent, phagocytic.

Polyneuritis Inflammation of several peripheral nerves at the same time.

Polyneuropathy Neuropathy involving a number of different nerves

Polyolefin The polyolefin polymer is probably one of the most economical

```
H           3      4      5      6
            CH3–CH2–CH2–CH3
 \1     2/   γ      δ      ε      ζ
   C = C
 /α     β\
H         H
```

1-hexene, an example of an alpha-olefin

Figure Polyolefin

and widely used classes of thermoplastics, including such materials as PB, PP, and PE. PB is a semicrystalline polymer based on polybutene, homopolymers, and either polybutene or polyethylene copolymers. The primary use of PB is pipe with hydrostatic pressure rating of 1,000 psi at 73°F. PP is a crystalline polymer that has good resistance to caustics, solvents, acids, and other organic chemicals, but is not resistant to oxidizing-type acids, detergents, alcohols, or chlorinated organic materials. It is suitable for pipe applications. The largest group of polyolefins is linear PE. It includes ULDPE, LLDPE, LDPE, HDPE, HMW-HDPE, and UHMWPE. These density descriptions generally refer to ASTM designations based on unmodified polymers. PE types of higher density have better permeation barrier properties, hardness, abrasion resistance, chemical resistance, and higher surface gloss.

Polyp A spheroidal mass that protrudes upwards or outwards from a normal surface. Polyps may be hyperplastic, inflammatory, or neoplastic, e.g. pedunculated polyp - a polyp attached by a thin stalk (peduncle), e.g. sessile polyp - a polyp with a broad base (sessile).

Polypectomy Surgery to remove a polyp.

Polypeptide A long chain of amino acids that are chemically linked to one another. Shorter chains of amino acids are referred to as peptides.

Polyphagia Excessive hunger; may be a symptom of uncontrolled diabetes.

Polyphenol A substance that is found in many plants and gives some flowers, fruits, and vegetables their color. Polyphenols have antioxidant activity.

Polyphenon E A substance that is being studied in the prevention of cancer. It is made from decaffeinated green tea, and contains chemicals called catechins, which are antioxidants. Also called green tea extract.

Polyphenon E topical ointment Other name for green tea extract.

Polypoid Resembling a polyp.

Polyposis The development of numerous polyps (growths that protrude from a mucous membrane).

Polysaccharide A type of carbohydrate. It contains sugar molecules that are linked together chemically.

Polyunsaturated fats A type of fat that comes from vegetables.

Polyuria Excessive urination; may be a symptom of uncontrolled diabetes.

Polyvalent melanoma vaccine A cancer vaccine consisting of whole irradiated heterologous melanoma cells which express multiple melanoma-related antigens. Polyvalent melanoma vaccine may stimulate an antitumoral cytotoxic T-cell immune response in the host, resulting in inhibition of tumor cell proliferation and tumor cell death.

Polyvalent vaccine A vaccine that combines multiple antigens. This type of vaccine may produce a stronger immune response or may provide protection from multiple strains of an infectious organism.

Pomegranate juice A natural juice isolated from the fruit of the plant Punica granatum with antioxidant, potential antineoplastic, and chemo-preventive activities. Pomegranate juice contains flavonoids which promote differentiation and apoptosis in tumor cells by down-regulating vascular endothelial growth factor (VEGF) and stimulating migration inhibitory factor (MIF), thereby inhibiting angiogenesis. The flavanoids in pomegranate juice also scavenge reactive oxygen species (ROS) and, in some cell types, may prevent ROS-mediated cell injury and death.

Pomegranate Punica granatum. A subtropical shrub or tree. Juice from the fruit may contain substances that decrease or slow the rise of prostate-specific antigen (PSA) levels. It is being studied for its ability to delay or prevent recurrent prostate cancer.

Pompholyx Eczema of the palms of the hands and soles of the feet, associated with intense itching.

Pons (brainstem) Portion of the central nervous system between the medulla oblongata and the mesencephalon, consisting of the pars dorsalis and pars ventralis.

The roof of the pons (the "tegmentum") forms the ventral/interior floor of the fourth ventricle. In a sagittal view, the pons looks like the "pot-belly" of an overweight man.

Pontic Replacement tooth mounted on a fixed or removal appliance.

Pontine Having to do with the pons (part of the central nervous system, located at the base of the brain, between the medulla oblongata and the midbrain).

Pooling Combining risks for groups into one risk pool.

Poor man's pump (basal/bolus insulin administration) Using several daily injections of clear insulin (either Regular or Lispro), at mealtimes – the bolus doses – together with one or more daily injections of cloudy insulin (either NPH or Ultralente insulin) – the basal doses – to achieve blood sugar control in a manner similar to that used by people who use insulin pumps.

Popliteal artery A continuation of the femoral artery that branches into the lateral and medial superior genicular, middle genicular, sural, lateral and medial inferior genicular, anterior and posterior tibial, genicular articular, and the patellar rete arteries.

Popliteal bursa The extension of the sheath of the synovial tendon of the popliteus muscle into the popliteal space.

Popliteal vein The vein that parallels the path of the popliteal artery, originating at the junction of the venae comitantes of the anterior and posterior tibial arteries and continuing into the femoral vein at the level of the adductor hiatus.

Population genetics The study of variation in genes among a group of individuals.

Population health Organized efforts focused on the health of defined populations in order to promote and maintain or restore health, to reduce the amount of disease, premature death and disease-produced discomfort and disability. Programs, services and institutions here emphasize the prevention of disease and the health needs of the population as a whole. Among a broad scope of disciplines, various knowledge and skills are utilized such as bio-statistics, epidemiology, planning, organization, management, financing and evaluation of health programs, environmental health, application of social and behavioral factors in health and disease, health promotion, health education and nutrition.

Porcelain crown All porcelain restoration covering the coronal portion of tooth (above the gum line).

Porcelain fused to metal (PFM) crown Restoration with metal coping (for strength) covered by porcelain (for appearance).

Porcelain inlay or onlay Tooth-coloured restoration made of porcelain, cemented or bonded in place.

Porcelain veneers A thin layer of porcelain, fabricated by a laboratory) bonded to a natural tooth to replace lost tooth structure, close spaces, straighten teeth or change colour and/or shape.

Porcine Of, relating to, or from swine (pigs) such as porcine growth hormone.

Porfimer sodium A synthetic derivative of hematoporphyrin with photodynamic properties. Absorbed selectively by tumor cells, porfimer produces oxygen radicals after activation by laser light, resulting in cytotoxicity.

Porfiromycin A substance that is being studied in the treatment of cancer. It belongs to the family of drugs called anticancer antibiotics.

Porous implant An implant having openings throughout to allow fibrous tissue ingrowth.

Port An implanted device through which blood may be withdrawn and drugs may be infused without repeated needle sticks. Also called a port-a-cath.

Port implanted A catheter connected to a quarter-sized disc that is surgically placed just below the skin in the chest or abdomen. The tube is inserted into a large vein or artery directly into the bloodstream. Fluids, drugs, or blood products can be infused, and blood can be drawn through a needle that is stuck into the disc. Examples: Port-o-cath, Infusaport, Lifeport.

Port peritoneal A catheter connected to a quarter-sized disc that is surgically placed in the abdomen. The catheter is inserted to deliver chemotherapy to the peritoneum (abdominal cavity).

Portal hypertension High blood pressure in the vein that carries blood to the liver from the stomach, small and large intestines, spleen, pancreas, and gallbladder. It is usually caused by a block in the blood flow through the liver due to cirrhosis (scarring) of the liver.

Portal vein A blood vessel that carries blood to the liver from the stomach, small and large intestines, spleen, pancreas, and gallbladder. Also called hepatic portal vein.

Portal-systemic encephalopathy Refers to a condition of mental status changes, ranging from mild confusion to a coma-state resulting from increased ammonia transferred to the brain because of the inability of the liver to remove this toxic compound from the circulation.

Portfolio-based learning or portfolios A collection of evidence that learning has taken place, usually set within agreed objectives or a negotiated set of learning activities. Some portfolios are developed in order to demonstrate the progression of learning, while others are assessed against specific targets of achievement. In essence, portfolios contain material collected by the learner over a period of time. They are the learner's practical and intellectual property and the learner takes responsibility for the portfolio's creation and maintenance. Because the portfolio is based upon the real experience of the learner, it helps to demonstrate the connection between theory and practice, accommodating evidence of learning from different sources, and enabling assessment within a framework of clear criteria and learning objectives. The use of portfolios encourages autonomous and reflective learning which is an integral part of professional education and development. Candidates are expected to produce evidence and process such evidence with relation to a pre-determined standard. Since the portfolio approach includes both content and a reflective component, one must first determine which components are to be assessed. Portfolios provide a process for both formative and summative assessment, based on either personally derived or externally set learning objectives or a model for lifelong learning and continuing professional development.

Positional cloning A technique used to identify genes, usually those that are associated with diseases, based on their location on a chromosome. This is contrast to the older, "functional cloning" technique that relies on some knowledge of a gene protein product. For most diseases, researchers have no such knowledge.

Positive airway pressure (PAP) Positive airway pressure adjuncts are used to mobilize secretions and treat conditions such as atelectasis, or to keep airways open and unobstructed in patients with sleep apnea. They include continuous positive airway pressure (CPAP), positive expiratory pressure (PEP), expiratory positive airway pressure (EPAP). and bilevel positive airway pressure (BiPAP)

Positive axillary lymph node A lymph node in the area of the armpit (axilla) to which cancer has spread. This spread is determined by surgically removing some of the lymph nodes and examining them under a microscope to see whether cancer cells are present.

Positive expiratory pressure (PEP) A method of mechanical ventilation in which pressure is maintained to increase the volume of gas remaining in the lung at the end of expiration, thus keeping alveoli open and improving gas exchange.

Sometimes called Positive end expiratory pressure (PEEP)

Positive pressure personnel suit Personnel protection equivalent to that provided by Class III (BSCs). It is a one-piece, ventilated suit worn by the laboratory worker when working with Biosafety

Level 3 (BL-3) or Biosafety Level 4 (BL-4) in a "suit area" and using Class I or II Biological Safety Cabinets (BSCs). The personnel suit is maintained under positive pressure with a life-support system to prevent leakage into the suit. In this containment system, the worker is isolated from the work materials. The personnel suit area must be entered through an airlock fitted with airtight doors. A chemical shower is provided as a "dunk tank" to decontaminate the surfaces of the suit as the worker leaves the area. The exhaust air from the suit area is filtered through two HEPA filters installed in series. The entire area must be under negative pressure.

Positive pressure ventilation (PPV) Process of forcing gases down a patient's trachea using either a manual control technique or using an automatic ventilator. PPV can be done using a manual resuscitator or the rebreathing bag on the anesthesia machine; for long term use an automatic ventilator is usually prescribed.

Positive relative accommodation (PRA) A measure of the maximum ability to stimulate accommodation while maintaining clear, single binocular vision.

Positive test result A test result that reveals the presence of a specific disease or condition for which the test is being done.

Post Thin metal rod inserted into the root of a tooth after root canal therapy; provides retention for a "coping" that replaces lost tooth structure and retains crown.

Post core Post and buildup to replace lost tooth structure and retain crown.

Post-crown Single structure that combines post-core and crown.

Post exposure prophylaxis (PEP) Administration of anti-HIV drugs within 72 hours of a high-risk exposure, including unprotected sex, needle sharing, or occupational needle stick injury, to help prevent development of HIV infection.

Post herpetic neuralgia (PHN) Literally "pain following herpes." The term is usually applied to the severe pain that sometimes follows the healing of herpes zoster lesions.

Post hoc analyses Analyses conducted after the results are available that were not defined before the start of the trial. Such analyses are particularly prone to false-positive claims or type I error.

Post marketing surveillance Term used by the Food and Drug Administration to characterize any procedure, implemented after licensure of a drug for a given indication, that is designed to provide information on the actual use of the drug for that indication and on the occurrence of related side effects. The surveillance usually involves survey techniques rather than controlled trials.

Post nasal discharge (PND) The sensation of mucus accumulation in the throat or a feeling that mucus is dripping downward from the back of the nose into the throat. Also called Postnasal Drip

Post partum After giving birth.

Post stratification The process of classifying patients into strata after they have been enrolled in the study‹usually for data analysis purposes.

Post void residual (PVR) volume A diagnostic test which measures how much urine remains in the bladder after urination. Specific measurement of PVR volume can be accomplished by catheterization, pelvic ultrasound, radiography, or radioisotope studies.

Posterior Rear side, or behind.

Posterior clinoid Two tubercles located on the superior sides of the dorsum sellae of the sphenoid bone, that are part of the attachment for the tentorium of the cerebellum.

Posterior rib Portion of the rib located on the dorsal side of the body.

Posterior surface The back of the prosthesis or under part of the eyelid.

Posterior tibial artery Artery originating from the popliteal artery and branching into the fibular circumflex branch, peroneal, medial plantar, and lateral plantar arteries.

Posthumous After Death.

Postmenopausal Having to do with the time after menopause. Menopause ("change of life") is the time in a woman's life when menstrual periods stop permanently.

Postmortem After death. Often used to describe an autopsy.

Postoperative After surgery.

Postpartum The time period after childbirth (refers to the mother).

Postprandial Occurring after a meal. Example: Blood taken 1-2 hours after eating to see the amount of glucose in the blood would be called a postprandial blood glucose test.

Postremission therapy Anticancer drugs given to kill cancer cells that survive after remission induction therapy.

Post-traumatic stress disorder (PTSD) An anxiety disorder that develops in reaction to physical injury or severe mental or emotional distress, such as military combat, violent assault, natural disaster, or other life-threatening events. Having cancer may also lead to PTSD. Symptoms interfere with day-to-day living and include reliving the event in nightmares or flashbacks; avoiding people, places, and things connected to the event; feeling alone and losing interest in daily activities; and having trouble concentrating and sleeping.

Potable Suitable for drinking.

Potassium A metallic element that is important in body functions such as regulation of blood pressure and of water content in cells, transmission of nerve impulses, digestion, muscle contraction, and heartbeat.

Potassium hydroxide A toxic and highly corrosive chemical used to make soap, in bleaching, and as a paint remover. It is used in small amounts as a food additive and in the preparation of some drugs.

Potent A substance that is "active" in relatively low doses or concentrations.

Potentiation In medicine, the effect of increasing the potency or effectiveness of a drug or other treatment.

Pouch A specialized collection bag worn over an ostomy to collect stool.

Power The probability of finding a treatment effect that actually exists, or of rejecting the null hypothesis when the alternative hypothesis is in fact true. In clinical trials, the power of the study design is the ability of the study to detect a postulated difference between treatment groups if it in fact exists. For example, if there is "something going on" in the study, does the study design have the power to demonstrate it.

PP (Polypropylene) A crystalline polymer with a melting point of 330°F (165°C), and heat deflection temperature ranging from 195°F (91°C) to 240°F (116°C) which is higher than other common plastics. Its key properties are high heat resistance (for piping an upper limit of 212°F (100°C)), a specific gravity of 0.91 if unmodified (the lightest of the most common thermoplastics), stiffness, and chemical resistance with respect to handling caustics, solvents, acids, and other organic chemicals. It is not recommended for use with oxidizing type acids, detergents, low boiling hydrocarbons, alcohols, and some chlorinated organic materials. Polypropylene is a relatively inert material and contributes little in the way of contamination to pharmaceutical water.

PPB (Parts per billion) Parts per billion, or micrograms per liter. One part per billion is like seeing a bottle cap on the earth's equator from an orbiting satellite.

PPF A blood plasma fraction. Identical to NHSA but containing not more than 15% w/w A and ß globulins. Dispensed as a 5% solution.

PPI 2458 A synthetic derivative of fumagillin with antineoplastic and cytotoxic properties. PPI-2458 irreversibly inhibits the enzyme methionine aminopeptidase type 2 (MetAP2), thereby preventing abnormal cell growth and angiogenesis. PPI-2458 is reported to have a better toxicity profile compared to other agents of its class.

PPLO Pleuropneumonia like organism.

PPM (Parts per million) The most common measure of dissolved ionized impurities in water. It is the same as milligrams per liter.

PR- (Progesterone receptor negative) Describes cells that do not have a protein to which the hormone progesterone will bind. Cancer cells that are PR- do not need progesterone to grow, and usually do not stop growing when treated with hormones that block progesterone from binding.

PR+ (Progesterone receptor positive) Describes cells that have a protein to which the hormone progesterone will bind. Cancer cells that are PR+ need progesterone to grow and will usually stop growing when treated with hormones that block progesterone from binding.

PR1 leukemia peptide vaccine A cancer vaccine consisting of PR1, a 9 amino-acid human leukocyte antigen (HLA)-A2 restricted peptide derived from proteinase 3. Vaccination with PR1 leukemia peptide vaccine stimulates the host immune system to mount a cytotoxic T lymphocyte (CTL) response against tumor cells expressing proteinase 3, resulting in tumor cell lysis. Proteinase 3 is often overexpressed in leukemic cells.

Practicability of assessment procedures As there are always restrictions on the resources available to conduct assessments, expertise and creativity are required to develop the best compromise between ideal and practical procedures and tools for assessment. Time and resources are required to develop a proper examination possessing minimally acceptable standards of validity and reliability. This applies particularly to the assessment of clinical skills where much longer or more frequent observations of student performance are required than are usually undertaken. The planning of exams should take into account the number of students to be assessed. An assessment procedure appropriate for 20 students may not be practical where 100-200 have to be evaluated. Important factors are the number of staff available, their status and specialties, number of available patients, available space or accommodation and the end-use of the assessment; for instance, if results are used to determine "pass or fail" status or to probe for areas of competence in which students are deficient.

Practical nurses Practical nurses, also known as vocational nurses, provide nursing care and treatment of patients under the supervision of a licensed physician or registered nurse.

Practice parameters, practice guidelines Systematically developed statements to standardize care and to assist in practitioner and patient decisions about the appropriate health care for specific circumstances. Practice guidelines are usually developed through a process that combines scientific evidence of effectiveness with expert opinion. Practice guidelines are also referred to as clinical criteria, protocols, algorithms, review criteria, and guidelines. Practice parameters may also be referred to as practice options, practice guidelines, practice policies, or practice standards.

Pravachol A drug that lowers the amount of cholesterol in the blood. It may also make tumor cells more sensitive to anticancer drugs, and is being studied in the treatment of cancer. It belongs to the families of drugs called HMG-CoA reductase inhibitors (statins) and chemosensitizers. Also called pravastatin.

Pravastatin A synthetic lipid-lowering agent. Pravastatin competitively inhibits hepatic hydroxymethyl-glutaryl coenzyme A (HMG-CoA) reductase, the enzyme which catalyzes the conversion of HMG-CoA to mevalonate, a key step in cholesterol synthesis. Pravastatin lowers plasma cholesterol and lipoprotein levels, and modulates immune responses by suppressing MHC II (major histocompatibility complex II) on interferon gamma-stimulated, antigen-presenting cells such as human vascular endothelial cells.

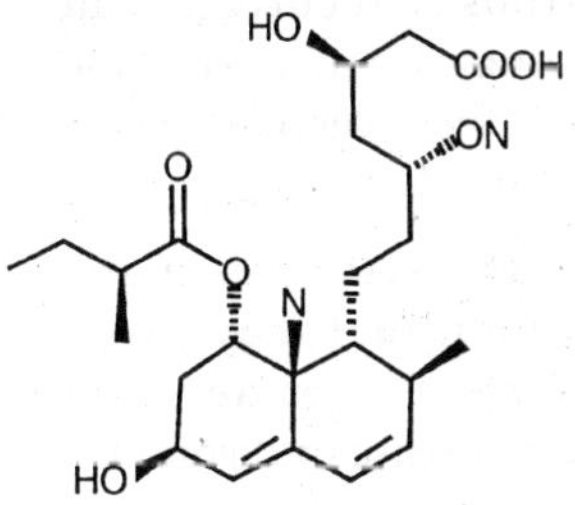

Figure Chemical structure of pravastatin

Pre clampsia The development of high blood pressure with protein in the urine or edema due to pregnancy. It occurs after the 20th week of pregnancy and usually with a woman's first pregnancy.

Pre conception counseling A specific type of health care for all women of childbearing age prior to pregnancy. Its purpose is to identify risks of pregnancy and childbirth for both mother and child, to provide education and counseling targeted to a woman's individual needs, and to treat or stabilize medical conditions prior to pregnancy in order to optimize the mother's and infant's health.

Precancerous A term used to describe a condition that may (or is likely to) become cancer. Also called premalignant.

Precancerous dermatosis A skin disease marked by scaly or thickened patches on the skin, and often caused by prolonged exposure to arsenic. The patches often occur on sunexposed areas of the skin and in older white men. These patches may become malignant (cancerous). Also called

Bowen's disease or precancerous dermatitis.

Precancerous polyps Growths that protrude from a mucous membrane. Precancerous polyps may (or are likely to) become cancer.

Precipitate An insoluble reaction product. When a solution reaches saturation, solute will begin to come out of solution, as when water precipitates from the air as rain, or calcium carbonate precipitates out of water to form scale, the chalky white substance deposited on the inside of tea kettles.

Preclinical Refers to the preliminary testing of investigational drugs in laboratory animals that occurs before human testing may begin.

Preclinical study Research using animals to find out if a drug, procedure, or treatment is likely to be useful. Preclinical studies take place before any testing in humans is done.

Precommission Preparing the plant for commissioning (start-up). This includes briefly starting (bumping) all pieces of equipment, verifying their shaft rotation is correct, verifying that valves, gauges, and other inline devices are installed in the correct orientation, and performing functionality runs on all equipment and material. This also includes leak tests.

Prediabetes Traditional definition:The stage before the development of diabetes, with normal glucose tolerance but with an increased risk of developing diabetes at some future time. Examples of increased risk might include family history of diabetes, prior diagnosis of gestational diabetes, presence of a positive antibody test for diabetes, or insulin resistance.

Revised definition: "Pre-diabetes is the state that occurs when a person's blood glucose levels are higher than normal but not high enough for a diagnosis of diabetes.Doctors sometimes refer to this state of elevated blood glucose levels as Impaired Glucose Tolerance or Impaired Fasting Glucose (IGT/IFG), depending on which test was used to detect it."

Predicate rules A previously published set of rules (such as GLPs, GCP, or cGMPs) that mandate what records must be maintained, the required contents of those records, whether signatures are necessary, and how long the record must be maintained.

Predictive factor A situation or condition that may increase a person's risk of developing a certain disease or disorder.

Predisposition Susceptibility to a disease that can be triggered under certain conditions. For example, some women have a family history of breast cancer and are therefore predisposed (but not necessarily destined) to develop breast cancer.

Prednicen M Other name for prednisone.

Prednisolone A synthetic glucocorticoid with anti-inflammatory and immun-omodulating properties. After cell surface receptor attachment and cell entry, prednisolone enters the nucleus where it binds to and activates specific nuclear receptors, resulting in an altered gene expression and inhibition of proinflammatory cytokine production. This agent also decreases the number of circulating lymphocytes, induces cell differentiation, and stimulates apoptosis in sensitive tumor cells populations.

Preeclampsia A condition that some women with diabetes have during the late stages of pregnancy. Two signs of this condition are high blood pressure and swelling because the body cells are holding extra water.

Pre-epiglottic recess The space between the posterior border of the tongue (at its root) and the anterior margin of the epiglottis.

Preferred provider organization (PPO) Some combination of hospitals and physicians that agrees to render particular services to a group of people, perhaps under contract with a private insurer. A health care delivery system that contracts with providers of medical care to provide services at discounted fees to members. Members may seek care form non-participating providers but generally are financially penalized for doing so by the loss of the discount and subjection to co-payments and deductibles. The services may be furnished at discounted rates and the insured population may incur out-of-pocket expenses for covered services received outside the PPO if the outside charge exceeds the PPO payment rate. A PPO can also be a legal entity or it may be a function of an already formed health plan. The entity may have a health benefit plan that is also referred to as a PPO. PPOs are a common method of managing care while still paying for services through an indemnity plan. Most PPO plans are point of service plans, in that they will pay a higher percentage for care provided by providers in the network. Many insurers will offer PPOs as well as HMOs. Generally PPOs will offer more choice for the patient and will provide higher reimbursement to the providers.

Prefilter A filter to trap gross particulates located upstream before a HEPA filter. The efficiency of initial prefilters is usually in the 20% to 30% range by the ASHRAE Atmospheric Dust Spot Efficiency, while intermediate prefilters usually have a collection efficiency of 80% to 90% by the same test.

Preleukemia A disease in which the bone marrow does not function normally. Also called myelodysplastic syndrome or smoldering leukemia.

Prelone Other name for prednisolone.

Premalignant Abnormal changes in cells that may, but not always, become cancer. Most of these early lesions respond well to treatment and result in cure. Also called precancerous.

Premarin Other name for conjugated estrogens.

Premature chromosome condensation (PCC) A method of studying chromosomes in the interphase stage of the cell cycle.

Premature ovarian failure A condition in which the ovaries stop working before age 40. Symptoms include hot flashes, mood swings, night sweats, vaginal dryness, and infertility. Some cancer treatments, such as chemotherapy, radiation therapy, and surgery can cause premature ovarian failure. Ovarian failure caused by cancer treatment may be temporary or permanent and may be treated with hormone replacement therapy. Also called primary ovarian insufficiency or early menopause.

Premature termination Early termination of a trial before data are sufficiently strong to be convincing.

Premenopausal Having to do with the time before menopause. Menopause ("change of life") is the time of life when a woman's menstrual periods stop permanently.

Premycotic phase A phase of mycosis fungoides in which a patient has areas of red, scaly, itchy skin on areas of the body that are usually not exposed to sun. This is early-phase mycosis fungoides, but it is hard to diagnose the rash as mycosis fungoides during this phase. The premycotic phase may last from months to decades.

Prenatal Period of time spanning conception to the begining of labour.

Preprandial Occurring before a meal. Example: Blood taken before eating to see the amount of glucose in the blood would be called a preprandial blood glucose test.

Prerandomization examination Any examination that is part of the evaluation process of a patient for enrollment into a trial and that is carried out before the randomization examination.

Prerandomization visit Any visit made to the clinic by a potential study patient for the purpose of evaluation for enrollment into the trial and that takes place prior to the randomization visit.

Presacral space The retro- and extra-peritoneal soft-tissues that are anterior to the sacrum.

Presbyopia Sometimes called the fourth refractive error, is not truly a refractive error. It is the natural process of the eye losing the ability to accommodate or change the shape of the natural crystalline lens inside the eye to see comfortably at near. This vision defect occurs with the advancement of age; the onset usually occurs between the ages of 40 to 45. Unlike the rest of the body, which stops growing by the age of twenty, the lens of the eye continues to grow throughout life. As the lens ages and grows, it becomes harder in consistency, loses its elasticity, and therefore is resistant to changes in shape. The result is a gradual reduction in accommodation (near eye focus), and a more dependence on reading glasses. A plus lens or multi-focal lens (such as a bifocal lens) is prescribed in the form of glasses or contact lenses. Vision therapy is not a treatment option.

Prescription A physician's order for the preparation and administration of a drug or device for a patient. A prescription has several parts. They include the superscription or heading with the symbol "R" or "Rx", which stands for the word recipe (meaning, in Latin, to take); the inscription, which contains the names and quantities of the ingredients; the subscription or directions for compounding the drug; and the signature which is often preceded by the sign "s" standing for signa (Latin for mark), giving the directions to be marked on the container.

Preservative A bacteriostatic or bacteriocidal agent added to some multiple dose parenterals and most cosmetics. Examples are benzalkonium chloride (BAC), formaldehyde, and thimerosol (merthiolate).

Pressure necrosis The localized wearing away of conjunctival tissue due to pressure from a poorly fitted prosthesis.

Pressure rating Pressure at which a system is designed to operate, allowing for applicable safety factors.

Pressure vessel A closed vessel designed to operate at pressures above 15 psig (103.4 kPa).

Presumptive Presumed. In the context of diagnosis, one that is not definitely made, but where signs and symptoms make it exceedingly likely to be the proper one, even without confirmatory evidence. Diagnosis of CMV retinitis by characteristic appearance, without using a biopsy is an example if a presumptive diagnosis.

Pretracheal space The area in front of the trachea (windpipe).

Pretreatment Initial water treatment steps performed prior to final processing to prolong the life of cartridges and filters and to protect downstream elements from premature failure.

Prevalence rate A measure of morbidity based on current sickness in a population, estimated either at a particular time (point prevalence) or over a stated period (period prevalence). It can be expressed either in terms of sick people (persons) or episodes of sickness per 1000 individuals at risk. Compare incidence rate.

Prevalence The number of cases of disease, infected persons, or persons with some other attribute, present at a particular time and in relation to the size of the population from which drawn. It can be a measurement of morbidity at a moment in time, e.g., the number of cases of hemophilia in the country as of the first of the year.

Prevascular space The area in the front part of the chest between the lungs. Also called anterior mediastinum.

Prevastein HC Other name for soy protein isolate.

Preventative maintenance A periodic evaluation of the orbital contents, and reglaze of the plastic ocular prosthesis.

Preventers Medicines (often based on steroids) that are usually breathed in from inhalers by people with asthma. Help to prevent the disease when taken on a regular basis.

Prevention The goals of medicine are to promote health, to preserve health, to restore health when it is impaired, and to minimize suffering and distress. These goals are embodied in the word prevention, which is easiest to define in the context of levels, customarily called primary, secondary and tertiary prevention:

Primary prevention refers to the protection of health by personal and community wide effects, such as preserving good nutritional status, physical fitness, and emotional well-being, immunizing against infectious diseases, and making the environment safe.

Secondary prevention can be defined as the measures available to individuals and populations for the early detection and prompt and effective intervention to correct departures from good health.

Tertiary prevention consists of the measures available to reduce or eliminate long-term impairments and disabilities, minimize suffering caused by existing departures from good health, and to promote the patient's adjustment to irremediable conditions. This extends the concept of prevention into the field of rehabilitation. There are no precise boundaries between these levels.

Preventive Used to prevent disease.

Preventive care Health care that emphasizes prevention, early detection and early treatment, thereby reducing the costs of healthcare in the long run. Health care that seeks to prevent or foster early detection of disease and morbidity and focuses on keeping patients well in addition to health them while they are sick.

Preventive HIV vaccine A vaccine designed to prevent HIV infection in people who are HIV negative. Preventive HIV vaccines are not designed to treat those already infected with HIV.

Preventive mastectomy Surgery to reduce the risk of developing breast cancer by removing one or both breasts before disease develops. Also called prophylactic mastectomy.

Preventive medicine A specialized field of medical practice composed of distinct disciplines that focus on the health of defined populations in order to promote and maintain health and well-being and prevent disease, disability and premature death. It aims at the application of preventive measures within all areas of clinical medicine. In addition to the knowledge of basic and clinical sciences and the skills common to all physicians, practitioners of preventive medicine possess knowledge of and competence in other disciplines. Among a broad scope of such disciplines are: biostatistics, epidemiology, planning, organization, management, financing, and evaluation of health programs, environmental health, application of social and behavioral factors in health and disease, health promotion, health education and nutrition.

Previous abnormality of glucose tolerance A term for people who have had above-normal levels of blood glucose (sugar) when tested for diabetes in the past but who show as normal on a current test. PrevAGT used to be called either "latent diabetes" or "prediabetes."

Prilosec Other name for omeprazole.

Primary air Air circulating through HEPA filters used to produce unidirectional flow in critical zones.

Primary biliary cirrhosis Chronic liver disease, most common in women, caused by inflammation of bile ductules leading to a raised serum alkaline phosphatase and serum bilirubin. Course may be prolonged over many years or may proceed to liver failure in 3-5 years.

Primary cancer The site where cancer begins. Primary cancer is usually named after the organ in which it starts (for example, breast cancer).

Primary care Basic or general health care usually rendered by general practitioners, family practitioners, internists, obstetricians and pediatricians – who are often referred to as primary care practitioners or PCPs. Professional and related services administered by an internist, family practitioner, obstetrician-gynecologist or pediatrician in an ambulatory setting, with referral to secondary care specialists, as necessary.

Primary care doctor A doctor who manages a person's health care over time. A primary care doctor is able to give a wide range of care, including prevention and treatment, can discuss cancer treatment choices, and can refer a patient to a specialist.

Primary care physician (PCP) A "generalist" such as a family practitioner, pediatrician, internist, or obstetrician. In a managed care organization, a primary care physician is accountable for the total health services of enrollees including referrals, procedures and hospitalization.

Primary care provider (PCP) The provider that serves as the initial interface between the member and the medical care system. The PCP is usually a physician, selected by the member upon enrollment, who is trained in one of the primary care specialties who treats and is responsible for coordinating the treatment of members assigned to his/her plan.

Primary central nervous system lymphoma Cancer that arises in the lymphoid tissue found in the central nervous system (CNS). The CNS includes the brain and spinal cord.

Primary ciliary dyskinesia (PCD) Condition where cilia in the body fail to beat effectively causing mucus to become trapped in various parts of the respiratory system.

Primary containment The first level of containment, consisting of the inside portion of that container which comes into immediate contact on its inner surface with the material being contained.

Primary drug resistance (PDR) Resistance of bacteria or other pathogens to drugs which exists prior to the beginning of treatment.

Primary endpoint The main result that is measured at the end of a study to see if a given treatment worked (e.g., the number of deaths or the difference in survival between the treatment group and the control group). What the primary endpoint will be is decided before the study begins.

Primary health care The World Health Organization defines primary health care as the principal vehicle for the delivery of health care at the most local level of a country's health system. It is essential health care made accessible at a cost the country and community can afford with methods that are practical, scientifically sound and socially acceptable. Everyone in the community should have access to it, and everyone should be involved in it. Beside an appropriate treatment of common diseases and injuries, provision of essential drugs, maternal and child health, and prevention and control locally endemic diseases and immunization, it should also include at least education of the community on prevalent health problems and methods of preventing them, promotion of proper nutrition, safe water and sanitation.

Primary immunodeficiency (PIDS) Primary immune deficiency diseases are inherited disorders in which part of the body's immune system is missing or fails to function properly. Often presenting as 'common' infections or conditions (such as asthma or sinusitus), PIDs can go undetected for many years resulting in permanent damage to organs, and even the patient's death.

Primary isolates Strains of HIV taken from an infected individual, as opposed to strains grown in the laboratory.

Primary lymphoid organs Organs in which the maturation of T and B lymphocytes take place and antigen-specific receptors are first acquired.

Primary medical care Primary medical care begins when a patient with a new health problem encounters the first-level provider of care. The provider initiates care, may screen for referral to a specialist, and secures overall responsibility for continuity of care provided by all medical personnel in both outpatient and in-patient settings.

Primary myelofibrosis A progressive, chronic disease in which the bone marrow is replaced by fibrous tissue and blood is made in organs such as the liver and the spleen, instead of in the bone marrow. This disease is marked by an enlarged spleen and progressive anemia. Also called chronic idiopathic myelofibrosis, agnogenic myeloid metaplasia, myelosclerosis with myeloid metaplasia, and idiopathic myelofibrosis.

Primary outcome 1. The event or condition the trial is designed to ameliorate, delay, or prevent.

2. The actual occurrence of a primary event in a study patient.

Primary outcome variable The outcome variable that is designated or regarded as key in the design or analysis of the results of a trial. Generally, the variable used for sample size calculations in the design of the trial or, when no sample size calculation is made, for the main avenue of data analyses. The primary outcome monitored in interim analyses.

Primary ovarian insufficiency A condition in which the ovaries stop working before age 40. Symptoms include hot flashes, mood swings, night sweats, vaginal dryness, and infertility. Some cancer treatments, such as chemotherapy, radiation therapy, and surgery can cause primary ovarian insufficiency. Ovarian insufficiency caused by cancer treatment may be temporary or permanent and may be treated with hormone replacement therapy. Also called premature ovarian failure or early menopause.

Primary physician capitation The amount paid to each physician monthly for services based on the age, sex and number of the Members selecting that physician.

Primary responses The immune response to a first encounter with antigen. The primary response is generally small, has a long induction phase or lag period, consists primarily of IgM antibodies, and generates immunologic memory.

Primary sclerosing cholangitis A liver disorder that most commonly occurs in patients with inflammatory bowel disease resulting in destruction of the bile ductules in the liver leading to a marked increase in the serum alkaline phosphatase and serum bilirubin. Ultimately leads to cirrhosis and liver failure.

Primary tumor The original cancer site. For example, breast cancer that has spread to the bone is still called breast cancer.

Primer Short preexisting polynucleotide chain to which new deoxyribonucleotides can be added by DNA polymerase.

Primitive neuroectodermal tumor (PNET) One of a group of cancers that develop from the same type of early cells, and share certain biochemical and genetic features. Some PNETs develop in the brain and central nervous system (CNS-PNET), and others develop in sites outside of the brain such as the limbs, pelvis, and chest wall (peripheral PNET).

Primordium An organ (eye) in its earliest stage of development.

Principal diagnosis The medical condition that is ultimately determined to have caused a patient's admission to the hospital. The principal diagnosis is used to assign every patient to a diagnosis related group. This diagnosis may differ from the admitting and major diagnoses.

Principal investigator 1. The designation used by the National Institutes of Health to denote the individual named on a grant who is responsible for directing the proposed research.

2. The lead scientist in a research project.

Principle of nonrepudiation The ability to say with confident assurance that only one user entered specific data or performed specific actions on a computer system and that the particular user is identifiable. If more than one user can get into the system in such a way that the audit trail cannot specify who performed what action, the principle of nonrepudiation has been violated.

Prinomastat A substance that is being studied in the treatment of cancer. It is a matrix metalloproteinase inhibitor and belongs to the family of drugs called angiogenesis inhibitors. Also called AG3340.

Prions Virus-like proteinaceous infectious agents. Prions differ from viruses in that they are not known to contain either DNA or RNA.

Prior authorization A formal process requiring a provider obtain approval to provide particular services or procedures before they are done. This is usually required for nonemergency services that are expensive or likely to be abused or overused. A managed care organization will identify those services and procedures that require prior authorization, without which the provider may not be compensated.

Prism A wedge-shaped lens which is thicker on one edge than the other. This plastic or glass lens bends light (opposite direction from its thicker end). Prisms can be used to measure an eye misalignment and/or treat a binocular dysfunction (eye teaming problem). A prism is sometimes added to glasses to help improve eyesight due to an eye misalignment or visual field loss.

Prismatic effect by lens When light goes through a wedge shaped lens which is called a prism, it bends. Light is also bent when it does not go through the center of a lens. This is an undesirable effect that can occur in glasses. It commonly occurs when the pupillary distance (PD) is not measured or made correctly.

Privacy notice Institution-wide notice describing the practices of the covered entity regarding protected health information. Health care providers and other covered entities must give the notice to patients and research subjects and should obtain signed acknowledgements of receipt. Internal and external uses of protected health information are explained. It is the responsibility of the researcher to provide a copy of the Privacy Notice to any subject who has not already received one. If the researcher does provide the notice, the researcher should also obtain the subject's written acknowledgement of receipt. These have become more common and visible in hospitals and physician offices due to HIPAA requirements.

Prn Abbreviation meaning "Take as needed:, usually applied to prescription drugs.

Pro oxidant A substance that can produce oxygen byproducts of metabolism that can cause damage to cells.

Probe Single-stranded DNA or RNA molecules of specific base sequence, labeled either radioactively or immunologically, that are used to detect the complementary base sequence by hybridization.

Probenecid A drug that is used to treat gout and is used together with some antibiotics to make them work better. It is being studied in the treatment of cancer. It belongs to the family of drugs called antibiotic therapy adjuncts.

Problem based learning (PBL) In this approach, students learn in small groups supported by a tutor. They initially explore a predetermined problem. The problem contains triggers designed to evoke objectives or concepts which are used to set the agenda for individual or group investigation and learning after the initial session. Subsequent group meetings permit students to monitor their achievements and to set further learning goals as required. The tutor's role is to offer support for learning and to help reach the expected outcomes. PBL enables students to develop the ability to translate knowledge into practice at an early stage, encourages individual participation in learning and also allows the development of teamwork skills. Students in PBL courses have been found to place more emphasis on "meaning" (understanding) than "reproduction" (memorization). Students must engage in a significant amount of self-directed learning; lectures are kept to a minimum. PBL originated at McMaster University in Canada, and then at Maastricht University, and is now widely adopted in medical schools in many countries. Each school makes its own adjustments to the basic model. It does require a heavy investment in resources (library books, IT, tutorial rooms) as well as requiring education and training for tutors.

Procarbazine A drug that is used to treat cancer. It belongs to the family of drugs called alkylating agents.

Procarbazine hydrochloride The hydrochloride salt of a methylhydrazine derivative with antineoplastic and mutagenic activities. Although the exact mode of cytotoxicity has not been elucidated, procarbazine, after metabolic activation, appears to inhibit the trans-methylation of methionine into transfer RNA (t-RNA), thereby preventing protein synthesis and consequently DNA and RNA synthesis. This agent may also undergo auto-oxidation, resulting in the formation of cytotoxic free radicals which damage DNA through an alkylation reaction.

Procedures A documented description of the operations to be carried out, the precautions to be taken and measures to be applied directly or indirectly related to the manufacture of an intermediate or API.

Process aids Materials, excluding solvents, used as an aid in the manufacture of an intermediate or API (Active Pharmaceutical Ingredient) which themselves do not participate in a chemical or biological reaction (e.g. filter aid, activated carbon, etc.).

Process limits Environmental limits that, if exceeded, may affect product quality adversely.

Process suitability The established capacity of the manufacturing process to produce effective and reproducible results consistently.

Process support systems Systems that do not contact product and are generally engineering systems.

Process systems Systems that may contact the drug substance or could otherwise directly impact product quality.

Process validation Establishing, through documented evidence, a high degree of assurance that a specific process will consistently produce a product that meets its predetermined specifications and quality characteristics.

Process validation protocol Documented plan for testing a pharmaceutical product and process to confirm that the production process used to manufacture the product performs as intended. This includes a review of process variables and operational limitations as well as providing the sampling plan under actual use conditions.

Prochlorperazine A synthetic propylpiperazine derivative of phenothiazine with antiemetic, antipsychotic, antihistaminic, and anticholinergic activities. Prochlorperazine antagonizes the dopamine D2-receptor in the chemoreceptor trigger zone (CTZ) of the brain and may prevent chemotherapy-induced emesis.

Procrit Brand name of Erythropoietin

Proctocort Other name for hydrocortisone.

Proctoscopy An examination of the rectum using a thin, lighted tube called a proctoscope.

Proctosigmoidoscopy An examination of the lower colon using a thin, lighted tube, called a sigmoidoscope, inserted into the rectum. Samples of tissues may be collected for examination under a microscope. Also called sigmoidoscopy.

Prodromal Pertaining to symptoms indicating the onset of a disease. May include symptoms prior to those adequate for accurate diagnosis.

Prodrug A chemical precursor of a drug that is converted into the desired substance in the body.

Product campaign The production of more than one product in a facility, with strict adherence to accepted cleaning procedures between these products. The products may be run in the same equipment, but not at the same time.

Product contact surface A surface that contacts raw materials, process materials, and/or product.

Product mix The types and number of different products produced in a facility.

Product water The water produced as a result of a treatment process.

Production All operations involved in the preparation of an API (Active Pharmaceutical Ingredient), from receipt of materials, through processing and packaging, to its completion as a finished API.

Productive cough A cough in which mucus or phlegm is dislodged, enabling a person to clear the lungs.

Professional review organization An organization that reviews the services provided to patients in terms of medical necessity professional standards; and appropriateness of setting.

Professionalism Adherence to a set of values comprising both a formally agreed-upon code of conduct and the informal expectations of colleagues, clients and society. The key values include acting in a patient's interest, responsiveness to the health needs of society, maintaining the highest standards of excellence in the practice of medicine and in the generation and dissemination of knowledge. In addition to medical knowledge and skills, medical professionals should present psychosocial and humanistic qualities such as caring, empathy, humility and compassion, as well as social responsibility and sensitivity to people's culture and beliefs. All these qualities are expected of members of highly trained professions.

The American Board of Internal Medicine's Project Professionalism indicates the most important elements of professionalism to be: altruism, accountability, duty, excellence, honour and integrity, and respect for others.

Professional Altruism: constitutes the essence of professionalism and is based on the rule that the best interest of patients and not self-interest is the professional obligation.

Professional Accountability is an important element of professionalism which is required of physicians at several levels: to their patients for fulfilling the implied contract governing the patient/physician relationship, to society for addressing the health needs of the public, and to their profession for adhering to medicine's time-honored ethical precepts.

Professional Duty can be expressed by the free acceptance of a commitment to service, availability and responsiveness when "on call," accepting inconvenience to meet the needs of ones patients, enduring unavoidable risks to oneself when a patient's welfare is at stake, and advocating the best possible care regardless of the patient's ability to pay. It is willingness to seek an active role in professional organizations and volunteering ones skills and expertise for the welfare of the community.

Professional Excellence entails a conscientious effort to exceed ordinary expectations. Commitment to excellence is an acknowledged goal for all physicians and includes a commitment to life-long learning.

Professional Honour and Integrity implies being fair, being truthful, keeping one's word, meeting commitments, and being straightforward. It also requires recognition of the possibility of conflict of interest and avoiding any situation in which the interest of the physician is placed above that of the patient or allowing personal gain to supersede the best interest of the patient. It constitutes an integral part of professionalism. The importance of professionalism in the patient/physician relationship cannot be overstated.

Professional Respect for Others is reflected in the respect towards the patients and their families, other physicians and professional colleagues such as nurses, medical students, and residents. It is the essence of humanism, and humanism is both central to professionalism and fundamental to enhancing collegiality among physicians.

Profunda femoris artery Atery which origintes from the femoral artery, and branches into the medial and later circumflex arteries of the thigh and perforating arteries.

Progeny Offspring; the product of reproduction or replication.

Progesterone A female sex hormone released by the ovaries to prepare the uterus for pregnancy and the breasts for milk production (lactation).

Progesterone receptor A protein found inside the cells of the female reproductive tissue, some other types of tissue, and some cancer cells. The hormone progesterone will bind to the receptors inside the cells and may cause the cells to grow.

Progesterone receptor assay A test that shows whether a breast cancer depends on progesterone for growth. Progesterone receptors are tested along with estrogen receptors for more complete information on the hormone sensitivity of a cancer, and how best to treat it.

Progesterone receptor negative PR– Describes cells that do not have a protein to which the hormone progesterone will bind. Cancer cells that are PR- do not need progesterone to grow, and usually do not stop growing when treated with hormones that block progesterone from binding.

Progesterone receptor positive PR+ Describes cells that have a protein to which the hormone progesterone will bind. Cancer cells that are PR+ need progesterone to grow and will usually stop growing when treated with hormones that block progesterone from binding.

Progesterone receptor test A lab test to find out if cancer cells have progesterone receptors (proteins to which the hormone progesterone will bind). If the cells have progesterone receptors, they may need progesterone to grow, and this can affect how the cancer is treated.

Progestin Any natural or laboratory-made substance that has some or all of the biologic effects of progesterone, a female hormone.

Prognosis A prediction of the course of disease; the prospects for the cure of the patient. For example, women with breast cancer that was detected early and received prompt treatment have a good prognosis.

Prognostic factor A situation or condition, or a characteristic of a patient, that can be used to estimate the chance of recovery from a disease or the chance of the disease recurring (coming back).

Programmed cell death A type of cell death in which a series of molecular steps in a cell leads to its death. This is the body's normal way of getting rid of unneeded or abnormal cells. The process of programmed cell death may be blocked in cancer cells. Also called apoptosis.

Programmer Not a person, but a computer-based equipment used to communicate with the pulse generator. It provides information during testing and follow-up exams. The doctor uses the programmer to adjust the pulse generator so that it senses and treats your arrhythmias. The programmer can, for example, help your doctor to determine when the pulse generator needs to be replaced.

Progression Increase in the size of a tumor or spread of cancer in the body.

Progression of disease A common endpoint used in AIDS clinical trials. The entity "progression of disease" usually consists of new occurrences of non-recurrent AIDS-defining illnesses or death.

Progression-free survival One type of measurement that can be used in a clinical study or trial to help determine whether a new treatment is effective. It refers to the probability that a patient will remain alive, without the disease getting worse.

Progressive multifocal leukoencephalopathy (PML) A rare brain and spinal cord disease caused by a virus and usually seen only in immunocompromised individuals, such as those with HIV. Symptoms vary, but include loss of muscle control, paralysis, blindness, speech problems, and an altered mental state. This disease often progresses rapidly and may be fatal. PML is considered an AIDS-defining condition in people with HIV.

Proinsulin The initial protein made by the beta cells of the pancreas that later is broken into several pieces. Proinsulin consists of three parts: C-Peptide and two long strands of amino acids (called the alpha and beta chains) that later become linked together to form the insulin molecule.

From every molecule of proinsulin, one molecule of insulin plus one molecule of C-Peptide are produced.

(It may be noted that commercial production of exogenous insulin purifies the original insulin, and removes any residual proinsulin and C-Peptide that might have been initially present.)

Project officer 1. The individual in the sponsoring agency who is responsible for dealing with technical, scientific, and programmatic aspects of a grant or contract-funded project.

2. Health scientist administrator in National Institutes of Health grant-funded projects.

Projection fibers One of three basic classifications of nerve fibers within the white matter (centrum ovale) of the cerebral hemispheres. Projection fibers (also known as itinerant fibers) project to widespread areas of the cerebral cortex from subcortical loci and from distant loci to the cortex.

Prokaryote A unicellular organism having a less complex structure than a eukaryote. It is characterized by the absence of a nucleus and by having the genetic material in the form of simple filaments of DNA. The sizes of most prokaryotes vary from 0.5μm to 3μm in equivalent radius. Different species have different shapes such as spherical or Coccus (for example, Staphylococci), cylindrical or bacillus (E. coli), or spiral or spirillum (Rhodospirillum).

Prokaryote Cell or organism lacking a membrane-bound, structurally discrete nucleus and other subcellular compartments. Bacteria are examples of prokaryotes.

Prokine Other name for sargramostim.

Prolactin A hormone released from the pituitary gland that prompts milk production (lactation.)

Prolapse When part of the body (for instance, a section of intestine) slips from its normal position.

Proleukin Other name for interleukin-2.

Proliferating Multiplying or increasing in number. In biology, cell proliferation occurs by a process known as cell division.

Proliferative index A measure of the number of cells in a tumor that are dividing (proliferating). May be used with the S-phase fraction to give a more complete understanding of how fast a tumor is growing.

Proliferative retinopathy A disease of the small blood vessels of the retina of the eye.

Prolymphocytic leukemia PLL A type of chronic lymphocytic leukemia (CLL), in which too many immature white blood cells (prolymphocytes) are found in the blood and bone marrow. PLL usually progresses more rapidly than classic CLL.

Promegapoietin A drug given during chemotherapy to increase blood cell regeneration. Promegapoietin is a colony-stimulating factor that stimulates the production of blood cells, especially platelets. It is a cytokine and belongs to the family of drugs called hematopoietic (blood-forming) agents.

Promoter A DNA site to which RNA polymerase will bind and initiate transcription.

Promyelocytic leukemia An aggressive (fast-growing) type of acute myeloid leukemia in which there are too many immature blood-forming cells in the blood and bone marrow. It is usually marked by an exchange of parts of chromosomes 15 and 17. Also called acute promyelocytic leukemia.

Prone Having the front or ventral surface downward; lying facedown.

Pronucleus The nucleus of a sperm or egg prior to fertilization.

Prophylactic cranial irradiation Radiation therapy to the head to reduce the risk that cancer will spread to the brain.

Prophylactic In medicine, something that prevents or protects.

Prophylactic mastectomy Surgery to reduce the risk of developing breast cancer by removing one or both breasts before disease develops. Also called preventive mastectomy.

Prophylactic oophorectomy Surgery intended to reduce the risk of ovarian cancer by removing the ovaries before disease develops.

Prophylactic surgery Surgery to remove an organ or gland that shows no signs of cancer, in an attempt to prevent development of cancer of that organ or gland. Prophylactic surgery is sometimes chosen by people who know they are at high risk for developing cancer.

Prophylactic trial A trial that is designed to assess the efficacy of a treatment procedure aimed at preventing the development or progression of a specific disease or condition.

Prophylaxis Treatment to prevent the onset of a particular disease or to prevent recurrence of symptoms of an existing infection that has been brought under control.

Proprius (fasciculus) An exclusively intrinsic spinal pathway that consists of short acsending and descending fibers interconnecting various spinal cord levels. This fasciculi proprii or spinospinal fasciculi system is located adjacent to the gray matter of the spinal cord and participates in intersegmental reflex activity.

Proptosis Protrusion of the eye.

Propylene glycol A common solvent for antibiotics, particularly the tetracyclines. Miscible (soluble) in water, but often filtered as pure propylene glycol prior to combination with the antibiotic. Its high viscosity controls absorption of the dissolved drug.

Prosencephalon The most rostral of the three primary vesicles of the mbryonic brain. The adult derivatives of the forebrain are the cerebral hemispheres, striatum, diencephalon, lateral and third ventricles.

Prospective cohort study A research study that follows over time groups of individuals who are alike in many ways but differ by a certain characteristic (for example, female nurses who smoke and those who do not smoke) and compares them for a particular outcome (such as lung cancer).

Prospective follow up study A study in which people with a specific attribute or characteristic are identified and then observed for some period of time thereafter for the occurrence of the outcome or condition of interest, usually disease or death. The study may or may not involve a comparison group. Clinical trials represent a special subset of prospective follow-up studies.

Prospective In medicine, a study or clinical trial in which participants are identified and then followed forward in time.

Prost 30 A monoclonal antibody that is being studied in the detection and treatment of cancer. Monoclonal antibodies are produced in the laboratory and can locate and bind to cancer cells.

Prostaglandin Any of various oxygenated unsaturated cyclic fatty acids of animals that have a variety of hormonelike actions (as in controlling blood pressure or smooth muscle contraction).

Prostate A gland in the male reproductive system. The prostate surrounds the part of the urethra (the tube that empties the bladder) just below the bladder, and produces a fluid that forms part of the semen.

Prostate cancer Cancer that forms in tissues of the prostate (a gland in the male reproductive system found below the bladder and in front of the rectum). Prostate cancer usually occurs in older men.

Prostate specific antigen test A blood test that measures the level of prostate-specific antigen (PSA), a substance produced by the prostate and some other tissues in the body. Increased levels of PSA may be a sign of prostate cancer.

Prostatectomy Surgical removal of the prostate. Suprapubic / Retropubic Prostatectomy This involves the removal of obstructing prostatic tissue through a supra-pubic incision (a cut below the belly button). The Prostate is not wholly removed. Suprapubic Prostatectomy requires incising the bladder to remove the obstructing tissue while a Retropubic approach involves incising the Prostatic capsule to remove the obstructing tissue. Both approaches utilize an abdominal incision.

Radical Retropubic Prostatectomy Removal of prostate through an abdominal incision. The prostate is completely removed. The advantage is that the lymph nodes can be sampled at the time of the operation and the nerve-sparing procedure is easier to do via this operation.

Perineal Prostatectomy A Perineal incision is utilized. The advantages are less blood loss, easier visualization of the bladder/ urethral anastomosis and decreased recovery time because the incision does not involve muscle or any other vital tissue

Prostate-specific antigen (PSA) A substance produced by the prostate that may be found in an increased amount in the blood of men who have prostate cancer, benign prostatic hyperplasia, or infection or inflammation of the prostate.

Prostatic acid phosphatase-sargramostim fusion protein A genetically-engineered protein formed by the fusion of prostatic acid phosphatase (PAP) and sargramostim (GM-CSF). Vaccination with antigen-presenting cells (APC) loaded with prostatic acid phosphatase-sargramostim fusion protein may elicit a cytotoxic T-cell response against tumor cells that express PAP.

Prostatic intraepithelial neoplasia Noncancerous growth of the cells lining the internal and external surfaces of the prostate gland. Having high-grade PIN may increase the risk of developing prostate cancer.

Prostatic stent Inserted through a cystoscope, it is a wire device that expands after placement thus pushing prostate tissue away from passageway allowing for easier urination.

Prostatic urethra Portion of the urethra that passes through the prostate.

Prostatitis Inflammation of the prostate gland.

Prostatron Also called TUMT or Transurethral Microwave Thermotherapy. A catheter is placed within the bladder and positioned within the prostate, then the antenna emits microwaves. This procedure increases the passageway allowing for easier urination.

Prosthesis A man-made substitute for a missing body part such as an arm or a leg; also an implant such as for the hip.

Prosthetic groups Organic and/or inorganic components other than amino acids, contained in proteins.

Prosthodontist A dentist who specializes in replacing missing teeth or other structures of the mouth to restore an individual's appearance, comfort, or health.

Prostvac Other name for vaccinia-PSA vaccine.

Protease An enzyme that breaks down long polypeptides into smaller protein units. HIV's protease enzyme cuts long chains of HIV polypeptide into the smaller, active proteins used in HIV replication.

Protease sparing regimen An anti-HIV drug regimen that does not include a PI.

Proteasome inhibitor A drug that blocks the action of proteasomes. A proteasome is a large protein complex that helps destroy other cellular proteins when they are no longer needed. Proteasome inhibitors are being studied in the treatment of cancer.

Protected health information Under HIPAA, this refers to individually identifiable health information transmitted or maintained in any form.

Protective factor Something that may decrease the chance of getting a certain disease. Some examples of protective factors for cancer are getting regular physical activity, staying at a healthy weight, and having a healthy diet.

Protein A large molecule composed of one or more chains of amino acids in a specific order; the order is determined by the base sequence of nucleotides in the gene that codes for the protein. Proteins are required for the structure, function, and regulation of the body's cells, tissues, and organs; and each protein has unique functions. Examples are hormones, enzymes, and antibodies. One of a group of substances constituting the greater part of the nitrogen-containing components of animal and vegetable tissues. They are of very complex constitution, all containing carbon, hydrogen, nitrogen, and oxygen and some containing in addition iron, phosphorous, or sulfur; chemically they are regarded as peptides (polypeptides) or combinations of amino acids and their derivatives. They are colorless, odorless, generally tasteless, and of varying degrees of solubility; they are putrefiable and readily undergo chemical change, hydrolysis, under the influence of ferments and on boiling with dilute acids or alkalis.

Protein deposits Dried tears, mucous, secretion build up on the surface of the prosthesis. It can be abrasive causing irritation to the conjunctival tissues.

Protein sequencer An instrument that will determine the sequence of amino acids, which make up a particular protein.

Proteinuria Too much protein in the urine. This may be a sign of kidney damage.

Proteoglycan A molecule that contains both protein and glycosaminoglycans, which are a type of polysaccharide. Proteoglycans are found in cartilage and other connective tissues.

Proteolysis Protein hydrolysis, the decomposition of protein.

Proteolytic enzymes Enzymes produced and secreted by the pancreas which aid in the proteolysis of proteins in the digestive tract. Pancreatic proteolytic enzymes include trypsin, chymotrypsin and carboxypeptidase; these enzymes are secreted as zymogens, inactive precursors of the enzymes, and are activated in the lumen of the digestive canal. Another proteolytic enzyme, enteropeptidase, is associated with the brush border of enterocytes; this enzyme catalyses the conversion of trypsinogen into trypsin which, in turn, can activate a number of other pancreatic zymogens.

Proteome Proteins expressed by a cell or organ at a particular time and under specific conditions.

Proteomic profile An evaluation of proteins in a sample of blood. This may help detect early cancer or cancer recurrence, or help predict response to treatment.

Proteomics A concept more than a defined technology, it refers to any protein-based approach that has the capacity to provide new information about proteins on a genomewide scale. 75% of the predicted proteins in multicellular organisms have no known cellular function.

Prothrombin time Test performed by laboratory that measures time required for a blood sample to clot. Reflects overall function of the liver.

Protocol The detailed plan for conducting an experiment such as a clinical trial. A clinical trial protocol is a lengthy document describing the trial's rationale, purpose, information about the drug or vaccine under study, participant inclusion/exclusion criteria, study endpoints, and details of the trial design.

Proton A small, positively charged particle of matter found in the atoms of all elements. Streams of protons generated by special equipment can be used for radiation treatment.

Proton beam radiation therapy A type of radiation therapy that uses protons generated by a special machine. A proton is a type of high-energy radiation that is different from an x-ray.

Proton magnetic resonance spectroscopic imaging A noninvasive imaging method that provides information about cellular activity (metabolic information). It is used along with magnetic resonance imaging (MRI) which provides information about the shape and size of the tumor (spacial information). Also called magnetic resonance spectroscopic imaging and 1H-nuclear magnetic resonance spectroscopic imaging.

Proton pump inhibitors Medicines that affect how acid is produced by the stomach's "proton pump" system, thereby decreasing stomach acid.

Protoplasm A semifluid, viscous, translucent mixture of water, proteins; lipids, carbohydrates, and inorganic salts found in all plant and animal cells.

Protozoa Nucleated microorganisms, some of which are large enough to be detected with the naked eye. They consist of a single cell and or an aggregation of nondifferentiated cells loosely held together and not forming tissues. The protozoa are divided into four classes: Sarcodina, Mastigophora, Sporozoa, and Infusoria (Ciliata).

Protozoal Having to do with the simplest organisms in the animal kingdom. Protozoa are single-cell organisms, such as ameba, and are different from bacteria, which are not members of the animal kingdom. Some protozoa can be seen without a microscope.

Provenge Other name for APC8015 vaccine.

Provera dosepak Other name for medroxyprogesterone.

Provigil Other name for modafinil.

Provirus Viral genetic material, in the form of DNA, that has been integrated into the host genome. HIV, when it is dormant in human cells, is in a proviral form

Proximal In medicine, refers to a part of the body that is closer to the center of the body than another part. For example, the knee is proximal to the toes. The opposite is distal.

Proximal vergence A convergence response attributed to the awareness of, or the impression of nearness of an object of regard.

Pruritic Causing itching

Pruritus Itching. Severe itching may be a side effect of some cancer treatments and a symptom of some types of cancers.

PS 341 A drug that is used to treat multiple myeloma and is being studied in the treatment of other types of cancer. It belongs to the families of drugs called proteosome inhibitors and dipeptidyl boronic acids. Also called Velcade and bortezomib.

Psaltarium A thin sheet of commissural fibers which bridges across the crura of the fornix beneath the splenium of the corpus callosum. It interconnects the hippocampal formations. It is also known as the hippocampal commissure.

Psammoma body A structure found in some benign (noncancerous) or malignant (cancerous) tumor cells. Psammoma bodies look like hardened concentric rings when viewed under a microscope. They can be a sign of chronic inflammation.

PSC 833 An analogue of cyclosporin-A. Valspodar inhibits p-glycoprotein, the multidrug resistance efflux pump, thereby restoring the retention and activity of some drugs in some drug-resistant tumor cells. This agent also induces caspase-mediated apoptosis.

Pseudo-allergy Reaction that mimics an allergy and does not involve the immune system.

Pseudoepitheliomatous hyperplasia Extreme irregular acanthosis with downward epidermal proliferation which may simulate a well differentiated squamous cell carcinoma.

Pseudogene A sequence of DNA similar to a gene but nonfunctional; probably the remnant of a once-functional gene that accumulated mutations.

Pseudohorn cyst Intraepidermal keratin-filled space which due to the plane of sectioning resembles a cyst, but actually represents an epidermal invagination.

Pseudomyopia The condition Accommodative Excess/Spasm causes an individual to experience blurry distance vision after prolonged near work such as reading or using a computer. The individual may appear to be nearsighted (myopia). Treatment options may include prescription lenses and/or vision therapy.

Pseudomyxoma peritonei A build-up of mucus in the peritoneal cavity. The mucus may come from ruptured ovarian cysts, the appendix, or from other abdominal tissues, and mucus-secreting cells may attach to the peritoneal lining and continue to secrete mucus.

Pseudonomas diminuta The bacterium used for validation of sterilizing filters. Recognized as the challenge organism for 0.2μm filters, its size is 0.3 x 0.8μm approximately. According to the HIMA (Health Industries Manufacturers Association) standard, filters must be successfully challenged to a titre of 107 per cm^2 to be validated as sterilizing grade 0.2μm rated.

Pseudoptosis A sagging or drooping of the upper eyelid. This is a result of orbital or global volume loss, but returns to normal elevation with a proper fitting ocular or scleral prosthesis.

Psoas muscle Originates at the lumbar vertebrae and fascia and inserts into the lesser trochanter of femur. It contributes to the flexion of the trunk and the flexion and medial rotation of the thigh.

Psoralen A substance from plants that is sensitive to light (or can be activated by light). Psoralens are used together with UV light to treat psoriasis, vitiligo, and skin nodules of cutaneous T-cell lymphoma. They are also being studied in the treatment of graft-versus-host disease. They belong to the family of drugs called furocoumarins. An example of a psoralen is methoxsalen.

Psoralen and ultraviolet A therapy (PUVA therapy) A type of photodynamic therapy used to treat skin conditions such as psoriasis, vitiligo, and skin nodules of cutaneous T-cell lymphoma. The patient receives psoralen (a drug that becomes active when it is exposed to light) by mouth or applied to the skin, followed by ultraviolet A radiation. PUVA therapy may increase the risk of getting skin cancer.

Psoriasis A chronic disease of the skin marked by red patches covered with white scales.

Psychological 'cure' Ability to restore cosmesis, to regain a normal appearance with the use of an ocular prosthesis or scleral shell. Being accepted by your peers as looking normal.

Psychologist A specialist who can talk with patients and their families about emotional and personal matters, and can help them make decisions.

Psychotherapy notes These include notes recorded by the health care provider who is a mental health professional during a counseling session, either in a private session or in a group. These notes are separate from documentation placed in the medical chart and do not include prescriptions. Specific patient authorization is required for use and disclosure of psychotherapy notes.

Psychrometer A hygrometer that uses the difference in readings between two thermometers, one having a wet bulb ventilated to cause evaporation and the other having a dry bulb, as a measure of atmospheric moisture.

Psychrophile An organism that requires temperatures below 20°C (68°F) for growth.

PTCD (Percutaneous transhepatic cholangiodrainage) A procedure to drain bile to relieve pressure in the bile ducts caused by a blockage. An x-ray of the liver and bile ducts locates the blockage of bile flow. Images made by ultrasound guide placement of a stent (tube), which remains in the liver. Bile drains through the stent into the small intestine or into a collection bag outside the body. This procedure may relieve jaundice before surgery. Also called percutaneous transhepatic biliary drainage.

PTFE (Polytetrafluoroethylene) teflon A fluoroplastic that is resistant to practically every known chemical or solvent in combination with the highest useful temperature limit of commercially available plastics. PTFE has a melt point of 620°F (327°C), a useful temperature range from -436°F (-260°C) to 500°F (260°C), high impact strength, and exceptionally low coefficient of friction. Usual processing techniques like injection molding are not possible with PTFE due to a very high molecular weight which results in a melt viscosity about 1 million times higher than is acceptable for conventional thermoplastics. PTFE resin is pressed into shapes under high pressure at room temperature and then heated to 700°F (371°C) to complete the molding (sintering process) and adjust the crystalline content.

PTH A substance made by the parathyroid gland that helps the body store and use calcium. Also called parathormone, parathyroid hormone, or parathyrin.

PTK787/ZK 222584 A substance that is being studied in the treatment of cancer. It belongs to the families of drugs called protein tyrosine kinase inhibitors and VEGF receptor kinase inhibitors. Also called vatalanib.

Ptosis Eyelid droop, caused by partial or complete loss of external orbital muscles. It is usually referring to the upper lid (UP). Lower lid (LL) would be a considered a prolapsed condition.

PTS (Computerized perceptual home vision therapy system) A home-based computerized perceptual therapy program, which was designed to enhance visual information processing. The therapy procedures address simultaneous processing, sequential processing and/or speed of information processing. This computer program contains 6 activities that are specifically for the following problems: a weakness with visual information processing skills such as figure-ground, form constancy, spatial relations, visual closure, visual discrimination, visual memory, and visualization skills, slow speed of information processing, and acquired brain injury with perceptual-cognitive deficits. This program is available only from a licensed eye care practitioner.

PTSD (Post-traumatic stress disorder) An anxiety disorder that develops in reaction to physical injury or severe mental or emotional distress, such as military combat, violent assault, natural disaster, or other life-threatening events. Having cancer may also lead to PTSD. Symptoms interfere with day-to-day living and include reliving the event in nightmares or flashbacks; avoiding people, places, and things connected to the event; feeling alone and losing interest in daily activities; and having trouble concentrating and sleeping.

Puberty The time of life when a child experiences physical and hormonal changes that mark a transition into adulthood. The child develops secondary sexual characteristics and becomes able to have children. Secondary sexual characteristics include growth of pubic, armpit, and leg hair; breast enlargement; and increased hip width in girls. In boys, they include growth of pubic, face, chest and armpit hair; voice changes; penis and testicle growth, and increased shoulder width.

Pubic symphysis The joining of the pubic bones, in the medial plane, by thick fibrocartilage.

Public health authority A National, state, local or tribal person or organization that is required to conduct public health activities.

Public health Organized efforts of society to protect, promote, and restore people's health. It is the combination of science, skills, and beliefs that is directed to the maintenance and improvement of the health of all the people through collective or social actions. The programs, services and institutions involved emphasize the prevention of disease and the health needs of the population as a whole. Public health activities change with variations in technology and social values but the goals remain the same: to reduce the amount of disease, premature death, and disease-produced discomfort and disability in the population. Public health is thus a social institution, a discipline, and a practice.

Pubovaginal sling A surgical procedure in which a man-made or cadaveric piece of material is placed under the bladder neck to support and immobilize. This technique improves sphincter function and decreases bladder neck movement, improving continence.

Pulmonary arteries and trunk The large vessel which originates from the conus arteriosus of the right ventricle (pulmonary trunk). It divides into the right and left pulmonary ateries. The pulmonary arteries deliver deoxygenated blood to the lungs for gas exchange.

Pulmonary Having to do with the lungs.

Pulmonary hypoplasia When the contents of the abdomen, including the stomach, intestine, liver, spleen and kidneys, move into the chest and prevent the lungs from growing to normal size. This can happen with congenital diaphragmatic hernia

(CDH) and congenital cystic adenomatoid malformation (CCAM).

Pulmonary rehabilitation education Education about behavior and lifestyle changes to help patients with chronic lung disease decrease breathing problems, return to daily activities, and improve quality of life. Education may include instruction about breathing exercises, nutrition, use of medicines, and ways for the patient to reduce stress and save energy.

Pulmonary sulcus tumorA type of lung cancer that begins in the upper part of a lung and spreads to nearby tissues such as the ribs and vertebrae. Most pulmonary sulcus tumors are non-small cell cancers. Also called Pancoast tumor.

Pulmonary veins The four veins (right/left superior and inferior) that return oxygenated blood from the lungs to the left atrium.

Pulp The nerves, blood vessels and connective tissue inside a tooth.

Pulp cap A medicated covering over a small area of exposed pulp tissue.

Pulp chamber The center or innermost portion of the tooth containing the pulp.

Pulpectomy Complete removal of the pulp (commonly done in children's teeth).

Pulpitis Inflammation of the pulp; common cause of toothache.

Pulpotomy Partial removal of the pulp tissue.

Pulse generator The part of the pacemaker or defibrillator system that contains the electronics and the battery. It is implanted under the skin in the abdominal or pectoral area.

Pulvinar The cushion-like nuclear mass in the posterior dorsal thalamus overhanging the geniculate bodies of the midbrain. It has reciprocal connections with areas of parietal, temporal and occipital cortex.

Pump (pump) A device that is used to give a controlled amount of a liquid at a specific rate. For example, pumps are used to give drugs (such as chemotherapy or pain medicine) or nutrients

Punch biopsy Removal of a small disk-shaped sample of tissue using a sharp, hollow device. The tissue is then examined under a microscope.

Pupil The opening at the center of the iris of the eye. It contracts (dilates) in the dark and when the eye is focused on a distant object.

Pupillary distance (PD) The distances between the pupils of the eyes, in millimeters — a necessary measurement for proper lens prescription.

Pupillary reflex The automatic contraction or enlargement of the pupil when confronted with the presence or absence of light, accommodation, or emotional change.

Pupillometer A device used to measure the distance between the pupils of the eyes, in millimeters, which is a necessary measurement for proper lens prescription. It also measures the diameter of the pupil.

Pure culture A culture containing only one species of microorganism.

Purification The removal of impurities of concern. The term has one meaning when applied to the preparation of drinking water, another when applied to reagent grade water for the laboratory, and still another when applied to water used to rinse ICs (Integrated Circuit devices).

Purified insulins Insulins with much less of the impure proinsulin. It is thought that the use of purified insulins may help avoid or reduce some of the problems of people with diabetes such as allergic reactions.

Purified protein derivative (PPD) A substance used in the tuburculin skin test to determine if a person has been exposed to Mycobacterium tuberculosis, the bacterium that causes tuberculosis (TB). PPD is usually injected just below the skin. A hard red bump or a swollen area at the injection site indicates that the person was exposed to the bacterium. Additional tests are required to determine if the person has active TB infection.

Purified water, Water rendered suitable for pharmaceutical purposes by processes such as distillation, ion-exchange treatment (deionization or demineralization), or reverse osmosis. It meets rigid specifications for chemical purity with respect to drinking water, and it contains no added substances. Cannot be used as raw material for parenterals. Common uses are: a rinse for equipment, vials, and ampoules, and as make up for cosmetics, bulk chemicals, and oral products.

Purine A nitrogen-containing, double-ring, basic compound that occurs in nucleic acids. The purines in DNA and RNA are adenine and guanine.

Purinethol A drug used to treat acute lymphatic leukemia. It belongs to the family of drugs called antimetabolites. Also called mercaptopurine.

Purity The ratio of desirable to undesirable components in a liquid as determined on a weight basis per unit volume of sample.

Purlytin Other name for tin ethyl etiopurpurin.

Purple clover Trifolium pratense. A plant whose flowers have been used in some cultures to treat certain medical problems. It is being studied in the relief of menopausal symptoms and may have anticancer effects. Also called red clover and wild clover.

Purpura 1. A hemorraghic disease characterized by extravasation of blood into the tissues producing spontaneous ecchymoses and petechiae.

2. Skin rash resulting from bleeding into the skin from small blood vessels; the individual

purple spots of the rash are called petechiae.

Pursuit dysfunction A condition in which the individual's ability to follow a moving target is inadequate. Vision therapy is an effective treatment option.

Pursuit test Measures the eyes ability to follow a moving target.

Purulent Infected and producing pus.

Pus A protein-rich liquid inflammation product comprised of leukocytes, a thin fluid and cellular debris.

Putamen The largest component of the lenticular nucleus, situated lateral to the globus pallidus and separated from it by the lateral medullary lamina. The putamen is continuous with the caudate nucleus rostrally.

PV701 An attenuated, replication-competent, oncolytic strain of Newcastle disease virus. PV701 selectively lyses tumor cells. The selectivity of this agent is related to defects in the interferon-mediated antiviral response found in tumor cells.

PVC (Polyvinyl chloride) The largest volume of the vinyl family of plastics. Overall it has excellent basic properties, may be easily processed and welded, and is exceptionally economical in cost. Homopolymers grades of PVC comprise over 80% of all PVC used, and contain 56.8% chlorine by weight. When the chlorine content is increased to about 67% its heat deflection temperature at 264 psi increases from 155°F (68°C) to 218°F (103°C). Because PVC is a thermally sensitive thermoplastic compounding ingredients such as heat stabilizers, lubricants, fillers, plasticizers, impact modifiers, pigments, and processing aids must be added to make it processible. PVC is prone to produce extractables during start-up in high purity water.

PVDF (Polyvinylidene fluoride) kynar, sygef, solef A thermoplastic fluoropolymer with a melt point of 352°F (178°C), and a wide service range from -40°F (-40°C) to 284°F (140°C). It has a very linear chemical structure, and is similar to PTFE with the exception of not being fully fluorinated, i.e. having 3% hydrogen by weight. Its drawbacks in the area of chemical resistance include unsuitability with strong alkalis, fuming acids, polar solvents, amines, ketones, and esters. It has a high tensile strength as well as a high heat deflection temperature. It is readily weldable, offers high purity qualities, and is resistant to permeation of gases. PVDF is a relatively inert material and contributes little in the way of contamination to pharmaceutical water.

Pyelonephritis (Nephropyelitis) Inflammation of the kidney and renal pelvis often by ascending bacterial infection.

Pyknosis Condensation of nuclear chromatin producing a dense, shrunken appearing nucleus.

Pyloric sphincter The muscle between the stomach and the small intestine.

Pyloric stenosis An enlargement of the muscle between the stomach and the small intestine, blocking the passage of food and liquids forward into the intestines.

Pyloric valve Fold of mucous membrane located at the pyloric orifice of the stomach.

Pyloroplasty An operation that enlarges the opening between the stomach and small intestine so food and liquid can move forward and be digested normally.

Pylorus Where the stomach connects to the small intestine.

Pyo Pus, e.g. pyometra - an accumulation of pus within the uterus, e.g. pyogranuloma - an infiltration of polymorphonuclear cells into an area of chronic inflammation characterized by mononuclear cells, macrophages, lymphocytes and even plasma cells.

Pyorrhea Older term for periodontal (gum) disease.

Pyramids (medullary) Two longitudinal eminences located on the ventral surface of the medulla oblongata formed by the corticospinal tract fibers.

Pyrazine diazohydroxide A substance that is being studied in the treatment of cancer.

Pyrazoloacridine A 9-methoxy acridine compound containing a reducible 5-nitro substituent. Pyrazoloacridine appears to intercalate into DNA and inhibit RNA synthesis, DNA synthesis, and the activities of topoisomerases I and II, thereby causing cytotoxicity.

Pyriform lobe A pear-shaped lobe that is prominent in macrosmatic animals. It includes the lateral olfactory gyrus, and areas (uncus, periamygdaloid, entorhinal) of the anterior parahippocampal gyrus. This corresponds to the primary and secondary olfactory areas of cortex.

Pyrimethamine (daraprim) An antibiotic used in treating toxoplasmosis, and rarely for the treatment or prophylaxis of PCP

Pyrimidine A nitrogen-containing, single ring, basic compound that occurs in nucleic acids. The pyrimidines in DNA are cytosine and thymine, in RNA, cytosine, and uracil.

Pyrogen A foreign substance that produces a fever response in humans and animals, hence the name pyrogen (heat producing). Chemically, the lipopolysaccharide outer layer of gram-negative bacteria. Bacterial pyrogens were at one time believed to be toxic substances released when bacterial cells disintegrate and are therefore still referred to as endotoxins. Parenteral drugs must be essentially pyrogen free. Pyrophoric A chemical that will spontaneously ignite in air at or below a temperature of 130°F (54.5°C).

Pyroxamide A substance that is being studied in the treatment of cancer. It belongs to the family of drugs called histone deacetylase inhibitors.

Pyuria The presence of pus in the urine; usually an indication of kidney or urinary tract infection.

Q.D. Once a day dosing instructions.

Q.I.D. Four times a day dosing instructions.

Q10 A substance found in most tissues in the body, and in many foods. It can also be made in the laboratory. It is used by the body to produce energy for cells, and as an antioxidant. It is being studied in the treatment of cancer and in the relief of side effects caused by some cancer treatments. Also called coenzyme Q10, CoQ10, vitamin Q10, and ubiquinone.

Q4H Common abbreviation for "every four hours". Also, q5h, would be every five hours, q6h would be every six, etc.

QC (Quality control) Checking or testing, that specifications are met, or the regulatory process through which the industry measures actual quality performance, compares it with standards, and acts on the difference.

QS21 A substance from plants that is being studied together with vaccine therapy for its ability to improve the way the immune system responds to disease. It belongs to the family of drugs called saponin adjuvants.

Quadrant One section of something that has been divided into four equal parts

Quadrantectomy Surgical removal of the region of the breast (approximately one quarter) containing cancer.

Quadriceps Collective name of the rectus femoris, vastus intermedius, vastus lateralis, and vastus medialis muscles, which all insert into the tuberosity of the tibia via a common tendon. They contribute to the extension of the leg upon the thigh.

Quadrigeminal plate and cistern The posterior part of the brainstem, at the mesencephalon (midbrain), has four knobby bit: two superior colliculi and two slightly smaller inferior collicul. The enlarged subarachnoid space posterior is called the Quadrigeminal Plate Cistern (QP or Kewpee Cister), and is contiguous with the ambient (circum-mesencephalic) cistern. The QP cistern looks like a smile. During brain herniation, the smile become crooked or disappears entirely, as the brainstem shifts and the subarachnoid space is obliterated.

Qualification Action of providing that equipment or ancillary systems are properly installed, work correctly, and actually lead to the expected results. Qualification is part of validation, but the individual qualification steps alone do not constitute process validation.

Qualitative Of, relating to, or expressed in relative or subjective terms‹impossible to precisely quantify.

Quality Quality is, according to the Institute of Medicine (IOM), the degree to which health services for individuals and populations increase the likelihood of desired health outcomes and are consistent with current professional knowledge. Quality can be defined as a measure of the degree to which delivered health services meet established professional standards and judgments of value to consumers. Quality may also be seen as the degree to which actions taken or not taken maximize the probability of beneficial health outcomes and minimize risk and other untoward outcomes, given the existing state of medical science and art. Quality is frequently described as having three dimensions: quality of input resources; quality of the process of services delivery (the use of appropriate procedures for a given condition); and quality of outcome of service use (actual improvement in condition or reduction of harmful effects). Quality programs are commonly called QA, TQM, QI, CQI all referring to the process of monitoring quality in systematic ways.

Quality assurance (QA) Activities and programs intended to assure the quality of care in a defined medical setting. Such programs include peer or utilization review components to identify and remedy deficiencies in quality. The program must have a mechanism for assessing its effectiveness and may measure care against pre-established standards. Also called quality improvement. A formal methodology and set of activities designed to access the quality of services provided. Quality assurance includes formal review of care, problem identification, corrective actions to remedy any deficiencies and evaluation of actions taken.

Quality function The entire collection of activities from which the industry achieves fitness for use, no matter where these activities are performed.

Quality of care A level of performance or accomplishment that characterizes health care. Ultimately, measures of the quality of care always depend upon clinical outcomes or value judgments, but there are ingredients and determinants of quality that can be measured objectively, such as structure, process or procedures, and outcomes.

Quality of life The degree to which individuals perceive themselves as able to function physically, emotionally and socially. In a general sense, it is that which makes life worth living. In a more "quantitative" sense it refers to a person's time remaining alive, free of impairment, disability, or handicap.

Quality unit (s) An organizational unit independent of production that fulfills both Quality Assurance and Quality Control responsibilities. This may be in the form of separate QA and QC units, a single individual (or group), depending upon the size and structure of the organization.

Quantitative Of, relating to, or expressed in terms of quantity.

Quarantine The status of materials isolated physically or by other effective means pending a decision on their subsequent approval or rejection.

Quick stop DNA mutants of E. coli cease replication immediately when the temperature is increased to 42°C.

R flurbiprofen An orally active synthetic enantiomer of flurbiprofen. R-flurbiprofen activates c-Jun N terminal kinase, increases AP-1 binding to DNA, and downregulates cyclin D1 expression, resulting in arrest of tumor cells in the G1 phase of the cell cycle and apoptosis. This agent also affects the expression of nuclear factor kappa B, a rapid response transcription factor that stimulates the immune response to tumor cells. R-flurbiprofen does not inhibit the enzyme cyclo-oxygenase.

R TPA (Recombinant tissue plasminogen activator) A protein that is made by the body and that helps dissolve blood clots. It can also be made in the laboratory and is used in the treatment of heart attack and stroke. It is also being studied in the treatment of cancer. r-tPA belongs to the family of drugs called systemic thrombolytic agents. Also called tissue plasminogen activator (TPA), Activase, and Alteplase.

R (+)XK469 The R-isomer of a synthetic quinoxaline phenoxypropionic acid derivative with proapoptotic and antiproliferative activities. R (+)XK469 selectively inhibits topoisomerase II-beta, blocks activation of MEK/MAPK signaling kinases, stimulates caspases, and upregulates p53-dependent proteins, including cyclins A and B1, thereby arresting cancer cells in the G2/M phase of the cell cycle. Both R (+) and S (-) isomers of this agent are cytotoxic, although the R-isomer is more potent.

R101933 A substance that is being studied for its ability to make cancer cells respond to drugs to which they have become resistant. It belongs to the family of drugs called multidrug resistance inhibitors.

R115777 A substance that is being studied in the treatment of cancer. It inhibits the transformation of normal cells into cancer cells. It belongs to the family of drugs called enzyme inhibitors. Also called tipifarnib.

R5 tropic virus Also known as M-tropic virus. A strain of HIV that uses the chemokine receptor CCR5 as a co-receptor to bind to and infect human cells. HIV is usually R5 tropic early on in infection, but the virus can switch to using a different co-receptor as the disease progresses.

Rabies A disease of the nervous system caused by the rabies virus. Rabies is marked by an increase in saliva production, abnormal behaviour, and eventual paralysis and death.

Radiation Energy released in the form of particles or electromagnetic waves. Common sources of radiation include radon gas, cosmic rays from outer space, and medical x-rays.

Radiation dermatitis A skin condition that is a common side effect of radiation therapy. The affected skin becomes painful, red, itchy, and blistered.

Radiation enteritis Inflammation of the small intestine caused by radiation therapy to the abdomen, pelvis, or rectum. Symptoms include nausea, vomiting, abdominal pain and cramping, frequent bowel movements, watery or bloody diarrhea, fatty stools, and weight loss. Some of these symptoms may continue for a long time.

Radiation fibrosis The formation of scar tissue as a result of radiation therapy.

Radiation hybrid A hybrid cell containing small fragments of irradiated human chromosomes. Maps of irradiation sites on chromosomes for the human, rat, mouse, and other genomes provide important markers, allowing the construction of very precise STS maps indispensable to studying multifactorial diseases.

Radiation nurse A health professional who specializes in caring for people who are receiving radiation therapy.

Radiation oncologist A doctor who specializes in using radiation to treat cancer.

Radiation physicist A person who makes sure that the radiation machine delivers the right amount of radiation to the correct site in the body. The physicist works with the radiation oncologist to choose the treatment schedule and dose that has the best chance of killing the most cancer cells.

Radiation sterilization Sterilization using gamma radiation emitted from radioactive materials such as cobalt-60, or cesium 137. If proper dosage of nuclear radiation can be documented, sterility testing is not required.

Radiation surgery A radiation therapy procedure that uses special equipment to position the patient and precisely deliver a large radiation dose to a tumor and not to normal tissue. This procedure does not use surgery. It is used to treat brain tumors and other brain disorders. It is also being studied in the treatment of other types of cancer, such as lung cancer. Also called radiosurgery, stereotactic external-beam radiation, stereotactic radiation therapy, stereotactic radiosurgery, and stereotaxic radiosurgery.

Radiation therapist A health professional who gives radiation treatment.

Radiation therapy The use of high-energy radiation from x-rays, gamma rays, neutrons, and other sources to kill cancer cells and shrink tumors. Radiation may come from a machine outside the body (external-beam radiation therapy), or it may come from radioactive material placed in the body near cancer cells (internal radiation therapy, implant radiation, or brachytherapy). Systemic radiation therapy uses a radioactive substance, such as a radiolabeled monoclonal antibody, that circulates throu-ghout the body. Also called radiotherapy.

Radical cystectomy Surgery to remove the bladder as well as nearby tissues and organs.

Radical hysterectomy Surgery to remove the uterus, cervix, and part of the vagina. The ovaries, fallopian tubes, and nearby lymph nodes may also be removed.

Radical lymph node dissection A surgical procedure to remove most or all of the lymph nodes that drain lymph from the area around a tumor. The lymph nodes are then examined under a microscope to see if cancer cells have spread to them.

Radical mastectomy Surgery for breast cancer in which the breast, chest muscles, and all of the lymph nodes under the arm are removed. For many years, this was the breast cancer operation used most often, but it is used rarely now. Doctors consider radical mastectomy only when the tumor has spread to the chest muscles. Also called the Halsted radical mastectomy.

Radical nephrectomy Surgery to remove an entire kidney, nearby adrenal gland and lymph nodes, and other surrounding tissue.

Radical perineal prostatectomy Surgery to remove all of the prostate through an incision between the scrotum and the anus. Nearby lymph nodes are sometimes removed through a separate incision in the wall of the abdomen.

Radical prostatectomy Surgery to remove the entire prostate. The two types of radical prostatectomy are retropubic prostatectomy (surgery through an incision in the wall of the abdomen) and perineal prostatectomy (surgery through an incision between the scrotum and the anus).

Radical retropubic prostatectomy Surgery to remove all of the prostate and nearby lymph nodes through an incision in the wall of the abdomen.

Radiculopathy Infection or other damage of the peripheral nerves and spinal roots, accompanied by weakness, numbness, and eventual -paralysis. Radiculopathy is distinguished from peripheral neuropathy frequently by its asymmetric presentation .

Radioactive Giving off radiation.

Radioactive drug A drug containing a radioactive substance that is used in the diagnosis and treatment of cancer and in pain management of bone metastases. Also called a radiopharmaceutical.

Radioactive fallout Airborne radioactive particles that fall to the ground during and after an atomic bombing, nuclear weapons test, or nuclear plant accident.

Radioactive implant A source of high-dose radiation that is temporarily placed right into and around a cancer to kill the cancer cells.

Radioactive iodine A radioactive form of iodine, often used for imaging tests or as a treatment for thyroid cancer and certain other cancers. For imaging tests, the patient takes a small dose of radioactive iodine that collects in thyroid cells and certain kinds of tumors and can be detected by a scanner. For treatment of thyroid cancer, the patient takes a large dose of radioactive iodine, which kills thyroid cells. Radioactive iodine is also used in internal radiation therapy for prostate cancer, intraocular (eye) melanoma, and carcinoid tumors. The radioactive iodine is given by infusion or sealed in seeds, which are placed in or near the tumor to kill cancer cells.

Radioactive material A material or combination of materials that spontaneously emits ionizing radiation.

Radioactive palladium A radioactive form of palladium (a metallic element that resembles platinum). When used to treat prostate cancer, radioactive seeds (small pellets that contain radioactive palladium) are placed in the prostate. Cancer cells are killed by the energy given off as the radioactive material decays (breaks down).

Radioactive seed A small, radioactive pellet that is placed in or near a tumor. Cancer cells are killed by the energy given off as the radioactive material decays (breaks down).

Radioallergosorbent test (RAST) A solid-phase radioimmunoassay for detecting IgE antibody specific for a particular allergen.

Radiofrequency ablation The use of electrodes to heat and destroy abnormal tissue.

Radiography The use of X-rays in diagnosis

Radioimmunoassay (RIA) A widely used technique for measurement of primary antigen-antibody interactions, and for the determination of the level of important biological substances in mixed samples. It takes advantage of the specificity of the antigen-antibody interaction and the sensitivity that derives from measurement of radioactively labelled materials.

Radioimmunoguided surgery A procedure that uses radioactive substances to locate tumors so that they can be removed by surgery.

Radioimmunotherapy Treatment with a radioactive substance that is linked to an antibody that will attach to the tumor when injected into thc body.

Radioisotope An isotope (portion of an atom) that is radioactive. In certain imaging procedures, radioisotopes are injected. They travel through the body in areas where the disease is active, showing up as highlighted areas on the images. In breast cancer, radioisotopes are used to check for metastasis to the bones or the liver.

Radiolabeled Any compound that has been joined with a radioactive substance.

Radiologic exam A test that uses radiation or other imaging procedures to find signs of cancer or other abnormalities.

Radiologic technologist A health professional (not a physician) trained to properly position patients for x-rays, to load film and take the images, and to develop and check the images for quality. Since mammograms (breast x-rays) are done on a machine that is used only for mammograms, the technologist must have special training in mammography. The films taken by the technologist are sent to a radiologist to be read.

Radiologist A doctor who specializes in creating and interpreting pictures of areas inside the body. The pictures are produced with x-rays, sound waves, or other types of energy.

Radiology The use of radiation (such as x-rays) or other imaging technologies (such as ultrasound and magnetic resonance imaging) to diagnose or treat disease.

Radionuclide scanning A test that produces pictures (scans) of internal parts of the body. The person is given an injection or swallows a small amount of radioactive material; a machine called a scanner then measures the radioactivity in certain organs.

Radiopharmaceutical A drug containing a radioactive substance that is used in the diagnosis and treatment of cancer and in pain management of bone metastases. Also called a radioactive drug.

Radiosensitization The use of a drug that makes tumor cells more sensitive to radiation therapy.

Radiosensitizer A drug that makes tumor cells more sensitive to radiation therapy.

Radiosurgery A radiation therapy procedure that uses special equipment to position the patient and precisely deliver a large radiation dose to a tumor and not to normal tissue. This procedure does not use surgery. It is used to treat brain tumors and other brain disorders. It is also being studied in the treatment of other types of cancer, such as lung cancer. Also called radiation surgery, stereotactic external-beam radiation, stereotactic radiation therapy, stereotactic radiosurgery, and stereotaxic radiosurgery.

Radiotherapy The use of high-energy radiation from x-rays, gamma rays, neutrons, and other sources to kill cancer cells and shrink tumors. Radiation may come from a machine outside the body (external-beam radiation therapy), or it may come from radioactive material placed in the body near cancer cells (internal radiation therapy, implant radiation, or brachytherapy). Systemic radiotherapy uses a radioactive substance, such as a radiolabeled monoclonal antibody, that circulates throughout the body. Also called radiation therapy.

Radius One of the two bones of the forearm, it has a large articulation with the carpal bones that form the wrist.

Radon A radioactive gas that is released by uranium, a substance found in soil and rock. Breathing in too much radon can damage lung cells and lead to lung cancer.

Rales Sounds in the lungs, often indicative of disease.

Raloxifene A selective benzothiophene estrogen receptor modulator (SERM). Raloxifene binds to estrogen receptors (ER) as a mixed estrogen agonist/antagonist; it displays both an ER-alpha-selective partial agonist/antagonist effect and a pure ER-beta-selective antagonist effect. This agent functions as an estrogen agonist in some tissues (bones, lipid metabolism) and as an estrogen antagonist in others (endometrium and breasts), with the potential for producing some of estrogen's beneficial effects without producing its adverse effects.

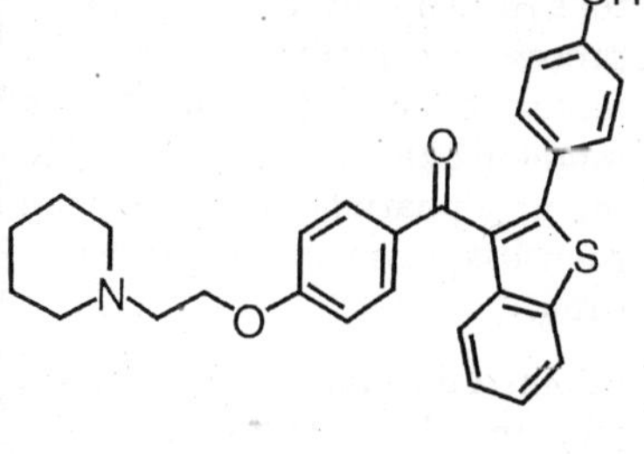

Figure The structure of Raloxifene

Raltitrexed An anticancer drug that stops tumor cells from growing by blocking the ability of cells to make DNA. Also called ICI D1694. It belongs to the family of drugs called thymidylate synthase inhibitors.

Rami (communicantes gray) Nerve bundles that extend from the sympathetic trunk to all 31 pairs of spinal nerves. They consist of unmyelinated postganglionic sympathetic fibers originating from cell bodies within the sympathetic trunk and distributed with the spinal nerves to cutaneous effectors (smooth muscle and glands).

Ramus A branch of the lateral fissure (of Sylvius) extending vertically from its stem into the inferior frontal gyrus and separating the pars triangularis from the pars opercularis.

R. (Anterior Horizontal): A horizontal branch of the lateral fissure (of Sylvius) extending forward from the stem of fissure and separating the pars orbitalis from the pars triangularis of the inferior frontal gyrus. It sometimes has a common origin with the anterior ascending ramus.

R. (Posterior): That branch of the lateral fissure (of Sylvius) distal to the point of origin of the anterior ascending and anterior horizontal rami.

Random (General) 1. Having no specific pattern or objective. Of or designating a chance process in which the occurrence of previous events is of no value in predicting future events. From Old French, random, meaning force, violence, impetuosity.

2. Sometimes used as a synonym for haphazard. Usage also refers to a formal process meeting, or believed to meet, the conditions specified under the statistical definition of random.

Random allocation A method for assigning patients to treatment using a random process.

Random number A number generated or drawn via some defined random process.

Random process Any method or procedure whose output is random (i.e., cannot be predicted by any means).

Random variable A variable that may assume any one of a number of different values, where the set of possible values is determined by a probability distribution, such as binomial or normal.

Randomization 1. The process of assigning patients to treatment using a random process, such as via use of a table of random numbers.

2. The process of deriving an order or sequence of items, determinations, specimens, readings, or the like using a random process.

Randomization visit The visit where the participant is randomly assigned to treatment.

Randomized clinical trial A study in which the participants are assigned by chance to separate groups that compare different treatments; neither the researchers nor the participants can choose which group. Using chance to assign people to groups means that the groups will be similar and that the treatments they receive can be compared objectively. At the time of the trial, it is not known which treatment is best. It is the patient's choice to be in a randomized trial.

Randomized controlled clinical trial A clinical trial that involves at least one test treatment and one control treatment, concurrent enrollment and follow-up of the test- and control-treated groups, and in which the treatments to be administered are selected by a random process, such that neither the patients nor the persons responsible for their selection or treatment can influence the assignments, and where the assignments remain unknown to the patients and clinic staff until the patients have been determined to be eligible for enrollment into the trial (and then in blinded trials may be revealed to patients and clinic personnel only by letter or number codes).

Randomized Having been assigned to a treatment via a random process. Normally considered to have occurred when the randomization schedule is sent to the unit pharmacist, so they can then dispense the appropriate drug.

Randomized trial A type of clinical trial in which participants are assigned by chance to one of two or more treatment or placebo groups. A randomized trial design helps researchers gather meaningful information and make valid statistical calculations.

Ranpirnase A natural homologue of ribonuclease A isolated from the eggs of the frog Rana pipiens. Ranpirnase primarily degrades cellular transfer RNA with a substrate specificity for uridine-guanidine base-pair sequences, resulting in inhibition of protein synthesis and cytotoxicity. This agent also activates caspase-9 in mitochondria, resulting in tumor cell apoptosis.

Rapamune Other name for sirolimus.

Rapamycin A drug used to help prevent the body from rejecting organ and bone marrow transplants. It is also being studied as a treatment for cancer. Rapamycin belongs to the family of drugs called immunosuppressants. It is now called sirolimus.

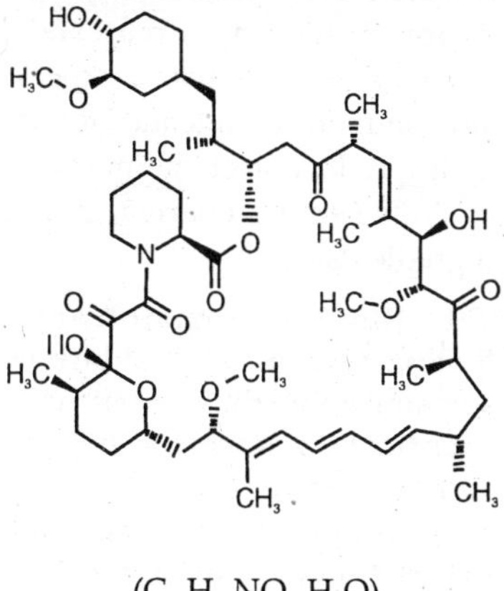

$(C_{44}H_{69}NO_{12}H_2O)$

Figure Rapamycin

Raphe The midline plane of the midbrain, pons, or medulla oblongata.

Raphe nuclei Cells groups located along the midline of the medulla, pons, and midbrain whose fibers are distributed widely in the neuraxis. They use serotonin as a neurotransmitter although not exclusively.

Rapid exchange (RX) A feature available on balloon catheters, also known as monorail or rail segment, which allows for easy exchange of the balloon catheter without removing the original guidewire.

Rapid hormone cycling A procedure in which drugs that block the production of male hormones are alternated with male hormones and/or drugs that promote the production of male hormones. This procedure is being studied in the treatment of prostate cancer.

Rapid onset opioid An opioid that relieves pain quickly. Opioids are drugs similar to opiates such as morphine and codeine but do not contain and are not made from opium.

Rapid test A type of HIV-1 ELISA test that can detect antibodies to HIV in the blood in less than 30 minutes with greater than 99% sensitivity and specificity. A positive rapid test result should be confirmed by an HIV Western blot test.

Ras gene A gene that has been found to cause cancer when it is altered (mutated). Agents that block its activity may stop the growth of cancer.

Ras peptide A short piece of the ras protein, which is made by the ras gene. The ras gene has been found to cause cancer when it is mutated (changed).

Ras peptide cancer vaccine A cancer vaccine containing a RAS oncogene-encoded peptide with potential antineoplastic activity. RAS peptide cancer vaccine may stimulate a RAS peptide-specific antitumoral T-cell cytotoxic immune response, resulting in an inhibition of tumor cell proliferation and tumor cell death.

Rasburicase A recombinant urate oxidase enzyme isolated from a genetically-modified strain of Saccharomyces cerevisae. Urate oxidase catalyzes the oxidation of uric acid to the excretable mebolite allantoin, a molecule that is 5-10 times more water-soluble than uric acid. An enzyme that occurs endogenously in most mammals, urate oxidase is not found in humans.

Rattlesnake root Cimicifuga racemosa. A substance obtained from the root of the plant has been used in some cultures to treat a number of medical problems. It is being studied in the treatment of hot flashes and other symptoms of menopause. The plant is also called black cohosh, black snakeroot, bugwort, and bugbane.

RAV12 A monoclonal antibody that is being studied in the treatment of some types of cancer. Monoclonal antibodies are made in the laboratory and can locate and bind to cancer cells. It binds to a carbohydrate (sugar) molecule that is found on gastric, colon, pancreatic, prostate, ovarian, breast, and kidney cancer cells.

Ravuconazole A triazole with antifungal activity. Ravuconazole inhibits 14a demethylase, an enzyme involved in sterol synthesis, resulting in lysis of the fungal cell wall and fungal cell death.

Raw data 1. Measurements and observations recorded on study data forms.

2. Unedited computer-generated listings of data from study data forms, prior to use of reduction and summary procedures needed for data analysis.

Raw material A general term used to denote starting materials, reagents, intermediates, process aids, and solvents intended for use in the production of intermediates or APIs (Active Pharmaceutical Ingredients).

RBST (Bovine somatotropin) Recom-binant bovine somatotropin (rBST) is virtually identical to a cow's natural somatotropin, a hormone produced in its pituitary gland that stimulates milk production. Treatment with rBST can increase a cow's milk production by 10 percent to 15 percent.

Reactive hypoglycemia A fall in blood sugar which causes symptoms during the period following meals. Simply put, the body has trouble braking the secretion of insulin after a meal, resulting in the blood sugar dropping further than it should. Reactive hypoglycemia is different from spontaneous hypoglycemia, which is not assoicated with meal ingestion. Reactive hypoglycemia generally has a benign prognosis.

Reading Requires the use of good visual skills, which are distance and near acuity, accommodation skills, binocularity skills (convergence), oculomotor skills (saccadic), peripheral vision, figure-ground, form constancy, spatial relations, visual closure, visual discrimination, visual memory, and visualization.

Reagent A substance used (as in detecting or measuring a component, in preparing a product, or in developing photographs) because of its chemical or biological activity.

Reagent grade water Water suitable for use in making up reagents or for use in sensitive analytical procedures. There are several grades of reagent grade water as defined by various professional organizations, such as ASTM, CAP, NCCLS, and ACS: 1. Type I: Used for procedures requiring maximum accuracy and precision, such as atomic spectrometry, flame photometry, enzymology, blood gas, pH and specific ion determinations; reference buffer solutions; and reconstitution of lyophilized materials used as standards. ASTM to produce Type I water specifies distillation pretreatment of feedwater.

2. Type II: Recommended for most analytical or general laboratory testing such as hematological, seralogical, and microbiological procedures as well as chemical methods not specifically stated or proven to require Type I quality. ASTM specifies preparation of Type II by distillation and recommends it whenever freedom from organic impurities is important.

3. Type III: Satisfactory for some general laboratory tests; for most qualitative analyses such as urinalysis, parasitology, and histological procedures; for rinsing of analytical samples; preparation of stock solutions; and for washing or rinsing of glassware (final glassware rinsing should be performed with the water type specified for the procedure performed). Distillation, mixed-bed deioni-zation, and reverse osmosis (with high quality feedwater) can be used to generate Type III.

Reagents, reagent strips Terms no longer used for diabetes blood and urine glucose or acetone test strips.

Reagin Allergist's term for IgE antibodies.

Real value Measurement of an economic amount corrected for change in price over time (inflation), thus expressing a value in terms of constant prices. A common term in economics.

Rebeccamycin A substance that is being studied in the treatment of cancer. It belongs to the family of drugs called antineoplastic antibiotics.

Rebeccamycin analogue A synthetic diethylaminoethyl analogue of the indolocarbazole glycoside antineoplastic antibiotic rebeccamycin. The rebeccamycin analogue intercalates into DNA and stabilizes the DNA-topoisomerase I complex, thereby interfering with the topoisomerase I-catalyzed DNA breakage-reunion reaction and initiating DNA cleavage and apoptosis.

Rebif Other name for recombinant interferon beta.

Rebound A swing to a high level of glucose (sugar) in the blood after having a low level.

Recalcification A technique producing serum from anticoagulated plasma. Citrate and oxalate act as anticoagulants because they are Ca^{++} (Calcium Ion) chelating agents; Ca^{++} as calcium chloride is added in excess (1/40 Molar). Ca^{++} is a coagulation co-factor (catalyst) and promotes clot formation.

Receptor A protein on the surface of a cell that serves as a binding site for substances outside the cell, such as HIV floating free in the blood.

Recessive allele A gene that is expressed only when its counterpart allele on the matching chromosome is also recessive (not dominant). Autosomal recessive disorders develop in persons who receive two copies of the mutant gene, one from each parent who is a carrier.

Recessive gene A gene which will be expressed only if there are 2 identical copies or, for a male, if one copy is present on the X chromosome.

Reciprocal translocation When a pair of chromosomes exchange exactly the same length and area of DNA. Results in a shuffling of genes.

Recirculation Continuous recirculation may be necessary to maintain uniformly high purity in larger water systems. Water is continuously recirculated and reprocessed to prevent stagnation and to rinse out residual impurities in the system. Bacteria flourish in stagnant water, especially if temperature is conducive to growth.

Recombinant Made through genetic engineering, which is also called gene splicing or recombinant DNA technology. By putting animal or plant genes into the genetic material of bacteria or yeast cells, these microorganisms can be turned into "factories" to make proteins for medical uses.

Recombinant clone Clone containing recombinant DNA molecules.

Recombinant DNA DNA that contains genes from different

sources that have been combined by the technique of genetic engineering rather than by breeding experiments Genetic engineering is therefore also known as recombinant DNA technology.

Recombinant DNA molecules In the context of the NIH Guidelines, recombinant DNA molecules are those constructed outside living cells by joining natural or synthetic DNA segments to DNA molecules that can replicate in a living cell, or molecules that result from the replication of those described above.

Recombinant DNA technology Procedure used to join together DNA segments in a cell-free system (an environment outside a cell or organism). Under appropriate conditions, a recombinant DNA molecule can enter a cell and replicate there, either autonomously or after it has become integrated into a cellular chromosome.

Recombinant fowlpox GM CSF vaccine A cancer vaccine consisting of a recombinant fowlpox virus encoding human granulocyte-macrophage colony-stimulating factor (GM-CSF). GM-CSF binds to specific cell surface receptors on various immuno-hematopoietic cell types, enhancing their proliferation and differentiation and stimulating macrophage and dendritic cell functions in antigen presentation and antitumor cell-mediated immunity. Administration of fowlpox-sargramostim may induce an immune response against tumor cells. Fowlpox virus is an attractive vector because its genome is easy to manipulate and it is replication incompetent in mammalian cells.

Recombinant interferon beta A recombinant protein which is chemically identical to or similar to endogenous interferon beta with antiviral and anti-tumor activities. Endogenous interferons beta are cytokines produced by nucleated cells (predominantly natural killer cells) upon exposure to live or inactivated virus, double-stranded RNA or bacterial products. These agents bind to specific cell-surface receptors, resulting in the transcription and translation of genes with an interferon-specific response element. The proteins so produced mediate many complex effects, including antiviral (the most important being inhibition of viral protein synthesis), antiproliferative and immune modulating effects. The recombinant therapeutic forms of interferon beta are interferon beta 1-a and interferon beta 1-b.

Recombinant interleukin 7 A recombinant protein which is chemically identical to or similar to endogenous interleukin-7 (IL-7) with hematopoietic and immunopotentiating properties. Produced by bone marrow, thymic stromal, and spleen cells, the cytokine interleukin-7 is a hematopoietic growth factor for progenitor B cells and T cells and stimulates proliferation and differentiation of mature T-cells and natural killer cells.

Recombinant tumor necrosis factor A recombinant therapeutic agent which is chemically identical to or similar to one of a number of endogenous tumor necrosis factor (TNF) proteins. TNF family cytokines bind to and activate specific cell-surface receptors, thereby mediating inflammatory processes, cell proliferation, immunity, angiogenesis, and tumor cell cytotoxicity. One primary antitumor effect of TNFs involves stimulation of T cell-mediated antitumor cytotoxicity.

Recombinant vaccinia CEA (D609)/MUC1 (L93)/TRICOM vaccine A cancer vaccine comprised of a recombinant vaccinia viral vector encoding the carcinoembryonic antigen (CEA), MUC-1, a transmembrane glycoprotein secreted by glandular tissues, and TRICOM, comprised of three co-stimulatory molecule transgenes (B7-1, ICAM-1 and LFA-3). This agent may enhance CEA and MUC-1 presentation to antigen presenting cells (APC) and activate a cytotoxic T-cells response against CEA- and MUC-1-expressing tumor cells.

Recombinant vaccinia NY ESO 1 vaccine A cancer vaccine consisting of a recombinant vaccinia viral vector encoding an immunogenic peptide derived from the cancer-testis antigen NY-ESO-1, an antigen found in normal testis and various tumors, including bladder, breast, hepatocellular, melanoma, and prostate cancers. Vaccination with recombinant vaccinia- NY-ESO-1 peptide vaccine may stimulate the host immune system to mount a humoral and cytotoxic T lymphocyte (CTL) response against tumor cells expressing NY-ESO-1 antigen, resulting in tumor cell lysis.

Recombination The process by which progeny derive a combination of genes different from that of either parent. In higher organisms, this can occur by crossing over.

Reconstructive surgeon A doctor who can surgically reshape or rebuild (reconstruct) a part of the body, such as a woman's breast after surgery for breast cancer.

Reconstructive surgery Surgery that is done to reshape or rebuild (reconstruct) a part of the body changed by previous surgery.

Record A paper or electronic document that contains or is designed to contain a set of facts related to some occurrence, transaction, or the like.

Recovery Any treatment of materials by a process intended to make them suitable for further use.

Recovery time The time after an upset in a room's HVAC environmental parameters for the room to return to "normal" conditions, such as a return to acceptable humidity levels after a room wash down. This occurs within a certain number of air changes after the upset source is removed, minimally six to ten, depending on the severity of the upset, the quality of the air supply, and the degree of mixing of room air.

Rectal By or having to do with the rectum. The rectum is the last several inches of the large intestine and ends at the anus.

Rectal manometry A test that measures the movements and strength of the rectal and anal sphincter muscles.

Rectocele A herniation of rectum into vagina

Rectoid Other name for hydrocortisone.

Rectum The distal portion of the large intestine, between the sigmoid colon and the anal canal. Functions as a storage cavity to collect fecal material prior to defecation.

Rectus Singular and plural for the muscles attached to the eyeball.

Rectus abdominus flap procedure A method of breast reconstruction in which tissue from the lower abdominal wall which receives its blood supply from the rectus abdominus muscle, is used. The tissue from this area is moved up to the chest to create a breast mound and usually does not require an implant. Moving muscle and tissue from the lower abdomen to the chest results in flattening of the lower abdomen (a 'tummy tuck'). Also called a TRAM flap.

Rectus femoris muscle Muscle which contributes to the extension of the leg and flexion of the thigh. It originates at the anterior inferior iliac spine and the rim of the acetabellum, and inserts into the patella and tubercle of tibia.

Recur To occur again.

Recurrence Cancer that has reoccurred, or reappeared after treatment. Local recurrence is at the same site as the original cancer. Metastasis means that the disease has recurred at a distant site. Regional recurrence is in the lymph nodes near the site.

Recurrent cancer Cancer that has returned after a period of time during which the cancer could not be detected. The cancer may come back to the same place as the original (primary) tumor or to another place in the body. Also called recurrence.

Red blood cells Cells in the blood that deliver oxygen to tissues and take carbon dioxide from them.

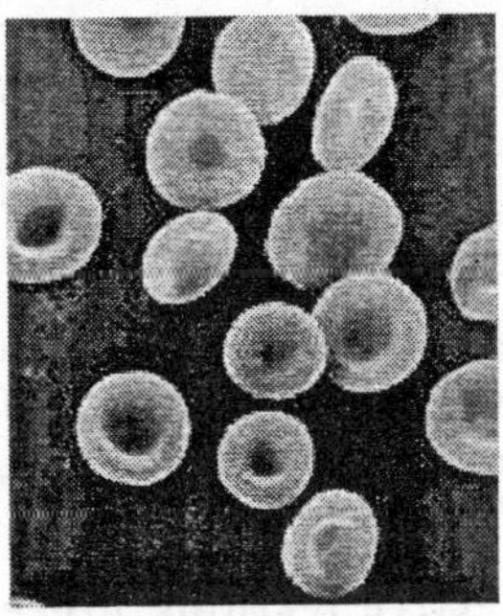

Figure RBC (Human red blood cells)

Red blood count (RBC) The number of red blood cells seen in a blood sample.

Red clover Trifolium pratense. A plant whose flowers have been used in some cultures to treat certain medical problems. It is being studied in the relief of menopausal symptoms and may have anticancer effects. Also called purple clover and wild clover.

Red date The fruit of the jujube plant. It has been used in some cultures to treat certain medical problems.

Red elm Ulmus fulva or Ulmus rubra. The inner bark of this plant has been used in some cultures to treat certain medical problems. It may have antioxidant effects. Also called slippery elm, gray elm, Indian elm, and sweet elm.

Reed-Sternberg cell A type of cell that appears in people with Hodgkin's disease. The number of these cells increases as the disease advances.

Referral The process of sending a patient from one practitioner to another for health care services. Health Plans may require that designated primary care providers authorize a referral for coverage of specialty services.

Referral services Medical Services arranged for by the physician and provided outside the physician's office other than Hospital Services.

Reflective learning process An important model of learning that is based on the principle of gaining from the learner's own experience; this is significantly different from the traditional model of undergraduate medical education. It has very clear links with the model of self-directed learning based on a portfolio which gives evidence of activity, reflection and the outcomes of learning. Students use their knowledge, skills and attitudes to solve problems in the workplace. However, many problems are ambiguous and create surprises. Recognition of these surprises causes the student to review problems and create alternative hypotheses, which is termed "reflection in action". This leads to a search for more information, seeking help from colleagues or experts, reading texts or searching on-line to solve the problem. In order to turn the new information into new learning, a further step is required, which takes place after the problem has been solved: Reflecting on action' involves looking back critically over the initial 'surprise' and the resolution of the problem. The process of reviewing and evaluating information leads to learning and this in turn adds to expertise. The process of learning itself tends to generate new questions and motivates the professional to undertake further inquiry, which results in the learning process being determined more by the learner than by the person who designed the activity. This process of reflection provides a stimulus for learning and helps learners to derive maximum benefit from their own experiences.

Reflux Digestive juices, food, and liquids moving backward from the stomach into the esophagus, and possibly into the mouth.

Reflux esophagitis Irritation of the lining of the esophagus due to movement of digestive juices backward from the stomach into the esophagus.

Reform prosthesis A description for a vacuum formed hollow glass eye. It also was used to describe the plastic stock eye. Today's terminology refers to an ocular prosthesis as compared to scleral shell prosthesis.

Refraction test Determines the eye's refractive error and the best corrective lenses to be prescribed. There are several methods of performing refraction: Retinoscopy, Automated Re-fractor, and Subjective Refraction.

Refractive error Defects in vision caused by the eye's inability to bend, or refract light and focus it clearly on the retina. Astigmatism, hyperopia, and myopia are common conditions of refractive error, also called ametropia.

Refractive media The parts of the eye that light travels through before being focused on the retina includes the cornea, crystalline lens, aqueous, and vitreous.

Refractive power A lens' ability to bend parallel light rays into focus, as measured by power diopters. In general, the greater the curvature of a lens and the greater the difference between center thickness and edge thickness, the higher the index of refraction and the greater its refractive power. Refractive power can also refer the strength of a person's contact lenses or glasses.

Refractory In medicine, describes a disease or condition that does not respond to treatment.

Refractory cancer Cancer that does not respond to treatment. The cancer may be resistant at the beginning of treatment or it may become resistant during treatment. Also called resistant cancer.

Refrigerants Fluids used for heat transfer in a refrigerating system; the refrigerant absorbs heat and transfers it at a higher temperature and higher pressure, usually with a change of state. Refrigerants can be: 1. Primary refrigerants. Liquids with low boiling points that change from a liquid to a gas after absorbing heat.

2. Secondary refrigerants. Substances that act only as heat carriers, such as brine, air, and water.

Regenerate Restore ion exchange of resins by reversing the process. An acid rinse is used to restore cation resin capacity and a sodium hydroxide rinse is used to restore anion resin capacity.

Regeneration In biology, regrowth of damaged or destroyed tissue or body part.

Regimen A strict, regulated plan of diet, exercise, or other activity designed to reach certain goals. In cancer treatment, a plan to treat cancer.

Regional In oncology, describes the body area right around a tumor.

Regional cancer Refers to cancer that has grown beyond the original (primary) tumor to nearby lymph nodes or organs and tissues.

Regional chemotherapy Treatment with anticancer drugs directed to a specific area of the body.

Regional enteritis Chronic inflammation of the gastro-intestinal tract, most commonly the small intestine and colon. Regional enteritis increases the risk for colorectal cancer and small intestine cancer. Also called Crohn's disease.

Regional involvement The spread of cancer from its original site to nearby areas such as muscles or lymph nodes, but not to distant sites such as other organs.

Regional lymph node In oncology, a lymph node that drains lymph from the region around a tumor.

Regional lymph node dissection A surgical procedure to remove some of the lymph nodes that drain lymph from the area around a tumor. The lymph nodes are then examined under a microscope to see if cancer cells have spread to them.

Registered dietitian A health professional with special training in the use of diet and nutrition to keep the body healthy. A registered dietitian may help the medical team improve the nutritional health of a patient.

Registered nurses Registered nurses are responsible for carrying out the physician's instructions. They supervise practical nurses and other auxiliary personnel who perform routine care and treatment of patients. Registered nurses provide nursing care to patients or perform specialized duties in a variety of settings from hospital and clinics to schools and public health departments. A license to practice nursing is required in all states.

Regitine Other name for phentolamine mesylate.

Regression 1. A decrease in the size of a tumor or in the extent of cancer in the body.

2. Any of several statistical techniques concerned with predicting some variables by knowing others. Regression is used to answers such questions as "how well can I predict the values of one variable, (such as survival) by knowing the value of another variable (such as treatment assignment)

Regression analysis Methods of explaining or predicting the variability of a dependent variable using information about one or more independent variables, or techniques for establishing a regression equation. The equation indicates the nature and closeness of the relationship between two or more variables, specifically the extent to which you can predicted some by knowing other, the extent to which some are associated with others. THe equation is often represented by a regression line, which is the straight line that comes closest to approximating a distribution of points in a scatter diagram.

Regression to the mean A phenomenon that occurs when a second determination or measurement is made only on those individuals with an extreme initial determination or measurement.

On average, the second determination or measurement tends to be less extreme than the initial one. Term originally coined by Sir Francis Galton (1886) to characterize the tendency for tall parents to produce shorter offspring and vice versa. Another example might be an imaginary trial that only enrolled people with fevers. Since the normal state ("mean") of humans is to be afebrile, even a placebo would appear effective. Regression to the mean is a particular concern with measures that are highly variable. Imagine a trial that required one low CD4 count for entry, say below 100. Chances are many eligible participants regularly have CD4 counts greater than 100, yet due to random error and variability were low that day. A measurement of the who e group two weeks later might shc w raised CD4 count averages, although there was no true gain. Perhaps best phrased as "everything is better by morning"

Regular follow up visit A required follow-up visit, the main purpose of which is to enable clinic personnel to carry out treatment assessment and data collection procedures, as specified in the study protocol. Called regular because such visits are normally required at fixed periods over the course of follow-up. Does not include visits done simply for treatment application or treatment adjustment.

Regular insulin A type of insulin that is fast actin.

Regulatory affairs Drug companies must show that their products consistently meet standards set by government agencies. Regulatory affairs departments document those activities, submit proposals, and follow those proposals through completion or approval.

Regulatory region or sequence A DNA base sequence that controls gene expression.

Rehabilitation Activities to adjust, heal and return to a full, productive life after injury or illness. This may involve physical restoration (such as the use of prostheses, exercises, and physical therapy), counseling, and emotional support.

Rehabilitation specialist A healthcare professional who helps people recover from an illness or injury and return to daily life. Examples of rehabilitation specialists are physical therapists and occupational therapists.

Reimplantation Insertion and temporary fixation of partially or completely avulsed tooth or teeth, resulting from traumatic injury.

Reject stream In reverse osmosis and ultrafiltration, those impurities not able to permeate the membrane are said to be rejected (removed). They are flushed away in the reject (waste) stream.

Relapse The return of signs and symptoms of cancer after a period of improvement.

Relative amblyopia Functional amblyopia can co-exit with a pathology abnormality. Treatment is possible.

Relative humidity (% RH) The ratio (measured in percent) of actual water vapor pressure in air to the pressure of saturated water vapor in air at the same temperature and pressure.

Relative survival rate A specific measurement of survival. For cancer, the rate is calculated by adjusting the survival rate to remove all causes of death except cancer. The rate is determined at specific time intervals, such as 2 years and 5 years after diagnosis.

Relaxation technique A method used to reduce tension and anxiety, and control pain.

Release The discharge of a microbiological agent or eukaryotic cell from a containment system.

Reliability Trust in the accuracy or provision of one's results; in the case of tests, it is an expression of the precision, consistency and reproducibility of measurements. Ideally, measurements should be the same when repeated by the same person or made by different assessors. In tests, contributing factors to reliability are the consistency of marking, the quality of test and test items, and the type and size of the sample. Satisfactory reliability of objective tests can be achieved by having large numbers of well-constructed test items marked by computer. Reliability is characterized by the stability, equivalence, and homogeneity of test.

Stability or test-retest reliability is the degree to which the same test produces the same results when repeated under the same conditions;

Equivalence or alternate-form reliability is the degree to which alternate forms of the same measurement instrument produce the same result

Homogeneity is the extent to which various items legitimately team together to measure a single characteristic, such as a desired attitude.

In a clinical examination, obtaining reliability depends on three variables: the students, the examiners and the patients. Such complexity makes it difficult to reproduce a comparable situation for tests of clinical skill and clinical problem-solving. In a reliable assessment procedure, the variability due to the patient and the examiner should be removed. Wherever possible, a subjective approach to marking should be replaced by a more objective one and students should be tested by a number of examiners. It is important to note that students are usually examined using different patients, which may enhance the performance of some students and harm the performance of others. Therefore, tests which aim to assess clinical skills and clinical problem-solving have to contain many samples of student performance if they are to achieve adequate levels of reliability. The development of the multi-station objective structured clinical examination (OSCE) represents an effort to do so.

Relievers Medicines based on Salbutamol that are used to treat the symptoms of an asthma attack by dilating the small airways.

Reline Acrylic restoration of denture base to compensate for bone loss; direct: done at chairside; indirect: in conjunction with a dental laboratory.

Remicade Other name for infliximab.

Remission A decrease in or disappearance of signs and symptoms of cancer. In partial remission, some, but not all, signs and symptoms of cancer have disappeared. In complete remission, all signs and symptoms of cancer have disappeared, although cancer still may be in the body.

Remission induction therapy Initial treatment with anticancer drugs to decrease the signs or symptoms of cancer or make them disappear.

Remote brachytherapy A type of internal radiation treatment in which the radioactive source is removed between treatments. Also called high-dose-rate remote brachytherapy or high-dose-rate remote radiation therapy.

Renal Relating to the kidneys. Wilson's Disease patients can sometimes cause the kidney to not function correctly.

Renal artery The main blood vessel that supplies blood to a kidney and its nearby adrenal gland and ureter. There is a renal artery for each kidney.

Renal capsule The fibrous connective tissue that surrounds each kidney.

Renal cell cancer The most common type of kidney cancer. It begins in the lining of the renal tubules in the kidney. The renal tubules filter the blood and produce urine. Also called hypernephroma.

Renal collecting tubule The last part of a long, twisting tube that collects urine from the nephrons (cellular structures in the kidney that filter blood and form urine) and moves it into the renal pelvis and ureters. Also called collecting duct.

Renal cortex The outer portion of the kidney, containing most of the glomeruli.

Renal dysplasia Abnormal, nonfunctioning kidney tissue.

Renal fascia A fibrous envelope of tissue that surrounds the kidney. Also called Gerota's fascia and Gerota's capsule.

Renal glomerulus A tiny, round cluster of blood vessels within the kidneys. It filters thꝏ blood to reabsorb useful materials and remove waste as urine.

Renal glycosuria Glycosuria occurring when there is a normal amount of sugar in the blood, due to an inherited inability of the kidneys to reabsorb glucose completely.

Renal hilus The inner medullary portion of the kidney, containing the urine collecting tubules.

Renal pelvis The area at the center of the kidney. Urine collects here and is funneled into the ureter, the tube that connects the kidney to the bladder.

Renal threshold When the blood is holding so much of a substance such as glucose (sugar) that the kidneys allow the excess to spill into the urine. This is also called "kidney threshold," "spilling point," and "leak point."

Renal tubular acidosis A rare disorder in which structures in the kidney that filter the blood are impaired, producing urine that is more acid than normal.

Renaturation The restoration of biological activity to a denatured protein or nucleic acid. The strands of a DNA duplex, for example, are denatured at high temperatures but can be correctly reformed by a slow cooling.

Reniform Shaped like a kidney.

Renova Other name for tretinoin.

Repaglinide A drug used as a treatment for Type 2 (noninsulin-dependent) diabetes; belongs to a class of drugs called meglitinides.

Repetitive DNA Sequences of varying lengths that occur in multiple copies in the genome; it represents much of the human genome.

Replicate To make a copy or duplicate of something.

Replication The action or process of reproducing exact copies of one's self.

Replication cycle In biology, refers to the reproduction cycle of viruses. A repliction cycle begins with the infection of a host cell and ends with the release of mature progeny virus particles.

Representative sample A sample that consists of a number of units that are drawn based on rational criteria such as random sampling and intended to assure that the sample accurately portraits the material being sampled.

Reprocessing Introducing an intermediate or API, including that which does not conform to standards or specifications, back into the process and repeating a crystallization step or other appropriate chemical or physical manipulation steps (e.g., distill-ation, filtration, chrom-atography, milling, etc.) that are part of the established manufacturing process. Conti-nuation of a chemical reaction after an in-process control test shows the reaction to be incomplete is considered to be part of the normal process, and not reprocessing.

Reproducibility of assessment Consistency in producing the same results if a test is repeated is a vital attribute of any test. It is important to know that if the same examinees were given the same test after some time and learned nothing in the interim, the same scores would result. Reproducibility is especially important in making licensure and certification decisions.

Reproductive cell An egg or sperm cell. Each mature reproductive cell carries a single set of 23 chromosomes.

Reproductive system In women, this system includes the ovaries, the fallopian tubes, the uterus (womb), the cervix, and the vagina (birth canal). The reproductive system in men includes the prostate, the testes, and the penis.

Reproductive toxicology Studies of whether exposure affects male or female fertility.

Research Scientific inquiry or an organized quest for new knowledge and better understanding, such as of the natural world or determinants of health and disease. Research can take several forms: empiric (observational), analytic, experimental, theoretical and applied.

Resectable Able to be removed by surgery.

Resection A procedure that uses surgery to remove tissue or part or all of an organ.

Residency The period of training in a specific medical specialty. It occurs after graduation from medical school and its length varies from three to seven years, depending upon the specialty.

Resident or resident physician An individual at any level in a Graduate Medical Education program, including subspecialty programs. Other terms used to refer to these individuals include interns, house officers, house staff, trainees, or fellows. The term "intern" is often used to denote physicians in their first year of training. The term "fellow" is frequently used to denote physicians in subspecialty programs (versus residents in specialty programs) or in Graduate Medical Education programs that are beyond the eligibility requirements for first board certification in the discipline.

Residual disease Cancer cells that remain after attempts to remove the cancer have been made.

Resilient Having the ability to return to an original shape after having been compressed or deformed.

Resin ion exchange resins are usually bead-like spherical materials with an affinity for particular ions. Cation exchange resins made of styrene and divinylbenzene containing sulfonic acid groups will exchange hydrogen ions for any cations they encounter. Similarly, anion exchange resins made of styrene and divinylbenzene containing quaternary ammonium groups will exchange a hydroxyl ion for any anions.

Resistance Refers to the ability of some pathogens to grow and multiply even in the presence of certain drugs which normally kill them. (Such strains are referred to as "drug resistant strains.")

Resistance The pressure drop across a filter at a stated flow and under given conditions; generally expressed in millimeters water gauge or PSI, or in SI units as N/m^2 or Pascals.

Resistant cancer Cancer that does not respond to treatment. The cancer may be resistant at the beginning of treatment, or it may become resistant during treatment. Also called refractory cancer.

Resistivity The reciprocal of conductivity (R=1/C). A measure of specific resistance to the flow of electricity. In water, provides an easy mean of continuously measuring the purity of very low Total Dissolved Solids (TDS), or ionic concentration. The fewer the dissolved ions in water, the higher its resistivity. Resistivity is normally expressed in Megohm-cm and is equivalent to one million ohms of resistance measured between two electrodes one centimeter apart. The theoretical maximum ionic purity of water is 18.3 Megohm-cm at 25°C.

Resolution Degree of molecular detail on a physical map of DNA, ranging from low to high.

Resorption A process in which a substance, such as tissue, is lost by being destroyed and then absorbed by the body.

Respirator In medicine, a machine used to help a patient breathe. Also called ventilator.

Respiratory burst Oxygen dependent increase in metabolic activity within phagocytic cells stimulated by bacteria or parasites, to be microbicidal.

Respiratory syncytial virus A virus that causes respiratory infections with cold-like symptoms.

Respiratory system The organs that are involved in breathing. These include the nose, throat, larynx, trachea, bronchi, and lungs. Also called the respiratory tract.

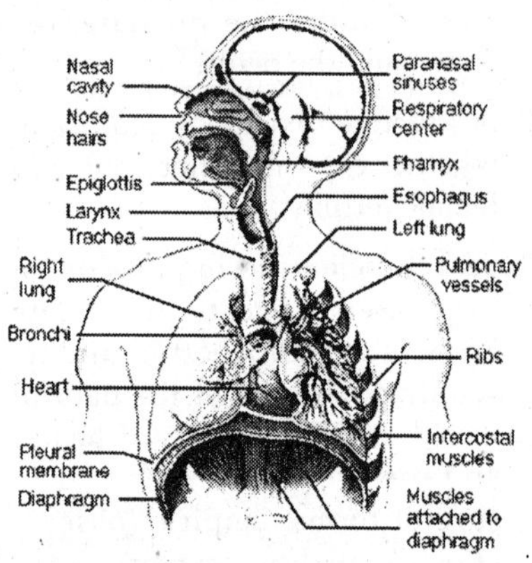

Respiratory therapy Exercises and treatments that help improve or restore lung function.

Respiratory tract The organs that are involved in breathing. These include the nose, throat, larynx, trachea, bronchi, and lungs. Also called the respiratory system.

Response In medicine, an improvement related to treatment.

Response rate The percentage of patients whose cancer shrinks or disappears after treatment.

Response variable Outcome variable.

Resting In biology, refers to a cell that is not dividing.

Restoration Replacement of portion of a damaged tooth.

Restriction enzyme, endonuclease A protein that recognizes specific, short nucleotide sequences and cuts DNA at those sites. Bacteria contain over 400 such enzymes that recognize and cut over 100 different DNA sequences.

Restriction fragment length polymorphism (RFLP) Variation between individuals in DNA fragments sizes cut by specific restriction enzymes; polymorphic sequences that result in RFLPs are used as markers on both physical maps and genetic linkage maps. RFLPs are usually caused by mutation at a cutting site.

Restriction-enzyme cutting site A specific nucleotide sequence of DNA at which a particular restriction enzyme cuts the DNA. Some sites occur frequently in DNA (e.g., every several hundred base pairs); others much less frequently (rare-cutter; e.g., every 10,000 base pairs).

Resveratrol A phytoalexin derived from grapes and other food products with antioxidant and potential chemopreventive activities. Resveratrol induces phase II drug-metabolizing enzymes (anti-initiation activity); mediates anti-inflammatory effects and inhibits cyclooxygenase and hydroperoxidase functions (anti-promotion activity); and induces promyelocytic leukemia cell differentiation (anti-progression activity), thereby exhibiting activities in three major steps of carcinogenesis. This agent may inhibit TNF-induced activation of NF-kappaB in a dose- and time-dependent manner.

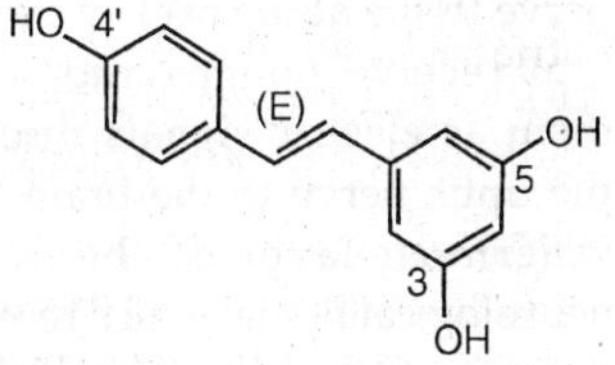

Figure Resveratrol ($C_{14}H_{12}O_3$)

Retained root Partial root structure remaining in jaw after extraction or fracture of a natural tooth.

Retest date The date when samples of the API (Active Pharmaceutical Ingredient) a material should be re-examined to ensure that material is still suitable for use.

Reticular degeneration A process in which severe intracellular edema results in bursting of keratinocytes and formation of multilocular bullae formed by remaining cell walls. It is seen in acute dermatitis and in viral blisters.

Reticuloendothelial system A network of phagocytic cells.

Retina The light-sensitive layers of nerve tissue at the back of the eye that receive images and sends them as electric signals through the optic nerve to the brain. The innermost layer of the eye, a neurological tissue, which receives light rays focused on it by the lens. This tissue contains receptor cells (rods and cones) that send electrical impulses to the brain via the optic nerve when the light rays are present.

Retinal detachment Separation of the retina from the inner wall of the eye. Retinal detachment can be a complication of cytomegalovirus (CMV) retinitis and can cause vision loss.

Retinitis Inflammation of the retina, the thin layer of tissue that lines the inside back wall of the eye and functions like the film of a camera. In people with HIV, retinitis can be caused by cytomegalovirus (CMV). If untreated, retinitis can lead to blindness. Symptoms include floating spots, flashing lights, blind spots, and blurred vision.

Retinoblastoma An eye cancer caused by the loss of a pair of tumor-suppressor genes; the inherited form typically appears in childhood, since one gene is missing from the time of birth.

Retinoid Vitamin A or a vitamin A-like compound.

Retinol Vitamin A, a nutrient essential for proper vision and healthy skin and mucous membranes. Retinol is being studied in the prevention of cancer. It belongs to the family of drugs called retinoids.

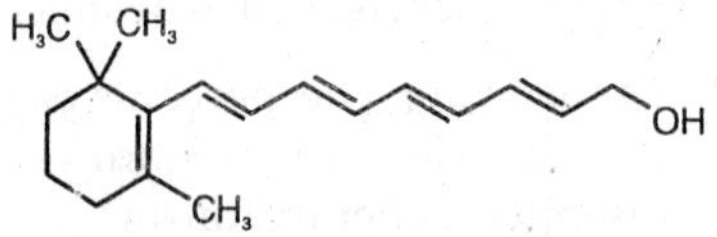

$(C_{20}H_{30}O)$

Figure Retinol

Retinopathy A disease of the small blood vessels in the retina of the eye.

Retinopathy of primaturity A retinal disease (ROP) in premature infants usually caused by excessive oxygen during the first few weeks of life.

Retinoscopy This technique determines the eye's refractive error and the best corrective lenses to be prescribed. An instrument called a retinoscope which consists of a light, lens, mirror, and handle, is used to shine light into a patient's eye. There are two types of retinoscope: streak and spot retinoscope. When light is shone into patient's eye, the light is reflected back ("reflex"). If the reflection is in the same direction ("with movement") of the retinoscope then the refractive error is hyperopia (farsightedness) and a plus lens is prescribed. If the reflection is in the opposite direction ("against movement") of the retinoscope then the refractive error is myopia (nearsightedness) and a minus lens is prescribed. The strength of the prescription is determined when the pupil is suddenly filled with light ("neutralized") with the appropriate lens powers (strength). There are other types of retinoscopy such as Static retinoscopy or Dynamic retinoscopy.

Retinyl palmitate A drug that is being studied in the prevention of cancer. It belongs to the family of drugs called retinoids.

Retrogastric area The area behind the stomach.

Retrolental fibroplasia A disease (RLF) first reported in 1942. Now categorized as (ROP)

Retroperitoneal Having to do with the area outside or behind the peritoneum (the tissue that lines the abdominal wall and covers most of the organs in the abdomen).

Retropubic prostatectomy Surgery to remove the prostate through an incision made in the wall of the abdomen.

Retrospective cohort study A research study in which the medical records of groups of individuals who are alike in many ways but differ by a certain characteristic (for example, female nurses who smoke and those who do not smoke) are compared for a particular outcome (such as lung cancer). Also called a historic cohort study.

Retrospective study A study that compares two groups of people: those with the disease or condition under study (cases) and a very similar group of people who do not have the disease or condition (controls). Researchers study the medical and lifestyle histories of the people in each group to learn what factors may be associated with the disease or condition. For example, one group may have been exposed to a particular substance that the other was not. Also called a case-control study.

Retrospective validation Establishing documented evidence that a system does what it purports to do based on review and analysis of historic information.

Retrotarsal atrophy The sinking in of the upper lid with loss or displacement of adipose tissue.

Retrovir Other name for zidovudine.

Retroviral infection The presence of retroviral vectors, such as some viruses, which use their recombinant DNA to insert their genetic material into the chromosomes of the host's cells. The virus is then propogated by the host cell.

Retroviral vector RNA from a virus that is used to insert genetic material into cells.

Retrovirus A type of virus that stores its genetic information in a single-stranded RNA molecule, then constructs a double-stranded DNA version of its genes using a special enzyme called reverse transcriptase. The DNA copy is then integrated into the host cell's own genetic material. HIV is an example of a retrovirus.

Revalidation Extent of validation necessary to assure that changes made to qualified or validated equipment, utilities, systems and process do not adversely affect the finished product. Implemented changes should be tracked and evaluated through a thorough, dynamic, change control program.

Revenue share The proportion of a practice's total revenue devoted to a particular type of expense. For example, the practice expense revenue share is that proportion of revenue used to pay for practice expense.

Reverse osmosis (RO) RO is one of two acceptable techniques for producing Water For injection (WFI), Procedure involves passing purified water across a semipermeable membrane against an osmotic gradient. R.O. is an excellent pretreatment for deionized water that will be subsequently filtered, because silt and colloids are removed. Usual performance of R.O. is removal of organics, multi-valent ions, and 90% of mono-valent ions.

Reverse transcriptase (RT) An enzyme found in HIV and other retroviruses. RT converts single-stranded HIV RNA into double-stranded HIV DNA. Some anti-HIV drugs interfere with this stage of HIV's life cycle.

Reverse transcriptase polymerase chain reaction (RT PCR) A laboratory test that measures the amount of HIV RNA (also known as viral load) in a blood sample by replicating HIV's genetic material to measurable levels. RT-PCR is the primary way that health care providers monitor HIV infection and its treatment.

Review group A group of individuals, normally recruited by the sponsoring agency or its representative, charged with the review of a specific research proposal or set of research proposals for scientific merit. Study section.

Revlimid Other name for lenalidomide.

RevM10 gene An antiviral gene that is being studied in the treatment of cancer in patients who have HIV, the virus that causes AIDS.

Reworking Subjecting an intermediate or API (Active Pharmaceutical Ingredient) that does not conform to standards or specifications, to one or more processing steps that are different from the established manufacturing process so that its quality may be made acceptable (e.g., recrystallizing with a different solvent).

A molecule consisting of a number of ribonucleotides attached together to form a long strand one nucleotide thick. Each nucleotide contains the sugar, ribose, and one of four different bases: cytosine, adenine and guanine (as in DNA) and uracil (as opposed to thymine in DNA). The major portion of cellular RNA occurs as ribosomal RNA (rRNA), to a lesser extent as transfer RNA (tRNA) and less still as messenger RNA (mRNA), all three forms being concerned with transformation of the DNA sequence into the complementary protein sequence. It also occurs in some viruses where it acts as the hereditary material.

Rf B7.1 vaccine A cancer vaccine comprised of a recombinant fowlpox virus vector encoding the stimulatory molecule transgene B7-1. Recombinant fowlpox-B7.1 (rF-B7.1) vaccine may enhance antigen presentation and activate antitumoral cytotoxic T-cells.

Rhabdoid tumor A malignant tumor of either the central nervous system (CNS) or the kidney. Malignant rhabdoid tumors of the CNS often have an abnormality of chromosome 22. These tumors usually occur in children younger than 2 years.

Rhabdomyosarcoma A malignant tumor of muscle tissue.

Rhage, rrhage, rrhagia (suffix) Discharge, e.g. hemorrhage - discharge of blood.

Rheumatism A group of disorders marked by inflammation or pain in the connective tissue structures of the body. These structures include bone, cartilage, and fat.

Rheumatoid factor An autoantibody (usually IgM) which reacts with the individual's own IgG. Present in rheumatoid arthritis.

Rheumatrex Other name for methotrexate.

Rhinencephalon Parts of the brain concerned with olfactory function (reception and integra-tion). In the narrow sense it refers to those parts directly involved with reception of olfactory stimuli only (olfactory bulbs, tract, striae, anterior olfactory nucleus, part of the amygdala and the pyriform cortex).

Rhinitis Irritation of the nose. Derived from the Greek word rhinos meaning of the nose.

Rhinorrhea A runny nose, usually with thin watery secretion.

Rhinoscopy A procedure in which a thin, lighted tube is inserted into the nose to look for abnormal areas. Also called nasoscopy.

Rhizoxin A substance that is being studied in the treatment of cancer. It comes from a fungus and is similar to vinca alkaloid drugs. It belongs to the family of drugs called antimitotic agents.

Rhombencephalon The hindbrain; most caudal of the three primary vesicles of the embryonic brain. The adult derivatives of which are the cerebellum and pons (metencephalon) and the medulla oblongata (myelencephal on).

Rhomboid fossa The diamond shaped fourth ventricle.

Rhubarb Rheum palmatum or Rheum officinale. The root of this plant has been used in some cultures to treat certain medical problems. It may have anti-inflammatory and anticancer effects. Also called da-huang, Chinese rhubarb, Indian rhubarb, and Turkish rhubarb.

Ribavirin One of a new class of drugs used to treat viral infections called nucleocide analogues. These drugs interfere in a specific way with the mechanisms used by viruses for multiplication.

Ribonucleic acid (RNA) A single stranded molecule that carries genetic information. In the human body, DNA is transcribed to RNA, which creates proteins. In HIV and other retroviruses, the process is reversed, and RNA (The native form of the virus) is transcribed to DNA for insertion in the human genome.

Ribonucleotide reductase inhibitor A family of anticancer drugs that interfere with the growth of tumor cells by blocking the formation of deoxyribonucleotides (building blocks of DNA).

Ribose The five-carbon sugar that serves as a component of RNA.

Ribosomal RNA A class of RNA found in the ribosomes of cells.

Ribosomes Small cellular components composed of specialized ribosomal RNA and protein; site of protein synthesis.

RIBS There are 12 pairs of thin curving bones, like struts, that extend around from the spine to support the chest cavity.

Rib Fx.

Rickettsias Gram-negative microorganisms that are often carried by arthropod vectors and may infect humans and other mammals. Generally smaller than other bacteria, they require living cells for growth.

Rifabutin (mycobutin) An antibiotic used as a component in the combination treatment of mycobacterium avium complex. Rifabutin is also the only drug currently approved for the prevention of MAC.

Rifadin Brand name of Rifampin.

Rifamate A combination of Rifampin and Isoniazid in one pill.

Rifampin A drug used in the treatment of infections caused by bacteria. It belongs to the family of drugs called antibiotics.

Right atrium Chamber on the right side of the heart that recieves blood from the superior and inferior vena cavi, directing it to the right ventricle.

Right colic artery Artery which originates from the superior mesenteric artery and supplies the ascending colon.

Right gastroepiploic artery Artery originating from the gastroduodenal artery and branching into the gastric and omental (epiploic) arteries.

Right mainstem bronchi Derived from the trachea, the right main bronchus that enters the right lung.

Right pulmonary artery Artery which originates from the pulmonary trunk and branches into the arteries of the superior, medial and inferior lobes of the lung.

Right ventricle Chamber of the heart that directs the blood to the pulmonary trunk and into the lungs.

Rimactane Brand name of Rifampin

Rinse The operation that follows regeneration, a flushing out of excess regenerant solution.

Risedronate A synthetic pyridinyl bisphosphonate agent. Risedronate binds to hydro-xyapatite crystals in bone and inhibits osteoclast-dependent bone resorption.

Risk The chance or possibility of loss. For example, physicians may be held at risk if hospitalization rates exceed agreed upon thresholds. Potential financial liability, particularly with respect to who or what is legally responsible for that liability.

Risk factor An aspect of personal behaviour or lifestyle, environmental exposure, or inborn or inherited characteristic, which on the basis of epidemiological evidence is known to be associated with an unfavourable health-related condition and considered important to prevent, if possible. It is used as an indication of increased probability of a specified health outcome such as the occurrence of a disease but is not necessarily a causal factor. The term risk factor is further used to mean a determinant that can be modified by intervention, thereby reducing the probability of occurrence of disease or other specified outcomes.

Risk load In underwriting, a factor that is multiplied into the rate to offset some adverse parameter of the group.

Ritalin Other name for methylphenidate hydrochloride.

Ritonavir A drug that belongs to the family of drugs called protease inhibitors. It interferes with the ability of a virus to make copies of itself.

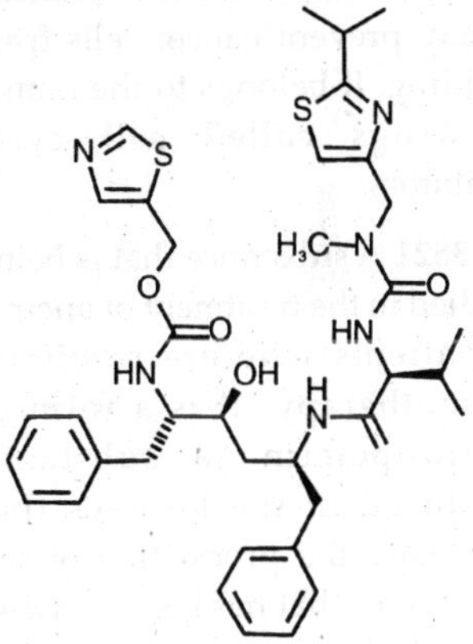

Figure Ritonavir

Rituximab A recombinant chimeric murine/human antibody directed against the CD20 antigen, a hydrophobic transmembrane protein located on normal pre-B and mature B lymphocytes.

Following binding, rituximab triggers a host cytotoxic immune response against CD20-positive cells.

RK 0202 An oral polymer matrix-based rinse formulation that contains N-acetylcysteine, an antioxidant amino acid derivative with antiinflammatory properties. RK-0202 may alleviate symptoms of radiation-induced oral mucositis.

RMP 7 A substance that is being studied for its ability to help other drugs reach the brain. It belongs to the family of drugs called bradykinin agonists. Also called lobradimil.

Ro 31-7453 A substance that is being studied in the treatment of cancer. It may prevent cancer cells from dividing. It belongs to the family of drugs called cell cycle inhibitors.

Ro 50-3821 A substance that is being studied in the treatment of anemia in patients who are receiving chemotherapy. It is a form of erythropoietin (a substance produced in the kidneys that stimulates the production of red blood cells) that has been changed in the laboratory. Also called methoxypolyethylene glycol epoetin beta.

Rocaltrol Other name for calcitriol.

Rod A receptor cell which is sensitive to light and is located in the retina of the eye. It is responsible for night vision (non-color vision in low level light).

Rofecoxib A synthetic, nonsteroidal derivative of phenyl-furanone with antiinflammatory, anti-pyretic and analgesic properties and potential antineoplastic properties. Rofecoxib binds to and inhibits the enzyme cyclooxygenase-2 (COX-2), resulting in an inhibition of the conversion of arachidonic acid to prostaglandins. COX-related metabolic pathways may represent key regulators of cell proliferation and neo-angiogenesis. Some epithelial tumor cell types overexpress pro-angiogenic COX-2.

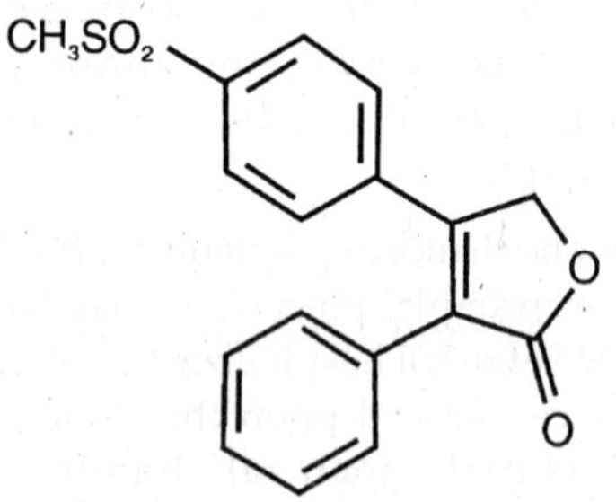

{4-[4- (methylsulfonyl)phenyl]-3-phenyl-2 (5H)-furanone}

Figure Rofecoxib

Roller bottles Small cylindrical bottles often used as bioreactors in the production of products by cell culture. The bottles are kept on a device that rotates them slowly to help assure proper growth. Automated systems may also be used for large arrays of roller bottles introducing sterile media and harvesting finished product automatically.

Roof of acetabulum The superior portion of the acetabulum.

Roof of orbit The superior wall formed by the "orbital process" of the frontal bone and lesser wing of the sphenoid bone.

Root canal Common term for root canal therapy, also the interior space of the tooth root.

Root canal therapy Process of removing pulp of a tooth and filling it with an inert material.

Root of penis The proximal, attached, portion of the penis.

Root resection Removal of a portion of diseased root structure, retaining the remaining natural tooth.

Root Tooth structure that connects the tooth to the jaw.

Roquinimex A quinoline-3-carboxamide with potential antineoplastic activity. Roquinimex inhibits endothelial cell proliferation, migration, and basement membrane invasion; reduces the secretion of the angiogenic factor tumor necrosis factor alpha by tumor-associated macrophages (TAMs); and inhibits angiogenesis. This agent is also an immune modulator that appears to alter cytokine profiles and enhance the activity of T cells, natural killer cells, and macrophages.

Rosiglitazone An orally-active thiazolidinedione with antidiabetic properties and potential antineoplastic activity. Rosiglitazone activates peroxisome proliferator-activated receptor gamma (PPAR-gamma), a ligand-activated transcription factor, thereby inducing cell differentiation and inhibiting cell growth and angiogenesis. This agent also modulates the transcription of insulin-responsive genes, inhibits macrophage and monocyte activation, and stimulates adipocyte differentiation.

Rostrum The most rostral part of the corpus callosum located below the septum pellucidum and extending from the genu to the lamina terminalis.

Rotator cuff The muscles and tendons of the upper arm and shoulder joint that form a 'cuff' about the glenohumeral joint.

Rotavirus A virus that causes diarrhea. It is the most common cause of infectious diarrhea, especially in children under 2 years old.

Rouge Form of surface corrosion that occurs in some stainless steel piping systems.

Roughness Consists of the finer irregularities of the surface texture, usually including those irregularities that result from the manufacturing process. These are considered to include traverse feed marks and other irregularities within the limits of the roughness sampling length.

RPI.4610 A substance that is being studied in the treatment of kidney cancer. It may prevent the growth of blood vessels from surrounding tissue to the tumor. It belongs to the families of drugs called VEGF receptor and angiogenesis inhibitors. Also called Angiozyme.

RPR 109881A A substance that is being studied in the treatment of cancer. It belongs to the family of drugs called taxanes.

Rrhea (suffix) Abnormal or excessive flow, e.g. steatorrhea - excessive lipid in the feces.

RSR13 A substance that is being studied for its ability to increase the effectiveness of radiation therapy. It belongs to the family of drugs called radiosensitizers. Also called efaproxiral.

RSV (Respiratory syncytial virus) A virus that causes respiratory infections with cold-like symptoms.

Rubber dam Soft latex sheet used to establish isolation of one or more teeth from contamination by oral fluids and to keep materials from falling to the back of the throat.

Ruthenium Ru 106 A radioactive isotope of the rare element ruthenium, a member of the light platinum group. A radioactive plaque containing ruthenium 106 may be inserted into the eye to irradiate ophthalmic tumors.

Rv B7.1 vaccine A recombinant vaccinia virus encoding the T-cell co-stimulatory molecule B7-1. Co-administration of recombinant vaccinia-B7.1 and a tumor-associated antigen in a cancer vaccine may enhance tumor-associated antigen-specific T-cell responses.

Rx Common abbreviation for "prescription".

S

S 1 An oral fluoropyrimidine antagonist composed of tegafur combined with two modulators of 5-flurouracil (5-FU) activity, 5-chloro-2,4-dihydro-xypyridine (CDHP) and potassium oxonate, in a molar ratio of 1:0.4:1. Tegafur is a prodrug of 5-fluorouracil, an antimetabolite that inhibits thymidylate synthase, thereby inhibiting DNA synthesis and cell division, and competes with uridine triphosphate, thus inhibiting RNA and protein synthesis. CDHP is a reversible inhibitor of dihydropyrimidine dehydrogenase (DPD), the liver enzyme responsible for rapid catabolism of 5-FU into inactive metabolites. Potassium oxonate preferentially localizes in the gut and inhibits the enzyme orotate phosphoribosyltransferase (the major enzyme responsible for 5-FU activation), thereby decreasing activation of 5-FU in the gut and activated 5-FU-related gastrointestinal toxicity.

S phase fraction A measure of the percentage of cells in a tumor that are in the phase of the cell cycle during which DNA is synthesized. The S-phase fraction may be used with the proliferative index to give a more complete understanding of how fast a tumor is growing.

Saccades The eye's ability to direct and coordinate movement as it quickly and voluntarily shift from one target to another.

Saccades dysfunction A condition in which the individual's ability to scan along a printed page and move his eyes from point to point is inadequate. Symptoms include frequent loss of place while reading, skip or transpose words, and have difficulty comprehending because of an inaccurate eye movement. Vision therapy is an effective treatment option.

Saccadic test Measures the eyes ability to move quickly and precisely from point to point.

Saccharin A man-made sweetener that people use in place of sugar because it has no calories.

Saccharomyces cerevisiae Better known as beer yeast, ordinary yeast. Yeast used in rDNA research.

Sacral ala The superior surface of the lateral portion of the sacrum.

Sacrococcygeal teratoma A tumor originating from the coccyx, or tailbone, and contains many different types of tissues.

Sacroiliac joint The joint made between the articular surfaces of the sacrum and ilium. Partly fibrous and partly synovial.

Sacrum The triangular bone made up of five fused vertebrae that is situated below the lumbar vertebrae and between the hip bones.

Safingol A substance that is being studied in the treatment of cancer. It belongs to the family of drugs called protein kinase C inhibitors.

Safranin A base, obtained from aniline; aniline pink; used as a stain in histology.

Sagittal view An anteroposterior (AP) vertical plane, parallel to the median plane of the body. The perspective is similar to a Lateral view.

Saline Relating to salt. As an adjective, "saline" means "salty, containing salt." As a noun "saline" is a salt solution, often adjusted to the normal salinity of the human body.

Salinity The concentration of soluble minerals (mainly salts of the alkali metals or of magnesium) in water.

Saliva The watery fluid in the mouth made by the salivary glands. Saliva moistens food to help digestion and it helps protect the mouth against infections.

Saliva ejector Suction tube placed in the mouth to remove saliva.

Salivary gland cancer A rare cancer that forms in tissues of a salivary gland (gland in the mouth that makes saliva). Most salivary gland cancers occur in older people.

Salmonella A large genus of the tribe Salmonellae, family Enterobacteriaceae, containing motile, gram-negative, rod-shaped organisms that ferment dextrose, forming acid and usually gas. Several species occur as intestinal pathogens in acute inflammations in humans and domestic animals. Salmonella typhimurium causes food poisoning in humans.

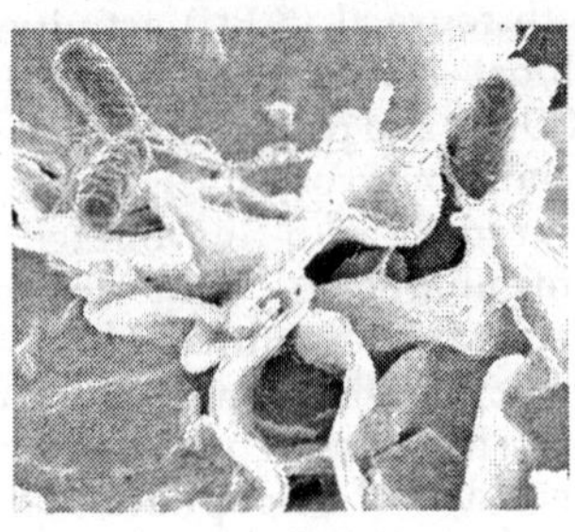

Scanning electron micrograph showing Salmonella typhimurium invading cultured human cells.

Figure Salmonella

Salmonella septicemia Salmonella is a bacterium that enters the body through ingestion of contaminated food or water. Symptoms of infection include nausea, vomiting, and diarrhea. Salmonella septicemia is a severe infection that circulates through the whole body. Recurrent Salmonella septicemia is considered an AIDS-defining condition in people with HIV.

Salpingo-oophorectomy Surgical removal of the fallopian tubes and ovaries.

Salt A compound formed by the interaction of an acid and a base, the hydrogen atoms of the acid being replaced by another positive ion derived from the base.

Salt rejection In reverse osmosis, the ratio of salts removed (rejected) to the original salt concentration.

Salvage plasma Plasma obtained by centrifugation of outdated (older than 21 days) whole blood. This type of plasma is difficult to convert to serum because most coagulation factors have lost their activity.

Salvage therapy Also known as rescue therapy. An HIV treatment regimen designed for people who have used many different anti-HIV drugs in the past, have failed at least two anti-HIV regimens, and have extensive drug resistance.

Samarium 153 A radioactive substance used in cancer therapy.

Sample size The number of patients required for a trial. In planning an interventional trial, a sample size is calculated , taking into account the frequency of the condition to be prevented or delayed, the anticipated effectiveness of the treatment thought to be clinically significant, and variables such as predicted drop outs and cross overs. The sample size is a calculated value that takes all of the above into account, and makes a statistically significant result likely within the prescribed amount of time.

Samster's triad The triad of asthma, aspirin sensitivity and nasal polyps.

Sanction Reprimand that gives binding force to a law or rule, or secures obedience to it, as the penalty for breaking it, or a reward for carrying it out. The government and its agencies can sanction hospitals, providers and health plans. Health plans sometimes seek to sanction hospitals and physicians. Medical staffs sometimes seek sanctions against its members.

Sandimmune Other name for cyclosporine.

Sandoglobulin Other name for immune globulin.

Sandostatin lar depot Other name for octreotide.

SangCya Other name for cyclosporine.

Sanger sequencing A widely used method of determining the order of bases in DNA.

Sanitization That part of decontamination that reduces viable microorganisms to a defined acceptance level, normally achieved by using a chemical agent or heat.

Saphenous vein (magna) The vein that extends from the dorsum of the foot to just below the inguinal ligament, making it the longest vein in the body. Used to supply vascular grafting material for cardiac (coronary artery) bypass surgery.

Saponification The hydrolysis of a fat by alkali with the formation of a soap and glycerol.

Saponin A substance found in soybeans and many other plants. Saponins may help lower cholesterol and may have anticancer effects.

Saquinavir (invirase) A protease inhibitor drug made by Hoffman-LaRoche.

Saquinavir mesylate A drug that belongs to the family of drugs called protease inhibitors. It interferes with the ability of a virus to make copies of itself.

Sarasar Other name for lonafarnib.

SarCNU An alkylating chloroethylnitrosourea with antineoplastic activity. Selectively accumulating in some tumor cells, SarCNU forms covalent linkages with nucleophilic centers in DNA, causing depurination, base pair miscoding, strand scission, and DNA-DNA cross-linking, which may result in cytotoxicity.

Sarcoid An inflammatory disease marked by the formation of granulomas (small nodules of immune cells) in the lungs, lymph nodes, and other organs. Sarcoid may be acute and go away by itself, or it may be chronic and progressive. Also called sarcoidosis.

Sarcoma A malignant tumor growing from connective tissues, such as cartilage, fat, muscle, or bone. Breast sarcoma is sarcoma occurring in the breast, but this happens only rarely. Sarcoma is often highly malignant when occurring outside the breast, but it has a better outlook when it occurs in the breast.

Sarcosinamide nitrosourea A substance that is being studied as a treatment for cancer. It belongs to the family of drugs called alkylating agents. Also called sarCNU.

Sargramostim A recombinant therapeutic agent which is chemically identical to or similar to endogenous human GM-CSF. Binding to specific cell surface receptors, sargramostim modulates the proliferation and differentiation of a variety of hematopoietic progenitor cells with some specificity towards stimulation of leukocyte production and may reverse treatment-induced neutropenias. This agent also promotes antigen presentation, up-regulates antibody-dependent cellular cytotoxicity (ADCC), and increases interleukin-2-mediated lymphokine-activated killer cell function; it may also augment host antitumoral immunity.

Sargramostim plasmid DNA hepatocellular carcinoma vaccine adjuvant A vaccine adjuvant consisting of a plasmid DNA encoding sargramostim (granulocyte-macrophage colony-stimulating factor). Upon administration, expressed sargramostim may stimulate a cytotoxic T cell response enhancing the host immune response to a concomitantly administered hepatocellular carcinoma vaccine.

Sartorius muscle Muscle which originates at the naterior superior iliac spine and inserts into the medial side of proximal end of tibia. It contributes to flexion of the thigh and leg. The "tailor's" muscle.

Satellite A chromosomal segment that branches off from the rest of the chromosome but is still connected by a thin filament or stalk.

Satraplatin A substance that is being studied in the treatment of cancer. It belongs to the family of drugs called platinum analogs. Also called BMS-182751 and JM 216.

Saturated air When there is a state of mutual equilibrium between the moist air and the liquid or solid phases of water. Saturated air holds as much water vapour as it can for a given temperature and pressure.

Saturated fat A type of fat that comes from animals.

Saturated fatty acids Fatty acids containing fully saturated alkyl chains.

Saturation humidity The air is saturated when the partial pressure of water vapor in the air at a given temperature equals the vapour pressure of water at the same temperature.

Saturation index The relation of calcium carbonate to the pH, alkalinity, and hardness of water to determine its scale-forming tendency.

SB 715992 A synthetic small molecule with antineoplastic properties. SB-715992 selectively inhibits kinesin spindle protein (KSP), resulting in inhibition of mitotic spindle assembly, induction of cell cycle arrest during the mitotic phase, and cell death in tumor cells that overexpress KSP.

SB AS02B adjuvant A proprietary oil-in-water emulsion specifically designed for combining protein preparations used in vaccines. SB-AS02B adjuvant contains monophosphoryl lipid A and QS21, a saponin extracted from the tree Quillaja saponaria Molina. This agent may be used for formulating cancer-specific vaccine preparations such as those containing MAGE-3 melanoma protein.

SB AS15 adjuvant A vaccine adjuvant containing CpG 7909, monophosphoryl lipid, and QS-21 with potential antineoplastic and immunostimulatory activities. CpG 7909 is a synthetic 24-mer oligonucleotide containing 3 CpG motifs that selectively targets Toll-like receptor 9 (TLR9), thereby activating dendritic and B cells and stimulating cytotoxic T cell and antibody responses against tumor cells bearing tumor antigens. Monophosphoryl lipid is a detoxified derivative of lipid A, a component of Salmonella minnesota lipopolysaccharide

(LPS); this agent may enhance humoral and cellular responses to various antigens. QS-21 is a purified, naturally occurring saponin derived from tree Quillaja saponaria Molina and exhibits various immunostimulatory activities. Combinations of monophosphoryl lipid and QS-21 may be synergistic in inducing humoral and cellular immune responses.

SC 70935 A substance that is being studied for its ability to stimulate the production of blood cells during chemotherapy. It belongs to the family of drugs called colony-stimulating factors. Also known as leridistim.

Scaffold In genomic mapping, a series of contigs that are in the right order but not necessarily connected in one continuous stretch of sequence.

Scale The mineral deposit that can coat the insides of boilers or the surfaces of RO membranes. It consists mainly of calcium carbonate that precipitates out of solution under certain conditions of pH, alkalinity, and hardness.

Scale up To take a biopharmaceutical manufacturing process from the laboratory scale to a scale at which it is commercially feasible.

Scaling and root planning Meticulous removal of plaque and calculus from tooth surfaces.

Scalpel A small, thin knife used for surgery.

Scan A picture of structures inside the body. Scans often used in diagnosing, staging, and monitoring disease include liver scans, bone scans, and computed tomography (CT) or computerized axial tomography (CAT) scans and magnetic resonance imaging (MRI) scans. In liver scanning and bone scanning, radioactive substances that are injected into the bloodstream collect in these organs. A scanner that detects the radiation is used to create pictures. In CT scanning, an x-ray machine linked to a computer is used to produce detailed pictures of organs inside the body. MRI scans use a large magnet connected to a computer to create pictures of areas inside the body.

Scanner In medicine, an instrument that takes pictures of the inside of the body.

Scaphoid A "boat shaped" bone of the hand and foot. Also called the navicular.

Scapula A complex flat bone that forms the shoulder girdle (joint). Also called the 'shoulder blade'.

SCH 54031 A drug used to treat hepatitis C infections. It is also being studied in the treatment and prevention of cancer. It is a cytokine that is modified in the laboratory. It belongs to the family of drugs called biological response modifiers. Also called PEG-Intron and PEG-interferon alfa-2b.

SCH 58500 A genetically-engineered adenovirus that contains the gene that encodes the human tumor-suppressor protein p53. This viral vector delivers p53 into tumor cells in order to initiate p53-dependent apoptosis and p53-induced cell cycle arrest.

SCH 66336 An anticancer drug that belongs to the family of drugs called enzyme inhibitors. Also called lonafarnib.

Schedule In clinical trials, the step-by-step plan for how patients are to be treated; for example, the drug or type of radiation therapy that is to be given, the method by which it is to be given, the amount of time between courses, and the total length of treatment.

Schiller test A test in which iodine is applied to the cervix. The iodine colors healthy cells brown; abnormal cells remain unstained, usually appearing white or yellow.

Schwann cell A type of glial cell of the peripheral nervous system that helps separate and insulate nerve cells.

Schwannoma A tumor of the peripheral nervous system that arises in the nerve sheath (protective covering). It is almost always benign, but rare malignant schwannomas have been reported.

Science A branch of knowledge that produces theoretical explanations of natural phenomena based on experimentation and observation.

Scientist A person who has studied science, especially one who is active in a particular field of investigation.

Scintillation camera Device used to enhance radiation and record the results for the diagnosis of cancer or other disorders.

Scintimammography A type of breast imaging test that is used to detect cancer cells in the breasts of some women who have had abnormal mammograms, or who have dense breast tissue. Scintimammography is not used for screening, or in place of a mammogram. In this test, a woman receives an injection of a small amount of a radioactive substance called technetium 99, which is taken up by cancer cells, and a gamma camera is used to take pictures of the breasts. Also called Miraluma test and sestamibi breast imaging.

Scirrhous cancer A breast cancer with a hard, firm, fibrous texture; usually an infiltrating ductal carcinoma.

Sclera The white protective covering of the eye.

Sclero Hard, e.g. scleroma - a hardened patch of skin or mucous membrane.

Scleroderma A chronic disorder marked by hardening and thickening of the skin. Scleroderma can be localized or it can affect the entire body (systemic).

Sclerosol intrapleural aerosol Other name for talc.

Scratch An elongated mark in the metal's surface not associated with the predominant surface texture pattern, which is visible to the unaided eye.

Screening The search for disease, such as cancer, in people without symptoms. Screening may refer to coordinated programs in large populations. The principal screening measure for breast cancer is mammography.

Screening mammogram X-rays of the breasts taken to check for breast cancer in the absence of signs or symptoms.

Scrotum In males, the external sac that contains the testicles.

Scutellaria barbata An herb that belongs to a group of herbs named the Scutellaria species or scullcap. Both the root and the above-ground part have been used to make herbal medicines. The root has been used in traditional Chinese medicine to treat lung cancer and other medical problems.

Scutum Latin for spur. The Tympanic scutum forms the bony division between the upper portion of the tympanic cavity and the mastoid cells.

SDX 102 A substance that is being studied in the treatment of cancer. It belongs to the family of drugs called antimetabolites. Also called alanosine.

SDX-105 A substance that is being studied in the treatment of cancer. It belongs to the family of drugs called alkylating agents. Also called bendamustine.

Sealants Thin resin material bonded in the pits and fissures of back teeth for the prevention of decay.

Seborrheic dermatitis A skin condition common in people with HIV. It is characterized by loose, greasy or dry, white to yellowish scales, with or without reddened skin. Seborrheic dermatitis may involve the skin of the scalp, eyebrows, eyelids, nasolabial creases, lips, behind the ears, in the external ear, and on the trunk, particularly over the sternum and along skin folds. The cause is unknown.

Sebum An oily substance produced by certain glands in the skin.

Second line therapy Treatment that is given when initial treatment (first-line therapy) doesn't work, or stops working.

Second look surgery Surgery performed after primary treatment to determine whether tumor cells remain.

Second phase insulin release Delayed release of insulin into the bloodstream from the beta cell after the blood glucose level rises. It is thought that this delayed release is due to release of insulin that is manufactured in the beta cell after the blood sugar starts to rise.

Second primary cancer Refers to a new primary cancer in a person with a history of cancer.

Second set rejection Accelerated rejection of an allograft in an already immune recipient.

Secondary cancer A term that is used to` describe either a new primary cancer or cancer that has spread from the place in which it started to other parts of the body.

Secondary care Services provided by medical specialists who generally do not have first contact with patients (e.g., cardiologist, urologists, dermatologists). However, there has been a trend toward self-referral by patients for these services, rather than referral by primary care providers.

Secondary containment Level of containment that is external to and separate from primary containment.

Secondary dentin Reparative tooth structure produced by the pulp in response to tooth irritation.

Secondary diabetes When a person gets diabetes because of another disease or because of taking certain drugs or chemicals.

Secondary lymphoid organs Organs in which antigen-driven proliferation and differentiation of B and T lymphocytes takes place.

Secondary outcome variable or secondary endpoint 1. An outcome variable that is known or believed to be related to the primary outcome variable and that is used, in addition to the primary outcome variable, for evaluation of treatments in the trial (e.g. the use of CD4 as a secondary endpoint in a antiretroviral trial with mortality as it's primary endpoint, where CD4 trends are presumed to be associated with survival)

2. Any other outcome variable, regardless of its relationship to the primary outcome variable, that is used for treatment evaluation. (e.g. use of the combined endpoint PCP or death as a secondary endpoint in a trial of PCP prophylaxis using PCP alone as the primary endpoint. This may give insight into the possible complicating factors, such as toxicity (bad) or activity against other organisms like Toxo (good) that may accompany the pure anti-PCP effect)

Secondary tumor A tumor that forms as a result of spread (metastasis) of cancer from its site of origin.

Secrete To make and give off such as when the beta cells make insulin and then release it into the blood so that the other cells in the body can use it to turn glucose (sugar) into energy.

Secretory component A surface receptor on epithelial cells lining mucosal surfaces which binds dimeric IgA and transports it through the cell into mucosal secretions.

Sedimentation A primary step in municipal water treatment. Water is allowed to stand long enough for solids to settle by gravity. Also called settling.

Sedimentation rate The distance red blood cells travel in one hour in a sample of blood as they settle to the bottom of a test tube. The sedimentation rate is increased in inflammation, infection, cancer, rheumatic diseases, and diseases of the blood and bone marrow. Also called erythrocyte sedimentation rate.

Sedimenters For sedimentation, batch and continuous centrifuges are available. There are three types of centrifuges for continuous sedimentation. (a) Disc - constructed on the vertical axis, disc centrifuges are solid-bowl units. All are capable of separating liquids from solids, solids from two immiscible liquids and two immiscible liquids. Disc-stack centrifuges differ in their ability to handle different volumes of solids in the feed stream, and in the way that the separated solids are removed from the separation vessel: solids-retaining, solids-ejecting, and nozzle-bowl separators. (b) Decanters - consists of a cylindrical settling section with a tapered end. Inside the bowl is a scroll conveyor that is driven usually at a slightly faster rate than the bowl and can be controlled by a differential speed device or back drive. (c) Tubular - a vertical solid-wall cylinder provided with caps on both ends; a tubular centrifuge generally has a bottom feed inlet. When two liquids of different specific gravities are fed, the heavier phase is concentrated against the wall, while the lighter phase "floats" on the heavier phase.

Sedoxantrone trihydrochloride A substance that is being studied as a treatment for cancer. It belongs to the family of drugs called DNA-intercalating compounds. Also called CI-958.

Seed Tank Industrial fermentations are generally started in tanks smaller than a 1,000 to 50,000 gallon main fermenter. This small "seed" tank may be up to 100 gallons and propagate enough organisms to "kick-off" the main fermentation. Often, a seed tank may be large enough to require its own seed tank.

Seed lot system A seed lot system is a system according to which successive batches of a product are derived from the same master seed lot at a given passage level. For routine production, a working seed lot is prepared from the master seed lot. The final product is derived from the working seed lot and has not undergone more passages from the master seed lot than the vaccine shown in clinical studies to be satisfactory with respect to safety and efficacy. The origin and the passage history of the master seed lot and the working seed lot are recorded.

Master Seed Lot - A culture of a microorganism distributed from a single bulk into containers in a single operation in such a manner as to ensure uniformity, to prevent contamination and to ensure stability. A master seed lot in liquid form is usually stored at or below -70°C. A freeze-dried master seed lot is stored at a temperature known to ensure stability.

Working Seed Lot - A culture of microorganism derived from the master seed lot and intended for use in production. Working seed lots are distributed into containers and stored as described above for master seed lots.

Seed stock The initial inoculum, or the cells placed in growth medium from which other cells will grow.

Segmental cystectomy The removal of cancer as well as some of the bladder tissue around the tumor. Sometimes called partial cystectomy.

Segmental mastectomy The removal of cancer as well as some of the breast tissue around the tumor and the lining over the chest muscles below the tumor. Usually some of the lymph nodes under the arm are also taken out. Also called partial mastectomy.

Segmental transplantation A surgical procedure in which a part of a pancreas that contains insulin-producing cells is placed in a person whose pancreas has stopped making insulin.

Segregated Storage in the same room or inside area, but physically separated by distance from incompatible materials.

Segregation The normal biological process whereby the two pieces of a chromosome pair are separated during meiosis and randomly distributed to the germ cells.

Seizure Convulsion; a sudden, involuntary movement of the muscles.

Selection bias An error in choosing the individuals or groups to take part in a study. Ideally, the subjects in a study should be very similar to one another and to the larger population from which they are drawn (for example, all individuals with the same disease or condition). If there are important differences, the results of the study may not be valid.

Selective estrogen receptor modulator (SERM) A drug that acts like estrogen on some tissues but blocks the effect of estrogen on other tissues. Tamoxifen and raloxifene are SERMs.

Selective serotonin reuptake inhibitor (SSRI) A type of drug that is used to treat depression. SSRIs slow the process by which serotonin (a substance that nerves use to send messages to one another) is reused by nerve cells that make it. This increases the amount of serotonin available for stimulating other nerves.

Selenium A nonmetallic chemical element found in trace amounts in human body. Selenium primarily occurs in vivo as seleno-compounds, mostly selenopro-teins such as glutathione peroxidase and thioredoxin reductase (enzymes responsible for detoxification). Alone or in combination with Vitamin E, selenocompounds act as antioxidants. These agents scavenge free radicals; prevent blood clots by inhibiting platelet aggregation; strengthen the immune system; and have been shown, in some instances, to inhibit chromosomal damage and mutations. Exhibiting chemopreventive activity, selenocompounds also inhibit the induction of protein kinase C.

Self assessment The process of evaluating ones own deficiencies, achievements, behaviour or professional performance and competencies. Self-assessment is an important part of self-directed and lifelong learning because it creates a need for improvement while it justifies confidence in ones competence.

Self assessment questionnaire (SAQ) Assessment completed by the learner about him or herself to provide indirect, inexpensive measures of skill attainment and real-life performance. SAQ's serve as an evaluation of ones own deficiencies and achievements, professional behavior, performance and competence. Though important as a tool in motivation for improvement of competence, it has the weakness of being subject to rating biases.

Self directed learning A form of education that involves the individual learner's initiative to identify and act on his or her learning needs (with or without assistance), taking increased responsibility for his or her own learning.

Self draining Capable of elimination of all fluid from the system due to the force of gravity alone.

Self monitoring of blood glucose A way as person can test how much glucose (sugar) is in the blood. Also called home blood glucose monitoring.

Self referral Ordering of laboratory tests, diagnostic procedures or treatment for a patient by a physician from businesses in which the physician has a financial interest. Many physicians who have such financial interests contend that their participation improves access or quality of care, but results of a number of studies suggest that physician-owned enterprises are detrimental, promoting excessive use of diagnostic tests and treatments and potentially increasing total costs of health care as well as harming the physical and financial well-being of the individual patient.

Sella turcica Refers to the configuration of the hypophysial fossa relative to the clinoid processes of the body of the sphenoid bone. The term is used interchangeably for the depression or fossa itself in the body of the sphenoid bone which lodges the pituitary gland.

SEM (Scanning electron microscopy) Utilizes an electron beam to produce images over a very broad magnification range of 10X to 105X. The technique is somewhat limited by the conductivity of the material but works very well to inspect 316L stainless steel. Typical magnification levels for surface defect evaluation are from 100 to 4,000.

Semaxanib A substance that has been studied in the treatment of cancer. It belongs to the families of drugs called angiogenesis inhibitors and tyrosine kinase inhibitors. Also called SU5416.

Semen The fluid that is released through the penis during orgasm. Semen is made up of sperm from the testicles and fluid from the prostate and other sex glands.

Semiautomatic arc welding Arc welding with equipment that controls only the filler metal feed. The advance of the welding is manually controlled.

Semicircular canals Three looped bone canals within the petrous pyramid, forming part of the bony labryrinth of the ear, that produce five openings into the vestibule.

Seminal fluid Fluid from the prostate and other sex glands that helps transport sperm out of the man's body during orgasm. Seminal fluid contains sugar as an energy source for sperm.

Seminal vesicles Paired pouches attached to the posterior portion of the bladder. The seminal ducts join with the ipsilateral ductus deferens to form the ejaculatory duct.

Seminal vesicle biopsy The removal of fluid or tissue with a needle from the seminal vesicles for examination under a microscope. The seminal vesicles are glands in the male reproductive tract that produce a part of semen.

Seminoma A type of cancer of the testicles. Seminomas may spread to the lung, bone, liver, or brain.

Semiparasitic In botany, a plant that gets food from a host but also contains chlorophyll and is capable of photosynthesis.

Semipermeable Membranes that do not have measurable pores but through which smaller molecules can pass.

Semustine An anticancer drug that belongs to the family of drugs called alkylating agents.

Senega root The root of an herb called Polygala senega. It has been used in some cultures to treat certain medical problems, including problems of the respiratory system.

Senile keratosis A precancerous condition of thick, scaly patches of skin. Also called solar or actinic keratosis.

Sensible heat (SH) Heat that causes a change of temperature without causing a change of state.

Sensible heat ratio The ratio of room sensible heat to room total heat as expressed in the formula: Sensible Heat ratio (SHR) = Room Sensible Heat (SH)/Room Total Heat (TH).

Sensitisation Alteration of the responsiveness of the body to the presence of foreign substances. In the development of allergy, an individual becomes sensitised to a particular allergen and reaches a state of hypersensitivity.

Sensitivity When referring to a medical test, sensitivity refers to the percentage of people who test positive for a specific disease among a group of people who have the disease. No test has 100% sensitivity because some people who have the disease will test negative for it (false negatives).

Sensitizer A chemical that causes a substantial proportion of exposed people or animals to develop an allergic reaction in normal tissue after repeated exposure to the chemical.

Sensor The part of a pacemaker system that senses the body's need for blood flow. The pacemaker uses sensor information to monitor body activity and provide the proper heart rate.

Sentinel event Adverse health events that may have been avoided through appropriate care or alternate interventions.

Sentinel lymph node The first lymph node to which cancer is likely to spread from the primary tumor. When cancer spreads, the cancer cells may appear first in the sentinel node before spreading to other lymph nodes.

Sentinel lymph node biopsy Removal and examination of the sentinel node(s) (the first lymph node(s) to which cancer cells are likely to spread from a primary tumor). To identify the sentinel lymph node(s), the surgeon injects a radioactive substance, blue dye, or both near the tumor. The surgeon then uses a scanner to find the sentinel lymph node(s) containing the radioactive substance or looks for the lymph node(s) stained with dye. The surgeon then removes the sentinel node(s) to check for the presence of cancer cells.

Sentinel lymph node mapping The use of dyes and radioactive substances to identify the first lymph node to which cancer is likely to spread from the primary tumor. Cancer cells may appear first in the sentinel node before spreading to other lymph nodes and other places in the body.

Seocalcitol A substance that is being studied as a treatment for cancer. It belongs to the family of drugs called vitamin D analogs.

Sepsis A serious blood-borne infection that is usually caused by bacteria. Immunocompromised people, such as those with HIV disease, are at increased risk for sepsis.

Septal area Paraterminal (subcallosal) gyrus and the medial and lateral septal nuclei located rostral to the anterior commissure and lamina terminalis.

Septate An organ or structure that is divided into compartments.

Septicemia Disease caused by the spread of bacteria and their toxins in the bloodstream. Also called blood poisoning.

Septra Other name for trimethoprim-sulfamethoxazole.

Septum pellucidum A thin lamerllar partition that extends between the corpus callosum and the fornix forming the medial wall of the anterior horn and body of the lateral cerebral ventricle.

Sequence assembly A process whereby the order of multiple sequenced DNA fragments is determined.

Sequence tagged site (STS) Short (200 to 500 base pairs) DNA sequence that has a single occurrence in the human genome and whose location and base sequence are known. Detectable by polymerase chain reaction, STSs are useful for localizing and orienting the mapping and sequence data reported from many different laboratories and serve as landmarks on the developing physical map of the human genome. Expressed sequence tags (ESTs) are STSs derived from cDNAs.

Sequencing Determination of the order of nucleotides (base sequences) in a DNA or RNA molecule or the order of amino acids in a protein.

Sequencing technology The instrumentation and procedures used to determine the order of nucleotides in DNA.

sequential treatment One treatment after the other.

Sequstrum Loosened spicule of bone pushed to the surface.

Sera One of the plural forms of serum.

Seroconversion The process by which a newly infected person develops antibodies to HIV. These antibodies are then detectable by an HIV test. Seroconversion may occur anywhere from days to weeks or months following HIV infection.

Serologic test A laboratory test to determine if an individual has antibodies to a particular foreign invader, such as a virus. A positive serologic test indicates that an individual is infected or has had an infection in the past.

Seroprevalence The number or proportion of people in a given population who have positive serologic tests for a particular infection.

Serosa The outer lining of organs and body cavities of the abdomen and chest, including the stomach. Also called serous membrane.

Serostatus Refers to the presence or absence of antibodies in the serum portion of blood.

Serotonin A hormone found in the brain, platelets, digestive tract,

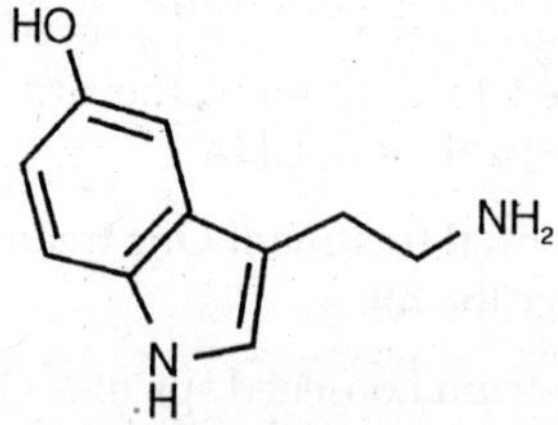

HO

NH$_2$

N
H

{5-Hydroxy-tryptamine or 3- (2-aminoethyl)-1 H-indol-5-ol}

Figure Serotonin

and pineal gland. It acts both as a neurotransmitter (a substance that nerves use to send messages to one another) and a vasoconstrictor (a substance that causes blood vessels to narrow). A lack of serotonin in the brain is thought to be a cause of depression. Also called 5-hydroxytryptamine.

Serous Having to do with serum, the clear liquid part of blood.

Serous membrane The membrane lining the walls of the body cavities and enclosing the contained organs. It is a mesothelium lying upon a connective tissue layer and secretes a watery serous fluid.

Serpiginous Having a wavy border.

Serrated Having a saw-like edge.

Serratia marcescens They are minute, rod-shaped or coccoid, aerobic, gram-negative organisms, found on various foodstuffs as a pink or reddish growth, nonpathogenic. Used to validate 0.45μm removal rated filters.

Sertoli leydig cell tumor of the ovary A rare type of ovarian tumor in which the tumor cells secrete a male sex hormone. This may cause virilization (the appearance of male physical characteristics in females). Also called andro-blastoma and arrhenoblastoma.

Sertraline The salt form of a synthetic derivative of naphthalenamine with anti-serotoninergic and anti-depressant properties. Sertraline appears to selectively inhibit the neuronal uptake of serotonin, raising serotonin levels in the CNS.

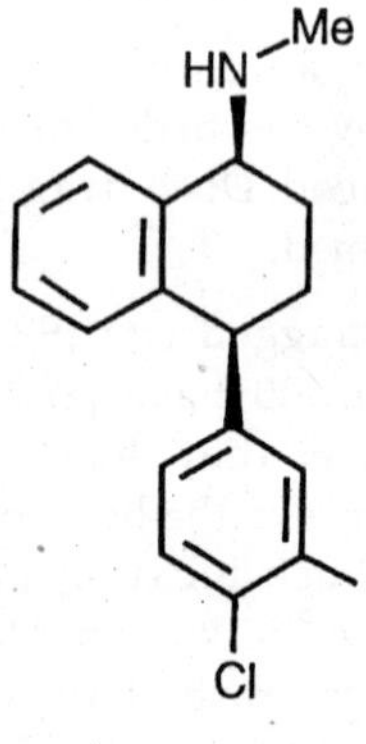

HN
Me

Cl

2{ (1S)-cis-4- (3,4-dichlorophenyl)-1,2,3,4-tetrahydro-N-methyl-1-naphthalenamine hydrochloride}

Figure Sertraline

Serum albumin The main protein in blood plasma. Low levels of serum albumin occur in people with malnutrition, inflammation, and serious liver and kidney disease.

Serum glutamate pyruvate transaminase (SGPT) An enzyme

found in the liver and other tissues. A high level of serum glutamate pyruvate transaminase released into the blood may be a sign of liver damage, cancer, or other diseases. Also called alanine transferase.

Serum glutamic-oxaloacetic transaminase (SGOT) An enzyme found in the liver, heart, and other tissues. A high level of serum glutamic-oxaloacetic transaminase released into the blood may be a sign of liver or heart damage, cancer, or other diseases. Also called aspartate transaminase.

Serum sickness A hypersensitivity reaction consisting of fever, rashes, joint pain and glomerulonephritis, resulting from localization of circulating, soluble, antigen-antibody complexes, which induce inflammatory reactions. Serum sickness was originally induced following therapy with large doses of antibody from a foreign source - e.g. horse serum.

Serum The clear liquid part of the blood that remains after blood cells and clotting proteins have been removed.

Serum tumor marker test A blood test that measures the amount of substances called tumor markers (or biomarkers). Tumor markers are released into the blood by tumor cells or by other cells in response to tumor cells. A high level of a tumor marker may be a sign of cancer.

Service life The life expectancy or number of cycles for which a processing unit will maintain its performance.

Sesamoid bone A bone within a tendon.

Sesquiterpene lactone A substance found in some plants. Sesquiterpene lactones may have anti-inflammatory and anticancer effects. Plants containing sesquiterpene lactones have been used in some cultures to treat certain medical problems.

Sessile Attached by a broad base.

Set point The viral load established within a few weeks to months after infection, after the initial burst of virus replication has subsided. The viral set point is thought to remain steady for an indefinite period of time if the infection is not treated with anti-HIV drugs. An individual's viral set point may determine how quickly HIV infection will progress without treatment. Higher set points suggest that disease will progress faster than lower set points.

Severe myelosuppression Severe reduction in the numbers of red blood cells, white blood cells, and platelets in the bone marrow. Severe myelosuppression is a side effect of some cancer treatments. Also called myeloablation.

Sex chromosome The X or Y chromosome in human beings that determines the sex of an individual. Females have two X chromosomes in diploid cells; males have an X and a Y chromosome. The sex chromosomes comprise the 23rd chromosome pair in a karyotype.

Sex linked Traits or diseases associated with the X or Y chromosome; generally seen in males.

Sexually transmitted disease (STD) Infections that are most commonly spread through sexual intercourse or genital contact.

Sézary syndrome A form of cutaneous T-cell lymphoma, a cancerous disease that affects the skin.

SGN 00101 A recombinant chimeric protein composed of the heat shock protein 65 (Hsp65) from Mycobacterium bovis, and the human papilloma viral (HPV) protein E7. Hsp65, similar to other members of its family of proteins, elicits a strong immune response and may be used to design vaccines against a number of different cancers. E7 protein is involved in carcinogenesis of anal and cervical tumors, and represents a tumor antigen that may be specifically targeted by lymphocytes.

SGN 15 A substance that is being studied in the treatment of cancer. It combines a monoclonal antibody with the anticancer drug doxorubicin. Monoclonal antibodies are substances that are made in the laboratory and that can locate and bind to cancer cells. SGN-15 belongs to the family of drugs called antibody drug conjugates. Also called cBR96-doxorubicin immunoconjugate.

SGN 30 A monoclonal antibody that binds to cells that have the CD30 antigen on their surface, including Hodgkin's disease cells and cells from anaplastic large cell lymphoma, and cutaneous T-cell lymphoma. SGN-30 is being studied in the treatment of cancer. It belongs to the family of drugs called monoclonal antibodies.

SGN 40 A monoclonal antibody that binds to cells that have the CD40 antigen on their surface, including cells from multiple myeloma, non-Hodgkin's lymphoma, and chronic lymphocytic leukemia. SGN-40 is being studied in the treatment of cancer. It belongs to the family of drugs called monoclonal antibodies.

Sham procedure A procedure designed to resemble the real one and that is performed on a patient for the purpose of masking the patient or the patient's study physician as to whether the patient has received the real procedure. A placebo procedure.

Sham therapy An inactive treatment or procedure that is intended to mimic as closely as possible a therapy in a clinical trial. Also called placebo therapy.

Shared risk pool for referral services In capitation, the pool established for the purpose of sharing the risk of costs for referral services among all participating providers. Commonly, this involves a group or specialty category of physicians and is based on utilization. Sometimes, risk pools are established in partnered or limited partner or foundation capitation systems, whereby both providers share risk in a limited way and health plans.

Shared savings A provision of most prepaid health care plans where at least part of the providers' income is directly linked to the financial performance of the plan. If costs are lower than projections, a percentage of these savings are referred to the providers.

Shark cartilage A nutritional supplement gleaned from the exoskeleton of the shark. Shark cartilage inhibits metalloproteinases (MMPs) and possesses antiangiogenic and antimetastatic properties.

Shave biopsy A procedure in which a skin abnormality and a thin layer of surrounding skin are removed with a small blade for examination under a microscope. Stitches are not needed with this procedure.

Sheep sorrel Rumex acetosella. A plant that has been used in some cultures to treat certain medical problems. It may have anticancer effects. Also called dock and sorrel.

Sheridan's formula A liquid that has been promoted as a treatment for a wide range of diseases, including cancer. The ingredients thought to be in Sheridan's Formula have been tested, and none of them has been shown to be effective in treating any form of cancer. Also called Entelev, Cancell, Jim's Juice, Crocinic Acid, JS–114, JS–101, 126–F, and Cantron.

Shielded metal-arc welding (SMAW) An arc welding process that produces coalescence of metals by heating them with an arc between a covered metal electrode and the work. Shielding is obtained from decomposition of the electrode covering. Pressure is not used and filler metal is obtained from the electrode.

Shiitake mushroom Lentinus edodes. A dark oriental mushroom widely used as a food. Several anticancer substances have been found in shiitake mushrooms, including lentinan, which has been studied in Japan as a treatment for stomach and colorectal cancer.

Shingles A disease caused by varicella zoster virus (VZV), which also causes chickenpox. VZV remains in the nerve roots of everyone who has had chickenpox and can become active years later to cause shingles. Shingles causes numbness, itching, or severe pain followed by clusters of blister-like lesions in a strip-like pattern on one side of the body. The pain can persist for weeks, months, or years after the rash heals.

Sho saiko to A Japanese formulation of seven Chinese herbs that is being studied as a treatment for cancer.

Shock A severe condition that causes severe low blood pressure, decreased level of consciousness, and is a threat to life.

Shock, insulin A term no longer used.

Short answer questions An assessment tool that requires students to construct short, written answers to presented questions; often used instead of multiple-choice questions to have students actually recall the answer rather than merely select it from a set of alternatives. As the answers must be constructed, it is reasonable to assume that there is little chance of guessing correctly. The questions are therefore cued-recall measures of memory for course material whereas multiple-choice questions require only recognition. Although the stem (question) could be the same in both exam formats and the answer could be quite short, even a single word, the short-answer version is likely to be more difficult than the multiple-choice version. Because the short-answer questions require students to construct answers, they provide more information about the students' knowledge than the selection of a multiple-choice alternative. The disadvantage of this form of exam is related to grading. Question vagueness can yield interpretive problems, and even with quite clear questions, scoring requires assessors with relevant knowledge, judgment and time.

Shotgun method Sequencing method that involves randomly sequenced cloned pieces of the genome, with no foreknowledge of where the piece originally came from. This can be contrasted with "directed" strategies, in which pieces of DNA from known chromosomal locations are sequenced. Because there are advantages to both strategies, researchers use both random (or shotgun) and directed strategies in combination to sequence the human genome.

Shoulder This is a ball and socket joint, without "weight bearing", formed by the distal clavicle, the scapula, and the proximal humerus.

Shunt In medicine, a passage that is made to allow blood or other fluid to move from one part of the body to another. For example, a surgeon may implant a tube to drain cerebrospinal fluid from the brain to the abdomen. A surgeon may also change normal blood flow by making a passage that leads from one blood vessel to another.

Sialic acid Any of a group of simple sugar molecules.

Sialyl Tn KLH A vaccine composed of a substance that enhances immunity plus an antigen found on some tumors of the colon, breast, lung, ovary, pancreas, and stomach.

Sickle cell anemia (SS) An inherited disorder of the red blood cells in which the hemoglobin (the red oxygen carrying pigment of the cell) is different from the usual type. This unusual hemoglobin results in the production of unusually shaped cells, which do not survive the usual length of time in the blood circulation. Thus, anemia results. Sickle cell anemia is the result of the inheritance of the gene for sickle hemoglobin (S) from both parents.

Sickle cell disease An inherited disorder of the red blood cells in which one gene is for sickle hemoglobin (S), and the other gene is for another unusual hemoglobin such as S, C, Thal. etc. The following are examples of sickle cell disease: SS, SC, SD, SßThal, etc.

Sickle cell trait (AS) The inheritance of one gene for the usual hemoglobin (A) and one gene for sickle hemoglobin (S). A person who has sickle cell trait (AS) is a carrier of the sickle gene, does not have the disease, does not have painful episodes, and is generally not affected by the sickle hemoglobin.

Sickle-cell anemia An inherited, potentially lethal disease in which a defect in hemoglobin, the oxygen-carrying pigment in the blood, causes distortion (sickling) and loss of red blood cells, producing damage to organs throughout the body.

Side effects The action or effect of a drug beyond what it is supposed to do. The term usually refers to undesired or negative effects, such as headache, skin irritation, or liver damage‹although side effects can be expected or unexpected, desired or undesired. Experimental drugs must be evaluated for both immediate and long-term side effects.

Side to end coloanal anastomosis A surgical procedure in which the side of the colon is attached to the anus after the rectum has been removed. A section of the colon about 2 inches long is formed into a mini-pouch in order to replace the function of the rectum and store stool until it can be eliminated. This procedure is similar to the J-pouch coloanal anastomosis but a much smaller pouch is formed.

Sideropenic dysphagia A disorder marked by anemia caused by iron deficiency, and a web-like growth of membranes in the throat that makes swallowing difficult. Having sideropenic dysphagia may increase the risk of developing esophageal cancer. Also called Paterson-Kelly syndrome and Plummer-Vinson syndrome.

Sigmoid colon S-shaped portion of the colon, extending from the pelvic brim to the third segment of the sacrum.

Sigmoid sinus An S-shaped dural venous sinus which extends along the the mastoid process of the temporal bone to the jugular foramen connecting the transverse sinus to the internal jugular vein.

Sigmoidoscopy Inspection of the lower colon using a thin, lighted tube called a sigmoidoscope. Samples of tissue or cells may be collected for examination under a microscope. Also called proctosigmoidoscopy.

Signal transduction inhibitor A drug that may prevent the ability of cancer cells to multiply quickly and invade other tissues.

Signed The record of who performed a particular action or review. This record may be initials, full handwritten signature, seal, or authenticated and secure electronic signature.

Signet ring cell carcinoma A highly malignant type of cancer typically found in glandular cells that line the digestive organs. The cells resemble signet rings when examined under a microscope.

Significance level (statistics) 1. The permissible type I error level for a test of the null hypothesis with a specified test statistic. The null hypothesis not rejected if the test statistic yields a p-value which is larger than the specified level and is rejected if it is equal to or less than this value.

2. p-value.

Significance test Test of significance.

Significance, clinical Statistical significance does not necessarily imply that the results have practical implications or are clinically significant from the clinician's point of view, and vice versa.

Significance, statistical Infers that an observation was unlikely to have occurred by chance alone. Statistical significance is often based on a p value <0.05. Below this level, the smaller the p value, the greater the statistical significance.

Significant In statistics, describes a mathematical measure of difference between groups. The difference is said to be significant if it is greater than what might be expected to happen by chance alone. Also called statistically significant.

Sildenafil The citrate salt of a pyrazolopyrimidinone derivative structurally related to zaprinast.

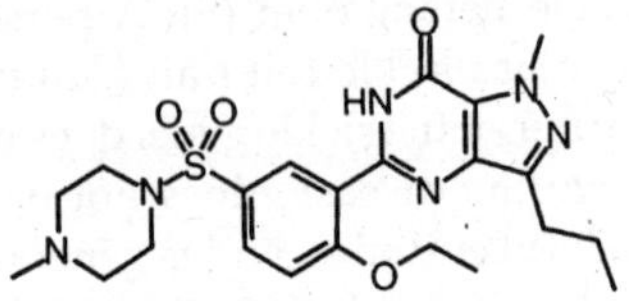

{1-[4-ethoxy-3- (6,7-dihydro-1-methyl-7-oxo- 3-propyl-1H-pyrazolo[4,3-d]pyrimidin-5-yl) phenylsulfonyl]-4-methylpiperazine citrate}

Figure Sildenafil

Sildenafil selectively inhibits cyclic guanosine monophosphate (cGMP) -specific type 5 phosphodiesterase, resulting in vasodilation in the corpus cavernosum of the penis and penile erection.

Silica Silicon dioxide (SiO_2) and its hydrated forms are classified as reactive and nonreactive. Generally, reactive Silica is removed by the anion exchange resin. Reactive Silica is only slightly ionized and is held lightly by the anion resin. It is for this reason that Silica is the first thing to break through when the resin nears exhaustion. Nonreactive Silica is generally considered to be particulate (colloidal) in nature.

Silicon phthalocyanine 4 A synthetic photosensitizer agent containing a large macrocyclic ring chelated with silicon. Silicon phthalocyanine 4 localizes primarily in mitochondrial cytosolic membranes and, after photoe-xcitation, forms reactive oxygen species that induce apoptosis.

Silicone gel Synthetic gel compound used in breast implants because of its flexibility, strength, and texture, which is similar to the texture of the natural breast. Silicone gel breast implants are available for women who have had breast cancer surgery, but only under the auspices of a clinical trial.

Silicone prosthesis remover A solid silicone prosthesis remover is similar to a suction cup and only requires you to hold it and make flush contact with the prosthesis (squeezing is not required) to remove it from the eye socket. It is for patients with arthritis, rheumatism or just stiffening of the finger joints and are unable to use a suction cup.

Silybum marianum A plant that has been used in some cultures to treat certain medical problems, including stomach, liver, and gallbladder disorders. The active extract of Silybum marianum seeds is called silymarin. It is being studied in the prevention of liver damage caused by some cancer treatments. Also called milk thistle.

Silymarin A mixture of flavonolignans isolated from the milk thistle plant Silybum marianum. Silymarin may act as an antioxidant, protecting hepatic cells from chemotherapy-related free radical damage. This agent may also promote the growth of new hepatic cells.

Simian immunodeficiency virus (SIV) A virus similar to HIV that can infect monkeys, chimpanzees, and macaques and can cause a disease similar to AIDS in some of these animals. Because the two viruses are closely related, researchers study SIV as a way to learn more about HIV. However, SIV cannot infect humans, and HIV cannot infect monkeys.

Simian virus 40 (SV40) A virus that infects some types of monkeys. It may also infect humans, and was found in some polio vaccines tested in the early 1960s. Although the virus has been shown to cause cancer in laboratory animals, there is no evidence that it causes cancer in people.

Simple mastectomy Removal of the breast. Also called total mastectomy.

Simple nephrectomy Surgery to remove one kidney.

Simple randomization Unrestricted randomization.

Simulated patient (SP) Simulated patients are healthy persons who have been trained to reliably reproduce the history and/or physical findings of typical clinical cases. Sometimes actors are used to accomplish this goal but more often, health care providers are used. Use of an SP is designed to assess students' clinical skills while making the examination as objective as possible.

Simulation In cancer treatment, a process used to plan radiation therapy so that the target area is precisely located and marked.

Simulations and models Tools for assessment of clinical performance in an environment closely resembling reality and imitating real clinical problems to rate the examinees' performance on clinical problems that are difficult or even impossible to evaluate effectively without harming a real patient. They permit examinees to make life-threatening errors and provide instant feedback so examinees can correct a mistaken action.

Models are mannequins constructed to respond realis-tically to actions, allowing examinees to reason through a clinical problem without risk to a real patient.

Simulation formats have been developed as paper-pencil patient management problems (PMP), computerized versions of PMP called clinical case simulations (CCX), role-playing situations, e.g., standardized patients (SP), clinical team simulations, anatomical models or mannequins, and combinations of all of the above formats.

Virtual reality simulations (VR) use computers sometimes combined with anatomical models to mimic realistic organ and surface images and the touch sensations a physician would expect examining a real patient. Written and computerized simulations have been used to assess clinical reasoning, diagnostic plans and treatment for a variety of clinical disciplines. They are expensive to create.

Single blind Where certain persons (e.g., study physicians) are informed of some fact or condition whereas other persons (e.g., patients) are purposefully denied information regarding that fact or condition. Used to minimize the placebo effect or different reporting of symptoms based on patient attitude toward the treatment they believe they are taking

Single blinded clinical trial 1. A clinical trial in which treatments are administered in such a manner that patients in the trial are not informed of whether they have been assigned to the test or control treatment, but clinic staff are.

2. A clinical trial in which the patient knows the treatment assigned, but the treating physician, examiner, or observer does not.

Single gene disorder Hereditary disorder caused by a mutant allele of a single gene (e.g., Duchenne muscular dystrophy, retinoblastoma, sickle cell disease).

Single nucleotide polymorphism (SNP) The most common type of change in DNA (molecules inside cells that carry genetic information). An SNP occurs when a single nucleotide (building block of DNA) is replaced with another. These changes may cause disease, and may affect how a person reacts to bacteria, viruses, drugs, and other substances.

Single photon emission computed tomography (SPECT) A special type of computed tomography (CT) scan in which a small amount of a radioactive drug is injected into a vein and a scanner is used to make detailed images of areas inside the body where the radioactive material is taken up by the cells. SPECT can give information about blood flow to tissues and chemical reactions (metabolism) in the body.

Single stream funding The consolidation of multiple sources of funding into a single stream. This is a key approach used in progressive mental health systems to ensure that "funds follow consumers."

Single-gene disorder Hereditary disorder caused by a mutant allele of a single gene (e.g., Duchenne muscular dystrophy, retinoblastoma, sickle cell disease).

Sino atrial (SA) node The small area in the upper right chamber of the heart that signals an electrical impulse to run through the heart to cause the heart to beat. It is often called the "pacemaker" of the heart.

Sinus rhythm The normal, regular rhythm of the heart, as seen on an ECG.

Sinusitis An infection of the sinus cavities in the head, often bacterial.

SIP (Steam in place) The introduction of steam to sanitize or sterilize a piece of equipment without relocating the equipment.

Siplizumab A monoclonal immunoglobulin G1 antibody with potential antineoplastic activity. Siplizumab binds to CD2, a specific receptor found in T cells and NK cells, thereby triggering a host immune response that results in lysis of CD2+ cells, selective suppression of the immune system, and control of activated T cell growth.

Sirolimus A natural macrocyclic lactone produced by the bacterium Streptomyces hygroscopicus, with immunosuppressant properties. In cells, sirolimus binds to the immunophilin FK Binding Protein-12 (FKBP-12) to generate an immunosuppressive complex that binds to and inhibits the activation of the mammalian Target Of Rapamycin (mTOR), a key regulatory kinase. This results in inhibition of T lymphocyte activation and proliferation that occurs in response to antigenic and cytokine (IL-2, IL-4, and IL-15) stimulation and inhibition of antibody production.

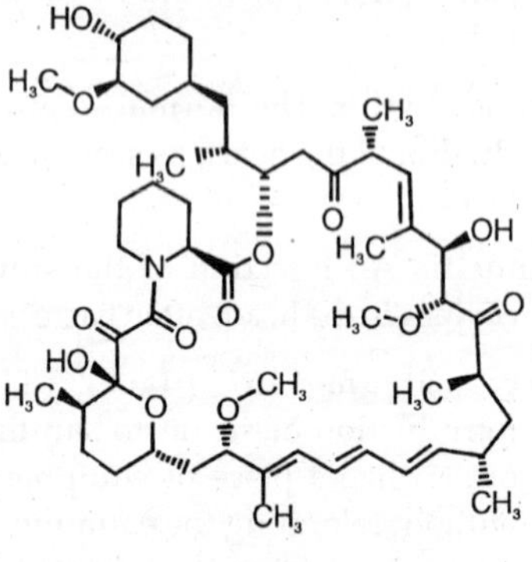

{[3S[3R[E (1S,3S,4S)],4S,5R,8S,9E,12R,14R,15S, 16R,18S,19S,26aR]]-5,6,8,11,12,13,14,15,16,17,18,19,24, 25,26,26a-hexadecahydro-5, 19-dihydroxy-3- [2- (4-hydroxy-3-methoxycyclohexyl) -1-methylethenyl]-14, 16-dimethoxy-4,10,12, 18-tetramethyl-8- (2-propenyl)-15, 19-epoxy-3H-pyrido[2,1-c][1,4] oxaazacyclotricosine-1,7,20, 21 (4H,23H)-tetrone, monohydrate.}

Figure Sirolimus

Site of service differential The difference in the monies paid when the same service is performed in different practice setting or by a different provider. One example would be an examination in an ER versus in a family doctor's office.

Site registration The process that must be completed by units and sites prior to participating in each NIAID-sponsored clinical trial. It is by this process that the Investigator of record (IoR) assures the Division of AIDS (DAIDS) that he/she has fulfilled all regulatory requirements necessary for participating in a specific protocol and that all required documents are on file with DAIDS.

Site visit A visit to a center or prospective center in a trial by personnel from outside that center for the purpose of assessing its performance or performance potential in the trial.

Size discordance A great difference in the size of twins.

SJG 136 A pyrrolobenzodiazepine dimer with potential antineoplastic activity. SJG-136 binds to the minor groove of DNA and induces interstrand cross-links between two N-2 guanine positions, thereby inhibiting DNA replication and transcription. With a preference for binding to purine-GATC-pyrimidine sequences, SJG-136 adducts do not appear to be subject to p53-mediated DNA excision repair mechanisms.

Sk dexamethasone Other name for dexamethasone.

Sk prednisone Other name for prednisone.

Skeletal Having to do with the skeleton (bones of the body).

Skeleton The framework that supports the soft tissues of vertebrate animals and protects many of their internal organs. The skeletons of vertebrates are made of bone and/or cartilage.

Skill The ability to perform a task well, usually gained by training or experience; a systematic and coordinated pattern of mental and/or physical activity.

Skilled nursing facility (SNF) A licensed institution, which is primarily engaged in the provision of skilled nursing care.

Skin cancer Cancer that forms in tissues of the skin. When cancer forms in cells that make pigment, it is called melanoma. When cancer forms in cells that do not make pigment it may begin in basal cells (small, round cells in the base of the outer layer of skin) or squamous cells (flat cells that form the surface of the skin). Both types of skin cancer usually occur in skin that has been exposed to sunlight, such as the skin on the face, neck, hands, and arms.

Skin graft Skin that is moved from one part of the body to another.

Skin patch A bandage-like patch that releases medicine into the body through the skin. The medicine enters the blood slowly and steadily.

Skin prick test An allergy test that involves putting a small amount of a known allergen on to a scratch in the skin, to see if the body reacts. Used to diagnose allergy to various pollens, house dust mite droppings and pet dander. Fresh food extracts may be used to accurately skin test for food allergy.

Skin stimulation The process of applying pressure, friction, temperature change, or chemical substances to the skin to lessen or block a feeling of pain.

Skin test A test for an immune response to a compound by placing it on or under the skin.

Sleep apnea The periodic interruption or delay in breathing during sleep.

Sliding scale Adjusting insulin on the basis of blood glucose tests, meals, and activity levels.

Sling procedures Surgical methods for treating urinary incontinence involving the placement of a sling, made either of tissue obtained from the person undergoing the sling procedure or a synthetic material. The sling is anchored to retropubic and/or abdominal structures.

Slippery elm Ulmus fulva or Ulmus rubra. The inner bark of this plant has been used in some cultures to treat certain medical problems. It may have antioxidant effects. Also called gray elm, Indian elm, red elm, and sweet elm.

Slit lamp (biomicroscope) This instrument can examine ocular tissue from the front of the cornea to the back of the lens. A narrow "slit" beam of very bright light produced by a lamp. This beam is focused on to the eye which is then viewed under magnification with a microscope. A joystick control is employed to enable instrument to be moved left-right and up-down. A chin rest, head rest and fixation target is also required. Some slit lamps have a tilting mechanism to enable the lamp to be directed from different angles.

Slope An incline or deviation from the horizontal. A tube or pipe installed in the horizontal plane is said to slope if one end is positioned higher than the other.

Slow-reacting substance of anaphylaxis A group of leukotrienes released by mast cells during anaphylaxis which induces a prolonged constriction of smooth muscle. This prolonged constriction is not reversible by treatment with antihistamines.

Small cell lung cancer An aggressive (fast-growing) cancer that usually forms in tissues of the lung and spreads to other parts of the body. The cancer cells look small and oval-shaped when looked at under a microscope. Also called oat cell cancer.

Small intestine The part of the digestive tract that is located between the stomach and the large intestine.

Small intestine cancer A rare cancer that forms in tissues of the small intestine (the part of the digestive tract between the stomach and the large intestine). The most common type is adenocarcinoma (cancer that begins in cells that make and release mucus and other fluids). Other types of small intestine cancer include sarcoma (cancer that begins in connective or supportive tissue), carcinoid tumor (a slow-growing type of cancer), gastrointestinal stromal tumor (a type of soft tissue sarcoma), and lymphoma (cancer that begins in immune system cells).

Small lymphocytic lymphoma An indolent (slow-growing) type of B-cell non-Hodgkin's lymphoma marked by swollen lymph nodes that usually occurs in people older than 50 years. It is very similar to a form of leukemia called chronic lymphocytic leukemia (CLL). Also called well-differentiated lymphocytic lymphoma.

Smoke control The use of physical barriers and mechanical ventilation to control the spread of smoke from a fire.

Smoke purge The use of mechanical ventilation to remove smoke resulting from fire.

Smoke test Visualization of airflow streams in a clean space using artificially generated smoke, such as Titanium smoke, CO_2, or glycol fog.

Smoldering leukemia A disease in which the bone marrow does not function normally. Also called preleukemia and myelodysplastic syndrome.

Smoldering myeloma A very slow-growing type of myeloma in which abnormal plasma cells (a type of white blood cell) make too much of a single type of monoclonal antibody (a protein). This protein buiids up in the blood or is passed in the urine. Patients with smoldering myeloma usually have no symptoms, but need to be checked often for signs of progression to fully developed multiple myeloma.

SnET2 An anticancer drug that is also used in cancer prevention. It belongs to the family of drugs called photosensitizing agents. Also called tin ethyl etiopurpurin.

SNX 111 A drug used in the treatment of chronic pain. Also called ziconotide.

Soblidotin A dolastatin-10 derivative. Soblidotin inhibits tubulin polymerization, resulting in cell cycle arrest and induction of apoptosis.

Social service A community resource that helps people in need. Services may include help getting to and from medical appointments, home delivery of medication and meals, in-home nursing care, help paying medical costs not covered by insurance, loaning medical equipment, and housekeeping help.

Social support A network of family, friends, neighbors, and community members that is available in times of need to give psychological, physical, and financial help.

Social worker A professional trained to talk with people and their families about emotional or physical needs, and to find them support services.

Sodium A mineral needed by the body to keep body fluids in balance. Sodium is found in table salt and in many processed foods. Too much sodium can cause the body to retain water.

Sodium borocaptate BSH A substance used in a type of radiation therapy called boron neutron capture therapy. Sodium borocaptate is injected into a vein and becomes concentrated in tumor cells. The patient then receives radiation treatment with atomic particles called neutrons. The neutrons react with the boron in sodium borocaptate and make radioactive particles that kill the tumor cells without harming normal cells.

Sodium salicylate The sodium salt of salicylic acid. As a nonsteroidal anti-inflammatory drug (NSAID), sodium salicylate irreversibly acetylates cyclooxygenases I and II, thereby inhibiting prostaglandin synthesis and associated inflammation and pain. This agent may also activate mitogen-activated protein kinase (p38MAPK), thereby inducing apoptosis in cancer cells.

Sodium sulphite A chemical used in photography, paper making, water treatment, and for other purposes.

Sodium thiosulphate A substance that is used in medicine as an antidote to cyanide poisoning and to decrease side effects of the anticancer drug cisplatin.

Sodothiol Other name for sodium thiosulphate.

Soft diet A diet consisting of bland foods that are softened by cooking, mashing, pureeing, or blending.

Soft outcome Any outcome measure that is subject to major errors of interpretation or measurement. Usually, a measurement or assessment that depends on clinical judgment, or is founded in symptom.

Soft palate The posterior fleshy portion of the horizntal partition separating the nasal from the oral cavity.

Soft tissue Refers to muscle, fat, fibrous tissue, blood vessels, or other supporting tissue of the body.

Soft tissue sarcoma A cancer that begins in the muscle, fat, fibrous tissue, blood vessels, or other supporting tissue of the body.

Softening A pretreatment process which uses cation exchange resin to remove hardness elements (calcium and magnesium) from water. The cation resin is regenerated with Sodium Chloride (NaCl) and during the exchange process, the calcium and magnesium are removed from the water and replaced with sodium ions (Na^+). The resulting sodium salts are much more soluble and do not precipitate, which provides better feed water to the RO system.

Solar keratosis A precancerous condition of thick, scaly patches of skin. Also called actinic or senile keratosis.

Soldering A metal joining process wherein coalescence is produced by heating to suitable temperatures and by using a nonferrous alloy fusible at temperatures below 427°C (800°F) and having a melting point below that of the base metals being joined. The filler metal is distributed between closely fitted surfaces of the joint by capillary attraction. In general, solders are lead-tin alloys and may contain antimony, bismuth, and other elements.

Solid tumor An abnormal mass of tissue that usually does not contain cysts or liquid areas. Solid tumors may be benign (not cancerous), or malignant (cancerous). Different types of solid tumors are named for the type of cells that form them.

Examples of solid tumors are sarcomas, carcinomas, and lymphomas. Leukemias (cancers of the blood) generally do not form solid tumors.

Solo practice, solo practitioner A physician who practices alone or with others but does not pool income or expenses. This form of practice is becoming increasingly less common as physicians band together for contracting, overhead costs and risk sharing.

Solu medrol Other name for methylprednisolone.

Soluble antigen Generally used in reference to vaccine production. As opposed to a whole live or attenuated virus, a soluble antigen is a fragment of the virus that produces immunity. Also refers to large molecular weight polysaccharides from some bacteria which can act as vaccines.

Solute The substance that dissolves to form ions in solution.

Solvent An inorganic or organic liquid used as a vehicle for the preparation of solutions or suspensions in the manufacture of an intermediate or API (Active Pharmaceutical Ingredient).

Somatic cell Any of the body cells except the reproductive (germ) cells.

Somatic cell gene therapy Incorporating new genetic material into cells for therapeutic purposes. The new genetic material cannot be passed to offspring.

Somatic cell genetic mutation A change in the genetic structure that is neither inherited nor passed to offspring. Also called acquired mutations.

Somatic mutation An alteration in DNA that occurs after conception. Somatic mutations can occur in any of the cells of the body except the germ cells (sperm and egg) and therefore are not passed on to children. These alterations can (but do not always) cause cancer or other diseases.

Somatostatin A hormone made by the delta cells of the pancreas (in areas called the islets of Langerhans). Scientists think it may control how the body secretes two other hormones, insulin and glucagon.

Somatostatin receptor scintigraphy (SRS) A type of radionuclide scan used to find carcinoid and other types of tumors. In SRS, radioactive octreotide, a drug similar to somatostatin, is injected into a vein and travels through the bloodstream. The radioactive octreotide attaches to tumor cells that have receptors for somatostatin. A radiation-measuring device detects the radioactive octreotide, and makes pictures showing where the tumor cells are in the body. This procedure is also called an octreotide scan.

Somnolence syndrome Periods of drowsiness, lethargy, loss of appetite, and irritability in children following radiation therapy treatments to the head.

Somoclonal variation Genetic variation produced from the culture of plant cells from a pure breeding strain; the source of the variation is not known.

Somogyi effect A swing to a high level of glucose (sugar) in the blood from an extremely low level, usually occurring after an untreated insulin reaction during the night. The swing is caused by the release of stress hormones to counter low glucose levels. People who experience high levels of blood glucose in the morning may need to test their blood glucose levels in the middle of the night. If blood glucose levels are falling or low, adjustments in evening snacks or insulin doses may be recommended. This condition is named after Dr. Michael Somogyi, the man who first wrote about it. Also called "rebound."

Sonogram A computer picture of areas inside the body created by bouncing high-energy sound waves (ultrasound) off internal tissues or organs. Also called an ultrasonogram.

SOP (Standard operating procedures) The description of necessary activities to respond to normal and abnormal situations in an operating system. The SOP may include a troubleshooting checklist, list of personnel to contact, etc. SOPs should also describe normal operation, maintenance, and cleaning of the system, and normal operating parameters. An SOP may be created for any system but an SOP must be created for each system requiring qualification.

Sorafenib A synthetic compound targeting growth signaling and angiogenesis. Sorafenib blocks the enzyme RAF kinase, a critical component of the RAF/MEK/ERK signaling pathway that controls cell division and proliferation; in addition, sorafenib inhibits the VEGFR-2/PDGFR-beta signaling cascade, thereby blocking tumor angiogenesis.

Sorbitol A sugar alcohol the body uses slowly. It is a sweetener used in diet foods. It is called a nutritive sweetener because it has four calories in every gram, just like table sugar and starch.

Sorbitol is also produced by the body. Too much sorbitol in cells can cause damage. Diabetic retinopathy and neuropathy may be related to too much sorbitol in the cells of the eyes and nerves.

Sorivudine An antiviral drug that is being studied as a treatment for herpesvirus. It belongs to the family of drugs called nucleic acid synthesis inhibitors.

Sorrel Rumex acetosella. A plant that has been used in some cultures to treat certain medical problems. It may have anticancer effects. Also called sheep sorrel and dock.

Source code An original computer program either in human readable or machine-readable form.

Southern blotting Transfer by absorption of DNA fragments separated in electrophoretic gels to membrane filters for detection of specific base sequences by radio-labeled complementary probes.

Soy Glycine max. A plant of Asian origin that produces beans used in many food products. Soy products contain isoflavones (estrogen-like substances) that are being studied for the prevention of cancer, hot flashes that occur with menopause, and osteoporosis (loss of bone density). Soy products in the diet may lower cholesterol levels and reduce the risk of heart disease. Also called soya and soybean.

Soy protein isolate A dietary protein isolated from soybeans that contains isoflavone phytoestrogens. Soy protein isolate has been shown to reduce tumor incidence and growth in some animal studies, possibly by modulating estrogen metabolism, reducing tumor cell proliferation, and inducing tumor cell apoptosis. Soy protein isolate may also inhibit endothelial cell proliferation. Isoflavone phytoestrogens display mild estrogen-like activities which may regulate hormone balance and reduce the risks of breast cancer, heart disease, and osteoporosis.

Space maintainer Dental device that holds the space lost through premature loss of baby teeth.

Spacer device A plastic tube that fits between the inhaler and the mouth to increase the delivery of atomised medication to the lungs.

Sparfloxacin An experimental flouroquinolone antibiotic active against mycobacterium avium complex.

Sparger A device used to agitate, oxygenate, aerate, or add a chemical to a liquid by means of compressed air or gas entering through small holes in a pipe below the liquid surface.

Spasm Movement of a muscle that causes cramping and pain.

Spatial relation The ability to judge the relative position of one object to another and the internal awareness of the two sides of the body. These skills allow the individual to develop the concepts of right, left, front, back, up, and down. This ability is needed in reading and math.

Specific conductance The reciprocal of specific resistance usually expressed in micromhos/cm.

Specific humidity Also known as Humidity Ratio, and Absolute Humidity, is the weight of water vapour in each pound of dry air expressed in grains of moisture per pound of dry air, or pounds of moisture per pound of dry air. Humidity of air mixtures is normally discussed in terms of grains of moisture per pound rather than the more common term of relative humidity because the grains of moisture in an air stream do not change when it is heated or cooled, unless condensation takes place.

Specific immune cell An immune cell such as a T or B lymphocyte that responds to a single, specific antigen.

Specific ion determinations Electrochemical measurement of trace ion levels in solution.

Specific resistance The resistance of a one-centimeter cube of water to the passage of electricity under standard conditions, expressed in ohms/cm. A measure of the Total Ionized Solids concentration.

Specific volume In Psychrometry, the cubic feet of the mixture per pound of dry air.

Specification A list of testes, references to analytical procedures, and appropriate acceptance criteria that are numerical limits, ranges, or other criteria for the test described. It establishes the set of criteria to which an intermediate or API (Active Pharmaceutical Ingredient) should conform to be considered acceptable for its intended use. "Conformance to Specifications" means that the intermediate or API, when tested according to the listed analytical procedures, will meet the listed acceptance criteria.

Specificity When referring to a medical test, specificity refers to the percentage of people who test negative for a specific disease among a group of people who do not have the disease. No test is 100% specific because some people who do not have the disease will test positive for it (false positive).

Spectral karyotype A graphic of all an organism's chromosomes, each labeled with a different color. Useful for identifying chromosomal abnormalities.

Speculum An instrument used to widen an opening of the body to make it easier to look inside.

Speech pathologist A specialist who evaluates and treats people with communication and swallowing problems. Also called a speech therapist.

Speech therapist A specialist who evaluates and treats people with communication and swallowing problems. Also called a speech pathologist.

Sperm The male reproductive cell formed in the testicle. A sperm unites with an egg to form an embryo.

Sperm banking Freezing sperm for use in the future. This procedure can allow men to father children after loss of fertility.

Sperm count A count of the number of sperm in a sample of semen. A sperm count may be used as a measure of fertility.

Sperm retrieval Removal of sperm from a man's testis or epididymis by a doctor using a fine needle or other instrument.

Spermatic cord The tissues extending from the abdominal inguinal ring to the testis, containing the ductus deferens, testicular artery, pampiniform (venous) plexus, and nerves.

Sphenoid sinus Made up of two cavities, separated by a bony septum, in the anterior portion of the body of the sphenoid bone. The sphenoid sinus communicates with the nasal cavity.

Sphere An ophthalmic lens with no cylindrical power or addition. It has the same power in all parts of the lens.

Sphincter A ring-shaped muscle that relaxes or tightens to open or close a passage or opening in the body. Examples are the anal sphincter (around the opening of the anus) and the pyloric sphincter (at the lower opening of the stomach).

Spiculated mass A lump of tissue with spikes or points on the surface.

Spilling point When the blood is holding so much of a substance such as glucose (sugar) that the kidneys allow the excess to spill into the urine.

Spina bifida Malformations that result from the defective development of the spinal cord and/or the encasing vertebrae of varying severity. They most commonly occur in the lower thoracic, lumbar and sacral regions.

Spinal column The bones, muscles, tendons, and other tissues that reach from the base of the skull to the tailbone. The spinal column encloses the spinal cord and the fluid surrounding the spinal cord. Also called spine, backbone, and vertebral column.

Spinal cord A column of nerve tissue that runs from the base of the skull down the back. It is surrounded by three protective membranes, and is enclosed within the vertebrae (back bones). The spinal cord and the brain make up the central nervous system, and spinal cord nerves carry most messages between the brain and the rest of the body.

Spinal tap Also known as lumbar puncture. A procedure in which cerebrospinal fluid from the lower spine is extracted with a needle for examination.

Spindle cell cancer Cancer that arises in cells that appear spindle-shaped when viewed under a microscope. These cancers can occur in various places in the body, including the skin, lungs, kidney, breast, gastrointestinal tract, bone, and muscle.

Spindle cell sarcoma A type of connective tissue cancer in which the cells are spindle-shaped when examined under a microscope.

Spine cancer Cancer that begins in the spinal column (backbone) or spinal cord. The spinal column is made up of linked bones, called vertebrae. The spinal cord is a column of nerve tissue that runs from the base of the skull down the back. It is surrounded by three protective membranes, and is enclosed within the vertebrae. Many different types of cancer may form in the bones, tissues, fluid, or nerves of the spine.

Spine of scapula Plate of bone attached to the back of the scapula, with the tip at the vertebral border and ending laterally as the acromion process.

Spinner flasks Small laboratory bioreactors used for the initial growth of mammalian cells lines.

Spinous process The portion of the vertebrae that projects backward from the arch and is a point of muscular attachment.

Spiral CT scan A detailed picture of areas inside the body. The pictures are created by a computer linked to an x-ray machine that scans the body in a spiral path. Also called helical computed tomography.

Spirituality Having to do with deep, often religious, feelings and beliefs, including a person's sense of peace, purpose, connection to others, and beliefs about the meaning of life.

Spirometer An instrument used for measuring the volume of air inhaled and exhaled.

Spleen Gland-like but ductless organ located on the left side of the upper abdominal cavity, lateral to the cardiac region of the stomach.

Splenectomy An operation to remove the spleen.

Splenic artery Originating from the celiac trunk and branching into the pancreatic and splenic branches, left gastro-omental, and short gastric arteries.

Splenic flexure Bend within the large intestine where the transverse colon becomes the descending colon.

Splenic portal vein confluence The point where these two veins merge into one.

Splenic vein The vein originating at the junction of several branches at the hilum of the spleen, and joining the superior mesenteric vein, to form the portal vein, at the neck of the pancreas.

Splenium The enlarged posterior portion of the corpus callosum. Fibers of the splenium contribute to the formation of the roof and lateral wall of the occipital horn of the lateral ventricle and the lateral wall of the temporal horn. Remaining fibers comprise the forceps major which interconnects the occipital lobes.

Splenomegaly Enlargement of the spleen.

Splice site Location in the DNA sequence where RNA removes the noncoding areas to form a continuous gene transcript for translation into a protein.

Splint Connection of two or more teeth so they function as a stronger single structure.

Split dose Division of a prescribed daily dose of insulin into two or more injections given over the course of a day. Also may be referred to as multiple injections. Many people who use insulin feel that split doses offer more consistent control over blood glucose (sugar) levels.

Spongiosis Intercellular epidermal edema seen as an increase in the width of spaces between cells.

Sporadic cancer Cancer that occurs randomly and is not inherited from parents. Caused by DNA changes in one cell that grows and divides, spreading throughout the body.

Spore A reproductive cell or seed of algae, fungi, or protozoa.

Spore, bacterial A bacterial spore is a resistant body formed as part of the life cycle of some bacteria. Bacterial spores are able to withstand severe environmental conditions (e.g., heat, drying, chemicals) for many years. When conditions are favourable, spores germinate into vegetative bacterial cells capable of replication.

Sporicide An agent that destroys bacterial and fungal spores.

Spotted thistle Cnicus benedictus. A plant whose leaves, stems, and flowers have been used in some cultures to treat certain medical problems. Spotted thistle may have anti-inflammatory and anticancer effects. Also called blessed thistle, St. Benedict's thistle, cardin, and holy thistle.

Spray drying Process by which a material in suspension is converted into droplets that may be coated by a substance, either melted or dissolved in the droplet's media. The action in spray drying is primarily that of evaporation, energy is applied to the droplet forcing evaporation of the media with both energy and mass transfer through the droplet. Examples of this technology include, pharmaceutical tablet granulation, and rapid drying which results in free-flowing powders on a continuous basis. Spray drying process consists of the following steps: 1. Formation of a slurry to be sprayed; this slurry may be a simple concentrated solution or the dispersion of an insoluble material in a solution.

2. Liquid atomization into droplets; this action is critical as the droplet size will dictate the equipment size as well as the final product size. There are four types of atomization devices: air, airless, disk (or rotary) spray, and ultrasonic.

3. Exposure of the droplet to a heated gas flow; this gas (normally air) supplies the energy required to vaporize the solvent. Collection

of the dry free-flowing powder or encapsulated liquid or solid.

Sputum Mucus and other matter brought up from the lungs by coughing.

Sputum analysis Method of detecting certain infections (especially tuberculosis) by analyzing sputum, the mucus matter that collects in the respiratory and upper digestive passages and is expelled by coughing.

Sputum cytology Examination under a microscope of lung cells found in sputum (mucus and other matter brought up from the lungs by coughing) to check for cancer.

Squalamine lactate A drug that belongs to the family of drugs called angiogenesis inhibitors. It prevents the growth of new blood vessels into a solid tumor.

Squamotization Replacement of the normally cuboidal or columnar basal cells with polygonal or flattened keratinocytes. This occurs mainly in lichenoid tissue reactions.

Squamous cell Flat cell that looks like a fish scale under a microscope. These cells cover inside and outside surfaces of the body. They are found in the tissues that form the surface of the skin, the lining of the hollow organs of the body (such as the bladder, kidney, and uterus), and the passages of the respiratory and digestive tracts.

Squamous cell carcinoma Cancer that begins in squamous cells, which are thin, flat cells that look like fish scales. Squamous cells are found in the tissue that forms the surface of the skin, the lining of the hollow organs of the body, and the passages of the respiratory and digestive tracts. Also called epidermoid carcinoma.

Squamous intraepithelial lesion (SIL) A general term for the abnormal growth of squamous cells on the surface of the cervix. The changes in the cells are described as low grade or high grade, depending on how much of the cervix is affected and how abnormal the cells appear.

Squint To be unable to direct both eyes simultaneously toward a point. Also known as strabismus (turned eye).

SR-29142 A drug that may protect healthy tissue from the toxic effects of anticancer drugs.

SR-45023A An anticancer drug that belongs to the family of drugs called bisphosphonates. It affects cancer cell receptors governing cell growth and cell death.

SR49059 A substance that is being studied in the treatment of cancer. It inhibits a hormone growth factor that causes some cancer cells to divide. It belongs to the family of drugs called vasopressin receptor antagonists.

SS1 (dsFv) PE38 immunotoxin A recombinant immunotoxin

consisting of the single chain anti-mesothelin monoclonal antibody SS1 (dsFv) linked to Pseudomonas exotoxin PE-38. The monoclonal antibody moiety of the agent binds to cells that express mesothelin, a cell surface glycoprotein which may be overexpressed in ovarian cancer, mesotheliomas, and some squamous cell carcinomas; after internalization, the exotoxin moiety inactivates eukaryotic translation elongation factor 2, thereby disrupting tumor cell protein synthesis.

St. Benedict's thistle Cnicus benedictus. A plant whose leaves, stems, and flowers have been used in some cultures to treat certain medical problems. St. Benedict's thistle may have anti-inflammatory and anticancer effects. Also called blessed thistle, cardin, holy thistle, and spotted thistle.

St. John's wort Hypericum perforatum, an herbal product sold as an over-the-counter treatment for depression. It is being studied for its ability to lessen certain side effects of cancer treatment.

ST1481 A substance that is being studied in the treatment of cancer. It belongs to the family of drugs called topoisomerase inhibitors. Also called gimatecan.

Stability Generally, stability refers to the physico-chemical condition of a parenteral, biological, or shelf life of labile drugs. Certain drugs must pass stability tests. For example, human serum albumin must pass certain limits of nephelometric turbidity. Also manufacturers must have documentation of potency of labile products under labeled storage conditions.

Stability index An empirical modification of the saturation index used to predict scaling or corrosive tendencies in water systems.

Stable disease Cancer that is neither decreasing nor increasing in extent or severity.

Stage The extent of a cancer in the body. Staging is usually based on the size of the tumor, whether lymph nodes contain cancer, and whether the cancer has spread from the original site to other parts of the body.

Stage 0 anal cancer Cancer is found in the innermost lining of the anus only. Also called carcinoma in situ.

Stage 0 bladder cancer Cancer is found on tissue lining the inside of the bladder only. Stage 0 is divided into stage 0a and stage 0is, depending on the type of the tumor. Stage 0a is also called papillary carcinoma, which may look like tiny mushrooms growing from the lining of the bladder. Stage 0is is also called carcinoma in situ, which is a flat tumor on the tissue lining the inside of the bladder.

Stage 0 cervical cancer Cancer is found in the first layer of cells lining the cervix only and has not invaded the deeper tissues of the cervix. Also called carcinoma in situ.

Stage 0 chronic lymphocytic leukemia There are too many lymphocytes in the blood, but there are no other symptoms of leukemia. Stage 0 is indolent (slow-growing).

Stage 0 colorectal cancer Cancer is found in the innermost lining of the colon and/or rectum only. Also called carcinoma in situ.

Stage 0 esophageal cancer Cancer is found in the innermost layer of cells lining the esophagus. Also called carcinoma in situ.

Stage 0 extrahepatic bile duct cancer Cancer is found only in the innermost layer of cells lining the extrahepatic bile duct. Also called carcinoma in situ.

Stage 0 gallbladder cancer In stage 0, cancer is found in the innermost (mucosal) layer of the gallbladder only. Stage 0 cancer is also called carcinoma in situ.

Stage 0 gastric cancer Cancer is found in the inside lining of the mucosal (innermost) layer of the stomach wall. Also called carcinoma in situ.

Stage 0 hypopharyngeal cancer Cancer is found only in the lining of the hypopharynx. Also called carcinoma in situ.

Stage 0 laryngeal cancer Cancer is found only in the cells lining the larynx. Stage 0 cancer is also called carcinoma in situ.

Stage 0 melanoma Cancer is found in the epidermis (outer layer of the skin) only. Also called melanoma in situ.

Stage 0 nasopharyngeal cancer Cancer is found in the lining of the nasopharynx (the upper part of the throat behind the nose) only. Also called carcinoma in situ.

Stage 0 non-small cell lung cancer Cancer is limited to the lung. It is found in a few layers of cells only, and has not grown through the top lining of the lung. Also called carcinoma in situ.

Stage 0 skin cancer Cancer is found in the epidermis (topmost layer of the skin) only, in the layer of cells in which the cancer began. Also called carcinoma in situ.

Stage 0 testicular cancer Abnormal cells are found only in the tiny tubules where the sperm cells begin to develop. The cells do not invade normal tissues; all tumor marker levels are normal. Sometimes called a precancerous condition. Also called carcinoma in situ.

Stage 0 transitional cell cancer of the renal pelvis and ureter (tran-ZIH-shu-nul sel KAN-ser of the REE-nul PEL-vus and yoo-REE-ter) Cancer is found only on tissue lining the inside of the renal pelvis or ureter. Stage 0 is divided into stages 0a and 0is, depending on the type of tumor. In stage 0a, the cancer may look like tiny mushrooms growing from the lining; also called noninvasive papillary carcinoma. In stage 0is, the tumor is flat on the lining; also called carcinoma in situ.

Stage 1 neuroblastoma Tumor is only found in one area; all of the tumor that can be seen is completely removed during surgery.

Stage 2 neuroblastoma Stage 2 is divided into stages 2A and 2B. In stage 2A, the tumor is in one area only and not all of the tumor that can be seen can be completely removed during surgery. In stage 2B, the tumor is in one area only and all of the tumor that can be seen may be completely removed during surgery, but cancer cells are found in nearby lymph nodes.

Stage 3 neuroblastoma In stage 3 neuroblastoma, the tumor (1) cannot be completely removed during surgery and has spread from one side of the body to the other side and may also have spread to nearby lymph nodes; or (2) is in one area of one side of the body only, but has spread to lymph nodes on the other side of the body; or (3) is in the middle of the body and has spread to tissues or lymph nodes on both sides of the body, and the tumor cannot be removed by surgery.

Stage 4 neuroblastoma Stage 4 neuroblastoma is divided into stages 4 and 4S. In stage 4, the tumor has spread to distant lymph nodes, the skin, and/or other parts of the body. In stage 4S, (1) the child is younger than 1 year; and (2) the cancer has spread to the skin, liver, and/or bone marrow; and (3) the tumor is in one area only and all of the tumor that can be seen may be completely removed during surgery; and/or (4) cancer cells may be found in the lymph nodes near the tumor.

Stage I adrenocortical cancer Cancer that is smaller than 5 centimeters (smaller than 2 inches) and has not spread into tissues around the adrenal gland.

Stage I adult Hodgkin's lymphoma Stage I is divided into stage I and stage IE. In stage I, cancer is found in a single group of lymph nodes. In stage IE, cancer is found in one area or organ other than the lymph nodes.

Stage I adult non-Hodgkin's lymphoma Stage I is divided into stage I and stage IE. In stage I, cancer is found in a single lymph node area. In stage IE, cancer is found in an organ or tissue other than the lymph nodes.

Stage I adult primary liver cancer There is one tumor and it has not spread to nearby blood vessels.

Stage I AIDS related lymphoma Stage I AIDS-related lymphoma is divided into stages I and IE. In stage I, cancer is found in one group of lymph nodes. In stage IE, cancer is found in one area of one organ or tissue that is not part of the lymph system.

Stage I anal cancer The tumor is no larger than 2 centimeters.

Stage I bladder cancer Cancer has spread to the connective tissue layer below the inner lining of the bladder.

Stage I breast cancer The tumor is 2 centimeters or smaller and has not spread outside the breast.

Stage I cancer of the uterus Cancer found in only the main part of the uterus, not the cervix.

Stage I cancer of the vulva Cancer found in the vulva only or the space between the opening of the rectum and the vagina (perineum). The tumor is 2 centimeters (about 1 inch) or smaller.

Stage I cervical cancer Cancer is found in the cervix only. Stage I is divided into stages IA and IB, based on the amount of cancer that is found. In stage IA, a very small amount of cancer that can only be seen with a microscope is found in the tissues of the cervix. The cancer is not deeper than 5 millimeters and not wider than 7 millimeters. In stage IB, the cancer is still within the cervix and either (1) can only be seen with a microscope and is deeper than 5 millimeters or wider than 7 millimeters; or (2) can be seen without a microscope and may be larger than 4 centimeters.

Stage I childhood liver cancer All of the cancer was removed by surgery.

Stage I childhood non-Hodgkin's lymphoma Cancer is found in a single area or lymph node outside of the abdomen or chest.

Stage I chronic lymphocytic leukemia There are too many lymphocytes in the blood and the lymph nodes are larger than normal.

Stage I colorectal cancer Cancer has spread beyond the innermost lining of the colon and/or rectum to the second and third layers and involves the inside wall of the colon and/or rectum, but it has not spread to the outer wall or outside the colon and/or rectum. Also called Dukes' A colorectal cancer.

Stage I cutaneous T-cell lymphoma May be either of the following: 1. Stage IA cancer affecting less than 10% of the skin's surface and appearing as red. dry, scaly patches;

2. Stage IB cancer affecting 10% or more of the skin's surface and appearing as red, dry, scaly patches.

Stage I endometrial cancer Cancer is found in the uterus only. Stage I is divided into stage IA, IB, and IC, based on how far the disease has spread. In stage IA, cancer is in the endometrium only; in stage IB, cancer has spread into the inner half of the myometrium (muscle layer of the uterus); in stage IC, cancer has spread into the outer half of the myometrium.

Stage I esophageal cancer Cancer has spread beyond the innermost layer of cells to the next layer of tissue in the wall of the esophagus.

Stage I extrahepatic bile duct cancer Stage I is divided into stage IA and IB. In stage IA, cancer is found only in the bile duct. In stage IB, cancer has spread through the wall of the bile duct.

Stage I gastric cancer Stage I is divided into stage IA and stage IB, depending on where the cancer has spread. In stage IA, cancer has spread completely through the mucosal (innermost) layer of the stomach wall. In stage IB, cancer has spread completely through the mucosal (innermost) layer of the stomach wall and is found in up to 6 lymph nodes near the tumor, or has spread to the muscularis (middle) layer of the stomach wall.

Stage I hypopharyngeal cancer The tumor is found only in one area of the hypopharynx and is 2 centimeters or smaller.

Stage I kidney cancer The tumor is 7 centimeters or smaller and is found in the kidney only. Also called stage I renal cell cancer.

Stage I laryngeal cancer Cancer is found only in the area where it started. Stage I laryngeal cancer depends on where cancer is found in the larynx. If it started in the supraglottis, then cancer is in one area of the supraglottis only and the vocal cords can move normally. If it started in the glottis, then cancer is in one or both vocal cords and the vocal cords can move normally. If it started in the subglottis, then cancer is in the subglottis only.

Stage I lip and oral cavity cancer Cancer that is no larger than 2 centimeters (about 1 inch) and has not spread to nearby lymph nodes.

Stage I malignant mesothelioma Cancer is found in the lining of the chest wall and may also be found in the lining of the lung, the lining of the diaphragm (the thin muscle below the lungs and heart that separates the chest from the abdomen), or the lining of the sac that covers the heart on the same side of the chest. Also called localized malignant mesothelioma.

Stage I melanoma Stage I is divided into stages IA and IB. In stage IA, the tumor is not more than 1 millimeter thick, with no ulceration. The tumor is in the epidermis (outer layer of skin) and upper layer of the dermis (inner layer of skin). In stage IB, the tumor is either not more than 1 millimeter thick, with ulceration, and may have spread into the dermis or the tissue below the skin; or 1 to 2 millimeters thick, with no ulceration.

Stage I multiple myeloma Relatively few cancer cells have spread throughout the body. There may be no symptoms of disease.

Stage I mycosis fungoides and the Sézary syndrome Stage I is divided into stages IA and IB. In stage IA, less than 10% of the skin surface is covered with patches and/or plaques (areas of abnormal tissue). In stage IB, 10% or more of the skin surface is covered with patches and/or plaques. Stage I may also be classified based on how many abnormal lymphocytes (white blood cells) are found in the blood.

Stage I nasopharyngeal cancer Cancer is found in the nasopharynx (the upper part of the throat behind the nose) only.

Stage I non-small cell lung cancer Cancer is in the lung only. Stage I is divided into stages IA and IB based on the size or location of the tumor.

Stage I oropharynx cancer Cancer that is no larger than 2 centimeters (about 0.75 inch) and is confined to the oropharynx.

Stage I ovarian cancer Cancer is found in one or both of the ovaries and has not spread. Stage I is divided into stage IA, stage IB, and stage IC. In stage IA, cancer is found in a single ovary. In stage IB, cancer is found in both ovaries. In stage IC, cancer is found in one or both ovaries and one of the following is true: cancer is found on the outside surface of one or both ovaries; the capsule (outer covering) of the tumor has ruptured (broken open); or, cancer cells are found in fluid from the peritoneal cavity (the body cavity that contains most of the organs in the abdomen).

Stage I pancreatic cancer Cancer is found in the pancreas only. Stage I is divided into stage IA and stage IB based on tumor size. In stage IA, the tumor is no larger than 2 centimeters and in stage IB, the tumor is larger than 2 centimeters.

Stage I prostate cancer Cancer is found in the prostate only. It cannot be felt during a digital rectal exam and is not visible by imaging. It is usually found accidentally during surgery for other reasons, such as benign prostatic hyperplasia (a condition in which an overgrowth of prostate tissue occurs). Also called stage A1 prostate cancer.

Stage I skin cancer The tumor is no larger than 2 centimeters.

Stage I testicular cancer Stage I is divided into stage IA, stage IB, and stage IS, and is determined after a radical inguinal orchiectomy (surgery to remove the testicle) is done. In stage IA, cancer is in the testicle and epididymis and may have spread to the inner layer of the membrane surrounding the testicle; all tumor marker levels are normal. In stage IB, the cancer is in the testicle and the epididymis and has spread to the blood or lymph vessels in the testicle; or has spread to the outer layer of the membrane surrounding the testicle; or is in the spermatic cord or the scrotum and may be in the blood or lymph vessels of the testicle; all tumor marker levels are normal. In stage IS, cancer is found anywhere within the testicle spermatic cord, or the scrotum, and either all tumor marker levels are slightly above normal or one or more tumor marker levels are moderately above normal or high.

Stage I transitional cell cancer of the renal pelvis and ureter Cancer has spread through the cells lining the renal pelvis and/or ureter, into the layer of connective tissue.

Stage I wilms' tumor Cancer that is found in the kidney only and can be completely removed by surgery.

Stage IA gallbladder cancer Stage I gallbladder cancer is divided into stages IA and IB. In stage IA, cancer has spread beyond the innermost (mucosal) layer to the connective tissue or to the muscle layer.

Stage IA soft tissue sarcoma Cancer in which the cells look very much like normal cells. The cancer is smaller than 5 centimeters (about 2 inches) and has not spread to lymph nodes or other parts of the body.

Stage IB gallbladder cancer Stage I gallbladder cancer is divided into stages IA and IB. In stage IB, cancer has spread beyond the muscle layer to the connective tissue around the muscle.

Stage IB soft tissue sarcoma Cancer in which the cells look somewhat different from normal cells. The cancer is larger than 5 centimeters (about 2 inches) and has not spread to lymph nodes or other parts of the body.

Stage II adrenocortical cancer Cancer that is larger than 5 centimeters (about 2 inches) and has not spread into tissues around the adrenal gland.

Stage II adult Hodgkin's lymphoma Stage II is divided into stage II and stage IIE. In stage II, cancer is found in two or more lymph node groups on the same side of the diaphragm (the thin muscle below the lungs that helps breathing and separates the chest from the abdomen). In stage IIE, cancer is found in one area or organ other than the lymph nodes and in the lymph nodes near that area or organ, and may have spread to other lymph node groups on the same side of the diaphragm.

Stage II adult non-Hodgkin's lymphoma Stage II is divided into stage II and stage IIE. In stage II, cancer is found in two or more lymph node areas on the same side of the diaphragm. In stage IIE, cancer is found in an organ or tissue other than the lymph nodes and may have spread to one or more lymph nodes on the same side of the diaphragm.

Stage II adult primary liver cancer There is either 1. One tumor that has spread to nearby blood vessels; or

2. There is more than one tumor, none of which is larger than 5 centimeters.

Stage II aids-related lymphoma Stage II AIDS-related lymphoma is divided into stages II and IIE. In stage II, cancer is found in two or more lymph node groups on the same side of the diaphragm (the muscle below the lungs and heart that separates the chest from the abdomen). In stage IIE, cancer is found in one area of one organ or tissue that is not part of the lymph system and in nearby lymph nodes. Cancer may also be found in other lymph node groups on the same side of the diaphragm.

Stage II anal cancer The tumor is larger than 2 centimeters.

Stage II bladder cancer Cancer has spread to either the inner layer or outer layer of the muscle wall of the bladder.

Stage II breast cancer Stage II is divided into stage IIA and stage IIB based on tumor size and whether it has spread to the axillary lymph nodes (the lymph nodes under the arm). In stage IIA, the cancer is either no larger than 2 centimeters and has spread to the axillary lymph nodes, or between 2 and 5 centimeters but has not spread to the axillary lymph nodes. In stage IIB, the cancer is either between 2 and 5 centimeters and has spread to the axillary lymph nodes, or larger than 5 centimeters but has not spread to the axillary lymph nodes.

Stage II cancer of the uterus Cancer that has spread to the cervix.

Stage II cancer of the vulva Cancer that is found in the vulva, the space between the opening of the rectum and the vagina (perineum), or both. The tumor is larger than 2 centimeters (larger than 1 inch).

Stage II cervical cancer Cancer has spread beyond the cervix but not to the pelvic wall (the tissues that line the part of the body between the hips). Stage II is divided into stages IIA and IIB, based on how far the cancer has spread. In stage IIA, cancer has spread to the upper two thirds of the vagina but not to tissues around the uterus. In stage IIB, cancer has spread to the upper two thirds of the vagina and to the tissues around the uterus.

Stage II childhood liver cancer All of the cancer was removed by surgery, except for a small amount of cancer that can be seen only with a microscope, or tumor cells that may have spilled into the abdomen during surgery.

Stage II childhood non-Hodgkin's lymphoma Cancer is found (1) in only one area and in the lymph nodes around it; or (2) in two or more areas or lymph nodes on one side of the diaphragm (the thin muscle under the lungs that divides the chest and abdominal cavity and helps with breathing); or (3) to have started in the stomach or intestines and has been completely removed by surgery, and lymph nodes in the area may or may not contain cancer.

Stage II chronic lymphocytic leukemia There are too many lymphocytes in the blood, the liver or spleen is larger than normal, and the lymph nodes may be larger than normal.

Stage II colorectal cancer Cancer has spread outside the colon and/or rectum to nearby tissue, but it has not gone into the lymph nodes. Also called Dukes' B colorectal cancer.

Stage II cutaneous T-cell lymphoma Stage II cutaneous T-cell lymphoma may be either of the following: 1. Stage IIA, in which the skin has red, dry, scaly patches but no tumors, and lymph nodes are enlarged but do not contain cancer cells;

2. Stage IIB, in which tumors are found on the skin, and lymph nodes are enlarged but do not contain cancer cells.

Stage II endometrial cancer Cancer has spread from the uterus to the cervix, but not beyond the cervix. Stage II is divided into stage IIA and IIB, based on how far the cancer has spread into the cervix. In stage IIA, cancer has spread to the glands where the cervix and uterus meet. In stage IIB, cancer has spread into the connective tissue of the cervix.

Stage II esophageal cancer Stage II is divided into stage IIA and stage IIB, depending on where the cancer has spread. In stage IIA, cancer has spread to the layer of esophageal muscle or to the outer wall of the esophagus. In stage IIB, cancer may have spread to any of the first three layers of the esophagus and to nearby lymph nodes.

Stage II extrahepatic bile duct cancer Stage II is divided into stage IIA and IIB. In stage IIA, cancer has spread to the liver, gallbladder, pancreas, and/or to either the right or left branches of the hepatic artery or of the portal vein (major blood vessels that carry blood to the liver). In stage IIB, cancer has spread to nearby lymph nodes and 1. Is found in the bile duct; or

2. Has spread through the wall of the bile duct; or

3. Has spread to the liver, gallbladder, pancreas, and/or the right or left branches of the hepatic artery or portal vein.

Stage II gastric cancer Cancer has spread 1. Completely through the mucosal (innermost) layer of the stomach wall and is found in 7 to 15 lymph nodes near the tumor, or

2. To the muscularis (middle) layer of the stomach wall and is found in up to 6 lymph nodes near the tumor, or

3. To the serosal (outermost) layer of the stomach wall but not to lymph nodes or other organs.

Stage II hypopharyngeal cancer The tumor is either 1. Larger than 2 centimeters but not larger than 4 centimeters and has not spread to the larynx (voice box); or

2. Found in more than one area of the hypopharynx or in nearby tissues.

Stage II kidney cancer The tumor is larger than 7 centimeters and is found in the kidney only. Also called stage II renal cell cancer.

Stage II laryngeal cancer Cancer that is found in the larynx. The exact definition of stage II depends on where the cancer started. If it started in the supraglottis, then cancer is in more than one area of the supraglottis or glottis or region near the supraglottis. If it started in the glottis, then cancer has spread to the supraglottis and/or the subglottis, and/or the vocal cords do not move normally. If it started in the subglottis, then cancer has spread to the vocal cords, which may not move normally.

Stage II lip and oral cavity cancer Cancer that is larger than 2 centimeters (about 1 inch) but smaller than 4 centimeters (about 2 inches) and has not spread to lymph nodes in the area.

Stage II malignant mesothelioma Cancer is found in the lining of the chest wall and the lymph nodes on the same side of the chest. Cancer may also be found in the lining of the lung, the lining of the diaphragm (the thin muscle below the lungs and heart that separates the chest from the abdomen), or the lining of the sac that covers the heart on the same side of the chest. Stages II, III, and IV malignant mesothelioma are also called advanced malignant mesothelioma.

Stage II melanoma Stage II is divided into stages IIA, IIB, and IIC. In stage IIA, the tumor is either 1 to 2 millimeters thick, with ulceration; or 2 to 4 millimeters thick, with no ulceration. In stage IIB, the tumor is either 2 to 4 millimeters thick, with ulceration; or more than 4 millimeters thick, with no ulceration. In stage IIC, the tumor is more than 4 millimeters thick, with ulceration.

Stage II multiple myeloma Cancer in which a moderate number of cancer cells have spread throughout the body.

Stage II mycosis fungoides and the Sézary syndrome Stage II is divided into stages IIA and IIB. In stage IIA, any amount of the skin surface is covered with patches and/or plaques (areas of abnormal tissue). Lymph nodes are enlarged but cancer has not spread to them. In stage IIB, one or more tumors (lumps of malignant cells) are found on the skin. Lymph nodes may be enlarged but cancer has not spread to them. Stage II may also be classified based on how many abnormal lymphocytes (white blood cells) are found in the blood.

Stage II nasopharyngeal cancer Stage II is divided into stage IIA and stage IIB. In stage IIA, cancer has spread from the nasopharynx (the upper part of the throat behind the nose) to the oropharynx (the middle part of the throat that includes the soft palate, the base of the tongue, and the tonsils), and/or to the nasal cavity. In stage IIB, cancer is found in the nasopharynx and has spread to lymph nodes on one side of the neck, or has spread to the area surrounding the nasopharynx and may have spread to lymph nodes on one side of the neck.

Stage II non small cell lung cancer Cancer has spread to nearby lymph nodes or to the chest wall, the diaphragm, the mediastinal pleura (the thin membrane that covers the outside of the lungs in the area near the heart), or the parietal pericardium (the outer layer of tissue that surrounds the heart). Stage II is divided into stage IIA and stage IIB based on the size of the tumor and whether it has spread to the lymph nodes.

Stage II oropharynx cancer Tumor that is between 2 and 4 centimeters (0.75 and 1.5 inches) and is confined to the oropharynx.

Stage II ovarian cancer Cancer is found in one or both ovaries and has spread into other areas of the pelvis. Stage II is divided into stage IIA, stage IIB, and stage IIC. In stage IIA, cancer has spread to the uterus and/or the fallopian tubes. In stage IIB, cancer has spread to other tissues within the pelvis. In stage IIC, cancer has spread to the uterus and/or fallopian tubes and/or other tissue within the pelvis and cancer cells are found in fluid from the peritoneal cavity (the body cavity that contains most of the organs in the abdomen).

Stage II pancreatic cancer Stage II is divided into stages IIA and IIB, based on where the cancer has spread. In stage IIA, cancer has spread to nearby tissue and organs but has not spread to nearby lymph nodes. In stage IIB, cancer has spread to nearby lymph nodes and may have spread to nearby tissue and organs.

Stage II prostate cancer Cancer is more advanced than in stage I, but has not spread outside the prostate. Also called stage A2, stage B1, or stage B2 prostate cancer.

Stage II skin cancer The tumor is larger than 2 centimeters.

Stage II testicular cancer Stage II is divided into stage IIA, stage IIB, and stage IIC, and is determined after a radical inguinal orchiectomy (surgery to remove the testicle) is done. In stage IIA, the cancer is anywhere within the testicle, spermatic cord, or scrotum; and has spread to up to 5 lymph nodes in the abdomen (none larger than 2 centimeters). In stage IIB, the cancer is anywhere within the testicle, spermatic cord, or scrotum; has spread to up to 5 lymph nodes in the abdomen (at least one of the lymph nodes is larger than 2 centimeters, but none is larger than 5 centimeters) or has spread to more than 5 lymph nodes (the lymph nodes are not larger than 5 centimeters). In stage

IIC, the cancer is anywhere within the testicle, spermatic cord, or scrotum; and has spread to a lymph node in the abdomen that is larger than 5 centimeters. All tumor marker levels are normal or slightly above normal.

Stage II transitional cell cancer of the renal pelvis and ureter Cancer has spread through the layer of connective tissue to the muscle layer of the renal pelvis and/or ureter.

Stage II wilms' tumor Cancer has spread to tissue near the kidney, to blood vessels, or to the renal sinus (a part of the kidney through which blood and fluid enter and exit). The cancer can be completely removed by surgery.

Stage IIA breast cancer Stage II breast cancer is divided into stages IIA and IIB. In stage IIA, 1. No tumor is found in the breast, but cancer is found in the axillary (under the arm) lymph nodes; or

2. The tumor is 2 centimeters or smaller and has spread to the axillary lymph nodes; or

3. The tumor is larger than 2 centimeters but not larger than 5 centimeters and has not spread to the axillary lymph nodes.

Stage IIA gallbladder cancer Stage II gallbladder cancer is divided into stages IIA and IIB. In stage IIA, cancer has spread beyond the tissue that covers the gallbladder and/or to the liver and/or to one nearby organ, such as the stomach, small intestine, colon, pancreas, or bile ducts outside the liver.

Stage IIA soft tissue sarcoma The cancer cells look somewhat different from normal cells. The cancer is larger than 5 centimeters (about 2 inches) and has not spread to lymph nodes or other parts of the body.

Stage IIB breast cancer Stage II breast cancer is divided into stages IIA and IIB. In stage IIB, 1. The tumor is larger than 2 centimeters but not larger than 5 centimeters and has spread to the axillary (under the arm) lymph nodes; or

2. The tumor is larger than 5 centimeters but has not spread to the axillary lymph nodes.

Stage IIB gallbladder cancer Stage II gallbladder cancer is divided into stages IIA and IIB. In stage IIB, cancer has spread in one of the following ways: 1. Beyond the innermost layer to the connective tissue and to nearby lymph nodes; or

2. To the muscle layer and nearby lymph nodes; or

3. Beyond the muscle layer to the connective tissue around the muscle and nearby lymph nodes; or

4. Through the tissue that covers the gallbladder and/or to the liver and/or to one nearby organ, such as the stomach, small intestine, colon, pancreas, or bile ducts outside the liver, and to nearby lymph nodes.

Stage IIB melanoma Melanoma in which the tumor is more than 4 millimeters thick. It has spread through the lower part of the inner layer of skin (dermis) and into subcutaneous (under the skin) tissue, but not to nearby lymph nodes.

Stage IIB soft tissue sarcoma The cancer cells look very different from normal cells. The cancer is smaller than 5 centimeters (about 2 inches) and has not spread to lymph nodes or other parts of the body.

Stage III adrenocortical cancer The cancer has spread into tissues around the adrenal gland or has spread to the lymph nodes around the adrenal gland.

Stage III adult Hodgkin's lymphoma Stage III is divided into stage III, stage IIIE, stage IIIS, and stage IIIS+E. In stage III, cancer is found in lymph node groups on both sides of the diaphragm (the thin muscle below the lungs that helps breathing and separates the chest from the abdomen). In stage IIIE, cancer is found in lymph node groups on both sides of the diaphragm and in a nearby area or organ other than the lymph nodes. In stage IIIS, cancer is found in lymph node groups on both sides of the diaphragm and in the spleen. In stage IIIE+S, cancer is found in lymph node groups on both sides of the diaphragm, in a nearby area or organ, and in the spleen. Stage III is also divided into stage III (1) and stage III (2). In stage III (1), cancer is limited to the upper abdomen above the renal vein. In stage III (2), cancer is found in lymph nodes in the pelvis and/or near the heart.

Stage III aids-related lymphoma Stage III AIDS-related lymphoma is divided into stages III, IIIE, IIIS, and IIIS+E. In stage III, cancer is found in lymph node groups on both sides of the diaphragm (the muscle below the lungs and heart that separates the chest from the abdomen). In stage IIIE, cancer is found in lymph node groups on both sides of the diaphragm and in one area of an organ or tissue that is not part of the lymph system. In stage IIIS, cancer is found in lymph node groups on both sides of the diaphragm and in the spleen. In stage IIIS+E, cancer is found in lymph node groups on both sides of the diaphragm, in the spleen, and in one area of an organ or tissue that is not part of the lymph system.

Stage III anal cancer Stage III anal cancer is divided into stage IIIA and IIIB. Stage IIIA anal cancer has spread to the lymph nodes around the rectum or to nearby organs such as the vagina or bladder. Stage IIIB cancer has spread to the lymph nodes in the middle of the abdomen or in the groin, or the cancer has spread to both nearby organs and the lymph nodes around the rectum.

Stage III bladder cancer Cancer has spread from the bladder to the fatty layer of tissue surrounding it, and may have spread to the reproductive organs (prostate, uterus, vagina).

Stage III breast cancer Stage III is divided into stages IIIA and IIIB. In stage IIIA breast cancer, the cancer 1. Is smaller than 5 centimeters (2 inches) and has spread to the lymph nodes in the armpit, which have grown into each other or into other structures and are attached to them; or

2. Is larger than 5 centimeters and has spread to the lymph nodes in the armpit. In stage IIIB breast cancer, the cancer (1) has spread to tissues near the breast (skin, chest wall, including the ribs and the muscles in the chest); or (2) has spread to lymph nodes inside the chest wall along the breast bone.

Stage III cancer of the uterus Cancer cells have spread outside the uterus to the vagina and/or lymph nodes in the pelvis but have not spread outside the pelvis.

Stage III cancer of the vulva Cancer is found in the vulva, perineum, or both. The cancer has also spread to nearby tissues such as the lower part of the urethra (the tube through which urine passes), the vagina, and the anus (the opening of the rectum); to nearby lymph nodes; or both.

Stage III cervical cancer Cancer has spread to the lower third of the vagina and may have spread to the pelvic wall (the tissues that line the part of the body between the hips), and nearby lymph nodes. Stage III is divided into stages IIIA and IIIB, based on now far the cancer has spread. In stage IIIA, cancer has spread to the lower third of the vagina but not to the pelvic wall. In stage IIIB, cancer has spread to the pelvic wall and/or the tumor has become large enough to block the ureters (the tubes that connect the kidneys to the bladder). This blockage can cause the kidneys to enlarge or stop working. Cancer may also have spread to lymph nodes in the pelvis.

Stage III childhood liver cancer Either 1. The tumor cannot be removed by surgery; or

2. Cancer that can be seen without a microscope remains after surgery; or

3. The cancer has spread to nearby lymph nodes.

Stage III childhood non-Hodgkin's lymphoma Cancer is found 1. In areas or lymph nodes on both sides of the diaphragm (the thin muscle under the lungs that divides the chest and abdominal cavity and helps with breathing); or

2. To have started in the chest; or
3. In more than one place in the abdomen; or

4. In the area around the spine.

Stage III chronic lymphocytic leukemia There are too many lymphocytes in the blood and there are too few red blood cells. The lymph nodes, liver, or spleen may be larger than normal.

Stage III colorectal cancer Tumor cells have spread to organs and lymph nodes near the colon/ rectum. Also called Dukes C colorectal cancer.

Stage III cutaneous T-cell lymphoma Nearly all of the skin is red, dry, and scaly; lymph nodes are either normal or enlarged but do not contain cancer cells.

Stage III endometrial cancer Cancer has spread beyond the uterus and cervix, but has not spread beyond the pelvis. Stage III is divided into stage IIIA, IIIB, and IIIC, based on how far the cancer has spread within the pelvis. In stage IIIA, cancer has spread to 1. The outermost layer of the uterus; and/or

2. Tissue just beyond the uterus; and/or

3. The peritoneum (tissue that lines the abdominal wall and organs). In stage IIIB, cancer has spread beyond the uterus and cervix, into the vagina. In stage IIIC, cancer has spread to lymph nodes near the uterus.

Stage III esophageal cancer Cancer has spread to the outer wall of the esophagus and may have spread to tissues or lymph nodes near the esophagus.

Stage III extrahepatic bile duct cancer Cancer has spread to 1. The portal vein (blood vessel that carries blood to the liver) or to both branches; or

2. The hepatic artery (blood vessel that carries blood to the liver); or 3. Other nearby organs or tissues, such as the colon, stomach, small intestine, or abdominal wall. Cancer may also have spread to nearby lymph nodes.

Stage III gallbladder cancer In stage III, cancer has spread to a main blood vessel in the liver or to nearby organs and may have spread to nearby lymph nodes.

Stage III gastric cancer Stage III is divided into stage IIIA and stage IIIB depending on where the cancer has spread. In stage IIIA, cancer has spread to 1. The muscularis (middle) layer of the stomach wall and is found in 7 to 15 lymph nodes near the tumor, or

2. The serosal (outermost) layer of the stomach wall and is found in 1 to 6 lymph nodes near the tumor, or

3. To organs next to the stomach but not to lymph nodes or other parts of the body. In stage IIIB, cancer has spread to the serosal (outermost) layer of the stomach wall and is found in 7 to 15 lymph nodes near the tumor.

Stage III hypopharyngeal cancer In stage III hypopharyngeal cancer the tumor is 1. Found only in one area of the hypopharynx and is 2 centimeters or smaller; cancer has also spread to a single lymph node on the same side of the neck and the lymph node is 3 centimeters or smaller; or

2. In more than one area of the hypopharynx, is in nearby tissues, or is larger than 2 centimeters but not larger than 4 centimeters and is not in the larynx; cancer has also spread to a single lymph node on the same side of the neck and the lymph node is 3 centimeters or smaller; or

3. Larger than 4 centimeters or has spread to the larynx; cancer may have spread to a single lymph node on the same side of the neck and the lymph node is 3 centimeters or smaller.

Stage III kidney cancer Cancer is found in either 1. The kidney and in 1 nearby lymph node; or

2. An adrenal gland or in the layer of fatty tissue around the kidney, and may be found in 1 nearby lymph node; or

3. The main blood vessels of the kidney and may be found in 1 nearby lymph node. Also called stage III renal cell cancer.

Stage III laryngeal cancer In stage III laryngeal cancer, one of the following is found: 1. Cancer is in the larynx only and the vocal cords do not move normally; cancer may have spread to tissues next to the larynx; cancer may have spread to one lymph node on the same side of the neck as the original tumor and the lymph node is smaller than 3 centimeters; or

2. Cancer is in one area of the larynx, the vocal cords move normally, and cancer is found in one lymph node on the same side of the neck as the original tumor; the lymph node is smaller than 3 centimeters; or

3. Cancer is in more than one area of the larynx or in the vocal cords (which may not move normally) and in one lymph node on the same side of the neck as the original tumor; the lymph node is smaller than 3 centimeters.

Stage III lip and oral cavity cancer The cancer is larger than 4 centimeters (about 2 inches); or the cancer is any size but has spread to only one lymph node on the same side of the neck as the cancer. The lymph node that contains cancer is no larger than 3 centimeters (just over one inch).

Stage III malignant mesothelioma Cancer has spread to the chest wall, mediastinum, heart, lining of the peritoneum, and/or beyond the diaphragm. Cancer may also have spread to lymph nodes on the other side of the chest or outside the chest. Stages II, III, and IV malignant mesothelioma are also called advanced malignant mesothelioma.

Stage III melanoma The tumor may be any thickness, with or without ulceration (formation of a break on the skin or surface of an organ), and 1. Has spread to 1 or more lymph nodes; or

2. Has spread into the nearby lymph system but not into nearby lymph nodes; or

3. Has spread to lymph nodes that are matted (not moveable); or

4. Satellite tumors (additional tumor growths within 2 centimeters of the original tumor) are present and nearby lymph nodes are involved.

Stage III multiple myeloma A relatively large number of cancer cells have spread throughout the body. There may be one or more of the following: 1. A decrease in the number of red blood cells, causing anemia;

2. The amount of calcium in the blood is very high, because the bones are being damaged;

3. More than three bone tumors (plasmacytomas) are found; or

4. High levels of M protein are found in the blood or urine.

Stage III mycosis fungoides and the Sézary syndrome In stage III, nearly all of the skin is reddened and there may be patches, plaques, or tumors. Lymph nodes may be enlarged but cancer has not spread to them. Stage III may also be classified based on how many abnormal lymphocytes (white blood cells) are found in the blood.

Stage III nasopharyngeal cancer Cancer 1. is found in the nasopharynx and has spread to lymph nodes on both sides of the neck; or

2. has spread into the soft tissues (oropharynx and/or nasal cavity) and to lymph nodes on both sides of the neck; or

3. has spread beyond the soft tissues into areas around the pharynx and to lymph nodes on both sides of the neck; or

4. Has spread to nearby bones or sinuses and may have spread to lymph nodes on one or both sides of the neck.

Stage III non-small cell lung cancer Cancer has spread to structures near the lung; to the lymph nodes in the area that separates the two lungs (mediastinum); or to the lymph nodes on the other side of the chest or in the lower neck. Stage III is further divided into stage IIIA (usually can be resected which is sometimes treated with surgery) and stage IIIB (usually cannot be resected which is rarely treated with surgery).

Stage III oropharynx cancer The tumor is larger than 4 centimeters (about 1.5 inches) in size and may involve a single lymph node on the same side of the neck.

Stage III ovarian cancer Cancer is found in one or both ovaries and has spread to other parts of the abdomen. Stage III is divided into stage IIIA, stage IIIB, and stage IIIC. In stage IIIA, the tumor is found in the pelvis only, but cancer cells have spread to the surface of the peritoneum. In stage IIIB, cancer has spread to the peritoneum but is not larger than 2 centimeters in diameter. In stage IIIC, cancer has spread to the peritoneum and is larger than 2 centimeters in diameter and/or has spread to lymph nodes in the abdomen. Cancer that has spread to the surface of the liver is also considered stage III disease.

Stage III pancreatic cancer Cancer has spread to the major blood vessels near the pancreas, and may have spread to nearby lymph nodes.

Stage III prostate cancer Cancer has spread beyond the outer layer of the prostate to nearby tissues and may be found in the seminal vesicles (glands that help produce semen). Also called stage C prostate cancer.

Stage III skin cancer Cancer has spread below the skin to cartilage, muscle, or bone and/or to nearby lymph nodes, but not to other parts of the body.

Stage III soft tissue sarcoma The cancer cells look very different from normal cells. The cancer is larger than 5 centimeters (about 2 inches) but has not spread to lymph nodes or other parts of the body.

Stage III testicular cancer Stage III is divided into stage IIIA, stage IIIB, and stage IIIC, and is determined after a radical inguinal orchiectomy (surgery to remove the testicle) is done. In stage IIIA, the cancer is anywhere within the testicle, spermatic cord, or scrotum; may have spread to one or more lymph nodes in the abdomen; and has spread to distant lymph nodes or to the lungs. In stage IIIB, the cancer is anywhere within the testicle, spermatic cord, or scrotum; and may have spread to one or more nearby or distant lymph nodes or to the lungs. In stage IIIC, the cancer is anywhere within the testicle, spermatic cord, or scrotum; and may have spread to one or more nearby or distant lymph nodes or to the lungs or anywhere else in the body. The level of one or more tumor markers may range from normal to very high.

Stage III transitional cell cancer of the renal pelvis and ureter Cancer has spread either 1. to the layer of fat outside the renal pelvis and/or ureter; or

2. into the wall of the kidney.

Stage III wilms' tumor Cancer has spread to tissues near the kidney and cannot be completely removed by surgery. The cancer may have spread to blood vessels or organs near the kidney or throughout the abdomen. The cancer may also have spread to lymph nodes near the kidney.

Stage IIIA adult primary liver cancer Stage III adult primary liver cancer is divided into stages IIIA, IIIB, and IIIC. In stage IIIA there is either 1. More than one tumor larger than 5 centimeters; or

2. One tumor that has spread to a major branch of blood vessels near the liver.

Stage IIIA anal cancer Stage III anal cancer is divided into stages IIIA and IIIB. In stage IIIA, the tumor may be any size and has spread to either 1. Lymph nodes near the rectum; or

2. Nearby organs, such as the vagina, urethra, and bladder.

Stage IIIA breast cancer Stage III breast cancer is divided into stages IIIA, IIIB, and IIIC. In stage IIIA, 1. No tumor is found in the breast, but cancer is found in axillary (under the arm) lymph nodes that are attached to each other or to other structures; or

2. The tumor is 5 centimeters or smaller and has spread to axillary lymph nodes that are attached to each other or to other structures; or

3. The tumor is larger than 5 centimeters and has spread to axillary lymph nodes that may or may not be attached to each other or to other structures.

Stage IIIB adult primary liver cancer Stage III adult primary liver cancer is divided into stages IIIA, IIIB, and IIIC. In stage IIIB, there are one or more tumors of any size that have either 1. Spread to nearby organs other than the gallbladder; or

2. Broken through the lining of the peritoneal cavity.

Stage IIIB anal cancer Stage III anal cancer is divided into stages IIIA and IIIB. In stage IIIB, the tumor may be any size and has spread to 1. Nearby organs and to lymph nodes near the rectum; or

2. Lymph nodes on one side of the pelvis and/or groin, and may have spread to nearby organs; or

3. Lymph nodes near the rectum and in the groin, and/or to lymph nodes on both sides of the pelvis and/or groin, and may have spread to nearby organs.

Stage IIIB breast cancer Stage III breast cancer is divided into stages IIIA, IIIB, and IIIC. In stage IIIB, the cancer may be any size, has spread to tissues near the breast (the skin or chest wall, including the ribs and muscles in the chest), and may have spread to lymph nodes within the breast or under the arm.

Stage IIIC adult primary liver cancer Stage III adult primary liver cancer is divided into stages IIIA, IIIB, and IIIC. In stage IIIC, the cancer has spread to nearby lymph nodes.

Stage IIIC breast cancer Stage III breast cancer is divided into stages IIIA, IIIB, and IIIC. In stage IIIC, cancer has spread to lymph nodes beneath the collarbone and near the neck; and may have spread to lymph nodes within the breast or under the arm and to tissues near the breast.

Stage IV adrenocortical cancer The cancer has spread to tissues or organs in the area and to lymph nodes around the adrenal cortex, or the cancer has spread to other parts of the body.

Stage IV adult Hodgkin's lymphoma The cancer is found in at least one organ other than the lymph nodes and may be in the lymph nodes near the organ (s); or the cancer is found in one organ other than the lymph nodes and has spread to lymph nodes far away from the organ.

Stage IV adult non-Hodgkin's lymphoma The cancer either 1. Is found in at least one organ or tissue other than the lymph nodes and may be in nearby lymph nodes; or

2. Has spread to one organ other than the lymph nodes and has spread to lymph nodes far away from that organ.

Stage IV adult primary liver cancer Cancer has spread beyond the liver to other places in the body, such as the bones or lungs. The tumors may be of any size and may also have spread to nearby blood vessels and/or lymph nodes.

Stage IV AIDS-related lymphoma In stage IV AIDS-related lymphoma, the cancer is found 1. In several areas throughout one or more organs that are not part of the lymph system, and it may be in nearby lymph nodes; or

2. In one organ that is not part of the lymph system, and it has spread to lymph nodes far away from that organ.

Stage IV anal cancer The tumor may be any size, and cancer has spread to distant parts of the body. It may also have spread to lymph nodes and nearby organs.

Stage IV bladder cancer Cancer has spread from the bladder to the wall of the abdomen or pelvis. Cancer may have spread to one or more lymph nodes or to other parts of the body.

Stage IV breast cancer Cancer has spread to other organs of the body, most often the bones, lungs, liver, or brain.

Stage IV cancer of the uterus Cancer cells have spread to the lining of the bladder or rectum or to distant parts of the body.

Stage IV cancer of the vulva Cancer has spread beyond the urethra, vagina, and anus into the lining of the bladder (the sac that holds urine) and the bowel (intestine); or it may have spread to the lymph nodes in the pelvis or to other parts of the body.

Stage IV cervical cancer Cancer has spread to the bladder, rectum, or other parts of the body. Stage IV is divided into stages IVA and IVB. In stage IVA, cancer has spread to the bladder or rectal wall and may have spread to lymph nodes in the pelvis. In stage IVB, cancer has spread beyond the pelvis and pelvic lymph nodes to other places in the body, such as the abdomen, liver, intestinal tract, or lungs.

Stage IV childhood liver cancer The cancer has spread to other parts of the body.

Stage IV childhood non-Hodgkin's lymphoma Cancer is found in the bone marrow, brain, or spinal cord. Cancer may also be found in other parts of the body.

Stage IV chronic lymphocytic leukemia There are too many lymphocytes in the blood and too few platelets. The lymph nodes, liver, or spleen may be larger than normal and there may be too few red blood cells.

Stage IV colorectal cancer Cancer may have spread to nearby lymph nodes and has spread to other parts of the body, such as the liver or lungs. Also called Dukes' D colorectal cancer.

Stage IV cutaneous T cell lymphoma Stage IV cutaneous T-cell lymphoma may be either of the following: in stage IVA cancer, the skin is red, dry, and scaly, and the lymph nodes contain cancer cells; in stage IVB cancer, the skin is red, dry and scaly, cancer cells may be found in lymph nodes, and cancer has spread to other organs in the body.

Stage IV endometrial cancer Cancer has spread beyond the pelvis. Stage IV is divided into stage IVA and IVB, based on how far the cancer has spread. In stage IVA, cancer has spread to the bladder or bowel wall. In stage IVB, cancer has spread to other parts of the body beyond the pelvis, including lymph nodes in the abdomen and/or groin.

Stage IV esophageal cancer Stage IV esophageal cancer is divided into stage IVA and stage IVB, depending on where the cancer has spread. In stage IVA, cancer has spread to nearby or distant lymph nodes. In stage IVB, cancer has spread to distant lymph nodes and/or organs in other parts of the body.

Stage IV extrahepatic bile duct cancer Cancer has spread to lymph nodes and/or organs far away from the extrahepatic bile duct.

Stage IV gallbladder cancer In stage IV, cancer has spread to nearby lymph nodes and/or to organs far away from the gallbladder.

Stage IV gastric cancer Cancer has spread 1. To organs next to the stomach and to at least one lymph node, or

2. To more than 15 lymph nodes, or

3. To other parts of the body.

Stage IV hypopharynx cancer The tumor has spread to nearby tissues and lymph nodes of the neck and may have spread to other parts of the body.

Stage IV kidney cancer Cancer has spread 1. Beyond the layer of fatty tissue around the kidney and may be found in 1 nearby lymph node; or

2. To 2 or more nearby lymph nodes; or

3. To other organs, such as the bowel, pancreas, or lungs, and may be found in nearby lymph nodes. Also called stage IV renal cell cancer.

Stage IV laryngeal cancer The cancer has spread to tissues around the larynx, such as the pharynx or the tissues in the neck. The lymph nodes in the area may contain cancer; the cancer has spread to more than one lymph node on the same side of the neck as the cancer, to lymph nodes on one or both sides of the neck, or to any lymph node that measures more than 6 centimeters (over 2 inches); or the cancer has spread to other parts of the body.

Stage IV lip and oral cavity cancer The cancer has spread to tissues around the lip and oral cavity (the lymph nodes in the area may contain cancer); the cancer is any size and has spread to more than one lymph node on the same side of the neck as the cancer, to lymph nodes on one or both sides of the neck, or to any lymph node that is larger than 6 centimeters (larger than 2 inches); or the cancer has spread to other parts of the body.

Stage IV malignant mesothelioma Cancer has spread to distant organs or tissues. Stages II, III, and IV malignant mesothelioma are also called advanced malignant mesothelioma.

Stage IV melanoma The tumor may be any thickness, with or without ulceration (formation of a break on the skin or surface of an organ), may have spread to 1 or more nearby lymph nodes, and has spread to other places in the body.

Stage IV mycosis fungoides and the Sézary syndrome Stage IV is divided into stages IVA and IVB. In stage IVA, most of the skin is reddened, and any amount of the skin is covered with patches and/or plaques (areas of abnormal tissue) or tumors (lumps of malignant cells). Cancer has spread to lymph nodes, and the lymph nodes may be enlarged. In stage IVB, most of the skin is reddened, and any amount of the skin is covered with lesions or tumors. Cancer has spread to other organs in the body. Lymph nodes may be enlarged and cancer may have spread to them. Stage IV may also be classified based on how many abnormal lymphocytes (white blood cells) are found in the blood.

Stage IV nasopharyngeal cancer Stage IV nasopharyngeal cancer is divided into stages IVA, IVB, and IVC. In stage IVA, cancer has spread beyond the nasopharynx and may have spread to the cranial nerves, the hypopharynx (bottom part of the throat), areas in and around the side of the skull or jawbone, and/or the bone around the eye. Cancer may also have spread to lymph nodes on one or both sides of the neck, and the involved lymph nodes are 6 centimeters or smaller. In stage IVB, cancer has spread to lymph nodes above the collarbone and/or the involved lymph nodes are larger than 6 centimeters. In stage IVC, cancer has spread beyond nearby lymph nodes to other parts of the body.

Stage IV non-small cell lung cancer Cancer has spread to other parts of the body or to another lobe of the lungs.

Stage IV oropharynx cancer The tumor has spread to the hard palate, tongue, or larynx, to nearby lymph nodes, and may have spread to other parts of the body.

Stage IV ovarian cancer Cancer is found in one or both ovaries and has metastasized (spread) beyond the abdomen to other parts of the body. Cancer that is found in tissues of the liver is considered stage IV disease.

Stage IV pancreatic cancer Cancer may be of any size and has spread to distant organs, such as the liver, lung, and peritoneal cavity (the body cavity that contains most of the organs in the abdomen), and may have also spread to organs and tissues near the pancreas or to lymph nodes.

Stage IV prostate cancer Cancer has metastasized (spread) to lymph nodes near or far from the prostate, or to other parts of the body, such as the bladder, rectum, bones, liver, or lungs. Metastatic prostate cancer often spreads to the bones. Also called stage D1 or stage D2 prostate cancer.

Stage IV skin cancer Cancer has spread to other parts of the body.

Stage IV soft tissue sarcoma The cancer has spread to lymph nodes in the area or other parts of the body (such as the lungs, head, or neck).

Stage IV transitional cell cancer of the renal pelvis and ureter Cancer has spread to a nearby organ and/ or to the layer of fat surrounding the kidney.

Stage IV wilms' tumor Cancer has spread to organs further away from the kidney (such as the lungs, liver, bone, and brain).

Stage IVA hypopharyngeal cancer Stage IV hypopharyngeal cancer is divided into stages IVA, IVB, and IVC. In stage IVA, the tumor is 1. Any size and has spread to nearby soft tissue, connective tissue, the thyroid, or the esophagus; cancer may be found either in one lymph node on the same side of the neck (the lymph node is 3 centimeters or smaller) or in one or more lymph nodes anywhere in the neck (all of these lymph nodes are 6 centimeters or smaller); or

2. In only one area of the hypopharynx, is 2 centimeters or smaller, and has also spread to one or more lymph nodes anywhere in the neck (all of these lymph nodes are 6 centimeters or smaller); or

3. In more than one area of the hypopharynx, is in nearby tissues, or is larger than 2 centimeters but not larger than 4 centimeters and has not spread to the larynx; cancer has spread to one or more lymph nodes anywhere in the neck (all of these lymph nodes are 6 centimeters or smaller); or

4. larger than 4 centimeters or has spread to the larynx; cancer has also spread to one or more lymph

nodes anywhere in the neck (all of these lymph nodes are 6 centimeters or smaller).

Stage IVA laryngeal cancer Stage IV is divided into stages IVA, IVB, and IVC. In stage IVA, one of the following is found: 1. Cancer has spread through the thyroid cartilage and/or has spread to tissues beyond the larynx such as the neck, trachea, thyroid, or esophagus; cancer may have spread to one lymph node on the same side of the neck as the original tumor and the lymph node is smaller than 3 centimeters; or

2. Cancer has spread to one or more lymph nodes anywhere in the neck and the lymph nodes are smaller than 6 centimeters; cancer may have spread to tissues beyond the larynx, such as the neck, trachea, thyroid, or esophagus. Vocal cords may not move normally.

Stage IVA pancreatic cancer Cancer has spread to organs that are near the pancreas (such as the stomach, spleen, or colon) but has not spread to distant organs (such as the liver or lungs).

Stage IVB hypopharyngeal cancer Stage IV hypopharyngeal cancer is divided into stages IVA, IVB, and IVC. In stage IVB, the tumor either 1. Has spread to nearby soft tissue, connective tissue, blood vessels, the thyroid, or the esophagus, and may have spread to lymph nodes of any size; or 2. Is any size and has spread to lymph nodes that are larger than 6 centimeters.

Stage IVB laryngeal cancer Stage IV is divided into stages IVA, IVB, and IVC. In stage IVB, one of the following is found: 1. Cancer has spread to the space in front of the spinal column and surrounds the carotid artery, or has spread to parts of the chest and may have spread to one or more lymph nodes anywhere in the neck (the lymph nodes may be any size); or

2. Cancer has spread to a lymph node that is larger than 6 centimeters and may have spread as far as the space in front of the spinal column, around the carotid artery, or to parts of the chest. Vocal cords may not move normally.

Stage IVB pancreatic cancer Cancer of the pancreas in which the cancer has spread to distant organs (such as the liver or lungs).

Stage IVC hypopharyngeal cancer Stage IV hypopharyngeal cancer is divided into stages IVA, IVB, and IVC. In stage IVC, cancer has spread beyond the hypopharynx to other parts of the body.

Stage IVC laryngeal cancer Stage IV is divided into stages IVA, IVB, and IVC. In stage IVC, cancer has spread beyond the larynx to distant parts of the body.

Stage V Wilms' tumor Cancer cells are found in both kidneys.

Staging Performing exams and tests to learn the extent of the cancer within the body, especially whether the disease has spread from the original site to other parts of the body. It is important to know the stage of the disease in order to plan the best treatment.

Standard Refers to a model, example or rule for the measure of quantity, weight, extent, value, or quality, established by authority, custom or general consent. It is also defined as a criterion, gauge or yardstick by which judgments or decisions may be made. A meaningful standard should offer a realistic prospect of determining whether or not one actually meets it.

Standards may be mandatory (required by law), voluntary (established by private and professional organizations and available for use), or de facto (generally accepted by custom or convention, such as standards of dress, manners, or behaviour).

Standard deviation A Statistic that shows the spread or dispersion of scores in a distribution of scores. in other words, a measure of dispersion. The more widely the scores are spread out, the greater the standard deviation. the standard deviation is the square root of the variance. For example. imagine trued groups of patients. In one CD4 cell counts range from 310-650, in the other they range from 43-700. The standard deviation would be much greater for the second group.

Standard dimensional ratio (SDR) The most commonly accepted means for providing a pipe wall thickness category and constant mechanical properties for many plastic materials. Used for solid, homogeneous pipe, the SDR is found by dividing the average outside diameter of a pipe by the wall thickness.

Standard error Short for "standard error of the mean", or "standard error of the estimate". A statistic indicating how greatly the mean score of a single sample is likely to differ from the mean score of the population. It is the standard deviation of a sampling distribution of the means. The Standard error of the mean indicates how much the sample mean differs from the expected value. The standard error of estimate is how much you are off when using a regression line to predict particular scores. In either case, the smaller the standard error, the better the sample statistic is an estimate of the population parameter. The standard error is a measure of sampling error, due to random fluctuations in the samples.

Standard in education A model design or formulation related to various aspects of medical education and presented in a manner that enables the assessment of graduates' performance in compliance with generally accepted professional requirements. They are set up by consent of experts or by decision of educational authority. Three types of interrelated educational standards can be envisaged:

Content standards or curriculum standards describe skills, knowledge, attitudes and values; what teachers are supposed to "teach" and students are expected to learn. Thus the content standards define what is to be taught and learned. Content standards can be also defined as "essential (core) requirements" that the medical curriculum should meet to equip physicians with the knowledge, skills and attitudes necessary at the time of graduation.

Performance or assessment standards define degrees of attainment of content standards and level of competencies in compliance with the professional requirements. Performance standards describe how well content has been learned.

Process or opportunity-to-learn standards define availability of staff and other resources necessary for the medical school so that students will be able to meet content and performance standards.

A standard can be also classified four ways:

An absolute standard refers to the knowledge and skills a student must possess in order to pass a given course. An absolute standard stays the same over multiple administrations relative to the content specifications of the test. The failure rate may vary due to changes in the group's ability, from one administration to the other.

A relative standard can be set at the mean performances of the candidates, or by defining the units of standard deviation from the mean. A relative standard may vary from year to year due to shifts in the ability of the group and may result in a fixed annual percentage of failing students, if the scores maintain a normal distribution across administrations.

A norm-referenced standard is a standard based on the representative group of the candidates' population. Credentialing organizations may use norm-referenced orientation, in which the standard is based on the performance of an external large representative sample (norm group) equivalent to the candidates taking the test. The norm-referenced standard will be somewhat unstable and will shift according to the performance of the norm group, as large as it may be. Shift of the standard over time is a concern.

A criterion-referenced standard is a fixed standard that may undergo periodic re-evaluation in view of shifts or trends in candidates' performance over time. The criterion reference orientation links the standard to the content of the level of competence.

Standard of care In medicine, treatment that experts agree is appropriate, accepted, and widely used. Health care providers are obligated to provide patients with the standard of care. Also called standard therapy or best practice.

Standard treatment The accepted mode of treatment for a given disease or condition. Equivalent to the control treatment in clinical trials when chosen to mimic standard medical practice.

Standardized oral examination (SOE) A performance assessment using realistic patient cases with a trained physician examiner questioning an examinee in a standardized manner. These exams assess clinical decision-making and the application or use of medical knowledge with realistic patients. The exam begins with the presentation of a clinical problem in the form of a patient case scenario with a request to the examinee to manage the case. An examinee can be tested on a selection of different clinical cases. The examiners need to be trained in how to provide patient data for each scenario, how to question the examinee, and how to evaluate and score the examinee's responses. To create such an exam, extensive resources and expertise are required.

Standardized patient (SP) Individuals who have been trained to reliably reproduce the history and/or physical findings of typical clinical cases. They can be real patients who have been "standardized" or they can be simulated patients, i.e. persons who are not sick but take on a patient's history and role. Sometimes health care providers or actors are used to accomplish this goal. This tool is designed to make examination and assessment of a student's clinical skills as objective as possible. To teach a standardized patient to simulate a new clinical problem takes eight to ten hours.

Standardized patient examination (SPE) An exam used to assess history-taking and physical examination skills, communication skills, differential diagnosis, laboratory utilization, and treatment. A standardized patient examination consists of multiple standardized patients, each presenting a different condition in a 10-12 minute encounter. The examinee performs a history-taking and physical examination, orders tests, provides diagnosis, develops a treatment plan, and counsels the patient. Using a checklist or rating form, the examiner or the Standardized Patient evaluates the student's performance and behavior. Reproducible scores are readily obtained for history-taking, physical examination, and communication skills. Thorough training of raters, whether they are physicians, patients or other types of observers, is critical to obtaining reliable scores. Development of such an examination is often time consuming.

Standpipe system A wet or dry system of piping, valves, outlets, and related equipment designed to provide water at specified pressures and installed exclusively for the fighting of fires.

Start Up The initial operation of equipment to prove that it is installed properly and operates as intended. Start-Up is considered complete when the selected equipment will adequately process prod··ct as specified.

Stasis (suffix) Standing still, e.g. hemostasis - arrest of blood circulation.

Statin Any of a group of drugs that lower the amount of cholesterol and certain fats in the blood. Statins inhibit a key enzyme that helps make cholesterol. Statin drugs are being studied in the prevention and treatment of cancer.

Statistical process control (SPC) A process control method to demonstrate mathematically that a process or system is operating within the limitations established for the parameter (s) in question.

Statistical test, analysis of variance (anova) A statistical technique used to test the difference among the means of two groups or more regarding continuous data. The purpose of ANOVA is to test whether the observed differences among the means of these groups is significant or due to chance.

Statistical test, chi square A statistical technique used to test the difference between groups regarding discrete (categorical) data. The purpose of chi square is to test whether differences between observed and expected frequencies are significant or due to chance.

Statistical test, multiple regression A statistical technique used to assess the relationship between one dependent variable and two or more input variables. The purpose of multiple regression analysis is to measure the degree of association between variables or predict the dependent variable as a function of the input variables.

Statistical test, t test A statistical technique used to test whether the means of two groups differ significantly regarding continuous data. The purpose of the t-test is to infer whether the difference between the means of two groups on one variable is statistically significant or due to chance.

Statistically significant Describes a mathematical measure of difference between groups. The difference is said to be statistically significant if it is greater than what might be expected to happen by chance alone. Also called significant.

Statistics, descriptive The intent of descriptive statistics is to summarize and present data, e.g., measures of central tendency (mean, mode, median) and measures of variability (standard deviation, variance, standard error of the mean).

Statistics, inferential Inference refers to making generalizations about a population on the basis of a sample from that population. The intent of inferential statistics is to determine whether differences between groups are real or due to chance.

Status asthmaticus A severe attack of asthma, which often follows a period of poorly controlled asthma.

Staurosporine A drug that belongs to the family of drugs called alkaloids. It is being studied in the treatment of cancer.

Stavudine A drug that belongs to the family of drugs called nucleoside analogs. It is used to treat infection caused by viruses.

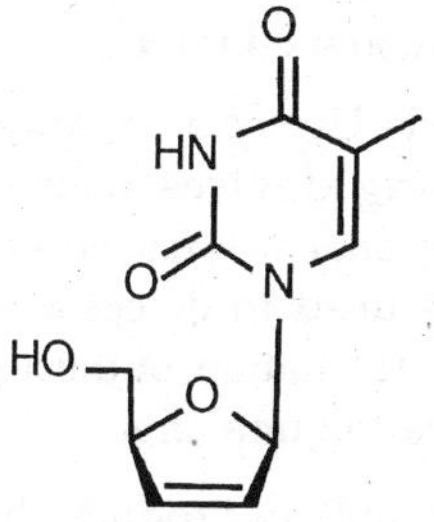

{2'-3'-didehydro-2'-3'-dideoxythymidine}

Figure Stavudine

Stea Lipid, e.g. steatorrhea excessive lipid in the feces.

Steatorrhea Loose, greasy bowel movements caused by an inability of the body to absorb fat.

Steering committee (SC) 1. A committee responsible for directing the activities of a designated project.

2. One of the key committees in the organizational structure of a multicenter clinical trial. Committee responsible for conduct of the trial and to which all other committees report, except the adverse experience committee and Data and Safety Monitoring Board or advisory-review and treatment effects monitoring committee.

Stellate Star shaped.

Stem cell A "generic" cell that can make exact copies of itself indefinitely, but can also produce specialized cells for various tissues in the body, such as heart muscle, brain tissue, and liver tissue.

Stem cell factor (SCF) A drug that is being studied for its ability to increase the number of stem cells in the blood. It belongs to the family of drugs called hematopoietic cell growth factors. Also called ancestim and Stemgen.

Stem Cell Transplantation A method of replacing immature blood-forming cells that were destroyed by cancer treatment. The stem cells are given to the person after treatment to help the bone marrow recover and continue producing healthy blood cells.

Stemgen A drug that is being studied for its ability to increase the number of stem cells in the blood. It belongs to the family of drugs called hematopoietic cell growth factors. Also called stem cell factor (SCF) and ancestim.

Stenosis A stricture of any canal.

Stent A device placed in a body structure (such as a blood vessel or the gastrointestinal tract) to provide support and keep the structure open.

Sterapred Other name for prednisone.

Stereopsis The ability to perceive a three dimensional depth which requires adequate fusion (union) of the images from each eye.

Stereopsis test Measures depth perception that is dependent on the accuracy of eye teaming.

Stereotactic biopsy A biopsy procedure that uses a computer and a 3-dimensional scanning device to find a tumor site and guide the removal of tissue for examination under a microscope.

Stereotactic body radiation therapy A radiation therapy technique that uses special equipment to position the patient and precisely deliver a large radiation dose to a tumor and not to normal tissue.

Stereotactic core needle biopsy A method of needle biopsy that is useful in some cases in which a mass can be seen on mammogram but cannot be located by touch. Computerized equipment maps the location of the mass and this is used as a guide for the placement of the needle.

Stereotactic external-beam radiation A radiation therapy procedure that uses special equipment to position the patient and precisely deliver a large radiation dose to a tumor and not to normal tissue. This procedure does not use surgery. It is used to treat brain tumors and other brain disorders. It is also being studied in the treatment of other types of cancer, such as lung cancer. Also called radiation surgery, radiosurgery, stereotactic radiation therapy, stereotactic radiosurgery, and stereotaxic radiosurgery.

Stereotactic injection A procedure in which a computer and a 3-dimensional scanning device are used to inject anticancer drugs directly into a tumor.

Stereotaxis Use of a computer and scanning devices to create 3-dimensional pictures. This method can be used to direct a biopsy, external radiation, or the insertion of radiation implants.

Sterile Unable to produce children. Also means free from germs.

Sterile engineering design (fermentation) The application of techniques to prevent contamination of a fermentation process by undesirable organisms. It includes three basic phases relating to the operation of the plant. First, the fermenter with the ancillary equipment, pipework, and valves must be brought to a sterile state. Secondly, the fermenter feed must be sterilized, and finally, sterile barriers at the interface between the fermenter and the outside environment must be maintained.

Sterile water For Injection, A form in which water is distributed in sterile packages. Sterile Water for Injection is intended mainly for use as a solvent for parenteral products such as sterile solids that must be distributed dry because of limited stability of their solutions. It must be packaged only in single-dose containers of not larger than 1-liter size.

Sterile water for irrigation, This form of water meets most, but not all, of the requirements for Sterile Water for Injection. The exceptions are with respect of container size (i.e., the container may contain a volume of more than 1 liter), container design (i.e., the container may be designed so as to empty rapidly the contents as a single dose), particulate matter requirements (i.e., need not meet the requirement for Large Volume Injections for single-dose infusions), and labeling requirements (e.g., the designation "For Irrigation Only" and "Not For Injection" appear prominently on the label).

Sterilization The act or process, physical or chemical, that destroys or eliminates all viable microbes including resistant bacterial spores from a fluid or a solid. Despite being stated as an absolute, the action of sterilization is usually stated in terms of probability. Examples of sterilization methods are: steam treatment at 121°C, dry heat at 450°F, flushing with a sterilizing solution such as Hydrogen Peroxide (H_2O_2) or ozone (O_3), irradiation, and filtration.

Sterilizing filter A filter that, when challenged with the microorganisms Brevundimonas diminuta, at a minimum concen-tration of 10^7 organisms per square centimeter of filter surface, produces a sterile effluent.

Steritalc Other name for talc.

Sternoclavicular articulation The joint formed by the junction of the sternal end of the clavicle, the clavicular notch of the manubrium, and the first costal cartilage.

Sternothyroid muscle Muscle which originates at the manubrium sterni, and inserts into the thyroid cartilage. It is responsible for the depression of the thyroid cartilage.

Sternotomy A lengthwise incision through the breastbone (sternum) that may be made when heart surgery is performed.

Sternum The longitudinal midline plate of bone that articulates with the clavicles and cartilages of the first seven ribs, forming the middle portion of the anterior chest wall of the thorax.

Steroid A general class of substances that are structurally related to one another and share the same chemical skeleton. Some hormones and drugs are steroids. For example, natural testosterone and its man-made derivatives help build muscle mass. Corticosteroid drugs are used to reduce swelling and pain.

Steroid drug A type of drug used to relieve swelling and inflammation. Some steroid drugs may also have antitumor effects.

Steroid therapy Treatment with corticosteroid drugs to reduce swelling, pain, and other symptoms of inflammation.

Stethoscope It is an acoustic medical device for auscultation, i.e. listening to internal sounds in the human body. It is most often used to listen to heart sounds and breathing (breath sounds), though it is also used to listen to intestines and blood flow in arteries and veins. The stethoscope was invented in France in 1816 by René-Théophile-Hyacinthe Laennec. It consisted of a hollow wooden tube and was monoaural. In 1851 Arthur Leared invented the binaural stethoscope which has become the standard ever since. By 1873, there were descriptions of a differential stethoscope that could connect to slightly different locations to create a slight stereo effect, though this did not become a standard tool in clinical practise.

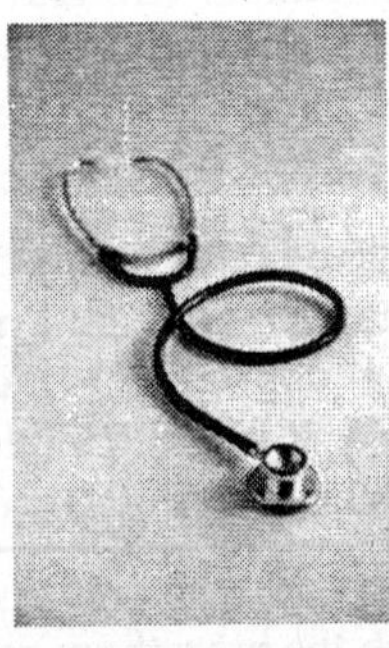

Figure Stethoscope

The stethoscope is used in aid of diagnosing certain diseases. The stethoscope is able to transmit certain sounds and exclude others. Before the stethoscope was invented, doctors placed their ear next to the patient's body in hopes of hearing something.

Stethoscopes are often considered as a symbol of the doctor's profession, as doctors are often seen or depicted with a stethoscope hanging around their neck.

Stethoscopes are also used by mechanics to isolate sounds of a particular moving engine part for diagnosis.

Acoustic stethoscopes are familiar to most people, and operate on the transmission of sound from the chestpiece, via air-filled hollow tubes, to the listener's ears. The chestpiece usually consists of two sides that can be placed against the patient for sensing sound - a diaphragm (plastic disc) or bell (hollow cup). If the diaphragm is placed on the patient, body sounds vibrate the diaphragm, creating acoustic pressure waves which travel up the tubing to the listener's ears. If the bell is placed on the patient, the vibrations of the skin directly produce acoustic pressure waves traveling up to the listener's ears. The bell transmits low frequency sounds, while the diaphragm transmits higher frequency sounds. This 2-sided stethoscope was invented by Rappaport and Sprague in the early part of the 20th century. The problem with acoustic stethoscope is that the sound level is extremely low, making diagnosis difficult.

Electronic stethoscopes overcome the low sound levels by amplifiying body sounds. Currently, a number of companies offer electronic stethoscopes, and it can be expected that within a few years, the electronic stethoscope will have eclipsed acoustic devices.

Electronic stethoscopes require conversion of acoustic sound waves to electrical signals which can then be amplified and processed for optimal listening. Unlike acoustic stethoscopes, which are all based on the same physics, transducers in electronic stethoscopes vary widely. The simplest and least effective method of sound detection is achieved by placing a microphone in the chestpiece. This method suffers from ambient noise interference and has fallen out of favor. Another method, used in Welch-Allyn's Meditron stethoscope, comprises placement of a piezoelectric crystal at the head of a metal shaft, the bottom of the shaft making contact with a diaphragm. 3M also uses a piezoelectric crystal placed within foam behind a thick rubber-like diaphragm. Thinklabs uses a stethoscope diaphragm with an electrically-conductive inner surface to form a capacitive sensor. This diaphragm responds to sound waves identically to a conventional acoustic stethoscope, with changes in an electric field replacing changes in air pressure. This preserves the sound of an acoustic stethoscope with the benefits of amplification.

Steven Johnson reaction A severe allergic drug reaction, Steven Johnson is characterized by high fevers and desquamating rash, and is frequently fatal.

Stevens Johnson syndrome (SJS) A severe and sometimes fatal form of skin rash characterized by red, blistered spots on the skin; blisters in the mouth, eyes, genitals, or other moist areas of the body; peeling skin that results in painful sores; and fever, headache, and other flu-like symptoms. Internal organs may also be affected. SJS may occur as a severe reaction to certain medications, including NNRTIs used to treat HIV infection.

STI571 A drug that is being studied for its ability to inhibit the growth of certain cancers. It interferes with a portion of the protein produced by the bcr/abl oncogene. Also called Gleevec and imatinib mesylate.

Stiff hand syndrome Thickening of the skin of the palm that results in loss of ability to hold hand straight. This condition occurs only in people with diabetes.

Stoma A surgically created opening in an organ, such as the stomach (gastrostomy) or intestine (colostomy).

Stomach An organ that is part of the digestive system. The stomach helps digest food by mixing it with digestive juices and churning it into a thin liquid.

Stomach cancer Cancer that forms in tissues lining the stomach. Also called gastric cancer.

Stomatitis Inflammation or ulcers of the lips, gums, tongue, palate, floor of the mouth or other tissues in the mouth. This condition can result as a side effect of some chemotherapies. A similar condition can occur in the vaginal tissues, as well.

Stool Waste products that remain after food is digested, including fiber, bacteria, mucus, undigested foods, and cells from the inside of the intestine. Passed through the rectum as a bowel movement.

Stool test A test to check for hidden blood in the bowel movement.

Stop condition 1. A condition encountered when carrying out a procedure (e.g., completing a data form, performing a patient examination) that requires the person performing the procedure to terminate the procedure until or unless the condition can be removed.

2. A defined condition that, when encountered for a patient enrolled in a trial, requires or permits clinic personnel to take some action related to that patient, such as instituting a change in treatment or terminating follow-up of that patient.

Stopping rule A rule, usually set before or shortly after the start of patient recruitment, that specifies a limit for the observed test-control treatment difference for the primary outcome, which, if exceeded, automatically leads to termination of the test or control treatment, depending on the direction of the observed difference.

Storiform A pattern of cellular arrangement which is seen in certain fibrous tumors when the elongated cells intersect or intertwine at various angles so as to resemble the weaving of a doormat.

Strabismus (clinical condition) Turned eye (s), the eyes are misaligned. It is caused by a reduction in visual acuity, reduced visual function, high refractive error, traumatic brain injury, oculomotor nerve lesion, or eye muscle injury. In strabismus, the eyes send conflicting images to the brain, and the brain cannot combine these images as it would in normal vision. The brain compensates by ignoring one image in favor of the other, causing a loss of depth perception. Strabismus in more common in children, and affects four percent of all children (although it may also appear later in life).

It is characterized by using the following categories:

Unilateral strabismus: Strabismus in which only one eye deviates.

Alternating strabismus. Strabismus in which the deviating eye can change.

Intermittent strabismus: Strabismus which is not present at all times.

Constant strabismus: Strabismus which is present at all times.

Periodic strabismus: Strabismus which occurs at one testing distance but not at another.

Strabismus is also known as squint. It may also be referred to as cross-eyes (convergent- turning inward) or wall eyes (divergent-turning outward). Treatment options may include one or more of the following: optical lenses, bifocal lenses, prisms, surgery, vision therapy, or Botulinum Toxin Type A (Oculinum, Botox) injections.

Straight sinus A large venous dural sinus, at the junction of the falx and the tentorium cerebelli.

Strain A population of cells all descended from a single cell.

Strata A series of distinct levels or layers. In this book, generally subgroups of patients formed by classification on some variable or set of variables, usually baseline variables.

Stratification 1. The process of classifying observation units into strata.

2. The process of classifying patients into strata as part of the randomization process or for purposes of data analysis.

Stratification variable A variable used to classify the experimental or observational units into strata.

Stratified allocation A method of treatment assignment in which patients are first classified into defined subgroups based on one or more baseline variables and then assigned to treatment within the defined subgroups.

Stratified randomization A treatment assignment process using stratified random allocation. Attempts to ensure balance by the stratification variable.

Stratum A layer, level, or defined subgroup.

Stratum zonale Thin plate of myelinated fibers covering the dorsal surface of the thalamus.

Streff syndrome Named after the optometrist who originally described it, Dr. John Streff. This functional vision loss is also known as Non-Malingering Syndrome. Signs include reduced visual acuity in both eyes at distance and near. The visual acuity at near is more reduced than the distance acuity. Frequently patients will have reduced stereopsis, large accommodative lag on dynamic retinoscopy, and a reduced visual field (tubular or spiral field). The syndrome is associated with a visual or emotional stress occurring in the child's life. It is more prominent in girls (ages 7-13) than boys. Treatment includes a low plus lens and/or vision therapy. This condition is sometimes incorrectly diagnosed by doctors as hysterical amblyopia.

Strength The concentration of the drug substance (for example, weight/weight, weight/volume, or unit dose/volume basis), and/or the potency, that is, the therapeutic activity of the drug product as indicated by appropriate laboratory tests or by adequately developed and controlled clinical data (expressed, for example, in terms of units by reference to a standard).

Streptavidin A small bacterial protein that binds with high affinity to the vitamin biotin. This streptavidin-biotin combination can be used to link molecules such as radioisotopes and monoclonal antibodies together. These bound products have the property of being attracted to, and attaching to, cancer cells, rather than normal cells. The radiolabeled products are more easily removed from the body, thus decreasing their toxicity.

Streptozocin A methylnitrosourea antineoplastic antibiotic isolated from the bacterium Streptomyces achromogenes. Streptozocin alkylates DNA, forming inter-strand DNA cross-links and inhibiting DNA synthesis. Due to its glucose moiety, this agent is readily taken up by pancreatic beta cells, inducing diabetes mellitus at high concentrations. Unlike other nitrosoureas, streptozocin causes little myelosuppression.

Stress test A diagnostic test using an ECG machine and a stationary bicycle or treadmill to look at areas of the heart that may have a decreased blood supply.

Stress ulcer An ulcer in the esophagus, stomach, or upper small intestine caused by excess acid produced as a result of surgery, major burns, head injury, or other trauma.

Stress urinary incontinence Urinary Incontinence The involuntary loss of urine during period of increased abdominal pressure. Such events include laughing, sneezing, coughing or lifting heavy objects.

Stria medullaris thalami Composite bundle of fibers that courses along the dorsomedial thalamus to the habenular nuclear complex. It conveys fibers that arise from the septal nuclei, lateral preoptic hypothalamus, and anterior thalamic nuclei to the habenular nuclei (interface between limbic, motor systems, and rostral midbrain.

Stria terminalis One of the extrinsic subcortical fiber systems of the amygdala that courses along the medial border of the caudate nucleus at its junction with the thalamus. It extends to the anterior hypothalamus, bed nucleus of the stria terminalis, and medial forebrain bundle.

Striate cortex Refers to the primary visual area of cortex (area 17) located in the walls of the calcarine sulcus of the occipital lobe. This is a thin cortical area (1.5-2.5 mm thick) which has striated appearance visible to the naked eye. This is due to presence of a conspicuous band of tangential fibers (outer band of Baillarger) located in cortical layer IV. In this region, this band is known as the band of Gennari which represents the terminal portions of the geniculo-calcarine tract.

Striations As referenced to the iris, it is the fine pigmented lines between the primary collarette (near the pupil) and the periphery of the diaphragm (limbus).

Striatum Refers to the neostriatum (caudate nucleus and putamen).

Stricture Abnormal narrowing of a part of an organ.

Stroke In medicine, a loss of blood flow to part of the brain, which damages brain tissue. Strokes are caused by blood clots and broken blood vessels in the brain. Symptoms include dizziness, numbness, weakness on one side of the body, and problems with talking, writing, or understanding language. The risk of stroke is increased by high blood pressure, older age, smoking, diabetes, high cholesterol, heart disease, atherosclerosis (a build-up of fatty material and plaque inside the coronary arteries), and a family history of stroke.

Stromagen A drug that is derived from a patient's stem cells (specialized cells in the bone marrow that form new blood cells) and may be given back to the patient to help restore bone marrow that has been damaged by high-dose chemotherapy.

Stromal tumor A tumor that arises in the supporting connective tissue of an organ.

Strontium 89 A radioactive compound that is absorbed by the bone. It is used to treat bone pain associated with prostate cancer.

Strontium chloride Sr 89 The chloride salt of a radioactive isotope of strontium. Strontium chloride Sr 89 is taken up and incorporated preferentially in metastatic lesions in bone where it emits cytotoxic beta radiation, resulting in an inhibition and/or reduction of tumor growth and so tumor-related bone pain.

Structural genomics The effort to determine the 3D structures of large numbers of proteins using both experimental techniques and computer simulation

Structured intermittent therapy (SIT) A type of structured treatment interruption that is characterized by time-based treatment cycles (weeks or months on and off anti-HIV drugs).

Structured treatment interruption (STI) Also known as a "drug holiday." A planned, doctor-supervised discontinuation of anti-HIV drugs. Goals of STI include reduced toxicity, reduced treatment costs, and improved quality of life.

Study 1. A general term used to refer to any one of a variety of research activities involving the collection, analysis, or interpretation of data.

2. Synonym for clinical trial.

3. A project involving multiple types of investigations, only one of which is a clinical trial (e.g., as in the Coronary Artery Surgery Study since it includes both a clinical trial and an uncontrolled prospective follow-up study.

Study agent A medicine, vitamin, mineral, food supplement, or a combination of them that is being tested in a clinical trial.

Study manual of operations A document or collection of documents that describes the procedures used in a center or set of centers in a clinical trial (e.g., manual of operations for study clinics, coordinating center manual of operations, protocol center manual of operations).

Study participant 1. A term sometimes used in place of study patient when there is a desire to avoid the connotation of illness, as in trials involving well people.

2. Study investigator.

Study patient Term used to characterize an individual considered for enrollment or actually enrolled into a trial regardless of whether or not there is a perceived need for medical care.

Study physician Any physician associated with a study clinic who is responsible for administering the study treatments to patients in the trial or who is responsible for patient care, as dictated by the study protocol.

Study population 1. The set of patients enrolled in a trial.

2. The entire set of patients considered for enrollment into the trial (not used in this context).

Study protocol A narrative document that describes the general design and operating features of a trial. Distinguished from the study manual of operations by its generality and absence of specific details needed for day-to-day execution of the trial.

Sturge-Weber syndrome (SWS) A rare, congenital disorder that affects the brain, skin, and eyes. Abnormal blood vessel growth occurs in the trigeminal nerve in the face and the meninges (covering) of the brain. This abnormal growth causes red or purple skin discoloration (sometimes called a port wine stain), usually on one side of the face, and can also cause seizures, learning disabilities, and glaucoma.

Styloid process A spike/penlike projection from the inferior portion of the temporal bone, anterior to the stylomastoid foramen, that allows for muscular attachment of the stylo-hyoid/ thyroid muscles.

SU006668 A substance that is being studied in the treatment of cancer. It belongs to the families of drugs called protein tyrosine kinase inhibitors and angiogenesis inhibitors. Also called SU6668.

SU011248 A substance that is being studied as a treatment for cancer. It belongs to the family of drugs called angiogenesis inhibitors.

SU101 An anticancer drug that works by inhibiting a cancer cell growth factor. Also called leflunomide.

SU5416 A substance that has been studied in the treatment of cancer. It belongs to the families of drugs called angiogenesis inhibitors and tyrosine kinase inhibitors. Also called semaxanib.

Subarachnoid cisternae Enlargements of the cerebrospinal fluid filled space between the pia and arachnoid mater (subarachnoid space). A number of these cisternae are identified at various locations (i.e. lumbar cistern, cisterna magnum etc.)

Subarachnoid space Cerebrospinal fluid filled space between the arachnoidea and the pia mater of the central nervous system.

Subcapitation An arrangement whereby a capitated health plan pays its contracted providers on a capitated basis.

Subclavian artery Artery which originates from the brachiocephalic artery on the right side and directly from the arch of aorta on the left side. They branch into the vertebral, internal thoracic arteries, thyrocervical and costocervical trunks.

Subclinical Describing a disease or condition that is suspected but not sufficiently developed to produce definite signs and symptoms in the patient.

Subclinical infection An infection, or phase of infection, without readily apparent symptoms or signs of disease.

Subconjunctival hemorrhage A blood spot on the eye. It occurs when a small blood vessel under the conjunctiva (the transparent coating that covers the inner eyelid and the white of the eye) breaks and bleeds. A common condition caused spontaneously from coughing, heavy lifting, or vomiting. In some cases, it may develop following eye surgery or trauma. It tends to be more common among those with diabetes, hypertension, and taking blood thinners (including aspirin). A subconjunctival hemorrhage is essentially harmless. The blood naturally absorbs within one to three weeks and no treatment is required. If a mild irritation is present, artificial tear drops can be used. You can speed up the healing process by applying cool compresses for the first two days and then warm compresses in the following days.

Subcutaneous (SC) Beneath the skin, or administration of a substance beneath the skin.

Subcutaneous adipose tissue (SAT) A type of adipose (fat) tissue found directly under the skin. Both loss (lipoatrophy) and gain (lipohypertrophy) of this fat tissue can occur as a side effect of HIV infection and some of the drugs used to treat HIV infection, especially PIs and NRTIs.

Subcutaneous injection Putting a fluid into the tissue under the skin with a needle and syringe.

Subcutaneous mastectomy Surgery to remove internal breast tissue. The nipple and skin are left intact.

Subcutaneous port A tube surgically placed into a blood vessel and attached to a disk placed under the skin. It is used for the administration of intravenous fluids and drugs; it can also be used to obtain blood samples.

Subdural space A potential space located between the innermost layer of the dura mater and the arachnoid mater. This interface is a site of rupture of delicate thin-walled veins following head injuries resulting in subdural hematomas which can have profound neurological consequences.

Subependymal Below the ependyma (the membrane that lines the ventricles of the brain and the central canal of the spinal cord).

Suberoylanilide hydroxamic acid A substance that is being studied as an anticancer drug.

Subglottic airway The airway below the "glottis", that is below the true vocal cords.

Subglottis The lowest part of the larynx; the area from just below the vocal cords down to the top of the trachea.

Subgroup A subpart of the study population distinguished by a particular characteristic or set of characteristics (e.g., males under age 45 at entry).

Subgroup analysis Any data analysis that focuses on a selected subgroup or patients. Generally, any analysis that is aimed at elucidating treatment differences within a defined subgroup of patients.

Subgrouping variable A variable, such as age, used to classify patients (treatment units) into subgroups. Usually a baseline characteristic for most subgroup analyses in clinical trials.

Subiculum Cortical zone along the medial parahippocampul gyrus. It is along with the presubiculum and prosubiculum transitional from the 6 layered parahippocampul cortex to the 3 layered cortex of the hippocampus and dentate gyri.

Subject based teaching A method of teaching in which each subject area of curriculum is addressed separately. In the past, this model had been very prominent in basic science education. Now, however, it is gradually being replaced with a problem-based learning (PBL) where knowledge and skills unfold as elements in cases that illustrate real life situations.

Subjective improvement An improvement that is reported by the patient, but cannot be measured by the healthcare provider (for example, "I feel better").

Subjective refraction The procedure in which the patient is asked to report on which lens combination provides the clearest vision. While this is the method of choice for determining prescription in those able to understand the task and respond to the examiner, it is less reliable in children.

Sublimation The process of vaporizing a solid substance by heat and then condensing it (without its having passed through a liquid state in either direction), a process of purification by separating the nonvaporizable impurities, a process analogous to the distillation of liquids.

Submandibular gland Paired salivary gland, located in the middle of the posterior half of the base of the mandible.

Submerged arc welding (SAW) An arc welding process that produces coalescence of metals by heating them with an arc or arcs between a bare metal electrode or electrodes and the work. A blanket of granular, fusible material on the work shields the arc. Pressure is not used and filler metal is obtained from the electrode and sometimes from a supplemental source (welding rod, flux, or metal granules).

Submucosa The layer of tissue under the mucosa (inner lining of some organs and body cavities that makes mucus).

Subscapularus muscle Muscle originating at the subscapular (ventral/anterior) fossa of the scapula and inserting at the lesser tubercle of the humerus.

Subserosa The layer of tissue under the serosa (outer lining of some organs and body cavities).

Subset analysis In a clinical study, the evaluation of results for some but not all of the patients who participated. The selected patients have one or more characteristics in common, such as the same stage of disease or the same hormone receptor status.

Substantia gelatinosa A cell column located at the apex of the dorsal horn throughout the length of the spinal cord. It corresponds to lamina II of Rexed and receives pain and temperature input from dorsal root afferents. This input is modified in this location by other sensory input and by excitatory and inhibitory input from the cerebral cortex. Lamina II neurons are entirely interneuronal; ascending or descending several segments in the dorsolateral fasciculus (of Lissauer) before re-entering lamina II.

Substantia nigra A large neuromelanin containing nuclear area ventral to the tegmentum extending throughout the rostrocaudal extent of the midbrain and into the caudal part of the ventral diencephalon. Consists of a ventral pars reticulata and a dorsal part called the pars compacta. Neurons in the pars compacta use dopamine as a neurotransmitter and project primarily to the neostriatum.

Substitution In genetics, a type of mutation due to replacement of one nucleotide in a DNA sequence by another nucleotide or replacement of one amino acid in a protein by another amino acid.

Substrate Reactive material - the substance on which an enzyme acts.

Subsurface carbon enrichment In metals, a rise in the carbon signal at depths from 15 to 20 angstroms (Å). This indicates that organic material is buried in cracks, crevices, pits, or smeared material. Subsurface carbon is most commonly found in materials having rough mor-phology generally associated with machining processes.

Subtenon Used to describe injections through the membrane covering the muscles and nerves at the back of the eyeball.

Subthalamus A subdivision of the diencephalon located ventral to the thalamus, medial to the internal capsule, and lateral and caudal to the hypothalamus. It consists of the subthalamic nucleus, sensory fiber tracts terminating in the thalamus, fibers from the cerebellum, corpus striatum, midbrain motor nuclei proceeding to the thalamus, and forward extensions of the zona incerta, red nucleus, and substantia nigra.

Subtype HIV is classified into two types, HIV-1 and HIV-2. Within HIV-1 are groups of similar viral strains. These are the major (M) subtype and non-M (new (N) and outlier (O)) subtypes. The majority of HIV-1 infections are by M-subtype viral strains. Subtype M HIV-1 is further broken down into nine genetically distinct strains known as clades.

Subunit HIV vaccine Also known as component vaccine. Subunit vaccines contain only part of the HIV virus (such as individual proteins or peptides) produced in the laboratory by genetic engineering techniques.

Sucralfate A drug used to treat ulcers. It adheres to proteins at the ulcer site and forms a protective coating over the ulcer. Sucralfate is also used to treat mucositis.

Sucrose Table sugar; a form of sugar that the body must break down into a more simple form before the blood can absorb it and take it to the cells.

Suction cup A small rubber or silicone vacuum device used in insertion and/or removal of the prosthesis.

Suction evacuation A surgical procedure in which the cervix is dilated (opened) and vacuum is used to remove tissue from the uterus. Also called suction aspiration or vacuum aspiration.

Sudden cardiac death (SCD) A death due to electrical problems in the heart. It is different from a heart attack, which is heart muscle damage from a blockage rather than an electrical problem. Sudden cardiac death usually is caused by ventricular tachycardia or fibrillation. An AICD system, however, greatly reduces the risk of sudden cardiac death.

Sudden infant death syndrome (SIDS) The sudden and unexpected death of a healthy child who is younger than one year old, usually during sleep. The cause of SIDS is not known. Also called crib death.

Sugar A class of carbohydrates that taste sweet. Sugar is a quick and easy fuel for the body to use. Types of sugar are lactose, glucose, fructose, and sucrose.

Sulcus The valleys or depressions that seperate cortical convolutions.

S. (Hypothalamic) A longitudinal groove that extends along each wall of the neural tube as far cranially as the mesencephalon. It serves to divide the neural tube into a dorsal half called the alar plate and a ventral half called the basal plate.

S. (Limitans) A longitudinal groove that extends along the medial wall of the diencephalon that divides the hypothalamus below from the thalamus above.

Sulfa drug A type of antibiotic used to treat infection. Also called sulfonamide.

Sulfadiazine A sulfa antibiotic, sometimes used in the treatment of Toxoplasmosis, especially in combination with pyrimethamine

Sulfadoxine A sulfa antibiotic, only occasionally used in AID.

Sulfonamide A type of antibiotic used to treat infection. Also called sulfa drug.

Sulfonylureas One of several different classes of pills that lower the level of glucose in the blood. Used in Type 2 diabetes.

There are several sulfonylurea pills available. Four, known as "first-generation" drugs, have been in use for some time. Three types, called "second-generation" drugs, have been developed recently. They are sometimes stronger than first-generation drugs and have fewer side effects. Each type of pill is sold under two names: one is the generic name; the other is the trade name given by the manufacturer. They are:

First-Generation Agents:

Generic Name: Tolbutamide

Trade Name: Orinase

Generic Name: Acetohexamide

Trade Name: Dymelor

Generic Name: Tolazamide

Trade Name: Tolinase

Generic Name: Chloropropamide

Trade Name: Diabinese

Second-Generation Agents:

Generic Name: Glipizide

Trade Name: Glucotrol, Glucotrol XL

Generic Name: Glyburide

Trade Name: Diabeta, Micronase, Glynase

Generic Name: Glimepiride

Trade Name: Amaryl .

Sulfuric acid A strong acid that, when concentrated, is extremely corrosive to the skin and mucous membranes. It is used in making fertilizers, dyes, electroplating, and industrial explosives.

Sulindac A sulfinylindene derivative prodrug with potential antineoplastic activity. Converted in vivo to an active metabolite, sulindac, a nonsteroidal anti-inflammatory drug (NSAID), blocks cyclic guanosine monophosphate-phosphodiesterase (cGMP-PDE), an enzyme that inhibits the normal apoptosis signal pathway; this inhibition permits the apoptotic signal pathway to proceed unopposed, resulting in apoptotic cell death.

Sulphamethoxazole A sulfa antibiotic, and half of the combination "trimethoprim-sulphamethoxazole", it is rarely used alone.

Summary plan description (SPD) In self-funded plans, a written explanation of the eligibility for and benefits available to employees required by ERISA

Summicort Other name for methylprednisolone.

Sun protection factor (SPF) A scale for rating the level of sunburn protection in sunscreen products. The higher the SPF, the more sunburn protection it gives. Sunscreens with an SPF value of 2 through 11 give minimal protection against sunburns. Sunscreens with an SPF of 12

through 29 give moderate protection. Those with an SPF of 30 or higher give high protection against sunburn.

Sunitinib malate The orally bioavailable malate salt of an indolinone-based tyrosine kinase inhibitor with potential antineoplastic activity. Sunitinib blocks the tyrosine kinase activities of vascular endothelial growth factor receptor 2 (VEGFR2), platelet-derived growth factor receptor b (PDGFRb), and c-kit, thereby inhibiting angiogenesis and cell proliferation. This agent also inhibits the phosphorylation of Fms-related tyrosine kinase 3 (FLT3), another receptor tyrosine kinase expressed by some leukemic cells.

Sunscreen A substance that helps protect the skin from the sun's harmful rays. Sunscreens reflect, absorb, and scatter both ultraviolet A and B radiation to provide protection against both types of radiation. Using lotions, creams, or gels that contain sunscreens can help protect the skin from premature aging and damage that may lead to skin cancer.

Superficial Affecting cells on the surface. Not invasive.

Superficial temporal artery Originating from the external carotid artery and branching into the parotid, auricular, and occipital rami, tranverse facial, zygomatico-orbital, and middle temporal arteries.

Superinfection A new infection acquired on top of an existing infection. For example, a person infected with one strain of HIV-1 can, if exposed to a different strain, become infected with the new strain in addition to the existing strain. Superinfection can complicate HIV treatment by requiring additional drugs to target the newly introduced HIV strain.

Superior gluteal artery Artery originating from the internal iliac artery and branching into the superficial and deep branches of the buttocks.

Superior mesenteric artery Artery which originates from the abdominal aorta and branches into the inferior pancreaticoduodenal, jejunal, ileal, ileocolic, right colic, and middle colic arteries.

Superior mesenteric vein The vein that parallels the superior mesenteric artery and joins the splenic vein to form the portal vein.

Superior pubic ramus Portion of the pubic bone that projects posterosuperolaterally to join the iliopubic eminence, to form part of the acetabulum.

Superior rectus muscle The muscle which originates at the lateral margin of the optic foramen, and inserts into the upper aspect of the sclera. It is responsible for the adduction and upward medial rotation of the eyeball.

Superior sagittal sinus (SSS) Venous sinus within the dura mater of the falx (at it's attachment to the sagittal suture), that extends from the crista galli to the junction with the tentorium and the torcular herophili.

Superior sulcus depression A loss or displacement of adipose tissue in the upper eyelid.

Superior thyroid artery Artery which originates from the external carotid artery and branches into the pharyngeal, esophageal, and tracheal rami, inferior laryngeal and ascending cervical arteries.

Superior vena cava The vein created by the joining of the two brachiocephalic veins and empties into the right atrium of the heart. It drains the head, neck, upper extremities and chest.

Superior vena cava syndrome A condition in which a tumor presses against the superior vena cava (the large vein that carries blood from the head, neck, arms, and chest to the heart). This pressure blocks blood flow to the heart and may cause coughing, difficulty in breathing, and swelling of the face, neck, and upper arms.

Superior vesicle artery Artery which stems from the umbilical artery, supplying the bladder urachus, and ureter.

Supernatant The material floating on the surface of a liquid mixture (often the liquid component that has the lowest density).

Supernumerary tooth Extra tooth.

Supine Lying on the back or with the face upward.

Supplemental nutrition A substance or product that is added to a person's diet. It may include vitamins, minerals, protein, or fat, and may be given by mouth, by tube feeding, or into a vein.

Supplemental services Optional services a health plan covers or provides.

Supplementation Adding nutrients to the diet.

Support group A group of patients and their family members coordinated by medial professionals. The AICD support group provides an opportunity for members to share their experiences with AICD therapy and to discuss any concerns.

Supportive care Care given to improve the quality of life of patients who have a serious or life-threatening disease. The goal of supportive care is to prevent or treat as early as possible the symptoms of the disease, side effects caused by treatment of the disease, and psychological, social, and spiritual problems related to the disease or its treatment. Also called palliative care, comfort care, and symptom management.

Suppression A mechanism for producing a specific state of immunologic unresponsiveness by the induction of suppressor T cells. This type of unresponsiveness is passively transferable by suppressor T cells or their soluble products.

Suppression of binocular vision When the brain ignores the image that is seen by one eye. It is the result of weak eye teaming skills (binocularity).

Suppression test Determines if there is any tendency for the visual processing center of the brain to ignore or suppress visual data from one eye.

Suppressor gene A gene that can suppress the action of another gene.

Suppuration Bacterial contamination of tissue exudate; pus.

Suppurative Containing pus.

Supraclavicular lymph node A lymph node located above the clavicle (collarbone).

Supraclavicular nodes Lymph nodes that are above the collarbone (clavicle).

Supraglottic laryngectomy An operation to remove the supraglottis, which is part of the larynx (voice box) above the vocal cords.

Supraglottis The upper part of the larynx (voice box), including the epiglottis; the area above the vocal cords.

Suprapatellar bursa A saclike cavity filled with a viscid fluid located between the distal end of the femur and the quadriceps tendon.

Suprasellar cistern The enlarged subarachnoid space just above the pituitary fossa, containing the arteries of the Circle of Willis and the infundibulum/pituitary stalk.

Supratentorial Having to do with the upper part of the brain.

Suramin A polysulphonated naphthylurea with potential antineoplastic activity. Suramin blocks the binding of various growth factors, including insulin-like growth factor I (IGF-I), epidermal growth factor (EGF), platelet-derived growth factor (PDGF), and tumor growth factor-beta (TGF-beta), to their receptors, thereby inhibiting endothelial cell proliferation and migration. This agent also inhibits vascular endothelial growth factor (VEGF)- and basic fibroblast growth factor (bFGF)-induced angiogenesis; retroviral reverse transcriptase; uncoupling of G-proteins from receptors; topoisomerases; cellular folate transport; and steroidogenesis.

Surface iron oxide layer Surface iron oxide layer present when the 316L stainless steel's iron composition signal is higher than its chromium signal at the surface.

Surface residual A foreign substance that adheres to a surface by chemical reaction, adhesion, adsorption, or ionic bonding (for example, corrosion, rouging, and staining).

Surface texture The repetitive or random deviations of the nominal metal surface from the three-dimensional topography of the surface. Surface texture includes roughness, waviness, lay, and flaws.

Surface water Any water where the source is above ground such as rivers, lakes, and reservoirs. Surface waters are usually higher in suspended matter and organic material and lower in dissolved minerals than well water.

Surfactant Any substance that changes the nature of a surface, such as lowering the surface tension of water.

Surgeon A doctor who removes or repairs a part of the body by operating on the patient.

Surgery A procedure to remove or repair a part of the body or to find out whether disease is present. An operation.

Surgical castration Surgical removal of the testicles (orchiectomy) or ovaries (oophorectomy) to stop the production of sex hormones. Decreasing the levels of hormones may stop the growth of certain cancers.

Surgical oncologist A doctor who performs biopsies and other surgical procedures in cancer patients.

Surrogate outcome variable (also called surrogate marker) A test, measurement, score, or some other similar variable that is used in place of a clinical event (e.g., use of blood pressure change in place of clinical hypertension) in the design of a trial, or in summarizing results from it. Used because the variable is believed to be correlated with the clinical event of interest and because of its perceived utility in yielding detectable treatment differences. CD4 was once believed to be a surrogate marker for death from AIDS.

Survival analysis 1. Any method of data analysis that focuses on the length of survival.

2. Lifetable analysis.

Survival rate A way of expressing how long, on average, people may live after diagnosis of disease or after treatment of the disease. It is expressed as the percentage of people who live a certain period of time, as opposed to the percentage of those who die. For example, the five-year survival rate for women with localized breast cancer (including all women living five years whether the patient was in remission, disease-free, or under treatment) was 78% in the 1940s, but in the 1990s it is 93%.

Survivin antigen A tumor-associated antigen. Vaccination with survivin antigen may result in a cytotoxic T-cell response against survivin antigen-expressing tumor cells, resulting in decreased tumor cell proliferation and tumor cell death. Overexpressed in many tumors, endogenous survivin inhibits tumor cell apoptosis.

Survivorship In cancer, survivorship covers the physical, psychosocial, and economic issues of cancer, from diagnosis until the end of life. It includes issues related to the ability to get health care and follow up treatment, late effects of treatment, second cancers, and quality of life.

Susceptible Having little resistance to a specific infectious disease. Also used to describe an HIV strain that is not resistant to a particular anti-HIV drug.

Suspended solids Undissolved solids that can be removed by filtration. Determined by a filter paper before and after filtration of a water sample.

Suspension A specific category of pharmaceutical product that must be in a colloidal dispersion (suspension) for proper action. For example, Kaolin/Pectin works as an adsorbant because its high surface area in suspension.

SV40 (Simian virus 40) A virus that infects some types of monkeys. It may also infect humans, and was found in some polio vaccines tested in the early 1960s. Although the virus has been shown to cause cancer in laboratory animals, there is no evidence that it causes cancer in people.

Sweet elm Ulmus fulva or Ulmus rubra. The inner bark of this plant has been used in some cultures to treat certain medical problems. It may have antioxidant effects. Also called slippery elm, gray elm, Indian elm, and red elm.

Sx Common abbreviation for "symptoms."

Sylvian fissure The deep cleft that begins at the anterior perforated substance, continuing between the frontal and temporal lobes, and then posteriorly between the temporal and parietal lobes. It is bound by the overhaning margins ("opercula") of the frontal, temporal, and parietal lobes, as well as deeply by the insular cortex.

Symbiosis The phenomenon of two entities performing a joint function that neither entity can perform alone.

Symblepharon Adhesion (s) between the bulbar and the palpebral conjunctiva.

Symmetric Equally divided, and identical on both sides of a middle line; mirror image

Sympathetic nervous system The thoracolumbar component of the autonomic nervous sytem. This system is widely distributed in the body and releases norepinephrine at most terminals. Stimulation of this system has the effect of quickly mobilizing the body for "flight or fight."

Symptom An indication that a person has a condition or disease. Some examples of symptoms are headache, fever, fatigue, nausea, vomiting, and pain.

Symptom management Care given to improve the quality of life of patients who have a serious or life-threatening disease. The goal of symptom management is to prevent or treat as early as possible the symptoms of the disease, side effects caused by treatment of the disease, and psychological, social, and spiritual problems related to the disease or its treatment. Also called palliative care, comfort care, and supportive care.

Symptomatic Showing clinical pathology or changes indica ve of disease, such as HIV disease. Often symptomatic HIV disease means clinical evidence of HIV infection in absence of an AIDS diagnosis, indicative of, relating to or constituting the aggregate of symptoms of a disease.

Synchronous At once; at the same time.

Syncope A temporary loss of consciousness due to insufficient cerebral blood flow; fainting.

Syncytia A mass of cells which fuse together to form one "giant cell." In HIV infection this condition leads to direct cell-to-cell infection and continued HIV replication.

Syncytium A giant cell formed by the fusing together of two or more smaller cells. HIV-infected cells can fuse with uninfected cells to form syncytia. The presence of so-called syncytia-inducing variants of HIV has been correlated with rapid disease progression in HIV-infected individuals.

Syndesmosis (Tibiofibular) A fibrous union between the fibular notch of the tibia and a triangular surface on the fibula.

Syndrome X An older phrase describing a combination of health conditions that place a person at high risk for heart disease. These conditions are Type 2 diabetes, hypertension (high blood pressure), hyperlipidemia (high levels of fat in the blood), and obesity. According to theory, all of these conditions are associated with high blood insulin levels, and it is claimed that the underlying problem in patients with Syndrome X is faulty insulin release from the beta cells of the pancreas.

Now usually called the Metabolic Syndrome.

Synergistic In medicine, describes the interaction of two or more drugs when their combined effect is greater than the sum of the effects seen when each drug is given alone.

Synergy An interaction between two or more drugs that produces an effect greater than the sum of their individual effects.

Syngeneic bone marrow transplantation A procedure in which a person receives bone marrow donated by his or her healthy identical twin.

Syngeneic Genetically identical members of the same species.

Syngeneic stem cell transplantation A procedure in which a patient receives blood-forming stem cells (cells from which all blood cells develop) donated by his or her healthy identical twin.

Syngraft Same as isograft.

Synovial Joint A joint in which the opposing bony surfaces are covered with a layer of hyaline cartilage or fibrocartilage, there is a joint cavity containing synovial fluid, lined with synovial membrane and reinforced by a fibrous capsule and ligaments, and there is some degree of free movement possible.

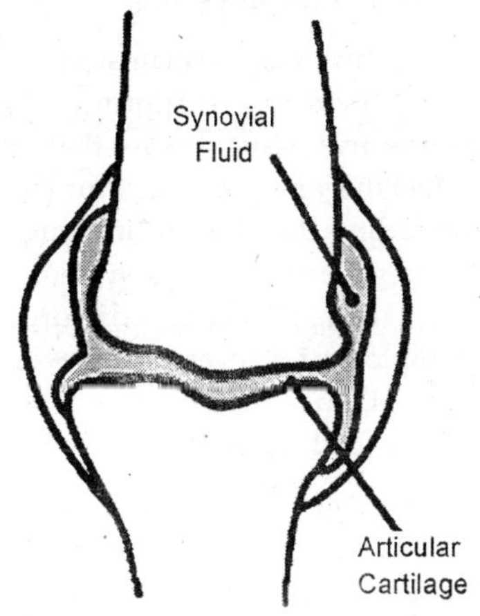

Figure Synovial joint

Synovial membrane A layer of connective tissue that lines the cavities of joints, tendon sheaths, and bursae (fluid-filled sacs between tendons and bones). The synovial membrane makes synovial fluid, which has a lubricating function.

Synovial sarcoma A malignant tumor that develops in the synovial membrane of the joints.

Synovir Other name for thalidomide.

Synovitis Inflammation (swelling, pain, and warmth) of a synovial membrane, which is a layer of connective tissue that lines a joint, such as the hip, knee, ankle, or shoulder. Synovitis is caused by some types of arthritis and other diseases.

Synteny Genes occurring in the same order on chromosomes of different species.

Synthesis Creating products through chemical and enzymatic reactions.

Synthetic peptide-based erythropoiesis stimulating agent A synthetic, non-recombinant, pegylated, peptidic erythropoiesis stimulating agent. Synthetic peptide-based erythropoiesis stimulating agent binds to and activates the erythropoietin (EPO) receptor on erythroid progenitor cells, thereby inducing their proliferation and differentiation into mature erythrocytes.

Synthetic protegrin analog A drug that may prevent oral mucositis (sores on the lining of the mouth), a side effect of some cancer treatments.

Synthetic retinoid A substance related to vitamin A that is produced in a laboratory.

Syphilis A sexually transmitted disease (STD) caused by the bacterium Treponema pallidum.

In the early stage of syphilis, a genital or mouth sore called a chancre develops, but eventually disappears on its own. However, if the disease is not treated, the infection can progress over years to affect the heart and central nervous system. Syphilis can also be transmitted from an infected mother to her fetus during pregnancy, with serious health consequences for the infant.

Syringe A device used to inject medications or other liquids into body tissues. The syringe for insulin has a hollow plastic or glass tube (barrel) with a plunger inside. The plunger forces the insulin through the needle into the body. Most insulin syringes now come with a needle attached. The side of the syringe has markings to show how much insulin is being injected.

System specifications Descriptions of how the system will meet the functional requirements.

Systemic A word used to describe conditions that affect the entire body. Diabetes is a systemic disease because it involves many parts of the body such as the pancreas, eyes, kidneys, heart, and nerves.

Systemic chemotherapy Treatment with anticancer drugs that travel through the blood to cells all over the body.

Systemic disease In breast cancer. this term means that the tumor that originated in the breast has spread to distant sites, such as the liver, chest, brain, bones or lungs.

Systemic inflammatory response syndrome (SIRS) A serious condition in which there is inflammation throughout the whole body. It may be caused by a severe bacterial infection (sepsis), trauma, or pancreatitis. It is marked by fast heart rate, low blood pressure, low or high body temperature, and low or high white blood cell count. The condition may lead to multiple organ failure and shock.

Systemic lupus erythematosus (SLE) A chronic, inflammatory, connective tissue disease that can affect the joints and many organs, including the skin, heart, lungs, kidneys, and nervous system. It can cause many different symptoms; however, not everyone with SLE has all of the symptoms. Also called lupus.

Systemic radiation Treatment with a radioactive substance, such as a radioactively-labeled monoclonal antibody, that travels through the blood to cells all over the body.

Systemic therapy Treatment using substances that travel through the bloodstream, reaching and affecting cells all over the body.

T

T 3 A thyroid hormone. Also called triiodothyronine or liothyronine sodium.

T cell A type of lymphocyte (disease-fighting white blood cell). The "T" stands for the thymus, where T cells mature. T cells include CD4 cells and CD8 cells, which are both critical components of the body's immune system.

T cell depletion Treatment to destroy T cells, which play an important role in the immune response. Elimination of T cells from a bone marrow graft from a donor may reduce the chance of an immune reaction against the recipient's tissues.

T cells (T lymphocytes) A thymus derived white blood cell that precipitates a variety of cell mediated immune reactions. Three fundamentally different types of T cells are recognized: helper, killer, and suppresser (each has many subdivisions).

T dependent antigen An immunogen that is able to induce antibody synthesis only in the presence of lymphokines released by helper T cells.

T helper cells Lymphocytes responsible for assisting other white blood cells in responding to infection, processing antigen, and triggering antibody production (also known as T4 cells, CD4 cells).

T independent antigen An immunogen which induces antibody synthesis in the absence of lymphokines released by T cells; the antibodies are generally only of the IgM isotype.

T ciller cells A major component of cytotoxic lymphocyte response (CTL), responsible for lysing infected or cancerous cells, T killer cells (not to be confused by natural killer cells) are a subset of CD8+ lymphocytes.

T lymphocyte cells Thymus dependent cells, coordinate the cell-mediated immune system.

T suppresser cells T lymphocytes responsible for turning the immune response off after infection is cleared, a subset of CD8+ lymphocytes.

T138067 An anticancer drug that belongs to the family of drugs called mitotic inhibitors. It inhibits the growth of cancer cells by preventing cell division.

T138067 sodium A synthetic pentafluorophenylsulfonamide with potential antineoplastic activity. T138067 covalently binds to and selectively modifies the beta 1, beta 2, beta 3, and beta 4 isotypes of beta tubulin at a conserved cysteine residue, resulting in disruption of microtubule polymerization, collapse of the cytoskeleton, an increase in chromosomal ploidy, cell cycle arrest, and tumor cell apoptosis.

T4N5 liposomal lotion A topical lotion that contains the enzyme T4-bacteriophage endonuclease V encapsulated within liposomes. With topical liposomal delivery, the DNA repair enzyme T4-bacteriophage endonuclease V is transported into skin cells, where the enzyme enters cell nuclei and binds to and incises pyrimidine dimers, thereby catalyzing the first reaction step of the cellular excision repair pathway for removing DNA replication-inhibiting pyrimidine dimers produced within duplex DNA through exposure to ultraviolet (UV) irradiation. In vitro and in vivo studies in indicate that T4N5 liposomes increases repair of DNA damage caused by UV irradiation.

T4N5 liposomal lotion Enzyme lotion used in treating xeroderma pigmentosum.

T900607 A pentafluorophenylsulfonamide compound with potential antineoplastic activity. T900607 inhibits tubulin polymerization by binding irreversibly to colchicine binding sites, resulting in cell cycle arrest and apoptosis.

Tabloid brand thioguanine Other name for thioguanine.

TAC 101 A retinobenzoic acid with potential antineoplastic activity. TAC-101 inhibits retinoblastoma-gene product (RB) phosphorylation and increases the presence of 2 cyclin-dependent kinase (CDK) inhibitors, resulting in cell cycle arrest. This agent also causes a cytotoxic decline in cyclin A and thymidylate synthase expression.

Tachyarrhythmias Abnormally fast heart rhythms.

Tachycardia Rapid beating of the heart, usually defined as greater than 100 beats per minute.

Tachyphylaxis A falling-off in the effects produced by a drug during continuous use.

Tacrolimus A macrolide isolated from the fungus Streptomyces

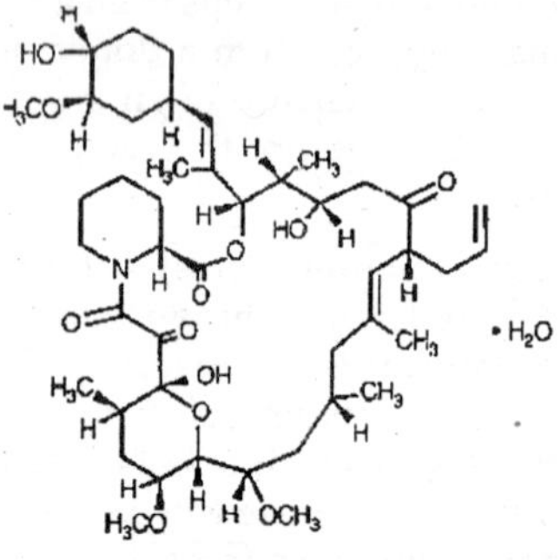

{[3S-[3R[E (1S,3S,4S)],4S,5R,8S,9E,12R, 14R,15S, 16R,18S,19S,26aR]]-5,6,8,11, 12,13,14, 15,16, 17,18,19,24,25,26,26a-hexadecahydro-5, 19-dihydroxy-3- [2-(4-hydroxy-3-methoxycyclohexyl) -1-methylethenyl]-14, 16-dimethoxy-4,10,12, 18-tetramethyl-8- (2-propenyl)-15, 19-epoxy-3H-pyrido[2,1-c][1,4] oxaazacyclotricosine-1,7,20, 21 (4H,23H)-tetrone, monohydrate. }

Figure Tacrolimus

tsukubaensis. Tacrolimus binds to the FKBP-12 protein and forms a complex with calcium-dependent proteins, thereby inhibiting calcineurin phosphatase activity and resulting in decreased cytokine production. This agent exhibits potent immunosuppressive activity in vivo and prevents the activation of T-lymphocytes in response to antigenic or mitogenic stimulation. Tacrolimus possesses similar immunosuppressive properties to cyclosporine, but is more potent.

Tactile Pertaining to the sense of touch.

TAG 72 antigen A protein/sugar complex found on the surface of many cancer cells, including breast, colon, and pancreatic cells.

Tail of pancreas The distal left extremity of the pancreas, next to the medial spleen and the junction between the transverse and descending colon.

Talampanel A synthetic derivative of dioxolo-benzodiazepine with anti-seizure activity. Talampanel noncompetitively binds to the AMPA (alpha-amino-3-hydroxy-5-methyl-4-isoxazolepropionic acid) subtype of glutamate excitatory amino acid receptors and may inhibit the growth of gliomas by interfering with neurotransmitters involved in brain tumor growth. This agent may also protect against traumatic brain injury.

Talaporfin sodium An agent consisting of chlorin e6, derived from chlorophyll, and L-aspartic acid with photosensitizing activity. After intratumoral activation by light emitting diodes, taporfin sodium forms an extended high energy conformational state that generates singlet oxygen, resulting in free radical-mediated cell death.

Talc Finely-powdered native hydrous magnesium silicate. When administered into the pleural space, talc initiates an inflammatory reaction, resulting in adhesion of the visceral pleura to the parietal pleura and fibrosis, thereby effectively closing the pleural space and preventing further accumulation of fluid. This agent exhibits no rtrinsic antineoplastic activity.

Talotrexin An antimetabolite analog of aminopterin with antineoplastic activity. As a folate antagonist, talotrexin binds to and inhibits the function of dihydrofolate reductase. Hydrosoluble, talotrexin is actively transported into cells by the reduced folate carrier (RFC) and, therefore, is unlikely to be associated with P-glycoprotein-mediated multidrug resistance.

Talus The highest tarsal bone which forms the ankle joint by articulating with the tibia and fibula.

Tamoxifen A drug that blocks estrogen; an antiestrogen drug. Blocking estrogen is desirable in some cases of breast cancer because estrogen feeds the growth of certain types of tumors. This drug is being tested in a large clinical trial to see if it will help prevent the recurrence of cancer.

Tamoxifen citrate The citrate salt of an antineoplastic nonsteroidal selective estrogen receptor modulator (SERM). Tamoxifen competitively inhibits the binding of estradiol to estrogen receptors, thereby preventing the receptor from binding to the estrogen-response element on DNA. The result is a reduction in DNA synthesis and cellular response to estrogen. In addition, tamoxifen up-regulates the production of transforming growth factor B (TGFb), a factor that inhibits tumor cell growth, and down-regulates insulin-like growth factor 1 (IGF-1), a factor that stimulates brast cancer cell growth.

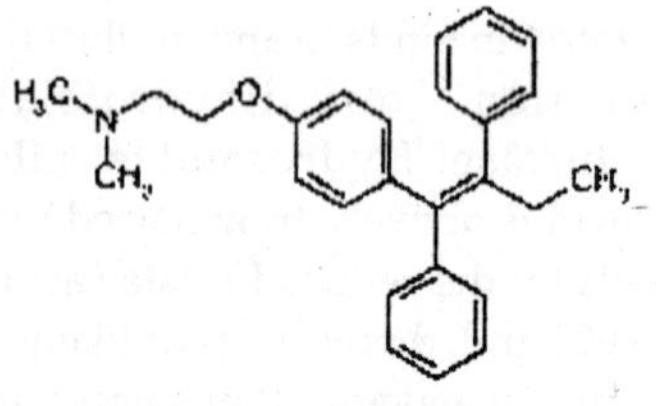

{ (Z)-2-[4- (1,2-diphenyl-1-butenyl)phenoxy]-N,N-dimethylethanamine}

Figure Tamoxifen citrate

Tandem repeat sequences Multiple copies of the same base sequence on a chromosome; used as markers in physical mapping.

Tangential flow filtration A separation method that transfers components of one system (stream) into another. The stream the product is being extracted from crosses the stream that the product is being transferred to, multiple times.

Tanner staging A method for determining an adolescent's stage of sexual development, irrespective of chronological age. In HIV treatment, Tanner staging is used to determine the appropriate treatment guidelines to follow: adult, adolescent, or pediatric.

Tanycytes Ependymal cell variants found only within circumscribed regions of the adult mammalian ventricular system. They are distinguished by the presence of a radially directed basal process that extends into the neuropil and terminates on blood vessels, neurons, glia, or the external glial limitans.

Tapetum Fibers of the corpus callosum which course laterally and inferiorly forming the roof and lateral walls of its posterior and inferior horns of thelateral ventricles. The fibers of the tapetum are located between lateral margin of the ventricle and the optic radiations.

Tarabine PFS Other name for cytarabine.

Tarceva Other name for erlotinib hydrochloride.

Targeted mutagenesis Deliberate change in the genetic structure directed at a specific site on the chromosome. Used in research to determine the targeted region's function.

Targeted therapy A type of treatment that uses drugs or other substances to identify and attack specific cancer cells without harming normal cells. A monoclonal antibody is a type of targeted therapy.

Tariquidar An anthranilamide derivative with multidrug resistance properties. Tariquidar non-competitively binds to the p-glycoprotein transporter, thereby inhibiting transmembrane transport of anticancer drugs. Inhibition of transmembrane transport may result in increased intracellular concentrations of an anticancer drug, thereby augmenting its cytotoxicity.

Tartar Common term for dental calculus, a hard deposit that adheres to teeth; produces rough surface that attracts plaque.

Taste alteration A temporary change in taste perception.

Taurolidine A substance that is being studied in the treatment of cancer. It belongs to the family of drugs called anti-infectives.

Tavocept Other name for dimesna.

Taxane A drug that inhibits cell growth by stopping cell division. Taxanes are used as treatments for cancer. Also called antimitotic or antimicrotubule agents or mitotic inhibitors. Docetaxel and paclitaxel are taxanes.

Taxol Other name for paclitaxel.

Taxonomy The development of approaches to organize and summarize our knowledge about the variety or organisms that exist.

Taxoprexin Other name for DHA-paclitaxel.

Taxotere Other name for docetaxel.

Tay sachs disease An inherited disease of infancy characterized by profound mental retardation and early death; it is caused by a recessive gene mutation.

Teacher centered education An educational system in which the teacher dictates what is being taught and how it is to be learned. The teacher is the central or key figure and activities such as the formal lecture and the formal laboratory are emphasized. Individual students have little control over what they learn, the order in which they learn and the methods they must use. In this approach, learning is rather more passive than active. It is the opposite of the learner-centered approach.

Technetium Tc 94m sestamibi A radioconjugate consisting of sestamibi labeled with the positron-emitting isotope Tc 94m. Sestamibi is a synthetic molecule of the isonitrile family that diffuses through cell membranes and may preferentially accumulate within mitochondria. Technetium Tc 94m sestamibi may be used in tumor-imaging studies utilizing positron emission tomography (PET).

Technetium Tc 99m dextran A radiolabeled substance that is used in cancer diagnosis.

Technetium Tc 99m sulfur colloid A gamma-emitting colloid used in scintillation scanning of the reticuloendothelial system (RES). After intravenous administration, technetium Tc 99m sulfur colloid is phagocytized by the reticuloendothelial system and concentrated in the liver, spleen, and bone marrow; detection/localization of phagocytized gamma ray-emitting colloid is performed with a gamma-ray scintillation camera. Scintillation scanning using technetium Tc 99m colloid sulfur helps determine the distribution and function of the RES and the extent to which tumor involves the RES. The RES includes cells types that can phagocytize and sequester inert particles and vital dyes; RES cell types include macrophages or macrophage precursors, specialized endothelial cells lining the sinusoids of the liver, spleen, and bone marrow, and reticular cells of lymphatic tissue and of bone marrow.

Technology transfer The process of transferring scientific findings from research laboratories to the commercial sector.

Tectum The part of the midbrain situated above the interventricular foramen consisting of the superior and inferior colliculi.

Tegafur An anticancer drug that belongs to the family of drugs called antimetabolites.

Tegmentum T. Midbrain: The part of the cerebral peduncle of the midbrain located between the basis pedunculi ventrally and the tectum dorsally.

T. Pontine: Small dorsal part of the pons located above the basilar region that forms the floor of the fourth ventricle.

Teicoplanin A glycopeptide antibiotic complex isolated from the bacterium Actinoplanes teichomyceticus. Teicoplanin inhibits peptidoglycan polymerization, resulting in inhibition of bacterial cell wall synthesis and cell death.

Tela choroidae A thin duplicated layer of pia mater with associated blood vessels that invaginates into the ventricles along with a modified ependymal epithelial lining to form the choroid plexuses.

Telangiectasia The permanent enlargement of blood vessels, causing redness in the skin or mucous membranes.

Telcyta A substance that is being studied in the treatment of cancer. It belongs to the family of drugs called glutathione analogs. Also called TLK286.

Telehealth, telemedicine, telehealth, e-health The use of telecommunications (i.e., wire, internet, radio, optical or electromagnetic channels transmitting text, x-ray, images, records, voice, data or video) to facilitate medical diagnosis, patient care, patient education and/or medical learning. Many rural areas are finding uses for telehealth and telemedicine in providing oncology, home health, ER, radiology and psychiatry among others. Telehealth services have been used between providers, to provide supervision of one another and to provide evaluation of patients. Telehealth is likely to serve greater purposes and populations in the future.

Telemedicine The application of communications technologies for the provision of health care services (diagnosis, treatment, prevention of diseases and injuries) over spatial distance in a situation where remoteness and/ or availability of professional expertise is a critical factor.

Telencephalon The rostral subdivision of the forebrain (prosencephalon) which in the adult gives rise to the cerebral cortex, medullary centre, corpus striatum, rhinencephalon, and lateral ventricle.

Telomerase The enzyme that directs the replication of telomeres.

Telomerase 540 548 peptide vaccine A recombinant peptide consisting of the amino acid residues 540 to 548 of the human telomerase reverse transcriptase (hTERT). Telomerase expression has been directly linked to tumor development; its catalytic subunit is expressed in the majority of human cancer cells, but infrequently in normal cells. Vaccination with telomerase:540-548 peptide may stimulate cytotoxic T cells to recognize and kill telomerase-expressing cells.

Telomere The end of a chromosome. This specialized structure is involved in the replication and stability of linear DNA molecules.

Temoporfin An anticancer drug that is also used in cancer prevention. It belongs to the family of drugs called photosensitizing agents.

Temozolomide A triazene analog of dacarbazine with antineoplastic activity. As a cytotoxic alkylating agent, temozolomide is converted at physiologic pH to the short-lived active compound, monomethyl triazeno imidazole carboxamide (MTIC). The cytotoxicity of MTIC is due primarily to methylation of DNA at the O6 and N7 positions of guanine, resulting in inhibition of DNA replication. Unlike dacarbazine, which is metabolized to MITC only in the liver, temozolomide is metabolized to MITC at all sites. Temozolomide is administered orally and penetrates well into the central nervous system.

Temperature A specific degree of heat intensity. There are three temperature designations associated with psychrometrics: 1. Dry Bulb (DB) - The air temperature as measured by a standard thermometer.

2. Wet Bulb (WB) - The air temperature measured by a thermometer with its reservoir bulb wrapped in a moistened cloth wick and exposed to an air stream moving at a velocity of 1,000 feet per minute.

3. Dewpoint temperature (DP) - Also called Saturation Temperature is the temperature at which condensation of moisture begins (air is holding 100% of the moisture it can) when the air is cooled, measured in °F.

Temporal lobe The lower lateral lobe of the cerebral hemisphere, containing the hippocampal formation and the amygdala.

Temporomandibular joint (TMJ) The joint formed by the condyle (head) of the mandible, the mandibular fossa, and the articular tubercle of the temporal bone.

Tempostatin Other name for halofuginone hydrobromide.

Temsirolimus An ester analog of rapamycin. CCI-779 binds to and inhibits the mammalian target of rapamycin (mTOR), resulting in decreased expression of mRNAs necessary for cell cycle progression and arresting cells in the G1 phase of the cell cycle. mTOR is a serine/threonine kinase which plays a role in the PI3K/AKT pathway that is upregulated in some tumors.

Tendocalcaneus (Achille's tendon) The tendon, located at the back of the heel, which connects the triceps surae muscle to the tuberosity of the calcaneus.

Teniposide An anticancer drug that is a podophyllotoxin derivative and belongs to the family of drugs called mitotic inhibitors.

Tentorium cerebelli A tent-like fold of dura mater that extends horizontally accross the transverse cerebral fissure between the occipital lobes of the cerebrum and the cerebellum forming a roof over the posterior-cranial fossa.

Teratocarcinoma A type of cancer that most commonly develops in the testes (testicles).

Teratogenic Causing harm to a fetus by interfering with normal prenatal development. Many drugs, including some anti-HIV drugs, are teratogenic when taken by pregnant women.

Teratogenicity The production of physical defects in offspring in utero.

Teratoma A type of germ cell tumor that may contain several different types of tissue, such as hair, muscle, and bone. Teratomas occur most often in the ovaries in women, the testicles in men, and the tailbone in children. Not all teratomas are malignant.

Terbinafine An antifungal drug used to treat severe ringworm. Trade name: Lamisil.

Terbutaline A bronchodilator drug used in the treatment of asthma. Trade name: Bricanyl.

Terminal disease Disease that cannot be cured and will cause death.

Terminal sterilization This term is a gross misnomer because it refers specifically to the terminal heat sterilization of LVPs usually by steam.

Terminally Ill For an individual, it means that the subject has a life expectancy of six months or less as stated in writing by his or her attending physician and surgeon.

Termination date Date that a group contract expires or an individual is no longer eligible for benefits.

Tertiary care Services provided by highly specialized providers such as neurosurgeons, thoracic surgeons and intensive care units. These services often require highly sophisticated technology and facilities.

Tespa Other name for thiotepa.

Test of significance 1. The evaluation of observed data by calculating a specified test statistic and then deriving the associated p-value.

2. Test statistic.

Test procedure A sequence of activities which when executed successfully provides documentary evidence that part of the system works as specified.

Test treatment The drug, device, or procedure to be evaluated in a particular trial.

Testicle One of two egg-shaped glands found inside the scrotum that produce sperm and male hormones. Also called a testis.

Testicular self examination (TSE) A simple manual self-examination of the testes.

Testimonial Information provided by an individual who claims to have been helped or cured by a particular product. The information provided lacks the necessary elements to be evaluated in a rigorous and scientific manner and is not used in the scientific literature.

Testosterone A hormone necessary for normal male sexual development and functioning and also important in maintaining muscle strength and mass. Testosterone is sometimes used for the treatment of HIV-related wasting syndrome and to increase muscle mass and decrease body fat in people with HIV. Testosterone replacement therapy is also used to raise testosterone levels in people with HIV-related hypogonadism.

Testro AQ Other name for therapeutic testosterone.

Tetanus peptide melanoma vaccine A vaccine consisting of peptides derived from melanoma-associated antigens and a modified T-cell epitope derived from tetanus toxoid. Vaccination with this agent may stimulate a host cytotoxic and helper T-cell response against tumor cells expressing melanoma-associated antigens, resulting in decreased tumor growth.

Tetanus toxoid A solution of formaldehyde-deactivated toxin isolated from the bacterium Clostridium tetani. Tetanus toxoid stimulates the production of antitoxin antibodies. This agent may be used as an adjuvant in cancer vaccines.

Tetanus toxoid helper peptide Obtained by genetic engineering from the bacterial Clostridium tetani toxoid, tetanus toxoid helper peptide QYIKANSKFIGITEL (amino acids 830-844) binds to class II MHC molecules as a nonspecific vaccine helper epitope (adjuvant) and induces an increased (and long term) immune response by increasing the helper T-cell response.

Tetracycline An antibiotic drug used to treat infection.

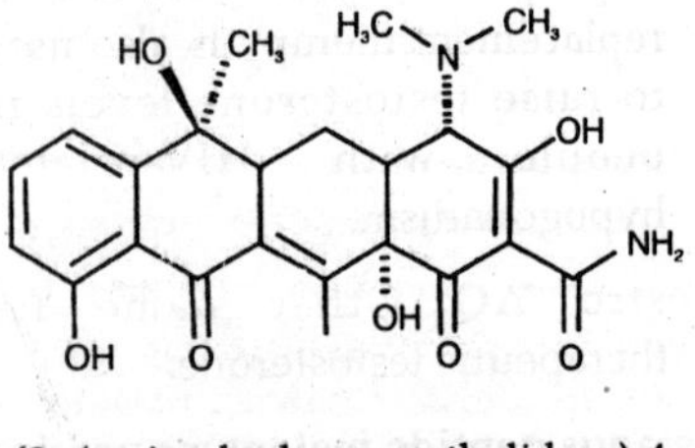

{2- (amino-hydroxy-methylidene)-4-dimethylamino-6,10,11,12a-tetrahydroxy-6-methyl-4,4a,5, 5a-tetrahydrotetracene-1,3,12-trione}

Figure Tetracycline

Tetrahydrouridine A synthetic pyrimidine nucleoside analogue with biomodulating activity. Tetrahydrouridine increases the efficacy of the radiosensitizer cytochlor (5-chloro-2'-deoxycytidine) by inhibiting the enzyme deoxycytidine monophosphate (dCMP) deaminase and preventing the premature deamination of the cytochlor metabolite 5-chloro-2'-deoxy-cytidine monophosphate (Cld-CMP) to 5-chloro-2'-deoxyuridine monophosphate (CldUMP); in turn, this increases tumor concentrations of CldUMP which is then further anabolized and incorporated selectively into tumor DNA as CldU (5-chloro-2'-deoxyuridine).

TG4010 A substance that is being studied as an anticancer drug.

TGFa PE38 immunotoxin A recombinant, chimeric toxin composed of human transforming growth factor alpha (TGF-alpha) fused to a fragment of Pseudomonas exotoxin (PE38) without its cell-binding domain. The TGF-alpha moiety of the agent attaches to tumor cells expressing the epithelial growth factor receptor (EGFR); the exotoxin induces caspase-mediated apop-tosis of tumor cells via a mechanism involving mitoch-ondrial damage; it also catalyzes the transfer of ADP ribose from nicotinamide adenine dinu-cleotide (NAD) to elongation factor-2 in eukaryotic cells, thereby inactivating elongation factor 2 and inhibiting protein synthesis.

TH1/TH2 cells Subsets of T-helper lymphocytes, involved in cell-mediated immune responses. TH1 cells secrete IL-1 and gamma interferon, which enhance cell-mediated responses and inhibit both TH2 subset cell activity and the humoral immune responses. TH2 cells, the other subset of T-helper cells, are also involved in cell-mediated immune responses. TH2 cell activity and secretions are thought to inhibit cell-mediated responses and to enhance the humoral response. TH2 cells secrete IL-4 and IL-10.

Thalamus The largest of the 4 subdivision of the diencephalon bordering the upper lateral wall of the third ventricle dorsal to the hypothalamic sulcus. It is consists of many nuclei with extensive cortical and subcortical connections. It functions as a motor and sensory relay station, and plays a role in arousal, attention, memory, consciousness, and expression of emotion.

Thalassemia An inherited disorder of the gene in the red blood cells which results in the impaired ability to produce hemoglobin.

Thalidomide A drug that belongs to the family of drugs called angiogenesis inhibitors. It prevents the growth of new blood vessels into a solid tumor.

Theophylline A drug used to improve breathing in people who are short of breath. It belongs to the family of drugs called bronchodilators or respiratory smooth muscle relaxants.

Theoretical yield The quantity that would be produced at any appropriate phase of manufacture, processing, or packing of a particular drug product, based upon the quantity of components to be used, in the absence of any loss or error in actual production.

Therapeutic Having to do with treating disease and helping healing take place.

Therapeutic alternatives Drug products that provide the same pharmacological or chemical effect in equivalent doses.

Therapeutic autologous dendritic cells A population of a type of antigen-presenting cell (APC), the dendritic cell (DC), harvested from a patient and grown in vitro in the presence of tumor-associated antigens (TAAs) derived from the patient's tumor (a technique known as 'pulsing') and then injected back into the patient; autologous DCs so manipulated may stimulate a specific cell-mediated antitumoral cytotoxicity. DCs derived from a patient may also be fused with the patient's tumor cells in vitro to combine sustained tumor antigen expression with the antigen-presenting and immunostimulatory capacities of DCs; when injected back into the patient, these autologous DC-tumor cell hybrids (fusion cells) may stimulate an active antitumoral immune response.

Therapeutic drug monitoring (TDM) Measurement of anti-HIV drug levels in an individual's blood. These measurements are then used to make appropriate adjustments to the dosage of the drug. TDM may help improve the drug's effect and reduce side effects by keeping the blood level in a specific target range. TDM is mainly used for drugs in which small changes in drug levels cause large changes in drug effect.

Therapeutic HIV vaccine Any HIV vaccine used for the treatment of an HIV-infected person. Therapeutic HIV vaccines are designed to boost an individual's immune response to HIV infection in order to better control the virus. This therapeutic approach is currently being tested in clinical trials.

Therapeutic index (TI) A measure of a drug's ability to achieve the desired effect in an individual. Many anti-HIV drugs have a narrow TI, meaning that small changes in levels of the drug may produce big effects. Doses of these drugs are sometimes adjusted using therapeutic drug monitoring (TDM).

Therapeutic scleral shell (TSS) A scleral shell whose thickness will restore lid and facial symmetry.

Therapeutic testosterone A synthetic form of the endogenous androgenic steroid testosterone. Due to rapid metabolism by the liver, therapeutic testosterone is generally administered as an ester derivative. This agent and its derivatives promote the maintenance of male sex characteristics.

Therapeutic trial A trial designed to test the safety and efficacy of a particular drug, device, or procedure that is considered to have therapeutic value.

Therapeutic tumor infiltrating lymphocytes A preparation of cells, consisting of autologous tumor infiltrating lymphocytes, that are manipulated in vitro and, upon administration in vivo, re-infiltrate the tumor to initiate tumor cell lysis. In vitro, therapeutic tumor-infiltrating lymphocytes (TILs) are isolated from tumor tissue and cultured with lymphokines such as interleukin-2; the therapeutic TILs are then infused into the patient, where, after re-infiltration of the tumor, they may induce lysis of tumor cells and tumor regression. The use of therapeutic TILs is considered a form of adoptive immunotherapy.

Therapy Any of the measures taken to treat a disease. Alternative therapy is any therapy that has not been scientifically tested and approved. Some alternative therapies are used along with standard therapy. Some are harmless, some may be helpful, and others can be dangerous, especially if they divert a person with cancer from receiving standard therapy. Also called questionable methods or unproven methods. Some people use alternative therapies along with standard therapy; in this approach, the health care team should be informed of the alternative method used. Experimental therapy is any new, as-yet-unproven method that is being tested for specific purposes in a scientific clinical trial. Standard therapy is any method that has been scientifically tested and proven useful for specific purposes, and is the standard treatment.

Thermal ablation A procedure using heat to remove tissue or a part of the body, or destroy its function. For example, to remove the lining of the uterus, a catheter is inserted through the cervix into the uterus, a balloon at the end of the catheter is inflated, and fluid inside the balloon is heated to destroy the lining of the uterus.

Thermography In medicine, a procedure in which a heat-sensing infrared camera is used to record the surface heat produced by different parts of the body. Abnormal tissue growth can cause temperature changes, which may show up on the thermogram. Thermography may be used to diagnose breast cancer and other tumors.

Thermophile An organism that grows best at greater than 50°C (122°F).

Thermophilic (of a microorganism) With optimum temperature for growth above 45°C, many thermophilic bacteria exist at high temperatures (greater than 80°C) and many of their enzymes which posses high thermal stability, are of great commercial interest.

Thiazolidinediones One of several different classes of pills that lower the level of glucose in the blood. Used in Type 2 diabetes. There are several thiazolidinedione pills available. This class of medications is also called "glitazones."

Each type of pill is sold under two names: one is the generic name; the other is the trade name given by the manufacturer. The thiazolidinediones that are presently available are:

Generic Name: Rosiglitazone

Trade Name: Avandia

Generic Name: Pioglitazone

Trade Name: Actos.

Thiofozil Other name for thiotepa.

Thioguanine A synthetic guanosine analogue antimetabolite. Phosphorylated by hypoxanthine-guanine phosphori-bosyl-transferase, thioguanine incor-porates into DNA and RNA, resulting in inhibition of DNA and RNA syntheses and cell death. This agent also inhibits glutamine-5-

phosphoribosylpyrophosphate amidotransferase, thereby inhibiting purine synthesis.

Thiotepa A synthetic alkylating agent. Related to nitrogen mustard, thiotepa alkylates and crosslinks DNA, resulting in the inhibition of DNA replication.

Third party administrator (TPA) An independent organization that provides administrative services including claims processing and underwriting for other entities, such as insurance companies or employers. Often insurance companies will contract as TPAs with other insurance companies or health plans. TPAs are not always insurance companies. TPAs are organizations with expertise and capability to administer all or a portion of the claims process. Self-insured employers will often contract with TPAs to handle their insurance functions. Insurance companies will sometimes outsource the claims, UR or membership functions to a TPA. Sometimes TPAs will only manage provider networks, only claims or only UR. Hospitals or provider organizations desiring to set up their own health plans will often outsource certain responsibilities to TPAs. TPAs are prominent players in the managed care industry.

Third-line therapy Treatment that is given when both initial treatment (first-line therapy) and subsequent treatment (second-line therapy) don't work, or stop working.

Thoracentesis A procedure to remove fluids from the area between the two layers (pleura) covering the lung.

Thoracic Having to do with the chest.

Thoracic duct The largest lymph channel in the body, which begins in the abdomen at the junction of the intestinal, lumbar, and descending intercostal trunks, and ends at the junction of the left subclavian and internal jugular veins.

Thoracic spine The portion of the vertebral column between the neck and thoracic diaphragm.

Thoracoscopy The use of a thin, lighted tube (called an endoscope) to examine the inside of the chest.

Thoracotomy An incision into the chest that may be made when heart or lung surgery is performed.

Throat (throte) The hollow tube inside the neck that starts behind the nose and ends at the top of the trachea (windpipe) and esophagus (the tube that goes to the stomach). The throat is about 5 inches long, depending on body size. Also called the pharynx.

Throat cancer Cancer that forms in tissues of the pharynx (the hollow tube inside the neck that starts behind the nose and ends at the top of the windpipe and esophagus). Throat cancer includes cancer of the nasopharynx (the upper part of the throat behind the nose), the oropharynx (the middle part of the pharynx), and the hypopharynx (the bottom part of the pharynx). Most throat cancers are squamous cell carcinomas (cancer that begins in flat cells lining the pharynx). Also called pharyngeal cancer.

Thrombin (Blood coagulation factor II) An enzyme (the activated thrombogen) formed in the blood, after this is shed, that converts fibrinogen into fibrin for clot formation. It is formed from conjunction of prothrombin and calcium salts. It is also a sterile protein substance prepared from prothrombin of bovine origin through interaction with thromboplastin in the presence of calcium. Bovine thrombin is often used to aid production of serum from "salvage" plasma.

Thrombocyte A type of blood cell that helps prevent bleeding by causing blood clots to form. Also called a platelet.

Thrombocytopenia A decrease in the number of platelets in the blood that may result in easy bruising and excessive bleeding from wounds or bleeding in mucous membranes and other tissues.

Thromboembolism The lesion created by a thromboembolus.

Thromboembolus A clot of material that breaks free from a primary site, is transported in the bloodstream and becomes lodged and adhered at a secondary site.

Thrombohemorrhagic event A process that involves either a blood clot or bleeding, such as a heart attack or stroke.

Thrombophlebitis Inflammation of a vein that occurs when a blood clot forms.

Thrombopoietin A colony-stimulating factor that stimulates the production of blood cells, especially platelets, during chemotherapy. It is a cytokine that belongs to the family of drugs called hematopoietic (blood forming) agents.

Thrombosis The use of drugs such as tPA or streptokinase, called thrombolytic agents, to dissolve (lyse) a clot (thrombus).

Throughput volume The amount of solution passed through an exchange bed before the resin is exhausted.

A pyrimidine component of nucleic acid first isolated from the thymus.

Thrush A condition in which Candida albicans, a type of yeast, grows out of control in moist skin areas of the body. It is usually a result of a weakened immune system, but can be a side effect of chemotherapy or treatment with antibiotics. Thrush usually affects the mouth (oral thrush); however, rarely, it spreads throughout the entire body. Also called Candidiasis or Candidosis.

Thymidine A chemical compound found in DNA. Also used as treatment for mucositis.

Thymidine analogue mutations Mutations in HIV's reverse transcriptase (RT) enzyme that can occur with the use of the NRTIs zidovudine and stavudine. TAMs make HIV resistant to these drugs and may limit a person's treatment options.

Thymidylate synthase inhibitor A drug that blocks DNA synthesis and may prevent tumor cell growth. It is being studied as a treatment for cancer.

Thymine (T) A nitrogenous base, one member of the base pair AT (adenine-thymine).

Thymitaq A substance that is being studied in the treatment of liver cancer. It belongs to the family of drugs called thymidylate synthase inhibitors. Also called AG337 and nolatrexed.

Thymoglobulin Other name for anti-thymocyte globulin.

Thymoma A tumor of the thymus, an organ that is part of the lymphatic system and is located in the chest, behind the breastbone.

Thymus An organ in the chest behind the breastbone. This organ is an essential part of the immune system because it is the site where infection-fighting T cells develop.

Thyrogen A form of thyroid-stimulating hormone (TSH) that is made in the laboratory. It is used to test for remaining or recurring cancer cells in patients who have been treated for thyroid cancer. Also called thyrotropin alfa.

Thyroglobulin The form that thyroid hormone takes when stored in the cells of the thyroid. If the thyroid has been removed, thyroglobulin should not show up on a blood test. Doctors measure thyroglobulin level in blood to detect thyroid cancer cells that remain in the body after treatment.

Thyroid An endocrine gland located in the neck, that makes two hormones (T4 or thyroxine and T3 or triiodothyronine, which are frequently simply called "thyroid hormone") that regulate the body's metabolic rate. Overactivity of the thyroid gland is called hyperthyroidism; underactivity is called hypothyroidism.

Both hyperthyroidism and hypothyroidism may have an autoimmune basis, and both are somewhat more common in people with Type 1 diabetes.

Thyroid cancer Cancer that forms in the thyroid gland (an organ at the base of the throat that makes hormones that help control heart rate, blood pressure, body temperature, and weight). Four main types of thyroid cancer are papillary, follicular, medullary, and anaplastic thyroid cancer. The four types are based on how the cancer cells look under a microscope.

Thyroid cartilage The largest cartilage of the larynx.

Thyroid follicular cell A type of cell in the thyroid. Thyroid follicular cells make thyroid hormone.

Thyroid gland A gland located beneath the voice box (larynx) that produces thyroid hormone. The thyroid helps regulate growth and metabolism.

Thyroid hormone A hormone that affects heart rate, blood pressure, body temperature, and weight. Thyroid hormone is made by the thyroid gland and can also be made in the laboratory.

Thyroid stimulating hormone (TSH) A hormone secreted by the anterior pituitary gland, that controls the production and release of the thyroid hormones (T4 and T3). Measurement of the TSH level in the bloodstream is commonly done as a screening tool for hypothyroidism and hyperthyroidism, and as an assessment of the adequacy of therapy in people who are taking thyroid hormone pills as therapy. Typically, high values of TSH are associated with hypothyroidism, and absence of TSH is associated with hyperthyroidism.

Thyroidectomy Surgery to remove part or all of the thyroid.

Thyrotropin alfa A form of thyroid-stimulating hormone (TSH) that is made in the laboratory. It is used to test for remaining or recurring cancer cells in patients who have been treated for thyroid cancer. Also called Thyrogen.

Tiazofurin An anticancer drug being studied to stop cell growth.

Tibia The large bone is the Tibia. The thin bone of the lower leg.

Tibial tuberosity Point of attachment for the patellar ligament, located distal to the intercondylar eminence.

TID Common abbreviation for "three times a day"

Time of enrollment The time point at which a patient (treatment unit) is regarded as having officially entered the trial and after which is regarded as a part of the study population. Operationally, the time point at which the treatment assignment is revealed to clinic staff, or when treatment is initiated when assignments are known in advance of enrollment.

Time stamp A part of the audit trail that clearly documents the sequence of events in human terms, helping to authenticate an electronic signature and minimizing the chances of signer repudiation. A local time stamp correlates with the whereabouts of the signer. With client-server data systems used by international companies and records accessed from remote sites (such as on business trips), time stamps that reflect the local time of only the user might make the sequence of actions for an individual record appear inconsistent. For example, the approval by a peer reviewer could be signed at 9:00 a.m. on a chromatographic analysis that was performed at 11:00 a.m. in a different time zone. Local time stamps should probably be supplemented consistently with the time stamp of a remote server, with one stamp clearly labeled as local.

Time to event A common manner of evaluating endpoints in clinical trials, time to event not only counts how many participants got a specified event, but how long it took to get it. Time to event allows patients to enroll non-simultaneously, and still derive valid conclusions

Time to progression A measure of time after a disease is diagnosed (or treated) until the disease starts to get worse.

Time window The permissible time interval for performing a specified baseline or follow-up examination.

Tin ethyl etiopurpurin A synthetic purpurin with photosensitizing activity. Tin ethyl etiopurpurin preferentially accumulates in tumor cells due to an increased rate of metabolism. Upon exposure to a light source, this agent absorbs light, forming an extended high energy conformational state that produces high quantum yields of singlet oxygen with local cytotoxic effects.

Tin Sn 117m dtpa A radioactive chemical being studied to treat bone pain associated with cancer.

Tincture of Iodine A germicidal solution of iodine in aqueous alcohol used primarily as antiseptic on skin and tissue.

Tinidazole A drug used to treat protozoal infections, such as amebiasis, giardiasis, and trichomoniasis. It belongs to a family of drugs called antiprotozoal agents. Tinidazole is also being evaluated in the treatment of Helicobacter pylori infections in people with low-grade gastric lymphoma.

Tinnitus Any noise (buzzing, ringing, etc.) in the ear. There are many causes including wax in the ear.

Tioguanine Other name for thioguanine.

Tipifarnib A nonpeptidomimetic quinolinone with potential antineoplastic activity. Tipifarnib binds to and inhibits the enzyme farnesyl protein transferase, an enzyme involved in protein processing (farnesylation) for signal transduction. By inhibiting the farnesylation of proteins, this agent prevents the activation of Ras oncogenes, inhibits cell growth, induces apoptosis, and inhibits angiogenesis.

Tirapazamine A drug that makes tumor cells more sensitive to radiation therapy.

Tirazone Other name for tirapazamine.

Tisseel Other name for fibrin sealant.

Tissue A collection of similar cells, united to perform a particular function. There are four basic types of tissue in the body: epithelial, connective, muscle and nerve.

Tissue culture Growing mammalian cells in the laboratory in a tissue culture medium (in vitro). For example, this allows researchers to determine the effects of various chemicals on mammalian cells without experimenting directly on live animals or man. Since a molecule of some toxic substances can harm a single mammalian cell, even one part-per-billion of some impurities can affect a tissue culture. Therefore, water used to make up tissue culture media should be extremely pure.

Tissue flap reconstruction A type of breast reconstruction in which a flap of tissue is surgically moved from another area of the body to the chest, and formed into a new breast mound.

Tissue plasminogen activator (TPA) A protein that is made by the body and that helps dissolve blood clots. It can also be made in the laboratory and is used in the treatment of heart attack and stroke. It is also being studied in the treatment of cancer. tPA belongs to the family of drugs called systemic thrombolytic agents. Also called recombinant tissue plasminogen activator (r-tPA), Activase, and Alteplase.

Titer A laboratory measurement of the amount of a given compound in solution. For example, an antibody titer is the measurement of the amount of a particular antibody in a sample of blood.

Titration Volumetric analysis by means of the addition of definite amounts of a test solution to a solution of a known amount of the substance analyzed.

TLK286 A modified glutathione analog. TLK286 is selectively activated by glutathione S-Transferase P1-1 into an alkylating metabolite which forms covalent linkages with nucleophillic centers in tumor cell DNA, thereby inducing a cellular stress response and cytotoxicity, and decreasing tumor proliferation. S-transferase P1-1 is an enzyme that is overexpressed in many human malignancies.

TMD (Temperomandibular disorder) Term given to condition characterized by facial pain and restricted ability to open or move the jaw.

TNFerade A gene therapy product that is being studied in combination with radiation therapy in the treatment of cancer.

TNM staging system A system for describing the extent of cancer in a patient's body. T describes the size of the tumor and whether it has invaded nearby tissue, N describes any lymph nodes that are involved, and M describes metastasis (spread of cancer from one body part to another).

TNP 470 A synthetic analog of fumagillin, an antibiotic isolated from the fungus Aspergillus fumigatus fresenius with antineoplastic activity. TNP-470 binds to and irreversibly inactivates methionine animopeptidase-2 (MetAP2), resulting in endothelial cell cycle arrest late in the G1 phase and inhibition of tumor angiogenesis. This agent may also induce the p53 pathway, thereby stimulating the production of cyclin-dependent kinase inhibitor p21 and inhibiting angiogenesis.

TNT (Tumor necrosis therapy) Therapeutic agents that target dead and dying cells found primarily at the core of the tumor.

Tobacco Nicotiana tabacum. A plant with leaves that have high levels of the addictive chemical nicotine. The leaves may be smoked (in cigarettes, cigars, and pipes), applied to the gums (as dipping and chewing tobacco), or inhaled (as snuff). Tobacco leaves also contain many cancer-causing chemicals, and tobacco use and exposure to secondhand tobacco smoke have been linked to many types of cancer and other diseases.

Tocladesine A substance that has been studied as an anticancer drug. It is an analog of a substance that occurs naturally in the body (cyclic adenosine monophosphate).

Toe of weld The junction between the face of a weld and the base material.

Tolbutamide A pill taken to lower the level of glucose (sugar) in the blood. Only some people with noninsulin-dependent diabetes take these pills.

Tolerability Term used to indicate how well a particular medication is tolerated or endured when taken by people at the usual dosage. Good tolerability means that medication side effects don't cause people to stop using the drug.

Tolerance Diminished or absent capacity to make a specific response to an antigen, usually produced as a result of contact with that antigen under nonimmunizing conditions.

Tomogram A blurring technique to create a radiograph of a selected plane (layer or cross-section) of the body. Both the location of the plane, and the thickness of tissue in "focus" are controlled by the type of blurring movements used. Largely supplanted by "computerized tomography" - that produces a similar cross-sectional image using a computer.

Tomography A series of detailed pictures of areas inside the body; the pictures are created by a computer linked to an x-ray machine.

Ton of refrigeration A unit used to indicate the size of a refrigeration unit. One ton of refrigeration effect is equivalent to removing 12,000 Btu/hr of heat, or melting one ton of ice in a 24-hour period.

Tongue cancer Cancer that begins in the tongue. When the cancer begins in the front two-thirds of the tongue, it is considered to be a type of oral cavity cancer; when the cancer begins in the back third of the tongue, it is considered to be a type of oropharyngeal or throat cancer.

Tonic Slow, smooth tension.

Tonic vergence Convergence due to the basic tonicity (tension) of the extraocular muscles, which are responsible, in part, for the distance phoria. Deficient tonic vergence would result in exophoria and excessive tonic vergence results in esophoria.

Tonometry An instrument that measures the pressure within the eye, which is known as intraocular pressure (IOP).

Tonsil One of two small masses of lymphoid tissue on either side of the throat.

Tooth One of the hard, bony appendages which are borne on the jaws, or on other bones in the walls of the mouth or pharynx of most vertebrates, and which usually aid in the prehension and mastication of food. The hard parts of teeth are principally made up of dentine, or ivory, and a very hard substance called enamel. These are variously combined in different animals. Each tooth consist of three parts, a crown, or body, projecting above the gum, one or more fangs imbedded in the jaw, and the neck, or intermediate part. In adult man there are thirty-two teeth, composed largely of dentine, but the crowns are covered with enamel, and the fangs with a layer of bone called cementum. Of the eight teeth on each half of each jaw, the two in front are incisors, then come one canine, cuspid, or dog tooth, two bicuspids, or false molars, and three molars, or grinding teeth. The milk, or temporary, teeth are only twenty in number, there being two incisors, one canine, and two molars on each half of each jaw. The last molars, or wisdom teeth, usually appear long after the others, and occasionally do not appear above the jaw at all.

Tooth bud Early embryonic structure that becomes a tooth.

Tooth whitening A chemical or laser process to lighten the colour of teeth.

Topical A medication applied to the skin, an ointment. Usually a medicament suspended in a carrier such as petrolatum or another oil based carrier. Filtration at elevated temperatures is usually possible.

Topical anesthetic Ointment that produces mild anesthesia when applied to tissue surface.

Topical chemotherapy Treatment with anticancer drugs in a lotion or cream applied to the skin.

Topical product A pharmaceutical product meant to be applied to the skin or soft tissue in the form of liquid, cream, or ointment, and therefore needs not be aseptic. Sterile ophthalmic products throughout are manufactured aseptically.

Topoisomerase inhibitor A substance that blocks topoisomerase enzymes, which are involved in DNA structure and cell growth. Certain topoisomerase inhibitors are used to treat some types of cancer.

Topotecan A semisynthetic derivative of camptothecin, a cytotoxic, quinoline-based alkaloid extracted from the Asian tree Camptotheca acuminata. Topotecan inhibits topoisomerase I activity by stabilizing the cleavable complex between topoisomerase I and DNA, resulting in DNA breaks that inhibit DNA replication and trigger apoptotic cell death. Because ongoing DNA synthesis is necessary for topotecan to exert its cytotoxic effects, it is classified as an S-phase-specific agent.

Torcular herophili Old term for the confluence of the sinuses located at the internal occipital protuberance first described by Herophilus.

Toremifene A nonsteroidal triphenylethylene antiestrogen. Chemically related to tamoxifen, toremifene is a selective estrogen receptor modulator (SERM). This agent binds competitively to estrogen receptors, thereby interfering with estrogen activity. Toremifene also has intrinsic estrogenic properties, which are manifested according to tissue type or species.

Torulopsis glabrata A fungal infection similar to Candida albicans, but less susceptible to many of the treatments used for candida.

Torus Common bony protuberance on the palate or lower jaw.

Torus tubarus The bottom lip of the pharyngeal opening of the auditory (Eustachian) tube.

Tositumomab A monoclonal antibody that is used in the treatment of certain types of non-Hodgkin's lymphoma. When tositumomab and iodine I 131 tositumomab (a form of tositumomab that has been chemically changed by adding radioactive iodine) are given together, the combination is called the Bexxar regimen.

Total adipose tissue (TAT) Adipose (fat) tissue is primarily located under the skin (subcutaneous adipose tissue), but also found around internal organs (visceral adipose tissue). Together, these two types of fat tissue are called total adipose tissue. Lipodystrophy, or changes in body fat, are a potential side effect of some anti-HIV drugs, especially PIs and NRTIs.

Total androgen blockade Therapy used to eliminate male sex hormones (androgens) in the body. This may be done with surgery, hormonal therapy, or a combination.

Total bacteria count An estimation of the total number of bacteria in a sample based usually on Standard Methods procedures for collecting, incubating, and counting colony-forming units (CFU).

Total budget Otherwise known as a "global" budget, a cap on overall health spending.

Total dissolved solids (TDS) The term used to describe inorganic ions in the water. Usually measured by electrical conductance of the water corrected to 25°C, and expressed as ppm (parts per million).

Total estrogen blockade Therapy used to eliminate estrogen in the body. This may be done with surgery, radiation therapy, chemotherapy, or a combination of these procedures.

Total heat (TH) The sum of sensible heat and latent heat.

Total hysterectomy Surgery to remove the entire uterus, including the cervix. Sometimes, not all of the cervix is removed. Also called complete hysterectomy.

Total Ionized solids Concentration of dissolved ions in solution expressed in concentration units of Sodium Chloride (NaCl). It determines the operating life of ion exchange resins and is calculated from measurements of Specific Resistance.

Total laryngectomy An operation to remove all of the larynx (voice box).

Total margin A measure that compares total hospital revenue and expenses for inpatient, outpatient, and non-patient care activities. The total margin is calculated by subtracting total expenses from total revenue and dividing by total revenue.

Total mastectomy Removal of the breast. Also called simple mastectomy.

Total nodal irradiation Radiation therapy to the mantle field, the spleen, the lymph nodes in the upper abdomen, and the lymph nodes in the pelvic area.

Total organic carbon (TOC) A measure of the level of organic impurities in water by their carbon content that determines the operating life of activated carbon beds. This is one of the parameters used to determine the purity of Semiconductor Grade water. Feed water will have TOC measured in ppm (parts per million), and ultrapure water (UPW) will have TOC measured in ppb (parts per billion).

Total pancreatectomy Surgery to remove the entire pancreas. Part of the stomach, part of the small intestine, the common bile duct, gallbladder, spleen, and nearby lymph nodes also are removed.

Total parenteral nutrition (TPN) A form of nutrition that is delivered into a vein. Total parenteral nutrition does not use the digestive system. It may be given to people who are unable to absorb nutrients through the intestinal tract because of vomiting that won't stop, severe diarrhea, or intestinal disease. It may also be given to those undergoing high-dose chemotherapy or radiation and bone marrow transplantation. It is possible to give all of the protein, calories, vitamins and minerals a person needs using total parenteral nutrition. Also known as hyperalimentation or parenteral nutrition.

Total quality management Related to quality management, TQM identifies required system elements to measure, design, and select processes that consistently deliver superior outcomes. These fundamentals make up the basis for TQM.

Total skin electron beam radiation therapy (TSEB therapy) A type of radiation therapy using electrons that is directed at the entire surface of the body. This type of radiation goes into the outer layers of the skin, but does not go deeper into tissues and organs below the skin.

Total solids Total solids in water include both dissolved and suspended solids. Determined by weighing sample before and after evaporation.

Total-body irradiation Radiation therapy to the entire body. It is usually followed by bone marrow or peripheral stem cell transplantation.

Totipotent Having to do with cells that are able to develop into any type of cell found in the body.

Toxemia of pregnancy A condition in pregnant women in which poisons such as the body's own waste products build up and may cause harm to both the mother and baby. The first signs of toxemia are swelling near the eyes and ankles (edema), headache, high blood pressure, and weight gain that the mother might confuse with the normal weight gain of being pregnant. The mother may have both glucose (sugar) and acetone in her urine. The mother should tell the doctor about these signs at once.

Toxic Having to do with poison or something harmful to the body. Toxic substances usually cause unwanted side effects.

Toxic epidermal necrolysis (TEN) A severe form of Stevens-Johnson syndrome involving at least 30% of the total body skin area.

Toxic hepatitis Hepatitis caused by an industrial chemical such as carbon tetrachloride or phosphorus.

Toxicity The extent, quality, or degree of being poisonous or harmful to the body.

Toxicogenomics The study of how genomes respond to environmental stressors or toxicants. Combines genome-wide mRNA expression profiling with protein expression patterns using bioinformatics to understand the role of gene-environment interactions in disease and dysfunction.

Toxicology A science that deals with poisons, their effects, and the problems involved.

Toxin Any poisonous agent, especially a poisonous substance produced by one living organism that is poisonous to other organisms. Toxins are usually very unstable, notably toxic when introduced into the tissues, and typically capable of inducing antibody formation.

Toxoid A nontoxic derivative of a toxin used as an immunogen for the induction of antibodies capable of cross-reacting with the toxin.

Toxoplasmosis An infection caused by the parasite Toxoplasma gondii. The parasite is carried by cats, birds, and other animals, and is also found in soil contaminated by cat feces and in meat, particularly pork. Infection can occur in the lungs, retina of the eye, heart, pancreas, liver, colon, testes, and brain. Toxoplasmosis of the brain is considered an AIDS-defining condition in people with HIV.

TP-38 immunotoxin A substance that combines a protein tha binds to certain tumor cells with a bacterial toxin that kills tumor cells. It is being studied in the treatment of brain tumors.

TPI 287 A synthetic, third generation taxane with potential antineoplastic activity. TPI 287 binds to tubulin and stabilizes microtubules, resulting in inhibition of microtubule assem-bly/disassembly dynamics, cell cycle arrest at the G2/M phase, and apoptosis.

Trabectedin A tetrahydroisoquinoline alkaloid isolated from the marine tunicate Ecteinascidia turbinate. Trabec-tedin, also known as ecteinascidin 743 (ET743), exhibits potent tumor cytotoxicity by prolonging the G2-M phase of the cell cycle. This agent interacts with the transcription-coupled nucleotide excision repair machinery to induce lethal DNA strand breaks.

Trabecular cancer A rare type of cancer that forms on or just beneath the skin and in hair follicles. Trabecular cancer is a type of Merkel cell cancer.

Trace analysis Analyzing constituents present in ppm and ppb concentrations. Trace analysis requires extremely pure reagents, made with ultrapure Type I reagent grade water.

Trace element A chemical found in very small amounts in a given substance. Organisms need certain trace elements to survive.

Traceability A prerequisite for trustworthy records, apart from data security. Traceability is the part of the laboratory data system audit trail that holds the evidence of who did what to a record and when.

Tracer A radioactively labeled nucleic acid component included in a reassociation reaction in amounts too small to influence the progress of reaction.

Trach tube A 2-inch- to 3-inch-long curved metal or plastic tube placed in a surgically created opening (tracheostomy) in the windpipe to keep it open. Also called a tracheostomy tube.

Trachea A cartilaginous and membranous tube beginning at the larynx and extending to the bifurcation, where it branches into the right and left main bronchi.

Tracheoesophageal fistula Caused by improper development of the baby's trachea (windpipe) and esophagus during pregnancy. The esophagus does not connect to the stomach, and there is also an abnormal connection between the esophagus and the trachea. Food cannot pass through to the stomach, and may pass into the trachea and then into the lungs, causing breathing problems.

Tracheoesophageal puncture A small opening made by a surgeon between the esophagus and the trachea. A valve keeps food out of the trachea but lets air into the esophagus for esophageal speech.

Tracheostomy Surgery to create an opening (stoma) into the windpipe. The opening itself may also be called a tracheostomy.

Tracheostomy button A 0.5-inch- to 1.5-inch-long plastic tube placed in a surgically created opening (tracheostomy) in the windpipe to keep it open.

Tracking of disclosures The HIPAA Privacy Rule gives individuals the right to request an accounting of disclosures of protected health information over the previous six years. If an individual authorizes uses or disclosures for research, the disclosures do not need to be tracked, but disclosures must be tracked if the researcher receives an IRB-approved waiver of authorization. The accounting of disclosures generally must include: the date of the disclosure, the name of the entity or person (and address if known) who received the protected health information, a brief description of the information disclosed, and a brief statement of the purpose of the disclosure. The Rule allows for an alternative tracking option is available for research involving 50 or more people.

Tranaglyph Red/green targets used with red/green glasses to develop eye teaming skills.

Transabdominal ultrasound A procedure used to examine the organs in the abdomen. The ultrasound device is pressed firmly against the skin of the abdomen. Sound waves from the device bounce off tissues and create echoes. A computer uses the echoes to make a picture called a sonogram.

Transcendental meditation (TM) A mental technique used to promote relaxation, reduce stress, and improve quality of life.

Transcription One of the steps in the HIV life cycle. Transcription is the process by which the HIV DNA provirus is used as a template to create copies of HIV's RNA genetic material, as well as shorter strands of HIV RNA called messenger RNA (mRNA). HIV mRNA is then used in a process called translation to create HIV proteins and continue the virus's life cycle.

Transcription factor A protein that binds to regulatory regions and helps control gene expression.

Transcriptome The full complement of activated genes, mRNAs, or transcripts in a particular tissue at a particular time.

Transcutaneous The passage of substances through unbroken skin, as in absorption.

Transcutaneous electric nerve stimulation (TENS) A technique in which mild electric currents are applied to some areas of the skin by a small power pack connected to two electrodes.

Transdermal Through the skin.

Transfection The introduction of foreign DNA into a host cell.

Transfer Movement of a patient between hospitals or between units in a given hospital. In managed care, transfers are often suggested by UR entities to move patients to lower cost care facilities.

Transfer RNA (tRNA) A class of RNA having structures with triplet nucleotide sequences that are complementary to the triplet nucleotide coding sequences of mRNA. The role of tRNAs in protein synthesis is to bond with amino acids and transfer them to the ribosomes, where proteins are assembled according to the genetic code carried by mRNA.

Transfer systems Equipment allowing the introduction and removal of material, toxic and/or sterile, with continuous protection to both operator and product.

Transferrin CRM107 A synthetic targeted protein toxin which consists of human transferrin (Tf) conjugated to a diphtheria toxin that contains a point mutation (CRM107). After binding to the transferrin receptor expressed on the tumor cell surface, transferrin-CRM107 is internalized, where the diphtheria toxin moiety exerts its cytotoxic effect intracellularly by inhibiting protein synthesis through ADP-ribosylation of elongation factor.

Transformation The change that a normal cell undergoes as it becomes malignant.

Transfusion The infusion of components of blood or whole blood into the bloodstream. The blood may be donated from another person, or it may have been taken from the person earlier and stored until needed.

Transgenic The alteration of a plant or animal's DNA such that it contains a gene from another organism. There are two types of cells in animal and plants, germ line cells (the sperm and egg in animals, pollen and ovule in plants) and somatic cells (all other cells). Transgenic animals have alterations in their germ line DNA so the alterations are passed on to the offspring. That is done to produce therapeutics, to study disease, and to improve farm animals. Transgenic plants have been created for increased resistance to disease and insects as well as to make biopharmaceuticals.

Transgenic lymphocyte immunization vaccine A vaccine consisting of a preparation of allogeneic lymphocytes that encode a gene for telomerase. In transgenic lymphocyte immunization, the transgenic cells are infused into the patient, where they serve as antigen- presenting cells (APCs) with the dual function of antigen synthesis and presentation. Vaccination produces an immune response targeting cancer cells expressing telomerase.

Transient Short-lived; passing; not permanent.

Transient urinary incontinence Temporary episodes of urinary incontinence that are gone when the cause of the episode is identified and treated.

Transitional cell A cell that varies in shape depending on whether the tissue is being stretched. Transitional cells may be stretched without breaking apart. They line hollow organs such as the bladder.

Transitional cell carcinoma A type of cancer that develops in the lining of the bladder, ureter, or renal pelvis (the part of the kidney that collects, holds, and drains urine).

Translation The step in the HIV life cycle that follows transcription. Translation is the process by which the genetic information contained in HIV mRNA is used to build HIV proteins using the host cell's protein-making machinery. Once these HIV proteins are produced, they can combine with copies of HIV's RNA genetic material to form new, complete copies of HIV.

Translocation A mutation in which a large segment of one chromosome breaks off and attaches to another chromosome.

TransMID Other name for transferrin-CRM107.

Transperineal biopsy A procedure in which a sample of tissue is removed from the prostate for examination under a microscope. The sample is removed with a thin needle that is inserted through the skin between the scrotum and rectum and into the prostate.

Transplacental Across or through the placenta. Usually refers to the exchange of nutrients, waste products, and other materials (for example, drugs or infectious organisms) between the mother and the fetus.

Transplant Placing a natural tooth in the empty socket of another tooth.

Transplant surgeon A doctor who specializes in transplantation surgery. The surgeon replaces a patient's organ with an organ from another person.

Transplantation The replacement of tissue with tissue from the person's own body or from another person.

Transposable element A class of DNA sequences that can move from one chromosomal site to another.

Transrectal biopsy A procedure in which a sample of tissue is removed from the prostate using a thin needle that is inserted through the rectum and into the prostate. Transrectal ultrasound (TRUS) is usually used to guide the needle. The sample is examined under a microscope to see if it contains cancer.

Transrectal ultrasound (TRUS) A procedure in which a probe that sends out high-energy sound waves is inserted into the rectum. The sound waves are bounced off internal tissues or organs and make echoes. The echoes form a picture of body tissue called a sonogram. TRUS is used to look for abnormalities in the rectum and nearby structures, including the prostate. Also called endorectal ultrasound.

Transurethral needle ablation A procedure that is used to treat benign prostatic hypertrophy (BPH). A small probe that gives off low-level radiofrequency energy is inserted through the urethra into the prostate. The energy from the probe heats and destroys the abnormal prostate tissue without damaging the urethra. Also called transurethral radiofrequency ablation.

Transurethral radiofrequency ablation A procedure that is used to treat benign prostatic hypertrophy (BPH). A small probe that gives off low-level radiofrequency energy is inserted through the urethra into the prostate. The energy from the probe heats and destroys the abnormal prostate tissue without damaging the urethra. Also called transurethral needle ablation.

Transurethral resection Surgery performed with a special instrument inserted through the urethra. Also called TUR.

Transurethral resection of the prostate (TURP) A surgical procedure to remove tissue from the prostate using an instrument inserted through the urethra.

Transvaginal sonography (TVS) A procedure used to examine the vagina, uterus, fallopian tubes, ovaries, and bladder. An instrument is inserted into the vagina that causes sound waves to bounce off organs inside the pelvis. These sound waves create echoes that are sent to a computer, which creates a picture called a sonogram. Also called transvaginal ultrasound.

Transvenous Passed into the heart through a vein.

Transverse Made at right angles to the long axis of the body.

Transverse colon The part of the intestine that lies horizontally in the abdomen, running straight across the abdomen from right to left.

Transverse process The lateral process of the vertebrae, which stems from the junction between the lamina and the pedicle.

Transverse rectus abdominal muscle flap Often called a TRAM flap, this is a type of breast reconstruction.

Transversus abdominus muscle Muscle responsible for the compression of the abdominal viscera. It originates at the cartilages of the six lower ribs, thoracolumbar fascia, iliac crest, and inguinal ligament, and inserts into the linea alba and conjoined tendon to pubis.

Trapezium One of the carpal bones of the wrist.

Trapezoid body The name given to secondary auditory fibers in the rostral medulla (specifically the ventral acoustic stria) as they cross the midline through parts of the medial lemniscus.

Trapezoid One of the carpal bones of the wrist.

Trastuzumab A recombinant humanized monoclonal antibody directed against the human epidermal growth factor receptor 2 (HER2). After binding to HER2 on the tumor cell surface, trastuzumab induces an antibody-dependent cell-mediated cytotoxicity against tumor cells that overexpress HER2. HER2 is overexpressed by many adenocarcinomas, particularly breast adenocarcinomas.

Trauma A wound, hurt, or injury to the body. Trauma can also be mental such as when a person feels great stress.

Traumeel S Diluted extracts isolated from plants and minerals, including belladonna, arnica, St. Johns wort, and Echinacea. As a homeopathic mouth rinse preparation, Traumeel S exhibits antiinflammatory activity; the mechanism of action has not been fully elucidated. This agent may reduce the severity and duration of treatment-related stomatitis.

Treatment 1. The act of treating, as in caring for a patient.

2. The specific regimen, method, or procedure being tested in a clinical trial.

Treatment allocation 1. The process of assigning patients to treatment.

2. The treatment assignment of a particular patient.

Treatment allocation design The plan for assigning patients to treatment.

Treatment arm Term sometimes used in place of study treatment, or study group, especially in AIDS and cancer trials.

Treatment assignment probability The probability associated with a specified treatment assignment. The value is fixed over the course of patient enrollment in trials with fixed allocation designs. It changes in trials using adaptive allocation designs.

Treatment assignment The treatment to be administered to a patient, but may also mean treatment assigned to some other larger unit such as all members of a family or members of a hospital ward) as indicated in the treatment allocation schedule.

Treatment block A block consisting of a prespecified number of patients, all enrolled in reasonably close proximity to one another and assigned to the various study treatments in such a way so as to satisfy a preset allocation ratio.

Treatment block size The number of allocations required for a specified treatment block. For example, a random allocation schedule for a trial involving two treatments constructed using blocks of size 8 and an allocation ratio of 1:1, would require constraints on the assignment process such that the specified allocation ratio is satisfied after every eighth assignment.

Treatment comparison Any comparison involving two or more of the study treatment groups for a designated outcome or follow-up variable.

Treatment compliance The degree to which a patient follows his assigned treatment regimen.

Treatment crossover Any change of treatment for a patient in a clinical trial involving a switch of study treatments. The switch may be planned, as in a crossover trial, or may be unplanned, as in the case of a noncrossover trial in which a patient assigned to one treatment is exposed to one of the other study treatments sometime during the trial. Unplanned crossovers are called "drop out" and "drop in."

Treatment difference 1. A difference observed between the test- and control-treated groups of patients for some specified outcome measure.

2. Any specified or observed difference for a designated outcome or follow-up variable involving two or more treatment groups in the trial.

Treatment effect 1. An effect attributed to the test treatment. Usually in clinical trials inferred from a comparison of the test- and control-treated groups of patients using observed results for a specified outcome measure.

2. The effect produced or assumed to be produced by a treatment in an individual patient. Can be assessed by measurements made before and after administration of the treatment in that individual, but most reliably assessed by evaluating treatment and control group responses.

Treatment episode The period of treatment between admission and discharge from a modality, e.g., inpatient, residential, partial hospitalization, and outpatient, or the period of time between the first procedure and last procedure on an outpatient basis for a given diagnosis.

Treatment experienced A term used to describe HIV-infected individuals who are currently being treated with anti-HIV drugs or who have taken anti-HIV drugs in the past.

Treatment failure A broad term describing failure of an anti-HIV treatment to adequately control HIV infection. The three types of HIV treatment failure are virologic, immunologic, and clinical failure. Factors contributing to treatment failure include poor adherence, drug resistance, and drug toxicity.

Treatment field In radiation therapy, the place on the body where the radiation beam is aimed.

Treatment group The group of patients assigned to receive a specified treatment.

Treatment IND See Treatment Investigational New Drug.

Treatment interaction A situation in which the effect exerted by a treatment is influenced by the level, or presence or absence, of some other factor or condition not related to treatment (e.g., one would say there is a treatment-sex interaction if the test-control treatment difference is in one direction for males and in the other direction, or is of a different order of magnitude, for females).

Treatment investigational new drug An Investigational New Drug that makes a promising new drug available to desperately ill patients as early in the drug development process as available.

Treatment lag The time required, or presumed to be required, for a treatment to exert its full effect.

Treatment naive A term used to describe HIV-infected individuals who have never taken anti-HIV drugs.

Treatment protocol A document that describes the treatment procedures used in a clinical trial.

Treatment side effect A by-product of treatment, either expected or unexpected, desired or undesired.

Treatment trial A trial in which the test treatment consists of a procedure used for treatment of a specific disease or health condition. Therapeutic trial.

Trench mouth Gum disease characterized by severe mouth sores and loss of tissue.

Trending Methods of estimating future costs of health services by reviewing past trends in cost and utilization of these services.

Treosulfan A substance that is being studied in the treatment of cancer. It belongs to the family of drugs called alkylating agents.

Trephine A surgical tool used to cut out circular pieces of bone or other tissue.

Tretinoin A naturally-occurring acid of retinol. Tretinoin binds to and activates retinoic acid receptors (RARs), thereby inducing changes in gene expression that lead to cell differentiation, decreased cell proliferation, and inhibition of tumorigenesis. This agent also inhibits telomerase, resulting in telomere shortening and eventual apoptosis of some tumor cell types. The oral form of tretinoin has teratogenic and embryotoxic properties.

Tretinoin liposome An intravenous formulation of tretinoin (vitamin A acid or all-trans retinoic acid) encased in liposomes. Tretinoin is a naturally occurring retinoic acid agent that binds to and activates retinoic acid receptors (RAR), effecting changes in gene expression that lead to cell differentiation, decreased cell proliferation, and inhibition of carcinogenesis. This agent also inhibits telomerase, leading to telomere shortening and eventual apoptosis of certain tumor cell types. Liposome encapsulation extends the half-life of intravenously administered tretinoin.

Triacetyluridine A synthetic uridine pro-drug that is converted to uridine in vivo. Uridine, a pyrimidine nucleotide, has been used in a variety of diseases including depressive disorders and inherited myopathies.

Triage Triage is the act of categorizing patients according to acuity and by determining that need services first. Most commonly occurs in emergency rooms, but, can occur in any healthcare setting. Classification of ill or injured persons by severity of condition. Designed to maximize and create the most efficient use of scarce resources of medical personnel and facilities. Managed care organizations, health plans and provider systems are setting up programs or clinics called "triage centers". These centers serve as an extension of the utilization review process, as diversions from emergency room care or as case management resources. These triage centers also serve to steer patients away from more costly care (for example, a child with a cold is steered away from an emergency room). Triage can also be handled on the telephone and be called a pre-authorization center, crisis center, call center or information line.

Triamcinolone A substance that is being studied for the prevention of nonmelanoma skin cancer. It is an anti-inflammatory drug that is applied to the skin to relieve irritation, rashes, and infections. It belongs to the family of drugs called topical corticosteroids.

Triangulation A method of assessment that is required when validity cannot be achieved with the use of a single assessment tool. If multiple testing methods are used to evaluate a single competence, one can be more certain that the competency has been appropriately assessed.

Triapine A substance that is being studied in the treatment of cancer. It belongs to the family of drugs called ribonucleotide reductase inhibitors. Also called 3-aminopyridine-2-carboxaldehyde thiosemicarbazone and 3-AP.

Tributyrin A triglyceride drug that may inhibit cell growth and induce cell differentiation. Differentiating agents may be effective in changing cancer cells back into normal cells.

Trichiasis An inward turning of the eyelashes.

Trichophyton Genus of fungi, parasitic to man, that frequently infects the skin, nails, and hair and cause ringworm.

Trichothiodystrophy A hereditary condition characterized by sparse and brittle hair, short stature, and mental retardation.

Trientine a copper chelator sometimes used in the treatment of Wilson's Disease.

Trifolium pratense A plant whose flowers have been used in some cultures to treat certain medical problems. It is being studied in the relief of menopausal symptoms and may have anticancer effects. Also called red clover, purple clover, and wild clover.

Trigeminal nerve The 5th and largest cranial nerve having three divisions (ophthalmic, maxillary and mandibular) and an asociated sensory ganglion (called the semilunar, gasserian or trigeminal ganglion). The sensory and motor roots of the nerve emerge from the lateral surface of the ventral pons and . The nerve is associated with nuclei located in the pons, midbrain, and medulla. It is the main sensory nerve of the head and innervates the muscles of matication.

Trigger Something that either sets off a disease in people who are genetically predisposed to developing the disease, or that causes a certain symptom to occur in a person who has a disease. For example, sunlight can trigger rashes in people with lupus.

Triglycerides Fat-like substances that help transfer energy from food into cells. Triglyceride levels that are too high increase the risk of heart disease and have been associated with diabetes and pancreatitis. Elevated triglyceride levels are a potential side effect of some PIs.

Trigone The triangular area between the temporal and occipital horns at the junction with the body of the lateral ventricle.

Trihalomethanes Compounds present in the feed water that are formed by the reaction of Chlorine and the organic material in the water. Activated carbon and degasification can reduce THMs.

Triiodothyronine A thyroid hormone. Also called liothyronine sodium or T-3.

Trimethoprim sulfamethoxazole A synthetic combination of two antibacterial agents, trimethoprim and sulfamethoxazole. This synergistic combination, also known as co-trimoxazole, inhibits two sequential steps in the bacterial metabolism of folic acid. Trimethoprim is a pyrimidine inhibitor of dihydrofolate reductase; sulfamethoxazole is a sulfamide inhibitor of bacterial dihydrofolate synthetase.

Trimetrexate A drug used for "salvage" therapy of pneumocystis carinii pneumonia, when other treatments have failed. Trimetrexate is enormously toxic unless administered with leucovorin, which "rescues" human cells from it's effects.

Trimetrexate glucuronate A lipid soluble methotrexate derivative with potential antineoplastic activity. Trimetrexate glucuronate inhibits the enzyme dihydrofolate reductase, thereby preventing the synthesis of purine nucleotides and thymidylate, with subsequent inhibition of DNA and RNA synthesis. Trimetrexate glucuronate also exhibits antiviral activity.

Triple blinded Sometimes used in a jocular fashion to characterize a situation in which neither the patient, physician, nor statistician knows how the trial is designed or operated.

Triple blinded clinical trial A double-blinded clinical trial in which data analyses done for treatment monitoring are presented to the individual or group responsible for such monitoring in a way that conceals the identity of the treatment groups.

Triptorelin A synthetic decapeptide agonist analog of luteinizing hormone releasing hormone (LHRH). Possessing greater potency than endogenous LHRH, triptorelin reversibly represses gonadotropin secretion. After chronic, continuous administration, this agent effects sustained decreases in LH and FSH production and testicular and ovarian steroidogenesis. Serum testosterone concentrations may fall to levels typically observed in surgically castrated men.

Triquetrum One of the carpal bones of the wrist.

Trisenox Other name for arsenic trioxide.

Trisomy Possessing three copies of a particular chromosome instead of the normal two copies.

Troglitazone A drug formerly used as a treatment for Type 2 (noninsulin-dependent) diabetes; belongs to a class of drugs called thiazolidinediones. Withdrawn from the market in March, 2000 because of rare liver problems.

Trophy (suffix) Nourish, e.g. dystrophy - defective or faulty nutrition.

Tropisetron An indole derivative with antiemetic activity. As a selective serotonin receptor antagonist, tropisetron competitively blocks the action of serotonin at 5HT3 receptors, resulting in suppression of chemotherapy-and radiotherapy-induced nausea and vomiting.

Troxacitabine A drug being studied for use as an anticancer agent.

True vocal cord The mucous membrane surrounding the vocalis muscle in the larynx, forming the inferior ventricular boundary. Air moving over this fold produces the vibrations of speech.

Tryptase Enzyme released in acute allergic reactions and during anaphylaxis, which can be measured on a blood test to confirm that an allergic reaction has definitely occurred.

TTI-237 A substance that is being studied in the treatment of cancer. It belongs to the family of drugs called mitotic inhibitors. Also called antimitotic or antimicrotubule agents.

Tubal ligation An operation to tie the fallopian tubes closed. This procedure prevents pregnancy by blocking the passage of eggs from the ovaries to the uterus.

Tube size Tube is sized by its nominal outside diameter. For bioprocessing equipment, tube does not include pipe.

Tubefeeding A type of enteral nutrition (nutrition that is delivered into the digestive system in a liquid form). For tubefeeding, a small tube may be placed through the nose into the stomach or the small intestine. Sometimes it is surgically placed into the stomach or the intestinal tract through an opening made on the outside of the abdomen, depending on how long it will be used. People who are unable to meet their needs with food and beverages alone, and who do not have vomiting or uncontrollable diarrhea may be given tubefeedings. Tubefeeding can be used to add to what a person is able to eat or can be the only source of nutrition.

Tuber cinereum A midline swelling on the ventral surface of the hypothalamus between the optic chiasma and the mammillary bodies. It tapers to form the median eminence from which the infundibular stem or stalk of the neurohypophysis takes oigin. The tuberal and arcuate nuclei are located in this region of the hypothalamus.

Tubercle Swelling on the dorsal surface of the rostral thalamus produced by the underlying anterior nuclear group. This complex serves as a relay nuclei of the limbic system receiving afferents from the mammillary nuclei (via the mammillothalamic tract) and projecting to the cingulate gyrus, mammillary nuclei and habenula. This complex plays a role in memory, learning, attention, and emotional behavior.

Tubercle of rib A small eminence on the posterior side, where the head and body of a rib join.

Tuberculin skin test A test performed by injecting purified protein derivative (PPD) extract under the skin. A person who receives this test must return to his or her health care provider after 48 to 72 hours so that the skin's reaction can be evaluated. A hard red bump or a swollen area at the injection site indicates that the person has been exposed to the bacterium that causes tuberculosis (TB). Additional tests are required to determine if the person has active TB infection.

Tuberculosis (TB) An infection caused by the bacterium Mycobacterium tuberculosis. TB bacteria are spread through the air when a person with active TB coughs, sneezes, or speaks. Breathing in the bacteria can lead to infection in the air sacs of the lungs. Symptoms of TB in the lungs include cough, tiredness, weight loss, fever, and night sweats. Although the disease usually occurs in the lungs, it may also affect the larynx, lymph nodes, brain, kidneys, or bones. A person with both TB and HIV is more likely to develop tubuerculosis disease than a person infected only with the TB bacterium, and TB is considered an AIDS-defining condition in people with HIV.

Tuberous sclerosis A genetic disorder in which benign (noncancerous) tumors form in the kidneys, brain, eyes, heart, lungs, and skin. This disease can cause seizures, mental disabilities, and different types of skin lesions.

Tubulovillous adenoma A type of polyp that grows in the colon and other places in the gastrointestinal tract and sometimes in other parts of the body. These adenomas may become malignant (cancerous).

Tumor An abnormal growth of cells. Also defined as a circumscribed growth, not inflammatory in character, arising from preexisting tissue, but independent of the normal rate or laws of growth of such tissue, and subserving no physiological function.

Tumor antigen vaccine A vaccine made of cancer cells, parts of cancer cells, or pure tumor antigens (substances isolated from tumor cells). A tumor antigen vaccine may stimulate the body's immune system to find and kill cancer cells.

Tumor board review A treatment planning approach in which a number of doctors who are experts in different specialties (disciplines) review and discuss the medical condition and treatment options of a patient. In cancer treatment, a tumor board review may include that of a medical oncologist (who provides cancer treatment with drugs), a surgical oncologist (who provides cancer treatment with surgery), and a radiation oncologist (who provides cancer treatment with radiation). Also called a multidisciplinary opinion.

Tumor burden Refers to the number of cancer cells, the size of a tumor, or the amount of cancer in the body. Also called tumor load.

Tumor debulking Surgically removing as much of the tumor as possible.

Tumor infiltrating lymphocyte A white blood cell that has left the bloodstream and migrated into a tumor.

Tumor initiation A process in which normal cells are changed so that they are able to form tumors. Substances that cause cancer can be tumor initiators.

Tumor load Refers to the number of cancer cells, the size of a tumor, or the amount of cancer in the body. Also called tumor burden.

Tumor marker A substance sometimes found in the blood, other body fluids, or tissues. A high level of tumor marker may mean that a certain type of cancer is in the body. Examples of tumor markers include CA 125 (ovarian cancer), CA 15-3 (breast cancer), CEA (ovarian, lung, breast, pancreas, and gastrointestinal tract cancers), and PSA (prostate cancer). Also called biomarker.

Tumor model Cells, tissues, or animals used to study the development and progression of cancer, and to test new treatments before they are given to humans. Animals with transplanted human tumors or other tissues are called xenograft models.

Tumor necrosis factor (TNF) A type of biological response modifier (a substance that can improve the body's natural response to disease). Three types of tumor necrosis factor have been identified: alpha, beta, and gamma. Tumor necrosis factor seems to play a role in the breakdown of cancer cells.

Tumor pathogenesis Morphological and physiological changes associated with tumor growth.

Tumor promotion A process in which existing tumors are stimulated to grow. Tumor promoters are not able to cause tumors to form.

Tumor suppressor gene A type of gene (unit of heredity passed from parent to offspring) that helps control cell growth. Blocking the action of tumor suppressor genes may lead to cancer.

Tumor vasculature-targeted tumor necrosis factor alpha A substance that is being studied in the treatment of cancer. It is made by linking tumor necrosis factor (TNF) to a peptide. The peptide binds to tumor blood vessels and TNF damages them. It belongs to the family of drugs called biological response modifiers. Also called NGR-TNF.

Tumor-derived Taken from an individual's own tumor tissue; may be used in the development of a vaccine that enhances the body's ability to build an immune response to the tumor.

Tumor-specific antigen A protein or other molecule that is unique to cancer cells or is much more abundant in them. These molecules are usually found in the plasma (outer) membrane, and they are thought to be potential targets for immunotherapy or other types of anticancer treatment.

Tunnel vision A constriction of the visual field that is commonly caused by chronic glaucoma, retinal degeneration, a tumor, or a brain disorder that interferes with the fibers that connect the optic nerve to the brain.

TUR Surgery Surgery performed with a special instrument inserted through the urethra. Also called transurethral resection.

Turbidity A suspension of fine particles that obscures light rays but requires many days for sedimentation because of small particle size.

Turbinate Delicate inner lining of the nasal passage that swells with nasal allergy and blocks nose.

Turkish rhubarb Rheum palmatum or Rheum officinale. The root of this plant has been used in some cultures to treat certain medical problems. It may have anti-inflammatory and anticancer effects. Also called rhubarb, da-huang, Chinese rhubarb, and Indian rhubarb.

Turnover package (TOP) A collection of pertinent design, construction, vendor, and operational documentation. This collection of documentation is used for the qualification and process validation activity, as well as reference and single source information for the life of any particular system, process, or piece of equipment.

Turtle lid syndrome Complete loss of adipose tissue causing the thin upper eyelid to conform closely to the anterior contour of the prosthesis and bony orbital wall.

Twenty four hour urine The total amount of a person's urine for a 24-hour period.

Two bed deionizer Separate beds or layers of cation and anion exchange resins. Results in lower purity than mixed-bed deionization, but provides higher capacity in terms of throughput.

Two step procedure A method in which breast biopsy for diagnosis and breast surgery for treatment (such as lumpectomy or mastectomy, if the diagnosis is indeed breast cancer) are performed as two separate procedures, after an interval of days or weeks. This method is strongly preferred by women and their health care team because it allows time to consider all options.

Two tailed test (statistics) A statistical test of significance based on the null value of no difference versus the set of all alternative values (i.e., those that lie to the right and left of the null value).

Tx Common abbreviation for "treatment".

Tympanites Swelling of the abdomen caused by gas in the intestines or peritoneal cavity. Also called meteorism.

Type 1 diabetes mellitus Type 1 diabetes has been subdivided into:

Immune-mediated diabetes (Type 1A). This form of diabetes results from a cellular-mediated autoimmune destruction of the beta cells of the pancreas. Markers of the immune destruction of the beta cell include islet cell autoantibodies and other antibodies. One and usually more of these autoantibodies are present in 85 - 90% of individuals when fasting hyperglycemia is initially detected. Also, the disease has strong HLA associations.

Idiopathic diabetes (Type 1B). Some forms of Type 1 diabetes have no known etiologies. Some of these patients have permanent insulin deficiency and are prone to ketoacidosis but have no evidence of autoimmunity. Although only a minority of patients with Type 1 diabetes fall into this category, of those who do, most are of African, Hispanic, or Asian origin. Individuals with this form of diabetes suffer from episodic ketoacidosis and exhibit varying degrees of insulin deficiency between episodes. This form of diabetes is strongly inherited, lacks immunological evidence for beta cell autoimmunity, and is not HLA associated. An absolute requirement for insulin replacement therapy in affected patients may come and go.

Type 1 diabetes used to be known as insulin-dependent diabetes mellitus, juvenile diabetes, juvenile-onset diabetes, and ketosis-prone diabetes.

Type 2 diabetes mellitus The most common form of diabetes mellitus; over 90 percent of people who have diabetes have Type 2 diabetes. The onset is usually in middle age and in most cases is thought to be due to some form of insensitivity to the action of insulin rather than to insulin deficiency. Many of the people who have this type of diabetes are overweight. Initial treatment is by weight reduction and excercise with the later addition of an increasing range of blood glucose lowering drugs. Ultimately it may be neccessary to give insulin. Increasingly, geneticists are defining specific subgroups such as Maturity Onset Diabetes in the

Young; but to date, this has not led to any change in treatment plans.

Type 2 diabetes used to be called noninsulin-dependent diabetes mellitus, adult-onset diabetes, maturity-onset diabetes, ketosis-resistant diabetes, and stable diabetes.

Type I error (alpha error) Deciding to reject the null hypothesis when the null hypothesis is in fact true. The investigator determines that there is something going on when in fact there is not.

Type II error (beta error) Failing to reject the null hypothesis when the alternative hypothesis is in fact true. The investigator determines that there is nothing going on when in fact there is.

Tyrosinase peptide One of a number of recombinant peptides consisting of amino acid residues of the enzyme tyrosinase, a protein frequently expressed by melanoma cells. Vaccination with tyrosinase peptide may stimulate cytotoxic T lymphocyte response against tyrosinase-expressing tumor cells, resulting in decreased tumor growth.

Tyrosinase-related protein 2 A recombinant therapeutic agent which is chemically identical to or similar to an endogenous non-mutated melanocyte differentiation antigen expressed by both normal and malignant melanocytes. Vaccinations with recombinant tyrosinase-related protein-2 may elicit an antitumoral cytotoxic T-cell response against tumor cells and some normal cells that express tyrosinase-related protein-2.

Tyrosine (TYR) A Phenolic alpha amino acid; a precursor of the hormones epinephrine, norepinephrine, thyroxine, and triiodothyronine, and of the black pigment melanin.

Tyrosine kinase inhibitor A drug that interferes with cell communication and growth and may prevent tumor growth. Some tyrosine kinase inhibitors are used to treat cancer.

TZT-1027 A substance that is being studied as a treatment for cancer. It belongs to the family of drugs called tubulin inhibitors. Also called soblidotin.

U

Ubiquinone A substance found in most tissues in the body, and in many foods. It can also be made in the laboratory. It is used by the body to produce energy for cells, and as an antioxidant. It is being studied in the treatment of cancer and in the relief of side effects caused by some cancer treatments. Also called coenzyme Q10, Q10, CoQ10, and vitamin Q10.

Ubiquitous Present everywhere: common and prevalent

UCN 01 A synthetic derivative of staurosporine with antineoplastic activity. 7-hydroxystaurosporine inhibits many phosphokinases, including the serine/threonine kinase AKT, calcium-dependent protein kinase C, and cyclin-dependent kinases. This agent arrests tumor cells in the G1/S of the cell cycle and prevents nucleotide excision repair by inhibiting the G2 checkpoint kinase chk1, resulting in apoptosis.

UGT1A1 A substance that is being studied as a treatment for cancer. It is an enzyme produced by the liver and intestine.

Ulcer A break in the skin; a deep sore. People with diabetes may get ulcers from minor scrapes on the feet or legs, from cuts that heal slowly, or from the rubbing of shoes that do not fit well. Ulcers can become infected.

Ulceration The formation of a break on the skin or on the surface of an organ. An ulcer forms when the surface cells die and are cast off. Ulcers may be associated with cancer and other diseases.

Ulcerative colitis Chronic inflammation of the colon that produces ulcers in its lining. This condition is marked by abdominal pain, cramps, and loose discharges of pus, blood, and mucus from the bowel.

Ulmus rubra Ulmus fulva. The inner bark of this plant has been used in some cultures to treat certain medical problems. It may have antioxidant effects. Also called slippery elm, gray elm, Indian elm, red elm, and sweet elm.

Ulna One of the two bones of the forearm, it has a large articulation with the distal humerus and protudes posteriorly as the olecranon process.

Ultra low penetration air filters (ULPA) Extended media dry filters in a rigid frame that have a minimum particle-collection efficiency of 99.999% for particles greater than or equal to 0.12µm in size. Most commonly used in microelectronics, few uses in pharmaceuticals.

Ultracentrifugation The separation of macromolecules on the basis of their density and shape using the gravitational field generated in a high-speed centrifuge. It is used in rDNA work for the separation of RNA and DNA, and for purification of plasmids.

Ultrafiltration Molecular sieves; membranes with pores small enough to remove large molecules. Rated in terms of nominal molecular weight cutoff. A 10,000 Dalton (molecular weight) UF membrane, for example, will remove bacterial pyrogens that are typically in the range of 20,000 Daltons.

Ultrafine particle Particle with an equivalent diameter less than 0.1µm.

Ultralente insulin A type of insulin that is long acting.

Ultrapure water Water with a specific resistance higher than 1 megohm-cm. In the laboratory, it usually refers to Type I reagent grade water. Anything in laboratory water that is not H_2O is an impurity. Although chemically pure water is not attainable, ultrapure water systems are now capable of reducing impurities down to the limits of detection.

Ultrasonogram A computer picture of areas inside the body created by bouncing high-energy sound waves (ultrasound) off internal tissues or organs. Also called a sonogram.

Ultrasonography An imaging method in which high-frequency sound waves are used to outline a part of the body. High-frequency sound waves are transmitted through the area of the body being studied. The soundwave echoes are picked up and displayed on a television screen. This painless method is used mainly to find out if a structure is solid or liquid. It is useful in detecting breasts cysts in young women with firm, fibrous breasts. No radiation exposure occurs.

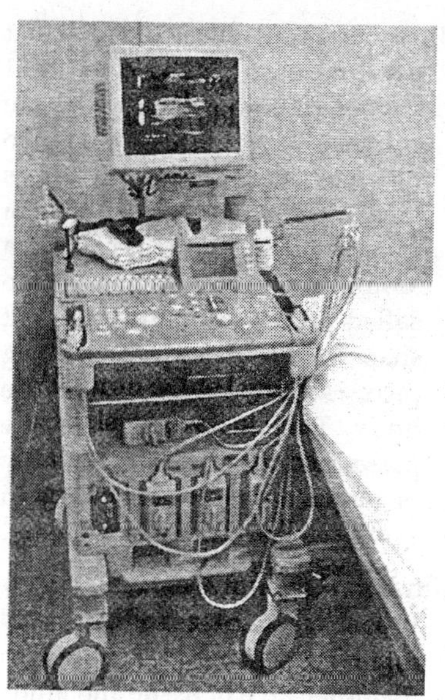

Figure Medical Sonographic Scanner

Ultrasound A procedure in which high-energy sound waves

(ultrasound) are bounced off internal tissues or organs and make echoes. The echo patterns are shown on the screen of an ultrasound machine, forming a picture of body tissues called a sonogram. Also called ultrasonography.

Ultrasound energy A form of therapy being studied as an anticancer treatment. Intensified ultrasound energy can be directed at cancer cells to heat them and kill them.

Ultrasound examination A test that utilizes ultrasound waves to bounce off internal organs of the body to construct a picture used by physicians as a non-invasive study of the liver.

Ultrasound transducer A device that produces sound waves that bounce off body tissues and make echoes. The transducer also receives the echoes and sends them to a computer that uses them to create a picture called a sonogram. Transducers (also called probes) come in different shapes and sizes for use in making pictures of different parts of the body. The transducer may be passed over the surface of the body or inserted into an opening such as the rectum or vagina.

Ultrasound-guided biopsy A biopsy procedure that uses an ultrasound imaging device to find an abnormal area of tissue and guide its removal for examination under a microscope.

Ultraviolet oxidation Ultraviolet radiation is employed in water purification for the photochemical oxidation of organic impurities resulting in HPLC grade water with organic impurity levels below 0.0005 absorbance units.

Ultraviolet radiation (UV radiation) Invisible rays that are part of the energy that comes from the sun. UV radiation also comes from sun lamps and tanning beds. UV radiation can damage the skin and cause melanoma and other types of skin cancer. UV radiation that reaches the Earth's surface is made up of two types of rays, called UVA and UVB rays. UVB rays are more likely than UVA rays to cause sunburn, but UVA rays pass deeper into the skin. Scientists have long thought that UVB radiation can cause melanoma and other types of skin cancer. They now think that UVA radiation also may add to skin damage that can lead to skin cancer and cause premature aging. For this reason, skin specialists recommend that people use sunscreens that reflect, absorb, or scatter both kinds of UV radiation.

Ultraviolet radiation therapy A form of radiation used in the treatment of cancer.

Ultraviolet sterilizer Ultraviolet lamps used to kill microorganisms in water.

Ultraviolet TOC reduction An ultraviolet source, which partially oxidizes organic compounds to ionic species that can be removed. It relies on 185 nm (nanometer) radiation from "ozone producing" mercury lamps (along with 254nm germicidal radiation). Generally has a longer contact time than sterilization alone.

Umbilical cord blood Blood from the umbilical cord of a newborn baby. This blood contains high concentrations of stem cells (cells from which all blood cells develop).

Umbilical cord blood transplantation The injection of umbilical cord blood to restore an individual's own blood production system suppressed by anticancer drugs, radiation therapy, or both. It is being studied in the treatment of cancer and severe blood disorders such as aplastic anemia. Cord blood contains high concentrations of stem cells needed to produce new blood cells.

Umbilicated Marked by depressed spots resembling the umbilicus.

Umbilicus The scar marking the site of entry of the umbilical cord into the fetus.

Unblind To reveal the treatment assignment of an individual patient or group of patients to an individual or group of individuals associated with the trial (e.g., patients, study physicians, treatment effects monitoring committee) who have heretofore been denied this information.

Uncinate process Literally a "hook". For the ethmoid bone, a plate of bone down and to the back from the anterior portion of the ethmoid labyrinth.

Uncinate process of pancreas The left and caudal portion of the head of the pancreas that "hooks" around.

Uncontrolled clinical trial A clinical trial that does not involve a control treatment. Any study that does not have a control group made up of patients treated and followed over the same time period as those in a treated group.

Uncontrolled study A clinical study that lacks a comparison (i.e., a control) group.

Unconventional cancer treatments Approaches that use substances or methods of treating cancer that have not been shown to be effective by accepted scientific methods, such as carefully designed clinical trials.

Undescended testicles A condition in which one or both testicles fail to move from the abdomen, where they develop before birth, into the scrotum. Undescended testicles may increase the risk for development of testicular cancer. Also called cryptorchidism.

Undetectable viral load The point at which levels of HIV RNA in the blood are too low to be detected with a viral load test. This does NOT mean that the virus has stopped replicating or has been removed from the body entirely, only that the small amount of virus remaining is below the test's ability to measure it. The viral load below which a test cannot detect the virus depends on the brand of the viral load test.

Undifferentiated A term used to describe cells or tissues that do not have specialized ("mature") structures or functions. Undifferentiated cancer cells often grow and spread quickly.

Unerupted tooth A tooth that has not pushed through the gum and assumed its correct position in the dental arch.

Unicellular Composed of only a single cell.

Unidirectional airflow Previously referred as "laminar" airflow, is the "rectified airflow through the entire cross section of a clean zone with a steady velocity and approximately parallel streamlines. This type of airflow results in a directed transport of particles from the clean zone".

Uniform treatment allocation A scheme in which the assignment probability of any one treatment group is the same as for every other treatment group in a trial.

Unilateral Affecting one side of the body. For example, unilateral breast cancer occurs in one breast only.

Unilateral salpingo-oophorectomy Surgery to remove the ovary and fallopian tube on one side of the body.

Unit dose Defines an SVP that must be administered in one dose. Unused contents must be discarded.

Unit of insulin The basic measure of insulin. U-100 insulin means 100 units of insulin per milliliter (mL) or cubic centimeter (cc) of solution.

United states medical licensing examination (USMLE) A 3-step examination procedure that provides a common evaluation system for United States medical licensure applicants. Results of the USMLE are reported to State Medical Boards granting the initial license to practice medicine. Each medical licensing authority requires, as part of its licensing procedure, a successful completion of an examination or other certifications demonstrating qualification for licensure.

Universal precautions Precautions taken when handling, storing, transporting, or shipping items or specimens containing, or contaminated with human blood and body fluids: all such materials are treated as infectious.

Unproven methods of cancer management Any therapy that has not been subjected to traditional scientific study and proved effective in clinical trials. Such methods range from harmless to life-threatening, especially if they are used in place of medically sound methods of treatment.

Unresectable Unable to be removed with surgery.

Unresectable gallbladder cancer Cancer that has spread to the tissues around the gallbladder (such as the liver, stomach, pancreas, intestine, or lymph nodes in the area) and cannot be surgically removed.

Unresected Describes an organ, tissue, or cancer that has not been either partly or completely removed by surgery.

Unresponsiveness Inability to respond to antigenic stimulus. Unresponsiveness may be specific for a particular antigen, or broadly nonspecific as a result of damage to the entire immune system, for example after whole body irradiation.

Unsaturated fatty acid A fatty acid containing one or more double bonds.

Unsealed internal radiation therapy Radiation therapy given by injecting a radioactive substance into the bloodstream or a body cavity, or by swallowing it. This substance is not sealed in a container.

Unstable (reactive) material A material other than an explosive, which in the pure state or as commercially produced will vigorously polymerize, decompose, condense or become self-reactive and undergo other violent chemical changes, including explosion, when exposed to heat, friction or shock, or in the absence of an inhibitor or in the presence of contaminants or in contact with noncompatible materials. Unstable, reactive materials are subdivided as follows: 1. Class 4 - Materials that in themselves are readily capable of detonation or of explosive decomposition or explosive reaction at normal temperatures and pressures. This class includes materials that are sensitive to mechanical or localized thermal shock at normal temperatures and pressures.

2. Class 3 - Materials that in themselves, are capable of detonation or of explosive decomposition or explosive reaction but which require a strong initiating source or which must be heated under confinement before initiation. This class includes materials that are sensitive to thermal or mechanical shock at elevated temperatures and pressures.

3. Class 2 - Materials that in themselves are normally unstable and readily undergo violent chemical change but do not detonate. This class includes materials which can undergo chemical change with rapid release of energy at normal temperatures and pressures and which can undergo violent chemical change at elevated temperatures and pressures.

4. Class 1 - Materials that in themselves are normally stable but which can become unstable at elevated temperatures and pressures.

Unstable diabetes A type of diabetes when a person's blood glucose (sugar) level often swings quickly from high to low and from low to high. Also called "brittle diabetes" or "labile diabetes."

Upper GI series A test that looks at the organs of the upper part of the digestive system: the esophagus, stomach, and duodenum (upper small intestine). A liquid that shows up well on x-rays called barium is swallowed. X-rays are then taken to evaluate the digestive organs.

Upper limit of normal The top of the normal range for a particular laboratory: helps assure between-lab comparability.

Upward compatibility Refers to software that runs not only on the computer for which it was designed, but also on newer and more powerful models. In the context of CFR 21 Part 11, compatibility plays an important role in ensuring that legacy data can be moved (copied) accurately and completely to a new system. Without it, legacy systems would have to be maintained as long as the records contained in them are kept.

Urachus A fibrous cord that connects the urinary bladder to the umbilicus (navel). The urachus is formed as the allantoic stalk during fetal development and lasts through life. Also called the median umbilical ligament.

Uracil A pyrimidine base important as a component of ribonucleic acid (RNA). Uracil is capable of forming a base pair with adenine.

Urea One of the chief waste products of the body. When the body breaks down food, it uses what it needs and throws the rest away as waste. The kidneys flush the waste from the body in the form of urea, which is in the urine.

Urea breath test A test that measures the amount of urease in the breath, which is an enzyme that the bacteria Helicobacter pylori makes. This helps diagnose H. pylori infection, which can help determine the cause for ulcers in the digestive tract.

Urea nitrogen A chemical in the blood produced by the breakdown of protein. Urea nitrogen is removed from the blood by the kidneys. Blood urea nitrogen (BUN) tests are sometimes done to see how well the kidneys are working.

Ureter A fibromuscular tube that transport urine from the collecting pelvis of the kidney to the base of the bladder, via a "stripping-wave" type of peristalsis.

Ureteronephrectomy Surgery to remove a kidney and its ureter. Also called nephroureterectomy.

Ureteroscopy An examination of the inside of the kidney and ureter. A thin, lighted tube (called a ureteroscope) is passed through the urethra into the bladder, ureter, and renal pelvis (part of the kidney that collects, holds, and drains urine).

Ureterostomy A surgical procedure consisting of cutting the ureters from the bladder and connecting them to an opening on the abdomen, allowing urine to flow into a collection bag.

Urethra A membraneous canal used in the transportion of urine from the bladder to the outside.

Uric acid A waste product left over from normal chemical processes in the body and found in the urine and blood. Abnormal buildup of uric acid in the body may cause a condition called gout. Increased levels of uric acid in the blood and urine can be a side effect of chemotherapy or radiation therapy.

Urinalysis A test that determines the content of the urine.

Urinary Having to do with the kidneys, ureters, and bladder. The urinary system represents the functional and anatomic aspects of the kidneys, ureters, and bladder.

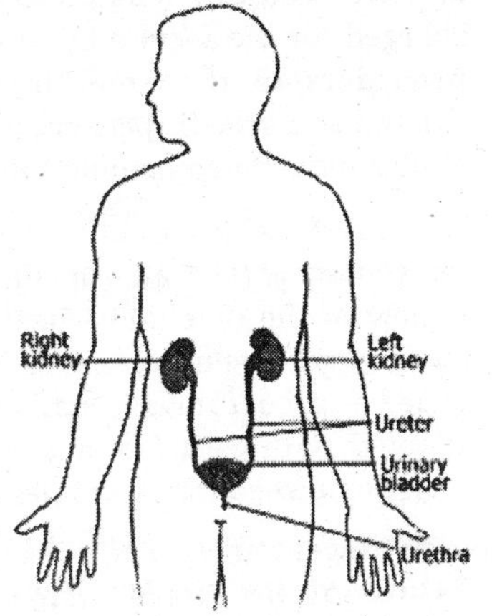

Figure Urinary system

Urinary incontinence Inability to hold urine in the bladder.

Urinary tract The organs of the body that produce and discharge urine. These include the kidneys, ureters, bladder, and urethra.

Urine Fluid containing water and waste products. Urine is made by the kidneys, stored in the bladder, and leaves the body through the urethra.

Urine cytology Tests performed on cells in urine to detect disease.

Urine testing Checking urine to see if it contains glucose (sugar) and ketones. Special strips of paper or tablets (called reagents) are put into a small amount of urine or urine plus water. Changes in the color of the strip show the amount of glucose or ketones in the urine. Urine testing is the only way to check for the presence of ketones, a sign of serious illness. However, urine testing is less desirable then blood testing for monitoring the level of glucose in the body.

Urogram (intra venous urogram or IVU) An imaging study to look at the structure and function of the kidneys, ureters, and bladder. Also called an IVU - intravenous urogram. This test requires the injection of a contrast agent.

Urokinase A drug that dissolves blood clots or prevents them from forming.

Urolene blue Other name for methylene blue.

Urologic oncologist A doctor who specializes in treating cancers of the urinary system.

Urologist A doctor who specializes in diseases of the urinary organs in females and the urinary and sex organs in males.

Urostomy An operation to create an opening from inside the body to the outside, making a new way to pass urine.

Urothelium The lining of the ureters, bladder, and urethra.

Ursodiol A synthetically-derived form of ursodiol, a bile acid produced by the liver and secreted and stored in the gallbladder. Also produced by the Chinese black bear liver, ursodiol has been used in the treatment of liver disease for centuries. This agent dissolves or prevents cholesterol gallstones by blocking hepatic cholesterol production and decreasing bile cholesterol. Ursodiol also reduces the absorption of cholesterol from the intestinal tract.

Urticaria A condition characterised by an itchy, bumpy rash. Often caused by an allergy. Also called hives or nettle rash.

Use Under HIPAA, th s term refers to the sharing of ındividually i 'entifiable health ınformation within a covered entity. For Partners' purposes, a use is the sharing of such information within the Partners affiliated covered entity.

User interface Dials, knobs, operating system commands, graphical display formats, and other devices provided by a computer or a program to allow users to communicate and use the computer or program. A Graphical User Interface (GUI) provides its user with a "picture oriented" way to interact with technology.

Usual, customary and reasonable (UCR) charges The amount a health plan will recognize for payment for a particular medical procedure. It is typically based on what is considered "reasonable" for that procedure in your service area. Commonly charged fees for health services in a certain area. The use of fee screens to determine the lowest value of provider reimbursement based on: 1. The provider's usual charge for a given procedure,

2. The amount customarily charged for the service by other providers in the area (often defined as a specific percentile of all charges in the community), and

3. The reasonable cost of services for a given patient after medical review of the case. Most health plans provide reimbursement for usual and customary charges, although no universal formula has been established for these rates.

Uterine cancer Cancer that forms in tissues of the uterus (small, hollow, pear-shaped organ in a woman's pelvis in which a baby grows). Two types of uterine cancer are endometrial cancer (cancer that begins in cells lining the uterus), and uterine sarcoma (a rare cancer that begins in muscle or other tissues in the uterus).

Uterine cavity The lumen within the uterus that is connected laterally to the uterine (fallopian) tubes and posteriorly/inferiorly with the cervix and vagina.

Uterine sarcoma A rare type of uterine cancer that forms in muscle or other tissues of the uterus (small, hollow, pear-shaped organ in a woman's pelvis in which a baby grows). It usually occurs after menopause. The two main types are leiomyosarcoma (cancer that begins in smooth muscle cells) and endometrial stromal sarcoma (cancer that begins in connective tissue cells).

Uterus The small, hollow, pear-shaped organ in a woman's pelvis. This is the organ in which a baby grows. Also called the womb.

Utility systems Facility wide systems not tailored to a specific process and that do not have contact with the drug substance or potential drug substance.

Utilization Use of services and supplies. Utilization is commonly examined in terms of patterns or rates of use of a single service or type of service such as hospital care, physician visits, and prescription drugs. Measurement of utilization of all medical services in combination is usually done in terms of dollar expenditures. Use is expressed in rates per unit of population at risk for a given period such as the number of admissions to the hospital per 1,000 persons over age 65 per year, or the number of visits to a physician per person per year for an annual physical.

Utilization review (UR), case management A formal review of utilization for appropriateness of health care services delivered to a member on a prospective, concurrent or retrospective basis. In a hospital, this includes review of the appropriateness of admissions, services ordered and provided, length of a stay, and discharge practices, both on a concurrent and retrospective basis. A peer review group, or a public agency can do utilization review. UR is a method of tracking, reviewing and rendering opinions regarding care provided to patients. Usually UR involves the use of protocols, benchmarks or data with which to compare specific cases to an aggregate set of cases. Those cases falling outside the protocols or range of data are reviewed individually. Managed care organizations will sometimes refuse to reimburse or pay for services that do not meet their own sets of UR standards. UR involves the review of patient records and patient bills primarily but may also include telephone conversations with providers. The practices of pre-certification, recertification, retrospective review and concurrent review all describe UR methods.

Utilization risk The risk that actual service utilization might differ from utilization projections.

UVA radiation A type of ultraviolet (UV) radiation. UV rays are invisible rays that are part of the energy that comes from the sun. UVA radiation also comes from sun lamps and tanning beds. Scientists think that UVA radiation may cause skin damage that can lead to skin cancer and premature aging. For this reason, skin specialists recommend that people use sunscreens that reflect, absorb, or scatter ultraviolet radiation.

Uvadex Other name for methoxsalen.

UVB radiation A type of ultraviolet (UV) radiation. UV rays are invisible rays that are part of the energy that comes from the sun. UVB radiation causes sunburn, and scientists have long thought that it can cause melanoma and other types of skin cancer. Skin specialists recommend that people use sunscreens that reflect, absorb, or scatter ultraviolet radiation.

Vaccinated Treated with a vaccine.

Vaccination Originally referred to immunization against smallpox with the less virulent cowpox (vaccinia) virus; more loosely used for any immunization against a pathogen.

Vaccine A preparation of microbial antigens that provokes an immune response (i.e. the production of antibodies) on injection, thus conferring immunity on the recipient. There are three types of vaccines: 1. Those containing material from a nonvirulent organism that retains its immunogenicity but does not result in infection.

2. Those containing a modified toxin (a toxoid) that has lost its toxic properties but retain its immunogenicity.

3. Those containing live, attenuated organisms (i.e. genetic variants of a virus or bacterium) that are antigenically similar to the original strain but lack virulence.

Recombinant DNA research has allowed the production of new and more specific vaccines. For example, the gene for the B antigen of hepatitis virus has been cloned in E. Coli, the protein expressed and a specific anti-B antiserum produced which can be used as a vaccine. A substance that stimulates the body's immune response in order to prevent or control an infection. A vaccine is typically made up of some part of a bacteria or virus that cannot itself cause an infection. Researchers are testing vaccines both to prevent and treat HIV/AIDS; however, there is currently no vaccine approved for use outside of clinical trials.

Vaccine adjuvant A substance added to a vaccine to improve the immune response so that less vaccine is needed.

Vaccine therapy A type of treatment that uses a substance or group of substances to stimulate the immune system to destroy a tumor or infectious microorganisms such as bacteria or viruses.

Vaccinia A cowpox virus that is used as a vaccine against smallpox infection and as a vector, or carrier, for other types of vaccine. In HIV vaccine clinical trials, vaccinia and other herpesviruses have been used as vectors.

Vaccinia cea tricom vaccine A vaccine consisting of recombinant vaccinia virus encoding the tumor-associated antigen carcin oembryonic antigen (CEA) and a triad of costimulatory molecules (B7-1, ICAM-1, and LFA-3; also called TRICOM). Vaccination with vaccinia-CEA-TRICOM stimulates the host immune system to mount a T-cell response against tumor cells expressing the CEA antigen. The use of TRICOM in the vaccine may elicit a greater antitumor cytotoxic T lymphocyte (CTL) immune response compared to the use of vaccinia-CEA alone.

Vaccinia psa tricom vaccine A vaccine formulation consisting of recombinant vaccinia virus encoding prostate specific antigen (PSA) and recombinant vaccinia virus encoding three co-stimulatory molecule transgenes B7.1, ICAM-1, and LFA-3 (TRICOM). Vaccination with PSA in combination with TRICOM may enhance antigen presentation, resulting in the augmentation of a cytotoxic T cell (CTL) immune response against tumor cells expressing PSA.S

Vaccinia tricom vaccine A vaccine consisting of recombinant vaccinia virus encoding a triad of costimulatory molecules (B7-1, ICAM-1, and LFA-3; also called TRICOM). Vaccination with vaccinia-TRICOM stimulates the host immune system to mount a non-specific T-cell response. With the addition of a tumor-associated antigen peptide, this vaccine may enhance a tumor-specific immune response.

Vacterl A syndrome involving birth defects affecting several organs. V stands for vertebral defects (spinal cord), A stands for anal deformities, C stands for cardiac problems, TE stands for tracheoesophageal fistula, R stands for renal abnormalities (urinary system and kidneys), and L stands for limb deformities (arms and legs).

Vacuoles Membrane-bound organelles of low density responsible for food digestion, osmotic regulation, and waste product storage. Vacuoles may occupy a large fraction of cell volume (up to 90% in plant cells).

Vacuum degasification The process of removing dissolved and entrained gases from the Reverse Osmosis (RO) product water by creating a vacuum in a tower through which this water flows. The degasifier may be located before the RO system but the majority of the time will be located after. The most prevalent gas present is Carbon Dioxide (CO_2), which may have been generated during pH adjustment of the RO feed water. The anion exchange resin can remove CO_2 but using the vacuum degasifier can reduce that load. The other gas of concern is Oxygen, which can also be removed by a vacuum degasifier.

Vagina The muscular canal extending from the uterus to the exterior of the body. Also called the birth canal.

Vaginal Having to do with the vagina (the birth canal).

Vaginitis Any inflammation of the vagina. Atrophic vaginitis is an inflammation of the vagina in which vaginal tissue becomes thin and dry. This condition occurs after menopause and is caused by lack of estrogen. An estrogen cream may be prescribed to relieve this problem. Vaginitis as a result of chemotherapy is similar to the mouth inflammation (stomatitis) that may result from some chemotherapies.

Valacyclovir A substance that is being studied in the prevention of fungal, bacterial, and viral infections in patients undergoing donor stem cell transplantation with cells that are infected with cytomegalovirus. It belongs to the family of drugs called antivirals.

Valcyte Other name for valganciclovir.

Valdecoxib A substance that is being studied as a treatment for pain and other side effects of cancer therapy. It belongs to the family of drugs called COX-2 inhibitors.

Valerian Valeriana officinalis. A plant whose roots are used as a sedative and to treat certain medical conditions. It is being studied as a way to improve sleep in cancer patients undergoing treatment. Also called garden valerian, Indian valerian, Pacific valerian, Mexican valerian, garden heliotrope, and Valerianac radix.

Valeriana officinalis An extract isolated from the root of the plant Valeriana officinalis. Valeriana officinalis extract inhibits the metabolic enzyme gamma-aminobutyric acid (GABA) transaminase and stimulates the synaptic release of GABA, an inhibitory neurotransmitter, resulting in sedation.

Valerianae radix Valeriana officinalis. A plant whose roots are used as a sedative and to treat certain medical conditions. It is being studied as a way to improve sleep in cancer patients undergoing treatment. Also called valerian, garden valerian, Indian valerian, Pacific valerian, Mexican valerian, and garden heliotrope.

Valganciclovir A synthetic prodrug of ganciclovir, a nucleoside analogue of 2'-deoxyguanosine, with antiviral activity. After phosphorylation, valganciclovir is incorporated into DNA, resulting in inhibition of viral DNA polymerase, viral DNA synthesis, and viral replication.

Validity A term that reflects a solid foundation or justification for bringing the intended results. In the case of assessment, validity means the degree to which a measurement instrument truly measures what it is intended to measure. The establishment of validity is the first priority in developing any form of assessment. Without it, all other attributes are of little consequence.

The assessment instrument should accurately represent the skills or characteristics it is designed to measure. Validity may be characterized in these four ways - content, concurrent, predictive or criterion-related validity:

Content validity is the one of greatest concern to teachers as the test must contain a epresentative sampling of the subject matter the student is expected to have learned. This sampling must be representative and should cross several categories of competence, a range of patient problems and a list of technical skills. Valid clinical examination should assess the components of clinical competence, including the ability to obtain from the patient a detailed and relevant history; carry out a physical examination of the patient; identify the patient's problems from the information obtained and reach a differential diagnosis; identify the appropriate investigations; interpret the results of the investigations; recommend and undertake appropriate management including patient education.

Concurrent validity considers the degree to which a measurement instrument produces the same results as another accepted or proven instrument which measures the same parameters.

Predictive validity examines the degree to which a measure accurately predicts expected outcomes; for instance, a measure of attitudes toward preventive care should correlate significantly with preventive care behaviors.

Criterion-related validity includes concurrent validity as well as predictive validity.

Validation A documented program that provides a high degree of assurance that a specific process, method, or system will consistently produce a result meeting pre-determined acceptance criteria.

Validation master plan The documented plan for qualification of a facility or part of a facility that identifies the layout of the operation, the associated utilities and systems, the equipment, and the processes to be validated. The validation master plan also provides preliminary information as to the extent of the qualification and validation (IQ, OQ, PQ), required documentation, SOPs, acceptance criteria and responsibilities. Validation Master Plans should also establish the cross reference of qualification projects by product, system, discipline, etc.

Validation protocol A written plan stating how validation will be conducted and defining acceptance criteria. For example, the protocol for a manufacturing process identifies processing equipment, critical process parameters/operating ranges, product characteristics, sampling, and test data to be collected, number of validation runs, and acceptable test results.

Vallecula A furrow located on the lateral and median glossoepiglottic folds.

Valproic acid A synthetic derivative of propylpentanoic acid with antiepileptic properties and potential antineoplastic and antiangiogenesis activities. In epilepsy, valproic acid appears to act by increasing the concentration of gamma-aminobutyric acid (GABA) in the brain. This agent's antitumor and antiangiogenesis activities may be related to the inhibition of histone deacetylases and nitric oxide synthase, which results in the inhibition of nitric oxide synthesis.

Valrubicin A drug that is used to treat bladder cancer that does not respond to BCG (Bacillus Calmette Guerin). It is an anthracycline and belongs to the family of drugs called antitumor antibiotics. Also called AD 32.

Value A term referring to what people believe in, or what they consider important about the way they live. Values influence behavior and culture as persons, groups and communities. Values therefore are an important determinant of individual and community health. They are, however, difficult to measure objectively.

Vanceril Other name for beclomethasone dipropionate.

Vancomycin An antibiotic drug used to fight resistant bacterial infections.

Vapour pressure Dalton's Law for a mixture of perfect gases states that the mixture pressure is equal to the sum of the partial pressures of the constituents. The partial pressure of moisture is called vapor pressure, and is expressed as: Total Pressure (Pt) = Partial Pressure of Air (Pa) + Partial Pressure of Moisture (Pv).

Vapreotide A substance that is being studied in the treatment of cancer. It belongs to the family of drugs called somatostatin analogs.

Vaqta Other name for hepatitis A vaccine.

Variability, range A measure of variability which describes the distribution as the difference between the largest and smallest values.

Variability, standard deviation A measure of variability which describes the average distance of the observations from their mean. For example in a normal distribution, +1 SD from the mean includes 68% of the observations; +2 SD from the mean includes 95% of the observations; +3 SD from the mean includes 99.7% of the observations.

Variability, standard error of the mean A measure of variability which describes the accuracy of the sample mean as an estimate of the population mean; SEM = SD / square root of the sample size.

Variable A quantity, attribute, phenomenon or event that may assume any one of a set of values:

Independent variable refers to a characteristic being observed or measured that is thought to influence an event or manifestation (the dependent variable) within the defined area of relationships under study. In medical education, it is a factor that could explain or predict the curriculum's outcomes such as the curriculum itself, previous or concurrent training, environmental factors.

Dependent variable is a manifestation or outcome whose variation we seek to explain or account for the influence of independent variables. It can be a program outcome, such as knowledge or skill attainment, real-life performance, and clinical outcomes.

It is prudent to focus on a few dependent variables that are most relevant to the main evaluation questions and similarly, to focus on the independent variables that are most likely to be related to the curriculum's outcomes.

Variable, continuous Continuous variables can assume all possible values along a continuum within a specified range, e.g., height, weight, blood pressure, CD4.

Variable, dependent A variable which has a value that is dependent upon the effect of one or more other independent variables. For example, diastolic blood pressure (dependent variable) can be dependent upon the effect of obesity (independent variable.)

Variable, discrete (categorical) Discrete variables have values that fall into a limited number of separate categories, e.g., gender (male/female),, survival status (alive/dead), exposure status (exposed/nonexposed), blood type (A/B/AB/O.)

Variable, independent A variable which influences the value of the dependent variable. For example, obesity (independent variable) can influence the level of diastolic blood pressure (dependent variable).

Variable, quantile A measure of variability which divides the distribution into equal, ordered subgroups. For example, terciles are thirds, quartiles are quarters, and quintiles are fifths.

Variance The degree to which a set of quantities vary: A measure of the spread of scores in a distribution of scores, that is, a measure of dispersion. The larger the variance, the further the individual cases are from the mean. The smaller the variance, the closer the individual score are to the mean. Specifically, the population variance is the mean of the sum of the squared deviations from the mean score. The Sample variance is computed by dividing the sum of squared deviations by the number in the sample minus 1. The Standard Deviation is the square root of the variance.

Variant A variation of a particular strain of virus or infective agent; slightly different in form or function.

Varicella zoster virus (VZV) A virus in the herpes family that causes chickenpox during childhood and may reactivate later in life to cause herpes zoster (shingles) in immunosuppressed individuals.

Varicose vein A condition in which a vein, most often in the legs, becomes permanently enlarged, twisted, and painful. This may be caused by valves in the vein that don't work properly or by weakness in the vein walls.

Varix A painfully enlarge blood vessel; plural is varices

Vas deferens A coiled tube that carries the sperm out of the testes.

Vascular endothelial growth factor (VEGF) A substance made by cells that stimulates new blood vessel formation.

Vascular Relating to the body's blood vessels (arteries, veins, and capillaries).

Vascular targeting agents (VTAs) Multifunctional agents that are home to the capillaries and vessels of solid tumors.

VasectomyAn operation to cut or tie off the two tubes that carry sperm out of the testicles.

Vasomax Other name for phentolamine mesylate.

Vasomotor Affecting the narrowing and widening of the blood vessels.

Vasomotor rhinitis Anon allergic rhinitis caused by changes in temperature, strong odours, or smoke.

Vatalanib An orally bioavailable anilinophthalazine with potential antineoplastic activity. Vatalanib binds to and inhibits the protein kinase domain of vascular endothelial growth factor receptors 1 and 2; both receptor tyrosine kinases are involved in angiogenesis. This agent also binds to and inhibits related receptor tyrosine kinases, including platelet-derived growth factor (PDGF) receptor, c-Kit, and c-Fms.

VEAs (Vasopermeation enhancement agents) A new generation of drugs that increase the uptake of therapeutic agents to solid tumors.

Vectogram A three-dimensional picture that is used to strengthen the binocularity system. Available in fixed and variable styles to provide base-in and/or base-out training.

Vector An agent, such as an insect, that can carry a disease-producing organism from one host to another; the agent used to carry new genes into cells. Plasmids currently are the vectors of choice, though viruses and other bacteria may sometimes be used. These molecules become part of the cell protoplasm.

VEGF trap A protein comprised of segments of the extracellular domains of human vascular endothelial growth factor receptors 1 (VEGFR1) and 2 (VEGFR2) fused to the constant region (Fc) of human IgG1. VEGF trap binds to vascular endothelial growth factor (VEGF), a pro-angiogenic growth factor, thereby preventing VEGF from binding to its cell receptors. Disruption of this cell receptor binding results in the inhibition of angiogenesis and metastasis, and tumor regression.

VEGFR tyrosine kinase inhibitor Vascular endothelial growth factor receptor tyrosine kinase inhibitor. A substance that blocks an enzyme needed to form blood vessels.

Vehicle Any solvent or carrier fluid in a pharmaceutical product that has no pharmacological role. For example, water is the vehicle for xilocaine and propylene glycol is the vehicle for many antibiotics.

Vein A blood vessel that carries blood to the heart.

Velban Other name for vinblastine.

Velcade A drug that is used to treat multiple myeloma and is being studied in the treatment of other types of cancer. It belongs to the families of drugs called proteosome inhibitors and dipeptidyl boronic acids. Also called bortezomib and PS-341.

Velsar Other name for vinblastine.

Vena cava The large venous channels that return blood to the heart. There is a superior vena cava (SVC above the heart - draining the head and upper extremities) and an inferior vena cava (IVC - below the heart, draining everything else).

Veneer Plastic or porcelain facing bonded directly to a tooth to improve its appearance.

Venipuncture Puncturing a vein in order to obtain blood samples, to start an intravenous drip, or to give medication.

Venlafaxine A synthetic phenethylamine bicyclic derivative with antidepressant activity. Venlafaxine and its active metabolite, O-desmethylvenlafaxine (ODV), are potent inhibitors of neuronal serotonin and norepinephrine reuptake and weak dopamine reuptake inhibitors. This agent may reduce hormone-related vasomotor symptoms.

Venoglobulin S Other name for immune globulin.

Venogram A radiograph or other image of veins, usually obtained by injecting a radiopaque liquid contrast material into a vein. Leg venograms are done to r/o DVT (Deep Vein Thrombosis) that can cause pulmonary embolism.

Venom A toxic substance secreted by an insect or a snake.

Ventak A family of implantable devices for patients with abnormal heart rhythms.

Ventavis Other name for iloprost.

Ventilator In medicine, a machine used to help a patient breathe. Also called respirator.

Figure Ventilator

Ventral Being or located near, on, or toward the front or anterior part of the human body.

Ventricle One of the two lower chambers of the heart. The right ventricle sends blood to the lungs, and the left ventricle passes blood carrying oxygen to the rest of the body. The ventricles contract at the same time.

Ventricular fibrillation (VF) A very fast, irregular heartbeat that is caused by abnormal impulses coming from several areas of the heart. These abnormal impulses take over the "pacemaker" function of the sino-atrial node. The heartbeat is so fast that the heart doesn't have time to pump enough blood to the brain and body tissue, which may lead to unconsciousness and heart arrest.

Ventricular tachycardia (VT) A fast heartbeat caused by abnormal impulses coming from a single area of the heart. These abnormal impulses also take over the "pacemaker" function of the sino-atrial node. The rapid heartbeat produces symptoms of fainting, dizziness, weakness, blind spots and, eventually, unconsciousness leading to heart arrest.

VePesid Other name for etoposide.

Vergence facility A measure of the ease and speed of the eyes to change from a converging to diverging position.

Vergence To turn the eyes horizontally (convergence- inward or divergence- outward). Accommodative vergence, fusional vergence, proximal vergence, and tonic vergence are needed to maintain single vision.

Verification The act of reviewing, inspecting, testing, checking, auditing, or otherwise establishing and documenting whether items, processes, services, or documents conform to specified requirements.

Verify To confirm or substantiate an item of information recorded in a data file or keyed for entry into the analysis database.

Verocay body An arrangement of Schwann cells nuclei forming palisading parallel rows that enclose a homogeneous material that is devoid of nuclei, and has scant or no collagen.

Verruca A wart.

Verrucous Rough; wart-like.

Vertebral artery Originating at the subclavian artery, passing vertically through the transverse foramina of the vertebrae, and providing branches for the spinal and muscular rami, anterior spinal artery, and posterior inferior cerebellar artery, before joining with the opposite side to form the basilar artery.

Vertebral body Only the main round, anterior portion of the vertebrae should be called the body. The part from which the other processes extend. However, often incorrectly used as a nickname for the entire vertebra.

Vertebral column The bones, muscles, tendons, and other tissues that reach from the base of the skull to the tailbone. The vertebral column encloses the spinal cord and the fluid surrounding the spinal cord. Also called spine, backbone, and spinal column.

Vertical dimension Arbitrary space between upper and lower jaws upon closure; may decrease over time due to wear, shifting or damage to the teeth.

Vertical transmission A term used to describe the transmission of a disease from parent(s) to offspring. For example, HIV can be spread vertically from mother to child during pregnancy, at birth, or through breastfeeding.

Vertigo A disordered state in which the individual is dizzy or feels that the surrounding environment is whirling.

Vesanoid Other name for tretinoin.

Vesicant A medication or agent that may cause blistering.

Vesicle A small bulla, generally less than 5 mm.

Vesicostomy A vesicostomy is an opening in the lower fetal abdomen that goes directly into the fetal bladder. This was used to treat fetuses with urinary tract obstruction.

Vestibule (of ear) The oval cavity within the bony laryrinth that is a confluence for the vestibular endolymphatic channels (semicircular canals).

Veterinary Referring to pharmaceuticals or biologicals intended for animal use. Historically veterinary products were made by less than "Good Manufacturing Products". Today, however, the GMP's refer to both human and veterinary products.

Viable living Viable Organism Capable of living and reproducing. Thus, nothing is sterile as long as it contains even a single viable organism.

Viadur Other name for leuprolide acetate.

Viagmox Other name for moxifloxacin hydrochloride.

Viagra A substance that is used to treat erectile dysfunction. Viagra relaxes the smooth muscle of the penis to allow increased blood flow and erection. It belongs to the family of drugs called phosphodiesterase inhibitors. Also called sildenafil.

Vial A final container for a parenteral or diagnostic product. Sealed with a rubber closure and over-seal. Generally required to be class I borosilicate glass.

Video assisted resection Surgery that is aided by the use of a video camera that projects and enlarges the image on a television screen. Also called video-assisted surgery.

Video assisted thoracic surgery (VATS) Thorascoscopy (aka VATS) is a minimally invasive keyhole surgical procedure which allows the surgeon to directly examine the chest cavity without a big incision.

Villous adenoma A type of polyp that grows in the colon and other places in the gastrointestinal tract and sometimes in other parts of the body. These adenomas may become malignant (cancerous).

Villus A dermal papilla extending into a bulla, vesicle, or lacuna which is covered with a single layer of epidermal cells resulting from suprabasalar acantholysis.

Vinblastine A natural alkaloid isolated from the plant Vinca rosea Linn. Vinblastine binds to tubulin and inhibits microtubule formation, resulting in disruption of mitotic spindle assembly and arrest of tumor cells in the M phase of the cell cycle. This agent may also interfere with amino acid, cyclic AMP, and glutathione metabolism; calmodulin-dependent Ca^{++} -transport ATPase activity; cellular respiration; and nucleic acid and lipid biosynthesis.

Vinca alkaloid An anticancer drug that inhibits cancer cell growth by stopping cell division. It is also called an antimitotic or antimicrotubule agent, or a mitotic inhibitor.

Vindesine A synthetic derivative of vinblastine, a naturally occurring vinca alkaloid. Vindesine binds to and stabilizes tubulin, thereby interrupting tubulin polymerization and preventing the formation of the mitotic spindle and cell division; treated cells are unable to undergo mitosis and are arrested in metaphase. This agent also disrupts macromolecular synthesis.

Vinorelbine An anticancer drug that belongs to the family of plant drugs called vinca alkaloids.

Vinyl chloride A substance used to make plastics. Exposure to vinyl chloride may increase the risk of developing liver, brain, and lung cancers; lymphoma; and leukemia.

Vioxx A drug that was being used for pain relief and was being studied for its ability to prevent cancer and to block the growth of new blood vessels to solid tumors. It belongs to the family of drugs called nonsteroidal anti-inflammatory drugs. Also called rofecoxib.

Viral antigens Specific proteins on the capsid of a virus that can act as inducers of antibody formation.

Viral burden/load The concentration of a virus in the body.

Viral Having to do with a virus.

Viral hepatitis Hepatitis caused by any of several known viruses for which physicians can perform tests.

Viral load (VL) The amount of HIV RNA in a blood sample, reported as number of HIV RNA copies per mL of blood plasma. The VL provides information about the number of cells infected with HIV and is an important indicator of HIV progression and how well treatment is working. The VL can be measured by different techniques, including branched chain DNA (bDNA) and reverse transcriptase-polymerase chain reaction (RT-PCR) assays. VL tests are usually done when an individual is diagnosed with HIV infection and at regular intervals after diagnosis.

Viral load test Test that measures the quantity of HIV RNA in the blood. Results are reported as the number of copies of HIV RNA per mL of blood plasma. The two types of HIV viral load test are reverse transcriptase-polymerase chain reaction (RT-PCR) and branched chain DNA (bDNA).

Viral rebound Reappearance of HIV in the blood after having been successfully suppressed to undetectable levels following anti-HIV drug treatment.

Viral vector A type of virus used in cancer therapy. The virus is changed in the laboratory and cannot cause disease. Viral vectors produce tumor antigens (proteins found on a tumor cell) and can stimulate an antitumor immune response in the body. Viral vectors may also be used to carry genes that can change cancer cells back to normal cells.

Viremia The presence of virus in the blood.

Viricide Any substance that can destroy or inactivate a virus.

Virion A fully formed, mature virus. Infection is initiated in a cell by a virion.

Viroid A very exotic type of virus-like particle that only infects plant cells and consists of a group of membraneless circular RNAs that neither code for nor contain any structural protein. They replicate without other viruses being present.

Virologic failure Inability of anti-HIV drug treatment to reduce viral load or to maintain suppression of viral load. Virologic failure is the most common type of treatment failure and may lead to immunologic and clinical failure.

Virology The study of viruses and viral disease.

Virtual colonoscopy A method under study to examine the colon by taking a series of x-rays (called a CT scan) and using a high-powered computer to reconstruct 2-D and 3-D pictures of the interior surfaces of the colon from these x-rays. The pictures can be saved, manipulated to better viewing angles, and reviewed after the procedure, even years later. Also called computed tomography colography.

Virucide An agent that destroys or inactivates viruses.

Virulence Refers to the ability of a microorganism to produce serious disease. Tuberculosis is a virulent organism. Some nontuberculous mycobacteria are virulent (e.g., M. kansasii), while others (e.g., M. gordonae) are not. (PATHOGENICITY is a related—though not identical—concept.)

Virulent Refers to the ability of a virus or a bacterium to cause damage to its host.

Virulizin A substance that activates some types of immune system cells, and is being studied as a treatment for cancer. It belongs to the family of drugs called biological therapy agents.

Virus A noncellular biological entity that can reproduce only within a host cell. Viruses consist of nucleic acid covered by protein; some animal viruses are also surrounded by membrane. Inside the infected cell, the virus uses the synthetic capability of the host to produce progeny virus. A simple, noncellular parasite that can reproduce only inside living cells. The simple structure of viruses is their most important characteristic. Most of them consist only of a genetic material - either DNA or RNA - and a protein coating. Some also have membranous envelopes. Viruses are "alive" in that they can reproduce themselves - although only by taking over a cell's synthetic machinery - but they have none of the other characteristics of living organisms. Viruses cause a large variety of significant diseases in plants and animals, including humans. A tiny infectious agent that is smaller than bacteria. The common cold is caused by a virus, and the herpes simplex virus causes cold sores.

Virus neutralizing antibody An antibody that binds to a virus and interferes with its ability to infect a cell.

Virus replication cycle The reproduction cycle of viruses. A replication cycle begins with the infection of a host cell and ends with the release of mature progeny virus particles.

Visagraph eye movement recording system Records and measures eye movements while an individual reads. The system also measures reading efficiency.

Viscera The soft internal organs of the body, including the lungs, the heart, and the organs of the digestive, excretory, and reproductive systems.

Visceral Having to do with the viscera, which are the soft internal organs of the body, including the lungs, the heart, and the organs of the digestive, excretory, reproductive, and circulatory systems.

Visceral adipose tissue (VAT) A type of adipose (fat) tissue that surrounds internal organs in the abdominal cavity. Accumulation of this fat is known as central fat deposition or visceral lipohypertrophy, and may occur as a side effect of some anti-HIV medications, especially PIs and NRTIs.

Visceral peritoneum The layers of tissue that cover the outer surface of most organs in the abdomen, including the intestines.

Viscosity The tendency of a fluid to resist flowing because of molecular attraction (cohesion).

Viscotoxin A member of a group of small proteins produced by mistletoe plants that are able to kill cells and may stimulate the immune system.

Viscous Thick, coagulated; sticky or gummy.

Visilizumab A monoclonal antibody that binds to CD3 (a substance found on T-cells) and that is being studied as a treatment for graft-versus-host disease (GVHD). It belongs to the family of drugs called monoclonal antibodies.

Vision The ability to take in information through our eyes and process the information so that it has meaning.

Vision therapist Optometrist or an optometric vision therapy technician who develops and administers vision therapy programs. (Typically this term is referring to a vision therapy technician rather than an optometrist.)

Vision therapy technician One who works under the supervision of an optometrist in evaluating clients and in planning and implementing vision therapy programs.

Visit driven data Data such as laboratory measurements or screening data that is collected on a fixed schedule.

Visual acuity Sharpness or clearness of eyesight.

Visual analysis Refers to figure-ground, form constancy, spatial relation, visual closure, visual discrimination, visual memory, and visualization.

Visual closure The ability to identify or recognize a symbol or object when the entire object is not visible.

Visual discrimination The ability to discriminate between visible likeness and differences in size, shape, pattern, form, position, and color. Such as the ability to distinguish between similar words like "ran" and "run".

Visual field The total area that can be seen while looking straight ahead.

Visual form dysfunction Difficulty with figure-ground, form constancy, visual closure, and visual discrimination. Symptoms include confusion with similar objects, words, or colors. Vision therapy is a treatment option.

Visual memory The ability to recall and use visual information from the past.

Visual memory dysfunction Difficulty with retention, recall, or recognition of things seen. Symptoms can include poor spelling and poor recall of visual information. Vision therapy is a treatment option.

Visual motor dysfunction The inability to process and reproduce visual images by writing or drawing. Symptoms can include poor pencil grip/writing, poor organization on written page, poor copying/spacing, and excessive erasing. Vision therapy is a treatment option.

Visual motor integration (VMI) After visual data is gathered, it is processed and combined in the brain with information from movement (eye hand coordination).

Visual motor skills The ability of our eyes to guide our hands (eye hand coordination, visual-motor integration).

Visual pathway Route of the nerve impulses from the retina along the optic nerve, and optic nerve radiations to the brain's sensory cortex that is located at the base of the skull.

Visual pathway glioma A rare, slow-growing tumor of the eye.

Visual perceptual disorders Information processing dysfunctions of the visual system. These dysfunctions can be a directionality/laterality disorder, visual form dysfunction, visual memory dysfunction, and visual-motor dysfunction. Vision therapy is a treatment option.

Visual perceptual skills The ability to organize and interpret information that is seen and give it meaning. These information-processing skills include figure-ground, form constancy, spatial relations, visual closure, visual discrimination, visual memory, and visualization.

Visual sensory integration After visual data is gathered, it is processed and combined in the brain with information from hearing (auditory-visual integration), balance (gross-motor/bilateral integration), posture, and movement (visual-motor integration).

Visual sequential memory Ability to recall a sequence of numbers, letters or objects in the order they were originally given.

Visual skills Are accommodation (eye focusing), binocularity (eye teaming), and oculomotor skills (eye movement), which are neuromuscular abilities that are controlled by muscles inside and outside of the eye and are networked with the brain.

Visualization The ability to crate and manipulate mental pictures of an object or concept on the basis of past visual experience and memory. Essential in reading and playing sports.

Visudyne Other name for benzoporphyrin derivative monoacid ring A.

Vital Necessary to maintain life. Breathing is a vital function.

Vital capacity (VC) The maximum volume of air that can be exhaled following a complete lung inflation. The difference between Total Lung Capacity (TLC) and Residual Volume (RV).

Vital statistics Statistics relating to births (natality), deaths (mortality), marriages, health, and disease (morbidity). Vital statistics can be obtained from CDC, state health departments, county health departments and other agencies. An individual patient's vital statistics in a health care setting may also refer simply to blood pressure, temperature, height and weight, etc.

Vitamin Term coined in 1911 (vita, Latin word for life, and the chemical term amine) by polish biochemist, Casimir Funk, represents one of a group of organic substances, some of which are of unknown composition, present in minute amount in natural foodstuffs which are essential to normal metabolism. A lack of which in the dietary causes deficiency diseases. Vitamins are commonly classified into two groups, the fat-soluble, and the water-soluble. Vitamins A, D, E, and K are fat-soluble. Vitamin C and members of the vitamin B complex group are water-soluble. In general, the vitamins play catalytic and regulatory roles in the body's metabolism. Among the water-soluble vitamins, the B vitamins apparently function as coenzymes. Vitamin's C coenzyme role, if any, has not been established. Part of the importance of vitamin C to the body may result from its strong antioxidant action. The actions of the fat-soluble vitamins are less well understood. Some of them, too, may contribute to enzyme activity, and some of them are essential to the functioning of cellular membranes.

Vitamin A Retinol, a nutrient essential for proper vision and healthy skin and mucous membranes. Vitamin A is being studied in the prevention of cancer. It belongs to the family of drugs called retinoids.

Vitamin B-6 Vitamin B-6 is used to counteract some of the side effects of Penicillamine.

Vitamin B12 A vitamin that is needed to make red blood cells and DNA (the genetic material in cells) and to keep nerve cells healthy. It is found in eggs, meat, poultry, shellfish, milk, and milk products. Vitamin B12, along with folate, may be given to help reduce side effects in cancer patients being treated with drugs called antimetabolites. Also called cobalamin.

Vitamin C A key nutrient that the body needs to fight infection, heal wounds, and keep tissues healthy, including the blood vessels, cartilage, ligaments, tendons, bones, muscle, skin, teeth, and gums. It is an antioxidant that helps prevent tissue damage caused by free radicals. The body does not make or store vitamin C, so it must be taken in every day. It is found in many fruits and vegetables, especially green peppers, citrus, strawberries, tomatoes, broccoli, leafy greens, potatoes, and cantaloupe. Also called ascorbic acid.

Vitamin D A nutrient that helps the body use calcium and phosphorus and make strong bones and teeth. It is found in fatty fish, eggs, and dairy products. The skin can also make vitamin D when exposed to sunshine. Not getting enough vitamin D can cause a bone disease called rickets. Vitamin D is being studied in the prevention and treatment of some types of cancer. Also called cholecalciferol.

Vitamin E A natural fat-soluble antioxidant with potential chemopreventive activity. Also known as tocopherol, vitamin E ameliorates free-radical damage to biological membranes, protecting polyunsaturated fatty acids (PUFA) within membrane phospholipids and within circulating lipoproteins. Peroxyl radicals react 1000-fold faster with vitamin E than with PUFA. In the case of oxygen free radical-mediated tumorigenesis, vitamin E may be chemopreventive.

Vitamin K A substance that promotes the clotting of blood.

Vitamin Q10 A substance found in most tissues in the body, and in many foods. It can also be made in the laboratory. It is used by the body to produce energy for cells, and as an antioxidant. It is being studied in the treatment of cancer and in the relief of side effects caused by some cancer treatments. Also called coenzyme Q10, Q10, CoQ10, and ubiquinone.

Vitrectomy Removing the gel from the center of the eyeball because it has blood and scar tissue in it that blocks sight. An eye surgeon replaces the clouded gel with a clear fluid.

Vitreous body The inner part of the eyeball located between the iris and retina that is made up of a transparent gel (actually a living tissue). Also known as the vitreous humour. The aqueous humour is the watery liquid between the cornea and the iris, in the anterior chamber of the eye.

Vitreous humor The clear jelly (gel) that fills the center of the eye.

VNP20009 A genetically modified Salmonella bacterium that is injected into the tumor. It is being studied for its ability to shrink solid tumors.

VNP40101M A sulfonyl hydrazine prodrug with antineoplastic activity. VNP40101M alkylates the 06 position of guanine, resulting in DNA crosslinking, strand breaks, chromosomal aberrations, and disruption of DNA synthesis. Intracellular metabolism of this agent also releases methyl isocyanate which inhibits 06-alkyl-guanine transferase, an enzyme involved with DNA repair.

Vocal cords Above the trachea, there are two pairs of fibromuscular "cords" - superiorly are the false cords, and inferiorly the true vocal cords. Between them is the laryngeal ventricle. Adduction (bringing together) the true cords causes vibration in the air column - speech or phonation. Abduction moves the cords apart.

Void To empty the bladder in order to obtain a urine sample for testing.

Volociximab A monoclonal antibody that is being studied in the treatment of some types of cancer. Monoclonal antibodies are made in the laboratory and can locate and bind to cancer cells. Volociximab binds to a protein that is found on cells that line some tumor blood vessels. It belongs to the family of drugs called angiogenesis inhibitors. Also called M200.

Volvulus A twisting of the stomach or large intestine that leads to blockage of the digestive tract.

Vomiting The release of stomach contents through the mouth; also known as throwing-up.

Von Hippel Lindau peptide vaccine A cancer vaccine composed of peptides derived from a tumor-associated protein encoded by a mutated Von Hippel-Lindau (VHL) oncogene. VHL peptide vaccine may stimulate a cytotoxic T cell response against tumor cells expressing the VHL tumor-associated protein.

Von Hippel Lindau syndrome A rare inherited disorder in which blood vessels grow abnormally in the eyes, brain, spinal cord, adrenal glands, or other parts of the body. People with von Hippel-Lindau syndrome have a higher risk of developing some types of cancer.

Voriconazole A synthetic triazole with antifungal activity. Voriconazole selectively inhibits 14-alpha-lanosterol demethylation in fungi, preventing the production of ergosterol, an essential constituent of the fungal cell membrane, and resulting in fungal cell lysis.

Vorinostat A synthetic agent with antineoplastic properties. Vorinostat, also known as suberoylanilide hydroxamic acid (SAHA), inhibits the enzyme histone deacetylase (HDAC), induces differentiation in some cell types, and has been shown to induce p53-independent apoptosis in a number of tumor cell lines. This agent crosses the blood-brain barrier.

Vorozole A hormone therapy drug used to decrease the production of estrogen.

VPHP Microbiodecontamination Technology used to decontaminate the exposed, internal surfaces within a sealed isolator and the exposed, external surfaces of materials and components placed within the sealed isolator. It consists of four distinctive phases: 1. Dehumidification - Lowers humidity and increases temperature

2. Conditioning - "Ramp-up" (VPHP) at or below saturation conditions

3. Sterilization - Steady-State (VPHP) at or below saturation conditions

4. Aeration - Reduces the VPHP to Safe Levels.

Vulva The external female genital organs, including the clitoris, vaginal lips, and the opening to the vagina.

Vulvar cancer Cancer of the vulva (the external female genital organs, including the clitoris, vaginal lips, and the opening to the vagina).

VX 853 A drug being studied to make cancer cells less resistant to the effects of chemotherapy.

VX-710 A drug being studied to make cancer cells less resistant to the effects of chemotherapy.

Waldenström's macroglobulinemia An indolent (slow-growing) type of non-Hodgkin's lymphoma marked by abnormal levels of IgM antibodies in the blood and an enlarged liver, spleen, or lymph nodes. Also called lymphoplasmacytic lymphoma.

Wallerian degeneration After cerebral infarction, when the cortical neuronal cell bodies have died, there is atrophy of their distal portions (dendrites). This is seen as atrophy in the white matter, especially in the cerebral peduncles.

Warfarin A synthetic anticoagulant. Warfarin appears to inhibit the regeneration of vitamin K1 epoxide and so the synthesis of vitamin K dependent clotting factors, which include Factors II, VII, IX and X, and the anticoagulant proteins C and S. This inhibition results in a sequential depression of Factors VII, IX, X and II activities. Vitamin K is an essential cofactor for the post ribosomal synthesis of the vitamin K dependent clotting factors. The vitamin promotes the biosynthesis of gamma-carboxyglutamic acid residues in these proteins which are essential for biological activity.

Wart A raised growth on the surface of the skin or other organ.

Wasting syndrome The involuntary loss of more than 10 percent of body weight, plus more than 30 days of either diarrhea or weakness and fever. Wasting refers to the loss of muscle mass, although part of the weight loss may also be due to loss of fat. HIV-associated wasting syndrome is considered an AIDS-defining condition.

Watchful waiting Closely monitoring a patient's condition but withholding treatment until symptoms appear or change. Also called observation.

Water hammer A tremendous force produced by rapid interruption of linear flow of a non-compressible fluid. Most commonly occurs when fast acting valves are closed in a high flow liquid system.

Water treatment Water treatment, also referred to as water conditioning, can consist of adding or removing chemicals to change the properties of water. In water softening, for example, sodium ions are substituted for metallic ions that cause "hardness" thus reducing the scale-forming tendencies of water. Water purification on the other hand, always consists of removing undesirable impurities.

Watercress Nasturtium officinale. Parts of the flowering plant have been used in some cultures to treat certain medical problems. It may have anticancer effects. Also called Indian cress.

Waviness The more widely spaced component of surface texture. Unless otherwise noted, waviness includes all irregularities whose spacing is greater than the roughness sampling length. Waviness may result from such factors as machine or work deflection, vibration, chatter, heat treatment or warping strains. Roughness may be considered as superimposed on a "wavy" surface.

Weal A raised bump on the skin that indicates an allergy in a skin prick test. Also seen on the skin as Urticaria.

Wedge resection A surgical procedure to remove a triangle-shaped slice of tissue. It may be used to remove a tumor and a small amount of normal tissue around it.

Welding disease A common term used to describe the symptoms of manganism as caused by excessive exposure to manganese from welding byproducts.

Well differentiated lymphocytic lymphoma An indolent (slow-growing) type of B-cell non-Hodgkin's lymphoma marked by swollen lymph nodes that usually occurs in people older than 50 years. It is very similar to a form of leukemia called chronic lymphocytic leukemia (CLL). Also called small lymphocytic lymphoma.

Wellbutrin Other name for bupropion hydrochloride.

Wellcovorin Other name for leucovorin calcium.

Wellness A dynamic state of physical, mental, and social well-being; a way of life which equips the individual to realize the full potential of his/her capabilities and to overcome and compensate for weaknesses; a lifestyle which recognizes the importance of nutrition, physical fitness, stress reduction, and self-responsibility. Wellness has been viewed as the result of four key factors over which an individual has varying degrees of control: human biology, environment, health care organization and lifestyle. Preventive medicine associated with lifestyle and preventive care that can reduce health- care utilization and costs. "Wellness" programs became popular with the advent of managed care in the 1980s, with the philosophy and business idea that health plans needed to emphasize keeping their beneficiaries well. However, there has been a drop off in these programs in the 1990s as health plans recognize the difficulty in assessing efficacy and they found that subscribers tend to change plans regularly, thus reducing benefit of keeping one population "well".

Wermer's syndrome A rare, inherited disorder that affects the endocrine glands and can cause tumors in the parathyroid and pituitary glands and the pancreas. These tumors (usually benign) cause the glands to secrete high levels of hormones, which can lead to other medical problems, such as kidney stones, fertility problems, and severe ulcers. In some cases, tumors inside the pancreas can become cancerous. Also called multiple endocrine adenomatosis and multiple endocrine neoplasia type 1 syndrome.

Western blot A procedure in which a mixture of proteins is separated on a polyacrylamide gel and then transferred to a nylon membrane. The membrane may then be treated with reagents such as specific antibodies to locate a protein of interest. A technique used to identify and locate proteins based on their ability to bind to specific antibodies.

Wet wrapping A treatment for eczema that involves applying emollients and corticosteroid creams to the affected parts of the body and then wrapping the body in wet bandages.

Wetted surface The surface (s) of any valve or component that will be exposed to a fluid (liquid or gas) when in service.

WFI (Water for injection), WFI is water purified by distillation or by reverse osmosis, it contains no added substance. WFI meets the purity requirements under Purified Water. Although not intended to be sterile, it meets a test for a limit of bacterial endotoxin. It must be produced, stored, and distributed under Sterile Water for Injection.

Wheatstone stereoscope An instrument designed to present separate images to each eye. Each eye can see independently. Two plane mirrors are joined at one edge at a 90-degree angle and two target holders, one opposite one mirror and the other, mounted on a screw base which, when turned, synchronously moves the targets toward or away from each other. The Amblyoscope, Troposcope, Synoptophore, and the Bernell Mirror Stereoscope are examples of this design.

Wheezing The sound made by air moving through partially obstructed airways.

Whipple procedure A type of surgery used to treat pancreatic cancer. The head of the pancreas, the duodenum, a portion of the stomach, and other nearby tissues are removed.

White blood cells (WBC) A name for several types of cells in blood that remain after red cells have been removed. Their purpose is to help defend against infection. T-cell lymphocytes and B-cell lymphocytes are two types of white blood cells that play a role in the immune system against cancer. White blood cells Also known as leukocytes. These cells make up the immune system and include lymphocytes, monocytes, neutrophils, eosinophils, macrophages, and mast cells. White blood cells are made by bone marrow and help the body fight infection and other diseases.

White blood count (WBC) The actual number of white blood cells seen in a blood sample.

White matter The white nervous tissue of the brain and spinal cord consisting of the conducting, myelinated fibers.

Whitmore jewett staging system A staging system for prostate cancer that uses ABCD. "A" and "B" refer to cancer that is confined to the prostate. "C" refers to cancer that has grown out of the prostate but has not spread to lymph nodes or other places in the body. "D" refers to cancer that has spread to lymph nodes or to other places in the body. Also called the ABCD rating or the Jewett staging system.

Whole cell vaccine Vaccine made from whole tumor cells that have been changed in the laboratory.

Wild clover Trifolium pratense. A plant whose flowers have been used in some cultures to treat certain medical problems. It is being studied in the relief of menopausal symptoms and may have anticancer effects. Also called red clover and purple clover.

Wild type The form of an organism that occurs most frequently in nature

Wild type virus 1. A term to describe virus strains (including strains of HIV) that have not acquired any genetic mutations that create special characteristics, such as resistance to particular drugs. 2. The customary type of a virus before genetic manipulation or mutation; virus isolated from an individual, as opposed to from a lab culture

Wilms ' tumor A kidney cancer that usually occurs in children younger than 5 years old.

Wilson's disease A genetic disorder leading to increased retention of copper in the liver resulting in chronic hepatitis and cirrhosis. If untreated, liver failure may occur.

Window period The time period between a person's infection with HIV and the appearance of detectable anti-HIV antibodies. Because antibodies to HIV take some time to form, an HIV antibody test will not be positive immediately after a person is infected. The time delay typically ranges from 14 to 21 days, but varies for different people. Nearly everyone infected with HIV will have detectable antibodies by 3 months after infection.

Windpipe The airway that leads from the larynx to the lungs. Also called the trachea.

WinRho SDF Other name for immune globulin.

Wisdom teeth Third (last) molars that usually erupt at age 18-25 (when "wisdom is attained").

Withdrawal 1. A technical term used to refer to the process of removing a specific individual from a lifetable analysis because of termination of follow-up, or because of the occurrence of an event that precludes further follow-up.

2. Dropout.

3. Also used to denote physiological symptoms produced by the discontinuation of an addictive drug.

Wobe mugos E A mixture made from an extract of the calf thymus gland and enzymes (proteins that speed up chemical reactions in the body) from the papaya plant, the pancreas of cows, and the pancreas of pigs. It has been used in Europe as a treatment for a variety of cancers and for herpes virus infections.

Wolfram syndrome A syndrome comprising diabetes insipidus, a mild form of diabetes mellitus, optic atrophy, and deafness. It is an autosomal recessive inherited disorder, with the chromosomal abnormality on the short arm of chromosome 4. Also called DIDMOAD, for diabetes insipidus, diabetes mellitus, optic atrophy and deafness.

Womb The small, hollow, pear-shaped organ in a woman's pelvis. This is the organ in which a baby grows. Also called the uterus.

Women's interagency HIV study (WIHS) A multicenter study established in 1993 to research the impact of HIV infection in women. The study's ultimate goal is to gain a better understanding of and provide adequate support for women who are currently HIV infected or who are at risk for HIV infection. The study is jointly supported by the National Institutes of Health (NIH) and the Centers for Disease Control and Prevention (CDC).

World federation for medical education (WFME) A non-governmental organization with ties to WHO and UNESCO, the WFME is concerned with global education and training of medical doctors and umbrella organization for six regional associations for medical education. . The WFME's general objective is to strive for the highest scientific and ethical standards in medical education and to take initiatives with respect to new methods, tools and management of medical education. The central office has been located at the University of Copenhagen, Denmark since 1996, in collaboration with Lund University in Sweden.

Worst case The highest or lowest value of a given control parameter actually evaluated in a validation exercise.

Wound (woond) A break in the skin or other body tissues caused by injury or surgical incision (cut).

Wrist The proximal part of the hand, composed of the carpal bones (Latin - 'carpe' to grasp or clutch, as in 'Carpe Diem').

Written interactive test Allows for assessment of clinical reasoning skills, understanding and knowledge of clinical and basic science and application of basic science to clinical problems. test methods such as essays and open-ended interviews are used, providing information about the respondent's perceptions, attitudes, feelings, and experiences. Examples of written objective-type tests are MCQ, PMP, MEQ. Such test should be designed to ensure that they are clinically coherent, containing questions from different disciplines, securing an appropriate discipline balance and ensuring that questions and answers reflect reasonable expectations of students. However, these test methods are often subjective and may contain rater biases. Presently, to enhance their validity and reliability, most of above mentioned methods are computerized with the addition of various audiovisual and holographic inputs (computer-interactive tests).

X chromosome A sex chromosome that usually occurs paired in each female cell and single in each male cell in species in which the male typically has two unlike cell chromosomes.

X4 tropic virus Also known as T-tropic virus. A strain of HIV that uses the chemokine receptor CXCR4 as a co-receptor to bind to and infect human immune cells. Although some HIV-1 strains are X4 tropic from the beginning of infection, it is more common for the virus to switch to using the CXCR4 co-receptor as the disease progresses.

Xantho Yellow, e.g. xanthoma - a yellow tumor.

Xanthotoxin Other name for methoxsalen.

Xcytrin Other name for motexafin gadolinium.

Xeloda Other name for capecitabine.

Xenobiotics Industrial chemicals that have a chemical structure not found in natural compounds that may resist degradation by microorganisms.

Xenograft Tissue or organs from an individual of one species transplanted into or grafted onto an organism of another species, genus, or family. A common example is the use of pig heart valves in humans.

Xeroderma A mild form of the hereditary disorder, ichthyosis in which the skin is dry and scaly.

Xeroderma pigmentosum A genetic condition marked by an extreme sensitivity to ultraviolet radiation, including sunlight. People with xeroderma pigmentosum are not able to repair skin damage from the sun and other sources of ultraviolet radiation, and have a very high risk of skin cancer.

Xerogram A picture of the body recorded on paper rather than on film. Also called a xeroradiograph.

Xeroradiography (xeromammography) An outdated form of mammography that records the image of the breast on paper rather than on film. This method is rarely used now.

Xerosis Abnormal dryness of the conjunctiva, the skin or mucous membrane.

Xerostomia Dry mouth. It occurs when the body is not able to make enough saliva.

Xinlay Other name for atrasentan hydrochloride.

Xiphoid process The cartilagenous process, with a bony core, connected to the inferior end of the of the sternum. The inferior tip of the sternum. (From the Greek "xiphias" - literally "sword")

XK469R The racemic form of a synthetic quinoxaline phenoxypropionic acid derivative with antineoplastic properties. XK469R selectively inhibits topoisomerase II by stabilizing the enzyme-DNA intermediates in which topoisomerase subunits are covalently linked to DNA through 5-phosphotyrosyl linkages, thereby interfering with DNA repair and replication, RNA and protein synthesis. This agent possesses unusual solid tumor selectivity and activity against multidrug-resistant cancer cells. XK469R is more water soluble and active than the pure isomers, R (+)XK469 and S (-)XK469.

XPS (X-ray photoelectron spectroscopy) or ESCA (Electron spectroscopy for chemical analysis) A surface-sensitive technique capable of detecting all elements with an atomic number greater than that of helium. ESCA provides data on the outermost several atomic layers of a material, and has a sensitivity in the order of 0.5 atomic percent. A primary advantage of ESCA is that it can both determine and quantify the chemical state of the elements detected (i.e. metallic state or oxide state).

XR9576 A substance that is being studied for its ability to overcome tumor-cell resistance to anticancer drugs. It belongs to the family of drugs called anthranilic acid derivatives. Also called tariquidar.

X-ray A type of high-energy radiation. In low doses, x-rays are used to diagnose diseases by making pictures of the inside of the body. In high doses, x-rays are used to treat cancer. High-energy electromagnetic radiation used to diagnose and treat disease. Diagnostic test using high energy to visualize internal body organs.

X-ray therapy The use of high-energy radiation from x-rays to kill cancer cells and shrink tumors. Radiation may come from a machine outside the body (external-beam radiation therapy) or from materials called radioisotopes. Radioisotopes produce radiation and can be placed in or near the tumor or in the area near cancer cells. This type of radiation treatment is called internal radiation therapy, implant radiation, interstitial radiation, or brachytherapy. Systemic radiation therapy uses a radioactive substance, such as a radiolabeled monoclonal antibody, that circulates throughout the body. X-ray therapy is also called radiation therapy, radiotherapy, and irradiation.

XRP9881 A semi-synthetic derivative of the taxane 10-deacetylbaccatin III with potential antineoplastic properties. XRP9881 binds to tubulin, promoting microtubule assembly and stabilization and preventing microtubule depolymerization, thereby inhibiting cell proliferation. As it represents poor substrate for P-glycoprotein-related drug resistance mechanisms, this agent may be useful for treating multi-drug resistant tumors. XRP9881 penetrates the blood brain barrier.

Xylitol A sweetener found in plants and used as a substitute for sugar; it is called a nutritive sweetener because it provides calories, just like sugar.

Xylocitin Other name for lidocaine.

Xyotax Other name for paclitaxel poliglumex.

Y chromosome A sex chromosome that is characteristic of male zygotes in species in which the male typically has two unlike sex chromosomes.

Yeasts Unicellular fungi belonging mainly to the Ascomycetes that usually multiply by budding. Their commercial significance lies in their ability to secrete enzymes. For example, in the brewing and baking industries, it is a source of vitamins and proteins. They can also be used as excipients in rDNA technology.

Yeast artificial chromosome A vector used to clone DNA fragments (up to 400 kb); it is constructed from the telomeric, centromeric, and replication origin sequences needed for replication in yeast cells.

Yield, expected The quantity of material or the percentage of theoretical yield anticipated at any appropriate phase of production based on previous laboratory, pilot scale, or manufacturing data.

Yield, theoretical The quantity that would be produced at any appropriate phase of manufacture, processing, or packing of a particular API (Active Pharmaceutical Ingredient) or intermediate, based upon the quantity of components to be used, in the absence of any loss or error in actual production.

YM598 A substance that is being studied as a treatment for advanced prostate cancer and for pain caused by prostate cancer that has spread to the bone. It belongs to the family of drugs called endothelin ETA receptor antagonists.

Yoked prisms A wedge-shaped lens which is thicker on one edge than the other. The prism bases (thicker end) are in the same direction for both eyes (up, down, left, or right). Yoked prisms are used to train or compensate for a binocular dysfunction (eye teaming problem) or a visual field loss. Sometimes used in optometric vision therapy programs.

Yttrium A rare elemental metal. A radioactive form of yttrium is used in radiation therapy and some types of immunotherapy.

Yttrium Y 90 DOTA biotin A compound that contains the radioisotope yttrium Y 90 linked to the chemical biotin. Biotin is a molecule that binds strongly to the chemical streptavidin. Yttrium Y 90 DOTA-biotin will find tumor cells in the body that have been targeted by an antibody linked to streptavidin and kill them. It is being studied together with CC49-streptavidin in the treatment of cancer.

Yttrium Y 90 DOTA monoclonal antibody hupam4 A radioimmunoconjugate comprised of the humanized monoclonal antibody HuPAM4, directed against the pancreatic cancer antigen MUC1, that is conjugated to the chelating agent tetra-azacyclodo-decane-tetra-acetic acid (DOTA) and radiolabeled with the beta-emitting radioisotope Yttrium Y90. Yttrium Y 90 DOTA monoclonal antibody HuPAM4 binds to tumor cells expressing MUC1 antigen, selectively delivering a cytotoxic dose of beta radiation.

Yttrium Y 90 dota tyr3 octreotide A radiotherapeutic agent consisting of an analogue of the octapeptide octreotide (SMT 487) chelated to the radioisotope yttrium-90. Yttrium Y 90-DOTA-tyr3-octreotide binds to somatostatin receptor-expressing tumor cells, selectively delivering a cytotoxic dose of beta radiation.

Yttrium Y 90 glass microspheres An injectable formulation of yttrium Y 90 consisting of glass microspheres containing the radioisotope yttrium Y 90. When injected into the tumor vascular bed, yttrium Y 90 glass microspheres occlude tumor blood vessels and deliver a cytotoxic dose of beta radiation to the tumor site, thereby reducing the tumor burden.

Yttrium Y 90 humanized epratuzumab A radioimmunotherapeutic humanized murine monoclonal antibody (LL2) directed against the CD22 pan-B-cell antigen and chelated to the radioisotope yttrium-90 (Y 90). Y 90 humanized monoclonal antibody LL2 binds to tumor cells expressing CD222, delivering a cytotoxic dose of beta radiation.

Yttrium Y 90 ibritumomab tiuxetan A radioimmunotherapeutic agent consisting of a murine monoclonal anti-CD20 antibody (ibritumomab) linked by the chelator tiuxetan to the radioisotope yttrium-90 (Y 90). Yttrium Y 90 ibritumomab tiuxetan binds to and specifically delivers beta radiation to CD20-expressing tumor cells, thereby minimizing the systemic effects of radiation.

Yttrium Y 90 monoclonal antibody bre 3 A radioimmunotherapeutic agent consisting of a monoclonal antibody (BrE-3) directed against the tumor-associated antigen epithelial glycoprotein mucin chelated to the radioisotope yttrium-90. Yttrium Y 90 monoclonal antibody BrE-3 binds to tumor cells expressing epithelial glycoprotein mucin, selectively delivering a cytotoxic dose of beta radiation.

Yttrium Y 90 monoclonal antibody Hu3S193 A radioimmunotherapeutic agent consisting of a humanized murine monoclonal antibody (hu3S193) directed against the tumor-associated Lewis Y epithelial antigen chelated to the radioisotope yttrium-90. Yttrium Y 90 monoclonal antibody Hu3S193 binds to Lewis Y epithelial antigen-expressing tumor cells, selectively delivering a cytotoxic dose of beta radiation.

Yttrium Y 90 monoclonal antibody MN 14 A radioimmu-notherapeutic monoclonal antibody (MN-14) directed against tumor-associated carcinoe-mbryonic antigen (CEA) and chelated to the radioisotope yttrium-90 (Y 90). Y 90 monoclonal antibody MN-14 binds to tumor cell expressing CEA, delivering a cytotoxic dose of beta radiation.

Yttrium Y 90 SMT 487 A substance that is being studied as a treatment for cancer. Also called yttrium Y 90-DOTA-tyr3-octreotide.

Z

Zarnestra Other name for tipifarnib.

ZD0473 A substance that is being studied in the treatment of cancer. It belongs to the family of drugs called platinum analogs.

ZD1839 A drug that is used to treat non-small cell lung cancer and is being studied in the treatment of other types of cancer. It belongs to the family of drugs called epidermal growth factor receptor (EGFR)-tyrosine kinase inhibitors. Also called gefitinib.

ZD4054 An orally available selective antagonist of the endothelin-A (ET-A) receptor with potential antineoplastic activity. ZD4054 binds selectively to the ET-A receptor, thereby inhibiting endothelin-mediated mechanisms that promote tumor cell proliferation.

ZD6474 An orally bioavailable 4-anilinoquinazoline. ZD-6474 selectively inhibits the tyrosine kinase activity of vascular endothelial growth factor receptor 2 (VEGF2), thereby blocking VEGF-stimulated endothelial cell proliferation and migration and reducing tumor vessel permeability. This agent also blocks the tyrosine kinase activity of epidermal growth factor receptor (EGFR), a receptor tyrosine kinase that mediates tumor cell proliferation and migration and angiogenesis.

Zemplar Other name for paricalcitol.

Zenapax Other name for daclizumab.

Zeolite Naturally occurring or synthetic permutite, a hydrated alkali-aluminum silicate that exhibits limited base exchange. Used as an ion exchange medium for the softening of hard water.

Zerit Brand name for Stavudine.

Zeta potential The charge or potential existing at the surface of a particle. It is the positive charge measured at the surface of the membrane across the pH range.

Zevalin Other name for yttrium Y 90 ibritumomab tiuxetan.

Ziconotide A drug used in the treatment of chronic pain. Also called SNX 111.

Zidovudine A synthetic dideoxy-nucleoside. After intracellular phosphorylation to its active metabolite, zidovudine inhibits DNA polymerase, resulting in the inhibition of DNA replication and cell death. This agent also decreases levels of available pyrimidines.

Zileuton A synthetic derivative of hydroxyurea with antiasthmatic properties. The leukotriene inhibitor zileuton blocks 5-lipoxygenase, which catalyzes the formation of leukotrienes from arachidonic acid; causes bronchodilation; decreases bronchial mucous secretion and edema; and may prevent or decrease the symptoms of asthma.

Zinc acetate A drug used in maintenance therapy for Wilson's Disease that works by blocking absorption of copper in the digestive system, therefore preventing further copper accumulation. A person must first be "decoppered" by a chelating agent.

Zinc oxide A compound that may enhance immune function, especially when administered by inhalation.

Zinc sulfate A salt of the essential trace metal zinc. Zinc is involved in tissue repair and is an important constituent of some proteins, including those involved in taste and smell. Zinc sulfate supplementation may prevent radiation-induced aguesia.

Zinc-finger protein A secondary feature of some proteins containing a zinc atom; a DNA-binding protein.

Zinecard Other name for dexrazoxane hydrochloride.

Zithromax Brand name for Azithromycin.

Zofran Other name for ondansetron.

Zoladex Other name for goserelin.

Zoledronate The brand name for zoledronic acid, a bisphosphonic imidazol compound which inhibits osteoclastic bone resorption. Although its mechanisms of action is yet to be fully characterized, zoledronic acid appears to directly inhibit osteoclast function and trigger osteoclast apoptotic cell death, thereby decreasing the osteoclast stimulation and bone calcium loss induced by various tumor-associated cytokines.

Zollinger Ellison syndrome A disorder in which tumors of the pancreatic islet cells produce large amounts of gastrin (a hormone), leading to excess acid in the stomach and, possibly, a peptic ulcer (ulcer of the stomach or the upper part of the small intestine).

Zoloft A drug that is used to treat depression. It belongs to the family of drugs called selective serotonin reuptake inhibitors (SSRIs). Also called sertraline.

Zolpidem A drug used to treat insomnia (inability to sleep), and anxiety. It belongs to a family of drugs known as imidazopyridines (sedative hypnotics). Also called Ambien.

Zolpidem tartrate The tartrate salt of a non-benzodiazepine of the imidazopyridine class with sedative-hypnotic activity. Zolpidem binds to the omega-1 subclass of the gamma-amino-butyric acid type A (GABA-A) receptor-chloride ionophore complex, thereby opening the chloride channel and resulting in hyperpolarization and inhibition of neuronal firing.

Zometa Other name for zoledronate.

Zoonosis Any disease in humans acquired from one of the lower animals, rabies is an example.

Zosuquidar trihydrochloride A difluorocyclopropyl quinoline. Zosuquidar trihydrochloride binds with high affinity to P-glycoprotein and inhibits P-glycoprotein-mediated multidrug resistance (MDR). P-glycoprotein, encoded by the MDR-1 gene, is a member of the ATP-binding cassette superfamily of transmembrane transporters and prevents the intracellular accumulation of many natural product-derived cytotoxic agents.

Zovirax Brand name for Acyclovir.

Zyflo Other name for zileuton.

Zygomatic arch The horizontal arch of the cheek bone, formed by the temporal process of the zygomatic bone and the zygomatic process of the temporal bone that attaches the masseter muscle.

Zygote Single cell formed from the conjugation of gametes (egg and sperm cells). The zygote has twice as many chromosomes as do gametes.

Zyloprim Other name for allopurinol.

YOUR SPACE